Fraud Investigation and Forensic Accounting in the Real World

Fraud Investigation and Forensic Accounting in the Real World

William L. Jennings, CPA/ABV, CFF, CFE, MBA, PD(IL)

CRC Press
Taylor & Francis Group
Boca Raton London New York

CRC Press is an imprint of the
Taylor & Francis Group, an **informa** business

First edition published 2022
by CRC Press
6000 Broken Sound Parkway NW, Suite 300, Boca Raton, FL 33487-2742

and by CRC Press
4 Park Square, Milton Park, Abingdon, Oxon, OX14 4RN

CRC Press is an imprint of Taylor & Francis Group, LLC

ISBN: 9780367639648 (hbk)
ISBN: 9781032244921 (pbk)
ISBN: 9781003121558 (ebk)

DOI: 10.1201/9781003121558

Typeset in Times
by KnowledgeWorks Global Ltd.

Contents

PART I   Fraud in the Real World

PART II   Forensic Accounting Investigations

Introduction

Congratulations on purchasing the most comprehensive practical guide to fraud investigation and forensic accounting in the real world. This is the textbook I wish I had had 40 years ago when I started my fraud investigation and forensic accounting career. This book will guide you, step by step, through a practical approach to address fraud from the perspective of a working fraud investigator and forensic accountant who has conducted hundreds of investigations over the past 40 years. I will be using my actual investigations to illustrate the concepts presented in this guide. With this guide you will be able to address the fraud risks you encounter every day with confidence. This guide will make you the fraud expert, a valuable new competency to enhance your career.

So, what is fraud investigation? Well, it's really a handy term that people use to describe every type of white-collar crime investigation. I suppose you could find a way to describe investigating a diversion of cash contributions made to a charity as a fraud, but most people would probably just call it theft (I worked several of these cases. How low will people go?).

Forensic accounting, on the other hand, involves applying accounting knowledge and skills to answer questions that may become the subject of a legal proceeding. I leave the definition intentionally broad because the myriad of ways in which forensic accountants apply their knowledge and skills in gathering, analyzing, and forming conclusions about information and data to assist a trier of fact's understanding is limitless.

I have been conducting fraud investigations, including audit committee investigations, for more than 40 years. I have worked with federal agencies on fraud and other criminal investigations including the US Attorneys' offices, the Securities and Exchange Commission (SEC), the US Marshals Service, the Federal Bureau of Investigation (FBI), and the Internal Revenue Service (IRS). I have worked directly on fraud investigations with the current Director of the FBI and two former Deputy Attorney Generals of the United States. I have conducted fraud investigations in virtually every industry on four continents.

This no-nonsense guide, based on my experiences, will give you the tools you need to tackle real fraud in the real world. You won't have to waste time wading through academic theories and jargon. I won't be sharing my "theories" about fraud investigation with you. I will be telling you what I learned, step by step, in my actual investigations. Also, while I have great respect for the Institute of Internal Auditors (IIA) and am a member, I am not an internal auditor; I am a fraud investigator. So, I won't be covering internal audit topics that have been covered by authors with far more internal audit education and experience than I have or repeating materials already available from the IIA. That would be a waste of your time. I will be giving you insights from an investigator's perspective. With that said, don't waste another minute; let's jump right in and get started! I hope it will be as much fun for you to read as it has been for me to write.

Acknowledgments

For Sarah, Victoria, Paul, Zoe, and Alexander who inspire me every day, and for my sister Anne, who is always there for me.

My great thanks to Kahler Hunter and Ralph Koch for their unselfish help in making this book better.

I would also like to thank Jacob Hou, Alice Ping and Sosie Ping for their constant support and encouragement.

Part I

Fraud in the Real World

What is fraud, anyway? You hear the term "fraud" thrown around a lot, but, what does it mean? One court wrote: "the law does not define fraud; it needs no definition; it is as old as falsehood and as versatile as human ingenuity."[1] A definition I and others often use is: Fraud is an intentional material misrepresentation or other deceit reasonably relied upon by a person or persons resulting in economic loss or other detrimental consequence to that person or persons in the case of business or other entities.

It is important to note that the deceit must be material, intentional, and reasonably relied upon in causing the loss or other damage. What does material mean? Let's say that I am selling you my car. I tell you that the car has brand new tires. The tires look great and perform well. However, after purchasing the car you are cleaning the interior and find a receipt for the tire purchase, which proves the tires were purchased six months earlier. The seller definitely made a knowing misrepresentation that you relied upon in purchasing the car but, was it material? The tires are in fine shape and look new; they function as well as any purchaser would expect. So, that would not be a material misrepresentation.

However, if for instance, you ask an audit client, "Why are you maintaining such high levels of this one raw material inventory item?" He answers, "Because we are getting such a great deal on this material; we want to buy as much as we can before our supplier increases the price. This raw material never degrades or becomes obsolete. All we have are some additional storage, insurance and time value of money costs. We have no risk because we also have a buyer who has committed to eventually purchasing all we can get at a nice profit for us." You rely on his answer in writing your report. Everything remains steady until year-end. At year-end, a physical inventory observation reveals that, instead of finding many large warehouses filled with the raw material bargain of the century, there is only one battered roll of the stuff in one small warehouse. Your audit client is stunned; having believed that the inventory was on hand. Did he defraud you? His misrepresentation was certainly material and you reasonably relied on it to your detriment and that of your company. However, because the audit client did not know the inventory did not exist, his misrepresentation was not intentional. So, he did not commit fraud.

The preceding example is based on an actual case I investigated. The victim was a large French company that had been ensnared in a huge commodity purchasing fraud. There were ten perpetrators spread over three states. The lead perpetrator presented a unique opportunity to the French

DOI: 10.1201/9781003121558-1

company; he told them that he could buy carpet fiber from the largest American supplier at lower prices than anyone else. He further represented that he had a number of carpet manufacturing customers who would buy all he could get at prices that would produce a hefty profit. The only problem he had was that the American supplier required a letter of credit in the amount of $10 million USD that he could not obtain on his own. If the French company would provide the letter of credit, he would split all profits with them 50/50. This was an unusual type of transaction for the French company. So, to be careful, they structured the letter of credit facility so it could only be drawn upon if nine sets of documents, each evidencing a completed step in the purchase and sale of the carpet fiber (e.g. purchase order from carpet manufacturer, purchase order to American supplier, bill of lading, invoice from American supplier, etc.), were presented. There were complex agreements drawn up to protect the French company; all happily executed by the lead perpetrator. At first, to keep up appearances, there was one 18-wheeler loaded with carpet fiber on an open flat-bed trailer, driven around to each of the other nine perpetrators who would each, in turn, create and deliver one of the required nine sets of documents. They drove that tractor-trailer around and around the same circle hundreds of times. So much so that, eventually, the one load of carpet fiber was getting beaten up badly and the cost of operating the 18-wheeler was becoming burdensome. So, they switched to using a car. When an internal auditor for the French company decided, at year-end, to physically inspect the inventory, the truth came out. By the time the music stopped, approximately $150 million USD had been drawn on the letter of credit and only $50 million USD had come back as the French company's share of the "profit."

Upon completing my investigation, I was asked to testify at the perpetrators' civil trial. They raised two interesting defenses. One was that these were normal random commodity transactions. In normal commodity transactions, one identifiable physical unit of goods (e.g. barrel of oil) is often sold, repurchased, and sold again many times. The problem with this defense was that these transactions were not random. The perpetrators did not trust one another. So, they developed a code embedded in each document number so that they could keep track of how many times the letter of credit was drawn on to make sure they got their correct share of the loot. I was able to use their own documents as trial exhibits to demonstrate how the code system worked. Goodbye to defense number one.

The second defense was trickier and is more relevant to our definition of fraud above. The perpetrators argued that the French company was quite large and sophisticated. It should, therefore, have had internal business and accounting controls in place to catch such a fraud, if in fact, that was what was proven at trial. Therefore, taken as a whole, the French company's reliance was not reasonable. So, the perpetrators' conduct did not constitute fraud. I was able to testify that the French company did have internal controls that were on a par with those of similar entities. Those controls did, in fact, operate properly, resulting in the ultimate discovery of the fraud. The reason that the fraud was not discovered sooner was that it was so cleverly concealed and executed that it continued to operate for some time. In my opinion, the French company's reliance was reasonable. The French company won at trial and was awarded all it sought in damages.

There are two other lessons to learn here. One is that good agreements will never protect you from bad people. Invest in knowing well the people with whom you are doing business. The second is that if something seems too good to be true; it often is. Take a closer look at anything that is performing far better than could be expected or easily explained. The salesman, who is lighting up the scoreboard, leads his peers by unexplainable margins. Be skeptical of division that is turning in results that cannot be achieved by any other division. It doesn't mean that your top performers are all defrauding you, but, as we shall see in the following pages, some likely are.

1 What Are You Up Against? A Bigger Problem than Most People Realize!

Forty years ago, I worked on my first fraud investigation. My firm was hired to assist a court-appointed receiver to investigate the causes of the failure of a privately owned financial institution. My job was to assist him in making recoveries. The US Attorney's Office and the FBI were conducting a parallel criminal investigation. I worked closely with a very talented FBI agent who taught me a great deal about how to conduct an investigation and preserve the evidence gathered in the investigation in a manner that would be suitable to be presented at trial. Our investigation revealed that the financial institution, established in the 1920s, had become one giant Ponzi scheme by the 1980s. The financial institution was licensed to make loans but not licensed to accept deposits. This did not, however, stop it from accepting deposits. The owners were Croatian immigrants who maintained relationships with influential people in the old country. Croatians emigrating to the United States would be directed to seek out the owners of this financial institution for help in getting settled. The owners of the financial institution would help the newly arrived immigrants to find employment in the oyster fishing industry and housing. In return, the grateful, newly arrived immigrants would set up savings accounts at the financial institution.

INVESTIGATOR NOTES

This, incidentally, is a classic example of the operation of an affinity fraud. Affinity frauds take advantage of the inherent trust that people who belong to ethnically distinct communities have for one another. They prey on human tribal instincts (i.e. people from the same place as me, who look and sound like me, are safe) that were necessary for self-preservation at a time in human history when people were only secure among members of their own tribe. This removes a natural barrier to approaches made by fraudsters (i.e. we tend to hold strangers at arms-length but embrace those we perceive to be friends.)

We started with a review of the cash records; a practice I have continued to this day. It's a cliché now, but "follow the money" is a tried and true friend that will, in most cases, get you to the truth in the shortest amount of time.

INVESTIGATOR NOTES

Always follow the money. Fraudsters deliberately create a variety of distractions to obscure their crimes from anyone who might come looking. But, the trail money leaves as it makes its way to the fraudster's pockets or purposes is always reliable. Once you track the money, collecting the other necessary evidence becomes much easier. This method also helps you to focus on gathering relevant evidence and avoiding journeys down interesting but unproductive rabbit holes.

DOI: 10.1201/9781003121558-2

Most of the cash had been loaned out. No surprise there for a financial institution. However, a review of the loan files revealed that depositors' money had been "loaned" to a small number of entities controlled by the financial institution's owners. Many of the loans had been originated decades earlier. At each maturity, the loan's principal and accrued interest were rolled into a new loan, a process known as evergreening. The scheme rocked along quietly for years. Croatian oyster fisherman, being a conservative lot, made new deposits sufficient to cover infrequent withdrawals, operating expenses, and the owners' lifestyles.

Disaster arrived in the form of a sharp increase in price of the largest direct operating cost input in the oyster fishing business: diesel fuel. The 1970's oil embargo had severely limited supply resulting in dramatically higher prices. This resulted in the proverbial run on the bank. The owners of the financial institution were prosecuted, convicted, and sent to prison; the expected happy ending. I remember thinking, at the time: why do people even try to get away with crimes? With the excellent government law enforcement resources and gifted private sector consulting detectives, like yours truly, no crime will ever go undetected and no criminal will ever escape justice. I'm afraid the past 40 years have changed my mind.

Even today, with all the technological advances that have been achieved in fraud prevention and detection, most frauds and other white-collar crimes are caught by accident. Something like, say, an oil embargo that causes a sharp rise in diesel prices resulting in economic pressure on oyster fisherman who then try to withdraw their hard-earned savings only to find that all the money is gone. To be sure, there were regulators regularly checking on the financial institution. The FBI agent and I watched bemused as a state bank examiner walked in one day and set about conducting the same examination he had likely conducted for the past 20 years. At the end of his examination, he informed the financial institution employee who had been helping him that everything appeared to be in order.

There are many statistics published about the direct cost of fraud and white-collar crime. Governments and numerous private sector entities take great pains to quantify the direct cost of fraud and white-collar crime. We take comfort in these statistics believing that they tell us the worst-case economic impact of these crimes. However, in the following paragraphs, I will prove that they represent the tiniest tip of the iceberg. What lies beneath the water should keep us all up at night.

First, let's take a look at the government statistics. The FBI publishes a useful data product called Uniform Crime Statistics or UCR. UCR purports to be a repository containing data on every crime committed in the United States. The FBI loves to collect and report data; it has been the key to the agency's success. William J. Flynn, former head of the Secret Service, became Director of the Bureau of Investigation in July 1919 and was the first to use that title. In October 1919, passage of the National Motor Vehicle Theft Act gave the Bureau of Investigation another tool by which to prosecute criminals who previously evaded the law by crossing state lines. That was the official story of the National Motor Vehicle Theft Act; the unofficial story is that it gave the Bureau a juicy statistic to present to Congress each year in budget hearings. The testimony went something like, "Last year we recovered $10 Million in stolen cars for US taxpayers." Back to the UCR, if you read the introductory language carefully, it says, "Figures used in this report were submitted voluntarily by law enforcement agencies throughout the country. Individuals using these tabulations are cautioned against drawing conclusions by making direct comparisons between cities." Hmm, submitted voluntarily and, of course, not checked in any way. What could possibly go wrong? Well, beyond the massive human error potential, there are the various federal, state, and local laws, regulations, and ordinances that govern the collection, classification, and sharing of this information. Don't get me wrong, the UCR is a useful tool that I consult regularly; it just won't answer the question: How big a problem is fraud and white-collar crime?

How about that annual report published by the worldwide professional organization dedicated to fraud investigation to which I, and likely you, belong? The report is very impressive and very useful for a variety of purposes. But, do you know where the data used to prepare the report comes from? Well, every year I get an email from that organization asking if there are any interesting cases that I investigated in the preceding year and would I be willing to share the details with them. Due to legal and ethical constraints, I never respond to those emails. So, that report never contains information about the cases I investigated and I have investigated some whales along the way. Do you think I am the only member who doesn't respond to those emails?

The other issue with measuring the cost of fraud and white-collar crime is that most of the published estimates are only attempting to quantify direct costs. They do not include all of the indirect costs, including: expenses associated with the investigation and subsequent litigation; loss of productivity; human resource costs (e.g. recruiting, training, etc.); loss of reputation and brand value (i.e. auto emissions cheating scandal); loss of business; and many others.

The point being that fraud and other white-collar crime is a much larger and more pervasive problem than most people imagine. I am sharing this with you because, in my experience, fraud and white-collar crime risk are not accorded to the appropriate level of attention in many organizations because they are not viewed as material to the organization's success. Nothing could be further from the truth.

Let's look at one example. Houston Natural Gas was a stable natural gas transmission and distribution company founded in 1940. It was acquired in 1985 by InterNorth. Under the leadership of convicted white-collar criminal Ken Lay, it became Enron. Lay, Fastow, and others perpetrated an accounting and financial reporting fraud that cost investors several billion USD, employees 5,600 jobs, and pension plans $2.1 billion USD. However, it also caused the failure of one of the largest accounting firms in the world and gave us the Sarbanes Oxley Act. What do you suppose those two indirect costs amounted to? My calculator doesn't have enough decimal places for that one.

SECTION I: INVISIBLE CRIMINALS

There's an old joke: "marriage is a great institution; it's people who give it a bad name." The same thing with fraud and white-collar crime. People commit crimes. It seems obvious, yet most companies ignore this simple fact. In addressing fraud and white-collar crime risk, most companies start by looking at commercial activities, contracts, transactions, systems, and controls. However, they fail to address the biggest risk of all: people.

Let me illustrate with an example from my case files. A friend of mine, who was the chief financial officer of a large agricultural and industrial machinery manufacturer, called me one day and asked me to come by for a chat. When I arrived, he ushered me into his office and asked me to keep what he was about to tell me confidential. He said that his company had quite the year and found themselves flush with more cash than they could put to work through normal channels. He said that he had shared this happy fact with his another friend who had proposed a great solution: invest the money in government-backed student debt. The interest rates were very favorable, and there was no principal default risk. His friend told him that he could set up the investment vehicle for him.

The Chief Financial Officer (CFO) raised one important concern, "Having never invested in something like this before, how do I protect against fraud?" His friend told him not to worry because he could obtain a fraud policy from Lloyd's of London to insure against fraud risk. My friend, the CFO, agreed to make the investment. He showed me a number of impressive agreements executed to create the mechanisms of the investment vehicle and, of course, the Lloyd's of London fraud policy. Basically, my friend's company was to purchase a traunch of student loans; a lock box was set up to receive payments, which would then be credited to my friend's company's account, simple enough. But, there was one problem: three months had elapsed and no payments had come to the lockbox. He had tried to contact his other friend to no avail. He didn't know what to do and wanted to hire me to help him sort all of this out, discreetly.

My investigation revealed that the money of my friend's company was transferred through various entities to a bank in Belize without coming within a hundred miles of a student loan. Belize has strict financial privacy laws and no tax treaties with the United States. In fact, prior to 2001, they didn't even have an extradition treaty with the United States. The Lloyd's of London policy was a fake, created on a laptop.

My point in telling you this story is that good contracts will never protect you from bad people. It's critically important to get the people right first. Just like you go to work every morning thinking about how you will make your company better, the bad guys go to work every morning thinking about how they will take what they want by any means possible.

INVESTIGATOR NOTES

Good contracts will never protect you from bad people. When somebody tells you, in order to answer to your inquiry about doing business with questionable people, "There's nothing to worry about because we have iron-clad agreements." That's when you should start worrying.

THE INVISIBLE CRIMINAL

What do criminals look like? Which of them is a photo of an actual criminal?

FIGURE 1.1

FIGURE 1.2

The guy in Figure 1.2 is Alexis Flores. He is on the FBI's Ten Most Wanted List. He kidnapped and murdered a five-year-old girl in Philadelphia, PA. The guy in Figure 1.1 is just criminally vain. It's even harder to spot white-collar criminals. For them to be successful at their criminal activities, they must, by necessity, fit in. They are often, although not always, charming and attractive people. They make friends easily and gain the trust of those with whom they form social bonds at work. However, many honest people who fit in at work are charming, attractive, make friends easily, and gain the trust of those around them.

INVESTIGATOR NOTES

This creates one of the most difficult problems you will have to deal with in conducting an internal investigation: denial. The people you report to, the witnesses you interview, and others who have worked closely with the fraudster will all be in denial about the fact that a crime has been committed. They will say things like, "That's impossible. I know Mr. Smith; there's no way he would ever do anything like that." or "That sort of thing just could not happen here." I believe that this is another manifestation of human tribal instinct. The internal narrative for denial goes something like, "If my friend, Mr. Smith, is a criminal what does that say about me?" or "I have worked for this company for 20 years; if something like that happened here, what does that say about me and my work friends?" Of course, I am not a trained psychologist. Although I have seen many sides to human nature that most people never see, I may be wrong about the underlying reasons for denial. But, that is not important; what is important is that you be prepared for it when it happens and to realize that just because people believe something does not make it true.

You can't tell who has or will commit a crime by the way they look. The fact is there are some people who, if given the opportunity, will always commit a crime. There are other people who, no matter what pressure they are feeling, will never commit a crime. Generally, these two groups of people comprise 10–20% of any population; then there are the rest of us.

The US military academy is named West Point. An atheist FBI agent friend of mine shared this line from the West Point Cadet Prayer with me:

"Make us to choose the harder right instead of the easier wrong"

This is a useful way to think about the rest of us. I coined a term many years ago to describe the remaining 80–90% of society: threshold criminals. Threshold criminals are persons who are not inherently disposed to commit a crime but given the proper motivation and opportunity will be drawn across a line that none of us should ever cross. Once across, it is very difficult for them to ever get back. This dynamic was present in almost every case I investigated and explained how, if left undetected, it caused small frauds to become enormous if given enough time. This relationship between motivation, opportunity, and fear had a powerful effect on my thinking about the people factor in fraud and white-collar crime. So much so that many years ago I developed a mathematical function, which I call the Fraud Function, to describe the operation of this relationship.

The Fraud Function

DESIRE > FEAR = ACT

When someone's desire to obtain something (e.g. travel, clothes, jewelry, real estate, aircraft, drugs, gambling, debt relief, medical care, revenge, etc.) not obtainable by ethical or legal means exceeds their fear of getting caught; the threshold criminal will act. Now stay with me here. The usefulness of the Fraud Function is in helping us to understand what happens following the first criminal act.

If you think about it, what happens after a person commits a crime and is not caught? The first thing that happens is the fear of getting caught drops dramatically; the person concludes, "Well that was easier than I thought; no one was even checking." I will be coming back to this important insight in Chapter 2. The second thing that happens is that the desire remains the same or even increases as is often the case with gambling problems. You don't think they are able to build all those giant casinos by letting the patrons walk out with their money, do you? In fact it is a mathematical certainty that if you continue gambling in a casino for long enough, no matter any interim winnings you may have, the casino will end up with all of your money. The reason is that the odds on all the games are in the casino's favor. The casino's advantage ranges, on average, from approximately 7% on slot machines to 1% for bets placed behind the come or pass lines at the craps table. The only exceptions are poker and the sports book that may reward individual skills such as bluffing. So, if you stay long enough you will lose; it is a mathematical certainty. Let me use the following case example to illustrate these principles.

There was a man named James who was the chief financial officer of a large nonprofit that served people with addiction problems. James was a quiet, nebbish fellow of small stature, balding with a weak chin and a pot belly. He was the picture of a trustworthy corporate officer. But, there was a darker side to James that no one knew about. James loved gambling in all its many splendid forms. He traveled, when possible, to casinos. However, on his limited income and tight schedule that was not often possible. So he also bet on dogs, football games, basketball games, the lottery, scratch off games, and many more. James would bet on anything. Unfortunately, James was not very good at gambling and lost far more often than he won. This led James to borrowing from increasingly shady lenders. He tried to win back enough money to pay off his debts, which only led to further losses. This downward spiral finally placed James in the clutches of lenders who use orthopedic surgery techniques to effect collections. James' **DESIRE** to avoid orthopedic damage was unbearable.

James' employer had a vision communicated in passionate terms to all donors. They wanted to build a sanctuary for the addicted people they served. It was to be a magnificent temple of safety and refuge for people who were often cast out by friends and family. Many years earlier, the organization had established a building fund account at their bank into which donor funds were deposited. They established a target of $50 million USD as the trigger to begin construction.

I entered the story shortly after the organization reached their $50 million USD target, or so they thought. There was a celebration at the board meeting. James had just distributed the building fund statements, which showed an account balance of $50.8 million USD. During the following discussion, James urged caution; "why rush into this" he said. James urged that they wait another quarter to establish a cushion, but the board would not be deterred. They voted unanimously to begin construction immediately. They instructed James to transfer control of the building fund to their payment agent, a local construction law firm. The general contractor undertook site preparation and filed the first payment application. The law firm contacted the president of the nonprofit, by telephone, to ask a fateful question, "When would the money be transferred into the building fund account?" The president, at first, didn't understand what he was hearing; he replied, "What are you talking about? There is more than $50 million USD in the account we transferred to your firm." The lawyer replied, "Sir, there was $48.67 in the account you transferred to us."

During a hastily called emergency board meeting, at which the lawyers and a representative of the bank were in attendance, the truth set in; the money was gone. James had been summoned to the meeting but failed to attend; no one could find him. The board voted to hire a lawyer who specialized in white-collar crime; that lawyer retained me to conduct the investigation.

My investigation found that James had transferred the entire $50 million USD, over the preceding ten years, from the building fund account to another account, with a name very similar to that of the nonprofit, at the same bank. The phony building fund statements he distributed at the board meetings were created on his home computer. After presenting my findings to the board, they asked that the attorney and I share them with the US Attorney's office in an effort to get them to agree to prosecute James, which they did. James entered into a plea agreement that required him to come to my office with any remaining records he had and to cooperate with me in attempting to make recoveries. When James arrived at my office, he had a stunningly beautiful woman with him. She introduced herself and handed me her card; she was a pediatric psychiatrist. She said that she wasn't able to stay but wanted to ask me when I thought James would get out of prison. She told me that she planned to marry James and wanted to know how long she would have to wait. I told her that I did not know but, thought to myself, "Lady, I don't know for sure, but, with the amount of money involved; the federal sentencing guidelines and the fact that there is no parole in the federal system, you may be walking down the aisle with a cane." She thanked me and left.

James proceeded to tell me that the whole thing started at the convergence of three unrelated events. First, he had just lost a large bet with a bookie to whom he already owed a great deal of money. Second, he had received a number of phone calls at the office and at home from a man who threatened to break his arms if he didn't pay the bookie the amounts owed. He was not sleeping well and had become increasingly confused and forgetful at work. One morning he walked several blocks to the nonprofit's bank to transfer a large amount of money from one account to another but had forgotten the check he had drawn, for that purpose, at the office. As he approached the teller, realizing that he did not have the check, he almost broke down as he explained his error to the teller. She took pity on him and told him that he did not need the official check to affect the transfer; he could simply fill out a counter check and she could use that to make the transfer. She reminded him to destroy the official check when he returned to his office that he agreed to do. But, in that moment, James felt that he had been delivered from his enemies by the divine hand of Providence. When he got back to his office, he spent the rest of the afternoon rolling the thing over in his mind. How could he do it? He would have to create the documents necessary to set up an account that he controlled; the account would have to have a name similar to that of the nonprofit to avoid any difficult questions at the bank. What if he got caught? Well, would that be any worse than getting his arms broken or worse? James' **FEAR** of getting caught was less than his **DESIRE** to avoid amateur orthopedic procedures.

The next morning, he arrived at the bank with the necessary paperwork and set up the account. At first, he transferred $100 USD just to see if anyone would notice (**ACT 1**); no one did. James' **FEAR** lessened substantially. Next, he transferred $500 USD (**ACT 2**), then $1,000 USD (**ACT 3**); still no one noticed. James' **FEAR** approached zero. Then he transferred $9,000 USD (**ACT 4**); no one noticed. James' **FEAR** now at zero, he kept on like this gradually increasing the amounts. No one ever noticed. He paid off the bookie but kept betting on everything he could think of to try to win enough money to replace the money he had stolen. In the interim, he would have to create false bank statements for the building fund account to distribute at the board meetings. He could create these easily enough on his home computer, but they were attached to a report reconciling them with contributions received during the preceding period. He knew the piper would have to paid one day; he just hoped he could put that day off until he had won enough money to put it all back. Eventually, he had transferred and gambled away $50 million USD. He said that the day of the fateful board meeting where the building fund goal was "reached" was the worst part of his life; he said that he felt like he was being strangled as he entered the boardroom.

On the day of James' sentencing hearing, I received a call from the Assistant U.S. Attorney prosecuting his case. He insisted I come to the US District Court where James was being sentenced. He said that James' lawyer had made a motion for a downward departure from the federal sentencing guidelines and he needed my help. When I arrived, the scene was surreal; on one side of the courtroom were all of the addicts from the organization James' had pilfered. They were lining up to make victim statements, many complaining that James had obviously lied to them about his own addictions to get them to give him a job. On the other side of the courtroom were James' new friends from Gamblers Anonymous who were prepared to testify that James' was unable to help himself due to his mental incapacity caused by his gambling addiction. The federal judge did not buy it. James was sentenced to serve seven years in federal prison.

We will come back to the Fraud Function in the chapters ahead. It is useful to think of the Fraud Function when designing systems to prevent fraud and when investigating fraud. For example, increasing fear increases the threshold to act and reduces its likelihood. When thought of in the context of the Fraud Function, each effective measure we consider can be evaluated from the standpoint of its likely effect on the operation of the Fraud Function versus its cost. So, the investment required to install cameras in an environment where people are likely to learn that the cameras are not actively monitored would likely not be worth the cost because of its negligible impact on the **FEAR** factor. However, a minimal investment in fake cameras and signs warning that activities are being monitored in a tightly controlled security environment could be worth their weight in gold; how much do cameras and signs weigh, anyhow? Well, you get the point.

The Fraud Function also provides a convincing proof that even small frauds left undetected can grow quite large over time. If crimes go undetected, criminals are emboldened and act again and again. Fraudulent transactions get larger and more frequent. When the cat's away, the rats will play.

INVESTIGATOR NOTES

A person's perception of reality is their reality. If you are able to create the perception, with employees and other stakeholders, that you are watching and will always catch any criminal conduct and violations of company policy, no matter how real that expectation is, it will raise the threshold for commission of an inappropriate act significantly. If, on the other hand, you create a perception of lax oversight and security, you will provide license to every employee and stakeholder who is motivated to commit fraud.

Another important thing to understand is that not all criminals are equal in terms of the threat they represent to your organization. We will deal with this issue in detail in Chapter 2; for now let's just think about the level of damage several different types of criminals can do to your organization. If you are a retailer, customers (i.e. outsiders) can shoplift. Shoplifting typically produces small individual losses; however, if it becomes pervasive, it can have a material impact on financial results but typically does not. If you are a public company and your chief accounting officer engages in accounting and financial reporting, fraud losses will always be material. This is an important concept to keep in mind when deciding how to deploy the limited resources at your disposal.

SECTION II: CRIMES

Fraud and other white-collar crime are a big problem. Worldwide, crime takes many different forms and is investigated and prosecuted by a wide variety of law enforcement agencies. For purposes of illustrating changes in the scope of criminal activity, I have chosen to present data for FBI prosecutions as a proxy for the evolution of crime and punishment (Table 1.1).

TABLE 1.1
FBI White-Collar Prosecutions[2]

Number year-to-date	2.001
Percent change from previous year	−6.8
Percent change from 5 years ago	−1.2
Percent change from 10 years ago	−45.2
Percent change from 20 years ago	−55.8

"Prosecutions of white-collar criminals recommended by the FBI are substantially down during the first ten months of Fiscal Year 2013, according to the latest available data obtained under the Freedom of Information Act from the Department of Justice."[3]

If the FBI's white-collar crime prosecutions continue at the same pace for the remaining two months of the current fiscal year, an analysis by the Transactional Records Access Clearinghouse estimates that the FY 2013 total will be nearly 7% (6.8%) lower than it was in the previous year, 1.2% lower than three years ago, and only about half what it was ten years ago – down 45.2%.[4]

While the FBI has long been considered the federal government's premier agency when it comes to white-collar crime, and the number of its criminal investigators has increased (from 11,097 in 2001 to 13,812 in 2012), the 9/11 attacks of 2001 prompted the agency to focus more and more of its investigative powers on trying to deal with international and domestic terrorism and weapons of mass destruction.[5]

Notice that while the number of FBI agents increased by approximately 25%, during this period, white-collar crime prosecutions declined by nearly 45%. This reflects the FBI's changing priorities, a shift away from white-collar investigations to international and domestic terrorism investigations. This provides a useful insight into federal white-collar crime investigation and prosecution. In order to draw the resources of the FBI and, by extension, US Attorneys offices, the crime against your organization usually must be a high-priority crime or represent a referral from another federal agency (e.g. Internal Revenue Service [IRS], Securities and Exchange Commission [SEC], etc.).

INVESTIGATOR NOTES

We will discuss the pros and cons of referring matters to the FBI and US Attorney's office later. But, if you do decide to go down that road, realize that just because something is a violation of law does not mean that the federal government will agree to investigate and prosecute it. These agencies answer to both the Legislative and Executive branches of government regarding the effectiveness of their use of budgeted funds; they need to show results in combatting crimes that are of current interest to those bodies. Your crime may just not be fashionable at the moment. So, here's a little secret to getting them to take on your matter: make it easy and rewarding for them. First, do as much of the investigation for them as you are able, using sound evidence gathering techniques. Deliver the investigation to them wrapped in a bow, ready for trial. Second, hire a lawyer who was a well-liked and respected former member of the relevant US Attorney's office; let them do an old pal a favor.

The long-term trend in white-collar crime prosecutions recommended by the FBI going back to FY 1993 is shown more clearly in Figure 1.3. The vertical bars in Figure 1.3 represent the number of these prosecutions recorded each fiscal year. "Projected figures for the current fiscal year are shown. Each presidential administration is distinguished by the color of the bars."[6]

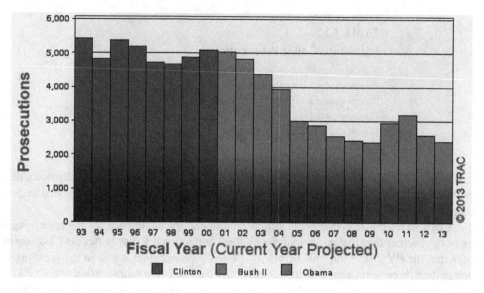

FIGURE 1.3[7]

The following table (Table 1.2) provides a window into how the FBI thinks about white-collar crime.

TABLE 1.2

FBI White-Collar Crime Program Categories[8]

Program Category	Prosecutions Filed	% of White-Collar Prosecutions Filed
-All-	2,001	100.0
Fraud-Financial Institution	355	17.7
Fraud-Other	341	17.0
Fraud-Mortgage	240	12.0
Fraud-Health Care	221	11.0
Fraud-Other Business	111	5.5
Fraud-Federal Program	99	4.9
Fraud-Computer	96	4.8
Fraud-Other Investment	81	4.0
Fraud-Tax	51	2.5
Fraud-Corporate	49	2.4
Fraud-Identity Theft-Other	45	2.2
Fraud-Consumer	35	1.7
Fraud-Identity Theft-Aggravated	34	1.7
Fraud-Federal Procurement	32	1.6
Fraud-Bankruptcy	28	1.4
Fraud-Against Ins. Provider	27	1.3
Fraud-Intellectual Property Violations	24	1.2
Fraud-Advance Fee Schemes	15	0.7
Fraud-Telemarketing	13	0.6
Fraud-Commodities	4	0.2
Antitrust-Other Finance Mkts.	2	0.1
Fraud-Insider Ins. Provider	1	0.0
Antitrust-Other	0	0.0

(Continued)

TABLE 1.2 *(Continued)*
FBI White-Collar Crime Program Categories[8]

Program Category	Prosecutions Filed	% of White-Collar Prosecutions Filed
Antitrust-Unspecified	0	0.0
Fraud-MEWA/MET	0	0.0
Fraud-Other Insurance	0	0.0
Fraud-Unspecified Insurance	0	0.0
Fraud-Unspecified	0	0.0

Let's begin by developing a common understanding of what crime is and what it is not. Depending on where you are, the words used to define the elements required to establish criminal conduct may vary but will likely include the following:

Criminal Act (actus reus)
Criminal Intent (mens rea)
Joint Operation (i.e. of 1 & 2) (concurrence)

Where I live; Title 16, Section 16-2-1 of the Georgia Criminal Code states:

(a) A crime is a violation of a statute of this state in which there is a joint operation of an act or omission to act and intention or criminal negligence.

Incidentally, the following are the white-collar crimes the FBI pays special attention to:

Falsification of financial information
False accounting entries and/or misrepresentations of financial condition
Fraudulent trades designed to inflate profits or hide losses
Illicit transactions designed to evade regulatory oversight
Self-dealing by corporate insiders
    Insider trading (trading based on material, non-public information)
Kickbacks
Misuse of corporate property for personal gain
Individual tax violations related to self-dealing
Fraud in connection with an otherwise legitimately operated mutual hedge fund
Late trading
Certain market timing schemes
Falsification of net asset values

Obstruction of justice designed to conceal any of the above-noted types of criminal conduct, particularly when the obstruction impedes the inquiries of the US SEC, Commodity Futures Trading Commission (CFTC), other regulatory agencies, and/or law enforcement agencies.[9]

INVESTIGATOR NOTES

Take a look at the previous box. The one that begins with "Obstruction of justice..." I would also add violations of Section 1001 of Title 18 of the US Code that makes it a felony, punishable by five years in federal prison, to make material false statements or knowing omissions in answer to questions asked by agents of the federal government. I have seen more people end up spending significantly more time in federal prison for violating one of these than they would have for the underlying crimes they were trying to conceal. Incidentally, the term "perjury trap" has been bantered about quite a bit lately. In my experience, there is no such thing. The FBI and other federal agents always have collected significant amounts of evidence ahead of conducting subject or target interviews. Most subjects and targets are not aware of that fact and choose to lie to the agents. Just because the federal agents already knew the truth does not make such an interview a perjury trap.

Let's look a little deeper at each of those before we move on.

Criminal acts can be either mala in se (i.e. evil in itself) or mala prohibita (i.e. wrong because it is prohibited). Examples of mala in se crimes include murder, kidnapping, theft, assault, etc. In other words, everyone knows these acts are wrong. Mala prohibita crimes, on the other hand, include things like use of illegal drugs, DUI, gambling, tax evasion, and certain white-collar crimes like books and records violations by SEC registrants. It is important to understand what appears, at first, to be an obvious distinction. Prosecutors of mala in se crimes do not have to first prove that the alleged criminal act is a crime. However, for mala prohibita crimes, the prosecutor must first prove that the alleged act is a crime under a statute and, if relevant, a related regulation or regulations.

INVESTIGATOR NOTES

Contrary to what you have learned from popular fiction books, television, and movies, motive is not a required element to establish criminal conduct. This is very fortunate for people who do what you and I do. You have heard the expression, "in order to truly understand someone you have to walk in their shoes." Believe me when I tell you that you cannot walk in many criminals' shoes; they are often only available in size bizarre. This is an important concept to understand if you are to be effective in your work. If you establish a requirement for yourself that you must first understand why a person would commit a crime against your organization in order to effectively investigate criminal conduct, you will waste a great deal of time and energy on a fool's errand.

Let me give you an example. Many years ago I was tasked with conducting acquisition due diligence for a large public company in its acquisition of a large private company. I had the great privilege of working directly with the CEO of the private company, a genius and early thought leader in the developing casual dining industry. The one dark cloud in my otherwise happy adventure in the casual dining business was that I discovered that the controller of the private company was stealing from the company by filing fraudulent expense reports. How I discovered that is a story to be told over a glass of wine, sometime, to those of you who meet me and remember to ask. It is not important to the lesson to be learned here.

I conducted an investigation of the controller and his expense reports. My background research on the controller revealed that he was unmarried, had no romantic attachments, and was not a gambler or extensive traveler. He lived in a modest home and drove an ordinary car and had no extravagant lifestyle tendencies whatsoever. His parents were recently deceased and had left him a not inconsiderable amount of money. Then, why steal? My investigation of his expense reports revealed something peculiar as well; he included fraudulent requests for reimbursement on almost every expense report, but the amounts were quite modest. Over a ten-year period, he had stolen less than $30 thousand USD. Why?

My discovery sent shock waves through the public company's C-suite and their SEC counsel. The public company desperately needed this acquisition. Their core business was operating cafeterias. Cafeterias, at this time, appealed to a market demographic with a mean age of 71; their customers were literally dying off. So, they needed to acquire their way into a younger demographic; this casual dining company acquisition was a key first step in that strategy. But, what to do? If they completed the acquisition and the truth about the controller's thefts were discovered, or worse, he engaged in new more egregious criminal conduct post acquisition after they were put on notice of his prior conduct, what would that mean? The only way to solve this problem was to have the controller quietly resign ahead of the completion of the acquisition. The CEO wanted to have the controller prosecuted so that he could exact justice and learn why he had been so cruelly betrayed by his trusted colleague. However, SEC counsel advised that that would be unwise and prevailed upon him to consider a different path to the same destination. They advised him to offer to not have the controller prosecuted in exchange for him submitting to psychological evaluation and allowing the psychologist to provide a copy of the report of findings to the company. The report clearly revealed the controller's motive; can you guess what it was? The report revealed that the controller had a pathological obsession with stealing; he enjoyed the thrill of regularly pilfering from the company and getting away with it. It gave him a sense of power and made him feel that he had this secret identity that would make him attractive to those around him. Try walking around in those shoes for a while.

As you consider the question of motive in your work, I would commend you to Franz Kafka's short story "A Hunger Artist." The protagonist in the story is a Hunger Artist; a person who fasts for long periods of time for public amusement. This was apparently a popular carnival sideshow attraction in the eighteenth century; basically, the Hunger Artist would be placed in a cage with no food. The cage would be placed where carnival guests could pass by and look at the Hunger Artist and marvel at the posted number of days he had lasted without food. Eventually, the Hunger Artist, the greatest in all Europe, pushes his skill too far and starves to death. In his last moments, he reveals that his skill was no skill at all; he simply was never able to find a food that he liked. It's true, people always do things for their own reasons; don't assume that you will be able to understand those reasons. Fortunately, your work does not require you to explain or prove motive unless you decide to be a movie star.

Not all crimes are created equal. This will become an important consideration in Chapter 2. For now, let's just consider the types of crimes that you will likely come up against. I will not bore you with a long list of crimes that would, in any case, be incomplete and would not serve any purpose other than to fill up space in this book. Instead, what I will do is to begin to give you a handy methodology to classify crime and to evaluate the level of harm it could represent to your organization. First, there are crimes against property and crimes against people; property you can replace, but people you cannot. Then, there are crimes that affect the value of your company's brand (i.e. Volkswagen's emission scandal) and crimes that affect the value of your company's market capitalization (i.e. Wirecard AG) think big numbers and, in the case of Wirecard AG, bet the company losses. Most of the largest crimes, in terms of cost to the company and stakeholders, are perpetrated by insiders. Then there are crimes that result in the loss of assets of the company (i.e. Home Depot's recent disclosure about its "shrink problem" harming financial results). These are often perpetrated by outsiders, sometimes with the help of insiders, and can result in significant losses, although usually less than crimes affecting brand or market capitalization. However, there are crimes that result in the loss of assets, perpetrated by outsiders that due to their nature result in a significant diminution of brand value and market capitalization (i.e. Equifax theft of consumer credit data); think big numbers and bet the company losses. In the age of cybercrime, losses to outside state-sponsored organized crime and other hacking can be enormous. We will develop these concepts more in Chapter 2. For now, I just want you to begin to think about how to evaluate your exposure to crime based on the level of harm it might cause to your organization in making decisions about how to allocate resources.

Let's take a brief look at some actual crimes that are being successfully prosecuted, as I write this book, to illustrate the concepts we have been discussing:

Department of Justice
US Attorney's Office

District of South Carolina

FOR IMMEDIATE RELEASE
Thursday, July 23, 2020

**Former SCANA Executive Pleads Guilty to Conspiracy
to Commit Mail and Wire Fraud**

Columbia, South Carolina – United States Attorney Peter M. McCoy, Jr. announced today that Stephen A. Byrne, 60, former Executive Vice President of SCANA, pleaded guilty in federal court to conspiracy to commit mail and wire fraud.

Byrne, who served as SCANA's Executive Vice President and SCE&G's President of Generation and Transmission and Chief Operating Officer, oversaw all nuclear operations for SCANA, including the construction of the two new nuclear units.

From its inception, substantial delays and cost overruns plagued the project. In late 2015 and early 2016, Byrne and others in SCANA's executive leadership were aware that without extraordinary progress, the project was at risk of not completing the construction of both units in time to qualify for the federal nuclear production tax credit, which will expire on December 31, 2020, and was worth up to $1.4 billion. In or around June 2016, Byrne became aware that efforts to improve the pace and productivity of the project were insufficient to meet the nuclear production tax credit deadline.

At that time he joined a conspiracy with other senior SCANA executives to defraud customers of money and property through material false and misleading statements and omissions.

Here, we have a C-suite level executive, definitely an insider, committing fraud by making material false and misleading statements to regulators and others, the direct result of which will cost shareholders and rate payers billions of dollars. This whole mess started when these executives tried to put a happy face on a doomed nuclear power plant construction project. If the truth had come out, based on what we can glean from public statements, these executives were probably looking at significant personal losses of compensation, stock value, and demotion or termination as a result of this debacle. In fairness to them, nuclear power plants are devilishly tricky to build correctly. I recently testified in an international arbitration in Asia related to a failed nuclear power plant construction project. The problems that plagued that construction project were legion. If we go back to the Fraud Function, we can see that when these executives' **DESIRE** (i.e. preventing loss of compensation, investment, and career) exceeded their **FEAR** (i.e. we won't get caught because this construction project is so massive and complex no one will ever figure it out) they **ACT**ed. Once they lied at the first public service commission hearing, they were locked in and had to continue to lie hoping that some miracle would make their lies true eventually. When they were not caught the first time the **FEAR** lessened, but the **DESIRE** remained and may have even grown, so they acted again and again. Had they told the truth at the beginning, billions of dollars could have been saved, but the operation of the Fraud Function is such that, if left unchecked long enough in an environment where significant amounts are at stake, losses will be enormous. Also, let's take a minute to think about the other costs to SCANA stakeholders: loss of brand value and trust with electric power customers and regulators, loss of market capitalization, criminal and civil litigation, professional fees, employee morale, and on and on.

INVESTIGATOR NOTES

This case illustrates an interesting phenomenon unique to the threshold criminal who crosses the line. This is a phenomenon I have dubbed magical rationalization; it's my little play on the term magical thinking. Like magical thinking, magical rationalization allows the threshold criminal to create a future in which he or she will somehow come up with enough money, or in this case, enough completed nuclear power plant to put things right before they are caught. But, of course, as is often said: hope is not a strategy.

Department of Justice
US Attorney's Office

Eastern District of Louisiana

FOR IMMEDIATE RELEASE

Friday, July 10, 2020

Three First NBC Executives Indicted for
Fraud against Failed $5 Billion Bank

NEW ORLEANS – The US Attorney's Office announced that a grand jury indicted **ASHTON J. RYAN**, age 72, of Kenner; **WILLIAM BURNELL**, age 70, of Kenner; **ROBERT BRAD CALLOWAY**, age 60, of Metairie; and **FRANK J. ADOLPH**, age 60, of Kenner, for defrauding First NBC Bank, the New Orleans-based bank that failed in April 2017.

According to the 46-count Indictment, from 2006 through April 2017 **RYAN, BURNELL, CALLOWAY**, and **ADOLPH** conspired to defraud First NBC Bank (the "Bank") through a variety of schemes. **RYAN** was the President and CEO of the Bank for most of its existence. **BURNELL** was the Chief Credit Officer. **CALLOWAY** was an Executive Vice President. **ADOLPH** was a borrower at the Bank who was charged with conspiring with the three Bank executives to obtain loans based on false statements and forged documents.

The Indictment alleges that **RYAN, RNELL, CALLOWAY, ADOLPH**, and others conspired to defraud First NBC Bank by disguising the true financial status of certain borrowers and their troubled loans, concealing the true financial condition of the Bank from the Board, auditors, and examiners. The borrowers included real estate developer Gary Gibbs, real estate developer Kenneth Charity, Bank general counsel Gregory St. Angelo, factoring business owner **FRANK ADOLPH**, hotel owner Arvind "Mike" Vira, contractor Warren Treme, and contractor Jeffrey Dunlap. **CALLOWAY** was Gibbs's loan officer, and **RYAN** served as the loan officer or oversaw the loan officers for all of those borrowers. **BURNELL** approved the risk rating for all of these borrowers' loans and was the gatekeeper tasked with protecting the safety and soundness of the Bank's loan portfolio. Dunlap, Charity, and St. Angelo have previously been charged in individual Bills of Information with conspiracy to commit bank fraud, and all three have pled guilty. Vira, Gibbs, and Treme have been charged more recently, in their own individual Bills of Information, with conspiring to defraud First NBC Bank. All six of these borrowers are listed in the Indictment as members of the bank fraud conspiracy with **RYAN, BURNELL, CALLOWAY,** and **ADOLPH.**

During the course of the conspiracy, **RYAN, BURNELL,** and **CALLOWAY** repeatedly extended loans to borrowers who were unable to pay their loans without relying on loan payments to keep them current. To hide this practice, **RYAN, BURNELL,** and **CALLOWAY** made false statements in loan documents and elsewhere about the purposes of loans, the borrowers' abilities to repay those loans, and the sources of funds used to pay those loans. When the borrowers were unable to pay those loans, **RYAN, BURNELL,** and **CALLOWAY** made new loans to these same borrowers and then used the proceeds from those new loans to pay the existing loans. This created the false impression that the borrowers were able to pay their loans, when in fact they would not have been able to pay their loans without going further into debt through new borrowing from the Bank. The new loans prevented these borrowers from appearing on lists that **RYAN** and **BURNELL** gave the Bank's Board each month, which would have highlighted that the borrowers were unable to make loan payments or had cash flow problems. **RYAN, BURNELL,** and **CALLOWAY** also made false statements about the purpose of those loans, misrepresenting in Bank documents that the borrowers were able to pay loans with cash generated from the borrowers' businesses, when in fact the borrowers were only able to pay those loans with proceeds from new Bank loans. The borrowers often spent the proceeds of these business loans on unrelated personal expenses, including by overdrawing their checking accounts at the Bank, and **RYAN, BURNELL,** and **CALLOWAY** paid these overdrafts by issuing new loans to the borrowers. This practice kept the borrowers off of month-end overdraft reports to the Board and hid the borrowers' inability to pay their own expenses without new loan proceeds.

For certain loans, **RYAN, BURNELL,** and **CALLOWAY** included borrower documents in loan files despite knowing that the documents were false. For example, even after **RYAN** and **BURNELL** learned that **ADOLPH** was submitting falsified documents to the Bank to inflate his collateral, **RYAN** and **BURNELL** continued to submit loans for **ADOLPH** that included the false documents. Similarly, even though **RYAN, BURNELL,** and **CALLOWAY** knew that Gibbs could not pay his loans with cash generated from his businesses, they continued to submit loan documents that included false documents showing that Gibbs's business earned enough cash to pay his loans at the Bank.

When members of the Board or the Bank's outside auditors or examiners asked about loans to these borrowers, **RYAN, BURNELL,** and **CALLOWAY** made false statements about the borrowers and their loans, and left out the truth about the borrowers' inability to pay their debts without getting new loans. As a result, the balance on these borrowers' loans continued to grow. By the time regulators closed First NBC Bank in April of 2017, Gibbs owed the Bank $123 million; Charity owed $18 million; St. Angelo owed $46 million; **ADOLPH** owed $6 million; Vira owed $39 million; Treme owed $6 million; and Dunlap owed $22 million. The Bank's failure cost the Federal Deposit Insurance Corporation deposit insurance fund just under $1 billion.

RYAN, BURNELL, and **CALLOWAY** each received millions of dollars in compensation from the Bank during the course of the conspiracy. **RYAN** also received personal benefits from three of the borrower relationships. Vira lent millions of dollars to **RYAN** at the same time Vira was a borrower at the Bank, and **RYAN** and Vira conspired to hide their business dealings from the Board, auditors, and examiners. Treme was **RYAN's** partner in several businesses and real estate development projects, and **RYAN** used Treme's borrowing from the Bank as a way to spend Bank loan proceeds on **RYAN's**

own projects. Even when parts of **RYAN's** business dealings with Vira and Treme were revealed to regulators, **RYAN** continued to conceal from regulators that he exercised authority over loans to Vira and Treme. Dunlap was a contractor for a business that **RYAN** and Treme ran, and **RYAN** used loan proceeds from Dunlap's business to benefit his own development project, Wadsworth Estates. **RYAN** never disclosed his business relationship with Dunlap to the Board, auditors, or examiners. **BURNELL** was aware of this business relationship and also never disclosed it to the Board, auditors, or examiners.

This case is being investigated by the Federal Bureau of Investigation, the Federal Deposit Insurance Corporation, Office of Inspector General.

Here, we have a more obvious illustration of the operation of the Fraud Function. These bankers, who are all insiders, **DESIRE** (i.e. millions of dollars in compensation from the bank and from borrowers) outweighed their **FEAR** (i.e. we will just keep evergreening these bad loans so no one will ever catch us) that led to a first **ACT** sometime in the past; my guess would be somewhere around 2009 related to the Great Recession. When they were not caught the first time the **FEAR** lessened, but the **DESIRE** remained and may have even grown, so they acted again and again until the enormity of their **ACT**s destroyed the bank. In terms of costs, the bank is gone, taken over by regulators, so the cost was something approaching everything every stakeholder had at risk with the bank. This was no small bank. In 1978, I worked in this bank's headquarters building in New Orleans. It was at the heart of what was then a thriving central business district with headquarters for large companies in the mining, transportation, and hospitality industries. First NBC was one of the top three banks in the city and was considered the business bank.

Department of Justice
US Attorney's Office

Southern District of New York

FOR IMMEDIATE RELEASE
Friday, June 26, 2020

Acting US Attorney Announces Extradition of Belgian Man Charged in $8 Million Aircraft Part Fraud Scheme

Audrey Strauss, the Acting US Attorney for the Southern District of New York, announced that STEFAN GILLIER, aka "Stephan Gillier," aka "Stefan R.R. Gillier," aka "Roland Gillier," aka "Roland Van Gorp," a Belgian citizen, was extradited today from Italy to the United States. GILLIER was arrested on May 26, 2019, for engaging in a scheme in which he and a co-conspirator fraudulently obtained millions of dollars' worth of aircraft parts through two aircraft part dealerships that they operated, RTF International, Inc. ("RTF") and UN Air Service, Inc. ("UAS"). GILLIER is expected be presented this afternoon in Manhattan federal court before Chief US Magistrate Judge Gabriel W. Gorenstein. GILLIER's case is assigned to US District Judge Richard M. Berman.

Acting US Attorney Audrey Strauss said: "As alleged, from 2004 until 2010, Stefan Gillier conspired to defraud manufacturers and distributors of aircraft parts out of millions of dollars' worth of aircraft parts. Gillier and his co-conspirator allegedly effectuated the scheme through fraudulent companies, phony references, stop orders on checks after they had received valuable parts, lucrative resales, and transferring criminal proceeds from corporate bank accounts to personal bank accounts once a victim company got wise to the fraud. Thanks to our partner agencies here and abroad, Gillier now faces justice in an American court."

According to the allegations in the Complaint and in the Indictment unsealed today: [1]

GILLIER and his co-conspirator ("CC-1") were co-presidents of RTF, a Delaware corporation that was registered to do business in New York, which dealt in aircraft parts. [2] GILLIER ran the day-to-day business activities of RTF and was a signatory on RTF's bank accounts. RTF began obtaining aircraft parts from Honeywell International, Inc. ("Honeywell") in June 2004. Starting in 2005, RTF began increasing the number of parts it ordered from Honeywell, paying for them by check. RTF paid with checks written for amounts well above the cost of the parts, which created an apparent credit balance in RTF's favor. RTF wrote approximately $16.6 million worth of checks to Honeywell, but stopped payment on approximately $15.8 million worth of them. As a result, RTF was able to obtain approximately $8 million worth of aircraft parts without paying for them, and RTF turned a profit when reselling those fraudulently obtained parts to customers for less than the price that Honeywell had charged RTF.

To execute the scheme, GILLIER signed checks to Honeywell on behalf of RTF but repeatedly caused stop payment orders to be placed after Honeywell shipped the parts to RTF. When questioned by Honeywell's employees about these stop payment orders, GILLIER, using an alias, falsely represented that the stop payment orders were the result of a misunderstanding with the bank and that he would check with RTF's finance department. In fact, as GILLIER knew, he had issued the stop payment orders, and RTF did not have a finance department. In June 2006, when Honeywell began seeking civil relief against RTF, GILLIER caused various large transfers of fraud proceeds into other bank accounts – accounts that, by way of example, belonged either to GILLIER, his relative, or CC-1's relatives.

After Honeywell discovered that it was being victimized by RTF, GILLIER and CC-1 continued their fraud scheme through a new corporate entity, UAS. (Despite its name, "UN Air Service, Inc." had no relation to the United Nations.) CC-1 was the president and owner of UAS, a Delaware corporation that dealt in aircraft parts, which CC-1 ran out of an apartment in Manhattan. GILLIER helped CC-1 obtain the Manhattan apartment that was used to continue the fraud scheme by providing a reference for CC-1 (using an alias) and by paying CC-1's initial rental fees. In 2006, UAS began obtaining aircraft parts from Pratt & Whitney Component Solutions, Inc. ("Pratt & Whitney"). Like RTF, UAS began stopping payment on checks it had written to Pratt & Whitney for the aircraft parts; like RTF, UAS sold those aircraft parts to third parties for less than the price that Pratt & Whitney had charged UAS.

GILLIER, 47, a citizen of Belgium, is charged with eight counts: (1) one count of conspiracy to commit mail fraud, wire fraud, interstate transportation of stolen property, and money laundering, which carries a maximum potential penalty of five years in prison; (2) one count of mail fraud, which carries a maximum potential penalty of 20 years in prison; (3) one count of wire fraud, which carries a maximum potential penalty of 20 years in prison; (4) one count of interstate transportation of stolen property, which carries a maximum potential penalty of 10 years in prison; and (5) and four counts of money laundering, each of which carries a maximum potential penalty of 10 years in prison.

---

[1] As the introductory phrase signifies, the entirety of the text of the Complaint and Indictment, and the descriptions of them set forth below, constitute only allegations, and every fact described should be treated as an allegation. The defendant is presumed innocent unless and until proven guilty.

[2] CC-1 died in March 2010, a few weeks after being arrested in this case and released on bail.

So, here we have outsiders (i.e. customers) defrauding Honeywell in a relatively simple fraud scheme. Basically, these fraudsters ordered aircraft parts from Honeywell, paid by check and then stopped payment on the checks. This is a different take on the old check kiting scheme; in this case, instead of writing and depositing multiple unfunded checks to a bank, they are writing them to a vendor. From what we can see, **DESIRE** (i.e. millions of dollars in aircraft parts at no cost) outweighed their **FEAR** (i.e. we will just keep sending and stopping payment on checks so no one will ever catch us) that led to a first **ACT** sometime in the past. When they were not caught the first time the **FEAR** lessened, but the **DESIRE** remained and may have even grown, so they acted again and again until Honeywell finally caught on to what was happening. I included this example to illustrate how outsiders normally cause less harm than insiders; here, Honeywell lost $8 million USD and probably had some additional professional fees, but that's probably about it. This sort of crime would likely not have resulted in any harm to Honeywell's brand, stakeholder trust, market capitalization, etc.

INVESTIGATOR NOTES

Notice that they wrote and stopped payment on $15.8 million USD, however, when the music stopped Honeywell was out $8 million USD. What this means is that they were sending replacement checks to Honeywell, to continue to conceal the scheme, on which they then stopped payment. We'll cover this in Chapter 2, but I want you to think about what sort of control you could have deigned to detect and stop this fraud.

Department of Justice
U.S. Attorney's Office

Central District of California

FOR IMMEDIATE RELEASE
Thursday, July 16, 2020

West L.A. Man Charged with Fraudulently Obtaining about $9 Million in COVID-Relief Loans, Some of Which He Gambled Away in Las Vegas

LOS ANGELES – A resident of the Beverly Grove neighborhood of Los Angeles was ordered held without bond this afternoon after being arrested on federal charges alleging he fraudulently obtained millions of dollars in Paycheck Protection Program (PPP) loans, some of which he used on gambling excursions to Las Vegas and transferred to his stock trading accounts.

Andrew Marnell, 40, was arrested this morning by federal authorities. Marnell made his initial court appearance this afternoon in United States District Court in Los Angeles, where he was ordered detained pending a hearing on Tuesday.

A criminal complaint unsealed in court this afternoon charges Marnell with one count of bank fraud and alleges he obtained more than $8 million in PPP loans through applications to insured financial institutions, and others, on behalf of different companies. During today's court hearing, prosecutors said they now believe Marnell received approximately $9 million in fraudulent loans – a number that could rise as the investigation continues.

The affidavit in support of the complaint alleges that Marnell submitted fraudulent loan applications that made numerous false and misleading statements about the companies' business operations and payroll expenses. The affidavit also alleges that Marnell, often using aliases, submitted fake and altered documents, including bogus federal tax filings and employee payroll records.

The complaint further alleges that Marnell then transferred millions of dollars from the fraudulently obtained loan proceeds to his brokerage accounts to make risky stock market bets. The affidavit also outlines how Marnell spent hundreds of thousands of dollars in fraudulently obtained loan proceeds at the Bellagio Hotel & Casino and other gambling establishments as recently as last weekend.

The Coronavirus Aid, Relief, and Economic Security (CARES) Act was designed to provide emergency financial assistance to millions of Americans who are suffering the economic effects resulting from the COVID-19 pandemic. One source of relief provided by the CARES Act is the authorization of up to $349 billion in forgivable loans to small businesses for job retention and certain other expenses through the PPP. In April, Congress authorized more than $300 billion in additional PPP funding.

So, here we have another outsider (i.e. borrower) defrauding a bank and the US Government in a bank fraud scheme. From what we can see, **DESIRE** (i.e. appears to be a gambling addict) outweighed their **FEAR** (i.e. if I can just win enough money betting in Vegas and on risky stocks I can pay it back before they catch me) that led to a first **ACT**. If he had not been caught the first time the **FEAR** would have lessened, but the **DESIRE** would have remained and surely would have grown as it always does with gambling addicts. I included this example to illustrate how outsiders normally cause less harm than insiders; here, the bank and the US Government lost $9 million USD and the bank probably had some additional professional fees, but that's about it. This sort of crime would likely not have resulted in any harm to the bank's brand, stakeholder trust, market capitalization, etc.

For one final illustration, let's look at a case I worked on. I conducted an audit committee investigation for a large publicly traded company. This was one of the largest companies in the country, operating in more than 10 states. Our investigation identified mortgage origination fraud as well as accounting and financial reporting fraud.

The mortgage origination fraud was carried out by executives in the company's mortgage lending subsidiary. A review of the mortgage loan files revealed two different types of fraud. One was the falsification of key borrower loan underwriting information: employment income, available assets, and employment status. The other was creating phony charitable grants to borrowers to fund down payments. Basically, the executives in the company would make a payment to a down payment assistance charity which would then make that money available to the borrower at closing. Of course, the company would recover the money it paid to the charity at the closing; everybody's happy, right? Well, sadly, no. You see the home buyers in those scenarios could not afford to make the mortgage payments. Also, having no economic stake in the home; the down payment having been provided by the company, the buyer would simply allow the mortgage to go into foreclosure and walk away from the home. This created startling levels of foreclosures and repossessed, empty homes in neighborhoods built by this company. So much so that a local newspaper in a city that incorporated several of the company's neighborhoods ran a series of articles about the unusually high rates of foreclosure in these neighborhoods. The FBI became interested in this story and opened an investigation. Then the local US Attorney got involved; a Grand Jury subpoena to the company followed. That's when I got involved; the company's audit committee hired its own counsel to investigate, as authorized by Sarbanes-Oxley, who in turn retained my firm to actually conduct the investigation.

The second shoe, accounting and financial reporting fraud, fell during counsel's review of the company's email. They discovered curiously detailed instructions from the company's chief accounting officer to its field controllers. Counsel forwarded examples of the emails to me while I was on a golf course in Scottsdale, AZ, enjoying the additional distance of my drives owing to the lower air density. They were quite insistent that I give them my thoughts immediately, so, sadly, I had to leave that excellent round of golf, duty first. After reviewing the emails, I called counsel and told them it looked like earnings management to me. However, I cautioned them that I was likely incorrect because no one in the age of Sarbanes-Oxley would be stupid enough to put this kind of damning evidence into emails. I also predicted Starbucks would go out of business because it was opening too many stores, so much for my ability to make predictions. Lucky I didn't pick fortune telling as a career.

The lawyers arranged for us to interview the chief accounting officer. The chief accounting officer apparently believed we would be interviewing him about mortgage fraud and prepared for those questions. When we showed him the emails he was caught off guard and answered our questions truthfully. He said that he was giving the field controllers directions on how to adjust profits to the correct amounts. We asked him how he was able to determine the correct amounts from HQ? He said that he used two methods to determine the correct profit per house amounts. The chief accounting officer said that his experience gave him the knowledge to determine how much profit the company should earn on each house. He said, based on this knowledge, he would apply margin-oriented accounting and economic profit to arrive at the amount of profit that should have been earned on each home sale in each of the company's neighborhood developments. Once having made those determinations, he would simply send emails to instruct each field controller to arrive at the profit amount he had determined for each house in each of their neighborhood developments. We asked him to explain how those methods squared with profits determined in accordance with Generally Accepted Accounting Principles (GAAP), the accounting principles required by the securities statutes. At that point, he became agitated, got up, and stormed out of the room. He never repeated the words "margin oriented accounting" or "economic profit" again to us or anyone else we ever learned about. What followed represents one of the dangers in investigating fraud and white-collar crime. Even though, following that interview, we believed we knew exactly what had happened; it took us three years to prove it. Following the interview, the chief accounting officer, a much-feared bully known for publicly dressing down his subordinates, circled the wagons and ordered his personnel not to cooperate with the investigation. This coupled with the fact that the company's operations, computerized management, and accounting systems were extremely complex, made the investigation difficult but not impossible.

When the chief accounting officer used the term "economic profits" in our interview, I assumed he was referring to the classical definition of profits that economists use. Wrong again; I am reminded that "assume" can be a useful anagram to keep in mind in my business. I learned, about six months into the investigation that economic profit was a defined term in the profit-sharing plan for the company's field employees. What the chief accounting officer was actually saying in the interview, although we did not realize it for some time, was that he used what he called margin-oriented accounting to calculate what he believed to be an ideal profit on each house sold. The chief accounting officer's "margin-oriented profit" amount was often smaller than the "economic profit" amount that would otherwise have been used in calculating bonuses for field employees and, as a result, created a constant tension between him and the field controllers. The various reserves the chief accounting officer was instructing the field controllers to use to adjust to his margin-oriented accounting profit were creating enormous amounts of what Arthur Leavitt, former chairman of the SEC, referred to in his famous "Numbers Game" speech as "Cookie Jar Reserves." The chief accounting officer later unwound these to prop up the company's earnings during a downturn.

Interestingly, the company's Big Four audit partner knew all about at least one of the schemes. The company established reserves against land inventory under development to provide for the cost of infrastructure requirements like electrical tie-ins, sewage lines, and permitting authority requirements. Most homebuilders try to keep land inventory at a minimum on their balance sheets because the rate at which they metabolize land inventory through development and sales is a key metric followed closely by analysts who specialize in the homebuilding industry.

At his criminal trial, the chief accounting officer's lawyer offered a defense that could be summed up as, "My client committed fraud to protect investors from the actual operating results of this company." The chief accounting officer was convicted of violating the federal securities laws and sentenced to over 15 years in federal prison. Incidentally, in the federal system, there is no parole, so inmates generally serve all or most of the sentence they receive.

The losses to legitimate owners of the company's homes were enormous. Imagine that you are a legitimate buyer of a home in a brand-new subdivision. You pay the same price as the other buyers; there have not been any resales yet to provide information about the actual value of the homes. Then, all of a sudden, your neighbors' homes begin to be foreclosed upon by the lenders and resold at much lower prices. Your new dream home has become a nightmare. How would it make you feel about the homebuilder when the truth comes out? When the accounting and financial reporting fraud was disclosed in a press release, investors lost billions of dollars. The company's market capitalization dropped by approximately $3 billion USD. Then there was the loss in brand value and reputation that were incalculable. The company, at one point, was advised by counsel to begin a plan of restructuring with a view to possible bankruptcy. The investigation cost in excess of $100 million USD. Then there was the increased audit fees for the Big 4 accounting firm; the audit partner was quietly let go when the litigation finally subsided.

In 2016, Wells Fargo retail banking opened more than a million unauthorized accounts and signed customers up for untold numbers of unnecessary products and services. The direct cost to Wells Fargo was $185 million USD, the amount of the Consumer Financial Protection Bureau fine. But, what about the other costs? Investors lost a bundle; following the disclosure, Wells Fargo's market capitalization dropped by over $20 billion USD. Its stock price continued to falter even as the rest of the market climbed to historic highs. Wells Fargo's CEO and head of retail banking were forced out, forfeiting tens of millions of dollars in compensation as they exited. What about the cost to Wells Fargo's reputation? Wells Fargo, founded in the nineteenth century and regarded as the embodiment of historic trust and stability, was suddenly recast as a nest of corruption. The board's internal investigation revealed poor leadership, a highly decentralized structure, and a corporate culture rife with perverse incentives. Employees were constantly pressured to achieve overly aggressive sales targets that were linked to generous bonuses and promotions.

INVESTIGATOR NOTES

Every organization has to be extremely careful in creating performance incentives; human nature is such that you may not avoid the results you punish, but you will always receive the results you reward. When you are making a preliminary evaluation of a unit you are investigating, take a look at the "superstars" in the unit. Make sure their incredible results are real.

SECTION III: THE IMPACT OF CRIME ON YOUR ORGANIZATION

In this section, we are going to inventory and drill down on all of the ways crime impacts your organization. This will help us to better plan and defend the strategies and actions we will lay out in Chapter 2. To paraphrase W. Edwards Deming, you will never get anyone to agree to pay the cost to be crime free until you can show them the true cost of crime.

Let's begin with a list of these impacts which become costs to organizations that fall victim to fraud and white-collar crime:

1. Direct Cost = Assets Lost + Encumbrances Incurred – Mitigation
2. Brand Value = Loss in Intrinsic Value of the Organization's Brand

3. Market Cap = Loss in the Value of Shares of the Company's Stock
4. Securities Litigation = Cost of Defending and Settling Shareholder Lawsuits
5. Internal Investigation = Cost of Professionals + Internal Resources to Conduct Internal Investigation
6. Personnel = Increased Recruiting, Training, and Monitoring Costs
7. Other Stakeholder = Increased Cost of Doing Business
8. Cost of Capital = Additional Cost of Raising Capital
9. Legal = Costs of Additional Regulatory or Legal Structures

It really adds up.

INVESTIGATOR NOTES

Human beings have a curious propensity to block out information that they perceive to be negative or which conflicts with their preferred beliefs. This propensity often causes people to accept greater levels of actual risk of harm than they realize because they have ignored evidence that they found unpleasant or inconvenient. As an example, are you more comfortable driving or flying? You are not alone; many people in the United States have a fear of flying. However, according to the US Department of Transportation, 83% of the US adult population regularly drives an automobile. US Census data puts the odds of dying in a plane crash at 1 in 205,552 while the odds of dying in an automobile crash are 1 in 102. So, even though you are 2,000 times more likely to die in an automobile crash than in an airplane crash, you happily hop in a car to make that four-hour drive to the plant in east Walla, Walla to avoid having to get on the scary airplane. We all do it; it's part of being human. The key is to recognize our instinctive reactions for what they are and to take a step back to evaluate the evidence before making decisions.

The FBI has a sobering message to all of us, about fraud and white-collar crime:

> "These are not victimless crimes. A single scam can destroy a company, devastate families by wiping out their life savings, or cost investors billions of dollars (or even all three). Today's fraud schemes are more sophisticated than ever, and the FBI is dedicated to using its skills to track down the culprits and stop scams before they start."[10]

We have touched on the impact of fraud and white-collar crime on organizations above. Now let's drill down on each of those to set the stage for Chapter 2. Let's begin with the largest companies in the world and work our way down. The reason is that fraud and white-collar crime tends to impact large organizations in many more different ways than smaller companies.

I am going to go over actual cases with you in order to stay away from the theoretical and keep it real. Truth is always stranger and more fun than fiction in any case.

UNITED STATES OF AMERICA
Before the
SECURITIES AND EXCHANGE COMMISSION

SECURITIES ACT OF 1933
Release No. 10701/September 26, 2019

SECURITIES EXCHANGE ACT OF 1934
Release No. 87129/September 26, 2019

ACCOUNTING AND AUDITING ENFORCEMENT
Release No. 4094/September 26, 2019

ADMINISTRATIVE PROCEEDING
File No. 3-19532

In the Matter of **PPG Industries, Inc.** **Respondent.**	**ORDER INSTITUTING CEASE-AND-DESIST PROCEEDINGS PURSUANT TO SECTION 8A OF THE SECURITIES ACT OF 1933 AND SECTION 21C OF THE SECURITIES EXCHANGE ACT OF 1934, MAKING FINDINGS, AND IMPOSING A CEASE-AND-DESIST ORDER**

I.

The Securities and Exchange Commission ("Commission") deems it appropriate that cease-and-desist proceedings be, and hereby are, instituted pursuant to Section 8A of the Securities Act of 1933 ("Securities Act") and Section 21C of the Securities Exchange Act of 1934 ("Exchange Act"), against PPG Industries, Inc. ("PPG" or "Respondent").

SUMMARY

1. PPG manufactures paint and other specialty industrial, automotive and architectural coating materials. From December 2016 through April 2018 (the "relevant period"), PPG maintained materially inaccurate books and records and insufficient internal accounting controls. The misstatements resulted from the conduct of a PPG senior accounting officer ("Officer A") and employees within PPG's finance division who manipulated accounting entries. The misstatements were designed to enable PPG to meet, or come closer to meeting, analysts' consensus earnings estimates.

2. Officer A made improper accounting determinations and directed subordinate personnel to delay recording or not to record certain expense accruals and to misclassify certain income as from continuing operations, in contravention of generally accepted accounting principles ("GAAP"). As a result, PPG's income from continuing operations in its published financial results was inflated for the years ended December 31, 2016 and December 31, 2017, and for certain quarters within that period. PPG included its misleading financial results in press releases and its filings with the Commission. Because of similar accounting misconduct, PPG's books and records contained intentional inaccuracies during the closing period for the first quarter of 2018; these inaccuracies were later corrected in PPG's Form 10-Q for that quarter.

3. PPG restated its financial statements for the relevant period on June 28, 2018 (the "Restatement"). The Restatement disclosed 14 instances of accounting misconduct during the relevant period, reduced PPG's previously reported GAAP pretax income from continuing operations by a cumulative $6 million USD for 2016 and 2017, and identified a material weakness in PPG's internal control over financial reporting.

4. Based on the foregoing and the conduct described below, PPG violated Section 17(a) of the Securities Act and Sections 10(b), 13(a), 13(b)(2)(A), and 13(b)(2)(B) of the Exchange Act and Rules 10b-5, 12b-20, 13a-1, 13a-11, and 13a-13 thereunder.

INVESTIGATOR NOTES

Notice that PPG, among other things, violated Rule 10b-5. Rule 10b-5 is what people are referring to when they say that securities fraud occurred with respect to a company whose securities are offered for sale and/or traded on a US Stock Exchange. Rule 10b-5 makes it unlawful for any person in connection with the offer or sale of securities to omit or misstate a material fact or to state a fact in a context that renders it misleading. The point I want you to take away from this is related to the difference in the threshold for criminal liability between our definition of crime, discussed earlier, and the threshold under Rule 10b-5. Our definition of crime, discussed earlier, requires mens rea or intent to commit a crime. Rule 10b-5 only requires intent to omit or misstate a fact or to present the fact in a misleading context. It does not require that a person do that in order to, for instance, steal from investors.

There are a number of interesting aspects to the PPG case. First, how the fraud was detected; following an announcement to lay off approximately 1,100 employees, a whistleblower filed a complaint in the company's internal reporting system. This whistleblower complaint made its way to PPG's audit committee that hired counsel and forensic accountants to conduct an internal investigation.

INVESTIGATOR NOTES

The fact is that, even with all of the advances in technology, most frauds are still discovered by accident. These detections result from a whistleblower complaint following an adverse HR incident. So, pay attention to those whistleblower hotlines and other reporting channels, especially following a layoff or similar disruptive HR event.

The second is the foolish way in which the PPG Controller blatantly makes entries and causes entries to be made to PPG's books and records to create the false impression that PPG met analyst's expectations. This is exactly the chicanery that SEC Chairman Leavitt was referring to in his "Numbers Game" speech. The SEC is so sensitized to this type of misconduct that you might just as well send in a plea agreement proffer when you decide to engage in it.

The third is that PPG's auditors missed these blatant violations entirely. How can this be? Were the auditor's crooked or stupid? It has to be one or the other. In two of my more complex investigations, the auditors were completely aware of the accounting misdeeds. In one case, the auditors rationalized turning a blind eye. During the audit, they discovered that their audit client, a manufacturing company, was computing cost of goods sold in a manner that was not in accordance with GAAP. This was a material error that concealed the company's dramatic obsolescence problem. However, they believed, incorrectly, that all users of the financial statements were insiders. So, they wrote a memo, to the audit file, taking note of the accounting error which, they concluded, resulted in the financial statements not being prepared in accordance with GAAP. But, they issued a clean opinion anyway because they thought all of the users of the financial statements knew about the error. The only problem was that those financial statements, prefaced by their clean opinion, were circulated to a host of naive investors in a pre-IPO capital raise. The investors lost millions of dollars as a result. In the other matter, the Big 4 audit partner stated that he was aware of the accounting irregularity, but because he believed "everybody else" in the industry was engaging in the same improper accounting practices, he turned a blind eye to it. Incidentally, the irregularity had the effect of artificially suppressing an asset account that analysts, specializing in this industry, pay a great deal of attention to because its metabolization is a great indicator of the company's quality of earnings. His firm paid a great deal of money for his vision problems. He is now an audit partner at a local CPA firm you have never heard of.

Here, we have the three horsemen of the apocalypse: Cultures that reward success at any cost. No internal control to detect the conduct. No auditor to uncover and report the conduct. What truer observation could you make than you get what you inspect, not what you expect, but more about that in Chapter 2.

Following the revelation, PPG's stock price dropped more than $20 USD/share; a decrease of more than 17%. That meant a loss of market capitalization of approximately $4.25 billion USD. Add to that the impact on the perception of the brand of a venerable company that came into existence in 1883 as the first successful US manufacturer of plate glass. Next comes the securities class-action litigation brought by shareholders. Also, what is the cost of the impact on employee morale and attitude toward compliance with company ethics and other policies? Of course, the fees of audit committee investigation professionals (i.e. lawyers and forensic accountants) were likely in the tens of millions of USD. There is also the auditors' 10A investigation and report. Then there is the cost of changes to internal control and accounting, employee training, etc.

All together it's a big number, much larger than the cost of preventing these kinds of shenanigans.

UNITED STATES OF AMERICA
Before the
SECURITIES AND EXCHANGE COMMISSION

SECURITIES ACT of 1933
Release No. 10684/September 16, 2019

SECURITIES EXCHANGE ACT OF 1934
Release No. 86971/September 16, 2019

ACCOUNTING AND AUDITING ENFORCEMENT
Release No. 4076/September 16, 2019

ADMINISTRATIVE PROCEEDING
File No. 3-19454

In the Matter of	**ORDER INSTITUTING CEASE-AND-DESIST PROCEEDINGS PURSUANT TO SECTION 8A OF THE SECURITIES ACT OF 1933 AND SECTION 21C OF THE SECURITIES EXCHANGE ACT OF 1934, MAKING FINDINGS AND IMPOSING A CEASE-AND-DESIST-ORDER**
Marvell Technology Group, Ltd.,	
Respondent.	

I.

The Securities and Exchange Commission ("Commission") deems it appropriate that cease- and-desist proceedings be, and hereby are, instituted pursuant to Section 8A of the Securities Act of

1933 ("Securities Act") and Section 21C of the Securities Exchange Act of 1934 ("Exchange Act") against Marvell Technology Group, Ltd. ("Marvell" or "Respondent").

A. Introduction

1. This matter concerns an undisclosed revenue management scheme by Marvell Technology Group. Faced with a substantial decline in customer demand in its core product markets, and concerned about the adverse consequences that would result from missing its public guidance, Marvell orchestrated a plan to accelerate, or pull-in, sales that had originally been scheduled for future quarters to the current quarter in order to close the gap between actual and forecasted revenue, meet publicly issued guidance, and mask declining sales. As a result, Marvell made materially misleading public statements and omitted to disclose certain facts regarding its financial results for the fourth quarter of fiscal year 2015 (Q4 FY2015) and first quarter of fiscal year 2016 (Q1 FY2016). In particular, Marvell made positive statements regarding its Q4 FY2015 results and met its revised public revenue guidance in Q1 FY2016 without disclosing the significant impact on revenues from its use of pull-ins. Marvell also failed to disclose that the pull- ins reduced future sales, thereby making it exceedingly difficult for Marvell to meet its revenue guidance in future quarters, particularly in a declining market.

2. From approximately January 2015 through July 2015 (the "Relevant Period"), Marvell's senior management directed the effort to pull-in sales for the purpose of meeting public revenue guidance. Marvell's senior management placed significant pressure on its sales employees to push customers to agree to accept products earlier than scheduled, and it closely tracked the gap between actual and forecasted revenue, and the use of pull-ins to bridge that gap.

    Marvell used the pull-ins despite internal concerns that the pull-ins were masking declining market conditions and also obfuscating the company's deteriorating financial results, thereby misleading investors. Senior management, however, refused to abandon its use of pull-ins, and those who raised concerns were ignored. Marvell's senior management also failed to inform the company's Board of Directors or its independent auditor of its pull-in scheme.

3. As a result of such conduct, Marvell violated Sections 17(a)(2) and 17(a)(3) of the Securities Act and Section 13(a) of the Exchange Act and Rules 13a-1, 13a-13, and 12b-20 thereunder.

INVESTIGATOR NOTES

Ah, a crime by any other name… The practice the SEC refers to as "pull-in sales" is also sometimes referred to as channel stuffing or trade loading. It's all the same practice. The seller either offers incentives or uses leverage to get buyers to purchase goods in advance of when they are needed and in quantities in excess of what can be metabolized through normal operations. The result is that one or two quarters look great and then sales drop through the floor. It occurs more often than most people realize. I have seen it occur most in non-US sales channels where, I imagine, the companies believe the SEC is less likely to look. I have worked on these investigations for the SEC and have been quite amazed that household name companies engage in these practices.

Well, as stated in an investigator note above, Marvell's senior management team engaged in some pretty reckless magical rationalization along with some pretty nasty conduct and cost Marvell's stakeholders a bundle. For starters, there was a 22% drop in Marvell's stock price which resulted in a $5.5 billion USD loss in market capitalization. Then there's the impact on Marvell's brand; if Marvell's senior executives are willing to go to these lengths to mislead investors, what about customers, vendors, governments, etc.? Next comes the securities class-action litigation brought by shareholders. Then there was the cost of the internal investigation. There was also a significant increase in audit fees to cover the required 10A work.

Then we have the big one (see Figures 1.4–1.10).

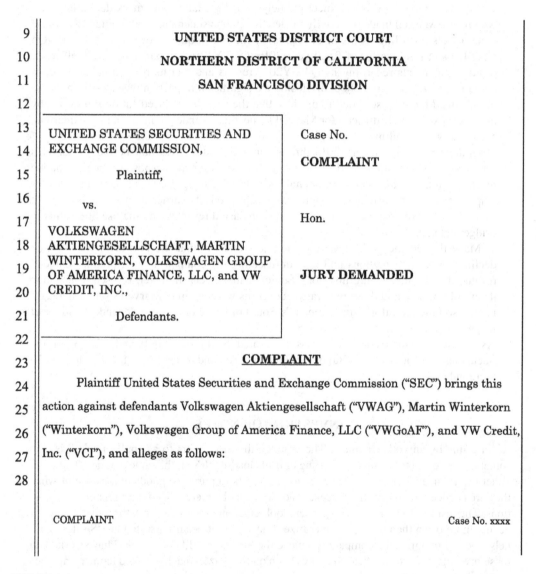

FIGURE 1.4

I.
SUMMARY

1.   From at least 2007 through September 2015, VW perpetrated a massive fraud.[1] VW, including its CEO Martin Winterkorn and numerous other senior officials, repeatedly lied to and misled United States investors, consumers, and regulators as part of an illegal scheme to sell its purportedly "clean diesel" cars and billions of dollars of corporate bonds and other securities in the United States. VW marketed these bonds and other securities without disclosing that its "clean diesel" cars used defeat devices to conceal substantial emissions problems.

2.   Winterkorn and other VW executives were made aware of the defeat device as early as November 2007, during a meeting with VW engineers, to discuss the emissions problems with VW's "clean diesel" vehicles. Although at least one meeting participant warned that putting the existing vehicles on the road in the U.S. would damage VW's reputation if the vehicles' high emissions were later discovered, those concerns were ignored.

3.   VW subsequently sold in the U.S. hundreds of thousands of "clean diesel" vehicles containing the defeat device. Meanwhile, it raised billions of dollars from U.S. investors to fund its expanding sales of "clean diesel" cars across the globe. Years later, when U.S. authorities began investigating emissions problems with VW vehicles, the company misled government investigators, concocted a sham software fix, and destroyed thousands of incriminating documents and other evidence.

4.   Eventually, U.S. regulators exposed the long-running fraud and ensuing cover-up, and VW was forced to admit its criminal behavior. On March 10, 2017, VW pled guilty in a United States District Court to conspiracy to commit fraud, obstruction of justice, and importing goods by false statements.

---

[1] Unless otherwise indicated, "VW" refers to VWAG including its subsidiaries and affiliated companies.

Complaint   2   Case No. XXXXXX

FIGURE 1.5

1   5.   Although the seeds of VW's "clean diesel" fraud were sown in 2005, the

2   scheme firmly took root in early 2007. That is when defendant Martin Winterkorn was

3   named CEO and Chairman of VWAG's Board of Management. Winterkorn, who had spent

4   decades climbing the corporate ladder at VW, announced a bold and aggressive plan to

5   make VW the biggest, most profitable, and most environmentally-friendly car company in

6   the world by 2018.

7   6.   The success of Winterkorn's plan—dubbed "Strategy 2018"—depended in

8   large part on VW's ability to develop, market, and sell its diesel vehicles, particularly in

9   the United States. Known historically for being more powerful and fuel efficient than their

10 gasoline counterparts, diesel engines emitted far more harmful pollutants into the

11 environment. Diesel vehicles, therefore, had difficulty complying with the strict vehicle

12 emissions laws in the United States and were unpopular with American consumers.

13   7.   But VW claimed to have developed a revolutionary solution to this problem—

14 the "clean diesel" engine. During Winterkorn's reign as CEO, VW unleashed a global

15 marketing campaign touting its groundbreaking "clean diesel" engines and its supposed

16 commitment to reducing toxic vehicle emissions. The successful production and sale of cars

17 with "clean diesel" engines was the cornerstone of Winterkorn's plan to dominate the

18 world auto industry.

19   8.   Over the next several years, Winterkorn's plan began bearing fruit. By the

20 end of 2013, VW increased its annual sales of diesel vehicles in the United States from

21 approximately 43,000 in 2009 to over 111,000 in 2013—a more than 150% increase in 4

22 years. Globally, sales of all VW vehicles increased 54% over the same period. And by mid-

23 2015, VW reached the first milestone of Winterkorn's ambitious goal. It surpassed Toyota

24 in global sales, becoming the largest carmaker in the world.

25   9.   To finance their ambitious Strategy 2018, VW and Winterkorn needed

26 money. And they relied on the U.S. capital markets to get it. From 2010 to 2015, VW sold

27 billions of dollars of corporate bonds and asset-backed securities ("ABS") in the United

28 States. In its offering documents, VW stressed its continuing commitment to and

Complaint   3   Case No. XXXXXX

FIGURE 1.6

Case 3:19-cv-01391   Document 1   Filed 03/14/19   Page 4 of 69

1   dependence upon developing energy-efficient vehicles and the reduction of vehicle

2   emissions. VW assured bond underwriters that its cars complied with all applicable

3   emissions laws and regulations.

4   10.   But it was all a lie. VW's "clean diesel" engines were a fraud. They did not

5   exist. In fact, the engines emitted pollutants, including nitrogen oxides ("NOx")—described

6   by the U.S. Environmental Protection Agency ("EPA") as a family of poisonous, highly

7   reactive gases—into the environment at levels nearly 40-times greater than U.S.

8   emissions limits.

9   11.   To hide this fact, VW installed illegal software (called a "defeat device") in 11

10 million diesel vehicles sold worldwide, including more than 580,000 in the United States.

11 The defeat device software recognized when the car was being tested on a treadmill and

12 then reduced the car's emissions to legal levels. When the defeat device sensed the car was

13 being driven in normal road conditions, it deactivated the car's emission control system,

14 causing it to emit excessive amounts of NOx gas into the environment.

15   12.   For years, VW lied and made misleading omissions to conceal the existence of

16 a defeat device. VW lied about its cars' compliance with environmental regulations and its

17 commitment to protecting the environment. It lied to U.S. investors, who then paid

18 artificially inflated prices for VW's bonds and ABS. These investors did not know that VW

19 was lying to consumers to fool them into buying its "clean diesel" cars and lying to

20 government authorities in order to sell cars in the United States that did not comply with

21 U.S. emission standards. The entire time, Winterkorn and other senior officials at VW

22 knew the truth: VW's "clean diesel" engine was a sham.

23   13.   VW's elaborate fraud started to unravel in March 2014. During an industry

24 conference held in San Diego, researchers from West Virginia University disclosed the

25 results of a study commissioned by the International Council on Clean Transportation

26 ("ICCT Study"). Using equipment capable of testing a car's emission levels while it was

27 being driven in normal road conditions (as opposed to on a treadmill), the researchers

28

Complaint   4   Case No. XXXXXX

FIGURE 1.7

1   announced that two of the three cars they tested discharged NOx pollutants at levels

2   greatly exceeding legal limits.

3   14.   Although the ICCT researchers did not reveal the makes and models of the

4   cars tested, VW employees in attendance knew immediately the two cars that

5   dramatically failed the emissions tests were Volkswagens. It was only a matter of time

6   before U.S. regulators began asking questions and demanding answers from VW about its

7   cars' elevated NOx emissions.

8   15.   Word of the ICCT Study spread quickly throughout VW. By May 2014,

9   multiple internal memos were circulating inside VW among its most senior officials,

10 including Winterkorn, detailing the depth of the problems VW was facing:

11   (a)   VW's "clean diesel" engines were emitting deadly NOx at levels nearly
                   40-times legal limits;
12

13   (b)   there was no way to fix the problem; and

14   (c)   U.S. regulators were investigating and would look for a defeat device.

15   16.   By VW's own assessment, its potential financial liability for the fraud

16 exceeded $20 billion. VW faced a choice. It could admit its scheme or cover it up. It chose a

17 cover-up.

18   17.   Senior VW employees and engineers repeatedly told U.S. regulators they did

19 not know what was causing VW's cars to exceed U.S. emissions limits; they implemented a

20 bogus software fix they knew would not solve the emissions problems with their cars; and,

21 when discovery of the fraud became inevitable, VW employees began destroying

22 documents and ditching their cell phones.

23   18.   At the same time VW was deceiving U.S. regulators, it pressed ahead with

24 Winterkorn's strategy of conquering the world automotive industry. And it needed more

25 and more money from U.S. investors to do it. Between May 2014 and June 2015, VW

26 conducted three separate bonding offerings in the U.S., selling over $8 billion of bonds to

27 U.S. investors. It also sold over $4.9 billion of ABS in the United States in 2014 and 2015.

28

FIGURE 1.8

Case 3:19-cv-01391   Document 1   Filed 03/14/19   Page 6 of 69

19.   The U.S. capital markets, including the corporate bond market, depend on true, complete, and honest disclosures by market participants. By keeping the defeat device and the scope of VW's legal exposure on this issue hidden from U.S investors, VW was able to pay lower interest rates on these securities, thereby defrauding investors out of hundreds of millions of dollars.

20.   Eventually, VW's "clean diesel" fraud and ensuing cover-up collapsed in August 2015. That is when one of its employees confessed unexpectedly to EPA and California state regulators that VW had been using a defeat device in its "clean diesel" cars. Following its employee's unauthorized confession, VW was forced to formally admit its fraud to U.S. regulators on September 3, 2015. The EPA issued a Notice of Violation ("NOV") to VW on September 18, 2015, and announced that it would not certify any of VW's model year 2016 vehicles for sale in the United States.

21.   When notice of VW's fraud became public, the price of its bonds and ABS fell in secondary market trading. Major ratings agencies downgraded VW's bonds. VW did not conduct another bond or public ABS offering in the United States for over three years.

22.   On March 10, 2017, VWAG pled guilty in a United States District Court to three criminal felony counts arising out of its massive "clean diesel" conspiracy. VW paid the Department of Justice a $2.8 billion penalty for its crimes. It paid billions more to resolve civil claims brought by the EPA, state attorneys general, and consumers who unwittingly purchased cars with defeat devices.

23.   VW, however, has never repaid the hundreds of millions of dollars in benefit it fraudulently obtained from the sale of its corporate bonds and ABS. Had the truth been known, VW never would have gotten away with charging U.S. investors artificially inflated prices for its bonds and ABS.

24.   The SEC brings this civil enforcement action seeking permanent injunctions, disgorgement with prejudgment interest, and civil penalties against the corporate defendants, as well as permanent injunctions, civil penalties and an officer-and-director bar against Winterkorn, as a result of their violations of Section 17(a) of the Securities Act

Complaint   6   Case No. XXXXXX

FIGURE 1.9

Case 3:19-cv-01391   Document 1   Filed 03/14/19   Page 7 of 69

1 of 1933 ("Securities Act") [15 U.S.C. § 77q(a)] and Section 10(b) of the Securities Exchange

2 Act of 1934 ("Exchange Act") [15 U.S.C. § 78j(b)] and Rule 10b-5 [17 C.F.R. § 240.10b-5]

3 thereunder.

FIGURE 1.10

INVESTIGATOR NOTES

Fraudsters always believe that they can control a universe that is beyond anyone's control. First, there was the unanticipated ICCT research project. Then there was the VW employee who confessed to the regulator. My point being, in fraud investigation, patience is a virtue. The fraudster's belief in their ability to control the universe is their greatest weakness. The universe unfolds as it chooses to unfold. If you will be patient and remain open to its unfolding, the solution will literally fall into your lap every time. I cannot count the number of times that I have run into what appeared to be a brick wall just before the entire case broke open for me. Be patient; continue to watch and you will be rewarded.

Wow! Well, this fraud is in a league all its own. This is the poster child for "go big or go home". Let's see, where to start with this one? VW's CEO Winterkorn either knew or was willfully blind to an outrageous scheme to make it appear that VW's dirty diesel engines represented the next quantum leap in green transportation technology: "clean diesel" engines. In order to finance the increased production of "clean diesel" engines demanded by the car buying public, VW sold billions of dollars of bonds in the US public debt markets. The public offerings were replete with claims of the better mousetrap that "clean diesel" represented. This fraud is beyond the realm of ordinary fraud. You willfully design software to defeat an honest analysis of the emissions your engine produces to dishonestly claim that you have discovered the holy grail of "clean diesel" which creates demand in an environmentally sensitive market, which you deceive, to create tremendous demand. Then you lie to bond investors about your phony "clean diesel" engine and the demand for it to make it possible for you to sell billions of dollars of bonds to finance production of the phony "clean diesel" engines. All I can say is That is bold! VW paid the Department of Justice a $2.8 billion USD penalty for its crimes. It paid billions more to resolve civil claims brought by the EPA, state attorneys general, and consumers who unwittingly purchased cars with defeat devices. VW estimates its total financial liability for the fraud to be in excess of $20 billion USD.

EXERCISES

1. What is fraud?
2. Using the definition of fraud in this chapter, identify and write down each element in the fraud definition that was present in a case you investigated or read about.
3. What does material mean?
4. Write down two examples of material misstatements from your own investigations or ones that you have read about.
5. What does "reasonably relied upon" mean?
6. What is an affinity fraud? Provide an example of an affinity fraud.

7. In trying to understand a fraud, what is a good place to start?
8. What do criminals look like?
9. With respect to criminal capacity, what three groups exist in society?
10. Write out the Fraud Function.
11. Describe what happens to each factor when a fraud is committed but not detected?
12. What is an actus reus?
13. What is mens rea?
14. What does concurrence mean with respect to the answers to questions 12 and 13?
15. What does "mala in se" mean? Provide examples of mala in se crimes.
16. What does "mala prohibita" mean? Provide examples of mala prohibita crimes.
17. What are the components of the cost of white-collar crime occurring in your company?

CHAPTER SUMMARY/KEY TAKEAWAYS

So, here are some things to think about:

- Fraud and white-collar crime represent a significant, persistent threat.
- People commit these crimes, and therefore, all of our prevention and investigation efforts must consider the human factor first.
- Most people will commit crimes (**ACT**) when their **DESIRE** for something they cannot legally possess exceeds their **FEAR** of getting caught. This is important because when they **ACT** the first time and are not caught; **DESIRE** usually remains the same or increases while their **FEAR** drops dramatically allowing them to act again and again.
- Crime remains a big problem that is not effectively addressed by existing law enforcement resources.
- The cost of crime can be enormous; the cost of crimes committed by insiders is often much larger the cost of crimes committed by outsiders.
- In addition to the Direct Cost of crime, we must add Brand Value, Market Cap, Securities Litigation, Internal Investigation, Personnel, Other Stakeholder, Cost of Capital, and Legal.

In Chapter 2, we will use these concepts to help us to construct an effective prevention architecture.

NOTES

1. Weiss v. US, 122 F.2d 675, 681 (5th Circuit 1941)
2. Transactional Records Access Clearinghouse at Syracuse University
3. Transactional Records Access Clearinghouse at Syracuse University
4. Transactional Records Access Clearinghouse at Syracuse University
5. Transactional Records Access Clearinghouse at Syracuse University
6. Transactional Records Access Clearinghouse at Syracuse University
7. Transactional Records Access Clearinghouse at Syracuse University
8. Transactional Records Access Clearinghouse at Syracuse University
9. Fbi.gov/investigate/white-collar-crime
10. Fbi.gov/investigate/white-collar-crime

2 An Ounce of Prevention

We discussed in Chapter 1 that once a fraud or other white-collar crime is committed, it requires more than a pound of cure. So, let's talk about what steps can be taken to prevent fraud and white-collar crime in your organization.

First, there is no "one size fits all" fraud prevention program. This is because each organization is unique and faces its own unique challenges. I once worked with a franchisor whose business operated primarily through cash only kiosks at shopping malls. I noticed that franchisees were not performing criminal background checks on new employees. In my report, I took note of this rather obvious lapse and recommended that it be fixed immediately. While going over my report with my client, we came to this recommendation. The client said that he could not implement this recommendation. I asked why? He said, "Look, who do you think would be willing to work at one of our kiosks for minimum wage? Most of our franchisees' employees probably have some problem in their background, that's why they are willing to come to work for us. We just don't want to know what problems they have had?" Well, that was not what I expected to hear but it reflected that organization's unique challenge. We had to accept that risk and focus on designing systems and controls to address it. That client situation also points up the most important issue in fraud prevention; you cannot design an effective control for a risk you have not identified. So, let's begin there.

SECTION I: HOW TO IDENTIFY, CODIFY, AND PRIORITIZE RISKS

It's important here to step outside the box and look at the risks confronting your organization as a scientist would. A scientist starts with a question whose answer has the following characteristics: it must be measurable, verifiable, and falsifiable. This means that when identifying and evaluating risk, it is important to be objective and unbiased. Don't just accept the judgments of the past without critical evaluation. Everything must be on the table. Be a skeptic; be a heretic; root out the real risks and deal with them effectively.

Shortly after 9/11, I was tasked with leading a team of experts in a variety of risk areas in evaluating the risks facing a large, highly centralized corporation. The C-Suite at this company was surprised that they were not targeted in the initial attacks and were certain that they would be high on the list for any future terrorist attack. They had always maintained command and control of their worldwide operations from their headquarters building. They were comfortable with everything inside HQ; they believed the threats were all outside. Not an uncommon view at the time.

Among the things we found when we conducted an unbiased, critical evaluation of risks facing the company was that all their executive officers, intellectual property, and mission critical systems were contained in that headquarters building. If they had been correct about being the target of a terrorist attack, the entire company could have been wiped from the face of the earth in one fell swoop. Heck, a catastrophic fire would produce the same outcome. Also, in an unfortunate design oversight, the company's main exit dumped people in front of the main garage exit. So, in the case of an event requiring evacuation, pedestrians would be forced to make their way through a stream of cars coming out of the garage in order to survive. We had many other findings; I just want to make this most important point about your initial evaluation of risk: accept nothing as given. Question everything!

Start by doing research. Start by researching your own organization. Even if you have worked at your organization for many years, you may not know all you need to know in order to properly identify the risks inside your organization.[1] Really drill down on all of the business processes in your organization. Read internal documents about business operations and processes. Read public filings. Read analysts' reports. Read media articles about your organization. Don't worry about understanding everything at this stage; you are simply gathering knowledge. What you should be doing is creating a list of questions to ask business operations and process owners. Next, research competitors and other companies in your industry with operations and processes similar to yours. Read public filings. Read analysts' reports. Read media articles about those organizations. Once again, you are just gathering knowledge; make a list of questions to ask employees of those corporations. Organize your findings in a way that works best for you; each of us process information, most effectively, in different ways. I like pictures and diagrams, so I use diagram software to organize the information I gather. But that's just because that's the way my mind works. See the following flowchart (Figure 2.1). I created this flowchart to help me understand a complicated process in an investigation I was working on.

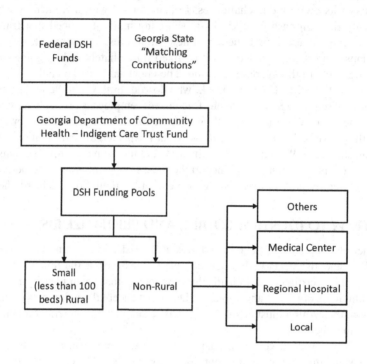

FIGURE 2.1

Of course, this was one small part of a much larger and complex process and I had to eliminate all the names and excerpts of interview notes to protect client confidentiality. So, it is not a complete illustration of my method, but I wanted to give you a glimpse of what I do. You, on the other hand, are free to use any approach that works for you: lists, narratives, recordings, or whatever. Do what works best for you.

Let's look at an actual company to walk through some of the steps I outlined above. There are a panoply of different types of risk we could identify and analyze, but we will restrict inquiry to fraud and white-collar crime risks since that is the subject of this book. We'll use Costco as an example because I am a card-carrying member of the Costco cult. In this case, because I do not work for Costco and don't have access to their internal documents, we will begin at their website. We learn some interesting things here. Costco is a membership warehouse club with hundreds of locations worldwide (Figure 2.2). Well, for a picture guy, like me, I want to create a picture of their geographic scope. Their annual report states:

> We are principally engaged in the operation of membership warehouses in the United States (U.S.) and Puerto Rico, Canada, United Kingdom (U.K.), Mexico, Japan, Korea, Australia, Spain, France, Iceland, China, and through a majority-owned subsidiary in Taiwan. Costco operated 782, 762, and 741 warehouses worldwide at September 1, 2019, September 2, 2018, and September 3, 2017, respectively.[2]

COSTCO **WHOLESALE** 785 locations as of December 31, 2019

Canada 100

United States and Puerto Rico 546

Mexico 39

UNITED STATES

COSTCO.COM

ALABAMA – 4
ALASKA – 4
ARIZONA – 18
CALIFORNIA – 128
COLORADO – 14
CONNECTICUT – 7
DELAWARE – 1
FLORIDA – 28
GEORGIA – 13
HAWAII – 7
IDAHO – 5
ILLINOIS – 20
INDIANA – 7
IOWA – 3
KANSAS – 3
KENTUCKY – 4
LOUISIANA – 3
MARYLAND – 11
MASSACHUSETTS – 6

MICHIGAN – 15
MINNESOTA – 12
MISSOURI – 6
MONTANA – 5
NEBRASKA – 3
NEVADA – 8
NEW HAMPSHIRE – 1
NEW JERSEY – 20
NEW MEXICO – 3
NEW YORK – 19
NORTH CAROLINA – 9
NORTH DAKOTA – 1
OHIO – 12
OKLAHOMA – 2
OREGON – 13
PENNSYLVANIA – 11
SOUTH CAROLINA – 6
SOUTH DAKOTA – 1
TENNESSEE – 5
TEXAS – 33
UTAH – 11
VERMONT – 1

VIRGINIA – 17
WASHINGTON – 32
WISCONSIN – 9
WASHINGTON, D.C. – 1
PUERTO RICO – 4

CANADA

COSTCO.CA

ALBERTA – 17
BRITISH COLUMBIA – 14
MANITOBA – 3
NEW BRUNSWICK – 3
NEWFOUNDLAND AND
 LABRADOR – 1
NOVA SCOTIA – 2
ONTARIO – 36
QUÉBEC – 21
SASKATCHEWAN – 3

MEXICO

COSTCO.COM.MX

AGUASCALIENTES – 1
BAJA CALIFORNIA – 4
BAJA CALIFORNIA SUR – 1
CHIHUAHUA – 2
CIUDAD DE MÉXICO – 4
COAHUILA – 1
GUANAJUATO – 3
JALISCO – 3
MÉXICO – 5
MICHOACÁN – 1

MORELOS – 1
NUEVO LEÓN – 3
PUEBLA – 1
QUERÉTARO – 1
QUINTANA ROO – 1
SAN LUIS POTOSÍ – 1
SINALOA – 1
SONORA – 1
TABASCO – 1
VERACRUZ – 2
YUCATÁN – 1

FIGURE 2.2[3]

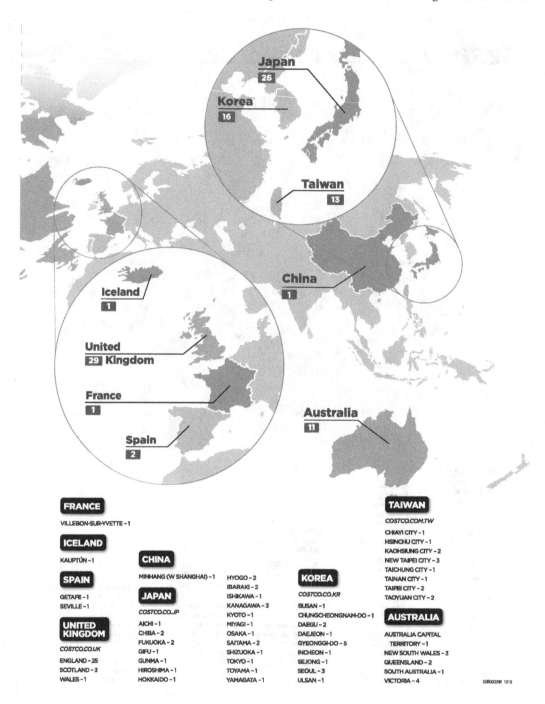

FIGURE 2.3[4]

The first thing that jumps out for me is that we are dealing with a number of different cultures and nations (Figure 2.3). So, we will need to develop questions for local business operations and process owners on business operations, processes, laws, and regulations. Those might include:

- What are your customer demographics?
- What are your employee demographics?
- Are you able to utilize the Costco supply chain for all real estate, equipment, and inventory?
- What purchases are accessed outside of the Costco supply chain?
- What is the process for those purchases?
- What is the process for selecting and approving new suppliers?
- What are the local laws and regulations that most impact your operations?

And so on.

You may have thought of other questions; that's good. There are no stupid questions at this point, except the ones you don't ask.

I was working on an internal investigation, in Costa Rica, of a company that was owned by another company in the UK. The UK parent believed that local management was engaged in a massive purchasing fraud scheme. I wanted to make a forensic copy of the email server, in Costa Rica, so that I could see what they were talking about (i.e. the modus operandi of the scheme) internally and with any outside accomplices. To be on the safe side, I asked my UK client to retain local counsel in Costa Rica to guide us in a lawful electronic data discovery and interrogation exercise. Local counsel determined that, while there were no laws or regulations preventing electronic discovery in Costa Rica, there were no less than three separate cases making their way to the Supreme Court of Costa Rica on the question of whether work email was protected by the country's constitutional guarantee of personal privacy. Had we proceeded as we would have in other jurisdictions, without asking that question, we would have, at least, ended up spending a great deal of time and money gathering evidence that would likely have been excluded at trial. But, back to the Costco example.

The annual report tells us who Costco considers its competitors (Figure 2.4):

We compete on a worldwide basis with global, national, and regional wholesalers and retailers, including supermarkets, supercenters, internet retailers, gasoline stations, hard discounters, department and specialty stores, and operators selling a single category or narrow range of merchandise. Walmart, Target, Kroger, and Amazon.com are among our significant general merchandise retail competitors. We also compete with other warehouse clubs (primarily Walmart's Sam's Club and BJ's Wholesale Club), and many of the major metropolitan areas in the U.S. and certain of our Other International locations have multiple club operations.[5]

This will give us a good list for our benchmarking research. For now, we will just capture this information and keep moving.

FIGURE 2.4

Now, let's look at who owns which business operation and process (Figure 2.5).

Information about our Executive Officers

The executive officers of Costco, their position, and ages are listed below. All executive officers have over 25 years of service with the Company.

Name	Position	Executive Officer Since	Age
W. Craig Jelinek	President and Chief Executive Officer. Mr. Jelinek has been President and Chief Executive Officer since January 2012 and a director since February 2010. He was President and Chief Operating Officer from February 2010 to December 2011. Prior to that he was Executive Vice President, Chief Operating Officer, Merchandising since 2004.	1995	67
Richard A. Galanti	Executive Vice President and Chief Financial Officer. Mr. Galanti has been a director since January 1995.	1993	63
Jim C. Klauer	Executive Vice President, Chief Operating Officer, Northern Division. Mr. Klauer was Senior Vice President, Non Foods and E-commerce merchandise, from 2013 to January 2018.	2018	57
Patrick J. Callans	Executive Vice President, Administration. Mr. Callans was Senior Vice President, Human Resources and Risk Management, from 2013 to December 2018.	2019	57
Russ D. Miller	Executive Vice President, Chief Operating Officer, Southern Division and Mexico. Mr. Miller was Senior Vice President, Western Canada Region, from 2001 to January 2018.	2018	62
Paul G. Moulton	Executive Vice President, Chief Information Officer. Mr. Moulton was Executive Vice President, Real Estate Development, from 2001 until March 2010.	2001	68
James P. Murphy	Executive Vice President, Chief Operating Officer, International. Mr. Murphy was Senior Vice President, International, from 2004 to October 2010.	2011	66
Joseph P. Portera	Executive Vice President, Chief Operating Officer, Eastern and Canadian Divisions. Mr. Portera has held these positions since 1994 and has been the Chief Diversity Officer since 2010.	1994	67
Timothy L. Rose	Executive Vice President, Ancillary Businesses, Manufacturing, and Business Centers. Mr. Rose was Senior Vice President, Merchandising, Food and Sundries and Private Label, from 1995 to December 2012.	2013	67
Ron M. Vachris	Executive Vice President, Chief Operating Officer, Merchandising. Mr. Vachris was Senior Vice President, Real Estate Development, from August 2015 to June 2016, and Senior Vice President, General Manager, Northwest Region, from 2010 to July 2015.	2016	54

FIGURE 2.5[6]

It's easier to start at the top of each business unit. Reaching out to the office of each of these business operations and process owners' offices will lead you to the designated experts to answer your questions. This list also gives us some insight into how Costco is organized from a command-and-control standpoint. At headquarters, 999 Lake Drive, Issaquah, WA, we have: Mr. Jelinek, CEO; Mr. Galanti, CFO; Mr. Klauer, COO Northern Division; Mr. Callans, EVP Risk Management; Mr. Miller, COO Southern Division and Mexico; Mr. Moulton, CIO; Mr. Murphy, COO International; Mr. Portera COO Eastern and Canada; Mr. Rose, COO Ancillary Business; Mr. Vachris, COO Merchandising (Figure 2.6).

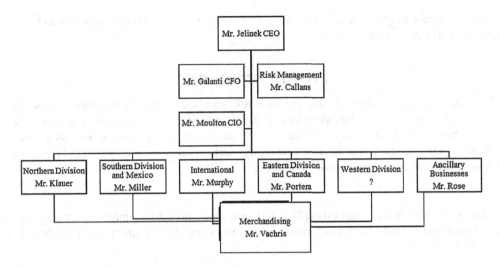

FIGURE 2.6

Now we have put four corners around our organization and know who owns which operation and process at the 30,000-foot level. From here we simply have to work our way down through each segment. But, we will not do that right away; it's time to step outside the box. Let's look at what other people are saying about us and what our competitors are up to.

Analysts say that a major risk factor for Costco is its dependence on memberships. Costco sets prices on merchandise just above cost. It relies on membership revenue to bolster profits, brand, exclusivity, and customer loyalty. In fact, when we look back at Costco's most recent annual report, we note that membership loyalty is listed as the first risk factor. We will note this issue and consider its many implications as we move through the balance of our analysis. Other risk factors noted in the press are shown in Figure 2.7.

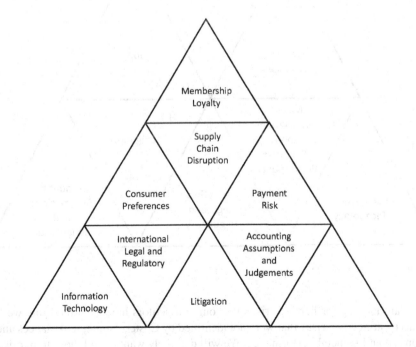

FIGURE 2.7

Here we have a good list of major categories of risk to use to frame our questions to business operations and process owners.

INVESTIGATOR NOTES

Even the best research can only unearth what is known and has been communicated. Never assume that your research has identified all the risks facing your organization. It is a good idea, when framing questions for business operations and process owners to develop a series of open-ended questions that have no previously identified answers (i.e. What am I missing? What other risks are you concerned about?).

Okay, so how about the competition? Walmart competes with Costco along two separate axes; it is a discount retailer and it has its own warehouse membership club. Walmart identifies the risks as shown in Figure 2.8.

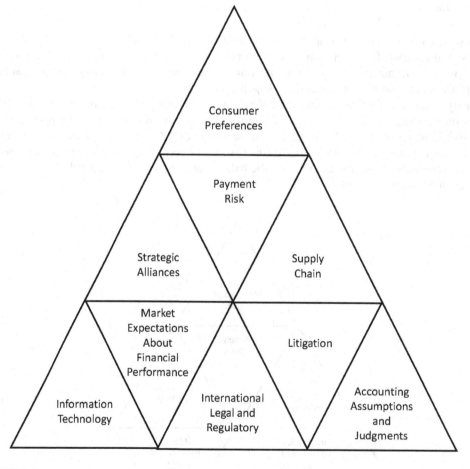

FIGURE 2.8

What we are looking for here are risks that our competitors have identified that we have not. Walmart has identified two risks that were not identified by Costco: Strategic Alliances and Market Expectations about Financial Performance. We will definitely want to add those to our list of questions for our own business operations and process owners.

Let's look at Target. Target has identified the risk factors as shown in Figure 2.9.

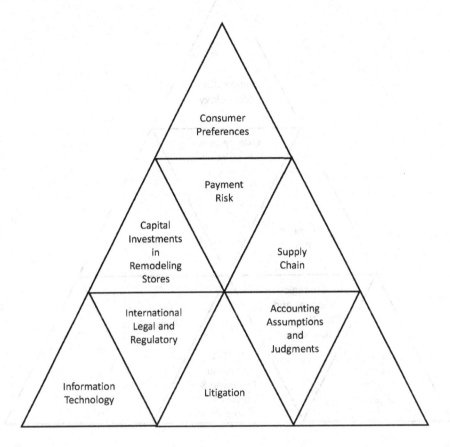

FIGURE 2.9

Target has added another risk to consider. Planning and executing store remodeling to support operations. Does Costco not have to remodel its stores?

Next up is Kroger; a little different business model, but there are definitely common elements. For one thing, Kroger only operates in the United States. However, Kroger operates out of physical stores and offers many of the same types of merchandise (focused mostly on groceries) as Costco albeit in a different format from Costco. Kroger sees its risks as shown in Figure 2.10.

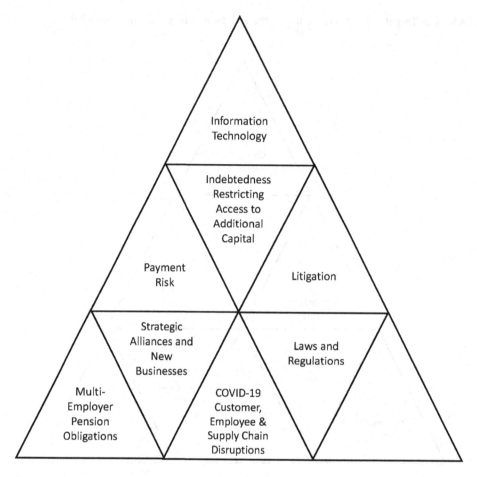

FIGURE 2.10

Kroger has an interesting way of presenting its risks. It looks like they are preparing to explain any bumps in the road in 2020 on COVID-19. Did they not have customer preference, supply chain, or labor risks prior to COVID-19? On the other hand, it's interesting that Costco did not mention COVID-19. This may be due to COVID-19 representing a huge boon to their 2020–21 sales and profits.

INVESTIGATOR NOTES

Two things often happen when widely distributed disruptive events (e.g. The Great Recession, COVID-19, etc.) occur. One is that you suddenly see a host of problems that were concealed by the high tide of revenue that preceded the event. It's like when the tide goes out and you see all the rocks that were hidden by the water. The second is that some of the people responsible for communicating about the financial condition and results of operations of entities blame every negative variance on the disruptive event, even when the disruptive event had nothing to do with the variance. I was hired by the finance committee of the board of a large museum to investigate a hedge fund they invested in following the onset of the Great Recession. The hedge fund wrote to the finance committee explaining that they had lost tens of millions of dollars due to the impact of the Great Recession on their investments. Originally, the hedge fund presented an investment strategy to the finance committee that was based on investing in a complex series of covered derivative instruments. What I found was that the hedge fund had used the museum's money to sell naked puts and calls, invest in a Ponzi scheme in Canada, and to prop up the hedge fund manager's failing tech start-up company.

Kroger mentions existing indebtedness restricting access to capital. Also, pension obligations, related accounting issues, union labor negotiations, and reputational risks (e.g. environmental, social, and governance). These definitely should be on our list of questions along with related questions about debt covenant compliance and all related accounting issues.

So, now let's take a stroll down brain-storming lane. What other risks might Costco be facing? Think through all they do and where they do it.

There is the Costco membership issue. The internal issue in operations would be whether Costco employees are somehow able to give memberships to family, friends or co-conspirators, for resale, without collecting payment. There are different membership levels, so there could also be an issue with selling a Gold Star membership for the basic membership price. Business memberships can add "affiliates"; how is that process controlled? The larger risk is with respect to Costco's accounting for membership numbers and revenue. The notes to Costco's financial statements tell us that Costco accounts for membership revenue, net of refunds, on a deferred basis (i.e. ratably over the membership period). What sorts of pressures exist, if any, to make sure those numbers steadily and predictably increase year over year? How could they be intentionally misstated in a way that might go undetected?

Next, Costco operates out of physical warehouse stores in countries around the world. How did Costco obtain permission to construct and operate those stores outside the United States? Were any payments or other emoluments given to any government official or agent, in any of those countries, to allow Costco to build and operate in those countries that would violate the Foreign Corrupt Practices Act (FCPA)? In case you are wondering what to even ask business operations and process owners, about possible FCPA violations, the SEC has put together a 130-page guide. It is available free of charge and gives you everything you need to know; just go to sec.gov and type in FCPA. They apparently didn't want any of their registrants claiming that they didn't know they were breaking the law.

INVESTIGATOR NOTES

The FCPA came into existence following the Spiro Agnew bribery scandal. Prior to being Richard Nixon's Vice President, Mr. Agnew was the Governor of Maryland. In that office he accepted hundreds of thousands of dollars in bribes from contractors; the bribes were made from off-book slush funds. Following this revelation, the SEC, IRS, and Congress became interested in whether other public companies had off-book assets, which were being used to make domestic or foreign bribes. They concluded that, while domestic bribery of public officials was limited, bribery of foreign public officials was rampant. So, Congress passed the FCPA that also modified portions of the Exchange Act to include what are called the books and records provision and the internal controls provision; this is why the FCPA is sometimes referred to as the internal audit full employment act.

Costco rightly views supply chain disruption as a critical risk. What could result in such a disruption? Well, first we would have to analyze Costco's supply chain architecture which is likely to be quite complex and difficult to find a one-size-fits-all approach to resolving. So, the best approach, in a situation like this, is to break it down into its component parts. There are the suppliers; have we performed our due diligence on them? Are they reliable, sustainable, legal, and regulatory compliant? What are the controls to have them approved and set up in our systems as an approved vendor? What controls are in place to ensure we only make valid payments to our suppliers? Do we track and evaluate our supplier performance over time?

INVESTIGATOR NOTES

Many years ago my firm was hired by the audit committee of a Fortune 500 company to investigate a worldwide purchasing fraud. That company invested heavily in the reliability and sustainability of their supply chain. They would identify the best suppliers for each of their many manufacturing inputs and enter very unique long-term supply contracts with them. Under the terms of these contracts, the Fortune 500 company would specify every detail of the supplier's manufacturing process for the items the company would be acquiring from them. They would specify the equipment to be used, operator qualifications and training, quality control protocols, etc. The company would make whatever investments were necessary in the supplier to make it possible to achieve its requirements. From that point on the supplier functioned like a division of the Fortune 500 company, subject to constant oversight and correction to assure that manufacturing inputs arrived exactly when needed and free of defects. This was an extraordinarily complex supply chain system that could only be analyzed by breaking it down into its component parts. By the way, it all worked great until a purchasing agent in the South Pacific had an affair, got caught by his wife, who blew the whistle about his purchasing fraud ring to the audit committee and, unfortunately, committed suicide. That's where I entered the story.

Well, you get the idea. Basically, you are using all available research sources to develop questions and resources to use in interviewing business operations and process owners to develop an accurate catalogue of the risks facing your organization. It is important to complete these steps and to collect whatever documentary evidence you can prior to conducting the interviews. This will accomplish two important things: First, it will demonstrate to the interviewee that you consider their work and their knowledge important. You will also be able to create a positive conversational tone for the interview by speaking the interviewee's language.

Second, it will help you to make sure that you cover all the areas you need to cover, not just the ones the interviewee is comfortable discussing. Also, you will be in a position to critically evaluate the answers you are getting and to push back when their response doesn't square with the information you developed in your research. This is extremely important making sure the interviewee is providing correct information. This allows you to control the interview in a way that will allow you to get what you need from it.

Before you begin the interviews, you need to do several things, some of these (e.g. selecting an appropriate venue, physical space preparation, decide whether or not to use a recording device, etc.) will be covered, in detail, in Chapter 8. First, you will want to write out your questions in advance of the interview, generally in a logical, sequential manner. Second, you will organize your documents so that you will be able to access them easily as you ask the questions.

Also, you will need to decide whether to make a sound recording of the interview or rely on written notes. If you decide on sound recording it is important to get the interviewee's permission well in advance of the interview. Be aware that sound recording can be very off-putting and/or intimidating to some people and can cause the interviewee to be less candid and open than they might be if they were not concerned about a voice recording device in the room. Also, some interviewees will adjust their responses to play to what they believe to be the interviewer's desired answers; this will create a sound recording of inaccurate interview answers. It will be difficult to later reconcile the interview to the truth. You are most often better off sticking to hand-written notes. I know, now you want to know whether I also want you to ride a dinosaur to the interview, but trust me, hand-written notes are still best. It is perfectly permissible to have another member of your staff take notes while you ask the questions. This is often great on-the-job training for more junior staff; they get to see the master (you) in action. However, be aware that a separate note-taker can create problems. First, it may make the interviewee uncomfortable. They may feel outnumbered and intimidated. Also, less experienced staff may not understand the objective of your questions and record answers in ways that convey meanings that neither you nor the interviewee intended. So, if you do intend to have a more junior staff member join you in the interview for the purpose of taking notes, make sure that he or she is thoroughly briefed in advance. Tell them that you will be the only one speaking to the interviewee; they are there only to observe and take copious notes. Also, be clear about dress code and decorum during the interview. Then go through the questions with them and make sure that they understand your objective for each question.

INVESTIGATOR NOTES

The FBI relies on handwritten notes when conducting witness interviews. They use their handwritten notes to create what they call a form 302 or FD-302 which is the FBI's standard interview report. When the 302 is completed, the agent puts the handwritten notes in an envelope which is attached to the 302. This is the gold standard of reports of interviews. I commend this approach to you. It has withstood the tests of time and trial.

Remember that the purpose of an interview is to help the interviewee share his or her knowledge with you in his or her own words. To do this you must put the interviewee at ease. Your questions should be designed as memory joggers to help the interviewee to provide you with complete information. Your research and documents should be shared with the interviewee only as an aide to recalling information accurately and never in a confrontational manner. An interview is never an interrogation.

Let's go back to Costco and construct a hypothetical set of interview questions for their head of merchandising based on a research item we came across:

Costco is the Latest Retailer to Drop Chaokoh Coconut Milk over Allegations of Forced Monkey Labor, PETA Says

Published 12:01 am EDT Oct. 28, 2020 | Updated 4:09 pm ET Oct. 30, 2020

Don't expect to find coconut milk on Costco shelves on your next shopping trip.

The retailer is the latest pledging not to stock coconut products from Thai suppliers who have been accused of using monkeys as forced labor, officials from the People for the Ethical Treatment of Animals (PETA) exclusively told USA TODAY.[7]

Remember, your objective is to put the interviewee at ease so that we can get as much accurate information as possible. The preceding information could create tension and conflict if presented improperly. A question like:

1. I want you to take a look at this article in USA Today.
2. How could you let something like this happen on your watch?

Such questions are likely to bring an abrupt end to the interview and your relationship or career with Costco.

A better approach is to figure out how to figuratively slide your chair around to the interviewee's side of the table. Become the interviewee's partner in getting to the right answers for the company. An example approach to designing your questions follows:

1. I am interested in learning about our supply chain operations and controls. I am told that no one knows more about than you.
2. Could you help me to better understand how our supply chain works?
3. What are our greatest strengths?
4. What issues give you the greatest concern?
5. How do we make sure that Costco suppliers deliver quality products that our customers will enjoy and feel good about?
6. I noticed this article in USA Today and wanted to tell you how much it means to me that you took swift and definitive action to protect our company and our customers.
7. This seems like a really difficult supplier issue to identify in our due diligence process.
8. What do you do in due diligence to identify issues like this one?
9. Do we have controls to unearth issues like this throughout our supplier life cycles?
10. Are you concerned that other suppliers might have similar issues?

Depending on your evaluation of the interviewee's personality, demeanor, etc. you may decide that different questions would be more appropriate. The point is to find ways to put interviewees at ease. To help them perceive you as a business partner and not an adversary. Remember, an effective interview is never an interrogation.

See Chapter 8 for further guidance on conducting and memorializing effective interviews.

PULLING IT ALL TOGETHER

Once you have completed your research and interviews it is time to correlate and analyze your findings. It is important to begin without preconceived notions or suppositions. Let the evidence you have collected guide you.

Let's start with the requirements for your risk analysis. Take a look at what senior management will be required to certify. From Costco's most recent 10-K we have the following:

Item 9—Changes in and Disagreements with Accountants on Accounting and Financial Disclosure
None.

Item 9A—Controls and Procedures

Evaluation of Disclosure Controls and Procedures
Our disclosure controls and procedures (as defined in Rules 13a-15(e) or 15d-15(e) under the Securities Exchange Act of 1934, as amended) are designed to ensure that information required to be disclosed in the reports that we file or submit under the Exchange Act is recorded, processed, summarized, and reported within the time periods specified in the rules and forms of the SEC and to ensure that information required to be disclosed is accumulated and communicated to management, including our principal executive and financial officers, to allow timely decisions regarding disclosure. The Chief Executive Officer and the Chief Financial Officer, with

assistance from other members of management, have reviewed the effectiveness of our disclosure controls and procedures as of August 30, 2020 and, based on their evaluation, have concluded that the disclosure controls and procedures were effective as of such date.

Management's Annual Report on Internal Control over Financial Reporting

Our management is responsible for establishing and maintaining adequate internal control over financial reporting as defined in Rule 13a-15(f) under the Exchange Act. Our internal control over financial reporting is designed to provide reasonable assurance regarding the reliability of financial reporting and the preparation of financial statements for external purposes in accordance with U.S. GAAP and includes those policies and procedures that: (1) pertain to the maintenance of records that in reasonable detail accurately and fairly reflect our transactions and the dispositions of our assets; (2) provide reasonable assurance that our transactions are recorded as necessary to permit preparation of financial statements in accordance with generally accepted accounting principles and that our receipts and expenditures are being made only in accordance with appropriate authorizations; and (3) provide reasonable assurance regarding prevention or timely detection of unauthorized acquisition, use or disposition of our assets that could have a material effect on our financial statements.

Because of its inherent limitations, internal control over financial reporting may not prevent or detect misstatements. Projections of any evaluation of effectiveness for future periods are subject to the risk that controls may become inadequate because of changes in conditions, or that the degree of compliance with the policies or procedures may deteriorate.

Under the supervision of and with the participation of our management, we assessed the effectiveness of our internal control over financial reporting as of August 30, 2020, using the criteria set forth by the Committee of Sponsoring Organizations of the Treadway Commission in Internal Control—Integrated Framework (2013).

Based on its assessment, management has concluded that our internal control over financial reporting was effective as of August 30, 2020. The attestation of KPMG LLP, our independent registered public accounting firm, on the effectiveness of our internal control over financial reporting is included with the consolidated financial statements in Item 8 of this Report.[8]

Let's break this down: *"Our management is responsible for establishing and maintaining adequate disclosure and internal controls over financial reporting as defined in Rule 13a-15(f) under the Exchange Act."* The SEC published following regarding Rule 13a-15F:

Final Rule:
Management's Report on Internal Control over Financial Reporting and Certification of Disclosure in Exchange Act Periodic Reports

SECURITIES AND EXCHANGE COMMISSION

17 CFR PARTS 210, 228, 229, 240, 249, 270 and 274

[RELEASE NOS. 33-8238; 34-47986; IC-26068; File Nos. S7-40-02; S7-06-03]

RIN 3235-AI66 and 3235-AI79

MANAGEMENT'S REPORT ON INTERNAL CONTROL OVER FINANCIAL REPORTING AND CERTIFICATION OF DISCLOSURE IN EXCHANGE ACT PERIODIC REPORTS

B. Summary of the Final Rules

The final rules require the annual report of every company that files periodic reports under Section 13(a) or 15(d) of the Exchange Act, other than reports by registered investment companies, to contain a report of management that includes:

- A statement of management's responsibility for establishing and maintaining adequate internal control over financial reporting for the company;
- A statement identifying the framework used by management to evaluate the effectiveness of the company's internal control over financial reporting;
- Management's assessment of the effectiveness of the company's internal control over financial reporting, as of the end of the most recent fiscal year; and
- A statement that the registered public accounting firm that audited the financial statements included in the annual report has issued an attestation report on management's evaluation of the company's internal control over financial reporting.

We are adding these requirements pursuant to the legislative mandate in Section 404 of the Sarbanes-Oxley Act. Under our final rules, a company also will be required to evaluate and disclose any change in its internal control over financial reporting that occurred during the fiscal quarter that has materially affected, or is reasonably likely to materially affect, the company's internal control over financial reporting.

We are also adopting amendments to require companies to file the certifications mandated by Sections 302 and 906 of the Sarbanes-Oxley Act as exhibits to their annual, semi-annual and quarterly reports. These amendments will enhance the ability of investors, the Commission staff, the Department of Justice and other interested parties to easily and efficiently access the certifications through our Electronic Data Gathering, Analysis and Retrieval ("EDGAR") system and facilitate better monitoring of a company's compliance with the certification requirements.[9]

So, the senior management of Costco is doing what it is required to do under Section 13(a) or 15(d) of the Exchange Act and Sections 302, 404, and 906 of the Sarbanes-Oxley Act. They are attesting to the adequacy of disclosure controls, internal controls, and their auditor's attestation as to management's evaluation of these controls. Well, that's the top of the pyramid, but how do we climb up there? One step at a time. Your job is to make sure that those assertions are accurate. You are responsible for making sure that the steps are reliable. Here is a great starting point:

> Under the supervision of and with the participation of our management, we assessed the effectiveness of our internal control over financial reporting as of August 30, 2020, using the criteria set forth by the Committee of Sponsoring Organizations of the Treadway Commission in Internal Control—Integrated Framework (2013).

Recall that Section 13(a) or 15(d) of the Exchange Act requires that management make:

- A statement identifying the framework used by management to evaluate the effectiveness of the company's internal control over financial reporting;

Costco management and pretty much everyone else has chosen the Committee of Sponsoring Organizations of the Treadway Commission in Internal Control—Integrated Framework (2013).

It is kind of the gold standard in terms of available frameworks. The Integrated Framework is a useful tool to help us to transcend binary or transactional thing about internal and disclosure controls.

So, let's think about how we might prioritize the risks you have identified. First, let's organize them in a way that will allow you to prioritize and decide how to address each. The following (Table 2.1) is a model that I find very useful in accomplishing these tasks.

TABLE 2.1
Risk Analysis Model

Frequency	Severity		
	Catastrophic	Moderate	Minor
Frequent	Hurricane Damage Risk at Hotel in South Florida.	Shoplifting at Retail Stores.	Low-Cost Inventory Shrinkage.
Recurring	Explosion Risk at Refinery in South Texas.	Purchasing Fraud.	Employees Bringing Home Office Supplies for Personal Use.
Infrequent	Financial Statement Fraud.	Embezzlement.	Broken Window or Door in Retail Store.
Remote	Terrorist Attack on Manufacturing Facility in Moab Utah.	Employee Violent Crime.	Failure to Recover Rebates on Infrequent Purchases.

Okay, now we have organized our risks by economic impact and expected frequency. Now we must decide how to address these risks. The following model is one way to think about these decisions. You can transfer the risk, for a price, to a third party, like an insurance company. You can use internal resources to mitigate the risk. Or you can accept the risk. The beauty of this type of analysis is that it removes bias from the process; you are simply using evidence to make rational decisions about how to address risk. Table 2.2 is an example of how this type of analysis may be employed to address risks that face your organization.

TABLE 2.2
Risk Decision Model

Transfer	1. Catastrophic/Frequent 2. Catastrophic/Recurring	1. Hurricane Damage Risk at Hotel in South Florida. 2. Explosion Risk at Refinery in South Texas.
Mitigate Internally	1. Catastrophic/Infrequent 2. Moderate/Frequent 3. Moderate/Recurring 4. Moderate Infrequent 5. Minor/Frequent	1. Financial Statement Fraud. 2. Shoplifting at Retail Stores. 3. Purchasing Fraud. 4. Embezzlement. 5. Low-Cost Inventory Shrinkage.
Accept	1. Catastrophic/Remote 2. Minor/Recurring 3. Minor/Infrequent 4. Minor/Remote	1. Terrorist Attack on Manufacturing Facility in Moab Utah. 2. Employees Bringing Home Office Supplies for Personal Use. 3. Broken Window or Door in Retail Store. 4. Failure to Recover Rebates on Infrequent Purchases.

To be sure, there may be disagreement about how you categorized and chose to address each risk. But with these two models and the evidence you collected, you will be in a position to have a rational conversation that relies on the evidence and not on your feelings. You may ultimately be overruled, but you will have a memorialized record of the recommendations you made and the evidence-based reasons you made them.

SECTION II: HOW TO GATHER AND EVALUATE CRITICAL DATA TO CREATE AN EARLY WARNING FRAUD DETECTION SYSTEM

We live in an amazing time. This will date me, but when I was an undergraduate, we still carried slide rules for advanced mathematics classes because electronic calculators, much less personal computers, had not yet been invented. Oh, the quantum leaps in information gathering and analysis we have made since then! My undergraduate computer science class had us programming by making holes in paper punch cards, which would be placed in a mechanical device that passed them "rapidly" over a light source to allow photoelectric receptor cells to record the commands they contained in 1s and 0s.

Early in my career, all evidence was provided on paper. Electronic data was not something anyone paid attention to and no judge would accept as evidence. Investigations were carried out by armies of people pouring over mountains of paper documents; often recording the results of their analyses on their own paper documents. This was a difficult environment in which to deduce anything of value in real time. Only in hindsight could anyone divine any useful information and analysis.

But, all that has changed. Electronic data has become the mainstream medium in which to capture and record all of life's coming and going; financial and otherwise. Much of this data is now available publicly and privately. There are many tools available to gather this data and to analyze it to answer all the questions we may ever choose to ask. We only need harvest it and analyze it to unlock the truth and to answer all the questions we need to answer.

INVESTIGATOR NOTES

Recently I was hired by a large, for profit, Institution that had been accused by the Department of Education of compensating its employees based on of the number of students recruited; a big no, no under **Title IV** of the Higher Education Act of 1965 (HEA) that covers the administration of the U.S. federal student financial aid programs. The Institution argued that associate dean compensation was based on performance evaluations, which measured many different performance metrics not related to the number of students recruited. On the face of it, this was a simple mathematical question, which could be answered by application of descriptive and analytic statistics. This is a favorite area of study for me, so I was excited to undertake the exercise. I requested the data that I would need to perform the analyses and waited to see what they would send. I could not have been more surprised. I received mountains of data, in a variety of formats, filled with duplications and inconsistencies; I was at a loss as to how to proceed. So, I retained a data scientist to assist me in making sense of this giant virtual shoebox of information. He introduced me to a Microsoft tool called Power BI that forever changed the way in which I viewed the ability to visualize, manipulate, analyze, and use electronic data to draw evidence-based conclusions. First, let me say that I have no financial interest in Power BI and that there are many other tools that do the same or similar things; that's not the point. The point is that there are tools available to you today that can literally transform your access to and use of information to do your job and fulfill your responsibilities. With this tool we were able to instantaneously collect in one database a cleaned version of all the data we had been provided, in any form, and, to visualize that data in a way that we could make informed judgments about it. We were then able to perform hypothesis tests and other descriptive and analytical analyses that not only allowed us to answer the Department of Education's complaints but also to provide the university with insights and guidance that allowed them to modify their performance evaluation and compensation systems in ways that made it less likely that the Department of Education would raise concerns in the future.

First, we must determine which risks represent the greatest threat to our organization. Then, we need to identify what data, properly measured and analyzed, would give us insight into whether the risk we were concerned about materialized. Next, we need to identify the metrics which, if increased or decreased unexpectedly, would alert us to an anomaly signaling one or more risks had materialized. We would need a way to establish a baseline for each metric and an acceptable range of variance for each. Finally, we would need a system to constantly monitor the metrics and automatically alert us if an anomaly had occurred. I am at a 30,000-foot level here because there is no one-size-fits-all for a system like this. However, there are some principles, protocols, and techniques that are generalizable.

BENCHMARK FROM EXTERNAL

Just as we did above, we should first look at our peers and competitors to gather two important types of information. First, what do they consider the greatest risks facing their organizations? Fortunately, they have been kind enough to tell us what those are. Let's look at an example from our friends at Costco:

> **Item 1A – Risk Factors**
> The risks described below could materially and adversely affect our business, financial condition and results of operations. We could also be affected by additional risks that apply to all companies operating in the U.S. and globally, as well as other risks that are not presently known to us or that we currently consider to be immaterial. These Risk Factors should be carefully reviewed in conjunction with Management's Discussion and Analysis of Financial Condition and Results of Operations in Item 7 and our consolidated financial statements and related notes in Item 8 of this Report.[10]
>
> **Business and Operating Risks**
> **We are highly dependent on the financial performance of our U.S. and Canadian operations.**
> Our financial and operational performance is highly dependent on our U.S. and Canadian operations, which comprised 87% and 83% of net sales and operating income in 2020, respectively. Within the U.S., we are highly dependent on our California operations, which comprised 29% of U.S. net sales in 2020. Our California market, in general, has a larger percentage of higher volume warehouses as compared to our other domestic markets. Any substantial slowing or sustained decline in these operations could materially adversely affect our business and financial results. Declines in financial performance of our U.S. operations, particularly in California, and our Canadian operations could arise from, among other things: slow growth or declines in comparable warehouse sales (comparable sales); negative trends in operating expenses, including increased labor, healthcare and energy costs; failing to meet targets for warehouse openings; cannibalizing existing locations with new warehouses; shifts in sales mix

toward lower gross margin products; changes or uncertainties in economic conditions in our markets, including higher levels of unemployment and depressed home values; and failing to consistently provide high quality and innovative new products.[11]

Okay, let's break this down: *"Our California market, in general, has a larger percentage of higher volume warehouses as compared to our other domestic markets. Any substantial slowing or sustained decline in these operations could materially adversely affect our business and financial results."* So, Costco definitely needs to identify some early warning data related to California Warehouse (i.e. Costco's euphemism for Store) sales. If you are a big-box discount retailer, do you have any markets or regions that are critical to your overall financial performance as an organization? If so, what types of data could provide an early warning of declining sales ahead? Let's start with the macro factors:

- Customers: What are the baseline customer demographics and key metrics for Costco customers in California (i.e. growing, shrinking, more white collar, blue collar, income rising or falling, older, younger). Are these demographics and key metrics for Costco customers in California changing?
- Economy: Is the economy of the regions of California where Costco has warehouses improving or declining? Are jobs being added or lost? Are household incomes rising or falling?
- Competition: Are other states offering opportunities that are causing a shift in population (i.e. recently, Utah, Texas, Alabama, and North Carolina were reported to have siphoned significant numbers of high-tech jobs away from California's Bay Area because they offered lower regulation, taxes, cost of living, and more diversity)?
- Climate Change and Related Effects: Are climate change and related effects displacing Costco customers (i.e. historically devastating fires and related electric power rationing)?
- Government: Are California's laws and regulations more likely to increase or decrease Costco customer purchases? Is the regulatory environment becoming more or less favorable to Costco current and/or potential new store locations?

All this data is publicly available. There are also third-party firms that are happy to assemble it for you for a fee. With tools like Power BI, Stata, Python, and others you can compile it, visualize it, and analyze it to form strong evidence-based conclusions about expected sales volume ahead of actual sales numbers rising or declining. It's like one of the three wishes most of us would ask a genie.

Now, here is the segue to the fraud alert part of our dashboard. All the preceding indicators are clearly leading indicators. But, let's say that all these metrics produce negative indications for more than two quarters and yet, California warehouse sales continue to rise throughout the subsequent quarter; what would this mean? Fraud? Not necessarily. Quantitative metric alerts are the beginning, not the end. This anomaly is simply an alert that an investigation should be initiated into the reason for the contrary dependent metric performance based on underlying independent underlying metrics. There are a variety of countervailing factors that could explain this apparent anomaly (i.e. there is an entirely new complement of Costco customers moving in to fill the gap left by the departing customers). The point is to use available data to get ahead of the issue. It's all out there waiting for you to access it and use it to your advantage.

DASHBOARD

Imagine if you were driving a car that had no speedometer or other gauges in constant view for you to monitor. Further imagine it had no alerts like low fuel, high engine temperature, low oil, etc. Oh, you could get all this information as you are driving along, but you would have to do something extraordinary to get each bit of information. You could stick a wind gauge out of the car window and convert the reading to miles or kilometers per hour to keep track of your speed then, based on what gear the car was in, you could calculate the engines revolutions per minute (RPMs) to make sure you were not above the engine's maximum safe RPM operating range. You could mount a thermometer on a rod and guide it through the firewall to get an idea of engine temperature. You could stop the car every so often and check the oil dipstick to make sure the engine oil was not too low. While you were under the hood you could also check the engine coolant level. You could walk around to the gas tank and stick a rod down the nozzle to gauge how much fuel you had on board. You could pull out your handy tire gauge and check the air pressure in each tire. Then you could get back in your car, confidence restored, to carry on with your journey.

But, how far would you be willing to drive before repeating your process to monitor the car's vital signs; how disruptive and time consuming would this be during your trip? How regularly would you go through your monitoring routine to make sure that none of the critical processes affecting your automobile's safe operation were within required parameters? How many speeding tickets do you think you might get because you didn't stick your wind gauge out of the car window often enough? How many engines would you destroy because you exceeded the engine's maximum safe RPM range? How many engines would you destroy because the oil or coolant levels got too low or the engine got too hot? How many times would you run out of gas?

Drivers of the earliest cars didn't have all those monitoring systems available and often came to disaster as a result. So, gradually, the automobile companies assembled all of these monitoring devices in a place that was convenient for the driver to monitor frequently simply by looking down; today there are even heads-up displays so you don't even have to look down. The place where all the monitoring gauges are assembled is called a dashboard and it makes driving a car an easily controlled process.

Now what does this have to do with you and your company? Well, if you think about it, operating a well-controlled organization is analogous to driving a car. You have to make sure the company remains in good operating condition and is rolling along in a controlled manner (i.e. revenue is growing along with cash flow; expenses remain under control to produce consistent profits; debt remains under control; etc.); you also have to make sure that the company and its stakeholders don't break any laws or do things that violate the will of the company's board of directors. You have an enormous role in making sure the company remains under control and operates in accordance with laws and the will of the board of directors.

Well, what sorts of indicators could you monitor on your dashboard? One good way would be to use tools that are designed to detect anomalies.

You may already know this, but six sigma is a term that was coined based on the work of a Russian mathematician we will talk about shortly. All business processes are controlled such that they should have an identifiable mean. Often, a business process is said to be well controlled if whatever it produces is within a stated tolerance with respect to an identified mean. An example would be a manufacturing process that produces tubes that are 1 meter long. So, the average length or mean tube length is one meter. The process is believed to produce tubes that are within 1 millimeter of the 1-meter mean length. Let's keep my simple example in mind as we learn about that Russian mathematician.

Pavroty Chebyshev, a Russian mathematician, found the proportions of data in a population that fall within each standard deviation from the population mean. Chebyshev's theorem states that for any data set, the proportion of data, which lie within k standard deviations of the mean is, at least, $1 - (1/k$ squared$)$. Therefore, if $k = 3$, the proportion of data, which we would expect to see, within three standard deviations of the mean, would be $1 - (1/3$ squared$) =$ (at least) 89% (Figure 2.11).[12]

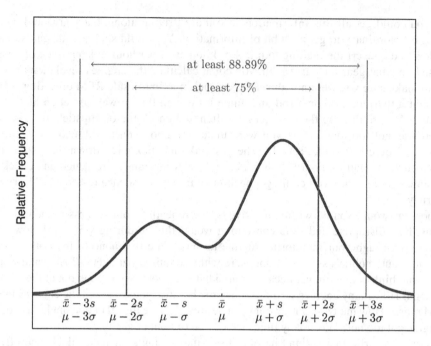

FIGURE 2.11[13]

The theorem is true for the entire population and any statistically valid sample drawn from the population. The proportions of data, which fall within each standard deviation, become even more precise if the population data has a normal, bell-shaped distribution. This is called the Empirical Rule and predicts that more than 99% of the data should be found within three standard deviations of the mean (Figure 2.12).

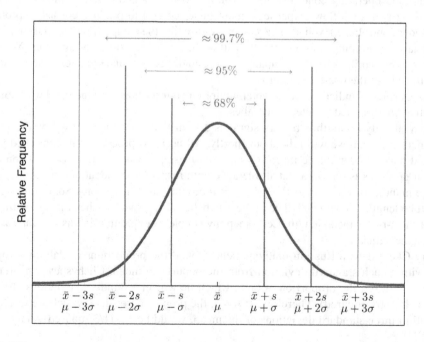

FIGURE 2.12[14]

This theorem is useful in understanding control and lack of control. It is often used to control uniformity and quality in manufacturing processes. The mathematical symbol for each standard deviation is called "sigma." Note that there are three standard deviations, or sigmas, to the right of the mean and three to the left; six sigmas in total. Chebyshev's theorem is quite useful in identifying anomalies. If you create or identify what you believe to be a population mean, then more than 89% of all observations should fall within three standard deviations of that mean in any type of population. If the population data is normally distributed (i.e. bell-shaped curve), then the expected proportion of data, within three standard deviations of the mean, rises to more than 99%.

So, if you determine the mean of the population (i.e. our tubes in the preceding example), at least 89% of the data (e.g. tube lengths) should fall within three standard deviations of that mean. If that is not the case, for example, if you discover that 20% of the tube lengths are beyond three standard deviations from the mean, there is only one possible conclusion; whatever you believed about the essential attributes of your population is incorrect. There is an unexplained variance between your beliefs about the characteristics of the population and the reality of the population characteristics.

I used this technique in an internal investigation of a large public company. The investigation of the principal allegations, which gave rise to the internal investigation, had been completed. However, the company's auditors wanted assurance that the company's accounts did not contain other fraudulent entries. I proposed using Chebyshev's theorem to identify anomalies for further investigation. Note that I did not say that I proposed using Chebyshev's theorem to identify the fraudulent entries the auditors were concerned about; these techniques are useful in identifying compliance or lack of compliance. The causes of noncompliance must be investigated thoroughly to be correctly understood.

In the 1930s, prior to the advent of electronic calculators or personal computers, physicist Frank Benford observed that the pages of an overused logarithm table were worn in a curious manner. The pages containing logarithms of the numbers 1 and 2 were more stained and frayed than those containing logarithms for the numbers 8 and 9. Benford noted that the logarithm tables were used in virtually every mathematic, engineering, and scientific analysis in which the subject of the analysis can be described using numbers.[15] Benford went on to carefully research and test this hypothesis, over a number of years, using a wide variety of data sets. This research and testing led to what is known as Benford's Law.

Benford's Law is best demonstrated in large data sets. If smaller data sets fail to satisfy the rule, combining data sets often produces a new sequence that will more closely approximate the distribution of first digits predicted by Benford's Law. Benford's Law is satisfied when the probability of observing a first digit of d (i.e. for digits 1–9) is log base 10 (d+1/d). The expected distribution of first digits, predicted by Benford's Law, describes what could be expected to occur in the natural world if human beings or mechanical systems did not intervene in the processes, which gave rise to them. The distribution of proportions of first digits, which are predicted by Benford's Law, follows:

1 = 30.0%
2 = 17.6%
3 = 12.5%
4 = 9.7%
5 = 7.9%
6 = 6.7%
7 = 5.8%
8 = 5.1%
9 = 4.6%[16]

This predictive capability is useful in being able to detect first digit distribution anomalies which may have been caused by artificial intervention.

I used this technique in fully investigating an accounts payable fraud perpetrated by the president of a division of a large public company. The fraud was so massive that the division was shut down due to the size of its recurring losses. There were numerous fake vendors, set up by the division president, which had submitted invoices for payment. Many were identified by other investigative techniques such as identifying vendors who shared a common address. However, it became clear that there were other fake vendors who could not be identified by these means. We were looking not for a needle in a haystack, but for a needle in a needle stack. How to identify the fake invoices among the tens of thousands of legitimate invoices? This was an impossible task for individual review. A more efficient technique had to be employed; enter Benford's Law.

The invoices received by the division often contained hundreds of line items. We loaded vendor names, number of items purchased, and price per item for each item included in the invoices received by the division, into a spreadsheet. We then had the spreadsheet multiply the number of items purchased by the dollar amount per item (i.e. we re-performed each extension on the odd chance that the extension had been falsified). Also, this was done to create a large data set from the mathematical combination of numbers from two distributions, more likely to satisfy Benford's Law. Next we separated the first digit in each result into a separate column. We then analyzed the proportions of the numbers 1–9 appearing as the first digit in our results. Note that we did not first sort by vendor. This exercise helped us identify vendor invoices, which contained line items that did not satisfy Benford's Law. The vendors who sent these invoices were then investigated. This investigation revealed another group of vendors, which turned out to be fraudulent. Why? Because you can't fake natural.

Of course, the preceding examples demonstrate how mathematical techniques can be used to investigate illegal conduct after the crime has occurred; however, these same techniques and others can be deployed as an integral part of any compliance system to detect anomalies in real time.

The great thing about electronic data is that it is available, in real time, twenty-four seven; all you need to do is to gather, organize, and analyze it to effectively answer your questions. Big data has become a buzz word used, imprecisely, to describe every current data analytics application. It's as though if you are not yet on the Big Data Train; you have missed your chance because the train has left the station. Nothing could be further from the truth. We are still very early in a technology revolution which will continue to evolve to allow us to do more with, well, more. Online transaction systems will become more effective. Technologies are developing which will allow broader and more seamless interactions with data warehouses. Also, technologies exist today to allow easier normalization of data for analysis purposes. The key, for using the available technologies today, is to create clarity around your control and compliance objectives and then identify the underlying processes you are attempting to control. Create a map of all relevant, internal and external, data, which relates to the subject process(es). Then decide which tools you will employ to analyze the data. From there, you will identify appropriate benchmarks and create analytical processes to support continuous monitoring.

But, then you need to find an effective way to get the results in front of the right people. If you include the raw analytical results in hourly, daily, weekly, monthly paper, or electronic reports, you will quickly overwhelm and then lose your constituency The reader may even try to do some additional analysis and form some preliminary conclusions but will likely lose interest quickly. However, because of the overwhelming scope and difficulty in using the information effectively, for its intended control objectives, recipients will quickly relegate these reports to the "to do" pile in favor of easier and more rewarding activities. That's why the concept of a dashboard is so powerful. A dashboard is simply a display of critical information in a format, which makes it instantly understandable and actionable. Think of the smoke alarm in your home. Basically, ionization type smoke detectors constantly monitor the ionization of air inside the device, when smoke is present it interrupts the ionization process and causes an alarm to sound. Now, what if instead, the device simply provided you with a constant count of ionized air particles present in the device? How likely do you believe you would notice the decline in the number of ionized air particles in the device in sufficient time to avoid being burned by the fire? This is the genius of a correctly designed dashboard; it presents the information a user needs, to make a correct investigative decision, at exactly the right moment and in a way in which it will not likely be missed.

EXERCISES

1. How do scientists go about designing experiments to answer questions?
2. What characteristics must answers to questions possess?
3. Let's do a research project.
   a. Do a critical objective review of your own organization.
   b. Really drill down on all the internal and external risks facing your organization. Also, review materials that contain information about the risks faced by your competitors.
   c. Develop questions about all the risks you identify. Develop interview questions that you would ask business process owners to learn all you could about each risk.
   d. List all the external and internal risks you can identify.
4. Based on your work in Exercise 3 above, create a Risk Analysis Model.
5. Based on your work in Exercises 3 and 4 above, create a Risk Decision Model.
6. Identify three companies that you could benchmark your company against.
7. For the companies, in Exercise 6 above, use analysts' reports and public filings to identify key performance indicators.
8. Create common size analyses (i.e. calculate percentages of totals for each key performance indicator to allow for easy comparison) for each key performance indicator.
9. Now, for your Company, identify the same key performance indicators and compare them to the key performance indicators for the benchmark companies. How do they compare? Can you explain any significant differences?
10. Now, use the key performance indicators to create a dashboard of the key performance indicators that you believe would alert you to potential issues for investigation.
11. What other things would you like to be able to monitor with your dashboard?
12. What are some ways in which you incorporate Chebyshev's theorem to make your dashboard more effective?
13. Download data from your company's records that can be used to create a derivative data set (e.g. invoice sales quantities and price per unit). If you can't download the data, you can just use any two strings of related data you may have available. Then multiply the data in one column by the data in the next column.
14. Calculate the percentage of the total number of first digits in the derivative column, from Exercise 13 above, for each first digit 1–9.
15. Compare the percentage of appearance of each digit, calculated in Exercise 14 above, to the percentages predicted by Benford's Law. (If you do download your company's data and the results do not correspond to the predictions in Benford's Law, you may want to investigate.)

CHAPTER SUMMARY/KEY TAKEAWAYS

So, here are some things to think about:

- You need to triage your company's white-collar crime risks.
- You need to decide which ones of those risks you will confront internally, which ones you will transfer to third parties, and which ones you will accept.
- You need to gather data to create an early warning system for your company.
- Use the analytical and data science tools available to you to create an effective dashboard.

In Chapter 3 you will learn what to do if your plan doesn't stop all white-collar crime.

NOTES

1. In fact, if you have worked at your organization for many years, it is highly likely you have become blind to many obvious weaknesses in your organization, akin to someone becoming "nose blind" to odors they are constantly exposed to. Obtaining a "cold eyes" objective review by an expert outside your organization will usually spot some major, obvious weaknesses.
2. Costco Annual Report, www.sec.gov/Archives/edgar/data/909832/000090983219000019/cost10k9119. htm
3. Costco Annual Report, www.sec.gov/Archives/edgar/data/909832/000090983219000019/cost10k9119. htm
4. Costco Annual Report, www.sec.gov/Archives/edgar/data/909832/000090983219000019/cost10k9119. htm
5. Costco Annual Report, www.sec.gov/Archives/edgar/data/909832/000090983219000019/cost10k9119. htm
6. Costco Annual Report, www.sec.gov/Archives/edgar/data/909832/000090983219000019/cost10k9119. htm
7. USA Today, Kelly Tyko, Published 12:01 am EDT, October 28, 2020, Updated 4:09 pm ET Oct 30, 2020.
8. Costco Annual Report, https://www.sec.gov/ix?doc=/Archives/edgar/data/909832/000090983220000017/ cost-20200830.htm#id2c7a27cc45a4341a7bdf88b9739d38b_187, 10/07/2020.
9. Final Rule: Management's Report on Internal Control Over Financial Reporting and Certification of Disclosure in Exchange Act Periodic Reports, SECURITIES AND EXCHANGE COMMISSION, August 14, 2003.
10. Costco Annual Report, https://www.sec.gov/ix?doc=/Archives/edgar/data/909832/000090983220000017/ cost-20200830.htm#id2c7a27cc45a4341a7bdf88b9739d38b_187, 10/07/2020.
11. Costco Annual Report, https://www.sec.gov/ix?doc=/Archives/edgar/data/909832/000090983220000017/ cost-20200830.htm#id2c7a27cc45a4341a7bdf88b9739d38b_187, 10/07/2020.
12. James R. Evans and David L. Olson (2003). *Statistics, Data Analysis, and Decision Modeling (Second Edition)*. Upper Saddle River, NJ: Pearson Education, Inc. p. 54.
13. http://statwiki.ucdavis.edu/Under_Construction/Descriptive_Statistics/2.5_The_Empirical_Rule_ and_Chebyshev%27s
14. http://statwiki.ucdavis.edu/Under_Construction/Descriptive_Statistics/2.5_The_Empirical_Rule_ and_Chebyshev%27s
15. Forensic and Investigative Accounting, D. Larry Crumbley, CPA, CFD, Cr.FA, Lester e. Heitger, CPA, G. Stevenson Smith, CPA, CMA, CCH: Chicago, IL, 2007, pp. 9–17, 9–18.
16. Forensic and Investigative Accounting, D. Larry Crumbley, CPA, CFD, Cr.FA, Lester e. Heitger, CPA, G. Stevenson Smith, CPA, CMA, CCH: Chicago, IL, 2007, pp. 9–17, 9–18.

Part II

Forensic Accounting Investigations

3 The Ounce of Prevention Didn't Work; Now What?

SECTION I: THE THINGS YOU SHOULD AND SHOULD NOT DO WHEN YOU LEARN OF POSSIBLE IRREGULARITY OR CRIME

As we discussed in Chapter 1, unfortunately many crimes and other irregularities are discovered by accident. So, be ready to be surprised. The next big investigation is likely to begin with an allegation that comes out of the blue. You must be ready to respond to virtually anything. It could be a major asset theft, accounting and financial reporting fraud, cyberattacks, alleged Foreign Corrupt Practices Act (FCPA) violations, and on and on. The best thing you can do is identify the people, tools, internal (e.g. head of compliance, head of security, general counsel, etc.) and external (e.g. law firm(s), forensic accounting firm, cyber consultants, etc.) you will pull together when something happens.

The first thing to do when you are told: something has gone missing; we've been hacked or we just received a grand jury subpoena, etc., is to make sure you do not react in a way that will make the problem worse.

For instance, if you are provided what you believe to be a credible tip that one of your company's employees has been selling trade secrets to a competitor and you do a little bit of snooping around and believe you have confirmed that this has happened, you report your concerns to the head of security who reports them to the general counsel. You attend a meeting where you share your findings and concerns with the general counsel. Following the meeting you all agree to immediately terminate the employee, which is carried out by human resources. In taking this hasty action you will have created a variety of problems. First, you have lost the ability to require the employee to cooperate with your investigation. Second, the employee will likely learn why you fired him or her and hire a lawyer to sue you for wrongful termination. This will also have the effect of ending your ability to communicate with the employee; you will only be able to speak to the employee's attorney following retention. If the employee was engaged in selling trade secrets to your competitor, he or she will likely alert them to your investigation.

Or, let's say that your company receives a grand jury subpoena requiring all persons associated with the company to maintain all documents and digital information. You are told that federal agents will be arriving to collect documents and digital information. You believe they will also want to interview a number of employees. You instruct IT to make sure that all documents that should have been destroyed in accordance with the company's document retention policy have, in fact, been destroyed. Also, you call a staff meeting to inform employees that they are entitled to have counsel present when they are interviewed and are not required to allow federal agents to interview them.

You have just committed two counts of obstruction of justice. Be prepared to experience the full weight of the federal government's prosecutorial force.

When you receive a grand jury subpoena the best thing to do is to comply with it and to not give any instructions to employees other than to comply with federal agents' requests. In other words don't create problems for yourself that don't already exist. Let the law enforcement folks do their job without hindrance. Everyone, including you, will be better off. Don't believe me? See below.

DOI: 10.1201/9781003121558-5

Deputy Attorney General Transcript

News Conference - Arthur Andersen Indictment
Thursday, March 14, 2002
DOJ Conference Center

MR. THOMPSON: Good afternoon — again. On October 17, the Securities and Exchange Commission launched an inquiry into the financial collapse of Enron, which had been considered the nation's seventh largest corporation. The SEC's inquiry focused attention on the role of Arthur Andersen LLP, Enron's long-time auditor and one of the nation's big five accounting firms. The Justice Department established a task force in January to investigate all the matters that have arisen from that collapse. Today we are unsealing an indictment obtained last week from a federal grand jury in Houston, Texas charging the Arthur Andersen partnership with obstruction of justice, for destroying literally tons of paper documents and other electronic information related to the Enron inquiries.

The indictment catalogues allegations of widespread criminal conduct by the Arthur Andersen firm, charging that the firm sought to undermine our justice system by destroying evidence relevant to the investigations. It alleges that at the firm's direction, Andersen personnel engaged in the wholesale destruction of tons of paperwork and attempted to purge huge volumes of electronic data or information.

The indictment further explains that at the time Andersen knew full well what — that these documents were relevant to the inquiries and to Enron's collapse. The indictment alleges that Andersen partners and others personally directed these efforts to destroy evidence.

As the indictment lays out, the destruction initiative began on or about October 10, 2001, as Andersen foresaw imminent government investigations and civil litigation. The destruction continued through the SEC's announcement that an investigation had been launched and only ended nearly one month later when the SEC officially served Andersen with a subpoena for Enron documents.

As charged in the indictment, on October 16th Enron issued a press release announcing a $618 million net loss for the third quarter of 2001.

The very next day, the SEC began an — began its Enron investigation. By October 19th, Enron notified Andersen that the SEC was investigating the Enron special-purpose entities that Andersen, itself, had helped to establish, enabling Enron to camouflage the true financial condition of the company.

The next morning, Andersen's high-level management discussed the SEC inquiry on a conference call. On October 23rd, Andersen partners ordered their employees to destroy Enron documents in Andersen's offices in Houston. The indictment alleges that in urgent and mandatory meetings, Andersen partners and others told employees to immediately destroy documents related to Enron. Dozens of large trunks were brought in to haul documents from Andersen's office in Enron's building to Andersen's firm office in Houston, in order to destroy literally tons of documents, the indictment alleges. Employees were told to work overtime, if necessary, to finish the job of destroying documents. The shredder at the Andersen office in the Enron building ran virtually constantly.

The indictment charges that destruction of evidence extended far beyond Andersen's Houston-based Enron engagement team. This is the indictment of a firm, of a partnership. As the indictment clearly outlines, the obstruction effort was not just confined to a few isolated individuals or documents. This was a substantial undertaking over an extended period of time with a very wide scope. The Andersen firm instructed Andersen firm in Portland, Oregon; Chicago, Illinois; and London, England, to join in the shredding. In London, Andersen partners and others orchestrated a parallel, coordinated effort to destroy Enron documents within days of notice of the SEC inquiry. The shredding apparently stopped only after the SEC officially served Andersen on November 8th with the anticipated subpoena for documents related to the firm's work on Enron.

Obstruction of justice is a grave matter and one that this department takes very seriously. Arthur Andersen is charged with a crime that attacks the justice system itself by impeding investigators and regulators from getting at the truth. This indictment alleges just such subversion of our justice system by a firm responsible for upholding the standards of the accounting profession on which hundreds of millions of investors rely.

Well, you get the point. Be thoughtful and professional in your approach. Do a quiet preliminary investigation to determine whether this appears to be a real issue or not. Then it's time to begin assembling a team. Normally, internal audit would contact the appropriate designated corporate officer or board member, depending on the nature of the issue, and then await further instructions. But, eventually, the corporate general counsel's office will likely get involved. Depending on the nature of the issue the general counsel's office will probably associate external counsel. This could be one or several law firms depending on complexity of the matter. As you can see, from the preceding examples, you need competent, experienced legal counsel to navigate these troubled waters successfully. Non-lawyers, no matter how experienced, just don't know what they don't know.

Things will likely go quiet as the lawyers try to wrap their heads around what has happened and to get things under control to the extent possible. But, lawyers are not forensic accountants or investigators; they are well aware of this and are not eager to undertake these tasks. So, they will either hire external forensic accountants and investigators or come to you or both. For the balance of the chapter let's assume they come to you.

SECTION II: HOW TO MAKE SURE YOU DO NOT BECOME ONE OF THE VICTIMS OF THE CRIME (I.E. INTERNAL AUDITORS ARE OFTEN PUNISHED FOR NOT REACTING CORRECTLY TO A SUSPECTED CRIME)

I personally have attended difficult audit committee meetings during which, following an incident which triggers an audit committee investigation, the chief audit executive is brought in to answer the audit committee's questions only to reveal that he or she had earlier detected the issues under investigation and had discussed them informally with the officer who owned the affected units only to be rebuffed. However, it was clear he or she had not brought these concerns to the designated internal reporting officer and/or the audit committee. In my experience, once the audit committee investigation is concluded, the chief audit executive is terminated. Don't let that be you. As that post 9/11 ad said: "If you see something, say something."

To be sure, you should follow your organization's official reporting lines. Also, make sure to document your reporting of detected incidents. However, if you feel that your information is being inappropriately withheld from those above your next-in-line direct report, you will find yourself in a difficult position. What you should do first is make sure that you have your facts straight; that you have interpreted the facts correctly as evidence of an incident that needs to be elevated (i.e. qualitatively or quantitatively material) and that your next-in-line direct report does not have some valid reasons for delaying their elevation (i.e. collecting additional evidence prior to elevating). However, your superior should be able to explain the delay to you in an open and professional manner. If not, you have a tough choice to make. I am reminded of the Cadet Prayer at West Point, the U.S. Army Academy, "Make us to choose the harder right instead of the easier wrong". The truth is that the truth will eventually come out. The choice you have make is whether you want to take some potentially difficult consequences now or face worse consequences including the loss of your good reputation down the road. I personally would and have taken the difficult consequences now.

INVESTIGATOR NOTES

Many years ago I was working for one of the Big 4. I was retained by a law firm representing a large Japanese company which had been victimized in a complex commodities fraud. Investigations are funny things; you never know where they will lead. In this case, after having been named an expert witness in a federal civil litigation proceeding, my investigation added a former client of my firm as a defendant. This former client did not take this well and demanded that my firm halt the investigation and resign from the engagement.

The pressure started when I got a call from the managing partner of the office that had serviced the former client. I explained that I had been named an expert in a federal trial and that we had collected millions of dollars in fees, so it would be impossible for me to resign from the engagement. I didn't think much more about it; I knew my firm would understand its ethical responsibilities and back me up. I was wrong. The former client dangled a new project worth several million dollars in front of certain partners of my firm in exchange for me resigning from the engagement and they crumpled like a cheap suit. I was called into an urgently arranged star chamber meeting where I was ordered to resign from the engagement and threatened with termination if I refused or even said anything to the lawyer who hired me. I explained again about my role as a named expert witness in a federal trial and the millions in fees we had collected from the Japanese company, which was a current and not former client. They told me it did not matter; I was to return to my office and keep quiet. They would hire lawyers to defend me if I agreed to do what they told me to do.

I flew back to my home on a Friday evening. I was up most of the night wrestling with what to do. At the time I was supporting a wife and three small children. But, Saturday morning I called the lawyer who had retained me on behalf of the Japanese company and asked her to meet that morning in violation of the direct orders I had been given. I told her everything.

Monday morning we were in front of the federal judge presiding over our case. After hearing what we had to say the judge instructed the clerk to contact the former client's law firm, which was in a different city, to instruct them to appear in his court at 4 pm that same day. The clerk returned to explain that the former client's attorneys had told him that they were too busy to appear today and asked if later in the week would work. The judge then instructed his clerk to telephone the lawyers and tell them that they could either agree to appear voluntarily at 4 pm or he would be forced to have the U.S. Marshals collect them and bring them to his court.

After hearing their statements about what their client had done, the judge instructed the lawyers to remind their client and my firm that tampering with a witness in a federal trial is a crime and to knock it off or there would be more serious consequences. As it was, the judge applied severe sanctions to the law firm's client. I knew my time with the firm would come to an abrupt end at the end of the trial and I was right. I was terminated as had been promised in the star chamber meeting.

This can, in many ways, be a dangerous business even when you are careful and do the right thing. But, I could get up in the morning and look myself in the mirror and feel okay about the person looking back at me. If I had taken that Faustian bargain, I would have been a pariah in the local legal community and would probably have been terminated anyway. As it turned out, I was contacted by a Canadian friend who asked if I would be interested in opening an office for them in my home city. I agreed and it turned out to be the best experience of my entire professional career. I just want you to know that like everything else in this book, I'm not offering abstract academic concepts; I learned most of this stuff the hard way.

SECTION III: CREATING AN EFFECTIVE INVESTIGATION AND RESOLUTION STRATEGY (THE KEY IS TO BEGIN WITH THE END IN MIND)

I was retained by a West Coast law firm representing a large vehicle manufacturer. The vehicle manufacturer told me one of their company-owned dealerships was losing a ton of money and they couldn't understand why. They wanted me to go in and find out. So, I traveled to a lovely town on the Pacific; I love the West Coast of the United States. My investigation first revealed that the dealership's CFO had just overseen a changeover from one accounting system to another system. Sadly, during the transition, all the data on the old system were lost. Also, the backup tapes had been mysteriously corrupted. I also learned that the CFO had not thought to run the two systems in parallel to confirm that the new system was producing reliable information. Funny how a man with the CFO's experience could make so many "mistakes". Also, by snooping around and engaging in conversation with as many of the dealership's lower-level employees (it pays to always have friends in low places) as I could, I learned that the dealership's president was quite the prolific gambler. Gamblers often have financial needs that can stretch far beyond their means. Also, the president wasn't gambling in legitimate casinos; he did most of his gambling in the bars that lined the docks. I did some surveillance and confirmed what I had been told.

At this point, I called the lawyers who had retained me to share my findings. They asked me what I thought it meant. I told them that I was reasonably certain that the CFO was engaged in some form of embezzlement or fraud but I had to do more work to learn exactly what he was doing. I asked them to ask the client whether they had some form of crime coverage available. I told them it would be useful to know what the policy terms were before I proceeded with the investigation. Those policies typically have tricky notice and exclusion provisions, which can void coverage if you're not careful. They said that they would, but I never heard any more about it.

My investigation eventually discovered that the CFO had compromised the President. The CFO had a brother who owned a vehicle leasing business. The CFO arranged for his brother to pay off the president's gambling debts in exchange for his cooperation and silence regarding the CFO's sales of vehicles to his brother. I discovered the CFO caused hundreds of vehicles to be sold to his brother at a price that was below the direct cost to manufacture the vehicles. This was a literal example of the widget business; the vehicle manufacturer was losing thousands of dollars on each vehicle sale to the CFO's brother. The president signed off on all these sales transactions. I was able to document these facts with respect to every sales transaction with the CFO's brother.

Hooray, time to declare victory and leave the field. Wrong! Our shared joy in solving the mystery of the declining dealership was short-lived.

The vehicle manufacturer tried to recover the money lost to the CFO's scheme by filing a claim on one of their insurance policies. Unfortunately, that policy only provided coverage for employees who either violated laws or written company policies. The unfortunate reality was that written company policy allowed the president to sell vehicles at any price he chose to "meet competition in the local market." There was also no law preventing the president from selling vehicles at any price he chose. So, the insurance company successfully denied coverage. The vehicle manufacturer's general counsel was livid. Who did he blame? Yours truly. After all, it was my investigation that revealed the evidence the insurance company used to deny the claim. At that point, the fact that I had specifically asked about the details of the vehicle manufacturer's insurance coverage before completing the investigation was ignored; just another annoying thing I had done.

I tell you this story to illustrate the fact that if you don't understand what the people paying you want to accomplish from your investigation, you can conduct the investigation perfectly and end up with a very disappointed employer. But, there is a way to avoid this calamity. Begin with the end in mind. What do I mean by that? Before I agree to undertake an investigation, I always ask whoever is paying me the same question, "If this were to turn out exactly as you would like it to, what would that look like?" I then walk them through a variety of scenarios and discuss the pros and cons of each. So, if a company has been a victim of embezzlement by a senior officer, I would go through the following possible approaches to investigation and resolution:

- We could do enough of an investigation to create a compelling package to deliver to law enforcement and let them take it from there. The big benefit of this approach is that it has a relatively low cost. Another benefit is that it sends a strong deterrent message to other employees who might contemplate similar conduct. However, once you turn a case over to law enforcement you lose control of the investigation and the evidence. Officer and director insurance policies usually exclude illegal acts from coverage. Any civil litigation you might bring to effect recovery will likely be stayed pending the outcome of the criminal trial. If the law enforcement agency makes recoveries from the defendant, they will often deduct a so-called "cost of law enforcement" charge. (I thought that was what the taxes we pay were for, but I am apparently wrong.)
- Another approach could be to do enough work to put together a notice of claim to our insurance carrier if we have crime coverage in one of our insurance policies. The benefit of this approach is that it can be relatively low cost. It does not have the same deterrent effect as turning the investigation over to law enforcement or conducting our own robust internal investigation. The message this sends is something like, "We view theft as a normal cost of doing business." The problem with this approach is that insurance companies don't like paying claims. The insurance company will demand a great deal more information that we will have to pay to gather, the cost of which they may or may not be willing to reimburse. The insurance carrier may also want to conduct its own investigation using its own claims agent. The insurance company will also likely actively try to deny coverage, so we will need to associate competent insurance coverage counsel to counter the insurance company's lawyer. If they do pay a claim, they may require us to cooperate in their subrogation efforts to recover monies from the perpetrator or other liable parties. This could result in uncontrollable disruption and costs to us. Because the insurance company, after paying the claim, would control the litigation against the perpetrator and other liable parties, we could potentially suffer reputational damage that we would have otherwise avoided. Our insurance premiums and other costs (e.g. controls reviews by an external consultant) may rise; our renewal policy may not contain the same coverage and may be cancelled.
- The third option would be for the company to conduct its own investigation. The benefit is that you are able to completely control the investigation, the evidence gathered, the preparation of the fidelity insurance claim, and the civil litigation. The company could mostly control

the dissemination of information and, by extension, impact on brand image. A properly conducted investigation also sends a strong deterrent message to employees, "The company has zero tolerance for crime and will spend the necessary resources to punish the perpetrator." The big downside of this approach is cost. Internal investigations are expensive. By the time you pay the outside lawyers, forensic accountants, other external resources and cover the cost of internal resources, the overall cost can be quite high. Think hundreds of thousands to millions. In working with clients, I always make sure that the negative surprises occur on the front end before anyone has worked an hour of billable time. The one other downside to this approach versus the law enforcement approach is that law enforcement has access to evidence discovery tools that those of us in the private sector can only dream about.

I answer any questions my employer may have and make myself available to discuss any open items. But, I do not allow my employer to make a decision during this discussion. Rather, I ask them to think it over and call me when they have a clear idea of the approach with which they are most comfortable. Only when my client and I have a meeting of the minds about their expectations for the outcome of the investigation and the approach to get that outcome will I agree to proceed.

EXERCISES

1. Identify the resources available to you today to respond to incidents of white-collar crime or violations of company policy.
2. Reach out to your resources and discuss how you would work together to respond to an incident.
3. Create a high-level response plan that lays out what you will do when you become aware of an incident.
4. Write out several incident scenarios for different types of incidents.
5. Develop a response plan for each type of incident.
6. What steps should you take when you become aware of an incident?
7. What should you not do when you become aware of an incident?
8. What types of actions can result in committing obstruction of justice?
9. Imagine you are speaking to the person asking you to initiate the investigation. What questions would you ask to make sure you fully understand the objectives and expectations for your investigation?
10. What are your lines of reporting?
11. What steps would you take if the business unit or process owner asks you to hold off on reporting your findings?

CHAPTER SUMMARY/KEY TAKEAWAYS

So, here are some things to think about:

- If you see something say something.
- Always be proactive and cautious when responding to an incident.
- Do not do anything that may worsen the problem.

In Chapter 4 you will learn to conduct an effective preliminary investigation.

4 Conducting an Effective Preliminary Investigation

SECTION I: IS IT MORE LIKELY THAN NOT THAT SOMETHING HAPPENED?

Once I was hired by a large international financial services company to investigate a borrower for which they had created a multi-hundred-million-dollar facility to purchase durable medical equipment to be leased to health-care providers in several different Latin American countries. The borrower was in serious default and my client believed it was due to some fraud committed by the borrower. After going through the steps above, my client decided that they wanted to do a robust investigation, which they would fund and control. Using their right to audit the borrower's lease files, my client got me access to those files at the borrower's headquarters. My review of those lease files produced some truly startling revelations. The original lease application, underwriting, and lease documentation all appeared to be in order. But, when I reviewed the servicing and amendment parts of the file, I was shocked. Many of the leases were to health-care providers in a country where the government had passed legislation to change the word dollar, in all financial contracts, to peso. In another country, where the borrower had many leases to health-care providers, the law provided that even when lessees were in payment default, they did not have to surrender the leased equipment until they were finished using it. Correlating these findings with the work being performed by an insolvency expert, it was clear that the borrower had not engaged in fraud. So, here, it was very clear that it was not likely that something had happened.

When I hear the details of an allegation, there are several questions I ask myself: Is the source of the allegation credible? The federal government would be at the top of my list and an outside competitor would be at the bottom. I also want to know if there is any evidence supporting the allegation and what type of evidence is it? Contemporaneous documentary evidence from an independent source (e.g. check image from a bank) would be very impactful to me. Hearsay testimony from a person with a conflict of interest (e.g. someone in line for the job held by person who is the subject of the allegation) would be less so. I also ask myself whether the thing alleged could have happened in the way it was alleged to have happened. However, while pondering that question I ask what business or internal controls would have had to fail for the thing to have occurred as alleged. I also ask myself if any one person had the access, authority, and opportunity to cause this thing to happen or if others would have needed to be involved. I then ask who these people might be. One thing we often fail to consider in the heat of the moment is that people commit crimes. Find the person(s) who had the access, authority, and opportunity to commit the alleged crime to find the key to a successful investigation outcome.

So, if the allegation came from a credible source, there is contemporaneous reliable evidence supporting the allegation, the conduct could have happened, or it could have happened if controls failed and there is a person or persons who could have committed the conduct, you should conclude that it is more likely than not that the alleged conduct occurred. This is usually an iterative process that follows a logical path; it usually doesn't all come together on the first day. But, it is a process that must be pursued deliberately and concluded as quickly as possible. Delay could allow the perpetrators cause more harm and, if they get wind of what you are doing, destroy valuable

DOI: 10.1201/9781003121558-6

evidence. Once you form your conclusion, communicate it and your support for it to your designated next-in-line report. Then wait, but not too long.

SECTION II: WHAT IS THE ACTUAL PROBLEM AND HOW WILL WE RESOLVE IT?

To answer this question the first thing I do is develop a working hypothesis of what happened and a list of questions that must be answered by the investigation to test the hypothesis. What questions you ask? You guessed it; knowing what the central allegations are, I want to craft questions, the answers to which will tell my employer the who, what, where, when, and why of the problem(s). Incidentally, the why can be the least important of these unless it somehow informs the answers to the other questions. The reason is that because my expert testimony will often be forensic accounting testimony where there is usually no requirement to establish motive, but this depends entirely on the case and the merits that have to be proven. I am thankful for this because, as many of you have heard in an old piece of wisdom, that to know why a person does something or other, "you need to be able to walk in their shoes." Well, believe me, I have been doing this work for more than 40 years and I'm here to tell you that it is impossible to walk in many of these people's shoes; you'll go crazy trying.

INVESTIGATOR NOTES

Many years ago I was hired by a large law firm in Chicago to investigate a strange occurrence at a recently shuttered Chicago subsidiary of a large metals company. It seems that upon closing the subsidiary the local bank was instructed to send any future statements etc. to the company's headquarters. As it turned out the first set of statements, delivered to headquarters, contained negotiated checks to vendors, which had check numbers not within the range of check numbers in the check register. My investigation revealed that the president of the subsidiary had set up a massive fictitious vendor fraud scheme that was so large it caused the parent company to shut down a profitable subsidiary and terminate hundreds of employees because the subsidiary president's thefts made it look unprofitable. Now, to get to my point about standing in someone else's shoes, do you know why the subsidiary president committed this monumental crime and cost all those people their jobs? He was obsessed with acquiring antique quilts and sea trunks that he could not afford. He literally had warehouses in neighboring Wisconsin filled with mostly worthless antique quilts and sea trunks. Stand in those shoes; I dare you.

But, I digress; back to the hypothesis, other questions and their answers. The first thing I do is to create a working hypothesis, based on the allegations, to explain what is currently believed to have occurred. Next, I do enough research to determine what questions must be answered to test the voracity of the hypothesis. Then I go over these questions with my employer and their attorney to make sure that we are in complete agreement about the working hypothesis and the questions that must be answered. I also confirm what access to facilities and person I will have and what evidence will be supplied versus what I will have to collect on my own.

Next, I decide on what resources I will need to get the questions answered. These could be more junior forensic accountants, investigators, data scientists, subject matter experts, etc. I also determine what equipment and software I will need. Then I determine what these things will cost and the most cost-effective way to acquire them.

Then I put together a preliminary workplan. Let me say that the preliminary workplan is a business document that cannot normally be shielded from discovery in litigation, so be very careful about what you include in it and the language you use to describe things.

Just because you are conducting a fraud investigation or forensic accounting engagement doesn't mean you get to leave your professional standards at the door. Let's take a look at what the professional standards require in terms of planning, execution, and supervision.

Here's what the IIA requires:

"2010 – Planning

2010.A2 – The chief audit executive must identify and consider the expectations of senior management, the board, and other stakeholders for internal audit opinions and other conclusions."[1]

Section 2010.A2 is important because it requires that the expectations of senior management, the board, and other stakeholders be considered. This is such an important step in planning your approach to and execution of the investigation. By doing this you will assure that you do not end up in the terrible situation where you do a great investigation that answers questions that management and the board do not care about.

"2201 – Planning Considerations

In planning the engagement, internal auditors must consider:

- The strategies and objectives of the activity being reviewed and the means by which the activity controls its performance.
- The significant risks to the activity's objectives, resources, and operations and the means by which the potential impact of risk is kept to an acceptable level.
- The adequacy and effectiveness of the activity's governance, risk management, and control processes compared to a relevant framework or model.
- The opportunities for making significant improvements to the activity's governance, risk management, and control processes.

2201.A1 – When planning an engagement for parties outside the organization, internal auditors must establish a written understanding with them about objectives, scope, respective responsibilities, and other expectations, including restrictions on distribution of the results of the engagement and access to engagement records.

2201.C1 – Internal auditors must establish an understanding with consulting engagement clients about objectives, scope, respective responsibilities, and other client expectations. For significant engagements, this understanding must be documented.

2230 – Engagement Resource Allocation

Internal auditors must determine appropriate and sufficient resources to achieve engagement objectives based on an evaluation of the nature and complexity of each engagement, time constraints, and available resources.

Interpretation

Appropriate refers to the mix of knowledge, skills, and other competencies needed to perform the engagement. Sufficient refers to the quantity of resources needed to accomplish the engagement with due professional care.

2240 – Engagement Work Program

Internal auditors must develop and document work programs that achieve the engagement objectives.

> **2240.A1** – Work programs must include the procedures for identifying, analyzing, evaluating, and documenting information during the engagement. The work program must be approved prior to its implementation, and any adjustments approved promptly.
>
> **2240.C1** – Work programs for consulting engagements may vary in form and content depending upon the nature of the engagement.

2300 – Performing the Engagement

Internal auditors must identify, analyze, evaluate, and document sufficient information to achieve the engagement's objectives.

2340 – Engagement Supervision

Engagements must be properly supervised to ensure objectives are achieved, quality is assured, and staff is developed."[2]

So, the IIA requires that the engagement be planned to achieve the objectives agreed upon with management and/or the board. There must be a work program that includes the procedures to be executed to achieve the objectives. Also, the investigation must be supervised to assure that the objectives are achieved, quality is assured, and staff are developed.

> **"Interpretation**
> *The extent of supervision required will depend on the proficiency and experience of internal auditors and the complexity of the engagement. The chief audit executive has overall responsibility for supervising the engagement, whether performed by or for the internal audit activity, but may designate appropriately experienced members of the internal audit activity to perform the review. Appropriate evidence of supervision is documented and retained."[3]*

"The IIA's Perspective is that internal auditing is an independent, objective assurance and consulting activity designed to add value and improve an organization's operations. Its role includes detecting, preventing, and monitoring fraud risks and addressing those risks in audits and investigations.

It should consider where fraud risk is present within the business and respond appropriately by auditing the controls of that area, evaluating the potential for the occurrence of fraud and how the organization manages fraud risk (Standard 2120.A2) through risk assessment, and audit planning. It is not internal audit's direct responsibility to prevent fraud happening within the business. This is the responsibility of management as the first line of defense.

The internal auditor should not be expected to have the expertise of a person whose primary responsibility is to investigate fraud. Such investigations are best carried out by those experienced to undertake such assignments.

Internal audit should use its expertise to analyze data sets to identify trends and patterns that might suggest fraud and funding abuse. Where the experience is not available within the internal audit team, the organization should consider recruiting or engaging resources with sufficient knowledge or expertise.

The organization should have a suitable anti-fraud response plan outlining key policies and investigation methodologies. The plan should make clear the role of internal audit when there is suspected fraud and associated control failure.

Operationally, internal audit should have sufficient knowledge of fraud to:

- Identify red flags indicating fraud may have been committed.
- Understand the characteristics of fraud and the techniques used to commit fraud, and the various fraud schemes and scenarios.
- Evaluate the indicators of fraud and decide whether further action is necessary or whether an investigation should be recommended.
- Evaluate the effectiveness of controls to prevent or detect fraud.

Where electronic evidence is collected, internal audit should provide assurance on whether necessary access rights and legislative requirements are being met.

Where fraud has occurred, internal audit should understand how the controls failed and identify opportunities for improvement. It should consider the probability of further errors, fraud, or noncompliance across the organization and reassess the cost of assurance in relation to potential benefits.

Many factors, including available resources, influence how organizations respond to fraud. Some organizations include fraud awareness (proactive) and response (reactive) mechanisms within the internal audit activity, and some internal auditors may investigate fraud.

FIVE QUESTIONS

Managing fraud risk is something every organization faces. Governing bodies and executive management can help clarify roles in fraud risk management, including internal audit's role.

Here are five key questions the governing body should be asking:

1. *Does the organization have a fraud response plan in place that outlines key policies and investigation methodologies?*
2. *Who carries out fraud investigations within the organization?*
3. *Is internal audit tasked with identifying where fraud risk is present, and does it audit controls in these areas?*
4. *When fraud has occurred, does internal audit investigate to understand how the controls failed and how they can be improved?*
5. *Is internal audit tasked to investigate fraud, and, if so, does it possess the proper skill sets to carry out such investigations?*

If internal audit is required to investigate fraud, the internal auditor should have the necessary skills and experience to undertake the investigation and discharge their professional responsibility without jeopardizing the investigation and associated evidence.

Investigation is not typically an internal audit task; therefore, internal auditors should exercise due professional care (Standard 1220) by considering the extent of work needed to achieve the engagement's objectives and the related complexity, materiality, or significance. They should decide if they are best placed to undertake the investigation or whether to engage internal legal counsel, human resources, qualified or certified fraud examiners, digital forensics, or outside legal and investigative expertise.

Conclusion: The threat of fraud is one of the most common challenges to governance that organizations face without regard to size, industry, or location. Having proper internal control procedures in place that include an appropriate response plan is fundamental to battling fraud. Internal audit possesses intimate control knowledge of the organization. A combined assurance approach is key in this regard to understand the gaps in controls to allow for the manifestation of fraud.

Fraud investigations are best carried out by those experienced to undertake such assignments. Organizations should not expect internal audit's skill set to include fraud investigation. Instead, internal audit should support the organization's anti-fraud management efforts by providing necessary assurance services over internal controls designed to detect and prevent fraud. If circumstances require internal audit to take on an investigatory role, internal auditors should exercise due professional care."[4]

So, the IIA doesn't preclude internal auditors from performing fraud investigations. It merely states that internal auditors should not be expected to possess the skills necessary to investigate fraud. It also reminds internal auditors that if they do decide to investigate fraud they are expected to have the necessary experience, skills, and exercise due professional care. Notice the following five key questions that the IIA require you to ask:

1. Do you have a fraud response plan?
2. Who will carry out fraud investigations?
3. Are you responsible for identifying fraud risk and do you have audit-related controls?
4. When fraud occurs, are you responsible for investigating related control failures?
5. Are you responsible for investigating fraud and do you have the necessary skills?

Now let's look at what the AICPA requires:

"Standards for Forensic Services

6. The general standards of the profession are contained in the "General Standards Rule" (ET sec. 1.300.001 and 2.300.001) and apply to all services performed by a member, including forensic services. They are as follows:

- *Professional competence.* Undertake only those professional services that the member or the member's firm can reasonably expect to be completed with professional competence.
- *Due professional care.* Exercise due professional care in the performance of professional services.
- *Planning and supervision.* Adequately plan and supervise the performance of professional services.
- *Sufficient relevant data.* Obtain sufficient relevant data to afford a reasonable basis for conclusions or recommendations in relation to any professional services performed.

7. A member must serve his or her client with integrity and objectivity, as required by the AICPA Code of Professional Conduct. A member performing forensic services should not subordinate his or her opinion to that of any other party.

8. A member performing forensic services must follow additional general standards, which are promulgated to address the distinctive nature of such services. These standards are established under the "Compliance With Standards Rule" (ET sec. 1.310.001 and 2.310.001):

- *Client interest.* Serve the client interest by seeking to accomplish the objectives established by the understanding with the client while maintaining integrity and objectivity.
  - *Integrity.* Integrity is described as follows: "Integrity requires a member to be, among other things, honest and candid within the constraints of client

confidentiality. Service and the public trust should not be subordinated to personal gain and advantage. Integrity can accommodate the inadvertent error and the honest difference of opinion; it cannot accommodate deceit or subordination of principle." (ET sec. 0.300.040)

- *Objectivity.* Objectivity is described as follows: "Objectivity is a state of mind, a quality that lends value to a member's services. It is a distinguishing feature of the profession. The principle of objectivity imposes the obligation to be impartial, intellectually honest, and free of conflicts of interest." (ET sec. 0.300.050)

- *Understanding with client.* Establish with the client a written or oral understanding about the responsibilities of the parties and the nature, scope, and limitations of services to be performed and modify the understanding if circumstances require a significant change during the engagement.

- *Communication with client.* Inform the client of (*a*) conflicts of interest that may occur pursuant to the "Integrity and Objectivity Rule" (ET sec. 1.100.001 and 2.100.001), (*b*) significant reservations concerning the scope or benefits of the engagement, and (*c*) significant engagement findings or events.

- The "Conflicts of Interest for Members in Public Practice" interpretation (ET sec. 1.110.010) under the "Integrity and Objectivity Rule" provides guidance about the identification, evaluation, disclosures, and consent related to conflict of interest. This section states, in part, the following:

  - In determining whether a professional service, relationship, or matter would result in a conflict of interest, a member should use professional judgment, taking into account whether a reasonable and informed third party who is aware of the relevant information would conclude that a conflict of interest exists.

9. A member engaged as an expert witness in a litigation engagement may not provide opinions pursuant to a contingent fee arrangement, unless explicitly allowed otherwise under the "Contingent Fees" (ET sec. 1.510).

10. The ultimate decision regarding the occurrence of fraud is determined by a trier of fact; therefore, a member performing forensic services is prohibited from opining regarding the ultimate conclusion of fraud. This does not apply when the member is the trier of fact. A member may provide expert opinions relating to whether evidence is consistent with certain elements of fraud or other laws based on objective evaluation.

Effective Date

11. This statement is effective for new engagements accepted on or after January 1, 2020. Early application of the provisions of this statement is permissible."[5]

So, the AICPA requires that the fraud investigator or forensic accountant who accepts a forensic accounting assignment be competent, plan the engagement, supervise the engagement, and collect sufficient relevant data to support any conclusions or opinions. They must perform the professional service with integrity and objectivity to serve the client interest by accomplishing the objectives agreed upon with the client.

A fraud investigation or forensic accounting engagement is in no sense an audit. Forensic accountants go to great lengths to make sure that clients and others who will be provided with their work product know that they absolutely did not conduct an audit. You should make sure to do this, also. Having said that the standards promulgated for auditors do provide useful guidance that allows fraud investigators and forensic accountants satisfy the legal standards for their expert testimony.

"AU Section 311

Planning and Supervision – the Standards of Field Work

(Supersedes SAS No. 22)

Source: SAS No. 108; SAS No. 114.

See section 9311 for interpretations of this section.

Effective for audits of financial statements for periods beginning on or after December 15, 2006. Earlier application is permitted.

.01 The first standard of field work states, "The auditor must adequately plan the work and must properly supervise any assistants." This section establishes standards and provides guidance to the independent auditor conducting an audit in accordance with generally accepted auditing standards on the considerations and activities applicable to planning and supervision. Planning and supervision continue throughout the audit.

.02 Audit planning involves developing an overall audit strategy for the expected conduct, organization, and staffing of the audit. The nature, timing, and extent of planning vary with the size and complexity of the entity, and with the auditor's experience with the entity and understanding of the entity and its environment, including its internal control.

.03 Obtaining an understanding of the entity and its environment, including its internal control, is an essential part of planning and performing an audit in accordance with generally accepted auditing standards.[1] The auditor must plan the audit so that it is responsive to the assessment of the risk of material misstatement based on the auditor's understanding of the entity and its environment, including its internal control. Planning is not a discrete phase of the audit, but rather an iterative process that begins with engagement acceptance and continues throughout the audit as the auditor performs audit procedures and accumulates sufficient appropriate audit evidence to support the audit opinion. As a result of performing planned audit procedures,[2] the auditor may obtain disconfirming evidence that might cause the auditor to revise the overall audit strategy.

.04 The auditor with final responsibility for the audit may delegate portions of the planning and supervision of the audit to other firm personnel.[3] For purposes of this section, (a) firm personnel other than the auditor with final responsibility for the audit are referred to as *assistants* and (b) the term *auditor* refers to either the auditor with final responsibility for the audit or assistants.

Planning
Appointment of the Independent Auditor

.05 Early appointment of the independent auditor has many advantages to both the auditor and the client. Early appointment enables the auditor to plan the audit prior to the balance-sheet date.

.06 Although early appointment is preferable, an independent auditor may accept an engagement near or after the close of the fiscal year. In such instances, before accepting the engagement, the auditor should ascertain whether circumstances are likely to permit an adequate audit and expression of an unqualified opinion and, if they will not, the auditor should discuss with the client the possible necessity for a qualified opinion or disclaimer of opinion. Sometimes the audit limitations present in such circumstances can be remedied. For example, the taking of the physical inventory can be postponed or another physical inventory, which the auditor can observe, can be taken.

.07 Section 315, *Communications Between Predecessor and Successor Auditors*, provides guidance concerning a change of auditors. Among other matters, it describes communications that a successor auditor should evaluate before accepting an engagement.

Establishing an Understanding with the Client

.08 The auditor should establish an understanding with the client[4] regarding the services to be performed for each engagement[5] and should document the understanding through a written communication with the client. Such an understanding reduces the risk that either the auditor or the client may misinterpret the needs or expectations of the other party. For example, it reduces the risk that the client may inappropriately rely on the auditor to protect the entity against certain risks or to perform certain functions that are the client's responsibility. The understanding should include the objectives of the engagement, management's responsibilities, the auditor's responsibilities, and limitations of the engagement.[6]

.09 An understanding with the client regarding an audit of the financial statements generally includes the following matters:

- The objective of the audit is the expression of an opinion on the financial statements.
- Management is responsible for the entity's financial statements and the selection and application of the accounting policies.
- Management is responsible for establishing and maintaining effective internal control over financial reporting.
- Management is responsible for designing and implementing programs and controls to prevent and detect fraud.
- Management is responsible for identifying and ensuring that the entity complies with the laws and regulations applicable to its activities.
- Management is responsible for making all financial records and related information available to the auditor.
- At the conclusion of the engagement, management will provide the auditor with a letter that confirms certain representations made during the audit.
- The auditor is responsible for conducting the audit in accordance with generally accepted auditing standards. Those standards require that the auditor obtain reasonable rather than absolute assurance about whether the financial statements are free of material misstatement, whether caused by error or fraud. Accordingly, a material misstatement may remain undetected. Also, an audit is not designed to detect error or fraud that is immaterial to the financial statements. If, for any reason, the auditor is unable to complete the audit or is unable to form or has not formed an opinion, he or she may decline to express an opinion or decline to issue a report as a result of the engagement.
- An audit includes obtaining an understanding of the entity and its environment, including its internal control, sufficient to assess the risks of material misstatement of the financial statements and to design the nature, timing, and extent of further audit procedures. An audit is not designed to provide assurance on internal control or to identify significant deficiencies. However, the auditor is responsible for ensuring that those charged with governance are aware of any significant deficiencies that come to his or her attention.
- Management is responsible for adjusting the financial statements to correct material misstatements and for affirming to the auditor in the management representation letter that the effects of any uncorrected misstatements[7] aggregated by the auditor during the current engagement and pertaining to the latest period

presented are immaterial, both individually and in the aggregate, to the financial statements taken as a whole.

These matters should be communicated in the form of an engagement letter.

.10 An understanding with the client also may include other matters, such as the following:

- The overall audit strategy (see paragraphs .13 through .18)
- Involvement of specialists or internal auditors, if applicable
- Involvement of a predecessor auditor
- Fees and billing
- Any limitation of or other arrangements regarding the liability of the auditor or the client, such as indemnification to the auditor for liability arising from knowing misrepresentations to the auditor by management (regulators may restrict or prohibit such liability limitation arrangements)
- Conditions under which access to audit documentation may be granted to others
- Additional services to be provided relating to regulatory requirements
- Other services to be provided in connection with the engagement, for example, nonattest services, such as accounting assistance and preparation of tax returns subject to the limitations of Ethics Interpretation No. 101–3, "Performance of Nonattest Services," [ET section 101.05], under Rule 101, *Independence*.

Preliminary Engagement Activities

.11 In addition to the procedures related to the appointment of the auditor and establishing an understanding of the terms of the engagement as discussed above, the auditor should perform the following activities at the beginning of the current audit engagement:

- Perform procedures regarding the continuance of the client relationship and the specific audit engagement.
- Evaluate the auditor's compliance with ethical requirements, including independence.

The auditor's consideration of client continuance and ethical requirements, including independence, occurs throughout the performance of the audit engagement as changes in conditions and circumstances occur. However, the auditor's initial procedures on both client continuance and evaluation of the auditor's ethical requirements (including independence) should be performed prior to performing other significant activities for the current audit engagement. For continuing audit engagements, such initial procedures often occur shortly after (or in connection with) the completion of the previous audit. See QC section 10B, *A Firm's System of Quality Control*. [Paragraph amended due to the issuance of SQCS No. 7, December 2008.]

.12 The purpose of performing these preliminary engagement activities is to consider any events or circumstances that may either adversely affect the auditor's ability to plan and perform the audit engagement to reduce audit risk to an acceptably low level or may pose an unacceptable level of risk to the auditor. Performing these preliminary engagement activities helps ensure that the auditor plans an audit engagement for which:

- The auditor maintains the necessary independence and ability to perform the engagement.
- There are no issues with management integrity that may affect the auditor's willingness to continue the engagement.
- There is no misunderstanding with the client as to the terms of the engagement.

The Overall Audit Strategy[8]

.13 The auditor should establish the overall audit strategy for the audit.

.14 In establishing the overall audit strategy, the auditor should:

a. Determine the characteristics of the engagement that define its scope, such as the basis of reporting, industry-specific reporting requirements, and the locations of the entity;

b. Ascertain the reporting objectives of the engagement to plan the timing of the audit and the nature of the communications required, such as deadlines for interim and final reporting, and key dates for expected communications with management and those charged with governance; and

c. Consider the important factors that will determine the focus of the audit team's efforts, such as determination of appropriate materiality levels, preliminary identification of areas where there may be higher risks of material misstatement, preliminary identification of material locations and account balances, evaluation of whether the auditor may plan to obtain evidence regarding the operating effectiveness of internal control, and identification of recent significant entity-specific, industry, financial reporting, or other relevant developments.

In developing the audit strategy, the auditor also should consider the results of preliminary engagement activities (see paragraphs .11 and .12) and, where practicable, experience gained on other engagements performed for the entity. The Appendix [paragraph .34] to this section lists examples of matters the auditor may consider in establishing the overall audit strategy for an engagement.

.15 The process of developing the audit strategy helps the auditor determine the resources necessary to perform the engagement, such as:

- The resources to assign for specific audit areas, such as the use of appropriately experienced team members for high-risk areas or the involvement of experts on complex matters;

- The amount of resources to assign to specific audit areas, such as the number of team members assigned to observe the inventory count at material locations, the extent of review of other auditors' work, or the audit budget in hours to allocate to high-risk areas;

- When these resources are to be assigned, such as whether at an interim audit period or at key cutoff dates;

- How such resources are to be managed, directed, and supervised, such as when team briefing and debriefing meetings are expected to be held, how the auditor with final responsibility and manager reviews are expected to take place (for example, on-site or off-site), and whether to complete engagement quality control reviews.

.16 The auditor should update and document any significant revisions to the overall audit strategy to respond to changes in circumstances.

.17 Once the audit strategy has been established, the auditor is able to start the development of a more detailed audit plan to address the various matters identified in the audit strategy, taking into account the need to achieve the audit objectives through the efficient use of the auditor's resources. Although the auditor may establish the audit strategy before developing the detailed audit plan, the two planning activities are not necessarily discrete or sequential processes but are closely interrelated since changes in one may result in consequential changes to the other. Paragraphs .19 through .21 provide further guidance on developing the audit plan.

.18 In audits of small entities, the entire audit may be conducted by a very small audit team. Many audits of small entities involve the auditor with final responsibility (who may be a sole practitioner) working with one audit team member (or without any audit team members). With a smaller team, coordination and communication between team members are easier. Establishing the overall audit strategy for the audit of a small entity need not be a complex or time-consuming exercise; it varies according to the size of the entity and the complexity of the audit. For example, a brief memorandum prepared at the completion of the previous audit, based on a review of the audit documentation and highlighting issues identified in the audit just completed, updated, and changed in the current period based on discussions with the owner-manager, can serve as the basis for planning the current audit engagement.

The Audit Plan

.19 The auditor must develop an audit plan in which the auditor documents the audit procedures to be used that, when performed, are expected to reduce audit risk to an acceptably low level.

.20 The audit plan is more detailed than the audit strategy and includes the nature, timing, and extent of audit procedures to be performed by audit team members in order to obtain sufficient appropriate audit evidence to reduce audit risk to an acceptably low level. Documentation of the audit plan also serves as a record of the proper planning and performance of the audit procedures that can be reviewed and approved prior to the performance of further audit procedures.

.21 The audit plan should include:

- A description of the nature, timing, and extent of planned risk assessment procedures sufficient to assess the risks of material misstatement, as determined under section 314, *Understanding the Entity and Its Environment and Assessing the Risks of Material Misstatement.*
- A description of the nature, timing, and extent of planned further audit procedures at the relevant assertion level for each material class of transactions, account balance, and disclosure, as determined under section 318, *Performing Audit Procedures in Response to Assessed Risks and Evaluating the Audit Evidence Obtained.* The plan for further audit procedures reflects the auditor's decision whether to test the operating effectiveness of controls, and the nature, timing, and extent of planned substantive procedures.
- A description of other audit procedures to be carried out for the engagement in order to comply with generally accepted auditing standards (for example, seeking direct communication with the entity's lawyers).

Planning for these audit procedures takes place over the course of the audit as the audit plan for the engagement develops. For example, planning of the auditor's risk assessment procedures may occur early in the audit process. However, planning of the nature, timing, and extent of specific further audit procedures depends on the outcome of those risk assessment procedures. The auditor should document changes to the original audit plan. In addition, the auditor may begin the execution of further audit procedures for some classes of transactions, account balances, and disclosures before completing the more detailed audit plan of all remaining further audit procedures.

Determining the Extent of Involvement of Professionals Possessing Specialized Skills

.22 The auditor should consider whether specialized skills are needed in performing the audit. If specialized skills are needed, the auditor should seek the assistance of a professional possessing such skills, who may be either on the auditor's staff or an outside professional. If the use of such a professional is planned, the auditor should determine whether that professional will effectively function as a member of the audit team. For example, a tax practitioner or a professional with valuation skills employed by the audit firm may be used to perform audit procedures as part of the audit team's work on the audit. If such a professional is part of the audit team, the auditor's responsibilities for supervising that professional are equivalent to those for other assistants (see paragraph .28). In such circumstances, the auditor should have sufficient knowledge to communicate the objectives of the other professional's work; to evaluate whether the specified audit procedures will meet the auditor's objectives; and to evaluate the results of the audit procedures applied as they relate to the nature, timing, and extent of further planned audit procedures.

.23 The use of professionals possessing information technology (IT) skills to determine the effect of IT on the audit, to understand the IT controls, or to design and perform tests of IT controls or substantive procedures is a significant aspect of many audit engagements. In determining whether such a professional is needed on the audit team, the auditor should consider such factors as the following:

- The complexity of the entity's systems and IT controls and the manner in which they are used in conducting the entity's business
- The significance of changes made to existing systems, or the implementation of new systems
- The extent to which data is shared among systems
- The extent of the entity's participation in electronic commerce
- The entity's use of emerging technologies
- The significance of audit evidence that is available only in electronic form

.24 Audit procedures that the auditor may assign to a professional possessing IT skills include inquiring of an entity's IT personnel how data and transactions are initiated, authorized, recorded, processed, and reported and how IT controls are designed; inspecting systems documentation; observing the operation of IT controls; and planning and performing tests of IT controls.

Communication with Those Charged with Governance

.25 Section 380, *The Auditor's Communication With Those Charged With Governance*, requires the auditor to communicate with those charged with governance an overview of the planned scope and timing of the audit. [As amended, effective for audits of financial statements for periods beginning on or after December 15, 2006, by Statement on Auditing Standards No. 114.]

Additional Considerations in Initial Audit Engagements

.26 The auditor should perform the following activities before starting an initial audit:

- *a.* Perform procedures regarding the acceptance of the client relationship and the specific audit engagement (see QC section 10B).
- *b.* Communicate with the previous auditor, where there has been a change of auditors (see section 315) [Paragraph amended due to the issuance of SQCS No. 7, December 2008.]

.27 The purpose and objective of planning the audit are the same whether the audit is an initial or recurring engagement. However, for an initial audit, the auditor may need to expand the planning activities because the auditor does not ordinarily have the previous experience with the entity that is considered when planning recurring engagements. For initial audits, additional matters the auditor should consider in developing the overall audit strategy and audit plan include the following:

- Arrangements to be made with the previous auditor, for example, to review the previous auditor's audit documentation.
- Any major issues (including the application of accounting principles or of auditing and reporting standards) discussed with management in connection with the initial selection as auditors, the communication of these matters to those charged with governance, and how these matters affect the overall audit strategy and audit plan.
- The planned audit procedures to obtain sufficient appropriate audit evidence regarding opening balances.
- The assignment of firm personnel with appropriate levels of capabilities and competence to respond to anticipated significant risks.
- Other procedures required by the firm's system of quality control for initial audit engagements (for example, the firm's system of quality control may require the involvement of another partner or senior individual to review the overall audit strategy prior to commencing significant audit procedures or to review reports prior to their issuance).

Supervision

.28 Supervision involves directing the efforts of assistants who are involved in accomplishing the objectives of the audit and determining whether those objectives were accomplished. Elements of supervision include instructing assistants, keeping informed of significant issues encountered, reviewing the work performed, and dealing with differences of opinion among firm personnel. The extent of supervision appropriate in a given instance depends on many factors, including the complexity of the subject matter and the qualifications of persons performing the work, including knowledge of the client's business and industry.

.29 The auditor with final responsibility for the audit should communicate with members of the audit team regarding the susceptibility of the entity's financial statements to material misstatement due to error or fraud, with special emphasis on fraud. Such discussion helps all audit team members understand the entity and its environment, including its internal control, and how risks that the entity faces may affect the audit. The discussion should emphasize the need to maintain a questioning mind and to exercise professional skepticism in gathering and evaluating evidence throughout the audit.[9]

.30 In addition, assistants should be informed of their responsibilities and the objectives of the audit procedures they are to perform. They should be informed of matters that may affect the nature, timing, and extent of audit procedures they are to perform, such as the nature of the entity's business as it relates to their assignments and possible accounting and auditing issues. The auditor with final responsibility for the audit should direct assistants to bring to his or her attention accounting and auditing issues raised during the audit that the assistant believes are of significance to the financial statements or auditor's report so the auditor with final responsibility may assess their significance. Assistants also should be directed to bring to the attention of appropriate individuals in the firm difficulties encountered in performing the audit, such as missing documents or resistance from client personnel in providing access to information or in responding to inquiries.

.31 The work performed by each assistant, including the audit documentation, should be reviewed to determine whether it was adequately performed and documented and to evaluate the results, relative to the conclusions to be presented in the auditor's report. The person with final responsibility for the audit may delegate parts of the review responsibility to other assistants, in accordance with the firm's quality control system.

See section 339, *Audit Documentation*, for guidance on documenting the review of audit documentation.

.32 Each assistant has a professional responsibility to bring to the attention of appropriate individuals in the firm disagreements or concerns with respect to accounting and auditing issues that the assistant believes are of significance to the financial statements or auditor's report, however those disagreements or concerns may have arisen. The auditor with final responsibility for the audit and assistants should be aware of the procedures to be followed when differences of opinion concerning accounting and auditing issues exist among firm personnel involved in the audit. Such procedures should enable an assistant to document his or her disagreement with the conclusions reached if, after appropriate consultation, he or she believes it necessary to disassociate himself or herself from the resolution of the matter. In this situation, the basis for the final resolution should also be documented.

Effective Date

.33 This section is effective for audits of financial statements for periods beginning on or after December 15, 2006. Earlier application is permitted."

---

[1] Section 314, *Understanding the Entity and Its Environment and Assessing the Risks of Material Misstatement*, establishes standards and provides guidance on obtaining an understanding of the entity and its environment, including its internal control, sufficient to assess the risks of material misstatement, whether due to error or fraud, at the financial statement and relevant assertion levels. Section 318, *Performing Audit Procedures in Response to Assessed Risks and Evaluating the Audit Evidence Obtained*, establishes standards and provides guidance on the auditor's overall responses and the nature, timing, and extent of further audit procedures that are responsive to the assessed risks.

[2] Paragraph .03 of section 314 provides guidance with respect to the procedures the auditor performs in obtaining an understanding of the entity and its environment to establish a frame of reference within which the auditor plans the audit and exercises professional judgment about assessing the risk of material misstatement of the financial statements.

[3] Paragraphs .14 through .20 of section 314 provide guidance about the discussion among the audit team. The objective of this discussion is for members of the audit team to gain a better understanding of the potential for material misstatements of the financial statements resulting from fraud or error in the specific areas assigned to them, and to understand how the results of the audit procedures that they perform may affect other aspects of the audit, including the decisions about the nature, timing, and extent of further audit procedures.

[4] Generally, the auditor establishes an understanding of the services to be performed with the entity's management. In some cases, the auditor may establish such an understanding with those charged with governance. The term *those charged with governance* means the person(s) with responsibility for overseeing the strategic direction of the entity and obligations related to the accountability of the entity. This includes overseeing the financial reporting and disclosure process. In some cases, those charged with governance are responsible for approving the financial statements (in other cases, management has this responsibility). For entities with a board of directors, this term encompasses the term *board of directors* or *audit committees* expressed elsewhere in generally accepted auditing standards.

[5] See paragraph .28 of QC section 10B, *A Firm's System of Quality Control*. [Footnote amended due to the issuance of SQCS No. 7, December 2008.]

[6] The objectives of certain engagements may differ. The understanding should reflect the effects of those objectives on the responsibilities of management and the auditor, and on the limitations of the engagement. The following are examples:

- Audits of an entity's compliance with applicable compliance requirements performed under section 801, *Compliance Audits*.
- Application of agreed-upon procedures to specified elements, accounts, or items of a financial statement (see AT section 201, *Agreed-Upon Procedures Engagements*).
- Engagements to examine the design and operating effectiveness of an entity's internal control over financial reporting that is integrated with an audit of the entity's financial statements (see AT section 501, *An Examination of an Entity's Internal Control Over Financial Reporting That Is Integrated With an Audit of Its Financial Statements*). [Footnote revised, December 2010, to reflect conforming changes necessary due to the issuance of SAS No. 117.]

[7] Paragraph .07 of section 312, *Audit Risk and Materiality in Conducting an Audit*, states that a misstatement can result from errors or fraud.

[8] See paragraphs .04 through .06 of section 318 for further guidance on the auditor's overall responses in performing an audit.

[9] For further guidance on the discussion among the audit team, see paragraphs .14 through .18 of section 316, *Consideration of Fraud in a Financial Statement Audit*, and paragraphs .14 through .20 of section 314.[6]

An example of a workplan and good faith fee estimate that I created follows in Figure 4.1.

Client
Fee Detail Estimate

	Low Range (USD)			High Range (USD)		
	Hours	Rate	Amount	Hours	Rate	Amount

PHASE I - INFORMATION GATHERING AND DOCUMENT REQUESTS

Purpose, Objectives and Deliverables:

Develop our understanding of the chronological sequence of relevant events (i.e. construction activities, project issues, work scope, non-conforming work, etc.) and all related information: oral, documentary or other; available to inform our analysis. This information will likely first come from Client personnel (until Defendant produces its records in the arbitration), and will be largely focused on the Defendant documentation that is in Client's possession. We will, of course, work closely with Client personnel and Law Firm to find the most effective means to develop this information. We will begin by analyzing real world activities on the project activities identified in invoices, and available supporting documentation, in order to compare it to what would commonly be expected in the industry under similar circumstances. This will inform our analysis of costs and damages, including amounts Defendant is seeking, the adequacy of Defendant's backup for its claims, and to confirm amounts that Client seeks through its counterclaims based on Defendant's own estimates to repair and/or complete its work. From these analyses we will construct Gantt or other appropriate models and related analyses to develop a basis for Mr. Jennings expert opinions and to inform Client & Law Firm.

1 Information Gathering, Evaluation and Analysis

	Hours	Rate	Amount	Hours	Rate	Amount
Senior Principal	160	$ 555	$ 88,800	240	$ 555	$133,200
Principal	16	$ 375	$ 6,000	24	$ 375	$ 9,000
Senior Manager	0	$ 350	$ -	0	$ 350	$ -
Manager	16	$ 325	$ 5,200	24	$ 325	$ 7,800
Senior Associate	0	$ 285	$ -	0	$ 285	$ -
Analyst	0	$ 150	$ -	0	$ 150	$ -
Total	192		$100,000	288		$150,000

Mr. Jennings will gather all documentation in Client's possession related to the claim under the supervision of Law Firm, with assigned Client personnel. Mr. Jennings expects to spend considerable time consulting with client personnel knowledgeable about the project and Defendant activities.

2 Assist in Identifying Documents to Request from Defendant

	Hours	Rate	Amount	Hours	Rate	Amount
Senior Principal	60	$ 555	$ 33,300	80	$ 555	$ 44,400
Principal	12	$ 375	$ 4,500	16	$ 375	$ 6,000
Senior Manager	0	$ 350	$ -	0	$ 350	$ -
Manager	12	$ 325	$ 3,900	20	$ 325	$ 6,500
Senior Associate	0	$ 285	$ -	0	$ 285	$ -
Analyst	0	$ 150	$ -	0	$ 150	$ -
Total	84		$ 41,700	116		$ 56,900

Mr. Jennings will assist Law Firm in drafting detailed document requests for Defendant to further development of the above-referenced opinions. Mr. Jennings may also assist Law Firm in developing objections to Defendant's document requests. Mr. Jennings may begin to provide additional services such as witness identification, witness interviews, and application of industry knowledge to emerging issues.

Total Phase I	276		$141,700	404		$206,900

PHASE II - REVIEW DOCUMENTS

Purpose, Objectives and Deliverables:

Analyze all of the relevant information Defendant produces, including information not necessarily admitted into evidence in the arbitration, but of the type normally relied on by experts like Mr. Jennings. Mr. Jennings will also rely on the work of other experts in arriving at his expert opinions, including Client's technical experts. Where possible, Mr. Jennings will employ electronic tools to make his document analysis more efficient. Mr. Jennings will refine the Gantt or other appropriate models and related analyses, and begin to construct his expert report of his opinions related to Defendant's claim and the amounts of Client's counterclaim damages.

3 Review of Documents Defendant Produces

	Hours	Rate	Amount	Hours	Rate	Amount
Senior Principal	160	$ 555	$ 88,800	220	$ 555	$122,100
Principal	32	$ 375	$ 12,000	40	$ 375	$ 15,000
Senior Manager	0	$ 350	$ -	0	$ 350	$ -
Manager	32	$ 325	$ 10,400	40	$ 325	$ 13,000
Senior Associate	40	$ 285	$ 11,400	40	$ 285	$ 11,400
Analyst	40	$ 150	$ 6,000	40	$ 150	$ 6,000
Total	304		$128,600	380		$167,500

Mr. Jennings will analyze Defendant's document production and use the results of this work to further refine the Gantt type model and expert findings.

4 Assist Law Firm in Drafting Client Statement of Defense and Identifying / Interviewing Potential Fact Witnesses

	Hours	Rate	Amount	Hours	Rate	Amount
Senior Principal	60	$ 555	$ 33,300	80	$ 555	$ 44,400
Principal	8	$ 375	$ 3,000	16	$ 375	$ 6,000
Senior Manager	0	$ 350	$ -	0	$ 350	$ -
Manager	8	$ 325	$ 2,600	16	$ 325	$ 5,200
Senior Associate	0	$ 285	$ -	0	$ 285	$ -
Analyst	0	$ 150	$ -	0	$ 150	$ -
Total	76		$ 38,900	112		$ 55,600

Mr. Jennings will assist Law Firm in incorporating expert finding into Law Firm's submissions to the Tribunal on behalf of Client. Mr. Jennings will also assist, under Law Firm's supervision and with Client approval, in identifying fact witnesses and developing questions for those witnesses for purposes of Client direct testimony and cross examination of Defendant witnesses.

5 Assist in Analyzing Fact Witness Statements and Reviewing/Editing Statement of Defense

	Hours	Rate	Amount	Hours	Rate	Amount
Senior Principal	80	$ 555	$ 44,400	100	$ 555	$ 55,500
Principal	16	$ 375	$ 6,000	16	$ 375	$ 6,000
Senior Manager	0	$ 350	$ -	0	$ 350	$ -
Manager	8	$ 325	$ 2,600	8	$ 325	$ 2,600
Senior Associate	0	$ 285	$ -	0	$ 285	$ -
Analyst	0	$ 150	$ -	0	$ 150	$ -
Total	104		$ 53,000	124		$ 64,100

Mr. Jennings will work with Law Firm and Client personnel to evaluate and analyze fact witness statements. In particular, Mr. Jennings will correlate fact witness statements with other evidence and Mr. Jennings' own expert findings. Mr. Jennings will continue to work with Law Firm on Client's statement of Defense and Counterclaims.

Total Phase II	484		$220,500	616		$287,200

PHASE III - EXPERT TESTIMONY

Purpose, Objectives and Deliverables:

Develop Mr. Jennings' written expert testimony, related exhibits and list of information relied upon in reaching his expert opinions. This work will also be subjected to appropriate peer review prior to issuance. The work will address Mr. Jennings' opinions related to the amount of Defendant's claims, the adequacy of supporting backup material for Defendant's claims, and the damages amounts of Client's counterclaims.

6 Drafting Expert Report

	Hours	Rate	Amount	Hours	Rate	Amount
Senior Principal	80	$ 555	$ 44,400	160	$ 555	$ 88,800
Principal	80	$ 375	$ 30,000	80	$ 375	$ 30,000
Senior Manager	0	$ 350	$ -	0	$ 350	$ -
Manager	16	$ 325	$ 5,200	16	$ 325	$ 5,200
Senior Associate	16	$ 285	$ 4,560	16	$ 285	$ 4,560
Analyst	0	$ 150	$ -	0	$ 150	$ -
Total	192		$ 84,160	272		$128,560

Mr. Jennings will work with Law Firm and Client personnel to complete all of his analyses and perform all required quality control procedures. Mr. Jennings will draft his expert report, integrating all relevant analyses and exhibits.

Total Phase III	192		$ 84,160	272		$128,560

Total Phases I - III	952		$446,360	1,292		$622,660

FIGURE 4.1

As you can see, whenever possible, I use generic descriptions for the workplan tasks. Again, this document is likely discoverable, so you want to be very careful to draft it in a way that won't get you into any trouble later.

SECTION III: DETERMINING WHETHER OTHER RELATED PROBLEMS EXIST

I worked on an audit committee investigation for a major public company that had acquired its largest competitor, a private company, a year earlier. All I knew when the investigation started was that a whistleblower had reported that he believed that the acquiree was overstating revenues by recording sales of products that had not been delivered to customers. Okay, I thought, that should be easy enough. However, before diving in on the ground investigation at the acquired subsidiary, I did some financial analysis work on the subsidiary's balance sheets, income statements, and statements of changes in cash for the current year and the year prior to the acquisition. The reasons I did this were:

- People who engage in fraud are usually what I call opportunity criminals; if any opportunity, unrelated to their central criminal conduct presents itself they act.
- This type of fraud comes into being because actual customers are not creating demand for the products being sold. The effects of this lack of demand, in a company that claims to be growing revenues, usually show up in a variety of other places: cash, accounts receivable, inventory, accounts payable, net revenue, gross profit, and many others.

Not surprisingly, accounts receivable started high, as a percentage of sales, and had grown significantly. The reserve for doubtful accounts was quite low. Inventory was quite high as a percentage of sales; there was a very small reserve for obsolescence. Net revenues were higher than gross revenues and there was the all too familiar hockey stick handle at the end of the period. Gross margin was not sufficient to cover below the line expenses; they were losing money. Cash flow from operations had declined significantly. There were other findings, but these were the most significant.

At this point the subsidiary still maintained its pre-acquisition headquarters, staff, operations, accounting systems, and records. When I arrived, I was greeted by the CFO who let me know that my presence was an unnecessary disruption and very annoying; I love it when they start that way. It makes their ultimate destruction less of a burden to my conscience. I asked to see the personnel records for the sales and accounting staff. That was my first step and it was very useful. I noted that most of the staff in key roles did not have a college education. Most had only worked for this company. That was a tip off to me that someone didn't want anyone who possessed independent knowledge pushing back against their instructions. I then asked to interview the employees and was granted access without a chaperone. I'm sure the CFO didn't expect me to interview the delivery truck drivers, but that what I did first. They provided more accurate information about the subsidiary's revenue accounting than the entire accounting department. They told me that, at the end of certain months, they were instructed to deliver customer orders to third-party warehouses that were approximately 10 miles from the subsidiary's main warehouse. Then later they were instructed to go to the third-party warehouses and pickup the products they had dropped off before month's end to deliver to the actual customers. How odd? The drivers let me make copies of their paperwork for the first and second shipments for the most recent year-end. Next, I interviewed the shipping clerk who confirmed what the drivers had told me. He said that he just thought the customers just weren't ready for the products at month's end and rather than clogging up their warehouse, they would first ship the products to the third-party warehouse. Ah the bliss of doing without knowing what you are supposed to be doing. I asked him whether he thought that substantially increased their shipping costs. He said he guessed so, but that wasn't really any of his business. This is the opposite of "if you see something say something." He was kind enough to also let me make copies of his paperwork.

Next, I made sure that I knew the sales contract terms for these customers. The contracts all reflected FOB the customer's dock. Then, I asked the revenue accountant to help me find the related sales. They were all recorded as revenue prior to year-end. I say accountant, but the revenue accountant had no accounting degree. She believed that all the revenue transactions were recorded properly. Incidentally, I asked the revenue accountant if she knew why net revenues were higher than gross revenues. She said that it had to do with the way they recorded vendor rebates. Basically, they allocated their vendor rebates to the customers who ordered the products that created the rebates; well, I guess a credit is a credit.

I then paid a visit to the manager of accounts receivable. A nice elderly woman who had never attended college and spent her entire career at the subsidiary. I went through a printout of the subsidiary's accounts receivable aging. I was expecting bad but nothing could have prepared me for what I saw on those pages. There were numerous accounts receivable adding up to tens of million dollars that were not days or months, but rather, years overdue. I asked her how there could be so many accounts so far overdue and yet there was no provision for doubtful accounts or bad debt expense. She told me it was because of their CFO's commitment to protecting their company's interests. I was perplexed by this answer, so I asked her what she meant by "his commitment to the company"? She said, "Well he never gives up on monies owed to the company. Many is the time I have gone to him with the notice of Chapter 7 dissolution of one of our customers. He always tells me the same thing; I don't care, we are never giving up and you are not to write it off!"

On to inventory. Remember there were no inventory write-offs or allowance for obsolescence. The warehouse was quite the journey through the history of health-care products. I pulled a statistically valid sample of the inventory records. I was able to conclude, with 95% certainty, that 43% of the inventory items in the warehouse had not been drawn since the acquisition.

With these preliminary results I went back to update the audit committee. Many of the audit committee members were confused by my findings, how could the due diligence have missed these things? They grumbled to one another until the committee chair, a storied investor, shouted: "I do not have time for this horse——! Bring me our internal audit director and the partner in charge of our audit. I want them to explain how they missed this." The internal audit executive said that he noted many of these problems and discussed them with the CFO but was rebuffed. He then backed off and did nothing else. Neither of them survived this event.

My point in telling you this story is twofold:

- If you see something say something.
- You cannot be transactional in your investigative mindset. You must consider what other things could be impacted by the identified conduct.

So, what can we take away from this example? Fraud is never a linear pattern of conduct. It is always a crime of opportunity. You must step back and consider all the areas that might be impacted by fraud.

In planning your investigation, you should always:

- Research the incident you have identified to learn everything you can about it.
  - You might consult internal company resources like training materials, policy and procedure documents, presentations, webinars, etc.
  - You could also do external research. Start with a search engine and use the most specific terms you can about the particular facet of the incident you are investigating; you

will be surprised how often you get relevant hits. From there you can use increasingly robust research tools or you can hire someone to do the research for you. It is amazing how many targeted research firms and online platforms there are out there. One caveat though, be careful not to reveal any information to third parties that you would not want to have to produce in response to a discovery request or that would create problems if it were leaked by the third party.

- Brainstorm with others about all the areas of your company that might be impacted by the conduct that created the incident.
  - Some of my best insights result from bouncing ideas off colleagues. I can't tell you how many times a colleague will say something, in one of these sessions, that will trigger a great insight into the problem at hand. This is a powerful investigative tool that I strongly encourage you to consider using. Make sure the colleagues are in your group and understand the importance of keeping all information confidential. No elevator brainstorming please!

INVESTIGATOR NOTES

Be careful about identifying "patterns of conduct" in your expert report or other testimony; it can lead to an easy impeachment of your testimony by an opponent who can identify all the instances where your pattern of conduct does not explain what happened at particular points in time (i.e. exceptions to your pattern of conduct). Criminals often simply take advantage of every opportunity, that presents itself, to steal. In hindsight, some of this conduct will appear to follow a pattern, but it actually is simply the criminal reacting to the opportunities to steal at different points in time.

The analogy I use is that it is like a table representing chronologic time. Magnets are placed under the table representing dates on which opportunities to steal existed. Then iron filings are scattered across the top of the table representing all conduct (i.e. criminal and not criminal conduct) that occurred during the time period. If you were to blow away the iron filings not held in place by the magnets, walked to the other end of the table and looked backward at the table top, you would perceive what appeared to be a pattern. However, what you would actually be looking at were the random intersections of the criminal with opportunities that existed on certain dates. Also, your pattern would not explain the activities represented by the iron filings that were blown away from the tabletop.

"Patterns of Conduct" are not necessary to prove most crimes. They may result in sentencing enhancements for certain crimes, but in my opinion, are way more trouble in providing expert testimony than they are worth.

- Do financial statement analyses; descriptive and analytical statistical analyses; or other appropriate analyses to identify other areas that may have been affected.
  - Use financial statement analyses that will identify anomalies related to the accounts that might have been affected by the conduct you are investigating. If you are investigating alleged revenue overstatement, you might consider a horizontal analysis of income statements where you are looking at the change in income statement accounts over several periods. You could also look at the timing of sales within the last month of the period you are interested in; there will usually be a hockey stick pattern (see Figure 4.2).

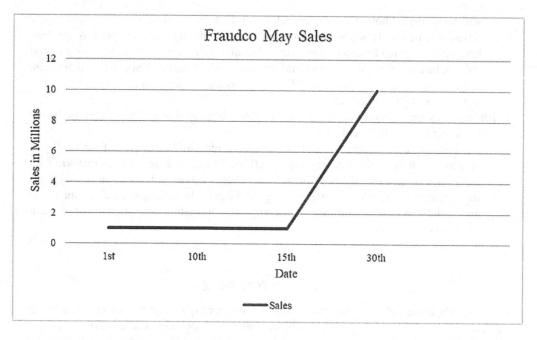

FIGURE 4.2

- Start thinking about the team you would need to investigate each of these areas. You will need people with a variety of skill sets. Also, you will have to decide whether to use internal or external resources. The questions you will need to answer here are:

  For employees:

  - Will working on the investigation take employees away from critical duties related to operating the company?
  - Will the work of employees not be covered by the attorney-client work product privilege, and therefore be discoverable?
  - Will employees be able to keep their work confidential?
  - Will employees be ostracized as a result of working on the investigation?
  - Will employees' work be viewed as independent?

  For outside contractors:

  - Will outside contractors be competent to perform the work (i.e. some large consulting firms' staff investigation projects with inexperienced personnel. Others advertise every professional service imaginable under one roof; is that possible? Others take the daring, "I always wanted to work on a _____.") You get my point. If you do use outside consultants; do thorough due diligence, including contacting references.
  - How much will external consultants cost? This is less of an issue with audit committee investigations; in those cases the audit committee has direct responsibility for financial arrangements.

A great way to control cost is to require the consultants to break their workplan into discreet segments that result in a reviewable deliverable and to make a good faith fee estimate for each segment. If they tell you that it is impossible to estimate the cost of each proposed segment, you will know that they have not done this type of work enough and are too inexperienced for your needs; it's time to say "thanks but no thanks"! If they exceed their fee estimate on the first one or two segments, you can either make them honor their original estimate or at least be in a position to recognize very early that they lack financial accountability. In the latter case I would advise, circumstances permitting, that you replace them.

Now look, sometimes there are unforeseeable circumstances that will cause one of your consultants to exceed their estimate and if the consultant can provide concrete evidence of what caused the unforeseeable circumstance, it would be perfectly reasonable for you to accept that evidence and move on. But, in my experience, unforeseeable circumstances are not common and may mean that your consultant wasn't experienced enough to foresee them or that they were simply trying to buy the work with a low bid. You must consider that possibility and, if you decide one of the two preceding reasons led to the overrun, you should consider immediately replacing the consultant if feasible. Otherwise, you will need to have a very direct conversation with the consultant where you put guardrails in place to prevent future overruns.

EXERCISES

1. If an allegation of fraud or other misconduct is made to you, what questions would you want answered before deciding what you will do?
2. If you conclude that the allegation is credible who would your report it to?
3. You are told that significant payments are being made to phony vendors.
   a. What questions do you want answered?
   b. What answers would cause you to conclude the allegation was credible?
   c. Based on your company, write a working hypothesis of what happened.
   d. Write questions to test the hypothesis.
   e. Write a workplan to get your questions answered.
4. You are told that your customer data has been stolen by cyber criminals.
   a. What is your strategy for responding to this crime?
   b. What specialized resources will you need internally?
   c. What specialized resources will you need externally?
5. Write a fraud response plan for your organization.
6. What are the key requirements imposed by the IIA on fraud investigators and forensic accountants?
7. What are the key requirements imposed by the AICPA on fraud investigators and forensic accountants?
8. You find credible evidence of a senior executive falsifying expense reports.
   a. What is your working hypothesis of what occurred?
   b. What questions would you want your investigation to answer?
   c. Write a workplan to get your questions answered.
   d. Make a list of persons (titles only please) who might be involved in this fraud.
   e. What other responsibilities and authorities do they possess?
   f. Make a list of the other areas where they might have committed fraud or other white-collar crimes.
9. You find credible evidence of accounts receivable lapping.
   a. What is your working hypothesis of what occurred?
   b. What questions would you want your investigation to answer?
   c. Write a workplan to get your questions answered.
   d. Make a list of persons (titles only please) who might be involved in this fraud.
   e. What other responsibilities and authorities do they possess?
   f. Make a list of the other areas where they might have committed fraud or other white-collar crimes.
10. You find credible evidence of fraudulent accounting entries to your company's books and records.
    a. What is your working hypothesis of what occurred?
    b. What questions would you want your investigation to answer?
    c. Write a workplan to get your questions answered.

    d. Make a list of persons (titles only please) who might be involved in this fraud.

    e. What other responsibilities and authorities do they possess?

    f. Make a list of the other areas where they might have committed fraud or other white-collar crimes.

CHAPTER SUMMARY/KEY TAKEAWAYS

- Did something requiring investigation happen?
- What is the scope of the problem?
- What does the scope of the investigation need to be?
- What other accounts may be affected by the fraud?

In Chapter 5 you will learn how to begin your investigation.

NOTES

1. https://na.theiia.org/standards-guidance/Public%20Documents/IPPF-Standards-2017.pdf, 2010.A2 Copyright © 2017 by The Institute of Internal Auditors, Inc. ("The IIA"). All rights reserved.
2. https://na.theiia.org/standards-guidance/Public%20Documents/IPPF-Standards-2017.pdf, 2201, 2201. A1, 2201.C1, 2230, 2240, 2240.A1, 2240.C1, 2300, 2340 Copyright © 2017 by The Institute of Internal Auditors, Inc. ("The IIA"). All rights reserved.
3. https://na.theiia.org/standards-guidance/Public%20Documents/IPPF-Standards-2017.pdf,2340Copyright© 2017 by The Institute of Internal Auditors, Inc. ("The IIA"). All rights reserved.
4. https://na.theiia.org/about-ia/PublicDocuments/Fraud-and-Internal-Audit.pdf pgs 2 & 3 Copyright © 2019 by The Institute of Internal Auditors, Inc. All rights reserved.
5. https://publication.cpa2biz.com/MainUI/PrintDocument.ashx?id=13 AICPA Standards Forensic Service ssfs-no-1
6. https://www.aicpa.org/Research/Standards/AuditAttest/DownloadableDocuments/AU-00311.pdf

5 Beginning the Investigation

SECTION I: PUTTING THE INVESTIGATION TEAM TOGETHER

A U.S. public company hired a large law firm to conduct an internal investigation for them. The company suspected that the president of a subsidiary they acquired was stealing from them. The subsidiary, a large-scale demolition company, had its field operations entirely under the control of individual project managers. The law firm was told that the company believed, based on a whistle-blower complaint, that the president was using change orders on demolition projects to pay for the construction of the building which the president owned and leased back to the client to serve as the subsidiary's headquarters. The company asked the lawyers to investigate the allegations and report their findings.

The law firm assigned former Justice Department lawyers, who had prosecuted famous criminal cases, to conduct the investigation. They were well-known and came highly recommended. But, the company's general counsel, who hired them, didn't think about the fact that at the Justice Department, these lawyers had FBI agents and other law enforcement investigators available to do the actual investigation work on the criminal cases they prosecuted. These lawyers had no or little experience in direct evidence collection and analysis, especially financial accounting records. It would be like me saying, "Well, I had a world-renowned pharmacologist assist me on an experimental drug theft case at a university research lab (true story) so, I am now capable of conducting audits of good clinical practice at pharmacies"; ridiculous.

The lawyers didn't know what evidence was available or even to ask for it. They took the few records provided to them by the general counsel and started interviewing project managers; they never spoke to lower-level employees or people in the accounting, HR, or finance departments. The lawyers were quickly told by the project managers that their bonuses were based on project profitability, so they would have no incentive to process phony unbillable change orders on their projects. The lawyers duly noted this excellent control and reported to the general counsel that he had nothing to worry about; the whistleblower must have been mistaken.

Case closed? Not so fast. It was later discovered, by yours truly, that the president of the subsidiary had stolen more than $50 million USD, which he used in the construction of "his" headquarters building through phony change orders on all the subsidiary's demolition projects.

Unfortunately, because of the lawyers' faulty conclusion, I was not given nearly so simple a task as the lawyers were. No one at the company told me about the whistleblower complaint or the lawyers' investigation and conclusion. My assignment was: "We believe that the president of our subsidiary and others may be stealing from us and we don't know how; go find out what they are doing and how they are doing it. We need hard evidence before we terminate anyone."

The General Counsel of the parent company asked that I travel to their headquarters in Chicago to present my findings directly to their outside law firm. When I arrived at the parent company's offices, I was directed to a large conference room where I was greeted by the general counsel and introduced to two very important looking senior partners from the parent company's white-shoe law firm. I attempted to engage in some polite conversation to get to know everyone better but was encouraged to move directly into my presentation, which I did. It was easy to tell the story because I had organized it in an easy to use and understand manner in my report. So, I was confidently moving through each finding and showing everyone the tightly-knit evidence package I assembled to support it.

The odd thing was that, as I moved through the presentation, I could see the more senior of the two outside lawyers becoming angrier and angrier; I couldn't figure out why. By the end of my presentation this guy was as red as a beet and both of his fists were tightly clenched. The moment I concluded, he stood straight up out of his chair and demanded that the general counsel fire every one of the project managers immediately. I thought to myself: wow, this guy really cares about his clients. But sadly, I was mistaken. The truth was that his white-shoe law firm was hired a year earlier to conduct exactly the same investigation I had just completed. Unfortunately for them, they had based their entire investigation on witness interviews that were devoid of documents with which to confront the witnesses. So, the same project managers who had admitted to me that the change orders were phony, when confronted with the documentary evidence, had lied to the lawyers because they had no documents with which to challenge them. (You will find the rest of this story in Chapter 8.)

I tell you this story for a couple of reasons. One is that, like in football (European or American), if you put the wrong team on the field you will lose. Also, you will likely allow conduct you need to stop immediately to continue. Finally, you will waste a lot of your company's money. To build a sound structure you need a solid foundation, your team is your foundation.

The investigation team composition will depend on the investigation. Before deciding on who will be on the team, you need to step back and think through who will be able to accomplish each required task most *competently, efficiently, and effectively* will flow from getting the first two right.

The nature of the matter under investigation dictates the composition of the team. Please discard all preconceived notions of who should be on your investigation team. Of course, first we need to consult the lawyers about whether or not we can use internal personnel; that's not your decision to make. So, for the balance of this section we will take that question out of our analysis. Instead, we will focus on the qualities of each team member.

First, we will need a leader or leaders, depending on whether we have one investigative team or several. We will talk more about who will do what in the next section. The leader has to be highly experienced in applying the investigative method to a wide variety of matters over enough time to be able to plan and supervise the investigation.

We also want a leader who has a track record of past success. Remember, it's not practice that makes perfect; it's perfect practice that makes perfect. If someone has a lot of experience but their track record suggests that their results have been spotty, you really want to look carefully at the reasons behind those past failures. Was it a failure to understand the matter correctly and plan and supervise properly or was there some external reason? A good team leader is not the best doer; the leader needs to be the person who charts the course, then inspires team members to go above and beyond to get to the truth as quickly as possible. Good leaders are people who others follow, not out of fear, but because they believe the leader will help them achieve their own goals while being mindful of their needs. A wise man once said, "You can get anything you want out of life as long as you can help enough other people get what they want."

A good leader is someone who has enough real-world experience to be a good storyteller. Stories have great power to address people's concerns and inspire them to give the investigation their all. Once I had a team that had serious doubts about our ability to carry out a large investigation in Asia where none spoke or could read the language. So, I told them a story about another large investigation I had led at a manufacturing company in a European country whose language none of us spoke. I told them that, while there were clearly disadvantages there could also be advantages. I told them that we had a team member from Australia, who looked and sounded like an Australian, who helped us interview witnesses. What the witnesses didn't know was that his parents were immigrants to Australia from the country in which we were working. They made sure that their children, including my Australian friend, learned their native tongue. As the witnesses spoke to one another, my Australian friend took detailed notes. It was almost not necessary to do the interviews. Understand, we never represented that there were no native speakers in our party and they never asked.

This story allowed my Asian team to move beyond their fear of being thrown into the deep end of the language pool and started to imagine how we could use our "foreign appearance" to advantage in our upcoming adventure. They even took it a step further, planning what we might do to get at information more quickly. They had the idea that by being the stupid Americans, it would be logical for us to ask for more help and explanation in understanding things. We could also ask witnesses to do things like draw pictures for us. We could ask if there was anyone who could explain what they were telling us about in English. Of course, we had actual translators at each interview.

Once, I led an investigation on behalf of a wrongly accused accounting executive in a large public company. I told the staff of another similar matter that I had worked on years ago. In that matter, the government had included 108 transactions and related accounting entries that they claimed to be fraudulent. In that case, we were able to clearly prove, from the available evidence, that 105 of the transactions were not fraudulent. However, the three we were not able to prove were not fraudulent cost that man his freedom. I told my team that we were not advocates, whether that man went to jail or not was not up to my team or me in that investigation. In that case, prosecutors and defense counsel presented their evidence to a trier of fact (i.e. jury or judge) who decided his fate. That was not the point of me telling my story to them. The point of my story was that our work was critically important to our client. If we didn't do our job to the very best of our ability, someone could lose their freedom. After a somber moment, everyone got to work.

The leader cannot be a project manager; that is, an instant formula for missing the forest for the trees. The leader must:

- Stay above the day-to-day work.
- Constantly adjust strategy to match new challenges.
- Be able to review the investigation's work product from a perspective not colored by participation in its creation.
- View the work product from the vantage point of how it fits into the overall strategy of the investigation.

So, the next team members we need are the project managers. A good project manager is able to manage team members to get them to complete investigative tasks effectively, accurately, and in a timely manner. In order to accomplish this, good project managers:

- Provide a detailed overview of the investigation, usually in the form of a chronologic story, highlighting the issues under investigation. This story must answer the known who, what, where, when, and why for the team members in their charge.
- They then go through the investigation plan and how the tasks will be divided between team members. At this point, great project managers tell team members that they are all equally responsible for the investigation's success and that there should be no such thing as "that's not my job." Every job is everyone's responsibility.
- Great project managers also make it clear that mistakes will happen and that, rather than being punished for mistakes, team members will be celebrated for identifying them early and working with the project manager and others to resolve them. If external consultants, they explain that if the mistakes result in fee estimate overruns, those will be handled by senior personnel in client billing adjustments and that they are not the team member's responsibility.
- Great project managers hold daily end-of-day sessions with all team members to hear the truth about that day's work: what went well, what didn't work, and how we plan to fix it tomorrow. Team members highlighting these opportunities for improvement are rewarded in some tangible way. A "Team Saver" certificate is enough, just something to tangibly demonstrate to other team members that people who highlight and help resolve mistakes are celebrated not punished.
  - Great team leaders make these sessions casual and even fun; you want everyone to feel comfortable sharing all they know.

- Project managers make sure that each investigative task is explained, in detail, to each team member directly involved in completing that task. They are then encouraged to ask any questions they have or make any comments they want to make. The team members are then encouraged to immediately raise their hand and are assured that they will be helped without any negative consequence.

INVESTIGATOR NOTES

When I was a junior auditor at what was the one of the Big 8 (I'm old, okay!) things were different. Our managers managed projects in an almost exactly opposite manner from the management system described above. Their explanation went something like, "It's an oil & gas company, okay?" and "You have been assigned receivables; you should be able to find everything you need to know in the permanent file, audit program and prior year's workpapers." If ever you deigned to ask a question it was usually met with, "You should already know that" or "I don't know; look it up." If mistakes were detected by performing junior auditors, they were often covered up and caught, if at all, in the partner review. And God forbid that you ever caused the audit to go over budget. Both things would result in severe punishment. Stupid! Any surprise we have so many audit failures by external auditors?

I am happy to report that my system has produced hundreds of investigative successes and only two failures. The first failure, resulting from not beginning with the end in mind, was discussed in Chapter 3. The second occurred because I failed to consider all areas that might be impacted by a discovered fraud.

I was hired by an east coast mezzanine level venture capital firm to investigate the president of a manufacturing company in the South that they had acquired. The president, installed after the former president had been fired, was also the owner of their largest raw material supplier; no conflict of interest was there. Sure enough, I completed the investigation and determined that the manufacturing company had paid for just in excess of $10 million USD in raw materials that were never delivered. I reported my findings to my client. They sent a lawyer to work with me in drafting a release for the president in exchange for him voluntarily resigning and writing a $10-million USD restitution check. The lawyer and I arranged a meeting with the president at the lawyer's office, our theory being that taking the president out of his sphere of power and into a foreign environment would make him feel more vulnerable and less hostile in our negotiation. The lawyer and I spent a lot of time developing a strategy to deal with the president who was known for his fulminate-type personality and frequent loud eruptions when pressed by anyone. We had a resignation letter and release letter prepared for his signature. The president arrived on time at 10 am. We began to go into my findings with him when he raised a hand to us, smiled, and asked, "Are these my resignation letter and release?" He asked for a moment and read the documents carefully. Then he took a checkbook out of his pocket and made out a $10-million USD check, drawn on his personal account, payable to the company. He signed two copies of each document, kept one set, rose, smiled again, and walked out, gently closing the door behind him as though he didn't want to alert anyone to the crime of the century that he had just gotten away with. No push back, no argument about my findings. He must have been thinking, "Here's your signed documents and my check. Now let me be on my way before you idiots figure out exactly how much I stole." I turned to the lawyer and said, "Oh my God; how much did this guy actually steal?" I was so focused on the raw materials fraud that I failed to consider other ways that he might have been stealing from the company.

Next, we need to consider what specialists and subject matter experts we will need to carry out our investigation. If this is an arcane area or if we need information that is beyond a Google search, we may want to add a professional researcher to the team. If you will have to recover electronic data, you should bring an electronic discovery expert on board. If you have massive amounts of data to access, clean, normalize, and analyze, you should consider adding a data scientist to the team. If your investigation involves whether complex regulations were violated or not, you should add a regulatory expert. If you are in a health-care setting and you are investigating alleged upcoding in patient billings, you need a billing and coding expert. Well, you get the idea; this is not a time to try to wing it. The reason is that, in any case, there will be strong push back against your findings. Any amateur gaff will be the basis for impeachment of your findings, no matter how otherwise accurate they may be.

Of course, the forensic accountants will normally comprise the bulk of the team. However, not all forensic accountants are created in the same way. Some will be current internal or external auditors. Some will have come from industry accounting positions. Some will have come from finance. Heck, I once hired an engineer to be a forensic accountant. He was the smartest, most capable intern I had ever had. He eventually went back to school to get his accounting hours, sat for and passed the CPA exam. But when he first came to work for me he had no accounting knowledge. My point being, if you are investigating alleged fraudulent accounting entries, don't select someone with a finance background to assist you. Likewise, if you are investigating alleged misrepresentations to external auditors, don't select a former industry accountant to help you. You get the idea; don't try to fit a square peg in a round hole. You will only create a lot of wasted time, wasted effort, and frustration.

It is also important to select individuals who can work well together. Everyone has strengths and weaknesses. It is important to recognize that and construct the team in a way that balances out those strengths and weaknesses. Also, it is important to select people who respect one another; notice I didn't say they must *like* one another but they must *respect* one another, the team's goals, and the organization. Otherwise, they will engage in infighting, back-stabbing, deliberately breaking the chain of command, and all manner of other mischief that will ultimately harm the investigation.

I once led an audit committee investigation of a large public company. Part of the investigation involved analyzing an extremely large number of paper documents. There were two project managers in two cities managing large teams of analysts for whom, as it turns out, they had little respect. So, they took to consoling one another by writing "funny" expletive laden emails critiquing each analyst. I did not discover these unique communications until I was on the stand in federal court. The opposing lawyer had great fun, for hours, cross-examining me about how the results of the analysts' work, laid out in my expert report, could possibly be credible if the work had been performed by expletive-deleted imbeciles. He put each email up on a huge projection screen in the courtroom and would then ask me to explain to the judge how my conclusions could be credible if they were based on work performed by that bleeping idiot Randy. It was a long day. We ultimately won the war, but this was a very irritating unforced error. This should never happen. Any team member performance issues should be dealt with confidentially in a one-on-one meeting with the team member. You must realize that anything you put in a text or email will be discovered and used against you or your team; don't do it.

SECTION II: DIVIDING RESPONSIBILITIES

When my oldest adult child was five, she played on a football (i.e. soccer) team that I coached. I had some great ideas about how the team should divide responsibilities to take advantage of their individual strengths and weaknesses plus controlling field position effectively against our opponents. We would practice these formations every week but on game day, the same thing always happened; the entire team would congregate around and chase the ball in a tight knot for the entirety of the game. The only exception was when one of them would discover a particularly interesting clover or insect which would cause them to abandon the ball in favor of the new curiosity. The other teams we played against were similarly motivated and organized resulting in the lowest scoring games imaginable, often ending nil/nil. What is the lesson in this story? If you are unable to deploy your assets effectively you will not be able to effectively complete the investigation.

Look, each team member needs to flexible enough to work on any assigned project. However, note the "assigned" in that last sentence. This means that team members need to stick to their knitting until reassigned. Every team member has to be indoctrinated into the importance of their role in the overall investigation. The first step is to tell the story of the incidents under investigation. This story is usually told in chronological order. You should encourage team members to ask questions and make comments during this briefing.

Next, it is time to assign tasks and responsibilities. This is the time to be strategic, not transactional. We want team member assignments to accomplish three unrelated but related goals:

1. We want the most competent people we have working on the tasks we have to complete.
2. We want to make sure that team members, working on the same task, work well together.
3. We want to cross train team members to prevent loss of momentum if a team member is unable to work (e.g. illness, family emergency, etc.).

So, competence is number one for a very good reason, the chain is only as strong as its weakest link. Make sure each team member has the intellectual tools for the task you are asking him or her to complete. This is not the same thing as experience. Experience is when you do something correctly over a period of time in a variety of different situations. Intellectual tools are the basic training competencies to perform the task competently. As an example, if you need to query a database using SQL, make sure the person(s) you assign to that task already know how to write SQL queries. If you are analyzing Generally Accepted Accounting Principles (GAAP) accounting entries and their underlying support, assign someone who already has an expert level understanding of GAAP and has the ability to research GAAP issues. If you need someone to normalize, visualize, and analyze very large data sets, hire a data scientist. My point being that this is no place for on-the-job training. Your team members must possess the requisite training prior to joining the investigation team. It perfectly fine to use more inexperienced staff as long as you properly plan the tasks they are to complete and supervise them.

You also want to make sure that team members assigned to a particular task can work well together. As long as team members respect one another, basic professionalism should take care of the rest. However, it is likely if you do this long enough, that you will end up with one or more troublemakers or malcontents on one or more of your teams. It is best to identify the problem and resolve it quickly. I had a team once which contained, unbeknownst to me, two members who were competing for a love interest, which competition had turned bitter. The easy resolution in that instance was simple: to separate them. In other cases, it is necessary to remove a disruptive team member from the investigation team. Now, please understand that I am not talking about team members who have legitimate complaints, if a team member complains of being discriminated against or harassed in any way that issue needs to be elevated to HR immediately. No punitive action must ever be taken against a person for filing a claim of discrimination or harassment.

Cross-training is good for the team as well as for its members. The team gets more robust and sustainable as more and more members are cross trained on more and more tasks. Team members benefit from learning new things and gaining new experience. Team members who cross-train are also less likely to get bored and burn out. Use this technique; it is remarkably powerful.

SECTION III: GETTING THE TEAM APPROPRIATE ACCESS

As one famous detective once noted, "Without clay I cannot make bricks." In other words, you can have the best people on your team armed with the best tools but, if you do not have access to the evidence related to the conduct you are investigating, it is all for nothing.

I was once hired by an insurance company to investigate a subsidiary that had been infiltrated by members of organized crime. The parent believed these individuals had co-opted members of management at the subsidiary and were causing them to issue financial guarantee bonds in violation of their state insurance license and the parent's policies. When we arrived at the subsidiary's office, we were told that we could not enter. We called the parent's general counsel to report the initial rebuff. She instructed us to wait outside and said she would see what was going on and get back to us. She called back about an hour later and said that the subsidiary's management would permit us to submit requests for documents we wanted to review. They would then make copies for us and we could pick them up and work on them offsite. She asked what I thought of this arrangement; I told her that I didn't think much of it. I asked her what she thought they might be hiding to be so afraid of our presence; she got my point immediately.

We wasted most of the day on these back-and-forth negotiations. Finally, at about 3 pm, we gained access to the office. A very rude man came into the room where we were working; I love it when they start out this way. It makes me far less conflicted about what will happen to them when I finish my work. He told us we were not to leave the room and that whatever we wanted should be made in the form of a request to him which he would then decide whether to honor. I told him that format would not work for us and called the poor general counsel again. I guess this time the gloves came off. About an hour later he came back in and said that we could move about as we chose, except that we were not permitted to enter one specific area in their offices.

He then informed us that it was now closing time so we should leave and resume in the morning. I told him that we had lost so much time with all the negotiation that we would have to work into the night to catch up. He said that this was impossible; back on the phone with my friend the general counsel. Thirty minutes later he came back in and sneered that we could stay. After I made certain that he and the other employees had left for the day I went straight to the off-limits area where I and the team began to look for evidence.

INVESTIGATOR NOTES

I need to make an important point about this type of evidence collection. First, you need to make sure that you have the authority to go through people's desks and filing cabinets without their permission or even knowledge. This is where you need to consult with the lawyers before proceeding, which I did with my friend the general counsel. In this case, the parent owned the office and all the equipment within it, so employees should have had no expectation of privacy. Interestingly, this would not be true in Costa Rica and other countries that have a Constitutional right to privacy wherever they happen to be. The point being, always consult local counsel before proceeding. The second point is that for this type of evidence collection to be effective in later witness interviews, you must make sure the employees never learn that you have gone through their desks and filing cabinets. This can be accomplished only if the team has been trained and practiced returning things to their exact original locations. We will talk more about this later but through careful observation, methodical order preservation, the use of dust patterns and tape, it can be done.

And wow, did we find evidence. We found all the correspondence, laying out how the scheme would work, between the organized crime figures and the subsidiary's management. We found the draft manuscripts for the new financial guarantee bonds and the list of "approved" guarantees. But we couldn't find any actual records of bonds having been issued or payments collected or made. Then it hit us; the dumpster. We spent the balance of the evening in the two dumpsters outside the subsidiary's office. Jackpot! All the issued bonds and related transaction documents were in the dumpster. We spent the rest of the day processing the evidence and creating a standard evidence log for all of it (see Chapter 7 for more on evidence collection).

The next day the witness interviews began working from the lowest level employees (i.e. people who are furthest from the conduct are usually the most forthcoming). All the witnesses were given

Upjohn warnings ahead of being interviewed. We used copies of the documents we had discovered the night before. Imagine the surprise and anger that were exhibited by the subsidiary's management when we showed them the documents. Of course, they demanded to know how we got the documents and demanded that they be returned immediately. I said no and referred them to the parent company's general counsel. I also reminded them that they had a fiduciary duty to cooperate with the investigation. They refused; I think it had something to do with their 5th Amendment rights.

INVESTIGATOR NOTES

A funny thing happened during the investigation I just described above. Our chief investigator decided that he and I should doorstep the main organized crime figure and see what we could learn. Door-stepping is when you go to someone's house, unannounced, to attempt to interview them. This tactic can be very effective because you catch people unprepared and, if you get lucky, they just might answer any question you ask. However, it does have some unique risks. So, we show up at this guy's house and ring the doorbell. A middle-aged woman in a maid's uniform answered the door. We asked if Mr. Made Man was at home and she said he was out running errands. My friend, the chief investigator, thinking quickly on his feet, says, "Well, he told us to come by and pick up an envelope <addressed to the subsidiary we were investigating> that he had on his desk." The maid said that she would go and look for the envelope and invited us to wait in the living room. At which point, we proceed to try to find any evidence we could. But we didn't make it very far. At that moment, two large Dobermans entered the room and confronted us with a very disturbing growl and baring of enormous teeth. I turned to our clever chief investigator and told him I did not think this would end well. But, fortunately, at that moment, the maid returned and scolded the bad doggies; thereby saving us from a terrible fate. We were able to exit with our pride damaged, but, otherwise, intact.

My point in telling you this story is that you must gain unrestricted access to the evidence (i.e. documents, electronic data, witnesses, etc.) in order to conduct a legitimate investigation. Be prepared to be in uncomfortable, awkward situations for long periods of time. You must resist the temptation to settle for anything less than all the available evidence. Imagine if I had caved in at the point where the subsidiary's management offered to evaluate requests for information and then, if they chose to comply, would have provided incomplete and sanitized versions of the evidence I was requesting. I would likely have ended up, unless I got a very lucky break, being forced to conclude that the allegations against the subsidiary and its management were false. And I would have been dead wrong. In fact, an investigation like that would have put my client in a worse situation than they were already in. So, when you are seeking access to evidence for your team, hang in there; we're all counting on you.

EXERCISES

1. What is the most important consideration when assembling an investigation team?
2. Assume you are investigating a massive embezzlement like the one I described in the opening paragraphs of this chapter:
   a. List the skills, credentials, and experience of an ideal team that you would assemble to conduct this investigation.
   b. What past experience questions would you have for each member?
   c. How would you assure that your team members could work well together?
3. What are the roles of each level of leadership in an investigation or forensic accounting team?

4. What is the role of the team leader?
5. What qualities would you want to see in the team leader?
6. What activities should the team leader participate in?
7. What activities should the team leader not participate in?
8. What is the role of the project manager?
9. What qualities would you want to see in the project manager?
10. What activities should the project manager participate in?
11. What structural dynamic should the project manager create with team members?
12. Make a list of non-monetary rewards that you would appreciate receiving and why?
13. Make a list of the other types of team members you would assemble for your investigation.
14. Create a plan to divide responsibilities among your team members. Who will be responsible for doing what?
15. What criteria would you use to make decisions about dividing responsibilities among your team members?
16. How would monitor team members progress toward completing objectives?
17. How would you handle disruptive team members?
18. Who (titles only please) would you reach out to gain appropriate access to persons, data, etc. for your team members?

CHAPTER SUMMARY/KEY TAKEAWAYS

- Leaders lead because others choose to follow.
- Leaders must remain strategic throughout the investigation.
- Project managers must put together teams by identifying members with the correct skill sets needed to complete the required tasks and who can work well together.
- Project managers must plan and supervise teams to assure that the work is carried out correctly, at the necessary pace and is producing valuable, accurate results.
- Project managers must create a work environment and rewards system that extracts the greatest contribution from each team member.
- Project managers must cross-train team members to avoid burnout and create sustainability of the overall investigation.
- Team members must possess the requisite training to complete assigned tasks competently. This will often require identifying team members with a variety of educational backgrounds.
- Tasks need to be assigned to team members based on competence, ability to work well with other team members assigned to the task and cross-training goals.
- Real troublemakers need to be quickly identified and reassigned if possible.
- Team members need to have access to all available relevant evidence.

In Chapter 6 you will learn about the legal issues you will face in conducting investigations.

6 Legal Issues

SECTION I: WORKING WITH LAWYERS

A wise man once said, "The law is a learned profession." What I believe that meant is that the law is a profession which requires continuing research and study to remain proficient. It strikes me that it also means that the lay person who acts as his or her own legal counsel has a fool for a client. Don't let that be you. Let me also say, at the outset of this chapter, that I am not a lawyer. What you will read here are simply my recollections about how I have intersected with various laws and regulations, over my long career, together with how attorneys saved the day, time and again, with their superior legal knowledge. The purpose of this chapter is to make you aware of how you might inadvertently run afoul of laws and regulations or lose the opportunity to accomplish your ultimate objectives and to strongly recommend that you hire competent attorneys to lead you away from those dangers and on to victory.

Years ago, I got a phone call from a good friend who was the CFO of a pharmaceutical company that was developing a new cancer medicine. The company was conducting its early clinical trials in the Bahamas to save money. My friend told me that he had just gotten a call from an FDA agent who said that he wanted to meet with him to answer a few questions the agent had about the pharmaceutical company's compliance with United States Food, Drug, and Cosmetic Act. My friend told me that he told the agent that he would be willing to meet to answer his questions because he had nothing to hide. He asked me what I thought? I told him to hang up with me and call another friend, a gifted criminal defense attorney whose name and number I had given him. Then, I told him to call the FDA agent back and tell him that he would be happy to meet, but wanted him to work through his lawyer to arrange the meeting. All my friend's colleagues at the pharmaceutical company, including physicians, ended up being indicted and/or convicted of felonies.

You see, the doctors, being above the laws the rest of us simple human beings have to obey, started sending their own cancer patients to the Bahamas to receive the new cancer drug. But, cancer being the debilitating disease that it is, many patients became too sick to travel to the Bahamas to receive treatment. So their doctors decided that no law would keep them from continuing to treat their patients in any way they chose. They simply had the research hospital in the Bahamas FedEx the unlicensed cancer drug directly to the patients' homes in the United States. The FDA found out about this little "Doctor's Special" detour and actually met with all the pharmaceutical company's management on the same day so that no one would be able to work out a story with anyone else. The only exception was my friend because he followed my advice and hired a talented lawyer. His lawyer developed a clever legal strategy that included having the cancer patients testify to the new drugs efficacy in a Congressional hearing. My friend was the only one who was never indicted. The other members of the pharmaceutical company concluded they had nothing to hide and decided to retain themselves to act as their legal counsel with a predictable, unfortunate result.

INVESTIGATOR NOTES

I am now going to share something with you that I have strongly encouraged my own children to do if ever they are contacted by an agent of the federal government who says that he or she wants to come by to ask them a few questions. When that happens, please tell them that you want to answer their questions and cooperate, but that you want them to set everything up through your attorney. If you do not have an attorney, tell them you will get back to them with the attorney's name and contact information.

DOI: 10.1201/9781003121558-8

Why do I so strongly recommend this? Well, first of all, federal agents don't come to you for normal business. If you have an ordinary issue with the IRS, they will set up an appointment at the local IRS office. Same thing with the State Department; you want a VISA, you set up an appointment to visit their office. Most federal employees, except when necessary to carry out a compelling government objective, like to stay in their own office. There are many reasons for this: no extra pay for extra effort, stingy expense reimbursement policies, it upsets the daily routine of people who are working for the government because they like having a daily routine, etc. So, if they are asking to come and spend time with you at your home or a coffee shop near your home, it's important and not in a good way.

The second thing is that you do have something to hide; you just may not know what it is, but rest assured, the federal agent knows. What you don't realize is, the federal agent has been using the awesome power of the federal government to gather data, documents, surveillance, and communications that feature you in some form or another. They already know a great deal about what they want to ask you questions about. They either want you to roll over on another subject of the investigation, confess to your own role in the matter you are investigating or catch you lying to them.

Then there are the actual interview questions (see Chapter 8 for details), which begin with the real softballs (e.g. where did you grow up, where did you go to school, how long have you lived here, etc.) and progress to questions about the things they are really interested in (e.g. did you direct Ms. Smith to make this accounting entry on March 31st? Why didn't you report this huge discrepancy in the bank reconciliation? What did you do when you received this email from the chief accounting officer talking about the "rainy day fund"?). This is the point where you begin to slow your answering pace and begin to stutter. It's at that point that the agent reminds you of Section 1001 of Title 18 of the US Code, which makes it a felony to make a false statement or a knowing omission in answering a question posed by an agent of the federal government.

Let's explore this topic by looking at a few examples from my case files. I feel that actual is better than theoretical in reinforcing concepts like this one.

Example 1

Years ago, I worked on a fraud investigation. The scheme revolved around drawing on a letter of credit created by a very large corporation. To draw on the letter of credit, documentary proof of purchase and sale of the commodity was required. The conspirators took the steps necessary to create the fraudulent documents required to draw on the letter of credit.

The scheme was uncovered by a very curious internal auditor who calculated the amount of warehouse space necessary to shelter their enormous inventory of this commodity. He was so curious that he decided to physically inspect the inventory which, of course, wasn't there. The scheme was easy enough to investigate. Most of the documentation was already in the victim's possession because it had been provided to draw on the letter of credit. But, how to get the money back? Once the scheme was uncovered, we not only did the forensic accounting analysis of the data and documents, but also began an on the ground investigation of the co-conspirators focused on establishing criminal intent and recovering assets. The conspirators, having realized they were caught, began trying to move assets beyond our reach. How to stop them? Enter the lawyers.

The victim hired a very gifted lawyer who came up with a very bold strategy. Using the work we had done, under her supervision, to establish the fraudulent nature of the scheme and the cash tracing work we did to trace the victim's money to assets purchased by the conspirators, she went into federal court and sought the very unusual remedy of establishing a constructive trust over the conspirators tainted assets. The judge granted the motion and just like that; the problem of disappearing assets vanished. Remember, your work, no matter how well done; only has value if it can be used to achieve your company's objectives. That often requires it being put to use by competent attorneys.

Example 2

In another case, the president of a subsidiary of a huge public company had stolen so much through a fake vendor fraud scheme that the subsidiary was shut down. The subsidiary's bank was instructed to forward all emails to the parent. The statements contained negotiated checks that were out of sequence. I was hired by the parent's external lawyers to investigate.

I uncovered the scheme and working with the lawyers developed the evidence they needed to get a civil judgment, against the former president, in a federal court. In a desperate attempt to avoid losing all of his assets the former president filed for bankruptcy protection from his creditors, which included my client. Bankruptcy Court functions very differently from US District court because Bankruptcy Court is a court of equity. Things move far more quickly in Bankruptcy Court.

At the first hearing, following completion of all the procedural requirements, the parent's lawyer walked me slowly through my expert testimony to the court. Using demonstrative exhibits I walked the judge step by step through the scheme. I showed her how much was stolen; how it was stolen and by whom. Next, I traced the stolen money into assets purchased and lavish expenses paid by the former president. Finally, I walked her through how the scheme caused many people to lose their jobs.

Following my testimony, the lawyer asked the court for an unusual remedy. Namely, that the judge dismiss the former president's bankruptcy. The judge ruled from the bench at the end of the hearing. I still remember exactly what she said, "Sir, I am hereby dismissing your bankruptcy. You not only bit the hand that fed you, you gnawed it to a bloody stump. I hope your creditors tear you apart like a pack of wild dogs."

Example 3

I worked on a two-part investigation for a very large construction company. They had been in contempt of a federal court for ten years. The court had ordered the company to demonstrate that they were in compliance with a consent decree they had entered into with the Department of Labor, which they had not done. I worked closely with the labor and employment attorneys the company hired to understand the requirements of the consent decree. Then, the lawyers and I conducted an internal investigation to identify all areas of noncompliance. Next, we worked together to develop a comprehensive plan to bring the company into compliance with the consent decree. We then went about gathering evidence of the company's compliance with the consent decree, which we presented to the judge who had issued the contempt order. The judge accepted our findings and removed the contempt order.

The other part of the investigation was focused on the allegations the Department of Labor had made in federal litigation brought against the construction company. The Department alleged that the construction company had committed "face of the records" violations by reducing employees' time, on their self-completed time records, so that the employees would not go over 40 hours per week and earn time and a half overtime pay. This investigation involved a forensic accounting analysis of ten years' worth of employee time and payroll data. It was a daunting task that required a great deal of time and effort to complete. I worked closely with the attorneys throughout to make sure that I was developing the evidence required and update them on the status of my work and any issues I identified.

Based on my forensic accounting investigation I concluded that, with a few exceptions, the construction company had not committed the "face of the records" violations the government alleged. I found, with a few exceptions, that none of the employees' time records had been changed or altered in any way.

This was one of the few times in my career that I was right and wrong at the same time. The trial started in federal court and the Department of Labor presented their case first. Their first witness, a tough-looking blue-collar fellow, took the stand and after answering questions about his background and employment by the construction company, was shown a time entry form that he had completed while employed by the construction company. The Department of Labor lawyer asked him if he was the person who completed the form? He said he was. Then the Department of Labor lawyer asked him if he could tell whether the form had been changed or altered in any way after he completed it? He said no it had not. Well, score one for Bill, I was certain the government lawyer must have been disappointed with the witness's answer since it perfectly aligned with my findings. Then the government lawyer had the witness look at one of the dates on the form and verify that the form contained eight hours worked by him on that date. He said that it did. Then the government lawyer asked him how many hours he had actually worked on that date? The witness stated that he had worked twelve hours on that date. Then the lawyer asked him why, if he worked twelve hours, did he only write eight in the form. The witness answered that his supervisor told him that if he wrote down any more than eight hours, he would have other men break his leg so that he couldn't work at all. At this point, I turned to the lawyer who had retained me and said, "We may have a problem here."

The Department of Labor put ten more witnesses, like that, on the stand. They each gave the same sort of testimony. The lawyers and I worked every night, after trial, to find out everything we could about these witnesses' work at the construction company. It turned out that they all worked on one project for a foreman who had been fired for other misdeeds. Based on my findings, the lawyers concluded that they could prove that the "face of the records" violations were limited to that one project and foreman.

I adjusted my expert report to take into account the impact of the testimony these witnesses had given. I changed my conclusions to reflect the fact that every employee who worked on that project, for that foreman, may have been similarly threatened to falsify their hours. I recalculated all the pay for all the employees who had worked on that project using the same relationship of false to valid hours as stated by the employees who testified. I now felt certain that my work would be unimpeachable, which it was. But that didn't stop the Department of Labor attorney from trying. My direct examination, in which I painstakingly went through my entire process and conclusions in detail, lasted six hours. My cross-examination, by the Department of Labor attorney, lasted eight days; the longest I have ever been on the stand. At the end of the day, our work held up. The construction company's liability was limited to the amount I calculated. But, without the lawyer's steering our ship through the rough waters, all would have been lost.

Example 4

I worked on an internal investigation in Costa Rica of a large resort property. The owners' attorneys, who hired me, were in the United States. The owners suspected the resort's general manager, with the help of other key employees, was stealing them blind. One of the things that I wanted to do, early in the investigation, was to make forensic images of the resort's email servers to see what the general manager and these employees were telling one another in emails. The lawyers did a bit of research of Costa Rican law to see if there were any laws or regulations that would prevent us from doing this type of electronic discovery; they found none. However, just to be safe, they hired local counsel in Costa Rica. As it turns out, in Costa Rica, citizens have an absolute right to privacy wherever they are, even at work. At that time, there were four separate cases making their way to the Costa Rican Supreme Court that were seeking damages and sanctions against people who had done exactly what I was proposing to do.

I could go on and on. The point of me telling you these stories is to illustrate the many ways in which attorneys can keep you from violating laws and regulations, as well as, achieving the ultimate objectives of your company's management using the evidence you gather in the investigation.

Lawyers, like other professionals, are not alike in education, experience, and style. It goes without saying that you should select the most competent lawyer available with the most experience in the type of matter you are working on. Style is an important factor, too. Lawyers must lead the investigation and supervise the investigation team. The reason for this is twofold. First, for the reasons I laid out above and many more, lawyers need to be in the lead to keep the investigative team from getting into trouble by inadvertently violating laws, regulations, or spoiling evidence and making sure that the investigation produces the evidence necessary to accomplish the company's legal objectives at trial or otherwise. Second, in the United States, only lawyers can assert the attorney-client communication privilege to protect the company's communication with the lawyers and the attorney-client work product privilege, which protects the investigative teams' work from discovery by adversaries.

Having said that, there are lawyers who are great leaders. They identify competent project leaders, like you, and let them do what they do best so the lawyer can do what he or she does best. These lawyers are typically there when needed, but not otherwise. They hold very detailed meetings up front to make sure everyone knows what they are responsible for delivering and when. Then they make themselves available to answer questions as they arise and schedule regular update meetings to go over findings with the investigations team. These are the Goldilocks lawyers, not too hot or cold.

Then there are lawyers who believe that they must be involved in every decision that is made and are constantly inserting themselves into the operations of the investigative team. These lawyers can be annoying, but otherwise can be very effective.

The third type of lawyer is completely hands off. Their approach is "you guys go and do whatever you need to do and call me when you are finished."

My advice is treasure the first kind, tolerate the second, and beware of the third; they will get you into trouble you didn't even know existed.

SECTION II: LAWS AND RULES RELATED TO ACCESSING THIRD PARTY INFORMATION

What the US government can't do or share:

OVERVIEW OF THE PRIVACY ACT: 2020 EDITION

INTRODUCTION

The Privacy Act of 1974, Pub Law No. 93–579, 88 Stat 1896 (Dec. 31, 1974), codified at 5 U.S.C. § 552a (2018), went into effect on September 27, 1975, when it became the principal law governing the handling of personal information in the federal government. Enacted in the wake of the Watergate and the Counterintelligence Program (COINTELPRO) scandals involving illegal surveillance on opposition political parties and individuals deemed to be "subversive," the Privacy Act sought to restore trust in government and to address what at the time was seen as an existential threat to American democracy. In the words of the bill's principal sponsor, Judiciary Chairman Senator Sam Ervin, "[i]f we have learned anything in this last year of Watergate, it is that there must be limits upon what the Government can know about each of its citizens." See S. Comm. on Gov't. Operations & H.R. Comm. on Gov't. Operations, 94th Cong., Legislative History of the Privacy Act of 1974 S. 3418 (Public Law 93–579)

In drafting the Privacy Act, Congress relied on a recently published and widely read report from an advisory committee of what was then the Department of Health, Education & Welfare (HEW). Records, Computers, and the Rights of Citizens: Report of the Secretary's Advisory Committee on Automated Personal Data Systems, DHEW Publication No. (OS) 73–94 (July 1973) (hereinafter HEW Report). The HEW Report represented the first comprehensive study of the risks to privacy presented by the increasingly widespread use of electronic information technologies by organizations, replacing traditional paper-based systems of creation, storage, and retrieval of information. To address these risks, the HEW Report developed what it called a "code of fair information practices," now more commonly called the Fair Information Practice Principles, or FIPPs.

As implemented in the Privacy Act, the FIPPs: allow individuals to determine what records pertaining to them are collected, maintained, used, or disseminated by an agency; require agencies to procure consent before records pertaining to an individual collected for one purpose could be used for other incompatible purposes; afford individuals a right of access to records pertaining to them and to have them corrected if inaccurate; and require agencies to collect such records only for lawful and authorized purposes and safeguard them appropriately. Exceptions from some of these principles are permitted only for important reasons of public policy. Judicial redress is afforded to individuals when an agency fails to comply with access and amendment rights, but only after an internal appeals process fails to correct the problem. Otherwise, liability for damages is afforded in the event of a willful or intentional violation of these rights.

The FIPPs are not only central to the framework of the Privacy Act, they have been the basis of almost every other privacy law and treaty in the world today. See, e.g., Regulation (EU) 2016/679 of the European Parliament and of the Council of 27 April 2016 on the Protection of Natural Persons with Regard to the Processing of Personal Data and on the Free Movement of Such Data (known as the General Data Protection Regulation ("GDPR")); The Gramm-Leach-Bliley Act, 15 U.S.C. § 6801; The Health Insurance Portability and Accountability Act ("HIPAA") of 1996, 42 U.S.C. § 320d-2; HIPPA Privacy Rule, 45 CFR Part 160 and Subparts A and E of Part 164 Directive 95/46/EC of the European Parliament and of the Council of 24 October 1995 (repealed and replaced by the GDPR); Org. for Econ. Coop. & Dev., Guidelines on the Protection of Privacy and Transborder Flows of Personal Data (rev. 2013). It is therefore helpful to understand something about their origins.

The FIPPs were the brainchild of three people, the HEW Secretary's Advisory Committee Chairman Willis Ware, Executive Director David B. H. Martin, and Associate Director Carole Parsons. Chairman Ware was a legendary computer scientist and pioneer in the field of information security who had worked with John Von Neumann and Claude Shannon building the first modern computer at the Institute for Advanced Study at Princeton. Chairman Ware later diagnosed fundamental vulnerabilities in what was then called the ARPANET (now renamed INTERNET), and is recognized as the founder of the field of information security. Executive Director Martin was the principal architect of the Cape Cod National Seashore, a multi-stakeholder collaborative governance structure, which became the model for the National Environmental Policy Act of 1970. Executive Director Martin would go on to devise other innovative collaborative governance frameworks like government-backed student loans. Associate Director Parsons was a Census Bureau expert in statistics and government record-keeping systems, who later served in the White House overseeing the legislative process leading to the enactment of the Privacy Act, and served as Executive Director of the Privacy Protection Study Commission.

As explained by the authors of the HEW Report, underlying the FIPPs was an understanding of the nature of electronic data as reflecting and mediating relationships in which both individuals and organizations have an interest, made for purposes that are shared by organizations and individuals. The concept of privacy had, at that point in time, been understood as a narrow, property-based concept of individual control. Unlike paper-based information systems, individuals cannot exercise the same level of physical control of information in electronic computer systems controlled by organizations. Accordingly, the authors of the HEW Report argued that the concept of privacy needed to be reimagined to recognize the mutual interests that institutions and individuals shared in the fair and appropriate management of personal information. This meant that instead of a property-based concept of individual control, what was needed was a governance framework designed to ensure the trust of the stakeholders in the information. These included the individuals about whom the information pertained and the agency with a public need to use the information, as well as others. As such, the model of the FIPPs developed in the HEW Report bears close similarities to the framework for management of shared common environmental resources, such as the Cape Cod National Seashore, which Executive Director Martin had helped design.

As implemented in the Privacy Act, the multi-stakeholder governance idea underlying the FIPPs can be seen in the fact that each of the individual rights that Congress created also serves the interests of any reasonable agency, and is consistent with the need for other legitimate secondary users, such as public health authorities, financial oversight agencies, law enforcement and national security agencies—indeed any stakeholder with a legitimate need to use the information in the public interest—to access and appropriately use the information. Just as loss of trust in the governance framework would harm the interests of all, so proper and appropriate use of personal information within a secure governance framework would maintain trust and benefit the interests of all.

The Ninety-Third United States Congress, facing a crisis of public trust, found the information governance model of the FIPPs, as presented in the HEW Report, to be an attractive approach. Following the breakdown of trust in the government after the Watergate and COINTELPRO scandals, Congress recognized that agency implementation of the FIPPs could help restore the most critical relationship of trust of all, that between the people and their government.

In the more than 45 years since the Privacy Act was enacted, information technologies have expanded in ways that the drafters of the HEW Report could never have imagined, and the risks associated with the collection and use of personal data have grown accordingly. But the basic principles of fair information practices as implemented in the Act have continued to do their work maintaining the relationship of trust between the people and their government. The Privacy Act was later modified by the Computer Matching and Privacy Protection Act of 1988, Pub. L. No. 100–503, 102 Stat. 2507, extending the Privacy Act's FIPPs-based protections to computer-matching activities by agencies, with requirements for certain additional internal agency procedures. The Privacy Act also has been supplemented by other structures of information governance, such as the E-Government Act of 2002, Pub. Law No. 107–347, 116 Stat. 2899, and the Federal Information Security Modernization Act of 2014, Pub. Law No. 113–283, 128 Stat. 3073. However, the original language of the Privacy Act, as drafted in 1974, has shown itself sufficiently flexible to adapt to those changes. More than any other law in the field, the Privacy Act has, to a remarkable extent, withstood the test of time.[1]

The Privacy Act grew out of the paranoia created by the Watergate scandal. It succeeded in placing limits on what data the government could collect, use, and share about individuals. It sought to balance the government's legitimate needs for data about individuals with the individual's right to privacy. Also, except in the case of some compelling public interest, governmental agencies cannot share information among themselves or with third parties. So, do not expect to be able to access information about a subject or target of your investigation from a governmental agency. However, note also that information about an individual in the government's possession can be accessed if the individual provides written consent. This can be enormously helpful in situations where the subject or target has a compelling need to trade consent for something he or she wants.

WHAT ABOUT THE EU?

The General Data Protection Regulation (GDPR) became effective on May 25th, 2018. GDPR defines a data subject as an EU citizen or other national physically present in the EU at the time data is collected. Any business or organization that offers services to EU data subjects that collects, processes, or stores the data of EU data subjects has to comply with GDPR regardless of their geographic location.

What is Personal Data under GDPR?

Personal data (also termed personally identifiable information) is any piece of information that contains an "identifier" that can be used to identify a specific individual or group of individuals. Personal data pertains to a person, rather than a business or other organization, which have their own set of data protection laws.

Personal data pertains to a person, rather than a business or other organization, which have their own set of data protection laws.

For example, the following data elements are considered personal data under GDPR:

1. Names (first, last, middle, maiden, etc.)
2. Dates of birth
3. Telephone numbers
4. Addresses
5. Photographs
6. Audio/visual recordings of an individual
7. Bank details
8. Opinions
9. Passport numbers
10. Location data

Anonymous data – Information that cannot easily be tied to a data subject – is not covered by GDPR.

GDPR requires that personal data only be stored for the time taken to achieve the purpose for which the data has been collected. Entities storing data must carefully consider how long data must be kept and also how to dispose of that information securely once the purpose for which the information was collected has been achieved.

There are particular pieces of information that are particularly sensitive and could result in individuals coming to harm in the event of a data breach. This data is treated as "special categories" data. If this type of data is collected or processed by an entity, greater levels of protection are required and extra levels of checks and justification for collecting and using those types of data are required (see GDPR Article 9).

Examples include the following:

a. Race or ethnicity
b. Religious or spiritual beliefs
c. Political or philosophical leanings
d. Trade union alliances
e. Biological/genetic data
f. Medical data
g. Sexuality/gender identity

There are three categories of entities and individuals covered by GDPR. The first, the Controller is a government agency or organization (public or private) that initiates the collection and processing of personal data. The controller is the entity that collects and uses personal data or shares that information. Processors are those contracted by the controller to process personal data. These are usually IT companies or marketing companies, but the term "data processor" can also relate to any software used to process data. Therefore, apps used to collect or process personal data are also subject to GDPR compliance. The same organization can be both a data controller and a data processor. Finally, there are the data subjects. These are the people whose personal information is being collected, used, and processed by the controllers and processors. These individuals retain the right to access their personal data, correct errors, and request the removal of information collected about them.

When GDPR refers to the processing of data, it means the handling, use, storage, and destruction of information. Processors and controllers are responsible for ensuring data security at every stage of its lifecycle.

In certain situations, individuals may request that their data not be processed, or that its processing is "restricted". This is also known as "the right to object".

There are three instances when an individual has the right to object:

- Processing of data for scientific/historical research
- Processing of data for direct marketing
- Processing that is based on profiling

If such requests are upheld, it means that any collected data cannot be used.

Not every organization that operates within the EU must comply with GDPR. Such exemptions are outlined in Articles 85 and 91, although member states may apply for specific exemptions (see Article 23).

If an individual poses a threat to the rights and freedoms of others their data may no longer be protected under GDPR.

Examples of when personal data may no longer be protected by GDPR include:

- Defense concerns
- Crime prevention
- Financial security
- Prosecution of a crime
- Suspected tax evasion
- Public health concerns
- Freedom of information

Privacy laws vary; what is legal in one country may not be legal in another. Additionally, data can be transmitted all around the world, which raises issues about how information can – and should be – protected. But, GDPR requires data to be protected for all of its citizens, regardless of where the data are located.

There is an existing agreement between the United States and the EU regarding privacy. In 2016, the EU-US Privacy Shield Framework came into being and allows private data to be transferred outside of the EU if the recipient organization is certified by the United States Department of Commerce or the EU Supervisory Authority. These organizations must process and use the data in accordance with the guidelines set out by the Framework. The United States Federal Trade Commission or Department for Transportation is responsible for enforcing these rules. To meet the criteria, organizations must conduct an annual review to self-certify that they are compliant.

The eight core GDPR privacy principles follow:

- Notification – Organizations must provide clear information to their customers about when and how their data are being used and if personal data are being transferred to a third party.
- Lawfulness – Consent is usually needed to share private data, although when consent is not necessary there must be a clear legal basis for sharing data.
- Limits – Personal data must only be disclosed when there is need for a disclosure. There are, however, exceptions that allow data to be used for purposes other than the reasons for which the information was originally collected.

- Security – Those who collect, use, and store personal information must employ reasonable measures to protect data.
- Accountability – Those who collect, use, and store personal data must comply with GDPR and its principles.
- Downstream Protection – As well as the initial collector of data, any party with whom the information is shared must also adhere to GDPR requirements.
- Access and Rights – Individuals should be able to access and use their own personal data, as well as withhold permission for certain uses of their data.
- Breach Notification – If an individual's data is breached, the individual must be notified as soon as possible and the supervisory authority notified within 72 hours of the breach's discovery.

This means that data must only be used for a predefined purpose and must be held securely within the EU and only accessed by those with adequate authorization. The data collected must also be accurate.[2]

The bottom line is that it is very difficult to get personal information about a subject or target of your investigation from the government without that individual's consent.

WHAT ABOUT THE BANKS?

Banks keep great independent transaction records. How about getting the transaction information for your subject or target directly from the banks they do business with? Not so fast, there are a few more laws we need to consider.

Gramm-Leach-Bliley Act of 1999

Title V of the Gramm-Leach-Bliley Act of 1999 established a set of comprehensive privacy laws at the federal level applicable to any firm that provides financial services. The new law established four new requirements regarding the nonpublic personal information of a consumer:

- *Annual Disclosure of Privacy Policy:* A financial institution must annually disclose to consumers its policy and practice regarding the protection and disclosure of nonpublic personal information to affiliates and nonaffiliated third-parties.
- *Customer "Opt-Out" of Disclosures to Third-Parties:* Consumers have the right to prevent the disclosure of nonpublic personal information to a nonaffiliated third-party - commonly referred to as the right to "opt-out." Third-parties may not re-disclose that information.

  There are important exceptions designed to resolve the practical problems with an opt-out provision. For example, opt-out does not apply in cases where information sharing is necessary to produce a consolidated customer statement, complete a transaction, or service the customer's account. It also does not apply to information disclosed to market the financial institution's own products or services offered through joint agreements with another financial institution.
- *Prohibition on Disclosure of Account Information:* A financial institution may not disclose account numbers to any nonaffiliated third-party for use in telemarketing, direct mail marketing, or other marketing through electronic mail to the consumer.
- *Regulatory Standards to Protect Security and Confidentiality:* Financial institution regulators are to establish "standards" (related to the physical security and integrity of customer records) that would (1) ensure the security and confidentiality of customer records; (2) protect against any anticipated threats to the security

of such records; and (3) to protect against unauthorized access to such records that could result in substantial harm or inconvenience to the customer.

The law also established rulemaking and enforcement authority for federal banking agencies, the National Credit Union Administration, the Securities Exchange Commission (SEC), the Treasury Department, and the Federal Trade Commission (FTC) each to prescribe implementing regulations for their respective institutions.

The law also makes it a federal crime to fraudulently obtain or cause to disclose customer information from a financial institution. This provision is aimed at the abusive practice of "pretext calling," in which someone misrepresents the identity of the person requesting the information or otherwise misleads an institution or customer into making an unwitting disclosure of customer information."[3]

Notice that ugly little note in the last paragraph. It is a federal crime to obtain information about a financial institution customer through pretext.

INVESTIGATOR NOTES

I still get calls from clients asking if I can get information from a bank about the subject or target of an investigation. Astonishingly, some of these calls come from licensed, practicing attorneys. I recently got a call from an attorney from whom I had earlier gotten this request, which I refused, citing Gramm-Leach-Bliley. In this phone call the lawyer told me that he had found a private investigator who told him he could get the information from the bank. He wanted to know if I still thought it was a bad idea. I asked him if he thought joining in a conspiracy to violate a federal criminal statute was a bad idea. I said if not, by all means proceed. Do me one favor before you do; lose my phone number.

Actually, before 1999, pretext calls and interviews were very common. If done correctly, they could be quite effective. I can remember being hired by one of the two largest competitors in a fast-growing industry. They were both private companies so their financial information was not publicly available. They were locked in high stakes intellectual property litigation; neither could survive a complete loss. So, my client wanted to negotiate a settlement. But first he wanted to learn more about his competitor's financial strength and wherewithal to sustain protracted litigation. So, I had one of my young staff members apply for an entry level financial analyst job the competitor was advertising. My plan was to have my young colleague go through the interview and when the interviewer asked the requisite: "Do you have any questions for me?" question, my young agent would pull out the list we had developed to learn everything he could about the competitor's finances. However, it never got to that point. When my young colleague checked in with the competitor's receptionist, he was told to wait in the lobby as the interviewer was not yet ready. Thinking on his feet he struck up a conversation with the receptionist. When he said that he was excited about working for this fine company, the receptionist motioned for him to come closer. She told my young colleague that he should not apply for the job because she had heard the company was about to run out of cash and was already laying large numbers of people off. My colleague thanked the receptionist earnestly and asked her to tell the interviewer that he was unable to wait any longer. Of course, he couldn't wait to tell us what he learned. Our client made a very modest offer to settle all the litigation. At first, the competitor pushed back arguing the merits of their case. But, my client had very valuable nonpublic information that suggested that the merit of a case you can't afford to litigate is of little practical value. My client held firm and was able to settle all the litigation at her number.

Well, OK, what about pulling a credit report on your subject or target? Credit reports have lots of information. Hold on; let's look at the law:

The Fair Credit Reporting Act

The Fair Credit Reporting Act (FCRA) contains many important privacy safeguards. It gives consumers the ability to stop the sharing of their credit application information or other personal information (obtained from third-parties, such as credit bureaus) with affiliated companies. The law permits sharing of information with affiliates regarding the consumer's performance on the loan or other "experience" resulting from the relationship between the consumer and the financial institution.

Moreover, it is important to note that the FCRA allows only *affiliated* companies to share such application or credit bureau information, after provision to the customer of notice and an opportunity to opt-out. If a financial institution were to share such information with an unaffiliated third-party, it could become a consumer reporting agency subject to burdensome, complex and onerous requirements of the existing FCRA.

The FCRA also mandates that other notices be provided to consumers in connection with the sharing of information. For example, financial institutions are required to notify consumers when adverse action is taken in connection with credit, insurance, or employment based on information obtained from an affiliate. This notice must inform the consumer that he or she also may obtain the information that led to the adverse action simply by requesting it in writing.

The FCRA also gives consumers the power to stop unwanted credit solicitations by blocking the use of their information from pre-screening by consumer reporting agencies. Pre-screening is the process in which a consumer reporting agency prepares a list of consumers who, based on the agency's review of its files, meet certain criteria specified by a creditor who has requested the prescreening. The FCRA also mandates that providers of credit include disclosures with every solicitation explaining that the offer results from a pre-screening and that the consumer has the right to be excluded from future pre-screenings by notifying the consumer reporting agency.[4]

Notice, above, that credit reporting agencies are not permitted to share credit reports or credit information about a person with any unaffiliated third party. Doing so would subject your employer to legal liability. Darn, stopped again.

Generally speaking your choices have two choices when trying to gather nonpublic third-party information about subjects and targets. You can access online public records (e.g. property, vital, litigation, criminal, etc.), social media information and whatever comes up on a search engine search (e.g. Google). You can continue to follow these threads on your own. Or, you can hire a professional research firm to do the work for you. (If you will drop me an email, I will give you the names and contact information for the best of the best.) If you have the funds this approach will yield the best results in the shortest time.

INVESTIGATOR NOTES

Some time back, I was hired by a health payor to investigate unusual claims related to a specific group of drugs filled by one large compounding pharmacy. These drugs had unusual names and were used to treat a specific genetic condition that tended to afflict family members. The pharmacy was recruiting people who used the drugs to recruit family members and then, with the help of a crooked physician, get them to fill prescriptions up to the amount of their lifetime cap with their health insurance company. There is no depth certain people will not sink to for a quick buck. Anyway, because of restrictions imposed by HIPPA and related laws and regulations, I had to interview the people who had been victimized to have any hope of putting together the necessary evidence. How to find the witnesses, though? I used a tool that looks for key words across all Facebook pages. It's not very useful for common words, returning a snowstorm of false hits. But, for very uncommon words, like the names of these drugs, it is extraordinarily effective. Presto, I had my witness list.

SECTION III: LAWS AND RULES RELATED TO ACCESSING DOCUMENTS

Here we are talking about accessing both electronic and paper records. Rule number one: break no laws or regulations. If you do, you may face criminal or civil liability and the documents you gather in this way will likely not be admissible as evidence or even as non-evidentiary support for your expert testimony. Rule number two: if you have several of the same document to choose from, choose the one that represents the best evidence of the conduct you are investigating (see Chapter 7). Rule number three: always maintain a carefully documented chain of custody log for all documents you gather (see Chapter 7).

So, for electronic documents, you must first have a legal right to seize them. There can be significant criminal and civil liability for collecting electronic documents or other evidence, which you are not authorized to collect. Computer forensics is still a relatively new field for the courts and many of the existing laws used to prosecute computer-related crimes, legal precedents, and practices are constantly evolving. New court rulings are issued frequently that affect how computer forensics is applied. The best source for this information is the United States Department of Justice's Cyber Crime website (www.cybercrime.gov). The site lists recent court cases involving computer forensics and computer crime, and it has guides about how to introduce computer evidence in court and what standards apply. In order to be useful, digital evidence must be collected in a way that is legally admissible. Also, as we discussed earlier, new laws require organizations to safeguard the privacy of personal data. It is becoming necessary to prove that your organization is complying with computer security best practices. There are three areas of law related to computer security that are important:

The first comes from the United States Constitution's Fourth Amendment, which protects against unreasonable search and seizure. The Fourth Amendment sets out, "The right of the people to be secure in their persons, houses, papers, and effects, against unreasonable searches and seizures, shall not be violated, and no Warrants shall issue, but upon probable cause, supported by Oath or affirmation, and particularly describing the place to be searched, and the persons or things to be seized."

From the US Justice Department's Searching and Seizing Computers and Obtaining Electronic Evidence in Criminal Investigations:

> "The Fourth Amendment limits the ability of government agents to search for and seize evidence without a warrant. This chapter explains the constitutional limits of warrantless searches and seizures in cases involving computers.
>
> The Fourth Amendment states:
>
>> The right of the people to be secure in their persons, houses, papers, and effects, against unreasonable searches and seizures, shall not be violated, and no Warrants shall issue, but upon probable cause, supported by Oath or affirmation, and particularly describing the place to be searched, and the persons or things to be seized.
>
> According to the Supreme Court, a "'seizure' of property occurs when there is some meaningful interference with an individual's possessory interests in that property,"

United States v. Jacobsen, 466 U.S. 109, 113 (1984), and the Court has also character-ized the interception of intangible communications as a seizure. *See Berger v. New York*, 388 U.S. 41, 59–60 (1967). Furthermore, the Court has held that a "'search' occurs when an expectation of privacy that society is prepared to consider reasonable is infringed." *Jacobsen*, 466 U.S. at 113. If the government's conduct does not violate a person's "reasonable expectation of privacy," then formally it does not constitute a Fourth Amendment "search" and no warrant is required. *See Illinois v. Andreas*, 463 U.S. 765, 771 (1983). In addition, a warrantless search that violates a person's reasonable expectation of privacy will nonetheless be constitutional if it falls within an established exception to the warrant requirement. *See Illinois v. Rodriguez*, 497 U.S. 177, 185–86 (1990). Accordingly, investigators must consider two issues when asking whether a gov-ernment search of a computer requires a warrant. First, does the search violate a reason-able expectation of privacy? And if so, is the search nonetheless permissible because it falls within an exception to the warrant requirement?"[5]

"1. General Principles

A search is constitutional if it does not violate a person's "reasonable" or "legitimate" expectation of privacy. *Katz v. United States*, 389 U.S. 347, 361 (1967) (Harlan, J., con-curring). This inquiry embraces two discrete questions: first, whether the individual's conduct reflects "an actual (subjective) expectation of privacy," and second, whether the individual's subjective expectation of privacy is "one that society is prepared to recog-nize as 'reasonable.'" *Id.* at 361. In most cases, the difficulty of contesting a defendant's subjective expectation of privacy focuses the analysis on the objective aspect of the *Katz* test, i.e., whether the individual's expectation of privacy was reasonable.

No bright line rule indicates whether an expectation of privacy is constitution-ally reasonable. *See O'Connor v. Ortega*, 480 U.S. 709, 715 (1987). For example, the Supreme Court has held that a person has a reasonable expectation of privacy in prop-erty located inside a person's home, *see Payton v. New York*, 445 U.S. 573, 589–90 (1980); in "the relative heat of various rooms in the home" revealed through the use of a thermal imager, see *Kyllo v. United States*, 533 U.S. 27, 34–35 (2001); in conversations taking place in an enclosed phone booth, *see Katz*, 389 U.S. at 352; and in the contents of opaque containers, *see United States v. Ross*, 456 U.S. 798, 822–23 (1982). In con-trast, a person does not have a reasonable expectation of privacy in activities conducted in open fields, *see Oliver v. United States*, 466 U.S. 170, 177 (1984); in garbage depos-ited at the outskirts of real property, *see California v. Greenwood*, 486 U.S. 35, 40–41 (1988); or in a stranger's house that the person has entered without the owner's consent in order to commit a theft, *see Rakas v. Illinois*, 439 U.S. 128, 143 n.12 (1978)."[6]

"2. Reasonable Expectation of Privacy in Computers as Storage Devices

To determine whether an individual has a reasonable expectation of privacy in informa-tion stored in a computer, it helps to treat the computer like a closed container such as a briefcase or file cabinet. The Fourth Amendment generally prohibits law enforcement from accessing and viewing information stored in a computer if it would be prohibited from opening a closed container and examining its contents in the same situation.

The most basic Fourth Amendment question in computer cases asks whether an indi-vidual enjoys a reasonable expectation of privacy in electronic information stored within computers (or other electronic storage devices) under the individual's control. For example, do individuals have a reasonable expectation of privacy in the contents of their laptop computers, USB drives, or cell phones? If the answer is "yes," then the government ordinarily must obtain a warrant, or fall within an exception to the warrant requirement, before it accesses the information stored inside.

When confronted with this issue, courts have analogized the expectation of privacy in a computer to the expectation of privacy in closed containers such as suitcases, footlockers, or briefcases. Because individuals generally retain a reasonable expectation of privacy in the contents of closed containers, *see United States v. Ross*, 456 U.S. 798, 822–23 (1982), they also generally retain a reasonable expectation of privacy in data held within electronic storage devices. Accordingly, accessing information stored in a computer ordinarily will implicate the owner's reasonable expectation of privacy in the information. *See United States v. Heckenkamp*, 482 F.3d 1142, 1146 (9th Cir. 2007) (finding reasonable expectation of privacy in a personal computer); *United States v. Buckner*, 473 F.3d 551, 554 n.2 (4th Cir. 2007) (same); *United States v. Lifshitz*, 369 F.3d 173, 190 (2d Cir. 2004) ("Individuals generally possess a reasonable expectation of privacy in their home computers."); *Trulock v. Freeh*, 275 F.3d 391, 403 (4th Cir. 2001); *United States v. Al-Marri*, 230 F. Supp. 2d 535, 541 (S.D.N.Y. 2002) ("Courts have uniformly agreed that computers should be treated as if they were closed containers."); *United States v. Reyes*, 922 F. Supp. 818, 832–33 (S.D.N.Y. 1996) (finding reasonable expectation of privacy in data stored in a pager); *United States v. Lynch*, 908 F. Supp. 284, 287 (D.V.I. 1995) (same); *United States v. Chan*, 830 F. Supp. 531, 535 (N.D. Cal. 1993) (same); *see also United States v. Andrus*, 483 F.3d 711, 718 (10th Cir. 2007) ("A personal computer is often a repository for private information the computer's owner does not intend to share with others. For most people, their computers are their most private spaces."[)7]

"Although courts have generally agreed that electronic storage devices can be analogized to closed containers, they have reached differing conclusions about whether a computer or other storage device should be classified as a single closed container or whether each individual file stored within a computer or storage device should be treated as a separate closed container. In two cases, the Fifth Circuit determined that a computer disk containing multiple files is a single container for Fourth Amendment purposes. First, in *United States v. Runyan*, 275 F.3d 449, 464–65 (5th Cir. 2001), in which private parties had searched certain files and found child pornography, the Fifth Circuit held that the police did not exceed the scope of the private search when they examined additional files on any disk that had been, in part, privately searched. Analogizing a disk to a closed container, the court explained that "police do not exceed the private search when they examine more items within a closed container than did the private searchers." *Id.* at 464. In a subsequent case, the Fifth Circuit held that when a warrantless search of a portion of a computer and zip disk had been justified, the defendant no longer retained any reasonable expectation of privacy in the remaining contents of the computer and disk, and thus a comprehensive search by law enforcement personnel did not violate the Fourth Amendment. *See United States v. Slanina*, 283 F.3d 670, 680 (5th Cir. 2002), *vacated on other grounds*, 537 U.S. 802 (2002), *aff'd*, 359 F.3d 356, 358 (5th Cir. 2004). *See also People v. Emerson*, 766 N.Y.S.2d 482, 488 (N.Y. Sup. Ct. 2003) (adopting intermediate position of treating computer folders rather than individual files as closed containers); *United States v. Beusch*, 596 F.2d 871, 876–77 (9th Cir. 1979) (holding that when a physical ledger contains some information that falls within the scope of a warrant, law enforcement may seize the entire ledger, rather than individual responsive pages).["8]

"Other appellate courts have treated individual computer files as separate entities, at least in the search warrant context. *See, e.g., Guest v. Leis*, 255 F.3d 325, 335 (6th Cir. 2001) (approving off-site review of a computer to "separate relevant files from unrelated files"). Similarly, the Tenth Circuit has refused to allow such exhaustive searches of a computer's hard drive in the absence of a warrant or some exception to the warrant requirement. *See United States v. Carey*, 172 F.3d 1268, 1273–75 (10th Cir. 1999) (ruling that agent exceeded the scope of a warrant to search for evidence of drug sales when he "abandoned that search" and instead searched for evidence of child pornography for five hours). In particular, the Tenth Circuit cautioned in a later case that "[b]ecause computers can hold so much information touching on many different areas of a person's life, there is greater potential for the 'intermingling' of documents and a consequent invasion of privacy when police execute a search for evidence on a computer." *United States v. Walser*, 275 F.3d 981, 986 (10th Cir. 2001).

Although individuals generally retain a reasonable expectation of privacy in computers under their control, special circumstances may eliminate that expectation. For example, an individual will not retain a reasonable expectation of privacy in information that the person has made openly available. *See Katz v. United States*, 389 U.S. 347, 351 (1967) ("What a person knowingly exposes to the public, even in his own home or office, is not a subject of Fourth Amendment protection."); *Wilson v. Moreau*, 440 F. Supp. 2d 81, 104 (D.R.I. 2006) (finding no expectation of privacy in documents user stored on computers available for public use in a public library); *United States v. Gines-Perez*, 214 F. Supp. 2d 205, 224–26 (D.P.R. 2002) (finding no reasonable expectation of privacy in information placed on the Internet); *United States v. Butler*, 151 F. Supp. 2d 82, 83–84 (D. Me. 2001) (finding no reasonable expectation of privacy in hard drives of shared university computers). Thus, several courts have held that a defendant has no reasonable expectation of privacy in files shared freely with others. *See United States v. King*, 509 F.3d 1338, 1341–42 (11th Cir. 2007) (holding that defendant did not have a legitimate expectation of privacy in the contents of a "shared drive" of his laptop while it was connected to a network); *United States v. Barrows*, 481 F.3d 1246, 1249 (10th Cir. 2007) (holding no reasonable expectation of privacy exists where defendant networked his computer "for the express purpose of sharing files"); *United States v. Stults*, 2007 WL 4284721, at *1 (D. Neb. Dec. 3, 2007) (finding no reasonable expectation of privacy in computer files that the defendant made available using a peer-topeer file sharing program). Similarly, in *United States v. David*, 756 F. Supp. 1385 (D. Nev. 1991), agents looking over the defendant's shoulder read the defendant's password from the screen as the defendant typed his password into a handheld computer. The court found no Fourth Amendment violation in obtaining the password because the defendant did not enjoy a reasonable expectation of privacy "in the display that appeared on the screen." *Id.* at 1390. *See also United States v. Gorshkov*, 2001 WL 1024026, at *2 (W.D. Wash. May 23, 2001) (holding that defendant did not have a reasonable expectation of privacy in use of a private computer network when undercover federal agents looked over his shoulder, when he did not own the computer he used, and when he knew that the system administrator could monitor his activities). Nor will individuals generally enjoy a reasonable expectation of privacy in the contents of computers they have stolen or obtained by fraud. *See United States v. Caymen*, 404 F.3d 1196, 1200 (9th Cir. 2005); *United States v. Lyons*, 992 F.2d 1029, 1031–32 (10th Cir. 1993)."[9]

"3. Reasonable Expectation of Privacy and Third-Party Possession

Individuals who retain a reasonable expectation of privacy in stored electronic information under their control may lose Fourth Amendment protections when they relinquish that control to third parties. For example, an individual may offer a container of electronic information to a third party by bringing a malfunctioning computer to a repair shop or by shipping a floppy diskette in the mail to a friend. Alternatively, a user may transmit information to third parties electronically, such as by sending data across the Internet, or a user may leave information on a shared computer network. When law enforcement agents learn of information possessed by third parties that may provide evidence of a crime, they may wish to inspect it. Whether the Fourth Amendment requires them to obtain a warrant before examining the information depends in part upon whether the third-party possession has eliminated the individual's reasonable expectation of privacy.

To analyze third-party possession issues, it helps first to distinguish between possession by a carrier in the course of transmission to an intended recipient and subsequent possession by the intended recipient. For example, if A hires B to carry a package to C, A's reasonable expectation of privacy in the contents of the package during the time that B carries the package on its way to C may be different than A's reasonable expectation of privacy after C has received the package. During transmission, contents generally retain Fourth Amendment protection. The government ordinarily may not examine the contents of a closed container in the course of transmission without a warrant. Government intrusion and examination of the contents ordinarily violates the reasonable expectation of privacy of both the sender and receiver. *See United States v. Villarreal*, 963 F.2d 770, 774 (5th Cir. 1992). *But see United States v. Young*, 350 F.3d 1302, 1308 (11th Cir. 2003) (holding that Federal Express's terms of service, which allowed it to access customers' packages, eliminated customer's reasonable expectation of privacy in package); *United States v. Walker*, 20 F. Supp. 2d 971, 973–74 (S.D.W.Va. 1998) (concluding that packages sent to an alias in furtherance of a criminal scheme do not support a reasonable expectation of privacy). This rule applies regardless of whether the carrier is owned by the government or a private company. *Compare Ex Parte Jackson*, 96 U.S. (6 Otto) 727, 733 (1877) (public carrier), *with Walter v. United States*, 447 U.S. 649, 651 (1980) (private carrier).

Government acquisition of an intangible electronic signal in the course of transmission may also implicate the Fourth Amendment. *See Berger v. New York*, 388 U.S. 41, 58–60 (1967) (applying the Fourth Amendment to a wire communication in the context of a wiretap). The boundaries of the Fourth Amendment in such cases remain hazy, however, because Congress addressed the Fourth Amendment concerns identified in *Berger* by passing Title III of the Omnibus Crime Control and Safe Streets Act of 1968 ("Title III"), 18 U.S.C. §§ 2510–2522. Title III, which is discussed fully in Chapter 4, provides a comprehensive statutory framework that regulates real-time monitoring of wire and electronic communications. Its scope encompasses, and in many significant ways exceeds, the protection offered by the Fourth Amendment. *See United States v. Torres*, 751 F.2d 875, 884 (7th Cir. 1984); Chandler v. United States Army, 125 F.3d 1296, 1298 (9th Cir. 1997). As a practical matter, then, the monitoring of wire and electronic communications in the course of transmission generally raises many statutory questions, but few constitutional ones."[10]

"Ordinarily, once an item has been received by the intended recipient, the sender's reasonable expectation of privacy in the item terminates. *See United States v. King*, 55 F.3d 1193, 1196 (6th Cir. 1995) (sender's expectation of privacy in letter "terminates upon delivery"). More generally, the Supreme Court has repeatedly held that the Fourth Amendment is not violated when information revealed to a third party is disclosed by the third party to the government, regardless of any subjective expectation that the third parties will keep the information confidential. For example, in *United States v. Miller*, 425 U.S. 435, 443 (1976), the Court held that the Fourth Amendment does not protect bank account information that account holders divulge to their banks. By placing information under the control of a third party, the Court stated, an account holder assumes the risk that the information will be conveyed to the government. Id. According to the Court, "the Fourth Amendment does not prohibit the obtaining of information revealed to a third party and conveyed by him to Government authorities, even if the information is revealed on the assumption that it will be used only for a limited purpose and the confidence placed in the third party will not be betrayed." *Id.* (citing *Hoffa v. United States*, 385 U.S. 293, 302 (1966)). *See also SEC v. Jerry T. O'Brien, Inc.*, 467 U.S. 735,

743 (1984) ("when a person communicates information to a third party … he cannot object if the third party conveys that information or records thereof to law enforcement authorities"); *Smith v. Maryland*, 442 U.S. 735, 743–44 (1979) (finding no reasonable expectation of privacy in phone numbers dialed by owner of a telephone because act of dialing the number effectively tells the number to the phone company); *Couch v. United States*, 409 U.S. 322, 335 (1973) (holding that government may subpoena accountant for client information given to accountant by client because client retains no reasonable expectation of privacy in information given to accountant).

Courts have applied these principles to electronic communications. For example, in *United States v. Horowitz*, 806 F.2d 1222 (4th Cir. 1986), the defendant emailed confidential pricing information relating to his employer to his employer's competitor. After the FBI searched the competitor's computers and found the pricing information, the defendant claimed that the search violated his Fourth Amendment rights. The Fourth Circuit disagreed, holding that the defendant relinquished his interest in and control over the information by sending it to the competitor for the competitor's future use. *See id.* at 1224–26. *See also Guest v. Leis*, 255 F.3d 325, 333 (6th Cir. 2001) (stating that sender of email "would lose a legitimate expectation of privacy in an e-mail that had already reached its recipient; at this moment, the e-mailer would be analogous to a letter-writer, whose 'expectation of privacy ordinarily terminates upon delivery' of the letter"); *United States v. Meriwether*, 917 F.2d 955, 959 (6th Cir. 1990) (defendant had no reasonable expectation of privacy in message sent to a pager); *United States v. Charbonneau*, 979 F. Supp. 1177, 1184 (S.D. Ohio 1997) (stating that a sender of an email "cannot be afforded a reasonable expectation of privacy once that message is received.").

Defendants will occasionally raise a Fourth Amendment challenge to the acquisition of account records and subscriber information held by Internet service providers where law enforcement obtained the records using less process than a search warrant. As discussed in Chapter 3.D, the Stored Communications Act permits the government to obtain transactional records with an "articulable facts" court order and specified subscriber information with a subpoena. *See* 18 U.S.C. §§ 2701–2712. These statutory procedures comply with the Fourth Amendment because customers of communication service providers do not have a reasonable expectation of privacy in customer account records maintained by and for the provider's business. *See United States v. Perrine*, 518 F.3d 1196, 1204 (10th Cir. 2008) ("Every federal court to address this issue has held that subscriber information provided to an internet provider is not protected by the Fourth Amendment's privacy expectation."); *Guest v. Leis*, 255 F.3d 325, 336 (6th Cir. 2001) (finding no Fourth Amendment protection for network account holder's basic subscriber information obtained from communication service provider).3 This rule accords with prior cases finding no Fourth Amendment protection in customer account records. *See, e.g., United States v. Fregoso*, 60 F.3d 1314, 1321 (8th Cir. 1995) (telephone records); *In re Grand Jury Proceedings*, 827 F.2d 301, 302–03 (8th Cir. 1987) (Western Union customer records). Similarly, use of a pen register to capture email to/from address information or Internet Protocol addresses of websites provided to an Internet service provider for routing communications does not implicate the Fourth Amendment. *See United States v. Forrester*, 512 F.3d 500, 510 (9th Cir. 2008) (email and Internet users have no reasonable expectation of privacy in to/from addresses of their messages or in IP addresses of websites visited).

Although an individual normally loses a reasonable expectation of privacy in an item delivered to a recipient, there is an exception to this rule when the individual can reasonably expect to retain control over the item and its contents. When a person leaves a package with a third party for temporary safekeeping, for example, she usually retains control of the package and thus retains a reasonable expectation of privacy in its contents. *See, e.g., United States v. James*, 353 F.3d 606, 614 (8th Cir. 2003) (finding that defendant retained Fourth Amendment rights in sealed envelope containing computer disks which he had left with a friend for storage); *United States v. Most*, 876 F.2d 191, 197–98 (D.C. Cir. 1989) (finding reasonable expectation of privacy in contents of plastic bag left with grocery store clerk); *United States v. Barry*, 853 F.2d 1479, 1481–83 (8th Cir. 1988) (finding reasonable expectation of privacy in locked suitcase stored at airport baggage counter); *United States v. Presler*, 610 F.2d 1206, 1213–14 (4th Cir. 1979) (finding reasonable expectation of privacy in locked briefcases stored with defendant's friend for safekeeping).

In some cases, the sender may initially retain a right to control the third party's possession, but may lose that right over time. The general rule is that the sender's Fourth Amendment rights dissipate as the sender's right to control the third party's possession diminishes. For example, in *United States v. Poulsen*, 41 F.3d 1330 (9th Cir. 1994), *overruled on other grounds, United States v. W. R. Grace*, 526 F.3d 499 (9th Cir. 2008) (en banc) computer hacker Kevin Poulsen left computer tapes in a locker at a commercial storage facility but neglected to pay rent for the locker. Following a warrantless search of the facility, the government sought to use the tapes against Poulsen. The Ninth Circuit held that the search did not violate Poulsen's reasonable expectation of privacy because under state law Poulsen's failure to pay rent extinguished his right to access the tapes. *See id.* at 1337. *See also United States v. Allen*, 106 F.3d 695, 699 (6th Cir. 1997) ("Once a hotel guest's rental period has expired or been lawfully terminated, the guest does not have a legitimate expectation of privacy in the hotel room."[11]

This is an important point for both electronic and paper documents or other electronic or physical evidence. This is because you would not believe what people throw away. There are people presently spending large amounts of money to search trash dump sites to recover the computer they carelessly discarded with their Bitcoin encryption key saved on its hard drive. Also, as I mentioned in an earlier story, office building dumpsters can be a treasure trove of evidence. It is a legal question as to whether control over materials contained in a garbage can physically located on a person's residential property has been relinquished; however, there are ways around that.

INVESTIGATOR NOTES

I have conducted many investigations where I needed to collect evidence that had been thrown into a residential garbage can. I came up with a simple solution to the relinquishing control question with regard to evidence recovered from the residential garbage of subjects and targets of investigations. Wait for it! I would strike up a conversation with the garbage truck guys two blocks ahead of the subject or target's home. I would say to them that I wanted to get the garbage bags from 1234 Smith Rd. I would give each of them a $10 bill and tell them that I would give each of them another $10 bill if they would deliver the bags to me two blocks down from where they picked them up. As an added incentive, I would tell them that I would be back tomorrow to offer them the same deal. Easy peasy; no trespassing or fights about whether control over the evidence had been relinquished. Obviously, this only works when the subject or target live in type of residence where residents place their bagged garbage in a garbage can left on a curb, in a driveway or service alley. But, my point is that clever beats illegal every time when conducting an investigation.

"4. Private Searches

The Fourth Amendment "is wholly inapplicable to a search or seizure, even an unreasonable one, effected by a private individual not acting as an agent of the Government or with the participation or knowledge of any governmental official." *United States v. Jacobsen*, 466 U.S. 109, 113 (1984) (internal quotation marks omitted). As a result, no violation of the Fourth Amendment occurs when a private individual acting on his own accord conducts a search and makes the results available to law enforcement. *See id.* According to *Jacobsen*, agents who learn of evidence via a private search can reenact the original private search without violating any reasonable expectation of privacy. What the agents cannot do without a warrant is "exceed[] the scope of the private search." *Id.* at 115. *See also United States v. Miller*, 152 F.3d 813, 815–16 (8th Cir. 1998); *United States v. Donnes*, 947 F.2d 1430, 1434 (10th Cir. 1991). *But see United States v. Allen*, 106 F.3d 695, 699 (6th Cir. 1997) (stating in dicta that *Jacobsen* does not permit law enforcement to reenact a private search of a private home or residence). This standard requires agents to limit their investigation to the scope of the private search when searching without a warrant after a private search has occurred. Where agents exceed the scope of the private warrantless search, any evidence uncovered may be vulnerable to a motion to suppress.

Private individuals often find contraband or other incriminating evidence on computers and bring that information to law enforcement, and the private search doctrine applies in these cases. In one common scenario, an individual leaves his computer with a repair technician. The technician discovers images of child pornography on the computer, contacts law enforcement, and shows those images to law enforcement. Courts have agreed that such searches by repairmen prior to their contact with law enforcement are private searches and do not implicate the Fourth Amendment. See *United States v. Grimes*, 244 F.3d 375, 383 (5th Cir. 2001); *United States v. Hall*, 142 F.3d 988, 993 (7th Cir. 1998); *United States v. Anderson*, 2007 WL 1121319 at *5–6 (N.D. Ind. Apr. 16, 2007); *United States v. Grant*, 434 F. Supp. 2d 735, 744–45 (D. Neb. 2006); *United States v. Caron*, 2004 WL 438685, at *4–5 (D. Me. Mar. 9, 2004); *see also United States v. Kennedy*, 81 F. Supp. 2d 1103, 1112 (D. Kan. 2000) (concluding that searches of defendant's computer over the Internet by an anonymous caller and employees of a private ISP did not violate Fourth Amendment because there was no evidence that the government was involved in the search).

One private search question that arises in computer cases is whether law enforcement agents must limit themselves to only files examined by the repair technician or whether all data on a particular storage device is within the scope of the initial private search. The Fifth Circuit has taken an expansive approach to this question. *See United States v. Runyan*, 275 F.3d 449, 464–65 (5th Cir. 2001) (police did not exceed the scope of a private search when they examined more files on privately searched disks than had the private searchers). Under this approach, a third-party search of a single file on a computer allows a warrantless search by law enforcement of the computer's entire contents. *See id.* Other courts, however, may not follow the Fifth Circuit's approach and instead rule that government searchers can view only those files whose contents were revealed in the private search. *See United States v. Barth*, 26 F. Supp. 2d 929, 937 (W.D. Tex. 1998) (holding, in a pre-*Runyan* case, that agents who viewed more files than private searcher exceeded the scope of the private search). Even if courts follow the more restrictive approach, the information gleaned from the private search will often provide the probable cause needed to obtain a warrant for a further search.

Importantly, the fact that the person conducting a search is not a government employee does not always mean that the search is "private" for Fourth Amendment purposes. A search by a private party will be considered a Fourth Amendment government search "if the private party act[s] as an instrument or agent of the Government." *Skinner v. Railway Labor Executives' Ass'n*, 489 U.S. 602, 614 (1989). The Supreme Court has offered little guidance on when private conduct can be attributed to the government; the Court has merely stated that this question "necessarily turns on the degree of the Government's participation in the private party's activities, ... a question that can only be resolved 'in light of all the circumstances.'" *Id*. at 614–15 (quoting *Coolidge v. New Hampshire*, 403 U.S. 443, 487 (1971)).

In the absence of a more definitive standard, the various federal Courts of Appeals have adopted a range of approaches for distinguishing between private and government searches. About half of the circuits apply a "totality of the circumstances" approach that examines three factors: whether the government knows of or acquiesces in the intrusive conduct; whether the party performing the search intends to assist law enforcement efforts at the time of the search; and whether the government affirmatively encourages, initiates, or instigates the private action. *See, e.g., United States v. Pervaz*, 118 F.3d 1, 6 (1st Cir. 1997); *United States v. Smythe*, 84 F.3d 1240, 1242–43 (10th Cir. 1996); *United States v. McAllister*, 18 F.3d 1412, 1417–18 (7th Cir. 1994); *United States v. Malbrough*, 922 F.2d 458, 462 (8th Cir. 1990). This test draws a line between situations where the government is a mere knowing witness to the search and those where the government is an active participant or driving force. However, this line can be difficult to discern. For example, in *United States v. Smith*, 383 F.3d 700 (8th Cir. 2004), police detectives participating in "parcel interdiction" at Federal Express removed a suspicious package from a conveyer belt, submitted it to a canine sniff, and delivered the package to the Federal Express manager, telling the manager that "if she wanted to open it that would be fine." However, because the police did not actually ask or order the manager to open the package, and because there was no evidence that the manager felt obligated to open the package, the Court found that the manager was not a "government agent" for Fourth Amendment purposes. *Id*. at 705. *See also United States v. Momoh*, 427 F.3d 137, 141–42 (1st Cir. 2005) (DHL employee's desire to comply with FAA regulations did not make her a government agent absent "affirmative encouragement"). By contrast, in *United States v. Souza*, 223 F.3d 1197 (10th Cir. 2000), the Court found that a UPS employee was a government agent. In *Souza*, the police identified and removed the package from the conveyer belt, submitted it to a canine sniff, and told the UPS employee that they suspected it contained drugs. The police then told the employee that they could not tell her to open the package, but they pointed to it and said "but there it is on the floor." *Id*. at 1200. The employee began to open the package, but when she had difficulty, the police assisted her. While the officers' actual aid in opening the package made this an easy case, the Court's analysis suggests that the officers' other actions—identifying the package and encouraging the employee to open it—might have made the employee a government agent, particularly without evidence that the employee had an independent motivation to open it. *See id*. at 1202.

Other circuits have adopted more rule-like tests that focus on only the first two factors. See, e.g., *United States v. Miller*, 688 F.2d 652, 657 (9th Cir. 1982) (holding that private action counts as government conduct if, at the time of the search, the government knew of or acquiesced in the intrusive conduct, and the party performing the search intended to assist law enforcement efforts); *United States v. Paige*, 136 F.3d 1012, 1017 (5th Cir. 1998) (same); *United States v. Lambert*, 771 F.2d 83, 89 (6th Cir. 1985) (holding that a private individual is a state actor for Fourth Amendment purposes if the police instigated, encouraged, or participated in the search, and the individual engaged in the search with the intent of assisting the police in their investigative efforts).

Two noteworthy private search cases involve an individual who hacked into computers of child pornographers for the purpose of collecting and disclosing evidence of their crimes. The hacker, who refused to identify himself or meet directly with law enforcement, emailed the incriminating evidence to law enforcement. In both cases, the evidence was admissible because when it was gathered, the individual was not an agent of law enforcement. In the first case, *United States v. Steiger*, 318 F.3d 1039 (11th Cir. 2003), the court had little difficulty in determining that the search did not implicate the Fourth Amendment. Because the relevant searches by the hacker took place before the hacker contacted law enforcement, the hacker was not acting as a government agent, and the private search doctrine applied. *See id.* at 1045. In the *Steiger* case, a law enforcement agent thanked the anonymous hacker, assured him he would not be prosecuted, and expressed willingness to receive other information from him. Approximately a year later (and seven months after his last previous contact with law enforcement), the hacker provided to law enforcement information he had illegally obtained from another child pornographer, which gave rise to *United States v. Jarrett*, 338 F.3d 339 (4th Cir. 2003). In Jarrett, the court ruled that although "the Government operated close to the line," the contacts in *Steiger* between the hacker and law enforcement did not create an agency relationship that carried forward to *Jarrett. Id.* at 346–47. Moreover, although the government created an agency relationship through further contacts with the hacker during the second investigation, that agency relationship arose after the relevant private search and disclosure. *See id.* at 346. Thus, the hacker's private search in *Jarrett* did not violate the Fourth Amendment."[12]

Your intersection with the "private search" guidelines, discussed earlier, can arise in a wide variety of ways. Your employee uses some form of social engineering to hack into data he or she was not authorized to access. Further, the data was stolen by the employee. The CIO sounds the alarm and you use your corporate authority to search for evidence and you discover the crime. You call the FBI and, initially, they repeat your search without a warrant. During the search they inadvertently discover that the employee has emails suggesting that she is blackmailing someone. The blackmail evidence would likely be outside the "private search" bounds and could not be seized as evidence by the FBI.

Remember that I said that it always better to be clever than illegal when conducting investigations. No matter how compelling, always resist the temptation to obtain evidence illegally. It never works out; no matter how safe you think you are, there is always something you didn't think about. It may take a little longer, but it is always easier to be clever than illegal. As we shall learn, consent is a beautiful thing. What if the subject or target will not give consent? Well, there may be others who can provide consent to access the evidence you are seeking. Let's look at what the law says.

"C. Exceptions to the Warrant Requirement in Cases Involving Computers

Warrantless searches that intrude upon a reasonable expectation of privacy will comply with the Fourth Amendment if they fall within an established exception to the warrant requirement. Cases involving computers often raise questions relating to how these "established" exceptions apply to new technologies.

1. Consent

Agents may search a place or object without a warrant or even probable cause if a person with authority has voluntarily consented to the search. *See Schneckloth v. Bustamonte*, 412 U.S. 218, 219 (1973). The authority to consent may be actual or apparent. *See United States v. Buckner*, 473 F.3d 551, 555 (4th Cir. 2007). The consent may be explicit or implicit. *See United States v. Milian-Rodriguez*, 759 F.2d 1558, 1563–64

(11th Cir. 1985). Whether consent was voluntarily given is a question of fact that the court must decide by considering the totality of the circumstances. While no single aspect controls the result, the Supreme Court has identified the following important factors: the age, education, intelligence, physical and mental condition of the person giving consent; whether the person was under arrest; and whether the person had been advised of his right to refuse consent. *See Schneckloth*, 412 U.S. at 226–27. The government carries the burden of proving that consent was voluntary. *See United States v. Matlock*, 415 U.S. 164, 177 (1974); *Buckner*, 473 F.3d at 554.

In computer crime cases, two consent issues arise particularly often. First, when does a search exceed the scope of consent? For example, when a target consents to the search of a location, to what extent does the consent authorize the retrieval of information stored in computers at the location? Second, who is the proper party to consent to a search? Do roommates, friends, and parents have the authority to consent to a search of another person's computer files?

Finally, consent to search may be revoked "prior to the time the search is completed." *United States v. Lattimore*, 87 F.3d 647, 651 (4th Cir. 1996) (quoting 3 Wayne R. LaFave, *Search and Seizure* § 8.2(f), at 674 (3d ed. 1996)). When agents obtain consent to remove computers for off-site review and analysis, the time required for review can be substantial. In such cases, law enforcement should keep in mind that before incriminating evidence is found, the consent may be revoked. In cases involving physical documents obtained by consent, courts have allowed the government to keep copies of the documents made by the government prior to the revocation of consent, but they have forced the government to return copies made after consent was revoked. *See Mason v. Pulliam*, 557 F.2d 426, 429 (5th Cir. 1977); *Vaughn v. Baldwin*, 950 F.2d 331, 334 (6th Cir. 1991). There is little reason for courts to distinguish copying paper documents from copying hard drives, and one district court recently stated that a defendant who revoked the consent to search his computer retained no reasonable expectation of privacy in a mirror image copy of his hard drive made by the FBI. *See United States v. Megahed*, 2009 WL 722481, at *3 (M.D. Fla. Mar. 18, 2009)."[13]

"a. Scope of Consent

"The scope of a consent to search is generally defined by its expressed object, and is limited by the breadth of the consent given." *United States v. Pena*, 143 F.3d 1363, 1368 (10th Cir. 1998) (internal quotation marks omitted). The standard for measuring the scope of consent under the Fourth Amendment is objective reasonableness: "[W]hat would the typical reasonable person have understood by the exchange between the [agent] and the [person granting consent]?" *Florida v. Jimeno*, 500 U.S. 248, 251 (1991). This requires a fact intensive inquiry into whether it was reasonable for the agent to believe that the scope of consent included the items searched. *Id.* Of course, when the limits of the consent are clearly given, either before or during the search, agents must respect these bounds. *See Vaughn v. Baldwin*, 950 F.2d 331, 333–34 (6th Cir. 1991).

Computer cases often raise the question of whether general consent to search a location or item implicitly includes consent to access the memory of electronic storage devices encountered during the search. In such cases, courts look to whether the particular circumstances of the agents' request for consent implicitly or explicitly limited the scope of the search to a particular type, scope, or duration. Because this approach ultimately relies on fact-driven notions of common sense, results reached in published opinions have hinged upon subtle (if not entirely inscrutable) distinctions. *Compare United States v. Reyes*, 922 F. Supp. 818, 834 (S.D.N.Y. 1996) (consent to "look inside" a car included consent to retrieve numbers stored inside pagers found in car's back seat), *with United States v. Blas*, 1990 WL 265179, at *20 (E.D. Wis. Dec. 4, 1990) (consent to "look at" a pager did not include consent to activate pager and retrieve numbers, because looking at pager could be construed to mean "what the device is, or how small it is, or what brand of pager it may be"). *See also United States v. Carey*, 172 F.3d 1268, 1274 (10th Cir. 1999) (reading written consent form extremely narrowly, so that consent to seizure of "any property" under the defendant's control and to "a complete search of the premises and property" at the defendant's address merely permitted the agents to seize the defendant's computer from his apartment, not to search the computer off-site because it was no longer located at the defendant's address); *United States v. Tucker*, 305 F.3d 1193, 1202 (10th Cir. 2002) (allowing computer search pursuant to parole agreement allowing search of "any other property under [defendant's] control"); *United States v. Lemmons*, 282 F.3d 920, 924–25 (7th Cir. 2002) (defendant expanded initial consent to search of cameras and recordings to include computer files when he invited officer to look at computer and failed to object to officer's search for pornographic images). Prosecutors can strengthen their argument that the scope of consent included consent to search electronic storage devices by relying on analogous cases involving closed containers. *See, e.g., United States v. Al-Marri*, 230 F. Supp. 2d 535, 540–41 (S.D.N.Y. 2002) (upholding search of computer in residence and citing principle that separate consent to search closed container in fixed premises is unnecessary); *United States v. Galante*, 1995 WL 507249, at *3 (S.D.N.Y. Aug. 25, 1995) (general consent to search car included consent to have officer access memory of cellular telephone found in the car, in light of circuit precedent involving closed containers); *Reyes*, 922 F. Supp. at 834.

When agents obtain consent for one reason but then conduct a search for another reason, they should be careful to make sure that the scope of consent encompasses their actual search. For example, in *United States v. Turner*, 169 F.3d 84 (1st Cir. 1999), the First Circuit suppressed images of child pornography found on computers after agents procured the defendant's consent to search his property for other evidence. In *Turner*, detectives searching for physical evidence of an attempted sexual assault obtained written consent to search the defendant's "premises" and "personal property." Before the defendant signed the consent form, the detectives discovered a large knife and blood stains in his apartment, and they explained to him that they were looking for more evidence of the assault that the suspect might have left behind. *See id.* at 85–86. While several agents searched for physical evidence, one detective searched the contents of the defendant's personal computer and discovered stored images of child pornography. The defendant was thereafter charged with possessing child pornography. On interlocutory appeal, the First Circuit held that the search of the computer exceeded the scope of consent and suppressed the evidence. According to the Court, the detectives' statements that they were looking for signs of the assault limited the scope of consent to the kind of physical evidence that an intruder might have left behind. *See id.* at 88. By transforming the search for physical evidence into a search for computer files, the detective exceeded the scope of consent. *See id.; see also Carey*, 172 F.3d at 1277 (Baldock, J., concurring) (concluding that agents exceeded scope of consent by searching computer after defendant signed broadly-worded written consent form, because agents told defendant that they were looking for drugs and drug related items rather than computer files containing child pornography) (citing *Turner*). Of course, as with other scope-of-consent cases, cases analyzing the reason for a search are fact specific, and courts' interpretations of the scope of consent are not always narrow. See *United States v. Marshall*, 348 F.3d 281, 287–88 (1st Cir. 2003) (finding that consent to search for "stolen items" did not preclude seizing and viewing video tapes where video equipment, but not video tapes, were reported stolen); *United States v. Raney*, 342 F.3d 551, 556–58 (7th Cir. 2003) (finding consent to search for "materials in the nature of" child exploitation and child erotica was broad enough to encompass search of homemade adult pornography where the defendant had expressed an intent to make similar homemade pornography with a minor).

Finally, the scope of consent usually relates to the target item, location, and purpose of the search, rather than the search methodology used. For example, in *United States v. Brooks*, 427 F.3d 1246 (10th Cir. 2005), an agent received permission to conduct a "complete search" of the defendant's computer for child pornography. The agent explained that he would use a "pre-search" disk to find and display image files, allowing the agent to easily ascertain whether any images contained child pornography. *Id.* at 1248. When the disk, for unexplained reasons, failed to function, the agent conducted a manual search for image files, eventually discovering several pieces of child pornography. *Id.* Although the agent ultimately used a different search methodology than the one he described to the defendant, the Court approved the manual search because it did not exceed the scope of the described disk search. *Id.* at 1249–50. *See also United States v. Long,* 425 F.3d 482, 487 (7th Cir. 2005) (finding that agent's use of "sophisticated" Encase forensic software did not exceed scope of consent to search laptop).

> It is a good practice for agents to use written consent forms that state explicitly that the scope of consent includes consent to search computers and other electronic storage devices.

Because the decisions evaluating the scope of consent to search computers have reached sometimes unpredictable results, investigators should indicate the scope of the search explicitly when obtaining a suspect's consent to search a computer. Moreover, investigators who have seized a computer based on consent and who have developed probable cause may consider obviating concerns with either the scope of consent or revocation of consent by obtaining a search warrant."[14]

Sample Consent Form for Computer Search

CONSENT TO SEARCH COMPUTER/ELECTRONIC EQUIPMENT

I, _____, have been asked to give my consent to the search of my computer/electronic equipment. I have also been informed of my right to refuse to consent to such a search.

I hereby authorize _____ and any other person(s) designated by [insert Agency/Department] to conduct at any time a complete search of:

¤ All computer/electronic equipment located at _____.
These persons are authorized by me to take from the above location: any computer hardware and storage media, including internal hard disk drive(s), floppy diskettes, compact disks, scanners, printers, other computer/electronic hardware or software and related manuals; any other electronic storage devices, including but not limited to, personal digital assistants, cellular telephones, and electronic pagers; and any other media or materials necessary to assist in accessing the stored electronic data.

¤ The following electronic devices:

[Description of computers, data storage devices, cellular telephone, or other devices (makes, models, and serial numbers, if available)]

I certify that I own, possess, control, and/or have a right of access to these devices and all information found in them. I understand that any contraband or evidence on these devices may be used against me in a court of law.

I relinquish any constitutional right to privacy in these electronic devices and any information stored on them. I authorize [insert Agency/Department] to make and keep a copy of any information stored on these devices. I understand that any copy made by [insert Agency/Department] will become the property of [insert Agency/Department] and that I will have no privacy or possessory interest in the copy.

This written permission is given by me voluntarily. I have not been threatened, placed under duress, or promised anything in exchange for my consent. I have read this form; it has been read to me; and I understand it. I understand the _____ language and have been able to communicate with the agents/officers.

I understand that I may withdraw my consent at any time. I may also ask for a receipt for all things turned over.

Signed: _____   Signature of Witnesses: _____

Date and Time:_____   Date and Time:_____[15]

Obviously, when relying on consent to access and collect electronic evidence it would be a very good idea for you to have the person providing the consent sign a form like the one above.

> *"b. Third-Party Consent*
> *i. General Principles*

It is common for several people to use or own the same computer equipment. If any one of those people gives permission to search for data, agents may generally rely on that consent, so long as the person has authority over the computer. In such cases, all users have assumed the risk that a co-user might discover everything in the computer and might also permit law enforcement to search this "common area" as well.

The watershed case in this area is *United States v. Matlock*, 415 U.S. 164 (1974). In *Matlock*, the Supreme Court stated that one who has "common authority" over premises or effects may consent to a search even if an absent co-user objects. *Id.* at 171. According to the Court, the common authority that establishes the right of third-party consent requires

> mutual use of the property by persons generally having joint access or control for most purposes, so that it is reasonable to recognize that any of the co-inhabitants has the right to permit the inspection in his own right and that the others have assumed the risk that one of their number might permit the common area to be searched.

Id. at 171 n.7.

Under the *Matlock* approach, a private third party may consent to a search of property under the third party's joint access or control. Agents may view what the third party may see without violating any reasonable expectation of privacy so long as they limit the search to the zone of the consenting third party's common authority.

See United States v. Jacobsen, 466 U.S. 109, 119–20 (1984) (noting that the Fourth Amendment is not violated when a private third party invites the government to view the contents of a package under the third party's control). This rule often requires agents to inquire into third parties' rights of access before conducting a consent search and to draw lines between those areas that fall within the third party's common authority and those areas outside of the third party's control. *See United States v. Block,* 590 F.2d 535, 541 (4th Cir. 1978) (holding that a mother could consent to a general search of her 23-year-old son's room, but could not consent to a search of a locked footlocker found in the room).

Co-users of a computer will generally have the ability to consent to a search of its files under *Matlock. See United States v. Smith,* 27 F. Supp. 2d 1111, 1115–16 (C.D. Ill. 1998) (concluding that a woman could consent to a search of her boyfriend's computer located in their house and noting that the boyfriend had not password-protected his files). However, when an individual protects her files with passwords and has not shared the passwords with others who also use the computer, the Fourth Circuit has held that the authority of those other users to consent to search of the computer will not extend to the password-protected files. *See Trulock v. Freeh,* 275 F.3d 391, 403 (4th Cir. 2001) (analogizing password-protected files to locked footlockers inside a bedroom, which the court had previously held to be outside the scope of common authority consent). Nevertheless, specific facts may overcome an individual's expectation of privacy even in password-protected files. In *United States v. Buckner,* 407 F. Supp. 2d 777 (W.D. Va. 2006), the Court held that the defendant's wife could validly consent to a search of the family computer, including her husband's password-protected files. The Court distinguished *Trulock* by noting that the computer was leased solely in the wife's name, the allegedly fraudulent activity that provoked the search had occurred through accounts in the wife's name, the computer was located in a common area of the house, none of the files were encrypted, and the computer was on even though the husband had apparently fled the area. *Id.* at 780–81. Furthermore, if the co-user has been given the password by the suspect, then she probably has the requisite common authority to consent to a search of the files under *Matlock. See United States v. Murphy,* 506 F.2d 529, 530 (9th Cir. 1974) (per curiam) (concluding that an employee could consent to a search of an employer's locked warehouse because the employee possessed the key, and finding "special significance" in the fact that the employer had himself delivered the key to the employee).

As a practical matter, agents may have little way of knowing the precise bounds of a third party's common authority when the agents obtain third-party consent to conduct a search. When queried, consenting third parties may falsely claim that they have common authority over property. In *Illinois v. Rodriguez,* 497 U.S. 177 (1990), the Supreme Court held that the Fourth Amendment does not automatically require suppression of evidence discovered during a consent search when it later comes to light that the third party who consented to the search lacked the authority to do so. *See id.* at 188–89. Instead, the Court held that agents can rely on a claim of authority to consent if based on "the facts available to the officer at the moment, ... a man of reasonable caution ... [would believe] that the consenting party had authority" to consent to a search of the premises. *Id.* (internal quotation marks omitted) (quoting *Terry v. Ohio,* 392 U.S. 1, 21–22 (1968)). When agents reasonably rely on apparent authority to consent, the resulting search does not violate the Fourth Amendment. For example, in *United States v. Morgan,* 435 F.3d 660 (6th Cir. 2006), investigators received consent from the defendant's wife to search a computer located in the common area of the home. The wife told police that she had access to the computer, that neither she nor her husband used individual usernames or passwords, and that she had recently installed spyware on the computer to monitor her husband's suspected viewing of child pornography. *Id.* at 663–64. She did not tell the police that she had her own, separate computer for her primary use. *Id.* at 662. Nevertheless, the Court found that the police could reasonably rely on her statements and conclude that she had authority to consent to the search. *Id.* at 664. *See also United States v. Andrus*, 483 F.3d 711, 720–21 (10th Cir. 2007) (holding that parent had apparent authority to consent to search of computer in room of adult child, where parent had unrestricted access to adult child's bedroom and paid for Internet access).

The Supreme Court has held, however, that investigators cannot rely on a third party's consent to search a residence when the target of the search is present and expressly objects to the search. *See Georgia v. Randolph*, 547 U.S. 103, 121 (2006). The court's conclusion was based on its determination that a "co-tenant wishing to open the door to a third party has no recognized authority in law or social practice to prevail over a present and objecting co-tenant." *Id.* at 114. Moreover, unless police remove a potential objector "for the sake of avoiding a possible objection," *Randolph* does not apply to "potential" objectors who have not taken part in the consent colloquy, even if the potential objector is nearby. *Id.* at 121. For example, in *United States v. Hudspeth*, 518 F.3d 954 (8th Cir. 2008) (en banc), officers arrested the defendant at his workplace for possession of child pornography, and the defendant refused to consent to a search of his home. Nevertheless, his wife subsequently consented to a search of a computer in their home. The Eighth Circuit upheld the search, explaining that "unlike *Randolph*, the officers in the present case were not confronted with a 'social custom' dilemma, where two physically present co-tenants have contemporaneous competing interests and one consents to a search, while the other objects." *Id.* at 960. *See also United States v. Crosbie*, 2006 WL 1663667, at *2 (S.D. Ala. June 9, 2006) (defendant's wife's consent to computer search was valid even though wife had ordered her husband out of the house, thus depriving him of the "opportunity to object").[16]

Every organization is different. So, it would probably be a good idea, if your organization has not already done so, to document the common usage spaces of your employees. This would apply to digital and physical data storage areas. Get the CIO and the general counsel's office and, perhaps, outside counsel to help with this important undertaking. Basically, you want to make sure that there are no private data spaces within the scope of your organization's operations; they all need to be common spaces. Examples of potential private spaces that should be eliminated include:

- Employees and contractors must carry out all work on company machines. This includes phones, iPads, laptops, desktops, flash drives, printers, etc.
- All employees should sign a written statement, as part of their onboarding process, which clearly establishes that they should not have any expectation of privacy within any workspace. (Note: With all the remote work being done, as part of the pandemic lockdown, this will be very difficult to enforce.)
- All employees should sign a written statement, as part of their onboarding process, which clearly establishes that all documents or other materials, physical or digital, are the property of the company and should be stored in authorized company storage spaces.

Also, do your homework. Do some digging; you may find disgruntled former business partners, unpaid contractors, or other aggrieved parties who share access to the storage spaces of your subjects or targets. They will often gleefully provide consent. But, have them sign a written consent form and get legal counsel involved to make sure what you are doing is legal.

"ii. Spouses and Domestic Partners

> Most spousal consent searches are valid.

Absent an affirmative showing that the consenting spouse has no access to the property searched, the courts generally hold that either spouse may consent to a search of all of the couple's property. *See, e.g., Trulock v. Freeh*, 275 F.3d 391, 398, 403–04 (4th Cir. 2001) (holding that woman did not have authority to consent to search of computer files of the man with whom she lived, when she had told agents that she did not know the password to access his files); *United States v. Duran*, 957 F.2d 499, 504–05 (7th Cir. 1992) (concluding that wife could consent to search of barn she did not use because husband had not denied her the right to enter barn); *United States v. Long*, 524 F.2d 660, 661 (9th Cir. 1975) (holding that wife who had left her husband could consent to search of jointly-owned home even though husband had changed the locks). For example, in *United States v. Smith*, 27 F. Supp. 2d 1111 (C.D. Ill. 1998), a man named Smith was living with a woman named Ushman and her two daughters. When allegations of child molestation were raised against Smith, Ushman consented to the search of his computer, which was located in the house in an alcove connected to the master bedroom. Although Ushman used Smith's computer only rarely, the district court held that she could consent to the search of Smith's computer. Because Ushman was not prohibited from entering the alcove and Smith had not password-protected the computer, the court reasoned, she had authority to consent to the search. *See id.* at 1115–16. Even if she lacked actual authority to consent, the court added, she had apparent authority to consent. *See id.* at 1116 (citing *Illinois v. Rodriguez*, 497 U.S. 177 (1990))."[17]

White-collar criminals often have a way of making their spouses very angry. They are often committing the crimes they are committing to support a mistress, keep ahead of a gambling or drug addiction, and countless other reasons. Many of these have the unintended consequence of turning their spouses into their worst enemies. Spouses can also provide perfectly valid consent. So, don't overlook them.

"iii. Parents

> Parents can consent to searches of their children's computers when the children are under 18 years old. If the children are 18 or older, the parents may or may not be able to consent, depending on the facts.

In some computer crime cases, the perpetrators are relatively young and reside with their parents. When the perpetrator is a minor, parental consent to search the perpetrator's property and living space will almost always be valid. *See 3* Wayne LaFave, *Search and Seizure: A Treatise on the Fourth Amendment* § 8.4(b) at 283 (2d ed. 1987) (noting that courts have rejected "even rather extraordinary efforts by [minor] child[ren] to establish exclusive use.").

When the sons and daughters who reside with their parents are legal adults, however, the issue is more complicated. Under *Matlock*, it is clear that parents may consent to a search of common areas in the family home regardless of the perpetrator's age. *See, e.g., United States v. Lavin*, 1992 WL 373486, at *6 (S.D.N.Y. Nov. 30, 1992) (recognizing right of parents to consent to search of basement room where son kept his computer and files). When agents would like to search an adult child's room or other private areas, however, agents cannot assume that the adult's parents have authority to consent. Although courts have offered divergent approaches, they have paid particular attention to three factors: the suspect's age; whether the suspect pays rent; and whether the suspect has taken affirmative steps to deny his or her parents access to the suspect's room or private area. When suspects are older, pay rent, and/or deny access to parents, courts have generally held that parents may not consent. *See United States v. Whitfield*, 939 F.2d 1071, 1075 (D.C. Cir. 1991) ("cursory questioning" of suspect's mother insufficient to establish right to consent to search of 29-year-old son's room); *United States v. Durham*, 1998 WL 684241, at *4 (D. Kan. Sept. 11, 1998) (mother had neither apparent nor actual authority to consent to search of 24-year-old son's room, because son had changed the locks to the room without telling his mother, and son also paid rent for the room). In contrast, parents usually may consent if their adult children do not pay rent, are fairly young, and have taken no steps to deny their parents access to the space to be searched. *See United States v. Andrus*, 483 F.3d 711, 713, 720–21 (10th Cir. 2007) (parent had apparent authority to consent to search of computer in room of 51-year-old son who did not pay rent, where parent had unrestricted access to adult child's bedroom and paid for Internet access); *United States v. Rith*, 164 F.3d 1323, 1331 (10th Cir. 1999) (suggesting that parents were presumed to have authority to consent to a search of their 18-year-old son's room because he did not pay rent); *United States v. Block*, 590 F.2d 535, 541 (4th Cir. 1978) (mother could consent to police search of 23-year-old son's room when son did not pay rent)."[18]

Many of your employees may still live at home and not pay rent. If so, their parents can provide valid consent to search for and recover evidence from storage paces, physical or digital, that are shared spaces. In this case the consent form should be expanded to include an affirmative statement of the arrangements that give rise to the shared spaces. By all means, consult legal before proceeding in reliance on this type of consent. But, this can be a perfectly legal way to access your employees shared storage spaces outside the company's offices.

"iv. Computer Repair Technicians

As discussed above in Section B.4, computer searches by repairman prior to contact with law enforcement are private searches and do not implicate the Fourth Amendment. Most commonly, law enforcement will use information revealed through a repairman's private search as a basis to secure a warrant for a full search of the computer. In some cases, however, law enforcement officers have relied on the consent of the repairman as the basis for a search of the computer that exceeds the scope of the initial private search. District courts have split on whether computer repairmen have the authority to authorize such searches. *Compare United States v. Anderson*, 2007 WL 1121319, at *6 (N.D. Ind. Apr. 16, 2007) (technicians had "actual and apparent authority" to consent to a search of computer brought in for repair because they had authority to access the computer), *with United States v. Barth*, 26 F. Supp. 2d 929, 938 (W.D. Tex. 1998) (repairman lacked actual or apparent authority to consent to search of hard drive because the defendant had given the hard drive to the technician only for a limited purpose unrelated to the specific files and only for a limited period of time)."[19]

Computer repair technicians can provide consent under some circumstances. When I have been able to access digital evidence in this way, it has literally broken the case wide open. These instances have primarily involved targets who believed that they had successfully destroyed storage spaces and their contents. Surprise! Gotcha!

"v. System Administrators

Computer network accounts, including the accounts provided by private employers to their employees, by government entities to public employees, and by large commercial service providers to their customers, often contain information relevant to criminal investigations. When investigators suspect that a computer network account contains relevant evidence, they may want to know whether the network's owner or manager has authority to voluntarily disclose information related to the account. As a practical matter, every computer network is managed by a "system administrator" or "system operator" whose job is to keep the network running smoothly, monitor security, and repair the network when problems arise. System operators have "root level" access to the systems they administer, which effectively grants them master keys to open any account and read any file on their systems. However, whether a system administrator (generally at the direction of an appropriate supervisory official) may voluntarily consent to disclose information from or regarding a user's account varies based on whether the network belongs to a communication service provider, a private business, or a government entity.

Regarding public commercial communication service providers (such as Google or Yahoo!), the primary barrier to voluntary disclosure by the service provider is statutory, not constitutional. As discussed in Chapter 3, any attempt to obtain a system administrator's consent to disclose information regarding an account must comply with the Stored Communications Act ("SCA"), 18 U.S.C. §§ 2701–2712. Section 2702 of the SCA prohibits public service providers from voluntarily disclosing to the government information pertaining to their customers except in certain specified situations—which often track Fourth Amendment exceptions—such as with the consent of the user, to protect the service provider's rights and property, or in an emergency. *See* Chapter 3.E, *infra*. Significantly for Fourth Amendment purposes, commercial service providers typically have terms of service that confirm their authority to access information stored on their systems, and such terms of service may establish a service provider's common authority over their users' accounts. *See United States v. Young*, 350 F.3d 1302, 1308–09 (11th Cir. 2003) (holding that Federal Express's terms of service, which authorized it to inspect packages, gave it common authority to consent to a government search of a package); *see also United States v. Beckett*, 544 F. Supp. 2d 1346, 1350 (S.D. Fla. 2008) ("where service providers have an agreement to share information under circumstances similar to those in our case (for investigation, to cooperate with law enforcement, and to take legal action), there is no objectively reasonable expectation of privacy and therefore no Fourth Amendment protection for subscriber information"). *But see Quon v. Arch Wireless Operating Co.*, 529 F.3d 892, 904–08 (9th Cir. 2008) (finding government employee had reasonable expectation of privacy in pager messages stored by provider of communication service based on "informal policy that the text messages would not be audited").

As discussed more fully in Section D.1.b below, private-sector employers generally have broad authority to consent to searches in the workplace, and this authority extends to workplace networks. For example, in *United States v. Ziegler*, 474 F.3d 1184 (9th Cir. 2007), the Ninth Circuit held that an employer could consent to a search of the computer it provided to an employee and stated that "the computer is the type of workplace property that remains within the control of the employer even if the employee has placed personal items in it." *Id.* at 1191 (internal quotation marks omitted). Thus, law enforcement can generally rely on the consent of an appropriate manager to search a private workplace network. In contrast, as discussed in Section D.2 below, the Fourth

Amendment rules for government computer networks differ significantly from the rules that apply to private networks. Searches of government computer networks are *not* evaluated under *Matlock*; instead, they are evaluated under the standards of *O'Connor v. Ortega*, 480 U.S. 709 (1987)."[20]

The System Administrator problem created by the Stored Communications Act ("SCA"), 18 U.S.C. §§ 2701–2712 makes a powerful argument in favor of maintaining an internal private network for your organization. If you do use such a network, then your system administrator has broad authority to grant access to the network for search and seizure purposes.

"c. Implied Consent

Individuals often enter into agreements with the government in which they waive some of their Fourth Amendment rights. For example, prison guards may agree to be searched for drugs as a condition of employment, and visitors to government buildings may agree to a limited search of their person and property as a condition of entrance. Similarly, users of computer systems may waive their rights to privacy as a condition of using the systems. When individuals who have waived their rights are then searched and challenge the searches on Fourth Amendment grounds, courts typically focus on whether the waiver eliminated the individual's reasonable expectation of privacy against the search. *See, e.g., United States v. Simons*, 206 F.3d 392, 398 (4th Cir. 2000) (government employee had no reasonable expectation of privacy in computer in light of computer use policy); *American Postal Workers Union, Columbus Area Local AFL-CIO v. United States Postal Service*, 871 F.2d 556, 559–61 (6th Cir. 1989) (postal employees retained no reasonable expectation of privacy in government lockers after signing waivers). For an expanded discussion of workplace searches, *see* Section D below.

A few courts have approached the same problem from a slightly different direction and have asked whether the waiver established implied consent to the search. According to the doctrine of implied consent, consent to a search may be inferred from an individual's conduct. For example, in *United States v. Ellis*, 547 F.2d 863 (5th Cir. 1977), a civilian visiting a naval air station agreed to post a visitor's pass on the windshield of his car as a condition of bringing the car on the base. The pass stated that "[a]cceptance of this pass gives your consent to search this vehicle while entering, aboard, or leaving this station." *Id.* at 865 n.1. During the visitor's stay on the base, a station investigator who suspected that the visitor had stored marijuana in the car approached the visitor and asked him if he had read the pass. After the visitor admitted that he had, the investigator searched the car and found 20 plastic bags containing marijuana. The Fifth Circuit ruled that the warrantless search of the car was permissible, because the visitor had impliedly consented to the search when he knowingly and voluntarily entered the base with full knowledge of the terms of the visitor's pass. *See id.* at 866–67.

Ellis notwithstanding, it must be noted that several circuits have been critical of the implied consent doctrine in the Fourth Amendment context. Despite the Fifth Circuit's broad construction, other courts have been reluctant to apply the doctrine absent evidence that the suspect actually knew of the search and voluntarily consented to it at the time the search occurred. *See McGann v. Northeast Illinois Regional Commuter R.R. Corp.*, 8 F.3d 1174, 1180 (7th Cir. 1993) ("Courts confronted with claims of implied consent have been reluctant to uphold a warrantless search based simply on actions taken in the light of a posted notice."); *Security and Law Enforcement Employees, Dist. Council 82 v. Carey*, 737 F.2d 187, 202 n.23 (2d Cir. 1984) (rejecting argument that prison guards impliedly consented to search by accepting employment at prison where consent to search was a condition of employment). Absent such evidence, these courts have preferred to examine general waivers of Fourth Amendment rights solely under the reasonable-expectation-of-privacy test."[21]

You need to work with legal to do this properly. But, getting employees to sign statements that create implied consents to legal searches and seizures will make your life much easier when conducting investigations. You don't want to wait until you need implied consent to find out that it does not exist.

The second area is codified in the United States Code: The Wiretap Act, 18 U.S.C. §§ 2510–2522, was first passed as Title III of the Omnibus Crime control and Safe Streets Act of 1968 and is generally known as "Title III". It was originally designed for wire and oral communications. The Electronic Communications Privacy Act of 1986 (ECPA) was enacted by the United States Congress to extend government restrictions on wire taps from telephone calls to include transmissions of electronic data by computer. It prohibits unauthorized government access to private electronic communications (see 18 U.S.C. § 2510(12)) in real time. The Stored Communications Act (SCA) [11], 18 U.S.C. §§ 2701–2712, is a law that was enacted by the United States Congress in 1986. SCA is a part of the ECPA. It protects the privacy of customers and subscribers of internet service providers (ISPs) and regulates the government access to stored content and noncontent records held by ISPs. The Pen Register Act [12], 18 U.S.C. §§ 3121–3127, also known as the Pen Registers and Trap and Trace Devices statute (Pen/Trap statute). A pen register device (see 18 U.S.C. § 3127(3)) records outgoing addressing information (such as a number dialed and receiver's email address); a trap and trace device (see 18 U.S.C. § 3127(4)) records incoming addressing information (such as incoming phone number and sender's email address). The Pen/Trap statute regulates the collection of addressing and other noncontent information such as packet size for wire and electronic communications.

From the US Justice Department's Searching and Seizing Computers and Obtaining Electronic Evidence in Criminal Investigations:

"A. Introduction

The SCA regulates how the government can obtain stored account information from network service providers such as ISPs. Whenever agents or prosecutors seek stored email, account records, or subscriber information from a network service provider, they must comply with the SCA. The SCA's classifications are summarized in the chart that appears in Section F of this chapter.

The Stored Communications Act, 18 U.S.C. §§ 2701–2712 ("SCA"), sets forth a system of statutory privacy rights for customers and subscribers of computer network service providers. There are three main substantive components to this system, which serves to protect and regulate the privacy interests of network users with respect to government, network service providers, and the world at large. First, § 2703 creates a code of criminal procedure that federal and state law enforcement officers must follow to compel disclosure of stored communications from network service providers. Second, § 2702 regulates voluntary disclosure by network service providers of customer communications and records, both to government and nongovernment entities. Third, § 2701 prohibits unlawful access to certain stored communications; anyone who obtains, alters, or prevents authorized access to those communications is subject to criminal penalties.

The structure of the SCA reflects a series of classifications that indicate the drafters' judgments about what kinds of information implicate greater or lesser privacy interests.

For example, the drafters saw greater privacy interests in the content of stored emails than in subscriber account information. Similarly, the drafters believed that computing services available "to the public" required more strict regulation than services not available to the public. (Perhaps this judgment reflects the view that providers available to the public are not likely to have close relationships with their customers, and therefore might have less incentive to protect their customers' privacy.) To protect the array of privacy interests identified by its drafters, the SCA offers varying degrees of legal protection depending on the perceived importance of the privacy interest involved. Some information can be obtained from providers with a subpoena; other information requires a special court order; and still other information requires a search warrant. In addition, some types of legal process require notice to the subscriber, while other types do not.

Agents and prosecutors must apply the various classifications devised by the SCA's drafters to the facts of each case to figure out the proper procedure for obtaining the information sought. First, they must classify the network service provider (e.g., does the provider provide "electronic communication service," "remote computing service," or neither). Next, they must classify the information sought (e.g., is the information content "in electronic storage," content held by a remote computing service, a non-content record pertaining to a subscriber, or other information enumerated by the SCA). Third, they must consider whether they are seeking to compel disclosure or seeking to accept information disclosed voluntarily by the provider. If they seek compelled disclosure, they need to determine whether they need a search warrant, a 2703(d) court order, or a subpoena to compel the disclosure. If they are seeking to accept information voluntarily disclosed, they must determine whether the statute permits the disclosure. The chart contained in Section F of this chapter provides a useful way to apply these distinctions in practice.

The organization of this chapter will follow the SCA's various classifications. Section B explains the SCA's classification structure, which distinguishes between providers of "electronic communication service" and providers of "remote computing service." Section C explains the different kinds of information that providers can divulge, such as content "in electronic storage" and "records ... pertaining to a subscriber." Section D explains the legal process that agents and prosecutors must follow to compel a provider to disclose information. Section E looks at the flip side of this problem and explains when providers may voluntarily disclose account information. A summary chart appears in Section F. Section G discusses important issues that may arise when agents obtain records from network providers: steps to preserve evidence, steps to prevent disclosure to subjects, Cable Act issues, and reimbursement to providers. Section H discusses the Fourth Amendment's application to stored electronic communications. Finally, Section I discusses the remedies that courts may impose following violations of the SCA."[22]

	Voluntary Disclosure Allowed?		How to Compel Disclosure	
	Public Provider	**Non-Public**	**Public Provider**	**Non-Public**
Basic subscriber, session, and billing information •	No, unless §2702(c) exception applies *§ 2702(a)(3)*	Yes *§ 2702(a)(3)*	Subpoena; 2703(d) order; or search warrant *§ 2703(c)(2)*	Subpoena; 2703(d) order; or search warrant *§ 2703(c)(2)*
Other transactional and account records	No, unless §2702(c) exception applies *§ 2702(a)(3)*	Yes *§ 2702(a)(3)*	2703(d) order or search warrant *§ 2703(c)(1)*	2703(d) order or search warrant *§ 2703(c)(1)*
Retrieved communications and the content of other stored files#	No, unless § 2702(b) exception applies *§ 2702(a)(2)*	Yes *§ 2702(a)(2)*	Subpoena with notice; 2703(d) order with notice; or search warrant* *§ 2703(b)*	Subpoena; SCA does not apply* *§ 2711(2)*
Unretrieved communications, including email and voice mail (in electronic storage more than 180 days) †	No, unless § 2702(b) exception applies *§ 2702(a)(1)*	Yes *§ 2702(a)(1)*	Subpoena with notice; 2703(d) order with notice; or search warrant *§ 2703(a), (b)*	Subpoena with notice; 2703(d) order with notice; or search warrant *§ 2703(a), (b)*
Unretrieved communications, including email and voice mail (in electronic storage 180 days or less) †	No, unless § 2702(b) exception applies *§ 2702(a)(1)*	Yes *§ 2702(a)(1)*	Search warrant *§ 2703(a)*	Search warrant *§ 2703(a)*

• See 18 U.S.C. § 2703(c)(2) for listing of information covered. This information includes local and long distance telephone connection records and records of session times and durations as well as IP addresses assigned to the user during the Internet connections.

† Includes the content of voice communications.

* For investigations occurring in the Ninth Circuit, *Theofel v. Farey-Jones*, 359 F.3d 1066 (9th Cir. 2004), requires use of a search warrant unless the communications have been in storage for more than 180 days. Some providers follow *Theofel* even outside the Ninth Circuit; contact CCIPS at (202) 514-1026 if you have an appropriate case to litigate this issue.

FIGURE 6.1[23]

The SCA Voluntary Disclosure chart provided in Figure 6.1 is a handy tool. You want to pay particular attention to columns 1–3. Do not assume that all those you seek to access and seize digital information from are expert in this area of the law that is complicated. Again, when in doubt, get the lawyers involved. Note that Public Providers, as we shall see in the following pages, must be classified as an Electronic Communication Service (ECS) or a Remote Computing Service (RCS) to properly apply the law.

"B. Providers of Electronic Communication Service vs. Remote Computing Service

The SCA protects communications held by two defined classes of network service providers: providers of "electronic communication service," *see* 18 U.S.C. § 2510(15), and providers of "remote computing service," *see* 18 U.S.C. § 2711(2). Careful examination of the definitions of these two terms is necessary to understand how to apply the SCA.

1. Electronic Communication Service

An electronic communication service ("ECS") is "any service which provides to users thereof the ability to send or receive wire or electronic communications." 18 U.S.C. § 2510(15). (For a discussion of the definitions of wire and electronic communications, see Chapter 4.D.2.) For example, "telephone companies and electronic mail companies" generally act as ECS providers. *See S.* Rep. No. 99–541 (1986), *reprinted in* 1986 U.S.C.C.A.N. 3555, 3568; *Quon v. Arch Wireless Operating Co.*, 529 F.3d 892, 900–03 (9th Cir. 2008) (text messaging service provider is an ECS); *In re Application of United States*, 509 F. Supp. 2d 76, 79 (D. Mass. 2007) (cell phone service provider is an ECS); *Kaufman v. Nest Seekers*, LLC, 2006 WL 2807177, at *5 (S.D.N.Y. Sept. 26, 2006) (host of electronic bulletin board is ECS); *Freedman v. America Online, Inc.*, 325 F. Supp. 2d 638, 643 n.4 (E.D. Va. 2004) (AOL is an ECS).

Any company or government entity that provides others with the means to communicate electronically can be a "provider of electronic communication service" relating to the communications it provides, regardless of the entity's primary business or function. See *Fraser v. Nationwide Mut. Ins. Co.*, 352 F.3d 107, 114–15 (3d Cir. 2004) (insurance company that provided email service to employees is an ECS); *Bohach v. City of Reno*, 932 F. Supp. 1232, 1236 (D. Nev. 1996) (city providing pager service to its police officers was a provider of ECS); *United States v. Mullins*, 992 F.2d 1472, 1478 (9th Cir. 1993) (airline that provides travel agents with computerized travel reservation system accessed through separate computer terminals can be a provider of ECS). In *In re Application of United States*, 349 F.3d 1132, 1138–41 (9th Cir. 2003), the Ninth Circuit held that a company operating a system that enabled drivers to communicate with designated call centers over a cellular telephone network was an ECS, though it also noted that the situation would have been entirely different "if the Company merely used wire communication as an incident to providing some other service, as is the case with a street-front shop that requires potential customers to speak into an intercom device before permitting entry, or a 'drive-thru' restaurant that allows customers to place orders via a two-way intercom located beside the drive-up lane." *Id.* at 1141 n.19.

A provider cannot provide ECS with respect to a communication if the service did not provide the ability to send or receive *that* communication. *See Sega Enterprises Ltd. v. MAPHIA*, 948 F. Supp. 923, 930–31 (N.D. Cal. 1996) (video game manufacturer that accessed private email of users of another company's bulletin board service was not a provider of electronic communication service); *State Wide Photocopy, Corp. v. Tokai Fin. Servs., Inc.*, 909 F. Supp. 137, 145 (S.D.N.Y. 1995) (financing company that used fax machines and computers but did not provide the ability to send or receive communications was not provider of electronic communication service).

Significantly, a mere user of ECS provided by another is not a provider of ECS. For example, a commercial website is not a provider of ECS, even though it may send and receive electronic communications from customers. In *Crowley v. CyberSource Corp.*, 166 F. Supp. 2d 1263, 1270 (N.D. Cal. 2001), the plaintiff argued that Amazon.com (to whom plaintiff sent his name, credit card number, and other identification information) was an electronic communications service provider because "without recipients such as Amazon. com, users would have no ability to send electronic information." The court rejected this argument, holding that Amazon was properly characterized as a user rather than a provider of ECS. *See id. See also United States v. Steiger*, 318 F.3d 1039, 1049 (11th Cir. 2003) (a home computer connected to the Internet is not an ECS); *In re Jetblue Airways Corp. Privacy Litigation*, 379 F. Supp. 2d 299, 309–10 (E.D.N.Y. 2005) (airline that operated website that enabled it to communicate with customers was not an ECS); *Dyer v. Northwest Airlines Corp.*, 334 F. Supp. 2d 1196, 1199 (D.N.D. 2004) (ECS "does not encompass businesses selling traditional products or services online"); *In re Doubleclick Inc. Privacy Litigation*, 154 F. Supp. 2d 497, 508–09 (S.D.N.Y. 2001) (distinguishing ISPs that provide ECS from websites that are users of ECS). However, "an online business or retailer may be considered an electronic communication service provider if the business has a website that offers customers the ability to send messages or communications to third parties." *Becker v. Toca*, 2008 WL 4443050, at *4 (E.D. La. Sept. 26, 2008)."[24]

"2. Remote Computing Service

The term "remote computing service" ("RCS") is defined by 18 U.S.C. § 2711(2) as "the provision to the public of computer storage or processing services by means of an electronic communications system." An "electronic communications system" is "any wire, radio, electromagnetic, photo-optical or photo-electronic facilities for the transmission of wire or electronic communications, and any computer facilities or related electronic equipment for the electronic storage of such communications." 18 U.S.C. § 2510(14).

Roughly speaking, a remote computing service is provided by an off-site computer that stores or processes data for a customer. See S. Rep. No. 99–541 (1986), *reprinted* in 1986 U.S.C.C.A.N. 3555, 3564–65. For example, a service provider that allows customers to use its computing facilities in "essentially a time-sharing arrangement" provides an RCS. H.R. Rep. No. 99–647, at 23 (1986). A server that allows users to store data for future retrieval also provides an RCS. *See Steve Jackson Games, Inc. v. United States Secret Service*, 816 F. Supp. 432, 442–43 (W.D. Tex. 1993) (provider of bulletin board services was a remote computing service), *aff'd on other grounds*, 36 F.3d 457 (5th Cir. 1994). Importantly, an entity that operates a website and its associated servers is not an RCS, unless of course the entity offers a storage or processing service through the website. For example, an airline may compile and store passenger information and itineraries through its website, but these functions are incidental to providing airline reservation service, not data storage and processing service; they do not convert the airline into an RCS. *See In re Jetblue Airways Corp. Privacy Litigation*, 379 F. Supp. 2d at 310; *see also United States v. Standefer*, 2007 WL 2301760, at *5 (S.D. Cal. Aug. 8, 2007) (holding that e-gold payment website was not an RCS because e-gold customers did not use the website "to simply store electronic data" or to "outsource tasks," but instead used e-gold "to transfer gold ownership to other users").

Under the definition provided by § 2711(2), a service can only be a "remote computing service" if it is available "to the public." Services are available to the public if they are available to any member of the general population who complies with the requisite procedures and pays any requisite fees. For example, Verizon is a provider to the public: anyone can obtain a Verizon account. (It may seem odd at first that a service can charge a fee but still be considered available "to the public," but this approach mirrors commercial relationships in the physical world. For example, movie theaters are open "to the public" because anyone can buy a ticket and see a show, even though tickets are not free.) In contrast, providers whose services are available only to those with a special relationship with the provider do not provide service to the public. For example, an employer that provides email accounts to its employees will not be an RCS with respect to those employees, because such email accounts are not available to the public. *See Andersen Consulting LLP v. UOP*, 991 F. Supp. 1041, 1043 (N.D. Ill. 1998) (interpreting the "to the public" clause in § 2702(a) to exclude an internal email system that was made available to a hired contractor but was not available to "any member of the community at large").

In *Quon v. Arch Wireless Operating Co.*, the Ninth Circuit held that a text messaging service provider was an ECS and therefore not an RCS. *See Quon*, 529 F.3d at 902–03. However, this "either/or" approach to ECS and RCS is contrary to the language of the statute and its legislative history. The definitions of ECS and RCS are independent of each other, and therefore nothing prevents a service provider from providing both forms of service to a single customer. In addition, an email service provider is certainly an ECS, but the House report on the SCA also stated that an email stored after transmission would be protected by a provision of the SCA that protects contents of communications stored by an RCS. See H.R. Rep. No. 99–647, at 65 (1986). One subsequent court has rejected the Ninth Circuit's analysis in *Quon* and stated that a provider "may be deemed to provide both an ECS and an RCS to the same customer." *Flagg, v. City of Detroit*, 252 F.R.D. 346, 362 (E.D. Mich. 2008). The key to determining whether the provider is an ECS or RCS is to ask what role the provider has played and is playing with respect to the communication in question."[25]

The thing that I want you to note, in the preceding sections, is that the definition of an ECS and RCS is very broad and complex. It also is fact and circumstance specific and can change if the company changes its offerings to customers and others. So, once again, when in doubt get the lawyers involved.

With respect to the handy chart, discussed earlier, ECSs and RCSs are both public providers.

"C. Classifying Types of Information Held by Service Providers

Network service providers can store different kinds of information relating to an individual customer or subscriber. Consider the range of information that an ISP may typically store regarding one of its customers. It may have the customer's subscriber information, such as name, address, and credit card number. It may have logs revealing when the customer logged on and off the service, the IP addresses assigned to the customer, and other more detailed logs pertaining to what the customer did while online. The ISP may also have the customer's opened, unopened, draft, and sent emails.

When agents and prosecutors wish to obtain such records, they must be able to classify these types of information using the language of the SCA. The SCA breaks the information down into three categories: (1) contents; (2) non-content records and other information pertaining to a subscriber or customer; and (3) basic subscriber and session information, which is a subset of non-content records and is specifically enumerated in 18 U.S.C. § 2703(c)(2). See 18 U.S.C. §§ 2510(8), 2703. In addition, as described below, the SCA creates substantially different protections for contents in "electronic storage" in an ECS and contents stored by a provider of RCS.

1. Basic Subscriber and Session Information Listed in 18 U.S.C. § 2703(c)(2)

Section 2703(c)(2) lists the categories of basic subscriber and session information:

(A) name; (B) address; (C) local and long distance telephone connection records, or records of session times and durations; (D) length of service (including start date) and types of service utilized; (E) telephone or instrument number or other subscriber number or identity, including any temporarily assigned network address; and (F) means and source of payment for such service (including any credit card or bank account number)[.]

In general, the items in this list relate to the identity of a subscriber, his relationship with his service provider, and his basic session connection records. In the Internet context, "any temporarily assigned network address" includes the IP address used by a customer for a particular session. For example, for a webmail service, the IP address used by a customer accessing her email account constitutes a "temporarily assigned network address." This list does not include other, more extensive transaction-related records, such as logging information revealing the email addresses of persons with whom a customer corresponded."[26]

2. Records or Other Information Pertaining to a Customer or Subscriber

Section 2703(c)(1) covers a second type of information: "a record or other information pertaining to a subscriber to or customer of such service (not including the contents of communications)." This is a catch-all category that includes all records that are not contents, including basic subscriber and session information described in the previous section. As one court explained, "a record means something stored or archived. The term information is synonymous with data." *In re United States*, 509 F. Supp. 2d 76, 80 (D. Mass. 2007).

Common examples of "record[s] ... pertaining to a subscriber" include transactional records, such as account logs that record account usage; cell-site data for cellular telephone calls; and email addresses of other individuals with whom the account holder has corresponded. *See* H.R. Rep. No. 103–827, at 10, 17, 31 (1994), *reprinted in* 1994 U.S.C.C.A.N. 3489, 3490, 3497, 3511. *See also In re Application of United States*, 509 F. Supp. 76, 80 (D. Mass. 2007) (historical cell-site information fall within scope of § 2703(c)(1)); *United States v. Allen*, 53 M.J. 402, 409 (C.A.A.F. 2000) (concluding that "a log identifying the date, time, user, and detailed internet address of sites accessed" by a user constituted "a record or other information pertaining to a subscriber or customer of such service" under the SCA); *Hill v. MCI WorldCom Commc'ns, Inc.*, 120 F. Supp. 2d 1194, 1195–96 (S.D. Iowa 2000) (concluding that the "names, addresses, and phone numbers of parties ... called" constituted "a record or other information pertaining to a subscriber or customer of such service," not contents, for a telephone account); *Jessup-Morgan v. America Online, Inc.*, 20 F. Supp. 2d 1105, 1108 (E.D. Mich. 1998) (holding that a customer's identification information is a "record or other information pertaining to a subscriber" rather than contents). According to the legislative history of the 1994 amendments to § 2703(c), the purpose of separating the basic subscriber and session information from other non-content records was to distinguish basic subscriber and session information from more revealing transactional information that could contain a "person's entire on-line profile." H.R. Rep. No. 103–827, at 17, 31–32 (1994), *reprinted in 1994* U.S.C.C.A.N. 3489, 3497, 3511–12."[27]

"3. Contents and "Electronic Storage"

The contents of a network account are the actual files (including email) stored in the account. See 18 U.S.C. § 2510(8) ("'contents,' when used with respect to any wire, oral, or electronic communication, includes any information concerning the substance, purport, or meaning of that communication"). For example, stored emails or voice mails are "contents," as are word processing files stored in employee network accounts. The subject lines of emails are also contents. *Cf. Brown v. Waddell*, 50 F.3d 285, 292 (4th Cir. 1995) (noting that numerical pager messages allow "an unlimited range of number-coded substantive messages" in the course of holding that the interception of pager messages requires compliance with Title III).

The SCA further divides contents into two categories: contents in "electronic storage" held by a provider of electronic communication service, and contents stored by a remote computing service. (In addition, contents that fall outside of these two categories are not protected by the SCA.) Importantly, "electronic storage" is a statutorily defined term. It does *not* simply mean storage of information by electronic means. Instead, "electronic storage" is "(A) any temporary, intermediate storage of a wire or electronic communication incidental to the electronic transmission thereof; and (B) any storage of such communication by an electronic communication service for purposes of backup protection of such communication." 18 U.S.C. § 2510(17). Moreover, the definition of "electronic storage" is important because, as explained in Section D below, contents in "electronic storage" for less than 181 days can be obtained only with a warrant.

Unfortunately, as a result of the Ninth Circuit's decision in *Theofel v. Farey-Jones*, 359 F.3d 1066 (9th Cir. 2004), there is now a split between two interpretations of "electronic storage"—a traditional narrow interpretation and an expansive interpretation supplied by the Ninth Circuit. Both interpretations are discussed below. As a practical matter, federal law enforcement within the Ninth Circuit is bound by the Ninth Circuit's decision in *Theofel*, but law enforcement elsewhere may continue to apply the traditional interpretation of "electronic storage."

As traditionally understood, "electronic storage" refers only to temporary storage made in the course of transmission by a service provider and to backups of such intermediate communications made by the service provider to ensure system integrity. It does not include post-transmission storage of communications. For example, email that has been received by a recipient's service provider but has not yet been accessed by the recipient is in "electronic storage." *See Steve Jackson Games, Inc. v. United States Secret Service*, 36 F.3d 457, 461 (5th Cir. 1994). At that stage, the communication is stored as a temporary and intermediate measure pending the recipient's retrieval of the communication from the service provider. Once the recipient retrieves the email, however, the communication reaches its final destination. If the recipient chooses to retain a copy of the accessed communication, the copy will not be in "temporary, intermediate storage" and is not stored incident to transmission. *See Fraser v. Nationwide Mut. Ins. Co.*, 352 F.3d 107, 114 (3d Cir. 2004) (stating that email in post-transmission storage was not in "temporary, intermediate storage"). By the same reasoning, if the sender of an email maintains a copy of the sent email, the copy will not be in "electronic storage." Messages posted to an electronic "bulletin board" or similar service are also not in "electronic storage" because the website on which they are posted is the final destination for the information. *See Snow v. DirecTV, Inc.*, 2005 WL 1226158, at *3 (M.D. Fla. May 9, 2005), *adopted by* 2005 WL 1266435 (M.D. Fla. May 27, 2005), *aff'd on other grounds*, 450 F.3d 1314 (11th Cir. 2006).

Furthermore, the "backup" component of the definition of "electronic storage" refers to copies made by an ISP to ensure system integrity. As one district court explained, the backup component "protects the communication in the event the system crashes before transmission is complete. The phrase 'for purposes of backup protection of such communication' in the statutory definition makes clear that messages that are in post-transmission storage, after transmission is complete, are not covered by part (B) of the definition of 'electronic storage.'" *Fraser v. Nationwide Mut. Ins. Co.*, 135 F. Supp. 2d 623, 636 (E.D. Pa. 2001), *aff'd in part on other grounds* 352 F.3d 107, 114 (3d Cir. 2004) (affirming the SCA portion of the district court's ruling on other grounds); *see also United States v. Weaver*, 2009 WL 2163478, at *4 (C.D. Ill. July 15, 2009) (interpreting "electronic storage" to exclude previously sent email stored by web-based email service provider); *In re Doubleclick Inc. Privacy Litigation*, 154 F. Supp. 2d 497, 511–13 (S.D.N.Y. 2001) (emphasizing that "electronic storage" should have a narrow interpretation based on statutory language and legislative intent and holding that cookies fall outside of the definition of "electronic storage" because of their "long-term residence on plaintiffs' hard drives"); H.R. Rep. No. 99–647, at 65 (1986) (noting congressional intent that opened email left on a provider's system be covered by provisions of the SCA relating to remote computing services, rather than provisions relating to communications in "electronic storage").

This narrow interpretation of "electronic storage" was rejected by the Ninth Circuit in *Theofel v. Farey-Jones*, 359 F.3d 1066 (9th Cir. 2004), in which the court held that email messages were in "electronic storage" regardless of whether they had been previously accessed, because it concluded that retrieved email fell within the backup portion of the definition of "electronic storage." Id. at 1075–77. Although the Ninth Circuit did not dispute that previously accessed email was not in temporary, intermediate storage within the meaning of § 2510(17)(A), it insisted that a previously accessed email message fell within the scope of the "backup" portion of the definition of "electronic storage," because such a message "functions as a 'backup' for the user." Id. at 1075. However, CCIPS has consistently argued that the Ninth Circuit's broad interpretation of the "backup" portion of the definition of "electronic storage" should be rejected. There is no way for a service provider to determine whether a previously opened email on its servers is a backup for a copy of the email stored by a user on his computer, as the service provider simply cannot know whether the underlying email remains stored on the user's computer. Essentially, the Ninth Circuit's reasoning in *Theofel* confuses "backup protection" with ordinary storage of a file.

Although prosecutors within the Ninth Circuit are bound by *Theofel*, law enforcement elsewhere may continue to apply the traditional narrow interpretation of "electronic storage," even when the data sought is within the Ninth Circuit. Recent lower court decisions addressing the scope of "electronic storage" have split between the traditional interpretation and the *Theofel* approach. *Compare United States v. Weaver*, 2009 WL 2163478, at *4 (C.D. Ill. July 15, 2009) (rejecting Theofel), *and Bansal v. Russ*, 513 F. Supp. 2d 264, 276 (E.D. Pa. 2007) (holding that access to opened email in account held by non-public service provider did not violate the SCA), *with Bailey v. Bailey*, 2008 WL 324156, at *6 (E.D. Mich. Feb. 6, 2008) (endorsing *Theofel*), *and Cardinal Health 414, Inc. v. Adams*, 482 F. Supp. 2d 967, 976 n.2 (M.D. Tenn. 2008) (same). Prosecutors confronted with *Theofel*-related issues should consult CCIPS at (202) 514–1026 for further assistance."[28]

"4. Illustration of the SCA's Classifications in the Email Context

An example illustrates how the SCA's categories work in practice outside the Ninth Circuit, where *Theofel* does not apply. Imagine that Joe sends an email from his account at work ("joe@goodcompany.com") to the personal account of his friend Jane ("jane@localisp.com"). The email will stream across the Internet until it reaches the servers of Jane's Internet service provider, here the fictional LocalISP. When the message first arrives at LocalISP, LocalISP is a provider of ECS with respect to that message. Before Jane accesses LocalISP and retrieves the message, Joe's email is in "electronic storage." Once Jane retrieves Joe's email, she can either delete the message from LocalISP's server or else leave the message stored there. If Jane chooses to store the email with LocalISP, LocalISP is now a provider of RCS (and not ECS) with respect to the email sent by Joe. The role of LocalISP has changed from a transmitter of Joe's email to a storage facility for a file stored remotely for Jane by a provider of RCS.

Next imagine that Jane responds to Joe's email. Jane's return email to Joe will stream across the Internet to the servers of Joe's employer, Good Company. Before Joe retrieves the email from Good Company's servers, Good Company is a provider of ECS with respect to Jane's email (just like LocalISP was with respect to Joe's original email before Jane accessed it). When Joe accesses Jane's email message and the communication reaches its destination (Joe), Good Company ceases to be a provider of ECS with respect to that email (just as LocalISP ceased to be a provider of ECS with respect to Joe's original email when Jane accessed it). Unlike LocalISP, however, Good Company does not become a provider of RCS if Joe decides to store the opened email on Good Company's server. Rather, for purposes of this specific message, Good Company is a provider of neither ECS nor RCS. Good Company does not provide RCS because it does not provide services to the public. See 18 U.S.C. § 2711(2) ("[T]he term 'remote computing service' means the provision to the public of computer storage or processing services by means of an electronic communications system." (emphasis added)); Andersen Consulting, 991 F. Supp. at 1043. Because Good Company provides neither ECS nor RCS with respect to the opened email in Joe's account, the SCA no longer regulates access to this email, and such access is governed solely by the Fourth Amendment. Functionally speaking, the opened email in Joe's account drops out of the SCA.

Finally, consider the status of the other copies of the emails in this scenario: Jane has downloaded a copy of Joe's email from LocalISP's server to her personal computer at home, and Joe has downloaded a copy of Jane's email from Good Company's server to his office desktop computer at work. The SCA governs neither. Although these computers contain copies of emails, these copies are not stored on the server of a third-party provider of RCS or ECS, and therefore the SCA does not apply. Access to the copies of the communications stored in Jane's personal computer at home and Joe's office computer at work is governed solely by the Fourth Amendment. As this example indicates, a single provider can simultaneously provide ECS with regard to some communications and RCS with regard to others, or ECS with regard to some communications and neither ECS nor RCS with regard to others."[29]

Section 4, discussed earlier, is a great illustration of how all the pieces of the law fit together in terms of classifying public providers and the type of digital evidence they possess.

"E. Voluntary Disclosure

Providers of services not available "to the public" may freely disclose both contents and other records relating to stored communications. The SCA imposes restrictions on voluntary disclosures by providers of services to the public, but it also includes exceptions to those restrictions.

The voluntary disclosure provisions of the SCA appear in 18 U.S.C. § 2702. These provisions govern when a provider of RCS or ECS can disclose contents and other information voluntarily, both to the government and non-government entities. If the provider may disclose the information to the government and is willing to do so voluntarily, law enforcement does not need to obtain a legal order to compel the disclosure. If the provider either may not or will not disclose the information, agents must rely on compelled disclosure provisions and obtain the appropriate legal orders.

When considering whether a provider of RCS or ECS can disclose contents or records, the first question is whether the relevant service offered by the provider is available "to the public." *See* Section B, above. If the provider does not provide the applicable service "to the public," then the SCA does not place any restrictions on disclosure. *See* 18 U.S.C. § 2702(a). For example, in *Andersen Consulting LLP v. UOP*, 991 F. Supp. 1041 (N.D. Ill. 1998), the petroleum company UOP hired the consulting firm Andersen Consulting and gave Andersen employees accounts on UOP's computer network. After the relationship between UOP and Andersen soured, UOP disclosed to the *Wall Street Journal* emails that Andersen employees had left on the UOP network. Andersen sued, claiming that the disclosure of its contents by the provider UOP had violated the SCA. The district court rejected the suit on the ground that UOP did not provide an electronic communication service to the public:

> [G]iving Andersen access to [UOP's] e-mail system is not equivalent to providing e-mail to the public. Andersen was hired by UOP to do a project and as such, was given access to UOP's e-mail system similar to UOP employees. Andersen was not any member of the community at large, but a hired contractor.

Id. at 1043. Because UOP did not provide services to the public, the SCA did not prohibit disclosure of contents belonging to UOP's "subscribers."

If the services offered by the provider *are* available to the public, then the SCA forbids both the disclosure of contents to any third party and the disclosure of other records *to any governmental entity* unless a statutory exception applies. Even a public provider may disclose customers' *non-content* records freely to any person other than a government entity. *See* 18 U.S.C. §§ 2702(a)(3), (c)(6). Section 2702(b) contains exceptions for disclosure of contents, and § 2702(c) contains exceptions for disclosure of other customer records.

The SCA allows the voluntary disclosure of contents when:

1) the disclosure is made to the intended recipient of the communication, with the consent of the sender or intended recipient, to a forwarding address, or pursuant to specified legal process, § 2702(b)(1)-(4);

2) in the case of a remote computing service, the disclosure is made with the consent of a subscriber, § 2702(b)(3);

3) the disclosure "may be necessarily incident to the rendition of the service or to the protection of the rights or property of the provider of that service," § 2702(b)(5);

4) the disclosure is submitted "to the National Center for Missing and Exploited Children, in connection with a report submitted thereto under section 2258A," § 2702(b)(6);

5) the disclosure is made to a law enforcement agency "if the contents … were inadvertently obtained by the service provider … [and] appear to pertain to the commission of a crime," § 2702(b)(7); or

6) the disclosure is made to a governmental entity, "if the provider, in good faith, believes that an emergency involving danger of death or serious physical injury to any person requires disclosure without delay of communications relating to the emergency." § 2702(b)(8)."[30]

"The SCA includes separate provisions for suits against the United States and suits against any other person or entity. Section 2707 permits a "person aggrieved" by SCA violations that result from knowing or intentional conduct to bring a civil action against the "person or entity, other than the United States, which engaged in that violation." 18 U.S.C. § 2707(a). Relief can include money damages no less than $

1,000 per person, equitable or declaratory relief, and a reasonable attorney's fee plus other reasonable litigation costs. 18 U.S.C. § 2707(b), (c). Willful or intentional violations can also result in punitive damages, see § 2707(c)."[31]

It is important to get legal counsel to help you sort through the labyrinth that is the Stored Communications Act.

The Wiretap Statute contains significant penalties for violations, so it is important to understand what we can and can't do.

"D. The Wiretap Statute ("Title III"), 18 U.S.C. §§ 2510–2522

1. Introduction: The General Prohibition

Since its enactment in 1968 and amendment in 1986, Title III has provided the statutory framework that governs real-time electronic surveillance of the contents of communications. When agents want to wiretap a suspect's phone, monitor a hacker breaking into a computer system, or accept the fruits of wiretapping by a private citizen who has discovered evidence of a crime, the agents first must consider the implications of Title III.

The structure of Title III is surprisingly simple. The statute's drafters assumed that every private communication could be modeled as a two-way exchange between two participating parties, such as a telephone call between A and B. At a fundamental level, the statute prohibits using an electronic, mechanical, or other device to intercept private wire, oral, or electronic communications between the parties unless one of several statutory exceptions applies. See 18 U.S.C. §§ 2510(4), 2511(1). Importantly, this prohibition is quite broad. Unlike some privacy laws that regulate only certain cases or specific places, Title III expansively prohibits eavesdropping (subject to certain exceptions and interstate requirements) essentially everywhere by anyone in the United States. Whether investigators want to conduct surveillance at a home, at a workplace, in government offices, in prison, or on the Internet, they must almost invariably make sure that the monitoring complies with Title III's prohibitions.

2. Key Phrases

Title III broadly prohibits the "interception" of "oral communications," "wire communications," and "electronic communications." These phrases are defined by the statute. See 18 U.S.C. §§ 2510(1), (2), (4), (12). In computer crime cases, agents and prosecutors planning electronic surveillance must understand the definition of "wire communication," "electronic communication," and "intercept." Surveillance of oral communications rarely arises in computer crime cases and will not be addressed directly here. Agents and prosecutors requiring assistance in cases involving oral communications should contact OEO at (202) 514–6809.

"Wire communication"

In general, telephone conversations are wire communications.

Title III defines "wire communication" as

any aural transfer made in whole or in part though the use of facilities for the transmission of communications by the aid of wire, cable, or other like connection between the point of origin and the point of reception (including the use of such connection in a switching station) furnished or operated by any person engaged in providing or operating such facilities for the transmission of interstate or foreign communications or communications affecting interstate or foreign commerce.

18 U.S.C. § 2510(1).

Within this complicated definition, the most important requirement is that the content of the communication must include the human voice. See § 2510(18) (defining "aural transfer" as "a transfer containing the human voice at any point between and including the point of origin and the point of reception"). If a communication does not contain a human voice, either alone or in a group conversation, then it is not a wire communication. See S. Rep. No. 99–541, at 12 (1986), reprinted in 1986 U.S.C.C.A.N. 3555; United States v. Torres, 751 F.2d 875, 885–86 (7th Cir. 1984) (concluding that "silent television surveillance" cannot lead to an interception of wire communications under Title III because no aural acquisition occurs).

The additional requirement that wire communications must be sent "in whole or in part ... by the aid of wire, cable, or other like connection" presents a fairly low hurdle. So long as the signal travels through wire at some point along its route between the point of origin and the point of reception, the requirement is satisfied. For example, all voice telephone transmissions, including those from satellite signals and cellular phones, qualify as wire communications. See H.R. Rep. No. 99–647, at 35 (1986). Because such transmissions are carried by wire within switching stations, they are expressly included in the definition of wire communication. See In re Application of United States, 349 F.3d 1132, 1138 n.12 (9th Cir. 2003) (cell phone communications are considered wire communications under Title III). Importantly, the presence of wires inside equipment at the sending or receiving end of a communication (such as an individual cellular phone) does not satisfy the requirement that a communication be sent "in part" by wire. The wire must transmit the communication "to a significant extent" along the path of transmission, outside of the equipment that sends or receives the communication. H.R. Rep. No. 99–647, at 35 (1986).

"Electronic communication"

Most Internet communications (including email) are electronic communications.

Title III originally covered only wire and oral communications, but Congress amended it in 1986 to include "electronic communications," defined as

any transfer of signs, signals, writing, images, sounds, data, or intelligence of any nature transmitted in whole or in part by a wire, radio, electromagnetic, photoelectronic or photooptical system that affects interstate or foreign commerce, but does not include—

(A) any wire or oral communication;
(B) any communication made through a tone-only paging device;
(C) any communication from a tracking device ...; or
(D) electronic funds transfer information stored by a financial institution in a communications system used for the electronic storage and transfer of funds.

18 U.S.C. § 2510(12).

As the definition suggests, "electronic communication" is a broad, catch-all category. See United States v. Herring, 993 F.2d 784, 787 (11th Cir. 1993). "As a rule, a communication is an electronic communication if it is neither carried by sound waves nor can fairly be characterized as one containing the human voice (carried in part by wire)." H.R. Rep. No. 99–647, at 35 (1986). Most electric or electronic signals that do not fit the definition of wire communications qualify as electronic communications. For example, almost all Internet communications qualify as electronic communications. *See, e.g., Konop v. Hawaiian Airlines, Inc.*, 302 F.3d 868, 876 (9th Cir. 2002) ("document" transmitted from web server); *In re Application of United States*, 416 F. Supp. 2d 13, 16 (D.D.C. 2006) ("there can be no doubt that [§ 2510(12)] is broad enough to encompass email communications and other similar signals transmitted over the Internet").

However, at least one district court has held that transmissions that occur within a single computer—such as the transmission of keystrokes from the keyboard to the central processing unit—are not "electronic communications" within the meaning of Title III. *See United States v. Ropp*, 347 F. Supp. 2d 831 (C.D. Cal. 2004). In *Ropp*, the defendant placed a piece of hardware between the victim's computer and her keyboard that recorded the signals transmitted between the two. *Id.* at 831. The court found that the acquired communications were not "electronic communications" because "the communications in question involved preparation of emails and other communications, but were not themselves emails or any other communication at the time of the interception." *Id.* at 835 n.1. Because the court found that the typing was a communication within the victim's own computer, it reasoned that "[a]t the time of interception, [the communications] no more affected interstate commerce than a letter, placed in a stamped envelope, that has not yet been mailed." *Id.* The court further stated that the acquired keystrokes could not be an "electronic communication" under Title III because these transmissions were not made by a "system that affects interstate or foreign commerce." *Id.* at 837. In the court's view, a computer is not a "system that affects interstate or foreign commerce" simply by virtue of the fact that it is connected to the Internet or to another external network at the time of the electronic transmission; rather, the relevant inquiry is whether the computer's network connection was involved in the transmission. *See id.* at 837–38. At least one court has criticized *Ropp* on the ground that it "seems to read the statute as requiring the communication to be traveling in interstate commerce, rather than merely 'affecting' interstate commerce." *Potter v. Havlicek*, 2007 WL 539534, at *8 (S.D. Ohio Feb. 14, 2007). The court explained that "keystrokes that send a message off into interstate commerce 'affect' interstate commerce." *Id.*

Notwithstanding the *Ropp* decision, investigators should use caution whenever they acquire the contents of communications on computers or internal networks in real time. For additional discussion of the statute and relevant legislative history as it relates to the meaning of "electronic communication," see U.S. Department of Justice, *Prosecuting Computer Crimes* (Office of Legal Education 2007), section II.A.4. Agents and prosecutors may call CCIPS at (202) 514–1026, OEO at (202) 514–6809, or the CHIP within their district (*see* Introduction, p. xii) for additional guidance in specific cases.

"Intercept"

The structure and language of the SCA and Title III require that the term "intercept" be applied only to communications acquired contemporaneously with their transmission.

Title III defines "intercept" as "the aural or other acquisition of the contents of any wire, electronic, or oral communication through the use of any electronic, mechanical, or other device." 18 U.S.C. § 2510(4). The statutory definition of "intercept" does not explicitly require that the "acquisition" of the communication be contemporaneous with the transmission of the communication. However, a contemporaneity requirement is necessary to maintain the proper relationship between Title III and the SCA's restrictions on access to stored communications. Otherwise, for example, a Title III order could be required to obtain unretrieved email from a service provider.

Most courts have held that both wire and electronic communications are "intercepted" within the meaning of Title III only when such communications are acquired contemporaneously with their transmission. An individual who obtains access to a stored copy of the communication does not "intercept" the communication. *See, e.g., Steve Jackson Games, Inc. v. United States Secret Service*, 36 F.3d 457, 460–63 (5th Cir. 1994) (access to stored email communications); *Fraser v. Nationwide Mut. Ins. Co.*, 352 F.3d 107, 113–14 (3d Cir. 2003) (same); *Konop v. Hawaiian Airlines, Inc.*, 302 F.3d 868, 876–79 (9th Cir. 2002) (website); *United States v. Steiger*, 318 F.3d 1039, 1047–50 (11th Cir. 2003) (files stored on hard drive); *United States v. Mercado-Nava*, 486 F. Supp. 2d 1271, 1279 (D. Kan. 2007) (numbers stored in cell phone); *United States v. Jones*, 451 F. Supp. 2d 71, 75 (D.D.C. 2006) (text messages); *United States v. Reyes*, 922 F. Supp. 818, 836–37 (S.D.N.Y. 1996) (pager communications); *Bohach v. City of Reno*, 932 F. Supp. 1232, 1235–36 (D. Nev. 1996) (same). However, the First Circuit has suggested that the contemporaneity requirement, which was developed during the era of telephone wiretaps, "may not be apt to address issues involving the application of the Wiretap Act to electronic communications." *United States v. Councilman*, 418 F.3d 67, 79–80 (1st Cir. 2005) (en banc) (citing *In re Pharmatrak, Inc. Privacy Litigation*, 329 F.3d 9, 21 (1st Cir. 2003)); *see also Potter v. Havlicek*, 2007 WL 539534, at *6–7 (S.D. Ohio Feb. 14, 2007) (finding "substantial likelihood" that the Sixth Circuit will find the contemporaneity requirement does not apply to electronic communications).

Notably, there is some disagreement between circuits about whether a computer communication is "intercepted" within the meaning of Title III if it is acquired while in "electronic storage," as defined in 18 U.S.C. § 2510(17). The Ninth Circuit has held that in order for a communication to be "intercepted" within the meaning of Title III, "it must be acquired during transmission, not while it is in electronic storage." *See Konop*, 302 F.3d at 878. The unstated implication of this holding is that communications in electronic storage are necessarily not in transmission. The First Circuit has held, however, that email messages are intercepted within the meaning of Title III when they are acquired while in "transient electronic storage that is intrinsic to the communication process." *United States v. Councilman*, 418 F.3d 67, 85 (1st Cir. 2005) (en banc). In so holding, the court suggested that an electronic communication can be in "electronic storage" and in transmission at the same time. *See id.* at 79. Exactly how close in time an acquisition must be to a transmission remains an open question. It is clear that "contemporaneous" does not mean "simultaneous." However, the Eleventh Circuit suggested that "contemporaneous" must equate with a communication "in flight." *United States v. Steiger*, 318 F.3d 1039, 1050 (11th Cir. 2003). By contrast, the First Circuit held the contemporaneity requirement could be read simply to exclude acquisitions "made a substantial amount of time after material was put into electronic storage." *In re Pharmatrak, Inc. Privacy Litigation*, 329 F.3d 9, 21 (1st Cir. 2003)"[32]

Significant portions of the Wire Tap Statute for our current purposes include:

- H.R. Rep. No. 99–647, at 35 (1986) amended Title III to include "Electronic communication" devoid of any oral or aural communication. Most email and other internet communication are electronic communications.
- Most courts have held that an individual who obtains access to a stored copy of the communication does not "intercept" the communication.

"3. Exceptions to Title III's Prohibition

Title III broadly prohibits the intentional interception, use, or disclosure of wire and electronic communications unless a statutory exception applies. See 18 U.S.C. § 2511(1).

In general, this prohibition bars third parties (including the government) from wiretapping telephones and installing electronic "sniffers" that read Internet traffic.

The breadth of Title III's prohibition means that the legality of most surveillance techniques under Title III depends upon the applicability of a statutory exception. Title III contains dozens of exceptions that may or may not apply in hundreds of different situations. In cases involving computer crimes or computer evidence, however, seven exceptions are especially pertinent:

a. interception pursuant to a § 2518 court order;
b. the 'consent' exceptions, § 2511(2)(c)-(d);
c. the 'provider' exception, § 2511(2)(a)(i);
d. the 'computer trespasser' exception, § 2511(2)(i);
e. the 'extension telephone' exception, § 2510(5)(a);
f. the 'inadvertently obtained criminal evidence' exception, § 2511(3)(b)(iv); and
g. the 'accessible to the public' exception, § 2511(2)(g)(i)."

For our purposes we will focus on the consent exception and the "accessible to the public" exceptions.

"b. Consent of a Party to the Communication, 18 U.S.C. § 2511(2)(c)-(d)

The second consent exception applies more generally:

It shall not be unlawful under this chapter for a person not acting under color of law to intercept a wire, oral, or electronic communication where such person is a party to the communication or where one of the parties to the communication has given prior consent to such interception unless such communication is intercepted for the purpose of committing any criminal or tortious act in violation of the Constitution or laws of the United States or of any State.

18 U.S.C. § 2511(2)(d). A criminal or tortious purpose must be a purpose other than merely to intercept the communication to which the individual is a party. *See Roberts v. Americable Int'l, Inc.*, 883 F. Supp. 499, 503 (E.D. Cal. 1995).

In general, both of these provisions authorize the interception of communications when one of the parties to the communication consents to the interception. For example, if an undercover government agent or informant records a telephone conversation between herself and a suspect, her consent to the recording authorizes the interception. *See, e.g., Obron Atlantic Corp. v. Barr*, 990 F.2d 861, 863–64 (6th Cir. 1993) (relying on § 2511(2)(c)). Similarly, if a private person records her own telephone conversations with others, her consent authorizes the interception unless the commission of a criminal or tortious act was at least a determinative factor in her motivation for intercepting the communication. *See United States v. Cassiere*, 4 F.3d 1006, 1021 (1st Cir. 1993) (interpreting § 2511(2)(d)).

Consent under subsections 2511(2)(c) and (d) may be express or implied. *See United States v. Amen*, 831 F.2d 373, 378 (2d Cir. 1987). The key to establishing implied consent in most cases is showing that the consenting party received actual notice of the monitoring and used the monitored system anyway. *See United States v. Workman*, 80 F.3d 688, 693 (2d Cir. 1996); *Griggs-Ryan v. Smith*, 904 F.2d 112, 116–17 (1st Cir. 1990) ("[I]mplied consent is consent in fact which is inferred from surrounding circumstances indicating that the party knowingly agreed to the surveillance.") (internal quotations omitted); *Berry v. Funk*, 146 F.3d 1003, 1011 (D.C. Cir. 1998) ("Without actual notice, consent can only be implied when the surrounding circumstances convincingly show that the party knew about and consented to the interception.") (internal quotation marks omitted). However, consent must be "actual" rather than "constructive." *See In re Pharmatrak, Inc. Privacy Litigation*, 329 F.3d 9, 19–20 (1st Cir. 2003) (citing cases). Proof of notice to the party generally supports the conclusion that the party knew of the monitoring. *See Workman*, 80 F.3d. at 693; *but see Deal v. Spears*, 980 F.2d 1153, 1157 (8th Cir. 1992) (finding lack of consent despite notice of possibility of monitoring). Absent proof of notice, the government must "convincingly" show that the party knew about the interception based on surrounding circumstances in order to support a finding of implied consent. *United States v. Lanoue*, 71 F.3d 966, 981 (1st Cir. 1995), *abrogated on other grounds by United States v. Watts*, 519 U.S. 148 (1997). Mere knowledge of the capability of monitoring does not imply consent. *Watkins v. L. M. Berry & Co.*, 704 F.2d 577, 581 (11th Cir. 1983)."[33]

Two very important points related to where the parties are located prior to and during the recording of the call. One is that consent can be given by you if you are a party to the communication. However, beware, whether you can record a telephone call without obtaining the consent of the other party(ies) to the call could be a state crime, depending on in which state the party initiating the communication resides. Where I live, one of the parties can give consent for the recording of the call. Fifteen other states do not permit one-party consent. The second important point is implied consent. We will look at this in more detail in the following paragraphs, but, note that, overall, a party can give their implied consent ahead of the communication. That's why you see those "Please Note That This Network is Monitored" banners on some networks. If you use the network, you are presumed to have given your implied consent.

"i. Bannering and Consent

Monitoring use of a computer network does not violate Title III after users view an appropriate network banner informing them that use of the network constitutes consent to monitoring.

In computer cases, a network banner alerting the user that communications on the network are monitored and intercepted may be used to demonstrate that a user consented to intercepting communications on that network. A banner is a posted notice informing users as they log on to a network that their use may be monitored, and that subsequent use of the system constitutes consent to the monitoring. Often, a user must click to consent to the terms of the banner before gaining further access to the system; such a user has explicitly consented to the monitoring of her communications. Even if no clicking is required, a user who sees the banner before logging on to the network has received notice of the monitoring. By using the network in light of the notice, the user impliedly consents to monitoring pursuant to 18 U.S.C. § 2511(2)(c)-(d). Numerous courts have held that explicit notices that prison telephones would be monitored generated consent to monitor inmates' calls. *See United States v. Conley*, 531 F.3d 56, 58–59 (1st Cir. 2008); *United States v. Verdin-Garcia*, 516 F.3d 884, 894–95 (10th Cir. 2008); *United States v. Workman*, 80 F.3d 688, 693–94 (2d Cir. 1996); *United States v. Amen*, 831 F.2d 373, 379 (2d Cir. 1987). In the computer context, one court rejected an employee's challenge to his employer's remote monitoring of his Internet activity based on a banner authorizing the employer to "monitor communications transmitted" by the employee. *United States v. Greiner*, 2007 WL 2261642, at *1 (9th Cir. 2007).

The scope of consent generated by a banner generally depends on the banner's language: network banners are not "one size fits all." A narrowly worded banner may authorize only some kinds of monitoring; a broadly worded banner may permit monitoring in many circumstances for many reasons. For example, a sensitive Department of Defense computer network might require a broad banner, while a state university network used by professors and students could use a narrow one. Appendix A contains several sample banners that reflect a range of approaches to network monitoring.

In addition to banners, there are also other ways to show that a computer user has impliedly consented to monitoring of network activity. For example, terms of service agreements and computer use policies may contain language showing that network users have consented to monitoring. *See, e.g., United States v. Angevine*, 281 F.3d 1130, 1132–34 (10th Cir. 2002) (university's computer use policy stated, *inter alia*, that the university would periodically monitor network traffic); United States v. Simons, 206 F.3d 392, 398 (4th Cir. 2000) (government employer's Internet usage policy stated that employer would periodically monitor users' Internet access as deemed appropriate); *Borninski v. Williamson*, 2005 WL 1206872, at *13 (N.D. Tex. May 17, 2005) (employee signed Application for Internet Access, which stated that use of system implied consent to monitoring)."[34]

Banner examples include:

"This computer network belongs to the Grommie Corporation and may be used only by Grommie Corporation employees and only for work-related purposes. The Grommie Corporation reserves the right to monitor use of this network to ensure network security and to respond to specific allegations of employee misuse. Use of this network shall constitute consent to monitoring for such purposes. In addition, the Grommie Corporation reserves the right to consent to a valid law enforcement request to search the network for evidence of a crime stored within the network.

Warning: Patrons of the Cyber-Fun Internet Café may not use its computers to access, view, or obtain obscene materials. To ensure compliance with this policy, the Cyber-Fun Internet Café reserves the right to record the names and addresses of World Wide Web sites that patrons visit using CyberFun Internet Café computers.

It is the policy of the law firm of Rowley & Yzaguirre to monitor the Internet access of its employees to ensure compliance with law firm policies. Accordingly, your use of the Internet may be monitored. The firm reserves the right to disclose the fruits of any monitoring to law enforcement if it deems such disclosure to be appropriate."[35]

So, as I said above, a banner alerts users that their use of the bannered network is subject to monitoring by the owner of the network. If they use the network anyway, they have given their implied consent to this monitoring of their activities.

Okay, here's the "public access" exception. It's pretty straightforward.

"g. The 'Accessible to the Public' Exception, 18 U.S.C. § 2511(2)(g)(i)

Section 2511(2)(g)(i) permits "any person" to intercept an electronic communication made through a system "that is configured so that … [the] communication is readily accessible to the general public." Congress intended this language to permit the interception of an electronic communication that has been posted to a public bulletin board, a public chat room, or a Usenet newsgroup. *See* S. Rep. No. 99–541, at 36 (1986), *reprinted in* 1986 U.S.C.C.A.N. 3555, 3590 (discussing bulletin boards). This exception may apply even if users are required to register and agree to terms of use in order to access the communication. See *Snow v. DirecTV, Inc.*, 450 F.3d 1314, 1321–22 (11th Cir. 2006) (electronic bulletin board that required visitors to register, obtain a password, and certify that they were not associated with DirecTV was accessible to the public)."[36]

For illustration purposes, a non-digital of this would be if you monitored and recorded a speech given at a public campaign rally, you would not be violating the Fourth Amendment's prohibition against eavesdropping or Title III. Because, the communication was always intended to be made public.

Okay, if you violate Title III, what's the worst that could happen? Well, it's pretty bad. Let's see what the Department of Justice thinks:

"E. Remedies For Violations of Title III and the Pen/Trap Statute

Agents and prosecutors must comply with Title III and the Pen/Trap statute when planning electronic surveillance. Violations can result in criminal penalties, civil liability, and (in the case of certain Title III violations) suppression of the evidence obtained. *See* 18 U.S.C. § 2511(4) (criminal penalties for Title III violations); 18 U.S.C. § 2520 (civil action for Title III violations); 18 U.S.C. § 3121(d) (criminal penalties for Pen/Trap statute violations); 18 U.S.C. § 2707(a), (g) (civil action for certain Pen/Trap statute violations); 18 U.S.C. § 2518(10)(a) (suppression for certain Title III violations). As a practical matter, however, courts may conclude that the electronic surveillance statutes were violated even after agents and prosecutors have acted in good faith and with full regard for the law. For example, a private citizen may wiretap his neighbor and later turn over the evidence to the police, or agents may intercept communications using a court order that the agents later learn is defective. Similarly, a court may construe an ambiguous portion of Title III differently than did the investigators, leading the court to find that a violation of Title III occurred. Accordingly, prosecutors and agents must understand not only what conduct the surveillance statutes prohibit, but also what the ramifications might be if a court finds that the statutes have been violated."[37]

Third, the US Federal rules of evidence about hearsay, authentication, reliability, and best evidence must be adhered to when collecting physical or digital evidence (also see Chapter 7).

Hearsay is simply a statement repeated by someone other than the person who made the statement. So, if I say that I heard from my friend John that Bob was seen stealing money from Jack, the statement I made would be hearsay. The reason for this is that I did not personally witness the conduct I am speaking about. Hearsay is generally not admissible under the federal rules of evidence but, there are exceptions. For your purposes, the most significant exception is the business records exception. Documents or computer records, created in the normal course of business, once authenticated, can be admitted as evidence.

Again, we will talk more about this in Chapter 7, but before a document or computer record can be admitted as evidence it must be authenticated. Authentication is achieved by offering sufficient evidence to establish that the document, computer record, or other evidence is what it purports to be. A chain of custody must be offered to demonstrate the what, who, where, and when the evidence was collected.

Documents, computer records, and other evidence must be reliable. Reliable evidence establishes the proof for which it is offered. A contemporaneous original contract, properly authenticated, would be reliable evidence of the agreement that existed between the signatories to the contract on its effective date. A contemporaneous original contract with obvious alterations not agreed to, in writing, by the signatories of the original contract would likely not be considered reliable evidence of the agreement between the signatories.

The Best Evidence Rule is simply that, unless unavailable, the original document, computer record, or other evidence would be the best evidence of what it is being offered to prove. This can be tricky with computer records because whenever they are accessed using normal computer operations, they and the metadata associated with them are altered. This is why it is necessary to restrict access to and, in many cases, unplug electronic devices until a forensic image can be made of the electronic records stored in the device.

SECTION IV: LAWS AND RULES RELATED TO ACCESSING WITNESSES

First, you must not break any criminal laws when interviewing witnesses. You cannot compel anyone to be interviewed. Do not threaten any physical violence or other harm to a potential witness who refuses to be interviewed. If you are interviewing a witness who suddenly stops the interview and wants to exit, let them go. You have no right to prevent them from leaving. Do not leave a concealed recording device anywhere you expect them to be.

Second, you must adhere to the same code of ethics that the lawyers adhere to. Therefore, you must not lie to the witness. If the witness is represented by a lawyer, you must only communicate with the witness after making arrangements through the witness's lawyer. If you are interviewing a witness not represented by a lawyer, you must make sure that they do not believe that the company's lawyer is representing them and that they understand that the company's lawyer represents the company and will act in the company's best interests (see Upjohn Warning in Chapter 8).

You must make a record of the interview. This could be a tape recording with or without videography. If you decide to use this technique, you must make the witness aware that interview will be recorded. You should make a record of the witness's knowledge and agreement. This can be done with a written form or in the form of the preliminary questions and answers, which are being recorded. I do not favor recording interviews. Too much of the context of the answers to questions can be lost especially in sound-only recordings. I prefer to take notes during the interview and then write a report of the interview to which I attach my notes (see Chapter 8).

EXERCISES

1. Which professional is most important to consult when beginning a fraud investigation or forensic accounting assignment?
2. What should you do if a federal agent contacts you and says that he or she wants to ask you a few questions?
3. How could you get around the Privacy Act restrictions with respect to an employee?
4. What is personal data under the GDPR?
5. Where in the world is GDPR personal data protected?
6. Under what circumstances may personal data not be protected under the GDPR?
7. What are the core GDPR privacy principles?
8. What will happen if you or your agent makes a pretext call to a bank to get customer information?
9. What two choices are available to you in investigating individuals?
10. Under what circumstances do persons have a reasonable expectation to privacy with respect to information stored in a computer?
11. Under what circumstances do persons not have a reasonable expectation to privacy with respect to information stored in a computer?
12. Under what circumstances can persons waive their reasonable expectation to privacy with respect to information stored in a computer?
13. What are ways that you can preserve your company's right to access information in employee computers, files, paper records, and other spaces on company property?
14. What are ways that you can preserve your company's right to access information in employee computers, files, and paper records when they are working remotely?
15. When do persons lose a reasonable expectation to privacy when they discard electronic storage devices or paper records?
16. How can you guarantee that you have a legal right to access discarded electronic storage devices or paper records from garbage or recycling bins left for waste pickup?
17. If a computer technician is servicing an employee's personal computer and finds contraband, can they turn the evidence over to law enforcement? What is this doctrine called?

18. If an employee steals your electronic data and you report it to law enforcement who then get a search warrant for the employee's computer, can the law enforcement agency also seize and use other evidence of unrelated crimes found on the computer?

19. How could you or law enforcement gain access to an employee's personal computer or other spaces where they do have a reasonable expectation to privacy?

20. If you or law enforcement do gain access to a person's personal computer or other spaces where they do have a reasonable expectation to privacy, what must you be certain to specify in the written consent form?

21. Which third parties can legally grant access to a person's personal computer or other spaces where they do have a reasonable expectation to privacy?

22. List the practical steps your company can take to limit the ability of employees to prevent access to information they create and control.

23. Should your company have an internal private network? Why?

24. What onboarding steps can you take to make it easier to access information in employees' personal computer or other spaces following employment?

25. Can you legally record a telephone conversation?

26. Under what circumstances can you legally record a telephone call?

27. What things must you never do when interviewing a witness?

CHAPTER SUMMARY/KEY TAKEAWAYS

- A competent lawyer is essential to a successful investigation result.
- The laws and regulations related to accessing third-party data, documents, electronic evidence, and witnesses are really complicated.
- Please consult with a competent lawyer.

In Chapter 7 you will learn how to properly gather and preserve information and evidence.

NOTES

1. https://www.justice.gov/opcl/overview-privacy-act-1974–2020-edition/introduction#LegHistory
2. https://gdpr-info.eu/
3. https://www.aba.com/banking-topics/consumer-banking/privacy/privacy-information-sharing
4. https://www.aba.com/banking-topics/consumer-banking/privacy/privacy-information-sharing
5. Searching and Seizing Computers and Obtaining Electronic Evidence in Criminal Investigations, Computer Crime and Intellectual Property Section Criminal Division Published by Office of Legal Education Executive Office for United States Attorneys January 2015 Page 1.
6. Searching and Seizing Computers and Obtaining Electronic Evidence in Criminal Investigations, Computer Crime and Intellectual Property Section Criminal Division Published by Office of Legal Education Executive Office for United States Attorneys January 2015 Page 2.
7. Searching and Seizing Computers and Obtaining Electronic Evidence in Criminal Investigations, Computer Crime and Intellectual Property Section Criminal Division Published by Office of Legal Education Executive Office for United States Attorneys January 2015 Page 3.
8. Searching and Seizing Computers and Obtaining Electronic Evidence in Criminal Investigations, Computer Crime and Intellectual Property Section Criminal Division Published by Office of Legal Education Executive Office for United States Attorneys January 2015 Page 4.
9. Searching and Seizing Computers and Obtaining Electronic Evidence in Criminal Investigations, Computer Crime and Intellectual Property Section Criminal Division Published by Office of Legal Education Executive Office for United States Attorneys January 2015 Pages 5–6.
10. Searching and Seizing Computers and Obtaining Electronic Evidence in Criminal Investigations, Computer Crime and Intellectual Property Section Criminal Division Published by Office of Legal Education Executive Office for United States Attorneys January 2015 Pages 5–6.

11. Searching and Seizing Computers and Obtaining Electronic Evidence in Criminal Investigations, Computer Crime and Intellectual Property Section Criminal Division Published by Office of Legal Education Executive Office for United States Attorneys January 2015 Pages 7–10.

12. Searching and Seizing Computers and Obtaining Electronic Evidence in Criminal Investigations, Computer Crime and Intellectual Property Section Criminal Division Published by Office of Legal Education Executive Office for United States Attorneys January 2015 Pages 11–14.

13. Searching and Seizing Computers and Obtaining Electronic Evidence in Criminal Investigations, Computer Crime and Intellectual Property Section Criminal Division Published by Office of Legal Education Executive Office for United States Attorneys January 2015 Pages 15–16.

14. Searching and Seizing Computers and Obtaining Electronic Evidence in Criminal Investigations, Computer Crime and Intellectual Property Section Criminal Division Published by Office of Legal Education Executive Office for United States Attorneys January 2015 Pages 15–19.

15. Searching and Seizing Computers and Obtaining Electronic Evidence in Criminal Investigations, Computer Crime and Intellectual Property Section Criminal Division Published by Office of Legal Education Executive Office for United States Attorneys January 2015 Pages 263–264.

16. Searching and Seizing Computers and Obtaining Electronic Evidence in Criminal Investigations, Computer Crime and Intellectual Property Section Criminal Division Published by Office of Legal Education Executive Office for United States Attorneys January 2015 Pages 19–22.

17. Searching and Seizing Computers and Obtaining Electronic Evidence in Criminal Investigations, Computer Crime and Intellectual Property Section Criminal Division Published by Office of Legal Education Executive Office for United States Attorneys January 2015 Pages 22–23.

18. Searching and Seizing Computers and Obtaining Electronic Evidence in Criminal Investigations, Computer Crime and Intellectual Property Section Criminal Division Published by Office of Legal Education Executive Office for United States Attorneys January 2015 Pages 23–24.

19. Searching and Seizing Computers and Obtaining Electronic Evidence in Criminal Investigations, Computer Crime and Intellectual Property Section Criminal Division Published by Office of Legal Education Executive Office for United States Attorneys January 2015 Pages 24–25.

20. Searching and Seizing Computers and Obtaining Electronic Evidence in Criminal Investigations, Computer Crime and Intellectual Property Section Criminal Division Published by Office of Legal Education Executive Office for United States Attorneys January 2015 Pages 25–26.

21. Searching and Seizing Computers and Obtaining Electronic Evidence in Criminal Investigations, Computer Crime and Intellectual Property Section Criminal Division Published by Office of Legal Education Executive Office for United States Attorneys January 2015 Pages 26–27.

22. Searching and Seizing Computers and Obtaining Electronic Evidence in Criminal Investigations, Computer Crime and Intellectual Property Section Criminal Division Published by Office of Legal Education Executive Office for United States Attorneys January 2015 Pages 115–117.

23. Searching and Seizing Computers and Obtaining Electronic Evidence in Criminal Investigations, Computer Crime and Intellectual Property Section Criminal Division Published by Office of Legal Education Executive Office for United States Attorneys January 2015 Page 138.

24. Searching and Seizing Computers and Obtaining Electronic Evidence in Criminal Investigations, Computer Crime and Intellectual Property Section Criminal Division Published by Office of Legal Education Executive Office for United States Attorneys January 2015 Pages 117–119.

25. Searching and Seizing Computers and Obtaining Electronic Evidence in Criminal Investigations, Computer Crime and Intellectual Property Section Criminal Division Published by Office of Legal Education Executive Office for United States Attorneys January 2015 Pages 119–120.

26. Searching and Seizing Computers and Obtaining Electronic Evidence in Criminal Investigations, Computer Crime and Intellectual Property Section Criminal Division Published by Office of Legal Education Executive Office for United States Attorneys January 2015 Pages 120–121.

27. Searching and Seizing Computers and Obtaining Electronic Evidence in Criminal Investigations, Computer Crime and Intellectual Property Section Criminal Division Published by Office of Legal Education Executive Office for United States Attorneys January 2015 Page 122.

28. Searching and Seizing Computers and Obtaining Electronic Evidence in Criminal Investigations, Computer Crime and Intellectual Property Section Criminal Division Published by Office of Legal Education Executive Office for United States Attorneys January 2015 Pages 122–125.

29. Searching and Seizing Computers and Obtaining Electronic Evidence in Criminal Investigations, Computer Crime and Intellectual Property Section Criminal Division Published by Office of Legal Education Executive Office for United States Attorneys January 2015 Pages 125–127.

30. Searching and Seizing Computers and Obtaining Electronic Evidence in Criminal Investigations, Computer Crime and Intellectual Property Section Criminal Division Published by Office of Legal Education Executive Office for United States Attorneys January 2015 Pages 135–136.

31. Searching and Seizing Computers and Obtaining Electronic Evidence in Criminal Investigations, Computer Crime and Intellectual Property Section Criminal Division Published by Office of Legal Education Executive Office for United States Attorneys January 2015 Page 149.

32. Searching and Seizing Computers and Obtaining Electronic Evidence in Criminal Investigations, Computer Crime and Intellectual Property Section Criminal Division Published by Office of Legal Education Executive Office for United States Attorneys January 2015 Page 161.

33. Searching and Seizing Computers and Obtaining Electronic Evidence in Criminal Investigations, Computer Crime and Intellectual Property Section Criminal Division Published by Office of Legal Education Executive Office for United States Attorneys January 2015 Pages 169–170.

34. Searching and Seizing Computers and Obtaining Electronic Evidence in Criminal Investigations, Computer Crime and Intellectual Property Section Criminal Division Published by Office of Legal Education Executive Office for United States Attorneys January 2015 Pages 170–171.

35. Searching and Seizing Computers and Obtaining Electronic Evidence in Criminal Investigations, Computer Crime and Intellectual Property Section Criminal Division Published by Office of Legal Education Executive Office for United States Attorneys January 2015 Pages 211–212.

36. Searching and Seizing Computers and Obtaining Electronic Evidence in Criminal Investigations, Computer Crime and Intellectual Property Section Criminal Division Published by Office of Legal Education Executive Office for United States Attorneys January 2015 Page 182.

37. Searching and Seizing Computers and Obtaining Electronic Evidence in Criminal Investigations, Computer Crime and Intellectual Property Section Criminal Division Published by Office of Legal Education Executive Office for United States Attorneys January 2015 Page 183.

7 Gathering Information and Evidence

In every investigation or forensic accounting analysis you should assume that there is a chance that your work will be presented to a trier of fact in criminal or civil litigation. So, you must collect information and evidence in a manner that will allow it to be used to support your expert opinions presented to a trier of fact. Fortunately, there are clear rules that have been set out for most litigation venues. The examples we will explore in this book are the Federal Rules of Evidence. This is necessary to prevent us from doing a ton of work gathering what we believe to be useful information and evidence that can't be used to support our expert opinions.

Information and evidence used at trial must be relevant to the issues being adjudicated.

"Rule 402. General Admissibility of Relevant
Evidence Relevant evidence is admissible unless any of the following provides otherwise:

- the United States Constitution;
- a federal statute;
- these rules; or
- other rules prescribed by the Supreme Court.

Irrelevant evidence is not admissible.
(As amended Apr. 26, 2011, eff. Dec. 1, 2011.)"[1]

Also, evidence must not unduly prejudicial, confusing, or a waste of the court's time.

"Rule 403. Excluding Relevant Evidence for Prejudice, Confusion, Waste of Time, or Other Reasons
The court may exclude relevant evidence if its probative value is substantially outweighed by a danger of one or more of the following: unfair prejudice, confusing the issues, misleading the jury, undue delay, wasting time, or needlessly presenting cumulative evidence.
(As amended Apr. 26, 2011, eff. Dec. 1, 2011.)"[2]

Evidence must be reliable. Evidence based on hearsay is often not admissible. But there are important exceptions related to physical and digital business records.

"Rule 803. Exceptions to the Rule Against Hearsay – Regardless of Whether the Declarant Is Available as a Witness
The following are not excluded by the rule against hearsay, regardless of whether the declarant is available as a witness:

(6) *Records of a Regularly Conducted Activity.* A record of an act, event, condition, opinion, or diagnosis if:
(A) the record was made at or near the time by – or from information transmitted by – someone with knowledge;
(B) the record was kept in the course of a regularly conducted activity of a business, organization, occupation, or calling, whether or not for profit;

    (C) making the record was a regular practice of that activity;

    (D) all these conditions are shown by the testimony of the custodian or another qualified witness, or by a certification that complies with Rule 902(11) or (12) or with a statute permitting certification; and

    (E) the opponent does not show that the source of information or the method or circumstances of preparation indicate a lack of trustworthiness.

(7) *Absence of a Record of a Regularly Conducted Activity.* Evidence that a matter is not included in a record described in paragraph (6) if:

    (A) the evidence is admitted to prove that the matter did not occur or exist;

    (B) a record was regularly kept for a matter of that kind;

    (C) the opponent does not show that the possible source of the information or other circumstances indicate a lack of trustworthiness."[3]

Public records are admissible.

"(8) *Public Records.* A record or statement of a public office if:

    (A) it sets out:

        (i) the office's activities;

        (ii) a matter observed while under a legal duty to report, but not including, in a criminal case, a matter observed by law-enforcement personnel; or

        (iii) in a civil case or against the government in a criminal case, factual findings from a legally authorized investigation; and

    (B) the opponent does not show that the source of information or other circumstances indicate a lack of trustworthiness.

(9) *Public Records of Vital Statistics.* A record of a birth, death, or marriage, if reported to a public office in accordance with a legal duty.

(10) *Absence of a Public Record.* Testimony – or a certification under Rule 902 – that a diligent search failed to disclose a public record or statement if:

    (A) the testimony or certification is admitted to prove that

        (i) the record or statement does not exist; or

        (ii) a matter did not occur or exist, if a public office regularly kept a record or statement for a matter of that kind; and

    (B) in a criminal case, a prosecutor who intends to offer a certification provides written notice of that intent at least 14 days before trial, and the defendant does not object in writing within 7 days of receiving the notice – unless the court sets a different time for the notice or the objection."[4]

Evidence must be authenticated to be admissible.

"Rule 901. Authenticating or Identifying Evidence

    (a) IN GENERAL. To satisfy the requirement of authenticating or identifying an item of evidence, the proponent must produce evidence sufficient to support a finding that the item is what the proponent claims it is.

    (b) EXAMPLES. The following are examples only – not a complete list – of evidence that satisfies the requirement:

        (1) *Testimony of a Witness with Knowledge.* Testimony that an item is what it is claimed to be.

        (2) *Nonexpert Opinion About Handwriting.* A nonexpert's opinion that handwriting is genuine, based on a familiarity with it that was not acquired for the current litigation.

        (3) *Comparison by an Expert Witness or the Trier of Fact.* A comparison with an authenticated specimen by an expert witness or the trier of fact.

(4) *Distinctive Characteristics and the Like.* The appearance, contents, substance, internal patterns, or other distinctive characteristics of the item, taken together with all the circumstances.

(5) *Opinion About a Voice.* An opinion identifying a person's voice – whether heard firsthand or through mechanical or electronic transmission or recording – based on hearing the voice at any time under circumstances that connect it with the alleged speaker.

(6) *Evidence About a Telephone Conversation.* For a telephone conversation, evidence that a call was made to the number assigned at the time to:

    (A) a particular person, if circumstances, including self-identification, show that the person answering was the one called; or

    (B) a particular business, if the call was made to a business and the call related to business reasonably transacted over the telephone.

(7) *Evidence About Public Records.* Evidence that:

    (A) a document was recorded or filed in a public office as authorized by law; or

    (B) a purported public record or statement is from the office where items of this kind are kept.

(8) *Evidence About Ancient Documents or Data Compilations.* For a document or data compilation, evidence that it:

    (A) is in a condition that creates no suspicion about its authenticity;

    (B) was in a place where, if authentic, it would likely be; and

    (C) is at least 20 years old when offered.

(9) *Evidence About a Process or System.* Evidence describing a process or system and showing that it produces an accurate result.

(10) *Methods Provided by a Statute or Rule.* Any method of authentication or identification allowed by a federal statute or a rule prescribed by the Supreme Court.

(As amended Apr. 26, 2011, eff. Dec. 1, 2011.)

Rule 902. Evidence That Is Self-Authenticating

The following items of evidence are self-authenticating; they require no extrinsic evidence of authenticity in order to be admitted:

(1) *Domestic Public Documents That Are Sealed and Signed.* A document that bears:

    (A) a seal purporting to be that of the United States; any state, district, commonwealth, territory, or insular possession of the United States; the former Panama Canal Zone; the Trust Territory of the Pacific Islands; a political subdivision of any of these entities; or a department, agency, or officer of any entity named above; and

    (B) a signature purporting to be an execution or attestation.

(2) *Domestic Public Documents That Are Not Sealed but Are Signed and Certified.* A document that bears no seal if:

    (A) it bears the signature of an officer or employee of an entity named in Rule 902(1)(A); and

    (B) another public officer who has a seal and official duties within that same entity certifies under seal – or its equivalent – that the signer has the official capacity and that the signature is genuine.

(3) *Foreign Public Documents.* A document that purports to be signed or attested by a person who is authorized by a foreign country's law to do so. The document

must be accompanied by a final certification that certifies the genuineness of the signature and official position of the signer or attester – or of any foreign official whose certificate of genuineness relates to the signature or attestation or is in a chain of certificates of genuineness relating to the signature or attestation. The certification may be made by a secretary of a United States embassy or legation; by a consul general, vice consul, or consular agent of the United States; or by a diplomatic or consular official of the foreign country assigned or accredited to the United States. If all parties have been given a reasonable opportunity to investigate the document's authenticity and accuracy, the court may, for good cause, either:

(A) order that it be treated as presumptively authentic without final certification; or

(B) allow it to be evidenced by an attested summary with or without final certification.

(4) *Certified Copies of Public Records.* A copy of an official record – or a copy of a document that was recorded or filed in a public office as authorized by law – if the copy is certified as correct by:

(A) the custodian or another person authorized to make the certification; or

(B) a certificate that complies with Rule 902(1), (2), or (3), a federal statute, or a rule prescribed by the Supreme Court.

(5) *Official Publications.* A book, pamphlet, or other publication purporting to be issued by a public authority.

(6) *Newspapers and Periodicals.* Printed material purporting to be a newspaper or periodical.

(7) *Trade Inscriptions and the Like.* An inscription, sign, tag, or label purporting to have been affixed in the course of business and indicating origin, ownership, or control.

(8) *Acknowledged Documents.* A document accompanied by a certificate of acknowledgment that is lawfully executed by a notary public or another officer who is authorized to take acknowledgments.

(9) *Commercial Paper and Related Documents.* Commercial paper, a signature on it, and related documents, to the extent allowed by general commercial law.

(10) *Presumptions Under a Federal Statute.* A signature, document, or anything else that a federal statute declares to be presumptively or prima facie genuine or authentic.

(11) *Certified Domestic Records of a Regularly Conducted Activity.* The original or a copy of a domestic record that meets the requirements of Rule 803(6)(A)–(C), as shown by a certification of the custodian or another qualified person that complies with a federal statute or a rule prescribed by the Supreme Court. Before the trial or hearing, the proponent must give an adverse party reasonable written notice of the intent to offer the record – and must make the record and certification available for inspection – so that the party has a fair opportunity to challenge them.

(12) *Certified Foreign Records of a Regularly Conducted Activity.* In a civil case, the original or a copy of a foreign record that meets the requirements of Rule 902(11), modified as follows: the certification, rather than complying with a federal statute or Supreme Court rule, must be signed in a manner that, if falsely made, would subject the maker to a criminal penalty in the country where the certification is signed. The proponent must also meet the notice requirements of Rule 902(11).

(As amended Mar. 2, 1987, eff. Oct. 1, 1987; Apr. 25, 1988, eff. Nov. 1, 1988; Apr. 17, 2000, eff. Dec. 1, 2000; Apr. 26, 2011, eff. Dec. 1, 2011; Apr. 27, 2017, eff. Dec 1, 2017.)"[5]

The best available evidence must be collected. Evidence should comprise originals created contemporaneously with the activity for which they are offered as proof.

"Rule 1001. Definitions That Apply to This Article
In this article:

(a) A "writing" consists of letters, words, numbers, or their equivalent set down in any form.

(b) A "recording" consists of letters, words, numbers, or their equivalent recorded in any manner.

(c) A "photograph" means a photographic image or its equivalent stored in any form.

(d) An "original" of a writing or recording means the writing or recording itself or any counterpart intended to have the same effect by the person who executed or issued it. For electronically stored information, "original" means any printout – or other output readable by sight – if it accurately reflects the information. An "original" of a photograph includes the negative or a print from it.

(e) A "duplicate" means a counterpart produced by a mechanical, photographic, chemical, electronic, or other equivalent process or technique that accurately reproduces the original.

(As amended Apr. 26, 2011, eff. Dec. 1, 2011.)

Rule 1002. Requirement of the Original
An original writing, recording, or photograph is required in order to prove its content unless these rules or a federal statute provides otherwise.
(As amended Apr. 26, 2011, eff. Dec. 1, 2011.)

Rule 1003. Admissibility of Duplicates
A duplicate is admissible to the same extent as the original unless a genuine question is raised about the original's authenticity or the circumstances make it unfair to admit the duplicate.
(As amended Apr. 26, 2011, eff. Dec. 1, 2011.)

Rule 1004. Admissibility of Other Evidence of Content
An original is not required and other evidence of the content of a writing, recording, or photograph is admissible if:

(a) all the originals are lost or destroyed, and not by the proponent acting in bad faith;

(b) an original cannot be obtained by any available judicial process;

(c) the party against whom the original would be offered had control of the original; was at that time put on notice, by pleadings or otherwise, that the original would be a subject of proof at the trial or hearing; and fails to produce it at the trial or hearing; or

(d) the writing, recording, or photograph is not closely related to a controlling issue.

(As amended Mar. 2, 1987, eff. Oct. 1, 1987; Apr. 26, 2011, eff. Dec. 1, 2011.)"[6]

Investigators are often carried away by leads and lose interest in gathering the evidence necessary to prove the subject of the lead. If carried too far, this can be a dangerous preoccupation. Let me illustrate with a true story.

INVESTIGATOR NOTES

Many years ago I was working on the forensic accounting part of a major investigation. There was another firm better known for its pure investigative capabilities doing the street level private investigation work. They had a team member stringing leads together faster than an industrial sewing machine could lay down thread. The lawyers, who hired us both, marveled at the amazing findings and associated stories spun by this guy each day. He led them around like the Pied Piper. We were basically ignored as we gathered evidence in an orderly and diligent manner.

The time came for the first hearing in US District Court. The week before the hearing the lawyers asked each of us to produce our findings together with the evidence supporting them. They had earlier included many of the Pied Piper's assertions in the pleadings leading up to the hearing. We submitted our evidence packages with chain of custody logs and conclusions. We wondered why we had been summoned first. The lawyers asked questions, which we were easily able to answer. They thanked us and we went back to our work. The next morning, we heard a great deal of yelling and rough language. We were confused, but it really didn't concern us. As it turned out, the Pied Piper had requested an extension, which was granted. Just days before the hearing he had to confess to the lawyers that he had little to no admissible evidence to support his stories that formed the basis for assertions that the lawyers included in pleadings to the court. The lawyers called us in and gave us a list of the presently unsupported assertions in the pleadings. They asked us to gather whatever evidence we could in support of those assertions. The Pied Piper was sent home and we assumed a new role in the investigation, effectively managing the other firm's personnel to make sure the unhappy episode would never be repeated.

SECTION I: PREVENTING THE INTENTIONAL OR, MORE OFTEN, UNINTENTIONAL DESTRUCTION OF EVIDENCE

Remember, I discussed with you in Chapter 6 that in order for your work to be able to be used in litigation, you must adhere to the same ethics rules as the lawyers who are supervising you. Well, there is an ethics rule for lawyers that states that a: "lawyer shall not unlawfully obstruct another party's access to evidence or unlawfully alter, destroy or conceal a document or other material having potential evidentiary value."[7]

Spoliation of evidence (physical or digital) means that the evidence has been deliberately, negligently, or accidentally destroyed. Spoliation of evidence can result in rather severe consequences. These could include anything from a court imposed monetary penalty to criminal indictment. Avoiding spoliation is a very serious obligation. You must first have a well-documented understanding of your company's email and network infrastructure to be able to competently identify, preserve, and collect relevant evidence. You must have a plan in place, before it is needed, to prevent spoliation of evidence. The first step in the process is issuing a litigation hold. The hold plan should identify your company's sources of potentially relevant electronically stored information (ESI) and set out procedures to preserve it. To ensure that electronic documents and data are properly preserved, the collection process should include interviews with document custodians to gain a better understanding of the location of all potentially relevant ESI. If your company is placed on a litigation hold, especially if your company receives a Grand Jury subpoena, you must make sure the hold goes into place immediately. If after the hold is in place, you discover something damaging to your company, resist the temptation to try to fix it. You must disclose what you find as you find it, through counsel, of course.

INVESTIGATOR NOTES

Does your company have a document retention policy? I once did an audit committee investigation for a public company. They had received a Grand Jury subpoena and immediately instituted a litigation hold. The lawyer and I worked closely with the company's chief information officer (CIO) to make sure that we had produced every physical and electronic record that was responsive to the subpoena. The company had a document retention policy which it followed faithfully. It was lucky, too, because a lot of the conduct the government was interested in occurred prior to the earliest year for which the company still retained physical and electronic records under their written retention policy. Following an exhaustive process and, satisfied that we had produced everything responsive to the subpoena, the lawyer contacted the US Attorney's office and certified that our production was complete.

About a week later, I was working alone at the company when the CIO came into the office where I was working. He asked me to come to his office so he could show me something that he was concerned about. He proceeded to tell me that he never liked the company's document-retention policy which, he felt, was forced on him by the company's general counsel. The CIO was concerned that someday someone would need information from electronic records that were no longer available because they had been destroyed in accordance with the document retention policy. So, he kept his own copies.

I asked him where he kept these copies? He made a grand sweep with his hand pointing to the massive lateral file cabinets, which lined the four walls of his office. I asked if he would mind showing me what was in the cabinet drawers. He agreed and walked to the one nearest me and opened the drawer. The drawer was packed with backup tapes. In fact, all the drawers were packed with backup tapes. What to do? The data in those backup tapes was bound to contain further incriminating evidence. I immediately called the lawyer with whom I was working and he immediately contacted the US Attorney's office to alert them about the additional digital evidence we found.

SECTION II: THE BEST EVIDENCE RULE AND HOW TO SELECT WHICH EVIDENCE TO GATHER

I was hired by lawyers representing the victim of a massive commodities fraud to investigate the fraud and give written and oral expert testimony about my findings. The defense had put forward two theories of the case. One was that these were normal commodities transactions and the victim just ended up on the wrong side of them. I was able to blow that up by showing that the ten other entities in the transactions were keeping secret records to assure they were coordinating their activities so that they would win and the victim to lose every time. Their other theory was that the victim, a large corporation, did not have sufficient internal controls such that its reliance on the defendant's representations was unreasonable.

I was testifying in the federal trial and it was, fortunately for me, very near the end of that day's proceedings. One of the defense lawyers walked up to the witness box and laid a seven-million-dollar check, drawn on the account of one of the victim's employees who had participated in the scheme, made payable, it appeared, to the victim. The check was written to cover up another accounts receivable problem that would have brought the crooked employee unwanted attention from internal audit. The lawyer asked me if I had seen the check before? I answered no. At that point, the Judge adjourned the trial for the day. This was bad news. I was obviously going to be asked if this should not have set off alarms at the victim corporation. Where would a relatively low-level employee get that kind of money and why would he be writing a check of that size to his employer? The inference being that the victim corporation's internal controls had such material weaknesses that the victim's supposed reliance on the perpetrator's representations was unreasonable. We spent the entire night at the victim company's offices trying to solve the mystery of the seven-million-dollar check. We found a seven-million-dollar deposit alright, but, it was made with a cashier's check which appeared to have been created by the customer with problem accounts receivable account.

I was back on the stand the next morning. The defense lawyer couldn't wait to ask me about the check. His first question was, "Mr. Jennings, how could a company with good internal controls receive a seven-million-dollar check from one of their lower-level employees and do nothing to investigate? When they saw that check, shouldn't they have known something was wrong?" I said, "Well maybe, if they had seen that check, but they didn't ever see that check." I could see the blood begin to drain from the lawyer's face. He sensed I was about to give him the expert testimony version of a pie in the face. I pulled out the cashier's check we had found the night before, which had the legitimate customer's name on it. I said, "You see, the check you are holding was used to purchase this cashier's check which is the only check the victim company saw." I think the lawyer's next line was: "No more questions."

As I explained earlier, the best evidence of the contents of a writing, recording, or a photograph is the original version. Interestingly, this principle came into existence under British Common Law long before modern copy machines or recording devices were available. At that time copies were made by hand and were notoriously unreliable. This is an ancient problem. Dual-entry accounting came into existence during the Renaissance because of the falsification of financial records in the mercantile trade based in Northern Italy (i.e. see The Merchant of Venice). Much earlier, the Masoretes were charged with replicating the sacred texts agreed upon at the Council of Jamnia. Importantly, written Hebrew does not include vowels. So, the Masoretes, in each reproduction would count from the first consonant character to the middle character and from that character to the last character to make sure that a character was not added or deleted. This ancient concern for faithful reproduction gave rise to the Best Evidence Rule today.

However, if the original document has been destroyed or is otherwise unattainable then a copy may be used. Further, there is an exception to the bar against hearsay if a physical or electronic record is created in the normal course of business and can be shown not to have been altered. This is why it is important to make a forensic image of all ESI before the electronic device it is stored in changes it in some way.

SECTION III: PROPERLY PRESERVING AND COLLECTING ELECTRONIC EVIDENCE

The first thing that I want to alert you to is that ESI can be altered and spoliated by the normal operation of the electronic devices on which it is stored. In most cases it is best to unplug electronic devices on which electronic records are stored until a forensic image of the records can be made.

A computer would, itself, be evidence of a crime if it contained child pornography or if it was stolen. However, the computer or other electronic device is more likely to contain evidence in the form of stored electronic records.

First, you need to make sure that you have legal access to the electronic device and its ESI. You would begin a chain of custody log for the ESI you will collect. Next you need to make sure that the electronic device is isolated and that the electronic storage cannot be altered. Then you need a plan to collect the data. This would be based on the type and location of the electronic device, the expected amount of stored data and the time available. Typically, you would use a trained and experienced specialist to collect the data because, even with a guide and the right computer forensic tools, there are many ways to find disaster. When finished collecting, you need a method to verify that the image you have created is exactly the same as the ESI on the device.

Let's take a look at how the Federal Bureau of Investigation (FBI) preserves and collects ESI:

"Computer evidence represented by physical items such as chips, boards, central processing units, storage media, monitors, and printers can be described easily and correctly as a unique form of physical evidence. The logging, description, storage, and disposition of physical evidence are well understood. Forensic laboratories have detailed plans describing acceptable methods for handling physical evidence. To the extent that computer evidence has a physical component, it does not represent any particular challenge. However, the evidence, while stored in these physical items, is latent and exists only in a metaphysical electronic form. The result that is reported from the examination is the recovery of this latent information. Although forensic laboratories are very good at ensuring the integrity of the physical items in their control, computer forensics also requires methods to ensure the integrity of the information contained within those physical items. The challenge to computer forensic science is to develop methods and techniques that provide valid and reliable results while protecting the real evidence – the information – from harm.

To complicate the matter further, computer evidence almost never exists in isolation. It is a product of the data stored, the application used to create and store it, and the computer system that directed these activities. To a lesser extent, it is also a product of the software tools used in the laboratory to extract it.

As an overall example, a laboratory may require that examinations be conducted, if possible and practical, on copies of the original evidence. This requirement is a principle of examination. It represents a logical approach taken by the computer forensic science community as a whole, and it is based on the tenet of protecting the original evidence from accidental or unintentional damage or alteration. This principle is predicated on the fact that digital evidence can be duplicated exactly to create a copy that is true and accurate.

Creating the copy and ensuring that it is true and accurate involves a subset of the principle, that is, policy and practice. Each agency and examiner must make a decision as to how to implement this principle on a case-by-case basis. Factors in that decision include the size of the data set, the method used to create it, and the media on which it resides. In some cases it may be sufficient to merely compare the size and creation dates of files listed in the copy to the original. In others, it may require the application of more technically robust and mathematical rigorous techniques such as a cyclical redundancy check (CRC) or calculating a message digest (MD).

CRC and MD are computer algorithms that produce unique mathematical representations of the data. They are calculated for both the original and the copy and then compared for identity. The selection of tools must be based on the character of the evidence rather than simply laboratory policy. It is likely that examiners will need several options available to them to perform this one function.

An examiner responsible for duplicating evidence must first decide an appropriate level of verification to weigh time constraints against large file types. The mathematical precision and discriminating power of these algorithms are usually directly proportional to the amount of time necessary to calculate them. If there were 1 million files to be duplicated, each less than 1 kilobyte in size, time and computational constraints would likely be a major determining factor. This circumstance would probably result in a decision to use a faster, but less precise and discriminating, data integrity algorithm.

Having decided how best to ensure the copy process will be complete and accurate, the next step is the actual task. This is a subset of the policy and practice, that is, procedures and techniques. These most closely represent the standard cookbook approach to protocol development. They are complete and contain required detailed steps that may be used to copy the data, verify that the operation was complete, and ensure that a true and accurate copy has been produced."[8]

Note that the FBI has a rigorous process that is documented and used for all their computer forensics projects. There is no freelancing.

The US Justice Department created a useful diagram to lay out the steps in a proper collection of ESI (see Figure 7.1).

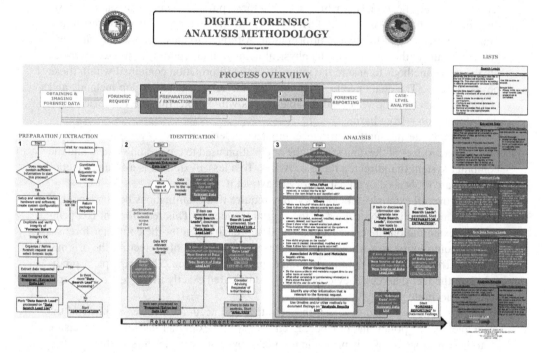

FIGURE 7.1[9]

The diagram has been broken out next for easier review. See Figures 7.2 through 7.7.

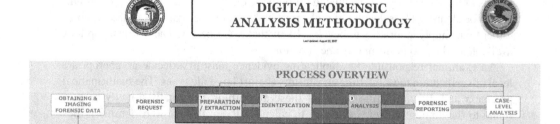

FIGURE 7.2[10]

PREPARATION / EXTRACTION

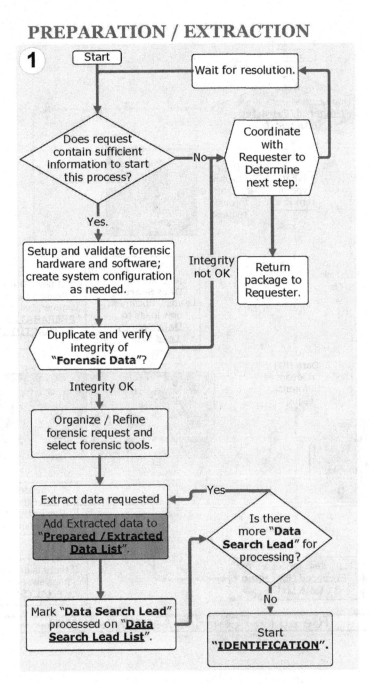

FIGURE 7.3[11]

IDENTIFICATION

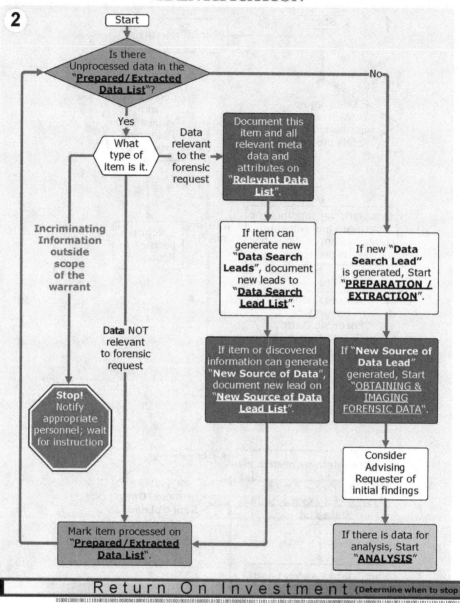

FIGURE 7.4[12]

ANALYSIS

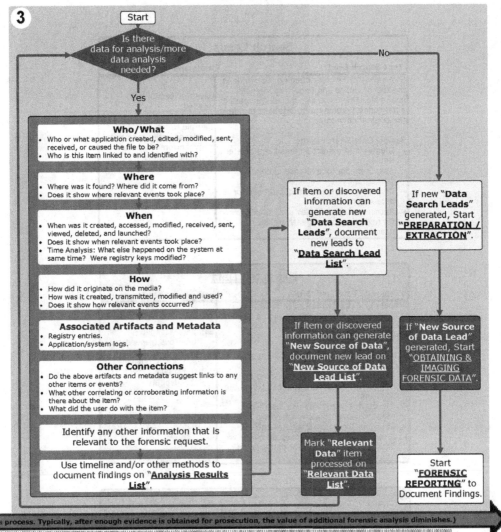

FIGURE 7.5[13]

LISTS

Search Leads

Data Search Leads	Comments/Notes/Messages
Generally this involves opening a case file in the tool of choice and importing forensic image file. This could also include recreating a network environment or database to mimic the original environment. Sample Data Search Leads: • Identify and extract all email and deleted items. • Search media for evidence of child pornography. • Configure and load seized database for data mining. • Recover all deleted files and index drive for review by case agent/forensic examiner.	Use this section as needed. Sample Note: • Please notify case agent when forensic data preparation is completed.

Extracted Data

Prepared / Extracted Data	Comments/Notes/Messages
Prepared / Extracted Data List is a list of items that are prepared or extracted to allow identification of Data pertaining to the forensic request. Sample Prepared / Extracted Data items: • Processed hard drive image using Encase or FTK to allow a case agent to triage the contents. • Exported registry files and installed registry viewer to allow a forensic examiner to examine registry entries. • A seized database files is loaded on a database server ready for data mining. •	Use this section as needed. Sample Message: • Numerous files located in c:\movies directory have .avi extensions but are actually Excel spreadsheets.

Relevant Data

Relevant Data	Comments/Notes/Messages
Relevant Data List is a list of data that is relevant to the forensic request. For example: • If the forensic request is finding information relating credit card fraud, any credit card number, image of credit card, emails discussing making credit card, web cache that shows the date, time and search term used to find credit card number program, Etc are Relevant Data as evidence. In addition, Victim information retrieved is also Relevant Data for purpose of victim notification.	Use this section as needed. Sample Note: • Attachment in Outlook.pst>message05 has a virus in it. Make sure an anti-virus software is installed before exporting and opening it. • Identified and recovered 12 emails detailing plan to commit crime.

FIGURE 7.6[14]

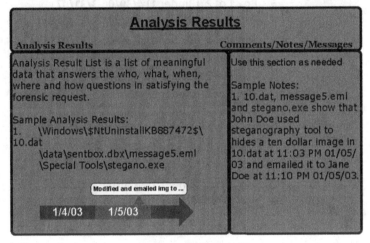

New Data Source Leads

New Source of Data Leads	Comments/Notes/Messages
New Source of Data Lead List is a list of data that should be obtained to corroborate or further investigative efforts. Sample New Source of Data Leads: • Email address: Jdoe@email.com. • Server logs from FTP server. • Subscriber information for an IP address. • Transaction logs from server.	This is self explanatory. Use this section as needed. Sample Notes: During forensic analysis of subject John Doe's hard drive image on credit card fraud, a email message revealed that Jane Doe asks John Doe for payment on credit card printing machine.

Analysis Results

Analysis Results	Comments/Notes/Messages

Analysis Result List is a list of meaningful data that answers the who, what, when, where and how questions in satisfying the forensic request.
 	
Sample Analysis Results:
1.   \Windows\$NtUninstallKB887472$\10.dat
        \data\sentbox.dbx\message5.eml
        \Special Tools\stegano.exe
 	
Modified and emailed img to ...
1/4/03   1/5/03
	Use this section as needed
	
	Sample Notes:
	1. 10.dat, message5.eml and stegano.exe show that John Doe used steganography tool to hides a ten dollar image in 10.dat at 11:03 PM 01/05/03 and emailed it to Jane Doe at 11:10 PM 01/05/03.

Department of Justice (DOJ)
Computer Crime and Intellectual Property Section (CCIPS)
Cybercrime Lab
http://www.cybercrime.gov
(202) 514-1026

FIGURE 7.7[15]

SECTION IV: PROPERLY PRESERVING AND COLLECTING NON-ELECTRONIC EVIDENCE

A while back, I worked on an investigation of the president of a large private company. The president was believed to have stolen a great deal of money from the company. Unfortunately, the company allowed the president to use his own computer for work, had no meaningful internal controls, and had no document retention policy. Also, they fired the president and let him take anything he desired unsupervised. This was one of the most difficult cases I have ever investigated because of the scarcity of remaining relevant physical and electronic records. The break in the case came when I found seventy-three boxes of paper records stored in the rat-infested attic of one of the company's buildings. I and one of my colleagues rented a van; hauled the boxes down from the attic and assigned a number to each box. We started an evidence log with each box number. When we got back to our office, we unloaded the boxes. We methodically went through each box and added the contents to our evidence log. Then and only then did we begin analyzing the documents. In this way we had created solid evidence to support the chain of custody for the documents. Figure 7.8 is an excerpt from that evidence log.

		Custody Log	
		Additional Original Documents 29July:	
		Two File Boxes	
Item #	Sub #		Binder Label / C
1	1	Box 1 of 2	(Binder 1) 4/30/06-3/31/07 (
2	2	Box 1 of 2	(Binder 1) 4/30/06-3/31/07 (
3	3	Box 1 of 2	(Binder 1) 4/30/06-3/31/07 (
4	4	Box 1 of 2	(Binder 1) 4/30/06-3/31/07 (
5	5	Box 1 of 2	(Binder 1) 4/30/06-3/31/07 (
6	6	Box 1 of 2	(Binder 1) 4/30/06-3/31/07 (
7	7	Box 1 of 2	(Binder 1) 4/30/06-3/31/07 (
8	8	Box 1 of 2	(Binder 1) 4/30/06-3/31/07 (
9	9	Box 1 of 2	(Binder 1) 4/30/06-3/31/07 (
10	10	Box 1 of 2	(Binder 1) 4/30/06-3/31/07 (
11	11	Box 1 of 2	(Binder 1) 4/30/06-3/31/07 (
12	12	Box 1 of 2	(Binder 1) 4/30/06-3/31/07 (
13	13	Box 1 of 2	(Binder 1) 4/30/06-3/31/07 (
14	14	Box 1 of 2	(Binder 1) 4/30/06-3/31/07 (
15	15	Box 1 of 2	(Binder 1) 4/30/06-3/31/07 (
16	16	Box 1 of 2	(Binder 1) 4/30/06-3/31/07 (

FIGURE 7.8

Again, you first need to make sure that you have legal access to the documents or other evidence. You would begin a chain of custody log for the documents you collect. It should contain the: date, location of the documents, type of document, and a description of the documents collected. These steps must be completed before you begin analyzing the documents.

Once you have completed those steps you must be careful not to alter any of the documents. If anyone needs to write anything on an evidentiary document, they should make a copy and return the original to your storage. You will also need to keep track of the documents you analyze in forming your conclusions. They will be listed on an exhibit to your report. We will discuss that further in Chapter 10.

EXERCISES

1. What type of evidence is admissible under the federal rules of evidence?
2. What are some reasons why relevant evidence might be excluded?
3. What is hearsay?
4. When is evidence, based on hearsay, admissible?
5. What is required to authenticate evidence?
6. What contains the best evidence of an evidentiary matter contained in a writing, recording, or photograph?

7. Can duplicates be admissible?
8. What is spoliation of evidence?
9. What's often the best way to avoid spoliation of evidence stored on an electronic device?
10. What is your company's document retention policy?
11. Are there controls in place to make sure it is followed?
12. If given a choice between a damaged original and a pristine duplicate, which would you choose to collect as evidence? Why?
13. What is a good process for collecting electronic evidence?
14. What steps should be followed in collecting electronic evidence?
15. What is a forensic image of evidentiary data?
16. What are some of the techniques used to assure you have an accurate and complete forensic image of the evidentiary data you have collected?
17. What is a chain of custody of evidence?
18. Why is creating a proper chain of custody of evidence log necessary to establish the chain of custody of evidence?
19. Create a proper chain of custody of evidence log form.
20. Develop a statement that you would use to authenticate evidence you have collected.

CHAPTER SUMMARY/KEY TAKEAWAYS

- Prevent spoliation of evidence at all costs.
- Originals are the best evidence of the contents of writings, recordings, and photographs.
- Physical and electronic records regularly created in the normal course of business are not barred from admissibility by the Hearsay Rule.
- ESI should be collected under rigorous protocols by trained and experienced specialists.
- Prove chain of custody by creating an evidence log.

In Chapter 8 you will learn the science and art of proper witness interviews.

NOTES

1. https://www.uscourts.gov/sites/default/files/Rules%20of%20Evidence Page 4.
2. https://www.uscourts.gov/sites/default/files/Rules%20of%20Evidence Page 4.
3. https://www.uscourts.gov/sites/default/files/Rules%20of%20Evidence Page 18.
4. https://www.uscourts.gov/sites/default/files/Rules%20of%20Evidence Page 19.
5. https://www.uscourts.gov/sites/default/files/Rules%20of%20Evidence Page 23-25.
6. https://www.uscourts.gov/sites/default/files/Rules%20of%20Evidence Page 26.
7. American Bar Association Model Rule 3.4.
8. https://archives.fbi.gov/archives/about-us/lab/forensic-science-communications/fsc/oct2020/computer.htm
9. https://www.justice.gov/sites/default/files/criminal-ccips/legacy/2015/03/26/forensics_chart.pdf
10. https://www.justice.gov/sites/default/files/criminal-ccips/legacy/2015/03/26/forensics_chart.pdf
11. https://www.justice.gov/sites/default/files/usao/legacy/2008/02/04/usab5601.pdf
12. https://www.justice.gov/sites/default/files/usao/legacy/2008/02/04/usab5601.pdf
13. https://www.justice.gov/sites/default/files/usao/legacy/2008/02/04/usab5601.pdf
14. https://www.justice.gov/sites/default/files/usao/legacy/2008/02/04/usab5601.pdf
15. https://www.justice.gov/sites/default/files/usao/legacy/2008/02/04/usab5601.pdf

8 Interviewing Witnesses

The easiest way to find out what actually happened, when conducting an investigation, is to get the people who witnessed the conduct to tell you what they saw and heard. I cannot count the number of times I cracked a case with an effective witness interview. But, notice I said that the witness interview must be effective. In this chapter I am going to teach you to conduct an effective witness interview, but, first, a story that illustrates the contrast between an effective and ineffective witness interview from an actual case I worked on.

A US public company in the Midwest had acquired a subsidiary in the Northeast. The subsidiary was in the demolition business. The founder of the subsidiary was kept on as president under a five-year earnout agreement. The president paid personally to construct a new headquarters building which he then leased back to the subsidiary on very generous terms. The subsidiary was maintaining revenue growth, but its earnings and cash flow were deteriorating. The parent company hired me to find out whether the president was ripping them off.

I traveled to the subsidiary and encountered a strong cult of personality. All the longtime employees were fiercely loyal to the president. They managed to find ways to answer my open-ended questions with one-word answers, very strange and frustrating. I persevered; running down every lead I could come up with. I found scrap metal thefts, accounts payable fraud, and any number of things that would be very difficult to connect to the president. One thing I discovered was that the bonuses paid to the demolition project managers were up even though earnings were declining. I noted it but had a hard time making the case that the president was getting enriched as a result. I was told that the project manager bonuses were based on project profitability and were not subjective. I requested the project manager bonus calculations and was told they had to be recovered from storage and would be provided.

Then it hit me; the new $50 million USD headquarters building. I asked to see the project manager for the construction of the building. I was told that it was his last day at the company and that he was retiring. He agreed to see me for five minutes. I asked him a series of open-ended questions and received the same one-word responses. My five minutes passed and he asked if there was anything else I wanted to know. I said, "Yes, there is: where are the payment applications for the construction of the building kept?" His body betrayed him. As I asked the question, he turned automatically to look at a wall of metal filing cabinets. I asked, "Are they in those cabinets?" He was silent. I told him that he was still an employee and that he owed a fiduciary duty to the company; lying to me would violate his fiduciary duty. I was making it up as I went along; this was my first truly promising lead. He admitted that the payment applications and supporting documents were in the filing cabinets. But he said that the documents in the filing cabinets were the personal property of the president and that I was not to open them under any circumstance. He then packed up his things and left the office.

Of course, my curiosity was overwhelming, but I remembered that curiosity killed the cat and did not want to meet a similar fate. So, I called the parent company's general counsel in Chicago and told him what I had discovered. His initial instinct was that since the filing cabinets were owned by the company and were on company property, there could be no reasonable expectation of privacy regarding their contents. However, out of an abundance of caution, he contacted the president's lawyer and worked out a deal for me to get access to the documents.

I first made an evidence log and an overall index of the payment application numbers and dates. Then I began going through the payment applications and supporting documents in order. A funny thing happened; I began discovering sheets containing only amounts and references to change orders from demolition projects embedded in the payment application supporting documentation. This struck me as extremely important. So, I immediately changed my focus to find all the demolition change orders embedded in the payment applications. There were over a hundred change orders referenced from all the demolition projects that were in progress during the time the headquarters building was under construction. I made a list of the information contained on the sheets and secured the payment application files; they were now important evidence and I had to maintain the chain of custody (see Chapter 7).

Next, I requested access to the demolition project files. I traced all the change order references and was surprised at what I found. For instance, the project file for the demolition of a large standalone department store building in Boston contained change orders for a three-story spiral staircase and a large custom sauna unit; strange things to install in a building you are demolishing. I was able to trace both these architectural elements into the new headquarters building. But something didn't add up; none of these change orders resulted in any additional revenue or payments from owners of the demolished structures. This would have been understandable but for the fact that each one of the change orders would have reduced the profitability on the demolition projects. That would mean that the bonuses to the project managers would be reduced as a result. Why weren't the project managers complaining? What sort of Svengali hold did the president have over them?

I set up interviews with each project manager. I followed the steps that I will lay out in the rest of this chapter including organizing the change order documents to show each project manager during the interview. Of course, I started each interview with questions designed to create rapport. But, when I got to the questions related to the change order documents, you could see the physical changes in the interviewee that we will discuss later in the chapter.

After admitting that the change orders had nothing to do with the demolition projects, each interviewee stated that all the referenced products were purchased using the demolition project budget at the direction of the president. Next, I asked if the phony change orders would have reduced profits on the demolition projects; each acknowledged they would have and did. I then asked wouldn't that have reduced their bonus because I was told that the project manager bonuses were based entirely on the demolition project revenues. They stated on the record that their bonuses were not based on demolition project profits, but instead were whatever amount the president decided to give them. So, the primary determinant of bonus amount was how happy you could make the president.

INVESTIGATOR NOTES

I have no idea why this is, but white-collar criminals often feel compelled to keep meticulous records of their criminal conduct. Always be on the lookout for these types of records; they have a tremendous impact on triers of fact at trial.

I also found that the president had caused some of the headquarters building vendors providing services, as compared to products, to be set up as vendors to the demolition company and had them invoice the demolition company for work actually performed on the president's "personally owned and paid for" headquarters building.

Well, at that point I correlated the documents I had gathered with my interview notes and wrote a report. The president was immediately terminated and litigation ensued. The general counsel of the parent company asked that I travel to their headquarters in Chicago to present my findings directly to their outside law firm. When I arrived at the parent company's offices, I was directed to a large conference room where I was greeted by the general counsel and introduced to two very important looking senior partners from the parent company's white shoe law firm. I attempted to engage in some polite conversation to get to know everyone better, but was encouraged to move directly into my presentation, which I did.

It was easy to tell the story because I had organized it in an easy to use and understand manner in my report. So, I was confidently moving through each finding and showing everyone the tightly knit evidence package I assembled to support it. The odd thing was that, as I moved through the presentation, I could see the more senior of the two outside lawyers becoming angrier and angrier; I couldn't figure out why. But, by the end of my presentation, this guy was as red as a beet and both his fists were tightly clenched. The moment I concluded, he stood straight up out of his chair and demanded that the general counsel fire every one of the project managers immediately. I thought to myself: wow, this guy really cares about his clients. But, sadly, I was mistaken. The truth was that his white shoe law firm was hired a year earlier to conduct exactly the same investigation I had just completed. Unfortunately for them, they had based their entire investigation on witness interviews that were devoid of documents with which to confront the witnesses. So, the same project managers who had admitted to me that the change orders were phony when confronted with the documentary evidence, had lied to the lawyers because they had no documents with which to challenge them. This is an important lesson about witness interviews: be thoroughly prepared or be prepared to be thoroughly embarrassed.

SECTION I: THE SCIENCE AND ART OF CONDUCTING WITNESS INTERVIEWS

WHAT SCIENCE TELLS US ABOUT WITNESS INTERVIEWS

There has been a lot of research done on the effectiveness (which I define as eliciting complete, detailed, reliable information from interviewees without violating laws and regulations or engaging in unethical conduct) of witness interview techniques. Some of the best research, I have seen, was published by the High-Value Detainee Interrogation Group (HIG). HIG is an interagency (i.e. FBI, CIA, and DOD) interrogation capability that brings together intelligence professionals, subject matter experts, and a team of researchers to improve the effectiveness of witness interviews and interrogations.[1]

One of the first tasks of an interviewer is to get an idea of how likely the subject will be to cooperate or resist providing useful, detailed, and reliable information to the interviewer. The three-dimensional Cylindrical Model of sensemaking provides a way to study the subject/interviewer interaction and evaluate the subject's level of cooperation or resistance at any point in time. The Cylindrical Model is based on research that evaluates successful versus unsuccessful negotiations in terms of the extent to which the interrogator and subject are in sync with one another at various points in time during the negotiation.[2]

The Cylindrical Model is employed as a means to understand the process of bringing a subject along a path from resistance to cooperation. Sensemaking is a process that helps the interviewer to understand the subject's resistance and what motivates that resistance. The orientation continuum ranges from cooperative to antagonistic to avoidant. This continuum is the vertical dimension of the Cylindrical Model, depicted in Figure 8.1.[3]

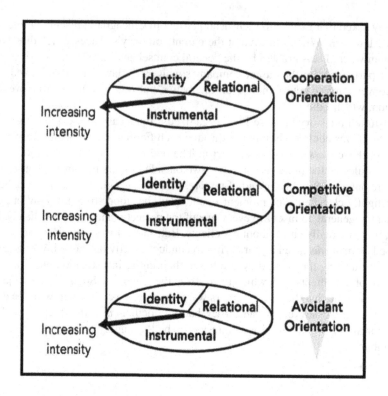

FIGURE 8.1[4]

The interactions between interviewer and interviewee depend on a variety of factors, including culture, individual differences, and power differentials. Communication within each level of the model's continuum may be motivated by different factors (e.g. interviewees may be motivated initially to establish personal and social identity with the interviewer). These motivations (Identity, Relational, and Instrumental) are represented along the horizontal axis in the model within each orientation level. The bulk of the research has been focused on instrumental motives in conflict resolution strongly influenced by game theory.[5]

INVESTIGATOR NOTES

As we shall see as we move through this chapter, game theory provides useful information even in the absence of complete, truthful responses to our questions. What is not said can provide as much information as what is said in an interview. A witness who is evasive and provides intentionally limited answers is telling us that he or she has something to hide. This often precedes a breakthrough in an investigation. For the interviewer who is perceptive and nimble, observing tells and shifting motivation can be the moment where victory is achieved. My story about the construction manager, above, is an illustration of these principles.

Identity motives relate to what may be thought of as "saving face". This is an interviewee's need to maintain a positive personal image. The strength of this motivation varies based on a number of factors including culture, personality type, and perception of power differentials.[6] In certain cultures saying "no" to someone in answer to a direct request is viewed as offensive and a cause for loss of face, so a person from that culture might refuse to answer or answer "yes" and then not do what was requested. A malignant narcissist might consistently lie in answer to questions with respect to which truthful answers would cast them in a bad light. There are effective techniques (i.e. creating the impression, with a witness, that their actions were understandable, albeit illegal) to manage identity motivations.

Relational motives arise in the context of affiliation and interdependence between interviewer and interviewee. Imagine an interviewee who has witnessed something they believe to be significant and wrong that his or her superiors insist did not happen. The interviewee will be motivated to form a positive relationship with an interviewer who is perceived to be a fair conduit to an impartial higher authority.[7] This motivation can be useful if properly managed. It is important, in this situation, to make it clear to the interviewee that what is important is the truth and that there is no need for embellishment or speculation.

Instrumental motives relate to a need to solve a problem. Driven by this motive, the interviewee will seek to manipulate the relationship with the interviewer to achieve a desired outcome (i.e. I am not cooperating because I don't believe this investigation is legitimate).[8]

A description of each motivational frame within each orientation follows:

- Avoidance – Identity: the subject directly attempts to deny involvement or knowledge; challenges the validity of the interrogation, blames the interrogator, and denies responsibility.[9]
- Avoidance – Relational: the subject continually interrupts with pejorative comments, withdraws, and is apathetic. These interactions reveal a lack of trust.
- Avoidance – Instrumental: the subject tries to take control and shift the conversation to irrelevant topics, contradicts previous statements, or is completely closed.
- Competitive – Identity: the subject speaks in a derogatory manner to the interrogator, makes unfounded laudatory statements about his position and himself.
- Competitive – Relational: the subject acquits him or herself, speaks threatening language as a means of asserting power over the situation.
- Competitive – Instrumental: the subject makes inappropriate demands or rejects reasonable demands, provides alternative offers favorable to himself, threatens to punish the interrogator for failing to agree to demands.
- Cooperative – Identity: the subject seeks agreement and a positive relationship with the interrogator, displays empathy, and reveals personal information or apologizes for previous actions.
- Cooperative – Relational: the subject praises the interrogator, while offering reassurances and promises about his own behaviors. Subject actively seeks to find common ground with the interrogator.
- Cooperative – Instrumental: the subject openly provides detailed relevant information; accepts responsibility, and seeks compromise.

Intensity is the third dimension of the Cylindrical Model. Intense language might include threats, derogatory language, and harsh criticism. High intensity dialogue stems from fear, high emotion, rigidity, and self-interest. Intense language has been shown to reduce the likelihood of a successful outcome in high-stakes situations. This suggests that low intensity behaviors may lead to more productive outcomes. It is, therefore, in the interest of the successful interrogator to remain calm and unemotional. The interrogator should take all necessary action or inaction to dial down the intensity of the interaction with the subject.[10]

Research has shown that sensemaking also occurs in coordination of verbal communication. Participants in negotiations tend to experience verbal communication convergence as they move toward agreement and divergence as they move away from agreement. Cooperation appears to correlate to the use of what are called "function" words. These include the use of articles, auxiliary verbs, and pronouns in ways that appear to be beyond the speaker's awareness and conscious control. This verbal communication phenomenon is called language style matching.[11] It can provide the skilled interviewer with a powerful tool to slip behind the interviewee's defenses, especially those driven by identity motives.

INVESTIGATOR NOTES

As we shall explore in more detail later, language style matching can be a powerful tool in successful witness interviewing. I always find out as much as I can about an interviewee's background ahead of conducting the interview. Then I engage the interviewee in casual chatting before proceeding with the actual interview questions. I do this to allow me to facilitate language style matching during the interview. This has to be done carefully and subtly so as not to come across as insincere or mocking to the interviewee. But, if I can match the interviewee's body language and speech patterns, I can often move into the cooperative identity-frame with the interviewee. This makes the interview easier and far more productive.

It is important to note that the Cylindrical Model does not allow for moving from an avoidant orientation to a cooperative orientation without moving through a competitive phase. So, if an interviewee presents at the opening of an interview in an avoidant orientation, it will be necessary to move into a competitive dynamic if there is to be any hope of reaching a cooperative orientation. However, the model also tells us that getting an interviewee to move from one orientation to another is best accomplished by lowering the intensity of interaction.[12] So, the competitive phase will have to be managed carefully by the interviewer.

One way to accomplish this with an identity avoidant interviewee is to focus on the identity motive. The interviewer, in this case, would take steps to raise the interviewee's self-esteem. Perhaps by verbally affirming the interviewee's expertise in a particular area. This could be followed by questions related to the area of expertise, "You know far more about X than I do; please help me to understand...." This could then be followed with clarifying questions to move the interviewee gently into the competitive orientation.

If the interviewee displays relational avoidance cues, the interviewer can redefine the relationship. There are a variety of ways to accomplish this paradigm shift. I have, at times, pointed out to the interviewee that our objectives were actually aligned against a common foe. Another technique I have used is storytelling, which I enjoy in any case. I tell the interviewee a story about someone from an earlier investigation who was in a circumstance very similar to the interviewee's situation and how I was actually able to help that person once we got into sync.

An interviewee will give very apparent signs of instrumental avoidance: arguing, changing the subject, and trying to take control of the interview. In order to move an interviewee from an initial instrumental avoidance frame, you have to employ a bit of wisdom. I once heard from a colleague, "Try getting someone to share a sandwich with you before inviting them to share a seven-course meal." What I mean by that is you need to try to get the interviewee to agree with you on something small; maybe just get them to agree that the interview can be awkward for both the interviewer and interviewee. Then move to small agreements about things that can make the situation less awkward. But don't try to immediately move to a cooperative frame. Once you get small agreements in place you will have to gently move through a competitive interaction before you will be able to move the interviewee to the cooperative frame.

A number of strategies can be employed to influence an interviewee to move from one orientation level to the next adjacent level on the continuum toward a cooperative orientation. The interviewer will select which strategy or strategies to employ based on the unique circumstances of each interview.

Since human beings are extremely social, reciprocity has been hypothesized to represent a virtually universal behavioral norm. Reciprocity can be expressed as the act of doing a small favor which engages the norm of reciprocity in the receiver of the favor triggering a felt obligation to return the favor.[13] The interviewer may provide the interviewee with valuable information that would not otherwise be available to the interviewee.

Humans are also self-interested; recall Adam Smith's "invisible hand of self-interest," the economic theoretical underpinning for the successful operation of free market economies. What I am talking about here is the power of incentives. A large body of research has shown how incentives can be made more effective by regulating the rate and amount of incentives.[14] However, it is important to keep in mind that incentives must not appear to of a nature (e.g. cash bribe) or be given in exchange for giving the answers that support the interviewers hypothesis of the case. These would surely be reason for impeachment of the witness's testimony in any adversarial venue. Also, the incentives must not violate laws or regulations (i.e. If you do not cooperate with the civilian interviewer you will be prosecuted). Instead, a legitimate incentive might be something like reminding an employee interviewee of his fiduciary obligations to him or employer to cooperate with the investigation and pointing out how failure to cooperate could result in monetary losses to the interviewee. Of course, in this circumstance it would be appropriate to provide the interviewee with, what is called in the United States, an Upjohn warning.

Creating the perception that the interviewer is a recognized expert or trustworthy person can be an effective tactic.[15] However, if used incorrectly, this tactic can produce compliance but not cooperation in the interviewee.

Human beings are very sensitive to social consensus information, what they believe others think or believe.[16] Telling the interviewee that many of their colleagues have already cooperated with the investigation and provided very helpful information can be a very effective tactic.

Engaging an interviewee's processes of commitment and consistency can be an effective tactic. People are compelled to align their behaviors with their beliefs.[17] A bit of research ahead of the interview can pay big bonuses here. Finding some earlier espoused belief or commitment and reminding an interviewee of his or her stated belief or commitment can be a powerful tactic.

Positive feelings and "liking" or friendliness can be brought about by the interviewer creating perceived similarities with the interviewee.[18] These can be anything that will appear genuine to the interviewee (i.e. The interviewer could say, "I heard that you enjoy fishing; I do quite a bit of fishing myself. Do you prefer fresh or salt water?" or, "I understand that you are a pilot; I am a pilot myself. What do you fly? How long have you been flying?"). Friendliness can also be enhanced by the interviewer's social presence, flattery, cooperation, and behavioral mimicry.[19] I use this last one quite often. I try to match the interviewee's body language and speech patterns, which tend to put the interviewee at ease and lowers instinctive natural defenses to strangers. To the extent possible I try to become a figurative member of their tribe. However, this must be done subtly and carefully or it could appear to be mocking or insulting to the interviewee that would like trigger negative identity motives and raise the interviewee's level of intensity.

Another effective technique is self-disclosure by the interviewer. A getting-to-know-you preamble to an interview in which the interviewer discloses personal, but non-actionable information about him or herself can enhance friendliness and trigger an obligation for reciprocity by the interviewee.[20] For instance, an interviewer might disclose that he or she has struggled with weight in the past and has started a new diet which has been difficult. They might add, "I hope we can get through this quickly so we can both get some lunch."

Rapport is the most important characteristic of a successful interview.[21] A team of UK researchers analyzed 418 recordings of interviews through the lens of the principles and strategies of motivational interviewing and identified the presence of the following motivational interviewing elements in each:

- Reflective listening. Reflecting interviewee disclosures back to them to encourage clarification.
- Rapport and Resistance. Developing rapport with and dealing with resistance from the interviewee without judgment.
- Summaries. Reflecting an overall summary of segments of testimony back to the interviewee for clarification.
- Discrepancies. Inconsistencies in the interviewee's testimony are reflected back to them to get clarification.
- Acceptance. Unconditional acceptance of the interviewee.
- Empathy. The interviewer's ability to demonstrate understanding of the interviewee's perspective.
- Adaption: The interviewer's ability to authentically adapt to the interviewee's communication characteristics (i.e. body language, speech cadence, volume, style, etc.).
- Evocation. The interviewer's ability to get the interviewee to express beliefs and views.
- Autonomy. The interviewer's ability to make it possible for the interviewee to disclose information without losing face.
- The UK researchers noted a strong positive correlation between the presence of these elements in an interview and interview yield.[22]

There are a variety of interview methods that can be employed depending upon the nature of the interviewee, the information sought and the context of the interview. We will explore some of these now.

The cognitive interview method is designed to give the interviewee incentives and a variety of avenues to recall the details of event(s) that the interviewee witnessed firsthand. This method requires the interviewer to engage in rapport building behaviors to place the interviewee in a positive and cooperative state of mind. These can take the form of the techniques discussed earlier (i.e. reflective listening, responding to resistance without judgment, summaries, and acceptance).[23] Although, it pays to be creative here; mimicking body language and speech patterns, identifying common experiences and objectives, affirming the interviewee's perspectives, are other ways rapport may be created. Once rapport is established, the interviewee is encouraged to take an active role in the interview discussion; providing information without waiting for questions to be asked. The interviewer encourages the interviewee to provide detailed narratives around the event(s) of interest. Interviewer questions do not follow a previously designed script but, rather, follow the narratives provided by the interviewee, mostly clarifying in form. These questions should not be asked until the interviewee finishes his or her narrative.[24] The only danger here is that the interviewee spins narratives that are irrelevant and unrelated to the subject(s) of inquiry. In this instance, the interviewer must tolerate some wandering, but be prepared to gently steer the interviewee back on course.

The cognitive method is based on scientific research into social dynamics, memory, and communication. The cognitive interview is based on the premise that individuals store, process, and recall memories in different ways. It opens up as many potential avenues of recall as possible. It can be very effective in obtaining detailed and context-rich testimony from interviewees. The only drawback is that it requires more time than a typical scripted-question interview.[25]

The Observing Rapport-Based Interview Technique (ORBIT) is based on UK researchers studying 600 hours of actual field interrogations. The researchers were able to identify specific interviewer behaviors and interviewee reactions to those behaviors. From this research they were able to create a model. The model broke down the observed behaviors and reactions into two interpersonal circles. They also added axes to the circles: a cooperation–confrontation axis and a control–capitulation axis (see Figure 8.2).

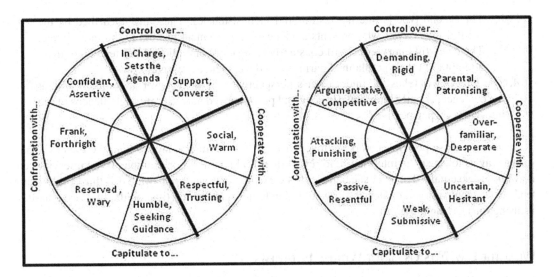

FIGURE 8.2[26]

Notice, first, that if you select the same triangle position from each circle you have a positive behavior (e.g. In Charge, Sets the Agenda) and a negative behavior (e.g. Demanding, Rigid). There was a strong statistical correlation between behaviors in each octant or quadrant of each circle. However, behaviors opposite one another were not highly correlated.[27]

Mathematical modeling revealed a complex relationship between rapport building behaviors and information yield. Generally, positive interviewer behaviors elicited positive interviewee behaviors and greater information yield.[28]

The secret to success with this method is for the interviewer to be self-aware and in control of their behaviors and to observe interviewee response to those behaviors. The interviewer must be constantly prepared to adjust as necessary to the interviewees observed behaviors.[29]

The Strategic Use of Evidence (SUE) method is based on an emerging body of scientific evidence focusing on the differences between liars and truth tellers' behaviors. There are four underlying principles to the SUE method:

1. The interviewee's perception of the evidence and the nature of the interview. Interviewee's who have something to hide will verbalize their thoughts about what the interviewer will be asking them. They will also share their perceptions of what evidence the interviewer may have.

2. The interviewees counter-interview strategy. Interviewees with something to hide will often plan their answers ahead of the interview. These answers may seem disingenuous or even nonsensical. In the latter case you will likely hear the interviewee say things like, "I can't explain it; that's just the way it is." They also will be hesitant to reveal information beyond what they perceive to be the minimum required to get the interviewer to move on. Interviewees with nothing to hide do not plan their answers. Also, they tend to be forthcoming in their answers; volunteering information they believe will be helpful to the interviewer and establish their good intentions.

3. The interviewee's responses. These can identify two types of deception:

   a. The first is testimony vs evidence inconsistencies. An example would be a situation in which the interviewee testifies that he or she has no knowledge of an event. The interviewer slides over a copy of an email describing the event sent by the interviewee. At this point, the interviewee usually says something like, "I didn't send that email; someone must have hacked into my account."

b. The second type is internal testimonial inconsistencies. These are unearthed by the skillful interviewer who presents evidence in a piecemeal fashion to the interviewee. The deceitful interviewee will constantly change or contradict earlier testimony in an attempt to fit their preplanned narrative to the evidence presented.

4. The interviewer takes the interviewee's perspective. The interviewer attempts to look at the evidence, counter interview strategy and preconceived narrative through the lens of the interviewee's perspective.[30]

SUE relies on these principles working together to enable the interviewer to plan the interview in such a way as to cause the interviewee to reveal their real nature.[31] For example, if the interviewee is aware of two emails that he or she believes to be exculpatory, but is not aware of a third email that tends to be inculpatory, the interviewer would plan to not spend much time on the first two emails, focusing, instead, on the third.

What the Law Tells Us about Witness Interviews

I need to begin this subsection with a disclaimer. I am not an attorney. I have no specialized education or licensing that would permit me to provide legal advice to anyone. What I am about to present in this subsection are the things I have heard and seen during my 40 years of conducting forensic accounting investigations. I do so, not to provide you with sound legal advice but, instead, to alert you to the issues that you should discuss with your own or the company's internal or external counsel.

First, it is important to respect and acknowledge the witness's rights and obligations. You should acquaint yourself with your company's policy on employees cooperating with internal investigations. Most organizations, of any size, have these and they usually require employees to cooperate with the company's internal investigation. You should make witnesses aware of these policies. However, that does not mean that you can compel anyone to testify or restrain them against their will. If after hearing the company's policy requiring cooperation with the internal investigation, they refuse to be interviewed and want to leave, let them go without further hindrance. Their refusal to be interviewed should be reported to internal or external counsel for further action.

If the employee does agree to be interviewed, it is important to inform the interviewee of the circumstances of the interview. The standard warning given to interviewees is called the Upjohn warning. The standard warning is named for a US Supreme Court case, Upjohn Co. vs United States, in which the court held that communications between company counsel and employees of the company are privileged, but the privilege is owned by the company and not the individual employee.[32] In an internal investigation, the company is the client and therefore controls the attorney client privilege. The purpose of the warning is to remove any doubt that the lawyer or the lawyer's supervised agent (i.e. you) speaking to the employee represents the company, and not the employee. I usually say that, "We represent the company and not you, Mr. or Ms. Interviewee." Anything revealed during the course of the interview is only privileged as between the lawyer and the company, not the interviewee. The interviewee has no control over whether the company decides to waive the privilege, which often may be done sometime in the future in the hope of obtaining cooperation credit from the government. I also say that the interviewee is not to discuss anything heard or said in the interview with anyone and that the interview must be kept completely confidential.

The Art of Witness Interviews

Now that we have been informed by the science, let's see how we apply this knowledge in the real world. Of course, I don't take advantage of every scientific principle in conducting witness interviews and neither will you. But it's important to be mindful of the science to inform our experiences and help us to improve our witness interview results. There is, however, also an art to properly conducting witness interviews and that's what we will talk about now.

How I Conduct Witness Interviews

As your experience and skill progress, you will develop your own method for conducting witness interviews; everyone does. It is a natural and usually beneficial process; in any case, you will not be able to prevent it. But, for starters, feel free to copy my method.

SECTION II: PREPARATION FOR THE INTERVIEW

Before I conduct a witness interview I try to learn everything I can about the witness and the circumstances I will be interviewing them about. I request relevant company records that can be shared with me. I do research to learn everything I can about the witness. I want to know about their background: where they're from, where did they go to school; what other positions have they held; are there any news stories about them; who are their friends, neighbors, immediate coworkers. I also analyze their job duties, authorities, and responsibilities. I want to know what they do; how they do it; whom do they do it with. All of this information will inform my interview plan for them.

I then gather all the documentary evidence I have in my possession that might be relevant to their firsthand knowledge of the subject(s) of the investigation. I organize all of this chronologically; I have found that witnesses tend to remember things in chronological order and those other contemporaneous events can actually improve their recall (i.e. "Oh yeah, I remember that now; I made the entry on the 31st; that also happens to be my birthday. I wanted to get it out of the way by the end of the day because I knew I would be celebrating pretty hard that night."). Of course, during the actual interview I often switch exhibits around to deal with changing answers and reactions from the witness. But I typically start with them in chronological order. I give unique identifiers to each exhibit (e.g. document name, date, or a number or letter).

Next, I begin to write either a list of topics I want to cover or actual questions I plan to ask the witness. This is done by reviewing the research I have done and my documentary evidence. The topics and questions, as we shall see later, are divided into the different phases of the interview but are still typically organized chronologically within each phase.

Finally, I make sure all the logistics are worked and that everyone is aware of them. I make sure the witness knows the date, place, and time of the interview. I visit the place where the interview will be conducted. Incidentally, there are pros and cons to interviewing a witness in their office or department versus a remote interview site. The pros to conducting the interview in the witness's office or department are lower expense and access to documents. The cons include: the witness believing he or she is in control of the interview; the interview could be overheard by coworkers; feel peer pressure to not cooperate with the investigation; identified for retaliation, etc. I have done both and all I can tell you is that you will have to be flexible, but be aware of the potential problems of each type of venue.

SECTION III: CONDUCTING THE INTERVIEW

I usually divide witness interviews into discreet phases. Each phase has a purpose and an objective. First, I make sure the room where the interview will be conducted is comfortable, well lit, quiet, and free of distractions. When the witness enters the room, I stand and introduce myself. I deliberately look the witness in the eye and try to move as close to the witness as possible without touching. After stating my name and introducing myself, I wait for the witness's response. What I am doing here is making careful note of the witness's baseline verbal and nonverbal communication characteristics. In particular, I want to observe the witness's:

- Willingness to be in close proximity with me;
- Ability to make and maintain eye contact with me;
- Response time;
- Body language (i.e. open with a relaxed demeanor or closed in a tense defensive posture);
- The speed, volume, cadence, and other characteristics of the witness's speech.

What I am calibrating is the witness's comfort or lack of comfort with my proximity to them, eye contact and overall state of relaxation or tension. When they respond to my introduction, I am listening for the speed of response, volume, cadence, pitch, and other observable characteristics.

At this point in our interaction, the witness should be somewhat tense, but without specific reason other than they are being interviewed. I make note of my observations for reference.

I will continue to make note of changes to these conditions throughout each phase of the interview. Changes in these characteristics indicate a change in the witness's reaction to the interview. They can identify information that the witness believes to be important or sensitive. These changes can also indicate points at which the witness is being deceptive.

Next, I ask the interviewee to sit, usually directly across from me. I immediately attempt to begin to build rapport. I ask the interviewee if he or she would like something to drink or anything else to make them more comfortable. I have everything I intend to use out of sight. I want the interviewee to focus on me, so I try to make sure there are no distractions in the room. I begin to make small talk. I will find something to compliment the interviewee about. I will ask them about their family, hobbies, job, likes, and dislikes. My demeanor is very casual and open. I often make some self-deprecating remark about myself. In addition to building rapport, I am gathering as much nonverbal communication information about the interviewee as I can. I will use the things I learn during this time to carefully mimic the interviewee's body language, speech patterns (e.g. accent, volume, cadence, timbre, etc.) to gain an understanding of the interviewee's likes and dislikes for use in presenting questions during the interview.

INVESTIGATOR NOTES

Mimicry in witness interviews is a powerful tool. It can allow the interviewer to slip behind the witness's instinctive native and other defenses to gather a great deal more useful detailed information than would have otherwise been possible. However, if done incorrectly, it can backfire and literally cause the witness to blow up in your face. Great witness interview mimicry is like great acting. Great actors all have one thing in common; they don't ever seem to be acting. We see them, on the screen, as the character they are portraying. My favorite recent example is Daniel Day Lewis' portrayal of Abraham Lincoln. I'm not saying you have to be that good, but, for every degree you feel you are missing the mark, you should increase your subtlety by two degrees. As with any skill, mimicry improves with correct practice. It's best to practice with others and to record the interaction for discussion and reflection. If you don't have anyone to practice with, you can record yourself.

Next, I pull out the materials I intend to use and make sure they are organized in the order I intend to present then to the witness. This also helps me to remember where documents are in case I need to show them to the witness out of order. I always make sure to have several tablets and pens available within easy reach.

I tell the witness that I would like our time together to be more like a conversation than an interview. I encourage the witness to make his or her answers as fulsome as possible and to interrupt me to provide information they think I should have about a question before moving to the next question. The purpose of an interview, which is very different from an interrogation, is to help the witness to communicate what they know in their own words.

I begin with easy questions about the witness's background. Things like: "Where were you born?" "Where did you go to college?" Once again, I am calibrating the witness's comfort or lack of comfort with my proximity to them, eye contact, and overall state of relaxation or tension. I am listening for the speed of response, volume, cadence, pitch, and other observable characteristics. This should be the time in the interview when the witness is most relaxed. So, the observations will form the baseline for my calibration of the witness's verbal and nonverbal reactions to my questions.

I gradually move to the questions that relate to the subjects at the heart of the investigation. Here I want to ask questions that will help the witness provide as much detailed information about the subjects of the investigation as possible. I use documents and other knowledge that I have gained to help the witness recover and communicate their memories about the events I am asking them about. I want to know:

- Who was involved?
- What happened?
- When did it happen?
- Where did it happen?
- Why did it happen?
- What the witness thought about the event(s)?

As I ask the questions, I continue to calibrate the witness's comfort or lack of comfort with my proximity to them, eye contact, and overall state of relaxation or tension.

Generally, if the witness's verbal and nonverbal reactions to my questions continue to be in line with the baseline I established earlier, I will continue at the same pace allowing the witness to communicate what they know in a relaxed open dialogue. The only thing I will do is if the witness seems to be getting significantly off track, I will gently steer them back to the information that is relevant to the investigation. I will also ask clarifying questions to make sure that I fully understand what the witness is telling me.

However, if the witness's verbal and nonverbal reactions begin to change, I will change my approach in response. First, I will slow down and continue to ask more open-ended questions about the matter that caused the change in the witness's reactions. I will take care not to let the witness steer us away from the troubling topic, but continue to come back to it with more open-ended questions. Questions like, "So, tell me more about this accounting entry." or "How do you know that Mr. Smith was the only person to have access to the terminal that night?" I also use silence. Human beings cannot stand silence when in conversation with others; they simply must fill the void with their words. Try this experiment: begin a conversation with someone; ask them an open ended question; let them respond and then remain silent; see what happens.

So, the technique is to ask an open-ended question and then just sit silently, maintaining eye contact with the witness. Continue this as long as the witness continues to speak. After the witness stops speaking, wait for thirty seconds or more to see if the witness will resume speaking. This will be a somewhat challenging, but ultimately rewarding exercise.

This is also the time to use the documents you have brought to use as exhibits. Ideally, you would ask open-ended questions based on the document you have selected. Let the witness finish his or her answer and note how the answer(s) does and does not square with the contents of the document. Once the witness finishes their answer, I begin to ask clarifying questions to make sure I understood exactly what they said. I also ask questions designed to lock them into the answers they have given me, such as, "Now, I want to make sure that I understand your answer; you're sure that the revenue you recorded was for products that were delivered to purchasers on December 26th?" I will also ask more open-ended questions like, "How did you know the products were, in fact, delivered on December 26th?" Once I have them staked out on the answers I know to be incorrect, I slide the document (e.g. bill of lading, other delivery records; often printed copies of electronic records) across to the witness. I ask them to review the document. Then, I ask them why their answers are different from the information contained in the document. This is a great time to be silent. Let the weight of what has just happened really sink in before you speak. After a sufficiently awkward time you can ask whether they would now like to change their earlier answers.

It is important to really nail these answers down. You want to leave no wiggle room for the witness later on. Remain friendly, even affirm the witness by saying things like, "I can see how it would be difficult for you to talk about this with me. I'm certain anyone would find this difficult. But, it's important for all of us to know the truth. So, please tell me in your own words exactly what did happen?" At this point, one of two things will happen: They will tell you what actually did happen or they will get up and say they want to end the interview. Either outcome is a victory for the interviewer. Either you get the testimony you have been seeking or, at least, an inference that if the witness answered the question truthfully, he or she would have provided testimony that would have been detrimental to them.

INVESTIGATOR NOTES

Notice that in the preceding paragraphs, I said nothing about the witness's testimony being truthful or a lie. The reason is, as we shall see later, it is not up to the investigator to opine on the voracity of testimony; that is the job of the ultimate trier of fact. We simply point out the discrepancies between the witness testimony and the other available evidence.

It is important to assign a specific identifier to each document shown to the witness. It is also important to clearly associate the correct document with the related witness testimony in your interview notes.

I always end my witness interviews with the same question. For the cooperative witness, this question is like a license to finally tell someone the thing(s) that they have had on their chest for a long time and have been dying to tell someone. It can often produce lightning in a bottle; very powerful. This question can literally be the key to discovering answers you didn't even know to ask questions about. So, what is this magical question? Here it is, "Is there anything I have not asked you about that you believe I should know or would like to tell me?" A simple, powerful question but, surprisingly, a question that is often not asked. Asking this question costs nothing; not asking it could cost a great deal.

SECTION IV: MEMORIALIZING THE INTERVIEW

I make sure that I have several notepads and at least two pens. I never record interviews for two important reasons: One is that, in the absence of the visual cues (e.g. expression, demeanor, body language, etc.) it can be easy to misunderstand the meaning of a witness's answer. For, example, think about someone asking you about your favorite opera; if you don't like opera, you might answer, "The ones I haven't seen or heard.", with a slight grin. Someone hearing that answer without the benefit of seeing the facial expressions might conclude that the witness has a budding passion for opera when the opposite is true.

The second reason is I want my notes to represent the best evidence of what was said by the witness during the interview. I usually begin with questions I believe will be easy for the witness to answer. I also often explain to the witness why I am asking certain types of questions. I often begin with questions about the witness's background. I also encourage the witness to tell me all they know about the subject of the answer to a particular question.

SECTION V: WRITING THE INTERVIEW REPORT

I normally type up my witness interview notes shortly after completing the interview. The reason I do this is because I want my memory of what occurred in the interview to be fresh. I find the ease of writing the report worth the effort of doing so shortly after the interview concludes. The header of the report usually is something like, "Interview of John Doe". In the upper right corner of the report, I include the date, place, and start and stop times for the interview. I usually use 12 pt, type with 1.5 line spacing. I put my handwritten interview notes into an envelope which I attach to a printed version of my typewritten interview report.

EXERCISES

1. What are the things you must never do when interviewing witnesses?
2. How can science help us to conduct more effective interviews?
3. What are some of the factors that determine the interactions between interviewer and witness?
4. What are some motives that drive witness behaviors?
5. What witness behaviors flow from these motivations?
6. Why is the intensity of responses important to guage?
7. What drives high intensity responses?
8. Do high intensity responses make it more or less likely to conduct an effective interview?
9. What is sensemaking and how can it help us to conduct more effective interviews?
10. Write down witness behaviors (i.e. motivational frame reactions and intensity) you recall from past interviews or can imagine.
11. Construct a Cylindrical Model. Now, identify, based on your answers to exercise 10, in which motivational frame and at what intensity level the witness behaviors would place them.
12. What does your work in exercise 11 tell you about the underlying motivations for the witness behaviors?
13. What does your work in exercise 11 tell you about the underlying motivations for the witness intensity level?
14. What is style matching? How can you use it to get more cooperation from witnesses?
15. What must happen in order for you to move an avoidant witness to a cooperative orientation?
16. What are ways in which you can help the witness to have a paradigm shift?
17. What is social reciprocity?
18. Write out an example of social reciprocity from an interview you can recall or imagine.
19. What is the cognitive interview method?
20. What is the strategic use of evidence method (SUE)?
21. Write down examples of SUE techniques you have or could imagine employing.
22. What is an Upjohn warning? Why must you provide one to witnesses you interview?
23. What are steps you could take to learn about the witness ahead of the interview?
24. Write a list of interview questions for an innocent witness to an expense report fraud?
25. What phases would you divide a witness interview into?
26. What do you want to observe about a witness in each phase of the interview?
27. What do you want to calibrate about the witness at the outset of the interview?
28. Mimicry is an intense form of style matching.
    a. What important benefits can it provide?
    b. What can go wrong and what would the consequences be?

29. List the key questions that must be answered by the interview?
30. What are open-ended questions?
31. Write an open-ended interview question.
32. How will you memorialize the interview?
33. Why is it important to prepare an interview report?

CHAPTER SUMMARY/KEY TAKEAWAYS

So, here are some things to think about:

- Always approach witness interviews in a completely professional manner.
- Be aware of and follow all laws, regulations, and ethical canons.
- Make sure the witness is made aware of the items in the Upjohn warning.
- Know the science of interviewing and use it to learn from your real world experiences.
- Do the research.
- Plan carefully for the interview.
- Conduct the interview in an environment that, to the extent possible, is free from distractions.
- Take handwritten notes. If someone insists on recording, request video as well.
- Calibrate verbal and nonverbal reactions; be alert to changes in reactions.
- When changes are noted, slow down and focus on questions about the topics that caused the changes.
- Use silence to leverage witness responses.
- Create questions that will lock the witness into answers that are inconsistent with information contained in documents.
- Identify specific discrepancies and run them to ground.
- Ask them if there is anything else they believe you should know.
- Write your report shortly after the interview and attach your handwritten notes.

In Chapter 9 you will learn to conduct a proper forensic analysis of the evidence.

NOTES

1. Interrogation: A Review of the Science; High-Value Detainee Interrogation Group; September 2016, Foreword page 1.
2. Interrogation: A Review of the Science; High-Value Detainee Interrogation Group; September 2016, Page 9.
3. Interrogation: A Review of the Science; High-Value Detainee Interrogation Group; September 2016, Page 9.
4. Interrogation: A Review of the Science; High-Value Detainee Interrogation Group; September 2016, Page 9.
5. Interrogation: A Review of the Science; High-Value Detainee Interrogation Group; September 2016, Page 9.
6. Interrogation: A Review of the Science; High-Value Detainee Interrogation Group; September 2016, Page 9.
7. Interrogation: A Review of the Science; High-Value Detainee Interrogation Group; September 2016, Page 9.
8. Interrogation: A Review of the Science; High-Value Detainee Interrogation Group; September 2016, Page 9.
9. Interrogation: A Review of the Science; High-Value Detainee Interrogation Group; September 2016, Page 10.
10. Interrogation: A Review of the Science; High-Value Detainee Interrogation Group; September 2016, Page 10.

11. Interrogation: A Review of the Science; High-Value Detainee Interrogation Group; September 2016, Page 10.
12. Interrogation: A Review of the Science; High-Value Detainee Interrogation Group; September 2016, Page 12.
13. Interrogation: A Review of the Science; High-Value Detainee Interrogation Group; September 2016, Page 14.
14. Interrogation: A Review of the Science; High-Value Detainee Interrogation Group; September 2016, Page 14.
15. Interrogation: A Review of the Science; High-Value Detainee Interrogation Group; September 2016, Page 15.
16. Interrogation: A Review of the Science; High-Value Detainee Interrogation Group; September 2016, Page 15.
17. Interrogation: A Review of the Science; High-Value Detainee Interrogation Group; September 2016, Page 15.
18. Interrogation: A Review of the Science; High-Value Detainee Interrogation Group; September 2016, Page 15.
19. Interrogation: A Review of the Science; High-Value Detainee Interrogation Group; September 2016, Page 15.
20. Interrogation: A Review of the Science; High-Value Detainee Interrogation Group; September 2016, Page 15.
21. Interrogation: A Review of the Science; High-Value Detainee Interrogation Group; September 2016, Page 17.
22. Interrogation: A Review of the Science; High-Value Detainee Interrogation Group; September 2016, Pages 18–19.
23. Interrogation: A Review of the Science; High-Value Detainee Interrogation Group; September 2016, Page 24.
24. Interrogation: A Review of the Science; High-Value Detainee Interrogation Group; September 2016, Page 24.
25. Interrogation: A Review of the Science; High-Value Detainee Interrogation Group; September 2016, Page 24.
26. Interrogation: A Review of the Science; High-Value Detainee Interrogation Group; September 2016, Page 25–26.
27. Interrogation: A Review of the Science; High-Value Detainee Interrogation Group; September 2016, Page 25–26.
28. Interrogation: A Review of the Science; High-Value Detainee Interrogation Group; September 2016, Page 25–26.
29. Interrogation: A Review of the Science; High-Value Detainee Interrogation Group; September 2016, Page 25–26.
30. Interrogation: A Review of the Science; High-Value Detainee Interrogation Group; September 2016, Page 27–28.
31. Interrogation: A Review of the Science; High-Value Detainee Interrogation Group; September 2016, Page 27–28.
32. Upjohn Co. v. United States, 449 U.S. 383 (1981).

9 Conducting a Forensic Analysis of the Evidence

SECTION I: FRAMING THE QUESTIONS THAT MUST BE ANSWERED WITH THE EVIDENCE

I received a phone call from defense lawyers representing a young woman, formerly a Big 4 auditor, who was the director of external reporting for a publicly traded company. I learned that, among other things, she had three small children and a husband who had serious health problems. She had never been in any trouble before. Her relevant conduct in this case, by all accounts, was limited to answering questions emailed to her by the company's chief financial officer related to the application of Generally Accepted Accounting Principles (GAAP) to specific transactions. Every company employee who testified said that when they wanted the correct GAAP answer, they would ask this young woman because she always gave the correct GAAP answer. Nevertheless, when the CFO was indicted for securities fraud and other crimes, she was indicted for securities fraud, wire fraud, and obstruction of justice.

The prosecutor's opening statement included the following:

> As accountants, the defendants' job was to get the numbers right. But that's not what they did, Your Honor. Instead of getting the numbers right, what the defendants did was engage in an accounting fraud scheme to make the numbers what they wanted them to be, not what the numbers should have been. The defendants reverse-engineered the numbers at the registrant to support a growth story and to make the numbers match what the registrant told the bank the numbers would be. How did they do it? They did it by exploiting the gray areas of accounting, those areas that require judgment. They did it by booking fraudulent, unsupported entries to increase earnings until they got to their number. And once they got to their number, Your Honor, they stopped.

Whoa, that's quite the scathing indictment; pardon the pun. So, what questions did I need to answer from the evidence? Well, the prosecutor laid out the direct questions in the indictment. Namely, did this woman cause a series of identified accounting entries to the books and records of this public company that were not in accordance with GAAP? But, there were other questions. Was this woman included in email chains in which her boss used unfortunate terms like: "cookie jar reserves," "a rainy-day fund," and other fun cooking the books terms? Did the whistleblower make his concerns known to this woman? Where were the auditors? Did their Consideration of Fraud steps unearth anything? What did they do about it?

My analysis of this woman's application of GAAP, to the transactions identified in the indictment, revealed that she faithfully applied GAAP as required by Section 108 of the Sarbanes-Oxley Act of 2002. She was not included in the bad email chains. The whistleblower even testified that when he had a question about GAAP, he always went to her because, "She always gave the correct answer." In the end, she was acquitted of securities fraud, wire fraud, and obstruction of justice. But can you think of another job that is more dangerous than being an accountant for a public company in America? You can get indicted for doing your job.

Every investigation is different and there will be different questions to answer depending on the nature of the issues you are investigating. However, you need to employ the discipline of writing out questions that your investigation or other forensic accounting analysis will seek to answer. The first reason to do this is to make sure that the lawyers supervising your efforts, and the management of

DOI: 10.1201/9781003121558-11

your company who commissioned the investigation or analysis, agree that you have identified the correct questions to answer. The other reason is that investigations uncover all sorts of interesting things that are irrelevant to the matter you are investigating.

INVESTIGATOR NOTES

Always begin your investigation with the end in mind. Make sure that you go over the questions that your investigation will answer with the person or persons who retained you to conduct the investigation. This is critical because you may be seeking to answer questions that are not relevant. Also, your client may want questions answered that you have not included in your list. Again, I always ask the following question: If this turns out exactly as you would like it to, what would that look like? Then I propose the questions that my investigation will be designed to answer. I go over these, in detail, with the client. Then I write them out and send them to the client to make sure we are in agreement before proceeding.

SECTION II: CREATING A FORENSIC ANALYSIS WORKPLAN

The IIA has specific requirements for internal audit engagement and supervision:

"2240 – Engagement Work Program
Internal auditors must develop and document work programs that achieve the engagement objectives.

2240.A1 – Work programs must include the procedures for identifying, analyzing, evaluating, and documenting information during the engagement. The work program must be approved prior to its implementation, and any adjustments approved promptly.

2240.C1 – Work programs for consulting engagements may vary in form and content depending upon the nature of the engagement.

2300 – Performing the Engagement
Internal auditors must identify, analyze, evaluate, and document sufficient information to achieve the engagement's objectives.

2340 – Engagement Supervision
Engagements must be properly supervised to ensure objectives are achieved, quality is assured, and staff is developed."[1]

So, the IIA requires that the engagement be planned to achieve the objectives agreed upon with management and/or the board. There must be a work program that includes the procedures to be executed to achieve the objectives. Also, the investigation must be supervised to assure that the objectives are achieved, quality is assured, and staff are developed.

"Interpretation
The extent of supervision required will depend on the proficiency and experience of internal auditors and the complexity of the engagement. The chief audit executive has overall responsibility for supervising the engagement, whether performed by or for the internal audit activity, but may designate appropriately experienced members of the internal audit activity to perform the review. Appropriate evidence of supervision is documented and retained."[2]

You will need to create a written workplan that sets out how you will go about collecting and analyzing the evidence you will use to answer the questions you have agreed to answer. The amount of detail in the workplan depends on two competing forces. The first is the experience level of your staff. Inexperienced staff will require a more detailed workplan than experienced staff. The other force is the concern about the amount of detail that would be revealed if the workplan were the subject of an effective discovery motion by the other side.

The following was a workplan I used for a major investigation (see Figure 9.1). In this case, I had a very experienced staff and there were severe concerns about discovery issues. So, the workplan was very spartan.

PHASE I - Gather and Analyze Available Evidence, Make Preliminary Recommendations		
Purpose, Objectives and Deliverables:		
1 Initial Information Gathering and Analysis		
Initial Information Gathering and Consulting with Attorney:	Meet with Attorney to obtain relevant materials to learn everything possible about the nature of the matter, the subject and the existing valuation report. Work with attorney to develop document request.	$
Initial Analyses and Recommendations:	Read all materials provided by attorney. Make preliminary analyses. Research available public information repositories and other resources to obtain relevant information. Consult with Attorney regarding observations.	$
2 Perform Business Valuation		
Gather Additional Evidence	Gather additional available evidence.	$
Analysis and Evaluation	Analyze and evaluate available evidence.	$
Site Visit	Travel to subject for inspection and interviews with management	$
Perform Research	Research relevant data for business valuation.	$
Business Valuation	Perform business valuation and write report.	$

FIGURE 9.1

I also had very experienced staff working on this case. However, since it was arbitration, the discovery concerns were less significant (see Figure 9.2).

PHASE I - INFORMATION GATHERING AND DOCUMENT REQUESTS

Purpose, Objectives and Deliverables:

Develop our understanding of the chronological sequence of relevant events (i.e. construction activities, project issues, work scope, non-conforming work, etc.) and all related information: oral, documentary or other; available to inform our analysis. This information will likely first come from Client personnel (until Defendant produces its records in the arbitration), and will be largely focused on the Defendant documentation that is in Client's possession. We will, of course, work closely with Client personnel and Law Firm to find the most effective means to develop this information. We will begin by analyzing real world activities on the project activities identified in invoices, and available supporting documentation, in order to compare it to what would commonly be expected in the industry under similar circumstances. This will inform our analysis of costs and damages, including amounts Defendant is seeking, the adequacy of Defendant's backup for its claims, and to confirm amounts that Client seeks through its counterclaims based on Defendant's own estimates to repair and/or complete its work. From these analyses we will construct Gantt or other appropriate models and related analyses to develop a basis for Mr. Jennings expert opinions and to inform Client & Law Firm.

1 **Information Gathering, Evaluation and Analysis**

Senior Principal
Principal
Senior Manager
Manager
Senior Associate
Analyst
Total

Mr. Jennings will gather all documentation in Client's possession related to the claim under the supervision of Law Firm, with assigned Client personnel. Mr. Jennings expects to spend considerable time consulting with client personnel knowledgeable about the project and Defendant activities.

2 **Assist in Identifying Documents to Request from Defendant**

Senior Principal
Principal
Senior Manager
Manager
Senior Associate
Analyst
Total

Mr. Jennings will assist Law Firm in drafting detailed document requests for Defendant to further development of the above-referenced opinions. Mr. Jennings may also assist Law Firm in developing objections to Defendant's document requests. Mr. Jennings may begin to provide additional services such as witness identification, witness interviews, and application of industry knowledge to emerging issues.

Total Phase I

PHASE II - REVIEW DOCUMENTS

Purpose, Objectives and Deliverables:

Analyze all of the relevant information Defendant produces, including information not necessarily admitted into evidence in the arbitration, but of the type normally relied on by experts like Mr. Jennings. Mr. Jennings will also rely on the work of other experts in arriving at his expert opinions, including Client's technical experts. Where possible, Mr. Jennings will employ electronic tools to make his document analysis more efficient. Mr. Jennings will refine the Gantt or other appropriate models and related analyses, and begin to construct his expert report of his opinions related to Defendant's claim and the amounts of Client's counterclaim damages.

3 **Review of Documents Defendant Produces**

Senior Principal
Principal
Senior Manager
Manager
Senior Associate
Analyst

Mr. Jennings will analyze Defendant's document production and use the results of this work to further refine the Gantt type model and expert findings.

Total

4 **Assist Law Firm in Drafting Client Statement of Defense and Identifying / Interviewing Potential Fact Witnesses**

Senior Principal
Principal
Senior Manager
Manager
Senior Associate
Analyst
Total

Mr. Jennings will assist Law Firm in incorporating expert finding into Law Firm's submissions to the Tribunal on behalf of Client. Mr. Jennings will also assist, under Law Firm's supervision and with Client approval, in identifying fact witnesses and developing questions for those witnesses for purposes of Client direct testimony and cross examination of Defendant witnesses.

5 **Assist in Analyzing Fact Witness Statements and Reviewing/Editing Statement of Defense**

Senior Principal
Principal
Senior Manager
Manager
Senior Associate
Analyst
Total

Mr. Jennings will work with Law Firm and Client personnel to evaluate and analyze fact witness statements. In particular, Mr. Jennings will correlate fact witness statements with other evidence and Mr. Jennings' own expert findings. Mr. Jennings will continue to work with Law Firm on Client's statement of Defense and Counterclaims.

Total Phase II

PHASE III - EXPERT TESTIMONY

Purpose, Objectives and Deliverables:

Develop Mr. Jennings' written expert testimony, related exhibits and list of information relied upon in reaching his expert opinions. This work will also be subjected to appropriate peer review prior to issuance. The work will address Mr. Jennings' opinions related to the amount of Defendant's claims, the adequacy of supporting backup material for Defendant's claims, and the damages amounts of Client's counterclaims

6 **Drafting Expert Report**

Senior Principal
Principal
Senior Manager
Manager
Senior Associate
Analyst

Mr. Jennings will work with Law Firm and Client personnel to complete all of his analyses and perform all required quality control procedures. Mr. Jennings will draft his expert report, integrating all relevant analyses and exhibits.

FIGURE 9.2

Here is another example of a workplan that is going to be executed by experienced staff.

TABLE 9.1
Workplan

Database analyses
Conversations to understand payroll data and choose appropriate compensation metric
Reconcile additional data upon receipt of new payroll and/or scorecard data
Clean and prepare database for analysis
Run regressions and analyze results
Confirm scorecard metrics in Excel documents using Access database and missing forms
Footnote outlying observations for qualitative metrics
Discussion of results with counsel and client
Subtotal

Summarize and report findings
Summarize and review results
Prepare opinions/report
Prepare supporting exhibits

The point being that the workplan only has to be detailed enough to allow you to appropriately communicate your requirements to staff. But not so detailed as to a problem if it is the subject of a successful discovery motion.

SECTION III: CREATING EFFECTIVE WORK PAPER SYSTEMS TO SUPPORT FINDINGS AND CONCLUSIONS

In criminal or civil litigation, you must be able to quickly access physical and electronic documents and other evidence to support your conclusions and opinions. You need an effective system to connect your conclusions and opinions, through intermediary analyses and summations, to the underlying detailed evidence. It should work like this.

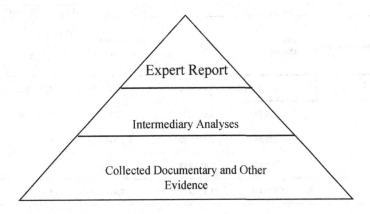

FIGURE 9.3

So at the top of the pyramid we have the Expert Report. The report is where all your conclusions and opinions will appear. The report would typically contain one or more summary exhibits like the one that follows.

This schedule was an actual exhibit to an expert report in a case that was brought in US District Court by a regulator. I was hired by the lawyers representing the defendant, a financial services firm. This exhibit was based on an analysis I prepared to demonstrate that the financial services firm had complied with the agreements it had signed with its investors.

	Actual			Hypothetical "2 and 20" Fee Method Based on NAV			Difference Between Actual and Hypothetical "2 and 20" Method Based on NAV
	Management Fee	Incentive Allocation	Total	Hypothetical Management Fee[1]	Hypothetical Incentive Allocation[2]	Total	
2013	$ -	$ 7,634,408	$ 7,634,408	$ 2,488,255	$ 9,818,382	$ 12,306,637	$ (4,672,228)
2014	-	6,920,232	6,920,232	3,204,658	3,445,286	6,649,944	270,288
2015	-	6,228,960	6,228,960	2,944,674	6,258,278	9,202,952	2,973,992
2016 through May	-	1,486,858	1,486,858	1,338,556	-	1,338,556	148,302
	$ -	$ 22,270,458	$ 22,270,458	$ 9,976,143	$ 19,521,946	$ 29,498,089	$ (1,279,646)

FIGURE 9.4

Now, let's see where these numbers came from. I am going to select cells and show you how they are cross-referenced to cells in intermediary analyses and summaries. Notice the $7,634,408 Incentive Allocation amount in the schedule above. I am going to show you the formula line that caused information from an intermediary schedule to be summarized to derive this amount.

D7   =SUMIF('Exhibit 1.2'!$C:$C,'Exhibit 1.1'!$A7,'Exhibit 1.2'!$L:$L)

	Actual			Hypothetical "2 and 20" Fee Method Based on NAV		
	Management Fee	Incentive Allocation	Total	Hypothetical Management Fee[1]	Hypothetical Incentive Allocation[2]	Total
2013	$ -	$ 7,634,408	$ 7,634,408	$ 2,488,255	$ 9,818,382	$ 12,306,637
2014	-	6,920,232	6,920,232	3,204,658	3,445,286	6,649,944
2015	-	6,228,960	6,228,960	2,944,674	6,258,278	9,202,952
2016 through May	-	1,486,858	1,486,858	1,338,556	-	1,338,556
	$ -	$ 22,270,458	$ 22,270,458	$ 9,976,143	$ 19,521,946	$ 29,498,088

FIGURE 9.5

Now let's look at the next level down in our pyramid. I will now show you the information in the next level down schedule that was summarized. Notice that the numbers in column L, in the schedule below, sum to $7,634,408.

Period	Month	Year	End of Month NAV	Realized Trading Gains/(Losses)	Change in Unrealized Gaines/(Losses)	Total Monthly Gains/(Losses)	Cummulative Change in Gains/(Losses)	Total Monthly Gains/(Losses) High Water Mark	Hypothetical Management Fee	Hypothetical Incentive Allocation	Actual Incentive Allocation	Difference Between Actual Incentive Allocation and Hypothetical "20 and 20" Method Based on NAV	Sum of Column L Values
Dec-12	Dec	2012	$ 79,379,541				$ 9,848,904	$ 9,261,223					
Jan-13	Jan	2013	96,409,215	1,919,556	13,887,296	15,806,851	25,655,756	6,545,629	160,682	1,309,126	←'Form (_NDGA-00015807)'!l114		
Feb-13	Feb	2013	108,128,047	1,496,309	5,349,303	6,845,612	32,501,368		180,213	1,369,122	299,262		
Mar-13	Mar	2013	104,078,401	3,761,269	(7,430,397)	(3,669,128)	28,832,240		173,464		752,254		
Apr-13	Apr	2013	110,033,590	3,739,625	6,157,128	9,896,753	38,728,993	6,227,625	183,389	1,245,525	747,925		
May-13	May	2013	103,593,911	3,486,731	(11,068,491)	(7,581,760)	31,147,233		172,657	-	697,346		
Jun-13	Jun	2013	120,667,510	2,332,347	15,232,886	17,565,233	48,712,466	9,983,473	201,113	1,996,695	466,469		
Jul-13	Jul	2013	129,369,438	3,985,849	231,460	4,217,309	52,929,775		215,616	843,462	797,170		
Aug-13	Aug	2013	132,440,738	3,333,755	(771,655)	2,562,100	55,491,875		220,735	512,420	666,751		
Sep-13	Sep	2013	135,489,321	3,353,810	(146,030)	3,207,780	58,699,655		225,816	641,556	670,762		
Oct-13	Oct	2013	147,449,833	3,590,021	(1,352,276)	2,237,745	60,937,400		245,750	447,549	718,004		
Nov-13	Nov	2013	149,609,681	2,319,449	(1,221,082)	1,098,367	62,035,767		249,349	219,673	463,890		
Dec-13	Dec	2013	155,683,033	4,853,320	1,312,590	6,166,270	68,202,037		259,472	1,233,254	970,664	$ (4,672,228)	7,634,408

FIGURE 9.6

Okay, now let's move down to the next level. Where did the numbers in column L, in the schedule above, come from? Let's look at the formula bar and see.

We will now move one more step down to "Form (_NDGA-00015807)."

		Beginning Capital	Capital Contribution	Capital Distribution	Revised Capital Account	Member Interest	Gross Realized Gain(Loss)	20% Expenses	Net Realiz
1	Prior Yrs		92,299,128	(16,997,716)			32,106,129	(6,421,224)	25,684,
2									
3	2013								
4	January	100,986,313	2,351,291	(1,700,840)	101,636,765	100.00%	1,919,556	(383,911)	1,535,
5	February	103,172,409	4,635,378	(3,028,644)	104,779,143	100.00%	1,496,309	(299,262)	1,197,
6	March	105,976,190	7,012,481	(1,840,000)	111,148,671	100.00%	3,761,269	(752,254)	3,009,
7	April	114,157,686	656,735	(285,000)	114,529,422	100.00%	3,739,625	(747,925)	2,991,
8	May	117,521,122	16,606,653	(19,800,291)	114,327,483	100.00%	3,486,731	(697,346)	2,789,
9	June	117,116,868	1,926,927	(87,500)	118,956,295	100.00%	2,332,347	(466,469)	1,865,
10	July	120,822,173	710,167	(735,331)	120,797,009	100.00%	3,985,849	(797,170)	3,188,
11	August	123,985,689	5,607,134	(323,000)	129,269,823	100.00%	3,333,755	(666,751)	2,667,
12	September	131,936,827	2,721,445	(1,545,494)	133,112,779	100.00%	3,353,810	(670,762)	2,683,
13	October	135,795,827	682,566	(171,000)	136,307,392	100.00%	3,590,021	(718,004)	2,872,
14	November	139,179,409	10,883,771	(443,000)	149,620,180	100.00%	2,319,449	(463,890)	1,855,
15	December	151,475,739	2,498,950	(973,580)	153,001,109	100.00%	4,853,320	(970,664)	3,882,
16	Jan 2014		49,999	(9,000)					
17	Total 2013		56,293,499	(30,933,680)			38,172,041	(7,634,408)	30,537,
18									
19	Grand Total		148,592,626	(47,931,396)			70,278,170	(14,055,633)	56,222,
20									
21	Curr Mo + 1		1,031,746	(154,000)					
21	YTD Adj		54,973,954	(29,386,840)					

FIGURE 9.7

Look at the numbers contained in the Form (_NDGA-00015807). This is an official form filed with the financial institution's regulator from whom we obtained it. This Form is prepared and filed on a regular basis as part of the normal operation of the financial institution's business, and therefore admissible under the federal rules of evidence as we discussed in Chapters 6 and 7. So, we have now worked our way from the report to the underlying individual pieces of evidence upon which it is based in an orderly easily reproducible fashion.

Each of these components has to be cross-referenced to the others. This allows you to move from the highest level of analysis and summation to the most discreet piece of underlying evidence. This is very important at trial where it is a requirement that you be able to produce the detailed evidence supporting your conclusions and opinions. In the example I presented above, the cross-referencing was accomplished by electronic means. If you are dealing with paper documents or other evidence you could not digitize, you would be required to accomplish the cross-referencing by hand.

SECTION IV: ANALYTICAL TOOLS COMMONLY USED IN FRAUD INVESTIGATION

The majority owner of a newspaper and cellist was quite the lyric opera devotee. As the fortunes of his newspaper sank slowly below the waves, he buoyed his spirits by immersing himself and his flagging company into the Pirates of Penzance and other lyric opera flights of fancy. At a time when the newspaper was facing financial ruin, he was spending enormous amounts of its money propping up the local lyric opera.

As a result, the large corporate minority shareholder filed suit against the newspaper and its directors alleging fraud, waste, and mismanagement. In this litigation, the forensic accountants were asked to formulate opinions in response to the following questions:

- Whether any transactions in the books and records of the newspaper demonstrated a wasting of corporate assets?
- Whether any such transactions indicate that corporate funds were being used to further the individual defendants' personal interests rather than the newspaper's corporate interests?
- Whether any transactions bore any "badges of fraud"?
- The amounts of damages sustained by the newspaper with respect to each of the transactions referred to above.

Through a review of thousands of documents, pages of sworn testimony and applying forensic accounting analytical tools to the financial records of the newspaper, the accountants were able to identify numerous transactions and entries in the records for which there was no clear business purpose. Those transactions amounted to tens of millions of dollars.

The forensic accountants were able to identify and testify regarding the following badges of fraud:

- Significant, unusual, or highly complex transactions that pose difficult "substance over form" questions.
- Significant related-party transactions not in the ordinary course of business.
- Overly complex organizational structure involving unusual legal entities or managerial lines of authority.
- Unrecorded transactions or missing records.
- Unusual financial statement relationships.
- Transactions not consistent with the entity's business.
- Employees in close association with suppliers or customers.
- Inadequate explanation to investors.
- Domination of management by a single individual or small group.

Specifically, the investigation revealed that the defendants had engaged in unusually significant and highly complex transactions that had no clear business purpose, which were recorded as "promotion" expenses. In reality, these "promotion" expenses provided the individual defendants with personal benefits at the expense of the newspaper's financial wellbeing. In one instance, $20 million was spent to purchase the naming rights to a planned lyric opera building long before it was even constructed.

Other interesting findings by the accountants included the determination that over fifty of the newspaper's employees were spending 100% of their time providing services to other entities and not to the newspaper. These employees received almost ten million US dollars in compensation during this period. In fact, the defendant gave testimony indicating that many of the lyric opera employees received their paychecks through the newspaper. The plaintiff, who was a shareholder with a 45% share in the newspaper, never received information about any of these activities.

Following a lengthy bench trial, the court found in favor of the plaintiff. The judge specifically ruled that there was a wasting of corporate assets and that the plaintiff had been defrauded.

When using forensic accounting analytical tools to identify where fraud might exist in a business, it is usually best to start at the outside and work inward. Beginning with the business' financial statements will often reveal areas to peer into more deeply. On a macro level, vertical analysis and horizontal analysis of financial statements are useful to identify unusual relationships in financial statements. Vertical analysis is a technique for evaluating the relationships between the items on the financial statements for one reporting period. The analysis highlights the relationships between components of the financial statements expressed as percentages that can then be compared across periods. Another term used for this technique is creating common size financial statements. In the vertical analysis of an income statement, net sales is assigned 100%; for a balance sheet, total assets is assigned 100% on the asset side, and total liabilities and equity is expressed as 100% on the other side. All other items in each of the sections are expressed as a percentage of these numbers.

Let's take a look at my favorite company Costco.

TABLE 9.2

Costco Wholesale Corp.

Common-Size Consolidated Balance Sheet: Assets

	Aug 30, 2020	Sep 1, 2019	Sep 2, 2018
Cash and cash equivalents	22.10%	18.47%	14.83%
Short-term investments	1.85%	2.33%	2.95%
Receivables, net	2.79%	3.38%	4.09%
Merchandise inventories	22.04%	25.10%	27.04%
Other current assets	1.84%	2.45%	0.79%
Current assets	**50.62%**	**51.73%**	**49.69%**
Property and equipment, net	39.25%	46.01%	48.20%
Operating lease right-of-use assets	5.02%	—	—
Other long-term assets	5.11%	2.26%	2.11%
Long-term assets	**49.38%**	**48.27%**	**50.31%**
Total assets	**100.00%**	**100.00%**	**100.00%**

Here, we can easily see the percentage of total assets that each asset account represents. We can see, for instance, that while current assets have maintained a relatively steady percentage of total assets, receivables, and inventory have decreased while cash has increased; a very positive trend.

TABLE 9.3

Costco Wholesale Corp.

Common-size Consolidated Balance Sheet: Liabilities and Stockholders' Equity

	Aug 30, 2020	Sep 1, 2019	Sep 2, 2018
Accounts payable	25.51%	25.72%	27.52%
Accrued salaries and benefits	6.49%	7.00%	7.33%
Accrued member rewards	2.51%	2.60%	2.59%
Deferred membership fees	3.33%	3.77%	3.98%
Current portion of long-term debt	0.17%	3.74%	0.22%
Other current liabilities	6.71%	8.35%	7.16%
Current liabilities	**44.72%**	**51.18%**	**48.80%**
Long-term debt, excluding current portion	13.53%	11.29%	15.89%
Long-term operating lease liabilities	4.60%	—	—
Other long-term liabilities	3.48%	3.20%	3.22%
Long-term liabilities	**21.61%**	**14.49%**	**19.11%**
Total liabilities	**66.33%**	**65.67%**	**67.91%**
Preferred stock $.01 par value; no shares issued and outstanding	—	—	—
Common stock $.01 par value	0.01%	0.01%	0.01%
Additional paid-in capital	12.06%	14.13%	14.96%
Accumulated other comprehensive loss	−2.33%	−3.16%	−2.94%
Retained earnings	23.18%	22.59%	19.32%
Total Costco stockholders' equity	**32.91%**	**33.57%**	**31.35%**
Noncontrolling interests	0.76%	0.75%	0.74%
Total equity	**33.67%**	**34.33%**	**32.09%**
Total liabilities and equity	**100.00%**	**100.00%**	**100.00%**

Once again, we see that current liabilities are decreasing as percentages of total liabilities and equity and accounts payable are declining, as well. This could be good or bad. It may simply mean that because Costco is collecting receivables more quickly, it is able to pay vendors sooner. On the other hand, Costco could be paying vendors too quickly, losing the ability to invest that cash to maximize returns.

Now, let's take a look at common size income statements.

TABLE 9.4

Costco Wholesale Corp.

Common-Size Consolidated Income Statement

12 months ended:	Aug 30, 2020	Sep 1, 2019	Sep 2, 2018
Net sales	100.00%	100.00%	100.00%
Merchandise costs	−88.80%	−88.98%	−88.96%
Gross margin	**11.20%**	**11.02%**	**11.04%**
Membership fees	2.17%	2.24%	2.27%
Selling, general and administrative	−10.01%	−10.04%	−10.02%
Preopening expenses	−0.03%	−0.06%	−0.05%
Operating income	**3.33%**	**3.17%**	**3.24%**

(Continued)

TABLE 9.4 (*Continued*)
Costco Wholesale Corp.
Common-Size Consolidated Income Statement

12 months ended:	Aug 30, 2020	Sep 1, 2019	Sep 2, 2018
Interest expense	−0.10%	−0.10%	−0.11%
Interest income	0.05%	0.08%	0.05%
Foreign-currency transactions gains (losses), net	—	0.02%	0.02%
Other, net	—	0.02%	0.02%
Interest income and other, net	**0.06%**	**0.12%**	**0.09%**
Other income (expense)	**−0.04%**	**0.02%**	**−0.03%**
Income before income taxes	**3.29%**	**3.19%**	**3.21%**
Provision for income taxes	−0.80%	−0.71%	−0.91%
Net income including noncontrolling interests	**2.49%**	**2.48%**	**2.30%**
Net income attributable to noncontrolling interests	−0.03%	−0.03%	−0.03%
Net income attributable to Costco	**2.45%**	**2.45%**	**2.26%**

The common size income statement measures each account as a percentage of total sales or revenues. In this common size income statement, all the relationships have remained stable. This is typically an indication of a stable business.

Common size financial statements can also be used to compare a small company's financial statements to a large benchmark company's financial statements. In that way, you can see how the smaller company's ratios compare to a large stable benchmark organization.

Horizontal analysis is a technique for analyzing the percentage change in individual financial statement items from one year to the next. The first period in the analysis is considered the base and the changes in the subsequent period are computed as a percentage of the base period. If more than two periods are presented, each period's changes are computed as a percentage of the preceding period. The resulting percentages are then studied in detail. It is important to consider the amount of change as well as the percentage in horizontal comparisons. A small change in an account with a very large dollar amount of activity may actually be much more of a change than a large change in an account with much lower dollar amount of activity. Both methods translate changes into percentages, which can then be compared to highlight areas where you need to look more closely.

There are also financial ratio analyses, which can identify areas for further investigation. When I am conducting an investigation, I always focus on the ratios that follow the cash. Except for companies focused on growth in their customer base, above all other factors, a healthy business converts its inventory (e.g. products, services, etc.) to cash within a predictable time period. Having said that, in cases of suspected financial statement fraud, you must pay attention to the accounts that analysts focus on. In a recent investigation of a public company in an industry where analysts focus on how quickly a company metabolizes inventory, I found that the company was using inventory reserves to artificially suppress the inventory shown on its balance sheet. In certain cases, there were actually negative inventory amounts embedded in the account. That would make an inventory observation pretty challenging, "Hey where are the 10 anti-widgets?" So, before deciding which ratios to focus on, think about what accounts might be implicated in what you are investigating.

Let's look at Costco again. Costco is a large stable company that does not need to drive customer growth at the cost of free cash flow. So, we would look at ratios that inform us about the creation of free cash flow.

TABLE 9.5

Costco Wholesale Corp.

Short-Term (Operating) Activity Ratios

	Aug 30, 2020	Sep 1, 2019	Sep 2, 2018
Turnover Ratios			
Inventory turnover	11.84	11.66	11.16
Receivables turnover	105.30	97.30	82.94
Payables turnover	10.23	11.38	10.96
Working capital turnover	49.82	602.22	381.36
Average No. of Days			
Average inventory processing period	31	31	33
Add: Average receivable collection period	3	4	4
Operating cycle	**34**	**35**	**37**
Less: Average payables payment period	36	32	33
Cash conversion cycle	**−2**	**3**	**4**

Notice that inventory turnover has increased. This ratio measures the number of times inventory turns over in sales. The receivables turnover ratio tells you how many times receivables are collected during a particular period. That ratio increased which is positive. Payables turnover has decreased which suggests that vendors are being paid more slowly. This could represent a conscious decision or it could represent a change in the vendor mix. Of some concern is the working capital turnover ratio that declined significantly. This ratio is measuring the amount of revenue a company is generating with its working capital. To calculate it, you divide revenue by average working capital for the period. In this case, the significant decline is probably explained by the effects of the pandemic.

The average inventory processing period is calculated by dividing average inventory by cost of goods sold and multiplying the result by 365 days. In this case the average inventory processing period has remained stable. The average receivable collection period has declined from 4 to 3 days. This is a good thing.

Now, here's where we get to my favorite measures for identifying a variety of types of fraud, everything from financial reporting fraud to revenue recognition fraud to massive accounts receivable lapping schemes: the cash conversion cycle (CCC) and its components. The CCC is measuring the time it takes to convert inventory to cash through sales. The CCC is calculated by adding days of inventory outstanding (DIO) to days sales outstanding (DSO) and subtracting days payables outstanding (DPO).

$$CCC = DIO + DSO - DPO$$

Of course, the components have to be calculated first. I want to focus first on days sales outstanding, which is calculated as accounts receivable divided by credit sales and multiplied by the number of days in the period. This is the "show me the money" calculation. It measures how quickly a company is collecting cash from its customers. Cash does not lie; either you are collecting it from your customers or you are not. If not, why not?

I did an investigation to uncover the reasons that my bank clients weren't being paid anything on the hard asset facility they had set up to finance telecommunications receivables. When I analyzed the DSO for the borrower, I noticed that it was continuously increasing. Without boring you with the whole tale, let me just say that witness interviews revealed that the CFO and his staff would have weekend pizza parties while lapping every receivable account they had to cover up their underlying crimes.

Let's now move down to the next level. What about individual account entries and balances? How can we discern which accounts bear more scrutiny?

Pavroty Chebyshev, a Russian mathematician, found the proportions of data in a population, which fall within each standard deviation from the population mean. Chebyshev's theorem states that for any data set, the proportion of data which lie within k standard deviations of the mean is, at least, $1 - (1/k$ squared). Therefore, if $k = 3$, the proportion of data which we would expect to see, within three standard deviations of the mean, would be $1 - (1/3$ squared$) = $ (at least) 89%.[7]

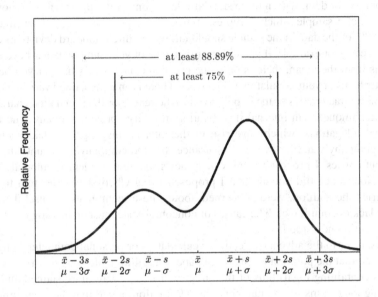

FIGURE 9.8[8]

The theorem is true for the entire population and any statistically valid sample drawn from the population. The proportions of data, which fall within each standard deviation, become even more precise if the population data has a normal, bell-shaped distribution. This is called the Empirical Rule and predicts that more than 99% of the data should be found within three standard deviations of the mean.

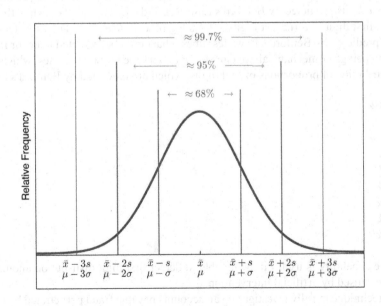

FIGURE 9.9[9]

This theorem is useful in understanding lack of compliance. It is used to control uniformity and quality in manufacturing processes. Incidentally, the mathematical symbol for each standard deviation is called "sigma." Note that there are three standard deviations, or sigmas, to the right of the mean and three to the left; six sigmas in total. Chebyshev's theorem is also quite useful in compliance applications. If you create or identify what you believe to be a population mean, then more than 89% of all observations should fall within three standard deviations of that mean in any type of population. If the population data is normally distributed (i.e. bell-shaped curve), then the expected proportion of data, within three standard deviations of the mean, rises to more than 99%.

So, if you select a sample which is representative of the population and determine the sample mean, at least 89% of the data in the sample should fall within three standard deviations of that mean. If that is not the case, for example, if you discover that 20% of your sample data is beyond three standard deviations from the mean, there is only one possible conclusion; whatever you believed about the essential attributes of your population is incorrect. There is an unexplained variance between your beliefs about the characteristics of the population and the reality of the population characteristics.

I used this technique in an internal investigation of a large public company. The investigation of the principal allegations, which gave rise to the internal investigation, had been completed. However, the company's auditors wanted assurance that the company's accounts did not contain other fraudulent entries. I proposed using Chebyshev's theorem to identify anomalies for further investigation. Note that I did not say that I proposed using Chebyshev's theorem to identify the fraudulent entries the auditors were concerned about; these techniques are useful in identifying compliance or lack of compliance. The causes of noncompliance must be investigated thoroughly in order to be correctly understood.

In the 1930s, prior to the advent of electronic calculators or personal computers, physicist Frank Benford observed that the pages of an overused paper logarithm table were worn in a curious manner. The pages containing logarithms of the numbers 1 and 2 were more stained and frayed than those containing logarithms for the numbers 8 and 9. Benford noted that the logarithm tables were used in virtually every mathematic, engineering, and scientific analysis in which the subject of the analysis can be described using numbers.[10] Benford went on to carefully research and test this hypothesis, over a number of years, using a wide variety of data sets. This research and testing led to what is known as Benford's Law.

Benford's Law is best demonstrated in large data sets. If smaller data sets fail to satisfy the rule, combining data sets often produces a new sequence, which will more closely approximate the distribution of first digits predicted by Benford's Law. Benford's Law is satisfied when the probability of observing a first digit of d (i.e. for digits 1–9) is log base 10 $(d + 1/d)$. The expected distribution of first digits, predicted by Benford's Law, describes what could be expected to occur in the natural world if human beings or mechanical systems did not intervene in the processes, which gave rise to them. The distribution of proportions of first digits, which are predicted by Benford's Law, follows:

1 = 30.0%
2 = 17.6%
3 = 12.5%
4 = 9.7%
5 = 7.9%
6 = 6.7%
7 = 5.8%
8 = 5.1%
9 = 4.6%[11]

This predictive capability is useful in being able to detect first digit distribution anomalies, which may have been caused by artificial intervention.

I used this technique in fully investigating an accounts payable fraud perpetrated by the president of a division of a large public company. The fraud was so massive that the division was shut down due to the size of its recurring losses. There were numerous fake vendors, set up by the division president, which had submitted invoices for payment. Many were identified by other investigative techniques such as identifying vendors who shared a common address. However, it became clear that there were other fake vendors, which could not be identified by these means. We were looking not for a needle in a haystack, but for a needle in a needle stack.

How to identify the fake invoices among the tens of thousands of legitimate invoices? This was an impossible task for individual review. A more efficient technique had to be employed; enter Benford's Law. The invoices received by the division often contained hundreds of line items. We loaded the vendor name, number of items purchased, and price per item for each item included in the invoices received by the division, into a spreadsheet. We then had the spreadsheet multiply the number of items purchased by the dollar amount per item (i.e. we re-performed each extension on the odd chance that the extension had been falsified). Also, this was done to create a large data set from the mathematical combination of numbers from two distributions, more likely to satisfy Benford's Law.

Next, we separated the first digit in each result into a separate column. We then analyzed the proportions of the numbers 1–9 appearing as the first digit in our results. Note that we did not first sort by vendor. This exercise helped us identify vendor invoices, which contained line items that did not comport with Benford's Law. The vendors who sent these invoices were then investigated. This investigation revealed another group of vendors, which turned out to be fraudulent. Why? Because you can't fake natural that is different from random.

INVESTIGATOR NOTES

These techniques can also be used as the basis for expert testimony you present at trial or in an arbitration proceeding. You just need to make sure that you apply them correctly. In one arbitration proceeding I was providing testimony about the fact that many invoices rendered to my client contained charges that did not conform to the contract between my client and the vendor. I then quantified the amount of the overbilling. The contract extended back more than 20 years. Most of the records were paper or picture type PDFs, so the analysis of the invoices had to be carried out manually. The population was entirely homogenous (i.e. it contained only invoices for the services described in the contract). I determined the size of the population and then drew a statistically significant sample for a 95% confidence level. I then extrapolated my results over the entire population. The opposing expert inexplicably decided to draw a judgmental sample from the population as the basis for his extrapolation and quantum conclusion. He testified that he did this because he was afraid that a statistically significant random sample would "Miss the large invoices." A quote from the arbitral proceeding in response to that testimony was: "Sir, you realize that a statistically significant sample, by definition, is designed to make sure that each member of the population is represented in the results."

SECTION V: USING DATA SCIENCE IN FRAUD INVESTIGATION AND FORENSIC ACCOUNTING

The great thing about electronic data is that it is available, in real time, twenty-four seven; all you need to do is to gather, organize, and analyze it to effectively answer your questions. Big data has become a buzz word used, imprecisely, to describe every current data analytics application. It's as though if you are not yet on the Big Data Train, you have missed your chance because the train has left the station. Nothing could be further from the truth. We are still very early in a technology revolution which will continue to evolve to allow us to do more with, well, more. Online transaction systems will become more effective. Technologies are developing, which will allow broader and more seamless interactions with data warehouses. There are technologies now available that allow easier normalization and visualization of data for analysis purposes. The key, for using the available technologies today, is to create clarity around your investigative objectives. Create a map of all relevant, internal and external, data, which relates to the subject process(es). Then decide which tools you will employ to analyze the data. From there, you will identify appropriate benchmarks and create analytical processes to identify areas to investigate. Remember that areas identified for additional scrutiny do not necessarily contain fraud. If you do identify anomalies, you must perform an actual investigation to identify if fraud exists and gather evidence to prove the fraud.

Recently, I was working on an investigation into allegations made by the Department of Education (DOE) against a college. Basically, the DOE was alleging that the college's associate deans were being compensated based on the number of students they recruited in violation of Title IV of the Higher Education Act of 1965. That is the act that created the federal part of college student financial aid including federally guaranteed student loans. The college insisted that their associate deans were only compensated based on their written performance evaluations, which evaluated a number of performance metrics not related to the number of students recruited that was intentionally left out of the performance evaluations. The student recruitment data, performance evaluation metrics, and compensation data were all digitized. I thought to myself: This is great; easiest fee I'll ever earn. All I have to do is run some descriptive and inferential statistics including a regression analysis and hypothesis testing to learn the truth to a definable degree of mathematical certainty. I was excited to begin, that is, until the data arrived. The data I received was like an enormous electronic shoebox of data in a variety of formats with duplicates and differing metrics. I was in a panic until I brought in a talented data scientist. The first thing he did was to use a tool (e.g. Power BI, Tableau, etc.) to normalize and visualize the data.

The first step, obviously, is to get the data. With the new data analysis tools, you can easily connect to the ever-expanding world of data. There are all sorts of data sources available. The following image shows how to connect to data, by selecting Get Data > Other > Web.

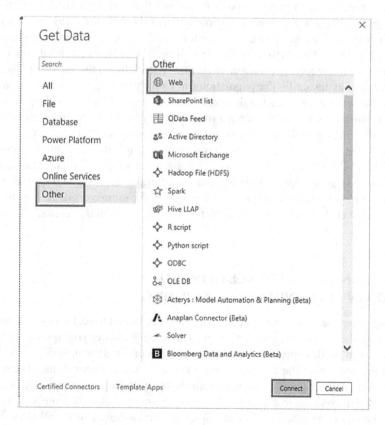

FIGURE 9.10[12]

So, that's how you access information on the web. But, notice on the left side of the chart above, that you can select File to download data from a data file; that's what we did.

The data, we received, came in like this.

Document	Remote IE	Fil	Received	Processed	Year	O	E E E	M	E	Begin2	Fo	End2	Mgr Oven	Mgr Oven	EE Overall	EE Overall	Active Lea	Active Lea	Communi	Communi	EE Engage	EE Engage	Job Know	Job Know
e60d7edc757b90e58	Zar	######	######			Dc	K Z U	R	R	2017-05-0		04/30/201	2.29	2.29	2.86	2.86	2	3	3	3	3	Expectatic	3	
1ddeea55f0ba11621	Zar	######	######	2017		Cc	N Z U	Br	B	2017-05-0		04/30/201	4.29	4.29	4.14	4.14	Rating:	4	4	4	4	4	4	4
20af2df182dc16a7bb	Zar	######	######	2017		Cc	N Z Fi	M	J	2017-05-0		04/30/201	2.86	2.86	3.29	3.29	Rating:	3	3	3	5	4	3	3
19b6992aa0a545396f	Zar	######	######	2017		Cc	P Z U	Tr	T	2017-05-0		04/30/201	3.57	3.57	3.71	3.71	Rating:	4	3	3	4	4	4	3
67b7c905edbf9b039	Zar	######	######	2017		G	S Z U	Vi	V	2017-05-0		04/30/201	3	3	3	3	Rating:	3	3	3	5	3	3	3
6b4bc14ecf54c81dbc	Zac	######	######	2017		Cc	B Z U	Br	B	2017-05-0		04/3	4	4	3.14	3.14	Rating:	4	3	4	3	3	4	3
9121129d83f6921c5f	Zac	######	######			M	C Z U	Cf	C	2017-05-0		04/30/201	3	3	3.86	3.86	Rating:	3	3	4	5	4	3	4
2f2d299463452ccedc	Zac	######	######			Cc	B Z U	Ni	N	2017-05-0		04/30/201	2.57	2.57	3.29	3.29	2	3	3	3	3	Expectatic	3	
9947ca27162701dcc4	Zac	######	######	2017		Cc	R Z U	St	S	2017-05-0		04/30/201	3.14	3.14	4	4	Rating:	3	5	4	4	3	3	4
5095cd13e2ffe3a2ba	Zac	######	######	2017		Dc	G Z U	Hc	H	2017-05-0		04/30/201	2.43	2.43	3.57	3.57	Rating:	3	3	4	3	3	3	4
4c5cbf47b2e1ab1561	Zac	######	######	2017		Cc	S Z U	Bc	B	2017-05-0		04/30/201	3.86	3.86	4	4	Rating:	3	4	4	5	5	4	4
a999afc47cccac5253c	Zar	######	######	2017		Cc	N Z Fi	M	J	2017-05-0		04/30/201	2.86	2.86	3.29	3.29	Rating:	3	3	3	3	4	3	3
c42e677284b3745871	Zar	######	######			Dc	K Z U	R	R	2017-05-0		04/30/201	2.29	2.29	2.86	2.86	2	3	3	3	3	Expectatic	3	
e3081da40365a2b1b	Zar	######	######	2017		Cc	N Z U	Br	B	2017-05-0		04/30/201	4.29	4.29	4.14	4.14	Rating:	4	4	4	4	4	4	4
b7ec2b060d5b44b77	Zar	######	######	2017		Cc	P Z U	Tr	T	2017-05-0		04/30/201	3.57	3.57	3.71	3.71	Rating:	4	3	3	4	4	4	3
50dc5f25f05aca7c677	Zac	######	######	2017		G	S Z U	Vi	V	2017-05-0		04/30/201	3	3	3	3	Rating:	3	3	3	5	3	3	3
765f3ad9dc612a3082	Zac	######	######			Cc	B Z U	Ni	N	2017-05-0		04/30/201	2.57	2.57	3.29	3.29	2	3	3	3	5	Expectatic	3	
9c82726273b20348f9	Zac	######	######	2017		M	C Z U	Cf	C	2017-05-0		04/30/201	3	3	3.86	3.86	Rating:	3	3	4	4	4	3	4
c641495ba57036002e	Zac	######	######	2017		Cc	S Z U	Bc	B	2017-05-0		04/30/201	3.86	3.86	4	4	Rating:	3	4	4	5	5	3	4
b37295bd25bb73ea7	Zac	######	######	2017		Cc	R Z U	St	S	2017-05-0		04/30/201	3.14	3.14	4	4	Rating:	3	3	5	4	3	3	4
bd955bf177810f798b	Zac	######	######	2017		Dc	G Z U	Hc	H	2017-05-0		04/30/201	2.43	2.43	3.57	3.57	Rating:	3	3	3	3	3	3	4
a2ff696a2a26b9cc45	Vc	######	######	2017		M	C X U	Kc	K	2017-05		04/30/201	3.86	3.86	3.71	3.71	Rating:	5						

FIGURE 9.11

Imagine this multiplied by thousands. The first step was to normalize, clean, and visualize the data. Next, we transformed the data by selecting Transform Data to load the table and launch the Power Query Editor. The Query Settings pane is displayed.[13] Here's what that looks like.

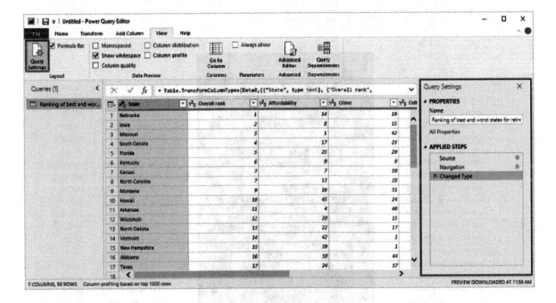

FIGURE 9.12

The next thing we had to do was link the data and set up the queries we wanted to run. This is what that looks like.

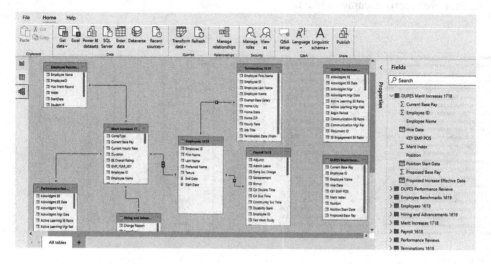

FIGURE 9.13

The next step was to analyze the results of the linkages and queries to see if we were getting what we needed or had to take additional steps. Here's what that looks like.

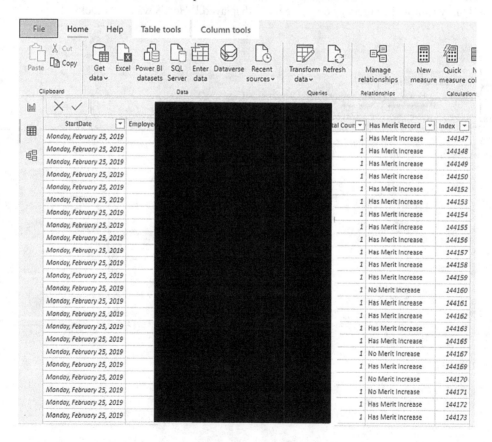

FIGURE 9.14

Following those steps here's what we turned that jumble of raw data into:

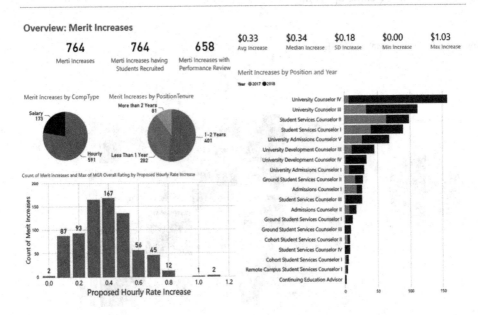

FIGURE 9.15

So, above we have an overview of every merit increase given during the period under review by the DOE. We also included some descriptive statistics like average increase, median increase, etc. We were further able to break down increases between salaried and hourly employees. We also summarized the amount of increases by position and year. This is the 30,000-foot level for the entire population of increases presented in a logical summarized format with some key metrics that allow the user to get a handle on all of the compensation increases on one sheet. It also helps us to see who the most impacted employees were.

The next logical thing to summarize? You guessed it, performance evaluation data. Here's what that looks like:

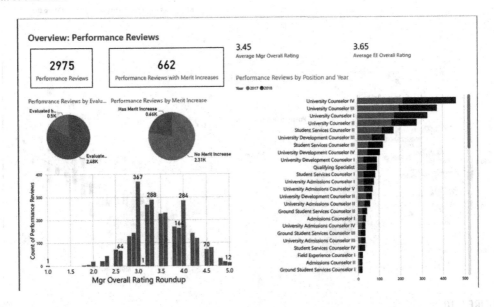

FIGURE 9.16

Next, we wanted to look at the influence a variety of potentially related metrics had on one another. Here's what we came up with:

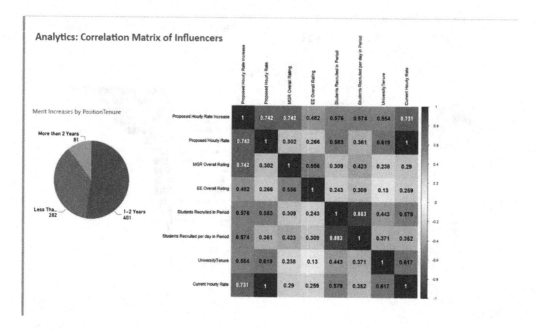

FIGURE 9.17

Next, we wanted to begin to look at the relative strength of correlation between compensation increases and students recruited versus manager ratings. We overlaid regression lines on a scatter plot so that the reader could easily see how the data broken out by length of tenure was distributed around the regression lines. This demonstrative also allows the user to easily visualize the goodness of fit of the data.

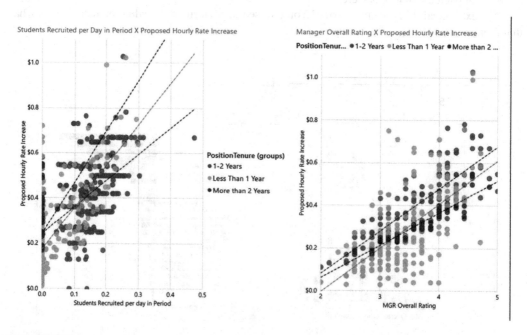

FIGURE 9.18

Looking at these you can easily see that the "Students Recruited" data has a low goodness of fit. The "MGR Overall Rating" has a higher goodness of fit, especially for employees with more than 2 years' tenure.

Next, we wanted to begin to look at inferential statistics. A multiple linear regression attempts to find an equation that explains the relationship between a single dependent variable and multiple independent variables.

- For example, one might wish to know how month over month car sales, percent electric cars in use, and diesel demand (independent variables) affect gasoline prices (dependent variable).

  Equation takes the form $Y = a + b_1X_1 + b_2X_2 + \cdots + b_nX_n + \varepsilon$

  From the above example: Gasoline price $= 3 + .5$ (MoM car sales) $- 1.3$ (% electric cars in use) $- .6$ (% diesel consumed)
- A regression requires finding the line of best fit.

  The regression line minimizes the sum of squared distances between itself and all independent points.

  A multiple regression will have multiple lines with different slopes.

  It looks like this:

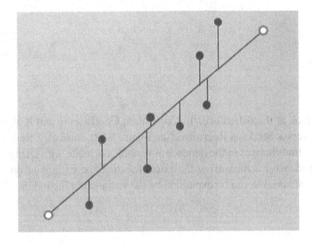

FIGURE 9.19

- There are different types of correlation:

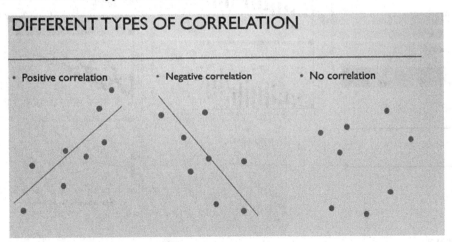

FIGURE 9.20

Regression analysis explains the relationship between independent variables (i.e. variables that have a suspected impact on other variables) and dependent variables (i.e. variables that are suspected to be impacted by other variables). See Figure 9.21.

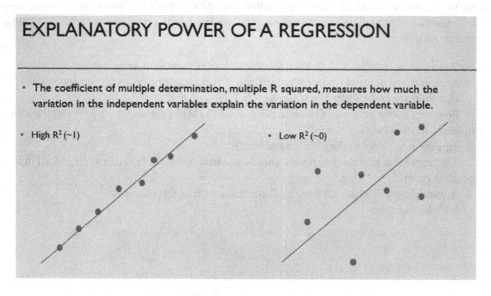

FIGURE 9.21

So, we wanted to look at the differences in Correlation Coefficients and R Squared factors for the MGR Overall Rating versus Students Recruited (see Figure 9.22). Basically, the correlation coefficient is measuring the extent that changes in the dependent variable correlate with changes in the independent variable. The R Squared factor is measuring the extent to which the variance from the least squares fitted line in the dependent variable can be explained by the variance in the independent variable.

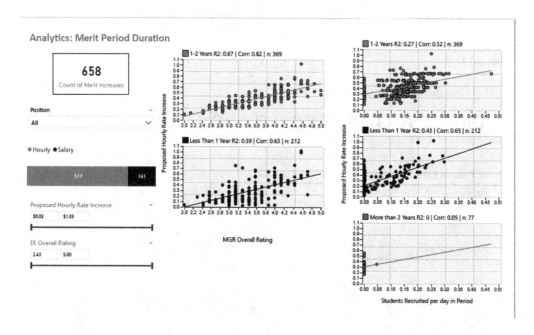

FIGURE 9.22

You can easily see that the MGR Overall Rating for employees with 1–2 years' tenure has a correlation coefficient of .67 and an R Squared of .82. That means that the movement in the independent variable (MGR Overall Rating) has a .67 impact on the dependent variable (Proposed Hourly Rate Increase). Also, for those employees the dependent variable's (Proposed Hourly Rate Increase) variance from the best fit line is 82% explained by the variance in the independent variable (MGR Overall Rating). However, the Students Recruited for employees with 1–2 years' tenure has a correlation coefficient of only .52 and an R Squared of .27. That means that the movement in the independent variable (Students Recruited) has a .52 impact on the dependent variable (Proposed Hourly Rate Increase). Also, for those employees the dependent variable's (Proposed Hourly Rate Increase) variance from the best fit line is 27% explained by the variance in the independent variable (Students Recruited). We also ran hypothesis test and were able to reject the null hypothesis for the relationship between the MGR Overall Rating and Compensation Changes, but were not able to reject the null hypothesis for the Students Recruited – Compensation Changes relationship. So, we were able to demonstrate with mathematical certainty that compensation changes were more explained by the performance evaluations than the number of students recruited.

Amazingly, using this tool, two of us were able to collect, normalize, clean, analyze, and draw conclusions about millions and millions of discrete data items in less than two weeks. That included a learning curve delay. Back in the Stone Age, when I started, a project like this would have taken a large team of people months to complete. We probably would have concluded that it would be cost prohibitive to analyze all the data and drawn a statistically significant sample from the data population. That would have required yet another hurdle to overcome with DOE, namely, was the sample drawn correctly. Now, you can just dump all the data into one of these tools and process it with previously unimaginable speed.

EXERCISES

1. Your company has been served with a Grand Jury Subpoena relating to alleged earnings management accounting entries. Develop a list of questions that you would want to be able to answer with the evidence.
2. What requirements does the IIA have for planning and supervising an internal audit engagement?
3. Your company has been served with a Grand Jury Subpoena relating to alleged earnings management accounting entries. The entries allegedly relate to inflated reserves for warranty claims. Develop a workplan to investigate these allegations.
4. Your company has been served with a Grand Jury Subpoena relating to alleged earnings management accounting entries. The entries allegedly relate to inflated reserves for warranty claims. Develop a theoretical model of the progression from evidence gathered to report.
5. What must your workplan and work papers accomplish to satisfy the IIA's requirements?
6. What are examples of Badges of Fraud?
7. Perform a vertical analysis of your company's financial statements.
8. What do the results of this analysis tell you about your company?
9. Write a list of questions you may want to investigate as a result of the issues you identified by performing this analysis.
10. Prepare common size income statements for your company and its three largest competitors.
11. Are there significant differences in the common size income statements you developed?
12. Can you explain the variances?
13. Develop a list of persons you would interview about the differences you could not explain. What questions would you ask them?
14. Perform a horizontal analysis of your company's financial statements.
15. Are there significant variances in your analysis?

16. Can you explain the variances?
17. If not, who would you ask to explain the variances? Make a list of the questions you would ask them.
18. Perform the following ratio analyses on your company's financial statements:
    a. Inventory turnover
    b. Receivables turnover
    c. Payables turnover
    d. Working capital turnover
    e. Average inventory processing period
    f. Average receivable collection period
    g. Average payables payment period
    h. Cash conversion cycle
19. Perform the following ratio analyses on your company's three largest competitor's financial statements:
    a. Inventory turnover
    b. Receivables turnover
    c. Payables turnover
    d. Working capital turnover
    e. Average inventory processing period
    f. Average receivable collection period
    g. Average payables payment period
    h. Cash conversion cycle
20. Are there significant differences between the ratio analyses you performed for your company versus its competitors?
21. Can you explain the differences?
22. If not, who would you as to explain the differences? What would you ask them?
23. What does Chebyshev's theorem tell us about what we should expect in a population for which we have calculated a mean?
24. What does Benford's Law tell us about what we should expect to see in the results of a naturally (i.e. not artificially created) created derivative distribution of data?
25. What is data visualization?
26. Do some research and list the tools that are currently available to allow us to normalize disparate data populations and create data visualizations.
27. What can we measure with a multiple regression analysis?
28. What are the three types of correlation?

CHAPTER SUMMARY/KEY TAKEAWAYS

So, here are some things to think about:

- Always start by writing out the questions that must be answered.
- Create a written workplan.
- Create an effective work paper system to support your findings.
- Use analytical tools to help you identify where to look.
- Use data science to improve the accuracy, speed, and effectiveness of your work.

In Chapter 10 you will learn how to properly document your findings, form conclusions and draft a proper report.

NOTES

1. https://na.theiia.org/standards-guidance/Public%20Documents/IPPF-Standards-2017.pdf. 2240, 2240. A1, 2240.C1, 2300, 2340 Copyright © 2017 by The Institute of Internal Auditors, Inc. ("The IIA"). All rights reserved.
2. https://na.theiia.org/standards-guidance/Public%20Documents/IPPF-Standards-2017.pdf 2340 Copyright © 2017 by The Institute of Internal Auditors, Inc. ("The IIA"). All rights reserved.
3. www.stock-analysis-on.net/NASDAQ/Company/Costco-Wholesale-Corp/Common-Size/Assets
4. www.stock-analysis-on.net/NASDAQ/Company/Costco-Wholesale-Corp/Common-Size/Assets
5. www.stock-analysis-on.net/NASDAQ/Company/Costco-Wholesale-Corp/Common-Size/Assets
6. www.stock-analysis-on.net/NASDAQ/Company/Costco-Wholesale-Corp/Common-Size/Assets
7. James R. Evans and David L. Olson (2003). *Statistics, Data Analysis, and Decision Modeling (Second Edition).* Upper Saddle River, NJ: Pearson Education, Inc. p. 54.
8. http://statwiki.ucdavis.edu/Under_Construction/Descriptive_Statistics/2.5_The_Empirical_Rule_and_Chebyshev%27s_Theorem
9. http://statwiki.ucdavis.edu/Under_Construction/Descriptive_Statistics/2.5_The_Empirical_Rule_and_Chebyshev%27s_Theorem
10. Forensic and Investigative Accounting, D. Larry Crumbley, CPA, CFD, Cr.FA, Lester e. Heitger, CPA, G. Stevenson Smith, CPA, CMA, CCH: Chicago, IL, 2007, pp. 9–17, 9–18.
11. Forensic and Investigative Accounting, D. Larry Crumbley, CPA, CFD, Cr.FA, Lester e. Heitger, CPA, G. Stevenson Smith, CPA, CMA, CCH: Chicago, IL, 2007, pp. 9–17, 9–18.
12. https://docs.microsoft.com/en-us/power-bi/connect-data/desktop-connect-to-data
13. https://docs.microsoft.com/en-us/power-bi/connect-data/desktop-connect-to-data

10 Documenting Findings, Forming Conclusions, and Writing the Investigation Report

It was literally a "bet the company" case. The founders of a very successful financial services firm that served only life insurance companies had, what could only be described as, a falling out. One was Mr. Inside who handled the operations of the financial services firm. The other was Mr. Outside, the face of the company who handled all sales and customer experience interfaces.

One day, Mr. Inside had had enough, so, he cancelled Mr. Outside's company phone, credit cards, etc. and changed the locks on the office doors. Mr. Outside was physically locked out of his own company. Realizing that the company wouldn't be much of a company without Mr. Inside and knowing there was no way to get Mr. Inside back onside, Mr. Outside decided to depart gracefully, but sought the compensation laid out in the company's operating agreement under such circumstances.

I was retained by counsel representing Mr. Outside to calculate the amount of compensation due Mr. Outside and to investigate the opposing experts hired by Mr. Inside and critique their work. I made my calculations and included them in an expert report that was produced to opposing counsel. Opposing experts did likewise. Upon investigation, I discovered that one of the key opposing experts had an undisclosed business partnership, related to the activities of the company at issue in this matter, with Mr. Inside. A clear conflict of interest. The other experts performed a business valuation, for reasons which are still not clear to me since the operating agreement contained a straight-forward easily calculable remedy in its four corners. Some people respond to their own insecurity by wasting time and money on the complex when the simple and straight forward would serve them much better. Even so, opposing experts selected incorrect reference sources for key factors in its business valuation calculation.

These findings were kept from opposing counsel ahead of the hearing. The previously undisclosed findings produced several dramatic moments in the hearing. But, that would make my story too long. So, suffice it to say, opposing experts' testimony was completely impeached; my testimony came in unopposed. The tribunal awarded Mr. Outside everything he sought including professional fees. When I saw opposing counsel, who had been up to this point a social friend, outside the hearing room, his face was a lovely shade of Elmo red. He looked me in the eye and spat: *"Could you have made the <expletive deleted> number any higher?"* I could have asked him the same question.

My point in telling you this story is that as you contemplate presenting your findings, especially in an adversarial setting, you have to be right. There is no room for error here. Your report, whatever form it takes, must be based entirely on evidence subjected to methods of analysis that are generally accepted in the profession to which you belong.

SECTION I: TYPES OF REPORTS

The type of report you use will depend entirely on your company's needs, the attorney's counsel, the type of service you performed, and the venue where the report will be presented as part of your testimony. You should always consult counsel and rely on the professional literature in selecting which type of report to use.

DOI: 10.1201/9781003121558-12

You could be conducting an internal investigation where you will present your findings to a Board Committee. In that case, the report can take any form that you believe will clearly communicate your findings to your audience in a compelling manner.

You might be conducting a forensic accounting analysis that will be presented as expert testimony in a civil proceeding in US District Court. In that case you will prepare your report in conformity with Rule 26 of the Federal Rules of Civil Procedure.

Maybe you are a Certified Public Accountant Accredited in Business Valuation (CPA/ABV) and you performed a business valuation. In preparing your report you would comply with the standards set out in the American Institute of Certified Public Accountant's (AICPA) Statement on Standards for Valuation Services No. 1 (SSVS 1).

Perhaps your work will be presented as expert testimony in an international arbitration before the Taiwan Arbitration Association. You would be required to follow the arbitral rules of that body in preparing your report.

Whatever form your report takes it must accomplish several important things, which we will discuss in the next section.

INVESTIGATOR NOTES

Many years ago, while working for one of the Big 8, I was retained by counsel representing a large public company that had been accused of committing criminal tax fraud. Two years and several million dollars in professional fees later, in consultation with the company's counsel, I came up with two very compelling demonstrative exhibits that were used by the company's counsel to persuade the person at the Department of Justice (i.e. Main Justice) who made the decision about whether to indict companies and their officers for criminal tax fraud. These were two exhibits that were primarily graphic in nature with very little text other than that necessary to identify the figures in the exhibits. Those exhibits and the talents of the company's excellent attorney carried the day. The company and its officers were not indicted. The attorney and the company's president were delighted with our work and the outcome; I received a great deal of praise from both.

However, because of the high-profile nature of the case, the managing partner of the office I worked in asked to do a post-issuance second partner review on the report. He called me into his office and I was trying to decide how to remain humble in the face of the laudatory praise he was likely to heap upon his returning hero. When I entered his office, he asked me to be seated. I could tell by his manner that something was wrong but for the life of me, I couldn't figure out why he was angry. He asked in a loud voice, "Where the hell is the report?". I said John, there is no report; that's not what their attorney wanted. He specifically instructed me not to prepare a narrative report. John then said, "I don't give a damn what their lawyer did or did not want. We charged one of our largest clients more than US$2 million in fees and what do they have to show for it? For that kind of money, they should have a report that is at least six inches thick." I never could get John to understand that what the client wanted was not to be indicted; they couldn't have cared less about a formal narrative report. In fact, the attorney specifically instructed me not to prepare a narrative report of my findings because it could potentially have been discoverable and might have contained information that would have been useful to prosecutors. Oh well, you can't please everyone.

SECTION II: WHAT THE INVESTIGATION REPORT MUST ACCOMPLISH

Your report must explain your findings in the simplest, clearest, and most compelling manner possible. Please eliminate as much jargon as possible. Write to persuade; not to impress. Use simple opening statements to communicate your highest level conclusions and opinions. You can then go on to provide the basis for your conclusion or opinion in the following paragraphs. Also, try to keep all quantitative analyses in the body of the report at the highest level of summation. Supporting quantitative analyses with detailed calculations can be included as exhibits.

Of course, your report must comply with the requirements of the venue in which it is to be presented. Make sure that you comply with all requirements. It would be very bad indeed, if your testimony got excluded because you failed to comply with all the requirements of the body where your expert testimony was to be presented.

The conclusions and opinions you offer must be supported by evidence, which has been analyzed by applying generally accepted methods within your profession. Your conclusions and opinions must be supported by analyses that are completely error free. If not, especially in an adversarial proceeding, get ready for a long-difficult cross-examination that will focus on even a single error. Lest you believe you will be able to cause your tormentor to move past the error because the error is a minor one and does not affect your overall conclusions or opinions, be prepared for this question, "What other errors may be present in your analyses that we have not yet found?"

INVESTIGATOR NOTES

I had a colleague who applied a generally accepted method to evidence using Excel. Unfortunately, a subtotal was added to the other amounts in the same column of the worksheet. This produced a relatively insignificant error in one of a number of quantifications of economic damages. The opposition discovered this error because they always do. My colleague spent over four hours of cross-examination on that one error. When the opposition got done with him the jury wouldn't have believed him if he had told them that the Sun was coming up the next morning.

SECTION III: THE ELEMENTS OF A GOOD INVESTIGATION REPORT

Let's work our way through a report that I prepared for an international arbitration. The first thing to cover is usually your own qualifications to provide this expert testimony:

I. Qualifications.

My name is William L. Jennings. My business address is Veritas Forensic Accounting, LLC, 1175 Peachtree Street, NE, Atlanta, GA, 30309.

I am a Member of Veritas Forensic Accounting, LLC. My previous positions included: Principal at AEA Group, LLC; Managing Director at Alvarez & Marsal in the Global Forensic and Dispute Services practice; Managing Director in the Disputes and Investigations Practice at Navigant Consulting, Inc.; Director in the National Forensic Accounting Practice at LECG, LLC; President of FFI, Inc.; Managing Director at Kroll, Inc., in charge of investigative accounting services for the Central Region; Principal-in-Charge of the Atlanta office of Lindquist, Avey, Macdonald, Baskerville, a multi-national independent forensic accounting firm; Director-in- Charge of Coopers & Lybrand's Fraud Investigation Services practice for the Southeast Region; and Partner in the public accounting firm of Brown & Jennings.

I have a Bachelor of Science degree in Accounting from the University of New Orleans and a Master's degree in Business Administration from Auburn University. I have been a Certified Public Accountant ("CPA") since 1981 and a Certified Fraud Examiner ("CFE") since 1991. I am also Certified in Financial Forensics ("CFF"), Accredited in Business Valuation ("ABV"), a member of the American Institute of Certified Public Accountants; a member of the Association of Certified Fraud Examiners, and a member of the Board of Governors for the Center for Ethics and Corporate Responsibility at Georgia State University.

For nearly 40 years, I have provided forensic accounting, investigation, asset recovery, business valuation, and business controls consulting services to a wide range of clients, including public companies, private companies, and government agencies, such as the US Attorney's Office for multiple districts, the US Securities and Exchange Commission, and the US Marshals Service. Over the course of my career, I have been engaged on hundreds of forensic accounting, audit and investigation assignments, including audit assignments for companies that engaged in significant derivative trading activities, such Good Hope (Refinery), Inc. and Freeport McMoRan, Inc., and I have gained substantial experience with and expertise on a variety of accounting, financial and investment-related topics, including US Generally Accepted Accounting Principles ("GAAP"); the Financial Account Standards Board's ("FASB") Accounting Standards Codification ("ASC") which codify GAAP; alternative investment vehicles, such as hedge funds, private equity funds, and venture capital funds; and a diverse range of financial instruments, including options, futures, stocks, and bonds. I have also personally traded stocks, bonds, options and futures in my own account.

I frequently speak and publish articles on accounting, financial and investment-related topics, such as forensic accounting, fraud investigations, white-collar crime, business ethics, and the valuation of financial instruments, among others.

In addition, I have often provided expert testimony in federal and state courts, as well as in many other dispute resolution venues. I have testified in matters that related to a variety of derivatives and hedge fund accounting, including: *Nodvin et al v. National Financial Services Corporation* (testimony regarding accounting for and reporting of values for IOs, POs, and inverse IO floaters given at NASD Arbitration Hearing); *Piedmont Family Office Fund, LP, et al. v. Robert L. Duncan, et al.* (testimony given at deposition).

Additional details regarding my qualifications, education, publications, speaking engagements and past expert testimony are included in my curriculum vitae, which is attached as Exhibit A.

This is where you set forth the educational, licensing, and experience credentials that qualify you to provide this testimony. This is an important section of the report. It will likely form the basis for much of the basis for your voir dire, which is the process in which your qualification to testify as an expert occurs. If you are in federal court, the other side will have likely already filed a Daubert motion and a motion in limine to limit or exclude your testimony based on your previously produced written expert report. However, if those failed or there is some shortcoming that the other side's lawyers would like the judge or jury to hear about you, it will be based on this section of your report. Above all, make sure that the information is correct (see Chapter 14).

Next, we want to provide a background for the matter that is the subject of the report. In this section of the report, we want to give the trier of fact (i.e. judge, jury, arbitrator, etc.) a simple clear understanding of what the matter being litigated is all about. The following is from a very interesting matter that I investigated and analyzed. Interestingly, it required me to apply the central limit theorem as we discussed in Chapter 9.

II. Case Background.

This case concerns two hedge funds, XXX Xxxxxxxxxxx, XXX ("XXX") and Xxxx Xxxxxxxxxxx, XXX (the "XX Fund") (together, the "Funds"), that primarily traded options on, options on futures on, and futures on broad-based indices, such as the S&P 500 Index.

On May 31, XXXX, the Securities and Exchange Commission (the "SEC") filed a complaint in the United States District Court for the Northern District of Georgia against Xxxx Xxxxxxxx, XXX ("Xxxx") and Xxxxx Xxxxxx ("Xx. Xxxxxx") alleging violations of the Securities Act of 1933, the Securities Exchange Act of 1934, and the Investment Advisers Act of 1940.[2] The SEC filed a First Amended Complaint on January 11, XXXX,[3] and a Second Amended Complaint on August 30, XXXX, which, among other things, added claims against Xxxx Xxxxxxx and Xxxx Xxxxxxx.[4]

The SEC alleges that Xxxx and Xx. Xxxxxx manipulated the trading strategy of the Funds to avoid realizing losses and to generate incentive allocations paid to Xx. Xxxxxx and Xxxx Xxxx Xxxxxxxxxx (the "Xxxx Xxxxxxxxxx") from at least January XXXX through May XXXX.[5] In addition, the SEC alleges that Xxxx and Xx. Xxxxxx misrepresented or omitted details about Xxxx's trading strategy.

This section should not be overly long. Also, you should probably track the language in your side's version of the pleadings. You do not want to insert your own legal theory of the case; you are not the lawyer.

Next you want to talk about what you were asked to do. Once again, this should be stated in clear declarative sentences.

III. Assignment.

I have been asked by counsel for Xxxx and Xxxxx Xxxxxx to provide my opinions on the accounting and related issues in this litigation, including background information on derivatives.

For my work on this matter, I am being compensated at my standard consulting rate of $595 per hour. My compensation is in no way contingent upon or based upon the content of my opinions or the outcome of this matter.

In this section you want to be as brief and clear as possible. You also need to say how and how much you are being paid for your services in this section.

The order that items appear in your report is up to you and the attorneys who are supervising your work. However, whenever possible, I like to put my conclusions and/or opinions right up front. The reason is that human beings have a finite attention span. I want the reader of the report to process and remember my conclusions and opinions. Then, based on their interest, they can read as much or as little of the balance of my report as they choose.

IV. Summary of Opinions.

Based on my review and analysis of the information described below, certain empirical analyses I have performed, and my skills, knowledge, education, training, and experience, I am of the following opinions, which are explained more fully in Part XI below:

- The Funds did not enter into any trades that were open for more than 90 days, which comports with the XX Fund's disclosures to investors.
- Xxxx applied correct accounting treatment to the Funds' classification of open and closed trading positions. In particular, as to options that expired and resulted in the assignment of the underlying financial instrument, on the date those options expired, Xxxx correctly classified the expired option as a closed position, and the resulting assignment of the underlying financial instrument as a separate, open position.
- With respect to the Xx Fund and the XXX Fund, the unrealized and net asset value ("NAV") of open positions and of the Funds were not particularly relevant (other than for margin and tax purposes). The XX Fund and the XXX Fund often

had open positions in an unrealized loss position, but that was not necessarily reflective of an actual risk of realized losses or the potential for realized gains. As investors in the Funds redeemed based on their percentage ownership of net realized gains and losses on closed positions, unrealized and net asset values that did not reflect the actual risk of realized losses or the potential for realized gains were not particularly relevant.

- Xxxx's investment strategy, in part, relied on the premise that, over time, it could reduce and eliminate trading losses that were caused by periods of unusual and extreme market volatility. This premise is supported by Chebyshev's Theorem and the Empirical Rule, including the tendency of reversion to the mean that is implied by both propositions.
- If the XX Fund utilized a fee structure more in line with the traditional "2 and 20" fee model based on NAV for hedge funds, XX. Xxxxxx and Xxxx Xxxxxxxxxx would have earned approximately $7.2 million *more* in fees and incentive allocations between January XXXX and May XXXX. In other words, the XX Fund's fee structure—with no management fee and an incentive allocation equal to 20% of net realized gains on closed positions—*saved* the investors approximately $7.2 million between January XXXX and May XXXX.

Now that we have communicated what we want everyone to remember, it's time to go into a little more detail. In this section we want to provide a detailed context for and explain the conclusions or opinions we have just stated.

V. The Complex and Volatile World of Options and Futures.[6]

Options, futures, and options on futures are types of financial instruments known as derivatives. According to Accounting Standards Codification ("ASC") No. 815, developed by the FASB, a derivative instrument is a financial instrument or other contract with each of the following characteristics: (a) one or more underlying and/or one or more notional amounts or payment provisions; (b) no or little initial net investment; and (c) the ability to be settled under contract terms, through a market mechanism, or by delivery of a derivative instrument or asset readily convertible to cash.[7]

An underlying may be, among other things, a security price, security price index, commodity price, or commodity price index.[8] In the case of options on S&P 500 Index Futures, the underlying is an S&P 500 Index futures contract. The S&P 500 Index is a market-cap-weighted stock market index that "includes 500 leading companies and captures approximately 80% coverage of available market capitalization."[9]

A notional amount is a number of currency units, shares, bushels, pounds, or other units specified in the contract.[10] Some derivative instruments require an initial net investment as compensation for either or both of the following: (a) the time value of the derivative instrument; or (b) terms that are more or less favorable than market conditions.[11] "An option generally requires that one party make an initial net investment ... because that party has the rights under the contract and the other party has the obligations."[12]

An option is the right or obligation to buy or sell a particular underlying financial instrument at a specified price on or before a certain date. A **call option** represents the right to buy or obligation to sell an underlying financial instrument, while a **put option** represents the right to sell or obligation to buy an underlying financial instrument. (*See* Table 10.1 later.) In the case of options on futures, the underlying financial instrument is a futures contract. The specified price at which an option may be exercised is called the **strike price**, and the date on or before which the option may be exercised is known as the **expiration date**, or expiry.[13]

Each option transaction consists of two parties – a buyer (who subsequently becomes a holder) and a seller (or writer). The buyer of a call option is said to take a "long" position in the market, while the seller of a call option takes a "short" position in the market. Similarly, the buyer of a put option has a "short" position, and the seller of a put option has a "long" position.[14]

TABLE 10.1

Rights (Obligations) of Option Holders (Writers)

	Call	Put
Holder	Has the **right** to **buy** the underlying financial instrument at the strike price.	Has the **right** to **sell** the underlying financial instrument at the strike price.
Writer	Has the **obligation** to **sell** underlying financial instrument at the strike price.	Has the **obligation** to **buy** the underlying financial instrument at the strike price.

The option buyer pays the seller a price which represents an initial net investment called a **premium**. The amount of premium the buyer pays depends on factors including the price of the underlying, the strike price, time remaining until expiration (i.e., time decay), and volatility of the underlying financial instrument. An option's premium generally increases as the option becomes further in the money and decreases as the option becomes more deeply out of the money. Generally, volatility of the underlying is positively correlated to changes in the premium. However, time remaining until expiration has a negative, exponential correlation to the premium. That is, the closer that an option gets to expiration, the lower the premium paid by the buyer and the faster the rate of reduction in the premium.[15]

At any given point in time, an option may be "**out of the money**" or "**in the money**."[16] For a call option, the option is said to be out of the money when the current market price of the underlying financial instrument is below the option strike price and in the money when the current market price of the underlying financial instrument is above the option strike price. The converse is true for a put option: the option is said to be out of the money when the current market price of the underlying financial instrument is above the option strike price and in the money when the current market price of the underlying financial instrument is below the option strike price.[17]

The value of an option has three components: (a) intrinsic value; (b) time value; and (c) volatility. An option has **intrinsic value** if it is in the money; the magnitude of this intrinsic value is based on the amount by which the option is in the money. The **time value** of an option is based on the amount of time remaining until expiry. Even when all other factors are held constant, time value erodes non-linearly the value of an option with each minute that passes.[18] As explained by the Options Industry Council, "Theta or time decay is not linear. The theoretical rate of decay will tend to increase as time to expiration decreases. Thus, the amount of decay indicated by Theta tends to be gradual at first and accelerates as expiration approaches. Upon expiration, an option has no time value and trades only for intrinsic value, if any."[19] The non-linear decay of the time value of an option is illustrated in Figure 10.1. Note, in particular, how the time value of an option decays more rapidly as the expiration date approaches—in this way, time value is always working in the favor of the option seller.

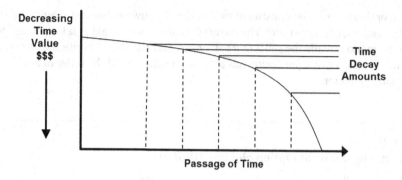

FIGURE 10.1[20]

Volatility measures how quickly and how much an option price moves in relation to the underlying financial instrument and may favor either the buyer or seller of the option.[21] The stock market moves constantly due to temporary differences in supply and demand stemming from a variety of reasons and economic indicators, including market sentiment, growth expectations, valuation, momentum, and central bank activity.[22] The value of an option based on the stock market likewise moves constantly due to instantaneous changes in both the price of the underlying and volatility, along with the ever-eroding time value.[23] Thus, option prices have the potential for more volatility than stock prices.

For option sellers, profit potential is limited to the premium collected upon the sale of the option and there is theoretically an unlimited risk of loss. However, a study published by *Futures* magazine in 2003 found that 76.5% of options held to expiration expire worthless and the Chicago Mercantile Exchange estimated in 2001 that approximately 74% of options held to expiration expire worthless. These proportions of options expiring worthless, along with the fact that the time value of an option is ever-eroding, indicate that the odds of gains on any option trade typically favor the option seller.[24]

There are two main styles of options – American-style options and European-style options. Both styles of options may be traded on American exchanges. The difference between the styles is the time at which they can be exercised. American-style options may be exercised by the option buyer at any time before or at expiration. European-style options, however, may only be exercised at expiration.[25] The buyer or seller of either an American style or European style option may "close" the position at any time. To close a position prior to expiration, an option seller or buyer must make an offsetting transaction; that is, a put or call buyer (seller) must sell (buy) a put or call with the same strike price and expiration date as the purchased (sold) put or call option, respectively.[26] Upon the execution of such an offsetting transaction, the position is closed.[27] Based upon my review of trading records for the Funds, I have found that the options that Xxxx traded were very rarely exercised prior to expiration.[28]

At expiry, the seller of an option of either style that is in the money is typically assigned or obligated to perform. When an option holder exercises a long call, an option seller is assigned the obligation to sell the underlying financial instrument at the strike price. This assignment results in a short position in the underlying financial instrument for the option seller. When an option holder exercises a long put, the option seller is assigned the obligation to buy the underlying financial instrument at the strike price. This assignment results in a long position in the underlying financial instrument for the option seller.[29] An assigned short or long position in the underlying financial instrument may be netted by an offsetting position; that is, a short position in the underlying financial instrument may be netted by a long position in the same underlying financial instrument, and vice versa.[30]

A futures contract is a legally binding agreement to buy or sell a specified commodity or financial instrument in a specified amount at a specified date in the future. One who buys a futures contract agrees to purchase the underlying commodity or financial instrument, while one who sells a futures contract agrees to sell the same. A futures contract includes the item being bought and sold, the contract size, the contract month (typically March, June, September, or December), and the manner of settlement. Stock index futures do not call for the delivery of the actual stocks associated with the stock index; rather, a cash settlement mechanism is used wherein subsequent to the final settlement day, positions expire and are settled at the spot (i.e., cash) value of the underlying index.[31]

Stock index futures, including S&P 500 futures, were introduced in 1982 on domestic futures exchanges. The original S&P 500 futures contract was based on a value of $500 times the index value. In 1997, the Chicago Mercantile Exchange found that the futures contract value was too high and halved the contract multiplier to $250. In the same year, realizing that the futures contract value was still high relative to many other futures contracts, the exchange introduced an alternative, electronically-traded "E-mini" S&P 500 contract based on a value of $50 times the index. The E-Mini S&P 500 design was "widely accepted and rapidly grew to become the most popular line of stock index futures available today."[32]

The SEC notes on its website that it "sometimes receive[s] questions and complaints about futures trading." It further notes that "[t]he SEC administers and enforces the federal laws that govern the sale and trading of securities, such as stocks, bonds, and mutual funds, but we do not regulate futures trading. We refer questions and complaints about futures to the Commodity Futures Trading Commission (CFTC)—the federal agency that does regulate futures trading."[33]

VI. An Overview of Hedge Funds.

A hedge fund is a privately offered fund that is administered by a professional investment management firm. Hedge fund managers seek and assume calculated risks to achieve investment returns. Globally, there are an estimated 8,200 active individual hedge funds with more than approximately $3.1 trillion in assets under management. The US accounts for approximately 72% of the global assets under management.[34]

One measure of value that is common among hedge funds is net asset value, or "NAV," which equals the hedge fund's total assets minus its liabilities. In other words, the NAV of a hedge fund is the value of the fund if it were closed at that moment. Daily changes in NAV occur due to changes in a fund's holdings, as well as mark-to-market accounting of its holdings. Under mark-to-market accounting (fair value accounting),[35] the value of an asset or liability is based on the current market price of the financial instrument, rather than the book value (i.e., the price paid for the financial instrument). The market price of an option moves constantly due to instantaneous changes in both the price of the underlying financial instrument and volatility, along with the ever-eroding time value. Accordingly, for hedge funds that trade options, the value of the fund's assets and liabilities (and, thus, its NAV) are constantly subject to change.[36]

For hedge funds that trade financial instruments without expiration or maturity dates, such as the stock of publicly-traded companies, NAV is a relevant data point for investors and it is strongly correlated to the profitability of the fund. If, however, a hedge fund trades financial instruments with expiration or maturity dates, such as options or futures, NAV is not nearly as relevant to investors nor is NAV strongly correlated with the profitability of the fund. For example, when a hedge fund sells an option, there is a potential for the fund to profit at expiration or maturity even if the option shows a paper loss at the moment NAV is calculated. In other words, an out of the money option may have a paper gain or loss at any given moment, but all else held constant, the option will be worthless at expiration. For example, suppose that the market price of Apple stock was $100 and that on January 1 a hedge fund sold one (1) call option on Apple stock for $20 with a strike price of $150 with an expiration date of February 15. This short call is out of the money by 50 points and has about 45 days until it expires. If, on January 31, the market price of Apple stock increased to $140, I would expect the price of the option to increase; in this case, suppose the price increases to $30. Since the stock price increased and is closer to the option's strike price, the value of the option would have increased. However, there has been 30 days that have passed and been a negative influence on the price of the option. The $10 price increase in the option is the net effect of the market driven increase and the decrease from time decay. Thus, this option is still out of the money, but would result in a $10 loss (−50%) if the fund decided to close it. If the fund chose not to close it, the option has a high probability that it will expire worthless in 15 days out of the money. If the option indeed expired worthless out of the money, the fund would realize a $20 gain (+100%) on the option. A calculation of the fund's NAV would not be able to capture or show to investors that, although the fund would lose money on certain positions if they were closed, the fund would be very likely to earn a profit on those positions when they mature or expire.

The traditional fee structure for hedge funds is the "2 and 20" structure based on NAV and subject to a high-water mark. Under this fee structure, hedge fund managers earn an annual management fee equal to 2% of the net asset value of the fund (irrespective of the fund's performance) plus 20% of gains, including both unrealized and realized gains and losses. In addition, many investors pay direct and indirect pass-through fund expenses under the typical hedge fund fee structure, such as administrative, legal, and audit fees.[37]

Despite its prevalence, many market commentators have criticized the traditional "2 and 20" fee structure for hedge funds. Warren Buffet, for example, has said that the "2 and 20" fee structure "borders on obscene."[38] As he explained, "how many hedge fund managers in the last 40 years have said 'I only want to get paid if I do something for you? Unless I actually deliver something beyond what you can get yourself, I don't want to get paid.' It just doesn't happen."[39]

VII. The Xxxx Entities.

Xxxx Xxxxxxxx, XXX ("Xxxx"), is a Xxxxxxxxx Limited Liability Company that was formed on March 23, XXXX. Xxxx is, or was, respectively, the investment advisor to Xxxx Xxxxxxxxxxx, XXX (the "XX Fund") and XXX Xxxxxxxxxxx, XXX (the "XXX Fund") (collectively, the "Funds"). Xxxx is registered with both the Commodity Futures Trading Commission ("CFTC") and the National Futures Association ("NFA") as a commodity pool operator and was registered as an investment advisor with the SEC from July XXXX until September 1, XXXX.[40]

Xxxx is wholly owned by Xxxxx Xxxxxx. Xx. Xxxxxx is an options trader and has served as President of Xxxx since March XXXX.[41] Xx. Xxxxxx received a bachelor's degrees in mathematics and accounting from the University of North Carolina, Chapel Hill, and holds an MBA from Wake Forest University. Xx. Xxxxxx previously held a CPA license, which is no longer active.[42] Xx. Xxxxxx became listed with the CFTC as a Principal of Xxxx, registered as an Associated Person of Xxxx, and became a member of NFA, in such capacities, on January 24, XXXX.[43] Xxxx Xxxxxxx and Xxxx Xxxxxxx are both employees of Xxxx. Xx. Xxxxxxx is a trader and Xx. Xxxxxxx is the controller, and previously served as the chief compliance officer.

Xxxx Xxxx Xxxxxxxxxx ("Xxxx Xxxxxxxxxx") is a Xxxxxxxxx-based tax-exempt 501(c)(3) private foundation.[44] Xx. Xxxxxx was the President of the Xxxx Xxxxxxxxxx in XXXX, XXXX and XXXX.[45] Xxx Xxxx Xxxxxxxxxx pays for all administrative expenses of Xxxx Xxxx Xxxxxxxxxxxxx ("Xxxx Xxxx"), which allows Xxxx Xxxx to use 100% of the donations it receives for project costs.[46]

Xxxx Xxxx is a Xxxxxxxx-based tax-exempt 501(c)(3) charitable organization founded by Xx. Xxxxxx.[47] Formed in XXXX – prior to Xxxx and the Funds – the organization "works to make an impact that lasts by empowering remarkable people to overcome some of the world's most difficult living conditions."[48] Xxxx Xxxx has served in many countries, including Nicaragua, Peru, Thailand, Malawi, Honduras, Uganda, Ghana, and Sierra Leone.[49] Xx. Xxxxxx believes that the best way for Xxxx Xxxx to make a real difference is to help people break the cycle of poverty themselves, which restores dignity and instills hope. The organization does development work, focusing on job creation and increased household income as the greatest potential for lasting change.[50]

The XXX Xxxx was a Xxxxxxxxx Limited Liability Company formed on or around April 3, XXXX and dissolved on or around August 6, XXXX.[51] On November 1, XXXX, the XXXX Xxxx ceased being a commingled commodity pool and became a single member limited liability company owned entirely by Xxxxx Xxxxx Xxxx, who was also the XXX Xxxx's managing member.[52] Xxx XXX Xxxx was originally formed by three individuals, Xxxxx Xxxxx Xxxx, X. Xxxxxxx Xxxxxx, and Xxxxx Xxxxxx, who previously worked together at Xxxxxxxxx Xxxxxxxxxx, Xxx., a limestone company based in Xxxxxxxxx, Xxxxxxxxx.[53] Xxxx became the investment advisor of the XXX Fund in XXXX, and ceased trading for the XXX Fund in XXXX[54]

<paragraph omitted>

The XX Fund has three classes of interests although only one, Class A, is offered to investors.[57] The Class B Interests are all held by Xxxx Xxxxxxxxxx and are entitled to a 10% incentive allocation, as defined in various documents described below.[58] This funding to the Xxxx Xxxxxxxxxx, among other things, "provides a permanent source of funds to pay the administrative costs" of Xxxx Xxxx.[59] Class C Interests are held by Xx. Xxxxxx, as the Managing Member of the XX Xxxx, and she is also entitled to a 10% incentive allocation as defined in various documents, described below.[60] Xx. Xxxxxx pays certain of the XX Xxxx's operating expenses as well as certain of Xxxx's operating expenses, including compensation for employees, such as Xxxx Xxxxxxx, Xxxx Xxxxxxx and others, from the 10% incentive allocation that she receives.[61]

For the period that is relevant to this proceeding, certain features of the XXX Fund and the XX Fund were somewhat unique, as compared to other hedge funds. First, many hedge funds operate under a "2 and 20" fee structure, as described above. In contrast, the XXX Fund and the XX Fund paid incentive allocations that were equal to 20% of net realized gains on closed positions. Second, investors who withdrew all or any portion of their investment from the Funds did so based upon capital account values that reflected only net realized gains and losses on closed positions. Thus, withdrawing members did not participate in unrealized gains and losses on open positions. The Funds' redemption practices contrasted with the redemption practices of certain other hedge funds, under which investors redeem at NAV, which includes realized and unrealized gains and losses.[62]

VIII. Information Provided to Prospective Investors in the XX Fund.

It is my understanding that prospective investors in the XX Fund were provided an XX Fund Confidential Private Placement Memorandum ("PPM"), XX Xxxx Operating Agreement (the "XX OA"), and Contribution Agreement (collectively, the "XX Fund Offering Materials"), which explained, among other things, the XX Fund's objectives and risks, the terms of investing in the XX Fund, as well as, fees and redemption terms.[63]

The original PPM was dated March 23, XXXX and updated on January 31, XXXX, January 31, XXXX, January 31, XXXX, and January 31, XXXX.[64] Each of the PPMs contained information that described the fund's investment objective, the manner in which incentive allocations would be earned and paid, the withdrawal process, tax information, suitability standards, and risk factors, among other things. Unless otherwise stated, this section quotes from the PPM dated January 31, XXXX.

Class A investors signed a Contribution Agreement for the XX Fund, wherein the investor, or "Subscriber," certified that he or she has reviewed and understands the risks of an investment <remaining paragraph omitted>.

<sections omitted>

... equity indexes [...]."[70] The XX OA similarly notes that, "[t]he purpose of the [XX Fund] is to use the funds provided by its Class A Members [...] for the sale, purchase, and trading of options on broad based equity indexes, options on futures on broad based equity indexes, and futures on broad based equity indexes [...]."[71]

The PPM cautioned investors, however, that "[t]here is no guarantee that the Fund will achieve its investment objective, and [investors] may lose [their] entire investment."[72] It continues, "**Investors must be able to bear the substantial risks of an investment in the Fund and be able to afford to lose his or her entire investment.**"[73] In addition, the PPM stated that "**[a]n investment in the Fund is speculative and involves a high degree of risk. Investors should be aware that an investment in the Fund is suitable only for persons who can afford to lose their entire investment.**"[74] The PPM further disclosed many specific risks that investors faced with an investment in the XX Fund.[75]

Moreover, the XX Fund Offering Materials cautioned investors that due to "the proprietary nature of the Investment Advisor's trading program, [investors] generally will not be advised if adjustments are made to the Investment Advisor's trading program," except that "to the extent that such changes are material, [investors] will be notified of such material changes, and [investors] will be given the opportunity to withdraw [their] investment."[76] While the XX Fund Offering Materials described the general trading objectives and strategy of the fund to prospective investors, Xxxx further informed its investors of updates to its strategy at various points from XXXX through XXXX, including updates in response to market volatility.[77] In addition, each Class A interest holder had the right to inspect the books and records of the XX Fund.[78]

B. The XX Fund's Fee Structure.

The XX Fund Offering Materials explained that the investors in the XX Fund, holders of Class A interests, do not pay a management fee to Xxxx, the XX Fund's investment advisor.[79] Rather, as described in the PPM, the XX Xxxx's operating expenses are paid for by Xx. Xxxxxx, except for brokerage commissions and trading fees, which are paid for by the XX Fund itself.[80] The PPM further described the incentive allocation, which is paid to Xxxx Xxxxxxxxxx, as the current holder of Class B interests, and Xx. Xxxxxx, as holder of Class C interests:

> An incentive allocation (the 'Incentive Allocation') equal to 20% of the New Trading Profits (as defined below) earned by the Fund accrues and is payable monthly to the holders of the Class B Interests and Class C Interests. [...] The holders of the Class B Interests receive 50% of the Incentive Allocation (i.e., 10% of the New Trading Profits), and the holder of the Class C Interests receives 50% of the Incentive Allocation (i.e., 10% of the New Trading Profits).
>
> The term "New Trading Profits" means net trading profits that have been realized on closed positions of trades made from the assets of the Fund [...], decreased proportionally by the Fund's brokerage fees and other transaction costs and increased by any interest income received by the Fund.[81]

Earlier iterations of the PPM stated the same by disclosing, inter alia, that the Class B and C interest holders would be compensated with 20% of "the profit realized by the [XX Fund] based upon the trades done by the [XX Fund] and/or the Investment Manager."[82]

As the Incentive Allocation was based on "net trading profits that have been realized on closed positions," the PPM further disclosed to investors that "it is possible that the Fund will pay an Incentive Allocation on New Trading Profits even though there are unrealized losses on open positions":

> The Fund pays an Incentive Allocation based upon the New Trading Profits generated by the Investment Advisor for the Fund. These New Trading Profits only include realized gains and losses on closed positions. Accordingly, it is possible that the Fund will pay an Incentive Allocation on New Trading Profits even though there are unrealized losses on open positions. Thus, there is an incentive for the Investment Advisor to realize gains and defer realization of losses; however, due to the type of trading in which the Investment Advisor engages, it is unlikely that the Investment Advisor will be able to defer realization of losses on positions for any extended period of time since most trades into which the Investment Advisor enters will only be open for 30- to 90-days at maximum.[83]

C. Withdrawals from the XX Fund.

As noted above, another aspect of the XX Fund that was somewhat unique, compared to other hedge funds, was that withdrawing members do not participate in unrealized gains and losses. That aspect of the XX Fund was also explained in the PPM:

> Upon the Withdrawal Date, the withdrawing Member shall only receive his or her *pro rata* portion of any net realized profits or losses on closed positions. Such Member will not receive the benefit of any unrealized gain that is subsequently realized by the Fund. Similarly, the withdrawing Member will not participate in any unrealized loss.
>
> Following such a Withdrawal by a Member, all other Members remaining in the Fund after the Withdrawal Date will receive the benefit of any gains realized subsequent to the Withdrawal Data; however, the Members remaining in the Fund will also participate in any losses subsequently realized on positions that were outstanding as of that Withdrawal Date and closed after the Withdrawal Date.[84]

The XX Fund Offering Materials note that an investor who wishes to withdraw some or all of his or her investment must give written notice of the withdrawal at least one month prior to a withdrawal of $5,000 to $25,000 and at least three months prior to a withdrawal of over $25,000. This notice requirement provides Xxxx with time to close out positions that "used and/or have relied upon the presence of the withdrawing Member's funds."[85] The PPM continues:

> The Fund will use its best efforts to close out positions that have relied upon the presence of the withdrawing Member's funds; however, upon the Withdrawal Date, the withdrawing Member will receive the *pro rata* portion of the realized gains or losses on all closed positions as of that date.[86]

D. Open and Closed Positions.

The XX Fund Offering Materials, as described above, disclosed to investors that withdrawals from the XX Fund and the incentive allocation were based on realized gains and losses on closed positions, and excluded any unrealized gains and losses on open positions. It is well-established that an options or futures position is closed when it expires or when Xxxx manually closes it by purchasing an offsetting position.[87] Otherwise, the position is open. As for options positions that expire in the money and result in the assignment of the underlying financial instrument, it is well-established that, in such a circumstance, the expired option is closed while the assigned futures position is open.[88]

IX. Account Information Provided to Investors in the Funds.
A. Monthly Account Statements.

The **XX Fund** Offering Materials state that as "promptly as practicable after the close of each calendar month, the Fund will distribute to each Class A Member a monthly Capital Account report with respect to such Class A Member's investment in the Fund."[89] The XX OA further states that, in accordance with 17 CFR 4.22 and 4.25:

> Xxxx Xxxxxxxx as the Investment Advisor for the Fund, is required to report gains and losses to Investors in its offered Funds monthly and annually based upon realized and unrealized gains and losses. Xxxx Xxxxxxxx will report monthly the Fund's unrealized gains and losses on open positions at month's end. Also monthly Xxxx Xxxxxxxx will report Net Realized Trading Profits and Losses on closed positions based upon the contractually agreed upon payment of the Incentive Allocation to the Class B and the Class C Members [...].
>
> ....
>
> The first monthly statement will be based upon realized gains and losses on closed positions [...]. Members will also receive a second monthly statement calculated according to the Commodity Futures Trading Commission Rule 4.22 found in 17 CFR Part 4, Subpart B in which unrealized gains and losses related to open positions at month end will be calculated according to accounting principles generally accepted in the United States.[90]

It is my understanding that monthly account statements were distributed to XX Fund investors in compliance with the XX Fund Offering Materials.[91]

From the beginning of the relevant period in January XXXX through August XXXX, Xxxx sent investors in the Funds monthly statements consistent with a contractual accounting method.[92] During this time, a typical XX Fund monthly capital account statement provided the following information, by month: (1) the Beginning Realized Capital Account balance as of the beginning of the month; (2) the amount of Capital Contributions made within the month; (3) the amount of Capital Distributions made within the month; (4) the Revised Capital Account balance; (5) the Member Interest in the Revised Capital Account; (6) the Gross Realized Gain/(Loss) for the month; (7) the 20% Expenses paid (or, Incentive Allocation) on the Gross Realized Gain/(Loss); (8) the Net Realized Gain/(Loss) after allocation of the 20% Expenses; (9) the Ending Realized Capital Account balance; and (10) the Net Monthly Realized ROI (Return on Investment). In addition to these financial metrics, the statement included a graph showing Cumulative Net Realized Gain/(Loss).[93] A typical XXX Fund monthly capital account statement from the beginning of the relevant period in January XXXX through August XXXX contained substantially the same information.

Xxxx expanded the investors' monthly statements for the XX Fund beginning with the statements for August XXXX to also include a statement prepared under regulatory accounting that showed both realized and unrealized gains and losses, as well as the one prepared under contractual accounting that showed realized gains and losses and an incentive allocation calculated based on the same. Beginning in August XXXX, the second page of a typical XX Fund capital account statement included a Statement of Operations for the period and a Statement of Changes in Net Asset Value for the period, each shown for each of the XX Fund in total, Class A Members, and the individual investor. The second page also includes a shaded box with a bold border that shows the calculation of current Net Asset Value based on: (1) the Realized Capital Account Balance; (2) Pending Contributions for NAV; (3) Pending Withdrawals for NAV; and (4) the Current Month Unrealized balance.[95] Put another way, beginning with the statements for August XXXX, Xxxx issued two-page monthly reports to XX Fund investors, with the first page showing realized gains/losses consistent with the participants' contractual investment terms and the second page showing the XX Fund's net asset value as well as realized and unrealized gains and losses, which complies with Regulation 4.22(d). Beginning with the statements for September XXXX, Xxxx also provided substantially similar two-page statements to investors in the XXX Fund.[96]

B. Year-End Audited Financial Statements and K-1s.

In addition to monthly account statements, the XX Fund Offering Materials indicate that investors would also receive as promptly as practicable after the close of each fiscal year an annual report containing audited financial statements for the fund.[97] It is my understanding that audited financial statements of the XX Fund were distributed to XX Fund investors in compliance with the XX Fund Offering Materials.[98] It is also my understanding that audited financial statements of the XXX Xxxx were distributed to XXX Fund investors until it ceased being a pool and became a single member Limited Liability Company managed account.[99] It is my understanding that the audited financial statements were distributed to investors after the close of the pool's fiscal year.[100]

I have reviewed the audited financial statements for XXX Fund and XX Fund for the years XXXX through XXXX. The financial statements of both the XX Fund and the XXX Fund were prepared in accordance with GAAP, as established by the FASB, and were audited by registered independent auditors each year during the relevant time period.[101] The financial statements of both Funds for the year ended December 31, XXXX were audited by Xxxxxxxx CPAs, P.C.[102] The financial statements of the XX Fund for the year ended December 31, XXXX were audited by XxXxxxxxx LLP, now known as XXX XX LLP.[103] The financial statements of the XX Fund for the year ended December 31, XXXX were audited by Xxxxxxx Xxxxx Xxxxxxxx, LLC.[104] Each of the foregoing companies is a public accounting firm currently registered with the PCAOB and was inspected by the PCAOB during the relevant period.[105]

In each audit report prepared for the XX Fund and the XXX Fund, the independent auditors stated that the audited financial statements included the current "statement of financial condition," "condensed schedule of investments," "statement of operations," statement of "changes in members' equity" for the year then ended, and "the related notes to the financial statements."[106] The auditor's opinion in each instance was that "the financial statements referred to above present fairly, in all material aspects, the financial position" of the audited Fund "and the results of its operations for the year then ended, in accordance with accounting principles generally accepted in the United States of America."[107]

The audited financial statements prepared for both the XX Fund and the XXX Fund reflected both realized and unrealized gains and losses for the Funds. The Statements of Operations that were prepared for each of the Funds in each year reflected both the "Net realized gain from derivative contracts" and the "Net unrealized increase (decrease) in value of derivative contracts." Further, the audited balance sheets for the Funds (the Statements of Financial Condition) reflected the fair value of both asset and liability derivative contacts as of the end of each year.[108] It is my understanding that all investors in both the XX Fund and the XXX Fund received the audited financial statements for the fund in which they were invested, and which reported all realized and unrealized gains and losses for the Funds.[109]

Investors in the XXX Fund and the XX Fund were also provided with Schedule K-1s.[110] I have reviewed a sample of K-1s that were prepared for investors in each of the years XXXX through XXXX.[111] The K-1s include the following information, which was specific to each investor: annual gains and losses calculated in accordance with GAAP, the annual increase or decrease in the investor's account based on GAAP accounting, and the investor's percentage ownership of the XX Fund.[112]

X. Xxxx's Investment Strategy.

Xxxx's investment strategy was to make a profit (realized gains), and minimize losses, for the investors of the XXX Fund and XX Fund.[113] The Funds were specifically designed to trade in options on, options on futures on, and futures on, broad based equity indexes, primarily the S&P 500 Index. The Funds, among other things, traded, bought, sold, spread, or otherwise acquired, held, or disposed of the aforementioned derivatives.[114] During the relevant period, Xxxx traded in options on S&P 500 Index Futures.[115]

To achieve its investment strategy, depending on a multitude of factors, including market conditions, the macroeconomic environment, world events, and the positions already in the portfolio, Xxxx deployed various tools that are widely utilized within the industry, including in the money expiration probabilities, analysis of market trends, moving averages, and Bollinger Bands.[116] Bollinger Bands are, "curves drawn in and around the price structure usually consisting of a moving average (the middle band), an upper band, and a lower band that answer the question as to whether prices are high or low on a relative basis."[117] Xxxx utilized these tools to evaluate the market, consider potential trades, and execute the trades that would create the most benefit for XX Fund and XXX Fund investors.[118]

One of the ways Xxxx executed its investment strategy for both the XX Fund and the XXX Fund was selling out of the money options.[119] But Xxxx also sold in the money options, purchased options, and purchased and sold futures,[120] depending on market conditions, macroeconomic conditions, world events, the positions in the portfolios, and a variety of other factors.[121]

In addition, Xxxx utilized a variety of tools to protect investors and help the Funds recover from periods of extreme or unusual market volatility, such as the October and December 2014 "V-bottom" events. A "V-bottom" event is characterized by a sharp decline in the market followed by a quick, sharp recovery.[122] In October 2014, the S&P 500 experienced such a "V-bottom" event, and the financial markets overall experienced significant turmoil. According to the Wall Street Journal, the October 2014 volatility was, "a 'bloodbath' for hedge funds, inflicting large losses at an array of multibillion-dollar firms in the industry's worst stretch since late 2011."[123] Those "V-bottom" events caused the Funds to experience trading losses, and realizing those losses at the end of the month would have caused a sharp decay in the value of each investor's capital account from which investor withdrawals are made. Xxxx believed that it could reduce and eliminate those losses over time and it executed trades that provided time in which it could work through and reduce the losses to an appropriate level.[124] Xxxx fully reduced the losses associated with the October and December 2014 market events by June Xxxx.[125]

XI. Opinion.

Based on my review and analysis of the materials identified above and certain empirical analyses I have performed, and my skills, knowledge, education, training, and experience, I am of the following opinions.

A. The Funds did not enter into trades that were open for more than 90 days.

Based on my review of the XX Fund's and the XXX Fund's trading records, I have not identified any trades that were open for more than 90 days.[126] With respect to the XX Fund, this conforms to the PPM, which noted that most trades into which Xxxx enters will be open for less than 90 days.[127]

B. Xxxx applied correct accounting treatment to the XX Fund's and the XXX Fund's open and closed trading positions.

Options contracts and futures contracts are examples of transferable derivative instruments. According to FASB ASC 815 on Derivatives and Hedging, which Xxxx was required to follow, "Derivative instruments that are transferable are, by their nature, separate and distinct contracts."[128] Thus, it was necessary for Xxxx to treat options contracts, on the one hand, and futures contracts that were assigned from options that expired in the money, on the other, as separate and distinct assets and liabilities.

Xxxx appropriately followed this mandatory guidance in preparing the monthly account statements for the XX Fund and the XXX Fund, and in calculating the XX Fund's and the XXX Fund's realized gains and losses on closed positions, as reflected in the monthly account statements. In particular, when Xxxx sold options for the XX Fund's account or the XXX Fund's account that expired in the money at the end of a particular month and resulted in the assignment of futures, Xxxx correctly classified the option as a closed position and the premium it received from the sale of that option as a realized gain, and Xxxx correctly classified the option as a closed position and the premium it received from the sale of that option as a realized gain, and Xxxx correctly classified the futures position that it was assigned as an open position and the gain or loss (depending on its mark-to-market value) on that futures position as unrealized.

Likewise, the XX Fund's and the XXX Fund's outside auditors appropriately followed this mandatory guidance in preparing annual audited financial statements for the XX Fund and XXX Fund.[129] The XX Fund's and the XXX Fund's outside auditors properly recorded options contracts and futures contracts as separate positions in the Funds' schedules of investments.[130] The schedules of investments were included in the audited financial statements that were distributed to the Funds' investors.[131] Regarding accounting treatment of gains and losses, ASC 815 states, "Gains and losses (realized and unrealized) on all derivative instruments [...] shall be shown net when recognized in the income statement, whether or not settled physically, if the derivative instruments are held for trading purposes."[132]

C. With respect to the XX Fund and the XXX Fund, Net Asset Value and unrealized gains and losses on open positions were not particularly relevant.

Other than for margin requirements and tax purposes,[133] with respect to the XX Fund and the XXX Fund, unrealized gains and losses on open positions and the NAV of the Funds were less relevant than realized gains and losses on closed positions. As explained in Part VI, the unrealized value or NAV of an open position measures the gain or loss the XX Fund or the XXX Fund would incur if it closed that position by purchasing or selling an offsetting position. In other words, unrealized value or NAV represents the value of a particular position or the Fund as a whole if that particular position or all of the Funds' positions were closed at the moment the unrealized value or NAV was measured.

As the Funds were a going concern and many of the Funds' investors were largely long-term investors;[134] however, the liquidation value of particular positions or the Funds as a whole was not particularly relevant. In addition, although it was not unusual for the Funds to have open positions with a negative unrealized value or NAV, such unrealized values were not particularly relevant because they did not necessarily reflect a risk of future realized losses or a potential for realized gains. As shown by the example in Part VI, even if the unrealized or net asset value of a position is negative, there could still be an extremely high likelihood that, at expiration, the XX Fund or XXX Fund will realize a gain on that position. Or, put differently, even when the unrealized or net asset value of a position is negative, there may be an extremely low likelihood that, at expiration, the XX Fund or the XXX Fund will incur a realized loss. As investor withdrawals from the XX Fund and XXX Fund were based on each investor's respective ownership of the XX Fund's or the XXX Fund's realized gains and losses, unrealized or net asset values of positions were not particularly relevant, since they did not necessarily reflect a risk of future realized losses or the potential for realized gains. Moreover, Xxxx primarily traded options on, options on futures on, and futures on the S&P 500 index, the value of which is constantly changing. As a result, the unrealized value or NAV of positions held by the XX Fund or the XXX Fund could increase or decrease instantaneously, which makes momentary unrealized gains and losses less relevant.[135]

D. Xxxx's premise that, over time, it could reduce and eliminate trading losses caused by periods of extreme and unusual market volatility is supported by Chebyshev's Theorem and the Empirical Rule.

As explained in Part X, during periods of unusual and extreme market volatility, such as the October and December 2014 "V-bottoms," the XX Fund and XXX Fund experienced trading losses, and realizing those losses at the end of the month would have caused a sharp decay in the value of each investor's capital account from which investor withdrawals are made. Xxxx's investment strategy, in part, relied on the premise that, over time, it could reduce and eliminate trading losses that were caused by periods of unusual and extreme volatility.[136] And, indeed, Xxxx fully reduced the losses associated with the October and December 2014 market events by June XXXX.[137]

This strategy is, in fact, supported by Chebyshev's Theorem, the Empirical Rule, and the tendency of reversion to the mean that is implied by both propositions. Chebyshev's Theorem states that for any set of data, regardless of the shape of the frequency distribution of the data, the proportion of values that lie within k standard deviations ($k > 1$) of the mean is at least $1 - (1/k$ squared). The standard deviation of a measurement is a calculation of distance from the mean, or the average of a data set. Given Chebyshev's Theorem, for $k = 2$, at least 75% of the data lie within two standard deviations of the mean; for $k = 3$, at least 89% of the data lie within three standard deviations of the mean.[138] Of course, all of the trades in stocks included in the S&P 500 index form a population with an easily identified mean.

Further, for data sets with frequency distributions that are symmetric and bell-shaped, these percentages are generally much higher than Chebyshev's Theorem specifies. The Empirical Rule applies to such data sets and predicts that 68%, 95%, and 99.7% of the data lie within one, two, and three standard deviations of the mean, respectively.[139] Figure 10.2 illustrates the operation of this principle.

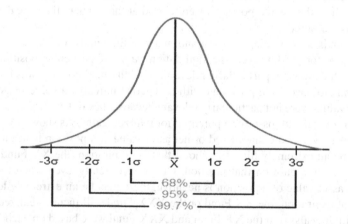

FIGURE 10.2

When Xxxx evaluated potential transactions involving the sale of out of the money options, it utilized various tools, including Bollinger Bands and in the money expiration probabilities that are based, in part, on Chebyshev's Theorem and the Empirical Rule and the probabilities that each puts forth. In particular, one of the ways Xxxx executed its investment strategy was selling out of the money options with a strike price that was at least two standard deviations from the current market price of the underlying financial instrument, which, according to Chebyshev's Theorem accounts for at least 75% of data. When selling that type of option, Xxxx utilized an in the money expiration probability threshold which was based, in part, Chebyshev's Theorem and the Empirical Rule.[140]

Reversion to the mean is "the tendency for stock returns to return to their long-term norms over time – periods of exceptional returns tend to be followed by periods of below average performance, and vice versa."[141] Dr. James Schultz notes that this tendency for reversion to the mean is the reason why options traders execute trades based on the probability of an option to expire in the money.[142] The stock market as a whole and the S&P 500 Index have historically shown an inexorable tendency for investors' returns to revert to the mean. Moreover, the mean returns for both the stock market and the S&P 500 Index are historically positive.[143]

Taken together in light of the S&P 500 Index, Chebyshev's Theorem, the Empirical Rule, and the tendency of reversion to the mean show that observations of extreme stock market returns, whether positive or negative, are infrequent, and that returns over time tend to revert to the mean. Because the historical mean of the S&P 500 Index is positive, it follows that periods of loss tend to eventually be offset by periods of gain, though the timing of reversion to the mean is unknown.[144] In other words, Chebyshev's Theorem, the Empirical Rule and the tendency of reversion to the mean support Xxxx's premise that it would be able to reduce trading losses caused by extreme market events to an appropriate level over time through its investment strategy, which included, among other things, selling options that have a high probability of expiring out of the money.

E. The traditional "2 and 20" method for hedge fund fees would have yielded approximately $7.2 million more in fees and incentive allocations.

Under the XX Fund fee structure, Xx. Xxxxxx and Xxxx Xxxxxxxxxx collectively received an incentive allocation equal to 20% of month-end realized gains on closed positions. From January 2013 through March 2016, the investors in the XX Fund earned $111,352,292 in net realized gains on closed positions, and Xx. Xxxxxx and Xxxx Xxxxxxxxxx were entitled to receive incentive allocations equal to 20% of that amount, which resulted in incentive allocations of $22,270,458 (see Figures 10.3–10.5).[145] Half of that amount ($11,135,229) was paid to the Xxxx Xxxxxxxxxx. The other half went to Xx. Xxxxxx, but she did not personally retain that amount. Instead, Xx. Xxxxxx used those funds to pay all expenses of the XX Fund (except for brokerage commissions and trading fees). In addition, as the sole owner of Xxxx, the XX Fund's investment advisor, Xx. Xxxxxx was also responsible for all of Xxxx's expenses, and she used her portion of the incentive allocation to pay for certain of Xxxx's expenses as well. I have performed an analysis of the XX Fund's records to determine the amount that Xx. Xxxxxx earned in salary and retained in incentive allocation after paying expenses as described above. I have determined that from January XXXX through May XXXX, this amounted to approximately $4.8 million, or approximately 22% of the $22,270,258 in incentive allocations paid by the XX Fund.[146]

I have also performed an analysis to determine whether Xx. Xxxxxx and Xxxx Xxxxxxxxxx would have earned more, less or the same amount from January XXXX through May XXXX if (i) the XX Fund charged an annual 2% management fee based on the XX Fund's NAV and (ii) the incentive allocation paid by the XX Fund was based on realized gains or losses on closed positions and unrealized gains or losses on open positions. This hypothetical fee structure would be more in line with the traditional "2 and 20" fee structure for hedge funds, as described in Part VI above.

As shown in Exhibits 1.1 and 1.2, under that hypothetical fee structure, XX. Xxxxxx and Xxxx Xxxxxxxxxx would have earned $9,976,143 in management fees and $19,521,946 in incentive allocations from January XXXX through May XXXX. In total, Xx. Xxxxxx and Xxxx Xxxxxxxxxx would have earned $29,498,088. That is $7,227,630 or approximately 32% more than Xx. Xxxxxx and Xxxx Xxxxxxxxxx actually earned in incentive allocations. In other words, the XX Fund's fee structure— with no management fee and an incentive allocation based on realized gains on closed positions only—saved the investors approximately $7.2 million, as compared to a fee structure more in line with the traditional "2 and 20" model that is common among hedge funds.[147]

XII. Other Considerations.

My report is issued in accordance with the Standards for Consulting Services issued by the American Institute of Certified Public Accountants. This report is to be used solely in connection with proceedings in the above-referenced matter, it should not be used for any other purpose, and it is designated Confidential pursuant to the Consent Confidentiality Order. Outside distribution of this report to others is not permitted without the written consent of Xxxxxxx Xxxxxxxx Xxxxxxxxxx, LLC. The information in this report is based on information learned through the date of this report. My review and analysis of the facts and circumstances of the case is ongoing, and I reserve the right to supplement and amend my opinions to consider information learned subsequent to the date of this report.

This concludes my report and it is respectfully submitted this fifth day of February XXXX.

By:_____
                                        William L. Jennings, CPA

XIII. Exhibits

Exhibit A – CV of William L. Jennings
William L. Jennings, BS, MBA, CPA, CFE, CFF

A. Background and Education

1. Present Position

- Veritas Forensic Accounting, LLC, Member

2. Other Positions Held

- Accounting, Economics & Appraisal Group, LLC, Principal, May 2016 to December 2017
- Alvarez & Marsal Global Forensic and Dispute Services, LLC, Managing Director, June 2012 to May 2016
- Navigant Consulting, Inc., Managing Director and Practice Segment Leader, Southeast – Disputes and Investigations, October 2005 to June 2012
- LECG, LLC, Director – National Forensic Accounting Practice, August 2004 to October 2005

- FFI, Inc., President, 2003 – 2004
- Kroll, Inc., Principal, 1995 – 2003
- Coopers & Lybrand, L.L.P., Director-in-Charge – Fraud Investigation services, 1989 – 1994
- Oxford Group, Ltd., Acting Chief Financial Officer, 1989
- Brown & Jennings, CPAs, Partner, 1984 – 1989
- Coopers & Lybrand, L.L.P., Supervisor – General Audit Practice, 1979 – 1983
- A.A. Harmon & Co., CPA's, Semi-Senior Accountant, 1978 – 1979

3. Education and Professional Certifications
- B.S., Accounting, University of New Orleans, 1976 – 1978
- Tulane University 1973 – 1975
- M.B.A., Auburn University, 2005
- CPA, American Institute of Certified Public Accountants, 1981
- CFE, Association of Certified Fraud Examiners, 1991
- CFF, American Institute of Certified Public Accountants, 2009
- Private Detective (Class A), 2000
- ABV, American Institute of Certified Public Accountants, 2015

B. Publications
- The Tangled Web: Unraveling the Badges of Fraud. (2007, March). *Investigations Quarterly Newsletter*
- The Mathematics of Compliance. (2014, December) *Compliance & Ethics Professional. (A publication of the Society of Corporate Compliance and Ethics)*

C. Speaking Engagements
- *High In-Fidelity – Corporate Theft and Recovery.* (2009, July)
  - Risk and Insurance Management Society 34th Annual Education Conference, Naples, FL
- *The New Hard Times: Business Crimes, Ponzi Schemes and Affinity Frauds.* (2009, August)
  - Georgia Society of CPA's 2009 Fraud and Forensic Accounting Conference, Atlanta, GA
- *High In-Fidelity – Corporate Theft and Recovery.* (2010, July)
  - Risk and Insurance Management Society 34th Annual Education Conference, Naples, FL
- *Asset Recovery: How to Get Your Stuff Back.* (2011, April)
  - Georgia Society of CPAs 2011 Spring Decision Makers Conference, Atlanta, GA
- *Hands-On, Real-Life Case Study on Succeeding in Tracing and Recovering Assets in a Multinational Fraud* Case (2011, June)
  - International Association for Asset Recovery 2011 Cross-Border Asset Tracing and Recovery Conference, London, England
- *Dissecting Bank, Business and Credit Card Records That Lead You to Hidden Assets and Fronts for Bad Guys* (2011, June)
  - International Association for Asset Recovery 2011 Cross-Border Asset Tracing and Recovery Conference, London, England
- *The Audit Leader's Role in Proactively Addressing Fraud: Keeping your Organization Out of the Headlines* (2013, January)
  - MIS Audit Leadership Institute, Miami, Florida

- *Fraud Prevention and Detection: What Chief Audit Executives Must Know* (2013, April)
  - MIS Training Institute SuperStrategies 2013 The Audit Best-Practices Conference, Orlando, Florida
- *Race to the Top: Issues Related to Rankings and External Data Misreporting in Higher Education* (2013, June)
  - Society of Corporate Compliance and Ethics Higher Education Compliance Conference, Austin, Texas
- *Keep Your Organization Out of the Headlines by Proactively Addressing Today's Threats* (2014, January)
  - Society for Corporate Compliance and Ethics Webinar, Atlanta, Georgia
- *Managing Fraud Risk with the Audit Committee* (2014, May)
  - MIS Training Institute SuperStrategies 2014 The Audit Best-Practices Conference, Chicago, Illinois.
- *Use of Forensic Audit as a Tool in Recovery* (2015, May)
  - FMO Special Operations Seminar 2015, Amsterdam, Netherlands
- *Managing Fraud Risk with the Audit Committee* (2016, May)
  - MIS Training Institute SuperStrategies 2016, Las Vegas, Nevada.

D. Expert Testimony
- US v. Wardlaw and Turpin
  - Evidence given at trial
- Nodvin et al v. National Financial Services Corporation
  - Evidence given at NASD Arbitration Hearing
- Curtis v. Morgan
  - Evidence given at trial and by affidavit
- Robert Reich, Secretary of Labor v. Davis Acoustical Corporation et al
  - Evidence given at trial and by affidavit
- US v. David Ramus
  - Evidence given at trial
- Alumax, Inc. v. David Mitchell, et al
  - Evidence given at trial and by affidavit
- Mitsubishi International Corporation v. Joseph Smith, et al
  - Evidence given at trial in evidentiary hearings, at depositions and by affidavit
- US v. Healthmaster, Jeannette Garrison, et al
  - Evidence given by affidavit
- Solnick v. Physicians Health Corporation, et al
  - Evidence given at American Arbitration Association hearing
- Errol O. Kendall v. Thomas Rosencrants
  - Evidence given at arbitration hearing and by affidavit
- Cimlinc v. Softech
  - Evidence given at arbitration hearing and by affidavit
- Merkel v. Pollard
  - Evidence given at trial and by affidavit
- Madison Gas & Electric v. Wisconsin Power & Light Arbitration Dispute
  - Evidence given at arbitration hearing and by affidavit
- Alla, et al v. Network Concepts, et al
  - Evidence given at trial

- Crown Theatres v. Milton Daily, et al
  - Evidence given by affidavit
- Ralph C. McCullough, III, as Plan Trustee for HomeGold, Inc., HomeGold Financial, Inc. and Carolina Investors, Inc. v. Elliott Davis, et al
  - Evidence given by written report
- Cox Enterprises, Inc. v. News-Journal Corporation and Others
  - Evidence given at deposition and at trial
- The State of Oregon, et al v. McKesson HBOC, et al
  - Evidence given at deposition
- Cendant Corporation, et al v. Ernst & Young, LLP
  - Evidence given at deposition
- MC Asset Recovery, LLC v. The Southern Company
  - Evidence given at deposition
- Securities & Exchange Commission v. Steven Forman
  - Evidence given at deposition
- Etowah Environmental Group LLC, et al. v Advanced Disposal Services, Inc., et al.
  - Evidence given at deposition and arbitration hearing
- CSX Transportation, Inc. v. Brian K. Leggett
  - Evidence given at trial
- Darryl S. Laddin, as Liquidating Trustee v. Steven A. Odom, et al.
  - Evidence given at deposition
- Piedmont Family Office Fund, LP; et al. v. Robert L. Duncan; et al.
  - Evidence given at deposition
- Heather Q. Bolinger, et al. v First Multiple Listing Service, Inc.
  - Evidence given at deposition
- United States of America, ex rel. v American Intercontinental University, Inc.
  - Evidence given at deposition
- Geveran Investments Limited v. Lighting Science Group Corporation, et al.
  - Evidence given at deposition and hearing
- United States of America v. D. Terry Dubose, et al.
  - Evidence given at deposition and trial
- US Tobacco Cooperative, Inc., US Flue-Cured Tobacco Growers, Inc., and Big South Distribution, Llc, v. Big South Wholesale of Virginia, Llc, d/b/a Big Sky
  - Evidence given at deposition
- Douglas Beal, et al vs. Royal Alliance Associates, Inc., et al
  - Evidence given at FINRA arbitration hearing
- Alice Caputo, et al vs. Royal Alliance Associates, Inc., et al
  - Evidence given at FINRA arbitration hearing
- United States of America v. Michael Kipp and Joanne Viard
  - Evidence given at trial
- United States of America v. Mark Hazelwood, Scott Wombold, Heather Jones and Karen Mann
  - Evidence given at trial

TABLE 10.2
Exhibit B – Materials Considered

Description	Beginning Bates or Range
Pleadings	
1 XXXX.05.31 Complaint	
2 XXXX.05.31 Consent Preliminary Injunction Order	
3 XXXX.09.01 Defendants' Motion to Dismiss for Failure to State a Claim	
4 XXXX.10.03 Plaintiffs' Opposition to Defendants' Motion to Dismiss	
5 XXXX.10.17 Defendants' Reply in Further Support of their Motion to Dismiss	
6 XXXX.01.11 First Amended Complaint	
7 XXXX.01.11 Order regarding Defendants' Motion to Dismiss	
8 XXXX.07.10 Response to First Interrogatories	
9 XXXX.07.10 Response to First Request to Admit	
10 XXXX.07.25 Redline of First Amended Complaint v Second Amended Complaint	
11 XXXX.07.25 Second Amended Complaint	
12 XXXX.08.22 Affidavit re Motion for Leave to File Second Amended Complaint	
13 XXXX.08.31 Order Granting Motion for Leave to File Second Amended Complaint	
14 XXXX.08.31 Second Amended Complaint	
15 XXXX.10.16 Defendants Xxxx Xxxxxxx and Xxxx Xxxxxxx's Motion to Dismiss	
16 XXXX.10.16 Defendants Xxxx's and Xxxxxx's Answer and Defenses to Second Amended Complaint	
17 XXXX.10.16 Defendants Xxxxxxx and Xxxxxxx's Answer and Defenses to Second Amended Complaint	
18 XXXX.10.20 Plaintiff's Opposition to Motion to Dismiss by Xxxxxxx and Xxxxxxx	
19 XXXX.11.08 - SEC's Response to Second Interrogatories of Xxxx Xxxxxxxx, XXX and Xxxxx Xxxxxx	
20 XXXX.11.13 Xxxxxxx and Xxxxxxx's Reply in Further Support of Motion to Dismiss	
21 Letter from Xxxxx Xxxxxx to Xxxx Xxxxxxxxxxx, XXX, Investor(s) dated March 25, XXXX (Dkt. No. XX-8)	
22 Letter from Xxxxx Xxxxxx to Xxxx Xxxxxxxxxxx, XXX, Investor(s) dated December 24, XXXX (Dkt. No. XX-9)	
23 Letter from Xxxxx Xxxxxx to Xxxx Xxxxxxxxxxx, XXX, Investor(s) dated June 4, XXXX (Dkt. No. XX-10)	
Deposition Transcripts and Exhibits	
24 Deposition of X. Xxxxxxx Xxxxxx dated June 8, XXXX and Exhibits 1–10	
25 Deposition of Xxxxx Xxxxxxx dated July 25, XXXX and Exhibits 7–9, 11–13	
26 Deposition of Xxxx Xxxxxxx dated December 13, XXXX and Exhibits 14–16 and W1–W9	
27 Deposition of Xxxx Xxxxxxx dated December 19, XXXX and Exhibits R1–R-10	
28 Deposition of Xxxxx Xxxxxx dated January 11, XXXX and Exhibits B001–B004	

(Continued)

TABLE 10.2 (*Continued*)
Exhibit B – Materials Considered

	Description	Beginning Bates or Range
	Public Documents, Statutes, Rules, Publications, and Books	
29	XXXX Xxxx Xxxx Xxxxxxxxxxxxx Form 990 - Guidestar	
30	XXXX Xxxx Xxxx Xxxxxxxxxxxxx Form 990 - Guidestar	
31	XXXX Xxxx Xxxx Xxxxxxxxxxxxx Form 990 - Guidestar	
32	XXXX Xxxx Xxxx Xxxxxxxxxx Form 990-PF - Guidestar	
33	XXXX Xxxx Xxxx Xxxxxxxxxx Form 990-PF - Guidestar	
34	XXXX Xxxx Xxxx Xxxxxxxxxx Form 990-PF - Guidestar	
35	Xxxxxxxxx Secretary of State Filing Information - Xxxx Xxxxxxxxxxx, XXX	
36	Xxxxxxxxx Secretary of State Filing Information - XXX Xxxxxxxxxxx, XXX	
37	15 U.S.C. 77q(a) - Use of interstate commerce for purpose of fraud or deceit	
38	15 U.S.C. 78j(b) - Manipulative and deceptive devices	
39	15 U.S.C. 80b-6 - Prohibited transactions by investment advisers	
40	17 CFR 4 (including 4.22 and 4.25)	
41	17 C.F.R. 240.10b-5 - Employment of manipulative and deceptive devices	
42	17 C.F.R. 275.206(4)-8 - Pooled investment vehicles	
43	17 CFR 279	
44	26 U.S.C. Sec. 475	
45	Form ADV Part 2	
46	ASC 210-20 - Balance Sheet Offsetting	
47	ASC 405-20-40 - Derecognition of Liabilities	
48	ASC 815-10 - Derivatives and Hedging Overall	
49	ASC 815-20 - Hedging General	
50	ASC 815-30 - Fair Value Hedges	
51	ASC 815-30 - Cash Flow Hedges	
52	ASC 820-10-35 - Subsequent Fair Value Measurement	
53	ASC 825-10-65 - Transition and Open Effective Date of Financial Instruments	
54	ASC 860-10-40 - Derecognition of Transfers and Servicing	
55	AU Section 623 "Special Reports." AICPA <https://www.aicpa.org/Research/Standards/AuditAttest/DownloadableDocuments/AU-00623.pdf>	
56	FASB Statement of Financial Accounting Standards No. 133	
57	FASB Statement of Financial Accounting Standards No. 168	
58	Public Company Accounting Oversight Board Firm Summaries for Xxxxxxxx XXXx, P.C., XxXxxxxxx LLP (now known as XXX XX LLP), and Xxxxxxx Xxxxx Xxxxxxx, LLC (accessed through PCAOB website 02/05/2018)	
59	http://www.cmegroup.com/trading/equity-index/us-index/e-mini-sandp500_quotes_globex_ options.html?optionProductId=138#optionProductId=138	
60	http://www.nasdaq.com/investing/glossary/m/mark-to-market-accounting	
61	https://xxxxxxxxxxxxxxxxxxxxxx.org/team/xxxxx-xxxxxx/	
62	https://xxxxxxxxxxxxxxxxxxxxxx.org/where-we-serve/	
63	https://xxxxxxxxxxxxxxxxxxxxxx.org/make-an-impact/	
64	https://xxxxxxxxxxxxxxxxxxxxxx.org/our-approach/	
65	https://www.bollingerbands.com/bollinger-bands	

(*Continued*)

TABLE 10.2 (*Continued*)

Exhibit B – Materials Considered

Description	Beginning Bates or Range
66	www.facebook.com/pg/xxxxxxxxxxxxxxxxxxxxx/about/	
67	http://us.spindices.com/indices/equity/sp-500	
68	https://www.theocc.com/education/futures/	
69	Acton, Gemma. "Number of hedge funds continues to shrink as launches fall to financial crisis levels." CNBC, December 16, 2016 <https://www.cnbc.com/2016/12/16/number-of-hedge-funds-continues-to-shrink-as-launches-fall-to-financial-crisis-levels.html>	
70	Baden, Ben. "5 Factors That Drive Stock Prices." U.S. News, 2011 <https://money.usnews.com/money/personal-finance/mutual-funds/articles/2011/07/14/5-factors-that-drive-stock-prices>	
71	Barlow, Joshua. "Hidden Fees in Hedge Funds." FINalternatives, July 30, 2013 <http://www.finalternatives.com/node/24322>	
72	Bogle, John C. The Little Book of Common Sense Investing: The Only Way to Guarantee Your Fair Share of Stock Market Returns. John Wiley & Sons, Inc.: Hoboken, NJ (2007)	
73	Bogle, John Co. "The Telltale Chart: Keynote Speech before the Morningstar Investment Forum, Chicago, IL, on June 26, 2002 <https://www.vanguard.com/bogle_site/sp20020626.html>	
74	Buhayar, Noah, et al. "Buffett Says Money Spent on Plumbers Better Than on Hedge Funds." Bloomberg, May 6, 2017 <https://www.bloomberg.com/news/articles/2017-05-06/buffett-says-money-spent-on-plumbers-better-than-on-hedge-funds>	
75	Chung, Juliet, et al. "Misery Widespread at Hedge Funds: Market Turmoil Inflicts Losses in Industry's Worst Period Since 2001." The Wall Street Journal, October 20, 2014 <http://www.wsj.com/articles/misery-widespread-at-hedge-funds-1413849220>	
76	Cordier, James and Gross, Michael. The Complete Guide to Option Selling: How Selling Options Can Lead to Stellar Returns in Bull and Bear Markets. McGraw-Hill, 2004	
77	Delevingne, Lawrence. "Struggling hedge funds still expense bonuses, bar tabs." Reuters, January 19, 2017 <https://www.reuters.com/article/us-hedgefunds-passthrough-insight/struggling-hedge-funds-still-expense-bonuses-bar-tabs-idUSKBN1530JL>	
78	Dr. James Schultz. "From Theory to Practice: The Central Limit Theorem." tastytrade (2016) <https://www.tastytrade.com/tt/shows/from-theory-to-practice/episodes/the-central-limit-theorem-09-30-2016>	
79	Durak, Robert. "New option a game changer for private companies." Journal of Accountancy, September 1, 2013 <https://www.journalofaccountancy.com/issues/2013/sep/20137921.html>	
80	Evans, James R. and Olson, David L. Statistics, Data Analysis, and Decision Modeling (Second Edition). Prentice Hall: Upper Saddle River, NJ (2003)	
81	Faccone, Erin. "The Essential Guide to Third-Party Valuations for Hedge Fund Investors." NEPC, LLC (2017) <https://cdn2.hubspot.net/hubfs/2529352/files/Third%20Party%20Valuations-%20White%20Paper-1.pdf?t=1513697342060>	

(*Continued*)

TABLE 10.2 (*Continued*)
Exhibit B – Materials Considered

	Description	Beginning Bates or Range
82	Fang, Jiali, et al. "Popularity versus Profitability: Evidence from Bollinger Bands." Auckland Centre For Financial Research, August 2014. <https://acfr.aut.ac.nz/__data/assets/pdf_file/0007/29896/100009-Popularity-vs-Profitability-BB-August-Final.pdf>	
83	Gad, Shan. "What Are Hedge Funds?" Forbes and Investopedia, October 22, 2013 <https://www.forbes.com/sites/investopedia/2013/10/22/what-are-hedge-funds/#7a653ff48ee3>	
84	Goonatilake, Rohitha. "The Volatility of the Stock Market and News." International Research Journal of Finance and Economics, 2007 <http://citeseerx.ist.psu.edu/viewdoc/summary?doi=10.1.1.124.5376>	
85	Gurdus, Elizabeth. "Hedge funds' 'obscene' fees make people rich – just not investors, says Buffett." CNBC, February 27, 2017 <https://www.cnbc.com/2017/02/27/buffett-hedge-funds-fees-border-on-obscene.html>	
86	Harmon, Michael and Kulsrud, William. "Sec. 475 Mark-to-Market Election." The Tax Adviser <https://www.thetaxadviser.com/issues/2010/feb/sec475mark-to-marketelection.html>	
87	Herbst-Bayliss, Svea. "Fewer hedge fund managers call it quits in 1st-half 2017." Reuters, September 18, 2017 <https://www.reuters.com/article/us-hedgefunds-closures/fewer-hedge-fund-managers-call-it-quits-in-1st-half-2017-idUSKCN1BT2C3>	
88	I.R.C. §475: Field Directive related to Mark-to-Market Valuation <https://www.irs.gov/businesses/irc-475-field-directive-related-to-mark-to-market-valuation>	
89	Jennings, William. "The mathematics of compliance." Compliance & Ethics Professional, December 2014	
90	Kirilenko, Andrei, et al. "The Flash Crash: The Impact of High Frequency Trading on an Electronic Market." February 21, 2014 <http://www.cftc.gov/idc/groups/public/@economicanalysis/documents/file/oce_flashcrash0314.pdf>	
91	Nielsen, Lars Tyge. "Understanding N(d1) and N(d2): Risk-Adjusted Probabilities in the Black-Scholes Model." Finance, Economics, and Mathematics. October 1992. <http://www.ltnielsen.com/wp-content/uploads/Understanding.pdf>	
92	Roman, Jan. "Chapter 15: Option Valuation." <http://janroman.dhis.org/finance/General/Option%20Valuation.pdf>	
93	Soled, Jay, et al. "The lure of a Sec. 475 election." Journal of Accountancy <https://www.journalofaccountancy.com/issues/2014/jul/sec-475-election-20149537.html>	
94	Staff of the Investment Adviser Regulation Office Division of Investment Management, U.S. Securities and Exchange Commission. "Regulation of Investment Advisers by the U.S. Securities and Exchange Commission." March 2013, p. 34-35 and footnote 181 <https://www.sec.gov/about/offices/oia/oia_investman/rplaze-042012.pdf>	
95	Summa, John. "Sellers vs Buyers: Who Wins? A Study of CME Options Expiration Patterns." OptionsNerd.com <http://app.topica.com/banners/forms/900067555/900031275/SELLERSVSBUYERSWHOWINS.doc>	

(Continued)

TABLE 10.2 (*Continued*)

Exhibit B – Materials Considered

Description	Beginning Bates or Range
96	Thorp, Wayne. "An Intro to Moving Averages: Popular Technical Indicators." American Association of Individual Investors Journal. August 1999. <https://www.aaii.com/journal/article/an-intro-to-moving-averages-popular-technical-indicators.touch>	
97	University of California, Davis Department of Statistics Lecture regarding Describing Data <http://www.stat.ucdavis.edu/~ntyang/teaching/12SSII/lecture02.pdf>	
98	"A Fascinating Look at How the Internet Has Changed the Stock Market." Vision Computer Solutions, 2016 <http://vcsolutions.com/a-fascinating-look-at-how-the-internet-has-changed-the-stock-market/>	
99	"About Hedge Funds" Hedge Fund Association <http://www.hedgefundassoc.org/about_hedge_funds/>	
100	"CME Group Options on Futures." CME Group <https://www.cmegroup.com/education/files/options-on-futures-brochure.pdf>	
101	"Fast Answers – Commodity Futures Trading Commission." U.S. Securities and Exchange Commission <https://www.sec.gov/fast-answers/answers-cftchtm.html>.	
102	"Fast Answers – Net Asset Value." U.S. Securities and Exchange Commission <https://www.sec.gov/fast-answers/answersnavhtm.html>	
103	"Financial Reporting Framework for Small- and Medium-Sized Entities." American Institute of Certified Public Accountants, 2013	
104	"Findings Regarding the Market Events of May 6, 2010." U.S. Securities and Exchange Commission and U.S. Commodities Futures Trading Commission, September 30, 2010 <https://www.sec.gov/news/studies/2010/marketevents-report.pdf>	
105	"Fundamentals of Options on Futures." CME Institute <https://institute.cmegroup.com/whitepapers/markets/fundamentals-of-options-on-futures>	
106	"Lessons in Clarity: Hedge Funds." CFA Institute <https://www.cfainstitute.org/programs/investmentfoundations/courseofstudy/Pages/lessons_in_clarity_hedge_funds.aspx>	
107	"Mark-to-Market Election for Hedge Funds." Capital Fund Law Blog <http://www.capitalfundlaw.com/blog/2015/05/21/mark-to-market-election-for-hedge-funds>	
108	"Preqin Special Report: Hedge Funds in the US." Preqin, October 2016 <http://docs.preqin.com/reports/Preqin-Special-Report-Hedge-Funds-in-the-US-October-2016.pdf>	
109	"S&P 500 Futures and Options on Futures." CME Group <https://www.cmegroup.com/trading/equity-index/files/sandp-500-futures-options.pdf>	
110	"Security Futures: An Introduction to Their Uses and Risks." National Futures Association <https://www.nfa.futures.org/members/member-resources/files/security-futures.pdf>	
111	"Stock Indexes: Understanding Stock Index Futures." CME Group, May 3, 2013 <https://www.cmegroup.com/education/files/understanding-stock-index-futures.pdf>	
112	"Technical Analysis." University of Cambridge. February 2, 2011. <https://www.mrao.cam.ac.uk/~mph/Technical_Analysis.pdf>	

(Continued)

TABLE 10.2 (*Continued*)

Exhibit B – Materials Considered

	Description	Beginning Bates or Range
113	"Theta." The Options Industry Council <https://www.optionseducation.org/strategies_advanced_concepts/advanced_concepts/understanding_option_greeks/theta.html>	
114	"Options Pricing." The Options Industry Council <https://www.optionseducation.org/getting_started/options_overview/options_pricing.html>	

Produced Documents

	Description	Beginning Bates or Range
115	Xxxx Xxxxxxxx, XXX Incentive Fees Schedule (SEC 801-78293, Question 45)	XX_001390
116	Xxxx Xxxxxxxxxxx rate of return schedule	Xxxx_NDGA-00004060-4061
117	December XXXX Xxxx Xxxxxxxxxxx spreadsheet	Xxxx_NDGA-00015807
118	December XXXX Xxxx Xxxxxxxxxxx spreadsheet	Xxxx_NDGA-00015819
119	December XXXX Xxxx Xxxxxxxxxxx spreadsheet	Xxxx_NDGA-00015934
120	May XXXX Xxxx Xxxxxxxxxxx spreadsheet	Xxxx_NDGA-00015844
121	Email string between Xxxx Xxxxxxxx, Xxxxx Xxxxxx, and Xxxx Xxxxxxx (April XXXX)	Xxxx_NDGA-00004412
122	XXXX XXX Year End Statement - Xxxxx Xxxx	XX_003122
123	XXXX XXX Year End Statement - Xxxx Xxxxxx	XX_006688
124	July XXXX XX Fund account statements	Xxxx_NDGA-00004453
125	August XXXX XX Fund account statements	Xxxx_NDGA-00004486
126	XXX Xxxxxxxxxxx, XXX Financial Statements for the Years Ended December 31, XXXX and XXXX	XX_002815
127	Xxxx Xxxxxxxxxxx, XXX Financial Statements for the Years Ended December 31, XXXX and XXXX	XX_002834
128	Xxxx Xxxxxxxxxxx, XXX Financial Statements for the Years Ended December 31, XXXX and XXXX	XX_002856
129	Xxxx Xxxxxxxx, XXX Investment Advisory Agreement dated January 24, XXXX	XX_000017
130	Xxxx Xxxxxxxx, XXX Investment Advisory Agreement dated January 24, XXXX	XX_000006
131	Xxxx Xxxxxxxx, XXX Investment Advisory Agreement dated January 24, XXXX with attached Schedule A	XX_002790
132	Contribution Agreement for Xxxx Xxxxxxxxxxx to be used in conjunction with the January 31, XXXX PPM	Xxxx_000228
133	Contribution Agreement for Xxxx Xxxxxxxxxxx to be used in conjunction with the Second Restated Operating Agreement	Xxxx_000217
134	Contribution Agreement for Xxxx Xxxxxxxxxxx to be used in conjunction with the original Operating Agreement, version 2	Xxxx_000207
135	Contribution Agreement for Xxxx Xxxxxxxxxxx to be used in conjunction with the original Operating Agreement	Xxxx_000197
136	Xxxx Xxxxxxxxxxx, XXX Subscription Booklet (XXXX PPM)	Xxxx_000253
137	Xxxx Xxxxxxxxxxx, XXX Subscription Booklet (XXXX PPM)	Xxxx_000293
138	Third Restated Operating Agreement of Xxxx Xxxxxxxxxxx, XXX dated January 31, XXXX	XX_000652
139	Amendment to the Third Restated Operating Agreement of Xxxx Xxxxxxxxxxx, XXX dated January 31, XXXX, Amendment dated August 25, XXXX	XX_000650

(*Continued*)

TABLE 10.2 (*Continued*)
Exhibit B – Materials Considered

	Description	Beginning Bates or Range
140	Confidential Private Placement Memorandum dated March 23, XXXX for Xxxx Xxxxxxxxxxx, XXX	Xxxx_000177
141	Confidential Private Placement Memorandum dated January 31, XXXX for Xxxx Xxxxxxxxxxx, XXX	Xxxx_000037
142	Confidential Private Placement Memorandum dated January 31, XXXX for Xxxx Xxxxxxxxxxx, XXX	Xxxx_000059
143	Confidential Private Placement Memorandum dated January 31, XXXX for Xxxx Xxxxxxxxxxx, XXX	XX_000681
144	Confidential Private Placement Memorandum dated January 31, XXXX for Xxxx Xxxxxxxxxxx, XXX	Xxxx_000115
145	January XXXX TD Ameritrade statement for XXX	SEC-AMERITRADE-E-0001504
146	February XXXX TD Ameritrade statement for XXX	SEC-AMERITRADE-E-0001587
147	March XXXX TD Ameritrade statement for XXX	SEC-AMERITRADE-E-0001603
148	April XXXX TD Ameritrade statement for XXX	SEC-AMERITRADE-E-0001590
149	May XXXX TD Ameritrade statement for XXX	SEC-AMERITRADE-E-0001510
150	June XXXX TD Ameritrade statement for XXX	SEC-AMERITRADE-E-0001452
151	July XXXX TD Ameritrade statement for XXX	SEC-AMERITRADE-E-0001554
152	August XXXX TD Ameritrade statement for XXX	SEC-AMERITRADE-E-0001544
153	September XXXX TD Ameritrade statement for XXX	SEC-AMERITRADE-E-0001503
154	October XXXX TD Ameritrade statement for XXX	SEC-AMERITRADE-E-0001507
155	November XXXX TD Ameritrade statement for XXX	SEC-AMERITRADE-E-0001597
156	December XXXX TD Ameritrade statement for XXX	SEC-AMERITRADE-E-0001548
157	January XXXX TD Ameritrade statement for XXX	SEC-AMERITRADE-E-0001599
158	February XXXX TD Ameritrade statement for XXX	SEC-AMERITRADE-E-0001446
159	March XXXX TD Ameritrade statement for XXX	SEC-AMERITRADE-E-0001550
160	April XXXX TD Ameritrade statement for XXX	SEC-AMERITRADE-E-0001442
161	May XXXX TD Ameritrade statement for XXX	SEC-AMERITRADE-E-0001449
162	June XXXX TD Ameritrade statement for XXX	SEC-AMERITRADE-E-0001594
163	July XXXX TD Ameritrade statement for XXX	SEC-AMERITRADE-E-0001456
164	August XXXX TD Ameritrade statement for XXX	SEC-AMERITRADE-E-0001489
165	September XXXX TD Ameritrade statement for XXX	SEC-AMERITRADE-E-0001565
166	October XXXX TD Ameritrade statement for XXX	SEC-AMERITRADE-E-0001463
167	November XXXX TD Ameritrade statement for XXX	SEC-AMERITRADE-E-0001458
168	December XXXX TD Ameritrade statement for XXX	SEC-AMERITRADE-E-0001644
169	January XXXX TD Ameritrade statement for XXX	SEC-AMERITRADE-E-0001468
170	February XXXX TD Ameritrade statement for XXX	SEC-AMERITRADE-E-0001529
171	March XXXX TD Ameritrade statement for XXX	SEC-AMERITRADE-E-0001513
172	April XXXX TD Ameritrade statement for XXX	SEC-AMERITRADE-E-0001181
173	May XXXX TD Ameritrade statement for XXX	SEC-AMERITRADE-E-0001120
174	June XXXX TD Ameritrade statement for XXX	SEC-AMERITRADE-E-0000643
175	July XXXX TD Ameritrade statement for XXX	XX_002008
176	August XXXX TD Ameritrade statement for XXX	XX_002043
177	September XXXX TD Ameritrade statement for XXX	XX_002063
178	October XXXX TD Ameritrade statement for XXX	XX_002094
179	November XXXX TD Ameritrade statement for XXX	XX_002130
180	December XXXX TD Ameritrade statement for XXX	XX_002156

(Continued)

TABLE 10.2 (*Continued*)
Exhibit B – Materials Considered

	Description	Beginning Bates or Range
181	January XXXX TD Ameritrade statement for XXX	XX_001857
182	February XXXX TD Ameritrade statement for XXX	XX_001883
183	March XXXX TD Ameritrade statement for XXX	XX_001909
184	April XXXX TD Ameritrade statement for XXX	XX_001932
185	May XXXX TD Ameritrade statement for XXX	XX_001954
186	June XXXX TD Ameritrade statement for XXX	XX_001978
187	July XXXX TD Ameritrade statement for XXX	XX_002014
188	August XXXX TD Ameritrade statement for XXX	XX_002050
189	September XXXX TD Ameritrade statement for XXX	XX_002076
190	October XXXX TD Ameritrade statement for XXX	XX_002106
191	November XXXX TD Ameritrade statement for XXX	XX_002136
192	December XXXX TD Ameritrade statement for XXX	XX_002161
193	January XXXX TD Ameritrade statement for XXX	XX_001874
194	February XXXX TD Ameritrade statement for XXX	XX_001901
195	March XXXX TD Ameritrade statement for XXX	XX_001926
196	April XXXX TD Ameritrade statement for XXX	XX_001948
197	May XXXX TD Ameritrade statement for XXX	XX_001971
198	June XXXX TD Ameritrade statement for XXX	XX_001997
199	July XXXX TD Ameritrade statement for XXX	XX_002034
200	August XXXX TD Ameritrade statement for XXX	SEC-AMERITRADE-E-0001320
201	September XXXX TD Ameritrade statement for XXX	SEC-AMERITRADE-E-0001343
202	October XXXX TD Ameritrade statement for XXX	SEC-AMERITRADE-E-0000860
203	November XXXX TD Ameritrade statement for XXX	SEC-AMERITRADE-E-0001332
204	December XXXX TD Ameritrade statement for XXX	SEC-AMERITRADE-E-0001374
205	January XXXX TD Ameritrade statement for XXX	Xxxx_NDGA-00000062
206	February XXXX TD Ameritrade statement for XXX	Xxxx_NDGA-00000077
207	March XXXX TD Ameritrade statement for XXX	Xxxx_NDGA-00000079
208	April XXXX TD Ameritrade statement for XXX	SEC-AMERITRADE-E-0001133
209	May XXXX TD Ameritrade statement for XXX	SEC-AMERITRADE-E-0001330
210	March XXXX TD Ameritrade statement for XX Fund	SEC-AMERITRADE-E-0001580
211	April XXXX TD Ameritrade statement for XX Fund	SEC-AMERITRADE-E-0001474
212	May XXXX TD Ameritrade statement for XX Fund	SEC-AMERITRADE-E-0001583
213	June XXXX TD Ameritrade statement for XX Fund	SEC-AMERITRADE-E-0001577
214	July XXXX TD Ameritrade statement for XX Fund	SEC-AMERITRADE-E-0001623
215	August XXXX TD Ameritrade statement for XX Fund	SEC-AMERITRADE-E-0001572
216	September XXXX TD Ameritrade statement for XX Fund	SEC-AMERITRADE-E-0001484
217	October XXXX TD Ameritrade statement for XX Fund	SEC-AMERITRADE-E-0001486
218	November XXXX TD Ameritrade statement for XX Fund	SEC-AMERITRADE-E-0001482
219	December XXXX TD Ameritrade statement for XX Fund	SEC-AMERITRADE-E-0001542
220	January XXXX TD Ameritrade statement for XX Fund	SEC-AMERITRADE-E-0001626
221	February XXXX TD Ameritrade statement for XX Fund	SEC-AMERITRADE-E-0001574
222	March XXXX TD Ameritrade statement for XX Fund	SEC-AMERITRADE-E-0001534
223	April XXXX TD Ameritrade statement for XX Fund	SEC-AMERITRADE-E-0001523
224	May XXXX TD Ameritrade statement for XX Fund	SEC-AMERITRADE-E-0001519
225	June XXXX TD Ameritrade statement for XX Fund	SEC-AMERITRADE-E-0001635
226	July XXXX TD Ameritrade statement for XX Fund	SEC-AMERITRADE-E-0001479
227	August XXXX TD Ameritrade statement for XX Fund	SEC-AMERITRADE-E-0001527

(Continued)

TABLE 10.2 (*Continued*)
Exhibit B – Materials Considered

	Description	Beginning Bates or Range
228	September XXXX TD Ameritrade statement for XX Fund	SEC-AMERITRADE-E-0001629
229	October XXXX TD Ameritrade statement for XX Fund	SEC-AMERITRADE-E-0001631
230	November XXXX TD Ameritrade statement for XX Fund	SEC-AMERITRADE-E-0001538
231	December XXXX TD Ameritrade statement for XX Fund	SEC-AMERITRADE-E-0001638
232	January XXXX TD Ameritrade statement for XX Fund	SEC-AMERITRADE-E-0001491
233	February XXXX TD Ameritrade statement for XX Fund	SEC-AMERITRADE-E-0001560
234	March XXXX TD Ameritrade statement for XX Fund	SEC-AMERITRADE-E-0001606
235	April XXXX TD Ameritrade statement for XX Fund	SEC-AMERITRADE-E-0000592
236	May XXXX TD Ameritrade statement for XX Fund	SEC-AMERITRADE-E-0000677
237	June XXXX TD Ameritrade statement for XX Fund	SEC-AMERITRADE-E-0001128
238	July XXXX TD Ameritrade statement for XX Fund	XX_002414
239	August XXXX TD Ameritrade statement for XX Fund	XX_002200
240	September XXXX TD Ameritrade statement for XX Fund	XX_002513
241	October XXXX TD Ameritrade statement for XX Fund	XX_002534
242	November XXXX TD Ameritrade statement for XX Fund	XX_002576
243	December XXXX TD Ameritrade statement for XX Fund	XX_002204
244	January XXXX TD Ameritrade statement for XX Fund	XX_002209
245	February XXXX TD Ameritrade statement for XX Fund	XX_002259
246	March XXXX TD Ameritrade statement for XX Fund	XX_002297
247	April XXXX TD Ameritrade statement for XX Fund	XX_002330
248	May XXXX TD Ameritrade statement for XX Fund	XX_002355
249	June XXXX TD Ameritrade statement for XX Fund	XX_002376
250	July XXXX TD Ameritrade statement for XX Fund	XX_002420
251	August XXXX TD Ameritrade statement for XX Fund	XX_002456
252	September XXXX TD Ameritrade statement for XX Fund	XX_002525
253	October XXXX TD Ameritrade statement for XX Fund	XX_002559
254	November XXXX TD Ameritrade statement for XX Fund	XX_002602
255	December XXXX TD Ameritrade statement for XX Fund	XX_002628
256	January XXXX TD Ameritrade statement for XX Fund	XX_002250
257	February XXXX TD Ameritrade statement for XX Fund	XX_002289
258	March XXXX TD Ameritrade statement for XX Fund	XX_002322
259	April XXXX TD Ameritrade statement for XX Fund	XX_002348
260	May XXXX TD Ameritrade statement for XX Fund	XX_002369
261	June XXXX TD Ameritrade statement for XX Fund	XX_002400
262	July XXXX TD Ameritrade statement for XX Fund	XX_002449
263	August XXXX TD Ameritrade statement for XX Fund	SEC-AMERITRADE-P-0000050
264	September XXXX TD Ameritrade statement for XX Fund	SEC-AMERITRADE-P-0000057
265	October XXXX TD Ameritrade statement for XX Fund	SEC-AMERITRADE-P-0000065
266	November XXXX TD Ameritrade statement for XX Fund	SEC-AMERITRADE-P-0000071
267	December XXXX TD Ameritrade statement for XX Fund	SEC-AMERITRADE-P-0000077
268	January XXXX TD Ameritrade statement for XX Fund	SEC-AMERITRADE-P-0000081
269	February XXXX TD Ameritrade statement for XX Fund	Xxxx_NDGA-00000116
270	March XXXX TD Ameritrade statement for XX Fund	Xxxx_NDGA-00000128
271	April XXXX TD Ameritrade statement for XX Fund	Xxxx_NDGA-00000140
272	May XXXX TD Ameritrade statement for XX Fund	Xxxx_NDGA-00000151
273	June XXXX TD Ameritrade statement for XX Fund	Xxxx_NDGA-00000162
274	July XXXX TD Ameritrade statement for XX Fund	Xxxx_NDGA-00000173

(Continued)

TABLE 10.2 (*Continued*)
Exhibit B – Materials Considered

	Description	Beginning Bates or Range
	Description	**Beginning Bates or Range**
275	August XXXX TD Ameritrade statement for XX Fund	Xxxx_NDGA-00000183
276	September XXXX TD Ameritrade statement for XX Fund	Xxxx_NDGA-00000192
277	October XXXX TD Ameritrade statement for XX Fund	Xxxx_NDGA-00000086
278	November XXXX TD Ameritrade statement for XX Fund	Xxxx_NDGA-00000096
279	December XXXX TD Ameritrade statement for XX Fund	Xxxx_NDGA-00000106
280	January XXXX TD Ameritrade statement for XX Fund	Xxxx_NDGA-00000203
281	Xxxxxxxxxxx-produced XX Fund Tax Returns and K-1s for XXXX	BCPAS000009-166, 175-332, 334-490
282	Xxxxxxxxxxx-produced XX Fund Tax Returns and K-1s for XXXX	BCPAS000555-742, 751-938, 940-1127
283	Xxxxxxxxxxx-produced XX Fund Tax Returns and K-1s for XXXX	BCPAS001202-1385, 1392-1575, 1578-1761, 1763-1944
284	Xxxxxxxxxxx-produced XX Fund Tax Returns and K-1s for XXXX	BCPAS00XXXX-2154, 2163-2300, 2302-2439
285	XX Fund account statements	Xxxx_NDGA-00005286-00015802
286	XXX account statements	Xxxx_NDGA-00019814-00019872
287	August XXXX statement for XXX	Xxxx_NDGA-00002955-2956
288	September XXXX statement for XXX	Xxxx_NDGA-00002964-2966
289	Employment information for Xxxxx Xxxxxx, Xxxx Xxxxxxx, Xxxx Xxxxxx, and Xxxx Xxxxxxx	XX_000002
290	List of Xxxx Xxxxxxxx, XXX employees and others who resigned or were eliminated during SEC examination period	XX_000003
291	List of threatened, pending, and settled litigation involving Xxxx Xxxxxxxx, XXX	XX_000004
292	List of joint ventures and other businesses in which Xxxx Xxxxxxxx, XXX, or its employees participate	XX_000043
293	Xxxx Xxxxxxxx, XXX, current fee schedule	XX_000045
294	Trade blotters for XXX, XX Fund, and Impact Capital fund	XX_000469 - XX_000472
295	Schedules of fund returns for XXX, XX Fund, and Impact Capital fund and comparisons to SPX returns	XX_000478
296	Xxxx Xxxxxxxx, XXX, balance sheets as of December 31, XXXX and July 31, XXXX; cash flow statements for January through December XXXX and January through July XXXX; profit and loss statements for January through December XXXX and January through July XXXX; trial balances as of December 31, XXXX and July 31, XXXX	XX_000479 - XX_000487
297	Xxxx Xxxxxxxx, XXX, general ledger as of July 31, XXXX and journal for cash receipts and disbursements from July XXXX through July XXXX	XX_000488 - XX_000582
298	Schedules of investors (balances, contributions, and withdrawals) for XXX for July XXXX through July XXXX; XX Fund for July XXXX through July XXXX; and Impact Capital for January XXXX through July XXXX	XX_000987 - XX_000990
299	XXX, XX Fund, and Impact Capital balance sheets, cash receipts and disbursements journals, general ledgers, income statements, trial balances, audited financial statements, and liquidation statements for various periods from XXXX through July XXXX	XX_000991 - XX_001329

Exhibit 1.1

U.S. Securities and Exchange Commission v. ▮▮▮ *et al.*

Comparison of Actual Fees and Hypothetical "2 and 20" Fee Method Based on NAV

	Actual			Hypothetical "2 and 20" Fee Method Based on NAV			Difference Between Actual and Hypothetical "2 and 20" Method Based on NAV
	Management Fee	Incentive Allocation	Total	Hypothetical Management Fee[1]	Hypothetical Incentive Allocation[2]	Total	
2013	$ -	$ 7,634,408	$ 7,634,408	$ 2,488,255	$ 9,818,382	$ 12,306,637	$ (4,672,228)
2014	-	6,920,232	6,920,232	3,204,658	3,445,286	6,649,944	270,288
2015	-	6,228,960	6,228,960	2,944,674	6,258,278	9,202,952	(2,973,992)
2016 through May	-	1,486,858	1,486,858	1,338,556	-	1,338,556	148,302
	$ -	$ 22,270,458	$ 22,270,458	$ 9,976,143	$ 19,521,946	$ 29,498,088	$ (7,227,630)

Sources: Monthly account statements for ▮▮▮ *-00005286-00015802), ▮▮▮ -00004961, and* ▮▮▮ *-00015807*

[1] Assumes a hypothetical management fee equal to 2% of the ▮▮▮'s end of month net asset value

[2] Assumes a hypothetical incentive allocation equal to 20% of the ▮▮▮'s end of month gains, including realized gains/(losses) on closed positions as well as the monthly change in unrealized gains/(losses) on open positions, subject to a monthly high-water mark based on the previous month's realized gains/(losses) on closed positions as well as the monthly change in unrealized gains/(losses) on open positions

Note: Immaterial differences may exist due to rounding.

FIGURE 10.3

U.S. Securities and Exchange Commission v. ▓▓▓▓ *et al.*

Exhibit 1.2

Comparison of Actual Fees and Hypothetical "2 and 20" Fee Method Based on NAV - Detail

Period	Month	Year	End of Month NAV	Realized Trading Gains/(Losses)	Change in Unrealized Gains/(Losses)	Total Monthly Gains/(Losses)[1]	Cumulative Change in Gains/(Losses)	Total Monthly Gains/(Losses) High- Water Mark[2]	Hypothetical Management Fee[3]	Hypothetical Incentive Allocation[4]	Actual Incentive Allocation	Difference Between Actual Incentive Allocation and Hypothetical "2 and 20" Method Based on NAV
Dec-12	Dec	2012	$ 79,379,541				$ 9,848,904	$ (9,261,223)				
Jan-13	Jan	2013	96,409,215 $	1,919,556 $	13,887,296	15,806,851 $	25,655,756	6,545,629 $	160,682 $	1,309,126 $	383,911 $	
Feb-13	Feb	2013	108,128,047	1,496,309	5,349,303	6,845,612	32,501,368		180,213	1,369,122	299,262	
Mar-13	Mar	2013	104,078,401	3,761,269	(7,430,397)	(3,669,128)	28,832,240		173,464	-	752,254	
Apr-13	Apr	2013	110,033,590	3,739,625	6,157,128	9,896,753	38,728,993	6,227,625	183,389	1,245,525	747,925	
May-13	May	2013	103,593,911	3,486,731	(11,068,491)	(7,581,760)	31,147,233		172,657	-	697,346	
Jun-13	Jun	2013	120,667,510	2,332,347	15,232,886	17,565,233	48,712,466	9,983,473	201,113	1,996,695	466,469	
Jul-13	Jul	2013	129,369,438	3,985,849	231,460	4,217,309	52,929,775		215,616	843,462	797,170	
Aug-13	Aug	2013	132,440,738	3,333,755	(771,655)	2,562,100	55,491,875		220,735	512,420	666,751	
Sep-13	Sep	2013	135,489,321	3,353,810	(146,030)	3,207,780	58,699,655		225,816	641,556	670,762	
Oct-13	Oct	2013	147,449,833	3,590,021	(1,352,276)	2,237,745	60,937,400		245,750	447,549	718,004	
Nov-13	Nov	2013	149,609,681	2,319,449	(1,221,082)	1,098,367	62,035,767		249,349	219,673	463,890	
Dec-13	Dec	2013	155,683,033	4,853,320	1,312,950	6,166,270	68,202,037		259,472	1,233,254	970,664	$ (4,673,228)
Jan-14	Jan	2014	164,668,358	4,382,872	1,245,546	5,628,418	73,830,455		274,447	1,125,684	876,574	
Feb-14	Feb	2014	153,782,500	2,994,120	(13,616,333)	(10,622,213)	63,208,242		256,304	-	598,824	
Mar-14	Mar	2014	158,728,669	4,448,431	1,948,613	6,397,044	69,605,286		264,548	-	889,686	
Apr-14	Apr	2014	168,089,580	1,223,264	2,188,518	3,411,782	73,017,068	6,850,866	280,149	1,370,173	244,653	
May-14	May	2014	174,963,675	2,251,901	5,412,352	7,664,253	80,681,321		291,606	-	450,380	
Jun-14	Jun	2014	167,871,366	3,390,133	(9,736,809)	(6,346,676)	74,334,645		279,786	-	678,027	
Jul-14	Jul	2014	174,657,357	5,008,227	2,647,491	7,655,718	81,990,363	1,309,042	291,096	261,808	1,001,645	
Aug-14	Aug	2014	161,574,286	2,413,014	(14,603,286)	(12,190,272)	69,800,091		269,290	-	482,603	
Sep-14	Sep	2014	177,313,801	5,578,087	10,050,289	15,628,376	85,428,467	3,438,104	295,523	687,621	1,115,617	
Oct-14	Oct	2014	144,118,572	1,833,768	(34,954,186)	(33,120,418)	52,308,049		240,198	-	366,754	
Nov-14	Nov	2014	138,658,823	864,279	(4,851,346)	(3,987,067)	48,320,982		231,098	-	172,856	
Dec-14	Dec	2014	138,367,876	213,065	191,429	404,494	48,725,476		230,613	-	42,613	**270,287.90**
Jan-15	Jan	2015	147,349,745	1,489,590	12,114,637	13,604,227	62,329,703		245,583		297,918	
Feb-15	Feb	2015	151,284,176	1,729,670	4,501,695	6,231,365	68,561,068		252,140		345,934	
Mar-15	Mar	2015	159,253,903	2,413,443	7,127,901	9,541,344	78,102,412		265,423		482,689	
Apr-15	Apr	2015	156,877,561	1,344,383	(630,921)	713,462	78,815,874		261,463		268,877	
May-15	May	2015	161,043,128	2,627,381	2,776,693	5,404,074	84,219,948		268,405		525,476	
Jun-15	Jun	2015	167,162,478	2,575,922	18,098,737	20,674,659	104,894,607	19,466,140	278,604	3,893,228	515,184	

FIGURE 10.4

U.S. Securities and Exchange Commission v. ▮▮▮ *et al.*

Exhibit 1.2

Comparison of Actual Fees and Hypothetical "2 and 20" Fee Method Based on NAV - Detail

Period Month	Year	End of Month NAV	Realized Trading Gains/(Losses)	Change in Unrealized Gains/(Losses)	Total Monthly Gains/(Losses)[1]	Cumulative Change in Gains/(Losses)	Total Monthly Gains/(Losses) High-Water Mark[2]	Hypothetical Management Fee[3]	Hypothetical Incentive Allocation[4]	Actual Incentive Allocation	Difference Between Actual Incentive Allocation and Hypothetical "20 and 20" Method Based on NAV
Jul-15	2015	176,499,345	3,227,226	8,598,022	11,825,248	116,719,855		294,166	2,365,050	645,445	
Aug-15	2015	118,138,653	4,102,702	(58,760,854)	(54,658,152)	62,061,703		196,898	-	820,540	
Sep-15	2015	140,778,692	2,805,003	20,501,036	23,306,039	85,367,742		234,631	-	561,001	
Oct-15	2015	122,440,810	2,856,734	(20,937,122)	(18,080,388)	67,287,354		204,068	-	571,347	
Nov-15	2015	135,013,807	2,938,797	9,954,600	12,893,397	80,180,751		225,023	-	587,759	
Dec-15	2015	130,962,278	3,033,950	(6,347,632)	(3,313,682)	76,867,069		218,270	-	606,790	(2,973,991.89)
Jan-16	2016	136,961,159	2,596,009	4,288,325	6,884,334	83,751,403		228,269	-	519,202	
Feb-16	2016	135,552,222	2,268,780	(2,446,275)	(177,495)	83,573,908		225,920	-	453,756	
Mar-16	2016	129,589,412	2,569,500	(7,749,460)	(5,179,960)	78,393,948		215,982	-	513,900	
Apr-16	2016	196,502,534	2,141,979	2,837,690	4,979,669	83,373,617		327,504	-	-	
May-16	2016	204,528,057	3,008,724	6,232,300	9,241,024	92,614,641		340,880	-	-	148,302
			$ 116,502,995		$ 82,765,737			$ 9,976,143	$ 19,521,946	$ 22,270,458	$ (7,227,630)

Sources: Monthly account statements for ▮▮▮ *-00005286-00015802),* ▮▮▮ *-00004061, and* ▮▮▮ *-00015807*

[1] Total monthly gain/(loss) is the sum of monthly realized trading gains/(losses) and the change in unrealized gains/(losses)

[2] Assumes a hypothetical monthly high-water mark, including realized trading gains/(losses) and the change in unrealized gains/(losses). Prior to January 2013, the total monthly gains/(losses) high-water mark was approximately $19,110,127, which occurred in May 2012. The cumulative gain/loss of approximately $9,848,904 in December 2012 was approximately $9,261,223 below the high-water mark

[3] Assumes a hypothetical management fee equal to 2% of the ▮▮▮'s end of month net asset value

[4] Assumes a hypothetical incentive allocation equal to 20% of the ▮▮▮'s end of month gains, including realized trading gains/(losses) as well as the change in unrealized gains/(losses), subject to the total monthly gains/(losses) high-water mark

Note: Immaterial differences may exist due to rounding.

FIGURE 10.5

I reproduced this report for you because it is an excellent example of a report prepared to meet the requirements of Rule 26 of the Federal Rules of Civil Procedure. Let's first examine Rule 26.

RULE 26 OF THE FEDERAL RULES OF CIVIL PROCEDURE: GENERAL PROVISIONS REGARDING DUSCOVERY; DUTY OF DISCLOSURE

(a) Required Disclosures; Methods to Discover Additional Matter.

(1) Initial Disclosures.
Except in categories of proceedings specified in Rule 26(a)(1)(E), or to the extent otherwise stipulated or directed by order, a party must, without awaiting a discovery request, provide to other parties:

(2) Disclosure of Expert Testimony.
    (A) In addition to the disclosures required by paragraph (1), a party shall disclose to other parties the identity of any person who may be used at trial to present evidence under Rules 702, 703, or 705 of the Federal Rules of Evidence.
    (B) Except as otherwise stipulated or directed by the court, this disclosure shall, with respect to a witness who is retained or specially employed to provide expert testimony in the case or whose duties as an employee of the party regularly involve giving expert testimony, be accompanied by a written report prepared and signed by the witness. The report shall contain a complete statement of all opinions to be expressed and the basis and reasons therefor; the data or other information considered by the witness in forming the opinions; any exhibits to be used as a summary of or support for the opinions; the qualifications of the witness, including a list of all publications authored by the witness within the preceding ten years; the compensation to be paid for the study and testimony; and a listing of any other cases in which the witness has testified as an expert at trial or by deposition within the preceding four years.
    (C) These disclosures shall be made at the times and in the sequence directed by the court. In the absence of other directions from the court or stipulation by the parties, the disclosures shall be made at least 90 days before the trial date or the date the case is to be ready for trial or, if the evidence is intended solely to contradict or rebut evidence on the same subject matter identified by another party under paragraph (2)(B), within 30 days after the disclosure made by the other party. The parties shall supplement these

(4) Form of Disclosures.
    Unless the court orders otherwise, all disclosures under Rules 26(a)(1) through (3) must be made in writing, signed, and served.[1]

OK, let's unpack Rule 26 and reconcile it with the report example above.

- First, it says: **"The report shall contain a complete statement of all opinions to be expressed and the basis and reasons therefore."** If you will look at paragraphs IV-II in the report above, you will see how these requirements were satisfied.
- Next, we have: **"the data or other information considered by the witness in forming the opinions."** This requirement is satisfied in Exhibit B (see Table 10.2) in the report above.
- The next requirement is: **"any exhibits to be used as a summary of or support for the opinions."** Exhibits 1.1 and 1.2 in the report above satisfies this requirement.

- The next requirement is: **"the qualifications of the witness, including a list of all publications authored by the witness within the preceding ten years; the compensation to be paid for the study and testimony; and a listing of any other cases in which the witness has testified as an expert at trial or by deposition within the preceding four years."** Paragraph III and Exhibit A, in the report above, satisfies this requirement.

So, the preceding report satisfies all of the requirements of Rule 26 of the Federal Rules of Civil Procedure, but it has to do more than that.

Let's look at how it does that. First, I lay out my qualifications to do the work that resulted in the report. This is where I communicate information necessary to confirm my role as expert to the reader of the report. Next, I provide background information to acquaint the reader with the context in which the matter that is the subject of the investigation occurred. Then I set out my expert opinions in simple clear language. I want to make sure that the reader understands and remembers my expert opinions. Having established those critical elements, upfront, I move into the detailed analyses supporting my opinions. What I am doing here is controlling how and when the reader encounters the information in the report to maximize the chances that the reader will remember my qualifications and my opinions in the context of the critical questions I am answering in the report.

Let's look at a different type of report. This report was prepared for an international arbitral panel. It conforms to the rules established by that arbitral panel (see Figures 10.6–10.110).

Expert Report of William L. Jennings

ICC Case No. ███████

12 April 2017

FIGURE 10.6

Table of Contents

FIGURE 10.7

I.   Introduction

1.   My name is William L. Jennings. My business address is Accounting, Economics and Appraisal Group, LLC, 1230 Peachtree Street NE, Suite 2440, Atlanta, GA 30309.

2.   I have been asked by counsel for respondent, in connection with the ████████████████ ████████████████ v. ████████████████████ arbitration under the Rules of Arbitration of the International Chamber of Commerce (ICC Case No. ████████ to provide my opinions on the accounting and damages issues in this arbitration. I have no relationship to the Parties to this arbitration, their legal advisors or the Arbitral Tribunal. I am independent and have no interest in the outcome of this matter. In connection with this work, my firm's billing rates for this engagement range from USD 150 to USD 555 per hour. I genuinely believe all statements and opinions in this report.

3.   I am a Principal of Accounting, Economics and Appraisal Group, LLC ("AEA Group"). Previously, my positions included: Managing Director at Alvarez & Marsal in the Global Forensic and Dispute Services practice; Managing Director in the Disputes and Investigations Practice at Navigant Consulting, Inc.; Director in the National Forensic Accounting Practice at LECG, LLC; President of FFI, Inc.; Managing Director at Kroll, Inc., in charge of investigative accounting services for the Central Region; Principal-in-Charge of the Atlanta office of Lindquist, Avey, Macdonald, Baskerville, a multi-national independent forensic accounting firm; Principal-in-Charge of Coopers & Lybrand's Fraud Investigation Services practice for the Southeast Region; and Partner in the public accounting firm of Brown & Jennings.

4.   I have a Bachelor of Science degree in Accounting and a Master's degree in Business Administration. I have been a Certified Public Accountant since 1981 and a Certified Fraud Examiner since 1991. I have more than 30 years of experience in forensic accounting, business controls development, public accounting and auditing for regulated utilities.

FIGURE 10.8

5. I have provided forensic accounting services to corporations, U.S. Attorneys' Offices, other government agencies, attorneys and their clients. I have also provided business controls consulting services to organizations. I have often provided expert testimony about the results of my work in federal and state courts as well as in many other dispute resolution venues. I have worked on hundreds of forensic accounting and investigation assignments. Further, I am a frequent public speaker on a variety of topics including white-collar crime, fraud investigation, forensic accounting and business ethics. I have also published articles relating to fraud and forensic accounting. Details regarding my background, education, publications, speaking engagements and expert testimony are included in my curriculum vitae, attached as Exhibit 1.

II.   Summary

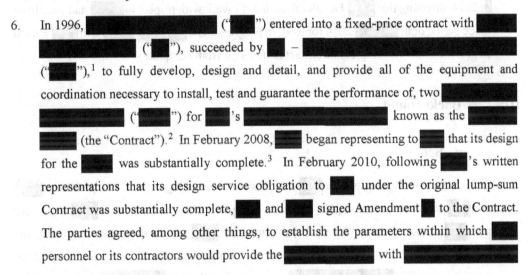

6. In 1996, ▮▮▮▮▮▮▮▮▮▮▮▮ ("▮▮▮") entered into a fixed-price contract with ▮▮▮ ▮▮▮▮▮▮▮▮▮ ("▮▮"), succeeded by ▮▮ – ▮▮▮▮▮▮▮▮▮▮▮▮▮▮▮▮ ("▮▮▮"),[1] to fully develop, design and detail, and provide all of the equipment and coordination necessary to install, test and guarantee the performance of, two ▮▮▮▮▮▮▮ ▮▮▮▮▮▮ ("▮▮▮") for ▮▮'s ▮▮▮▮▮▮▮▮▮▮▮▮▮ known as the ▮▮▮ ▮▮▮ (the "Contract").[2] In February 2008, ▮▮▮ began representing to ▮▮ that its design for the ▮▮▮ was substantially complete.[3] In February 2010, following ▮▮▮'s written representations that its design service obligation to ▮▮ under the original lump-sum Contract was substantially complete, ▮▮▮ and ▮▮▮ signed Amendment ▮ to the Contract. The parties agreed, among other things, to establish the parameters within which ▮▮▮ personnel or its contractors would provide the ▮▮▮▮▮▮▮▮▮ with ▮▮▮▮▮▮▮▮▮

---

[1] ▮▮▮▮▮▮▮▮▮▮▮▮▮▮▮ (▮▮▮), is a company duly incorporated and existing in accordance with the laws of the State of Delaware, United States of America. ▮▮▮ is a global ▮▮▮ alliance created by the ▮▮▮▮▮▮▮▮ ("▮▮") and ▮▮▮▮.

[2] Effective ▮▮▮, 2011, ▮▮, ▮ and ▮▮ entered into an Assignment and Assumption Agreement whereby ▮▮ assigned and ▮▮ assumed ▮▮'s rights under the Contract.

[3] *See* Exhibit R-584.

FIGURE 10.9

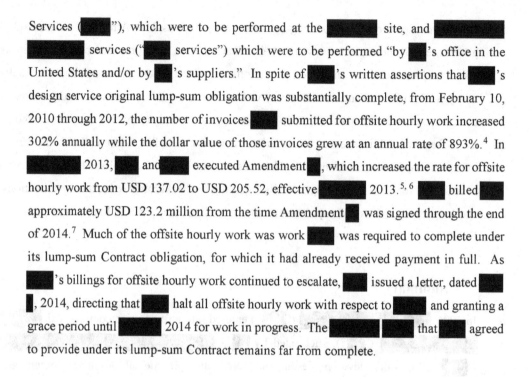

Services (█████ ”), which were to be performed at the ██████ site, and ████████ ████████ services (“ ████ services”) which were to be performed “by ██’s office in the United States and/or by ██’s suppliers.” In spite of ████’s written assertions that ████’s design service original lump-sum obligation was substantially complete, from February 10, 2010 through 2012, the number of invoices ████ submitted for offsite hourly work increased 302% annually while the dollar value of those invoices grew at an annual rate of 893%.[4] In ████████ 2013, ██ and ███ executed Amendment ██, which increased the rate for offsite hourly work from USD 137.02 to USD 205.52, effective ████████ 2013.[5, 6] ████ billed ████ approximately USD 123.2 million from the time Amendment ██ was signed through the end of 2014.[7] Much of the offsite hourly work was work ████ was required to complete under its lump-sum Contract obligation, for which it had already received payment in full. As ████’s billings for offsite hourly work continued to escalate, ████ issued a letter, dated ████ █, 2014, directing that ████ halt all offsite hourly work with respect to █████ and granting a grace period until ██████ 2014 for work in progress. The ████████████ that ██ agreed to provide under its lump-sum Contract remains far from complete.

III.   Background

a. Scope

7.   I have been asked by counsel for ████ to perform an accounting of the contract between ████ and ███ and evaluate subsequent claims by █████, including assessment of ████’s invoices and ████’s counterclaims for work performed by █████ which does not conform to the Contract or work that remains incomplete. I have also been asked to review and comment upon the report of ██████████████, Inc. submitted by Mr. █████████ .

---

[4] *See* Appendix 3.

[5] All currency amounts throughout this report are in U.S. Dollars (“USD”) unless otherwise specified.

[6] *See* Appendix 2.

[7] *See* Appendix 3.

FIGURE 10.10

b. Relevant Parties and the Contract

8. █████ is a global █████ alliance created by ██ and █████ that provides advanced █████ and ████ services.[8]

9. ████ is a █████, 96.92% of which is owned by █████████, and is the sole █████ company in Taiwan.[9]

10. ████ and ██ executed a fixed price contract dated █████████ (the "Contract"), in which ███ agreed to pay ██ a lump sum, and ██ agreed to fully develop, design and detail, and provide all of the equipment and coordination necessary to install, test and guarantee the performance of, ██ █████████████ ("████") for Taiwan's █████ ██████ known as the █████ Project. Under the Contract, ████ was to provide, among other things, complete engineering and project support; equipment, mandatory spare parts and special tools for installation, ████, operation and maintenance; technology transfer services; regular training services and █████ training (████'s "Lump-sum Obligations"), in exchange for payment by ███ of USD 1,655,007,000 and NTD 786,516,000.[10, 11]

11. █████████ of the ████ were initially scheduled for completion 91 and 103 months after the commencement date, respectively.[12] The lump-sum Contract was subsequently amended numerous times, impacting both the lump-sum price and completion date. In monthly reports beginning in █████ 2008, ████ represented to ████ that its design for the █████ was substantially complete, excluding only "plans for rationalizing designs to final vendor information received after issuance of deliverables by ████" and "plans to finish ████'s

---

[8] *See, e.g.,* █████'s Request for Arbitration dated █████████, 2015 p. 2.

[9] *Id.* at p. 3.

[10] *See* Contract No. M001-1 for █████ ████████████████ *System and Related Systems, Equipment and Services* between █████ and █████ █████ and amendments thereto.

[11] NTD refers to New Taiwan dollars, the currency of Taiwan.

[12] *See* Contract No. M001-1 for █████ ████████ ███████████ *and Services* between █████ and █████ and amendments thereto.

FIGURE 10.11

work and address associated outstanding design and resultant technical issues with ███'s issued designs."[13]

12.   ███ agreed to promptly correct, replace or reperform any equipment or services that were determined not to be in accordance with the Contract. Paragraph 2.33.3 of the Contract specifically states that, "[i]n the event the Equipment or items of Equipment or services furnished by [███] under the Contract are determined prior to Commercial operation not to be in conformance with the Contract, [███] shall promptly correct or replace or otherwise disposition in accordance with Paragraph 3.2.8.7 any such defect or deficiency in the Equipment and reperform any non-conforming services." In addition, Paragraph 2.33.3 of the Contract specifies that upon ███'s failure or refusal to correct the Work, ███ may elect to "make correction, replace Equipment/materials, or reperform services by itself or by engaging a third party by the most expeditious means available to it and backcharge the Supplier for all the costs."

13.   In addition, ███ agreed to certain performance guarantees and expressly stated that ███, at its cost, would repair or replace work until those performance guarantees were met. Specifically, in Paragraph 3.1.8 of the Contract, ███ agreed that "[███] shall be solely responsible for all costs involved in effecting all alterations, modifications, replacements, changes, and/or adjustments to the Work or any part thereof as may be necessary or desirable for strict compliance with the guaranteed performance specified in the Contract" and "[███] guarantees ███ fully licensable [███████] prevailing as of the date of Notice of Award. The Contractor shall bear full costs of changes in the ██ information or criteria to meet licensing requirements."[14] Further, in paragraph 2.24.5 of the lump-sum Contract, ███ agreed that if ███'s work was the cause of any failure to meet those performance guarantees, ███ would be "solely responsible for all costs involved, including transportation, ███, duties, etc., in effecting all reasonable alterations, modifications,

---

[13] *See, e.g.,* Exhibit R-584.

[14] *See* Paragraph 3.1.8 of the Contract.

FIGURE 10.12

changes, and/or adjustments to the Work or any part thereof as may be necessary for strict compliance with the guaranteed performance specified in the Contract."[15]

14. The Contract called for payment of the lump-sum price in installments called "milestone payments." Separate payment terms were delineated for the engineering, equipment and other portions of the Contract in paragraph 1.18. After Contract signing, ▮ was to make a first payment of 10% of the total contracted price for both the engineering portion and the portion of equipment provided by suppliers or manufacturers located outside the Republic of China.

15. 4% of the engineering portion was to be paid after the Commercial Operation Date for each ▮ and 1% of the engineering portion was to be held as retention and paid after all Work was completed and all required documents had been submitted to ▮. The remaining 85% of the engineering portion was to be paid every three months after the Notice to Proceed Date in accordance with the corresponding milestone schedule.

16. Payment for equipment was further bifurcated between that manufactured or provided by suppliers located outside the Republic of China (the "Foreign Equipment") and that manufactured in the Republic of China (the "Local Equipment"). With respect to the Foreign Equipment, 85% of the Contract price of embedment and anchor bolts for the ▮▮▮ ▮ and 50% of the remaining contract price of Foreign Equipment were to be paid based upon respective shipment values after ▮ provided that equipment. 35% of the Foreign Equipment contract price (excluding embedment and anchor bolt materials) was to be paid every three months after the first payment in accordance with the designated milestone schedule, provided that ▮ had achieved the corresponding milestone. 5% of the contract price of equipment value was to be withheld as retention and paid after ▮▮▮ and after ▮ actually completed provision of Equipment for ▮▮▮.

---

[15] *See* Paragraph 2.24.5 of the Contract.

FIGURE 10.13

17. Payment of the Contract price for 95% of the Local Equipment was to be made after ▮ provided the respective equipment to the job site. 5% of the value of all Local Equipment shipments was to be withheld as retainage.

18. Payment for certain technology transfer and training services was to be made upon completion of each technology transfer package and training program. Payment for Technical Advisory Services performed at the Jobsite, for which ▮ was to be compensated based on hourly service rates for its service engineers, was to be made quarterly.

19. Amendment ▮ to the Contract was entered into as of ▮▮, 2010. Pursuant to Amendment ▮ the parties agreed, among other things, to release and discharge certain claims against one another; amend project milestones; and establish the parameters within which ▮ personnel or its contractors would provide two new categories of hourly services referred to as ▮ and ▮ Services.

20. Section 6.2 of Amendment ▮ defined ▮ as those services performed at the jobsite as requested by ▮:

> To investigate, review, evaluate, and resolve, or propose solutions for, all engineering and design-related issues and problems, including design conflicts and interferences, in or pertaining to ▮'s Work which ▮ has found during construction, installation, pre-operation and ▮, including maintenance and operation issues, ▮ and tapping problems;
>
> To work with ▮'s Home Office (defined in Section 6.8) to review, verify, incorporate and certify (where requested by ▮) modifications made by ▮ to resolve design issues and/or interferences in ▮'s Work found by ▮ in ▮ and ▮ during construction, installation or ▮ of the ▮;

FIGURE 10.14

> To review, verify and incorporate (if deemed necessary) the ▮▮▮▮ vendor data into ▮ 's design documents, and, to the extent necessary as agreed by the Parties, to coordinate with ▮ 's Home Office to formally revise and issue the revised design documents.

> To review, verify and modify (if deemed necessary) ▮ 's design inputs to ▮▮▮ system of the ▮▮▮ , necessary for incorporating the updated ▮ input data; and

> Other work or services related to the Project within ▮ 's scope of Work or such other consulting services as referred by the ▮ Manager from time to time…

21. Amendment ▮ expressly granted ▮ the discretion whether or not to request ▮ and the right to approve the engineers and technicians ▮ assigned to the project.[16] ▮ were priced at an agreed upon hourly rate. Amendment ▮ contained provisions relating to reimbursement to ▮ for certain travel costs and assumption by ▮ of resignation and replacement costs related to its personnel and for certain unauthorized absences.[17]

22. Section 6.8 of Amendment ▮ provided that with respect to ▮ , " ▮ may by written notice to ▮ state that supporting engineering services by ▮ 's office in the United States (" ▮ 's Home Office") and/or by ▮ 's suppliers are needed" and established those services as ▮▮▮ (" ▮ services"). As more fully described below, ▮ was required to submit a proposal for contemplated ▮ services, along with the estimated resources and time required to render the work. Under Amendment ▮ , ▮ had the right to authorize or not authorize ▮ requests to perform ▮ services, and processes for ▮ to do so were established. The rate specified in the Agreement was 50% of a "list" rate provided by ▮ plus an additional 12% charge.[18]

---

[16] *See* Amendment ▮ Sections 6.2 and 6.3.

[17] *See* Amendment ▮ Section 6.7.

[18] *See* Amendment ▮ Section 6.9.

FIGURE 10.15

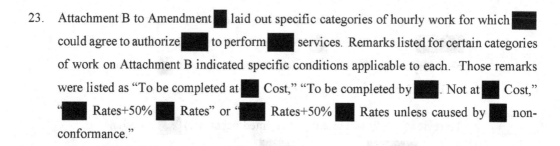

23. Attachment B to Amendment ▮ laid out specific categories of hourly work for which ▮ could agree to authorize ▮ to perform ▮ services. Remarks listed for certain categories of work on Attachment B indicated specific conditions applicable to each. Those remarks were listed as "To be completed at ▮ Cost," "To be completed by ▮. Not at ▮ Cost," "▮ Rates+50% ▮ Rates" or "▮ Rates+50% ▮ Rates unless caused by ▮ non-conformance."

24. On ▮ 2013, Amendment ▮ was modified further by Amendment ▮ with an effective date of ▮, 2013, which served to adjust some of the terms for ▮'s offsite hourly work and explicitly stated that "[a]ll provisions of the Contract remain unchanged except as expressly set forth in this Amendment 29."[19]

25. The lump-sum Contract was ultimately amended ▮ times (as amended through Amendment ▮, the "Contract") and the parties engaged in negotiations for a ▮, ▮ and ▮ amendment to which none was ever agreed.[20]

c. ▮ Invoices for Offsite Services Mount

26. Despite ▮'s representation that its design of the ▮ was substantially complete in February of ▮, between the execution of Amendment ▮ and the end of 2012, ▮ had invoiced ▮ for approximately USD 41.9 million for offsite hourly work.[21] During 2013, ▮ charged ▮ an additional USD 35.4 million, bringing the total offsite hourly work charges to more than USD 77.2 million.[22]

27. From the inception of Amendment ▮ on or about ▮, 2010 through 2012, the number of invoices ▮ issued each year for offsite hourly work increased approximately

---

[19] *See* Amendment ▮ p. 2.

[20] *See, e.g.,* First Witness Statement of ▮ ¶ 55.

[21] *See* Appendix 3.

[22] *Ibid.*

FIGURE 10.16

302% while the dollar value of those invoices grew at an annual rate of 893%.[23] On or about 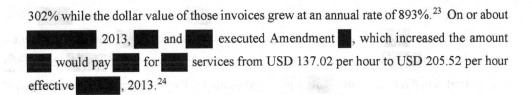 2013, ▮ and ▮ executed Amendment ▮, which increased the amount ▮ would pay ▮ for ▮ services from USD 137.02 per hour to USD 205.52 per hour effective ▮, 2013.[24]

28. The ▮ invoices for offsite hourly work continued to escalate in 2014 in both number and amount, and by the end of the year ▮ had billed ▮ a total of more than USD 123.0 million.[25] The following chart reflects the amount of ▮ charges for offsite hourly work from 2010 through 2016:[26]

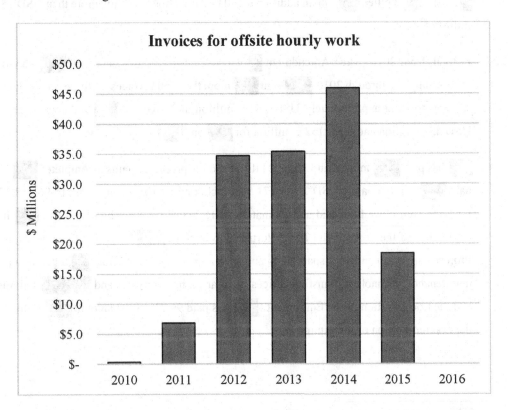

_____

[23] _See_ Appendix 3.

[24] _See_ Appendix 2.

[25] _See_ Appendix 3.

[26] _Ibid._

FIGURE 10.17

Expert Report of William Jennings
Page 11 of 48

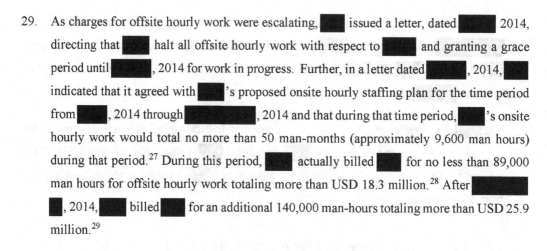

29. As charges for offsite hourly work were escalating, ▮ issued a letter, dated ▮ 2014, directing that ▮ halt all offsite hourly work with respect to ▮ and granting a grace period until ▮, 2014 for work in progress. Further, in a letter dated ▮, 2014, ▮ indicated that it agreed with ▮'s proposed onsite hourly staffing plan for the time period from ▮, 2014 through ▮, 2014 and that during that time period, ▮'s onsite hourly work would total no more than 50 man-months (approximately 9,600 man hours) during that period.[27] During this period, ▮ actually billed ▮ for no less than 89,000 man hours for offsite hourly work totaling more than USD 18.3 million.[28] After ▮, 2014, ▮ billed ▮ for an additional 140,000 man-hours totaling more than USD 25.9 million.[29]

30. In total, from 2010, when Amendment ▮ was executed and the concept of ▮ services was established, through 2016, ▮ sent ▮ more than 550 invoices for these offsite hourly services totaling approximately USD 141.6 million and invoiced ▮ for approximately USD 43.5 million and USD 152.2 million for ▮ and ▮, respectively.[30]

31. ▮ has paid ▮ more than USD 2.2 billion and the project remains incomplete. ▮ has paid ▮ approximately USD 2,244,771,583, including approximately USD 1,996,158,375 for lump-sum obligations and approximately USD 248,613,208 for hourly work. ▮ has paid 100% of the Foreign and Local Portions of amounts ▮ billed for Engineering and Project Support; mandatory spare parts and special tools for installation, ▮, operation and maintenance; technology transfer services; regular training services and ▮ training; and the Local Portion of the Equipment. ▮ has paid 99.7% of the amount ▮ billed for the Foreign Portion of the Equipment.[31]

---

[27] *See* ▮ Exhibits C-12 and C-116.

[28] *See* Appendix 3.1.

[29] *Ibid.*

[30] *See* Appendix 3.1 and Exhibit R-892.

[31] *See, e.g.,* Exhibit R-892.

FIGURE 10.18

32. Despite ███'s payment of more than USD 2.2 billion, the ██████ project remains incomplete. Critical safety components ███ was contractually obligated to provide remain inoperable. For example, the ████████████████████████ ("█████"), which "contains the ██████████ that are used to monitor the status of the ███ and remotely control equipment," includes equipment supplied by ███'s suppliers ███ and ██████ that was delivered with and still contains numerous problems inhibiting the equipment's performance.[32] Similarly, there are critical pieces of equipment and associated documentation within the ██████ ██████ and mechanical systems that currently do not conform to Contract and regulatory requirements.[33] These nonconformances prevent ███ from seeking or gaining ROC ███ approval with respect to the impacted Work.

d. Regulatory Environment and Market for ██████████

i. Regulatory Environment

33. "████████████████████████ of the Republic of China ("ROC ███") exercises regulatory control over the ████████, ████████████, operation and environmental effects of ████████████ operation" in Taiwan.[34] ROC ███, as the primary ████████ regulator in Taiwan, possesses authority over performance of the Work delineated in the Contract between ███ and ███. The design, construction and operation of ███ ██████ must comply with the provisions of the safety design and quality assurance criteria of ██████████ facilities prescribed by ROC ███.

34. Prior to construction of a ██████████ facility in Taiwan, an application for construction permit is required to be filed, and construction may not commence until the application has been reviewed and approved by the regulator. Among the requirements for approval are that the equipment and facilities are sufficient to ████████████████████████; the

---

[32] *See, e.g.*, Expert Report of ██████████.

[33] *See, e.g.*, Expert Report of ██████████; Expert Report of ██████████.

[34] *See, e.g.*, Chapter 1 of Exhibit 1 to the Contract p. 1-8.

FIGURE 10.19

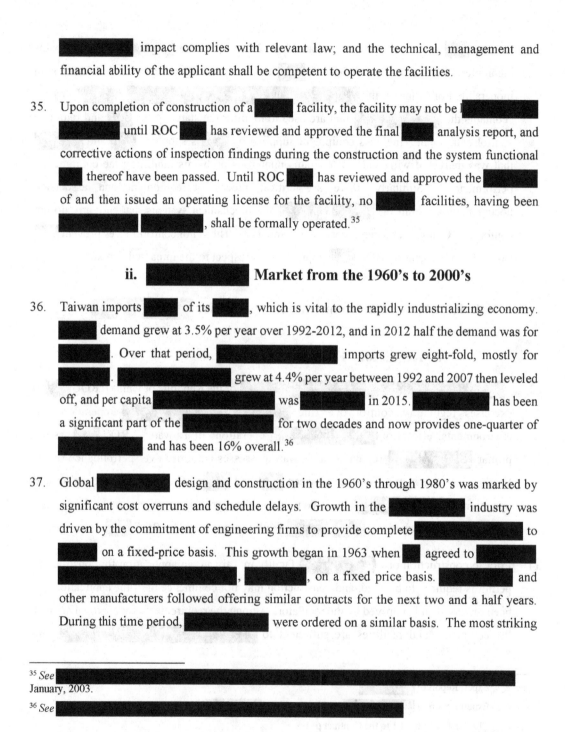

███████████ impact complies with relevant law; and the technical, management and financial ability of the applicant shall be competent to operate the facilities.

35. Upon completion of construction of a █████ facility, the facility may not be ██████████ ███████ until ROC ████ has reviewed and approved the final ████ analysis report, and corrective actions of inspection findings during the construction and the system functional ████ thereof have been passed. Until ROC ████ has reviewed and approved the ██████████ of and then issued an operating license for the facility, no █████ facilities, having been ███████████ ████████, shall be formally operated.[35]

ii. ██████████████ **Market from the 1960's to 2000's**

36. Taiwan imports █████ of its █████, which is vital to the rapidly industrializing economy. ███████ demand grew at 3.5% per year over 1992-2012, and in 2012 half the demand was for ███████. Over that period, ██████████████████ imports grew eight-fold, mostly for ████████. ██████████████ grew at 4.4% per year between 1992 and 2007 then leveled off, and per capita █████████████ was ████████████ in 2015. ██████████████ has been a significant part of the █████████████ for two decades and now provides one-quarter of ████████████ and has been 16% overall.[36]

37. Global ████████████ design and construction in the 1960's through 1980's was marked by significant cost overruns and schedule delays. Growth in the ██████████ industry was driven by the commitment of engineering firms to provide complete ████████████████ to ██████ on a fixed-price basis. This growth began in 1963 when ██ agreed to ████████████ ████████████████████████████, ████████, on a fixed price basis. ███████████ and other manufacturers followed offering similar contracts for the next two and a half years. During this time period, ████████████ were ordered on a similar basis. The most striking

---

[35] *See* ██
January, 2003.

[36] *See* ██

FIGURE 10.20

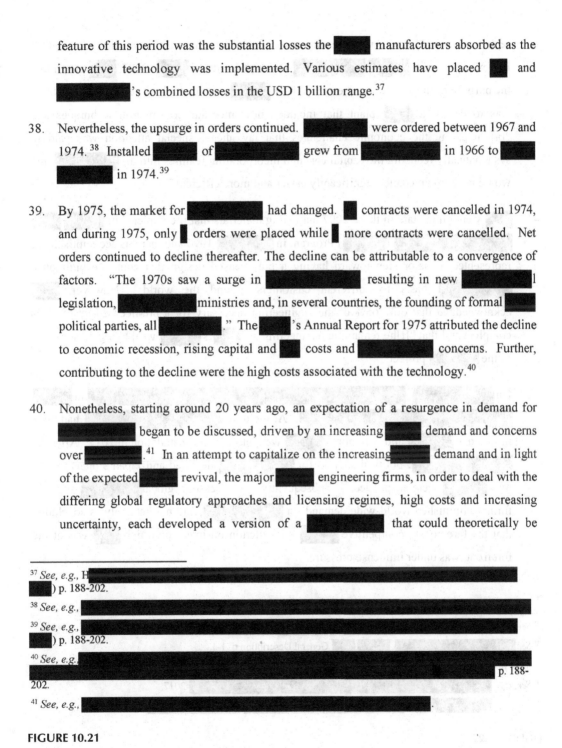

FIGURE 10.21

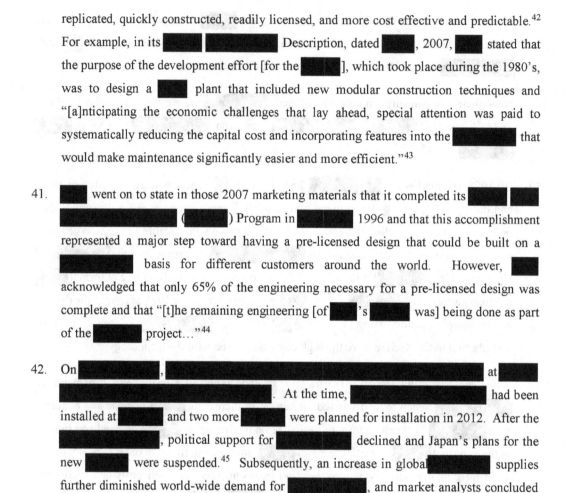

Expert Report of William Jennings
Page 15 of 48

replicated, quickly constructed, readily licensed, and more cost effective and predictable.[42] For example, in its ████ █████████ Description, dated ████, 2007, ████ stated that the purpose of the development effort [for the █████], which took place during the 1980's, was to design a ████ plant that included new modular construction techniques and "[a]nticipating the economic challenges that lay ahead, special attention was paid to systematically reducing the capital cost and incorporating features into the █████████ that would make maintenance significantly easier and more efficient."[43]

41.   ████ went on to state in those 2007 marketing materials that it completed its ████ ████ ██████████████ (████████) Program in ████████ 1996 and that this accomplishment represented a major step toward having a pre-licensed design that could be built on a ██████████ basis for different customers around the world. However, ████ acknowledged that only 65% of the engineering necessary for a pre-licensed design was complete and that "[t]he remaining engineering [of ████ 's ██████ was] being done as part of the █████████ project..."[44]

42.   On ██████████ , ███ at ██████ ██████████████████████████████████ . At the time, ████████████████████ had been installed at ████████ and two more ████████ were planned for installation in 2012. After the ██████████████ , political support for ██████████ declined and Japan's plans for the new ████████ were suspended.[45] Subsequently, an increase in global █████████ supplies further diminished world-wide demand for ██████████ , and market analysts concluded that the ferociously competitive ████████ construction business, of which ████ was at the forefront, was under immense pressure.[46]

---

[42] *See, e.g.,* ████████████████████████████████████ , 2010.
[43] *See* ████████████████████ , ████ ████ General Description p. 1-4.
[44] *Id.* at p. 1-5 and 6.
[45] *See, e.g.,* ████████████████████████████████████ 2017.
[46] *See, e.g.,* ██████████████████████████████████████ , 2017.

FIGURE 10.22

43. In ███████ of 2017, █████████████████ announced plans to stop building its competing █████████████ ████ and was set to announce plans to exit the ██████ construction business altogether after "incurring billions of dollars in losses trying to complete long-delayed projects in the U.S...."[47] In ███████ of 2017, ████ announced the lay-off of an undisclosed number of employees from its █████████████████████ headquarters. On ████████, 2017, █████████████████████████████████████, filed for bankruptcy protection as ███████ expected to lose USD 9 billion for the fiscal year ending ███████ primarily as a result of guaranteeing USD 6 billion of █████████████ obligations.[48]

44. "The alliance with ███ is a key partnership for ██████ in its aim of expanding its business globally and opens up possibilities for various different collaborations that can be realized in the future. Based on a belief that ██████████ will play a key role in solving global █████████ issues, the ████████ companies involved in the ██████ business intend to work together to exploit the future potential of ██████████."[49]

45. However, "[f]our global ██████ industry giants – █████████████████████████ (████) and ████, US-based █████████████ and ████████████████████ – face crippling debts and possible bankruptcy because of their investments in █████████."[50]

46. "A ██████████ piece in the ████████████ noted: 'Hopes of a ██████ renaissance have largely disappeared. For many suppliers, not least ████████, Simply avoiding a ██████ dark ages would be achievement enough."

47. "'There's billions and billions of dollars at stake here.' said Gregory Jaczko, former head of the US █████████████ Commission. 'This could take down ████████ and it certainly means the end of new ██████ construction in the US.'"

---

[47] *See, e.g.,* ███████████████████████████████████████, 2017.
[48] *See, e.g.,* ███, 2017.
[49] *See, e.g.,* █████████████████████████████████), 2009.
[50] *See, e.g.,* ███
██, 2017.

FIGURE 10.23

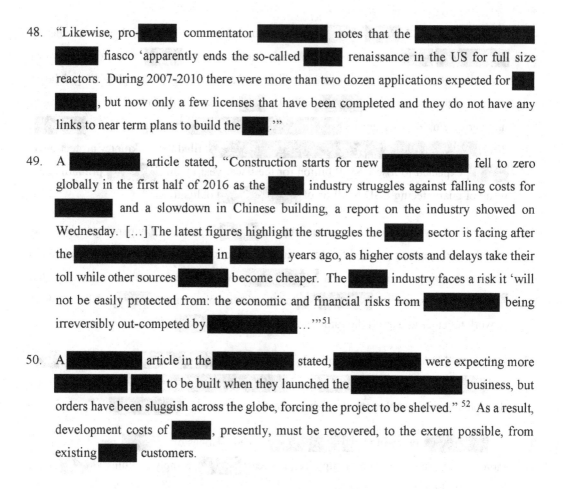

48. "Likewise, pro-███ commentator ███████ notes that the ████████████ ████ fiasco 'apparently ends the so-called ████ renaissance in the US for full size reactors. During 2007-2010 there were more than two dozen applications expected for ███ ████, but now only a few licenses that have been completed and they do not have any links to near term plans to build the ███.'"

49. A ████████ article stated, "Construction starts for new ████████████ fell to zero globally in the first half of 2016 as the ████ industry struggles against falling costs for ████████ and a slowdown in Chinese building, a report on the industry showed on Wednesday. [...] The latest figures highlight the struggles the ████ sector is facing after the ███████████████ in ███████ years ago, as higher costs and delays take their toll while other sources ██████ become cheaper. The ████ industry faces a risk it 'will not be easily protected from: the economic and financial risks from ████████ being irreversibly out-competed by ██████████...'"[51]

50. A ████████ article in the ██████████ stated, ████████████ were expecting more ████████████ to be built when they launched the ██████████████ business, but orders have been sluggish across the globe, forcing the project to be shelved."[52] As a result, development costs of ██████, presently, must be recovered, to the extent possible, from existing ████ customers.

e. Construction Contracts and Project Controls

51. In order to mitigate some of the risks associated with diverging incentives, owners and contractors enter into agreements tailored to mitigate the specific risks about which the parties are concerned. The type of contract used is generally based upon the availability of information, the capabilities and requirement of the parties and the preferences of the owner and contractor and may include fixed-price, cost-plus-fee and time and materials contracts.

---

[51] *See, e.g.,* ████████████████████████████████, 2016.
[52] *See, e.g.,* ████████████████████████████████, 2017.

FIGURE 10.24

The ███████████████████████████ describes fixed-price contracts as follows:

> A fixed-price contract is sometimes referred to as a lump-sum or stipulated-sum contract. This type of contract obligates the contractor to perform the work required by the contract for a fixed dollar amount. This type of contract permits the owner to fix the exact cost of construction in advance and, therefore, helps to minimize the owner's construction cost risk. On the other hand, the contractor must commit to the price of the work in advance and, thus, is subject to performance and productivity cost risk.
>
> The price is established through the process of estimating the cost of each work segment required by the contract. The contractor, therefore, must be able to accurately estimate the quantities of material required, the labor, the equipment necessary to install the materials, and the time the job will take. Since the price will be based on the estimate, the contractor's estimating skills are crucial. Other factors that increase the contractor's risk include weather conditions, site conditions, labor problems, and the potential for escalation in the cost of material, equipment, supplies, and labor.[53]

52. Inherent in a fixed-price arrangement, the contractor agrees to comply with all of the contractual provisions, including any warranty, guarantee, or compliance provisions, in exchange for payment of the agreed upon lump sum.

53. According to the ████████████████████, pursuant to time and materials contracts, the owner pays the contractor for direct labor hours at specified fixed hourly rates, and material at cost. This contract type is utilized when it is not possible at the time of award to estimate

---

[53] *See, e.g.,* 1 Financial Management and Accounting for the Construction Industry, Ch. 1, §1.04 (Construction Financial Management Association ed., Matthew Bender 2013).

FIGURE 10.25

costs with any degree of confidence or the nature of the work is known at the time of award but not its extent or duration. These types of contracts place a "[h]eavy burden on technical personnel to perform surveillance to preclude inefficiency or waste" and there is "[n]o positive profit incentive for [the] contractor to control costs." [54]

54. In addition, processes are typically agreed between the contracting parties with respect to how to deal with changes that arise during construction that were not contemplated as part of the original contract.

55. Construction and cost records should be kept in such detail to enable a determination that costs are complete, accurate and properly billable under a particular contract or provision of a contract, as applicable for purposes of regulatory compliance (as described above), licensing considerations, financial reporting (including determination of percentage of completion status), fraud prevention, and claim valuation.

56. As discussed above, in order to obtain a license and operate ████ █████ in accordance with the laws of Taiwan and under the authority of ROC ████, accurate construction records must be maintained by the operator of a ██████████ in such a manner that the operator can prove that the design, construction and operation comply with the safety design and quality assurance criteria proscribed by ROC ████.

57. In order to comply with laws and regulations surrounding financial markets, contractors must be capable of accurately assessing costs incurred to date and estimating costs to complete. Both of these amounts are necessary to properly determine a contract's status, and therefore fairly reflect the financial position of the contracting parties. For example, as ██ states in its █████████████ filed with the ███████████████████:

> We recognize revenue on agreements for sales of goods and services
> under ██████████ unit and uprate contracts, ██████████
> assemblies, larger ██████████████ projects, ██████████

---

[54] *See, e.g.,* ████████████████████████████████████ p. 37.

FIGURE 10.26

unit contracts, military development contracts, locomotive production contracts, and long-term construction projects, using long-term construction and production contract accounting. We estimate total long-term contract revenue net of price concessions as well as total contract costs.[55]

58. Costs must be sufficiently recorded and determinable in order to prevent and detect fraud. For example, "cost shifting" is a type of fraud in which costs incurred pursuant to one contract or provision are billed under another contract or provision. Usually, when perpetrating cost shifting, contractors "shift" costs they incurred in the course of performing their obligations under a fixed-price contract to a different contract that allows for billing on an "hourly rate," "time and materials" or cost-plus-a-fee basis. To evaluate the propriety of the charges and prevent fraud, costs must be recorded in a manner that is sufficiently detailed to allow an evaluation of the underlying activities in conjunction with the associated charges. [56]

59. Accurately recorded costs are vital to appropriately determining and, if necessary, pricing work performed pursuant to or outside a contract's scope. [57] Inherent in contracting scenarios are instances in which work must be performed that was not specifically discussed or delineated at the outset. It is not unusual for the contractor and owner to have divergent views over whether the work is included in the original contract or is an addition to the original arrangement and the pricing of such work may be determined prior to or after the work has been performed.

60. In accordance with the Contract, from the outset, ▆▆▆ was to perform substantially all of its obligations in exchange for the agreed upon lump-sum price. Amendment ▆ created two new but limited arrangements under which discrete types of work were to be performed pursuant to an hourly compensation arrangement only under particular circumstances.

---

[55] See, e.g., ▆▆▆▆▆▆▆ p.142.

[56] See, e.g., Association of Certified Fraud Examiners, 2016 Fraud Examiners' Manual §1.1428-1.1433.

[57] See, e.g., Proving and Pricing Construction Claims §13.03.

FIGURE 10.27

Accordingly, accurate determination of the obligations of the parties and associated cost is critical to price compensable work performed by ▮▮ and value the assets obtained by ▮▮ .

61. Specifically, ▮▮ and ▮▮ entered into ▮ amendments modifying the ▮▮ Contract and attempted to negotiate three more. Amendment ▮, while maintaining all provisions of the original Contract and previous amendments unless expressly indicated, established services ▮▮ would provide and associated payment terms not present in the original Contract as well as processes and provisions to mitigate the attendant risks. For example, Section 6.8 of Amendment ▮ stated that ▮▮, by written notice to ▮▮, may state that a particular category of supporting engineering services that could only be provided by ▮▮'s home office in the United States or ▮▮'s suppliers might be needed. Pursuant to such notice, the parties were to discuss the services needed, the engineers and technicians to carry out such services, the length of time required to render such services and an estimate of the associated total cost and schedule. If ▮▮ agreed to authorize those offsite hourly services, ▮▮ would execute a written Authorization form with respect to the category of services discussed.

62. In that regard, Attachment C to Amendment ▮ allowed for ▮▮'s examination of, and agreement or non-agreement to, ▮▮'s requests for authorization to perform certain categories of ▮▮ or ▮▮ services in the United States. Section 6.8 of Amendment ▮ explicitly provided that ▮▮ was to ensure that personnel maintained time entries and detailed description of the services it contended were provided within the category of services described in a written Authorization form:

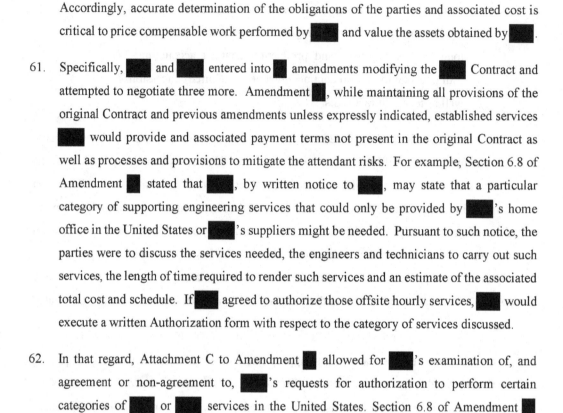

> With respect to any ▮▮▮▮▮▮ by ▮'s ▮▮
> Team pursuant to this Article ▮, ▮▮ may by written notice to ▮▮
> that supporting engineering services by ▮▮'s office in the United
> States [...] and/or by ▮▮'s suppliers are needed. Upon receipt of
> such notice, the Parties shall in good faith immediately discuss the
> circumstances or events giving rise to such need, and discuss and
> agree on the engineers and technicians of ▮▮'s Home Office and
> ▮▮'s suppliers deemed necessary, qualified and experienced to

FIGURE 10.28

render such supporting services […], the supporting services to be rendered by the ██████████████████████ ("██████████ ███████████████"), the length of time required to render such supporting services in support of any ███'s ████████████████ ████ under this Article █, and an estimate of the total costs of an schedule for the ████████████████████████ proposed by ██ to render the ██████████████████████████. Attachment C contains a guideline for use by ████ to examine these issues and estimates and to give ████'s authorization for any [████ ██████]…

63. Under Amendment █, ████ was required to keep complete, detailed records of all services that ████ might claim were billable under a category of ████ or ████ work described in a signed Authorization form. ████ was entitled to audit all records and other documents, including those related to time entries, kept by the ████ Team and ████ Team. Section 6.10 of Amendment █ stated:

> ████ shall ensure that each engineer or technician of ████'s ████ Team and the ██████████████████ Team (where applicable) will keep (a) time entries of the time actually spent on providing ████████████ ██████████████ (in the case of ███'s ████ Team) or ██████████ ██████████████ (in the case of the ████████████████ Team) and (b) detailed description of the ████████████████ Services or ██████████████████ Services such engineer or technician performed.

> ████ shall have the right to audit or cause to be audited, at ████'s cost, all records (including time entries) and other documents kept by each engineer and technician of ███'s ████ Team and of the ██████████████████ Team (where applicable) related to the services rendered by such engineer or technician hereunder and the

FIGURE 10.29

time actually spent on such services. ███ shall, at it [sic] cost, make or cause to be made available to ███ all such records and other documents and provide to ███ such assistance, as ███ may need or request in conducting such audit.

IV.   Opinions

64. Based on my review and analysis of the Contract, certain amendments thereto, ███'s Invoices (including those for ███, ███ and ███ Services and their supporting documentation), meeting minutes, monthly progress reports, other project documentation, witness statements and pleadings, briefings and other filings in this matter, I am of the following opinions.

1.   ███ Failed to Deliver a Complete ████████████████
   ███) and Related Systems, Equipment and Service in Accordance with the Contract

65. ███ failed to perform or deficiently performed work that was required as part of ███'s lump-sum obligations valued at approximately USD 283.0 million.[58] ███ now seeks additional duplicative payments.[59]

a.   ███ failed to meet certain lump-sum obligations

66. I understand that ███'s position is that, despite ███'s payment of substantially all of the lump sum Contract price, ███ has failed to perform all of its lump-sum obligations.[60]

---

[58] *See* Appendix 5.

[59] *Ibid.*

[60] *See, e.g.,* ███ 's Witness Statement.

FIGURE 10.30

67. I have accounted for amounts associated with certain lump-sum obligations ▮▮ has failed to deliver in accordance with the Contract totaling approximately USD 283.0 million.[61]

68. ▮▮ has identified more than 900 problems attributable to ▮▮'s deficient work that ▮▮ is unwilling or unable to address despite its contractual obligation to do so. I have conducted interviews with ▮▮ personnel, reviewed the ▮▮ witness statements and analyzed associated project documentation regarding those problems. For example:[62, 63]

    a. ▮▮ provided various pieces of equipment, totaling approximately USD 138.8 million that do not meet ROC ▮▮'s requirements regarding the amount of ▮▮▮▮ the equipment could withstand in the event of ▮▮▮▮. Therefore ▮▮ cannot gain ▮▮▮▮ approval for the equipment.[64, 65] Included in this amount is approximately USD 95.2 million ▮▮ paid ▮▮ for the ▮▮▮▮▮▮▮▮ ("▮▮▮▮") that perform critical ▮▮ functions. However, the ▮▮▮▮s cannot be used because of ▮▮'s inadequate performance, which may preclude licensing of the ▮▮.

    b. ▮▮ provided equipment sourced from its suppliers ▮▮ and ▮▮▮▮, valued at approximately USD 50.7 million, that comprises the ▮▮▮▮▮▮ ("▮▮▮") and is nonconforming, which prevents operators from reliably ▮▮▮▮▮▮.[66, 67]

---

[61] *See* Appendix 5.

[62] *See, e.g.*, Expert Report of ▮▮▮▮ ¶ 5.27.5.

[63] *See, e.g.*, Expert Report of ▮▮▮ ¶ 50.

[64] *See, e.g.*, Expert Report of ▮▮▮ ¶ 5.23 and 5.26.

[65] *See, e.g.*, First Witness Statement of ▮▮▮▮.

[66] *See, e.g.*, Expert Report of ▮▮▮ ¶ 52 – 59.

[67] *See* Appendix 5.3.

FIGURE 10.31

     c. █████ provided █████ 200 butterfly valves valued at approximately USD 7.4 million that were manufactured improperly and do not conform to contract requirements.[68, 69]

     d. I have identified at least an additional USD 86.0 million associated with either work █████ failed to perform or more than 300 other pieces of equipment █████ provided that do not conform to the Contract requirements.[70, 71, 72, 73]

69.   Not used.

70.   Not used.

b. █████ seeks additional duplicative payments

71.   █████ now seeks payment for an additional USD 90.0 million it has billed for █████, █████ and offsite hourly work that █████ has not yet paid. Approximately USD 7.4 million is related to █████ and █████ and approximately USD 82.7 million is purportedly for offsite hourly work.[74] Of the combined USD 82.7 million, I have identified invoices totaling more than USD 42.5 million clearly attributable to work required under █████'s lump-sum obligations, and that the remaining invoices lack sufficient documentation to warrant payment.[75] For example:

     a. Approximately USD 42.5 million of the invoices claimed by █████ are attributable to work performed resolving problems with the █████, █████, and █████ equipment, which comprises key components of the █████.[76] Prior to execution of Amendment

---

[68] *See, e.g.,* Expert Report of █████████ ¶ 5.11.

[69] *See* Appendix 5.4.

[70] *See, e.g.,* First Witness Statement of █████.

[71] *See, e.g.,* Expert Report of █████████ ¶ 5.1-6.26.

[72] *See* Appendices 5.2 through 5.9.

[73] See, e.g., Expert Report of █████████ ¶ 107-108.

[74] *See* Appendix 6.

[75] *Ibid.*

[76] *Ibid.*

FIGURE 10.32

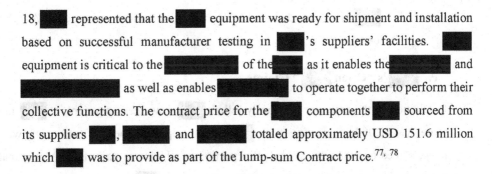

18, ▮▮ represented that the ▮▮ equipment was ready for shipment and installation based on successful manufacturer testing in ▮▮'s suppliers' facilities. ▮▮ equipment is critical to the ▮▮▮▮ of the ▮▮ as it enables the ▮▮▮▮ and ▮▮▮▮▮▮ as well as enables ▮▮▮▮ to operate together to perform their collective functions. The contract price for the ▮▮ components ▮▮ sourced from its suppliers ▮▮, ▮▮▮ and ▮▮▮ totaled approximately USD 151.6 million which ▮▮ was to provide as part of the lump-sum Contract price.[77, 78]

b. With respect to the remaining USD 40.2 million and as more fully described below, ▮▮ has not provided sufficient evidence to allow a determination of whether the work ▮▮ allegedly performed is or is not included in ▮▮'s lump-sum obligations. Specifically:

    i. ▮▮ claims USD 10.6 million it billed under the Attachment B category I.1. As indicated on Attachment B, responsibility for the cost of work performed pursuant to this category is subject to determination of the party responsible for the cause of the underlying problem.[79] Specifically, the "Remark" column on Attachment B states "▮▮ Rates+50% ▮▮ Rates unless caused by ▮▮ non-conformance issues."[80]

    ii. ▮▮ billed an additional USD 18.8 million under Attachment B category I.3.C for work allegedly performed to review and verify the as-built drawings and perform reconciliation analysis as needed.[81]

---

[77] *See, e.g.,* Expert Report of ▮▮▮ ¶ 38-48 and 138-148.

[78] *See, e.g.,* Exhibit R-830

[79] *See* Appendix 3.1.

[80] *See, e.g.,* Expert Report of ▮▮▮ ¶ 5.27.1-5.27.5.

[81] *See* Appendix 3.1.

FIGURE 10.33

    iii.   ██ billed an additional USD 10.8 million under various other Attachment B categories.

c.   ██'s "Open ██" Claims

72. In addition to the amounts previously billed, ██ now seeks payment, at ██ rates, for more than 86,000 engineering hours ██ or its suppliers expended performing work ██ never agreed to authorize, a substantial portion of which was part of ██'s original lump sum obligations (the "Unauthorized Offsite Work").[82] ██ has not been invoiced for these hours and ██ admits the work was performed without obtaining ██'s authorization pursuant to Attachment C of Amendment ██. I have identified that approximately USD 14.7 million of ██'s USD 18 million claim for Unauthorized Offsite Work relates to work required under ██'s original lump sum obligations.[83] For example:

    a. At least 70,000 of the more than 86,000 Unauthorized Offsite Work hours claimed by ██ relate to correcting problems with ██ equipment;[84]

    b. An entire sub-category of ██'s claim for Unauthorized Offsite Work -- "Open ██ – ██," which totals more than USD 6.3 million, is attributable to one of ██'s ██ suppliers that provided equipment that was never conforming and remains non-conforming;[85] and

    c. Included in the documents that purportedly validate ██'s claim for Unauthorized Offsite Work are Non-conformance Reports ("NCR") and Non-conformance Documents ("NCD"), which are records generated by ██ notifying ██ that that equipment provided does not comport with ██'s lump sum obligations.[86]

---

[82] *See* Appendix 4.

[83] *Ibid.*

[84] *Ibid.*

[85] *Ibid.*

[86] *See, e.g.,* Exhibit R-646.

FIGURE 10.34

2. ███'s Amendment ███ Invoices are Deficient

73. In order to assess whether or not amounts ███ invoiced ███, pursuant to Amendment ███, were appropriate and not the responsibility of ███, ███ must be able to determine whether the work was allocable to the ███ project, properly allocable to a specific Attachment B category and compensable by ███. The payment terms of Attachment B categories included "To be performed at ███ Cost," "To be completed by ███. Not at ███ Cost," " ███ Rates+50% ███ Rates" or " ███ Rates+50% ███ Rates unless caused by ███ non-conformance." Where the Contract specified payment terms at " ███ Rates+50% ███ Rates unless caused by ███ non-conformance," a determination that the work was caused by a ███ non-conformance would render ███ invoices improper to the extent of such work. Further, Section 6.11 of Amendment ███ specifically stated that to the extent Equipment or services provided by ███ were not in conformance with the Contract, the ███ cost of that work would be the responsibility of ███. Accordingly, work performed by ███ addressing its nonconforming services or Equipment is not properly allocable to Amendment ███.

d. ███'s Claim for ███, ███ and Offsite Hourly Work Lacks Sufficient Detail

74. Under Section 6.10.1 of Amendment ███, ███ is entitled to examine ███'s invoices and to review ███'s back-up documentation to determine whether the subject services are in fact chargeable under Amendment ███, whether they fall within a category of services described in a signed Authorization form, and whether they were timely and meet the other requirements of Amendment ███ and the applicable Authorization form. ███ has failed to provide ███ with records that would allow an accurate determination of whether the hours included in ███'s invoices were spent in furtherance of work a) contemplated under the Contract, b) caused by ███ or other parties' non-conforming work, c) devoted to further development of the ███ standard ███ design for ███'s continued commercialization at

FIGURE 10.35

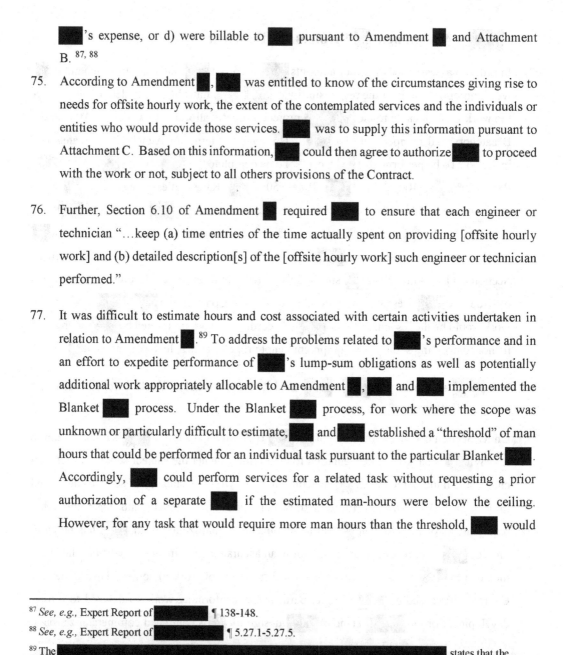

███ 's expense, or d) were billable to ███ pursuant to Amendment ██ and Attachment B. [87, 88]

75. According to Amendment ██, ██ was entitled to know of the circumstances giving rise to needs for offsite hourly work, the extent of the contemplated services and the individuals or entities who would provide those services. ████ was to supply this information pursuant to Attachment C. Based on this information, ████ could then agree to authorize ████ to proceed with the work or not, subject to all others provisions of the Contract.

76. Further, Section 6.10 of Amendment ██ required ████ to ensure that each engineer or technician "…keep (a) time entries of the time actually spent on providing [offsite hourly work] and (b) detailed description[s] of the [offsite hourly work] such engineer or technician performed."

77. It was difficult to estimate hours and cost associated with certain activities undertaken in relation to Amendment ██.[89] To address the problems related to ████ 's performance and in an effort to expedite performance of ████ 's lump-sum obligations as well as potentially additional work appropriately allocable to Amendment ██, ████ and ████ implemented the Blanket ████ process. Under the Blanket ████ process, for work where the scope was unknown or particularly difficult to estimate, ████ and ████ established a "threshold" of man hours that could be performed for an individual task pursuant to the particular Blanket ████. Accordingly, ████ could perform services for a related task without requesting a prior authorization of a separate ████ if the estimated man-hours were below the ceiling. However, for any task that would require more man hours than the threshold, ████ would

---

[87] *See, e.g.,* Expert Report of ████████ ¶ 138-148.

[88] *See, e.g.,* Expert Report of ████████ ¶ 5.27.1-5.27.5.

[89] The ██ states that the ██

FIGURE 10.36

submit a separate authorization request. This did not alter the approval process or alter determination of the party responsible for bearing the cost.

78. In order to determine which party would bear responsibility for the associated cost and the payment terms, it is necessary to determine under which Attachment B Item and Work Description the work was categorized, as well as the underlying cause for the necessity of ▆▆, ▆▆ or offsite hourly work, because ▆▆ did not have to pay for ▆▆ to address nonconformances.

79. The information ▆▆ has produced to date is insufficient to substantiate whether payment of ▆▆'s invoices is warranted.[90, 91] ▆▆ has provided limited detail of man hours allegedly incurred providing Amendment ▆ services with only general descriptions vaguely indicating the subject of the work. Those descriptions do not provide any evidence regarding the underlying cause of problems or evidence that the amounts were appropriately allocated to an Attachment B category that would substantiate that the work was properly billable.[92] Based upon my experience, the information that I would expect to see could include documentation such as certificates of compliance and conformance, certified ▆▆ reports, product certification reports, ▆▆▆▆, ▆▆▆ and ▆▆▆ certificates, ▆▆▆ examination forms, ▆▆▆ reports, ▆▆▆ certificates, ▆▆▆▆ ▆▆ or ▆▆▆▆ reports.

80. After removing from ▆▆'s USD 90.0 million claim the aforementioned invoices for inappropriate offsite ▆▆ work, of the remaining USD 47.5 million, I have identified a substantial portion of the invoices that fall into an Attachment B category that would require evaluation of the underlying cause for the necessity to perform the work. For example, approximately USD 10.6 million of ▆▆'s claim is associated with category I.1 of Attachment B.[93] Category I.1 specifically states that work performed resolving design and

---

[90] *See, e.g.,* Expert Report of ▆▆▆ ¶ 138-148.

[91] *See, e.g.,* Expert Report of ▆▆▆ ¶ 5.27.1-5.27.5.

[92] *Ibid.*

[93] *See* Appendix 3.1.

FIGURE 10.37

equipment related issues found during construction/installation" is to be performed at "███ Rates+50% ██ Rates unless caused by ██ non-conformance issues." Further, as discussed below, Section 6.11 of Amendment ██ requires that ███ bear responsibility for correction of nonconforming work.

81.   ███'s invoices lack sufficient information to determine whether the work was properly allocable to the ██████ project, properly allocable to a specific Attachment B category or compensable by ███.[94] As described above, ███'s invoices do not contain sufficient information that would allow ███ to determine whether or not the work was attributable to ███'s deficient work. Attachment B specifically reiterated in Section 6.11, that: "in the event the Equipment or items of Equipment furnished or services by [███] under the contact are determined prior to Commercial Operation not to be in conformance with the Contract [...] [███] shall promptly correct or replace or otherwise disposition in accordance with Paragraph 3.2.8.7 any such defect or deficiency in the Equipment and reperform any non-conforming services in accordance with the provisions of Paragraph 2.33."

82.   Accordingly, ███ has failed to adequately support its claims for ███, ███ and offsite hourly work and Unauthorized Offsite Work and offers the report of ██████, which attempts to buttress ███'s claims.

e. Mr. ██████'s Analysis is Incomplete

83.   Mr. ██████'s opinion regarding the invoice claims of ███ is unreliable as his analysis is anecdotal and fails to address contractual provisions regarding limitations on ███'s responsibility to pay by the hour for services necessary to fulfill ███'s lump-sum obligations and ███'s limitation from seeking suspension costs arising out of offsite hourly work.

84.   Counsel for ███ instructed Mr. ██████ to review ███'s claim and "[o]ffer an opinion regarding the reasonableness of the quantum basis used to develop and fully support the

---

[94] *See, e.g.,* Expert Report of ██████ ¶ 5.27.1-5.27.5.

FIGURE 10.38

Expert Report of William Jennings
Page 32 of 48

Claims related to: (i) unpaid invoices for..." Amendment ▇ Services (the "Unpaid Invoices Claim") and "additional ▇ provided by ▇ to ▇ but not invoiced (the "Open ▇ Claim")." In reaching such an opinion, Mr. ▇ selected for review 23 invoices out of the total 380 included in the Unpaid Invoices Claim and 61% of the Open ▇ Claim. Both selections were based on an unspecified selection methodology.

85. Mr. ▇ stated that he reconciled the invoice cover letter and summary to the invoice details or reconciled the amounts claimed in ▇'s Application To Introduce Additional Claims dated ▇, 2016 with documentation and other backup..." as applicable and evaluated the deliverables and ▇ Services of the specific invoice, reviewing "deliverables for assignment of appropriate Amendment ▇, Attachment B Scope of Work as authorized by ▇, ▇ and cost category."

86. Mr. ▇ concluded after his review that "[t]he Engineering Services performed were responsive to the Attachment B work to be performed in accordance with Amendment ▇, and as amended, and as otherwise directed by ▇."

87. To conclude that the work was "responsive" to Attachment B is insufficient for purposes of supporting ▇'s claims. [95] As discussed above, it is necessary to determine under which Attachment B Item and Work Description the work was categorized, as well as identify the underlying cause for the necessity of Amendment ▇ services in order to opine which party would bear responsibility for the associated cost. As described by ▇'s engineering experts:

> Thus, in addition to finding that the time-card descriptions are inadequate for determining whether work purportedly performed under Amendment ▇, Attachment B, Sections II.5, II.6, and II.7, is eligible for payment, I find that the invoices I reviewed in more detail lack supporting evidence for determining if payment for said work is warranted. More specifically, the supporting material

---

[95] *See, e.g.,* Expert Report of ▇ ¶ 138-163.

FIGURE 10.39

supplied by ▮▮▮ along with its invoices for offsite hourly work on the ▮▮▮ generally includes a conclusory statement that the work was performed according to the relevant section of Attachment B to Amendment ▮ but lacks sufficient evidence to support this statement. There is simply no actual evidence provided of why the work, or the problems being address by said work, falls within a discrete category of work eligible for payment under Attachment B to Amendment ▮.[96]

I reviewed the descriptions that ▮▮▮ provided for tasks and work for which the invoice seeks additional compensation. It is my opinion that the majority of items listed on this invoice do not contain sufficient information in order to determine whether the associated work warrants payment pursuant to Amendment ▮.[97]

It is also my opinion that in the cases where I have been able to identify work associated with an item listed on invoice ▮▮▮▮▮▮ 569 that arise out of one of the problems with the ▮▮▮, said work is not contemplated by Amendment ▮, Attachment B, Sections I.1 because it was caused by a ▮▮▮ non-conformance.[98]

88.   Mr. ▮▮▮ claims to have determined under which Attachment B Item and Work Description the work was categorized. Included in the documentation Mr. ▮▮▮ reviewed were ▮▮▮s and ▮▮▮s, which are both documents created by ▮▮ alerting ▮▮ to problems ▮▮ identified with the Work ▮▮ provided. However, despite the fact that he was in possession of documents which raise questions regarding the party responsible for the underlying

---

[96] *See, e.g.,* Expert Report of ▮▮▮▮▮ ¶ 148.
[97] *See* Expert Report of ▮▮▮▮▮ ¶ 5.27.4
[98] *Ibid.*

FIGURE 10.40

problem, he has made no assertion and provided no evidence regarding any attempt to determine fault.

89. The conclusions Mr. ███ drew based upon his anecdotal and judgmental "samples" provide no basis upon which to project his conclusions to the remaining invoices for which ███ seeks payment. By only judgmentally selecting 23 of 380 invoices, Mr. ███ has not established a statistically valid sample upon which conclusions can be extrapolated to a larger population.[99] Accordingly, Mr. ███'s conclusions are limited to the individual invoices and amounts he reviewed and inapplicable to more than USD 60.7 million of ███'s Unpaid Invoices Claim.[100, 101, 102, 103]

90. Despite the inapplicability of Mr. ███'s judgmental "samples" to the remaining populations, the conclusions Mr. ███ drew from those samples are also flawed. For example, of the only 23 invoices Mr. ███ reviewed, 9 relate to work performed relative to ███'s ███ suppliers ███, ███ and ███ and related equipment.[104] Each ███ supplier is listed on Attachment B in Sections II.5, II.6 and II.7, respectively. Each section specified that ███ was to be compensated at "███ Rates+50% ███ Rates" for "perform[ing] design changes after delivery." However, ███ never delivered conforming ███ equipment.[105, 106] Accordingly, the work billed under these categories could not be "responsive" to Attachment B.[107]

---

[99] *See* Appendix 6.

[100] *See, e.g.,* ███████████

[101] *See* ███████████

[102] *See, e.g.,* PCAOB AU Section 350: Audit Sampling.

[103] *See* Appendix 6.

[104] *Ibid.*

[105] *See, e.g.,* Expert Report of ███ ¶ 6, 7, 49, 50 and 157.

[106] *See, e.g.,* First Witness Statement of ███.

[107] *Ibid.*

FIGURE 10.41

91. Similarly, Mr. ███ concluded that ███'s claim for Unauthorized ███ was fully "supported, allowable, and allocable to the Project," despite the fact that the overwhelming majority of the claim is attributable to the ███ or other nonconforming Work supplied by ███. Further, Mr. ███ acknowledges that the work was performed without obtaining the authorization of ███ pursuant to the Contract.

92. In order to reach his flawed conclusions, Mr. ███ utilized: ███'s internal accounting system, including its enterprise resource planning system, vouchers, labor distribution reports, and manual timesheets; ███ accounting and human resources policies; interviews with ███ employees; and ███H's suppliers' internal time keeping systems. ███ does not have access to that information. Accordingly, ███ was not in a position to meaningfully exercise its rights to thoroughly review ███'s invoices to consider the purpose and cause of the work reflected, whether the work was properly allocable to Amendment ███ and if so, which party should bear the cost. Mr. ███ did not talk to ███ personnel to evaluate information in ███'s possession.

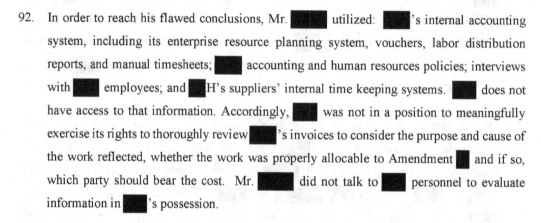

3.   ███H's "Suspension" Claim Lacks Economic Basis

93. ███'s suspension claim and Mr. ███'s analysis thereof makes no sense in light of the factual context in which the activities purportedly generating those costs occurred.

94. Amendment ███, Section 6.9 states, "███ shall in no event be liable to ███ (including ███ suppliers) for any other amount, payment, fees, charges or other costs or expenses of any kind with respect or related to the personnel of the ███████████ Team or an ███████████ Services."

95. Amendment ███ specified that the associated rates included any and all related costs, including but not limited to the expenses of management, demobilization and/or reorganization, and that payment of those rates included full compensation for all management, demobilization, reorganization or other similar costs of the kind that ███ is now claiming as "suspension" costs.

FIGURE 10.42

96. ██ and ██ clearly agree that ██ was not required to request, or to allow ██ to perform, any offsite hourly services. Instead, ██ had the right, but not the obligation, to allow ██ to perform offsite hourly services.

97. ██'s suspension claim is comprised of "Personnel Cost," "Severance/Restructuring Costs," "Demobilization Costs," "Preservation and Disposition" costs and subcontractor costs. Personnel cost portions of ██'s suspension claim is calculated based on hourly services using man hours generated at the Home Office and ██ Services rates while at the same time acknowledging that ██ directed them to halt performing those optional services. ██ issued ██ multiple letters identifying these amounts; the amounts grew with each letter.

98. However, the documentation ██ produced (and Mr. ██ reviewed) generally appear to be nothing more than spreadsheet summaries of costs allegedly incurred. For example, the documentation purportedly "validating" USD 9.2 million of ██'s USD 10.3 million claim for "██ ██ & Direct ██ Cost Claim" are nothing more than spreadsheets describing activities of "██ Taipei Office Operations," ██ Project Office Operations," "Engineering Operations," "Supporting Functions" and ██'s vendors that reflect a total number of hours claimed.[108] There is no meaningful evidence that the amounts were actually costs ██ incurred or paid.[109]

99. ██ made it clear that Amendment ██ did not release ██ from its original lump-sum obligations for which it was compensated by payment of the lump-sum price. Based on my experience with other commercial construction projects, ██ could have avoided "suspension costs" by deploying any affected personnel to complete the work required of ██ under its original lump-sum obligations.

---

[108] *See* ██-2016-0048.
[109] *See* Report of ██ p. 30 – 36.

FIGURE 10.43

4. ███'s Other Commercial Claims Lack Meaningful Support

100. The documentation ███ produced purportedly substantiating its "Other Commercial Claims" are insufficient summaries unsupported by meaningful evidence.

101. The documentation ███ produced (and Mr. ███ reviewed) generally appear to be nothing more than spreadsheet summaries of what ███ describes as "Open ███ Assignments," "Unreimbursed Engineering Processes," "Unreimbursed Supplier Audits for ███," "Unreimbursed Routine Material Shipments," "Unreimbursed Hardware and Material" and a claim "Related to 'Good Faith Effort' Work for 13 Category 'C' Alleged Nonconformances and IMS Server ███ Issue[s]." ███ has produced no meaningful evidence, beyond those summary level spreadsheets and letters to which they were attached, that the amounts listed were actually costs ███ incurred or that ███ is obligated to reimburse ███ for them. For example, the documentation "validating" USD 1.8 million of ███'s USD 2.3 million claim consists of a transmittal letter, an attached ███ invoice to ███ and Excel spreadsheets which appear to have been generated more than 10 months after ███ filed its Request for Arbitration. [110]

5. No evidence of ███'s "cost-sharing"

f. No evidence of ███'s "cost-sharing"

102. Despite repeated ███ references to "cost-sharing" throughout the project and in its claim, I have seen no evidence of actual payments to third parties. ███ has produced no contemporaneous documentation that would indicate ███ bore any cost that was not reimbursed by ███ in such a manner that would generate anything other than profit for ███. In my experience, if ███ were truly sharing costs; instead of the ███ invoices rendered to ███, I would have expected to see detailed records evidencing costs allegedly borne by ███.

---

[110] *See, e.g.,* ███ P-2016-0041 and ███ 2016-0044.

FIGURE 10.44

g. 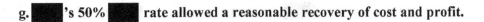's 50% ███ rate allowed a reasonable recovery of cost and profit.

103. Amendment ███ provided that ███ and ███ which were both services provided on-site, would be reimbursed by ███ at a rate calculated annually using USD 218 per hour and adjusted based on the current year and an escalation percentage using 2009 as the base year. With respect to offsite hourly work, ███ agreed to a 50% reduction against a "blended" rate of USD 240 per hour for ███ and its suppliers' personnel performing offsite hourly services.[111] Offsite hourly rates were also adjusted upward annually. ███ and ███ services were not reduced. Under Amendment ███, which became effective on ███ 2013, ███ agreed to pay 75% of the applicable ███ rate after ███ represented it was losing money performing offsite hourly work at the 50% reduced rate.

104. Application of the 50% reduction resulted in a rate of USD 120 per hour for straight-time offsite hourly work performed by ███ personnel. ███ was allowed to charge 150% of this rate (USD 180 per hour) for "overtime" hours. ███ was also allowed to add a 12% surcharge on hours provided by engineers or technicians employed by ███'s suppliers. This resulted in a USD 134.40 rate for straight time of supplier personnel, and a USD 201.60 rate for overtime of supplier personnel.

105. Many variables must be considered to determine whether hourly services are profitable for a company providing them. For personnel employed directly by ███, the variables would include factors such as the availability and capacity of ███'s salaried-work force, ███'s fixed costs for salaried labor and benefits, ███'s variable costs for hourly labor and burdens, and its actual overtime costs. For personnel employed by ███'s suppliers, ███'s margin (or loss) would depend primarily on the rate it actually paid to the supplier.

106. I have seen no cost justification provided by ███ for either its original "list" rate, the reduced rates, or what ███ expected to earn (or lose) as a result of the rates. In my experience, contractors normally apply a markup to labor cost to earn a profit. Depending upon the

---

[111] ███ actually charged ███ USD 248 per hour for ███ *See, e.g.,* Exhibit R-647.

FIGURE 10.45

capacity and cost structure of ███, it is entirely possible that ███ earned a positive margin on all "discounted" offsite work hours.

107. According to the American Society of Civil Engineers' 2012 The Engineering Income and Salary Survey:[112]

    a. 2010 total annual income of engineers ranged from approximately USD 60,000 for the 10th percentile up to USD 150,600 for the 90th percentile and averaged USD 100,603 or approximately USD 48 per hour a 2,080 hour year.

    b. Assuming 2010 offsite hourly rates of USD 240 per hour reduced by 50% and 2,000 billable hours, ███ was profiting by approximately USD 89,000 annually for each engineer if every engineer was paid at the 90th percentile. Assuming all ███ engineers providing ███ Services were not paid in the 90th percentile, ███'s annual profit per year for each engineer likely ranged from USD 89,000 to USD 180,000.

Submitted April 12, 2017:

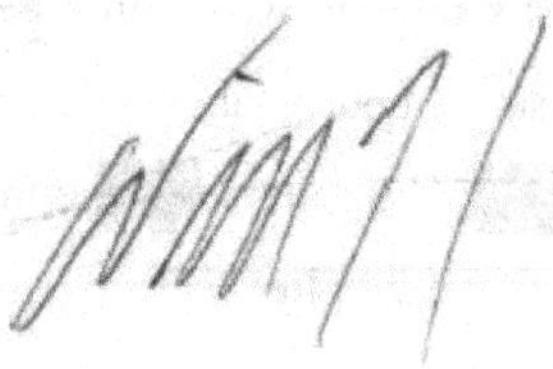

William L. Jennings

---

[112] *See* The Engineering Income and Salary Survey Standard Report: Trends Analysis, Policies, and Practices as of April 1, 2012.

FIGURE 10.46

Expert Report of William Jennings
Page 40 of 48

EXHIBITS

FIGURE 10.47

Expert Report of William Jennings
Page 41 of 48

Exhibit 1 – CV of William L. Jennings

William L. Jennings, BS, MBA, CPA, CFE, CFF

A. Background and Education

1. Present Position

- Accounting, Economics and Appraisal Group, LLC, Principal

2. Other Positions Held

- Alvarez & Marsal Global Forensic and Dispute Services, LLC, Managing Director, June 2012 to May 2016
- Navigant Consulting, Inc., Managing Director and Practice Segment Leader, Southeast – Disputes and Investigations, October 2005 to June 2012
- LECG, LLC, Director – National Forensic Accounting Practice, August 2004 to October 2005
- FFI, Inc., President, 2003 – 2004
- Kroll, Inc., Principal, 1995 – 2003
- Coopers & Lybrand, L.L.P., Director – Fraud Investigation services, 1989 – 1994
- Oxford Group, Ltd., Acting Chief Financial Officer, 1989
- Brown & Jennings, CPAs, Partner, 1984 – 1989
- Coopers & Lybrand, L.L.P., Supervisor – General Audit Practice, 1979 – 1983
- A.A. Harmon & Co., CPA's, Semi-Senior Accountant, 1978 – 1979

FIGURE 10.48

3. Education and Professional Certifications

- B.S., Accounting, University of New Orleans, 1976-1978

- Tulane University 1973-1975

- M.B.A., Auburn University, 2005

- CPA, American Institute of Certified Public Accountants, 1981

- CFE, Association of Certified Fraud Examiners, 1991

- CFF, American Institute of Certified Public Accountants, 2008

- Private Detective (Class A), 2000

B. Publications – Previous Ten Years

- The Tangled Web: Unraveling the Badges of Fraud. (2007, March). *Investigations Quarterly Newsletter.*

C. Speaking Engagements – Previous Ten Years

- *Financial Statement Fraud.* (2002 – 2003). Crouching Profits Hidden Debts, Kroll, Inc., Chicago, IL; Seattle, WA; San Francisco, CA; Dallas, TX; and Atlanta, GA.

- *Financial Statement Fraud.* (May 2003). FSG International Training Conference, Kroll, Inc., Collingwood, Ontario.

- *Fraud Investigation.* (August 2003). Association of Certified Fraud Examiners National Conference, Chicago, IL.

- *Uncovering Investigative Issues-Methods and Tools.* (May 2004). Southern Institute for Business and Professional Ethics Summer Seminar Series, Atlanta, GA.

- *Using Forensic Accounting to Catch the Bad Guys.* (2005, April). Southeastern Corporate Law Institute 42nd Annual Meeting, Point Clear, AL.

- *The Risk Detector: What You Don't Know About Your Organization Can Hurt You.* (2005, April). Georgia Society of CPAs Spring Decision Makers Series, Atlanta, GA.

- *Internal Investigations.* (2005, September). Institute of Continuing Legal Education in Georgia: White Collar Crime, Atlanta, GA.

FIGURE 10.49

- *Building an Ethical Culture: Strategies for Effective Recruitment and Orientation.* (2006, August). Southern Institute for Business and Professional Ethics 2006 Summer Seminar Series, Atlanta, GA.
- *High In-Fidelity – Corporate Theft and Recovery.* (2009, July). Risk and Insurance Management Society 34th Annual Education Conference, Naples, FL.
- *The New Hard Times: Business Crimes, Ponzi Schemes and Affinity Frauds.* (2009, August). Georgia Society of CPA's 2009 Fraud and Forensic Accounting Conference, Atlanta, GA.
- *High In-Fidelity – Corporate Theft and Recovery.* (2010, July). Risk and Insurance Management Society 34th Annual Education Conference, Naples, FL.
- *Asset Recovery: How to Get Your Stuff Back.* (2011, April). Georgia Society of CPAs 2011 Spring Decision Makers Conference, Atlanta, GA.
- *Hands-On, Real-Life Case Study on Succeeding in Tracing and Recovering Assets in a Multinational Fraud* Case (2011, June). International Association for Asset Recovery 2011 Cross-Border Asset Tracing and Recovery Conference, London, England.
- *Dissecting Bank, Business and Credit Card Records That Lead You to Hidden Assets and Fronts for Bad Guys* (2011, June). International Association for Asset Recovery 2011 Cross- Border Asset Tracing and Recovery Conference, London, England.
- *The Audit Leader's Role in Proactively Addressing Fraud: Keeping Your Organization Out of the Headlines* (2013, January). MIS Audit Leadership Institute. Miami, Florida.
- *Fraud Prevention and Detection: What Chief Audit Executives Must Know* (2013, April). MIS Training Institute SuperStrategies 2013, The Audit Best Practices Conference, Orlando, FL.
- *Race to the Top: Issues Related to Rankings and External Data Misreporting in Higher Education* (2013, June). Society of Corporate Compliance and Ethics Higher Education Compliance Conference, Austin, TX.

D. Expert Testimony – Previous Four Years

- Heather Q. Bolinger, *et al.* v. First Multiple Listing Service, Inc., *et al.*
  - o Evidence given at deposition

- U.S.A. *ex. Rel.* Melissa Simms Powell, *et al.* v. American Intercontinental University, Inc., *et al.*
  - o Evidence given at deposition

FIGURE 10.50

- Securities & Exchange Commission v. Steven Forman
  - o Evidence given at deposition

- Etowah Environmental Group LLC, et al. v Advanced Disposal Services, Inc., et al.
  - o Evidence given at deposition and arbitration hearing

- CSX Transportation, Inc. v. Brian K. Leggett
  - o Evidence given at trial

- Darryl S. Laddin, as Liquidating Trustee v. Steven A. Odom, et al.
  - o Evidence given at deposition

- Piedmont Family Office Fund, LP; et al. v. Robert L. Duncan; et al.
  - o Evidence given at deposition

FIGURE 10.51

Exhibit 2 – Materials Reviewed

Contract No. ▇▇▇ between ▇▇ and ▇▇▇ and Amendments No. ▇, ▇ and ▇ thereto;

▇▇ Statement of Claim and all Witness Statements, Appendices Exhibits, Reports and documents attached thereto and referenced therein;

First witness statement of ▇▇ ;

First witness statement of ▇▇ ;

First witness statement of ▇▇ ;

First witness statement of ▇▇ ;

First witness statement of ▇▇ ;

First witness statement of ▇▇ ;

First witness statement of ▇▇ ;

First witness statement of ▇▇ ;

First witness statement of ▇▇ ;

First witness statement of ▇▇ ;

First witness statement of ▇▇ ;

First witness statement of ▇▇ ;

First witness statement of ▇▇ ;

First witness statement of ▇▇ ;

First witness statement of ▇▇ ;

First witness statement of ▇▇ ;

First witness statement of ▇▇ ;

Expert Report of ▇▇ , Ph.D.;

Expert Report of ▇▇ , Ph.D., P.E., FASM;

Response and Counterclaim;

▇▇'s Response to ▇▇'s Application for Bifurcation;

▇▇'s Rejoinder in Further Opposition to ▇▇'s Application for Bifurcation;

▇▇'s Reply on Bifurcation;

▇▇'s Application for Bifurcation;

Exhibit R-023;

Exhibit R-024;

Exhibit R-060;

Exhibit R-062;

Exhibit R-063;

Exhibit R-064;

Exhibit R-067;

Exhibit R-068;

Exhibit R-092;

Exhibit R-120;

Exhibit R-121;

Exhibit R-122;

Exhibit R-124;

Exhibit R-131;

Exhibit R-144;

Exhibit R-168;

Exhibit R-191;

Exhibit R-194;

Exhibit R-196;

Exhibit R-198;

FIGURE 10.52

Exhibit R-223;	Exhibit R-450;
Exhibit R-239;	Exhibit R-451;
Exhibit R-241;	Exhibit R-477;
Exhibit R-242;	Exhibit R-481;
Exhibit R-243;	Exhibit R-487;
Exhibit R-244;	Exhibit R-489;
Exhibit R-245;	Exhibit R-490;
Exhibit R-246;	Exhibit R-491;
Exhibit R-248;	Exhibit R-492;
Exhibit R-266;	Exhibit R-514;
Exhibit R-269;	Exhibit R-515;
Exhibit R-287;	Exhibit R-516;
Exhibit R-288;	Exhibit R-517;
Exhibit R-289;	Exhibit R-552;
Exhibit R-305;	Exhibit R-576;
Exhibit R-306;	Exhibit R-579;
Exhibit R-318;	Exhibit R-580;
Exhibit R-327;	Exhibit R-584;
Exhibit R-328;	Exhibit R-620;
Exhibit R-335;	Exhibit R-621;
Exhibit R-351;	Exhibit R-622;
Exhibit R-352;	Exhibit R-623;
Exhibit R-378;	Exhibit R-624;
Exhibit R-394;	Exhibit R-625;
Exhibit R-419;	Exhibit R-626;
Exhibit R-420;	Exhibit R-627;
Exhibit R-437;	Exhibit R-628;

FIGURE 10.53

Exhibit R-629;	Exhibit R-650;
Exhibit R-630;	Exhibit R-651;
Exhibit R-631;	Exhibit R-652;
Exhibit R-632;	Exhibit R-654;
Exhibit R-633;	Exhibit R-656;
Exhibit R-634;	Exhibit R-657;
Exhibit R-635;	Exhibit R-658;
Exhibit R-636;	Exhibit R-659;
Exhibit R-637;	Exhibit R-660;
Exhibit R-638;	Exhibit R-669;
Exhibit R-639;	Exhibit R-679;
Exhibit R-639;	Exhibit R-785;
Exhibit R-640;	Exhibit R-812;
Exhibit R-641;	Exhibit R-813;
Exhibit R-642;	Exhibit R-820;
Exhibit R-643;	Exhibit R-822;
Exhibit R-646;	Exhibit R-824;
Exhibit R-647;	Exhibit R-830;
Exhibit R-649;	Exhibit R-892

FIGURE 10.54

Appendices

Appendix 1 – █████ v. █████

Appendix 1.1 – █████ v. █████ Claims

Appendix 2 – Offsite Hourly Work Billing Rates

Appendix 3 – Growth Rate of Invoices for Offsite Hourly Work

Appendix 3.1 – Invoices for Offsite Hourly Work

Appendix 4 – Analysis of "Open █████ Claims

Appendix 4.1 – "Open █████ Hours Analysis

Appendix 5 – ███ Claim Summary

Appendix 5.1 – ███ Claim Summary by Problem

Appendix 5.2 – Outstanding ████ Lump-Sum Obligations

Appendix 5.3 – Select Contract Pricing – ████

Appendix 5.4 – Non-Conforming ████████████

Appendix 5.5 – Non-Conforming ██████████████

Appendix 5.6 – Overpayment for ████████████████

Appendix 5.7 – Non-Conforming ██████████

Appendix 5.8 – ████ Out of Pocket Cost to Correct Non-Conforming Work

Appendix 5.9 – Duplicative Payments to ████

Appendix 6 – Summary of Amendment No. ██ Invoices

Appendix 6.1 – ████ Offsite Hourly Work Claim

Appendix 6.2 – ████ ████████ Claim Per ████████

Appendix 6.3 – Offsite Hourly Work

FIGURE 10.55

Appendix 1

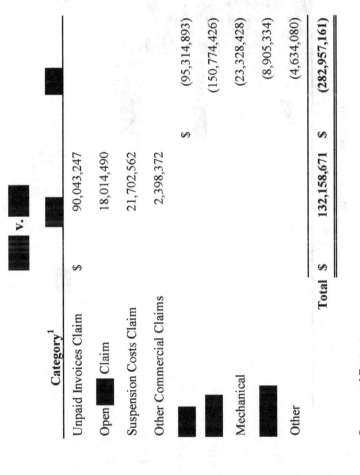

Category[1]	v. ▮		
Unpaid Invoices Claim	$	90,043,247	(95,314,893)
Open ▮ Claim		18,014,490	(150,774,426)
Suspension Costs Claim		21,702,562	(23,328,428)
Other Commercial Claims		2,398,372	(8,905,334)
	$		(4,634,080)
Mechanical			
Other			
Total $		**132,158,671** $	**(282,957,161)**

Sources and Footnotes:

Report of ▮▮▮, Table 3, submitted by ▮▮

Appendix 5

1) I understand that ▮ and ▮ have resolved the issues surrounding ▮'s Spare Parts Contracts Claim.

1 of 1

FIGURE 10.56

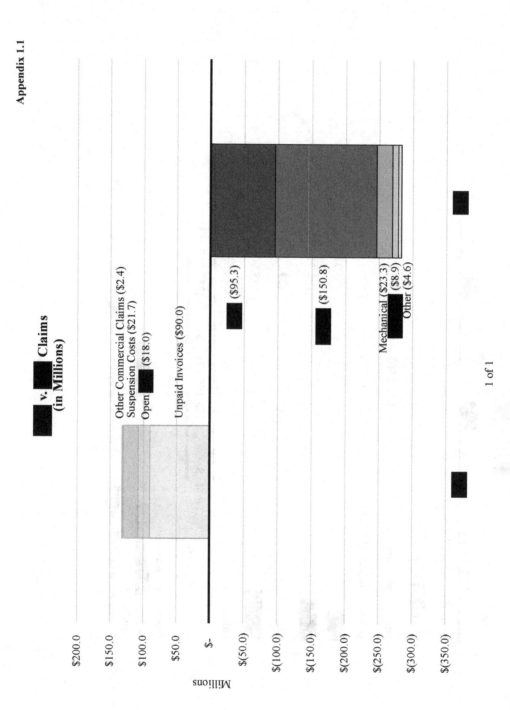

FIGURE 10.57

Appendix 2

Offsite Hourly Work Billing Rates

Contractual Billing Rates

Am. No.[1]	Year	Base Rate	Maximum Escalation %	Adjusted Hourly Rate	Discount	Effective Rate (USD/hr)
▮	2009	$ 240.00	0.00%			
▮	2010	240.00	3.37%	$ 248.09	50%	$ 124.04
▮	2011	240.00	6.85%	256.44	50%	128.22
▮	2012	240.00	10.45%	265.08	50%	132.54
▮	2013	240.00	14.18%	274.03	50%	137.02
▮	2013	240.00	14.18%	274.03	25%	205.52
▮	2014	240.00	18.02%	283.25	25%	212.44

Actual Billing Rates

Am. No.[1]	Year	Rate (USD/hr)	Discount	Effective Rate (USD/hr)
▮	2010	$ 248.00	50%	$ 124.00
▮	2011	256.00	50%	128.00
▮	2012	258.00	50%	129.00
▮	2013	259.00	50%	129.50

1 of 2

FIGURE 10.58

Appendix 2

Am. No. [1]	Year	Rate (USD/hr)	Discount	Effective Rate (USD/hr)
■	2013	259.00	25%	194.25
■	2014	264.00	25%	198.00

Sources and Footnotes:

Contractual billing rates are Pursuant to §6.6.2 of Amendment No. ■

Actual billing rates appear as reflected in ■'s invoices to ■ .

1) Effective ■ 1, 2013, the discount changed from 50% to 25%, pursuant to Amendment No. ■ .

2 of 2

FIGURE 10.59

Growth Rate of Invoices for Offsite Hourly Work

	Invoiced Amounts (Excluding 5% VAT)	Cumulative	Annual % Change	CAGR	Number of Invoices	Cumulative	Annual % Change	CAGR
2010	$ 351,833	$ 351,833			8	8		
2011	6,835,246	7,187,079	1843%		55	63	588%	
2012	34,665,661	41,852,740	407%	893%	129	192	135%	302%
2013	35,385,362	77,238,102	2%	365%	110	302	-15%	140%
2014	45,935,499	123,173,601	30%	238%	162	464	47%	112%
2015	18,423,127	141,596,728	-60%		94	558	-42%	
2016	12,723	141,609,450	-100%		1	559	-99%	
	$ 141,609,450				559			

Sources:
Appendix 3.1

1 of 1

FIGURE 10.60

Appendix 3.1

Invoices for Offsite Hourly Work

No.	No.	Category	Attachment B Item	Invoice No.	Js (Issue Date)	Total invoiced M-H	Invoiced amounts (exclude 5% VAT)	actually paid (exclude 5% VAT)	Amount Outstanding
2010-0001	-2010-0744	Other	I.1.A.X	100423.036	8/2/2010	1,699	$ 225,913	$ 217,833	$ 8,080
2010-0001	-2011-1762	Other	I.19.M	100423.098	9/14/2011	3,106	422,179	422,179	-
2010-0002	-2014-1776	Other		100423.621	12/1/2014	384	53,330	-	53,330
2010-0005	N/A		I.1.P	no invoice	N/A	-	-	-	-
2010-0006	-2014-1399	Other	I.1.H	100423.581	7/11/2014	375	52,156	-	52,156
2010-0007	-2015-0118	Other	I.2.A	100423.683	10/17/2011	83	11,279	-	11,279
2010-0007	-2011-2057	Other	I.2.A	100423.107	9/25/2012	68	8,370	8,370	-
2010-0007	-2012-1520	Other	I.2.A	100423.251	11/14/2012	39	4,986	4,154	832
2010-0007	-2012-1855	Other	I.2.A	100423.292	8/1/2013	242	31,192	24,710	6,482
2010-0008	-2013-1439	Other	I.2.B	100423.386	3/25/2015	196	25,323	12,294	13,029
2010-0008	-2014-1605	Other	I.2.B	100423.605	10/18/2011	2,879	526,488	-	526,488
2010-0008	-2014-1861	Other	I.2.B	100423.640	9/25/2012	1,052	208,336	-	208,336
2010-0008	-2014-1861	Other	I.2.B	100423.641	9/25/2012	2	396	-	396
2010-0008	-2015-0043	Other	I.2.B	100423.657	12/3/2012	109	24,172	-	24,172
2010-0008	-2015-0123	Other	I.2.B	100423.686	12/3/2012	85	16,889	-	16,889
2010-0008	-2011-2064	Other	I.2.B	100423.108	10/16/2013	145	18,575	18,575	-
2010-0008	-2012-1521	Other	I.2.B	100423.252	9/24/2014	163	20,864	20,864	-
2010-0008	-2012-1522	Other	I.2.B	100423.253	12/31/2014	328	41,926	39,942	1,984
2010-0008	-2012-1958	Other	I.2.B	100423.298	12/31/2014	530	68,338	65,577	2,761
2010-0008	-2012-1959	Other	I.2.B	100423.299	1/29/2015	451	58,211	54,025	4,186
2010-0009	-2013-1915	Other	I.2.C	100423.417	3/26/2015	1,260	162,592	133,283	29,309
2010-0009	-2015-0119	Other	I.2.C	100423.684	10/18/2011	135	22,416	-	22,416
2010-0009	-2015-0120	Other	I.2.C	100423.685	9/28/2012	196	38,877	-	38,877
2010-0009	-2011-2069	Other	I.2.C	100423.110	9/28/2012	596	73,867	35,923	37,944
2010-0009	-2012-1550	Other	I.2.C	100423.256	11/16/2012	343	43,872	37,152	6,720
2010-0009	-2012-1551	Other	I.2.C	100423.257	8/1/2013	597	76,454	49,907	26,547
2010-0009	-2012-1867	Other	I.2.C	100423.295	3/25/2015	510	65,803	32,121	33,682
2010-0009	-2013-1438	Other	I.2.C	100423.385	3/25/2015	109	14,016	-	14,016
2010-0010	-2012-0040	Other	I.19.K	100423.149	1/10/2012	334	47,013	47,013	-
2010-0011	-2010-1171	Other	I.2.B	100423.047	11/4/2010	40	5,555	5,555	-
2010-0012	-2012-0536	Other	V.6	100423.192	4/16/2012	827	114,854	114,854	-
2010-0015	-2012-0074	1.3.C	I.3.C	100423.152	1/16/2012	8,184	1,096,578	1,096,578	-
2010-0017	-2012-0036	Other	I.1.P	100423.147	1/9/2012	1,674	232,727	232,727	-
2010-0018 & 21	-2010-1157	Other	I.2.A	100423.043	11/2/2010	88	12,221	12,221	-
2010-0019	-2010-1071	I.1	I.1	100423.044	10/13/2010	80	11,110	11,110	-
2010-0020	-2010-1158	I.1	I.1	100423.045	11/2/2010	24	3,333	3,333	-
2010-0022	-2010-1159	I.1	I.1	100423.046	11/2/2010	16	2,222	2,222	-
2010-0023	-2010-1160	Other	I.2.A		11/2/2010	70	9,722	9,722	-

FIGURE 10.61

Appendix 3.1

Invoices for Offsite Hourly Work

No.	No.	Category	Attachment B Item	Invoice No.	's (Issue Date)	Total invoiced M-H	Invoiced amounts (exclude 5% VAT)	actually paid (exclude 5% VAT)	Amount Outstanding
2010-0024	N/A			no invoice	N/A		-	-	-
2010-0025	-2010-1316	Other	I.1.Q	100423.049	12/6/2010	613	81,756	81,756	-
2010-0028	-2015-0037F	Other	II.19.A	100423.653	1/29/2015	164	22,776		22,776
2010-0029	-2011-1680	I.1	I.1	100423.094	9/7/2011	2,395	333,850	333,850	-
2010-0029	-2012-0260	I.1	I.1	100423.171	2/27/2012	116	16,630	16,630	-
2010-0030	-2012-1733	I.1	I.1	100423.276	10/26/2012	47	6,527	6,527	-
2010-0031	-2012-0097	I.3.C	I.3.C	100423.157	1/25/2012	5,500	739,300	739,300	-
2010-0032	-2011-0111	Other	I.2.B	100423.048	1/24/2011	120	16,666	12,777	3,889
2010-0034	N/A	Other	I.1.H	no invoice	N/A	-	-	-	-
2010-0035	-2012-0897	Other	V.6	100423.213	6/12/2012	92	13,050	13,050	-
2010-0037	-2011-1731	I.1	I.1	100423.095	9/13/2011	811	115,692	115,405	287
2010-0037	-2012-1581	I.1	I.1	100423.261	12/2/2011	277	39,893	39,893	-
2010-0038	-2011-2338	I.3.C	I.3.C	100423.132	12/2/2011	661	83,517	83,517	-
2010-0039	-2011-1651	I.3.C	I.3.C	100423.086	9/1/2011	1,625	229,573	229,573	-
2010-0040	-2011-1949	I.3.C	I.3.C	100423.105	10/6/2011	175	25,088	25,088	-
2010-0042	-2012-0365	Other	II.19.N	100423.185	3/14/2012	44	6,111	6,111	-
2010-0043	-2011-2063	I.3.C	I.3.C	100423.109	10/17/2011	3,921	528,423	528,423	-
2010-0044	-2011-1610	Other	II.19.C	100423.078	8/29/2011	332	46,771	46,771	-
2010-0045	-2011-1946	I.3.C	I.3.C	100423.104	10/6/2011	259	35,970	35,970	-
2010-0046	-2011-1132	I.1	I.1	100423.066	7/6/2011	4,495	589,748	581,832	7,916
2010-0046	-2011-2238	I.1	I.1	100423.118	11/10/2011	6,560	870,445	862,405	8,040
2010-0046	-2012-0323	I.1	I.1	100423.119	3/7/2012	5,149	679,825	667,281	12,544
2010-0046	-2014-1390	I.1	I.1	100423.569	2/14/2012	29,368	5,669,066	5,669,066	5,669,066
2010-0046	-2014-1785	I.1	I.1	100423.624	2/16/2012	7,829	1,633,973	-	1,633,973
2010-0046	-2014-1785	I.1	I.1	100423.625	2/17/2012	247	49,643	-	49,643
2010-0046	-2015-0262	I.1	I.1	100423.728	3/7/2012	170	36,775		36,775
2010-0046	-2012-0177	I.1	I.1	100423.159	12/3/2012	5,844	788,669	762,701	25,969
2010-0046	-2012-0196	I.1	I.1	100423.160	5/15/2013	6,194	834,474	784,361	50,113
2010-0046	-2012-0215	I.1	I.1	100423.162	7/25/2013	7,300	985,558	899,785	85,773
2010-0046	-2012-0320	I.1	I.1	100423.178	7/11/2014	5,577	751,677	416,220	335,457
2010-0046	-2012-1960	I.1	I.1	100423.300	12/5/2014	14,801	2,006,091	1,857,986	148,105
2010-0046	-2013-0915	I.1	I.1	100423.363	12/5/2014	45	5,580	3,100	2,480
2010-0046	-2013-1402	I.1	I.1	100423.382	9/2/2015	14,223	1,940,655	1,937,123	3,532
2010-0047	-2011-1637	Other	II.19.D	100423.085	8/31/2011	1,269	178,488	178,488	-
2010-0047	-2012-0711	Other	II.19.D	100423.203	5/11/2012	231	33,116	33,116	-
2010-0048	-2012-0059	Other	II.19.D	100423.151	1/12/2012	310	44,442	44,442	-
2010-0048	-2012-0709	Other	II.19.D	100423.200	5/11/2012	608	87,091	87,091	-
2010-0049	-2011-2000	Other	II.19.D	100423.106	10/12/2011	129	18,493	18,493	-

FIGURE 10.62

Appendix 3.1

Invoices for Offsite Hourly Work

No.	No.	Category	Attachment B Item	Invoice No.	's (Issue Date)	Total invoiced M-H	Invoiced amounts (exclude 5% VAT)	actually paid (exclude 5% VAT)	Amount Outstanding
2010-0050	2011-1621	Other	II.19.D	100423.079	8/30/2011	494	69,040	69,040	-
2010-0051	2011-1609	I.3.C	I.3.C	100423.077	8/29/2011	1,784	255,754	255,754	-
2010-0051	2012-0707	I.3.C	I.3.C	100423.199	5/11/2012	184	26,378	26,378	-
2010-0052	2011-1653	I.3.C	I.3.C	100423.088	9/1/2011	310	43,053	43,053	-
2010-0053	2011-1628	I.3.C	I.3.C	100423.083	8/30/2011	1,071	153,539	153,539	-
2010-0053	2012-1584	I.3.C	I.3.C	100423.263	10/3/2012	129	18,493	18,493	-
2010-0054	2011-1627	I.3.C	I.3.C	100423.080	8/30/2011	459	65,731	65,731	-
2010-0056	2011-1655	I.3.C	I.3.C	100423.090	9/1/2011	248	34,608	34,608	-
2010-0057	2011-1654	I.3.C	I.3.C	100423.089	9/1/2011	1,359	191,453	191,453	-
2010-0058	2011-1652	I.3.C	I.3.C	100423.087	9/1/2011	559	79,188	79,188	-
2010-0059	2011-1733	I.3.C	I.3.C	100423.097	9/13/2011	264	37,533	37,533	-
2010-0060	2011-1629	I.3.C	I.3.C	100423.084	8/30/2011	3,291	464,005	464,005	-
2010-0060	2012-0672	I.3.C	I.3.C	100423.201	5/11/2012	96	13,763	13,763	-
2010-0060	2012-0869	I.3.C	I.3.C	100423.210	6/7/2012	2,178	311,638	311,638	-
2010-0061	2011-2449	I.3.C	I.3.C	100423.142	12/22/2011	245	35,123	35,123	-
2010-0061	2012-0338	I.3.C	I.3.C	100423.182	3/9/2012	227	32,543	32,543	-
2010-0062	2013-0411	I.1	I.1	100423.331	2/26/2013	773	104,356	104,356	-
2010-0063	2011-0238	Other	I.2.B	100423.055	2/18/2011	128	17,777	17,777	-
2010-0064	2011-1509	Other	I.1.Q	100423.075	8/16/2011	263	35,986	35,986	-
2010-0065	2012-0175	I.3.C	I.3.C	100423.158	2/14/2012	1,498	191,002	191,002	-
2010-0066	2011-1732	Other	II.19.G	100423.096	9/13/2011	1,308	185,835	185,835	-
2010-0067	2011-2321	I.3.C	I.3.C	100423.125	11/30/2011	632	90,402	90,402	-
2010-0069	2012-1684	I.1	I.1	100423.272	10/19/2012	449	63,921	63,921	-
2010-0070	2011-1481	I.3.C	I.3.C	100423.072	8/11/2011	169	21,458	21,458	-
2010-0071	2011-1662	I.3.C	I.3.C	100423.091	9/2/2011	319	40,804	40,804	-
2010-0072	2012-0058	I.3.C	I.3.C	100423.150	1/12/2012	252	33,122	32,235	887
2010-0073	2011-2202	I.3.C	I.3.C	100423.117	11/7/2011	466	61,453	61,453	-
2010-0074	2012-0522	I.1	I.1	100423.195	4/12/2012	200	28,508	28,508	-
2011-0001	2014-1139	Other	II.19.D	100423.550	5/19/2014	139	26,149	-	26,149
2011-0001	2015-0042	Other	II.19.D	100423.656	1/29/2015	8	1,774	-	1,774
2011-0002	2012-0236	I.3.C	I.3.C	100423.164	2/22/2012	234	33,546	33,546	-
2011-0004	2012-0237	I.1	I.1	100423.165	2/22/2012	85	12,186	12,186	-
2011-0006	2012-0524	I.1	I.1	100423.194	4/12/2012	280	39,791	39,791	-
2011-0007	2012-0706	I.3.C	I.3.C	100423.198	5/11/2012	280	40,340	40,340	-
2011-0008	2011-2312	I.3.C	I.3.C	100423.123	11/29/2011	324	46,449	46,449	-
2011-0009	2012-2450	I.3.C	I.3.C	100423.137	12/22/2011	100	14,264	14,264	-
2011-0010	2011-2310	Other	II.19.D	100423.121	11/29/2011	1,111	159,201	159,201	-
2011-0011	2012-0277	I.3.C	I.3.C	100423.174	2/29/2012	257	36,844	36,844	-

FIGURE 10.63

Appendix 3.1

Invoices for Offsite Hourly Work

No.	No.	Category	Attachment B Item	Invoice No.	's (Issue Date)	Total invoiced M-H	Invoiced amounts (exclude 5% VAT)	actually paid (exclude 5% VAT)	Amount Outstanding
2011-0012	-2012-0525	Other	V.6	I00423.193	4/12/2012	1,944	278,692	278,692	-
2011-0013	-2014-0068	Other	II.19.C	I00423.465	1/16/2014	267	38,277		38,277
2011-0014	-2012-0280	I3.C	I3.C	I00423.177	2/29/2012	276	39,567	39,567	-
2011-0015	-2012-0258	I3.C	I3.C	I00423.169	2/27/2012	389	55,767	55,767	-
2011-0016	-2011-2188	I.1	I.1	I00423.116	11/4/2011	132	18,862	18,862	-
2011-0017	-2012-0037	Other	II.19.C	I00423.148	1/9/2012	186	26,665	26,665	-
2011-0018	-2012-0364	Other	II.19.D	I00423.184	3/14/2012	122	17,490	17,490	-
2011-0019	-2012-1326	Other	II.19.C	I00423.234	8/27/2012	927	132,895	132,895	-
2011-0019	-2012-1794	Other	II.19.C	I00423.283	11/2/2012	432	62,415	62,415	-
2011-0019	-2013-0505	Other	II.19.C	I00423.338	3/12/2013	218	31,497	31,497	-
2011-0020	-2012-0259	I3.C	I3.C	I00423.170	2/27/2012	215	30,822	30,822	-
2011-0021	-2012-0870	I.1	I3.C	I00423.212	6/7/2012	594	85,156	85,156	-
2011-0022	-2015-0132	I.1	I.1	I00423.694	4/2/2015	105	13,461		13,461
2011-0023	-2012-1040	Other	II.19.D	I00423.223	7/5/2012	143	20,551	20,551	(0)
2011-0024	-2012-0213	I3.C	I3.C	I00423.161	2/17/2012	255	36,485	36,485	-
2011-0026	-2012-0278	I3.C	I3.C	I00423.175	2/29/2012	228	32,686	32,686	-
2011-0027	-2011-2311	I3.C	I3.C	I00423.122	11/29/2011	337	48,312	48,312	-
2011-0030	-2015-0028	Other	III.2	I00423.644	1/28/2015	3,924	852,105		852,105
2011-0031	-2012-0987	I3.C	I3.C	I00423.216	6/22/2012	837	119,921	119,921	-
2011-0032	-2012-0238	I3.C	I3.C	I00423.166	2/22/2012	390	55,680	55,680	-
2011-0033	-2013-0075	I3.C	I3.C	I00423.317	1/16/2013	7,330	972,617	972,617	-
2011-0034	-2011-2447	I3.C	I3.C	I00423.140	12/22/2011	165	23,583	23,583	-
2011-0035	-2012-0255	I3.C	I3.C	I00423.168	2/27/2012	382	54,764	54,764	-
2011-0036	-2012-0898	I.1	I.1	I00423.214	6/12/2012	270	38,707	38,707	-
2011-0037	-2011-1925	Other	III.2	I00423.103	10/4/2011	104	13,139	13,139	-
2011-0038	-2011-2444	I3.C	I3.C	I00423.138	12/22/2011	183	26,235	26,235	-
2011-0038	-2011-2331	I3.C	I3.C	I00423.129	12/1/2011	321	45,947	45,947	-
2011-0039	-2015-0177	Other	III.2	I00423.706	5/6/2015	2,392	332,470		332,470
2011-0040	-2015-0177	I3.C	III.2	I00423.707	5/6/2015	6	768		768
2011-0040	-2011-2320	Other	III.2	I00423.124	11/30/2011	450	64,512	64,512	-
2011-0041	-2012-0321	Other	II.5	I00423.179	3/9/2012	460	56,978	51,398	5,580
2011-0042	-2012-2095F		II.5	I00423.309	8/23/2013	2,411	337,292		337,292
2011-0042	-2012-2096F		II.5	I00423.310	8/23/2013	4,645	647,961		647,961
2011-0042	-2013-0148		II.5	I00423.322	1/28/2013	11,940	1,669,931		1,669,931
2011-0042	-2013-0226		II.5	I00423.328	2/5/2013	14,444	2,025,189		2,025,189
2011-0042	-2013-2368		II.5	I00423.454	12/13/2013	11,931	1,687,915		1,687,915
2011-0042	-2015-0192		II.5	I00423.717	5/13/2015	22,994	1,560,944		1,560,944
2011-0042	-2015-0192		II.5	I00423.718	5/13/2015		3,078,958		3,078,958

FIGURE 10.64

Appendix 3.1

Invoices for Offsite Hourly Work

No.	No.	Category	Attachment B Item	Invoice No.	J's (Issue Date)	Total invoiced M-H	Invoiced amounts (exclude 5% VAT)	actually paid (exclude 5% VAT)	Amount Outstanding
2011-0042	-2015-0211		II.5	100423.722	6/4/2015	11,243	198,255	-	198,255
2011-0042	-2015-0211		II.5	100423.723	6/4/2015		2,240,904	-	2,240,904
2011-0042	-2015-0312		II.5	100423.739	11/26/2015	886	193,713	-	193,713
2011-0043	-2012-0340		II.6	100423.180	3/9/2012	220	27,249	15,903	11,346
2011-0043	-2012-1063		II.6	100423.224	7/10/2012	7,427	1,037,832	-	1,037,832
2011-0043	-2012-1070		II.6	100423.225	7/10/2012	9,042	1,263,420	-	1,263,420
2011-0043	-2012-1330		II.6	100423.237	7/10/2012	3,894	546,852	-	546,852
2011-0043	-2012-1332		II.6	100423.238	7/10/2012	2,171	301,508	-	301,508
2011-0043	-2012-1549		II.6	100423.258	9/27/2012	7,323	1,032,902	-	1,032,902
2011-0043	-2013-0507		II.6	100423.339	3/12/2013	12,806	1,826,105	-	1,826,105
2011-0043	-2013-2312		II.6	100423.453	12/10/2013	9,278	1,314,420	-	1,314,420
2011-0043	-2014-1578		II.6	100423.602	9/11/2014	21,689	4,380,750	-	4,380,750
2011-0043	-2014-1606		II.6	100423.606	9/24/2014	8,912	1,950,747	-	1,950,747
2011-0043	-2014-1846		II.6	100423.632	12/22/2014	2,287	501,783	-	501,783
2011-0043	-2015-0320		II.6	100423.740	12/30/2015	7	1,426	-	1,426
2011-0044	-2012-0341		II.7	100423.181	3/9/2012	143	17,670	17,670	-
2011-0044	-2012-1749		II.7	100423.277	10/24/2012	2,285	306,427	-	306,427
2011-0044	-2012-1750		II.7	100423.278	10/29/2012	3,096	431,558	-	431,558
2011-0044	-2012-1751		II.7	100423.279	10/29/2012	4,376	600,770	-	600,770
2011-0044	-2012-1757		II.7	100423.280	10/29/2012	3,390	461,312	-	461,312
2011-0044	-2013-0509		II.7	100423.341	10/30/2012	13,393	1,877,373	-	1,877,373
2011-0044	-2014-1847		II.7	100423.633	3/12/2013	12,638	1,770,851	-	1,770,851
2011-0044	-2014-1847		II.7	100423.634	12/22/2014	-	6,400	-	6,400
2011-0044	-2014-1848		II.7	100423.635	12/22/2014	4,363	746,630	-	746,630
2011-0044	-2014-1848		II.7	100423.636	12/22/2014	-	76,178	-	76,178
2011-0044	-2015-0127		II.7	100423.687	12/22/2014	3,106	610,741	-	610,741
2011-0044	-2015-0127		II.7	100423.688	4/2/2015	-	47,698	-	47,698
2011-0044	-2015-0264		II.7	100423.730	4/2/2015	453	96,616	-	96,616
2011-0044	-2012-1712		II.7	100423.274	9/7/2015	1,232	158,874	158,874	-
2011-0045	-2011-2329	I.3.C	I.3.C	100423.127	12/1/2011	188	26,952	26,952	-
2011-0047	-2011-2330	I.3.C	I.3.C	100423.128	12/1/2011	251	35,912	35,912	-
2011-0048	-2012-0511	Other	III.2	100423.191	4/11/2012	251	64,128	64,128	-
2011-0058A	-2012-1281	Other	III.2	100423.233	8/20/2012	1,246	178,458	171,290	7,168
2011-0058A	-2012-1792	Other	III.2	100423.285	11/2/2012	2,092	302,252	302,252	-
2011-0058B	-2012-0463	Other	III.2	100423.188	4/3/2012	1,784	511,508	511,508	-
2011-0058B	-2012-1792	Other	III.2	100423.286	11/2/2012	843	243,593	243,593	-
2011-0059	-2012-0712	I.3.C	I.3.C	100423.204	5/11/2012	8,047	1,153,546	1,153,546	-
2011-0059	-2012-1323	I.3.C	I.3.C	100423.235	8/24/2012	3,953	571,129	571,129	-

FIGURE 10.65

Appendix 3.1

Invoices for Offsite Hourly Work

No.	No.	Category	Attachment B Item	Invoice No.	's (Issue Date)	Total invoiced M-H	Invoiced amounts (exclude 5% VAT)	actually paid (exclude 5% VAT)	Amount Outstanding
2011-0061	2012-0845	I.3.C	I.3.C	I00423.211	6/6/2012	836	108,236	108,236	-
2011-0062	2012-1041	I.3.C	I.3.C	I00423.219	7/5/2012	727	93,134	93,134	-
2011-0063	2011-2328	I.3.C	I.3.C	I00423.126	12/1/2011	207	29,676	29,676	-
2011-0064	2014-0740	Other	II.19.D	I00423.534	3/19/2014	571	84,513	-	84,513
2011-0066	2011-2346	I.3.C	I.3.C	I00423.133	12/5/2011	451	64,584	64,584	-
2011-0067	2012-1042	I.3.C	I.3.C	I00423.220	7/5/2012	185	23,640	23,640	-
2011-0068	2012-1280	I.3.C	I.3.C	I00423.232	8/20/2012	581	74,582	74,582	-
2011-0071	2012-1624	Other	III.2	I00423.268	10/10/2012	44	5,590	5,590	-
2011-0072	2014-0395	Other	I.2.E.b1	I00423.489	9/16/2013	-	65	65	-
2011-0072	2013-1679	Other	I.2.E.b1	I00423.406	2/17/2014	189	24,123	24,123	-
2011-0073	2013-0945	Other	II.10	I00423.366	5/21/2013	1,343	169,033	169,033	-
2011-0074	2012-1279	Other	II.10	I00423.231	8/20/2012	1,010	129,407	129,407	-
2011-0076	2011-2241	Other	I.2.A	I00423.120	11/10/2011	48	6,881	6,308	573
2011-0078	2012-0214	Other	II.19.C	I00423.163	2/17/2012	86	12,329	12,329	-
2011-0081	2011-2448	I.3.C	I.3.C	I00423.141	12/22/2011	446	63,939	63,939	-
2011-0082	2011-2446	I.3.C	I.3.C	I00423.139	12/22/2011	434	62,218	62,218	-
2011-0084	2015-0130	Other	I.2.A	I00423.691	4/2/2015	48	6,881	-	6,881
2011-0094	2013-0210	I.1	I.1	I00423.325	2/1/2013	581	83,916	83,916	-
2011-0095	2012-0602	I.3.C	I.3.C	I00423.197	4/25/2012	376	53,832	53,832	-
2011-0099	2013-0074	I.3.C	I.3.C	I00423.312	1/16/2013	4,741	637,536	637,536	-
2011-0101	2012-1583	I.1	I.1	I00423.262	10/3/2012	350	50,053	50,053	-
2011-0102	2012-0713	I.1	I.1	I00423.205	5/11/2012	111	15,913	15,913	-
2011-0107	2012-0254	I.3.C	I.3.C	I00423.167	2/27/2012	229	32,829	32,829	-
2011-0108	2012-0262	I.3.C	I.3.C	I00423.173	2/27/2012	485	69,530	69,530	-
2011-0109	2011-2443	I.3.C	I.3.C	I00423.136	12/22/2011	852	122,143	122,143	-
2011-0110	2011-2442	I.3.C	I.3.C	I00423.135	12/22/2011	137	19,640	19,640	-
2011-0111	2012-1658	I.3.C	I.3.C	I00423.270	10/16/2012	147	19,011	19,011	-
2011-0112	2015-0204	Other	I.2.B	I00423.721	5/27/2015	13	1,664	-	1,664
2011-0113	2012-1341	I.3.C	I.3.C	I00423.239	8/29/2012	4,350	626,679	626,679	-
2011-0114	2013-0079	I.3.C	I.3.C	I00423.313	1/16/2013	2,278	312,042	312,042	-
2011-0115	2013-0412	Other	I.2.C	I00423.332	2/26/2013	46	5,920	5,920	-
2011-0116	2011-2175	Other	I.2.B	I00423.115	11/2/2011	35	4,972	4,972	-
2011-0119	2013-1440	Other	I.2.B	I00423.387	8/1/2013	803	102,918	102,790	128
2011-0120	2012-0261	I.1	I.1	I00423.172	2/27/2012	55	7,885	7,885	-
2011-0121	2012-1820	Other	I.2.B	I00423.287	11/9/2012	47	6,327	5,508	819
2011-0122	2014-1735	Other	II.10	I00423.614	11/11/2014	1,061	179,720	-	179,720
2011-0123	2014-0734	I.1	I.1	I00423.528	3/19/2014	196	25,064	-	25,064
2011-0124	2013-0097	I.3.C	I.3.C	I00423.314	1/18/2013	938	127,765	127,765	-

6 of 15

FIGURE 10.66

Appendix 3.1

Invoices for Offsite Hourly Work

No.	No.	Category	Attachment B Item	Invoice No.	's (Issue Date)	Total invoiced M-H	Invoiced amounts (exclude 5% VAT)	actually paid (exclude 5% VAT)	Amount Outstanding
2011-0125	-2012-2006	I.3.C	I.3.C	100423.304	12/11/2012	358	46,169	46,169	-
2011-0126	-2012-0710	I.3.C	I.3.C	100423.202	5/11/2012	298	42,827	42,827	-
2011-0127	-2012-0986	I.3.C	I.3.C	100423.215	6/22/2012	438	62,822	62,822	(0)
2011-0128	-2012-0342	I.3.C	I.3.C	100423.183	3/9/2012	541	77,558	77,558	-
2011-0129	-2012-0279	I.3.C	I.3.C	100423.176	2/29/2012	74	10,609	10,609	-
2011-0131	-2015-0129	Other	III.2	100423.645	4/2/2015	1,311	275,918	-	275,918
2011-0133	-2013-2063		II.7	100423.425	10/30/2013	2,619	378,844	378,844	-
2011-0134	-2012-1531	I.1	I.1	100423.254	9/26/2012	42	6,021	6,021	-
2011-0135	-2014-1795	I.1	I.1	100423.627	12/11/2014	1,379	255,849	-	255,849
2011-0137	-2014-1304	I.1	I.1	100423.556	6/25/2014	664	93,034	-	93,034
2011-0138	-2012-0714	Other	II.19.D	100423.206	5/11/2012	613	87,880	87,880	-
2011-0141	-2012-0515	Other	III.2	100423.190	4/11/2012	103	27,187	27,187	-
2011-0143	-2012-0535	I.1	I.1	100423.196	4/16/2012	250	63,899	63,899	-
2011-0147	-2012-1039	I.3.C	I.3.C	100423.222	7/5/2012	646	92,935	92,935	-
2011-0148	-2012-1585	I.3.C	I.3.C	100423.264	10/3/2012	77	11,125	11,125	-
2011-0149	-2012-1868	I.3.C	I.3.C	100423.296	11/16/2012	438	56,472	56,472	-
2011-0151	-2012-1043	I.3.C	I.3.C	100423.221	7/5/2012	180	23,256	23,256	-
2011-0153	-2013-1691	Other	II.19.G	100423.400	9/17/2013	275	39,742	39,742	-
2011-0154	-2013-1678		II.5	100423.407	9/16/2013	421	60,657	-	60,657
2011-0155	-2013-1510		II.6	100423.389	8/16/2013	487	69,993	69,993	-
2011-0158	-2013-1856F		II.7	100423.412	2/6/2014	421	60,501	60,501	-
2011-0159	-2013-1857F		II.7	100423.413	10/9/2013	399	57,311	57,311	-
2011-0160	-2014-1860	I.3.C	I.3.C	100423.639	12/30/2014	432	61,932	-	61,932
2011-0162	-2012-1324	I.3.C	I.3.C	100423.236	8/24/2012	2,770	391,763	391,763	-
2011-0165	-2012-1583	I.3.C	I.3.C	100423.265	10/3/2012	291	42,044	42,044	-
2011-0166	-2012-1587	I.3.C	I.3.C	100423.266	10/3/2012	173	24,995	24,995	-
2012-0001	-2012-0514	Other	III.2	100423.189	4/11/2012	100	25,671	25,671	-
2012-0002	-2012-1532	I.3.C	I.3.C	100423.255	9/28/2012	380	54,902	54,902	-
2012-0004	-2015-0140	Other	I.2.C	100423.695	4/13/2015	600	77,352	-	77,352
2012-0005	-2012-1350	I.3.C	III.2	100423.240	8/30/2012	21,055	3,051,750	3,051,750	-
2012-0006	-2015-0175	Other	III.2	100423.704	5/5/2015	2,719	461,020	-	461,020
2012-0006	-2015-0259	Other	III.2	100423.705	5/5/2015	55	8,941	-	8,941
2012-0006	-2015-0259	Other	III.2	100423.726	9/1/2015	-	178,893	-	178,893
2012-0007	-2015-0142	I.1	I.1	100423.727	4/13/2015	254	33,562	-	33,562
2012-0008	-2012-1588	I.3.C	I.3.C	100423.267	10/3/2012	89	12,859	12,859	-
2012-0009	-2013-0098	I.3.C	I.3.C	100423.315	1/18/2013	1,911	251,700	251,700	-
2012-0010	-2012-1957	I.3.C	I.3.C	100423.301	12/3/2012	498	71,483	71,483	-

FIGURE 10.67

Appendix 3.1

Invoices for Offsite Hourly Work

No.	No.	Category	Attachment B Item	Invoice No.	's (Issue Date)	Total invoiced M-H	Invoiced amounts (exclude 5% VAT)	actually paid (exclude 5% VAT)	Amount Outstanding
2012-0011	-2013-1194	I.1	I.1	100423.375	1/9/2014	943	134,215	-	134,215
2012-0011	-2014-0038	I.1	I.1	100423.459	6/28/2013	42	6,068	-	6,068
2012-0012	-2013-1268	Other	V.6	100423.377	7/8/2013	2,200	317,856	317,856	-
2012-0013	-2012-1795	I.1	I.1	100423.282	11/2/2012	318	45,945	45,945	-
2012-0014	-2014-1580	I.1	I.1	100423.604	9/11/2014	1,848	240,807	-	240,807
2012-0015	-2013-2078	I.1	II.7	100423.426	10/31/2013	947	136,334	-	136,334
2012-0017	-2012-1821	I.3.C	I.3.C	100423.288	11/9/2012	239	30,876	30,876	-
2012-0018	-2013-0450	I.1	I.1	100423.334	3/4/2013	617	80,904	80,904	-
2012-0019	-2013-1263	Other	V.6	100423.376	7/8/2013	225	32,508	32,508	-
2012-0020	-2014-0725	I.3.C	I.3.C	100423.521	10/3/2013	-	291	291	-
2012-0020	-2013-1829	I.3.C	I.3.C	100423.408	3/19/2014	93	12,007	12,007	-
2012-0021	-2012-1796	I.3.C	I.3.C	100423.284	11/2/2012	192	27,740	27,740	-
2012-0022	-2012-1859	I.3.C	I.3.C	100423.293	11/15/2012	2,421	349,786	349,786	-
2012-0023	-2013-1913	I.3.C	II.7	100423.416	10/16/2013	2,147	317,073	-	317,073
2012-0024	-2014-1807	I.3.C	II.6	100423.628	12/17/2014	2,305	377,499	-	377,499
2012-0025	-2013-1946	Other	III.2	100423.297	11/30/2012	1,184	340,390	204,395	135,994
2012-0025	-2014-0459	Other	III.2	100423.516	1/9/2014	569	123,642	-	123,642
2012-0025	-2014-1366	Other	III.2	100423.562	2/20/2014	72	15,967	-	15,967
2012-0025	-2015-0038	Other	III.2	100423.654	7/8/2014	234	51,892	-	51,892
2012-0025	-2014-0036	Other	III.2	100423.457	1/28/2015	1,533	392,600	528,594	(135,994)
2012-0026	-2012-1718	I.3.C	I.3.C	100423.275	10/24/2012	63	8,172	8,172	-
2012-0027	-2012-2053	I.3.C	I.3.C	100423.306	12/19/2012	2,720	392,986	392,986	-
2012-0027	-2013-0504	I.3.C	I.3.C	100423.337	3/12/2013	3,006	434,307	434,307	-
2012-0027	-2014-0406	I.3.C	I.3.C	100423.499	12/17/2013	-	3,699	3,699	-
2012-0027	-2013-1633F	I.3.C	I.3.C	100423.393	2/17/2014	1,458	211,468	211,468	-
2012-0028	-2013-2233	I.3.C	I.3.C	100423.449	11/26/2013	2,779	402,892	-	402,892
2012-0028	-2014-0208	I.3.C	I.3.C	100423.472	1/28/2014	-	114,364	-	114,364
2012-0029	-2012-1797	I.3.C	I.3.C	100423.281	11/2/2012	434	62,704	62,704	-
2012-0030	-2012-2004	I.3.C	I.3.C	100423.305	12/11/2012	164	23,695	23,695	-
2012-0031	-2013-0642	I.6	II.6	100423.352	3/27/2013	557	80,475	80,475	-
2012-0032	-2013-2104	I.1	I.1	100423.436	11/1/2013	226	29,150	-	29,150
2012-0035	-2013-0080	I.3.C	I.3.C	100423.316	1/16/2013	120	15,739	15,739	-
2012-0036	-2013-0221	I.1	I.1	100423.326	2/5/2013	117	15,145	15,145	-
2012-0037	-2013-0448	I.1	I.1	100423.333	3/4/2013	481	69,495	69,495	-
2012-0037	-2014-0460	I.1	I.1	100423.517	2/20/2014	38	8,267	-	8,267
2012-0037	-2014-1368	Other	I.1	100423.564	7/8/2014	8	1,774	-	1,774
2012-0038	-2012-1564	I.3.C	I.2.B	100423.260	10/1/2012	60	8,483	8,483	-
2012-0039	-2012-1905	I.3.C	I.3.C	100423.291	11/27/2012				
						13,757	1,998,197	1,998,197	

FIGURE 10.68

Appendix 3.1

Invoices for Offsite Hourly Work

No.	No.	Category	Attachment B Item	Invoice No.	's (Issue Date)	Total invoiced M-H	Invoiced amounts (exclude 5% VAT)	actually paid (exclude 5% VAT)	Amount Outstanding
2012-0039	2013-1269	I.3.C	I.3.C	100423.378	7/8/2013	3,412	492,091	492,091	-
2012-0040	2014-1021	I.3.C	I.3.C	100423.549	5/1/2014	1,421	249,623	-	249,623
2012-0040	2014-0461	I.3.C	I.3.C	Cancelled	2/20/2014	-	-	-	-
2012-0040	2014-0811	I.3.C	I.3.C	Cancelled	3/31/2014	-	-	-	-
2012-0041	2014-1502	I.3.C	I.3.C	100423.589	8/14/2014	1,082	194,951	-	194,951
2012-0042	2015-0128	I.1	I.1	100423.689	4/2/2015	273	54,472	-	54,472
2012-0043	2014-0738	I.3.C	I.3.C	100423.532	3/19/2014	1,611	292,134	-	292,134
2012-0045	2014-1505	I.3.C	I.3.C	100423.590	8/14/2014	2,268	443,727	-	443,727
2012-0046	2014-0739	I.3.C	I.3.C	100423.533	3/19/2014	1,942	360,374	-	360,374
2012-0047	2014-0438	I.3.C	I.3.C	100423.508	12/13/2013	-	65	65	-
2012-0047	2013-1689F	I.3.C	I.3.C	100423.398	2/19/2014	1,230	158,678	158,678	-
2012-0048	2014-0401	I.3.C	I.3.C	100423.495	10/16/2013	-	73	73	-
2012-0048	2013-1918	I.3.C	I.3.C	100423.420	2/17/2014	78	11,279	11,279	-
2012-0049	2012-2005	I.3.C	I.3.C	100423.303	12/11/2012	379	54,758	54,758	-
2012-0050	2013-0641	Other	II.19.B	100423.351	3/27/2013	22	3,179	3,179	-
2012-0050	2014-1140	Other	II.19.B	100423.551	5/19/2014	11	2,393	-	2,393
2012-0051	2013-2226	I.1	I.1	100423.444	11/26/2013	302	43,358	-	43,358
2012-0051	2014-0443	I.1	I.1	100423.513	2/19/2014	-	874	-	874
2012-0051	2014-1520	I.1	I.1	100423.593	8/18/2014	24	4,134	-	4,134
2012-0052	2013-0565	I.3.C	II.7	100423.345	3/18/2013	134	19,360	19,360	-
2012-0053	2016-0008	I.1	I.1	100423.742	1/22/2016	66	12,723	-	12,723
2012-0056	2012-0845	I.1	I.1	100423.358	5/2/2013	665	92,363	92,363	-
2012-0057	2015-0178	I.1	I.1	100423.708	5/7/2015	705	105,948	-	105,948
2012-0058	2012-1860	I.3.C	I.3.C	100423.294	11/15/2012	6,838	988,884	988,884	-
2012-0058	2013-0225	I.3.C	I.3.C	100423.327	2/5/2013	5,068	730,429	730,429	-
2012-0059	2013-1682F	I.1	I.1	100423.405	9/24/2013	298	41,859	-	41,859
2012-0059	2014-0439	I.1	I.1	100423.509	2/19/2014	-	356	-	356
2012-0060	2013-0508	I.3.C	I.3.C	100423.340	3/12/2013	13,411	1,937,621	1,937,621	-
2012-0060	2013-1056	I.3.C	I.3.C	100423.370	6/10/2013	1,184	171,727	171,727	-
2012-0061	2013-0561	I.3.C	I.3.C	100423.343	3/18/2013	400	57,792	57,792	-
2012-0062	2013-0640	I.3.C	I.3.C	100423.350	3/27/2013	147	21,239	21,239	-
2012-0063	2014-1561	I.1	II.7	100423.596	9/3/2014	2,529	392,119	-	392,119
2012-0064	2014-1777	I.3.C	II.7	100423.622	12/1/2014	1,962	299,930	-	299,930
2012-0065	2013-0916	I.3.C	II.7	100423.364	5/15/2013	289	44,156	44,156	-
2012-0066	2013-1615	I.3.C	I.3.C	100423.391	9/5/2013	8,126	1,172,018	1,172,018	-
2012-0066	2014-0396	I.3.C	I.3.C	100423.490	2/17/2014	-	37,420	-	37,420
2012-0068	2012-1984	I.1	I.1	100423.302	12/7/2012	62	7,992	7,992	-
2012-0069	2013-0560	I.1	I.1	100423.342	3/18/2013	412	59,526	59,526	-

FIGURE 10.69

Appendix 3.1

Invoices for Offsite Hourly Work

No.	No.	Category	Attachment B Item	Invoice No.	's (Issue Date)	Total invoiced M-H	Invoiced amounts (exclude 5% VAT)	actually paid (exclude 5% VAT)	Amount Outstanding
2012-0070	2013-0150	Other	I.2.B	I00423.323	1/28/2013	32	4,623	4,623	-
2012-0072	2014-0437	I.3.C	I.3.C	I00423.507	12/13/2013	-	45,060		45,060
2012-0072	2013-1688F	I.3.C	I.3.C	I00423.397	2/19/2014	1,555	201,110	201,110	-
2012-0073	2015-0276		II.7	I00423.733	9/14/2015	914	136,078		136,078
2012-0074	2013-0502	I.3.C	I.3.C	I00423.335	3/12/2013	641	92,612	92,612	-
2012-0074	2014-1370	I.3.C	I.3.C	I00423.565	7/8/2014	24	3,481		3,481
2012-0075	2013-2086	I.3.C	I.3.C	I00423.429	10/31/2013	43	6,215	6,215	-
2012-0076	2015-0181	I.1	I.1	I00423.711	5/7/2015	86	14,706		14,706
2012-0077	2014-1577	Other	V.6	I00423.601	9/11/2014	108	20,135		20,135
2012-0080	2014-1521	Other	V.6	I00423.594	8/18/2014	217	43,099		43,099
2012-0081	2015-0143	Other	I.2.B	I00423.698	4/13/2015	170	21,949		21,949
2012-0082	2013-1919		I.6	I00423.421	10/8/2013	71	10,155		10,155
2012-0083	2013-1858	I.3.C	I.3.C	I00423.510	10/16/2013	-	19,639		19,639
2012-0083	2014-0440	I.3.C	I.3.C	I00423.414	2/19/2014	444	60,908	60,908	-
2012-0084	2013-0805F	I.1	I.1	I00423.356	4/29/2013	158	20,356	20,356	-
2012-0085	2014-0207	I.3.C	I.3.C	I00423.471	1/28/2014	1,649	278,940		278,940
2012-0086	2015-0180	Other	III.5	I00423.336	5/7/2015	936	144,752		144,752
2012-0088	2013-0503	I.3.C	I.3.C	I00423.433	3/12/2013	1,600	231,168	231,168	-
2012-0088	2013-2099	I.3.C	I.3.C	I00423.493	11/1/2013	313	45,398		45,398
2012-0088	2014-0399	I.3.C	I.3.C	I00423.482	2/17/2014	-	4,279		4,279
2012-0089	2014-0286	I.3.C	I.3.C	I00423.349	2/7/2014	2,389	404,863	404,863	-
2012-0090	2013-0639	I.3.C	I.3.C	I00423.404	3/27/2013	543	78,453	78,453	-
2012-0090	2013-1683	I.3.C	I.3.C	I00423.492	9/16/2013	447	64,833	64,833	-
2012-0090	2014-0398	I.3.C	I.3.C	I00423.399	2/17/2014	-	10,153		10,153
2012-0092	2013-1690	Other	I.2.B	I00423.511	9/17/2013	1,349	194,752	194,752	-
2012-0092	2014-0441	Other	I.2.B	I00423.330	2/19/2014	154	56,907		56,907
2012-0093	2013-0309	Other	I.2.B	I00423.344	2/14/2013	185	22,033	22,033	-
2012-0094	2013-0562	I.1	I.1	I00423.469	3/18/2013		26,729	26,729	-
2012-0094	2014-0175	I.1	I.1	I00423.455	1/24/2014	849	149,536		149,536
2012-0096	2013-2370	I.3.C	I.3.C	I00423.434	12/13/2013	760	136,346		136,346
2012-0100	2013-2101		II.7	I00423.512	11/1/2013	2,856	441,961		441,961
2012-0100	2014-0442		II.7	I00423.514	2/19/2014	-	181,080		181,080
2012-0101	2014-0444	I.1	I.1	I00423.430	10/31/2013	-	10,295		10,295
2012-0101	2013-2087	I.1	I.1	I00423.542	2/19/2014	360	46,992	46,992	-
2012-0103	2014-0814	I.3.C	I.3.C	I00423.483	3/31/2014	1,673	294,844		294,844
2012-0109	2014-0298	I.3.C	I.3.C	I00423.659	2/7/2014	1,833	333,137		333,137
2012-0110	2015-0046		II.7	I00423.346	1/30/2015	1,440	207,117		207,117
2012-0111	2013-0568	I.1	I.1		3/18/2013	150	21,672	21,672	-

FIGURE 10.70

Appendix 3.1

Invoices for Offsite Hourly Work

No.	No.	Category	Attachment B Item	Invoice No.	's (Issue Date)	Total invoiced M-H	Invoiced amounts (exclude 5% VAT)	actually paid (exclude 5% VAT)	Amount Outstanding
2012-0111	2013-2088	I.1	I.1	100423.431	10/31/2013	161	23,351	23,351	-
2012-0113	2014-1397	I.1	I.1	100423.579	7/11/2014	512	73,974	-	73,974
2012-0114	2014-1778		II.7	100423.623	12/1/2014	3,005	561,786	-	561,786
2012-0115	2013-1057	I.3.C	I.3.C	100423.371	6/10/2013	104	15,026	15,026	-
2012-0115	2014-0404	I.3.C	I.3.C	100423.497	11/11/2013	-	5,076	-	5,076
2012-0115	2013-2165	I.3.C	I.3.C	100423.443	2/17/2014	293	42,497	42,497	-
2012-0116	2013-1974	I.3.C	I.3.C	100423.424	10/22/2013	36	5,208	5,208	-
2012-0117	2013-1916		II.7	100423.418	10/16/2013	945	142,221	-	142,221
2012-0117	2014-0759		II.7	100423.535	3/20/2014	-	22,069	-	22,069
2012-0118	2013-2231	Other	II.19.G	100423.447	11/26/2013	5,485	795,415	-	795,415
2012-0118	2014-0212	Other	II.19.G	100423.475	1/28/2014	-	297,205	-	297,205
2012-0120	2013-1653	I.3.C	I.3.C	100423.395	9/11/2013	2,464	356,693	356,693	-
2012-0120	2014-0402	I.3.C	I.3.C	100423.496	2/17/2014	-	4,786	-	4,786
2012-0121	2014-0808	I.3.C	I.3.C	100423.537	3/31/2014	2,030	379,673	-	379,673
2012-0128	2015-0197		II.7	100423.719	5/21/2015	1,239	191,669	-	191,669
2012-0131	2014-0813	I.1	I.1	100423.541	3/31/2014	356	56,052	-	56,052
2013-0001	2013-1650	I.3.C	I.3.C	100423.394	9/11/2013	6,186	897,145	897,145	-
2013-0001	2014-0210	I.3.C	I.3.C	100423.473	1/28/2014	-	116,540	-	116,540
2013-0002	2013-1971	I.3.C	I.3.C	100423.422	10/22/2013	7,617	1,104,467	1,104,467	-
2013-0002	2014-0122	I.3.C	I.3.C	100423.468	1/20/2014	-	535,481	-	535,481
2013-0003	2013-1855	I.3.C	I.3.C	100423.411	10/8/2013	5,238	759,647	759,647	-
2013-0003	2014-0067	I.3.C	I.3.C	100423.464	12/11/2013	394	85,719	-	85,719
2013-0003	2014-0215	I.3.C	I.3.C	100423.477	1/16/2014	-	411,080	-	411,080
2013-0003	2014-0283	I.3.C	I.3.C	100423.480	1/29/2014	-	379,824	-	379,824
2013-0003	2013-2234F	I.3.C	I.3.C	100423.450	2/6/2014	5,669	822,159	822,159	-
2013-0005	2014-0462	I.3.C	I.3.C	100423.519	2/20/2014	3,910	850,660	850,660	-
2013-0007	2014-0214	I.3.C	I.3.C	100423.476	11/26/2013	-	290,080	-	290,080
2013-0007	2013-2229	I.3.C	I.3.C	100423.446	1/29/2014	4,000	580,160	580,160	-
2013-0008	2013-1692F	I.3.C	I.3.C	100423.401	11/26/2013	164	23,787	23,787	-
2013-0008	2014-0405	I.3.C	I.3.C	100423.498	2/17/2014	-	6,237	-	6,237
2013-0009	2013-1694	I.3.C	I.3.C	100423.402	9/18/2013	122	17,695	17,695	-
2013-0009	2014-0400	I.3.C	I.3.C	100423.494	2/17/2014	-	2,683	-	2,683
2013-0010	2014-1141	I.3.C	I.3.C	100423.552	5/19/2014	23	5,004	-	5,004
2013-0011	2014-1142	I.3.C	I.3.C	100423.553	5/19/2014	44	9,573	-	9,573
2013-0012	2013-2158	Other	V.6	100423.440	11/11/2013	1,312	190,292	-	190,292
2013-0012	2014-0729	Other	V.6	100423.524	3/19/2014	-	61,841	-	61,841
2013-0012	2014-1501	Other	V.6	100423.588	8/14/2014	1,312	285,493	-	285,493
2013-0013	2014-0035	Other	II.19.G	100423.456	1/9/2014	953	182,533	-	182,533

FIGURE 10.71

Appendix 3.1

Invoices for Offsite Hourly Work

No.	No.	Category	Attachment B Item	Invoice No.	's (Issue Date)	Total invoiced M-H	Invoiced amounts (exclude 5% VAT)	actually paid (exclude 5% VAT)	Amount Outstanding
2013-0015	2014-1497	Other	III.2	100423.584	8/14/2014	751	153,896	-	153,896
2013-0016	2014-1143	Other	II.19.B	100423.554	5/19/2014	212	44,849	-	44,849
2013-0017	2013-2103		II.7	100423.435	11/1/2013	1,412	217,046	-	217,046
2013-0017	2014-0727		II.7	100423.523	3/19/2014	-	91,859	-	91,859
2013-0019	2013-2161	I.3.C	I.3.C	100423.441	11/11/2013	95	12,303	-	12,303
2013-0019	2014-0726	I.3.C	I.3.C	100423.522	3/19/2014	-	3,917	-	3,917
2013-0022	2014-0445	I.3.C	I.3.C	100423.515	11/26/2013	-	13,634	-	13,634
2013-0022	2013-2227	I.3.C	I.3.C	100423.445	2/19/2014	198	28,718	28,718	-
2013-0024	2013-1695		II.6	100423.403	9/18/2013	379	54,887	-	54,887
2013-0024	2014-0436		II.6	100423.506	2/19/2014	-	8,806	-	8,806
2013-0025	2013-1655	I.3.C	I.3.C	100423.396	9/11/2013	2,431	352,592	352,592	-
2013-0025	2014-0211	I.3.C	I.3.C	100423.474	1/28/2014	-	136,120	-	136,120
2013-0026	2014-0735	Other	I.2.B	100423.529	3/19/2014	453	86,134	-	86,134
2013-0027	2014-0736		II.6	100423.530	3/19/2014	210	45,602	-	45,602
2013-0028	2014-0308	Other	II.19.G	100423.485	2/11/2014	478	103,994	-	103,994
2013-0029	2013-2085	Other	I.2.B	100423.428	10/31/2013	60	7,802	7,802	-
2013-0029	2014-0428	Other	I.2.B	100423.500	5/7/2015	-	2,412	-	2,412
2013-0030	2015-0429		II.7	100423.709	2/19/2014	4,197	908,706	-	908,706
2013-0031	2015-0184		II.7	100423.712	5/8/2015	7,229	1,635,480	-	1,635,480
2013-0033	2013-2105	I.1	I.1	100423.437	11/1/2013	120	16,162	16,162	-
2013-0033	2014-0435	I.1	I.1	100423.505	2/19/2014	-	7,951	-	7,951
2013-0035	2013-1973	I.3.C	I.3.C	100423.423	10/22/2013	12,746	1,844,857	1,844,857	-
2013-0035	2014-0284	I.3.C	I.3.C	100423.481	2/6/2014	-	922,429	-	922,429
2013-0037	2015-0141	Other	I.2.C	100423.696	4/13/2015	160	31,111	-	31,111
2013-0039	2014-1812	Other	I.2.B	100423.629	12/17/2014	857	142,777	-	142,777
2013-0042	2014-0737	I.1	I.1	100423.531	3/19/2014	320	62,160	-	62,160
2013-0043	2013-2084	Other	I.2.B	100423.427	10/31/2013	141	18,221	18,221	-
2013-0043	2014-0434	Other	I.2.B	100423.504	2/19/2014	-	9,110	-	9,110
2013-0046	2015-0052	I.1	I.1	100423.663	2/5/2015	538	110,205	-	110,205
2013-0052	2015-0071		II.6	100423.671	2/17/2015	272	59,491	-	59,491
2013-0055	2013-2089	I.3.C	I.3.C	100423.432	10/31/2013	5,067	729,321	729,321	-
2013-0055	2013-2232	I.3.C	I.3.C	100423.448	11/26/2013	15,913	2,307,369	2,307,369	-
2013-0055	2014-0281	I.3.C	I.3.C	100423.478	2/6/2014	-	354,870	-	354,870
2013-0055	2014-0282	I.3.C	I.3.C	100423.479	2/6/2014	6,339	1,153,684	-	1,153,684
2013-0055	2014-0733	I.3.C	I.3.C	100423.527	3/19/2014	-	1,373,250	1,373,250	-
2013-0056	2015-0292	Other	I.2.B	100423.737	10/9/2015	29	5,536	-	5,536
2013-0057	2015-0185		II.7	100423.713	5/8/2015	1,264	271,624	-	271,624
2013-0058	2013-2163	I.1	I.1	100423.442	11/11/2013	86	11,085	-	11,085

12 of 15

FIGURE 10.72

Appendix 3.1

Invoices for Offsite Hourly Work

No.	No.	Category	Attachment B Item	Invoice No.	's (Issue Date)	Total invoiced M-H	Invoiced amounts (exclude 5% VAT)	actually paid (exclude 5% VAT)	Amount Outstanding
2013-0058	2014-0431	I.1	I.1	100423.502	2/19/2014	-	5,543	-	5,543
2013-0059	2014-1365	I.3.C	I.3.C	100423.561	7/8/2014	964	192,875	-	192,875
2013-0060	2014-1394	Other	I.2.B	100423.576	7/11/2014	184	40,514	-	40,514
2013-0061	2014-1754	Other	I.1.G	100423.616	11/17/2014	230	45,056	-	45,056
2013-0064	2013-1364	I.3.C	I.3.C	100423.560	7/22/2013	386	73,342	-	73,342
2013-0065	2013-2107	Other	I.2.B	100423.438	11/1/2013	61	7,861	7,861	-
2013-0065	2014-0432	Other	I.2.B	100423.503	2/19/2014	-	3,930	-	3,930
2013-0066	2014-0807	Other	I.2.B	100423.536	3/31/2014	315	61,092	-	61,092
2013-0067	2014-1761	Other	I.10	100423.620	11/17/2014	300	57,666	-	57,666
2013-0068	2014-0066	I.3.C	I.3.C	100423.463	1/16/2014	132	28,718	-	28,718
2013-0072	2015-0144	I.1	I.1	100423.699	4/13/2015	200	39,375	-	39,375
2013-0073	N/A	Other	I.2.B	no invoice	N/A	-	-	-	-
2013-0075	2013-1917	Other	I.2.B	100423.419	10/16/2013	129	16,706	16,706	-
2013-0075	2014-0430	Other	I.2.B	100423.501	2/19/2014	-	8,353	-	8,353
2013-0077	2015-0284	Other	I.2.B	100423.735	9/21/2015	99	19,231	-	19,231
2013-0078	2014-1393	I.1	I.1	100423.575	7/11/2014	45	9,627	-	9,627
2013-0081	2015-0066	Other	II.6	100423.667	2/13/2015	242	52,887	-	52,887
2013-0082	2015-0186	Other	II.17	100423.714	5/8/2015	1,093	217,493	-	217,493
2013-0083	2014-1372	Other	II.19.G	100423.567	7/8/2014	430	94,361	-	94,361
2013-0083	2015-0041	Other	II.19.G	100423.655	1/29/2015	60	13,306	-	13,306
2013-0085	2014-1564	I.3.C	I.3.C	100423.598	9/3/2014	382	84,190	-	84,190
2013-0090	2014-0309	I.1	I.1	100423.486	2/11/2014	357	77,669	-	77,669
2013-0090	2014-1498	I.1	I.1	100423.585	8/14/2014	86	18,731	-	18,731
2013-0091	2014-0118	I.1	I.1	100423.466	1/20/2014	107	20,785	-	20,785
2013-0092	2015-0072	I.1	I.1	100423.672	2/17/2015	119	16,664	-	16,664
2013-0094	2014-0121	I.1	I.1	100423.467	1/20/2014	100	19,367	-	19,367
2013-0097	2015-0295	II.5	II.5	100423.738	10/21/2015	2,929	634,383	-	634,383
2013-0098	2014-0463	I.3.C	I.3.C	100423.520	2/20/2014	2,350	511,266	511,266	-
2013-0099	2014-0310	I.3.C	I.3.C	100423.487	2/11/2014	499	108,562	-	108,562
2013-0100	2014-0311	Other	II.19.G	100423.488	2/11/2014	450	97,902	-	97,902
2013-0101	2014-1858	Other	III.2	100423.637	12/30/2014	1,844	404,308	-	404,308
2013-0102	2014-1367	I.1	I.1	100423.563	7/8/2014	35	7,428	-	7,428
2013-0103	2014-1144	Other	I.2.B	100423.555	5/19/2014	281	54,536	-	54,536
2013-0104	2013-2235	I.3.C	I.3.C	100423.451	11/26/2013	396	57,436	-	57,436
2013-0104	2014-0397	I.3.C	I.3.C	100423.491	2/17/2014	-	28,718	-	28,718
2013-0105	2014-1391	I.3.C	I.3.C	100423.570	5/1/2014	5,056	1,116,609	-	1,116,609
2013-0105	2014-1020	I.3.C	I.3.C	100423.548	7/11/2014	5,026	1,090,935	1,090,935	-
2013-0106	2014-1398	I.1	I.1	100423.580	7/11/2014	423	88,151	-	88,151

FIGURE 10.73

Appendix 3.1

Invoices for Offsite Hourly Work

No.	No.	Category	Attachment B Item	Invoice No.	's (Issue Date)	Total invoiced M-H	Invoiced amounts (exclude 5% VAT)	actually paid (exclude 5% VAT)	Amount Outstanding
2013-0108	2014-0809	I.3.C	I.3.C	100423.538	3/31/2014	3,129	680,745	680,745	-
2013-0109	2014-0037	I.3.C	I.3.C	100423.458	1/9/2014	429	93,333	-	93,333
2013-0110	2014-1373	I.3.C	I.3.C	100423.568	7/8/2014	331	72,012	-	72,012
2013-0111	2015-0295	Other	III.2	100423.738	10/21/2015	181	35,789	-	35,789
2013-0112	2014-1371	I.1	I.1	100423.566	7/8/2014	43	9,355	-	9,355
2013-0113	2014-1813	Other	V.6	100423.630	12/7/2014	2,180	483,381	-	483,381
2013-0113	2015-0111	Other	V.6	100423.679	3/20/2015	621	137,713	-	137,713
2013-0114	2014-1305	I.3.C	I.3.C	100423.557	6/25/2014	819	179,937	-	179,937
2013-0115	2015-0069		I1.6	100423.669	2/17/2015	120	26,092	-	26,092
2013-0116	2015-0285	Other	I.2.B	100423.736	9/21/2015	1,200	235,040	-	235,040
2013-0116	2015-0321	Other	I.2.B	100423.741	12/30/2015	362	79,196	-	79,196
2013-0119	2014-0732	I.3.C	I.3.C	100423.526	3/19/2014	4,890	1,063,868	1,063,868	-
2013-0120	2014-0731	I.3.C	I.3.C	100423.525	3/19/2014	900	195,804	-	195,804
2013-0121	2015-0131	I.1	I.1	100423.692	4/2/2015	229	44,744	-	44,744
2013-0121	2015-0131	I.1	I.1	100423.693	4/2/2015	55	10,605	-	10,605
2013-0122	2014-0812	Other	II.19.G	100423.540	3/31/2014	6,127	1,332,990	-	1,332,990
2013-0123	2015-0067		I1.6	100423.668	2/13/2015	179	39,186	-	39,186
2013-0124	2014-1759	I.1	I.1	100423.618	11/17/2014	275	53,551	-	53,551
2013-0126	2014-1392	I.1	I.1	100423.571	7/11/2014	225	43,937	-	43,937
2013-0127	2014-1518	I.3.C	I.3.C	100423.591	8/18/2014	19,515	4,322,110	-	4,322,110
2013-0127	2014-1579	I.3.C	I.3.C	100423.603	9/11/2014	2,494	553,069	-	553,069
2013-0131	2015-0187	Other	I.2.B	100423.715	5/11/2015	1,320	260,781	-	260,781
2013-0132	2014-1306	I.3.C	I.3.C	100423.558	6/25/2014	446	98,397	-	98,397
2013-0134	2014-1565	I.3.C	I.2.B	100423.599	9/3/2014	385	76,158	-	76,158
2013-0138	2014-1308	I.3.C	I.3.C	100423.559	6/25/2014	553	120,311	-	120,311
2013-0138	2014-1519	I.3.C	I.3.C	100423.592	8/18/2014	4,436	983,616	-	983,616
2014-0002	2014-1859	Other	III.2	100423.638	12/30/2014	449	98,810	-	98,810
2014-0005	2015-0054	Other	I.2.B	100423.665	2/5/2015	183	36,185	-	36,185
2014-0007	2014-1560	I.3.C	I.3.C	100423.595	9/3/2014	297	58,895	-	58,895
2014-0012	2015-0129	Other	I.2.B	100423.690	4/2/2015	73	14,405	-	14,405
2014-0013	2014-1395	Other	II.19.B	100423.577	7/11/2014	353	77,487	-	77,487
2014-0014	2015-0145	I.1	I.1	100423.700	4/13/2015	447	88,411	-	88,411
2014-0016	2015-0047	Other	II.17	100423.660	2/2/2015	283	57,485	-	57,485
2014-0019	2015-0274	Other	I.2.B	100423.732	9/14/2015	150	29,687	-	29,687
2014-0020	2015-0070		I1.6	100423.670	2/17/2015	154	34,051	-	34,051
2014-0021	2014-1396	Other	III.2	100423.578	7/11/2014	77	17,076	-	17,076
2014-0022	2014-1499	Other	III.2	100423.586	8/14/2014	95	21,067	-	21,067
2014-0023	2014-1500	I.1	I.1	100423.587	8/14/2014	235	51,842	-	51,842

FIGURE 10.74

Appendix 3.1

Invoices for Offsite Hourly Work

No.	No.	Category	Attachment B Item	Invoice No.	's (Issue Date)	Total invoiced M-H	Invoiced amounts (exclude 5% VAT)	actually paid (exclude 5% VAT)	Amount Outstanding
2014-0025	2015-0048		I1.6	100423.661	2/2/2015	190	40,638	-	40,638
2014-0026	2015-0053		I1.7	100423.664	2/5/2015	218	48,066	-	48,066
2014-0029	2015-0188	Other	I1.10	100423.716	5/11/2015	115	22,770	-	22,770
2014-0030	2015-0049		I1.5	100423.662	2/2/2015	162	34,066	-	34,066
2014-0032	2014-1745	I3.C	I3.C	100423.608	11/13/2014	612	121,245	-	121,245
2014-0033	2015-0263	I3.C	I3.C	100423.729	9/14/2015	115	22,721	-	22,721
2014-0034	2015-1608	I3.C	I3.C	100423.607	9/24/2014	610	120,839	-	120,839
2014-0038	2014-1833	I3.C	I3.C	100423.631	12/18/2014	440	87,021	-	87,021
2014-0039	2015-0273	I3.C	I3.C	100423.731	9/14/2015	337	66,677	-	66,677
2014-0040	2014-1734	I3.C	I3.C	100423.615	11/11/2014	671	132,868	-	132,868
2014-0041	2014-1562F	I3.C	I3.C	100423.597	9/12/2014	5,562	1,231,024	-	1,231,024
2014-0042	2015-0199	Other	III.2	100423.720	5/21/2015	105	20,905	-	20,905
2014-0043	2015-0073	I.1	I.1	100423.673	2/17/2015	68	13,365	-	13,365
2014-0045	2015-0045	I3.C	I3.C	100423.658	1/30/2015	52	11,532	-	11,532
2014-0047	2015-0055	Other	I2.B	100423.666	2/5/2015	173	34,244	-	34,244
2014-0048	2015-0098	Other	I2.B	100423.675	3/12/2015	275	54,391	-	54,391
2014-0056	2015-0035	I3.C	I3.C	100423.651	1/28/2015	106	23,507	-	23,507
2014-0058	2015-0099	I.1	I.1	100423.676	3/12/2015	194	39,572	-	39,572
2014-0063	2015-0112	I.1	I.1	100423.680	3/20/2015	679	150,575	-	150,575
2014-0065	2015-0112	I.1	I.1	100423.681	3/20/2015	9	1,996	-	1,996
2014-0066	2015-0030	I3.C	I3.C	100423.646	1/28/2015	125	27,720	-	27,720
2014-0068	2015-0031	I3.C	I3.C	100423.647	1/28/2015	128	28,193	-	28,193
2014-0070	2015-0117	I.1	I.1	100423.682	3/25/2015	110	22,461	-	22,461
2014-0071	2015-0034	I.1	I.1	100423.650	1/28/2015	70	15,523	-	15,523
2014-0073	2015-0036	I.1	I.1	100423.652	1/28/2015	20	4,293	-	4,293
2014-0075	2015-0106	I.1	I.1	100423.677	3/17/2015	33	6,435	-	6,435
2014-0076	2015-0032	I.1	I.1	100423.648	1/28/2015	260	57,658	-	57,658
2014-0080	2015-0033	I.1	I.1	100423.649	1/28/2015	61	13,527	-	13,527
2014-0085	2015-0074	Other	III.2	100423.674	2/17/2015	153	30,334	-	30,334
2014-0087	2015-0283	I.1	I.1	100423.734	9/25/2015	27	5,306	-	5,306
N/A	2015-0107	I.1	I.1	100423.678	3/17/2015	18	3,643	-	3,643
N/A	N/A	Other	N/A	100423.617	N/A	-	-	-	-
N/A	N/A	Other	N/A	100423.619	N/A	-	-	-	-
Total						**832,915**	**$ 141,609,450**	**$ 58,813,089**	**$ 82,796,361**

Sources:
Exhibit R-830

15 of 15

FIGURE 10.75

Appendix 4

Analysis of "Open ▮" Claims

Category	Hours				▮ $	Supplier	Total	▮ Total
	▮	Other	Total	%				
Anticipated Amendment 30 ▮	2,947	2,302	5,250	56.1%	$ 720,605	$ 369,718	$ 1,090,323	$ 612,135
Deferred ▮	3,861	95	3,956	97.6%	69,825	781,279	851,104	830,771
Revision Not Submitted to ▮	230	5,362	5,592	4.1%	167,130	853,497	1,020,627	41,908
Pre-Authorized	1,512	94	1,605	94.2%	73,194	275,662	348,856	328,494
Unapproved ▮ R0 (▮ not in agreement with scope)	-	1,860	1,860	0.0%	314,297	88,676	402,973	-
Unapproved R0 (▮ not in agreement with total man-hours)	20,547	194	20,742	99.1%	319,960	4,196,284	4,516,244	4,473,938
Unapproved R1 or Higher (▮ not in agreement with revision man-hours)	2,105	613	2,719	77.4%	116,869	441,813	558,682	432,628
Unapproved R1 or Higher (▮ not in agreement with revision scope)	32	-	32	100.0%	5,442	887	6,329	6,329
Open ▮ - Alleged Nonconformance Claim	4,306	4,698	9,004	47.8%	838,298	1,039,789	1,878,087	898,161
Open ▮ Claim	34,917	-	34,917	100.0%			6,333,652	6,333,652
Project Management - Claim Management & Assembly	-	978	978	0.0%			149,783	-
Value Added Tax (5%) - Per ▮ [1]							857,830	697,901
Total	**70,457**	**16,196**	**86,653**	**81.3%**			**$ 18,014,490**	**$ 14,655,918**

Sources and Footnotes:

Appendix 4.1

Report of ▮, Tables 10, 11, 12, and 13 submitted by ▮

1) VAT is calculated as 5% of $17,156,657.

1 of 1

FIGURE 10.76

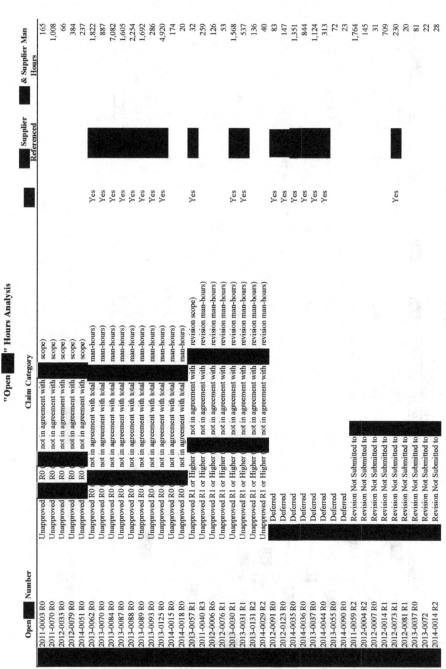

Appendix 4.1

1 of 2

FIGURE 10.77

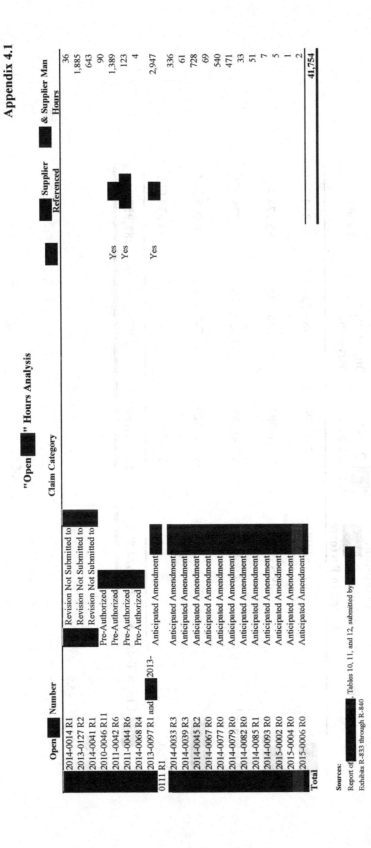

FIGURE 10.78

Appendix 5

Claim Summary

System	Lump-sum Obligations Failed to Perform	Out of Pocket Costs	Duplicative Payments	Total
	$ 91,164,981	$ 3,761,179	$ 388,733	$ 95,314,893
	148,551,751	2,014,083	208,592	150,774,426
Mechanical	14,908,163	5,790,388	2,629,876	23,328,428
	-	8,162,020	743,314	8,905,334
Other	-	4,634,080	-	4,634,080
Claim Total	**$ 254,624,895**	**$ 24,361,750**	**$ 3,970,515**	**$ 282,957,161**

Sources:
Appendices 5.1 - 5.9

1 of 1

FIGURE 10.79

Appendix 5.1

Claim Summary by Problem

Problem	Lump-sum Obligations Failed to Perform		Out of Pocket Costs		Duplicative Payments		Total	
System	$	75,111,924	$	-	$	-	$	75,111,924
Problem		-		121,849		-		121,849
Problem		-		517,285		-		517,285
Problem		-		166,496		-		166,496
Problem		-		2,276,464		-		2,276,464
Problem		-		220,913		-		220,913
Problem		-		220,016		-		220,016
Problem		-		155,352		-		155,352
Problem	See Footnote 1		-		-		-
Problem	See Footnote 2		-		-		-
Problem		-		27,328		-		27,328
Problem		-		16,807		384,506		401,313
Problem		-		11,068		1,407		12,475
Problem		-		16,533		1,410		17,943
Problem		15,958,497		-		-		15,958,497
Problem		-		11,068		1,410		12,478
End-to-End Problem		94,560		-		-		94,560
Total	$	91,164,981	$	3,761,179	$	388,733	$	95,314,893
Problem		641,084		65,587		-		706,671

1 of 3

FIGURE 10.80

Claim Summary by Problem

Problem	Lump-sum Obligations Failed to Perform	Out of Pocket Costs	Duplicative Payments	Total
Problem	See Footnote 3	3,416	-	3,416
Problem	7,920	564,596	-	572,516
Problem	346,500	102,981	-	449,481
Problem	-	221,068	30,937	252,005
Problem	3,352,000	992,828	130,663	4,475,491
Problem	5,439,868	9,292	-	5,449,160
Problem	138,764,379	54,314	46,992	138,865,685
Total $	**148,551,751** $	**2,014,083** $	**208,592** $	**150,774,426**
Problem	-	577,310	11,394	588,704
Problem	5,733,610	46,457	-	5,780,067
Problem	-	853,664	-	853,664
Problem	-	182,148	206,651	388,799
Problem	1,506,271	97,288	26,208	1,629,767
Problem	-	85,547	-	85,547
Problem	-	82,531	-	352,933
Problem	270,402			
Problem	7,397,881	392,160	41,184	7,831,225
Caused Problem	-	255,243	1,127,368	1,382,611
Problem	-	718,210	45,945	764,155
Problem	-	1,969,165	-	1,969,165

2 of 3

FIGURE 10.81

Appendix 5.1

Claim Summary by Problem

Problem	Lump-sum Obligations Failed to Perform	Out of Pocket Costs	Duplicative Payments	Total
Problem	-	338,276	92,363	430,639
t Problem	-	192,389	1,078,763	1,271,152
Mechanical Total $	14,908,163	$ 5,790,388	$ 2,629,876	$ 23,328,428
Problem		1,184,952	350,479	1,535,431
rawings Problem		467,815	207,000	674,815
Problem		6,338,620	185,835	6,524,455
Problem		170,633	-	170,633
Electrical Total $	-	$ 8,162,020	$ 743,314	$ 8,905,334
Problems	-	4,008,018	-	4,008,018
Problems		626,062	-	626,062
Other Total $	-	$ 4,634,080	$ -	$ 4,634,080
Claim Total $	254,624,895	$ 24,361,750	3,970,515	$ 282,957,161

Sources and Footnotes:

Appendices 5.2 - 5.9

1) ████'s Lump-Sum Obligations include update of ████ Manuals. That work, valued at $1,864,107, is included in the $75,111,924 contract price for the ████ System for purposes of conservatism.

2) ████ paid $24,460,000 for the ████, which had a critical system hardware error and remains inoperable. This amount has been included in the $75,111,924 contract price for the ████ System. See Appendix 5.3

3) The ████ Problem), for which ████ paid $95,170,628, do not conform to ████'s design specifications and therefore cannot be used. They also do not meet ROC ████'s requirements regarding the amount of ████ Problem). To avoid double-counting the ████, they have been included in the $138,764,379 of equipment associated with the ████ Problem.

FIGURE 10.82

Appendix 5.2

■ Outstanding　■ Lump-sum Obligations

System	Problem[1,2]	Witness Statement	Equipment	Quantity	Cost	Source
■	■ Problem		Various	100	15,958,497	Witness Statement
■	■ End-to-End Problem		Various	0	94,560	Witness Statement
Subtotal				**100**	**$ 16,053,057**	
■	■ Problem			2	$ 3,352,000	Am. 7, Ex. 2
■	■ Problem			16	5,439,868	Am. 7, Ex. 2
■	■ Problem	■		1	641,084	Witness Statement
■	■ Problem	■		0	7,920	Witness Statement
■	■ Problem	■	System	0	346,500	Witness Statement
Subtotal				**19**	**$ 9,787,372**	
Mechanical	■ Problem	■	■	9	270,402	Appendix 5.5
Mechanical	■ Problem	■	■	12	5,733,610	Appendix 5.6
Mechanical	■ r Problem	■	■	144	1,052,927	Appendix 5.7
Mechanical	■ Problem	■	■	62	453,344	Appendix 5.7
Mechanical Subtotal				**227**	**$ 7,510,283**	
Total Cost of ■				**346**	**$ 33,350,712**	

Footnotes:

1) ■'s Lump-Sum Obligations include update of ■ Manuals. That work, valued at $1,864,107, is included in the $75,111,924 contract price for the ■ System for purposes of conservatism.

2) The ■ ■'s requirements regarding the amount of ■ paid $95,170,628, do not conform to ■'s design specifications, and therefore cannot be used. They also do not meet ROC■'s requirements regarding the amount of ■, they have been included in the $138,764,379 of equipment associated with the ■ System). To avoid ■ Problem.

1 of 1

FIGURE 10.83

Appendix 5.3

Select Contract Pricing - ▮

Engineered	Source	Supplier	Unit 1		Unit 2		Total
Actuation System			**Base Price**	**Price Increase**	**Base Price**	**Price Increase**	
H12 Equipment Part 1	Am. ▮, Ex. 2	▮	$ 2,500,000	$ 312,371	$ 2,500,000	$ 312,371	$ 5,624,742
H12 Equipment Part 2	Am. ▮, Ex. 2	▮	3,000,000	374,845	3,000,000	374,845	6,749,690
H12 Equipment Part 3	Am. ▮, Ex. 2	▮	5,400,000	674,721	5,400,000	674,721	12,149,442
H12 Equipment Part 4	Am. ▮, Ex. 2	▮	5,000,000	624,742	5,000,000	624,742	11,249,484
H12 Equipment Part 5	Am. ▮, Ex. 2	▮	4,500,000	562,267	4,500,000	562,267	10,124,534
H12 Equipment Part 6	Am. ▮, Ex. 2	▮	2,113,000	264,016	2,113,000	264,016	4,754,032
Subtotal			**22,513,000**	**2,812,962**	**22,513,000**	**2,812,962**	**50,651,924**
Information Management System - Execution of IMS	Ch. 2, Ex. 2		5,214,000	-	2,235,000	-	7,449,000
Information Management System - Software	Ch. 2, Ex. 2		4,815,000	-	2,064,000	-	6,879,000
Hardware	Ch. 2, Ex. 2	▮	10,132,000	-	-	-	10,132,000
							$ 75,111,924

Sources:
Exhibit R-831
Exhibit R-832

1 of 1

FIGURE 10.84

Appendix 5.4

Non-Conforming ▮

Shipment No.	Contract Price per Shipment	Shipped Units	Average Price per Unit	Non-Conforming Units	Price for Non-Conforming Units
28	$ 755,640	30	$ 25,188	30	$ 755,640
29/29A[1]	1,343,360	36	37,316	36	1,343,360
124	1,949,634	39	49,991	21	1,049,803
158	755,640	30	25,188	30	755,640
161	480,958	13	36,997	13	480,958
172	168,408	6	28,068	6	168,408
207	1,343,360	38	35,352	38	1,343,360
227	305,167	8	38,146	8	305,167
353	2,618,574	48	54,554	30	1,636,609
Total	**$ 9,720,741**	**248**	**$ 36,755**	**212**	**$ 7,838,945**
Less: 12 repaired ▮				(12)	(441,064)
Total Non-Conforming ▮[2]				**200**	**$ 7,397,881**

Sources:

Exhibit R-817

First Witness Statement of ▮

1) Per Exhibit R-817, there was no charge for shipment batch 29A.

2) As calculated, the average price per unit would be $39,196.54 (Total Contract Price / Total Units Shipped), which decreases the contract price of non-conforming ▮ by $29,000.

1 of 1

FIGURE 10.85

Appendix 5.5

Non-Conforming

Shipment No.	Contract Price per Shipment	Shipped Units	Average Price per Unit	Non-Conforming Units	Price for Non-Conforming Units
635	$ 297,101	61	$ 4,871	3	$ 14,612
417	1,357,813	31	43,800	5	219,002
470	484,141	16	30,259	5	151,294
689	953,871	49	19,467	3	58,400
755	988,830	47	21,039	2	42,078
Total	$ 4,081,756	204	$ 23,887	18	$ 485,386
Less: 9 repaired █				(9)	(214,984)
Total Non-Conforming █				9	$ 270,402

Sources:
Exhibit R-817
First Witness Statement of █

1 of 1

FIGURE 10.86

Appendix 5.6

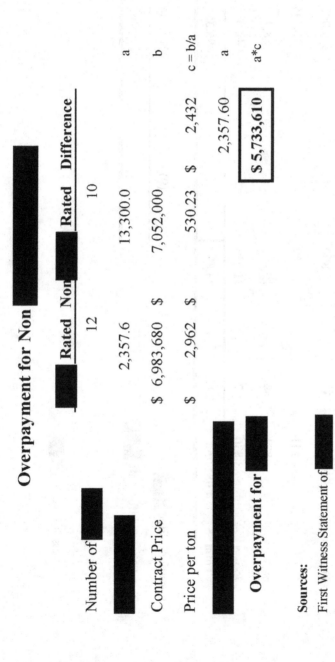

Overpayment for Non[▮]

	Rated Non[▮]	Rated	Difference	
Number of ▮	12	10		
	2,357.6	13,300.0		a
Contract Price	$ 6,983,680	$ 7,052,000		b
Price per ton	$ 2,962	$ 530.23	$ 2,432	c = b/a
			2,357.60	a
Overpayment for ▮			**$ 5,733,610**	a*c

Sources:
First Witness Statement of ▮

1 of 1

FIGURE 10.87

Appendix 5.7

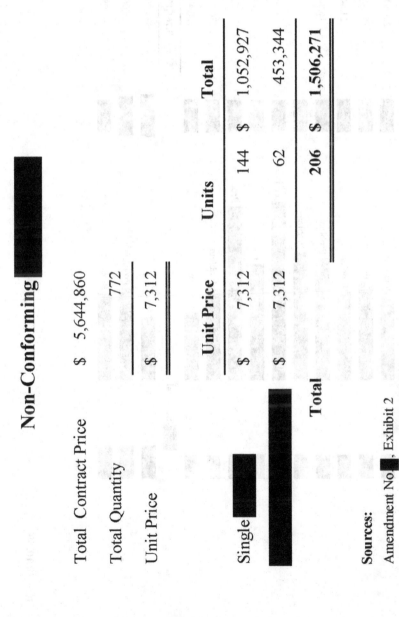

Non-Conforming

Total Contract Price	$	5,644,860
Total Quantity		772
Unit Price	$	7,312

	Unit Price	Units	Total
Single	$ 7,312	144	$ 1,052,927
	$ 7,312	62	453,344
Total		**206**	**$ 1,506,271**

Sources:

Amendment No ▮, Exhibit 2

First Witness Statement of ▮▮▮

1 of 1

FIGURE 10.88

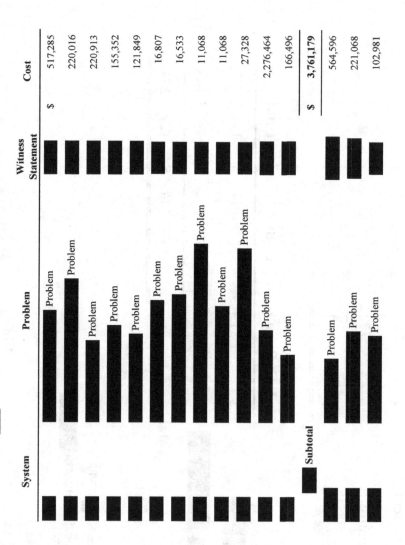

1 of 3

FIGURE 10.89

Appendix 5.8

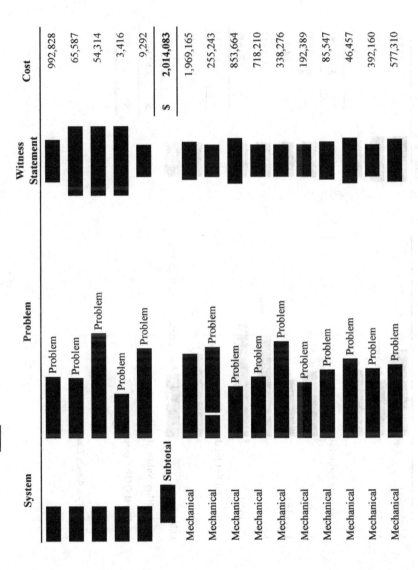

Out-of-Pocket Cost to Correct Non-Conforming Work

System	Problem	Witness Statement	Cost
	Problem		992,828
	Problem		65,587
	Problem		54,314
	Problem		3,416
	Problem		9,292
Subtotal			**$ 2,014,083**
Mechanical	Problem		1,969,165
Mechanical	Problem		255,243
Mechanical	Problem		853,664
Mechanical	Problem		718,210
Mechanical	Problem		338,276
Mechanical	Problem		192,389
Mechanical	Problem		85,547
Mechanical	Problem		46,457
Mechanical	Problem		392,160
Mechanical	Problem		577,310

FIGURE 10.90

Appendix 5.8

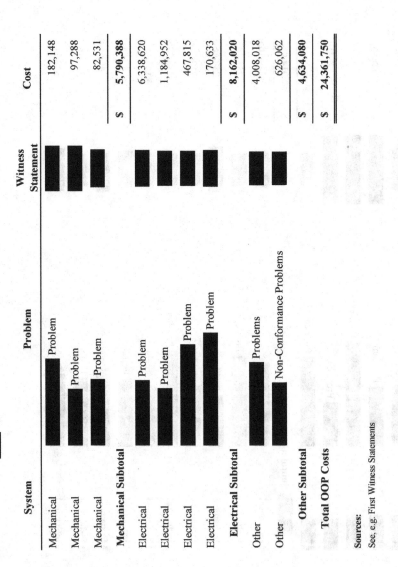

Out-of-Pocket Cost to Correct Non-Conforming Work

System	Problem	Witness Statement	Cost
Mechanical	Problem		182,148
Mechanical	Problem		97,288
Mechanical	Problem		82,531
Mechanical Subtotal			$ **5,790,388**
Electrical	Problem		6,338,620
Electrical	Problem		1,184,952
Electrical	Problem		467,815
Electrical	Problem		170,633
Electrical Subtotal			$ **8,162,020**
Other	Problems		4,008,018
Other	Non-Conformance Problems		626,062
Other Subtotal			$ **4,634,080**
Total OOP Costs			$ **24,361,750**

Sources:

See, e.g. First Witness Statements

3 of 3

FIGURE 10.91

Appendix 5.9

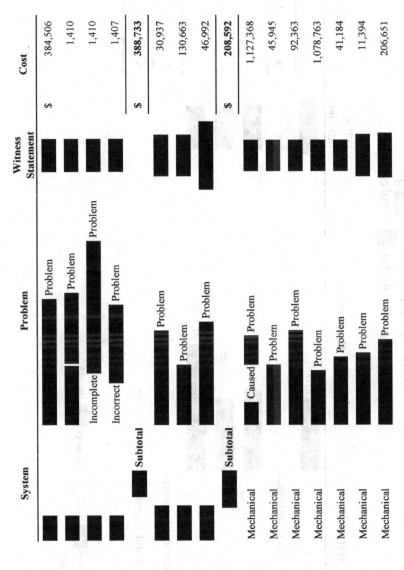

FIGURE 10.92

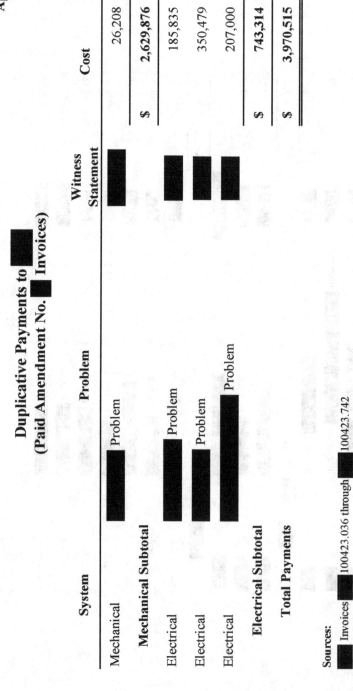

Appendix 5.9

Duplicative Payments to
(Paid Amendment No. ▪ Invoices)

System	Problem	Witness Statement	Cost	
Mechanical	Problem	▪		26,208
Mechanical Subtotal			$	**2,629,876**
Electrical	Problem	▪		185,835
Electrical	Problem	▪		350,479
Electrical	Problem	▪		207,000
Electrical Subtotal			$	**743,314**
Total Payments			$	**3,970,515**

Sources:
▪ Invoices 100423.036 through ▪ 100423.742
Exhibit R-830

2 of 2

FIGURE 10.93

Appendix 6

Summary of ▮▮ Amendment No. ▮ Invoices

Attachment B Item	Single Invoices	Value Multi Invoices[1]	Total	Reviewed by ▮▮
II.5	$ 14,370,167	$ -	$ 14,370,167	$ 8,568,721
II.6	14,918,384	-	14,918,384	6,688,419
II.7	13,247,283	-	13,247,283	1,635,480
Offsite ▮ subtotal	$ 42,535,835	$ -	$ 42,535,835	$ 16,892,620
I.3.C As-built reconciliation	18,807,676	- ▮	18,807,676	4,322,110
I.1 Design and Equipment Related Issues Found During Fieldwork	9,917,815	650,602	10,568,417	6,319,669
Other	10,654,183	126,084	10,780,267	-
Offsite ▮ subtotal	$ 39,379,673	$ 776,686	$ 40,156,359	$ 10,641,779
Total Offsite Hourly Services	$ 81,915,508	$ 776,686	$ 82,692,194	$ 27,534,399
Other ▮▮	7,351,054	-	7,351,054	1,761,496
Grand Total ▮▮	$ 89,266,561	$ 776,686	$ 90,043,247	$ 29,295,894

1 of 3

FIGURE 10.94

Appendix 6

Summary of ▮ Amendment No. ▮ Invoices

Attachment B Item	Count of Invoices			Reviewed by ▮
	Single	Multi	Navigant[2]	
II.5	13	-	13	4
II.6	23	-	23	4
II.7	31	-	31	1
Offsite **subtotal**	**67**	**-**	**67**	**9**
I.3.C As-built reconciliation	73	-	73	1
I.1 Design and Equipment Related Issues Found During Fieldwork	61	9	70	10
Other	88	9	97	-
Offsite ▮ **subtotal**	**222**	**18**	**240**	**11**
Total Offsite Services	**289**	**18**	**307**	**20**
Other	73	-	73	3
Grand Total	**362**	**18**	**380**	**23**

2 of 3

FIGURE 10.95

Appendix 6

Summary of ▮ Amendment No. ▮ Invoices

Attachment B Item	Man Hours		
	Total	Reviewed by ▮	
II.5	84,005	34,926	
II.6	89,177	38,274	
II.7	79,471	7,229	
Offsite ▮ subtotal	252,653	80,429	31.8%
I.3.C As-built reconciliation	69,551	19,515	
I.1 Design and Equipment Related Issues Found During Fieldwork	122,377	99,510	
Other	58,080	-	
Total Offsite Services	502,661	199,455	39.7%

Sources and Footnotes:

Appendix 6.1 - 6.2

Report of ▮, submitted by ▮

1) In ▮ Exhibit NC-002, several invoices are grouped together as "Multi." Invoices ▮ 100423.066, 118, 119, 159, 160, 162, 178, 300, 382 total $650,602 and are categorized by ▮ as "I.1." Invoices ▮ 100423.256, 257, 295, 385 total $71,478 and are categorized as "Other." Invoices ▮ 100423.292, 386 total $18,350 and are categorized as "Other." Invoices ▮ 100423.298, 299, 417 total $36,255 and are categorized as "Other."

2) In ▮ Exhibit NC-002, there are 77 line items representing 58 unique invoice numbers. In calculation of its 380 invoices, ▮ has excluded 4 of the 19 duplicative invoice numbers (▮ 100423.613, .701, .702, .703).

3) Invoice ▮ 100423.738 is associated with two ▮ Nos.: ▮ 2013-0097 ($634,383 - Attachment B Item II.5) and ▮ 2013-0111 ($35,789 - Attachment B Item III.2). The invoice is included in the count of Category II.5 for purposes of this Appendix.

3 of 3

FIGURE 10.96

Appendix 6.1

Offsite Hourly Work Claim

Category No.	Invoice No.[1]	Type	Supplier's letter (Issue Date)	Attachment B Item	Category	Invoiced amounts (Exclude 5% VAT)	Outstanding per	Invoiced M-H	Reviewed by	Single/Multi	Invoiced Amount	Credit	Amount Outstanding
						$	$				$	$	$
5	100423.066		7/6/2011	I.1	I.1	589,747.72	7,916.16	4,494.55	Yes	Multi	-	-	-
5	100423.118		11/10/2011	I.1	I.1	870,445.28	8,040.16	6,560.30	Yes	Multi	-	-	-
5	100423.119		3/7/2012	I.1	I.1	679,825.04	12,543.84	5,148.50	Yes	Multi	-	-	-
5	100423.159		12/3/2012	I.1	I.1	788,669.44	25,968.64	5,843.60	Yes	Multi	-	-	-
5	100423.160		5/15/2013	I.1	I.1	834,474.24	50,113.28	6,193.65	Yes	Multi	-	-	-
5	100423.162		7/25/2013	I.1	I.1	985,557.76	85,772.80	7,300.25	Yes	Multi	-	-	-
5	100423.178		7/11/2014	I.1	I.1	751,677.44	335,457.28	5,577.40	Yes	Multi	-	-	-
2	100423.180		3/9/2012	I1.6		27,249.00	11,346.00	219.75	Yes	Single	11,346.00	-	11,346.00
2	100423.224		7/10/2012	I1.6		1,037,831.68	1,037,831.68	7,427.00	No	Single	1,037,831.68	-	1,037,831.68
2	100423.225		7/10/2012	I1.6		1,263,420.16	1,263,420.16	9,042.05	Yes	Single	1,263,420.16	-	1,263,420.16
2	100423.237		7/10/2012	I1.6		546,851.84	546,851.84	3,894.40	No	Single	546,851.84	-	546,851.84
2	100423.238		7/10/2012	I1.6		301,508.48	301,508.48	2,171.00	No	Single	301,508.48	-	301,508.48
6	100423.256		11/16/2012	I2.C	Other	43,872.00	6,720.00	342.75	No	Multi	-	-	-
6	100423.257		8/1/2013	I2.C	Other	76,454.40	26,547.20	597.30	No	Multi	-	-	-
2	100423.258		9/27/2012	I1.6		1,032,902.40	1,032,902.40	7,323.30	Yes	Single	1,032,902.40	-	1,032,902.40
3	100423.277		10/24/2012	I1.7		306,426.88	306,426.88	2,285.15	No	Single	306,426.88	-	306,426.88
3	100423.278		10/29/2012	I1.7		431,558.40	431,558.40	3,096.00	No	Single	431,558.40	-	431,558.40
3	100423.279		10/29/2012	I1.7		600,770.30	600,770.30	4,376.40	No	Single	600,770.30	-	600,770.30
3	100423.280		10/29/2012	I1.7		461,312.26	461,312.26	3,389.55	No	Single	461,312.26	-	461,312.26
6	100423.292		8/1/2013	I2.A		31,192.20	6,482.25	241.80	No	Multi	-	-	-
6	100423.295		3/25/2015	I2.C		65,802.90	33,681.90	510.10	No	Multi	-	-	-
6	100423.298		12/31/2014	I2.B		68,337.75	2,760.60	529.75	No	Multi	-	-	-
6	100423.299		1/29/2015	I2.B		58,211.25	4,186.05	451.25	No	Multi	-	-	-
5	100423.300		12/5/2014	I.1		2,006,090.61	148,104.84	14,800.97	Yes	Multi	-	-	-
1	100423.309		8/23/2013	I1.5		337,292.24	337,292.24	2,410.68	No	Single	337,292.24	-	337,292.24
1	100423.310		8/23/2013	I1.5		647,960.93	647,960.93	4,644.59	No	Single	647,960.93	-	647,960.93
1	100423.322		1/28/2013	I1.5		1,669,931.06	1,669,931.06	11,939.52	No	Single	1,669,931.06	-	1,669,931.06
1	100423.328		2/5/2013	I1.5		2,025,188.60	2,025,188.60	14,443.82	No	Single	2,025,188.60	-	2,025,188.60
2	100423.339		3/12/2013	I1.6		1,826,104.65	1,826,104.65	12,805.85	No	Single	1,826,104.65	-	1,826,104.65
3	100423.341		10/30/2012	I1.7		1,877,373.38	1,877,373.38	13,392.60	No	Single	1,877,373.38	-	1,877,373.38
5	100423.363		12/5/2014	I.1		5,580.00	2,480.00	45.00	No	Single	2,480.00	2,480.00	-
5	100423.375		1/9/2014	I.1	I.1	134,215.47	134,215.47	942.75	Yes	Single	134,215.47	-	134,215.47
5	100423.382		9/2/2015	I.1	I.1	1,940,655.36	3,532.38	14,223.40	No	Multi	-	-	-
6	100423.385		3/25/2015	I2.C	Other	14,015.85	14,015.85	108.65	No	Multi	-	-	-
6	100423.386		3/25/2015	I2.A	Other	25,322.70	13,029.00	196.30	No	Multi	-	-	-
6	100423.387		8/1/2013	I2.B	Other	102,918.10	128.00	802.90	No	Single	128.00	128.00	-

1 of 9

FIGURE 10.97

Appendix 6.1

Offsite Hourly Work Claim

Category No.	Invoice No.	Type	's letter (Issue Date)	Attachment B item	Category	Invoiced amounts (Exclude 5% VAT)	Outstanding per	Invoiced M-H	Reviewed by	Single/Multi	Invoiced Amount	Credit	Amount Outstanding
2	100423.403		9/18/2013	II.6		54,887.05	54,887.05	379.30	No	Single	54,887.05	-	54,887.05
5	100423.405		9/24/2013	I.1	I.1	41,858.72	41,858.72	297.75	No	Single	41,858.72	-	41,858.72
1	100423.407		9/16/2013	II.5		60,656.83	60,656.83	420.90	No	Single	60,656.83	-	60,656.83
3	100423.416		10/16/2013	II.7		317,072.97	317,072.97	2,147.25	No	Single	317,072.97	-	317,072.97
6	100423.417		3/26/2015	I.2.B	Other	162,591.60	29,308.80	1,260.40	No	Multi	-	-	-
3	100423.418		10/16/2013	II.7		142,221.31	142,221.31	944.65	No	Single	142,198.85	-	142,198.85
2	100423.421		10/16/2013	II.6		10,154.88	10,154.88	70.50	No	Single	10,154.88	-	10,154.88
3	100423.426		10/31/2013	II.7		136,333.65	136,333.65	947.10	No	Single	136,333.65	-	136,333.65
4	100423.433		11/1/2013	13.C	13.C	45,397.52	45,397.52	313.00	No	Single	45,397.52	-	45,397.52
3	100423.434		11/1/2013	II.7		441,960.73	441,960.73	2,856.15	No	Single	441,849.16	-	441,849.16
3	100423.435		11/1/2013	II.7		217,046.27	217,046.27	1,412.30	No	Single	216,992.79	-	216,992.79
5	100423.436		11/1/2013	I.1	I.1	29,149.50	29,149.50	225.95	No	Single	29,149.50	-	29,149.50
6	100423.440		11/11/2013	V.6	Other	190,292.48	190,292.48	1,312.00	No	Single	190,292.48	-	190,292.48
4	100423.441		11/11/2013	13.C	13.C	12,302.50	12,302.50	95.00	No	Single	12,302.50	-	12,302.50
5	100423.442		11/11/2013	I.1	I.1	11,085.20	11,085.20	85.60	No	Single	11,085.20	-	11,085.20
1	100423.444		11/26/2013	I.1	I.1	43,358.49	43,358.49	301.50	No	Single	43,358.49	-	43,358.49
6	100423.447		11/26/2013	II.19.G	Other	795,414.90	795,414.90	5,485.00	No	Single	795,414.90	-	795,414.90
4	100423.449		11/26/2013	13.C	13.C	402,892.00	402,892.00	2,779.00	No	Single	402,892.00	-	402,892.00
4	100423.451		11/26/2013	13.C	13.C	57,435.84	57,435.84	396.00	No	Single	57,435.84	-	57,435.84
2	100423.453		12/10/2013	II.6		1,314,419.70	1,314,419.70	9,277.90	No	Single	1,314,419.70	-	1,314,419.70
1	100423.454		12/13/2013	II.5		1,687,914.84	1,687,914.84	11,991.38	Yes	Single	1,687,914.84	-	1,687,914.84
4	100423.455		12/13/2013	13.C	13.C	136,345.80	136,345.80	759.50	No	Single	136,345.80	-	136,345.80
6	100423.456		1/9/2014	II.19.G	Other	182,532.84	182,532.84	953.00	No	Single	182,532.84	-	182,532.84
4	100423.458		1/9/2014	13.C	13.C	93,333.24	93,333.24	429.00	No	Single	93,333.24	-	93,333.24
5	100423.459		6/28/2013	I.1	I.1	6,068.16	6,068.16	42.00	No	Single	6,068.16	-	6,068.16
4	100423.463		1/16/2014	13.C	13.C	28,717.92	28,717.92	132.00	No	Single	28,717.92	-	28,717.92
4	100423.464		12/11/2013	13.C	13.C	85,718.64	85,718.64	394.00	No	Single	85,718.64	-	85,718.64
6	100423.465		1/16/2014	II.19.C	Other	38,277.12	38,277.12	267.00	No	Single	38,277.12	-	38,277.12
5	100423.466		1/20/2014	I.1	I.1	20,784.75	20,784.75	107.00	No	Single	20,784.75	-	20,784.75
5	100423.467		1/20/2014	I.1	I.1	19,366.73	19,366.73	99.70	No	Single	19,366.73	-	19,366.73
4	100423.468		1/20/2014	13.C	13.C	535,481.22	535,481.22	-	No	Single	535,481.22	-	535,481.22
5	100423.469		1/24/2014	I.1	I.1	149,536.24	149,536.24	849.00	No	Single	149,536.24	-	149,536.24
4	100423.471		1/28/2014	I.1	I.1	278,939.83	278,939.83	1,648.95	No	Single	278,939.83	-	278,939.83
4	100423.472		1/28/2014	13.C	13.C	114,364.04	114,364.04	-	No	Single	114,364.04	-	114,364.04
4	100423.473		1/28/2014	13.C	13.C	116,539.64	116,539.64	-	No	Single	116,539.64	-	116,539.64
4	100423.474		1/28/2014	13.C	13.C	136,120.04	136,120.04	-	No	Single	136,120.04	-	136,120.04

FIGURE 10.98

Appendix 6.1

■ Offsite Hourly Work Claim

Category No.	Invoice No.	Type	"s" letter (Issue Date)	Attachment B Item	Category	Invoiced amounts (Exclude 5% VAT)	Outstanding per	Invoiced M-H	Reviewed by	Single/Multi	Invoiced Amount	Credit	Amount Outstanding
6	100423.475	■	1/28/2014	II.19 G	Other	297,205.09	297,205.09	-	No	Single	297,205.09	-	297,205.09
4	100423.476	■	11/26/2013	1.3.C	1.3.C	290,080.00	290,080.00	-	No	Single	290,080.00	-	290,080.00
4	100423.477	■	1/16/2014	1.3.C	1.3.C	411,079.63	411,079.63	-	No	Single	411,079.63	-	411,079.63
4	100423.478	■	2/6/2014	1.3.C	1.3.C	354,870.15	354,870.15	-	No	Single	354,870.15	-	354,870.15
4	100423.479	■	2/6/2014	1.3.C	1.3.C	1,153,684.42	1,153,684.42	-	No	Single	1,153,684.42	-	1,153,684.42
4	100423.480	■	1/29/2014	1.3.C	1.3.C	379,823.51	379,823.51	-	No	Single	379,823.51	-	379,823.51
4	100423.481	■	2/6/2014	1.3.C	1.3.C	922,428.50	922,428.50	-	No	Single	922,428.50	-	922,428.50
4	100423.482	■	2/7/2014	1.3.C	1.3.C	404,862.92	404,862.92	2,388.70	No	Single	404,862.92	-	404,862.92
4	100423.483	■	2/7/2014	1.3.C	1.3.C	333,136.56	333,136.56	1,832.65	No	Single	333,136.56	-	333,136.56
6	100423.485	■	2/11/2014	II.19 G	Other	103,993.68	103,993.68	478.00	No	Single	103,993.68	-	103,993.68
5	100423.486	■	2/11/2014	1.1	1.1	77,668.92	77,668.92	357.00	No	Single	77,668.92	-	77,668.92
4	100423.487	■	2/11/2014	1.3.C	1.3.C	108,562.44	108,562.44	499.00	No	Single	108,562.44	-	108,562.44
6	100423.488	■	2/11/2014	II.19 G	Other	97,902.00	97,902.00	450.00	No	Single	97,902.00	-	97,902.00
6	100423.489	■	9/16/2013	I2.E.b1	Other	64.75	-	-	No	Single	64.75	-	64.75
4	100423.490	■	2/17/2014	1.3.C	1.3.C	37,420.32	37,420.32	-	No	Single	37,420.32	-	37,420.32
4	100423.491	■	2/17/2014	1.3.C	1.3.C	28,717.92	28,717.92	-	No	Single	28,717.92	-	28,717.92
4	100423.492	■	2/17/2014	1.3.C	1.3.C	10,152.80	10,152.80	-	No	Single	10,152.80	-	10,152.80
4	100423.493	■	2/17/2014	1.3.C	1.3.C	4,278.68	4,278.68	-	No	Single	4,278.68	-	4,278.68
4	100423.494	■	2/17/2014	1.3.C	1.3.C	2,683.24	2,683.24	-	No	Single	2,683.24	-	2,683.24
4	100423.495	■	10/16/2013	1.3.C	1.3.C	72.52	-	-	No	Single	72.52	-	72.52
4	100423.496	■	2/17/2014	1.3.C	1.3.C	4,786.32	4,786.32	-	No	Single	4,786.32	-	4,786.32
4	100423.497	■	11/11/2013	1.3.C	1.3.C	5,076.40	5,076.40	-	No	Single	5,076.40	-	5,076.40
4	100423.498	■	2/17/2014	1.3.C	1.3.C	6,236.72	6,236.72	-	No	Single	6,236.72	-	6,236.72
4	100423.499	■	12/17/2013	1.3.C	1.3.C	3,698.52	3,698.52	-	No	Single	3,698.52	-	3,698.52
6	100423.500	■	5/7/2015	I2.B	Other	2,411.94	2,411.94	-	No	Single	2,411.94	-	2,411.94
6	100423.501	■	2/19/2014	I2.B	Other	8,352.75	8,352.75	-	No	Single	8,352.75	-	8,352.75
5	100423.502	■	2/19/2014	1.1	1.1	5,542.60	5,542.60	-	No	Single	5,542.60	-	5,542.60
6	100423.503	■	2/19/2014	I2.B	Other	3,930.33	3,930.33	-	No	Single	3,930.33	-	3,930.33
6	100423.504	■	2/19/2014	I2.B	Other	9,110.33	9,110.33	-	No	Single	9,110.33	-	9,110.33
5	100423.505	■	2/19/2014	1.1	1.1	7,951.30	7,951.30	-	No	Single	7,951.30	-	7,951.30
2	100423.506	■	2/19/2014	II.6	■	8,806.00	8,806.00	-	No	Single	8,806.00	-	8,806.00
4	100423.507	■	12/13/2013	1.3.C	1.3.C	45,059.53	45,059.53	-	No	Single	45,059.53	-	45,059.53
4	100423.508	■	12/13/2013	1.3.C	1.3.C	64.75	64.75	-	No	Single	64.75	-	64.75
5	100423.509	■	2/19/2014	1.1	1.1	356.13	356.13	-	No	Single	356.13	-	356.13
4	100423.510	■	10/8/2013	1.3.C	1.3.C	19,638.68	19,638.68	-	No	Single	19,638.68	-	19,638.68
6	100423.511	■	2/19/2014	I2.B	Other	56,907.48	56,907.48	-	No	Single	56,907.48	-	56,907.48

FIGURE 10.99

Appendix 6.1

Offsite Hourly Work Claim

Category No.	Invoice No.	Type	's letter (Issue Date)	Attachment B Item	Category	Invoiced amounts (Exclude 5% VAT)	Outstanding per	Invoiced M-H	Reviewed by	Single/Multi	Invoiced Amount	Credit	Amount Outstanding
3	100423.512		2/19/2014	II.7	I.1	181,079.78	181,079.78	-	No	Single	181,079.78	-	181,079.78
5	100423.513		2/19/2014	I.1	I.1	874.13	874.13	-	No	Single	874.13	-	874.13
5	100423.515		10/31/2013	I.1	I.1	10,295.25	10,295.25	-	No	Single	10,295.25	-	10,295.25
4	100423.515		11/26/2013	13.C	13.C	13,633.76	13,633.76	-	No	Single	13,633.76	-	13,633.76
6	100423.516		1/9/2014	III.2	Other	123,642.07	123,642.07	568.95	No	Single	123,642.07	-	123,642.07
5	100423.517		2/20/2014	I.1	I.1	8,267.28	8,267.28	38.00	No	Single	8,267.28	-	8,267.28
4	100423.521		10/3/2013	13.C	13.C	291.38	291.38	-	No	Single	291.38	-	291.38
3	100423.522		3/19/2014	13.C	13.C	3,917.38	3,917.38	-	No	Single	3,917.38	-	3,917.38
6	100423.523		3/19/2014	II.7		91,859.22	91,859.22	-	No	Single	91,859.22	-	91,859.22
4	100423.524		3/19/2014	V.6	Other	61,841.43	61,841.43	-	No	Single	61,841.43	-	61,841.43
5	100423.525		3/19/2014	13.C	13.C	195,804.00	195,804.00	900.00	No	Single	195,804.00	-	195,804.00
6	100423.528		3/19/2014	I.1	I.1	25,064.20	25,064.20	195.55	No	Single	25,064.20	-	25,064.20
2	100423.529		3/19/2014	I.2.B	Other	86,133.69	86,133.69	453.15	No	Single	86,133.69	-	86,133.69
5	100423.530		3/19/2014	II.6		45,602.13	45,602.13	209.80	No	Single	45,602.13	-	45,602.13
4	100423.531		3/19/2014	I.1	I.1	62,160.00	62,160.00	320.00	No	Single	62,160.00	-	62,160.00
4	100423.532		3/19/2014	13.C	13.C	292,133.86	292,133.86	1,610.65	No	Single	292,133.86	-	292,133.86
6	100423.533		3/19/2014	13.C	13.C	360,374.28	360,374.28	1,942.00	No	Single	360,374.28	-	360,374.28
3	100423.534		3/19/2014	II.19.D	Other	84,512.96	84,512.96	571.00	No	Single	84,512.96	-	84,512.96
6	100423.535		3/20/2014	II.7		22,069.02	22,069.02	-	No	Single	22,069.02	-	22,069.02
4	100423.536		3/31/2014	I.2.B	Other	61,091.63	61,091.63	314.50	No	Single	61,091.63	-	61,091.63
5	100423.537		3/31/2014	13.C	13.C	379,673.06	379,673.06	2,029.50	No	Single	379,673.06	-	379,673.06
4	100423.540		3/31/2014	II.19.G	Other	1,332,990.12	1,332,990.12	6,127.00	No	Single	1,332,990.12	-	1,332,990.12
5	100423.541		3/31/2014	I.1	I.1	56,052.15	56,052.15	356.00	No	Single	56,052.15	-	56,052.15
4	100423.542		3/31/2014	13.C	13.C	294,844.45	294,844.45	1,673.05	No	Single	294,844.45	-	294,844.45
4	100423.549		5/1/2014	13.C	13.C	249,623.36	249,623.36	1,421.00	No	Single	249,623.36	-	249,623.36
6	100423.550		5/19/2014	II.19.D	Other	26,149.20	26,149.20	139.00	No	Single	26,149.20	-	26,149.20
6	100423.551		5/19/2014	II.19.B	Other	2,393.16	2,393.16	11.00	No	Single	2,393.16	-	2,393.16
4	100423.552		5/19/2014	13.C	13.C	5,003.88	5,003.88	23.00	No	Single	5,003.88	-	5,003.88
4	100423.553		5/19/2014	13.C	13.C	9,572.64	9,572.64	44.00	No	Single	9,572.64	-	9,572.64
6	100423.554		5/19/2014	II.19.B	Other	44,848.72	44,848.72	212.00	No	Single	44,848.72	-	44,848.72
6	100423.555		5/19/2014	I.2.B	Other	54,535.69	54,535.69	280.75	No	Single	54,535.69	-	54,535.69
5	100423.556		6/25/2014	I.1	I.1	93,033.57	93,033.57	664.05	No	Single	93,033.57	-	93,033.57
4	100423.557		6/25/2014	13.C	13.C	179,937.24	179,937.24	819.00	No	Single	179,937.24	-	179,937.24
4	100423.558		6/25/2014	13.C	13.C	98,396.76	98,396.76	446.00	No	Single	98,396.76	-	98,396.76
4	100423.559		6/25/2014	13.C	13.C	120,310.68	120,310.68	553.00	No	Single	120,310.68	-	120,310.68
4	100423.560		7/22/2013	13.C	13.C	73,342.33	73,342.33	385.60	No	Single	73,342.33	-	73,342.33

FIGURE 10.100

Appendix 6.1

Offsite Hourly Work Claim

Category No.	Invoice No.	Type	's letter (Issue Date)	Attachment B item	Category	Invoiced amounts (Exclude 5% VAT)	Outstanding per	Invoiced M-H	Reviewed by	Single/Multi	Invoiced Amount	Credit	Amount Outstanding
4	100423.561		7/8/2014	I3.C	I3.C	192,874.71	192,874.71	963.55	No	Single	192,874.71	-	192,874.71
6	100423.562		2/20/2014	III.2	Other	15,966.72	15,966.72	72.00	No	Single	15,966.72	-	15,966.72
5	100423.563		7/8/2014	I.1	I.1	7,428.12	7,428.12	35.00	No	Single	7,428.12	-	7,428.12
5	100423.564		7/8/2014	I.1	I.1	1,774.08	1,774.08	8.00	No	Single	1,774.08	-	1,774.08
4	100423.565		7/8/2014	I3.C	I3.C	3,480.96	3,480.96	24.00	No	Single	3,480.96	-	3,480.96
5	100423.566		7/8/2014	I.1	I.1	9,355.08	9,355.08	43.00	No	Single	9,355.08	-	9,355.08
6	100423.567		7/8/2014	II.19.G	Other	94,361.40	94,361.40	430.00	No	Single	94,361.40	-	94,361.40
4	100423.568		7/8/2014	I3.C	I3.C	72,012.36	72,012.36	331.00	No	Single	72,012.36	-	72,012.36
5	100423.569		2/14/2012	I.1	I.1	5,669,066.46	5,669,066.46	29,367.75	Yes	Single	5,669,066.46	-	5,669,066.46
4	100423.570		5/1/2014	I3.C	I3.C	1,116,609.12	1,116,609.12	5,056.00	No	Single	1,116,609.12	-	1,116,609.12
5	100423.571		7/11/2014	I.1	I.1	43,937.06	43,937.06	224.75	No	Single	43,937.06	-	43,937.06
5	100423.575		7/11/2014	I.1	I.1	9,627.03	9,627.03	45.00	No	Single	9,627.03	-	9,627.03
6	100423.576		7/11/2014	I2.B	Other	40,514.04	40,514.04	184.00	No	Single	40,514.04	-	40,514.04
6	100423.577		7/11/2014	II.19.B	Other	77,487.48	77,487.48	353.00	No	Single	77,487.48	-	77,487.48
5	100423.578		7/11/2014	III.2	Other	17,075.52	17,075.52	77.00	No	Single	17,075.52	-	17,075.52
5	100423.579		7/11/2014	I.1	I.1	73,973.76	73,973.76	512.00	No	Single	73,973.76	-	73,973.76
5	100423.580		7/11/2014	I.1	I.1	88,150.65	88,150.65	422.60	No	Single	88,150.65	-	88,150.65
6	100423.581		7/11/2014	I.1.H	Other	52,156.16	52,156.16	375.00	No	Single	52,156.16	-	52,156.16
6	100423.584		8/14/2014	III.2	Other	153,896.04	153,896.04	751.20	No	Single	153,896.04	-	153,896.04
5	100423.585		8/14/2014	I.1	I.1	18,731.16	18,731.16	86.00	No	Single	18,731.16	-	18,731.16
6	100423.586		8/14/2014	III.2	Other	21,067.20	21,067.20	95.00	No	Single	21,067.20	-	21,067.20
5	100423.587		8/14/2014	I.1	I.1	51,842.40	51,842.40	235.00	No	Single	51,842.40	-	51,842.40
6	100423.588		8/14/2014	V.6	Other	285,493.11	285,493.11	1,312.25	No	Single	285,493.11	-	285,493.11
4	100423.589		8/14/2014	I3.C	I3.C	194,951.30	194,951.30	1,081.75	No	Single	194,951.30	-	194,951.30
4	100423.590		8/18/2014	I3.C	I3.C	443,727.21	443,727.21	2,267.80	No	Single	443,727.21	-	443,727.21
4	100423.591		8/18/2014	I3.C	I3.C	4,322,110.32	4,322,110.32	19,515.00	Yes	Single	4,322,110.32	-	4,322,110.32
4	100423.592		8/18/2014	I3.C	I3.C	983,616.48	983,616.48	4,435.50	No	Single	983,616.48	-	983,616.48
5	100423.593		8/18/2014	I.1	I.1	4,133.64	4,133.64	24.00	No	Single	4,133.64	-	4,133.64
6	100423.594		8/18/2014	V.6	Other	43,099.04	43,099.04	216.50	No	Single	43,099.04	-	43,099.04
4	100423.595		9/3/2014	I3.C	I3.C	58,895.10	58,895.10	297.45	No	Single	58,895.10	-	58,895.10
3	100423.596		9/3/2014	IL7		392,118.89	392,118.89	2,529.45	No	Single	392,118.89	-	392,118.89
4	100423.597		9/12/2014	I3.C	I3.C	1,231,023.60	1,231,023.60	5,562.00	No	Single	1,231,023.60	-	1,231,023.60
4	100423.598		9/3/2014	I3.C	I3.C	84,189.90	84,189.90	382.15	No	Single	84,189.90	-	84,189.90
6	100423.599		9/3/2014	I2.B	Other	76,158.34	76,158.34	384.50	No	Single	76,158.34	-	76,158.34
6	100423.601		9/11/2014	V.6	Other	20,134.80	20,134.80	108.00	No	Single	20,134.80	-	20,134.80
2	100423.602		9/11/2014	I1.6	Other	4,380,749.97	4,380,749.97	21,689.05	Yes	Single	4,380,749.97	-	4,380,749.97

FIGURE 10.101

Appendix 6.1

Offsite Hourly Work Claim

Category No.	Invoice No.[1]	Type	's letter (Issue Date)	Attachment B Item	Category	Invoiced amounts (Exclude 5% VAT)	Outstanding per	Invoiced M-H	Reviewed by	Single/Multi	Invoiced Amount	Credit	Amount Outstanding
4	100423.603		9/11/2014	I3.C	I3.C	553,069.44	553,069.44	2,494.00	No	Single	553,069.44	-	553,069.44
5	100423.604		9/11/2014	I.1	I.1	240,806.88	240,806.88	1,848.00	No	Single	240,806.88		240,806.88
6	100423.605		10/18/2011	I.2.B	Other	526,488.08	526,488.08	2,878.50	No	Single	526,488.08	-	526,488.08
2	100423.606		9/24/2014	I1.6		1,950,747.48	1,950,747.48	8,912.00	No	Single	1,950,747.48	-	1,950,747.48
4	100423.607		9/24/2014	I3.C	I3.C	120,839.40	120,839.40	610.30	No	Single	120,839.40	-	120,839.40
4	100423.608		11/13/2014	I3.C	I3.C	121,245.30	121,245.30	612.35	No	Single	121,245.30	-	121,245.30
6	100423.614		11/11/2014	I1.10	Other	179,720.16	179,720.16	1,061.05	No	Single	179,720.16	-	179,720.16
4	100423.615		11/11/2014	I3.C	I3.C	132,867.90	132,867.90	671.05	No	Single	132,867.90	-	132,867.90
6	100423.616		11/17/2014	I1.G	Other	45,056.25	45,056.25	230.00	No	Single	45,056.25	-	45,056.25
6	100423.617		#N/A		Other	-	-	-	No	Single	-	-	-
5	100423.618		11/17/2014	I.1	I.1	53,551.35	53,551.35	275.20	No	Single	53,551.35	-	53,551.35
6	100423.619		#N/A		Other	-	-	-	No	Single	-	-	-
6	100423.620		11/17/2014	I1.10	Other	57,666.30	57,666.30	300.20	No	Single	57,666.30	-	57,666.30
6	100423.621		12/1/2014	I1.19 M	Other	53,329.92	53,329.92	384.00	No	Single	53,329.92	-	53,329.92
3	100423.622		12/1/2014	I1.7		299,929.65	299,929.65	1,962.00	No	Single	299,929.65	-	299,929.65
3	100423.623		12/1/2014	I1.7		561,786.37	561,786.37	3,004.75	No	Single	561,786.37	-	561,786.37
5	100423.624		2/16/2012	I.1	I.1	1,633,973.22	1,633,973.22	7,828.85	No	Single	1,633,973.22	-	1,633,973.22
5	100423.625		2/17/2012	I.1	I.1	49,642.56	49,642.56	247.00	No	Single	49,642.56	-	49,642.56
5	100423.627		12/11/2014	I.1	I.1	255,849.27	255,849.27	1,378.65	No	Single	255,849.27	-	255,849.27
2	100423.628		12/17/2014	I1.6	Other	377,498.52	377,498.52	2,305.10	No	Single	377,498.52	-	377,498.52
6	100423.629		12/17/2014	I.2.B	Other	142,776.99	142,776.99	856.60	No	Single	142,776.99	-	142,776.99
6	100423.630		12/7/2014	I1.7	Other	483,381.36	483,381.36	2,179.75	No	Single	483,381.36	-	483,381.36
4	100423.631		12/18/2014	V.6	I3.C	87,021.00	87,021.00	439.50	No	Single	87,021.00	-	87,021.00
2	100423.632		12/22/2014	I1.6		501,783.48	501,783.48	2,286.70	No	Single	501,783.48	-	501,783.48
3	100423.633		3/12/2013	I1.7		1,770,851.11	1,770,851.11	12,637.60	No	Single	1,770,825.31	-	1,770,825.31
3	100423.634		12/22/2014	I1.7		6,399.69	6,399.69	-	No	Single	6,399.69		6,399.69
3	100423.635		12/22/2014	I1.7		746,630.32	746,630.32	4,363.40	No	Single	746,630.32	-	746,630.32
3	100423.636		12/22/2014	I1.7		76,178.39	76,178.39	-	No	Single	76,178.39	-	76,178.39
6	100423.637		12/30/2014	III.2	Other	404,307.96	404,307.96	1,843.50	No	Single	404,307.96	-	404,307.96
6	100423.638		12/30/2014	III.2	Other	98,809.92	98,809.92	449.00	No	Single	98,809.92	-	98,809.92
4	100423.639		12/30/2014	I3.C	I3.C	61,931.52	61,931.52	432.00	No	Single	61,931.52	-	61,931.52
6	100423.640		9/25/2012	I.2.B	Other	208,335.60	208,335.60	1,052.20	No	Single	208,335.60	-	208,335.60
6	100423.641		9/25/2012	I.2.B	Other	396.00	396.00	2.00	No	Single	396.00	-	396.00
6	100423.644		1/28/2015	III.2	Other	852,105.10	852,105.10	3,924.45	No	Single	852,105.10	-	852,105.10
6	100423.645		4/2/2015	III.2	Other	275,918.35	275,918.35	1,310.95	No	Single	275,918.35	-	275,918.35
4	100423.646		1/28/2015	I3.C	I3.C	27,720.00	27,720.00	125.00	No	Single	27,720.00	-	27,720.00

6 of 9

FIGURE 10.102

Appendix 6.1

Offsite Hourly Work Claim

Category No.	Invoice No.	Type	"A" letter (Issue Date)	Attachment B Item	Category	Invoiced amounts (Exclude 5% VAT)	Outstanding per	Invoiced M-H	Reviewed by	Single/Multi	Invoiced Amount	Credit	Amount Outstanding
4	100423.647		1/28/2015	I3.C	I3.C	28,193.22	28,193.22	127.75	No	Single	28,193.22	-	28,193.22
5	100423.648		1/28/2015	I.1	I.1	57,657.60	57,657.60	260.00	No	Single	57,657.60	-	57,657.60
5	100423.649		1/28/2015	I.1	I.1	13,527.36	13,527.36	61.00	No	Single	13,527.36	-	13,527.36
5	100423.650		1/28/2015	I.1	I.1	15,523.20	15,523.20	70.00	No	Single	15,523.20	-	15,523.20
4	100423.651		1/28/2015	I3.C	I3.C	23,506.56	23,506.56	106.00	No	Single	23,506.56	-	23,506.56
5	100423.652		1/28/2015	I.1	I.1	4,292.64	4,292.64	20.00	No	Single	4,292.64	-	4,292.64
6	100423.653		1/29/2015	I1.19-A	Other	22,776.32	22,776.32	164.00	No	Single	22,776.32	-	22,776.32
6	100423.654		7/8/2014	III.2	Other	51,891.84	51,891.84	234.00	No	Single	51,891.84	-	51,891.84
6	100423.655		1/29/2015	II.19.G	Other	13,305.60	13,305.60	60.00	No	Single	13,305.60	-	13,305.60
6	100423.656		1/29/2015	II.19.D	Other	1,774.08	1,774.08	8.00	No	Single	1,774.08	-	1,774.08
6	100423.657		12/3/2012	I2.B	Other	24,171.84	24,171.84	109.00	No	Single	24,171.84	-	24,171.84
4	100423.658		1/30/2015	I3.C	I3.C	11,531.52	11,531.52	52.00	No	Single	11,531.52	-	11,531.52
3	100423.659		1/30/2015	I1.7		207,116.71	207,116.71	1,439.55	No	Single	207,116.71	-	207,116.71
6	100423.660		2/2/2015	I1.17	Other	57,485.34	57,485.34	283.25	No	Single	57,485.34	-	57,485.34
2	100423.661		2/2/2015	I1.6		40,637.52	40,637.52	190.00	No	Single	40,637.52	-	40,637.52
1	100423.662		2/2/2015	I1.5		34,065.50	34,065.50	162.40	No	Single	34,065.50	-	34,065.50
5	100423.663		2/5/2015	I.1	I.1	110,205.15	110,205.15	537.50	No	Single	110,205.15	-	110,205.15
3	100423.664		2/5/2015	I1.7		48,066.48	48,066.48	218.25	No	Single	48,066.48	-	48,066.48
6	100423.665		2/5/2015	I2.B	Other	36,184.50	36,184.50	182.75	No	Single	36,184.50	-	36,184.50
6	100423.666		2/5/2015	I2.B	Other	34,244.10	34,244.10	172.95	No	Single	34,244.10	-	34,244.10
2	100423.667		2/13/2015	I1.6		52,887.35	52,887.35	242.00	No	Single	52,887.35	-	52,887.35
2	100423.668		2/13/2015	I1.6		39,186.06	39,186.06	178.55	No	Single	39,186.06	-	39,186.06
2	100423.669		2/17/2015	I1.6		26,091.67	26,091.67	120.10	No	Single	26,091.67	-	26,091.67
2	100423.670		2/17/2015	I1.6		34,051.00	34,051.00	154.10	No	Single	34,051.00	-	34,051.00
2	100423.671		2/17/2015	I1.6		59,490.79	59,490.79	271.70	No	Single	59,490.79	-	59,490.79
5	100423.672		2/17/2015	I.1	I.1	16,664.03	16,664.03	118.65	No	Single	16,664.03	-	16,664.03
5	100423.673		2/17/2015	I.1	I.1	13,365.00	13,365.00	67.50	No	Single	13,365.00	-	13,365.00
6	100423.674		2/17/2015	III.2	Other	30,333.60	30,333.60	153.20	No	Single	30,333.60	-	30,333.60
6	100423.675		3/12/2015	I2.B	Other	54,390.60	54,390.60	274.70	No	Single	54,390.60	-	54,390.60
5	100423.676		3/12/2015	I.1	I.1	39,572.20	39,572.20	193.90	No	Single	39,572.20	-	39,572.20
5	100423.677		3/17/2015	I.1	I.1	6,435.00	6,435.00	32.50	No	Single	6,435.00	-	6,435.00
5	100423.678		3/17/2015	I.1	I.1	3,643.20	3,643.20	18.40	No	Single	3,643.20	-	3,643.20
6	100423.679		3/20/2015	V.6	Other	137,712.96	137,712.96	621.00	No	Single	137,712.96	-	137,712.96
5	100423.680		3/20/2015	I.1	I.1	150,575.04	150,575.04	679.00	No	Single	150,575.04	-	150,575.04
5	100423.681		3/20/2015	I.1	I.1	1,995.84	1,995.84	9.00	No	Single	1,995.84	-	1,995.84
5	100423.682		3/25/2015	I.1	I.1	22,461.12	22,461.12	110.20	No	Single	22,461.12	-	22,461.12

FIGURE 10.103

Appendix 6.1

Offsite Hourly Work Claim

Category No.	Invoice No.[1]	Type	Letter (Issue Date)	Attachment B Item	Category	Invoiced amounts (Exclude 5% VAT)	Outstanding per	Invoiced M-H	Reviewed by	Single/Multi	Invoiced Amount	Credit	Amount Outstanding
6	100423.683	▓	10/17/2011	I.2.A	Other	11,279.46	11,279.46	82.85	No	Single	11,279.46	-	11,279.46
6	100423.684	▓	10/18/2011	I.2.C	Other	22,416.46	22,416.46	134.55	No	Single	22,416.46	-	22,416.46
6	100423.685	▓	9/28/2012	I.2.C	Other	38,877.30	38,877.30	196.35	No	Single	38,877.30	-	38,877.30
6	100423.686	▓	12/3/2012	I.2.B	Other	16,889.40	16,889.40	85.30	No	Single	16,889.40	-	16,889.40
3	100423.687	▓	12/22/2014	II.7	▓	610,740.90	610,740.90	3,105.70	No	Single	610,740.90	-	610,740.90
3	100423.688	▓	4/2/2015	II.7	▓	47,698.20	47,698.20	-	No	Single	47,698.20	-	47,698.20
5	100423.689	▓	4/2/2015		I.1	54,471.84	54,471.84	272.75	No	Single	54,471.84	-	54,471.84
6	100423.690	▓	4/2/2015	I.2.B	Other	14,404.50	14,404.50	72.75	No	Single	14,404.50	-	14,404.50
6	100423.691	▓	4/2/2015	I.2.A	Other	6,881.28	6,881.28	48.00	No	Single	6,881.28	-	6,881.28
5	100423.692	▓	4/2/2015	I.1	I.1	44,744.48	44,744.48	228.95	No	Single	44,744.48	-	44,744.48
5	100423.693	▓	4/2/2015	I.1	I.1	10,605.38	10,605.38	54.50	No	Single	10,605.38	-	10,605.38
5	100423.694	▓	4/2/2015	I.1	I.1	13,461.30	13,461.30	104.65	No	Single	13,461.30	-	13,461.30
6	100423.695	▓	4/13/2015	I.2.C	Other	77,352.38	77,352.38	600.00	No	Single	77,352.38	-	77,352.38
6	100423.696	▓	4/13/2015	I.2.C	Other	31,110.94	31,110.94	160.00	No	Single	31,110.94	-	31,110.94
5	100423.697	▓	4/13/2015	I.1	I.1	33,561.60	33,561.60	253.50	No	Single	33,561.60	-	33,561.60
6	100423.698	▓	4/13/2015	I.2.B	I.1	21,948.55	21,948.55	170.00	No	Single	21,948.55	-	21,948.55
5	100423.699	▓	4/13/2015	I.1	I.1	39,375.00	39,375.00	200.00	No	Single	39,375.00	-	39,375.00
5	100423.700	▓	4/13/2015	I.1	I.1	88,410.90	88,410.90	447.05	No	Single	88,410.90	-	88,410.90
6	100423.704	▓	5/5/2015	III.2	Other	461,019.50	461,019.50	2,719.00	No	Single	461,019.50	-	461,019.50
6	100423.705	▓	5/5/2015	III.2	Other	8,940.75	8,940.75	55.00	No	Single	8,940.75	-	8,940.75
6	100423.706	▓	5/6/2015	III.2	Other	332,469.99	332,469.99	2,391.50	No	Single	332,469.99	-	332,469.99
6	100423.707	▓	5/6/2015	III.2	Other	768.00	768.00	6.00	No	Single	768.00	-	768.00
5	100423.708	▓	5/7/2015	I.1	I.1	105,948.17	105,948.17	704.80	No	Single	105,948.17	-	105,948.17
3	100423.709	▓	2/19/2014	II.7	▓	908,706.04	908,706.04	4,197.00	No	Single	908,706.04	-	908,706.04
6	100423.710	▓	5/7/2015	III.5	I.1	144,751.68	144,751.68	936.45	No	Single	144,751.68	-	144,751.68
5	100423.711	▓	5/7/2015	I.1	▓	14,706.00	14,706.00	86.00	No	Single	14,706.00	-	14,706.00
3	100423.712	▓	5/8/2015	II.7	▓	1,635,480.14	1,635,480.14	7,229.45	Yes	Single	1,635,480.14	-	1,635,480.14
3	100423.713	▓	5/8/2015	II.7	▓	271,623.67	271,623.67	1,263.50	No	Single	271,623.67	-	271,623.67
6	100423.714	▓	5/8/2015	II.17	Other	217,492.67	217,492.67	1,092.75	No	Single	217,492.67	-	217,492.67
6	100423.715	▓	5/11/2015	I.2.B	Other	260,780.63	260,780.63	1,320.00	No	Single	260,780.63	-	260,780.63
6	100423.716	▓	5/11/2015	II.10	Other	22,770.00	22,770.00	115.00	No	Single	22,770.00	-	22,770.00
1	100423.717	▓	5/13/2015	II.5	▓	1,560,944.32	1,560,944.32	22,994.25	Yes	Single	1,560,944.32	-	1,560,944.32
1	100423.718	▓	5/13/2015	II.5	▓	3,078,957.83	3,078,957.83		Yes	Single	3,078,957.83	-	3,078,957.83
3	100423.719	▓	5/21/2015	II.7	Other	191,668.76	191,668.76	1,239.35	No	Single	191,668.76	-	191,668.76
6	100423.720	▓	5/21/2015	III.2	Other	20,904.84	20,904.84	104.50	No	Single	20,904.84	-	20,904.84
6	100423.721	▓	5/27/2015	I.2.B	Other	1,664.00	1,664.00	13.00	No	Single	1,664.00	-	1,664.00

FIGURE 10.104

Appendix 6.1

■ Offsite Hourly Work Claim

Category No.	Invoice No.¹	Type	■ letter (Issue Date)	Attachment B Item	Category	Invoiced amounts (Exclude 5% VAT)	Outstanding per	Invoiced M-H	Reviewed by	Single/Multi	Invoiced Amount	Credit	Amount Outstanding
1	100423.722	■	6/4/2015	II.5	■	198,255.42	198,255.42	11,242.62	No	Single	198,255.42	-	198,255.42
1	100423.723	■	6/4/2015	II.5	■	2,240,903.89	2,240,903.89	-	Yes	Single	2,240,903.89	-	2,240,903.89
6	100423.726	■	9/1/2015	III.2	Other	178,892.81	178,892.81	-	No	Single	178,892.81	-	178,892.81
6	100423.727	■	9/1/2015	III.2	Other	3,582.75	3,582.75	-	No	Single	3,582.75	-	3,582.75
5	100423.728	■	3/7/2012	I.1	I.1	36,774.54	36,774.54	170.25	No	Single	36,774.54	-	36,774.54
4	100423.729	■	9/14/2015	I.3.C	I.3.C	22,720.50	22,720.50	114.75	No	Single	22,720.50	-	22,720.50
3	100423.730	■	4/2/2015	II.7	■	96,616.08	96,616.08	452.95	No	Single	96,616.08	-	96,616.08
4	100423.731	■	9/14/2015	I.3.C	I.3.C	66,676.50	66,676.50	336.75	No	Single	66,676.50	-	66,676.50
6	100423.732	■	9/14/2015	I.2.B	Other	29,686.88	29,686.88	150.00	No	Single	29,686.88	-	29,686.88
3	100423.733	■	9/14/2015	II.7	I.1	136,077.94	136,077.94	914.45	No	Single	136,077.94	-	136,077.94
5	100423.734	■	9/25/2015	I.1	I.1	5,306.40	5,306.40	26.80	No	Single	5,306.40	-	5,306.40
6	100423.735	■	9/21/2015	I.2.B	Other	19,230.75	19,230.75	99.00	No	Single	19,230.75	-	19,230.75
6	100423.736	■	9/21/2015	I.2.B	Other	235,040.06	235,040.06	1,200.00	No	Single	235,040.06	-	235,040.06
6	100423.737	■	10/9/2015	I.2.B	Other	5,536.13	5,536.13	28.50	No	Single	5,536.13	-	5,536.13
1	100423.738	■	10/21/2015	II.5	■	634,383.47	634,383.47	2,928.68	No	Single	634,383.47	-	634,383.47
6	100423.738	■	10/21/2015	III.2	Other	35,788.50	35,788.50	180.75	No	Single	35,788.50	-	35,788.50
1	100423.739	■	11/26/2015	II.5	■	193,712.51	193,712.51	885.85	No	Single	193,712.51	-	193,712.51
2	100423.740	■	12/30/2015	I.6	■	1,425.60	1,425.60	7.20	No	Single	1,425.60	-	1,425.60
6	100423.741	■	12/30/2015	I.2.B	Other	79,195.83	79,195.83	361.75	No	Single	79,195.83	-	79,195.83
3	100423.742	■	1/22/2016	II.7	■	12,722.63	12,722.63	66.00	No	Single	12,722.63	-	12,722.63
						$ 92,033,065.89	$ 82,728,318.36	502,661.06			$ 81,918,115.94	$ 2,608.00	$ 81,915,507.94

Sources:
Exhibit R-830
Report of ■ Exhibit NC-002, submitted by ■
Report of ■ Table 6, submitted by ■
Amendment ■ Nos. ■ 2013-0097 ($634,383 - Attachment B Item II.5) and ■ 2013-0111 ($35,789 - Attachment B Item III.2).
Attachment B
1) Invoice ■ 100423.738 is associated with two Nos. ■

FIGURE 10.105

Appendix 6.2

Invoice No.	Type	Reviewed by	Claim (Per) Invoiced Amount	Credit	Amount Outstanding
100423.061		No	$ 17,456.45	$ 13,779.90	$ 3,676.55
100423.062		No	8,617.29	4,490.09	4,127.20
100423.073		No	10,427.21	4,721.61	5,705.60
100423.074		No	11,073.28	-	11,073.28
100423.081		No	3,943.86	-	3,943.86
100423.082		No	9,983.34	6,277.54	3,705.80
100423.092		No	29,494.29	21,187.42	8,306.87
100423.093		No	986.76	136.64	850.12
100423.099		No	10,232.61	1,367.41	8,865.20
100423.100		No	19,299.98	8,792.74	10,507.24
100423.130		No	16,665.10	10,584.85	6,080.25
100423.131		No	16,087.84	6,506.47	9,581.37
100423.143		No	337,596.07	58,040.46	279,555.61
100423.143		No	Included in above	-	Included in above
100423.153		No	90,062.76	36,089.42	53,973.34
100423.153		No	Included in above	-	Included in above
100423.155		No	2,283.14	-	2,283.14
100423.186		No	2,544.94	1,980.74	564.20
100423.187		No	7,836.06	3,700.02	4,136.04
100423.207		No	212,094.44	78,858.00	133,236.44
100423.207		No	Included in above	-	Included in above
100423.208		No	78.79	-	78.79
100423.226R2		No	198,484.37	-	198,484.37
100423.229		No	276.83	276.83	-
100423.230		No	990.69	458.34	532.35
100423.271		No	2,645.05	1,872.00	773.05

1 of 4

FIGURE 10.106

Appendix 6.2

Invoice No.	Type	Reviewed by	Claim (Per ▮) Invoiced Amount	▮ Credit	▮ Amount Outstanding
100423.271		No	Included in above	-	Included in above
100423.273		No	203,642.76	28,080.00	175,562.76
100423.273		No	Included in above	-	Included in above
100423.289		No	88.00	88.00	-
100423.290		No	657.62	657.62	-
100423.318		No	8,612.98	4,003.64	4,609.34
100423.319		No	1,305.90	1,305.90	-
100423.320		No	5,759.02	-	5,759.02
100423.320		No	Included in above	-	Included in above
100423.324		Yes	338,034.19	54,288.00	283,746.19
100423.324		Yes	Included in above	-	Included in above
100423.355		No	663,039.60	455,761.69	207,277.91
100423.355		No	Included in above	-	Included in above
100423.360		No	377,012.77	375,144.96	1,867.81
100423.360		No	Included in above	-	Included in above
100423.361		No	3,012.21	-	3,012.21
100423.361		No	Included in above	-	Included in above
100423.379		No	5,627.90	3,760.00	1,867.90
100423.381		No	190,331.02	10,340.00	179,991.02
100423.381		No	Included in above	-	Included in above
100423.392		No	703.45	266.17	437.28
100423.410		No	67,007.68	-	67,007.68
100423.410		No	Included in above	-	Included in above

FIGURE 10.107

Appendix 6.2

Invoice No.	Type	Reviewed by	Invoiced Amount	Credit	Amount Outstanding
100423.415		No	242,906.05	1,880.00	241,026.05
100423.415		No	Included in above	-	Included in above
100423.439		No	1,057.99	1,057.99	-
100423.460		No	10,171.70	0.02	10,171.69
100423.460		No	Included in above	-	Included in above
100423.461		Yes	177,253.39	5,816.50	171,436.89
100423.461		Yes	Included in above	-	Included in above
100423.470		No	2,233.16	623.91	1,609.25
100423.484		No	310.03	310.03	-
100423.544		No	68,825.83	-	68,825.83
100423.545		No	203,927.31	5,720.00	198,207.31
100423.546		No	30,032.52	4,447.58	25,584.94
100423.547		No	2,318.66	243.64	2,075.02
100423.573		No	10,220.56	480.00	9,740.56
100423.574		Yes	1,306,312.44	0.02	1,306,312.42
100423.600		No	16,431.89	-	16,431.89
100423.611		No	1,423.64	-	1,423.64
100423.612		No	3,002,826.00	-	3,002,826.00
100423.613		No	56,375.19	-	56,375.19
100423.613		No	-	-	-
100423.642		No	280,127.27	-	280,127.27
100423.643		No	162,081.28	-	162,081.28
100423.701		No	102,030.59	19,476.70	82,553.89
100423.701		No	-	-	-
100423.702		No	6,648.22	1,420.23	5,227.99

3 of 4

FIGURE 10.108

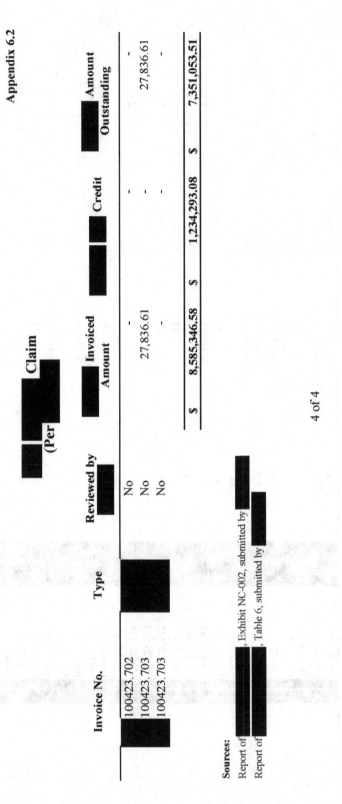

FIGURE 10.109

Appendix 6.3

Offsite Hourly Work

Attachment B Item	Category		Unreconciled Difference	Amount Outstanding
II.5		$ 14,370,167	$ -	$ 14,370,167
II.6		14,918,384	0.41	14,918,384
II.7		13,247,496	213	13,247,283
	Subtotal	42,536,048	214	42,535,834
I.3.C	As-built reconciliation	18,803,549	(4,127)	18,807,676
I.1	Design and Equipment Related Issues Found During Fieldwork	10,597,744	29,327	10,568,417
	Other	10,790,978	10,711	10,780,267
	Total	$ 82,728,318	$ 36,125	$ 82,692,194

Sources:

Exhibit R-830

Report of ███████████, Exhibit NC-002, submitted by ███████

1 of 1

FIGURE 10.110

The structure of this report is quite different. It is designed to conform to the rules and structure of the arbitral panel. Whereas the Rule 26 report, discussed earlier, was designed to communicate my opinions to a jury, this report is designed to communicate my work and opinions to the members of an arbitral panel. The members of the panel were trained lawyers and a construction industry expert. These men were far more sophisticated than a typical jury member and, therefore, the information in the report had to be presented in a different manner.

- Here we begin with an introduction that identifies me, the arbitral organization, my independence with respect to the parties, the amount of my compensation and a statement attesting to my genuine belief in the statements and opinions I intend to present to the arbitral panel.
- Next, I set out my employment history, education, licensing, and experience.
- Next, I provide a high-level summary of the significant events that led to the arbitration proceeding.
- Then I set out the background. I describe the parties and the contract.
- Then I begin to set out the details that created the dispute. I also talk about external factors that contributed to the disagreement.
- Next, I describe the override of and failings in controls that allowed the dispute to spiral out of control.
- Only then do I present my expert opinions.
- In the exhibits I include my curriculum vitae, the evidence I relied on and the analyses supporting my opinions.

Well, there you have it, the elements of two of the most common types of expert reports. Please keep in mind that expert reports may take different forms, but must comply with the rules of the venue in which they are presented and tell a clear, compelling story to the audience for which they are intended.

SECTION IV: FACT AND COMPUTATION CHECKING

Many years ago, I had a colleague who prepared an expert report that was produced to opposing counsel and ultimately at trial. The report contained an economic damage calculation that was based on computations performed in an Excel spreadsheet. The spreadsheet contained a column summarizing the results of the computations, which included subtotals. Unfortunately, my colleague's staff had included one of the subtotals in the sum of the individual amounts overstating the grand total. My colleague, unfortunately, did not recheck the results of the calculation in the spreadsheet believing that Excel was so robust that rechecking the results of the computations would be a waste of time. Opposing counsel did not perceive rechecking my colleague's spreadsheet as a waste of time. At the trial, my colleague's direct examination went smoothly. On cross-examination, after locking my colleague completely into the position that his computations were flawless, opposing counsel sprung the trap. My colleague endured almost eight hours of withering cross-examination about his error. Opposing counsel asked questions like, "Well, if that computation is incorrect, how many of your other computations are incorrect?" and "How can this jury have faith that any of your work is correct?" I cannot overemphasize how critical it will be to your success to have a colleague who did not work on the report recheck every computation and every piece of evidence upon which you rely in forming the expert opinions set out in your report.

EXERCISES

1. What types of reports have you seen?
2. What factors must be considered in choosing the type of report to be used?

3. What objectives must the investigation report achieve?
4. What are the elements of a good investigation report?
5. Write a qualifications section about yourself.
6. Write a case background about a case you worked on. Please be careful to anonymize (i.e. change the details so no one can identify the actual case you are writing about) your work.
7. Write an assignment section for an investigation you worked on.
8. Write out conclusions and opinions for a case you worked on.
9. What are the requirements of Rule 26 of the Federal Rules of Civil Procedure as they pertain to expert reports?
10. Construct a Rule 26 report based on an investigation you worked on.

CHAPTER SUMMARY/KEY TAKEAWAYS

So, here are some things to think about:

- The type of report you choose to create depends on the rules in the venue where you are providing expert testimony and the expected audience for the expert testimony.
- The elements of your report must satisfy the rules of the venue in which you are giving expert testimony, but, you and the attorneys have control over what, how and in what order you present the information in your report.
- Always have an independent colleague fact- and math-check every bit of evidence and computation in your report before it is released.

In Chapter 11 you will learn about the quantification of economic damages.

NOTE

1. https://www.ilnd.uscourts.gov/_assets/_documents/_forms/_legal/frcpweb/FRC00029.HTM

11 Quantification of Economic Damages

Lest you believe the measurement of economic damages is a minor aspect of the civil litigation process, overshadowed by the investigation and forensic accounting analysis of liability issues, I offer the following story from the NY Times:

> A month ago, Texaco Inc. was one of the nation's strongest companies. Today, the oil giant is reeling and on the ropes.
>
> Texaco suffered the body blow because a Houston jury decided that it owed $10.53 billion in damages to the Pennzoil Company for improperly luring Getty Oil from a merger with Pennzoil in January 1984.
>
> The huge judgment shocked the nation's corporate and legal communities: Few people outside the courtroom had been following the twists and turns of the complex four-month-long trial. When the jury delivered its verdict on Nov. 19, the question from all quarters was, what evidence did the 12-member panel hear that led it to hit Texaco with the biggest civil judgment in American legal history?
>
> During the trial, Pennzoil argued that it had suffered an actual loss of $7.53 billion because it did not get its share of the Getty Oil reserves it had acquired in the deal. In addition, it wanted another $7.53 billion in punitive damages.
>
> Pennzoil figured it would cost $10.96 billion to find and develop 1.008 billion barrels – the amount of reserves it thought it had acquired in its agreement with Getty. Pennzoil then subtracted the $3.43 billion it would have paid for the Getty reserves from the $10.96 billion, arriving at $7.53 billion.
>
> Thomas D. Barrow, a former vice-chairman of Sohio, testified for Pennzoil at the trial that those calculations were "conservative."
>
> Texaco's lawyers chose not to respond directly with testimony to refute the Barrow testimony or Pennzoil's claim for damages.
>
> He said the Texaco lawyers gambled that if the jury found Texaco had interfered with a Pennzoil-Getty contract, they would naturally conclude that Pennzoil should get no more than $15.50 a share for the Getty stock it anticipated buying. Mr. Miller maintained that the trial record was "replete" with those calculations.
>
> "When you have a strong defense on liability as we did," Mr. Miller said, "it is very defeatist to put on evidence of damages." Acknowledging that the tactic has since drawn a torrent of criticism, he said: "You're going to get second-guessed if you lose on whatever you did. That just comes with the territory."[1]

The jury only heard Pennzoil's damages case. Texaco put up no damages case, relying on what they perceived as the strength of their liability case. This was an unfortunate decision, indeed. As a result of this verdict, Texaco was forced to declare bankruptcy. The stakes don't get any higher than that.

At times you will be asked to provide expert testimony on liability issues and economic damages. I was retained by the minority owner of a media organization. At a time when the company was facing financial ruin, the majority owner who was also its CEO was spending enormous amounts of its money propping up his favorite hobby, a local art museum that had nothing to do with its media business.

As a result, the large corporate minority shareholder filed suit against the media company, its CEO, and its directors alleging a wasting of corporate assets. In this litigation, I was asked to formulate opinions in response to the following questions: Whether any transactions in the books and records of the media company represented a wasting of corporate assets? Whether any such transactions indicate that corporate funds were being used to further the individual defendants' personal interests rather than the media company's corporate interests? Whether any transactions bore any "badges of fraud"? The amounts of damages sustained by the newspaper with respect to each of the transactions referred to above. Through a review of thousands of documents and pages of sworn testimony, I was able to identify numerous transactions and entries in the records for which there was no clear business purpose. Those transactions amounted to tens of millions of dollars.

DOI: 10.1201/9781003121558-13

Specifically, the investigation revealed that the defendants had engaged in unusually significant and highly complex transactions that had no clear business purpose. In reality, these expenses provided the individual defendants with personal benefits at the expense of the media company's financial well-being.

Following a lengthy bench trial, the court found in favor of the plaintiff. The judge specifically ruled that there was a wasting of corporate assets and that the plaintiff had been defrauded.

Now came the second part of my expert testimony. In the work I performed above, I identified specific expense transactions that provided no benefit to the media company, but, did benefit the defendants. So, I put together a summary schedule of those amounts together with the supporting evidence. When I added judicial interest to this amount, the result was greater than $70 million USD. Of course my client was only entitled to that amount multiplied by his ownership percentage.

I tell you this story to illustrate that your work on the merits of your company's matter (i.e. the investigation of what happened) may also be used to determine the amount of economic damages. It is important to keep this in mind so that you do not have to analyze the evidence twice. That will make you more efficient and effective in conducting your investigation or forensic accounting analysis. Remember to always begin with the end in mind.

SECTION I: GAME THEORY AND SETTLEMENT

Before we begin describing about the quantification of economic damages let's discuss about settlement. Look, litigation exists for a reason. There are some disputes that cannot be resolved by mutual agreement. Mediators have a term for this best alternative to a negotiated agreement (BATNA). But, litigation is expensive. It is not uncommon for emotionally attached litigants to spend more in legal fees than the amount at stake. There is also the uncertainty associated with litigation. For those reasons, unless your company is bound and determined to litigate to avenge some wrong committed against you, explore whether settlement is possible.

The other benefit to exploring settlement is that if you pursue it intelligently, you can actually learn a great deal about the other side's perception of the strength of the merits of their case. Some time ago I developed a settlement model based on basic Game Theory. Work through the steps provided in Table 11.1 and I believe you will understand the tremendous value of going through this exercise in any settlement negotiation.

TABLE 11.1

Positive Theory of Litigation and Settlement

Settlement Advantages			
Lower out – of – pocket costs.			
Surplus monies available to the parties to use for settlement as a result of cost savings.			
Lower risk of catastrophic adverse outcome.			
Avoidance of collateral consequences; potentially including: criminal liability; regulatory issues; loss of business relationships; damage to brand; loss of market capitalization, and others.			

(Continued)

TABLE 11.1 (*Continued*)

Positive Theory of Litigation and Settlement

	Plaintiff	Defendant
A Simple Quantitative Example to Illustrate these Concepts:		
Assumptions:		
(a) The amount at issue equals $100,000.		
(b) The plaintiff believes there is a 75% probability that the defendant will be held liable.		
(c) Litigation costs are expected to equal $10,000 for each party.		
(d) Both parties are risk neutral.		
Expected Outcome of Litigation		
Risk Adjusted Value of Award ($100,000 × 75%)	$75,000	$75,000
Costs	$10,000	$10,000
Expected Cost Recovery ($10,000 × 50% × 75%)	$3,750	$0
Expected Total Risk Adjusted Outcome	$68,750	$85,000
Rational parties, in this instance, should be willing to settle at an amount between $68,750 and $85,000.		
In the preceding example, any amount between $68,750 and $85,000 would result in both parties profiting from settlement over litigation.		
This may explain why, in the USA, 95% of filed lawsuits settle ahead of trial.		
Questions, which naturally arise, include:		
Why do cases go to trial?		
What factors are present in cases that go to trial?		
If the case settles, what determines the amount that the parties ultimately agree on?		
What information can be gathered from settlement offers made by each party?		
Determinants of Choice for Settlement vs Litigation		
Determinants include to following:		
The quality of information, available to each party, about their chance of prevailing in litigation and the benefits vs costs of not prevailing.		
The underlying motivation of each party (i.e. Parties with unique sensitivities may settle for less than optimal amounts. Conversely, parties who have entered a dispute for a larger purpose, such as protecting a trademark, may be far less likely to settle on otherwise acceptable terms).		
Whether the parties are able to identify a risk adjusted amount that they perceive to be superior to what they expect to receive/pay in litigation.		
What the parties perceive to be their chance of prevailing in litigation.		

(Continued)

TABLE 11.1 (*Continued*)

Positive Theory of Litigation and Settlement

	Plaintiff		Defendant
What the parties perceive to be their cost of not prevailing in litigation.			
The extent to which the parties have asymmetric information about the case.			
Another simple example will demonstrate, quantitatively, how the quality and symmetry of information impacts settlement negotiations:			
Assumptions:			
(a) The amount at issue equals $100,000.			
(b) The plaintiff believes there is a 75% probability that the defendant will be held liable. However, defendant believes there is only a 25% chance of being held liable.			
(c) Litigation costs are expected to equal $10,000 for each party			
(d) Both parties are risk neutral.			
Expected Outcome of Litigation:	*Plaintiff*		*Defendant*
Risk Adjusted Value of Award: P($100,000 × 75%) vs D ($100,000 × 25%)	$75,000		$25,000
Costs	$10,000		$10,000
Expected Cost Recovery ($10,000 × 50% × 75%)	$3,750		$0
Expected Total Risk Adjusted Outcome	$68,750		$35,000
In this example Plaintiff should not be willing to accept anything less than $68,750, but defendant should not offer anything above $35,000. Clearly the parties have very different perceptions about the likely result of litigation. Two questions follow from this:			
Which party's perception is informed by superior information?			
Would it be in the best interest of the party, in possession of superior information, to educate the other party or to hold back the information to gain an advantage at trial? ($100,000 × 75%)			
Game Theory			

(*Continued*)

TABLE 11.1 (*Continued*)
Positive Theory of Litigation and Settlement

In the preceding example, quality and symmetry aside, each party can gain valuable information from the other's offer. Rational Choice theory suggests that each party should revise his own assessment of perceived risk adjusted litigation outcome based on the other party's offer. If, for example, the other party makes a significantly lower than expected offer; one of three things may have occurred. Either the other party has no motivation to settle; the other party has inferior information or the other party has superior information. It would be in the rational interest of each party to answer these questions to the best of their ability.			
Asymmetric information creates a measurable bias in favor of litigation over settlement.			
A simple example will illustrate, quantitatively, why this is the case:			
Assumptions:			
(a) The amount at issue equals $100,000.			
(b) If plaintiff has a strong case it will be worth $100,000 on a risk adjusted basis. However, if plaintiff has a weak case it will only be worth $30,000 on a risk adjusted basis.			
(c) Litigation costs are expected to equal $10,000 for each party.			
(d) Both parties are risk neutral.			
(e) Plaintiff has superior information about whether the claim is strong or weak. Defendant knows only that there are two possible claim qualities (i.e. strong or weak).			
(f) Defendant will make a take it or leave it offer.			
Expected Outcome of Litigation:			
		Strong	*Weak*
Risk Adjusted Value of Award: Strong ($100,000) vs Weak ($30,000)		$100,000	$30,000
Costs		$10,000	$10,000
Expected Cost Recovery		$5,000	$0
Expected Total Risk Adjusted Outcome		$95,000	$20,000
As can be seen, in the preceding example, if the case is weak plaintiff should be willing to accept $20,000, but, if the case is strong, plaintiff should not be willing to accept anything less than $95,000.			
However, the defendant has no information other than, due to the binary nature of the outcomes, that there is a 50%/50% chance of plaintiff having a strong vs. weak case. If the defendant definitely wants to settle; he/she will have to offer $95,000 in order to ensure plaintiff's acceptance. But, with a little mathematical reasoning, the defendant would conclude that the risk adjusted "worst case scenario" cost of making the lower offer is less. This can be demonstrated as follows: ($110,000 × 50%) + (40,000 × 50%) = $75,000.			
We can see from this example that, even in a situation where either party is at a disadvantage with respect to the other party's perception of the strength of their case, a great deal can be learned from the other party's behavior. This assumes that both parties are rational and are motivated by their respective financial interests.			

By going through this exercise, you will learn several things that are very useful. First, you may actually be able to settle the case in a manner that satisfies both parties' objectives. If you can reach settlement, you will save enormous professional fees and costs related to trying a case. Second, you may learn that your opponent is committed to litigation as a result of asymmetric information. In other words, you may know something incredibly significant that they do not know. If that occurs, you have an important strategic decision to make. Do you share the information with your opponent or do you save it for trial where it could do devastating damage to their case? On the other hand, you may learn that your opponent is not thinking rationally about the litigation. Finally, if nothing else, you will gain insight into your opponent's view of the merits of their case. All this information will inform your strategy in ways that will improve your chances of success. Also, you have, and your general counsel will have, evidence of your quantitative evaluation of each side's perception of the strengths of the merits of their case ahead of making strategic litigation decisions.

INVESTIGATOR NOTES

Once I was hired by a lawyer representing a bank that had inadvertently violated a large business customer's signature card instructions. The business had a CFO who entered the early stages of dementia. The CFO had been with the company for 40 years and other members of management could not bring themselves to discharge him. So, they created another position to which they transferred his duties and then quietly removed his ability to transfer company assets, incur liabilities, or enter into contracts.

To accomplish this at their bank, they changed the signature cards to remove his name. Unfortunately, the memo apparently didn't get to the bank employees whom the CFO normally dealt with. They allowed him to transfer almost $10 million USD to a broker through whom he acquired a number of risky securities, which lost a great deal of value by the time that company management discovered what had happened.

The company informed the bank that it intended to pursue litigation to recover its losses. The bank had a right to audit the company for compliance with loan covenants related to the company's debt with the bank. It was under this authority that the bank sent me to the company. At first, I was not permitted to proceed past the company's reception desk. Eventually, I was admitted to the president's office.

He expressed his anger about what had happened and the bank's refusal to make the company whole. I just listened (a good approach in situations like this one) and noted that as he continued to talk, he revealed that the company needed to maintain a good business relationship with the bank. He expressed no intention to move the company's business to another bank. After we spoke, I asked for a brief recess to call the bank's attorney. I called the lawyer and explained what I had learned in my conversation with the company's president. It's too long of a story to repeat here, but eventually we arrived at a settlement agreement between the bank and the company.

A structure was created where the bank contributed $9 million USD to an account that I controlled. The company created the authority for me to liquidate the securities acquired by the CFO. I liquidated the securities for as much as I could recover. Then I prepared an accounting of the company's losses and provided it to the bank and the company. Once both agreed, I transferred funds equal to the amount of the company's losses from the account the bank set up to the company. Then I transferred the remaining balance in the account to the bank. This is admittedly not a common remedy structure, but, in this case saved both parties millions of dollars in litigation costs and loss exposure.

SECTION II: DETERMINING THE PROPER MEASURE OF ECONOMIC DAMAGES

First, we need to understand the legal standards related to economic damages. These are the standards that be met to support the economic damages claim. These legal standards are important as they affect determinations of culpability. If evidence of the merits of the lawsuit does not satisfy these legal standards, the lawsuit may prove the defendant's wrongful conduct, but may not provide a remedy for the plaintiff. The legal standards that I am describing about are (1) causation, (2) reasonable certainty, (3) economic loss doctrine, (4) proximate cause, (5) foreseeability, and (6) duty to mitigate.[2]

Loss causation represents the connection between the defendant's wrongful acts and the damages suffered by the plaintiff. Causation is proved only when the wrongful acts of the defendant are the primary reason for the plaintiff's damages and there are no other factors that could have caused or contributed to the plaintiff's damages. Courts have challenged admissibility of the expert's testimony because the expert did not convincingly establish the link between (1) the defendant's wrongful act and (2) the plaintiff's economic damages. It is also important to understand that a plaintiff's economic damages may not be caused entirely by the defendant's wrongful act. For example, if several different entities caused the harm suffered by plaintiff there is, sometimes, a question of apportionment of damages between several defendants.[3]

Economic damages must not exceed an amount that an analysis of the evidence establishes with reasonable certainty. In other words, damages cannot be speculative. This is one place where you may need to counsel the counselors. If the attorneys are pushing for a damages amount that, in your expert opinion, is not supported by the evidence, you must push back. I have had to do this many times over the years. I always take the same approach. I tell the attorneys that I would be happy to testify to the amount they have put forward. I tell them that we could even likely get through direct examination. I then point out that I will likely get destroyed on cross-examination and that my testimony would then likely be excluded by the judge. They normally see reason at that point.[4]

The economic loss doctrine defines the extent of loss a plaintiff can recover in a tort case. A tort case involves a breach of a civil duty to another party. Torts can include: assault, battery, false imprisonment, defamation of character, interference with business, unfair competition, tortious interference with contract, trespass, negligence, and infringement of protected intellectual property rights. The plaintiff can only recover the losses related to a tort based on the economic loss doctrine. Recovery of actual monetary losses is precluded under tort law based on the economic loss doctrine. Victims are only allowed to recover personal injury or property losses.[5]

Proximate cause limits plaintiff's economic damages to the point at which the defendant's actions cease to "proximately cause" harm to the plaintiff. Proximate cause exists only when damages result from the defendant's conduct. In other words, if there were no defendant, there would be no damages to the plaintiff.[6]

Foreseeability means that the results or consequences of the defendant's wrongful acts are reasonably foreseeable. Foreseeability is related to the legal standard of proximate cause. Foreseeability is one of the fundamental tests that can be applied to aid in determining proximate cause.[7]

The duty to mitigate requires the plaintiff to take reasonable steps to reduce or altogether eliminate the loss that was caused by the defendant's wrongful act. Failure to take reasonable steps to mitigate damages will likely result in a reduced amount being awarded to plaintiff.[8]

There are three basic types of claims: contract, tort, or statutory.

A contract claim relates to a dispute that arises between parties to a contract. Parties to the contract and third parties identified in the contract are the only entities that have standing to bring a contract claim. External parties may, however, seek remedies through a tort case or a statutory case. A material breach of the contract is normally alleged by the plaintiff. Damages awards in breach of contract cases are meant to place the injured party in substantially the same position as the party would have been in had the contract been performed and not breached. At times the contract itself will contain language defining damages to be awarded to an injured party in the event of certain types of contract breaches.[9]

I described about the following example earlier, but I would like to describe about it in the context of our contract claim. Two mentally competent, adult parties can agree to anything that is legal. Contracts that are written do not contain provisions that are illegal and signed by mentally competent adults in exchange for consideration are normally upheld by courts.

The founders of a very successful financial services firm that served only life insurance companies had, what could only be described as, a falling out. One was Mr. Inside who handled the operations of the financial services firm. The other was Mr. Outside, the face of the company who handled all sales and customer experience interfaces.

One day, Mr. Inside had had enough, so he cancelled Mr. Outside's company phone, credit cards, etc. and changed the locks on the office doors. Mr. Outside was physically locked out of his own company. Realizing that the company wouldn't be much of a company without Mr. Inside and knowing there was no way to get Mr. Inside back onside, Mr. Outside decided to depart gracefully but sought the compensation laid out in the company's operating agreement under such circumstances.

I was retained by counsel representing Mr. Outside to calculate the amount of compensation due Mr. Outside and to investigate the opposing experts hired by Mr. Inside and critique their work. I made my calculations and included them in an expert report that was produced to opposing counsel. Opposing experts did likewise. Upon investigation, I discovered that one of the key opposing experts had an undisclosed business partnership, related to the activities of the company at issue in this matter, with Mr. Inside. A clear conflict of interest. The other experts performed a business valuation, for reasons which are still not clear to me since the operating agreement contained a straight-forward easily calculable remedy in its four corners. Some people respond to their own insecurity by wasting time and money on the complex when the simple and straight forward would serve them much better. Even so, opposing experts selected incorrect reference sources for key factors in its business valuation calculation.

These findings were kept from opposing counsel ahead of the hearing. The previously undisclosed findings produced several dramatic moments in the hearing. But, that would make my story too long. So, suffice it to say, opposing experts' testimony was completely impeached; my testimony came in unopposed. The tribunal awarded Mr. Outside everything he sought including professional fees. When I saw opposing counsel, who had been up to this point a social friend, outside the hearing room, his face was a lovely shade of candy apple red. He looked me in the eye and spat: *"Could you have made the <expletive deleted> number any higher?"* I could have asked him the same question.

What I want you to notice is that opposing counsel and experts tried to create a remedy that was in direct opposition to the black letter language of the signed written contract. That approach was rejected by the arbitral panel. Be careful that you and the attorneys you are working with understand what your expert testimony on damages must include to satisfy the legal standards of damages.

A tort claim damages award seeks to place the injured party in the same position they occupied prior to the tortious activity. The three common elements that should be present in every tort claim are: the existence of a legal duty to the plaintiff, the breach of that legal duty by the defendant, and the plaintiff experienced harm or damages due to a breach of duty. Tort claims include: defamation, tortious interference with contract, theft of trade secrets, breach of fiduciary duty, negligence, infringement, wrongful termination, and others.[10]

A statutory claim arises when the wrongful act is performed in violation of a federal or state law. There is usually a statutory definition of damages in these cases.[11]

Damages in matters which you investigate or provide forensic accounting analyses for will probably, over time, include all three categories of damages. Work closely with the attorneys to decide which category of damages you are calculating, the legal standards you must satisfy, and the remedies that are available.

Okay, now that you know the technical requirements for recovering economic damages, we will delve into how to measure economic damages. The preceding discussion may have made it seem that there are a relatively small number of techniques to measure economic damages. Nothing could be further from the truth. In fact, there are often many heads of damages which mean that there can be several different types of damages caused by the conduct that is the subject of the litigation. We'll take a look at some of those now.

SECTION III: PROPER TECHNIQUES FOR MEASURING ECONOMIC DAMAGES

The first thing to do when considering how to measure economic damages is to read the pleadings, if available, or consider what is known about a matter under investigation. Then, think about all the ways in which your company might have been harmed by the conduct. Think also about the types of claims your company may have available. Is there a contract claim, a tort, or a statutory claim? Then think through the legal standards that would need to be satisfied to prevail in the claim. Obviously, you are not an attorney, but I have given you enough information to begin thinking about these things.

We'll go over how to think about measuring economic damages for each type of claim, so let's assume you know how to do that and will include that in your thinking. Next, schedule a brainstorming session with the attorneys to hear their ideas and to share yours. The results of this exercise are that you should have a good starting point for your economic damages measurement work. The examples below are intended to illustrate some of the many forms economic damages measurements may take; it is not intended to be exhaustive. I leave the other ways in which damages may be measured to you. You will find that following the process I outlined, and, with a bit of research, you will find the correct manner to identify each head of economic damages and measure it correctly.

Now, let's take a simple example from my case files to illustrate how we might think about measuring several heads of economic damages resulting from one tort. This case concerned clever employees of a large corporation who set up their own business within the corporation. The corporation essentially bought raw materials, converted them to products and resold them through intermediaries. The clever employees recognized that the products could be sold for higher prices than the corporation was selling them. So, they simply inserted an entity, owned and controlled by them, in the sales process. They would sell the products at the higher price, pay the corporation what it was expecting and pocket the difference.

Following my earlier advice, we will begin with my damages opinions in my expert report and work backward through the economic damages measurement techniques I employed. Remember that this is a tort case, so recoverable economic damages were limited to property losses.

Expert Report of William L. Jennings
Page XX

IV. WORK PERFORMED AND OPINIONS

18. In order to calculate damages associated with the various allegations in this case, I reviewed bank statements, checks, and other items from 2008 to 2014 for various entities and people, which were produced during discovery in this case. All of the information contained in these bank statements, checks (e.g., payor, payee, date, amount, account number), and other items was entered into a database, which I used to trace cash flows and run analyses. See Exhibit 3 for a list of all of the bank accounts that I reviewed and included in the database.

19. I also reviewed other information and documents produced during discovery to further understand the transactions and cash flows. This information included, but was not limited to, emails, invoices, rebate statements, employment/consulting contracts, tax returns, check images, paystubs, PowerPoint presentations, Board presentations, warehouse inventory reports, and QuickBooks data. In my analyses below and in the exhibits to this report, I reference the specific documents that I used in analyzing specific transactions and cash flows.

20. In my opinion, XXX were damaged in the amount of $21,706,066 by the defendants' actions in this case.

21. The damages calculated represent actual damages incurred by the plaintiffs related to defendants' actions. These damages do not include any other damages or remedies that the plaintiffs may be entitled to, such as pre- or post-judgment interest, attorneys' fees, punitive damages, or treble damages.

22. My damage calculations are summarized in Table 11.2, and each category of damages is subsequently discussed in more detail. See Exhibit 4 for more detail.

So, here is my summary of the four heads of damages I identified resulting from the torts these defendants committed. There were profits on the illicit sales, rebates on the same sales, compensation paid to the defendants during a period in which they had violated their fiduciary duties to the company and losses resulting from their misrepresentations to the company.

TABLE 11.2

Damages Category	Damages Amount ($)	Reference
A. Profits from XXX **See A Below**	14,761,334	Exhibit 5
B. Rebates to XXX **See B Below**	1,191,352	Exhibit 6
C. Compensation Paid to Pete & RePete **See C Below**	1,066,394	Exhibit 7
D. XXX Misrepresentations **See D Below**	4,686,986	Exhibit 8
Total Damages	**21,706,066**	

In A., above, I am measuring the profits that XXX was entitled to which were diverted by defendants for their personal use. In B., above, I am measuring the rebates that XXX was entitled to which were diverted by defendants for their personal use. Because defendants violated their employment contracts and their fiduciary duty to XXX, they were not entitled to the compensation they received and I am measuring that head of damages in C., above. Finally, in D., above, I am measuring the damage XXX as a result of relying on the misrepresentations made by defendants in furtherance of their scheme.

In addition to the damages categorized above, I also conducted additional analyses of transactions that, while not directly leading to damages, did not seem consistent with normal commercial business practices:

a. I noted a large number of transactions labeled as counter checks, checking debits, and checking withdrawals. Further details about these counter check withdrawals are discussed in Section E of this report. I noted 136 such transactions totaling $15,476,277. See Exhibit 9.

b. I conducted a cash tracing exercise to follow the flow of funds into and out of the three primary bank accounts used by the defendants in the alleged schemes. Further details about this cash tracing are discussed in Section F of this report. See Exhibit 10.

c. I noted $473,932 in payments made to Jack & XXX. Further details about these payments are discussed in Section G of this report. See Exhibit 11.

A. Damages: Profits from Illicit Sales to XXX ($14,761,334)

2. Per the XXX, XXX purchased substantially all the assets of XXX and XXXVA and hired all of the employees of XXX and XXXVA as of May 1, 2011.[12] However, both XXXVA and XXX continued to sell Italian Shoes to XXX at marked up prices, inflating the costs incurred by XXX and depriving XXX of the lower prices at which XXXVA and XXX were able to acquire Italian Shoes.[13] Rather than XXX buying directly from the supplier, Pete and RePete – who, post-XXX, were a consultant and employee, respectively, at XXX – caused XXX to continue purchasing Italian Shoes from their companies, XXXVA and XXX.[14]

3. To calculate the amount that XXX and XXXVA created in profits on the inflated cost of the Italian Shoes sold to XXX, I analyzed XXX's and XXXVA's accounting records produced in this case for the period May 2011 to September 2015 and identified Italian shoe sales from XXX and XXXVA to XXX.

4. For each sale, I compared the sales transaction from XXX or XXXVA to XXX (i.e., the amount recorded in XXX or XXXVA's Accounts Receivable for that sale) with the amount that XXX or XXXVA had recorded for the purchase of that same inventory (i.e., the amount recorded in the XXX or XXXVA's Inventory Asset account). The difference between these two amounts is the "profit" that XXX or XXXVA recorded on these sales. See Exhibit 5.

5. I also reviewed supporting documentation, such as invoices, checks, bank statements, and emails produced in this case, for each of the transactions, which provided information about the nature and amounts of the transactions.[15] In addition, the emails provided information about the roles of each person in directing and approving the transactions.[16] Supporting documentation for each transaction can be found in the supporting documentation produced with this report in the folder corresponding with the "Reference" column in Exhibit 5.

6. Based on XXX and XXXVA's accounting data in QuickBooks, XXX's "profit" recorded on sales to XXX, identified by me, totaled $4,176,905 after May 1, 2011, and XXXVA's "profit" recorded on sales to XXX, identified by me, totaled $1,500,784 after May 1, 2011. See Exhibit 5, profits "As Recorded."

7. However, these profits are understated because XXX and XXXVA included abnormal charges (e.g., charitable contributions, sales commissions, employee bonuses) in

---

[12] XXX Recitals and Section 1.5, CCCC-EXPERT-012364-12482. Deposition of Tinkerbell dated 2/25/16, pp. 43:6 - 43:25.

[13] Deposition of Tinkerbell dated 2/25/16, pp. 44:8 - 46:1, 51:5 - 52:15, 54:4 - 57:10, 59:25 - 62:25, 66:16 - 67:9, 70:1 - 70:8, 72:5 - 73:20, 74:3 - 76:12. Deposition of Amerigo RePete dated 10/27/15, pp. 71:6 - 71:23, 147:23 - 148:10, 211:21 - 212:7, 220:24 - 222:2, 259:12 - 260:15.

[14] Deposition of Tinkerbell dated 2/25/16, pp. 44:8 - 46:1, 49:23 - 51:4, 51:5 - 52:15, 54:4 - 57:10, 59:25 - 62:25, 66:16 - 67:9, 70:1 - 70:8, 72:5 - 73:20, 74:3 - 76:12, 77:5 - 78:11, 78:18 - 79:24, 80:7 - 81:2, 81:8 - 81:21, 82:10 - 83:12. Deposition of Amerigo RePete dated 10/27/15, pp. 147:23 - 148:10, 220:24 - 222:2, 259:12 - 260:15. Deposition of Argo Pete dated 11/17/15, pp. 82:11 - 87:18.

[15] Deposition of Amerigo RePete dated 10/27/15, pp. 254:2 - 254:5, 254:10 - 254:14, 258:9 - 258:23, 259:2 - 259:9, 259:12 - 260:15.

[16] Deposition of Amerigo RePete dated 10/27/15, pp. 71:6 - 71:23, 132:4 - 135:16, 258:9 - 258:23. Deposition of Tinkerbell dated 2/25/16, pp. 49:23 - 51:4, 59:25 - 62:25.

the Inventory asset account,[17] which are not permitted to be recorded as inventory under generally accepted accounting principles ("GAAP"). These artificially high inventory values led to lower profit margins. To account for this, I recalculated XXX and XXXVA's profits after reducing their inventory values to reflect the actual value of inventory based on accounting records and testimony.

8. With regard to recording inventory, GAAP state that "[t]he primary basis of accounting for inventories is cost, which has been defined generally as the price paid or consideration given to acquire an asset."[18] In addition, "[un]allocated overheads shall be recognized as an expense in the period in which they are incurred. Other items such as abnormal freight, handling costs, and amounts of wasted materials (spoilage) require treatment as current period charges rather than as a portion of the inventory cost."[19] "Also, under most circumstances, general and administrative expenses shall be included as period charges …. Selling expenses constitute no part of inventory costs. … General and administrative expenses ordinarily shall be charged to expense as incurred …."[20]

9. After recalculating XXX and XXXVA's profit margins, XXX's "profit" on sales to XXX, identified by me, totaled $11,930,965 after May 1, 2011, and XXXVA's "profit" on sales to XXX, identified by me, totaled $2,830,369 after May 1, 2011. Thus, the total profits earned by XXX and XXXVA after May 1, 2011, were $14,761,334. Therefore, total damages for this category are $14,761,334. See Exhibit 5, profits As Corrected (see Figures 11.1 and 11.2).

So, the following schedules are the ones I used to calculate the profits from the illicit sales. It was a simple matter of identifying the transactions and finding the accounting entries related to each. Then I was able to calculate the revenues and costs as recorded by the bad guys and correct the amounts to their true values. This allowed me to calculate the difference between the profits that were recorded and the true profits from the illicit sales.

Exhibit 5 - Profit Analysis - Total Profit
Schedule 1

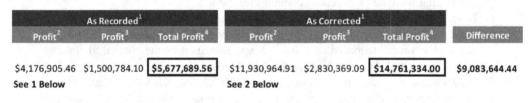

As Recorded[1]			As Corrected[1]			
Profit[2]	Profit[3]	Total Profit[4]	Profit[2]	Profit[3]	Total Profit[4]	Difference
$4,176,905.46	$1,500,784.10	**$5,677,689.56**	$11,930,964.91	$2,830,369.09	**$14,761,334.00**	$9,083,644.44
See 1 Below			See 2 Below			

FIGURE 11.1

Profit Analysis - Profit
Schedule 2

Type	Date	Numaret	Split	Debit		Accounts Receivable[2] ent	##	Profit[3]	e	ventor	Profit[7]
						As Recorded[1]				**As Corrected[1]**	
Invoice	10/17/2011	102	Big -SPLIT-	$	336,000.00	$ 336,000.00	##	$ 33,814.10	c	###	$ 126,000.00
Invoice	11/7/2011	104	Big -SPLIT-	$	329,310.00	$ 329,310.00	##	$ 84,150.00	e	###	$ 304,353.00
Invoice	11/18/2011	106	Big -SPLIT-	$	336,960.00	$ 336,960.00	##	$ 131,040.00	f	###	$ 131,040.00
Invoice	12/19/2011	108	Big -SPLIT-	$	831,600.00	$ 831,600.00	##	$ 110,430.00	g	###	$ 693,792.00
Invoice	12/19/2011	109	Big -SPLIT-	$	755,850.00	$ 755,850.00	##	$ 133,950.00	h	###	$ 618,345.00
Invoice	12/19/2011	110	Big -SPLIT-	$	657,000.00	$ 657,000.00	##	$ 26,726.76	i	###	$ 219,000.00
Invoice	1/16/2012	114	Big -SPLIT-	$	802,800.00	$ 802,800.00	##	$ 225,447.25	j	###	$ 267,600.00
Invoice	2/3/2012	118	Big -SPLIT-	$	12,015.00	$ 12,015.00	##	$ (3,741.00)	l	###	$ 4,005.00
Invoice	2/6/2012	117	Big -SPLIT-	$	855,360.00	$ 855,360.00	##	$ 380,160.00	m	###	$ 715,176.00
Invoice	3/6/2012	119	Big -SPLIT-	$	758,400.00	$ 758,400.00	##	$ 94,800.00	n	###	$ 618,570.00
Invoice	3/19/2012	125	Big -SPLIT-	$	782,100.00	$ 782,100.00	##	$ 260,700.00	o	###	$ 260,700.00
Invoice	3/19/2012	126	Big Sales	$	184,320.00	$ 184,320.00	##	$ 23,040.00	p	###	$ 161,280.00
Invoice	3/19/2012	127	Big Sales	$	160,000.00	$ 160,000.00	##	$ 60,000.00	q	###	$ 130,500.00
Invoice	5/13/2012	132	Big -SPLIT-	$	747,492.00	$ 747,492.00	##	$ 255,132.00	r	###	$ 613,212.00
Invoice	5/15/2012	133	Big -SPLIT-	$	1,503,130.00	$ 1,503,130.00	##	$ 597,630.00	s	###	$ 1,236,007.50
Invoice	5/18/2012	135	Big Income	$	9,990.00	$ 9,990.00	##	$ 3,846.00	t	###	$ 3,846.00
Invoice	6/11/2012	138	Big Sales	$	1,349,568.00	$ 1,349,568.00	##	$ 19,008.00	v	###	$ 1,069,200.00
Invoice	6/11/2012	139	Big Sales	$	338,040.00	$ 338,040.00	##	$ 38,040.00	w	###	$ 107,028.00
Invoice	6/26/2012	140	Big Sales	$	36,660.00	$ 36,660.00	##	$ 15,660.00	x	###	$ 15,660.00
Invoice	7/16/2012	141	Big -SPLIT-	$	760,320.00	$ 760,320.00	##	$ 190,080.00	y	###	$ 620,136.00
Invoice	7/23/2012	142	Big Sales	$	184,680.00	$ 184,680.00	##	$ 7,212.72	z	###	$ 7,212.69
Invoice	7/31/2012	143	Big Sales	$	372,000.00	$ 372,000.00	##	$ 71,006.04	aa	###	$ 71,006.04
Invoice	8/22/2012	147	Big Sales	$	372,000.00	$ 372,000.00	##	$ 72,000.00	bb	###	$ 72,000.00
Invoice	8/27/2012	148	Big Sales	$	355,200.00	$ 355,200.00	##	$ 133,200.00	cc	###	$ 289,710.00
Invoice	9/3/2012	149	Big Sales	$	405,120.00	$ 405,120.00	##	$ 151,920.00	dd	###	$ 330,426.00
Invoice	9/21/2012	150	Big Sales	$	162,000.00	$ 162,000.00	##	$ 5,604.00	ee	###	$ 5,604.00
Invoice	10/8/2012	152	Big Sales	$	363,000.00	$ 363,000.00	##	$ 61,000.00	ff	###	$ 61,599.96
Invoice	10/10/2012	153	Big Sales	$	712,800.00	$ 712,800.00	##	$ 142,560.00	gg	###	$ 572,616.00
Invoice	10/10/2012	154	Big Sales	$	176,400.00	$ 176,400.00	##	$ 25,200.00	hh	###	$ 50,400.00
Invoice	10/10/2012	155	Big Sales	$	2,132.00	$ 2,132.00	##	$ (2,768.38)	ii	###	$ (3,198.00)
Invoice	11/1/2012	156	Big Sales	$	570,240.00	$ 570,240.00	##	$ 142,560.00	jj	###	$ 430,056.00
Invoice	12/17/2012	157	Big -SPLIT-	$	665,280.00	$ 665,280.00	##	$ 525,096.00	kk	###	$ 525,096.00
Invoice	12/21/2012	158	Big -SPLIT-	$	783,000.00	$ 783,000.00	##	$ 132,120.00	ll	###	$ 243,000.00
Invoice	1/25/2013	161	Big Sales	$	260,253.00	$ 260,253.00	##	$ 29,681.97	nn	###	$ 58,293.00
Total				$	**16,931,020.00**	$ **16,931,020.00**	##	$ **4,176,905.46**		###	$ **10,629,272.19**

Type	Date	Numaret	Split	Debit		Accounts Receivable[2] ent	##	Profit[3]	e	ventor	Profit[7]
						As Recorded[1]				**As Corrected[1]**	
Invoice	9/1/2011	100	Big -SPLIT-	$	1,092,000.00	$ 1,092,000.00			a	###	$ 500,760.00
General Jou	9/1/2011	2	B E DLG 2008 I	$	652,400.00	$ 652,400.00			b	$-	$ 652,400.00
Invoice	10/17/2011	103	Big -SPLIT-	$	630,000.00	$ 630,000.00			d	###	$ 142,752.60
Invoice	1/31/2012	116	Big -SPLIT-	$	20,800.00	$ 20,800.00			k	$-	$ 20,800.00
Invoice	5/18/2018	136	-SPLIT-	$	3,370.80	$ 3,370.80			u	$-	$ 3,370.80
Invoice	1/1/2018	160	Sales	$	65,835.00	$ 65,835.00			mm	###	$ 15,800.40
Invoice	1/1/2018	163	Sales	$	27,864.00	$ 27,864.00			oo	###	$ (33,540.00)
Invoice	1/1/2018	164	-SPLIT-	$	4,941.00	$ 4,941.00			pp	###	$ (5,947.50)
Invoice	1/1/2018	166	Income	$	5,296.42	$ 5,296.42			qq	$-	$ 5,296.42
Total				$	**2,502,507.22**	$ **2,502,507.22**	##	$ **-**		###	$ **1,301,692.72**
Total Profit								$ **4,176,905.46**			$ **11,930,964.91**

See 1 Above   See 2 Above

FIGURE 11.2

B. Damages: CCCC, DDDD, & Shady Rebates to XXX & XXX/XXXVA ($1,191,352)

10. After the XXX, CCCC, DDDD, and Shady paid marketing rebates to XXX and XXXVA, companies Pete and RePete continued to own and operate in contravention of the XXX and related agreements.[21]

11. I identified all marketing rebates paid from CCCC or DDDD to XXX, XXX, and XXXVA. I identified these rebate payments in XXX and XXXVA's accounting records produced in this case, where they were noted as "DDDD Marketing Funds" or "Marketing Funds." I also identified these rebate payments in supporting documents, such as DDDD payment memos, emails, invoices, and checks. Supporting documentation can be found in the folder corresponding with each transaction, as denoted in the "Reference" column in Exhibit 6.

12. CCCC, DDDD, and Shady paid the following marketing rebates (transactions identified by me) from May 2011 to March 2012: $997,128 to XXX and $194,224 to XXX/XXXVA, for total rebate damages of $1,191,352. See Exhibit 6.

13. In addition to the damages listed above, I also noted that CCCC paid $1,239,926 in marketing rebates to XXX from May 2011 to November 2012. See Exhibit 6. Although XXX is a plaintiff in this matter, Pete and RePete both received 15% of XXX's net income as incentive compensation under their consulting and employment agreements. Thus, any activity that artificially increased XXX's net income would have also increased their incentive compensation.

C. Damages: Compensation Paid to Pete & RePete ($1,066,394)

14. As part of the XXX's closing conditions,[22] Pete entered into a consulting agreement with XXX and RePete entered into an employment agreement with XXX.[23]

15. Per the terms of the XXX, the consulting agreement, and the employment agreement, Pete and RePete each agreed to not compete with DDDD or XXX.[24]

16. Pete's consulting agreement included compensation of $8,334 per month plus 15% of XXX's net income paid quarterly.[25]

17. RePete's employment agreement included compensation of $8,334 per month plus 15% of XXX's net income paid quarterly.[26]

18. From May 2011 to April 2013, XXX paid Pete $532,588 in total compensation (regular monthly payment plus quarterly incentives) and paid RePete $533,806 in total compensation. See Exhibit 7.

19. Thus, in total, XXX paid $1,066,394 in compensation to Pete and RePete after the XXX was executed. Therefore, total compensation damages are $1,066,394.

D. Damages: XXX Misrepresentations ($4,686,986)

20. This category of damages represents the difference between what was purportedly being transferred in the XXX from XXX and XXXVA to DDDD and XXX and what DDDD and XXX actually received.

---

[21] Second Amended Complaint, para. 95. Argo Pete Consulting & Compensation Agreement, Section 3.1, CCCC-EXPERT-011977-011985. Amerigo RePete Employment Agreement, Section 3.2, CCCC-EXPERT - 011967-011976. Deposition of Argo Pete dated 11/17/15, p. 186:10 - 186:19.

[22] XXX, Section 7.1, CCCC-EXPERT-012364-12482.

[23] Argo Pete Consulting & Compensation Agreement, XXX00009450-9458. Amerigo RePete Employment Agreement, CCCC0001457-1466.

[24] XXX, Section 5.5, CCCC-EXPERT-012364-12482. Argo Pete Consulting & Compensation Agreement, Section 5(b), at XXX00009452. Amerigo RePete Employment Agreement, Section 6.3, at CCCC0001461-62.

[25] Argo Pete Consulting & Compensation Agreement, Section 2, CCCC-EXPERT-011977-011985.

[26] Amerigo RePete Employment Agreement, Section 3, CCCC-EXPERT-011967-011976.

21. On April 29, 2011, Jesse James sent an email to Dumb and Dumber and attached "a copy of the presentation made to the DDDD Board and the underlying information used for the valuation process."[27] In the "Key Acquisition Terms" section, the presentation shows that DDDD and XXX would be purchasing two things in the proposed transactions (1) "the following assets from XXX Texas, New Mexico" and (2) "Payment for Value of Business."

22. The assets of XXX and XXXVA to be purchased included Sellable Inventory (At XXX cost or realizable value); Collectable Accounts Receivable; Furniture Fixtures and Equipment; and Prepaid Expenses and Supplies. As discussed below, the value of the Sellable Inventory included in the XXX was overstated.

23. The value of the inventory transferred in the XXX appears to have been overstated for two reasons: (1) incorrect accounting for the value of the inventory, and (2) overstating the value of the business due to misrepresentations regarding the business' normalized earnings.

24. With regard to incorrect accounting for inventory, GAAP state that "[t]he primary basis of accounting for inventories is cost, which has been defined generally as the price paid or consideration given to acquire an asset."[28] In addition, "[un]allocated overheads shall be recognized as an expense in the period in which they are incurred. Other items such as abnormal freight, handling costs, and amounts of wasted materials (spoilage) require treatment as current period charges rather than as a portion of the inventory cost."[29] "Also, under most circumstances, general and administrative expenses shall be included as period charges .... Selling expenses constitute no part of inventory costs. ... General and administrative expenses ordinarily shall be charged to expense as incurred ...."[30]

25. Thus, costs such as freight costs, commission payments, employee bonuses, prepayment of utilities, and charitable contributions should not be included in inventory. However, it appears that XXX/XXXVA did include such costs in their inventory.[31] For example, a series of emails from Pete shows that XXX/XXXVA recorded 47,520 cartons of Italian Shoes at $12.00 per carton ($570,240), although it purchased the Italian Shoes for only $2.95 per carton from Giuseppe USA ($140,184).[32] In testimony, defendants stated that the "cost" of the Italian Shoes included various other costs such as tens of thousands of dollars in contributions to several civic and charitable groups; a $2 per carton commission to Cersei; purchases and prepayments of bulk snack items and beverages; and freight charges.[33] All of these costs should have been expensed in the period incurred rather than included in inventory under GAAP.

26. With regard to the inflated valuation of the XXX/XXXVA business, the Board presentation (dated February 2, 2011 in the filename) contained a slide entitled

---

[27] Email dated April 29, 2011, from Jesse James to Dumb and Dumber, copying Rabbit, including the attached file "DDDD Board Presentation of XXX Companies Board Presentation Version 02 02 2011.ppt". CCCC - EXPERT-012013-012050. Deposition of Argo Pete dated 11/17/15, pp. 45:6 - 47:19.

[28] XXX 330-10-30-1.

[29] XXX 330-10-30-7.

[30] XXX 330-10-30-8.

[31] Deposition of Amerigo RePete dated 10/27/15, pp. 254:2 - 254:5, 254:10 - 254:14, 259:2 - 259:9, 259:12 - 260:15. Deposition of Argo Pete dated 11/17/15, pp. 136:9 - 138:22.

[32] CCCC-EXPERT-011613-011618 at 011617. Although the emails were sent in 2013, I assumed that this inflation of inventory values is representative of XXX/XXXVA's normal course of business even before the XXX. *See* Deposition of Tinkerbell dated 2/25/16, pp. 91:18 - 92:9. Deposition of Amerigo RePete dated 10/27/15, pp. 254:2 - 254:5, 254:10 - 254:14, 259:2 - 259:9, 259:12 - 260:15.

[33] Deposition of Amerigo RePete dated 10/27/15, pp. 254:2 - 254:5, 254:10 - 254:14, 259:2 - 259:9, 259:12 - 260:15. Deposition of Argo Pete dated 11/17/15, pp. 136:9 - 138:22.

"Potential Target Valuation of the Business Operations," which calculated XXX/XXXVA's "Value of Business Operations" at $3,594,039 based on an "excess earnings" valuation methodology.[34]

27. The business value of XXX and XXXVA to be purchased represents the value of the businesses over and above the expected return from the companies' assets (i.e., goodwill). As discussed below, the business value included in this presentation – and embedded in the purchase price in the XXX – was overstated.

28. The excess earnings methodology is meant to represent the value of a business' operations in excess of the expected return from the investment in its tangible assets (e.g., accounts receivable, inventory, furniture and fixtures). In the presentation to DDDD's Board, XXX/XXXVA reported that it had "normalized net income before taxes" of $2,458,013, which exceeded the $1,260,000 required return on its investment in tangible assets (18% × $7,000,000) by $1,198,013 annually. The Board presentation then uses a multiple of 3.0 (i.e., three years' worth of these excess earnings) to arrive at a $3,594,039 valuation of the business operations ($1,198,013 × 3).

29. However, the "normalized net income before taxes" used in the presentation was inflated because it was based on artificially inflated sales and artificially low product costs.[35]

30. First, the "normalized net income before taxes" figure of $2,458,013 is incorrect because these earnings were based on artificial, "churning account" sales transactions that could not be replicated in normal commercial operations.[36] In fact, Pete testified that all of XXX and XXXVA's post-XXX sales were the result of churning account transactions.[37] Thus, the businesses' actual "normalized net income before taxes" should have been zero, which would in turn lead to a business value of zero under the excess earnings methodology. Second, even if such churning sales did continue after the XXX transaction, the normalized net income reported in the Board presentation would not have been achievable by XXX because XXX would have had a much higher cost of goods sold.[38]

31. Finally, I noted that a February 17, 2011, email believed to be from Pete to RePete and Tim Pete states: "[t]he Board was presented a bogus profit & loss."[39] This statement appears in a section of the email entitled "Meet the demands of and promises to DDDD." Thus, it appears that Pete and RePete were aware that the information presented to the DDDD Board was incorrect at the time it was presented.

32. As part of the Closing Payment made under the XXX, XXX paid $5,519,220 to XXX and XXXVA for "Estimated Inventory Value", which purportedly represented the estimated value of Italian Shoes in warehouses in Texas and New Mexico.[40]

33. I reviewed the documents provided by the Defendants to support the value of the inventory included in the XXX.[41]

---

[34] "DDDD Board Presentation of XXX Companies Board Presentation Version 02 02 2011.ppt", slide 20 (entitled "Potential Target Valuation of the Business Operations"). CCCC-EXPERT-012013-012050 at 012041.

[35] Deposition of Argo Pete dated 11/17/15, pp. 82:11 - 87:18.

[36] Deposition of Tinkerbell dated 2/25/16, pp. 51:5 - 52:15.

[37] Deposition of Argo Pete dated 11/17/15, pp. 93:23 - 94:2. Deposition of Tinkerbell dated 2/25/16, pp. 51:5 - 52:15.

[38] Deposition of Tinkerbell dated 2/25/16, pp. 91:18 - 92:9, 131:2 - 132:1. Deposition of Argo Pete dated 11/17/15, pp. 82:11 - 87:18.

[39] Email dated February 17, 2011, from Slim Shady to RePete and Tim Pete, CCCC-EXPERT- 012011-012012. Deposition of Argo Pete dated 11/17/15, pp. 54:20 - 60:16.

[40] XXX, Section 2.1(a), CCCC-EXPERT-012364-12482. Deposition of Stephen Jesse James dated 9/22/15, pp. 173:20 – 177:5, 178:15 – 181:16, 190:23 – 193:5, 322:19 – 323:13. Deposition of Amerigo RePete dated 10/27/15, pp. 110:9 – 111:4, 112:19 – 114:13.

[41] Exhibits to Defendant's Supplemental Responses to Plaintiff's First Request for Production.

34. Defendants only provided supporting documentation for $832,235 of Italian Shoes, but did not provide supporting documents related to the remaining $4,686,986 of inventory. See Exhibit 8. Therefore, damages due to misrepresentations in the XXX are $4,686,986.

E. XXX, XXXVA, & XXX Counter Check Withdrawals ($15,476,277)

35. Within the database, I identified all transactions after May 1, 2011, labeled as counter checks, checking debits, and checking withdrawals from the bank accounts associated with XXX, XXXVA, and XXX (listed in Tables 11.3 & 11.4).

TABLE 11.3

Account Holders	Bank	Account Ending in
XXXVA/XXX	Regions	1297
XXX/XXX	Regions	2214
XXX/Marketing Group	Regions	2222
XXXVA/RePete	Regions	2568
XXXVA Management Account	Regions	2928
XXX Holdings, LLC	Regions	3939
XXX/Pete	Regions	5159
XXXVA	Regions	6580

---

36. Counter checks are not written to a specific payee. Therefore, in the case of counter checks, I identified the person making the counter check as the signer. This signer was authorizing the transaction and able to leave the bank with cash or use the counter check to fund a cashier's check.

37. I also reviewed supporting documentation associated with the counter checks, such as emails, corresponding cashier's checks, and bank statements, for each of the transactions, which provided additional context regarding the nature of the transaction.

38. I determined that there were 136 transactions after May 1, 2011, totaling $15,476,277 where money was withdrawn from a bank account associated with XXX, XXXVA, and/or XXX. See Exhibit 9.[42]

39. Of these transactions, I was able to trace 55 transactions totaling $5,795,294 to the ultimate recipient of the funds via cashier's checks. See Exhibit 9.

F. Transaction Tracing

40. I traced the flow of funds into and out of the following three bank accounts after the date of the XXX.[43] These three accounts contained the great majority of transaction activity in terms of both number of transactions and dollar volume. In addition, I calculated a running account balance based on such inflows and outflows for each account as shown in Table 11.4. See Exhibit 10.

---

[42] Deposition of Tinkerbell dated 2/25/16, pp. 43:6 – 43:25, 44:8 – 46:1, 117:7 – 118:6, 119:20 – 123:12, 131:2 – 134:1.

[43] "[T]racing refers to the search for evidence showing what has happened to property, identifying the proceeds of property, and identifying those who have handled property or the proceeds of property. That is, tracing involves accounting for the movement of assets in and out of accounts." 2015 Fraud Examiner's Manual, p. 3.909, Association of Certified Fraud Examiners.

TABLE 11.4

Account Holders	Bank	Account Ending in
XXXVA/XXX	Regions	1297
XXXVA Management Account	Regions	2928
XXXVA	Regions	6580

41. Funds from various plaintiff sources flowed into these accounts as a result of the defendants' activities described above, including: proceeds of the XXX; rebates from CCCC, DDDD, and/or Shady; and income generated from inventory sales to XXX.[44]

42. Funds flowed out of these accounts via various methods, including counter checks, checking debits, and checking withdrawals. Where supporting documentation was available, i.e., the purchase of related cashier's checks, I noted the identified payee of each counter check, checking debit, and/or checking withdrawal.[45]

43. In conducting this analysis, I used a method of tracing known as the Bank Deposits Method.[46] If an account was funded from comingled sources, including allegedly illegitimate sources (e.g., proceeds from profits from XXX and XXXVA sales to XXX), creating a balance sufficient to cover expenditures; then any expenditure from that account was deemed to have been made with the Plaintiff's funds.

G. Payments to Dewey Cheatum & How Consulting ($473,932)

44. Jesse James was an executive at DDDD at the same time that he owned and operated Dewey Cheatum & How.

45. Within the database, I identified all payments to Dewey Cheatum & How.[47] I also included all payments to Jesse James, as all such checks were deposited into a Dewey Cheatum & How bank account.[48] Jesse James and Dewey Cheatum & How held a joint SunTrust bank account.[49]

46. I determined that Dewey Cheatum & How received 7 checks and cashier's checks totaling $473,932 from May 2011 to October 2012. See Exhibit 11.[50]

<signature>
<Source> William Jennings
March XX, XXXX

Okay, so that's a nice simple example of how you can identify and measure multiple heads of economic damages. Now let's turn to something a bit more complex.

The following report was used to quantify economic damages in an arbitration hearing about construction defects in a pipeline project. The matter was complicated because the plaintiff was a regulated utility. So, I had to explain not only the direct cause of the economic damages, but also the complex regulatory issues that created further economic damages for LZU Company.

<Report Head> **Expert Report of**
<Report_AU> **By: William L. Jennings**

In the Matter of Arbitration Between:
LZU Company, Claimant
v.
Glove Company, Respondent

As of MM/DD/YYYY
AAA Case No. XX

<page break>

Table of Contents

I. INTRODUCTION

1. My name is William L. Jennings.
2. I have been asked by counsel for claimant, in connection with the LZU Services Company v. Glove Construction Company arbitration under the Construction Industry Arbitration Rules of the American Arbitration Association, to provide my opinions on the accounting and damages issues present in this arbitration. I have also been asked to provide background on the regulatory environment in which LZU operates. My firm's billing rates for this engagement range from $XX to $XX per hour.
3. I am the Managing Member of Verite' Forensic Accounting ("Verite"). Previously, my positions included: Managing Director at Alvarez & Marsal in the Global Forensic and Dispute Services practice; Managing Director in the Disputes and Investigations Practice at Navigant Consulting, Inc.; Director in the National Forensic Accounting Practice at LECG, LLC; President of FFI, Inc.; Managing Director at Kroll, Inc., in charge of investigative accounting services for the Central Region; Principal-in-Charge of the Madison office of Lindquist, Avey, Macdonald, Baskerville, a multi-national independent forensic accounting firm; Principal-in-Charge of Coopers & Lybrand's Fraud Investigation Services practice for the Southeast Region; and Partner in the public accounting firm of Brown & Jennings.
4. I have a Bachelor of Science degree in Accounting and a Master's degree in Business Administration. I have been a Certified Public Accountant since 1981 and a Certified Fraud Examiner since 1991. I have more than 30 years of experience in forensic accounting, business controls development, public accounting and auditing.
5. I have substantial experience in forensic accounting, investigation, asset recovery, business valuation, business controls development, public accounting and auditing

for regulated utilities. I have provided forensic accounting services to corporations, U.S. Attorneys' Offices, other government agencies, attorneys and their clients. I have also provided business controls consulting services to organizations. I have often provided expert testimony about the results of my work in federal and state courts as well as in many other dispute resolution venues. I have worked on hundreds of forensic accounting and investigation assignments. Further, I am a frequent public speaker on a variety of topics including white-collar crime, fraud investigation, forensic accounting and business ethics. I have also published articles relating to fraud and forensic accounting. Details regarding my background, education, publications, speaking engagements and expert testimony are included in my curriculum vitae, attached as Exhibit A.

II. BACKGROUND

6. On September 25, 2018, LZU Services Company ("LZU" or the "Company"), as the Claimant, and Glove Construction Company ("Glove"), as the Respondent, jointly filed a Demand for Arbitration and Request for Mediation ("Demand for Arbitration") with the American Arbitration Association. The parties agreed that disputes not resolved informally through mediation would be resolved through binding arbitration under the Construction Industry Arbitration Rules of the American Arbitration Association.[1]

7. The following is based on my review of the Demand for Arbitration, contracts related to the dispute, various Wisconsin Public Service Commission ("PSC") public filings, research I conducted related to the parties and the regulation of public utilities, and my skills, knowledge, education, training, and experience.

THE PARTIES

8. LZU is a wholly owned subsidiary of LZU Resources Inc., which is one of the oldest natural gas-only distribution companies in the United States, providing for the energy needs of millions of American households and businesses. Headquartered in Madison, Wisconsin, LZU has more than 150 years of experience and owns thousands of miles of underground pipeline in the United States for transporting natural gas, including thousands of miles of pipeline in Wisconsin.[2]

9. Glove is a construction company that has served the natural gas transmission pipeline industry for over 65 years. Headquartered near Madison, Wisconsin, and with roots in Illinois and Michigan, Glove has completed numerous projects involving the construction of large diameter cross-country transmission pipelines.[3]

10. The dispute between the parties arises from work Glove performed on LZU's Lake Michigan Pipeline Project ("LMPP" or the "Project").[4] The Project was an effort to replace a 35AT mile segment of buried natural gas transmission bare steel pipeline that runs through suburban Madison neighborhoods from Kenosha County, through Madison County, to a connection point in Racine County.[5] LZU and PSC

---

[1] *See, e.g.,* LZU Services Company v. Glove Construction Company Demand for Arbitration and Request for Mediation dated September 25, 2016.

[2] *Id.,* p. 2–3.

[3] *See, e.g.,* Glove Construction Company website (www.Gloveconstruction.com).

[4] *See* LZU Services Company v. Glove Construction Company Demand for Arbitration and Request for Mediation dated September 25, 2016, p. 1.

[5] *See* LZU Services Company v. Glove Construction Company Demand for Arbitration and Request for Mediation dated September 25, 2016, p. 1; GSPC DN 8516 Document Filing No. 151511: Staff's Letter Concerning PRP Issues dated January 23, 2014, p. 2.

Pipeline Safety Staff agreed to include the LMPP as part of its large-scale Pipeline Replacement Program ("PRP") in December 2009. The deadline to complete the bare steel pipe portion of the PRP was December 31, 2017.[6]

11. According to the Demand for Arbitration, "LZU hired Glove to install the new pipeline, and in doing so, to ensure that the integrity of the protective coating remained intact during the installation, among other responsibilities."[7] Glove performed its work on the Project pursuant to a Master Agreement dated July 3, 2017 and a related Statement of Work dated August 15, 2017.[8] LZU supplied the pipe for the Project, and "Glove assumed care, custody and control, and all risk of loss or damage to the pipe."[9]

12. Glove agreed to provide its "best efforts" to properly install the pipe, to supervise the installation using its "best skill and attention," and to conduct daily "Best Management Practices" inspections of the installation.[10] LZU alleges that Glove breached its contractual obligations to LZU by:

> [A]mong other things: [f]ailing to adequately inspect the pipe coating prior to the pipe's installation and to correct any defects in the coating; [f]ailing to ensure that the coating was not damaged during the pipe's installation; [f]ailing to identify and advise of the lack of a temporary cathodic protection system; and [f]ailing to install the pipe in a manner that complied with the Project drawings and specifications, best industry practices, or even reasonable industry practices.[11]

LZU alleges that these failures resulted in widespread external deterioration throughout large segments of the new pipeline.[12]

13. Glove commenced its work installing the new pipeline in late 2012 and was to complete its work on the Project by the agreed upon Completion Date of September 30, 2017.[13] LZU states that in the summer of 2017, before natural gas had ever been introduced into the new pipeline, it discovered that large portions of the pipeline had suffered extensive external deterioration damage. LZU then launched an investigation into the damage. The Company found that the protective coating had been damaged during the pipeline's installation, which enabled widespread external deterioration across large segments of the new pipeline.[14] LZU closed the PRP on December 31, 2017 without having completed construction of the LMPP.[15] The Company subsequently undertook efforts to excavate and replace several thousand

---

[6] *See, e.g.,* WISC DN 8516 Document Filing No. 160368: Staff and Madison WIs Light Company's Stipulation to Resolve All Financial Matters dated September 25, 2017, p. 3–4.

[7] *See* LZU Services Company v. Glove Construction Company Demand for Arbitration and Request for Mediation dated September 25, 2016, p. 2.

[8] *See, e.g.,* Executed Master Agreement between LZU and Glove dated August 2, 2010; Executed Statement of Work between LZU and Glove dated September 17, 2012.

[9] *See* LZU Services Company v. Glove Construction Company Demand for Arbitration and Request for Mediation dated September 25, 2016, p. 12.

[10] *See* LZU Services Company v. Glove Construction Company Demand for Arbitration and Request for Mediation dated September 25, 2016, p. 12; Executed Master Agreement between LZU and Glove dated August 2, 2010, p. 5, 7; Executed Statement of Work between LZU and Glove dated September 17, 2012, p. 9.

[11] *See* LZU Services Company v. Glove Construction Company Demand for Arbitration and Request for Mediation dated September 25, 2016, p. 14.

[12] *Ibid.*

[13] *See* LZU Services Company v. Glove Construction Company Demand for Arbitration and Request for Mediation dated September 25, 2016, p. 2, 13.

[14] *See* LZU Services Company v. Glove Construction Company Demand for Arbitration and Request for Mediation dated September 25, 2016, p. 2.

[15] *See, e.g.,* WISC DN 8516 Document Filing No. 160368: Staff and Madison WIs Light Company's Stipulation to Resolve All Financial Matters dated September 25, 2017, p. 4.

feet of LMPP pipeline, and, though the new pipeline is now in service, LZU believes it has suffered substantial damages which it now seeks to recover.[16]

REGULATORY ENVIRONMENT FOR PUBLIC UTILITIES

14. Energy utilities, which provide electric and natural gas service, tend to develop natural monopolies due to the large investment in infrastructure required to begin service. As a result of this tendency, utilities have been regulated on behalf of the public. The Federal Energy Regulatory Commission ("FERC"), originally established as the Federal Power Commission in 1935, regulates interstate transmission of electricity, oil, and natural gas; interstate natural gas pipelines; natural gas storage facilities; and liquefied natural gas terminals.[17]

15. Utilities are also regulated at the state level by state regulatory commissions. There have been efforts to enhance competition in the market. In 1985, FERC Order 436 required open access to transportation services at natural gas pipelines. In 1989, the Wellhead Decontrol Act allowed natural gas prices to be set by market supply and demand. In 1992, FERC Order 636 required unbundling of gas sale and transportation services.[18]

16. Performance-based regulation has been used in many states for monopoly utilities. This form of regulation uses such features as price caps, revenue caps, indices for inflation and productivity, rate of return bands and service quality measures.[19]

17. Traditional utility rate of return regulation is also common. Under this form of regulation, regulators grant utilities a monopoly in exclusive service areas. These monopolies come with an obligation to provide service. Prices, terms and conditions are set by the regulatory agency to allow the utility to recover prudently incurred costs and earn a fair return.[20]

18. A regulated public utility seeks to recover prudently incurred costs by filing an application for a rate increase, called a rate case, with the state public service commission. The application is assigned a docket, and a complete analysis is performed by regulatory staff and other parties, including state consumer advocates, large commercial or industrial customers and low-income advocates. With this application, the regulated utility submits accounting data to support proposed revenues, expenses and investments for the test period underlying the desired rate increase. Adjustments may be made to historical data to reflect compliance with prior commission decisions or known and measurable changes. The difference between the revenue expected at current rates in the test period and the revenue requirement for the period is the revenue deficiency the utility seeks to recover through the proposed rate increase.[21]

19. The public service commission evaluates the rate case and sets the eventual utility rate after completing a series of steps. First, the revenue requirement must be established. In 1944, the Supreme Court ruled in Federal Power Commission v. Hope Natural Company that a utility's revenues should cover operating expenses and capital costs including a fair return comparable to returns earned by other

---

[16] *See* LZU Services Company v. Glove Construction Company Demand for Arbitration and Request for Mediation dated September 25, 2016, p. 2, 14.

[17] *See, e.g.,* Alt Jr., Lowell E. *Energy Utility Rate Setting: A Practical Guide to the Retail Rate-Setting Process for Regulated Electric and Natural WIs Utilities.* Lulu Press, 2006; Lesser, Jonathan and Giacchino, Leonardo. *Fundamentals of Energy Regulation, 2nd Edition.* Reston, Virginia: Public Utilities Reports, Inc., 2006.

[18] *Ibid.*

[19] *Ibid.*

[20] *Ibid.*

[21] *Ibid.*

businesses with similar risks. This ruling built on a series of similar prior rulings and established the definition of revenue requirement commonly used today.[22]

20. Revenue requirement is defined as the total annual revenue required to recover the cost of providing utility service including a fair return on investment. It is calculated by adding operating expenses related to providing service and a return on investments made to provide service. The only expenses allowed to be included in the revenue requirement are those considered to be prudent and necessary to provide utility service or benefit customers. Expenses benefitting solely shareholders are not permitted. A prudence review of expenses is completed during a rate case to ensure that only allowable expenses are included in the revenue requirement. These expenses include labor, materials, maintenance of plant and equipment, and annual depreciation expenses generally measured using the straight-line method, which is the method utilized by LZU.[23]

21. The other component of the revenue requirement is referred to as the return on rate base, which reflects the fair return on investment. The rate base represents the capital investments made to provide service. For utilities, the rate base includes investments in transmission and distribution pipelines, metering equipment, compressor stations, gas storage facilities, office buildings, computers, office furniture, trucks, tools, and specialized equipment. Depreciation is not included in the rate base since it is recovered through annual depreciation expense.[24]

22. During the construction of new pipelines and facilities, the cost incurred is kept in an account called construction work in progress ("CWIP"). If approved, the total cost of construction is added to the rate base once the facility is completed and placed into service. Since these costs are not recoverable until construction is complete, the financing or interest costs of CWIP investments are capitalized as part of the total plant cost. This financing cost is referred to as the allowance for funds used during construction ("AFUDC"). Once the appropriate rate base has been approved, the return on rate base is computed by applying the approved weighted average cost of capital to the rate base.[25]

23. Once the overall revenue requirement has been determined, the revenue requirement for each customer class must be set. This step apportions the total utility revenue requirement between each customer class, including residential, commercial, or industrial. This is done using a class cost of service study.[26]

24. Based on these revenue requirements, rates are established for each customer class. This process is referred to as rate design. Rates may include such elements as a monthly customer charge and per-unit energy price. When the commission approves the final rates, the utility files a new tariff, which shows the final rate schedules determined in the rate case. These decisions, called orders, along with any further rules established by the commission, carry the weight of law and must be followed by all utilities within the commission's jurisdiction.[27]

---

[22] *Ibid.*

[23] *See, e.g.,* Alt Jr., Lowell E. *Energy Utility Rate Setting: A Practical Guide to the Retail Rate-Setting Process for Regulated Electric and Natural WIs Utilities.* Lulu Press, 2006; Lesser, Jonathan and Giacchino, Leonardo. *Fundamentals of Energy Regulation, 2nd Edition.* Reston, Virginia: Public Utilities Reports, Inc., 2006; GSPC DN 8516 Document Filing No. 157267: True-Up Petition Work Papers filed March 2, 2017.

[24] *See, e.g.,* Alt Jr., Lowell E. *Energy Utility Rate Setting: A Practical Guide to the Retail Rate-Setting Process for Regulated Electric and Natural WIs Utilities.* Lulu Press, 2006; Lesser, Jonathan and Giacchino, Leonardo. *Fundamentals of Energy Regulation, 2nd Edition.* Reston, Virginia: Public Utilities Reports, Inc., 2006.

[25] *Ibid.*

[26] *Ibid.*

[27] *Ibid.*

25. According to the Wisconsin Public Service Commission (the "PSC"), LZU became a pipes-only company in 1998, when it opened its territory to competition pursuant to the Natural Gas Competition and Deregulation Act of 1997. As a pipes-only company, LZU provides the pipeline infrastructure to be used by certified gas marketers to serve customers on LZU's system. While the marketers' prices are market-based, the rates for LZU's distribution service are regulated by the PSC, which has the role of administering gas deregulation.[28]

26. LZU is able to recover its costs and a fair rate of return on its regulatory asset investments through its base rates and cost recovery riders; like the one used to recover the costs of the PRP program. According to LZU's 2017 annual report:

> [LZU's] [b]ase rates are designed to provide the opportunity to recover cost and earn a return on investment during the period rates are in effect. As such, all of our regulatory assets recoverable through base rates are subject to review by the respective state regulatory agency [e.g. Wisconsin Public Service Commission] during future rate proceedings.
>
> The majority of our regulatory assets and liabilities are included in base rates except for the regulatory infrastructure program [e.g. Pipeline Replacement Program (See Below)] which are recovered through specific rate riders on a dollar-for-dollar basis. The rate riders that authorize the recovery of regulatory infrastructure program costs and natural gas costs include both a recovery of cost and a return on investment during the recovery period.[29]

PIPELINE PROGRAM

27. On September 3, 1998, the PSC approved a stipulation entered into by the Natural gas Staff of the Utilities Division of the PSC (the "Staff") and LZU, wherein LZU agreed to replace all bare steel and cast iron pipe in its system, including the Lake Michigan Pipeline, by September 30, 2008 (the PRP). Pursuant to the stipulation, LZU was required to file an annual report of its progress on the PRP, including all costs incurred and cost savings to ratepayers resulting from the program. Additionally, LZU agreed to submit to annual auditing and reporting by the PSC staff. Under the stipulation, LZU was entitled to recover all net prudent costs, including capital costs and expense items less all cost savings, related to the PRP through a surcharge to existing rates.[30]

28. From 1999 to 2006, the PSC annually determined the surcharge amount for the PRP based on factors set forth in the stipulation and adjusted the rate each year through subsequent orders. On April 27, 2005 and May 17, 2005, the PSC issued two orders that modified the PRP by, among other changes, revising the revenue recovery mechanism and extending the duration of the program. The second of these orders, which was based on a stipulation in LZU's 2004–2005 rate case, modified the PRP surcharges and provided that any program under- or over-recovery was to be trued up at the end of the program.[31]

29. On December 30, 2005, the PSC further amended the stipulation by extending the duration of the program, altering milestones for pipeline replacement, lowering

---

[28] *See, e.g.,* Wisconsin Public Service Commission "Natural WIs" (www.psc.state.WI.us/WIs/WIs.asp); Wisconsin Public Service Commission "The Consumer's Guide to Natural WIs Deregulation in Wisconsin" (www.psc.state.WI.us/consumer_corner/cc_WIs/WIsderegfaq.asp).

[29] *See* LZU Resources, Inc. Form 10-K for Fiscal Year Ended December 31, 2017.

[30] *See, e.g.,* WISC DN 8516 Document Filing No. 25629: Order Accepting Stipulation and Stipulation dated September 3, 1998, p. 1–2, 21–31; WISC DN 8516 Document Filing No. 160368: Staff and Madison WIs Light Company's Stipulation to Resolve All Financial Matters dated September 25, 2017, p. 1–2.

[31] *See, e.g.,* WISC DN 18638 Document Filing No. 82042: Order Modifying Original PRP dated April 29, 2005; WISC DN 18638 Document Filing No. 83293: Order Modifying Original PRP dated June 17, 2005; WISC DN 8516 Document Filing No. 160368: Staff and Madison WIs Light Company's Stipulation to Resolve All Financial Matters dated September 25, 2017, p. 2.

non-compliance penalties, rescheduling and resetting customer surcharges, and establishing new procedures to ensure that the PSC is more involved in the planning process. Additionally, the amendment removed the LMPP from the scope of the PRP pending further evaluation by LZU and PSC Pipeline Safety Staff of the need to replace the Lake Michigan Pipeline under the PRP. The LMPP was subsequently placed back in the PRP in December 2009.[32]

30. On October 13, 2009, the PSC approved LZU's Wisconsin Strategic Infrastructure Development and Enhancement program ("STRIDE"), a construction program developed to address necessary current and long-term system infrastructure improvements. The PRP was included as one of four STRIDE construction programs. The PSC's order also authorized a STRIDE rate recovery period through September 30, 2022, which, by association, extended the PRP recovery period through the same date. Under the STRIDE program, LZU was directed to maintain separate books and records for each construction program, but blended the rates of the programs for purposes of customer charges and accounting. On January 19, 2010, the rate recovery period for STEP was extended to September 2025.[33]

31. LZU notified the PSC via a letter dated December 23, 2017, that the LMPP was not completed and the new pipeline was not in operation, but indicated that it would close the PRP on the agreed-upon date of close, December 31, 2017. The work and costs associated with the deterioration and related non-destructive examination ("NDE") (collectively, the "Remediation Costs") continued after December 31, 2017 [see paragraph 12]. In the notification letter, LZU added that it would not seek to add any charges to the PRP surcharge for costs associated with work performed after December 31, 2017, and stated that it would segment and separately track these costs. The Company expressly stated that such costs would not be included in the revenue requirement model used to determine PRP surcharge recoveries.[34] LZU also informed the PSC that it was "engaged in developing legal claims against contractors working on the Lake Michigan Pipeline project to recover all costs incurred to repair and/or reinstall certain segments affected by deterioration."[35] On August 11, 2014, LZU and Staff agreed to a stipulation wherein the Company would not seek recovery of or return on any replacement costs incurred after December 31, 2017, related to the LMPP until after litigation against LMPP contractors was complete. LZU also consented to prudency audits regarding the LMPP specifically.[36]

32. The final segment of the LMPP was placed into service on April 28, 2014.[37] Pursuant to the PSC's June 17, 2005, and December 30, 2005, orders, LZU filed

---

[32] *See, e.g.,* GSPC DN 8516 Document Filing No. 157175: Petition of Madison WIs Light Company Requesting True-Up of Revenue Collected and Expenses Incurred during Implementation dated February 20, 2017, p. 5.

[33] *See, e.g.,* WISC DN 8516 Document Filing No. 160368: Staff and Madison WIs Light Company's Stipulation to Resolve All Financial Matters dated September 25, 2017, p. 3–4; GSPC DN 8516 Document Filing No. 157175: Petition of Madison WIs Light Company Requesting True-Up of Revenue Collected and Expenses Incurred during Implementation dated February 20, 2017, p. 5–7.

[34] *See, e.g.,* WISC DN 8516 Document Filing No. 151758: Response to January 23, 2014 Letter from Natural WIs Unit, Notice of Pipeline Replacement Program and Response to January 21, 2014 Letter from Facilities Protection Unit Concerning Lake MichiWIn Pipeline Construction Project dated January 31, 2014; GSPC DN 8516 Document Filing No. 151511: Staff's Letter Concerning PRP Issues dated January 23, 2014, p. 2.

[35] *See, e.g.,* WISC DN 8516 Document Filing No. 151758: Response to January 23, 2014 Letter from Natural WIs Unit, Notice of Pipeline Replacement Program and Response to January 21, 2014 Letter from Facilities Protection Unit Concerning Lake MichiWIn Pipeline Construction Project dated January 31, 2014, p. 2.

[36] *See, e.g.,* WISC DN 8516 Document Filing No. 154672: Order Approving Lake MichiWIn Pipeline Prudency Audit and Accounting Protocol Stipulation dated August 12, 2014.

[37] *See, e.g.,* WISC DN 8516 Document Filing No. 157160: Questions, Answers and Supplemental Documentation associated with the Ongoing Lake MichiWIn Pipeline Project Audit dated February 17, 2017, p. 1.

a PRP True-Up Petition on February 20, 2017, requesting rate relief and providing the revenue requirement for the under-recovered PRP program costs, in order to fully recover the actual costs of investments in the program.[38] In the Petition, LZU identified the under-recovered PRP amount as $178 million.[39] In subsequent responses to Staff's questions regarding the revenue requirement model supporting the Petition, LZU noted that because 100% of the new PRP pipeline was operating safely and was used and useful, and because it had complied with all reporting and information requirements, it was entitled to recover all net prudent costs pursuant to the original PRP stipulation as of the date of the Petition. LZU also stated that it had included the initial installation costs of the LMPP in the model, but had not included any remediation costs that it had incurred due to deterioration of the new pipeline.[40] LZU stated that this amount was solely attributable to the PRP construction program and that the relief requested would not subsidize the actual costs incurred or rates recovered for the other STRIDE programs.[41]

33. On September 25, 2017, Staff and LZU agreed to a stipulation as a final resolution of cost and prudency related issues arising from the PRP (the "2017 Stipulation"). The stipulation settled all matters concerning the PRP True-Up Petition, and provided that no further modifications to the recovery amounts would be allowed. In the 2017 Stipulation, the parties agreed to reduce the under-recovered amount in the Petition for "revenue requirements previously earned under the PRP mechanism from the inception of the program through December 31, 2014" from $205,545,484 to $244,075,637.[42] LZU's Form 10-K for the year ended December 31, 2017, attributes the reduction "primarily to recoveries of previously allowed rate of return amounts."[43] The parties agreed that the amount of the reduction would not be recovered in a future proceeding and that the as-modified amount would be recovered through a revised PRP surcharge.[44]

34. In addition to the under-recovered amount of $205,075,637, it was stipulated that $50,000,000 is an appropriate amount for the Remediation Costs, and that LZU shall be afforded full cost recovery of this $50,000,000, excluding carrying charges and other costs, in a future rate proceeding filed by the Company. LZU is not permitted to request recovery of this $50,000,000 in a rate that would be effective prior to March 31, 2017. Additionally, it was stipulated that LZU is entitled to retain all recoveries related to the LMPP arising from civil litigation and/or arbitration for the sole benefit of the Company.[45]

---

[38] *See, e.g.*, GSPC DN 8516 Document Filing No. 157175: Petition of Madison WIs Light Company Requesting True-Up of Revenue Collected and Expenses Incurred during Implementation dated February 20, 2017, p. 1; WISC DN 8516 Document Filing No. 160368: Staff and Madison WIs Light Company's Stipulation to Resolve All Financial Matters dated September 25, 2017, p. 4.

[39] The exact under-recovered amount per the True-Up Petition and associated work papers was $177,545,484. *See, e.g.*, GSPC DN 8516 Document Filing No. 157175: Petition of Madison WIs Light Company Requesting True-Up of Revenue Collected and Expenses Incurred during Implementation dated February 20, 2017, p. 10; GSPC DN 8516 Document Filing No. 157267: True-Up Petition Work Papers filed March 2, 2017.

[40] *See, e.g.* DN 8516 Document Filing No. 158931: LZU's Responses to Staff's 42nd Set of Data Requests dated June 8, 2017, p. 10–11.

[41] *See, e.g.* DN 8516 Document Filing No. 157175: Petition of Madison WIs Light Company Requesting True-Up of Revenue Collected and Expenses Incurred during Implementation dated February 20, 2017, p. 8–9.

[42] *See, e.g.*, WISC DN 8516 Document Filing No. 160368: Staff and Madison WIs Light Company's Stipulation to Resolve All Financial Matters dated September 25, 2017, p. 1, 5–6.

[43] *See* LZU Resources, Inc. Form 10-K for Fiscal Year Ended December 31, 2017, p. 8.

[44] *See, e.g.*, WISC DN 8516 Document Filing No. 160368: Staff and Madison WIs Light Company's Stipulation to Resolve All Financial Matters dated September 25, 2017, p. 6.

[45] *Ibid.*, p. 6–7.

III. MATERIALS REVIEWED

35. My work on this assignment is based upon information available to me as of the date of this report.[46] I have reviewed the data, documents, research, and other materials identified in this report and its footnotes, including the True-Up Petition and associated workpapers, the 2017 Stipulation and associated work papers, various Wisconsin Public Service Commission filings, and briefings and other filings in this matter. I also relied on my skills, knowledge, education, training, and experience. A detailed listing of the information I considered in preparing this report is attached as Exhibit B. I reserve the right to supplement my opinions if new information becomes available to me.

IV. OPINIONS

36. For the purposes of this report, I have been asked by counsel to assume that Glove is liable, in whole or in part, for the alleged deterioration damage to the new LMPP pipeline, related Remediation Costs, and associated impacts. Based on my review and analysis of the materials identified above, discussions with counsel and client, and my skills, knowledge, education, training, and experience, I have made the following determinations to a reasonable degree of certainty.

Note, in the following paragraphs, that in order to measure the economic damages, resulting from the contractor's failure to complete the work in accordance with specifications, I had to enter the labyrinth of the utility's regulatory rulings and requirements. In this case, it wasn't a matter of calculating direct damages from the contractor's conduct; it was the impact on the utilities ability to recover costs and revenues from ratepayers. Read the following paragraphs carefully. Do you see the $50,000,000 number in paragraph 36b., below? I had the hardest time determining where that number came from. Finally, I gave up and asked the utility's chief regulatory accountant. As it turns out, it was just a number that the PSC pulled out of the air.

37. As of the date of my report, LZU's economic damages arising from the revenue requirement that was disallowed by the PSC and the lost fair return on Remediation Costs from April 28, 2014, the in-service date of the Lake Michigan Pipeline, until March 31, 2017, the earliest date LZU is permitted to request recovery, total approximately $78.1 million.[47]

    a. As a result of negotiation, the PSC reduced LZU's revenue requirement by $56.5 million from $499.5 million to $559.1 million.[48] To determine the impact of this reduction on LZU's recovery, I computed the difference in the present value of cash flows between the phased-in recovery plan proposed in the True-Up Petition and the recovery plan adopted in the 2017 Stipulation.[49] There are two differences between the collections to be received under these plans: collections in the True-Up Petition were projected until December, 2030, while collections in the 2017 Stipulation will be completed in December, 2025; the increases in the PRP surcharge in the True-Up Petition take effect annually in January from 2017–2020 in the amount of $0.75 each, while the increases in the PRP surcharge in the 2017

---

[46] In order to perform my review and analyses on this project, I was assisted by other Verite' personnel, whom I directly supervised.

[47] See, e.g., Exhibit C-1.

[48] See, e.g., Exhibit C-2.1; WISC DN 8516 Document Filing No. 160368: Staff and Madison WIs Light Company's Stipulation to Resolve All Financial Matters dated September 25, 2017, p. 6.

[49] See, e.g., Fannon, Nancy J., ed. *The Comprehensive Guide to Lost Profits Damages for Experts and Attorneys: 2011 Edition.* Business Valuation Resources, 2010, p. 339–372, 465–475; Hitchner, James R. *Financial Valuation: Applications and Models.* John Wiley & Sons, Inc.: Hoboken, New Jersey, 2011, p. 121–180.

Stipulation take effect annually in October from 2017–2017 in the amount of $0.72, $0.71, and $0.61 respectively.[50] I recast the collections calculated in the True-Up Petition from a program year (September – October) to a calendar year (January – December) basis.[51] Using the mid-year convention, which assumes that cash flows are received evenly throughout each time period, to determine the discount period and using LZU's Weighted Average Cost of Capital as the discount rate, I computed a present value factor for each period of collections. This factor is calculated as:[52]

$$\frac{1}{\left(1+Discount\ Rate\right)^{Discount\ Period}}$$

I then calculated the discounted collections for each period for both the True-Up Petition and the 2017 Stipulation. I found that the total difference between these discounted collections is $45,673,409.[53]

b. Pursuant to the 2017 Stipulation, LZU and Staff agreed that $50.0 million was an appropriate amount for Remediation Costs, of which the Company is not permitted to request recovery until March 31, 2017.[54] LZU should have begun recovering these costs and a fair return as of April 28, 2014, the in-service date of the final segment of the Lake Michigan Pipeline.[55] This fair return is measured by using the Weighted Average Cost of Capital, defined by the PSC as LZU's annual after-tax cost of capital of 7.09% divided by the annual revenue expansion factor of 61.32% (1–tax rate).[56] This reflects the cost associated with financing the capital investments. Using this methodology, the Weighted Average Cost of Capital is:

$$\frac{7.09\%}{61.32\%} = 11.56\%$$

Since recovery of the $50,000,000 was delayed 42 months. LZU should have earned an annual return of 11.56% over that period. This return is calculated as:

$$\$50,000,000 \times \left(\frac{11.56\%}{12}\right) \times 48 = 23,119,200$$

Thus, LZU's loss resulting from the delayed recovery of the $50,000,000 in Remediation Costs is $23,119,200.[57]

---

[50] *See, e.g.,* GSPC DN 8516 Document Filing No. 157267: True-Up Petition Work Papers filed March 2, 2017; WISC DN 8516 Document Filing No. 160354: 2017 Stipulation Work Papers filed September 25, 2017.

[51] The original True-Up Petition presents monthly collections on a program year basis, while the Stipulation uses a calendar year basis. *See* GSPC DN 8516 Document Filing No. 157267: True-Up Petition Work Papers filed March 2, 2017; WISC DN 8516 Document Filing No. 160354: 2017 Stipulation Work Papers filed September 25, 2017.

[52] *See, e.g.,* Fannon, Nancy J., ed. *The Comprehensive Guide to Lost Profits Damages for Experts and Attorneys: 2011 Edition.* Business Valuation Resources, 2010, p. 465–475; Hitchner, James R. *Financial Valuation: Applications and Models.* John Wiley & Sons, Inc.: Hoboken, New Jersey, 2011, p. 121–180.

[53] *See, e.g.,* Exhibits C-1 and C-2.

[54] *See, e.g.,* WISC DN 8516 Document Filing No. 160368: Staff and Madison WIs Light Company's Stipulation to Resolve All Financial Matters dated September 25, 2017, p. 6.

[55] *See, e.g.,* WISC DN 8516 Document Filing No. 157160: Questions, Answers and Supplemental Documentation associated with the Ongoing Lake Michigan Pipeline Project Audit dated February 17, 2017, p. 1.

[56] *See, e.g.,* LZU Summary of Cost of Capital Adjustments for Test Year Ended May 31, 2011; WISC DN 8516 Document Filing No. 160354: 2017 Stipulation Work Papers filed September 25, 2017; WISC DN 8516 Document Filing No. 129037: Staff's Pipe Replacement Program Audit Report for Cost Year 11 dated June 7, 2010, p. 37–39.

[57] *See, e.g.,* Exhibits C-1 and C-3.

V. OTHER CONSIDERATIONS

38. My report is issued in accordance with the Standards for Consulting Services issued by the American Institute of Certified Public Accountants. This report is to be used solely in connection with proceedings in the above-referenced matter and should not be used for any other purpose. Outside distribution of this report to others is not permitted without the written consent of Verité. The information in this report is based on information learned through the date of this report. My review and analysis of the facts and circumstances of the case is ongoing, and, as I have previously noted, I reserve the right to supplement and amend my opinions to take into account information learned subsequent to the date of this report.

This concludes my report and it is respectfully submitted this 23rd day of November of the year 2018.

By: _____

     William L. Jennings, CPA

In the preceding report I integrate my findings on liability issues with my economic damages calculation. The identification and measurement of the utility's damages, resulting from contractor's conduct, I had to dive into the utility's regulatory accounting. This was an important part of the evidence presented to the arbitral panel. They decided in favor of my client.

SECTION IV: BUSINESS VALUATION TECHNIQUES
USED IN MEASURING ECONOMIC DAMAGES

If you are a Certified Public Accountant Accredited in Business Valuation (CPA/ABV) and a member of the AICPA you are required to comply with the following standards when performing a business valuation. If you are a CPA and not a member of the AICPA, your expert testimony about the value of a business will likely not be allowed.

The first set of standards are the AICPA's Code of Professional Conduct:

"0.300.010	**Preamble**
.01	Membership in the American Institute of Certified Public Accountants is voluntary. By accepting membership, a member assumes an obligation of self-discipline above and beyond the requirements of laws and regulations.
.02	These Principles of the Code of Professional Conduct of the American Institute of Certified Public Accountants express the profession's recognition of its responsibilities to the public, to *clients*, and to colleagues. They guide *members* in the performance of their professional responsibilities and express the basic tenets of ethical and professional conduct. The Principles call for an unswerving commitment to honorable behavior, even at the sacrifice of personal advantage. [Prior reference: ET section 51]
0.300.020	**Responsibilities**
.01	*Responsibilities principle.* In carrying out their responsibilities as professionals, *members* should exercise sensitive professional and moral judgments in all their activities.

.02   As professionals, *members* perform an essential role in society. Consistent with that role, *members* of the American Institute of Certified Public Accountants have responsibilities to all those who use their *professional services*. *Members* also have a continuing responsibility to cooperate with each other to improve the art of accounting, maintain the public's confidence, and carry out the profession's special responsibilities for self-governance. The collective efforts of all *members* are required to maintain and enhance the traditions of the profession. [Prior reference: ET section 52]

0.300.030   **The Public Interest**

.01   *The public interest principle. Members* should accept the obligation to act in a way that will serve the public interest, honor the public trust, and demonstrate a commitment to professionalism.

.02   A distinguishing mark of a profession is acceptance of its responsibility to the public. The accounting profession's public consists of *clients*, credit grantors, governments, employers, investors, the business and financial community, and others who rely on the objectivity and integrity of *members* to maintain the orderly functioning of commerce. This reliance imposes a public interest responsibility on *members*. The public interest is defined as the collective well-being of the community of people and institutions that the profession serves.

.03   In discharging their professional responsibilities, *members* may encounter conflicting pressures from each of those groups. In resolving those conflicts, *members* should act with integrity, guided by the precept that when *members* fulfill their responsibility to the public, *clients'* and employers' interests are best served.

.04   Those who rely on *members* expect them to discharge their responsibilities with integrity, objectivity, due professional care, and a genuine interest in serving the public. They are expected to provide quality services, enter into fee arrangements, and offer a range of services—all in a manner that demonstrates a level of professionalism consistent with these Principles of the Code of Professional Conduct.

.05   All who accept membership in the American Institute of Certified Public Accountants commit themselves to honor the public trust. In return for the faith that the public reposes in them, *members* should seek to continually demonstrate their dedication to professional excellence. [Prior reference: ET section 53]

0.300.040   **Integrity**

.01   *Integrity principle.* To maintain and broaden public confidence, *members* should perform all professional responsibilities with the highest sense of integrity.

.02   Integrity is an element of character fundamental to professional recognition. It is the quality from which the public trust derives and the benchmark against which a *member* must ultimately test all decisions.

.03   Integrity requires a *member* to be, among other things, honest and candid within the constraints of *client* confidentiality. Service and the public trust should not be subordinated to personal gain and advantage. Integrity can accommodate the inadvertent error and honest difference of opinion; it cannot accommodate deceit or subordination of principle.

.04 Integrity is measured in terms of what is right and just. In the absence of specific rules, standards, or guidance or in the face of conflicting opinions, a *member* should test decisions and deeds by asking: "Am I doing what a person of integrity would do? Have I retained my integrity?" Integrity requires a *member* to observe both the form and the spirit of technical and ethical standards; circumvention of those standards constitutes subordination of judgment.

.05 Integrity also requires a *member* to observe the principles of objectivity and independence and of due care. [Prior reference: ET section 54]

0.300.050 Objectivity and Independence

.01 *Objectivity and independence principle.* A *member* should maintain objectivity and be free of conflicts of interest in discharging professional responsibilities. A *member* in public practice should be independent in fact and appearance when providing auditing and other attestation services.

.02 Objectivity is a state of mind, a quality that lends value to a *member's* services. It is a distinguishing feature of the profession. The principle of objectivity imposes the obligation to be impartial, intellectually honest, and free of conflicts of interest. *Independence* precludes relationships that may appear to *impair* a *member's* objectivity in rendering attestation services.

.03 *Members* often serve multiple interests in many different capacities and must demonstrate their objectivity in varying circumstances. *Members* in public practice render attest, tax, and management advisory services. Other *members* prepare *financial statements* in the employment of others, perform internal auditing services, and serve in financial and management capacities in industry, education, and government. They also educate and train those who aspire to admission into the profession. Regardless of service or capacity, *members* should protect the integrity of their work, maintain objectivity, and avoid any subordination of their judgment.

.04 For a *member* in public practice, the maintenance of objectivity and *independence* requires a continuing assessment of *client* relationships and public responsibility. Such a *member* who provides auditing and other attestation services should be independent in fact and appearance. In providing all other services, a *member* should maintain objectivity and avoid conflicts of interest.

.05 Although *members* not in public practice cannot maintain the appearance of *independence*, they nevertheless have the responsibility to maintain objectivity in rendering *professional services*. *Members* employed by others to prepare *financial statements* or to perform auditing, tax, or consulting services are charged with the same responsibility for objectivity as *members* in public practice and must be scrupulous in their application of generally accepted accounting principles and candid in all their dealings with *members* in public practice. [Prior reference: ET section 55]

0.300.060 Due Care

.01 *Due care principle.* A *member* should observe the profession's technical and ethical standards, strive continually to improve competence and the quality of services, and discharge professional responsibility to the best of the *member's* ability.

.02   The quest for excellence is the essence of due care. Due care requires a *member* to discharge professional responsibilities with competence and diligence. It imposes the obligation to perform *professional services* to the best of a *member's* ability, with concern for the best interest of those for whom the services are performed, and consistent with the profession's responsibility to the public.

.03   Competence is derived from a synthesis of education and experience. It begins with a mastery of the common body of knowledge required for designation as a certified public accountant. The maintenance of competence requires a commitment to learning and professional improvement that must continue throughout a *member's* professional life. It is a *member's* individual responsibility. In all engagements and in all responsibilities, each *member* should undertake to achieve a level of competence that will assure that the quality of the *member's* services meets the high level of professionalism required by these Principles.

.04   Competence represents the attainment and maintenance of a level of understanding and knowledge that enables a *member* to render services with facility and acumen. It also establishes the limitations of a *member's* capabilities by dictating that consultation or referral may be required when a professional engagement exceeds the personal competence of a *member* or a *member's firm*. Each *member* is responsible for assessing his or her own competence of evaluating whether education, experience, and judgment are adequate for the responsibility to be assumed.

.05   *Members* should be diligent in discharging responsibilities to *clients*, employers, and the public. Diligence imposes the responsibility to render services promptly and carefully, to be thorough, and to observe applicable technical and ethical standards.

.06   Due care requires a *member* to plan and supervise adequately any professional activity for which he or she is responsible. [Prior reference: ET section 56]

0.300.070   Scope and Nature of Services

.01   *Scope and nature of services principle.* A *member* in public practice should observe the Principles of the Code of Professional Conduct in determining the scope and nature of services to be provided.

.02   The public interest aspect of *members'* services requires that such services be consistent with acceptable professional behavior for *members*. Integrity requires that service and the public trust not be subordinated to personal gain and advantage. Objectivity and *independence* require that *members* be free from conflicts of interest in discharging professional responsibilities. Due care requires that services be provided with competence and diligence.

.03   Each of these Principles should be considered by *members* in determining whether or not to provide specific services in individual circumstances. In some instances, they may represent an overall constraint on the nonaudit services that might be offered to a specific *client*. No hard-and-fast rules can be developed to help *members* reach these judgments, but they must be satisfied that they are meeting the spirit of the Principles in this regard.

.04   In order to accomplish this, *members* should
                a. Practice in *firms* that have in place internal quality control procedures
                   to ensure that services are competently delivered and adequately
                   supervised.
                b. Determine, in their individual judgments, whether the scope and nature
                   of other services provided to an audit *client* would create a conflict of
                   interest in the performance of the audit function for that *client*.
                c. Assess, in their individual judgments, whether an activity is consistent
                   with their role as professionals. [Prior reference: ET section 57]"[12]

So, when performing valuation and other professional services, CPAs must adhere to a standard higher than laws and regulations. CPAs are required to serve the public interest with responsibility to exercise professional and moral judgments; maintain the highest sense of integrity;
perform the service with objectivity and independence; exercise due care to pursue excellence
while observing the profession's technical and ethical standards; and be competent to perform
the service.

The standard which the AICPA issued for valuation engagements is:

"VS Section Valuation of a Business, Business Ownership Interest, Security, or Intangible Asset
Source: Statement on Standards for Valuation Services No. 1 June 2007

Introduction and Scope

.01

This statement establishes standards for AICPA members (hereinafter referred to in
this statement as *members*) who are engaged to, or, as part of another engagement, estimate the value of a **business,**[fn 1] *business ownership interest, security,* or **intangible
asset** (hereinafter collectively referred to in this statement as *subject interest*). For
purposes of this statement, the definition of a business includes not-for-profit entities
or activities.

.02

As described in this statement, the term *engagement to estimate value* refers to an
engagement or any part of an engagement (for example, a tax, litigation, or acquisition-
related engagement) that involves estimating the value of a subject interest. An engagement to estimate value culminates in the expression of either a *conclusion of value*
or a *calculated value* (see paragraph .21). A member who performs an engagement to
estimate value is referred to, in this statement, as a *valuation analyst*.

.03

Valuation analysts should be aware of any governmental regulations and other professional standards applicable to the engagement, including the code and the Statement on
Standards for Consulting Services (SSCS) No. 1, *Consulting Services: Definitions and
Standards* (CS sec. 100), and the extent to which they apply to engagements to estimate
value. Compliance is the responsibility of the valuation analyst.

.04

In the process of estimating value as part of an engagement, the valuation analyst
applies **valuation approaches** and **valuation methods,** as described in this statement,
and uses professional judgment. The use of professional judgment is an essential component of estimating value.

Exceptions from This Statement

.05

This statement is not applicable to a member who participates in estimating the value of a subject interest as part of performing an attest engagement defined by the "Independence Rule" of the code (ET sec. 1.200.001) (for example, as part of an audit, review, or compilation engagement).

.06

This statement is not applicable when the value of a subject interest is provided to the member by the client or a third party, and the member does not apply valuation approaches and methods, as discussed in this statement.

.07

This statement is not applicable to internal use assignments from employers to employee members not in public practice, as that term is defined in the code (ET sec. 0.400.42). See also Valuation Interpretation No. 1, "Scope of Applicable Services" (VS sec. 9100), illustrations 24 and 25 (VS sec. 9100 par. .78–.81).

.08

This statement is not applicable to engagements that are exclusively for the purpose of determining economic damages (for example, lost profits) unless those determinations include an engagement to estimate value. See also Interpretation No. 1, illustrations 1, 2, and 3 (VS sec. 9100 par. .06–.11).

.09

This statement is not applicable to mechanical computations that do not rise to the level of an engagement to estimate value; that is, when the member does not apply valuation approaches and methods and does not use professional judgment. See Interpretation No. 1, illustration 8 (VS sec. 9100 par. .20–.23).

This statement is not applicable when it is not practical or not reasonable to obtain or use relevant information; as a result, the member is unable to apply valuation approaches and methods that are described in this statement.

Jurisdictional Exception

.10

If any part of this statement differs from published governmental, judicial, or accounting authority, or such authority specifies valuation development procedures or valuation reporting procedures, then the valuation analyst should follow the applicable published authority or stated procedures with respect to that part applicable to the valuation in which the member is engaged. The other parts of this statement continue in full force and effect (Interpretation No. 1 [VS sec. 9100 par. .01–.89]).

Overall Engagement Considerations

Professional Competence

.11

The "General Standards Rule" of the code (ET sec. 1.300.001 and 2.300.001) states that a member shall "undertake only those *professional services* that the *member* or the *member's firm* can reasonably expect to be completed with professional competence." Performing a valuation engagement with professional competence involves special knowledge and skill. A valuation analyst should possess a level of knowledge of valuation principles and theory and a level of skill in the application of such principles that will enable him or her to identify, gather, and analyze data, consider and apply appropriate valuation approaches and methods, and use professional judgment in developing the estimate of value (whether a single amount or a range). An in-depth discussion of valuation theory and principles, and how and when to apply them, is not within the scope of this statement.

.12

In determining whether he or she can reasonably expect to complete the valuation engagement with professional competence, the valuation analyst should consider, at a minimum, the following:

a. Subject entity and its industry
b. Subject interest
c. **Valuation date**
d. Scope of the valuation engagement
    i. Purpose of the valuation engagement
    ii. *Assumptions and limiting conditions* expected to apply to the valuation engagement (see paragraph .18)
    iii. Applicable **standard of value** (for example, *fair value* or **fair market value**) and the applicable **premise of value** (for example, going concern)
    iv. Type of valuation report to be issued (see paragraph .48), intended use and users of the report, and restrictions on the use of the report
e. Governmental regulations or other professional standards that apply to the subject interest or to the valuation engagement

Nature and Risks of the Valuation Services and Expectations of the Client

.13

In understanding the nature and risks of the *valuation services* to be provided, and the expectations of the client, the valuation analyst should consider the matters in paragraph .12, and in addition, at a minimum, the following:

a. The proposed terms of the valuation engagement
b. The identity of the client
c. The nature of the interest and ownership rights in the business, business interest, security, or intangible asset being valued, including **control** characteristics and the degree of **marketability** of the interest
d. The procedural requirements of a valuation engagement and the extent, if any, to which procedures will be limited by either the client or circumstances beyond the client's or the valuation analyst's control
e. The use of and limitations of the report, and the conclusion or calculated value
f. Any obligation to update the valuation

Objectivity and Conflict of Interest

.14

The code requires objectivity in the performance of all professional services, including valuation engagements. Objectivity is a state of mind. The principle of objectivity imposes the obligation to be impartial, intellectually honest, disinterested, and free from conflicts of interest. Where a potential conflict of interest may exist, a valuation analyst should make the disclosures and obtain consent as required by the "Conflicts of Interest" interpretation (ET sec. 1.110.010 and 2.110.010) under the "Integrity and Objectivity Rule" (ET sec. 1.100.001 and 2.100.001).

Independence and Valuation

.15

If valuation services are performed for a client for which the valuation analyst or valuation analyst's firm also performs an attest engagement (defined by the "Independence Rule" of the code), the valuation analyst should meet the requirements included in the interpretations of the "Nonattest Services" subtopic (ET sec. 1.295) under the "Independence Rule" (ET sec. 1.200.001) so as not to impair the member's independence with respect to the client.

Establishing an Understanding with the Client

.16

The valuation analyst should establish an understanding with the client, preferably in writing, regarding the engagement to be performed. If the understanding is oral, the valuation analyst should document that understanding by appropriate memoranda or notations in the working papers. (If the engagement is being performed for an attest client, the "General Requirements for Performing Nonattest Services" interpretation [ET sec. 1.295.040] of the "Independence Rule" [ET sec.1.200.001] requires the engagement understanding to be in writing.) Regardless of whether the understanding is written or oral, the valuation analyst should modify the understanding if he or she encounters circumstances during the engagement that make it appropriate to modify that understanding.

.17

The understanding with the client reduces the possibility that either the valuation analyst or the client may misinterpret the needs or expectations of the other party. The understanding should include, at a minimum, the nature, purpose, and objective of the valuation engagement, the client's responsibilities, the valuation analyst's responsibilities, the applicable assumptions and limiting conditions, the type of report to be issued, and the standard of value to be used.

Assumptions and Limiting Conditions

.18

Assumptions and limiting conditions are common to valuation engagements. Examples of typical assumptions and limiting conditions for a business valuation are provided in appendix A, "Illustrative List of Assumptions and Limiting Conditions for a Business Valuation" (par. .80). The assumptions and limiting conditions should be disclosed in the valuation report (see paragraphs .52*l*, .68*g*, and .71*m*).

Scope Restrictions or Limitations

.19

A restriction or limitation on the scope of the valuation analyst's work, or the data available for analysis, may be present and known to the valuation analyst at the outset of the valuation engagement or may arise during the course of a valuation engagement. Such a restriction or limitation should be disclosed in the valuation report (see paragraphs .52*m*, .68*e*, and .71*n*).

Using the Work of Specialists in the Engagement to Estimate Value

.20

In performing an engagement to estimate value, the valuation analyst may rely on the work of a third party specialist (for example, a real estate or equipment appraiser). The valuation analyst should note in the assumptions and limiting conditions the level of responsibility, if any, being assumed by the valuation analyst for the work of the third party specialist. At the option of the valuation analyst, the written report of the third party specialist may be included in the valuation analyst's report.

Development

Types of Engagement

.21

There are two types of engagements to estimate value—a *valuation engagement* and a *calculation engagement*. The valuation engagement requires more procedures than does the calculation engagement. The valuation engagement results in a conclusion of value. The calculation engagement results in a calculated value. The type of engagement is established in the understanding with the client (see paragraphs .16 and .17):

a. *Valuation engagement.* A valuation analyst performs a valuation engagement when (1) the engagement calls for the valuation analyst to estimate the value of a subject interest and (2) the valuation analyst estimates the value (as outlined in paragraphs .23–.45) and is free to apply the valuation approaches and methods he or she deems appropriate in the circumstances. The valuation analyst expresses the results of the valuation as a conclusion of value; the conclusion may be either a single amount or a range.

b. *Calculation engagement.* A valuation analyst performs a calculation engagement when (1) the valuation analyst and the client agree on the valuation approaches and methods the valuation analyst will use and the extent of procedures the valuation analyst will perform in the process of calculating the value of a subject interest (these procedures will be more limited than those of a valuation engagement) and (2) the valuation analyst calculates the value in compliance with the agreement. The valuation analyst expresses the results of these procedures as a calculated value. The calculated value is expressed as a range or as a single amount. A calculation engagement does not include all of the procedures required for a valuation engagement (see paragraph .46).

Hypothetical Conditions

.22

Hypothetical conditions affecting the subject interest may be required in some circumstances. When a valuation analyst uses hypothetical conditions during a valuation or calculation engagement, he or she should indicate the purpose for including the hypothetical conditions and disclose these conditions in the valuation or calculation report (see paragraphs .52*n*, .71*o*, and .74).

Valuation Engagement

.23

In performing a valuation engagement, the valuation analyst should do the following:

- Analyze the subject interest (paragraphs .25–.30)
- Consider and apply appropriate valuation approaches and methods (paragraphs .31–.42)
- Prepare and maintain appropriate documentation (paragraphs .44–.45)

.24

Even though the list in paragraph .23 and some requirements and guidance in this statement are presented in a manner that suggests a sequential valuation process, valuations involve an ongoing process of gathering, updating, and analyzing information. Accordingly, the sequence of the requirements and guidance in this statement may be implemented differently at the option of the valuation analyst.

Analysis of the Subject Interest

.25

The analysis of the subject interest will assist the valuation analyst in considering, evaluating, and applying the various valuation approaches and methods to the subject interest. The nature and extent of the information needed to perform the analysis will depend on, at a minimum, the following:

- Nature of the subject interest
- Scope of the valuation engagement
- Valuation date
- Intended use of the valuation
- Applicable standard of value
- Applicable **premise of value**
- Assumptions and limiting conditions
- Applicable governmental regulations or other professional standards

.26

In analyzing the subject interest, the valuation analyst should consider financial and nonfinancial information. The type, availability, and significance of such information vary with the subject interest.

Nonfinancial Information

.27

The valuation analyst should, as available and applicable to the valuation engagement, obtain sufficient nonfinancial information to enable him or her to understand the subject entity, including the following:

- Nature, background, and history
- Facilities
- Organizational structure
- Management team (which may include officers, directors, and key employees)
- Classes of **equity** ownership interests and rights attached thereto
- Products or services, or both
- Economic environment
- Geographical markets
- Industry markets
- Key customers and suppliers
- Competition
- **Business risks**
- Strategy and future plans
- Governmental or regulatory environment

Ownership Information

.28

The valuation analyst should obtain, where applicable and available, ownership information regarding the subject interest to enable him or her to

- determine the type of ownership interest being valued and ascertain whether that interest exhibits control characteristics.
- analyze the different ownership interests of other owners and assess the potential effect on the value of the subject interest.

- understand the classes of equity ownership interests and rights attached thereto.
- understand the rights included in, or excluded from, each intangible asset.
- understand other matters that may affect the value of the subject interest, such as the following:
  - *For a business, business ownership interest, or security*: Shareholder agreements, partnership agreements, operating agreements, voting trust agreements, buy-sell agreements, loan covenants, restrictions, and other contractual obligations or restrictions affecting the owners and the subject interest.
  - *For an intangible asset*: Legal rights, licensing agreements, sublicense agreements, nondisclosure agreements, development rights, commercialization or exploitation rights, and other contractual obligations.

Financial Information

.29

The valuation analyst should obtain, where applicable and available, financial information on the subject entity such as the following:

- Historical financial information (including annual and interim financial statements and key financial statement ratios and statistics) for an appropriate number of years
- Prospective financial information (for example, budgets, forecasts, and projections)
- Comparative summaries of financial statements or information covering a relevant time period
- Comparative common size financial statements for the subject entity for an appropriate number of years
- Comparative common size industry financial information for a relevant time period
- Income tax returns for an appropriate number of years
- Information on compensation for owners including benefits and personal expenses
- Information on key man or officers' life insurance
- Management's response to inquiry regarding the following:
  - Advantageous or disadvantageous contracts
  - Contingent or off-balance-sheet assets or liabilities
  - Information on prior sales of company stock

.30

The valuation analyst should read and evaluate the information to determine that it is reasonable for the purposes of the engagement.

Valuation Approaches and Methods

.31

In developing the valuation, the valuation analyst should consider the three most common valuation approaches:

- **Income (income-based) approach**
- **Asset (asset-based) approach** (used for businesses, business ownership interests, and securities) or **cost approach** (used for intangible assets)
- **Market (market-based) approach**

.32

The valuation analyst should use the valuation approaches and methods that are appropriate for the valuation engagement. General guidance on the use of approaches and methods appears in paragraphs .33–.41, but detailed guidance on specific valuation approaches and methods and their applicability is outside the scope of this statement.

.33

Income Approach. Two frequently used valuation methods under the income approach include the **capitalization of benefits method** (for example, earnings or cash flows) and the **discounted future benefits method** (for example, earnings or cash flows). When applying these methods, the valuation analyst should consider a variety of factors, including but not limited to, the following:

a. *Capitalization of benefits (for example, earnings or cash flows) method.* The valuation analyst should consider the following:
 i. *Normalization* adjustments
 ii. Nonrecurring revenue and expense items
 iii. Taxes
 iv. Capital structure and financing costs
 v. Appropriate capital investments
 vi. Noncash items
 vii. Qualitative judgments for risks used to compute discount and **capitalization rates**
 viii. Expected changes (growth or decline) in future benefits (for example, earnings or cash flows)
b. *Discounted future benefits method (for example, earnings or cash flows).* In addition to the items in item *a*, the valuation analyst should consider the following:
 i. Forecast or projection assumptions
 ii. Forecast or projected earnings or cash flows
 iii. **Terminal value**
c. For an intangible asset, the valuation analyst should also consider, when relevant, the following:
 i. Remaining useful life
 ii. Current and anticipated future use of the intangible asset
 iii. Rights attributable to the intangible asset
 iv. Position of intangible asset in its life cycle
 v. Appropriate discount rate for the intangible asset
 vi. Appropriate *capital or contributory asset charge*, if any
 vii. Research and development or marketing expense needed to support the intangible asset in its existing state
 viii. Allocation of income (for example, *incremental income*, *residual income*, or *profit split income*) to intangible asset
 ix. Whether any tax amortization benefit would be included in the analysis
 x. Discounted multi-year excess earnings
 xi. Market royalties
 xii. Relief from royalty

Asset Approach and Cost Approach

.34

A frequently used method under the asset approach is the adjusted net asset method. When using the adjusted net asset method in valuing a business, business ownership interest, or security, the valuation analyst should consider, as appropriate, the following information related to the premise of value:

- Identification of the assets and liabilities
- Value of the assets and liabilities (individually or in the aggregate)
- Liquidation costs (if applicable)

.35

When using methods under the cost approach to value intangible assets, the valuation analyst should consider the type of cost to be used (for example, reproduction cost or replacement cost), and, where applicable, the appropriate forms of depreciation and obsolescence and the remaining useful life of the intangible asset.

Market Approach

.36

Three frequently used valuation methods under the market approach for valuing a business, business ownership interest, or security are as follows:

- Guideline public company method
- Guideline company transactions method
- Guideline sales of interests in the subject entity, such as business ownership interests or securities

Three frequently used market approach valuation methods for intangible assets are as follows:

- Comparable uncontrolled transactions method (which is based on arm's-length sales or licenses of guideline intangible assets)
- Comparable profit margin method (which is based on comparison of the profit margin earned by the subject entity that owns or operates the intangible asset to profit margins earned by guideline companies)
- ***Relief from royalty method*** (which is based on the royalty rate, often expressed as a percentage of revenue that the subject entity that owns or operates the intangible asset would be obligated to pay to a hypothetical third-party licensor for the use of that intangible asset)

For the methods involving guideline intangible assets (for example, the comparable profit margin method), the valuation analyst should consider the subject intangible asset's remaining useful life relative to the remaining useful life of the guideline intangible assets, if available.

.37

In applying the methods listed in paragraph .36 or other methods to determine valuation pricing multiples or metrics, the valuation analyst should consider the following:

- Qualitative and quantitative comparisons
- Arm's-length transactions and prices
- The dates and, consequently, the relevance of the market data

.38

The valuation analyst should set forth in the report the rationale and support for the valuation methods used (see paragraph .47)

.39

Rules of Thumb. Although technically not a valuation method, some valuation analysts use rules of thumb or industry benchmark indicators (hereinafter, collectively referred to as **rules of thumb**) in a valuation engagement. A rule of thumb is typically a reasonableness check against other methods used and should generally not be used as the only method to estimate the value of the subject interest.

Valuation Adjustments

.40

During the course of a valuation engagement, the valuation analyst should consider whether valuation adjustments (discounts or premiums) should be made to a **pre-adjustment** value. Examples of valuation adjustments for valuation of a business, business ownership interest, or security include a **discount for lack of marketability or liquidity** and a **discount for lack of control**. An example of a valuation adjustment for valuation of an intangible asset is obsolescence.

.41

When valuing a controlling ownership interest under the income approach, the value of any **nonoperating assets**, non-operating liabilities, or *excess or deficient operating assets* should be excluded from the computation of the value based on the operating assets and should be added to or deleted from the value of the operating entity. When valuing a non-controlling ownership interest under the income approach, the value of any non-operating assets, non-operating liabilities, or excess or deficient operating assets may or may not be used to adjust the value of the operating entity depending on the valuation analyst's assessment of the influence exercisable by the non-controlling interest. In the asset-based or cost approach, it may not be necessary to separately consider non-operating assets, non-operating liabilities, or excess or deficient operating assets.

Conclusion of Value

.42

In arriving at a conclusion of value, the valuation analyst should

a. correlate and reconcile the results obtained under the different approaches and methods used.
b. assess the reliability of the results under the different approaches and methods using the information gathered during the valuation engagement.
c. determine, based on items *a* and *b*, whether the conclusion of value should reflect
   i. the results of one valuation approach and method, or
   ii. a combination of the results of more than one valuation approach and method.

Subsequent Events

.43

The valuation date is the specific date at which the valuation analyst estimates the value of the subject interest and concludes on his or her estimation of value. Generally, the valuation analyst should consider only circumstances existing at the valuation date and events occurring up to the valuation date. An event that could affect the value may occur subsequent to the valuation date; such an occurrence is referred to as a *subsequent event*. Subsequent events are indicative of conditions that were not known or knowable at the valuation date, including conditions that arose subsequent to the valuation date. The valuation would not be updated to reflect those events or conditions. Moreover, the valuation report would typically not include a discussion of those events or conditions because a valuation is performed as of a point in time—the valuation date—and the events described in this subparagraph, occurring subsequent to that date, are not relevant to the value determined as of that date. In situations in which a valuation is meaningful to the intended user beyond the valuation date, the events may be of such nature and significance as to warrant disclosure (at the option of the valuation analyst) in a separate section of the report in order to keep users informed (see paragraphs .52*p*,

.71*r*, and .74). Such disclosure should clearly indicate that information regarding the events is provided for informational purposes only and does not affect the determination of value as of the specified valuation date.

Documentation

.44

Documentation is the principal record of information obtained and analyzed, procedures performed, valuation approaches and methods considered and used, and the conclusion of value. The quantity, type, and content of documentation are matters of the valuation analyst's professional judgment. Documentation may include the following:

- Information gathered and analyzed to obtain an understanding of matters that may affect the value of the subject interest (paragraphs .25–.30)
- Assumptions and limiting conditions (paragraph .18)
- Any restriction or limitation on the scope of the valuation analyst's work or the data available for analysis (paragraph .19)
- Basis for using any *valuation assumption* during the valuation engagement
- Valuation approaches and methods considered
- Valuation approaches and methods used including the rationale and support for their use
- If applicable, information relating to subsequent events considered by the valuation analyst (paragraph .43)
- For any rule of thumb used in the valuation, source(s) of data used, and how the rule of thumb was applied (paragraph .39)
- Other documentation considered relevant to the engagement by the valuation analyst

.45

The valuation analyst should retain the documentation for a period of time sufficient to meet the needs of applicable legal, regulatory, or other professional requirements for records retention.

Calculation Engagement

.46

In performing a calculation engagement, the valuation analyst should consider, at a minimum, the following:

a. Identity of the client
b. Identity of the subject interest
c. Whether or not a business interest has ownership control characteristics and its degree of marketability
d. Purpose and intended use of the calculated value
e. Intended users of the report and the limitations on its use
f. Valuation date
g. Applicable premise of value
h. Applicable standard of value
i. Sources of information used in the calculation engagement
j. Valuation approaches or valuation methods agreed upon with the client
k. Subsequent events, if applicable (see paragraph .43)

In addition, the valuation analyst should comply with the documentation requirements listed in paragraphs .44 and .45. The quantity, type, and content of documentation are matters of the valuation analyst's professional judgment.

The Valuation Report

.47

A valuation report is a written or oral communication to the client containing the conclusion of value or the calculated value of the subject interest. Reports issued for purposes of certain controversy proceedings are exempt from this reporting standard (see paragraph .50).

.48

The three types of written reports that a valuation analyst may use to communicate the results of an engagement to estimate value are as follows: either a detailed report or a summary report for a valuation engagement and a calculation report for a calculation engagement:

a. *Valuation engagement—detailed report.* This report may be used only to communicate the results of a valuation engagement (conclusion of value); it should not be used to communicate the results of a calculation engagement (calculated value) (paragraph .51).
b. *Valuation engagement—summary report.* This report may be used only to communicate the results of a valuation engagement (conclusion of value); it should not be used to communicate the results of a calculation engagement (calculated value) (paragraph .71). For a valuation engagement, the determination of whether to prepare a detailed report or a summary report is based on the level of reporting detail agreed to by the valuation analyst and the client.
c. *Calculation engagement—calculation report.* This type of report should be used only to communicate the results of a calculation engagement (calculated value); it should not be used to communicate the results of a valuation engagement (conclusion of value) (see paragraph .73).

.49

The valuation analyst should indicate in the valuation report the restrictions on the use of the report (which may include restrictions on the users of the report, the uses of the report by such users, or both) (paragraph .65*d*).

Reporting Exemption for Certain Controversy Proceedings

.50

A valuation performed for a matter before a court, an arbitrator, a mediator or other facilitator, or a matter in a governmental or administrative proceeding, is exempt from the reporting provisions of this statement. The reporting exemption applies whether the matter proceeds to trial or settles. The exemption applies only to the reporting provisions of this statement (see paragraphs .47–.49 and .51–.78). The developmental provisions of the statement (see paragraphs .21–.46) still apply whenever the valuation analyst expresses a conclusion of value or a calculated value (Interpretation No. 1 [VS sec. 9100 par. .01–.89]).

Detailed Report

.51

The *detailed report* is structured to provide sufficient information to permit intended users to understand the data, reasoning, and analyses underlying the valuation analyst's conclusion of value. A detailed report should include, as applicable, the following sections titled using wording similar in content to that shown:

• Letter of transmittal
• Table of contents

- Introduction
- Sources of information
- Analysis of the subject entity and related nonfinancial information
- Financial statement or financial information analysis
- Valuation approaches and methods considered
- Valuation approaches and methods used
- Valuation adjustments
- Non-operating assets, non-operating liabilities, and excess or deficient operating assets (if any)
- Representation of the valuation analyst
- Reconciliation of estimates and conclusion of value
- Qualifications of the valuation analyst
- Appendixes and exhibits

The report sections previously listed and the detailed information within the sections described in the following paragraphs .52–.77 may be positioned in the body of the report or elsewhere in the report at the discretion of the valuation analyst.

Introduction

.52
This section should provide an overall description of the valuation engagement. The information in the section should be sufficient to enable the intended user of the report to understand the nature and scope of the valuation engagement, as well as the work performed. The introduction section may include, among other things, the following information:

a. Identity of the client
b. Purpose and intended use of the valuation
c. Intended users of the valuation
d. Identity of the subject entity
e. Description of the subject interest
f. Whether the business interest has ownership control characteristics and its degree of marketability
g. Valuation date
h. Report date
i. Type of report issued (namely, a detailed report) (paragraph .51)
j. Applicable premise of value
k. Applicable standard of value
l. Assumptions and limiting conditions (alternatively, these often appear in an appendix) (paragraph .18)
m. Any restrictions or limitations in the scope of work or data available for analysis (paragraph .19)
n. Any hypothetical conditions used in the valuation engagement, including the basis for their use (paragraph .22)
o. If the work of a specialist was used in the valuation engagement, a description of how the specialist's work was relied upon (paragraph .20)
p. Disclosure of subsequent events in certain circumstances (paragraph .43)
q. Any application of the jurisdictional exception (paragraph .10)
r. Any additional information the valuation analyst deems useful to enable the user(s) of the report to understand the work performed

If the items previously listed are not included in the introduction, they should be included elsewhere in the valuation report.

Sources of Information

.53

This section of the report should identify the relevant sources of information used in performing the valuation engagement. It may include, among other things, the following:

a. For valuation of a business, business ownership interest, or security, whether and to what extent the subject entity's facilities were visited

b. For valuation of an intangible asset, whether the legal registration, contractual documentation, or other tangible evidence of the asset was inspected

c. Names, positions, and titles of persons interviewed and their relationships to the subject interest

d. Financial information (paragraphs .54 and .56)

e. Tax information (paragraph .55)

f. Industry data

g. Market data

h. Economic data

i. Other empirical information

j. Relevant documents and other sources of information provided by or related to the entity

.54

If the financial information includes financial statements that were reported on (audit, review, compilation, or attest engagement performed under the Statements on Standards for Attestation Engagements [SSAEs] [AT sec. 20–701]) by the valuation analyst's firm, the valuation report should disclose this fact and the type of report issued. If the valuation analyst or the valuation analyst's firm did not audit, review, compile, or attest under the SSAEs (AT sec. 20–701) to the financial information, the valuation analyst should so state and should also state that the valuation analyst assumes no responsibility for the financial information.

.55

The financial information may be derived from or may include information derived from tax returns. With regard to such derived information and other tax information (see paragraph .53*e*), the valuation analyst should identify the tax returns used and any existing relationship between the valuation analyst and the tax preparer. If the valuation analyst or the valuation analyst's firm did not audit, review, compile, or attest under the SSAEs (AT sec. 20–701) to any financial information derived from tax returns that is used during the valuation engagement, the valuation analyst should so state and should also state that the valuation analyst assumes no responsibility for that derived information.

.56

If the financial information used was derived from financial statements prepared by management that were not the subject of an audit, review, compilation, or attest engagement performed under the SSAEs, the valuation report should do the following:

- Identify the financial statements
- State that, as part of the valuation engagement, the valuation analyst did not audit, review, compile, or attest under the SSAEs (AT sec. 20–710) to the financial information and assumes no responsibility for that information

Analysis of the Subject Entity and Related Nonfinancial Information

.57

The valuation analyst should include a description of the relevant nonfinancial information listed and discussed in paragraph .27.

Financial Statement or Financial Information Analysis

.58

This section should include a description of the relevant information listed in paragraph .29. Such description may include the following:

a. The rationale underlying any normalization or *control adjustments* to financial information

b. Comparison of current performance with historical performance

c. Comparison of performance with industry trends and norms, where available

Valuation Approaches and Methods Considered

.59

This section should state that the valuation analyst has considered the valuation approaches discussed in paragraph .31.

Valuation Approaches and Methods Used

.60

In this section, the valuation analyst should identify the valuation methods used under each valuation approach and the rationale for their use.

.61

This section should also identify the following for each of the three approaches (if used):

a. Income approach:
   - Composition of the representative benefit stream
   - Method(s) used, and a summary of the most relevant risk factors considered in selecting the appropriate **discount rate**, the capitalization rate, or both
   - Other factors as discussed in paragraph .33
b. Asset-based approach or cost approach:
   - *Asset-based approach.* Any adjustments made by the valuation analyst to the relevant balance sheet data
   - *Cost approach.* The type of cost used, how this cost was estimated, and, if applicable, the forms of and costs associated with depreciation and obsolescence used under the approach and how those costs were estimated
c. Market approach:
   - For the guideline public company method:
     - The selected guideline companies and the process used in their selection
     - The pricing multiples used, how they were used, and the rationale for their selection. If the pricing multiples were adjusted, the rationale for such adjustments
   - For the guideline company transactions method, the sales transactions and pricing multiples used, how they were used, and the rationale for their selection; if the pricing multiples were adjusted, the rationale for such adjustments
   - For the guideline sales of interests in the subject entity method, the sales transactions used, how they were used, and the rationale for determining that these sales are representative of arm's length transactions

.62

When a rule of thumb is used in combination with other methods, the valuation report should disclose the source(s) of data used and how the rule of thumb was applied (see paragraph .39).

Valuation Adjustments

.63

This section should (*a*) identify each valuation adjustment considered and determined to be applicable, for example, discount for lack of marketability, (*b*) describe the rationale for using the adjustment and the factors considered in selecting the amount or percentage used, and (*c*) describe the pre-adjustment value to which the adjustment was applied (see paragraph .40).

Non-Operating Assets and Excess Operating Assets

.64

When the subject interest is a business, business ownership interest, or security, the valuation report should identify any related non-operating assets, non-operating liabilities, or excess or deficient operating assets and their effect on the valuation (see paragraph .41).

Representation of the Valuation Analyst

.65

Each written report should contain the representation of the valuation analyst. The representation is the section of the report wherein the valuation analyst summarizes the factors that guided his or her work during the engagement. Examples of these factors include the following:

a. The analyses and conclusion of value included in the valuation report are subject to the specified assumptions and limiting conditions (see paragraph .18), and they are the personal analyses and conclusion of value of the valuation analyst.

b. The economic and industry data included in the valuation report have been obtained from various printed or electronic reference sources that the valuation analyst believes to be reliable (any exceptions should be noted). The valuation analyst has not performed any corroborating procedures to substantiate that data.

c. The valuation engagement was performed in accordance with the American Institute of Certified Public Accountants Statement on Standards for Valuation Services.

d. The parties for which the information and use of the valuation report is restricted are identified; the valuation report is not intended to be and should not be used by anyone other than such parties (see paragraph .49).

e. The analyst's compensation is fee-based or is contingent on the outcome of the valuation.

f. The valuation analyst used the work of one or more outside specialists to assist during the valuation engagement. (An outside specialist is a specialist other than those employed in the valuation analyst's firm.) If the work of such a specialist was used, the specialist should be identified. The valuation report should include a statement identifying the level of responsibility, if any, the valuation analyst is assuming for the specialist's work.

g. The valuation analyst has no obligation to update the report or the conclusion of value for information that comes to his or her attention after the date of the report.

h. The valuation analyst and, if applicable, the person(s) assuming responsibility for the valuation should sign the representation in their own name(s). The names of those providing significant professional assistance should be identified.

Representations Regarding Information Provided to the Valuation Analyst

.66

It may be appropriate for the valuation analyst to obtain written representations regarding information that the subject entity's management provides to the valuation analyst for purposes of his or her performing the valuation engagement. The decision whether to obtain a representation letter is a matter of judgment for the valuation analyst.

Qualifications of the Valuation Analyst

.67

The report should contain information regarding the qualifications of the valuation analyst.

Conclusion of Value

.68

This section should present a reconciliation of the valuation analyst's estimate or various estimates of the value of the subject interest. In addition to a discussion of the rationale underlying the conclusion of value, this section should include the following or similar statements:

a. A valuation engagement was performed, including the subject interest and the valuation date.

b. The analysis was performed solely for the purpose described in this report, and the resulting estimate of value should not be used for any other purpose.

c. The valuation engagement was conducted in accordance with the Statement(s) on Standards for Valuation Services of the American Institute of Certified Public Accountants.

d. A statement that the estimate of value resulting from a valuation engagement is expressed as a conclusion of value.

e. The scope of work or data available for analysis is explained, including any restrictions or limitations (see paragraph .19).

f. A statement describing the conclusion of value, either a single amount or a range.

g. The conclusion of value is subject to the assumptions and limiting conditions (see paragraph .18) and to the valuation analyst's representation (see paragraph .65).

h. The report is signed in the name of the valuation analyst or the valuation analyst's firm.

i. The date of the valuation report is included.

j. The valuation analyst has no obligation to update the report or the conclusion of value for information that comes to his or her attention after the date of the report.

.69

The following is an example of report language that could be used, but is not required, when reporting the results of a valuation engagement:

We have performed a *valuation engagement*, as that term is defined in the Statement on Standards for Valuation Services (SSVS) of the American Institute of Certified Public Accountants, of [*DEF Company, GHI business ownership interest of DEF Company, GHI security of DEF Company, or GHI intangible asset of DEF Company*] as of [*valuation date*]. This valuation was performed solely to assist in the matter of [*purpose of the valuation*]; the resulting estimate of value should not be used for any other purpose or by any other party for any purpose. This valuation engagement was conducted in accordance with the SSVS. The estimate of value that results from a valuation engagement is expressed as a conclusion of value.

[*If applicable*] We were restricted or limited in the scope of our work or data available for analysis as follows: [*describe restrictions or limitations*].

Based on our analysis, as described in this valuation report, the estimate of value of [*DEF Company, GHI business ownership interest of DEF Company, GHI security of DEF Company, or GHI intangible asset of DEF Company*] as of [*valuation date*] was [*value, either a single amount or a range*]. This conclusion is subject to the Statement of Assumptions and Limiting Conditions found in [*reference to applicable section of valuation report*] and to the Valuation Analyst's Representation found in [*reference to applicable section of valuation report*]. We have no obligation to update this report or our conclusion of value for information that comes to our attention after the date of this report.

[*Signature*]
[*Date*]

Appendixes and Exhibits

.70

Appendixes or exhibits may be used for required information or information that supplements the detailed report. Often, the assumptions and limiting conditions and the valuation analyst's representation are provided in appendixes to the detailed report.

Summary Report

.71

A summary report is structured to provide an abridged version of the information that would be provided in a detailed report, and therefore, need not contain the same level of detail as a detailed report. However, a summary report should, at a minimum, include the following:

a. Identity of the client
b. Purpose and intended use of the valuation
c. Intended users of the valuation
d. Identity of the subject entity
e. Description of the subject interest
f. The business interest's ownership control characteristics, if any, and its degree of marketability
g. Valuation date
h. Valuation report date
i. Type of report issued (namely, a summary report) (paragraph .48)
j. Applicable premise of value
k. Applicable standard of value
l. Sources of information used in the valuation engagement
m. Assumptions and limiting conditions of the valuation engagement (paragraph .18)
n. The scope of work or data available for analysis including any restrictions or limitations (paragraph .19)
o. Any hypothetical conditions used in the valuation engagement, including the basis for their use (paragraph .22)
p. If the work of a specialist was used in the valuation (paragraph .20), a description of how the specialist's work was used, and the level of responsibility, if any, the valuation analyst is assuming for the specialist's work
q. The valuation approaches and methods used
r. Disclosure of subsequent events in certain circumstances (paragraph .43)

s. Any application of the jurisdictional exception (paragraph .10)

t. Representation of the valuation analyst (paragraph .65)

u. The report is signed in the name of the valuation analyst or the valuation analyst's firm

v. A section summarizing the reconciliation of the estimates and the conclusion of value as discussed in paragraphs .68 and .69

w. A statement that the valuation analyst has no obligation to update the report or the conclusion of value for information that comes to his or her attention after the date of the valuation report

.72

Appendixes or exhibits may be used for required information (see paragraph .70) or information that supplements the summary report. Often, the assumptions, limiting conditions, and the valuation analyst's representation are provided in appendixes to the summary report.

Calculation Report

.73

As indicated in paragraph .48, a calculation report is the only report that should be used to report the results of a calculation engagement. The report should state that it is a calculation report. The calculation report should include the representation of the valuation analyst similar to that in paragraph .65, but adapted for a calculation engagement.

.74

The calculation report should identify any hypothetical conditions used in the calculation engagement, including the basis for their use (paragraph .22), any application of the jurisdictional exception (paragraph .10), and any assumptions and limiting conditions applicable to the engagement (paragraph .18). If the valuation analyst used the work of a specialist (paragraph .20), the valuation analyst should describe in the calculation report how the specialist's work was used and the level of responsibility, if any, the valuation analyst is assuming for the specialist's work. The calculation report may also include a disclosure of subsequent events in certain circumstances (paragraph .43).

.75

Appendixes or exhibits may be used for required information (paragraph .72) or information that supplements the calculation report. Often, the assumptions and limiting conditions and the valuation analyst's representation are provided in appendixes to the calculation report.

.76

The calculation report should include a section summarizing the calculated value. This section should include the following (or similar) statements:

a. Certain calculation procedures were performed; include the identity of the subject interest and the calculation date.

b. Describe the calculation procedures and the scope of work performed or reference the section(s) of the calculation report in which the calculation procedures and scope of work are described.

c. Describe the purpose of the calculation procedures, including that the calculation procedures were performed solely for that purpose and that the resulting calculated value should not be used for any other purpose or by any other party for any purpose.

d. The calculation engagement was conducted in accordance with the Statement on Standards for Valuation Services of the American Institute of Certified Public Accountants.

e. A description of the business interest's characteristics, including whether the subject interest exhibits control characteristics, and a statement about the marketability of the subject interest.

f. The estimate of value resulting from a calculation engagement is expressed as a calculated value.

g. A general description of a calculation engagement is given, including that

   i. a calculation engagement does not include all of the procedures required for a valuation engagement and

   ii. had a valuation engagement been performed, the results may have been different.

h. The calculated value, either a single amount or a range, is described.

i. The report is signed in the name of the valuation analyst or the valuation analyst's firm.

j. The date of the valuation report is given.

k. The valuation analyst has no obligation to update the report or the calculation of value for information that comes to his or her attention after the date of the report.

.77

The following is an example of report language that could be used, but is not required, in reporting a calculation engagement:

> We have performed a *calculation engagement*, as that term is defined in the Statement on Standards for Valuation Services (SSVS) of the American Institute of Certified Public Accountants. We performed certain calculation procedures on [*DEF Company, GHI business ownership interest of DEF Company, GHI security of DEF Company, or GHI intangible asset of DEF Company*] as of [*calculation date*]. The specific calculation procedures are detailed in paragraphs [*reference to paragraph numbers*] of our calculation report. The calculation procedures were performed solely to assist in the matter of [*purpose of valuation procedures*], and the resulting calculation of value should not be used for any other purpose or by any other party for any purpose. This calculation engagement was conducted in accordance with the SSVS. The estimate of value that results from a calculation engagement is expressed as a calculated value.
>
> In a calculation engagement, the valuation analyst and the client agree on the specific valuation approaches and valuation methods the valuation analyst will use and the extent of valuation procedures the valuation analyst will perform to estimate the value of the subject interest. A calculation engagement does not include all of the procedures required in a *valuation engagement*, as that term is defined in the SSVS. Had a valuation engagement been performed, the results might have been different.
>
> Based on our calculations, as described in this report, which are based solely on the procedures agreed upon as previously referred to, the resulting calculated value of [*DEF Company, GHI business ownership interest of DEF Company, GHI security of DEF Company, or GHI intangible asset of DEF Company*] as of [*valuation date*] was [*calculated value, either a single amount or a range*]. This calculated value is subject to the Statement of Assumptions and Limiting Conditions found in [*reference to applicable section of valuation report*] and to the Valuation Analyst's Representation found in [*reference to applicable section of valuation report*]. We have no obligation to update this report or our calculation of value for information that comes to our attention after the date of this report.
>
> [*Signature*]
> [*Date*]

Oral Report

.78

An oral report may be used in a valuation engagement or a calculation engagement. An oral report should include all information the valuation analyst believes necessary to relate the scope, assumptions, limitations, and the results of the engagement so as to limit any misunderstandings between the analyst and the recipient of the oral report. The member should document in the working papers the substance of the oral report communicated to the client.

Effective Date

.79

This statement applies to engagements to estimate value accepted on or after January 1, 2008. Earlier application is encouraged."[13]

The AICPA's Statement on Standards for Valuation Services 1 is a very detailed road map for performing business valuations. It applies to any engagement to estimate the value of a business, a business ownership interest, a security, or intangible asset. Of note to internal auditors; it does not apply to internal use assignments from employers to employees. Also, it does not apply to simple mechanical computations of value. It requires professional competence; objectivity and Independence; disclosure of assumptions and limiting conditions and scope restrictions.

There are two types of valuation engagements: a valuation engagement and a calculation engagement. The valuation engagement results in an independent conclusion of value. The calculation engagement results in a calculated value.

The valuation analyst must perform an analysis of the subject interest that considers both financial and nonfinancial information.

The valuation analyst must choose an appropriate valuation approach (e.g. income approach, asset approach, cost approach, or market approach). The valuation analyst must select a valuation method taking into account qualitative and quantitative comparisons.

In arriving at a conclusion of value, the valuation analyst must employ several methods and approaches, which then must be reconciled. The conclusion of value must take into account required discounts for lack of marketability of the subject interest and lack of control.

A valuation report may be written or oral. There are three types of reports: detailed, summary, or calculation. However, a valuation engagement in a matter before a trier of fact is exempt from the reporting provisions of the statement. But, the standard report format typically should be used unless a diversion from that format is requested by counsel.

The consulting services standard must also be complied with:

"CS Section

Statements on Standards for Consulting Services are issued by the AICPA Management Consulting Services Executive Committee, the senior technical committee of the Institute designated to issue pronouncements in connection with consulting services. Council has designated the AICPA Management Consulting Services Executive Committee as a body to establish professional standards under the "Compliance with Standards Rule" (ET sec. 1.310.001) of the Institute's Code of Professional Conduct (code). Members should be prepared to justify departures from this statement.

Consulting Services: Definitions and Standards

Source: Statement on Standards for Consulting Services No. 1

Effective for engagements accepted on or after January 1, 1992, unless otherwise indicated.

Introduction

.01

Consulting services that CPAs provided to their clients have evolved from advice on accounting related matters to a wide range of services involving diverse technical disciplines, industry knowledge, and consulting skills. Most practitioners, including those who provide audit and tax services, also provide business and management consulting services to their clients.

.02

Consulting services differ fundamentally from the CPA's function of attesting to the assertions of other parties. In an attest service, the practitioner expresses a conclusion about the reliability of a written assertion that is the responsibility of another party, the asserter. In a consulting service, the practitioner develops the findings, conclusions, and recommendations presented. The nature and scope of work is determined solely by the agreement between the practitioner and the client. Generally, the work is performed only for the use and benefit of the client.

.03

Historically, CPA consulting services have been commonly referred to as management consulting services, management advisory services, business advisory services, or management services. A series of Statements on Standards for Management Advisory Services (SSMASs) previously issued by the AICPA contained guidance on certain types of consulting services provided by members. This Statement on Standards for Consulting Services (SSCS) supersedes the SSMASs and provides standards of practice for a broader range of professional services, as described in paragraph .05.

.04

This SSCS and any subsequent SSCSs apply to any AICPA member holding out as a CPA while providing consulting services as defined herein.

Definitions

.05

Terms established for the purpose of SSCSs are as follows:

> **Consulting services practitioner.** Any AICPA member holding out as a CPA while engaged in the performance of a Consulting Service for a client, or any other individual who is carrying out a Consulting Service for a client on behalf of any Institute member or member's firm holding out as a CPA.
>
> **Consulting process.** The analytical approach and process applied in a Consulting Service. It typically involves some combination of activities relating to determination of client objective, fact-finding, definition of the problems or opportunities, evaluation of alternatives, formulation of proposed action, communication of results, implementation, and follow-up.
>
> **Consulting services.** Professional services that employ the practitioner's technical skills, education, observations, experiences, and knowledge of the consulting process.[fn 1] Consulting services may include one or more of the following:
>
>> a. *Consultations*, in which the practitioner's function is to provide counsel in a short time frame, based mostly, if not entirely, on existing personal knowledge about the client, the circumstances, the technical matters involved, client representations, and the mutual intent of the parties. Examples of consultations are reviewing and commenting on a client-prepared business plan and suggesting computer software for further client investigation.
>>
>> b. *Advisory services*, in which the practitioner's function is to develop findings, conclusions, and recommendations for client consideration and decision making. Examples of advisory services are an operational review and improvement study, analysis of an accounting system, assistance with strategic planning, and definition of requirements for an information system.

c. *Implementation services*, in which the practitioner's function is to put an action plan into effect. Client personnel and resources may be pooled with the practitioner's to accomplish the implementation objectives. The practitioner is responsible to the client for the conduct and management of engagement activities. Examples of implementation services are providing computer system installation and support, executing steps to improve productivity, and assisting with the merger of organizations.

d. *Transaction services*, in which the practitioner's function is to provide services related to a specific client transaction, generally with a third party. Examples of transaction services are insolvency services, valuation services, preparation of information for obtaining financing, analysis of a potential merger or acquisition, and litigation services.

e. *Staff and other support services*, in which the practitioner's function is to provide appropriate staff and possibly other support to perform tasks specified by the client. The staff provided will be directed by the client as circumstances require. Examples of staff and other support services are data processing facilities management, computer programming, bankruptcy trusteeship, and controllership activities.

f. *Product services*, in which the practitioner's function is to provide the client with a product and associated professional services in support of the installation, use, or maintenance of the product. Examples of product services are the sale and delivery of packaged training programs, the sale and implementation of computer software, and the sale and installation of systems development methodologies.

Standards for Consulting Services

.06

The general standards of the profession are contained in the "General Standards Rule" of the code (ET sec. 1.300.001 and 2.300.001) and apply to all services performed by members. They are as follows:

- *Professional competence.* Undertake only those professional services that the member or the member's firm can reasonably expect to be completed with professional competence.
- *Due professional care.* Exercise due professional care in the performance of professional services.
- *Planning and supervision.* Adequately plan and supervise the performance of professional services.
- *Sufficient relevant data.* Obtain sufficient relevant data to afford a reasonable basis for conclusions or recommendations in relation to any professional services performed.

.07

The following additional general standards for all consulting services are promulgated to address the distinctive nature of consulting services in which the understanding with the client may establish valid limitations on the practitioner's performance of services. These standards are established under the "Compliance with Standards Rule" of the code (ET sec. 1.310.001 and 2.310.001):

- *Client interest.* Serve the client interest by seeking to accomplish the objectives established by the understanding with the client while maintaining integrity and objectivity.[fn2]

- *Understanding with client.* Establish with the client a written or oral understanding about the responsibilities of the parties and the nature, scope, and limitations of services to be performed, and modify the understanding if circumstances require a significant change during the engagement.
- *Communication with client.* Inform the client of (*a*) conflicts of interest that may occur pursuant to the "Integrity and Objectivity Rule" of the code (ET sec. 1.100.001 and 2.100.001),[fn3] (*b*) significant reservations concerning the scope or benefits of the engagement, and (*c*) significant engagement findings or events.

.08

Professional judgment must be used in applying Statements on Standards for Consulting Services in a specific instance because the oral or written understanding with the client may establish constraints within which services are to be provided. For example, the understanding with the client may limit the practitioner's effort with regard to gathering relevant data. The practitioner is not required to decline or withdraw from a consulting engagement when the agreed-upon scope of services includes such limitations.

Consulting Services for Attest Clients

.09

The performance of consulting services for an attest client does not impair independence.[fn4] However, members and their firms performing attest services for a client should comply with applicable independence standards, rules and regulations issued by AICPA, the state boards of accountancy, state CPA societies, and other regulatory agencies.

Effective Date

.10

This section is effective for engagements accepted on or after January 1, 1992. Early application of the provisions of this section is permissible.

[Revised, January 2015, to reflect the revised Code of Professional Conduct.]

Footnotes (CS Section 100—Consulting Services: Definitions and Standards):

[fn1] The definition of consulting services excludes the following:

a. Services subject to other AICPA professional standards such as Statements on Auditing Standards (SASs), Statements on Standards for Attestation Engagements (SSAEs), or Statements on Standards for Accounting and Review Services (SSARSs). (These excluded services may be performed in conjunction with consulting services, but only the consulting services are subject to the Statement on Standards for Consulting Services [SSCS].)

b. Engagements specifically to perform tax return preparation, tax planning or advice, tax representation, personal financial planning or bookkeeping services, or situations involving the preparation of written reports or the provision of oral advice on the application of accounting principles to specified transactions or events, either completed or proposed, and the reporting thereof.

c. Recommendations and comments prepared during the same engagement as a direct result of observations made while performing the excluded services.

[fn2] In "Integrity" (ET sec. 0.300.040), *integrity* is described as follows: "Integrity requires a member to be, among other things, honest and candid within the constraints of client confidentiality. Service and the public trust should not be subordinated to personal gain and advantage. Integrity can accommodate the inadvertent error and the honest difference of opinion; it cannot accommodate deceit or subordination of principle."

In "Objectivity and Independence" (ET sec. 0.300.050), *objectivity* and *independence* are differentiated as follows: "Objectivity is a state of mind, a quality that lends value to a member's services. It is a distinguishing feature of the profession. The principle of objectivity imposes the obligation to be impartial, intellectually honest, and free of conflicts of interest. *Independence* precludes relationships that may appear to impair a member's objectivity in rendering attestation services."

fn 3 The "Conflict of Interest Rule" (ET sec. 1.110.010) states, in part, the following:

> A conflict of interest may occur if a *member* or the *member's firm* has a relationship with another person, entity, product, or service that, in the member's professional judgment, the client or other appropriate parties may view as impairing the *member's* objectivity...
>
> A *member* may perform the *professional service* if he or she determines that the service can be performed with objectivity because the *threats* are not significant or can be reduced to an *acceptable level* through the application of *safeguards*...

fn 4 AICPA independence standards relate only to the performance of attestation services; objectivity standards apply to all services. See footnote 2."[14]

The AICPA's Statement on Standards for Consulting Services requires that CPAs adhere to the General Standards (e.g. Competence, Due Care, Planning and Supervision, and Consider Sufficient Relevant Data). The CPA must seek to serve the client interest by accomplishing the objectives of the professional service agreed upon with the client while maintaining integrity and objectivity. There must be a written or oral understanding of the nature, scope, and limitations of the service to be performed, which should be updated if circumstances change significantly. The CPA is required to inform the client of any conflict of interest, significant reservations concerning the scope or benefits of the engagement, and significant engagement finings or events.

Finally, when performing a business valuation, you must comply with the AICPA's Statement on Standards for Forensic Services:

> "STATEMENT ON STANDARDS FOR FORENSIC SERVICES
> Statements on Standards for Forensic Services (SSFSs) are issued by the Forensic and Valuation Services Executive Committee (FVS Executive Committee). The FVS Executive Committee provides guidance and establishes enforceable standards for *members* performing certain forensic and valuation services. The AICPA Council has designated the FVS Executive Committee as a body to establish professional standards under the "Compliance With Standards Rule," found in ET sections 1.310.001 and 2.310.001 of the AICPA Code of Professional Conduct. Members should be prepared to justify departures from this statement (ET sec. 0.100.010).
> Statement on Standards for Forensic Services No. 1
> Effective for engagements accepted on or after January 1, 2020.

WHY ISSUED

The term *forensic* is defined as "used in, or suitable to, courts of law or public debate."[1] Forensic accounting services[2] generally involve the application of specialized knowledge and investigative skills by a member[3] to collect, analyze, and evaluate certain evidential matter, and to interpret and communicate findings (forensic services).

The FVS Executive Committee has issued this standard to protect the public interest by preserving and enhancing the quality of practice of a member performing forensic services. Practice aids and other guidance issued at the direction of the FVS Executive Committee continue to serve as nonauthoritative guidance on the application of professional standards.[4] Authoritative standards and nonauthoritative guidance are not a substitute for the use of professional judgment.

---

[1] Bryan A. Garner, ed. *Black's Law Dictionary*, 10 ed., St. Paul, MN: Thomson West Publishing Co., 2014.

[2] ET section 1.295.140.01.

[3] ET section 0.400.31.

[4] Professionals should be aware of any governmental regulations and other professional standards applicable to the engagement.

Introduction and Scope—Forensic Services

1. This statement establishes standards for a member providing services to a client[5] as part of the following engagements:

- *Litigation.* An actual or potential legal or regulatory proceeding before a trier of fact or a regulatory body as an expert witness, consultant, neutral, mediator, or arbitrator in connection with the resolution of disputes between parties. The term *litigation* as used herein is not limited to formal litigation but is inclusive of disputes and all forms of alternative dispute resolution.
- *Investigation.* A matter conducted in response to specific concerns of wrongdoing in which the member is engaged to perform procedures to collect, analyze, evaluate, or interpret certain evidential matter to assist the stakeholders (for example, client, board of directors, independent auditor, or regulator) in reaching a conclusion on the merits of the concerns.

2. For purposes of this statement, forensic services consist of either litigation or investigation engagements. When an engagement meets the definition of *forensic services*, CS section 100, *Consulting Services: Definitions and Standards*,[6] does not apply. This statement applies when services provided under VS section 100, *Valuation of a Business, Business Ownership Interest, Security, or Intangible Asset*,[7] are provided as part of a litigation or investigation engagement.

Except as provided hereunder, this statement does not apply to a member who performs forensic services as part of an attest engagement (for example, as part of an audit, review, or compilation) or under TS section 100, *Tax Return Positions*.[8]

When a member is engaged as an expert witness by one party in a litigation engagement to provide expert opinions, the member may not perform the work under AT-C section 215, *Agreed-Upon Procedures Engagements*[9] (AUP standard). When performing services under the AUP standard, "the member does not perform an examination or a review and does not provide an opinion or conclusion." However, results may be reported under the AUP standard in an engagement in which a member is engaged by the trier of fact or both sides of the dispute jointly, or both. In each scenario, this statement and the AUP standard applies.

3. The key consideration of this statement's applicability is the purpose for which the member was engaged (for example, litigation or investigation) as opposed to the skill set employed or services provided. As an example, a member may provide data analysis services in a client engagement that does not constitute a litigation or investigation engagement. Conversely, similar data analysis services may also be performed in a client engagement, which constitutes a litigation or investigation engagement. This statement would apply under the second scenario and would not apply under the first scenario.

4. This statement applies when a member, who may have been engaged originally to perform services under another set of standards, discovers that the original scope of the engagement has been modified or amended and has become a litigation or investigation

---

[5] See ET section 0.400.07 for the definition of *client*, which indicates there may be multiple clients for one engagement.
[6] All CS sections can be found in AICPA *Professional Standards*.
[7] All VS sections can be found in AICPA *Professional Standards*.
[8] All TS sections can be found in AICPA *Professional Standards*.
[9] AT-C section 215, *Agreed-Upon Procedures Engagements*, can be found in AICPA *Professional Standards*.

engagement. The member should modify his or her understanding with the client if such an engagement converts to a forensic services engagement.

5. This statement is not applicable to internal use assignments from employers to employee members not in public practice. *Public practice* is defined as the performance of professional services for a client by a member or member's firm (ET sec. 0.400.42). The definition of a *client* specifically excludes a member's employer (ET sec. 0.400.07).

Standards for Forensic Services

6. The general standards of the profession are contained in the "General Standards Rule" (ET sec. 1.300.001 and 2.300.001) and apply to all services performed by a member, including forensic services. They are as follows:

- *Professional competence.* Undertake only those professional services that the member or the member's firm can reasonably expect to be completed with professional competence.
- *Due professional care.* Exercise due professional care in the performance of professional services.
- *Planning and supervision.* Adequately plan and supervise the performance of professional services.
- *Sufficient relevant data.* Obtain sufficient relevant data to afford a reasonable basis for conclusions or recommendations in relation to any professional services performed.

7. A member must serve his or her client with integrity and objectivity, as required by the AICPA Code of Professional Conduct. A member performing forensic services should not subordinate his or her opinion to that of any other party.

8. A member performing forensic services must follow additional general standards, which are promulgated to address the distinctive nature of such services. These standards are established under the "Compliance With Standards Rule" (ET sec. 1.310.001 and 2.310.001):

- *Client interest.* Serve the client interest by seeking to accomplish the objectives established by the understanding with the client while maintaining integrity and objectivity.
  - *Integrity.* Integrity is described as follows: "Integrity requires a member to be, among other things, honest and candid within the constraints of client confidentiality. Service and the public trust should not be subordinated to personal gain and advantage. Integrity can accommodate the inadvertent error and the honest difference of opinion; it cannot accommodate deceit or subordination of principle." (ET sec. 0.300.040)
  - *Objectivity.* Objectivity is described as follows: "Objectivity is a state of mind, a quality that lends value to a member's services. It is a distinguishing feature of the profession. The principle of objectivity imposes the obligation to be impartial, intellectually honest, and free of conflicts of interest." (ET sec. 0.300.050)
- *Understanding with client.* Establish with the client a written or oral understanding about the responsibilities of the parties and the nature, scope, and limitations of services to be performed and modify the understanding if circumstances require a significant change during the engagement.

- *Communication with client.* Inform the client of (*a*) conflicts of interest that may occur pursuant to the "Integrity and Objectivity Rule" (ET sec. 1.100.001 and 2.100.001), (*b*) significant reservations concerning the scope or benefits of the engagement, and (*c*) significant engagement findings or events.

  The "Conflicts of Interest for Members in Public Practice" interpretation (ET sec. 1.110.010) under the "Integrity and Objectivity Rule" provides guidance about the identification, evaluation, disclosures, and consent related to conflict of interest. This section states, in part, the following:

  - In determining whether a professional service, relationship, or matter would result in a conflict of interest, a member should use professional judgment, taking into account whether a reasonable and informed third party who is aware of the relevant information would conclude that a conflict of interest exists.

9. A member engaged as an expert witness in a litigation engagement may not provide opinions pursuant to a contingent fee arrangement, unless explicitly allowed otherwise under the "Contingent Fees" (ET sec. 1.510).

10. The ultimate decision regarding the occurrence of fraud is determined by a trier of fact; therefore, a member performing forensic services is prohibited from opining regarding the ultimate conclusion of fraud. This does not apply when the member is the trier of fact. A member may provide expert opinions relating to whether evidence is consistent with certain elements of fraud or other laws based on objective evaluation.

Effective Date

11. This statement is effective for new engagements accepted on or after January 1, 2020. Early application of the provisions of this statement is permissible."[15]

This statement provides standards for CPAs performing litigation or investigation services. The statement does not apply to consulting services but does apply to business valuation services. Of note, this statement does not apply to internal use assignments from employer to employee. Otherwise, the statement requires CPAs to exhibit; wait for it: professional competence, due care, planning and supervision, as well as, gathering sufficient relevant data as the basis for findings or conclusions. It also requires that the CPA serve the client with integrity and objectivity. Any conflicts of interest must be disclosed to the client. Generally, CPAs must not enter into contingent-fee arrangements when engaged to provide expert testimony and may not opine on the ultimate question of whether a fraud occurred or not.

Example: Economic Damages

In this first example we will look at how to measure economic damages in a case where an investor in a pre-IPO transaction was provided materially false information about the entity in which he was making the investment. Here we have a couple of different types of actions. One seeks a rescission remedy that would result in the investor's money being returned to him in exchange for him surrendering his shares in the pre-IPO entity; an easy calculation. But, if that remedy would have been unavailable, it was necessary to determine the difference in the value of the entity that the investor believed he was investing in versus the value of the entity as it really was. So, a business valuation needed to be performed comparing the entity's value as it was presented to the investor compared to the entity's value adjusted for the impact of all the misrepresentations. This is an excellent example of a report that deals with both liability and economic damages. The evidence was only processed once for both purposes. Study this report carefully. You will be rewarded with the confidence to be able to tackle even the most complex questions.

<Report_head> Expert Report of William L. Jennings

Viking Investments Limited v. Mirage, Inc., et al.

Circuit Court for the Ninth Judicial Circuit in and for Tombstone County, Arizona

August 24, 2018

<Report_source> Expert Report of William Jennings

Table of Contents

Even though my expert testimony was offered in state court the state court rules of civil procedure were similar to Rule 26. So, my report generally followed the format of a Rule 26 report.

Expert Report of William Jennings

I Introduction

1. My name is William L. Jennings. My business address is Veritaf, LLC.
2. I have been asked by counsel for plaintiff, in connection with the Viking Investments Limited v. Mirage, *et al.* litigation, to provide my opinions on the accounting and damages issues present in this litigation. In connection with this work, I am charging a fee of $550 per hour.
3. I am a Managing Director at Veritaf, LLC ("V") in the Global Forensic and Dispute Services practice. Previously, my positions included: Managing Director in the

Expert Report of William Jennings

Disputes and Investigations Practice at Navigant Consulting, Inc.; Director in the National Forensic Accounting Practice at LECG, LLC; President of FFI, Inc.; Managing Director at Kroll, Inc., in charge of investigative accounting services for the Central Region; Principal-in-Charge of the Atlanta office of Lindquist, Avey, Macdonald, Baskerville, a multinational independent forensic accounting firm; Principal-in-Charge of Coopers & Lybrand's Fraud Investigation Services practice for the Southeast Region; and Partner in the public accounting firm of Brown & Jennings.

4. I have a Bachelor of Science degree in Accounting and a Master's degree in Business Administration. I have been a Certified Public Accountant since 1981 and a Certified Fraud Examiner since 1991. I have more than 30 years of experience in forensic accounting, business controls development, public accounting and auditing. I am a member of the American Institute of Certified Public Accountants and the Association of Certified Fraud Examiners.

5. I have provided forensic accounting services to corporations, U.S. Attorneys' Offices, other government agencies, attorneys and their clients. I have also provided business controls consulting services to organizations. I have often provided expert testimony about the results of my work in federal and state courts as well as in many other dispute resolution venues. I have worked on hundreds of forensic accounting and investigation assignments. Further, I am a frequent public speaker on a variety of topics including white-collar crime, securities fraud, fraud investigation, forensic accounting, business ethics, accounting and financial reporting fraud. I have also published articles relating to fraud and forensic accounting. Details regarding my background, education, publications, speaking engagements and expert testimony are included in Exhibit 1.

6. Mirage, Inc. ("MIRAGE, INC.") is a company based in Satellite Beach, Florida that designs, manufactures, and markets Radar products.

7. Medusa Capital Advisors, L.P. ("Medusa") is a private equity fund manager based in Connecticut. At all times relevant to my analysis, Medusa (and its affiliates) owned approximately 80–90% of MIRAGE, INC.[1]

8. Banco Nazionale Securities, LLC ("BNS") is an international investment banking firm with offices all over the world, including various offices in Florida.

9. Viking Investments Limited ("Viking") is an investment company based in Germany. Viking's representative in the MIRAGE, INC. investment was Jack Beanstalk ("Jack Beanstalk").

II Materials Reviewed

10. My work on this assignment[2] is based upon information available to me as of the date of this report. I have reviewed the data, documents, testimony and other materials identified in this report and its footnotes. In addition, I have relied on the sworn testimony (and associated exhibits) in this matter. I also relied on my education, training and experience. A listing of the information I considered in preparing this report is attached as Exhibit 2. I reserve the right to supplement my opinions if new information becomes available to me.

My opinions are offered in Section III of the report. This is still very early and hopefully soon enough to capture the readers' full attention. My opinions begin with the most significant

---

[1] *See, e.g.,* Exhibit 359, at ABC00010652.

[2] In order to perform my review and analyses on this project, I was assisted by other V personnel, who I directly supervised.

Expert Report of William Jennings

misrepresentations made to Viking. Basically, Mirage hid significant costs of goods sold below the line (i.e. general and administrative expenses). Remember, this was an early stage growth company story. So, a healthy gross profit percentage could be applied to ever growing future sales over many periods in the future. On the other hand, below the line expenses would be expected to remain relatively stable for many future periods. I also point out that Mirage had material weaknesses in its internal controls which allowed incorrect accounting entries to be made to its books and records; another source of misrepresentations to Viking. I then discuss a transaction that further diluted Viking's investment in Mirage. Finally, I discuss the remedies available to Viking and the quantification of economic damages associated with each. Note that I also satisfy the legal standards in my opinions (i.e. (1) causation, (2) reasonable certainty, (3) economic loss doctrine, (4) proximate cause, (5) foreseeability, and (6) duty to mitigate). The misrepresentations were the cause of the loss. Economic damages were calculated with reasonable certainty. The remedies sought relate to property losses satisfying the economic loss doctrine. Defendants could foresee that their misrepresentations would result in Viking's loss. Viking had no opportunity to mitigate its losses.

Expert Report of William Jennings

III Opinions

11. Gross margin is a key operational and financial metric for a manufacturing company like MIRAGE, INC. It represents the amount of revenue remaining after deducting cost of goods sold ("COGS") (i.e., all direct costs associated with producing the products sold) to cover operating and other expenses as well as produce net income. Gross margin is a key metric that a reasonable investor would evaluate in making investment decisions about a manufacturing company like MIRAGE, INC.

12. For a manufacturing company like MIRAGE, INC., accurate inventory accounting is critical in calculating COGS, which is critical in calculating gross margin. MIRAGE, INC.'s inventory accounting was incorrect.

13. MIRAGE, INC. falsely reported its historical COGS and, as a result, gross margins. In addition, the Subscription Agreement falsely represented that MIRAGE, INC.'s financial statements were prepared in accordance with Generally Accepted Accounting Principles ("GAAP").

14. For a manufacturing company like MIRAGE, INC., COGS and gross margin are key elements in financial models of results of future operations. If any errors in historical COGS or gross margin percentages are used in models of results of future operations that show increasing revenues, then those errors will be magnified over time in the projected results of operations. Viking was provided models that contained such magnified errors.

15. Incorrect gross margins were material to Viking's investment decision and would have been material to any reasonable investor.

16. MIRAGE, INC.'s books and records were not in compliance with GAAP as a result of material internal control weaknesses. Thus, MIRAGE, INC. falsely represented in the Subscription Agreement that its financial statements had been prepared in accordance with GAAP is important to investors because it allows investors and other users of financial statements to rely on those statements. "Reliability and relevance are the two primary qualities that make accounting information useful for decision making."[3]

---

[3] Kieso, Weygandt, and Warfield. *Intermediate Accounting*, 12th Edition (John Galey & Sons, 2014), pp. 32–33. Comparability is another quality that makes accounting information useful.

Expert Report of William Jennings

17. As a result of incorrect accounting for the valuation of some of its warrants, MIRAGE, INC. falsely reported the amount of its liabilities, earnings, and earnings per share in its 10-Qs for the first three quarters of 2016. MIRAGE, INC. did not note in the 2016 10-K that the previous 10-Qs contained errors nor did it inform Viking of the errors. The first public disclosure of this error did not come until a public filing on May 16, 2018 – after the Subscription Agreement was signed – when MIRAGE, INC. included a note in its 10-Q for the first quarter of 2018. MIRAGE, INC. then subsequently restated its second and third quarter 2016 financial statements in its second and third quarter 2018 10-Qs, which were months after Viking's investment.

18. The Life Insurance, Inc. transaction, together with its resulting consequences, resulted in an approximately $203 million reduction in MIRAGE, INC.'s paid-in capital and the constructive creation in 2019 of two classes of MIRAGE, INC. common stock: (1) a controlling shareholder class, which included MIRAGE, INC.C Holdings LLC (a Medusa Capital Fund), and (2) a non-controlling shareholder class that included Viking. In 2019, the non-controlling shares were allocated an additional $0.45 per share of losses compared to the controlling shares. This made the non-controlling shareholders' (including Viking) common stock less valuable than the controlling shareholders' stock.

19. Based on a review of the material presented to Viking, MIRAGE, INC. was presented as a growth company. However, if accurate numbers had been reported in the 2016 10-K and to Viking, any reasonable investor would have been much more skeptical of MIRAGE, INC.'s potential for growth, as the poor performance in 2016 could not be explained as an outlier following better years in 2017 and 2015 (e.g., the restatement switched MIRAGE, INC.'s 2017 gross margin from positive to negative). The gross margin errors were material and the SEC forced a restatement. Indeed, the pre-IPO contemplated in the Subscription Agreement to be completed soon after Viking's investment still has not occurred nearly three years later. From the First Amended Complaint, Viking is seeking rescission. The magnitude of the differences between MIRAGE, INC.'s statements of operations and financial position *as represented* compared to its actual results supports the rescission request.

20. Alternatively, performing a damages calculation leads to the conclusion that the non-marketable, non-controlling common shares held by Viking are currently worth pennies, if anything. A valuation analysis also shows that if the truth about MIRAGE, INC.'s gross margins had been disclosed to Viking at the date of investment and BNS's models had been adjusted accordingly, then MIRAGE, INC.'s equity value – and therefore the value of Viking's shares – would have been reduced by at least 48%, or almost $12 million (plus prejudgment interest) by virtue of the gross margin misstatement issue alone, looking solely at the date Viking purchased the shares. Viking's damages attributable to this error alone are likely even greater than 48% due to the fact that the valuation analysis did not account for the differences in rights and preferences between Viking's common stock and the numerous more preferred and beneficial classes of equity present in MIRAGE, INC.'s capital structure (i.e., Viking holds the least valuable class of shares). For example, there are several classes of preferred shares senior to common stock that have priority rights to dividends, redemption rights, conversion rights, voting rights, and significant liquidation rights. Thus, the common stock portion of the company's overall equity value is likely small which would result in a significantly larger reduction than 48%. Moreover, this damage does not take into account the restatements of

the Series B and C warrants which damaged earnings (see Section VI), MIRAGE, INC.'s understatement of its inventory reserves (see Section V.D), or the post-investment conduct damaging Viking (see Section VIII). Please see Exhibit 3 for supporting schedules.[4]

21. Expanding the analysis to take into account additional restatements and conduct by MIRAGE, INC. and Medusa after the Subscription Agreement was executed confirms that Viking's shares are currently virtually worthless and unsaleable. MIRAGE, INC. continued to reduce the value of common shares through a number of dilutive transactions, including the Life Insurance, Inc. transaction. This 2019 transaction alone, the disclosure of which was questioned by the SEC because of its negative impact on non-controlling shareholders like Viking, caused a $0.45 per share differential between controlling and minority shares in 2019.

22. Under rescission or if the analysis in paragraphs 20 and 21 indicate that MIRAGE, INC.'s shares are worthless, then Viking's damages are equal to the amount of its initial investment, $25 million, plus attendant prejudgment interest calculated under Florida state law from May 18, 2018 to August 24, 2014, in an amount of $3,404,795. Please see Exhibit 4 for calculation of prejudgment interest. All calculations herein are exclusive of any attorneys' fees, costs, punitive or other damages the Court may award.

23. In the alternative, if the reported stock price of MIRAGE, INC.'s shares at the close of business on Friday, August 21, 2014 ($0.39 per share) is used as a proxy for the value of Viking common shares, then the value of Viking's 6.25 million shares is $2,437,500 and Viking's damages are equal to $22,562,500. This is a conservative estimate of damages because the value of a Viking common share may be less than the reported stock price due to the fact that the reported stock price may include sales of controlling shares, which may be more valuable due to their additional anti-dilution protections (as revealed in MIRAGE, INC. Amendment No. 3 to Form S-1, 2/14/14), and/or may not have the restrictions that Viking shares do.

Notice that my opinions 1–21, above, are concerned entirely with liability and loss causation issues. Opinions 21 and 22 are based on two entirely different economic damages measures. These measures were chosen in consultation with the attorneys. The first calculation is based on a measure of economic damages and judicial interest that would result from the court granting a rescission remedy. Basically, the court would set aside the investment transaction and restore the investor's investment plus judicial interest from the date of the investment. Opinion 23, as we shall see, is a bit more complicated. This assumes that the court does not grant the rescission remedy. In this case, the economic damages would be calculated by measuring the impact of the misrepresentations and other bad acts of defendants on the value of the business that was the subject of the investment. While the information and the calculations were complex, they are fully explained in the pages that follow.

Next, I provide a detailed background of all the circumstances that led to Viking's loss. This is necessary to give the reader of the report the context in which I offer my opinions. Here I let the evidence tell the story. This is so that the trier of fact can see that my expert testimony is solidly based on the evidence offered in this case.

---

[4] A valuation analysis was performed by V to calculate damages to Viking's investment in MIRAGE, INC.'s common shares as a result of the restatement of MIRAGE, INC.'s financials due to the inventory obsolescence misclassification issues. The analysis is attached as Exhibit 3.

Expert Report of William Jennings

IV Background

24. From an accounting perspective, materiality is "the magnitude of an omission or misstatement of accounting information that, in light of surrounding circumstances, makes it probable that the judgment of a reasonable person relying on the information would have been changed or influenced by the omission or misstatement."[5] Auditors are required to determine a materiality level for the financial statements during the audit planning process. In doing so, they use their professional judgment and consider all relevant quantitative and qualitative factors.[6]

25. I C Little, LLC ("I C Little") is an independent, registered, licensed public accounting firm that served as MIRAGE, INC.'s auditor for the years ended December 31, 2014, 2017, 2015, and 2016. I C Little set the following materiality levels for its audits of MIRAGE, INC.:

- 2016: $850,000[7]
- 2017: $950,000[8]
- 2018: $999,999[9]

26. RCMP is an independent registered, licensed public accounting firm that served as MIRAGE, INC.'s auditor for the years ended December 31, 2018. RCMP set the materiality level for its 2018 audit of MIRAGE, INC. at $1.5 million.[10]

27. In May 2018, Viking purchased $25 million of MIRAGE, INC. common stock – 6.25 million shares at $4 per share – in a private placement arranged by BNS.[11]

28. On August 19, 2016, the Chair of MIRAGE, INC.'s Audit Committee sent an email to the Audit Committee stating "[i]t's very clear that we have consistently overestimated our revenues and underestimated our COGS [cost of goods sold] and Operating Expenses."[12] He also agrees that "all our forecasts are overstated" and shares a chart comparing previous financial forecasts to actual results.

29. On August 30, 2016, at a meeting of the MIRAGE, INC. Audit Committee, MIRAGE, INC.'s CFO and Corporate Controller told the Audit Committee that accounting for COGS was "being done by 'the seat of the pants' rather than based on data."[13]

30. In late 2016, BNS approached Viking with an investment opportunity, namely a private placement of MIRAGE, INC. stock ahead of a planned public offering of MIRAGE, INC. stock.[14]

31. On August 10, 2018, MIRAGE, INC. a Form S-1 (i.e., IPO prospectus) with the U.S. Securities and Exchange Commission ("SEC").[15] This filing contained incorrect gross margins for fiscal years 2017 and 2015 due to MIRAGE, INC.'s incorrect misclassification of obsolete inventory into research and development ("R&D") expense rather than as COGS.

32. In March, April, and May 2018, BNS and MIRAGE, INC. provided Viking with various MIRAGE, INC. financial, accounting, and operational reports and models

---

[5] Statement of Financial Accounting Concepts No. 2 (CON-2), p. 10.
[6] AICPA Audit and Attest Standards, AU 312, "Audit Risk and Materiality in Conducting an Audit."
[7] M-MIRAGE, INC.-007664-7666, at 7665.
[8] M-MIRAGE, INC.-002222-2226, at 2225.
[9] M-MIRAGE, INC.-004346-4353, at 4352.
[10] RCMP.MIRAGE, INC. 002074-2081, at 2080.
[11] Exhibit 378, ABC00001670-1680.
[12] Exhibit 354, DE000523023.
[13] Exhibit 355, MIRAGE, INC.-000409-412 at 411 (also ABC00013645-13648 at 13647).
[14] First Amended Complaint, para. 44.
[15] Exhibit 359, ABC00010630-10818.

for Viking to review in relation to the pre-IPO private placement opportunity. These included historical reports and models of future results for various metrics, including revenues, COGS, gross margins, and earnings. Some examples of the materials that BNS provided to Viking include:

a. On March 16, 2018, BNS Jack Beanstalk financial models for MIRAGE, INC. and a MIRAGE, INC. investor presentation.[16]
b. On March 21, 2018, BNS Jack Beanstalk financial models for MIRAGE, INC. and a headcount summary for MIRAGE, INC.[17]
c. On April 2, 2018, BNS Jack Beanstalk a valuation analysis of MIRAGE, INC. that included various financial models, key highlights of those models, and financial comparisons of MIRAGE, INC. to peer companies.[18]
d. On May 9, 2018, BNS Jack Beanstalk a summary and explanation of MIRAGE, INC.'s April financial and operational results prepared by MIRAGE, INC.'s CFO.[19] (As discussed later in this report, BNS omitted key information from the CFO's email, such as the fact that MIRAGE, INC. missed its gross margin target for April, when it forwarded the CFO's email.)

33. The historical reports inflated MIRAGE, INC.'s past gross margins due to MIRAGE, INC.'s incorrect accounting treatment of write-downs of obsolete inventory. The models of MIRAGE, INC.'s future revenue, gross margins, and earnings were based on this false financial data and turned out to be wildly optimistic relative to MIRAGE, INC.'s actual financial performance. Please see Exhibit 5 for a comparison of MIRAGE, INC.'s performance, as depicted in the 2018 and 2019 models provided to Viking by BNS, to MIRAGE, INC.'s actual performance in those years. Highlights include:

- *Revenue*
  - *2018*: Forecast $200+ million. Actual $109 million.
  - *2019*: Forecast $440+ million. Actual $127 million.
- *Gross Margins*
  - *2018*: Forecast $39 million, or 18–19%. Actual ($20) million, or −18%.
  - *2019*: Forecast $134 million, or 30%. Actual ($19.7) million, or −15%.
- *EBITDA*
  - *2018*: Forecast ($4.6–5.3) million. Actual ($83) million.
  - *2019:* Forecast $72 million. Actual ($98) million.

In addition (and discussed in greater detail below), BNS was informed that the SEC was challenging MIRAGE, INC.'s accounting treatment of gross margins by at least late April but did not make Viking aware of this information.

34. On April 1, 2018, MIRAGE, INC. its 10-K for the fiscal year ended December 31, 2016.[20] MIRAGE, INC. would later amend this filing – *after* Viking's investment

---

[16] Exhibit 311, ABC00000168-170.
[17] Exhibit 312, ABC00000562-566.
[18] Exhibit 369, ABC00000209-215.
[19] Exhibit 521, BNS_00034308-34311
[20] Exhibit 366, DE000303928-304022.

in MIRAGE, INC. – and file a 10-K/A on June 29, 2018.[21] The amended filing described MIRAGE, INC.'s incorrect accounting treatment for obsolete inventory in fiscal years 2017 and 2015 and reported significantly lower gross margins for those years than had previously been reported.

35. On April 4, 2018, representatives of MIRAGE, INC., BNS, and Medusa met at MIRAGE, INC.'s headquarters with a representative of Viking (Jack Beanstalk) to discuss Viking's potential investment in MIRAGE, INC.[22]

36. On April 20, 2018, MIRAGE, INC. a Form S-1/A (i.e., amended IPO prospectus) with the SEC.[23] This S-1/A reported the same incorrect gross margins as the original S-1 August 10, 2018, and the 10-K April 1, 2018. MIRAGE, INC.'s outside counsel this S-1/A to Viking's outside counsel (copying various MIRAGE, INC., BNS, and Medusa executives) on May 7, 2018,[24] in lieu of a private placement memorandum just days before Viking's investment was finalized.

37. On April 28, 2018, the SEC transmitted a Comment Letter dated April 29, 2018, to MIRAGE, INC.'s counsel, which relayed the results of the SEC's review of MIRAGE, INC.'s Form S-1/A. MIRAGE, INC.'s counsel immediately the Comment Letter to over 60 recipients, including executives at MIRAGE, INC., BNS, and Medusa, as well as MIRAGE, INC.'s auditors and various investment banks and law firms involved in MIRAGE, INC.'s IPO plans. In the letter, the SEC commented on the S-1/A's section on inventories and stated that "[n]otwithstanding the stage of development of certain products or your focus on research and development during 2015 and 2017, we believe expenses incurred as a result of write-downs of products held for sale should be recorded within cost of goods sold."[25] I did not see any contemporaneous documents that MIRAGE, INC., BNS, or Medusa ever made Viking aware of this SEC Comment Letter prior to Viking's investment. In addition, I did not see any indication that this letter was made available to the public before Viking's investment.

38. On April 29, 2018, BNS a draft Subscription Agreement to Viking. This email does not disclose to Viking the SEC Comment Letter received by MIRAGE, INC. the previous afternoon.[26]

39. On May 3, 2018, the SEC transmitted to MIRAGE, INC.'s counsel a Comment Letter dated May 3, 2018, which relayed the results of the SEC's review of MIRAGE, INC.'s 10-K for FY2018. MIRAGE, INC.'s counsel immediately the Comment Letter to over 60 recipients, including executives at MIRAGE, INC., BNS, and Medusa, as well as MIRAGE, INC.'s auditors and various investment banks and law firms involved in MIRAGE, INC.'s IPO plans. In the letter, the SEC commented on the 10-K's section on inventories and stated that "[n]otwithstanding the stage of development of certain products or your focus on research and development during 2015 and 2017, we believe expenses incurred as a result of write-downs of products held for sale should be recorded within cost of goods sold."[27] I did not see any contemporaneous documents that MIRAGE, INC., BNS, or Medusa ever made Viking aware of this SEC

---

[21] Exhibit 385, DE000007233-7359.

[22] First Amended Complaint, para. 77. *See also* Exhibit 368, DE000338608.

[23] Exhibit 373, BNS_00058319-58504.

[24] Exhibit 373, BNS_00058319-58504.

[25] Exhibit 370, BNS_ 00044494-44500 at 44499.

[26] Exhibit 329, ABC00000279-289.

[27] Exhibit 331, BNS_00044502-44508 at 44507.

Comment Letter prior to Viking's investment. In addition, I did not see any indication that this letter was made available to the public before Viking's investment.

40. On May 5, 2018, the MIRAGE, INC. Board of Directors approved Viking's proposed investment.[28] The notes of this meeting also confirm BNS's role in bringing Viking into this investment: "[MIRAGE, INC.'s CFO] also noted the identities of potential participants in the Proposed Investment, including … a potential investor introduced to the Company by J.P. Prince."[29]

41. As noted above, on May 7, 2018, counsel for MIRAGE, INC. sent to counsel for Viking a copy of the April 20, 2018, S-1/A, along with a draft Subscription Agreement. This email does not disclose either of the SEC Comment Letters received by MIRAGE, INC. on April 28 and May 3, 2018.[30] The S-1/A contained the same incorrect gross margins as the original S-1 August 10, 2018, and the 10-K April 1, 2018.

42. On May 10, 2018, Viking and MIRAGE, INC. entered into a Subscription Agreement for Viking to purchase $25 million in MIRAGE, INC. common stock: 6.25 million shares at a price of $4.00 per share.[31] BNS acted as MIRAGE, INC.'s placement agent for this transaction and received a fee from MIRAGE, INC. equal to 4.5% of the value of the deal ($1.125 million), as out in the engagement letter between MIRAGE, INC. and BNS.[32] This engagement letter, however, was entered into after the Viking transaction, yet contained an indemnity by which MIRAGE, INC. agreed to pay for a number of items, including BNS's fees in litigation.

43. On May 12, 2018 – after the Subscription Agreement had been signed but prior to Viking making payment – MIRAGE, INC.'s Audit Committee held a meeting at which they discussed both the SEC Comment Letter on MIRAGE, INC.'s 10-K and Viking's $25 million investment.[33] There is no indication in the meeting notes that the Audit Committee ever discussed informing Viking of the SEC Comment Letter.

44. On May 16, 2018, Jack Beanstalk authorized Viking to wire $25 million to MIRAGE, INC. to fund the share purchase.[34] Jack Beanstalk then informed BNS that the funds were being transferred to MIRAGE, INC.[35]

45. On May 16, 2018, MIRAGE, INC. its 10-Q for the quarter ending March 31, 2018. As discussed in greater detail later in this report, this 10-Q included a Correction of Immaterial Prior Period Error disclosure that MIRAGE, INC. had previously valued its Series D warrants incorrectly, and thus underreported its liabilities and net loss for the quarter ended March 31, 2016.[36]

   MIRAGE, INC. had underreported its liabilities by $1.4 million (63.5%), over-reported its accretion of preferred stock by $19,000 (9.3%), and underreported its net loss by $1.4 million (11.2%) for the quarter ended March 31, 2016. Then, on August 15, 2018, MIRAGE, INC. its 10-Q for the quarter ending June 30, 2018.[37] This 10-Q included a Restatement of Financial Statements because MIRAGE, INC. had also previously valued its Series E warrants incorrectly. MIRAGE, INC. had

---

[28] Exhibit 547, MIRAGE, INC.-000070-72 (also ABC00013306-13308)
[29] Exhibit 547, at MIRAGE, INC.-000070.
[30] Exhibit 373, BNS_00058319-58504.
[31] Exhibit 378, ABC00001670-1681.
[32] Exhibit 388, BNS_00035008-35014.
[33] RCMP.MIRAGE, INC. 002453-2456.
[34] Def. Exh. 7(t), ABC00001526-1528.
[35] Def. Exh. 7(u), BNS_00000769.
[36] BNS_00034542-34572, at 34549.
[37] DE000518872-518949, at 518888-889.

Expert Report of William Jennings

underreported its liabilities by $11.0 million (13.9%), its accretion of preferred stock by $85,000 (10.9%), and its net loss by $11.1 million (9.6%) for the six months ended June 30, 2016. Finally, on November 14, 2018, MIRAGE, INC. its 10-Q for the quarter ending September 30, 2018.[38] This 10-Q also included a Restatement of Financial Statements, which showed that MIRAGE, INC. had underreported its liabilities by $3.8 million (6.7%), its accretion of preferred stock by $24.5 million (50.6%), and its net loss by $28.3 million (18.2%) for the nine months ended September 30, 2016. Please see Exhibit 6 for details of these restatements. The knowledge that MIRAGE, INC. had incorrectly underreported its net losses for the first three, six, and nine months of 2016 by 11.2%, 9.6%, and 18.2%, respectively, would have been important to a reasonable investor. All three of these net loss misstatements were in excess of I C Little's materiality threshold for 2016.

46. On May 18, 2018, $25 million was wired from an entity related to Viking to MIRAGE, INC. to fund the share purchase.[39]

47. On or about May 26, 2018, MIRAGE, INC.'s largest shareholder, MIRAGE, INC.C Holdings LLC ("Holdings"), a Medusa Capital Fund that owned approximately 90% of MIRAGE, INC.'s shares, issued its own senior preferred membership interests (Class C Preferred Interests) and distributed 15,000,000 Class C Preferred Interests and 562,500 shares of MIRAGE, INC.'s common stock to Life Insurance, Inc. Company ("CCC") in exchange for $15 million.[40] As part of this transaction, Holdings agreed to redeem CCC's investment plus interest if certain events were triggered. Holdings used the proceeds to purchase 3,750,000 shares of MIRAGE, INC. common stock issued through a private placement. In January 2019, CCC purchased 5,000 units of Series G, in exchange for $5 million directly from MIRAGE, INC.[41] Also, Holdings and CCC agreed to modify the terms of the Class C Preferred Interests, including by adding another trigger for redemption. This trigger would require Holdings to redeem CCC's $15 million investment, plus interest, if MIRAGE, INC. issued over $80 million of preferred equity.[42] At the same time, MIRAGE, INC. agreed to indemnify Holdings for that obligation.[43] This indemnification obligation was triggered in May 2019, resulting in MIRAGE, INC. paying approximately $16.2 million (in cash and preferred stock) directly to CCC on behalf of Holdings.[44] This transaction resulted in a "deemed dividend" to Holdings, which effectively created two separate classes of common stock. The class held by Viking and other minority investors absorbed all of MIRAGE, INC.'s subsequent losses up to the amount of the "deemed dividend," while the class held by Holdings absorbed no losses up to the amount of the "deemed dividend."[45]

48. On June 22, 2018, MIRAGE, INC. an 8-K announcing that it would need to restate its financial statements for fiscal years 2017 and 2015 due to its misclassification of write-offs for obsolete inventory.[46] On June 29, 2018, MIRAGE, INC. an amended

---

[38] DE000099751-99797, at 99770-771.

[39] Def. Exh. 9(h), ABC00002311.

[40] RCMP.MIRAGE, INC. 000144-154; Exhibit 434, DE000603295-603352, at 603308.

[41] DE000017621-17624.

[42] DE000692466-692494.

[43] Exhibit 435, DE000017617-17620.

[44] Exhibit 436, DE000445058-445070, at 445063.

[45] Exhibit 434, DE0000603295-603352, at 603308-603310.

[46] Exhibit 395, ABC00007467-7469.

10-K disclosing that it had misclassified $4.1 million of obsolete inventory in 2015 and $4.5 million of obsolete inventory in 2017 as research and development costs rather than as COGS.[47] Therefore, MIRAGE, INC.'s gross margins were overstated by these same amounts in MIRAGE, INC.'s previously-issued financial reports. Both of these misstatements were in excess of I C Little's materiality thresholds for 2017 and 2015.

49. MIRAGE, INC. has never completed the IPO associated with the S-1 and S-1/A and specifically referenced in Section 3(i) the Subscription Agreement: "The Company intends to list its shares of Common Stock on the NASDAQ stock market ..., which is currently to occur on or before July 31, 2018.[48] In its 10-Q for the quarter ended September 30, 2018, MIRAGE, INC. noted "the extended postponement of the proposed offering" and, in accordance with SEC rules, expensed the $1.3 million of legal and accounting costs associated with the offering, which it had previously capitalized.[49]

50. In fact, MIRAGE, INC. subsequently two additional versions of the S-1/A, one in September 2019 and another on August 14, 2014. The S-1/A this month reveals that MIRAGE, INC.'s pattern of systematically destroying the value of Viking's shares has continued over the past several years. The reduced value of common shares, such as those held by Viking, can also be seen in the value over time of the common stock issued to MIRAGE, INC. employees under the company's employee stock purchase plan. In 2018, shares were issued to employees at prices ranging from $1.62 to $2.32, in 2019 at prices ranging from $0.58 to $1.34, in 2013 at prices ranging from $0.29 to $0.57, and in 2014 at prices ranging from $0.31 to $0.32.[50] MIRAGE, INC. common stock closed at $0.39 per share on August 21, 2014, when 8,950 shares were traded on the OTC Bulletin Board.[51]

Now, I drill down on the central misrepresentation. This is the fact that Mirage's Cost of Goods Sold was repeatedly understated to hide the fact that they were in the widget business.

V MIRAGE, INC.'s Falsely Reported Gross Margins
A. Gross Margin and Cost of Goods Sold

51. Gross margin equals a company's revenue minus its COGS. It reflects the amount of revenue remaining after deducting all of the direct costs required to produce the revenue.

52. For a manufacturing company, such as MIRAGE, INC.:

COGS = Beginning Inventory + Purchases + Other cost inputs – Ending Inventory

Therefore, inventory accounting is critical in accurately calculating COGS and gross margin, and ultimately, profitability and forecasts of operating results for a company like MIRAGE, INC.

---

[47] Exhibit 385, DE0007233-7359.
[48] Exhibit 378, ABC00001670-1681, at 1672.
[49] MIRAGE, INC. Form 10-Q for the quarterly period ended September 30, 2018, DE000099751-99797 at 99781.
[50] MIRAGE, INC. Form S-1/A August 14, 2014, Item 15 (Recent Sales of Unregistered Securities).
[51] Downloaded on August 22, 2014, at http://www.otcmarkets.com/stock/MIRAGE/quote.

Expert Report of William Jennings

53. Gross margins affect a company's current earnings and models of future earnings because they represent the revenue remaining, after deducting all direct costs associated with producing the revenue, to pay operating expenses and produce earnings. Thus, the greater the gross margins, the more revenue that is available to drop to the company's "bottom line." As revenues increase in future periods, if gross margin percentages remain the same or increase and operating expenses remain consistent, there will be an ever greater surplus available to increase EBITDA (earnings before interest, taxes, depreciation, and amortization) and net income.

54. To illustrate this point, consider two hypothetical companies: Company A and Company B. Company A and Company B have the same net earnings in Year 1 and are alike in all respects except that Company A has 20% gross margins while Company B has 5% gross margins. If revenue increases in the same amount for each company, Company A's net earnings will grow much faster than Company B's because more of that revenue will be available to drop down to the "bottom line."

55. Thus, all else remaining equal, a company with positive gross margins will see its earnings increase as its revenue increases (even if it currently produces net losses) and the larger the gross margin percentage, the quicker its earnings will improve. A company with negative gross margins may never see its earnings increase no matter how much revenue is generated.

B. MIRAGE, INC. Reported Inflated Gross Margins for 2017 and 2015

56. MIRAGE, INC.'s financial statements for 2017 and 2015 understated COGS, thus artificially inflating the gross margins reported to users of those financial statements. The resulting misstated gross margin percentages were also included in the financial models provided to Viking prior to Viking's investment in MIRAGE, INC.

57. MIRAGE, INC. annual financial statements (Form 10-K) with the SEC each year from 2017–2016. In addition, MIRAGE, INC. an IPO prospectus (Form S-1) on August 10, 2018, and an amended IPO prospectus (Form S-1/A) on April 20, 2018. An S-1 is a registration statement that a company must file with the SEC prior to an initial public offering of its stock. The S-1 serves as a prospectus for the offering and is designed to provide potential investors with relevant information that they will need in making an investment decision, such as detailed financial results and information, in-depth descriptions of the company's business model and risks, the planned use of the capital being raised, and any dilution that will occur to the company's other listed securities.

58. A representative of MIRAGE, INC. the S-1/A to a Viking representative on May 7, 2018, just days before Viking's investment was finalized.[52] In this transaction, the S-1/A also served as the registration statement for the offering, substituting for the private placement memo that one would normally see in a private placement of stock.[53]

59. In both the S-1 and S-1/A, MIRAGE, INC. reported the gross margins and gross margin percentages as shown in Table 11.5 (as a percentage of revenue).

---

[52] Exhibit 373, email (and attachments) from Ryan Cox of the law firm Dewey Cheatum & How, BNS_00058319-58504.
[53] Exhibit 373, at BNS_00058320.

Expert Report of William Jennings

TABLE 11.5

Year Ended	Gross Margin ($)	Gross Margin (%)
2017	4,069,993	19.6
2015	6,621,997	21.1
2016	(5,852,838)	(11.0)

Source: MIRAGE, INC. 10-Ks 7/1/09, 4/13/10, and 4/1/11.

    MIRAGE, INC. described the 2016 gross margin in its public filings as an anomaly due to greater than expected costs related to new products, primarily due to greater than expected demand.[54] In other words, MIRAGE, INC. described itself as a company with solid, positive gross margins that experienced a dip in gross margins in 2016 due to costs related to keeping up with increasing demand.

60. GAAP requires that "inventory markdowns ... be classified in the income statement as a component of cost of goods sold."[55] Such inventory markdowns include writeoffs of obsolete or slow-moving inventory and have the effect of increasing COGS and reducing gross margin.

61. I C Little noted during its interoffice inspection[56] of the 2015 audit that MIRAGE, INC. had misclassified its obsolete inventory losses as operational costs (i.e., research and development) rather than as COGS in both the 2017 and 2015 financial statements. I C Little's analysis of this issue was memorialized in an audit workpaper memo "SAB 99 Analysis – Classification of Inventory Obsolescence Loss in the Statement of Operations."[57] This memo states that MIRAGE, INC. management concluded that the misclassification of obsolete inventory and the resulting effect on COGS and gross margins was not material, and therefore MIRAGE, INC. was not required to restate its financial statements. I C Little concurred with this conclusion.

62. The same issue was noted again during the 2016 audit by a new I C Little audit team, and again it was deemed immaterial by MIRAGE, INC. management. This is documented in a June 21, 2018, audit workpaper "Record of Consultation – Restatement of Previously Issued F/S."[58]

63. However, after reviewing MIRAGE, INC.'s S-1/A and 2016 10-K, the SEC issued Comment Letters to MIRAGE, INC. on April 29 and May 3, 2018, respectively, which both stated that "[n]otwithstanding the stage of development of certain products or your focus on research and development during 2015 and 2017, we believe expenses incurred as a result of write-downs of products held for sale should be recorded within cost of goods sold."[59]

---

[54] Exhibit 366, DE000303928-304022 at 303957.

[55] ASC 420-10-S99-3.

[56] Interoffice inspections, where partners review each other's work, are a normal part of an accounting firm's quality control processes and procedures.

[57] There are two versions of this memo in the record, both with the same conclusion: (1) Exhibit 356, M-MIRAGE, INC.-000499-501, dated September 20, 2016, and (2) M-MIRAGE, INC.-003950-52, dated March 30, 2018.

[58] Exhibit 393, M-MIRAGE, INC.-003124-3129.

[59] Exhibit 370, BNS_00044494-44500; Exhibit 331, BNS_00044502-44508.

MIRAGE, INC., BNS, and Medusa personnel (as well as various investment bankers and attorneys) were forwarded copies of the Comment Letters immediately after MIRAGE, INC.'s counsel received them.[60] However, I did not see any contemporaneous documents showing that Viking, which was in the final stages of negotiating a $25 million purchase of MIRAGE, INC. stock, was ever notified of these letters or their content.

64. After discussions with its counsel, auditors, and Audit Committee and phone calls with the SEC in which it attempted to explain why it believed the misclassification was immaterial, MIRAGE, INC. management finally decided to restate its 2017 and 2015 financials.[61] Again, I did not see any contemporaneous documents showing that Viking was ever notified of any of these discussions regarding a potential restatement of the financial statements that it was relying upon in making its investment decision.

65. MIRAGE, INC. issued an amended 2016 10-K on June 29, 2018 – after Viking had made its $25 million payment – which restated MIRAGE, INC.'s financial results for 2017 and 2015.[62] In particular, MIRAGE, INC. reclassified its provision for excess and obsolete inventory from an operating expense (Research and Development) to COGS. By increasing COGS, this reclassification reduced MIRAGE, INC.'s reported gross margins and gross margin percentages for 2017 and 2015. With lower gross margin percentages, MIRAGE, INC.'s future revenues would produce less future earnings, thus making MIRAGE, INC. stock less valuable. In other words, keeping everything else constant, a MIRAGE, INC. with lower gross margins is less valuable than a MIRAGE, INC. with higher gross margins.

66. In the amended 2016 10-K, MIRAGE, INC. reported the gross margins and gross margin percentages as shown in Table 11.6.

TABLE 11.6

Year Ended	Gross Margin ($)	Gross Margin (%)
2017	(448,110)	(2.2)
2015	2,495,867	8.0
2016	(5,852,838)	(11.0)

Source: MIRAGE, INC. 10-K/A 6/29/11.

By correcting its accounting for obsolete inventory, MIRAGE, INC.'s gross margin percentage for 2017 decreased from 19.6% to (2.2%) and for 2015 decreased from 21.1% to 8.0%. By any reasonable measure, misstatements of this magnitude

---

[60] Exhibit 370, BNS_00044494-44500; Exhibit 331, BNS_00044502-44508. Dozens of other attorneys and investment bankers - apparently all those involved in the planned IPO, nicknamed Project Nosedive - were also copied on the same emails that forwarded the SEC Comment Letters.

[61] The history of the misclassification issue is described in I C Little's documentation of the restatement. Exhibit 393, M-MIRAGE, INC.-003124-3129. *See also* Exhibit 565, DE000435020-435025; Exhibit 566, DE000435046; Exhibit 567, DE000387718-387722.

[62] Exhibit 385, MIRAGE, INC. 2016 10-K/A June 29, 2018, DE000007233-7359.

would be considered material to users of the financial statements, including potential investors.

67. It is clear that the gross margin accounting issue was well known by MIRAGE, INC.'s management, Board of Directors, and auditors well before Viking's potential investment. In addition, it is clear that this issue was being discussed among these parties in April and May 2018 during the same period of time that MIRAGE, INC. and BNS were providing incorrect financial and operational data to Viking to facilitate and finalize Viking's potential investment. For example, Board members, MIRAGE, INC.'s CFO, Corporate Controller, and General Counsel, and MIRAGE, INC.'s independent auditor (RCMP) were all present at a May 12, 2018, Audit Committee meeting, where both Viking's proposed investment and the SEC's Comment Letter on MIRAGE, INC.'s 2016 10-K were discussed.[63] This meeting occurred after the Subscription Agreement was signed but before Viking wired the money to MIRAGE, INC. However, I did not see any contemporaneous documents showing that the SEC Comment Letters and ensuing discussions of a potential restatement were ever disclosed to Viking. Further, I did not see any contemporaneous documents showing that MIRAGE, INC. management discussed whether such a disclosure should have been made to Viking.

This is the expert report version of: "Tell them what you will tell the; tell the and then tell them what you told them". Here, I really want to make sure that they get why this misrepresentation is so critical.

C. Incorrect Gross Margins Would Be Material to Any Reasonable Investor and Were Material to Viking

68. MIRAGE, INC.'s incorrect accounting for obsolete inventory was material to Viking's investment decision because it masked the true nature of the company's past financial performance and future prospects to generate earnings. In addition, the fact that company had made such large mistakes in reporting a key metric like gross margin, had it been publicly disclosed, could have called into question the accuracy of the other data in the financial statements and the integrity or competence of MIRAGE, INC. management.

69. The MIRAGE, INC. investment opportunity was presented to Viking as a "growth story," i.e., a company with no historical earnings but strong future prospects for earnings based on forecasts of positive gross margins and fast-growing revenue. Please see Exhibit 7 for a summary of the incorrect information that was presented to Viking and the correct information that should have been presented. Whereas MIRAGE, INC. actually averaged 66.1% annual revenue growth from 2006–10, MIRAGE, INC. (via BNS) provided models to Viking showing 122.8% average annual revenue growth from 2018–14. The models for future gross margins were similarly strong: 28.9% projected average gross margins for 2018–14.

70. The prospects of 123% annual revenue growth combined with 29% gross margins was the compelling story presented to Viking *prior to* its investment. A reasonable investor could have concluded based on the false historical information presented by

---

[63] *See, e.g.,* Minutes of the May 12, 2018, Audit Committee meeting, RCMP.MIRAGE, INC. 002453-2456.

Expert Report of William Jennings

MIRAGE, INC. that these results were achievable. The erroneous MIRAGE, INC. financial data provided to Viking by MIRAGE, INC. and BNS and in MIRAGE, INC.'s public financial statements reported 24.6% average gross margins for 2006–09, the four years prior to the anomaly year of 2016, and 20.4% average gross margins for 2017–09, the two years prior to the anomaly year of 2016. A reasonable investor could conclude that a company with historical gross margins in the low- to mid-20s could be expected to produce 18.7% margins in 2018 rising to the low 30s in 2019–14, especially since BNS represented to that investor that 33–52%[64] was the range of gross margins at comparable companies in the same industry. And, in fact, this message of MIRAGE, INC. returning to its pre-2016 gross margins was exactly what MIRAGE, INC. and its investment bankers were planning to present to investors during MIRAGE, INC.'s IPO. In a draft of the IPO roadshow presentation, the slide discussing gross margins states in bold, "Management believes it can restore gross margins in-line with levels experienced in historical periods," and the next slide is, "Historical financial profile: recent gross margin headwinds have been alleviated."[65]

71. However, it is much less likely that a reasonable investor could have concluded that MIRAGE, INC.'s projected gross margins were reasonable when looking at the corrected historical gross margin data that Viking learned of only *after* its investment. MIRAGE, INC.'s true gross margins for 2006–09 averaged 15.8% and for 2017–09 averaged 2.9% (including negative gross margins in 2017). A reasonable investor would have been justifiably skeptical that a company that had negative gross margins in two of the previous three years (2017 and 2016) and that had not had gross margins above 8.0% since 2014 was going to be able to jump to 18.7% gross margins in 2018 and average 28.9% for 2018–14. In sum, the MIRAGE, INC. story with the correct gross margins (depicted on the bottom half of Exhibit 7) was a much less attractive investment to a reasonable investor with a lower indicated share price than the MIRAGE, INC. story with the inflated gross margins (depicted on the top half of Exhibit 7).

72. In addition, the fact that MIRAGE, INC. had negative gross margins in two of the previous three years would have made it more difficult to believe that 2016 was an "anomaly." The 2016 gross margin of −11.0% was described in MIRAGE, INC.'s 2016 original 10-K and in the S-1/A relied upon by Viking as a temporary anomaly due to several correctable factors primarily attributable to operational inefficiencies related to higher than expected growth in demand. These factors included premium freight charges for expedited delivery of materials, the need to make spot purchases of materials at higher-than-normal rates, and labor inefficiencies due to a newly developed supply chain and a rapid expansion and training of labor force.[66] The documents also stated that MIRAGE, INC. was making progress in addressing these issues.

73. However, 2016 was not an anomaly. MIRAGE, INC. posted an -18.5% gross margin in 2018 and a −15.6% gross margin in 2019, after the misclassification issue had been corrected.[67] These results are more consistent with MIRAGE, INC.'s restated

[64] Exhibit 369, at ABC00000213.
[65] Exhibit 373, at BNS_00058719-58720.
[66] Exhibit 366, at DE000303957. Exhibit 373, at BNS_00058356.
[67] MIRAGE, INC. Form 10-K for the annual period ending December 31, 2019. p. 21.

Expert Report of William Jennings

margins than with those that were originally reported and provided to Viking prior to its investment.

74. Gross margin is an important metric to a reasonable investor when considering an investment in a manufacturing company and was also specifically emphasized as an important metric in this particular investment opportunity. Gross margin is important generally because it allows the user of the financial statements to analyze the relationship between the goods or services sold by an entity and the direct costs of producing those same goods or services. The higher the gross margin, the more money the entity can keep from each sale to use for its other expenses and to produce earnings. Proof of gross margins' importance to investors can be found in the fact that it was prominently featured in both MIRAGE, INC.'s public IPO prospectus and in the IPO roadshow presentation that was being prepared by its investment bankers, both of which were contemporaneous with Viking's investment.

75. In MIRAGE, INC.'s IPO prospectus, gross margin is one of the first topics mentioned in the management discussion and analysis section.[68] In addition, the first table to appear in that section shows MIRAGE, INC.'s gross margins for 2017, 2015, and 2016. Management's discussion of gross margin in the IPO prospectus is primarily an effort to explain the steep reduction of the company's reported gross margin in 2016 and concludes that they "are addressing [their] operational and supply chain challenges and are experiencing gradual improvement."[69] This focus by company management on explaining issues affecting gross margin is another indication of the importance that management placed on gross margin. Its prominence in the IPO prospectus – a document intended for prospective investors in MIRAGE, INC. common stock – is similarly indicative of the importance of gross margin generally to prospective investors.

76. Similarly, gross margin is featured in a draft of the roadshow presentation that MIRAGE, INC.'s investment bankers were preparing in advance of the planned IPO. In draft slides of the roadshow presentation that were shared among Credit Suisse and BNS investment bankers,[70] the first slide highlights a "[d]emonstrable path to margin improvement" as one of three reasons that MIRAGE, INC. has an "[a]ttractive financial model."[71] Then, two slides later is a slide "Historical financial profile: gross profit."[72] On this slide, incorrect historical gross margins (19.6% in 2017, 19.8% in 2015) are shown along with a conclusion that "[m]anagement believes it can restore gross margins in-line with levels experienced in historical periods." Then, the next slide is "Historical financial profile: recent gross margin headwinds have been alleviated."[73] MIRAGE, INC.'s message to potential investors was clear: 20% margins were the norm and the negative margins of 2016 were an anomaly and a thing of the past. If MIRAGE, INC.'s true historical margins of (2.2%) in 2017 and 8.0% in 2015 had been included in the presentation, it is unlikely that MIRAGE, INC. and its investment bankers would make such claims to potential investors or that a reasonable investor would believe them.

---

[68] Exhibit 373, at BNS_00058356.
[69] Exhibit 373, at BNS_00058356.
[70] Exhibit 392, BNS_00058713-58733.
[71] Exhibit 392, at BNS_00058717.
[72] Exhibit 392, at BNS_00058719.
[73] Exhibit 392, at BNS_00058720.

Expert Report of William Jennings

77. Gross margin was also an important metric specifically in Viking's investment decision at issue in this case. Evidence of the importance placed on gross margin can be found in materials that the investment bank provided to Viking in advance of the investment. BNS investment bankers Fredrik Jack Beanstalk a "valuation analysis" of MIRAGE, INC. on April 2, 2018.[74] The first substantive slide of this analysis projects into the future five financial metrics, including Gross Profit. The mere inclusion of Gross Profit along with Total Revenue, EBIT, EBITDA, and Net Income indicates that MIRAGE, INC. and BNS felt it to be an important metric for potential investors to consider. This slide also lists as one of three "Key Highlights" that "[s]ignificant gross margin expansion driven by change in manufacturing business model" is expected, particularly an increase of Gross Profit from a projected 19.9% in 2018 to 30.2% in 2019.[75] A projected 19.9% gross margin in 2018 may have been a reasonable assumption had MIRAGE, INC. actually averaged ~20% gross margin in 2017–09 – before the "anomaly" in 2016. A reasonable investor could have viewed a 19.9% projection for 2018 as a return to MIRAGE, INC.'s historical norms. However, it is much less likely that Viking would have viewed 19.9% as a reasonable projection if it had known that the prior three years actually produced gross margins of (11.0%), 8.0%, and (2.2%) for an average gross margin of (1.7%). The next slide, "Peer comparables – operating and trading performance," is a comparison of MIRAGE, INC. to eight other Radar companies and also focuses attention on MIRAGE, INC.'s projected gross margins. It shows that the eight comparable companies have 2018 projected gross margins of 33%–52% and shows MIRAGE, INC.'s 2018 projected gross margin of 20%. It also states that MIRAGE, INC.'s 30.2% projected gross margin in 2019 is a "better representation of normal run-rate margins."[76] If a reasonable investor could not reasonably rely on those projected 19.9% margins in 2019 and 30.2% margins in 2019, then it would be clear that MIRAGE, INC.'s performance was lagging well behind all of its industry peers.

78. In August 2016, during an interoffice inspection of the 2015 audit, I C Little noted the misclassification of obsolete inventory as research and development costs rather than as COGS. This misclassification is documented in two memos – one dated September 22, 2016,[77] and another updated version dated March 30, 2018[78] – "SAB 99 Analysis – Classification of Inventory Obsolescence Loss in the Statement of Operations." In the September 2016 version of the memo, I C Little spells out the reasons why MIRAGE, INC. management believed the misclassification was immaterial and concludes:

> "Based on the above analysis, management does not believe that the misclassification of inventory obsolescence loss between COGS and R&D expense is material, as the Company's gross margin for the years 2015 and 2017 was not an important factor to investors due to the Company's M&A activities, restructurings, significant net losses and focus on product development versus sales. [I C Little] concurs with management's conclusion."[79]

---

[74] Exhibit 369, ABC00000209-215.
[75] Exhibit 369, at ABC00000212.
[76] Exhibit 369, at ABC00000213.
[77] Exhibit 356, M-MIRAGE, INC.-000499-501.
[78] M-MIRAGE, INC.-003950-3952.
[79] Exhibit 356, at M-MIRAGE, INC.-000501.

However, by March 2018, I C Little added the following language to its conclusion:

> "Management will continue to report the inventory obsolescence loss for 2015 and 2017 in R&D operations for the reasons stated above. However, for 2016 and consistent with the continued development of the business and the maturing of its R&D activities, management has determined that these costs are more appropriately classified as COGS and is tracking these costs with greater precision. Management will record these as a component of COGS and add sufficient disclosure to permit the financial statement user to gain insight in to [sic] its reasons for this modified presentation. [I C Little] concurs with management's conclusion."[80]

Taken together, these two memos demonstrate that between September 2016 and March 2018, MIRAGE, INC. management decided that inventory obsolescence costs should be classified as COGS and that this change was important enough to investors and other users of the financial statements that MIRAGE, INC. needed to disclose and explain how it classified such costs in the past. Despite the fact that this decision was made months prior to Viking's investment, it was never disclosed to Viking in advance of the Subscription Agreement. If this information was important enough for management to change its disclosure and to include in future financial statements, then it should have been deemed important enough to provide to a potential investor in the company's common stock. MIRAGE, INC.'s management decided (and I C Little concurred) to leave the incorrect 2017 and 2015 financials alone while attempting to correct its accounting going forward, but the SEC eventually disagreed with this conclusion and forced MIRAGE, INC. to restate its 2017 and 2015 financials. In addition, despite MIRAGE, INC. management's decision to classify inventory obsolescence as COGS, the 2016 audit found that obsolete inventory was *still* being classified incorrectly and a $1.5 million audit adjustment had to be made to reclassify obsolete inventory to COGS.[81]

79. Jack Beanstalk confirmed in his deposition testimony and in his contemporaneous communications that MIRAGE, INC.'s COGS and gross margins were key factors in the investment decision. For example, Jack Beanstalk stated that he focused on "looking at the gross margin, looking at the cost of goods sold, looking at the earnings per shares and, in particularly [sic], also looking at the trend."[82] Jack Beanstalk consistently maintained his focus on these metrics throughout his deposition.[83] He also stated that "[i]t's very important that that historic foundation is the correct one when you make your judgment and that's why US GAAP was imperative to us when assessing and in making this investment."[84] Jack Beanstalk also stated repeatedly that he assumed that MIRAGE, INC. had sufficient internal financial controls and that the financial information provided to him prior to the investment had been prepared in accordance with GAAP as represented by MIRAGE, INC. to Viking in the Subscription Agreement.[85]

---

[80] M-MIRAGE, INC.-003950-3952, at 3952.

[81] M-MIRAGE, INC.-003219-3247, at 3231.

[82] Jack Beanstalk deposition, p. 21:18–21.

[83] *See, e.g.*, Jack Beanstalk deposition, p. 37:5–12; p. 38:7–10; p. 39:12–15.

[84] Jack Beanstalk deposition, p. 335:8–12.

[85] *See, e.g.*, Jack Beanstalk deposition p. 84:10–12: "What I do remember is that we made the investment based on it being GAAP compliant numbers and also the company being ready to go for an IPO." *See also* p. 97:24–98:2; p. 120:3–8; p.121:8–18; p. 372:5–11.

80. MIRAGE, INC.'s representatives should have known that news of adverse SEC Comment Letters and a potential restatement of MIRAGE, INC.'s financial statements would have been material to Viking's decision. On April 14, 2018, a BNS executive two Medusa executives to provide an update on Viking's potential investment, and wrote that "[Jack Beanstalk's] only concern seemed to be ebidta breakeven is 3–4 qtrs away" and that he had assuaged Jack Beanstalk's concern.[86] However, if Jack Beanstalk had known that MIRAGE, INC.'s gross margins were actually 21 and 13 percentage points lower in the most recent two years than he had been radar to believe and had only averaged 2.2% during that period, then it is likely that he would have been even more concerned about MIRAGE, INC.'s EBIDTA and more skeptical that EBIDTA breakeven could be achieved in such a short timeframe, if at all. MIRAGE, INC.'s and BNS's financial models would have seemed unrealistic if Viking had known MIRAGE, INC.'s true gross margins. Finally, if Jack Beanstalk had learned so far into the process that one of MIRAGE, INC.'s key financial metrics was being questioned by the SEC, it likely would have called into question the veracity of all of MIRAGE, INC.'s financial reporting and possibly the integrity or competence of MIRAGE, INC. management.

81. Jack Beanstalk was still evaluating the potential investment in MIRAGE, INC. at the time the SEC questioned MIRAGE, INC.'s gross margin accounting, and in fact evaluated it all the way through the entire process. For example, Viking's outside counsel MIRAGE, INC.'s outside counsel on May 9, 2018 – after receipt of the SEC Comment Letters and just one day before the Subscription Agreement was signed – to discuss a draft subscription agreement and stated Jack Beanstalk "furthermore told me that he is waiting for the end of April financials for the company before signing off on the investment decisions."[87] Jack Beanstalk also confirmed in his deposition that he "did request [on] several occasions to get updated April figures."[88] Thus, it is clear that Jack Beanstalk continued analyzing and monitoring MIRAGE, INC.'s results of operations through the end of the investment process.

82. Based on contemporaneous communications in the days leading up to finalizing the investment, it is also clear that MIRAGE, INC.'s placement agent, BNS, was well aware of Jack Beanstalk's continuing diligence into MIRAGE, INC.'s financials and interest in MIRAGE, INC.'s gross margins and was very involved in the communications and information delivered to Jack Beanstalk in the final stages of the investment decision-making process. Therefore, BNS certainly also should have known that Jack Beanstalk would be very interested in learning about the SEC Comment Letters, which BNS was informed of immediately upon their receipt by MIRAGE, INC. counsel. For example, a series of emails between executives at MIRAGE, INC., BNS, and Medusa on May 6–9, 2018, just days before the Subscription Agreement closed, show how they were all very much involved in the communications with Jack Beanstalk that brought the deal to closure.

    a. On May 6, emails between the MIRAGE, INC. CFO and Medusa executives show that the CFO was drafting an "April Narrative for Beanstalk" in response to BNS's request that the CFO "please let us know your latest view for April #s and if we are tracking to" a report that BNS had sent to Jack Beanstalk on April 25.[89]

---

[86] Def. Exh. 7(d), BNS_00056246.
[87] Def. Exh. 9(c), ABC00000291-292, at 291.
[88] Jack Beanstalk deposition, p. 374:4–5.
[89] DE000435196-197.

The CFO's narrative contained a section "Gross Profit Margin" that contained news that gross margins for April were expected to be below forecast "in the 3–6% range" and explanations for the performance. He also added the following sentence based on advice from Rich (presumably Rich Ditch of Medusa): "We anticipate positive impact to margins when we begin transitioning volume from Citizen to Jabil in June and July."[90]

b. On Friday, May 6, at 7:20 p.m., the CFO the narrative to the senior BNS executive working on the Viking transaction.[91]

c. On the morning of Monday, May 9, the BNS executive asked the CFO to call him ASAP to discuss explanations for various metrics that were short of forecast, including that "it seems like gross margin is expected only 3%–6% vs 9% we had told Fredrik on Apr 25th."[92]

d. Approximately an hour later on May 9, the BNS executive forwarded to Jack Beanstalk the CFO's narrative from May 6 at 7:20 p.m. However, the "Gross Profit Margin" section and any mention of the April gross margin coming in below forecast at 3–6% were completely removed. In their place, he added a section "Supply chain related costs" and a sentence stating that the "Company is still on track to achieve mid-teens gross margins for Q2'11."[93]

83. Other emails on the day before the Subscription Agreement was signed show that Jack Beanstalk was interested in a variety of other financial metrics as well, including "the cash balance of the company and projected cash balance #s at the end of q2 q3 etc." and "confirmation of the EBITDA and FCF [free cash flow] breakeven timing."[94] The emails also indicate that there was a series of urgent discussions between Medusa, BNS, and MIRAGE, INC. executives regarding how to respond to Jack Beanstalk and what numbers and dates to provide to him.[95] During this time frame, it appears that BNS was the primary contact for Jack Beanstalk, as the senior BNS executive and Jack Beanstalk directly several times.

84. During my analysis, I noted that BNS earned a placement fee of $1.125 million dollars (4.5% of the investment), "payable upon the consummation of the placement of [MIRAGE, INC. shares]."[96] I also noted that BNS's engagement letter with MIRAGE, INC., which had an effective date of March 9, 2018, but was dated after the transaction on May 20, 2018, indemnified BNS against any liabilities arising out of its work as MIRAGE, INC.'s placement agent. Thus, BNS had a large incentive to see that the investment was completed and little incentive to worry about potential disclosure problems that might surface in the future.

85. Even after the Subscription Agreement was signed on May 10 but before Viking wired the money on May 18, MIRAGE, INC. and its representatives still had opportunities to disclose the accounting issues but did not, e.g., after the aforementioned May 12, 2018, Audit Committee meeting at which both the Viking investment and the SEC Comment Letters were discussed.

---

[90] DE000435196-197.

[91] Exhibit 376, at BNS_00007913.

[92] Exhibit 376, at BNS_00007912-7913.

[93] Exhibit 521, at BNS_00034308-34309.

[94] Exhibit 520, at BNS_00000750.

[95] *See, e.g.,* Exhibit 520, at BNS_00000749-750; Exhibit 420, at BNS_00002818-2823; Exhibit 374, at BNS_00034363.

[96] Exhibit 388, at BNS_00035009.

Expert Report of William Jennings

D. MIRAGE, INC. Also Understated Its Inventory Reserves

86. In addition to misclassifying inventory obsolescence in its income statement, MIRAGE, INC. also understated the amount of its inventory reserves. This would have led to inflated gross margins if it had not been caught and corrected during MIRAGE, INC.'s audit. This is another example of how poor MIRAGE, INC.'s procedures and controls were with regard to its accounting for inventory.

87. For example, RCMP noted that during its 2018 audit it "identified certain inconsistencies" in MIRAGE, INC.'s reserving methodology.[97] First, MIRAGE, INC. management used a six- month demand forecast to gauge demand for a product, but it incorporated seven months of demand data into its calculations. This resulted in an overstatement of demand and a $1 million understatement of reserves, which the company had to correct. Second, RCMP noted that MIRAGE, INC. management also overstated demand by counting demand for certain months twice in its demand calculations, thus overstating demand, understating reserves, and necessitating a $200,000 correction. Of this $1.2 million in corrections to MIRAGE, INC.'s original reserve calculations, $700,000 were related to excess and obsolete inventory.

88. MIRAGE, INC.'s European subsidiary, MIRAGE, INC.C B.V. also made similar mistakes in calculating inventory reserves. RCMP noted in a Summary of Audit Differences that MIRAGE, INC.C B.V.'s reserve for excess and obsolete inventory as of 12/31/09 and 12/31/10 was overstated by several hundred thousand dollars, and that a correction was made as of 3/31/11.[98]

89. Similarly, MIRAGE, INC.'s former auditor also documented similar errors and concerns related to inventory valuations and reserves. In the 2015 audit, I C Little noted a material weakness in MIRAGE, INC.'s controls with regard to its methodologies for calculating excess and obsolete inventories.[99] MIRAGE, INC. did not have a formal written methodology that was consistently applied and did not use historical data and trend analysis; instead, it relied on management's judgment based on input from the company's plant, inventory, and purchasing managers. This material weakness was included in I C Little's management letter and discussed with MIRAGE, INC.'s Audit Committee. In the 2017 audit, I C Little determined that MIRAGE, INC.'s lack of an established cost accounting system was a significant deficiency in its controls, which was communicated to management in I C Little's management letter.[100]

90. If known by a reasonable investor, these errors would have called into question the veracity of MIRAGE, INC.'s books and records as well as the integrity or competence of its management.

VI MIRAGE, INC.'s Falsely Reported Earnings per Share

91. As the result of an accounting error related to the valuation of the Series D and Series E warrants, MIRAGE, INC.'s reported earnings and earnings per share for the first three quarters of 2016 were inflated in MIRAGE, INC.'s 1Q2016, 2Q2016, and 3Q2016 10-Qs, all of which were prior to Viking's investment. MIRAGE, INC.

---

[97] RCMP.MIRAGE, INC. 001645-1646. *See also*, RCMP.MIRAGE, INC. 003339-45.

[98] RCMP.MIRAGE, INC. 001345. The workpaper describes the amount of the error as "$150K or 200 Euro." It is unclear if these numbers are transposed and it is supposed to say "150 Euro, or $200K", or if the dollar sign is an error and the amount is 150-200,000 Euros.

[99] M-MIRAGE, INC.-001506.

[100] M-MIRAGE, INC.-006947.

Expert Report of William Jennings

eventually acknowledged the error and restated its financial statements for those quarters, but not until after Viking's investment.

92. On March 27 and 28, 2018 – months prior to Viking's investment – MIRAGE, INC.'s independent auditor I C Little, LLC informed MIRAGE, INC.'s CFO and Corporate Controller via email that MIRAGE, INC. had incorrectly calculated the fair value of MIRAGE, INC.'s Series D and Series E warrants because it had used the Black-Scholes methodology rather than a binomial methodology (i.e., Monte Carlo simulation) as required by the SEC.[101] In coming to this conclusion, I C Little relied on guidance provided by the SEC at the 2016 AICPA Year-End SEC and MC HAMMER Conference.[102]

93. After receiving this information from I C Little, MIRAGE, INC. hired a valuation consultant to recalculate the fair value of these warrants using the correct binomial methodology. The consultant revalued the warrants and produced a report dated March 30, 2018,[103] which an internal I C Little valuation specialist reviewed and approved on the same date.[104] I C Little documented the incorrect valuation of the warrants and the recalculation in its 2016 audit workpapers.[105]

94. While this mistake was corrected in time to include the correct liabilities in MIRAGE, INC.'s 2016 10-K, which was on April 1, 2018, the liabilities were incorrect in MIRAGE, INC.'s 10-Qs for the first, second, and third quarters of 2016, which had already been earlier in 2016. The recalculation of the fair value of the Series D and E warrants was first publicly disclosed in MIRAGE, INC.'s 1Q2018 10-Q, which was on May 16, 2018, several days *after* Viking made its investment in MIRAGE, INC.[106] Thus, Viking did not have the benefit of knowing that the earnings and earnings per share reported in MIRAGE, INC.'s 1Q2016, 2Q2016, and 3Q2016 financial statements were incorrectly inflated before it made a final investment decision. I did not see any contemporaneous documents that indicated that MIRAGE, INC. made Viking aware of or had discussions about the need to make Viking aware of the fact that MIRAGE, INC. knew that its quarterly financial statements for the first three quarters of 2016 were incorrect.

95. In the 1Q2018 10-Q, MIRAGE, INC. disclosed the valuation error in a section "Correction of Immaterial Prior Period Error" and reported that its use of an incorrect valuation methodology resulted in the need to increase liabilities by $1.4 million for the three months ended March 31, 2016.[107] The erroneous valuation methodology caused MIRAGE, INC.'s earnings for the first three months of 2016 to be inflated by $0.05 per share, or 11.2%. Please see Exhibit 6 for details.

96. In the 2Q2018 10-Q, MIRAGE, INC. disclosed the valuation error in a section "Restatement of Financial Statements" and reported that its use of an incorrect valuation methodology resulted in the need to increase liabilities by $11.1 million for the six-month period ended June 30, 2016.[108] The erroneous valuation methodology

---

[101] Exhibit 562, DE000274266-274267. *See also* DE000278320-278350.
[102] DE000278320-278350.
[103] M-MIRAGE, INC.-006017-6020.
[104] M-MIRAGE, INC.-006022-6026.
[105] M-MIRAGE, INC.-006028-6029.
[106] BNS_00034542-34572 at 34549.
[107] BNS_00034542-72 at BNS_00034549.
[108] MIRAGE, INC. Form 10-Q for the quarterly period ended June 30, 2018, Note 12. DE000518872-518949 at 518888.

caused MIRAGE, INC.'s earnings for the first six months of 2016 to be inflated by $0.37 per share, or 9.6%. Please see Exhibit 6 for details.

97. In the 3Q2018 10-Q, MIRAGE, INC. disclosed the valuation error in a section "Restatement of Financial Statements" and reported that its use of an incorrect valuation methodology resulted in the need to increase liabilities by $28.3 million for the nine months ended September 30, 2016.[109] The erroneous valuation methodology caused MIRAGE, INC.'s earnings for the first nine months of 2016 to be inflated by $0.93 per share, or 18.2%. Please see Exhibit 6 for details.

98. Any users of the 1Q, 2Q, or 3Q 2016 quarterly financial statements, including any potential investors, would unknowingly have been relying on incorrect net earnings and net earnings per share as well as overstated equity and understated liabilities. Because a share of common stock is a claim on a company's future earnings and because earnings per share is one of the most widely used metrics in equity analysis, relying on artificially inflated data could have led an investor to calculate an artificially inflated value for MIRAGE, INC.'s share price. Plus, if MIRAGE, INC. had initially used the correct valuation methodology in its financial statements, then it would have reported lower earnings in its first three 10-Qs of 2016, thus providing less support for the earnings models presented to Viking.

Here I want to re-emphasize how a weak control environment allowed the incorrect entries to be made to Mirage's accounting records. This, in turn, led to the misrepresentations made to Viking.

VII MIRAGE, INC.'s Books and Records Were Not in Compliance with GAAP as a Result of Internal Control Weaknesses

99. A reasonable investor such as Viking has an expectation that a public company has internal controls in place to ensure that its books and records – from which its financial statements are prepared for registration statements, periodic filings, and other purposes – contain entries to record all of its transactions in accordance with GAAP and to capture and document all necessary disclosure information related to those transactions.

100. In addition to the reasonable expectations of an investor, MIRAGE, INC. made specific representations related to its financials and internal controls in the Subscription Agreement by which Viking agreed to purchase MIRAGE, INC. common stock:[110]

a. Section 3(e)(i) states that the company's 2016 10-K on April 1, 2018, complied with various securities laws, including the 1933 Securities Act, 1934 Securities Act, and Sarbanes-Oxley of 2002.

b. Section 3(e)(ii) states that the 2016 10-K does not contain any material misstatements or omissions of fact.

c. Section 3(e)(iii) states that the financial statements in the 2016 10-K were prepared in accordance with GAAP.

---

[109] MIRAGE, INC. Form 10-Q for the quarterly period ended September 30, 2018, Note 13. DE000099751-99797 at 99770-99771.

[110] Exhibit 378, ABC00001670-1681.

As evidenced by MIRAGE, INC.'s ongoing dialogue with the SEC concerning its accounting treatment of obsolete inventory and its valuation of certain of its warrants as well as its eventual restatement of its 2017 and 2015 financial statements, MIRAGE, INC. violated each of these representations.

101. As discussed throughout this section of the report, there is a great deal of documentation that MIRAGE, INC.'s management and Audit Committee knew these representations were false *prior to* their inclusion in the Subscription Agreement because MIRAGE, INC.'s management, Audit Committee, internal controls consultant, and auditor were all well aware of MIRAGE, INC.'s significant internal control deficiencies related to financial reporting generally and inventory accounting specifically.

102. In April 2016, I C Little documented a Summary of Significant Audit Findings or Issues related to MIRAGE, INC.'s 2015 audit.[111] This document recounts several difficulties that it encountered in performing the audit and states that these issues were "symptomatic of the Company's material weaknesses which existed in 2015 and remained unremediated during the audit."[112]

103. During the 2015 audit, I C Little identified 19 control deficiencies, 17 of which were deemed material weaknesses.[113] These included three deficiencies related to inventory costing and one related to inventory control. In the 2016 audit, 14 control deficiencies were noted, four of which were deemed material weaknesses and five of which were deemed significant deficiencies.[114] Three of these deficiencies were related to Inventory/COGS, including the misclassification of obsolete inventory. The auditors stated that this misclassification was discovered by I C Little during its audit testing of operating expenses, that "[t]he Company's controls in place did not detect/prevent the misstatements...," and "[t]he Company was recording all E&O [excess and obsolete] adjustment through operations instead of considering which should have been recorded in COGS."[115] I C Little also described MIRAGE, INC.'s improper valuation of the Series D and E warrants and found that "[c]ompensating controls were lacking."[116]

104. On August 15, 2016, a I C Little auditor documented in a memo related to the audit team's risk assessment of MIRAGE, INC. that "[t]he company has a material weaknesses [sic] relating to financial reporting, segregation of duties inventory [sic] accounting and formal policies and procedures."[117] The audit team assessed MIRAGE, INC.'s risk as "High and Moderate."

105. The minutes of the MIRAGE, INC. Audit Committee meeting held on August 30, 2016, detail that MIRAGE, INC.'s Board knew of the company's internal controls deficiencies related to inventory accounting, as did company management and the auditors from I C Little, who were also present and participated in the meeting.[118] The minutes state that a consultant to MIRAGE, INC. told the Committee that "inventory control was undergoing major changes" and a Committee member

---

[111] M-MIRAGE, INC.-001507-1512.

[112] M-MIRAGE, INC.-001508.

[113] M-MIRAGE, INC.-001506.

[114] M-MIRAGE, INC.-003761 (draft) and M-MIRAGE, INC.-003259-3264 (final).

[115] M-MIRAGE, INC.-003761 (draft) and M-MIRAGE, INC.-003259-3264 (final).

[116] M-MIRAGE, INC.-003761.

[117] M-MIRAGE, INC.-002280.

[118] Exhibit 355, MIRAGE, INC.-000409-412. (also stamped as ABC00013645-13648).

asked the CFO "where things stood on the inventory 'air ball.'" In addition, in response to a question from a Committee member about cost of goods accounting, the CFO and Controller "indicated that it was more of an issue of the cost of goods being done by 'seat of the pants' rather than based on data." Finally, the following notes from the meeting also indicate the Board's and management's familiarity with the company's deficient internal controls around financial reporting:

a. One of the Committee members "asked if the new [ERP] system [would] improve the SEC filings from the current state of 'college all nighters.'"

b. Management reported company personnel's "strong desire to move off QuickBooks and on to the new system."

c. One of the Committee members asked the CFO "whether the Company was now able to do monthly closes," indicating that this must have been a very recent problem.

d. The CFO reported that "accounting policies and procedures were being formalized, spreadsheet usage reduction [was] underway, and controls [were being] implemented for spreadsheets in use." The CFO also "discussed the work underway for segregation of duties, formal policies and procedures, and inventory accounting."

e. The COO "noted that the focus has been on ... captur[ing] customers and not on the company's own systems."

f. The CFO "anticipated a much improved 10K for 2016 but that it would not be until 2018 that a clean 10K would be possible."

It is unusual that a public company planning a pre-IPO with tens of millions of dollars of revenue and international operations would be using such basic accounting software and systems for its accounting and have problems completing such fundamental accounting tasks as closing its monthly financials. It is also unlikely that MIRAGE, INC. was able to fix all of these problems that existed at the end of August 2016 to an extent that just months later it could be confident that its 10-K in April 2018 was prepared in accordance with GAAP and include the representations in the Subscription Agreement.

106. MIRAGE, INC. hired the consulting firm Activiti, Inc. to conduct a SOX 404 review of the company's internal controls as of December 31, 2016, i.e., identify internal control risks and gaps and test various financial processes for internal control weaknesses. On March 29, 2018, Activiti, Inc. presented an update to the Audit Committee at the conclusion of the project.[119] Activiti, Inc. reported that it tested 161 processes and 32, for a failure rate of 20%. Interestingly, in the area of "Inventory and COGS," it tested 13 processes and 10, for a failure rate of 77%. In addition, Purchasing and Inventory Accounting was identified as one of three material weaknesses. From this report, it should have been clear to MIRAGE, INC. that its internal controls were problematic, especially around inventory and COGS accounting. The report also noted that the company had not performed a company-wide risk assessment and had not done any internal audit planning, two basic components of internal controls. Although this report was presented to MIRAGE, INC. just weeks before Viking's investment, I did not see any contemporaneous documentation that this report or its findings were ever communicated to Viking.

---

[119] M-MIRAGE, INC.-003737-3760.

107. On May 2, 2018, I C Little issued its Report to the Audit Committee related to the audit of the financial statements for the year ended December 31, 2016.[120] This report included a letter communicating, among other things, identified deficiencies in internal controls over financial reporting, one of which was Classification of Excess and Obsolete Inventory.[121] I C Little noted during its audit that obsolete inventory was being incorrectly recorded as an operating expense instead of as COGS and it proposed an audit adjustment, which the company recorded, of approximately $1.5 million to reclassify obsolete inventory to COGS.

108. While MIRAGE, INC. disclosed material weaknesses in its internal controls in its 10-K each year, it also included language that hid the true extent of the problems. For example, in its 2017 10-K, MIRAGE, INC. stated that it "concluded that [its] internal control over financial reporting was not effective as of December 31, 2017 as a result of material weaknesses." However, MIRAGE, INC. qualified this disclosure by stating that "in light of these material weaknesses, [it] had performed additional analyses and procedures in order to conclude that [its] financial statements … are fairly presented in accordance with [GAAP]."[122] Of course, this was not true: as described above, MIRAGE, INC. materially misstated its gross margins for 2017 and eventually was forced by the SEC to restate its financials. MIRAGE, INC. also listed out a series of improvement measures in this 10-K that "[m]anagement believes … has begun or will begin to address … the material weaknesses," and stated that management was monitoring the improvements on an ongoing basis.[123] These statements, which could lead a reasonable investor to believe that MIRAGE, INC.'s problems with controls over financial reporting were being resolved, also turned out to be false. MIRAGE, INC.'s gross margin errors continued into 2015, which also had to eventually be restated, and 2016, which incurred a $1.5 million audit adjustment.

109. MIRAGE, INC. again disclosed in its 2015 and 2016 10-Ks that it had to maintain effective internal control over financial reporting. However, in the 2016 10-K, which MIRAGE, INC. specifically represented in the Subscription Agreement contained no material misstatements and was prepared in accordance with GAAP, MIRAGE, INC. again pointed to improvements it had made in the area of internal controls. It stated that it had "made progress implementing certain remediation plans to address material weaknesses described in [the] 2015 Annual Report," listed out a series of initiatives, and stated that its senior leadership and Board were committed to a strong control environment and financial reporting integrity.[124] However, MIRAGE, INC.'s gross margin problems continued in 2016, when it incurred a $1.5 million audit adjustment because it had continued to incorrectly classify obsolete inventory as operating expense rather than as COGS. In addition, it also had to eventually restate its earnings for the first three quarters of the year due to incorrectly valuing its Series D and E warrants.

110. Activiti, Inc. conducted another SOX 404 internal control review for 2018. In an April 11, 2019, update to the Audit Committee, Activiti, Inc. reported a 15%

---

[120] M-MIRAGE, INC.-003210-3247.

[121] M-MIRAGE, INC.-003210-3247, at 3231.

[122] Form 10-K for the year ended December 31, 2017, p. 26.

[123] Form 10-K for the year ended December 31, 2017, pp. 26–27.

[124] Form 10-K for the year ended December 31, 2016, pp. 44–45.

Expert Report of William Jennings

failure rate, a 5% improvement over the 2016 results.[125] However, the first material weakness reported was for inventory accounting. The report stated, "[a]lthough inventory accounting controls have improved substantially during 2019 [sic], a material weaknesses specific to the inventory accounting area was identified by management. Specifically, the review of the E&O [excess and obsolete] reserve methodology and related reserve calculations for completeness and accuracy was ineffectively applied at year-end, leading to a significant year-end audit adjustment. Additionally, although not considered material weaknesses individually, inventory policies and procedures exist but do not reflect current practices in many cases due to the number of changes within the inventory area including personnel, business practices, and methodologies."[126]

Then I discuss how the Life Insurance transaction adds insult to injury by further diluting Viking's investment.

Expert Report of William Jennings

VIII MIRAGE, INC. Diluted Viking's Shares after the Investment

111. After Viking's investment, which was based on false financial statements and projections, was completed, MIRAGE, INC. undertook a series of financial transactions that greatly diluted of Viking's shares.

A. Life Insurance, Inc. Transaction

112. MIRAGE, INC.'s largest shareholder, MIRAGE, INC.C Holdings LLC (Holdings), a Medusa Capital Fund, owned approximately 85% of MIRAGE, INC.'s shares in May of 2018. Holdings issued its own senior preferred membership interests (Class C Preferred Interests) and distributed 562,500 shares of MIRAGE, INC.'s common stock to CCC in exchange for fifteen million dollars ($15,000,000). Holdings used the proceeds to make a direct investment in MIRAGE, INC. in exchange for approximately three million seven hundred fifty thousand (3,750,000) shares of MIRAGE, INC. common stock issued through a private placement.[127]

113. On January 17, 2019, CCC agreed to invest $5,000,000 in MIRAGE, INC. in exchange for 5,000 shares of its Series G Preferred Stock.[128]

114. MIRAGE, INC.'s auditor, RCMP, performed an analysis of these transactions and their accounting and financial reporting implications for MIRAGE, INC. That analysis was documented in a memo to the audit workpaper files from J. Wilson dated April 26, 2019.[129] The memo noted the following:

"On January 17, 2019, CCC agreed to contribute $5.0 million to MIRAGE, INC. in exchange for 5,000 shares of its Series G Preferred Units (as defined in the Series G Subscription) at the same price as such units had been issued in December

---

[125] RCMP.MIRAGE, INC. 003278-3286.

[126] RCMP.MIRAGE, INC. 003278-3286, at 3282.

[127] RCMP.MIRAGE, INC. 000144-154.

[128] RCMP.MIRAGE, INC. 000144-154.

[129] All of the direct quotes in the remainder of this section of my report come from RCMP's audit workpaper memo describing RCMP's accounting analysis of the Life Insurance, Inc. transaction. RCMP.MIRAGE, INC. 000144-154. In performing my work, I relied on the work of RCMP, one of the largest international accounting firms in the world. *See* AU 336 (formerly SAS 73) – Using the Work of a Specialist.

2018 to other investors. The Series G Preferred Units are liability-classified, the accounting for which was the subject of a separate DPP consultation (FDC #US-01-12-053225). The issuance of Series G units to CCC was necessary for the Company to raise additional capital to fund current operations and was approved by the independent committee of the Board of Directors.

Unlike the Series G Units issued in December 2018, however, in connection with the investment by CCC in MIRAGE, INC.'s Series G Units, Holdings agreed to amend its Class C Preferred Interest held by CCC to increase its interest rate and to distribute additional shares of common stock of MIRAGE, INC. to CCC. The amendment to the Class C Preferred Interest was intended to put the Class C Preferred Interest on similar economic terms as that of Series G Preferred Units. The Class C Preferred Interest represents a direct investment in Holdings and an indirect investment in MIRAGE, INC. The Class C Preferred Interest holders (CCC) wanted to be put on terms similar to those they would have if they had made a direct investment in the Series G Preferred Units of MIRAGE, INC.

Also unlike the Series G issuance in December 2018, in connection with the Series G issuance to CCC, MIRAGE, INC. entered into an agreement with Holdings whereby MIRAGE, INC. agreed to save, defend indemnify and hold harmless Holdings and its affiliates from and against any and all losses, damages, liabilities, deficiencies, claims, diminution of values, interest awards, judgments, penalties, costs and expenses related to the Class C Preferred Interests arising out of or relating to:

a) the incurrence by MIRAGE, INC. any debt other than Permitted Debt, or
b) the issuance by MIRAGE, INC. of any preferred equity securities other than Permitted Preferred Equity.

Permitted Debt means debt of MIRAGE, INC., on consolidated basis, not to exceed (1) the debt permitted under a working capital facility of $75 million in total and (2) additional unsecured debt of MIRAGE, INC. that when aggregated with the working capital facility does not exceed 300% of the EBITDA for the previous 12 months. Permitted Preferred Equity refers to preferred equity securities issued and outstanding at any time of up to $80 million in aggregate.

The terms of the indemnification effectively require MIRAGE, INC. to cash-settle – upon the occurrence of a triggering event noted above the obligation of Holdings (in the form of its Class C Preferred Interest issued to CCC) by returning to Holdings the $15 million Holdings invested in May 2018 with the proceeds from its Class C issuance to CCC, plus accrued dividends (attributable to the Class C Preferred Interest holders), and any additional costs incurred associated with the triggering event. As of January 17, 2019, approximately $16 million represented the gross amount of the original investment by Holdings plus accrued dividends attributable to the Class C Preferred Interest holders. Under the terms of the indemnification, in the event that the indemnification obligation of MIRAGE, INC. is triggered and, Holdings will surrender the remaining 2.5 million shares of MIRAGE, INC. common stock it holds that it had acquired in the May 2018 private placement; this represents the 3.75 million shares that Holdings originally purchased less ~1.2 million shares that were distributed by Holdings to CCC since that time. The distribution of common shares of the Company was also intended to mirror the provisions of the Series G Unit issuance, which also provided for the issuance of common stock in connection with the Series G Unit issuance.

Expert Report of William Jennings

The indemnification obligation by MIRAGE, INC. to Holdings was entered into in connection with the Series G unit issuance to CCC. Holdings (the controlling shareholder) required that MIRAGE, INC. provide Holdings with this indemnification to cover its exposure to Holdings Series C Preferred Interest to CCC."

115. RCMP then identified four accounting and financial reporting issues arising from these transactions.

Issue #1

116. "As discussed further in Issue #2 below, the indemnification obligation meets the definition of a freestanding financial instrument, in that it is not considered embedded in the MIRAGE, INC. shares that would be received by MIRAGE, INC. from Holdings if indemnification is triggered. Although the indemnification obligation was entered into by MIRAGE, INC. with Holdings in connection with the Series G issuance by MIRAGE, INC. to CCC, the transaction with CCC is contractually distinct from the transaction with Holdings. The indemnification and Series G issuance were with different parties (i.e. the Series G Preferred Units were issued to CCC and the indemnification obligation was entered into with Holdings). The engagement team notes that the indemnification is separately detachable from that transaction as any settlement required under the indemnification would be paid at the time that it is triggered, as discussed above, and that payment would be made to Holdings, while the Series G Units may continue to remain outstanding at that time. Additionally, [RCMP] considered that Holdings is the controlling shareholder of MIRAGE, INC. and that, although CCC is an investor in Holdings, CCC is a distinct third party that is not in control of Holdings (as noted above, Holdings is controlled by Medusa Capital)."

117. "[RCMP] also considered that the issuance price for the Series G Preferred Units was consistent with the price paid by other investors in December 2018 (i.e. one month prior). Allocating proceeds received from CCC to the indemnification agreement between MIRAGE, INC. and Holdings would result in an unusually high interest rate on that instrument that would not reflect the economic substance of CCC's direct investment in MIRAGE, INC."

118. "Based on the above, management and the engagement team concluded **that proceeds received for the issuance of Series G Preferred Units to CCC should be allocated entirely to the issuance of the Series G Preferred Units**, the accounting for which was the subject of a separate consultation with DPP, as noted above." *(emphasis added)*

Issue #2

119. "Under what measurement basis should the indemnification obligation be recorded initially and subsequently? [RCMP] considered whether the indemnification arrangement is within the scope of the measurement guidance of ASC Topic, 460, Guarantees (previously FIN 45). However, ASC 460-10-25-I-h3 (paragraph 7h of FIN 45) excludes from the guidance on recognition/initial measurement an entity's guarantee of its parent's obligations. Because MIRAGE, INC.'s indemnification obligation indemnifies the contingent obligation of its parent (Holdings), it would not be subject to the recognition/initial measurement guidance of ASC 460. ASC 460 does not prescribe subsequent measurement, instead states the following:

- 35-1: This Subsection does not describe in detail how the guarantor's liability for its obligations under the guarantee would be measured after its initial recognition. The liability that the guarantor initially recognized under paragraph 460-10-25-4 would typically be reduced (by a credit to earnings) as the guarantor is released from risk under the guarantee,

- 35-2: Depending on the nature of the guarantee, the guarantor's release from risk has typically been recognized over the term of the guarantee using one of the following three methods:
  a) Only upon either expiration or settlement of the guarantee,
  b) By a systematic and rational amortization method,
  c) As the fair value of the guarantee changes.

Although those three methods are currently being used in practice for subsequent accounting, this Subsection does not provide comprehensive guidance regarding the circumstances in which each of those methods would be appropriate."

120. "A guarantor is not free to choose any of the three methods in deciding how the liability for its obligations under the guarantee is measured subsequent to the initial recognition of that liability. A guarantor shall not use fair value in subsequently accounting for the liability for its obligations under a previously issued guarantee unless the use of that method can be justified under generally accepted accounting principles (GAAP). For example, fair value is used to subsequently measure guarantees accounted for as derivatives under Topic 815.

35-3 For guidance on credit losses for financial instruments with off-balance-sheet credit risk (including financial guarantees and financial standby letters of credit), see paragraphs 825-10-35-2 through 35-3.

35-4 The discussion in paragraph 460-10-35-2 about how a guarantor typically reduces the liability that it initially recognized does not encompass the recognition and subsequent adjustment of the contingent liability related to the contingent loss for the guarantee. The contingent aspect of the guarantee shall be accounted for in accordance with Subtopic 450-20 unless the guarantee is accounted for as a derivative under Topic 815.

Next it was considered whether the indemnification obligation is a liability within the scope of ASC Topic 480. Management and the engagement team first considered whether it is freestanding or embedded in the shares to be received upon potential settlement of the indemnification (i.e. the remaining g 2.5 million shares referenced above). ASC 480-10-20 (Glossary) specifies that "A freestanding financial instrument is an instrument that is entered into (1) separately and apart from any of the entity's other financial instruments or equity transactions, or (2) is entered into in conjunction with another transaction and is legally detachable and separately exercisable." [RCMP] considered the guidance in chapter 6 of RCMP's book, Accounting for Certain Financial Instruments with Characteristics of Both Liabilities and Equity. Paragraph 6.008 states, in part, "For many instruments that require physical settlement in an entity's own shares (e.g., written put options and forward purchase contracts that require physical settlement), the shares or other financial instruments transferred at settlement of the contract are fungible. That is, the party required to deliver shares in physical settlement of a financial instrument (e.g., the holder of a written put option) can often use the shares it held when the put option was purchased, shares subsequently purchased from another investor, or shares subsequently purchased directly from the entity.

In those instances, the physically settled financial instrument is not linked to specifically identified shares, which may indicate that the instrument would be

Expert Report of William Jennings

considered a freestanding financial instrument for purposes of applying Statement ISO. However, in situations where a financial instrument requires settlement by physical delivery of specifically identified shares or financial instruments, the financial instrument would not be considered legally detachable and separately exercisable." Given the amount of time that had lapsed between the two transactions (i.e. May 2018 to January 2019) and the fact that the obligation was a separate instrument and not tied directly to any specific shares (meaning, although 2.5 million shares must be returned, the specific shares constituting that 2.5 million shares are not identified and the Company's shares are publicly traded), the instrument is considered freestanding. **Furthermore, [RCMP] believe[s] that the substance of the transaction is to create a separate class of common stock for all stock held by the controlling shareholders** (see Issue #4 below); consequently, while ~2.5 million shares of MIRAGE, INC. will be returned to MIRAGE, INC. if the indemnification is triggered, **the substance of the transaction is more broadly applicable to all shares held by the controlling shareholders rather than pertaining solely to those 2.5 million shares."** *(emphasis added)*

121. "ASC 480-10-25-8 to -12 specifies criteria pursuant to which a financial instrument is required to be classified as a liability, as follows:

25-8 An entity shall classify as a liability (or an asset in some circumstances) any financial instrument, other than an outstanding share, that, at inception, has both of the following characteristics:

a) It embodies an obligation to repurchase the issuer's equity shares or is indexed to such an obligation

b) It requires or may require the [sic] to settle the obligation by transferring assets."

122. "Management and the [RCMP] engagement team considered the indemnification obligation vis-a-vis these characteristics as follows:

1) The indemnification does not represent an outstanding share of the issuer (MIRAGE, INC.).

2) The indemnification represents a conditional obligation that may require the Company to make a payment to Holdings in the event the Permitted Debt or Preferred Equity provisions are triggered and at settlement the Company will receive the remaining shares held by Holdings related to the original equity transaction in May 2018. However, as noted above, while ~2.5 million shares of MIRAGE, INC. will be returned to MIRAGE, INC. if the indemnification is triggered, the substance of the transaction is more broadly applicable to all shares held by the controlling shareholders rather than pertaining solely to those 2.5 million shares.

3) The indemnification requires the Company to transfer cash to satisfy the obligation, if triggered."

123. "[RCMP] noted that the contingent event triggering indemnification is MIRAGE, INC. raising capital in certain transactions, which are in the control of MIRAGE, INC. **Furthermore, as noted above, [RCMP] believe[s] that the substance of the transaction is to create a separate class of common stock for all stock held by the controlling shareholders (see Issue #4 below); consequently, while ~2.5 million shares of MIRAGE, INC. will be returned to MIRAGE, INC. if the indemnification is triggered, the substance of the transaction is**

more broadly applicable to all shares held by the controlling shareholders rather than pertaining solely to those 2.5 million shares. Therefore, [RCMP] do[es] not believe that the indemnification is a liability within the scope of ASC Topic 480.

Considering the above, [RCMP] concluded that GAAP does not prescribe initial or subsequent measurement guidance for this transaction. Accordingly, analogy to the above literature would be acceptable for initial and subsequent measurement guidance, including to either ASC Topic 460 or ASC Topic 480. (Note: See Issue #3 below for discussion regarding the corresponding debit to be recorded to the financial statements). In regards to the indemnification obligation, the liability will be recorded in the financial statements at fair value and will continue to be carried at fair value in each subsequent reporting period until the obligation is settradar, by analogy to ASC Topic 480." (emphasis added)

Issue #3

124. "Does the indemnification of Holdings by MIRAGE, INC. of the original $15 million investment plus accrued dividends represent a capital transaction with Holdings or should MIRAGE, INC. record a charge to the income statement associated with a financing transaction?

The indemnification if triggered will result in MIRAGE, INC. making a payment to Holdings of approximately $15 million plus the accrued dividends on the Series C Preferred interest and the Company will receive the remaining shares held by Holdings related to the initial transaction in May 2018. **As this transaction was entered into with a 85% controlling shareholder, management and the engagement team concluded this to be a capital transaction as it is effectively providing a return of capital to its controlling shareholder.**

The engagement team notes that the amount that would be paid if the indemnification was triggered was approximately $16 million at January 17, 2019, which is a price that was significantly in excess of the fair value of the 2.5 million shares (as of January 17, 2019) that would be received at the settlement of the obligation; this fact and the likelihood of a triggering event occurring cause the indemnification obligation (written put option) to have significant fair value!

Management and the engagement team concluded that the fair value of the written put option is considered a "deemed dividend". MIRAGE, INC. will record this "deemed dividend" as a reduction of additional paid in capital as MIRAGE, INC. has an accumulated deficit rather than retained earnings. Subsequent changes in fair value of the obligation recorded on the financial statements will be recorded as "deemed dividends" similar to the initial accounting treatment.

Additionally, the repurchase of the treasury stock will be recorded at the fair value of the common stock at the date of the trigger of the indemnification obligation (i.e. immediately prior to the redemption occurring, the combined value of the shares and the repurchase obligation should equal the cash settlement amount)." *(emphasis added)*

125. "In reaching this conclusion, management and the engagement team considered the guidance of ASC Topic 505-30-30 in regards to this transaction, specifically the guidance in former FTB 85-6, Accounting for a Purchase of Treasury Shares at a Price Significantly in Excess of the Current Market Price of the Shares and

Expert Report of William Jennings

the Income Statement Classification of Costs Incurred in Defending against a Takeover Attempt. Following are excerpts from FTB 85-6:

> 3. A purchase of shares at a price significantly in excess of the current market price creates a presumption that the purchase price includes amounts attributable to items other than the shares purchased. For example, the selling shareholder may agree to abandon certain acquisition plans, forego other planned transactions, settle litigation, settle employment contracts, or restrict voluntarily the ability to purchase shares of the company or its affiliates within a stated time period. If the purchase of treasury shares includes the receipt of stated or unstated rights, privileges, or agreements in addition to the capital stock, only the amount representing the fair value of the treasury shares at the date the major terms of the agreement to purchase the shares are reached should be accounted for as the cost of the shares acquired. The price paid in excess of the amount accounted for as the cost of treasury shares should be attributed to the other elements of the transaction and accounted for according to their substance. If the fair value of those other elements of the transaction is more clearly evident, for example, because a company's shares are not publicly traded, that amount should be assigned to those elements and the difference recorded as the cost of treasury shares. If no stated or unstated consideration in addition to the capital stock can be identified, the entire purchase price should be accounted for as the cost of treasury shares. The allocation of amounts paid and the accounting treatment for such amounts should be disclosed.

> 14. An enterprise offering to repurchase shares only from a specific shareholder (or group of shareholders) suggests that the repurchase may involve more than the purchase of treasury shares. Also, when an enterprise repurchases shares at a price that is different from the price obtainable in transactions in the open market or transactions in which the identity of the selling shareholder is not important, some portion of the amount being paid presumably represents a payment for stated or unstated rights or privileges that should be given separate accounting recognition.

> **Based upon the engagement team's review of the indemnity letter as well as their inquiries of MIRAGE, INC. management, the independent committee of the Board of Directors (which is also the Audit Committee and represents members of the Board of Directors that are independent of Medusa) and external counsel, there are no stated or unstated rights such as those described in paragraph 3 of FTB 85-6 associated with this transaction that require separate accounting treatment (e.g. no acquisition plans, no litigation, no settlement of employment contracts, etc.). Rather, the benefit to the Company of this overall arrangement was an immediate cash infusion from CCC for the Series G Units, while the controlling shareholders were provided an instrument that will contingently return to them the cash contributed to MIRAGE, INC. in May 2018 (along with a specified return) upon the occurrence of specified future potential capital raises.** Therefore, the indemnification obligation was concluded to be a deemed dividend from MIRAGE, INC. to Holdings." *(emphasis added)*

126. "As noted above under Issue #2, [RCMP] believe[s] that the substance of the transaction is to create a separate class of common stock for all stock held by the controlling shareholders (see Issue #4 below); consequently, while ~2.5 million shares of MIRAGE, INC. will be returned to MIRAGE, INC. if the indemnification is

triggered, the substance of the transaction is more broadly applicable to all shares held by the controlling shareholders rather than pertaining solely to those 2.5 million shares. This class of common stock held by the controlling shareholders has received a preferential return as compared to the stock held by the noncontrolling shareholders. Thus, [RCMP] will not object to management recording subsequent changes in measurement of the obligation as deemed dividends as well, as they will reflect the impact of adjusting the original deemed dividend, by analogy to the guidance for dividends on redeemable preferred stock. KARG provides the following guidance about classification of dividends and adjustments to the balance of redeemable preferred stock:

> 19.026 - Regardless of the accounting method selected, the resulting increases or decreases in the carrying amount of redeemable should be treated in the same manner as on nonredeemable and should be effected by charges against retained earnings or, in the absence of retained earnings, by charges against paid-in capital. (EITF D-98). Entities should also consider the impact of redeemable on earnings per share as discussed in EITF D-98 Earnings per Share.
>
> 19.029 - Classification of Dividends on Preferred Stock. Dividends on preferred stock classified as equity should be charged against retained earnings or, in the absence of retained earnings, against additional paid-in capital. Dividends on preferred stock classified as a liability should be charged against income and should be presented separately from interest due and payments to other creditors in the results of operations and statement of cash flows."

Issue #4

127. "Does the 'deemed dividend' to Holdings have any impact on the Earnings per Share calculation or presentation?"

128. "ASC 260-10-45-59A to 60A states that the capital structure of some entities includes a class of common stock with different dividend rates from those of another class of common stock. The two class method is an earnings allocation that treats a participating security as having rights to earnings that otherwise would have been available to common shareholders. All securities that meet the definition of a participating security shall be included in the basic EPS computation using the two class method. Additionally, Cathy J. Cole, Associate Chief Accountant in the SEC's Office of the Chief Accountant, clarified in her Remarks Before the 2006 AI CPA National Conference on Current SEC and MC HAMMEROB Developments that the SEC staff believes that "a company with two classes of common stock must actually present both a basic and diluted earnings per share number for each class of common stock"

129. **"The 'deemed dividend' created by this transaction was only to the benefit of Holdings, which is led by Medusa Capital (the Parent). This effectively created two classes of common stock of MIRAGE, INC. under ASC 260. MIRAGE, INC. will present two classes of common stock for EPS purposes, one being those shares owned by Holdings (the "Controlling Shareholders") and the other being the holders of common stock that did not receive this benefit (the "Noncontrolling Shareholders"). For the EPS calculation, the Company will allocate the earnings based upon the respective percentages of ownership of MIRAGE, INC. held by the Controlling Shareholders (approximately 85%) and the Noncontrolling Shareholders (approximately 15%), and then will reflect the effect of the entire deemed dividend (i.e. that will be a**

charge to the Noncontrolling Shareholders for the benefit of the Controlling Shareholders). In the case of MIRAGE, INC., this will reduce the allocated losses for the Controlling Shareholders by the amount of the deemed dividend and will increase the loss per share for the Noncontrolling Shareholders.

The computation could also be described as:

- **Distributed earnings allocation: The deemed dividend represents a distribution received by the Controlling Shareholders.**
- **Undistributed earnings allocation: The effect of the deemed dividend increases the undistributed loss to be allocated between the 2 classes of common stock. Neither class is required to fund losses of the Company but both are classes of common stock so losses should be allocated. From a contractual participation perspective, however, the Controlling Shareholders were not required to participate in the losses resulting from the deemed dividend. Thus, the allocation of net losses to Controlling Shareholders should be made excluding the effect of the deemed dividend, and that effect should be allocated entirely to the Noncontrolling Shareholders."** *(emphasis added)*

130. These transactions, from an accounting and financial reporting standpoint, resulted in a "deemed dividend" to Holdings and CCC, which effectively created two separate classes of common stock. The class held by Viking and other minority investors absorbed all of MIRAGE, INC.'s subsequent losses, up to the amount of the deemed dividend, as a reduction of paid in capital while the class held by Holdings and CCC absorbed no losses.

    Dean Wormer, MIRAGE, INC.'s Controller, testified as follows:

    Q. Okay. And you agree with the statement that the, "This preferential dividend was considered in concluding that the common stock held by Medusa Capital and its affiliates was 'a class of common stock' at different dividend rates from those of another class of common stock but without prior or senior rights." Do you see where I'm reading from?
    A. Yes.
    Q. And you agree with that?
    A. Yes. Yes.
    Q. And the class of common stock without prior senior rights is what the non-controlling shareholders had?
    A. Correct.
    Q. Like Viking.
    A. Yes. And everybody else.
    Q. And everybody else. And the all other holders of common stock which would be the non-controlling stockholders as you stated here?
    A. Mm-hmm."[130]

131. In an 8-K dated May 25, 2019, MIRAGE, INC. reported the following:

    On May 25, 2019 (the "Issuance Date"), Mirage, Inc. (the "Company") entered into a Preferred Stock Subscription Agreement (the "Subscription Agreement")

---

[130] Dean Wormer Deposition, December 5, 2019, pp. 240:19–241: 13.

with RW MIRAGE, INC. Holdings LLC ("Wormwood Holdings," an affiliate of Wormwood MIRAGE, INC. Management Holdings LLC ("Wormwood
Management") and Wormwood Capital Partners L.P. ("Wormwood Capital," and
together with Wormwood Holdings, Wormwood Management and their affiliates,
"Wormwood")) and certain other purchasers identified on the signature pages
thereto.

Pursuant to the Subscription Agreement, the Company issued an aggregate of
60,705 shares of Series H Convertible Preferred Stock ("Series H Preferred Stock")
and 6,364 shares of Series I Convertible Preferred Stock ("Series I Preferred
Stock," and together with the Series H Preferred Stock, the "Preferred Shares")
at a price of $1,000 (the "Stated Value") per Preferred Share (the "Preferred
Offering"). The Company raised gross proceeds of approximately $67.1 million in
the Preferred Offering.

The Rollover Offering

The consummation of the Preferred Offering, and the issuance of the Preferred
Shares in connection therewith, constituted a subsequent transaction (as such
term is defined in the Certificate of Designation (the "Series G Certificate of
Designation") governing the Company's Series G Preferred Stock (the "Series G
Preferred Stock")). As a result, MC HAMMER MIRAGE, INC. Holdings, LLC
("MC HAMMER Holdings"), MIRAGE, INC.C Holdings II LLC ("Holdings II"),
Mr. L Redbone, who is a member of the Board (as defined below) (together with
MC HAMMER Holdings and Holdings II, the "Related Party Holders"), Life
Insurance, Inc. Company ("CCC") and certain other holders of the Company's
Series G Preferred Stock (the "Additional Holders," and together with the Related
Party Holders and CCC, the "Series G Holders") were to elect to convert (the
"Conversion Right") all or less than all of their shares of Series G Preferred Stock
into a number of shares of Series H Preferred Stock or Series I Preferred Stock
equal to the aggregate liquidation value (as defined in the Series G Certificate of
Designation) of the outstanding shares of Series G Preferred Stock held by each
of the Series G Holders (rounding down to avoid fractional shares) (the "Rollover
Offering").

Pursuant to the Conversion Right, (a) each of MC HAMMER Holdings and
Holdings II agreed to cause all 17,650 and 14,958 of their shares of Series G
Preferred Stock, respectively, to be converted into 18,316 and 15,577 shares of
Series I Preferred Stock, respectively; (b) Mr. Wood elected to convert all 6,500
of his shares of Series G Preferred Stock into 6,651 shares of Series I Preferred
Stock, (c) CCC elected to convert all 5,000 of its shares of Series G Preferred
Stock into 5,176 shares of Series I Preferred Stock and (d) the Additional Holders
collectively elected to convert all 8,627 of the shares of Series G Preferred Stock
held by such Additional Holders into 4,346 shares Series H Preferred Stock and
4,281 shares of Series I Preferred Stock. In total, the Company issued 4,346 shares
of Series H Preferred Stock and 50,001 shares of Series I Preferred Stock pursuant
to the Rollover Offering (the "Rollover Shares").

The Independent Committee reviewed and approved the Rollover Offering as it
related to the Related Party Investors.[131]

---

[131] MIRAGE, INC. Form 8-K, May 25, 2019.

These transactions resulted in MIRAGE, INC.'s preferred equity exceeding $80,000,000. As a result, MIRAGE, INC. reported the following:

Exchange and Redemption Agreement
Following consummation of the Preferred Offering, the amount of preferred equity issued by the Company exceeded $80.0 million, and, as a result, MIRAGE, INC.C Holdings LLC ("MIRAGE, INC.C Holdings") was required to redeem 15,000,000 of its issued and outstanding senior preferred member interests held by CCC (the "Class C Interests") pursuant to an existing agreement between such parties. As previously disclosed, pursuant to that certain letter agreement, dated January 17, 2019, from the Company to MIRAGE, INC.C Holdings (the "Letter Agreement"), the Company agreed to indemnify MIRAGE, INC.C Holdings for, among other things, the cost of redeeming the Class C Interests in the event that the Company issued preferred equity securities in excess of $80.0 million. Additionally, under the terms of the Letter Agreement, in the event that the Company would be required to indemnify MIRAGE, INC.C Holdings under the Letter Agreement, MIRAGE, INC.C Holdings agreed to surrender 3,750,000 shares of Common Stock to the Company less any shares of Common Stock previously distributed by MIRAGE, INC.C Holdings to CCC.

On May 25, 2019, the Company, MIRAGE, INC.C Holdings and CCC entered into that certain Exchange and Redemption Agreement (the "Exchange Agreement") to, among other things, facilitate the redemption of the Class C Interests and Common Stock held by CCC and MIRAGE, INC.C Holdings, respectively, and the indemnification payments to be made in accordance with the Letter Agreement. Pursuant to the Exchange Agreement, (a) the Company made an indemnification payment directly to CCC in the amount of $16,228,543.12, representing the cost to redeem the Class C Interests, consisting of: (i) a cash payment of $10,228,543.12, and (ii) in lieu of an additional $6,000,000 in cash, 6,000 shares of Series I Preferred Stock, deliverable within 20 days following the date of the Exchange Agreement (the "CCC Offering"); (b) CCC surrendered all of the Class C Interests to MIRAGE, INC.C Holdings; and (c) MIRAGE, INC.C Holdings surrendered a total of 2,505,000 shares of Common Stock to the Company. The Independent Committee reviewed the terms of, and approved of the Company's entering into and consummation of the transactions contemplated by, the Exchange Agreement.

The foregoing description of the Exchange Agreement does not purport to be complete and is qualified in its entirety by reference to the full text of Exchange Agreement, which is as Exhibit 10.2 to this Current Report on Form 8-K and is incorporated herein by reference.[132]

132. The unequal allocation of net losses between the share classes is reflected in MIRAGE, INC.'s financial statements beginning in 2019. For the year 2019, MIRAGE, INC.'s 10-K reported that MIRAGE, INC.'s controlling shareholders (i.e., those representing shares beneficially owned and controlled by Medusa Capital and its affiliates) incurred a net loss of $1.47 per share for the year, while noncontrolling shareholders incurred a net loss of $1.92 per share.[133] Thus, Viking

---

[132] MIRAGE, INC. Form 8-K, May 25, 2019.
[133] MIRAGE, INC. Form 10-K for the annual period ended December 31, 2019, Note 13.

and other noncontrolling shareholders absorbed an additional $0.45 per share of losses compared to Medusa and other controlling shareholders. This is due to the fact that approximately $12.5 million of deemed dividends reduced the controlling shareholders' net losses while the noncontrolling shareholders' net losses were increased by that same amount.

B. Series J Transaction

133. MIRAGE, INC.'s Amendment No. 3 to Form S-1, on August 14, 2014, contained the following disclosures:

Series J Preferred Offering

Between September 11, 2013 and January 14, 2014, we issued an aggregate of 37,394 units of our securities (the "Series J Securities") at a purchase price of $1,000 per Series J Security and raised gross proceeds of $37.4 million (the "Series J Offering"). We issued an aggregate of 8,500 Series J Securities to MC HAMMER Holdings, 19,657 Series J Securities to Holdings II, 5,254 Series J Securities to Wormwood Holdings and 2,570 Series J Securities to Puke. Each Series J Security consists of (A) one share of Series J Preferred Stock and (B) a warrant to purchase 2,650 at an exercise price of $0.001 per share shares of common stock (the "Series J Warrants"). The Company has offered each holder of shares of Series H Preferred Stock, Series I Preferred Stock and Series J Preferred Stock the right to purchase a pro-rata share of the Series J Securities issued in the Series J Offering. *(emphasis added)*

Series H, Series I and Series J Convertible Preferred Stock

In conjunction with the Wormwood Offering, on May 25, 2019 (the "Series H-I Issuance Date"), we the Series H Certificate of Designation and Series I Certificate of Designation with the Secretary of State of the State of Delaware setting forth the designations, preferences, dividends, voting rights and other special rights of the Series H Preferred Stock and Series I Preferred Stock, respectively. In conjunction with the Series J Offering, on September 11, 2013 (the "Series J Issuance Date"), we the Series J Certificate of Designation with the Secretary of State of the State of Delaware setting forth the designations, preferences, dividends, voting rights and other special rights of the Series J Preferred Stock. In conjunction with the Follow-On Offering, on January 8, 2014 we amended and restated the Series H Certificate of Designation, Series I Certificate of Designation and Series J Certificate of Designation (collectively, the "Amended and Restated Certificates of Designation").

We have designated 135,000 shares of our preferred stock as Series H Preferred Stock, 90,000 shares of our preferred stock as Series I Preferred Stock and **90,000 shares of our preferred stock as Series J Preferred Stock.** *(emphasis added)*

The Series J Preferred Stock is senior to the Series H Preferred Stock, the Series I Preferred Stock and the Common Stock. The Series H Preferred Stock and the Series I Preferred Stock are senior to the common stock. The Preferred Shares are to dividends of the same type as any dividends or other distribution of any kind payable or to be made on outstanding shares of common stock, on an as converted basis. *(emphasis added)*

Upon the consummation of an underwritten public offering (a "QPO") where

(i) the gross proceeds received by us and any selling stockholders in the offering are no less than $100 million and

(ii) our market capitalization immediately after consummation of the offering is no less than $500 million, each outstanding Preferred Share will automatically convert into the number of shares of common stock equal to the greater of (a) the number of Optional Conversion Shares or (b) the quotient obtained by dividing (i) the Returned Value (as defined below) by (ii) the price per share of common stock paid by the public in the QPO.

In addition, the Series H Certificate of Designation and the Series I Certificate of Designation each contain certain rights exercisable by Wormwood and Medusa Capital, respectively, as the "primary investor" of such series. At any time on or after September 25, 2015, so long as the primary investor of the respective series of Series H Preferred Stock or Series I Preferred Stock beneficially owns any shares of such series of Preferred Shares, the respective primary investor will have the right to require the company to redeem all or a portion of such primary investor's Series H Preferred Stock or Series I Preferred Stock for an amount in cash equal to the Liquidation Amount (as defined below) of such Series H Preferred Stock or Series I Preferred Stock (the "Optional Redemption Right"). If the primary investor of the Series H Preferred Stock or Series I Preferred Stock elects to exercise its Optional Redemption Right, all other holders of such series will have the right to have all or any portion of their Series H Preferred Stock or Series I Preferred Stock redeemed for an amount in cash equal to the Liquidation Amount of such series.

We must redeem all outstanding shares of Series J Preferred Stock for an amount in cash equal to the Liquidation Amount of such shares upon our receipt of a notice from the holders of Series H Preferred Stock that would require us to redeem the shares of Series H Preferred Stock pursuant to the Series H Certificate of Designation. The redemption of any shares of Series J Preferred Stock would be senior and prior to any redemption of Series H Preferred Stock or Series I Preferred Stock and any holder of shares of Series J Preferred Stock may elect to have less than all or none of such holder's Series J Preferred Stock redeemed. After we have redeemed any shares of Series H Preferred Stock, at any time thereafter each holder of shares of Series J Preferred Stock may elect to have all or a portion of such holder's Series J Preferred Stock redeemed for an amount in cash equal to the Liquidation Amount of such share or Series J Preferred Stock. *(emphasis added)*

134. The Series J Preferred stock offering appears to result in at least three negative consequences for Viking. First, it creates yet another class of security senior in claims to Viking's common shares. Second, it creates another MIRAGE, INC. redemption obligation similar to the obligation in the Life Insurance, Inc. transactions described above. Third, in addition to its other dilutive qualities, each Series J Security has a warrant attached for the purchase of 2,650 MIRAGE, INC. common shares at a price of $.001 per share. So, a holder of a Series J Security, in addition to its other preferences and superior claims, can purchase 2,650 MIRAGE, INC. common shares for $2.65. These same shares were sold to Viking for $4.00 per share. So, Viking paid $10,600 for each block of 2,650 MIRAGE, INC. common shares which Series J warrant holders can now purchase for $2.65.

C. Performance of MIRAGE, INC. Common Shares after the Investment

135. The price of MIRAGE, INC.'s common stock after Viking's investment has declined steadily as MIRAGE, INC. entered into more and more capital transactions that diluted the value of common shareholders, such as Viking.

136. Although MIRAGE, INC. common stock is not listed on one of the major exchanges, it is publicly traded on the OTC Bulletin Board. The market for MIRAGE, INC.'s common shares is not efficient because the stock is so thinly traded. Below are the high and low prices for common shares of MIRAGE, INC. for each quarter in 2016–12, as reported in MIRAGE, INC.'s 2018 and 2019 10-Ks.[134] A steady decline in share price can be seen in Table 11.7 beginning in mid-2018.

TABLE 11.7

Period	Low	High
2016		
1Q	$0.78	$1.69
2Q	$1.25	$1.75
3Q	$1.55	$2.25
4Q	$2.10	$2.25
2018		
1Q	$3.05	$5.55
2Q	$2.96	$3.78
3Q	$2.33	$3.66
4Q	$1.22	$2.44
2019		
1Q	$1.02	$1.66
2Q	$0.92	$1.51
3Q	$0.81	$1.22
4Q	$0.48	$0.88

137. MIRAGE, INC. shares have continued to decline. On the last trading day before this report was issued, August 21, 2018, 8,800 shares of MIRAGE, INC.'s common shares traded on the OTC Bulletin Board at prices ranging from $0.33 to $0.44 per share. The closing price was $0.38 per share.[135]

Submitted August 24, 2019:

<signature>

William L. Jennings

---

[134] Form 10-K for the annual period ended December 31, 2017, on April 1, 2018, Item 5. Form 10-K for the annual period ended December 31, 2018, on April 16, 2019, Item 5.
[135] Downloaded on August 22, 2018, at http://www.otcmarkets.com/stock/quote

Now, that I have made the points I needed to make, in the body of the report, I lay out my detailed analyses in the exhibits. The decision was made to put the detailed quantitative analyses in the Exhibit section because there was so much evidence to cover in the body of the report that we didn't want to make it more difficult than it would already be for the reader to get through it.

Expert Report of William Jennings

EXHIBITS <section cover page>

Exhibit 1 – CV of William L. Jennings, BS, MBA, CPA, CFE, CFF
<insert current Rule 26 CV>

Exhibit 2 – Materials Reviewed
<list of all documents received, filings reviewed, research sources, etc.>

In this section we measure the impact of the misrepresentations on the value of Mirage. We did this to quantify the economic damages under our alternative remedy if rescission turned out not to be available.

Expert Report of William Jennings

Exhibit 3 – Valuation Analysis of Equity

(Schedules Follow)

<page break>

Viking Investments Limited v. Mirage, Inc., et al.
Analysis of Impact of Restated Financial Statements on Equity Value
Exhibit 3

Procedures Performed
1. In order to analyze the impact of the restatement which impacted gross margins, V first sought to determine a baseline value of MIRAGE, INC.'s equity as of May 10, 2018, the date of valuation based on the date of Viking's investment in MIRAGE, INC.
2. V considered the three general approaches for business valuation (income, market, and asset-based approach) and determined that the discounted cash flow ("DCF") method of the income approach was the most appropriate to estimate the value of MIRAGE, INC.
3. In creating the DCF model, V used the latest comprehensive financial forecast that was provided to Viking by J.P. Prince on April 6, 2018, and assumed it was correct (see Schedule 2; Table 11.9 attached hereto). V did, however, correct "Operating Income" (also earnings before interest and taxes, or "EBIT") and earnings before interest, taxes, depreciation, and amortization ("EBITDA") in the forecast, as both were overstated, since the amounts included depreciation and amortization twice.
4. V then calculated the future cash flows that would be available to debt and equity holders ("Debt-Free Cash Flow") by adding back non-cash expenses (depreciation and amortization) and subtracting taxes, capital expenditures, and reduction in working capital from EBIT.
5. Next, V determined a discount rate (weighted average cost of capital, or "WACC") based on guideline lighting companies to apply to the future cash flows in order to value them as of May 10, 2018 (see Schedule 5, attached hereto).

Expert Report of William Jennings

Viking Investments Limited v. Mirage, Inc., et al.
Analysis of Impact of Restated Financial Statements on Equity Value
Exhibit 3

6. V then calculated a terminal value of the Company by dividing the estimated post-2016 perpetual annual Debt-Free Cash Flow by the result of the WACC minus the assumed terminal growth rate of 3% and discounted the terminal value back to May 10, 2018.

7. V subsequently added the present values of the future cash flows and terminal value to calculate the enterprise value based on J.P. Prince's forecast ("Indicated Enterprise Value from Operations").

8. Next, V added cash and cash equivalents, working capital surplus, amortization benefit beyond discrete period, and the net present value of net operating loss carry-forwards to calculate the enterprise value on a control, marketable basis of approximately $510,000,000.

9. V subtracted interest-bearing debt from the enterprise value to calculate the equity value of approximately $500,300,000 on a control, marketable basis (see Schedules 1 and 2, attached hereto, "Original BNS Scenario").

10. V then applied discounts for lack of control ("DLOC") and lack of marketability ("DLOM"), which were required to adjust the control, marketable basis of the equity value calculated. The DLOC was based on control premium studies and was needed to reflect the nature of Viking's minority interest investment. The DLOM was based on restricted stock and pre-initial public offering studies and was required to reflect the lack of marketability of Viking's investment. Although there were several different classes of equity as of the valuation date, all were treated as common for the simplified purpose of calculating the relative value differences of the scenarios analyzed. Had each class of equity been valued separately, the common equity that Viking purchased would have had a lower relative value than senior classes to common, due primarily to liquidation rights, voting rights, and preferences, and thus an even larger percentage difference between scenarios. Applying the DLOC and DLOM to calculate a minority, non-marketable equity basis resulted in a value of approximately $405,200,000 (see Schedule 1; Table 11.8).

11. The next objective was to calculate the equity value using the same J.P. Prince forecast, DCF model data, and methodology of the Original BNS Scenario, but adjusting only the forecasted gross profit margins an appropriate in light of the restatement and true historical financial performance of the Company (see Schedule 3, attached hereto, "Adjusted BNS Scenario").

12. V applied the same methodology outlined in paragraphs 2 through 10 above, but adjusted the gross profit margins as a reasonable investor would, based on the new information contained in the restatement. In addition, V adjusted the DLOM to reflect a longer time horizon for a potential IPO, reduced likelihood of dividends, reduced reliability of financial information, and overall lower marketability expectations in light of the restatement. In addition to restricted stock and pre-initial public offering studies, the adjusted DLOM was also based on analysis of an implied DLOM using a European protective put model. The result was a reduced equity value of approximately $212,400,000 (see Schedules 1 and 3, attached hereto).

13. V then prepared a third DCF analysis, using the same J.P. Prince forecast, DCF model data, and methodology of the Adjusted BNS Scenario, but adjusting only

Expert Report of William Jennings

Viking Investments Limited v. Mirage, Inc., et al.
Analysis of Impact of Restated Financial Statements on Equity Value
Exhibit 3

the forecasted gross profit margins to reflect available *ex post* information, using MIRAGE, INC.'s actual gross margins for the fiscal years ended December 31, 2018 and 2019 (see Schedule 4, attached hereto, "Actual BNS Scenario").

14. V applied the same methodology outlined in paragraphs 2 through 10 above, but adjusted the gross profit margins to reflect actual gross margins for comparison purposes, and calculated a reduced equity value of approximately $145,000,000 (see Schedules 1 and 4, attached hereto).

15. V calculated the percentage difference between the overall equity value derived under the Original BNS Scenario and the Adjusted BNS Scenario to estimate the impact of the restatement (*i.e.,* if the restatement information had been available as of the date of valuation, how would that have impacted the original J.P. Prince forecast and valuation). In addition, V calculated the percentage difference between the overall equity value derived under the Original BNS Scenario and the Actual BNS Scenario for comparative purposes.

Summary of Conclusions

16. The reduction in MIRAGE, INC.'s gross margins attributable to the restatement would require a reduction of certain gross margins in J.P. Prince's forecast, which would, in turn, have a significant adverse impact on the value of the Company's equity as of May 10, 2018.

17. The reduction in the value of the Company's overall equity (including all tranches) attributable to the restatement is approximately 48% by virtue of the gross margin misstatement issue alone, looking solely at the date Viking purchased the shares. However, this analysis does not take into account the restatements of the Series D and E warrants that damaged earnings, MIRAGE, INC.'s understatement of its inventory reserves, or the post-investment conduct damaging Viking. The reduction attributable to the gross margin misstatement error alone are likely even greater than 48% due to the fact that the valuation analysis did not account for the differences in rights and preferences between Viking's common stock and the numerous more preferred and beneficial classes of equity present in MIRAGE, INC.'s capital structure (i.e., Viking holds the least valuable class of shares). Thus, the common stock portion of the company's overall equity value is likely small which would result in a significantly larger reduction than 48%.

18. Since Viking invested in common equity, the riskiness of the residual future cash flows available to it was greater than that of other equity holders, such as those holding preferred equity. For example, there are several classes of preferred shares senior to common stock that have priority rights to dividends, redemption rights, conversion rights, voting rights, and significant liquidation rights. As described in paragraph 10 above had each class of equity been valued separately, the common equity that Viking purchased would have had a lower relative value and thus an even larger percentage difference between scenarios. Accordingly, V estimates that the reduction in common equity value is at least 48%.

19. Substituting actual gross margins for the fiscal years ended December 31, 2018 and 2019 would result in a reduction in common equity value of at least 64%.

Viking Investments Limited v. Mirage, Inc., et al.
Analysis of Impact of Restated Financial Statements on Equity Value
Exhibit 3

20. Applying the estimated reduction in common equity value of approximately 48% to Viking's $25 million investment would yield a decline in value of approximately $12 million (48% × $25 million) (see Figure 11.3 below).

TABLE 1

	Original	Adjusted	Actual
Fair market value of equity - minority, non-marketable	$ 405,200,000	$ 212,400,000	$ 145,000,000
Percent Difference	-	-47.6%	-64.2%
Viking Investment	$25,000,000	$25,000,000	$25,000,000
Reduction in Value of Viking Investments	$0	($11,900,000)	($16,050,000)

FIGURE 11.3

21. In addition to the reduction in common equity value, the restatement also had an adverse impact on Viking's time horizon to earn its anticipated return.
22. Under the Adjusted BNS Scenario, the Company would not earn positive equity cash flows until the fiscal year ended December 31, 2014, as opposed to December 31, 2019, under the Original BNS Scenario.
23. V understands that the restatement also had an adverse impact on the timing of the Company's planned initial public offering, which also adversely impacted Viking's time horizon to earn its anticipated return (see Figures 11.4–11.14 and Tables 11.10–11.12).

TABLE 11.8
Schedule 1

Viking Investments Limited vs Mirage, Inc., et al.
Analysis of Impact of Restated Financial Statements on Equity Value
Valuation Summary (1)
US$

Schedule 1
Valuation Date: May 10, 2018

	Original BNS Scenario (2) Fair Market Value Indication of Invested Capital	Adjusted BNS Scenario (3) Fair Market Value Indication of Invested Capital	Actual BNS Scenario (4) Fair Market Value Indication of Invested Capital
Indicated Fair Market Value of Invested Capital - Control, Marketable Basis (Rounded)	$ 510,000,000	$ 403,100,000	$ 278,300,000
Less: Interest-Bearing Debt (5)	$ 9,651,078	$ 9,651,078	$ 9,651,078
Indicated Fair Market Value of Equity - Control, Marketable Basis (Rounded)	**$ 500,300,000**	**$ 393,400,000**	**$ 268,600,000**
Less: Discount for Lack of Control (6)	$ (50,030,000)	$ (39,340,000)	$ (26,860,000)
	10.0%	10.0%	10.0%
Indicated Fair Market Value of Equity - Minority, Marketable Basis (Rounded)	$ 450,270,000	$ 354,060,000	$ 241,740,000
Less: Discount for Lack of Marketability (7)	$ (45,027,000)	$ (141,624,000)	$ (96,696,000)
	10.0%	40.0%	40.0%
Indicated Fair Market Value of Equity - Minority, Non-Marketable Basis (Rounded)	**$ 405,200,000**	**$ 212,400,000**	**$ 145,000,000**

	Original	Adjusted	Actual
Percent Difference (Rounded)	-	-47.6%	-64.2%
Viking Investment	$25,000,000	$25,000,000	$25,000,000
Reduction in Value of Viking Investment	$0	($11,900,000)	($16,050,000)

Footnotes:

(1) This schedule has been prepared on the basis of the information and assumptions set forth in our report and the attached schedules. It must be read in conjunction with all of the other schedules included herein.

(2) The only changes in the scenarios are adjustments to the cost of revenue margin. All other factors are kept consistent across scenarios. Cost of revenue margins are based on the JP Prince model through December 31, 2014. See Exhibit 320, ABC00000221 (Pages 6–7 of 14). See Schedule 2.

(3) The only changes in the scenarios are adjustments to the cost of revenue margin. All other factors are kept consistent across scenarios. Cost of revenue margins in the Adjusted BNS Scenario reflect a slower ramp-up period from 2018 through 2013 than in the Original BNS Scenario. See Schedule 3.

(4) The only changes in the scenarios are adjustments to the cost of revenue margin. All other factors are kept consistent across scenarios. Cost of revenue margins in the Actual BNS Scenario reflects actual margins for 2018 and 2019 and a smoothed margin for 2013. See Schedule 4.

(5) Interest-bearing debt includes the Company's short-term debt and current installment of long-term debt.

(6) Based on our informed judgment and MergerStat/BVR control premium studies. See Schedule 9.

(7) Based on our informed judgment and marketability studies and research. See Schedules 10 through 13.

TABLE 11.9
Schedule 2

Viking Investments Limited vs Mirage, Inc., et al.
Analysis of Impact of Restated Financial Statements on Equity Value
Discounted Debt-Free Cash Flow ("DCF") Method – Original BNS Scenario (1)
US$

Schedule 2

Valuation Date: May 10, 2018

	7.7 Months Dec 31, '11	Dec 31, '12	Dec 31, '13	Dec 31, '14	Dec 31, '15	Dec 31, '16	Terminal
Net Revenue	$ 135,589,927	$ 444,959,274	$ 658,058,912	$ 895,585,295	$ 922,452,854	$ 950,126,439	$ 978,630,233
% Revenue Growth Rate	NA	111.3%	47.9%	36.1%	3.0%	3.0%	3.0%
Cost of Goods Sold	110,205,503	310,406,691	441,203,163	593,722,877	611,534,563	629,880,600	648,777,018
Gross Profit	25,384,423	134,552,583	216,855,749	301,862,418	310,918,291	320,245,839	329,853,214
Gross Profit Margin	18.7%	30.2%	33.0%	33.7%	33.7%	33.7%	33.7%
Operating Expenses:							
Sales & Marketing	10,378,073	25,201,471	35,672,737	47,419,215	48,841,791	50,307,045	51,816,257
Operations	10,673,775	25,127,298	35,698,937	46,479,718	47,874,110	49,310,333	50,789,643
General & Administrative	7,294,533	11,461,695	14,553,301	17,551,385	18,077,927	18,620,264	19,178,872
Research & Development			-				-
Depreciation	2,035,389	5,877,144	8,620,001	13,105,715	13,498,887	13,903,853	14,320,969
Amortization (2)	1,040,979	1,616,840	1,616,840	1,616,840	1,616,840	1,616,840	-
Total Operating Expenses	31,422,749	69,284,448	96,161,816	126,172,873	129,909,554	133,758,335	136,105,741
Operating Expense Margin	23.2%	15.6%	14.6%	14.1%	14.1%	14.1%	13.9%
Earnings Before Interest & Taxes (EBIT) (3)	$ (6,038,326)	$ 65,268,135	$ 120,693,933	$ 175,689,545	$ 181,008,737	$ 186,487,504	$ 193,747,474
EBIT Margin	NA	14.7%	18.3%	19.6%	19.6%	19.6%	19.8%
Blended Income Taxes	-	(25,177,184)	(46,557,685)	(67,772,242)	(69,824,121)	(71,937,555)	(74,738,088)
Blended Income Tax Rate	0.0%	38.6%	38.6%	38.6%	38.6%	38.6%	38.6%
Debt-Free Net Income	$ (6,038,326)	$ 40,090,951	$ 74,136,248	$ 107,917,303	$ 111,184,616	$ 114,549,949	$ 119,009,385
Cash Flow Adjustments:							
Depreciation & Amortization	3,076,368	7,493,984	10,236,841	14,722,555	15,115,726	15,520,693	14,320,969
Capital Expenditures (4)	(6,931,202)	(19,010,564)	(19,200,000)	(31,400,000)	(31,400,000)	(31,400,000)	(14,320,969)
Net Change in Non-Cash Debt-Free Working Capital	(10,135,782)	(23,436,215)	(21,309,964)	(23,752,638)	(2,686,756)	(2,767,359)	(2,850,379)
Debt-Free Cash Flow	$ (20,028,942)	$ 5,138,156	$ 43,863,125	$ 67,487,219	$ 92,213,587	$ 95,903,283	$ 116,159,006

(Continued)

TABLE 11.9 (Continued)
Schedule 2

Viking Investments Limited vs Mirage, Inc., et al.

Analysis of Impact of Restated Financial Statements on Equity Value

Discounted Debt-Free Cash Flow ("DCF") Method – Original BNS Scenario (1)

US$

Schedule 2

Valuation Date: May 10, 2018

	7.7 Months Dec 31, '11	Dec 31, '12	Dec 31, '13	Dec 31, '14	Dec 31, '15	Dec 31, '16	Terminal
Discount Period	0.32	1.14	2.14	3.14	4.14	5.14	
Present Value Factor (5)	0.9481	0.8275	0.7013	0.5943	0.5037	0.4268	0.4268
Present Value of Debt-Free Cash Flows	$ (18,989,692)	$ 4,251,930	$ 30,760,711	$ 40,108,491	$ 46,443,794	$ 40,934,006	
		Terminal Growth Rate					3.0%
Sum of the Present Value of Discrete Year Cash Flows	$ 143,509,239	Residual Value at Terminal Year				$ 774,393,373	
Present Value of Terminal Cash Flow	330,531,153	Present Value Factor					
Indicated Enterprise Value from Operations	**$ 474,040,392**	**Present Value of Terminal Cash Flow**				**$ 330,531,153**	
Add: Cash & Cash Equivalents (6)	9,540,605						
Add: Working Capital Surplus / (Deficit) (7)	4,011,612						
Add: Amortization Benefit Beyond Discrete Period (8)	1,014,665						
Add: Net Present Value of NOL Carryforwards (9)	21,400,000						
Indicated Enterprise Value - Control, Marketable Basis (Rounded)	**$ 510,000,000**						

18.0%

Footnotes:

(1) Forecast for MIRAGE, INC. obtained from BNS model. See Exhibit 320, ABC00000221 (Pages 6–7 of 14). Figures for 2015–16 were based on 2014 (see Schedule 6). Note that figures may not be exact due to rounding.

(2) Amortization represents estimated tax amortization which differs slightly from the BNS model for 2018–14.

(3) The EBIT calculation (operating income) in the BNS model was incorrect, as it was overstated by the depreciation and amortization amount. This schedule presents the corrected amounts.

(4) Capital expenditures for 2015–16 were assumed constant at the 2014 level in the BNS model.

(5) See Schedule 5.

(6) See Schedule 8.

(7) Net working capital surplus has been estimated based on an assumed net working capital requirement of 10% of revenue based on an analysis of the guideline companies' requirements.

(8) Represents the estimated tax amortization of intangibles and goodwill. Amortization tax benefit is projected to continue through 2023 and has not been included in the terminal value due to the fact that this benefit would not exist into perpetuity. However, we have included an add-back for the tax benefit through 2023.

(9) Based on the December 31, 2016 NOL carry forward balance.

Viking Investments Limited v. Mirage, Inc., et al.
Analysis of Impact of Restated Financial Statements on Equity Value
Discounted Debt-Free Cash Flow ("DCF") Method – Adjusted BNS Scenario (1)
US$

Schedule 3
Valuation Date: May 10, 2018

	7.7 Months Dec 31, '11	Dec 31, '12	Dec 31, '13	Dec 31, '14	Dec 31, '15	Dec 31, '16	Terminal
Net Revenue	$ 135,589,927	$ 444,969,274	$ 658,068,912	$ 895,585,295	$ 922,452,854	$ 950,126,439	$ 978,630,233
% Revenue Growth Rate	NA	111.3%	47.9%	36.1%	3.0%	3.0%	3.0%
Cost of Goods Sold	135,589,927	400,463,347	526,447,130	593,722,877	611,534,563	629,880,600	648,777,018
Gross Profit	-	44,495,927	131,611,782	301,862,418	310,918,291	320,245,839	329,853,214
Gross Profit Margin	0.0%	10.0%	20.0%	33.7%	33.7%	33.7%	33.7%
Operating Expenses:							
Sales & Marketing	10,378,073	25,201,471	35,672,737	47,419,215	48,841,791	50,307,045	51,816,257
Operations	10,673,775	25,127,298	35,696,937	46,479,718	47,874,110	49,310,333	50,789,643
General & Administrative	7,294,533	11,461,695	14,553,301	17,551,385	18,077,927	18,620,264	19,178,872
Research & Development							
Depreciation	2,035,389	5,877,144	8,620,001	13,105,715	13,498,887	13,903,853	14,320,969
Amortization (2)	1,040,979	1,616,840	1,616,840	1,616,840	1,616,840	1,616,840	
Total Operating Expenses	31,422,749	69,284,448	96,161,816	126,172,873	129,909,554	133,758,335	136,105,741
Operating Expense Margin	23.2%	15.6%	14.6%	14.1%	14.1%	14.1%	13.9%
Earnings Before Interest & Taxes (EBIT) (3)	$ (31,422,749)	$ (24,788,521)	$ 35,449,966	$ 175,689,545	$ 181,008,737	$ 186,487,504	$ 193,747,474
EBIT Margin	NA	(5.6%)	5.4%	19.6%	19.6%	19.6%	19.6%
Blended Income Taxes	0.0%	0.0%	(13,674,825)	(67,772,242)	(69,924,121)	(71,937,555)	(74,738,088)
Blended Income Tax Rate			38.6%	38.6%	38.6%	38.6%	38.6%
Debt-Free Net Income	$ (31,422,749)	$ (24,788,521)	$ 21,775,141	$ 107,917,303	$ 111,184,616	$ 114,549,949	$ 119,009,385
Cash Flow Adjustments:							
Depreciation & Amortization	3,076,368	7,493,984	10,236,841	14,722,555	15,115,726	15,520,693	14,320,969
Capital Expenditures (4)	(6,931,202)	(19,010,564)	(19,200,000)	(31,400,000)	(31,400,000)	(31,400,000)	(14,320,969)
Net Change in Non-Cash Debt-Free Working Capital	(19,135,782)	(23,438,215)	(21,309,966)	(23,752,638)	(2,686,756)	(2,767,359)	(2,859,379)
Debt-Free Cash Flow	$ (45,413,365)	$ (59,741,316)	$ (9,497,981)	$ 67,487,219	$ 92,213,587	$ 95,903,283	$ 116,159,006
Discount Period		0.32	1.14	2.14	3.14	4.14	5.14
Present Value Factor (5)	16.0%	0.9481	0.8275	0.7013	0.5943	0.5037	0.4268
Present Value of Debt-Free Cash Flows		$ (43,058,982)	$ (49,437,168)	$ (5,599,538)	$ 40,108,491	$ 46,443,794	$ 40,924,008

Sum of the Present Value of Discrete Year Cash Flows	$ 29,032,603
Present Value of Terminal Cash Flow	330,531,152
Indicated Enterprise Value from Operations	$ 359,563,766
Add: Cash & Cash Equivalents (6)	9,540,605
Add: Working Capital Surplus / (Deficit) (7)	4,011,612
Add: Amortization Benefit Beyond Discrete Period (8)	1,014,665
Add: Net Present Value of NOL Carryforwards (9)	29,000,000
Indicated Enterprise Value - Control, Marketable Basis (Rounded)	$ 403,100,000

Terminal Growth Rate		3.0%
Residual Value at Terminal Year		$ 774,393,373
Present Value Factor		0.4268
Present Value of Terminal Cash Flow		$ 330,531,152

Footnotes:

(1) Forecast for MIRAGE obtained from BNS model. See Exhibit 320, ABC00000221 (Pages 6-7 of 14). COGS has been adjusted in 2016 through 2013, and then mirrors BNS model beginning in 2014. Figures for 2015-16 were based on 2014 (see Schedule 6). Note that figures may not be exact due to rounding.
(2) Amortization represents estimated tax amortization which differ slightly from the BNS model for 2016-14.
(3) The EBIT calculation (operating income) in the BNS model was incorrect, as it was overstated by the depreciation and amortization amount. This schedule presents the corrected amounts.
(4) Capital expenditures for 2015-16 was assumed constant at the 2014 level in the BNS model.
(5) See Schedule 5.
(6) See Schedule 5.
(7) Net working capital surplus has been estimated based on an assumed net working capital requirement of 10% of revenue based on an analysis of the guideline companies' requirements.
(8) Represents the estimated tax amortization of intangibles and goodwill. Amortization tax benefit is projected to continue through 2023 and has not been included in the terminal value due to the fact that this benefit would not exist into perpetuity. However, we have included an add-back for the tax benefit through 2023.
(9) Based on the December 31, 2016 NOL carryforward balance.

FIGURE 11.4

Viking Investments Limited v. Mirage, Inc., et al.

Analysis of Impact of Restated Financial Statements on Equity Value

Discounted Debt-Free Cash Flow ("DCF") Method – Actual BNS Scenario (1)

Schedule 4

Valuation Date: May 10, 2018

	7.7 Months Dec 31, '11	Dec 31, '12	Dec 31, '13	Dec 31, '14	Dec 31, '15	Dec 31, '16	Terminal
Net Revenue	$ 135,589,927	$ 444,959,274	$ 658,058,912	$ 895,585,295	$ 922,452,854	$ 950,126,439	$ 978,630,233
% Revenue Growth Rate	NA	111.3%	47.9%	36.1%	3.0%	3.0%	3.0%
Cost of Goods Sold	160,728,760	514,240,198	598,388,004	563,722,877	611,534,563	629,880,600	648,777,018
Gross Profit	(25,138,833)	(69,280,924)	59,670,908	301,862,418	310,918,291	320,245,839	329,853,214
Gross Profit Margin	(18.5%)	(15.6%)	9.1%	33.7%	33.7%	33.7%	33.7%
Operating Expenses:							
Sales & Marketing	10,378,073	25,201,471	35,672,737	47,419,215	48,841,791	50,307,045	51,816,257
Operations	10,673,775	25,127,298	35,698,637	46,479,718	47,874,110	49,310,333	50,789,643
General & Administrative	7,294,533	11,461,685	14,563,301	17,561,385	18,077,927	18,620,264	19,178,872
Research & Development							
Depreciation	2,035,389	5,877,144	8,620,001	13,105,715	13,498,887	13,903,853	14,320,969
Amortization (2)	1,040,979	1,616,840	1,616,840	1,616,840	1,616,840	1,616,840	
Total Operating Expenses	31,422,749	69,284,448	96,161,816	126,172,873	129,909,554	133,758,335	136,105,741
Operating Expense Margin	23.2%	15.6%	14.6%	14.1%	14.1%	14.1%	13.9%
Earnings Before Interest & Taxes (EBIT) (3)	$ (56,561,583)	$ (138,565,372)	$ (36,490,908)	$ 175,689,545	$ 181,008,737	$ 185,487,504	$ 193,747,474
EBIT Margin	NA	(31.1%)	(5.5%)	19.6%	19.6%	19.6%	19.8%
Blended Income Taxes				(67,772,242)	(69,824,121)	(71,937,555)	(74,738,088)
Blended Income Tax Rate	0.0%	0.0%	0.0%	38.6%	38.6%	38.6%	38.6%
Debt-Free Net Income	$ (56,561,583)	$ (138,565,372)	$ (36,490,908)	$ 107,917,303	$ 111,184,616	$ 114,549,949	$ 119,009,385
Cash Flow Adjustments:							
Depreciation & Amortization	3,076,368	7,493,984	10,236,841	14,722,555	15,115,726	15,520,693	14,320,969
Capital Expenditures (4)	(6,931,202)	(19,010,564)	(19,200,000)	(31,400,000)	(31,400,000)	(31,400,000)	(14,320,969)
Net Change in Non-Cash Debt-Free Working Capital	(10,135,762)	(23,436,215)	(21,309,864)	(23,752,638)	(2,686,756)	(2,767,358)	(2,850,379)
Debt-Free Cash Flow	$ (70,552,199)	$ (173,518,168)	$ (66,764,031)	$ 67,487,219	$ 92,213,587	$ 95,903,283	$ 116,159,006
Discount Period		0.32	1.14	2.14	3.14	4.14	5.14
Present Value Factor (5)	18.0%	0.9481	0.8275	0.7013	0.5943	0.5037	0.4268
Present Value of Debt-Free Cash Flows	$ (66,891,426)	$ (143,589,854)	$ (46,820,855)	$ 40,108,491	$ 46,443,794	$ 40,834,006	

Terminal Growth Rate   3.0%

Sum of the Present Value of Discrete Year Cash Flows	$ (129,815,845)
Present Value of Terminal Cash Flow	330,531,153
Indicated Enterprise Value from Operations	$ 200,715,308
Add: Cash & Cash Equivalents (6)	9,540,605
Add: Working Capital Surplus / (Deficit) (7)	4,011,612
Add: Amortization Benefit Beyond Discrete Period (8)	1,014,665
Add: Net Present Value of NOL Carryforwards (9)	63,000,000
Indicated Enterprise Value – Control, Marketable Basis	$ 278,300,000

Residual Value at Terminal Year $ 774,393,373

Present Value Factor   0.4268

Present Value of Terminal Cash Flow $ 330,531,153

Footnotes:
(1) Forecast for MIRAGE obtained from BNS model. See Exhibit 320, ABC00000271 (Pages 6-7 of 14). COGS have been adjusted to reflect the actual COGS percentage for 2018-12, and then mirror the BNS model beginning in 2014.
(2) Figures for 2015-16 were based on 2014 (see Schedule 6). Note that figures may not be exact due to rounding.
(2) Amortization represents estimated tax amortization which differ slightly from the BNS model for 2018-14.
(3) The EBIT calculation (operating income) in the BNS model was incorrect, as it was overstated by the depreciation and amortization amount. This schedule presents the corrected amounts.
(4) Capital expenditures for 2015-16 was assumed constant at the 2014 level in the BNS model.
(5) See Schedule 5.
(6) See Schedule 8.
(7) Net working capital surplus has been estimated based on an assumed net working capital requirement of 10% of revenue based on an analysis of the guideline companies' requirements.
(8) Represents the estimated tax amortization of intangibles and goodwill. Amortization tax benefit is projected to continue through 2023 and has not been included in the terminal value due to the fact that this benefit would not exist into perpetuity. However, we have included an add-back for the tax benefit through 2023.
(9) Based on the December 31, 2016 NOL carryforward balance.

FIGURE 11.5

Viking Investments Limited v. Mirage, Inc., et al. — Schedule 5
Analysis of Impact of Restated Financial Statements on Equity Value
Beta, Capital Asset Pricing Model ("CAPM") & Weighted Average Cost of Capital ("WACC") Analyses — Valuation Date: May 10, 2018
US$, except per share amounts

Selected Public Guideline Companies (1)	Total Debt	Total Preferred Equity	Month End Stock Price	Total Shares Outstanding	Market Value of Common Equity	Total Capital	Book Value of Debt to Equity	Book Value of Debt to Capital (Wd)	TTM Income Taxes	TTM Pre-Tax Income	Effective Income Tax Rate (2)	5 Year Monthly Equity Raw Beta	5 Year Monthly Asset Raw Beta (Ba)
Airdron SE	$ — $	— $	— $	40.69	NA	NA	NA	NA	NA	$ 134,342 $	436,324	30.8%	2.60	NA
Acuity Brands, Inc.	353,400	—	59.21	43,306	2,564,154	2,917,554	13.0%	12.1%	46,400	139,200	33.3%	1.33	1.22
Cree, Inc.	—	—	39.23	108,942	4,273,795	4,273,795	0.0%	0.0%	45,773	225,313	20.3%	0.86	0.86
Eaton Corporation plc	3,451,000	—	52.02	341,200	17,749,224	21,200,224	19.4%	16.3%	117,000	1,184,000	35.0%	1.40	1.24
Hubbell Inc.	597,800	—	68.57	60,258	4,131,877	4,729,677	14.5%	12.6%	106,300	336,800	31.6%	1.12	1.02
Veeco Instruments Inc.	97,567	—	51.80	40,739	2,110,280	2,207,847	4.6%	4.4%	34,888	325,677	35.0%	2.45	2.38
Zumtobel AG	336,077	—	34.21	42,815	1,464,860	1,800,936	22.9%	18.7%	10,382	(39,440)	35.0%	1.47	1.28
EPISTAR corporation	506,490	—	3.13	854,809	2,677,261	3,183,751	18.9%	15.9%	15,058	191,095	35.0%	1.26	1.13
High	$ 3,451,000 $	— $	— $	68.57	854,809	$ 17,749,224	$ 21,200,224	22.9%	18.7%	$ 134,342 $	1,184,000	35.0%	2.60	2.38
Low	$ — $	— $	— $	3.13	40,739	$ 1,464,860	$ 1,800,936	0.0%	0.0%	$ 10,382 $	(39,440)	20.3%	0.86	0.86
Mean	$ 667,792 $	— $	— $	43.41	213,153	$ 4,995,922	$ 5,759,112	13.5%	11.4%	$ 63,768 $	349,871	32.0%	1.57	1.39
Median	$ 344,738 $	— $	— $	46.25	60,258	$ 2,677,261	$ 3,183,751	14.5%	12.6%	$ 46,087 $	275,495	34.2%	1.36	1.22

Selected as Most Comparable to Subject Company

| | | | | | | **14.4%** | **12.6%** | | | **38.6%** | | **1.22** |

Cost of Equity Calculation:

		Source:
Risk-Free Rate (Rf)	4.1%	Risk-free rate of return (20-year Treasury Bond yield) as of May 10, 2018 as published in Federal Reserve Statistical Release, H.15.
Plus Equity Premiums:		
Equity Risk Premium (Rm-Rf)	6.00%	The expected return of the market in excess of the risk-free rate (3)
Relevered Equity Beta (Be)	1.33	Be = Ba x [1 + (Wd / We) x (1 - T)]
Industry - Adjusted Equity Risk Premium	8.0%	Be x (Rm - Rf)
Size Premium (SP)	4.1%	2018 Ibbotson SBBI Valuation Yearbook, Morningstar, Inc.; 9-10 decile
Additional Risk Premium (ARP)	3.8%	Additional risk premium based on perceived uncertainties associated with operating forecast
Cost of Equity (Re) Discount Rate (rounded)	19.9%	Re = Rf + Be (Rm - Rf) + SP + ARP

Cost of Debt Calculation:

Pre-Tax Weighted Cost of Debt	5.6%	Moody's Baa Interest Rate as of May 10, 2018
Premium	2.2%	Estimated additional required rate of return associated with a debt investment in the subject
Adjusted Pre-tax Cost of Debt (Rounded)	8.0%	
Estimated Tax Rate	38.6%	Effective combined State and Federal income tax rate (Federal + [(1 - Federal) x State])
After-Tax Cost of Debt (Rd)	4.9%	Rd = Rd x (1 - T)

Weighted Average Cost of Capital Calculation:

Debt % of Capital	12.6%	Wd
Cost of Debt	4.9%	Rd
Weighted Cost of Debt	0.6%	Wd x Rd
Equity % of Capital	87.4%	We
Cost of Equity	19.9%	Re
Weighted Cost of Equity	17.4%	We x Re
Weighted Average Cost of Capital (rounded)	18.0%	
Less Long-term Sustainable Growth Rate (G)	(3.0%)	Based on a combination of the Company's and its industry's historical and potential growth rates, and the overall economic environment in which it competes.
Capitalization Rate (rounded)	15.0%	

Footnotes:
(1) Source: Capital IQ.
(2) Effective income tax rates for the selected public guideline companies are normalized at 35% if the effective tax rate is a) below 15%, or b) above 55%, in order to offset the use of NOL carryforwards, R&D tax credits, etc.
(3) The estimated Equity Risk Premium (ERP) of 6.00 percent, which equals Rm - Rf, incorporates perspective provided by recent long-term market return studies and historical data compiled by Morningstar (formerly Ibbotson Associates).

FIGURE 11.6

Viking Investments Limited v. Mirage, Inc., et al. — Schedule 6
Analysis of Impact of Restated Financial Statements on Equity Value Income Statements (1) — Valuation Date: May 10, 2018
US$ — Page 1 of 2

	SEC Filing Dec 31, '08	SEC Filing Dec 31, '09	SEC Filing Dec 31, '10	Estimated Internal TTM May 10, '11	Dec 31, '11	Dec 31, '12	Forecast (2) Dec 31, '13	Dec 31, '14	Dec 31, '15	Dec 31, '16	Terminal
% Revenue Growth	NA	51.2%	69.5%	NA	295.1%	111.3%	47.9%	36.1%	3.0%	3.0%	3.0%
Net Revenue	$ 20,758,593	$ 31,376,816	$ 53,169,013	$ 109,239,298	$ 210,597,120	$ 444,959,274	$ 658,058,912	$ 895,585,265	$ 922,452,854	$ 950,126,439	$ 978,630,233
Total Cost of Revenue	21,206,703	28,880,949	59,021,851	98,965,116	171,170,250	310,406,691	441,203,163	593,722,877	611,534,563	629,880,600	648,777,018
Gross Profit	(448,110)	2,495,867	(5,852,838)	10,274,181	39,426,870	134,552,583	216,855,749	301,862,418	310,918,291	320,245,839	329,853,214
Operating Expenses:											
Sales & Marketing	5,847,833	7,200,329	11,107,379	12,893,388	16,119,135	25,201,471	35,872,737	47,419,215	48,841,791	50,307,045	51,816,257
Operations	6,006,872	6,243,968	4,634,592	9,017,324	16,578,416	25,127,298	35,696,937	46,479,718	47,874,110	49,310,333	50,789,643
General & Administrative	23,224,581	20,753,513	17,753,656	15,485,710	11,329,807	11,481,695	14,553,301	17,551,385	18,077,927	18,620,264	19,178,872
Research & Development	3,259,188	4,395,320	10,246,511	6,597,069							
Depreciation	1,200,000	1,300,000	1,400,000	2,027,330	3,161,349	5,877,144	8,620,001	13,105,715	13,498,887	13,903,853	14,320,969
Amortization	3,154,028	4,027,033	1,487,886		1,616,840	1,616,840	1,616,840	1,616,840	1,616,840	1,616,840	
Total Operating Expenses	42,694,482	43,920,157	46,810,004	45,999,820	48,805,547	69,284,448	96,161,816	126,172,873	129,909,554	133,758,335	136,105,741
Operating Income (Loss)	(43,142,592)	(41,424,290)	(52,662,842)	(35,725,639)	(9,378,677)	65,268,135	120,693,933	175,689,545	181,008,737	186,487,504	193,747,474
Other Income (Expense):											
Impairment of Intangibles	(53,110,133)	—	(11,548,650)	(7,435,432)							
Restructuring Expenses	—	(1,111,189)	(1,101,992)	(709,502)							
Interest Income	188,460	1,104	3,450	7,088	13,665	28,872	42,700	56,112	59,856	61,651	63,501
Interest Expense	(1,365,295)	(2,378,544)	(616,545)	(1,286,733)	(2,442,073)	(5,159,724)	(7,630,816)	(10,385,159)	(10,696,713)	(11,017,615)	(11,348,143)
Related Party Interest Expense	(60,151)	(3,860,149)	(2,884,511)	(1,857,151)							
Derivative Contracts Fair Value	415,628	2,731	(150,557,529)	(96,934,299)							
Dividends on Preferred Stock	(533)	(37,356)	(3,534,796)	(2,276,827)							
Accretion of Preferred Stock	(94,607)	(126,017)	(73,077,280)	(47,049,756)							
Other Income	(1,740)	203,781	(281,352)	(578,057)	(1,114,407)	(2,354,570)	(3,482,220)	(4,739,127)	(4,881,301)	(5,027,740)	(5,178,572)
Total Other Income (Expense)	(54,028,371)	(7,125,639)	(243,599,204)	(158,099,666)	(3,542,815)	(7,485,422)	(11,070,336)	(15,066,174)	(15,518,159)	(15,983,704)	(16,463,215)
Earnings (Loss) Before Income Taxes	(97,170,963)	(48,549,929)	(296,262,046)	(193,825,307)	(12,921,492)	57,782,713	109,623,597	160,623,371	165,490,578	170,503,800	177,284,259
Provision for Income Taxes (Benefit)	(2,207,507)	(413,002)	(1,123,107)	(2,307,499)	(4,448,514)	(9,399,025)	(13,900,400)	(18,917,750)	(19,486,283)	(20,069,841)	(20,671,937)
Minority Interest											
Net Income (Loss)	$ (94,963,456)	$ (48,136,927)	$ (295,138,939)	$ (191,517,808)	$ (8,472,978)	$ 67,181,738	$ 123,523,998	$ 179,541,122	$ 184,976,861	$ 190,573,642	$ 197,956,196
EBIT	(43,142,592)	(41,424,290)	(52,662,842)	(35,725,639)	(9,378,677)	65,268,135	120,693,933	175,689,545	181,008,737	186,487,504	193,747,474
EBITDA	(38,788,564)	(36,097,257)	(49,794,976)	(33,698,309)	(4,600,488)	72,762,119	130,930,774	190,412,100	196,124,463	202,008,197	208,068,443
Supplemental Data:											
Distributions											
Interest Expense	1,365,295	2,378,544	616,545	1,286,733	2,442,073	5,159,724	7,630,816	10,385,159	10,696,713	11,017,615	11,348,143
Depreciation & Amortization Expense	4,354,028	5,327,033	2,887,886	2,027,330	4,778,189	7,493,984	10,236,841	14,722,555	15,115,726	15,520,693	14,320,969
Total Capital Expenditures	(1,671,303)	(1,111,656)	(6,651,591)	(8,116,813)	(10,765,484)	(19,010,564)	(19,200,000)	(31,400,000)	(31,400,000)	(31,400,000)	(14,320,969)

Footnotes:
(1) The historical financial information presented above was obtained from the Company's SEC Filings, after restatement. We have not audited, reviewed, or compiled these financials and express no assurance on them.
(2) Obtained from BNS Model. See Exhibit 320, ABC00000221 (Pages 6-7 of 14). Revenue for 2015-16 assumed to grow at 3% and 2014 expenses or expenses as a percentage of revenue assumed constant.

FIGURE 11.7

Viking Investments Limited v. **Mirage, Inc., et al.**

Analysis of Impact of Restated Financial Statements on Equity Value

Schedule 6 — Valuation Data: May 10, 2018 — Page 2 of 2

	SEC Filing Dec 31, '08	SEC Filing Dec 31, '09	SEC Filing Dec 31, '10	Internal TTM May 10, '11	Dec 31, '11	Dec 31, '12	Forecast (2) Dec 31, '13	Dec 31, '14	Dec 31, '15	Dec 31, '16	Terminal
Net Revenue	100.0%	100.0%	100.0%	100.0%	100.0%	100.0%	100.0%	100.0%	100.0%	100.0%	100.0%
Total Cost of Revenue	102.2%	92.0%	111.0%	90.6%	81.3%	69.8%	67.0%	66.3%	66.3%	66.3%	66.3%
Gross Profit	(2.2%)	8.0%	(11.0%)	9.4%	18.7%	30.2%	33.0%	33.7%	33.7%	33.7%	33.7%
Operating Expenses:											
Sales & Marketing	28.2%	22.9%	20.9%	11.8%	7.7%	5.7%	5.4%	5.3%	5.3%	5.3%	5.3%
Operations	28.9%	19.9%	9.1%	8.3%	7.9%	5.6%	5.4%	5.2%	5.2%	5.2%	5.2%
General & Administrative	111.9%	66.1%	33.4%	14.2%	5.4%	2.6%	2.2%	2.0%	2.0%	2.0%	2.0%
Research & Development	15.7%	14.0%	19.3%	6.0%	0.0%	0.0%	0.0%	0.0%	0.0%	0.0%	0.0%
Depreciation	5.8%	4.1%	2.6%	1.9%	1.5%	1.3%	1.3%	1.5%	1.5%	1.5%	1.5%
Amortization	15.2%	12.8%	2.8%	0.0%	0.8%	0.4%	0.2%	0.2%	0.2%	0.2%	0.0%
Total Operating Expenses	205.7%	140.0%	88.0%	42.1%	23.2%	15.6%	14.6%	14.1%	14.1%	14.1%	13.9%
Operating Income (Loss)	(207.8%)	(132.0%)	(99.0%)	(32.7%)	(4.5%)	14.7%	18.3%	19.6%	19.6%	19.6%	19.8%
Other Income (Expense):											
Impairment of Intangibles	(255.8%)	0.0%	(21.7%)	(6.8%)	0.0%	0.0%	0.0%	0.0%	0.0%	0.0%	0.0%
Restructuring Expenses	0.0%	(3.5%)	(2.1%)	(0.6%)	0.0%	0.0%	0.0%	0.0%	0.0%	0.0%	0.0%
Interest Income	0.9%	0.0%	0.0%	0.0%	0.0%	0.0%	0.0%	0.0%	0.0%	0.0%	0.0%
Interest Expense	(6.6%)	(7.6%)	(1.2%)	(1.2%)	(1.2%)	(1.2%)	(1.2%)	(1.2%)	(1.2%)	(1.2%)	(1.2%)
Related Party Interest Expense	(0.3%)	(11.7%)	(5.4%)	(1.7%)	0.0%	0.0%	0.0%	0.0%	0.0%	0.0%	0.0%
Derivative Contracts Fair Value	2.0%	0.0%	(283.2%)	(88.7%)	0.0%	0.0%	0.0%	0.0%	0.0%	0.0%	0.0%
Dividends on Preferred Stock	(0.0%)	(0.1%)	(6.6%)	(2.1%)	0.0%	0.0%	0.0%	0.0%	0.0%	0.0%	0.0%
Accretion of Preferred Stock	(0.5%)	(0.4%)	(137.4%)	(43.1%)	0.0%	0.0%	0.0%	0.0%	0.0%	0.0%	0.0%
Other Income	(0.0%)	0.6%	(0.5%)	(0.5%)	(0.5%)	(0.5%)	(0.5%)	(0.5%)	(0.5%)	(0.5%)	(0.5%)
Total Other Income (Expense)	(260.3%)	(22.7%)	(458.2%)	(144.7%)	(1.7%)	(1.7%)	(1.7%)	(1.7%)	(1.7%)	(1.7%)	(1.7%)
Earnings (Loss) Before Income Taxes	(468.1%)	(154.7%)	(557.2%)	(177.4%)	(6.1%)	13.0%	16.7%	17.9%	17.9%	17.9%	18.1%
Provision for Income Taxes (Benefit)	(10.6%)	(1.3%)	(2.1%)	(2.1%)	(2.1%)	(2.1%)	(2.1%)	(2.1%)	(2.1%)	(2.1%)	(2.1%)
Minority Interest	0.0%	0.0%	0.0%	0.0%	0.0%	0.0%	0.0%	0.0%	0.0%	0.0%	0.0%
Net Income (Loss)	(457.5%)	(153.4%)	(555.1%)	(175.3%)	(4.0%)	15.1%	18.8%	20.0%	20.1%	20.1%	20.2%
EBIT	(207.8%)	(132.0%)	(99.0%)	(32.7%)	(4.5%)	14.7%	18.3%	19.6%	19.6%	19.6%	19.8%
EBITDA	(186.9%)	(115.0%)	(93.7%)	(30.8%)	(2.2%)	16.4%	19.9%	21.3%	21.3%	21.3%	21.3%
Supplemental Data:											
Distributions	0.0%	0.0%	0.0%	0.0%	0.0%	0.0%	0.0%	0.0%	0.0%	0.0%	0.0%
Interest Expense	6.6%	7.6%	1.2%	1.2%	1.2%	1.2%	1.2%	1.2%	1.2%	1.2%	1.2%
Depreciation & Amortization Expense	21.0%	17.0%	5.4%	1.9%	2.3%	1.7%	1.6%	1.6%	1.6%	1.6%	1.5%
Total Capital Expenditures	(8.1%)	(3.5%)	(12.5%)	(7.4%)	(5.1%)	(4.3%)	(2.9%)	(3.5%)	(3.4%)	(3.3%)	(1.5%)

Footnotes:
(1) The historical financial information presented above was obtained from the Company's SEC Filings, after restatement. We have not audited, reviewed, or these financials and express no assurance on them.
(2) Obtained from BNS Model. See Exhibit 320, ABC00000221 (Pages 6-7 of 14). Revenue for 2015-16 assumed to grow at 3% and 2014 expenses as a percentage of revenue assumed constant.

FIGURE 11.8

TABLE 11.10
Schedule 7.1–2

Viking Investments Limited vs Mirage, Inc., et al.
Analysis of Impact of Restated Financial Statements on Equity Value
Comparison of Original and Restated Financial Statements (1)
US$

Schedule 7
Valuation Date: May 10, 2018
Page 1 of 2

	Original as		Restated	
	Dec 31, '08	Dec 31, '09	Dec 31, '08	Dec 31, '09
% Revenue Growth	*NA*	*51.2%*	*NA*	*51.2%*
Net Revenue	$ **20,758,593**	$ **31,376,816**	$ **20,758,593**	$ **31,376,816**
Total Cost of Revenue	16,688,600	24,754,818	21,206,703	28,880,949
Gross Profit	4,069,993	6,621,998	(448,110)	2,495,867
Operating Expenses:				
Sales & Marketing	5,847,833	7,248,311	5,847,833	7,200,323
Operations	13,786,163	15,170,029	6,008,872	6,243,968
General & Administrative	23,224,561	21,412,103	23,224,561	20,753,513
Research & Development			3,259,188	4,395,320
Depreciation	1,200,000	1,300,000	1,200,000	1,300,000
Amortization	3,154,028	4,027,033	3,154,028	4,027,033
Total Operating Expenses	47,212,585	49,157,476	42,694,482	43,920,157
Operating Income (Loss)	**(43,142,592)**	**(42,535,478)**	**(43,142,592)**	**(41,424,290)**
Other Income (Expense):				
Impairment of Intangibles	(53,110,133)	-	(53,110,133)	(1,111,189)
Restructuring Expenses	-			
Interest Income	188,460	1,104	188,460	1,104
Interest Expense	(1,365,295)	(2,378,544)	(1,365,295)	(2,378,544)
Related Party Interest Expense	(60,151)	(3,680,149)	(60,151)	(3,680,149)
Derivative Contracts Fair Value	415,628	2,731	415,628	2,731
Dividends on Preferred Stock	(533)	(37,356)	(533)	(37,356)
Accretion of Preferred Stock	(94,607)	(126,017)	(94,607)	(126,017)
Other Income	(1,740)	203,781	(1,740)	203,781
Total Other Income (Expense)	(54,028,371)	(6,014,450)	(54,028,371)	(7,125,639)

(Continued)

TABLE 11.10 (Continued)
Schedule 7.1-2

Viking Investments Limited vs Mirage, Inc., et al.
Analysis of Impact of Restated Financial Statements on Equity Value
Comparison of Original and Restated Financial Statements (1)
US$

Schedule 7

Valuation Date: May 10, 2018
Page 1 of 2

	Original as		Restated	
	Dec 31, '08	Dec 31, '09	Dec 31, '08	Dec 31, '09
Earnings (Loss) Before Income Taxes	(97,170,963)	(48,549,928)	(97,170,963)	(48,549,929)
Provision for Income Taxes (Benefit)	(2,207,507)	(413,002)	(2,207,507)	(413,002)
Minority Interest	-	-		
Net Income (Loss)	$ (94,963,456)	$ (48,136,926)	$ (94,963,456)	$ (48,136,927)
EBIT	(43,142,592)	(42,535,478)	(43,142,592)	(41,424,290)
EBITDA	(38,788,564)	(37,208,445)	(38,788,564)	(36,097,257)
Supplemental Data:				
Distributions	-	-		-
Interest Expense	1,365,295	2,378,544	1,365,295	2,378,544
Depreciation & Amortization Expense	4,354,028	5,327,033	4,354,028	5,327,033
Total Capital Expenditures	(1,671,303)	(1,111,656)	(1,671,303)	(1,111,656)

Footnote:

(1) The historical financial information presented above was obtained from the Company's SEC Filings, as originally, in its 2016 10-K and after restatement (2016 10-K/A). We have not audited, reviewed, or compiled these financials and express no assurance on them.

TABLE 11.11
Schedule 7.2–2

Schedule 7

Viking Investments Limited vs Mirage, Inc., et al.
Analysis of Impact of Restated Financial Statements on Equity Value
Comparison of Original and Restated Financial Statements (1): Common Size

Valuation Date: May 10, 2018

Page 2 of 2

	Original as		Restated	
	Dec 31, '08	Dec 31, '09	Dec 31, '08	Dec 31, '09
Net Revenue	100.0%	100.0%	100.0%	100.0%
Total Cost of Revenue	80.4%	78.9%	102.2%	92.0%
Gross Profit	19.6%	21.1%	(2.2%)	8.0%
Operating Expenses:				
Sales & Marketing	28.2%	23.1%	28.2%	22.9%
Operations	66.4%	48.3%	28.9%	19.9%
General & Administrative	111.9%	68.2%	111.9%	66.1%
Research & Development	0.0%	0.0%	15.7%	14.0%
Depreciation	5.8%	4.1%	5.8%	4.1%
Amortization	15.2%	12.8%	15.2%	12.8%
Total Operating Expenses	227.4%	156.7%	205.7%	140.0%
Operating Income (Loss)	(207.8%)	(135.6%)	(207.8%)	(132.0%)
Other Income (Expense):				
Impairment of Intangibles	(255.8%)	0.0%	(255.8%)	0.0%
Restructuring Expenses	0.0%	0.0%	0.0%	(3.5%)
Interest Income	0.9%	0.0%	0.9%	0.0%
Interest Expense	(6.6%)	(7.6%)	(6.6%)	(7.6%)
Related Party Interest Expense	(0.3%)	(11.7%)	(0.3%)	(11.7%)
Derivative Contracts Fair Value	2.0%	0.0%	2.0%	0.0%
Dividends on Preferred Stock	(0.0%)	(0.1%)	(0.0%)	(0.1%)

(Continued)

TABLE 11.11 (Continued)
Schedule 7.2-2

Viking Investments Limited vs Mirage, Inc., et al.   Schedule 7
Analysis of Impact of Restated Financial Statements on Equity Value
Comparison of Original and Restated Financial Statements (1): Common Size   Valuation Date: May 10, 2018

Page 2 of 2

	Original as		Restated	
	Dec 31, '08	Dec 31, '09	Dec 31, '08	Dec 31, '09
Accretion of Preferred Stock	(0.5%)	(0.4%)	(0.5%)	(0.4%)
Other Income	(0.0%)	0.6%	(0.0%)	0.6%
Total Other Income (Expense)	(260.3%)	(19.2%)	(260.3%)	(22.7%)
Earnings (Loss) Before Income Taxes	(468.1%)	(154.7%)	(468.1%)	(154.7%)
Provision for Income Taxes (Benefit)	(10.6%)	(1.3%)	(10.6%)	(1.3%)
Minority Interest	0.0%	0.0%	0.0%	0.0%
Net Income (Loss)	**(457.5%)**	**(153.4%)**	**(457.5%)**	**(153.4%)**
EBIT	**(207.8%)**	**(135.6%)**	**(207.8%)**	**(132.0%)**
EBITDA	**(186.9%)**	**(118.6%)**	**(186.9%)**	**(115.0%)**
Supplemental Data:				
Distributions	0.0%	0.0%	0.0%	0.0%
Interest Expense	6.6%	7.6%	6.6%	7.6%
Depreciation & Amortization Expense	21.0%	17.0%	21.0%	17.0%
Total Capital Expenditures	(8.1%)	(3.5%)	(8.1%)	(3.5%)

Footnote:
(1) The historical financial information presented above was obtained from the Company's SEC Filings, as originally, in its 2016 10-K and after restatement (2016 10-K/A). We have not audited, reviewed, or compiled these financials and express no assurance on them.

Viking Investments Limited v. Mirage, Inc., et al.
Analysis of Impact of Restated Financial Statements on Equity Value
Balance Sheets (1)
US$

Schedule 8
Valuation Date: May 10, 2018
Page 1 of 2

	Dec. 31, '08	Dec. 31, '09	Dec. 31, '10	May 10, '11 (2)
Assets				
Cash & Equivalents	$ 254,538	$ 267,048	$ 14,489,700	$ 9,540,605
Marketable Securities				
Accounts Receivable, Net				
Trade & Other	6,633,888	5,020,226	15,722,762	17,174,867
Related Party				
Inventories	12,202,774	8,064,624	23,046,912	44,775,510
Prepaid Expenses and Other Current Assets	1,517,690	1,472,018	5,724,899	7,720,089
Deferred Income Tax	671,782	682,227		
Total Current Assets	21,280,672	15,506,143	58,984,273	79,211,071
Property, Plant & Equipment				
Construction-in-process				
Tooling, Production, and Test Equipment	5,892,385	5,959,658	997,112	1,524,598
Office Furniture and Equipment	4,219,098	4,495,919	7,334,068	8,129,735
Leasehold Improvements	2,668,566	2,727,334	3,906,000	3,137,336
			500,244	1,057,381
Gross Property, Plant & Equipment	12,780,049	13,182,911	12,737,424	13,849,050
Less: Depreciation	(9,149,161)	(9,891,615)	(4,907,083)	(3,798,313)
Net Property, Plant & Equipment	3,630,888	3,291,296	7,830,341	10,050,737
Other Assets				
Goodwill	6,799,962	5,770,245	1,626,482	1,626,482
Intangible Assets, Net	17,452,632	13,482,736	3,952,927	3,802,469
Other	389,113	418,394	99,340	137,506
Total Other Assets	24,641,707	19,671,375	5,678,749	5,566,457
Total Assets	$ 49,553,267	$ 38,468,814	$ 72,493,363	$ 94,828,265
Liabilities & Equity				
Short-term Debt	$ 24,426,991	$ 56,400,173	$ 6,075,679	$ 9,573,877
Current Installments of Long-Term Debt	142,262	110,322	93,193	77,201
Accounts Payable	6,419,248	7,496,633	37,236,525	50,478,951
Accrued Expenses	4,163,156	6,190,129	4,267,944	4,042,793
Unearned Revenue	1,001,704	12,631	132,010	213,180
Total Current Liabilities	36,153,361	70,209,888	47,805,351	64,386,002
Long-Term Liabilities				
Liability under Derivatives Contracts				
Deferred Income Taxes	2,049,074	1,805,334		
Capital Leases				
Long-Term Debt, Noncurrent	96,443	117,447	6,501	
Total Long-Term Liabilities	2,145,517	1,922,781	6,501	
Total Liabilities	38,298,878	72,132,669	47,811,852	64,386,092
Shareholders' Equity				
6% Convertible Preferred Stock	459,532	585,549		
Series B Preferred Stock	2,000	2,000		
Series C Preferred Stock	252	252		
Common Stock	28,960	29,874	125,595	186,449
APIC	112,505,607	116,447,080	471,255,918	493,174,404
Accumulated Deficit	(99,865,725)	(148,002,652)	(443,141,591)	(459,503,383)
Accumulated OCI	(1,876,263)	(2,725,958)	(3,558,411)	(3,415,207)
Total Shareholders' Equity	11,254,389	(33,663,855)	24,681,511	30,442,263
Total Liabilities & Equity	$ 49,553,267	$ 38,468,814	$ 72,493,363	$ 94,828,265

Footnotes:
(1) The historical financial information presented above was obtained from the Company's SEC Filings, after restatement. We have not audited, reviewed, or compiled these financials and express no assurance on them.
(2) Balance sheet data as of the Valuation Date assumed equivalent to the March 31, 2018 figures.

FIGURE 11.9

Viking Investments Limited v. Mirage, Inc., et al.
Analysis of Impact of Restated Financial Statements on Equity Value
Balance Sheets (1): Common Size

Schedule 8
Valuation Date: May 10, 2018
Page 2 of 2

	Dec. 31, '08	Dec. 31, '09	Dec. 31, '10	May 10, '11 (2)
Assets				
Cash & Equivalents	0.5%	0.7%	20.0%	10.1%
Marketable Securities	0.0%	0.0%	0.0%	0.0%
Accounts Receivable, Net				
Trade & Other	13.4%	13.1%	21.7%	18.1%
Related Party	0.0%	0.0%	0.0%	0.0%
Inventories	24.6%	21.0%	31.6%	47.2%
Prepaid Expenses and Other Current Assets	3.1%	3.6%	7.9%	8.1%
Deferred Income Tax	1.6%	1.6%	0.0%	0.0%
Total Current Assets	42.9%	40.3%	61.4%	63.2%
Property, Plant & Equipment				
Construction-in-process	0.0%	0.0%	1.4%	1.6%
Tooling, Production, and Test Equipment	11.9%	15.5%	10.1%	8.6%
Office Furniture and Equipment	8.5%	11.7%	5.4%	3.3%
Leasehold Improvements	5.4%	7.1%	0.2%	1.1%
Gross Property, Plant & Equipment	25.8%	34.3%	17.6%	14.6%
Less: Depreciation	(18.5%)	(25.7%)	(6.6%)	(4.0%)
Net Property, Plant & Equipment	7.2%	8.6%	10.8%	10.6%
Other Assets				
Goodwill	13.7%	15.0%	2.2%	1.7%
Intangible Assets, Net	35.2%	33.0%	5.5%	4.0%
Other	0.8%	1.1%	0.1%	0.1%
Total Other Assets	49.7%	51.1%	7.8%	5.9%
Total Assets	100.0%	100.0%	100.0%	100.0%
Liabilities & Equity				
Short-term Debt	49.3%	146.6%	8.4%	10.1%
Current Installments of Long-Term Debt	0.3%	0.3%	0.1%	0.1%
Accounts Payable	13.0%	19.5%	51.4%	53.2%
Accrued Expenses	8.4%	16.1%	5.5%	4.3%
Unearned Revenue	2.0%	0.0%	0.2%	0.2%
Total Current Liabilities	73.0%	182.5%	65.9%	67.9%
Long-Term Liabilities				
Liability under Derivatives Contracts	0.0%	0.0%	0.0%	0.0%
Deferred Income Taxes	4.1%	4.7%	0.0%	0.0%
Capital Leases	0.0%	0.0%	0.0%	0.0%
Long-Term Debt, Noncurrent	0.2%	0.3%	0.0%	0.0%
Total Long-Term Liabilities	4.3%	5.0%	0.0%	0.0%
Total Liabilities	77.2%	187.5%	66.0%	67.9%
Shareholders' Equity				
6% Convertible Preferred Stock	0.9%	1.5%	0.0%	0.0%
Series B Preferred Stock	0.0%	0.0%	0.0%	0.0%
Series C Preferred Stock	0.0%	0.0%	0.0%	0.0%
Common Stock	0.1%	0.1%	0.2%	0.2%
APIC	227.0%	302.7%	650.1%	520.1%
Accumulated Deficit	(201.5%)	(384.7%)	(611.3%)	(484.6%)
Accumulated OCI	(3.6%)	(0.1%)	(4.9%)	(3.6%)
Total Shareholders' Equity	22.7%	(87.5%)	34.0%	32.1%
Total Liabilities & Equity	100.0%	100.0%	100.0%	100.0%

Footnotes:
(1) The historical financial information presented above was obtained from the Company's SEC Filings, after restatement. We have not audited, reviewed, or compiled these financials and express no assurance on them.
(2) Balance sheet data as of the Valuation Date assumed equivalent to the March 31, 2018 figures.

FIGURE 11.10

Viking Investments Limited v. Mirage, Inc., et al.
Analysis of Impact of Restated Financial Statements on Equity Value
Control Issues (1) (2)
US$

Schedule 9
Valuation Date: May 10, 2018

Year	(A) Average Control Premium	(A) / [1 + (A)] Implied Minority Interest Discount	(B) Median Control Premium	Implied Minority Interest Discount
1994	41.9%	29.5%	35.0%	25.9%
1995	44.7%	30.9%	29.2%	22.6%
1996	36.6%	26.8%	27.3%	21.4%
1997	35.7%	26.3%	27.5%	21.6%
1998	40.7%	28.9%	30.1%	23.1%
1999	43.3%	30.2%	34.6%	25.7%
2000	49.2%	33.0%	41.1%	29.1%
2001	57.2%	36.4%	40.5%	28.8%
2002	59.7%	37.4%	34.4%	25.6%
2003	62.3%	38.4%	31.6%	24.0%
2004	30.7%	23.5%	23.4%	19.0%
2005	34.5%	25.7%	24.1%	19.4%
2006	31.5%	24.0%	23.1%	18.8%
2014	31.5%	24.0%	24.7%	19.8%
2017	56.5%	36.1%	36.5%	26.7%
2015	58.7%	37.0%	39.8%	28.5%
2016	51.5%	34.0%	34.6%	25.7%
2018	54.1%	35.1%	37.8%	27.4%
2019	46.2%	31.6%	37.1%	27.1%
Descriptive Statistics				
Max	62.3%	38.4%	39.8%	28.5%
Min	30.7%	23.5%	23.1%	18.8%
Selected Control Premium (3)				11.0%
Implied Minority Interest Discount (Rounded)				10.0%

Footnotes:

(1) Purchasers of controlling interests in companies will often pay a premium for the right or ability to elect board members, determine company strategies, set compensation levels for key employees, and otherwise control the business enterprise. Several studies have been conducted analyzing purchases of controlling interests in companies compared to the market prices at which minority interests in the stock of these companies previously traded.

(2) For more information on the above control premium/discounts, see Mergerstat Review 2013, Factset Mergerstat, LLC, p. 25.

(3) It should be noted that control premium data included in the MergerStat/BVR studies include synergistic and investment value premiums associated with the transactions in the sample. Some valuation practitioners believe that strategic considerations can account for as much as 50% of the observed premium paid. Consequently, in selecting a control premium, the excess synergistic and investment premiums should be excluded to isolate the control premium. Accordingly, a control premium below the minimum premium of the studies was chosen in order to exclude the excess premiums.

FIGURE 11.11

Viking Investments Limited v. Mirage, Inc., et al.
Analysis of Impact of Restated Financial Statements on Equity Value
Lack of Marketability Studies: Restricted Stock Studies

Schedule 10
Valuation Date: May 10, 2018

US$

Summary of Lack of Marketability Studies: Restricted Stock Studies

Lack of Marketability Studies	Year	Period Covered	Mean Discount (1)	Range Low	Range High	Type of Study
SEC Overall Studies (2)	1971	1966 - 1969	25.8%	-15.0%	80.0%	Discounts on Restricted vs. Unrestricted Stocks
SEC Nonreporting OTC Companies (2)	1971	1966 - 1969	32.6%	N/A	N/A	Discounts on Restricted vs. Unrestricted Stocks
Milton Gelman (3)	1972	1968 - 1970	33.0%	<15.0%	>40.0%	Prices Paid by Four Investment Co.'s for Restricted Stocks
Robert R. Trout (4)	1972	1968 - 1972	33.5%	N/A	N/A	Letter Stocks Purchased by Mutual Funds
Robert E. Moroney (5)	1973	1969 - 1972	35.6%	-30.0%	90.0%	Restricted Stocks Purchased by Ten Registered Investment Companies
Michael J. Maher (6)	1976	1969 - 1973	35.4%	2.7%	75.7%	Discounts on Restricted vs. Unrestricted Stocks
Standard Research Consultants (7)	1983	1978 - 1982	45.0%	7.0%	91.0%	An Update of the SEC Study by Studying Recent Private Placements
Willamette Management Associates (8)	1984	1981 - 1984	31.2%	N/A	N/A	Restricted vs. Unrestricted Stocks in the Marketplace
William L. Silber (9)	1991	1981 - 1988	33.8%	-13.0%	84.0%	Private Placements of Restricted Common Stock
FMV Study (10)	1994	1980 - Mar 2005	22.1%	N/A	N/A	Over 100 Restricted Stock Transactions
Bruce Johnson (11)	1999	1991 - 1995	20.0%	-10.0%	60.0%	72 Restricted Stock Transactions
Management Planning, Inc. (12)	2000	1980 - 2000	27.4%	0.0%	57.6%	Private Placements of 49 Restricted Common Stock Transactions
Columbia Financial Advisors (13)	2000	1996 - Feb. 1997	21.0%	0.8%	67.5%	Private Placements of 23 Restricted Common Stock Transactions
Columbia Financial Advisors (13)	2000	May 1997 - 1998	13.0%	0.0%	30.0%	Private Placements of 15 Restricted Common Stock Transactions
FMV Restricted Stock Study (14)	2001	1980 - 2001	22.1%	N/A	N/A	Private Placements of 243 Restricted Common Stock Transactions
LiquiStat (15)	2014	2005 - 2006	32.8%	N/A	N/A	Private Sales Transactions
Trugman Valuation Advisors, Inc. (16)	2015	2014 - 2017	18.1%	1.5%	73.5%	80 Restricted Stock Transactions
		Low Mean =	13.0%			
		High Mean =	45.0%			

Footnotes:
(1) Some of the indicated discounts denote median.
(2) Discounts Involved in Purchases of Common Stock (1966-1969), Institutional Investor Study Report of the Securities and Exchange Commission, H.R. Doc. No., Part 5, 92d Cong. 1st Sess. 1971, pp. 2444-2456.
(3) Milton Gelman, *An Economist-Financial Analyst's Approach to Valuing Stock of a Closely-Held Company*, Journal of Taxation, June 1972, p. 354.
(4) Robert R. Trout, *Estimation of the Discount Associated with the Transfer of Restricted Securities*, Taxes, June 1977, pp. 381-85.
(5) Robert E. Moroney, *Most Courts Overvalue Closely Held Stocks*, Taxes, March 1973, pp. 144-55.
(6) J. Michael Maher, *Discounts for Lack of Marketability for Closely-Held Business Interests*, Taxes, September 1976, pp 562-71.
(7) Standard Research Consultants, *Revenue Ruling 77-287 Revisited*, SRC Quarterly Reports, Spring 1983, pp. 1-3.
(8) Willamette Management Associates 1981-1984 Study (unpublished).
(9) William L. Silber, *Discounts on Restricted Stock: The Impact of Illiquidity on Stock Prices*, Financial Analysts Journal, July-August 1991, pp. 60-64.
(10) Lance Hall and Timothy Polacek, *Strategies for Obtaining the Largest Valuation Discounts*, Estate Planning, Jan./Feb. 1994, pp. 38-44.
(11) Bruce Johnson, *Restricted Stock Discounts, 1991-1995*, Shannon Pratt's Business Valuation Update, March 1999, pp. 1-3.
(12) Robert P. Oliver and Roy H. Meyers, *Discounts Seen In Private Placements of Restricted Stock: The Management Planning, Inc., Long-Term Study (1980-1996)* (Chapter 5) in Robert F. Reilly and Robert P. Schweihs, eds. The Handbook of Advanced Business Valuation.
(13) Kathryn Aschwald, *Restricted Stock Discounts Decline as a Result of 1-Year Holding Period*, Shannon Pratt's Business Valuation Update, May 2000, pp. 1-5.
(14) Espen Roback, *FMV Introduces DetaraStar Restricted Stock Study*, Shannon Pratt's Business Valuation Update, November 2001, pp. 1-3.
(15) Espen Roback, *Discounts for Illiquid Shares and Warrants: The LiquiStat Database of Transactions on the Restricted Securities Trading Network*, Pluris Valuation Advisors White Paper, January 2014, pp. 22-32.
(16) William Harris, *Trugman Valuation Advisors, Inc. (TVA), Restricted Stock Study*, Business Valuation Review, Fall 2015, pp. 128-139.

FIGURE 11.12

Viking Investments Limited v. Mirage, Inc., et al.
Analysis of Impact of Restated Financial Statements on Equity Value
Lack of Marketability Studies: Pre-IPO Sales
US$

Schedule 11
Valuation Date: May 10, 2018

Summary of Lack of Marketability Studies: Pre-IPO Sales

Lack of Marketability Studies	Period Covered	Mean Discount	Median Discount	Number of Transactions
Robert W. Baird & Company (Emory Studies) (1)	1980-1981	59.0%	68.0%	12
	1985-1986	43.0%	43.0%	19
	1987-1989	43.0%	43.0%	21
	1989-1990	46.0%	40.0%	17
	1990-1992	34.0%	33.0%	30
	1991-1993	45.0%	44.0%	49
	1994-1995	45.0%	45.0%	45
	1996-1997	43.0%	42.0%	84
	1997-2000 (2)	50.0%	42.0%	266
Willamette Management Associates (3)	1975-1978	34.0%	52.5%	31
	1979	55.6%	62.7%	17
	1980-82	48.0%	56.5%	113
	1983	50.1%	60.7%	214
	1984	43.2%	73.1%	33
	1985	41.3%	42.6%	25
	1986	38.5%	47.4%	74
	1987	36.9%	43.8%	40
	1988	41.5%	51.8%	19
	1989	47.3%	50.3%	19
	1990	30.5%	48.5%	23
	1991	24.2%	31.8%	34
	1992	41.9%	51.7%	75
	1993	46.9%	53.3%	10
	1994	31.9%	42.0%	48
	1995	32.2%	58.7%	66
	1996	31.5%	44.3%	22
	1997	28.4%	35.2%	44
	1998	35.0%	49.4%	21
	1999	26.4%	27.7%	28
	2000	18.0%	31.9%	15
Valuation Advisors (4)				
1999 Study	1-90 Days	32.5%		166
	91-180 Days	52.1%		163
	181-270 Days	65.8%		99
	271-365 Days	73.7%		84
	1-2 Years	77.2%		167
2000 Study	1-90 Days	30.4%		129
	91-180 Days	41.5%		176
	181-270 Days	56.8%		116
	271-365 Days	64.6%		91
	1-2 Years	71.8%		141
2001 Study	1-90 Days	18.0%		15
	91-180 Days	14.2%		17
	181-270 Days	14.0%		19
	271-365 Days	43.1%		17
	1-2 Years	49.3%		49
2002 Study	1-90 Days	14.6%		9
	91-180 Days	25.8%		13
	181-270 Days	33.6%		7
	271-365 Days	37.9%		16
	1-2 Years	50.2%		36
	Low	14.0%	27.7%	
	High	77.2%	73.1%	

Footnotes:
(1) John D. Emory [Robert W. Baird & Company], *The Value of Marketability as Illustrated in Initial Public Offerings of Common Stock--January 1980 through April 1997*, Business Valuation Review, September 1997.
(2) John D. Emory Sr.; F.R. Dengel III and John D. Emory Jr., *Expanded Study of the Value of Marketability as Illustrated in Initial Public Offerings of Common Stock--May 1997 through December 2000*, Business Valuation Review, December 2001, pp. 4-30.
(3) Willamette Management Associates (unpublished studies), 1975-2000.
(4) The Valuation Advisors, *Discount for Lack of Marketability Database*, www.bvmarketdata.com, 2002.

FIGURE 11.13

TABLE 11.12
Schedule 12

Viking Investments Limited vs Mirage, Inc., et al.
Analysis of Impact of Restated Financial Statements on Equity Value
Implied Discount for Lack of Marketability (DLOM): European Protective Put Model

Schedule 12

Valuation Date: May 10, 2018

Concept:

A method to determine an estimate of the marketability discount is the put option valuation method. By utilizing a Black-Scholes Option Pricing Model, one can determine the price an investor would pay to guarantee a given stock price of on a future date. The value of the put option as a percent of the stock price represents the amount of the marketability discount.

Grant Date	Stock Price	Exercise Price	Date Of Liquidity Event (1)	Term (In Years)	Estimate of Volatility (2)	Risk-Free Rate (3)	Dividend Yield	Value of Put Option
May 10, '11	$4.00	$4.00	May 10, '14	3.0	68.5%	1.0%	0.0%	$ 1.70

	Implied DLOM	42.5%

Footnotes:

(1) Assumes a 3-year horizon for a liquidity event.

(2) Based on performing a detailed volatility analysis on Mirage, Inc. and the selected guideline companies. We selected 68.5% for purposes of this analysis. See Schedule 13.

(3) Risk-free rate derived from U.S. government securities with the same term as the option, as of the grant date. Data pulled from Federal Reserve H.15 statistical release.

| Viking Investments Limited v. Mirage, Inc., et al.Analysis of Impact of Restated Financial Statements on Equity Value Historical Volatility Analysis (1) (2) | | | | | | | | | | | | | Schedule 13 Valuation Date: May 10, 2018 |

						Historical Volatility Over Horizon								
Horizon	MIRAGE	AIXG	AYI	CREE	ETN	VECO	ZAG	2448	High	75th %	Mean	Median	25th %	Low
0.50 Yrs	90.1%	41.1%	23.5%	43.9%	22.9%	47.4%	42.4%	37.1%	90.1%	44.8%	43.6%	41.8%	33.7%	22.9%
1.00 Yrs	91.6%	48.2%	31.9%	48.6%	27.6%	60.9%	39.6%	39.1%	91.6%	51.7%	48.4%	43.9%	37.3%	27.6%
1.50 Yrs	104.6%	49.9%	30.5%	48.2%	27.4%	58.9%	38.4%	40.7%	104.6%	52.1%	49.8%	44.4%	36.4%	27.4%
2.00 Yrs	140.2%	54.9%	32.6%	46.6%	29.4%	63.6%	43.2%	44.6%	140.2%	57.1%	56.9%	45.6%	40.5%	29.4%
2.50 Yrs	170.3%	61.8%	40.1%	51.2%	36.8%	76.1%	51.5%	49.9%	170.3%	65.4%	67.2%	51.4%	47.4%	36.8%
3.00 Yrs	162.7%	67.1%	44.7%	54.3%	39.7%	73.7%	52.3%	53.7%	162.7%	68.8%	68.5%	54.0%	50.4%	39.7%

						Historical Volatility over Calendar Year								
Year	MIRAGE	AIXG	AYI	CREE	ETN	VECO	ZAG	2448	High	75th %	Mean	Median	25th %	Low
2018	93.9%	39.3%	23.5%	45.9%	24.8%	39.4%	40.1%	41.0%	93.9%	42.2%	43.5%	39.7%	35.7%	23.5%
2016	103.4%	52.4%	33.5%	51.2%	29.0%	66.3%	38.4%	40.4%	103.4%	55.9%	51.8%	45.8%	37.2%	29.0%
2015	234.1%	70.2%	43.6%	47.7%	42.2%	84.1%	61.4%	55.5%	234.1%	73.7%	79.8%	58.4%	46.7%	42.2%
2017	149.6%	79.8%	59.7%	68.5%	48.2%	72.0%	58.1%	67.3%	149.6%	74.0%	75.4%	67.9%	59.3%	48.2%
2014	124.8%	63.3%	52.2%	52.1%	29.8%	35.4%	43.8%	50.2%	124.8%	55.0%	56.4%	51.1%	41.7%	29.8%

Footnotes:
(1) Volatility information was computed based on stock price information from Capital IQ.
(2) Volatility percentages reflect a daily volatility.

FIGURE 11.14

Next, we calculate prejudgment interest that is owed to a prevailing plaintiff by statute. The interest rate varies by jurisdiction; so, make sure that you check with the attorneys before making this calculation. The period during which the interest is calculated begins with the date the harm occurred through the judgment date. Most jurisdictions only allow simple interest (see Figures 11.15–11.18).

Exhibit 4 – Prejudgment Interest Calculations

Florida statutory rates[1] (simple interest):

1/1/2018 - 9/30/2018	6.00%
10/1/2018 - present	4.75%
Date of damage	5/18/2018
Present	2/24/2014

Start	End	# of Days
05/18/11	09/30/11	135
10/01/11	12/31/11	92
01/01/12	12/31/12	366
01/01/13	12/31/13	365
01/01/14	02/24/14	54

Judgment Amount	2018		2019	2013	2014	Total
	5/18 - 9/30	10/1 - 12/31				
$ 25,000,000	$ 554,795	$ 299,315	$ 1,187,500	$ 1,187,500	$ 175,685	$ 3,404,795

Source:

1. Downloaded on 2/23/14 at
http://www.myfloridacfo.com/Division/AA/Vendors/default.htm#.UwrGMvldUrV and
http://www.myfloridacfo.com/Division/AA/Vendors/JudgmentInterestRates.htm#.UwrDEPldUrU.

Note:

The calculation of prejudgment interest can be updated as necessary as this litigation proceeds to account for interest through future dates and for any judgments greater than or less than $25 million.

FIGURE 11.15

Exhibit 5 – Financial Models vs. MIRAGE, INC.'s Actual Financial Performance

| | Fiscal Year 2018 | | | | | Fiscal Year 2019 | | | |
	March 16, 2018 Model Provided to Viking[1]	April 6, 2018 Model Provided to Viking[2]	April 25, 2018 Model Provided to Viking[3]	Actual MIRAGE , INC. Results[4]		March 16, 2018 Model Provided to Viking[1]	April 6, 2018 Model Provided to Viking[2]	April 25, 2018 Model Provided to Viking[3]	Actual MIRAGE , INC. Results[4]
Revenues									
COGS									
Gross Profit	$ 210,597,120	$ 210,597,120	$ 206,608,485	$ 108,981,588		$ 444,959,274	$ 444,959,274	n/a	$ 127,111,351
Gross Profit %	171,896,536	171,170,250	165,812,893	129,187,145		310,405,498	310,406,691	n/a	146,902,807
EBITDA*	$ 38,700,584	$ 39,426,870	$ 40,795,592	$ (20,205,557)		$ 134,553,776	$ 134,552,583	n/a	$ (19,791,456)
EBITDA %	18.4%	18.7%	19.7%	-18.5%		30.2%	30.2%	n/a	-15.6%

Note:
* The financial models provided to Viking included EBITDA models. MIRAGE, INC. does not report EBITDA in its 10-Ks. To calculate EBITDA, I added MIRAGE, INC.'s reported Depreciation & Amortization and Income Tax Benefit back into MIRAGE, INC.'s reported Net Loss:

2018[4]	
Net loss	$ (90,434,568)
Interest expense	2,016,388
Income tax benefit	-
Depreciation and amortization	4,895,74_
EBITDA	$ (83,522,438)

2019[4]	
Net loss	$ (111,340,409)
Interest expense	4,646,628
Income tax benefit	-
Depreciation and amortization	8,411,18_
EBITDA	$ (98,282,594)

Sources:
1. Exhibit 311, MIRAGE, INC.C Financial Models from J.P. Prince to Fredrik Jack Beanstalk on 3/16/11, at ABC00000171.
2. Exhibit 320, MIRAGE, INC. Financial Models from J.P. Prince to Fredrik Jack Beanstalk on 4/6/11, ABC00000221 (and attachments), at pp. 5-6 of attachment.
3. Def. Exhibit 6E, MIRAGE, INC. Financial Models from J.P. Prince to Fredrik Jack Beanstalk on 4/25/11, BNS_00057471-57472.
4. MIRAGE, INC. Form 10-K for 2019, 4/1/13.

FIGURE 11.16

Exhibit 6 – Revaluation of Series D and E Warrants

| | Three Months Ended 3/31/10 | | | | | Six Months Ended 6/30/10 | | | | | Nine Months Ended 9/30/10 | | | |
	As Originally Reported[1]	As Restated[2]	Difference	% Difference		As Originally Reported[3]	As Restated[3]	Difference	% Difference		As Originally Reported[4]	As Restated[4]	Difference	% Difference
Increase in fair value of liabilities under derivatives contracts	$ (2,234,471)	$ (3,654,374)	$ (1,419,903)	-63.5%		$ (79,097,242)	$ (90,115,544)	$ (11,018,302)	-13.9%		$ (56,007,778)	$ (59,774,455)	$ (3,766,677)	-6.7%
Accretion of preferred stock	$ (206,835)	$ (187,527)	19,308	9.3%		$ (781,542)	$ (866,785)	$ (85,243)	-10.9%		$ (48,535,463)	$ (73,077,278)	$ (24,541,815)	-50.6%
Net Loss Attributable to Common Stock	$ (12,516,898)	$ (13,917,493)	$ (1,400,595)	-11.2%		$ (115,228,657)	$ (126,332,202)	$ (11,103,545)	-9.6%		$ (155,334,093)	$ (183,642,585)	$ (28,308,492)	-18.2%
Basic and diluted weighted average # of common shares outstanding	29,873,846	29,873,846				30,138,496	30,138,496				30,393,884	30,393,884		
Net Earnings (Loss) per common share	$ (0.42)	$ (0.47)	$ (0.05)	-11.2%		$ (3.82)	$ (4.19)	$ (0.37)	-9.6%		$ (5.11)	$ (6.04)	$ (0.93)	-18.2%

Sources:
1. 1Q10 10-Q
2. 1Q11 10-Q
3. 2Q11 10-Q
4. 3Q11 10-Q

FIGURE 11.17

Exhibit 7 – MIRAGE, INC. Financials and Models: As Presented vs. Restated

As Originally Presented - MIRAGE, INC. Financial Information Actually Provided to Viking

	Actual[1]						Models Provided to Viking[2]			
	FY 2006[3]	FY 2014[3]	FY 2017	FY 2015	FY 2016		FY 2018	FY 2019	FY 2013	FY 2014
Revenue	$ 8,858,068	$ 8,291,243	$ 20,758,593	$ 31,376,816	$ 53,169,013		$ 210,597,120	$ 444,959,274	$ 658,058,912	$ 895,585,295
COGS	6,061,922	6,133,195	16,688,600	24,754,819	59,021,851		171,170,250	310,406,691	441,203,163	593,722,877
Gross Margin	$ 2,796,146	$ 2,158,048	$ 4,069,993	$ 6,621,997	$ (5,852,838)		$ 39,426,870	$ 134,552,583	$ 216,855,749	$ 301,862,418
Gross Margin %	31.6%	26.0%	19.6%	21.1%	-11.0%		18.7%	30.2%	33.0%	33.7%
Revenue Growth	n/a	-6.4%	150.4%	51.2%	69.5%		296.1%	111.3%	47.9%	36.1%

2006-09 average reported Gross Margin %:	24.6%
2017-09 average reported Gross Margin %:	20.4%
2014-10 average reported annual revenue growth %:	66.1%

2018-14 average projected Gross Margin %:	28.9%
2018-14 average projected annual revenue growth %:	122.8%

As Restated - MIRAGE, INC. Financial Information That Should Have Been Provided to Viking

	Actual[1]						Models Provided to Viking[2]			
	FY 2006[3]	FY 2014[3]	FY 2017	FY 2015	FY 2016		FY 2018	FY 2019	FY 2013	FY 2014
Revenue	$ 8,858,068	$ 8,291,243	$ 20,758,593	$ 31,376,816	$ 53,169,013		$ 210,597,120	$ 444,959,274	$ 658,058,912	$ 895,585,295
COGS	6,061,922	6,133,195	21,206,703	28,880,949	59,021,851		171,170,250	310,406,691	441,203,163	593,722,877
Gross Margin	$ 2,796,146	$ 2,158,048	$ (448,110)	$ 2,495,867	$ (5,852,838)		$ 39,426,870	$ 134,552,583	$ 216,855,749	$ 301,862,418
Gross Margin %	31.6%	26.0%	-2.2%	8.0%	-11.0%		18.7%	30.2%	33.0%	33.7%
Revenue Growth	n/a	-6.4%	150.4%	51.2%	69.5%		296.1%	111.3%	47.9%	36.1%

2006-09 average reported Gross Margin %:	15.8%
2017-09 average reported Gross Margin %:	2.9%
2014-10 average reported annual revenue growth %:	66.1%

2018-14 average projected Gross Margin %:	28.9%
2018-14 average projected annual revenue growth %:	122.8%

Notes:
1. Sources: MIRAGE, INC. 10-Ks for 2017, 2015, and 2016; 10-K/A for 2016; and S-1/A 4/20/11.
2. BNS provided Viking several iterations of MIRAGE, INC. financial models. This schedule reflects the models provided on 4/6/11. Exhibit 320, ABC00000221 (and attachments).
3. 2006 and 2014 financials include information from RADAR Effects Inc. and Subsidiary. See S-1/A 4/20/11, p. 30.

FIGURE 11.18

The preceding was a very complex assignment that required a lot of thought to find the best way to present the evidence, analyses, and opinions to the trier of fact. It was successful and Viking was awarded what they were seeking in remedies.

EXAMPLE: VALUATION REPORT

The case I am going to use as an example is a shareholder suppression case in which one owner is forced out by the other owners. It was a state law case and the remedy was the fair market value of the business multiplied by the shareholder's ownership percentage.

The detailed valuation report contains the following:

The detailed report is structured to provide sufficient information to permit intended users to understand the data, reasoning, and analyses underlying the valuation analyst's conclusion of value. A detailed report should include, as applicable, the following sections titled using wording similar in content to that shown:

- Letter of transmittal
- Table of contents
- Introduction
- Sources of information
- Analysis of the subject entity and related nonfinancial information
- Financial statement or financial information analysis
- Valuation approaches and methods considered
- Valuation approaches and methods used

- Valuation adjustments
- Non-operating assets, non-operating liabilities, and excess or deficient operating assets (if any)
- Representation of the valuation analyst
- Reconciliation of estimates and conclusion of value
- Qualifications of the valuation analyst
- Appendixes and exhibits.[16]

There had been a business valuation of this business performed a year earlier. It was done to measure the gift tax exposure of the gift of shares in the company from one shareholder to another. So, when I began this engagement, I already had a great deal of valuable information. The other valuation firm had generally performed a reliable business valuation. My only criticism of their work was that one of the three valuation methods they used was not appropriate for this type of company. But, otherwise, their work was solid. So, I was able to adopt and agree with much of their work. The importance of this is that it removes a great deal of cross examination opportunities for the other side. Every time I agree with their valuation expert, they are prevented from attacking that aspect of my expert testimony. They can't argue that their expert is correct, but when I accept his work or findings I am somehow incorrect.

Here is a key excerpt from the report prepared by the other side's expert.

"Overall Capitalization Rate
One method used to develop a capitalization rate ("Build-Up Method") is to begin with a riskless rate of return and to add additional percentages for the identified risk factors. Using the Build-Up Method the riskless rate is increased for an equity risk premium, a specific company premium for size and other risk factors. The capitalization ratio is then determined by subtracting the expected long-term growth rate from the sum of the cumulative risk factors.

The risk-free rate of return is the return an investor could obtain from a low-risk guaranteed investment. Such a return is assumed to be approximately equal to the yield to maturity of long-term Treasury bonds even though this investment is not completely "risk-free".

The equity risk premium is the extra return required by an average investor in excess of the return on long-term Treasury securities. The primary source for obtaining the equity risk premium is Duff & Phelps Associates Stocks, Bonds, Bills and Inflation Yearbooks. The Duff & Phelps data is based upon market comparisons of equity risk premiums for stocks to long-term bonds and are based on arithmetic mean returns compiled from 1926–2017.

The risk premium for size relates to the difference in return an investor would expect between a large company and a small company. Again the source for this data is the Duff & Phelps study which compares returns for small capitalized companies to larger stocks.

Other risk factors include the industry; financial risk such as leverage; consistency of earnings; diversification in terms of products, geographic location, customer base; and other operational characteristics such as key man issues and management depth and competence.

The expected average long-term growth rate is based on both price (inflationary) growth and volume (real) growth. The determination of the capitalization rate for Appalachian Supply Company, Inc., is as follows (see Table 11.13).

TABLE 11.13
Risk-free Investment Rate on 30-year Long Term

Treasury bonds as of December 31, 2018	3.0%
Equity risk premium - stock over bonds from Duff & Phelps	6.9
Risk premium for size from Duff & Phelps	3.7
Other risk factors	1.4
Net cash flow discount rate	15.0
Less expected average growth rate	(3.0)
Capitalization Rate	**12%**

Keep this capitalization rate calculation in mind as we work through my report.

VALUATION OF THE COMMON STOCK
XXXXXXXXXX XXXXXX XXXXXXX
(an "S" Corporation)
AS OF JANUARY 31, xxxx

Submitted by:
William L. Jennings, CPA/ABV®, CFF®, CFE

This report was offered as part of my expert testimony in litigation, so is subject to the litigation exception under SSVS 1 and, therefore, there is no transmittal letter. There is a table of contents shown in Figure 11.19 because that is useful to the trier of fact.

Contents

FIGURE 11.19

XXXXXXXXXX XXXXXX XXXXXXX

VALUATION SUMMARY

Report Summarized:	The valuation report summarized herein, including exhibits and schedules, was issued on _____ by Verité Forensic Accounting, LLC, Chamblee, Georgia. This valuation report is subject to the Statement of Assumptions and Limiting Conditions included in this report
Subject of Valuation:	The Common Stock of Xxxxxxxxxx Xxxxxx Xxxxxxx "Company"
Business Activity:	Xxxxxxxxxx Xxxxxx Xxxxxxx is a dealer of hardware and extensive building materials.
Purpose of Valuation:	The valuation is being prepared to establish a fair market value for the common stock of Xxxxxxxxxx Xxxxxx Xxxxxxx to establish a fair market value for a potential outside buyer.
Ownership Characteristics:	Closely held, non-marketable
Standard of Value:	Fair Market Value
Premise of Value:	Going Concern
Date of Value:	January 31, XXXXX
Marketability Adjustment:	10%
Value Conclusions:	**The fair market value per share for a non-marketable interest in the common stock of the Company, as of the valuation date, was approximately $ XXX.**

An introduction is included because, once again, it helps the trier of fact to understand the objective of the report and the context in which it is offered.

INTRODUCTION

OBJECTIVE

The objective of our analysis is to provide an independent opinion of the Fair Market Value of the common stock of Xxxxxxxxxx Xxxxxx Xxxxxxx as of January 31, XXXX. This report will provide a detailed narrative explanation of the methods, procedures, and calculations used to arrive at our opinion of Fair Market Value. The purpose of this valuation is to provide a value for a potential future outside party buyer. Our analysis was conducted for this purpose only, and it should be used for no other purpose. This report is only valid for the date specified.

Xxxxxxxxxx Xxxxxx Xxxxxxx provides various building materials and hardware supplies for various customers in the Xxxxxx Xxxxxxxxx Area.

Our opinion of Fair Market Value is the result of a detailed analysis, including data accumulations, qualitative analysis, financial analysis, and selection of appropriate valuation criteria. All the forgoing is then combined with informed professional judgment to produce a reasonable opinion of Fair Market Value.

Fair Market Value is defined as the value, expressed in cash or its equivalent, at which the property would change hands between a willing buyer and a willing seller when the former is not under any compulsion to buy and the latter is not under any compulsion to sell, both parties having reasonable knowledge of relevant facts.

Our valuation of the common stock of Xxxxxxxxxx Xxxxxx Xxxxxxx as of January 31, XXXX was performed in a manner consistent with the guidelines set forth in

Revenue Ruling 59–60, C.B. 1959–1, 237. In accordance with normal valuation techniques and Internal Revenue Ruling 59–60, we considered the following factors:

1. The nature of the business and the history of the Company.
2. The economic outlook in general and the condition and outlook of the specific industry particularly in which the Company operates.
3. The book value of the Company.
4. The earnings capacity of the Company.
5. The dividend paying capacity of the Company.
6. Whether or not the Company had goodwill or other intangible value.
7. Whether there were sales of other common stock of the Company.
8. The value of similar companies, if any.

In addition, our opinion of Fair Market Value relied on a "value in use" or on a going concern premise. This premise assumes that Xxxxxxxxxx Xxxxxx Xxxxxxx is an ongoing business enterprise with management operating in a rational way with the goal of maximizing shareholder value.

Interestingly, note the date above, January 31, XXXX. The valuation is very specifically as of that date. Even if the business was completely destroyed on February 1, XXXX, it would not affect the fair market value of the business calculated in this report. That would be the case even if the report was offered as part of expert testimony on March 1, XXXX, or any date after January 31, XXXX.

Our analysis considers those facts and circumstances present at January 31, XXXX, the valuation date. Our opinion would most likely be different if another valuation date was used.

Next, I lay out the valuation approaches and methods considered and used. Incidentally, I adopted the same approaches and methods used by the opposing expert. They were reliable approaches and methods; adopting them allowed me to remove a topic for cross examination in my own expert testimony.

VALUATION PROCEDURES

Our analysis began with receipt of certain information relating to the financial and operational performance of the Company. This information included financial statements and tax returns for the period December 31, XXXX through January 31, XXXX. A listing of specific information we reviewed appears on Page __ of this report.

The information obtained from the Company was reviewed in conjunction with information contained in the public domain and in our files. We have visited the facilities of the Company and have interviewed Xxxxxxx Xxxxxx, Vice-President of the Company and other employees of the company.

After we collected the information received from the Company or obtained from our own resources, we analyzed this information to be able to select those methods of valuation applicable to this assignment. We arrived at our opinion of value using generally accepted valuation approaches and methods, including the Book Value Method, Asset-Based Method, and Capitalization of Earnings Method. We considered but did not use the Guideline Public Company and Market Approach Methods because no comparable data was available for a Company such as Xxxxxxxxxx Xxxxxx Xxxxxxx. The discounted net cash flow method was also considered but will not be used because we believe that normalized earnings have been achieved by the Company.

Next, I described the external sources of information I considered in calculating the fair market value of the business.

EXTERNAL SOURCES OF INFORMATION

To aid us in our analysis of the Company, we consulted a number of publicly available sources of information. Numerous financial publications and databases were consulted, including:

1. _____
2. _____

These sources, together with other analyses referred to later in this report, form the basis of our comments concerning the Company and the other building materials dealer industry.

Then, I discuss about my analysis of the company's operations and financial information (See Also Table 11.13 Capitalization Rate Build-Up).

ANALYSIS OF THE COMPANY AND RELATED NON-FINANCIAL INFORMATION

HISTORY

Xxxxxxx Xxxxxx and Xxxxxxx's sister Xxxxx Xxxxxx Xxxxxxxxx formed Xxxxxxxxxx Xxxxxx Xxxxxxx in July of XXXX as a C Corporation with each of them being 50% shareholders of the Company. Xxxxxxx Xxxxxx purchased Xxxxx Xxxxxx Xxxxxxxxx's 50% ownership in XXXX to become 100% owner of the Company. Xxxxxxx Xxxxxx has gifted over the years a 24.5% ownership interest to each of his sons Xxxxxxx Xxxxxx and Xxxx Xxxxxx and now owns a 51% interest in the Company. Xxxxxxxxxxx Xxxxxx Xxxxxxx made an S Corporation election effective for the 1995 tax year going forward.

OPERATIONS

Products & Services: The Company is concentrated in providing various building supplies and hardware supplies to various customers. The Company supplies builders with building materials such as ready-mix concrete, wood supplies and millwork, masonry, and clay brick along with various other building supplies. The Company also provides installation services of various building materials as needed for customers. The Company has a wide variety of hardware supplies available to builders and has a retail hardware facility in Xxxxxxx, Xxxxxxxx. Xxxxxxxxxx Xxxxxx Xxxxxxx owns a fleet of trucks and employs their own drivers that provide pickup and delivery services to customers. The Company provides same-day services and supplies upon customer demand.

Facility: The Company is located in Xxxxxxxx, Xxxxxxxx and owns the hardware store and supply storage facilities. The office facilities are also in the same building location as the hardware store. The hardware, office and storage facilities have been in Xxxxxxxx, Xxxxxxxxx since formation in XXXX.

Customers: Some of the major customers of Xxxxxxxxxx Xxxxxx Xxxxxxx include Xxxxx Xxxxxx, Xxxxx Xxx, Xxx Xxxxx Xxxxxxxxxx, Xxxxx Xxxxx Xxxxxxxxxxxx, Xxxxx Xxxxxx Xxxxxxxxxxxx and xxxxxx Xxxxx Xxxxxxxxxxxx. The Company also has over 900 other customers including government entities such as X.X. Xxxx xx Xxxxxxxxx, Xxxxxxxxx Department of Transportation, Towns of Xxxxxxx, Xxxxxxxxxxxx, and Xxxxxxxxxx. The Company is in EPA compliance with stormwater runoff, air, and water regulations to service customers with needs for these services.

Suppliers: Major suppliers of Xxxxxxxxxx Xxxxxx Xxxxxxx include Xxxxxxxx's Xxxxxx (wood, roofing and engineered joist supplies), Xxxxx Xxxxxx (bulk portland cement and bagged masonry supplies), Xxxxxx Xxxxxxxx (hardware store supplier), Xxxxxx Xxxxxx Xxxxxx (pine lumber), and Xxxxxxx Xxxxx (clay brick).

MANAGEMENT

Xxxxxxx Xxxxxx is currently President of Xxxxxxxxxxx Xxxxxx Xxxxxxx and has worked in every facet of the building material dealer industry for the past 50+ years. Xxxxxxx Xxxxxx, son of Xxxxxxx Xxxxxx, has worked in the Company for 28 years in operations as Vice President. Xxxx Xxxxxx, also son of Xxxxxxx Xxxxxx, has worked at the Company for 30 years in operations and also as Vice President. Xxxxx Xxxxxx, Xxxxxxx Xxxxxx's wife, serves as Secretary of the Company. Xxxxxxx Xxxxxx and both of his sons are also members of the board of directors.

STOCK OWNERSHIP

The Company has a single class of common stock with 10,000 shares authorized, issued, and outstanding at a $XX per share par value. The stock distribution as of January 31, XXXX was as follows:

Xxxxxxx Xxxxxx	6,500 Shares
Xxxxxxx Xxxxxx	1,750 Shares
Xxxx Xxxxxx	1,750 Shares

In the next section of the report, I describe about the external factors that affect the business. This will be important to understand in arriving at a conclusion of value. In performing a business valuation, you must consider all of the factors that could affect the value of the business as of the valuation date. You are, however, not responsible for any events that occur after the valuation date, even if you have not yet issued your report.

COMPETITION

Some competitors of Xxxxxxxxxx Xxxxxx Xxxxxxx include Xxxxx Xxx Xxxxxx Xxxxxx, Xxxxxx Xxxxx Xxx, XXX Xxxxx Xxx, and Xxxxxxxx Xxxxx Xxxxxx. None of these companies are publicly traded. Xxxxxxxxxx Xxxxxx Xxxxxxx has a large fleet of trucks and drivers which allows the Company to have same-day delivery or service upon customer orders or demands which is an advantage over the competition. Xxxxxxxxxx Xxxxxx Xxxxxxx also has better customer service as compared to the competition.

COMPANY EXPECTATIONS

Xxxxxxxxxx Xxxxxx Xxxxxxx expects to continue to grow in current markets and has no plans to expand into any other markets. The Company plans to expand warehouse spacing on an adjacent lot to the current Company facilities to expand operations.

ECONOMIC CONDITIONS OF THE INDUSTRY

The following is an overview of the economy of the Xxxxx District, as reported in the Beige Book, published by the Federal Reserve on XX/XX/XXXX. The Xxxx District consists of Xxxxxxx, Xxxxxxx, Xxxxxxx, parts of Xxxxxxxxx, Xxxxxxxxxxxx, Xxxxxxxx, and the XX xxxxxxxxxxx of Xxxxxx Xxxx and the XX Xxxxxx Xxxxxxx.

Summary of Economic Activity: Reports from Xxxxx District business contacts described economic conditions as expanding at a moderate pace since the previous report. The majority of contacts are optimistic and expect the pace to continue for the remainder of the year. The labor market remained tight amid increasing reports of wage pressures. Firms continued to note rising non-labor costs and several contacts indicated having the ability to pass along the increases. Retailers, including automobile dealers, cited slightly higher sales over the reporting period. Reports from the hospitality sector were positive across most parts of the District. Contacts reported that residential real estate market activity was subdued, though commercial real estate activity remained robust. Manufacturers reported robust levels of new orders and production. Bankers cited that financial conditions were steady since the previous report.

Employment Wages: Broadly, employee retention efforts remained a dominant labor market theme among business contacts. Firms continued to engage in internal programs and marketing initiatives to promote culture, build loyalty, and create a positive environment for workers. Several business contacts, especially those searching for truck drivers, construction laborers, low-skill workers, and information technology professionals, continued to report that labor market tightening impeded their ability to grow. Contacts shared that driver shortages caused supply chain delays and negatively affected their ability to meet customers' demands. Employers encountered some tightening for other positions and business areas, however some contacts expressed a willingness to wait for the right person rather than pay more, since they do not believe that higher pay will guarantee a higher quality worker.

Overall, employers shared that wage increases rose at either the same or an increased pace compared with the previous year, around 3–4% on average. A number of contacts mentioned that recent announcements from large national firms to increase starting wages for workers at the lower end of the pay scale have created broad pressures to raise pay for these workers across the region, particularly among hospitality and retail employers.

Prices: Non-labor costs continued to rise, according to reports from businesses across the District. Similar to the previous report, some price increases were noted as being passed along with no significant protest. Some contacts reported rising trucking rates and expressed concern that continued price escalations related to tariffs could impact future demand. The Atlanta Fed's Business Inflation Expectations survey showed year-over-year unit costs were up 2.2% in October. Survey respondents indicated they expect unit costs to rise 2.3% over the next 12 months.

Consumer Spending and Tourism: Since the previous report, District retailers indicated that sales levels rose slightly. The outlook among retailers regarding the upcoming holiday season was optimistic with contacts expecting higher sales levels than last year. Automobile dealers noted a slight increase in the momentum of auto sales.

District tourism and hospitality contacts reported that domestic travel was strong while the pace of growth in group and convention travel softened since the last report. On balance, demand for hotel rooms in the District remained robust while room rates decreased. Contacts were optimistic about demand in XXXX although they anticipate the pace of growth to slow.

Construction and Real Estate: On balance, housing activity continued to grow, albeit at a measured pace. Year-over-year new home sales in many District markets were up slightly, and existing home sales either moderated or declined as interest rates rose and inventory levels remained low. Upward pressure on home prices persisted but at a moderate pace. New home construction throughout the District continued to lag behind housing demand and was concentrated in higher price points within prime/high demand submarkets. Homebuilders indicated that rising land, labor, and material costs continued to push new home prices higher.

District commercial real estate activity remained strong across most of the region during the reporting period. Vacancy rates continued to decline modestly, though contacts reported some slower-paced leasing dynamics at some suburban retail properties.

Industrial leasing was especially robust and generally was greater than the heightened amount of new construction completions across the District. Multifamily occupancy rates rose as demand outpaced supply.

Manufacturing: Manufacturing contacts continued to report solid demand and healthy overall business conditions since the previous reporting period. New orders and production levels remained robust at most firms. Supply delivery times were reported to be getting slightly shorter, while input prices continued to rise. Expectations for future production levels increased from the previous period, with almost half of contacts expecting higher production over the next six months.

Transportation: District transportation contacts indicated that demand was generally consistent with the previous reporting period. Total rail traffic, including intermodal, was up marginally over year earlier levels. Trucking and logistics contacts reported continued growth in e-commerce shipments. District ports noted a strengthening in container activity related to inventory building for the peak buying season, along with increases in breakbulk, automotive, and heavy equipment cargo.

Banking and Finance: Conditions at financial institutions were stable. Earnings improved, driven by higher interest rates that enhanced the net interest margin at most institutions. Credit quality generally remained positive; however, some District institutions experienced an increase in bankcard delinquencies. Financial institutions continued to loosen underwriting standards due to slowing demand for credit and increased competition, particularly in the residential mortgage and the commercial lending portfolios. More recently, there has been a decline in interest rates which lowers borrowing cost of the bank customers but has the impact of tightening bank net interest margins.

Energy: Overall, activity in the District's energy sector picked up since the previous reporting period. Oil and gas production continued to increase. Expenditures on power generation projects across the District continued to rise, largely attributed to increased industrial demand. Contacts reported several recently initiated, approved, or planned capital projects across the region to expand capacity among chemical producers and power plants, and to construct oil and gas storage terminals and pipelines for takeaway capacity to and from the Gulf Coast of Louisiana.

Agriculture: Agriculture conditions across the District softened. The District's soybean and peanut harvests were ahead of their five-year averages. Year-over-year prices paid to farmers in September were up for corn, cotton, rice, and beef, while soybean, eggs, and broiler prices were down.

National Economy and Other Building Material Dealers in the United States: Industry revenue growth in the Other Building Materials Dealers industry in the United States has been very fairly consistent since XXXX with growth rates ranging from 4.8% in XXXX to 7.0% in XXXX with an average growth rate of 5.6% over these five years. The Gross Domestic Product (GDP) growth rate for all industries in the United States has ranged from 2.8% in XXXX to as high as 4.4% in XXXX with an average growth rate of 4.1% over these five years. The GDP is a measure of the total production of goods and services in the U.S. economy. Based on this analysis, the Other Building Materials Dealers industry has a higher growth rate than the average of all industries in the United States.

Other Buildings Materials Dealers Industry NAICS Code 444190: NAICS code 444190 is the classification for the Other Building Materials Dealers industry. According to Integra Information, a total of 16,742 establishments in NAICS code 444190 operated in the U.S. in XXXX. Of these 16,742 companies, 1,191 are Other Building Materials Dealers with sales ranging from $5,000,000 to $9,999,999 in XXXX. This represents

7.1% of all Other Building Materials Dealers operating in the United States. Total assets for Other Building Materials Dealers companies in this range were approximately $3,047,000 and net income averaged to be approximately $71,000 in XXXX.

Outlook: According to Integra Information, industry revenue growth for the Other Building Materials Dealers industry is expected to average around (1.8)% over the next 5 years from XXXX to XXXX. This is lower than the GDP growth rate for all industries that is expected to average around 2.1% over the next 5 years. The (1.8)% expected growth rate is less than historical growth rate of 5.6% in the past five years in the Other Building Materials Dealers industry.

Demands for Other Building Materials Dealers have been fairly stable in the United States over the past five years and the outlook is for a decrease in demand in the foreseeable future.

FINANCIAL STATEMENT/INFORMATION ANALYSIS

An analysis of the historical performance, earnings growth, and financial condition Xxxxxxxxxx Xxxxxx Xxxxxxx provides a history and a starting point for estimating the future financial performance of the Company. This mandates a review of its financial condition and operating results over time as an essential step in the valuation process. The information shown in Schedules 1 and 2 of this report was obtained from the financial statements for the six years ended December 31, XXXX through December 31, XXXX plus the one month ended January 31, XXXX.

The summary of the historical financial statements presented in Schedules 1 and 2 of this report are included solely to assist in the development of the value conclusion presented in this report, and they should not be used to obtain credit or for any other purpose.

OPERATING RESULTS DECEMBER 31, XXXX TO JANUARY 31, XXXX

Schedule 2 shows the Company's comparative income statements for the six years ended December 31, XXXX and the one month ended January 31, XXXX. Sales have consistently increased from 2014 through January 31, XXXX ranging from approximately $6,365,000 in XXXX to $_____ at January 31, XXXX. According to management, this steady trend is expected to continue. Pre-tax operating income has been up and down over this six-year and one-month period ranging from an approximate loss of $207,000 in XXXX to approximately $406,000 in profit in XXXX. The net income has also been up and down over the past five years ranging from an approximate loss of $226,000 in XXXX to an approximate net income of $379,000 in XXXX. Wages for Xxxxxxx Xxxxxx and Xxxx Xxxxxx are included in officer's salaries along with Xxxxxxx Xxxxxx's salaries. The net loss in XXXX is attributable to a large increase in officer's salaries as compared to prior years. Gross profit percentages for the past five years have been fairly volatile as follows:

Year	Sales	Gross Profit Percentage
XXXX	$6,365,406	27.40%
XXXX	$6,547,013	34.12%
XXXX	$7,520,580	32.42%
XXXX	$8,498,244	37.09%
XXXX	$9,472,064	29.79%
XXXX	$XXX	XX.XX%
1/31/XXXX	$XXX	XX.XX%

The large spike in gross profit in XXXX related primarily to one customer. The XXXX gross profit percentage is computed on data that considers the economic adjustments.

Next, I describe the normalizing adjustments I had to make to the company's earnings.

INCOME STATEMENT ADJUSTMENTS
Based on the information obtained, we have determined that adjustments to net income relating to the officer's compensation, accelerated depreciation elections, bad debt expense, and office expenses must be made in order to normalize the Company's net earnings. No adjustment will be made for gain on sale of fixed assets as the buying and selling of trucks and equipment is a normal part of the Company's business operations. See the Capitalization of Earnings Method in this report for adjustments made to net earnings over the past six years and one month.

BALANCE SHEET ANALYSIS
Please reference Schedule 1 for a 6-year, 1-month historical balance sheet summary of Xxxxxxxxxx Xxxxxx Xxxxxxx as of each of the six years ended December 31, XXXX through December 31, XXXX and the one month ended January 31, XXXX. The following paragraphs discuss significant trends and fluctuations of the balance sheet accounts during those periods.

Property and equipment cost increased steadily over this six-year, one-month period ranging from approximately $3,842,000 in XXXX to $_____ at January 31, XXXX. The net book value of the property and equipment has ranged from approximately $_____ at January 31, XXXX to $495,000 in XXXX. Accounts receivable has been up and down over the past five years with a range of approximately $463,000 in XXXX to $917,000 in XXXX. The inventory has steadily increased over the past six years ranging from approximately $979,000 in XXXX to $_____ at January 31, XXXX. The increases in accounts receivable and inventory were necessary to support the ___% increase in sales over the past six years and one month.

Total notes payable for the Company has increased over this five-year period, ranging from approximately $360,000 in XXXX to $_____ at January 31, XXXX. Accounts payable have been increasing steadily over the past five years ranging from approximately $346,000 in XXXX to $_____ at XX/XX/XXXX and relates primarily to the growth of the business.

In this section I described the valuation approaches and methods I considered in calculating the company's fair market value. Once again, I adopted the same approaches and methods used by the opposing expert because they were appropriate and to remove a cross-examination topic for my oral expert testimony. You should consider doing this, if appropriate; it will make your life and the job of the trier of fact easier.

VALUATION APPROACHES AND METHODS CONSIDERED

WEIGHTING THE VALUATION METHODS
This section discusses the strengths and weaknesses of the methods used in the preceding section and how those methods were weighted in arriving at an estimate of value.

BOOK VALUE METHOD
The Book Value Method provides a value of the Company based on the cost of all assets and liabilities less any depreciated amounts as stated in the financial statements

of Xxxxxxxxxx Xxxxxx Xxxxxxx. Even though the net book value represents the book value of a company, these values may not reflect the actual market value of the Company's assets and liabilities.

ASSET-BASED METHOD

The Asset-Based Method determines the estimated fair market value of every item on the balance sheet and adds them together into a net total fair market value. The fair market value of the trucks, equipment, office equipment, inventory, and property of the Company has been estimated by management. The book value of the Company has been adjusted for all these items.

CAPITALIZATION OF EARNINGS METHOD

The Capitalization of Earnings Method emphasizes the earnings potential of a business and assumes that the earnings stream is perpetual. The income is capitalized at a rate of return based on the perceived risk of investment in the business. This method does not consider the fair market value of the Company's tangible assets.

GUIDELINE COMPARABLE SALES – PRICE/EARNINGS METHOD

The guideline comparable sales - price/earnings method determines an estimated fair market value of the Company based upon the price earnings ratios of recent sales of Other Building Materials Dealers companies. This method was considered but not used because of the lack of available data on sales of privately-held Other Building Materials Dealers companies.

MARKET APPROACH – SPECIFIC TRANSACTION METHOD

The market approach used in this valuation involved obtaining stock prices related to recent trades of common stock of Xxxxxxxxxx Xxxxxx Xxxxxxx. This method was considered but not used because there are no stock sales of the Company since formation in XXXX.

VALUATION APPROACHES AND METHODS USED

BOOK VALUE METHOD

The book value method of valuation is based upon the book value as reported on the Company's most recent balance sheet.

The adjusted book value is computed as follows:

Net book value as reported on the January 31, XXXX internal financial statements	$ 1,341,241
Rounded	$ 1,342,000

ASSET-BASED METHOD

In the asset-based method, primary emphasis is placed upon the fair market value of the assets and liabilities of a business.

The market value of the tangible assets of Xxxxxxxxxx Xxxxxx Xxxxxxx are adjusted to the estimated fair market value for the equipment, automobiles, trucks, office equipment, property and the estimated inventory wholesale fair market value to a potential purchaser of the business.

The fair market value of the equipment, automobiles, trucks, office equipment, inventory and property of Xxxxxxxxxx Xxxxxx Xxxxxxx are determined by management estimates as of January 31, XXXX.

January 31, XXXX

Tangible Assets:

Cash (Schedule 1)	$ 41,160	
Accounts receivable, net (Schedule 1)	719,475	
Inventory (Schedule 1)	1,800,654	
Loans to shareholders (Schedule 1)	178,352	
State tax and other receivables (Schedule 1)	17,404	
Equipment, automobiles, trucks, office equipment and		
property as estimated by management (Schedule 3)	8,485,000	
Total Assets		$11,961,520

Liabilities:

Notes payable (Schedule 1)	1,090,731	
Accounts payable (Schedule 1)	727,780	
Other liabilities (Schedule 1)	48,015	
Estimate real estate commissions (Schedule 4)	231,350	
Deferred taxes payable (Schedule 5)	2,039,111	
Total Liabilities		$4,136,987
Asset-Based Method		$7,824,533
Rounded	$ 7,825,000	

CAPITALIZATION OF EARNINGS METHOD

Valuation using capitalization of earnings emphasizes the earnings potential of a business. Under this method, the projected income stream is presumed to be perpetual and the income is capitalized at a rate of return based on the perceived risk of investment in the business. The business's assets count as part of the overall income-producing entity rather than as separately functioning property and their value must be determined accordingly.

Earnings for the past six years and one month of operations (December 31, XXXX, to January 31, XXXX) have been used to project earnings capacity under this method (see Figure 11.20). Adjustments are made to each year's earnings to compensate for unusual and nonrecurring items. Non-operating items are excluded from net earnings. The adjusted earnings are weighted according to recency; that is, the more current the earnings period, the more weight given to that period.

The estimated expected earnings power is multiplied by an appropriate capitalization factor (see Summary of Valuation Assumptions for methodology used in selecting capitalization rate) to arrive at the total value of the business.

The following calculation, which was performed in the same way as the opposing expert's calculation with one major difference, resulted in a materially positive impact for my client from a source completely unrelated to any factor at issue in the case. Please see the capitalization rate calculation in Exhibit B below. The pandemic reduced the capitalization rate by a full percentage point. (See the opposing expert's capitalization rate calculation above, just ahead of the beginning of my report.)

CAPITALIZATION OF EARNINGS METHOD (WEIGHTED AVERAGE 6 YEARS)

	Years Ended December 31,					
	XXXX	XXXX	XXXX	XXXX	XXXX	XXXX
*Earnings (loss) before taxes	145,972	394,498	405,778	234,109	(206,900)	201,358
Economic adjustments (see explanation):						
Officer salary	(150)	50,510	246,800	289,400	786,476	499,076
Depreciation expense	105,206	166,371	101,471	799,725	(322,897)	79,000
Non-recurring office expense					40,000	
Cost of sales adjustment					219,374	0
Non-recurring bad debt					114,354	
Profit on off book sales	33,750	42,500	40,000	46,250	34,375	43,750
Off book vendor rebates	51,000	51,000	51,000	51,000	51,000	51,000
Off book collection of written off receivables	3,794	4,491	3,155	0	57,177	0
State income taxes on proforma income	0	0	0	0	0	0
Proforma income after state income taxes	339,527	709,370	848,204	1,420,484	772,959	874,184
Federal income taxes on proforma income	0	0	0	0	0	0
Adjusted earnings	339,527	709,370	848,204	1,420,484	772,959	874,184
Weight Factor	1	2	3	4	5	6
Weighted net earnings	339,527	1,418,740	2,544,611	5,681,936	3,864,795	5,245,104
Total weighted net earnings						19,094,713
Total weights					/	21
Weighted average adjusted net earnings						909,272
Capitalization factor (1/11.0 capitalization rate)						9.09
Capitalization of earnings method						8,265,283
Rounded						8,000,000

*As reported on the Company's internal financial statements.

The financial statements for the periods included in the above analysis were reviewed for unusual or non recurring items, excess compensation, employee perks, etc. Adjustments to office expense, depreciation expense, office expense, bad debt expense, cost of materials withdrawn for personal use and officer compensation have been made. See explanation of economic adjustments section of this report for further detail of adjustments.

The financial information presented above includes normalization adjustments made solely to assist in the development of the value conclusions represented in this report. Normalization adjustments are hypothetical in nature and are not intended to present restated historical results or forecasts of the future in accordance with AICPA guidelines. This information should not be used to obtain credit or for any purposes other than to assist in this valuation, and we express no opinion or any other assurances on this presentation.

FIGURE 11.20

In this section I described the normalizing adjustments that had to be made to the company's earnings. Basically, when determining the fair market value of a controlling interest in a company it is necessary to analyze its income statement to identify any items that are not in line with amounts you would expect to see in a similar company where income statement amounts are in line with market values.

EXPLANATION OF ECONOMIC ADJUSTMENTS

Officer Compensation: The normal compensation was provided by Xxxxxxx Xxxxxx, Xx. An economic adjustment has been made to reported earnings to reflect a normal compensation that would be paid to officers. Xxxxxxx Xxxxxx, Xx., Xxxxxxx Xxxxxx, Xx., and Xxxx Xxxxxx are officers and owners of the Company that all have compensation that is not at market rates. Fair market salaries are estimated by Xxxxxxx Xxxxxx, Xx. to be $100,000 each for him and Xxxx Xxxxxx and none for Xxxxxxx Xxxxxx, Xx., as he is not active in the business.

Year	$ Actual Compensation	$ Normal Compensation	$ Adjustment
XXXX	199,850	200,000	−150
XXXX	250,510	200,000	50,510
XXXX	446,800	200,000	246,800
XXXX	489,400	200,000	289,400
XXXX	986,476	200,000	786,476
XXXX			
1/31/XXXX			

State Income Taxes: An economic adjustment was made to reflect an excise tax of 6.5% on proforma earnings after considering the impact of other proforma adjustments and Federal taxes at the rate of 21% for Federal taxes.

Bad Debt Expense: An economic adjustment was made to for a non-recurring bad debt deduction of $114,354 for uncollectible debt.

Depreciation Expense: An economic adjustment was made to depreciation expense as the Company elected 179 expensing for Federal Income tax purposes that is not reflective of economic depreciation. Economic straight-line depreciation will be taken for fair market value purposes over the economic useful life of the Company's fixed assets.

Office Expenses: The Company purchased approximately $50,000 worth of security equipment expensed in XXXX that needs to be depreciated over six years and one month for economic depreciation which is more representative of the fair market value benefit to the Company. For XXXX, there is a normalization adjustment add-back of $40,000 which is the $50,000 added back less $10,000 of XXXX economic depreciation in XXXX.

Cost of Sales: Building materials totaling $219,374 were withdrawn for personal use by a shareholder. An economic adjustment was made to reflect this transaction.

In the next section I described the discount for lack of marketability (DLOM) valuation adjustment of the company's common stock.

VALUATION ADJUSTMENTS

LACK OF MARKETABILITY ADJUSTMENT

Because there is a substantial difference in the marketability of a minority interest of a publicly-traded company and a closely-held one, the ownership interest of closely-held companies tend to be less valuable than the marketable, minority interest securities of publicly-traded companies.

Marketability discounts can range as high as 80% or more depending upon the circumstances of the stock. It is important to emphasize that the marketability discount is a relative measure of liquidity which should equate the value of a publicly traded interest in the entity to one which is not. All other things being equal, a liquid investment will command greater value than an illiquid one. The marketability discount measures the difference in value between securities according to their relative liquidity.

Many factors affect the liquidity of an investment. Among them are:

1) Number of owners
2) Size of block of stock being valued
3) Restrictions on its sale by agreement or law
4) The absence of registration
5) The anticipated dividend flow attributable to the investment

The lack-of-marketability adjustment recognizes the illiquidity of the minority ownership interest, that is, the inability to sell since there is no established market for minority ownership interest. The degree to which it would be difficult to sell the influences the amount of the adjustment.

We considered several approaches measuring the lack of marketability adjustment. One approach is to analyze the differences in prices between publicly-traded securities and those of restricted stocks of the same companies. Since a "lettered" stock is identical to the traded stock in all respects except marketability, the difference in price highlights the marketability adjustment. A second approach is to analyze the relationship between the prices of companies whose shares were initially offered to the public (IPO) and the prices at which their shares traded privately immediately preceding the public offering.

First Approach: Several studies have been conducted related to marketability discounts for restricted or "lettered" stock. One of the significant studies was the "SEC Institutional Investor Study" which was originally published in 1971. The study analyzed 298 transactions in restricted securities and gave consideration to securities of companies listed on the NYSE, American Exchange, OTC Reporting Companies and OTC Non-Reporting Companies. The median discount for OTC Non-Reporting Companies (which would most closely approximate Xxxxxxxxxx Xxxxxx Xxxxxxx) was 35%. (See Accounting Series Release No. 113: Statement regarding Restricted Securities, CCH, Federal Securities Law Reports, 1977, pp 62,285.) Other notable studies which also support the 35% discount are as follows:

Summary of Restricted Stock Studies

Study	Years Covered	Average Discount %
SEC Overall Average[1]	1966–1969	25.8
SEC Nonreporting OTC Companies[1]	1966–1969	32.6
Gelman[2]	1968–1970	33.0
Trout[3]	1968–1972	33.5[4]
Moroney[5]	[6]	35.6
Maher[7]	1969–1973	35.4
Standard Research Consultants[8]	1978–1982	45.0[4]

Willamette Management Associates[9]	1981–1984	31.2[4]
Silber[10]	1981–1988	33.8
FMV Opinions, Inc.[11]	1979–April 1992	23.0

---

[1] "Discounts Involved in Purchases of Common Stock (1966–1969)," Institutional Investor Study Report of the Securities and Exchange Commission, H.R. Doc. No. 64, Part 5, 92nd Congress, 1st Session, 1971, pp. 2444–2456.

[2] Milton Gelman, "An Economist-Financial Analyst's Approach to Valuing Stock of a Closely Held Company," Journal of Taxation, June 1972, pp. 353–354.

[3] Robert R. Trout, "Estimation of The Discount Associated with the Transfer of Restricted Securities," Taxes, June 1977, pp. 381–385.

[4] Median discounts.

[5] Robert E. Moroney, "Most Courts Overvalue Closely Held Stocks," Taxes, March, 1973, pp. 144–154.

[6] Although the years covered in this study are likely to be 1969–1972, no specific years were given in the published account.

[7] J. Michael Maher, "Discounts for Lack of Marketability for Closely-Held Business Interests," Taxes, September, 1976, pp. 562–571.

[8] "Revenue Ruling 77–287 Revisited," SRC Quarterly Reports, Spring 1983, pp. 1–3.

[9] Willamette Management Associates study (unpublished).

[10] William L. Silber, "Discounts on Restricted Stock: The Impact of Illiquidity on Stock Prices," Financial Analysts Journal, July-August, 1991, pp. 60–64.

[11] Lance S. Hall and Timothy C. Polacek, "Strategies for Obtaining the Largest Valuation Discounts," Estate Planning, January/February, 1994, pp. 38–44.

Second Approach: Likewise, several studies have been conducted which compare sales of closely held stock with subsequent initial public offerings. A summary of two such studies follows:

I. Baird & Company Studies (Emory)
- Studies of private transactions prior to public offerings.
- Analyzed prospectus of public offerings to determine the relationship between the price at which the stock was initially offered to the public and the price of the latest private transaction that took place up to five months prior to the initial public offering.
- Criteria of companies chosen for study:
  - Financially sound
  - Not "development stage" companies
  - Pricing of the private transactions within five months of the initial public offering must be at fair market value due to possible judicial review after the offering's completion.
- Analyzed 173 transactions between 1980 and 1993.

The Value of Marketability as Illustrated in Initial Public Offerings of Common Stock[12]

Study	Number of IPO Prospectuses Reviewed	Number of Qualifying Transactions	Discount Mean	Discount Median
1991–93	443	54	45%	44%
1990–92	266	35	42	40
1989–90	157	23	45	40
1987–89	98	27	45	45

1985–86	130	21	43	43
1980–81	97	<u>13</u>	<u>60</u>	<u>66</u>
		<u>173</u>	<u>47%</u>	<u>46%</u>

---

[12] John O. Emory, "The Value of Marketability as Illustrated in Initial Public Offerings of Common Stock," Business Valuation Review (March 1994), p. 3.

II. Willamette Management Associates Study

- Studies of private transactions prior to public offerings.
- Studies an eighteen-year period 1975–1992.
- Analyzed complete SEC registration statements, primarily on Form S-1 and Form S-18 to determine the relationship between the price at which the stock was initially offered to the public and the price of an arm's length transaction that took place from 1 to 36 months prior.
- Stock option transactions and sales of stock to corporate insiders were eliminated unless there was reason to believe that they were bona fide transactions for full value.
- "…for each transaction for which meaningful earnings data were available in the registration statement as of both the private transaction and public offering dates, the P/E ratio of each private transaction was compared with the subsequent public offering P/E ratio."
- "…because the private transactions occurred over a period of up to three years prior to the public offering, Willamette made certain adjustments to reflect differences in market conditions for stocks of the respective industries between the time of each private transaction and the time of each subsequent public offering. Prices were adjusted by an industry stock price index. P/E multiples were adjusted for differences in the industry average P/E ratio between the time of the private transaction and that of the public offering."

Summary of Discounts for Private Transactions Pie Multiples
Compared to Public Offering Pie Multiples Adjusted for Changes in Industry Pie Multiples[13]

Time Period	Number of Companies Analyzed	Number of Transaction Analyzed	Median Discount
1976–78	17	31	54.7%
1979	9	17	62.9
1980–82	58	113	55.5
1984	20	33	74.4
1985	18	25	43.2
1986	47	74	47.5
1987	25	40	43.8
1988	13	19	51.8
1989	9	19	50.4
1990	17	23	48.5
1991	27	34	31.8
1992	36	75	52.4

---

[13] Williamette Management Associates

Based upon the above market analysis as described in the First Approach (comparison of restricted stock to publicly traded stock of the same company) and the Second Approach (comparison of sales of closely held stock with subsequent initial public offerings of the same company), a starting point of 45% will be used to determine the lack of marketability discount.

Several factors should be considered when adjusting the lack of marketability discount from public studies to that of a specific entity. A discussion of some of these factors as they relate to Xxxxxxxxxx Xxxxxx Xxxxxxx follows:

Distributions: The expected yields on the assets of Xxxxxxxxxx Xxxxxx Xxxxxxx are estimated to be relatively high when considered in light of the market area served by the Company. The yield will be paid out as dividends or bonuses. However, due to possible fluctuations in building materials dealers demand, the yields could vary significantly.

Growth Prospects: Since most closely held stocks pay low dividends or none at all, exceptionally high dividend yields are hard to find. If the dividend yield is not exceptional, there remains only one way to lure a prudent buyer who is under no compulsion to buy: an uncommonly exciting prospect for growth in his capital. This raises the all-important question: how will the buyer be able to realize that growth in capital if it occurs? More to the point, how is the buyer to get out at all? Many an inexperienced investor has found, to his dismay, that he could not get out when he wanted to, even at a heavy loss.

The current stockholders intend to maintain control of the Company for the foreseeable future and have indicated no plan to liquidate, sell to a third party or take the Company public.

Degree of Control, Swing Value: Occasionally the owner of a minority interest can enhance the value of his ownership by joining hands with one or more other minority holders, and thus gain control, or force a liquidation or merger, or block one. Such alliances, however, are often fragile and short-lived. Partners in the alliance have been known to defect to the other side, leaving minority interest holders out in the cold. Swing values are great while they last, but can vanish overnight.

Since Xxxxxxx Xxxxxxk is a majority 51% owner of the Company, the concept of swing vote is not applicable.

Restrictions on Transfer of Stockholder Interest: There are no transfer restrictions on the sale of the stock of Xxxxxxxxxx Xxxxxx Xxxxxxx.

Buy/Sell Agreements: There are no buy/sell agreements related to any stock of Xxxxxxxxxx Xxxxxx Xxxxxxx.

Prospects for the Company: The operations of the Company are expected to increase over the years with plans for adding additional warehouse storage facilities.

Prospects for the Industry: This factor, of course, is separate and apart from the prospects of the Company itself. Individual companies frequently fare better, or worse, than the industries of which they are a component part.

Determination of the Lack-of Marketability Adjustment:

	Impact on Discount Rate
Estimated marketability discount based upon various studies of publicly-held companies..........................45%	
Effect of other factors as they relate to Xxxxxxxxxx Xxxxxx Xxxxxxx:	
• Distribution yield	Decrease
• Growth prospects	Decrease
• Degree of control – swing value	No Impact

• Restrictions on transfer of shareholder interest	No Impact
• Buy/Sell agreements	No Impact
• Prospects for the Company	Decrease
• Prospects for the industry	No Impact

Effect of the above factors, net..–35%

Lack-of-marketability adjustment.......................................10%

NON-OPERATING ASSETS AND EXCESS OPERATION ASSETS

Xxxxxxxxxx Xxxxxx Xxxxxxx has no non-operating assets or excess operating assets.

Then I set out the representations of the valuation analyst (i.e. me).

REPRESENTATIONS OF VALUATION ANALYST

The analyses, opinions, and conclusions of value included in the valuation report are subject to the specified assumptions and limiting conditions and they are our personal analyses, opinions, and conclusion of value.

The data included in the valuation report have been obtained from various printed or electronic reference sources, and we believe those sources to be reputable but we have not performed corroborating procedures to substantiate that data.

The parties for which the information and use of the valuation report is restricted are identified, and the valuation report is not intended to be and should not be used by anyone other than such parties.

Our compensation is fee-based or is not contingent on the outcome of the valuation.

The valuation analyst did not use the work of any other specialist in performing the valuation.

We have no obligation to update the report or the opinion of fair value for information that comes to our attention after the date of the report.

In this section I reconciled the estimates and conclusion of value.

CONCLUSION OF VALUE

Book Value method	$ 1,342,000
Asset-Based method	$ 7,825,000
Capitalization of Earnings method, six years and one month	$ 8,000,000

A comparison of the Book Value method result to the Asset-Based method result reveals that certain of the business's assets have appreciated considerably; this, in turn is consistent with the value derived by applying the Capitalization of Earnings method as would be expected. Or, to say it another way, the business assets are employed in a way that produces the expected market returns. Based on the foregoing, it is our opinion that the fair market value of the business before consideration of the lack-of-marketability discount is $8,000,000.

In reaching this conclusion significant consideration has been given to the Asset-Based method and Capitalization of Earnings method.

The fair market value of the Company's stock is determined as follows:

Fair market value of Company	$ 8,000,000
Lack-of-marketability discount @ 10%	($ 800,000)
Value of the Company's Common Stock	$ 7,200,000

ASSUMPTIONS AND STATEMENT OF LIMITING CONDITIONS

The valuation is subject to the following assumptions and limiting conditions:

Legal, Tax or Accounting Advice: No opinion, counsel or interpretation is intended in matters that require legal, tax, accounting or other appropriate professional advice. It is assumed that such opinions, counsel or interpretations have been or will be obtained from the appropriate professional sources.

The valuator assumes no responsibility for matters of a legal nature affecting the property appraised, nor is any opinion of title rendered.

No opinion of the tax consequences resulting from a possible sale or transfer is expressed by Verité Forensic Accounting, LLC.

Future Services: Future services regarding the subject matter of this valuation report, including but not limited to, testimony or attendance in court, shall not be required of Verité Forensic Accounting, LLC unless previous arrangements have been made therefore in writing.

The valuator is not required to give testimony in court or be in attendance during any hearings or depositions with reference to the matters herein stated, directly or indirectly, unless prior satisfactory arrangements have been made with valuator.

Limitation of Projections: Some assumptions inevitably will not materialize, and unanticipated events and circumstances may occur. Therefore, the actual performance in any areas forecasted/projected will vary from the forecast/projection, and the variations may be material. Verité Forensic Accounting, LLC will not express any form of assurance on the likelihood of achieving the forecast/projection or on the reasonableness of the used assumptions. Any such forecast/projection is presented as part of the valuation and is not intended to be used separately.

Independence and Objectivity: In accordance with recognized professional ethics, the professional fee for this service is not contingent upon our conclusion of value, and neither Verité Forensic Accounting, LLC nor any of its employees has a present or intended financial interest in the Company.

The fee for this report is for the expressed opinion of value on the appraisal's effective date, without warranties or guarantees as to the outcome at any future date, or any contrary opinion of value as of the same date.

Limited Purpose and Date: The opinion of value expressed herein is valid only for the stated purpose and date of the valuation.

Entity Supplied Information: Financial statements and other information provided by the Entity or its representatives in the course of this investigation have been accepted, without further verification, as correctly reflecting the Entity's business conditions and operating results for the respective periods, except as specifically noted herein.

The valuation report, relying upon management's representations, assumes there are no litigious, regulatory compliance, environmental hazard, or similar problems. Therefore, no representations or warranties are expressed or implied regarding such conditions and no consideration has been given, within this report, to the possible effects of any such conditions.

The valuation is based upon information obtained from sources that, with exceptions as noted herein, the valuator believes to be reliable. However, the valuator has not made a specific effort to confirm the validity of any of the information, and accordingly, its accuracy or completeness cannot be guaranteed. Had procedures to independently confirm representations made to the valuator, been performed, significant matters that would alter the amounts used in the determination of the final valuation might have come to the attention of the valuator.

Public Information Used: Public information and industry and statistical information are from sources we deem to be reliable; however, we make no representation as to the accuracy or completeness of such information and have accepted the information without further verification.

If Sold, Sale Price Mav Be Different: The opinion of value expressed within this valuation report is applicable only to the type of value stated within the report, and then only based upon the referenced definition of that type of value. Should this valuation be based upon Fair Market Value, that value assumes a hypothetical sale, and unless stated otherwise, an all-cash sale. Any actual transaction may be concluded at a price that is higher or lower than the opinion of value, depending upon the circumstances of the actual transaction. Such circumstances should include, but not be limited to, changes in the economy, leveraging, cost of capital, the parties' individual perception of risk, knowledge, motivation, negotiating skills, quality of counsel, and other individual or interrelated factors.

Related Party Transactions: The Company has no related party transactions. We have relied upon management's representations that this is the case.

Business Expansion: We have been informed that the Company does plan to expand the business a small amount but that the business will not start any new operations. Accordingly, we have considered future plans of the business in our valuation. We have assumed that the existing facility will operate a little more than the current levels into the foreseeable future.

Other Assumptions and Limiting Conditions within the Report: This report is further subject to any other contingencies, assumptions, and limiting conditions that may be set out elsewhere within this report.

Environmental Issues: Regarding any real properties owned or leased by the subject business, we have not undertaken to discover any toxic substances or other environmental hazards which may exist at any of the properties. Such investigation is beyond the scope of this valuation and outside the scope of our expertise.

Management Continuation: The conclusions are based upon the assumption that present management would continue to maintain the character and integrity of the enterprise through any sale, reorganization, or diminution of the owners' participation.

Restricted Use: This valuation report and the conclusions arrived at herein are for the exclusive use of our client. Furthermore, the letter and conclusions are not intended by the author, and should not be construed by the reader, to be investment advice in any manner whatsoever. The conclusions reached herein represent the considered opinion of Verité Forensic Accounting, LLC based upon information furnished to them by the Company and other sources. The extent to which the conclusions and valuations arrived at herein should be relied upon, should be governed and weighted accordingly.

While the client has not informed Verité Forensic Accounting, LLC of any intent to do so, any third parties to whom this report is shown may be assured that this report, while performed in the employ of the client, was materially prepared on a nonadvocacy basis. Any third persons, however, are cautioned that Verité Forensic Accounting, LLC has no duty to you and, therefore, no warranty is expressed or implied. Nothing in this report is intended to replace your independent sole judgment, due diligence, or decision to seek professional legal, accounting, or valuation counsel.

This valuation was made and this valuation report has been prepared for the purpose and function stated herein. Neither the report nor the information it contains should be used for any other purpose or function, and they are invalid if so used. Neither this valuation nor any part of it shall be used in connection with any other valuation.

Publication of Report: Neither all nor any part of the contents of this valuation should be conveyed to the public through advertising, public relations, news, sales, mail direct transmittal, or other media, without the prior written consent and approval of Verité Forensic Accounting, LLC. No third parties are to be benefited.

Possession of this valuation report, or a copy hereof, does not carry with it the right of publication of all or any part of this report without the expressed written consent of the valuator and the client.

Next, I set out the qualifications of the valuation analyst (i.e. me).

STATEMENT OF QUALIFICATIONS OF VALUATION ANALYST

William L. Jennings, CPA/ABV, CFF, CFE, PI

William Jennings is the Managing Member of Verité' Forensic Accounting, LLC. He is responsible for providing forensic accounting, investigation and asset recovery services to corporations, government agencies, attorneys and their clients. Additionally, he offers business controls consulting services to organizations. When required, Mr. Jennings provides expert testimony about the results of his work.

With more than 30 years of experience in public accounting and auditing, forensic accounting, business valuation, investigation, asset recovery and business controls development, Mr. Jennings has worked on hundreds of forensic accounting and investigation assignments. He has been retained to conduct investigations by the Securities and Exchange Commission, the Justice Department and the U.S. Marshals Service. Mr. Jennings is a CPA/ABV, CFF, CFE and a licensed private detective. He is also a private pilot.

Mr. Jennings is a member of the Board of Directors for the Atlanta Women's Foundation. He is also a member of the Atlanta Chapter of the March of Dimes where he served as Chairman for the 2012 Walk for Babies.

Mr. Jennings has been a guest speaker at numerous industry events and educational forums in the United States and Europe. He has written many articles on the specialized field of forensic accounting and is currently writing a book due to be published in 2021.

Professional Certifications:

- Certified Public Accountant (CPA), Accredited in Business Valuation (ABV®)
- Certified in Financial Forensics (CFF®)
- Certified Fraud Examiner (CFE)
- Private Detective, Illinois

Professional Affiliations:

- American Institute of Certified Public Accountants (AICPA)
- Georgia Society of Certified Public Accountants (GSCPA)
- Association of Certified Fraud Examiners (ACFE)
- Institute of Internal Auditors (IIA)
- Atlanta International Arbitration Society (AtlAS)
- American Bar Association (ABA), Affiliated Professional, Criminal Justice Section

Education:

- Master of Business Administration – Auburn University
- Bachelor of Science, Accounting – University of New Orleans

Finally, I included my appendices and exhibits setting out the significant sources of information and calculation of factors used in the business valuation.

EXHIBIT A – Source of Information Relied Upon in this Valuation
January 31, XXXX

EXTERNAL DOCUMENTS

1) Federal Reserve Board Beige Book _____<DATE>
2) Industry Summary and outlook reports by Integra Information
3) Wall Street Journal
4) Duff & Phelps <DATE> Valuation Handbook-Guide to Cost of Capital

INTERNAL DOCUMENTS

5) Internal financial statements for Xxxxxxxxxx Xxxxxx Xxxxxxx for the years ended December 31, XXXX through December 31, XXXX and the one month ended January 31, XXXX.
6) Management's estimated fair market values of office/computer equipment, construction equipment, trucks/cars, and real property buildings and land.
7) Corporate by-laws and minutes.
8) Company History Summary
9) Sales reports by customer
10) Tax returns for Xxxxxxxxxx Xxxxxx Xxxxxxx for the years ended December 31, XXXX through December 31, XXXX.

We have relied on information from management or others without verification.

EXHIBIT B – Determination of the Capitalization Rate Using the Build-Up Method
Overall Capitalization Rate: One method used to develop a capitalization rate ("Build-Up Method") is to begin with a riskless rate of return and to add additional percentages for the identified risk factors. Using the Build-Up Method the riskless rate is increased for an equity risk premium, a specific company premium for size and other risk factors. The capitalization ratio is then determined by subtracting the expected long-term growth rate from the sum of the cumulative risk factors.

The risk-free rate of return is the return an investor could obtain from a low-risk guaranteed investment. Such a return is assumed to be approximately equal to the yield to maturity of long-term Treasury bonds even though this investment is not completely "risk-free".

The equity risk premium is the extra return required by an average investor in excess of the return on long-term Treasury securities. The primary source for obtaining the equity risk premium is Duff & Phelps Associates Stocks, Bonds, Bills and Inflation Yearbooks. The Duff & Phelps data is based upon market comparisons of equity risk premiums for stocks to long-term bonds and are based on arithmetic mean returns compiled from 1926-XXXX.

The risk premium for size relates to the difference in return an investor would expect between a large company and a small company. Again, the source for this data is the Duff & Phelps study which compares returns for small capitalized companies to larger stocks.

Other risk factors include the industry; financial risk such as leverage; consistency of earnings; diversification in terms of products, geographic location, customer base; and other operational characteristics such as key man issues and management depth and competence.

The expected average long-term growth rate is based on both price (inflationary) growth and volume (real) growth. The determination of the capitalization rate for Xxxxxxxxxx Xxxxxx Xxxxxxx is as follows:

Risk-free investment rate on 30-year long-term Treasury Bonds
as of December 31, XXXX.   3.0%
Equity risk premium- stock over bonds from Duff & Phelps   6.9%
Risk premium for size from Duff & Phelps   3.7%
Other risk factors   1.4%

Net cash flow discount rate:	15.0%
Less expected average growth:	(3.0%)
Net earnings capitalization rate for next year's earnings:	12.0%

SCHEDULES
Xxxxxxxxxx Xxxxxx Xxxxxxx

Schedule 1   (see Figure 11.21) Comparative Balance Sheets - December 31, XXXX – January 31, XXXX

Schedule 2   (see Figure 11.22) Comparative Income Statements - December 31, XXXX – January 31, XXXX

Schedule 3   (see Figure 11.23) Management fair market value estimates of office/computer equipment, construction equipment, trucks/cars, and real property buildings and land as of January 31, XXXX

Schedule 4   Real Estate Items in Schedule 3

Schedule 5   Deferred Taxes Payable

SCHEDULE 1 – Comparative Balance Sheets

	January 31	December 31	December 31	December 31	December 31	December 31	December 31
Cash	$ -	-	41,160	331,461	134,977	193,556	68,808
Accounts receivable, net	-	-	719,475	916,527	540,254	462,707	729,635
Inventory	-	-	1,800,654	1,605,055	1,160,069	1,031,520	978,520
Other receivables	-	-	268	-	-	-	-
Loans to Shareholders	-	-	178,352	209,552	226,352	-	-
State tax receivable	-	-	17,136	-	-	-	-
Total Current Assets	-	-	2,757,045	3,062,595	2,061,652	1,687,783	1,776,963
Land	-	-	197,295	197,295	197,295	197,295	197,295
Depreciable assets	-	-	5,213,021	5,203,020	4,324,987	4,113,122	3,841,854
Less accumulated depreciation	-	-	4,958,888	4,930,022	4,057,002	3,831,149	3,543,617
Net Property and Equipment	-	-	451,428	470,293	465,280	479,268	495,532
Total Assets	$ -	-	3,208,473	3,532,888	2,526,932	2,167,051	2,272,495
Accounts payable			727,780	566,392	459,723	345,778	456,305
State franchise & excise payable			-	25,081	17,053	11,624	12,491
Sales tax payable			48,015	58,268	36,003	43,452	46,691
Total Current Liabilities			775,795	649,741	512,779	400,854	515,487
Notes payable			1,090,731	1,315,616	600,000	610,000	360,000
Total Long Term Liabilities	-	-	1,090,731	1,315,616	600,000	610,000	360,000
Common stock			50,000	50,000	50,000	50,000	50,000
Additional paid-in capital			37,862	37,862	37,862	37,862	37,862
Retained earnings			1,254,085	1,479,669	1,326,291	1,068,335	1,309,146
Total Owners' Equity			1,341,947	1,567,531	1,414,153	1,156,197	1,397,008
Total Liabilities & Owners' Equity	$ -	-	3,208,473	3,532,888	2,526,932	2,167,051	2,272,495

FIGURE 11.21

SCHEDULE 2 – Comparative Income Statements

	January 31	December 31	December 31	December 31	December 31	December 31	December 31
Income							
Sales, net of returns	$ -	-	9,472,064	8,498,244	7,520,580	6,547,013	6,365,406
Cost of goods sold	-	-	6,869,131	5,345,964	5,082,542	4,312,992	4,621,073
Gross Profit	$ -	-	2,602,933	3,152,280	2,438,038	2,234,021	1,744,333
Expenses							
Compensation to officers			986,476	489,400	446,800	250,510	199,850
Other wages & salaries			835,372	743,169	683,891	639,704	641,163
Repairs & maintenance			84,903	42,385	87,684	44,723	61,939
Bad debts			114,354	-	6,309	8,982	7,497
Taxes & licenses			159,887	152,369	100,545	114,456	104,893
Interest expense			25,094	27,536	37,663	33,877	23,200
Depreciation expense			28,866	976,020	225,855	287,532	173,971
Insurance			121,168	122,312	114,802	126,855	124,414
Truck/car expenses			219,598	197,297	184,511	195,108	234,531
Office expense			163,145	111,572	97,706	86,267	57,978
Office supplies			11,016	15,645	1,910	1,983	13,826
Legal & professional			6,637	4,902	4,959	4,364	4,169
Garbage fee			2,247	2,034	2,046	1,881	1,498
Dues & subscriptions			1,303	-	-	-	-
Miscellaneous			19	2,230	5,086	-	699
Utilities			49,748	41,456	41,475	43,339	39,998
Total Expenses	$ -	-	2,809,833	2,928,327	2,041,242	1,839,581	1,689,626
Other Income							
Gain on sale of fixed assets	-	-	-	10,000	-	-	67,000
Miscellaneous income	-	-	-	156	8,982	58	24,265
Total Other Income	$ -	-	-	10,156	8,982	58	91,265
Earnings(loss) before income taxes	-	-	(206,900)	234,109	405,778	394,498	145,972
State income taxes expense	-	-	18,684	48,731	30,174	15,309	3,000
Net earnings (loss)	$ -	-	(225,584)	185,378	375,604	379,189	142,972
Distributions	-	-	-	32,000	117,648	620,000	124,000
Retained Earnings, BOY	-	-	1,479,669	1,326,291	1,068,335	1,309,146	1,290,174
Retained Earnings, EOY	$ -	-	1,254,085	1,479,669	1,326,291	1,068,335	1,309,146

FIGURE 11.22

SCHEDULE 3- **Management fair market value estimates of office/computer equipment, construction equipment, trucks/cars, and real property buildings and land as of January 31,** ■

2011 KW-W9	75,000	
Bulk Tanker 1	40,000	
Bulk Tanker 2	30,000	
Flatbed Trailer	15,000	
Fencing	10,000	
Hyster	7,000	
Total Block Yard $	177,000	177,000
Structure	1,200,000	
Office Equipment	50,000	
Computers	100,000	
Fixtures/shelves/racks	50,000	
Hardware Bldg/Office 60'x200x12 $	1,400,000	1,400,000
Warehouse (G,H) 150'x85x18 $	1,275,000	1,275,000
Mortar Bldg 65'x50x12 $	200,000	200,000
Side Sheds Break room,A,B,C,D 285'x40x16 $	855,000	855,000
Structure	200,000	
Fuel Tanks	15,000	
Racks	25,000	
Saw	5,000	
Wall Racks	20,000	
Total Trim Building 40'x65x16 $	265,000	265,000
Plant	850,000	
Cat Loader	40,000	
Bins	100,000	
Trk Front 1	240,000	
Trk Front 2	240,000	
Trk Front 3	240,000	
Trk Front 4	240,000	
Trk Rear 1	85,000	
Trk Rear 1	85,000	
Dump trk 1	65,000	
Dump trk 2	35,000	
Shop (70'x160x18)	420,000	
Heater House	50,000	
Tub Bldg (60'x60x16)	180,000	
Shop contents/parts	250,000	
Total Concrete Plant Facility $	3,120,000	3,120,000
Ford Tractor	5,000	
Moffett 1■	200,000	
Moffett 2■	150,000	
Moffett 3■)	65,000	
Ton 1	15,000	
Ton 2	15,000	
Freightliner	20,000	
Hyster 1	7,000	
Hyster 2	7,000	
Hyster 3	7,000	
■ Car	5,000	
Other Vehicles/Eqpt $	496,000	496,000
21 acres land	672,000	
Fencing	25,000	
Total Property $	697,000	697,000
Total: Prop/Bldgs/Trucks/Equip	**$ 8,485,000**	**8,485,000**

FIGURE 11.23

SCHEDULE 4 - Real Estate Items in Schedule 3

Hardware Building/Office	$ 1,400,000
Warehouse (G, H)	1,275,000
Mortar Building	200,000
Side Sheds Break Room	855,000
Trim Building	200,000
Property 21 Acres	697,000
Total Real Estate Items	4,627,000
Estimated Commission Rate	5%
Estimated Commission Cost	$ 231,350

SCHEDULE 5 - Deferred Taxes Payable

Estimated fair market value of final assets - Schedule 3	$ 8,485,000
Cost Basis - Schedule 1	(451,428)
Commissions on Real Estate - Schedule 4	(231,350)
Estimated Gain	7,802,222
Estimated Effective Federal and State Income Tax Rate	26.135%
Deferred Taxes Payable	$ 2,039,111

The preceding report, as part of my testimony, was used to quantify the remedy that was available to the plaintiff under state law. It is important to first understand what remedies are available under relevant laws before deciding on an approach to measure damages.

EXERCISES

1. Let's work through the following settlement model as shown in Table 11.14.

TABLE 11.14

Settlement Model

Assumptions:				
a) The amount at issue equals $100,000				
b) The plaintiff believes there is a 75% probability that the defendant will be held liable				
c) Litigation costs are expected to equal $10,000 for each party				
d) Both parties are risk neutral				
		Plaintiff		**Defendant**
Expected Outcome of Litigation:				
Risk Adjusted Value of Award		$		$

(Continued)

TABLE 11.14 (*Continued*)

Settlement Model

Costs	$	$
Expected Cost Recovery	$	$
Expected Total Risk Adjusted Outcome	$	$
Rational parties, in this instance, should settle at what amount?		

2. What are the legal standards that must be met for economic damages to be sustained?
3. What must you demonstrate to meet the loss causation standard?
4. What is reasonable certainty?
5. What is the economic loss doctrine?
6. How do you establish proximate cause?
7. How could you demonstrate foreseeability?
8. What would indicate a failure to satisfy the duty to mitigate?
9. What impact would a failure to mitigate have on plaintiff's economic damages?
10. What are the most common types of economic damages?
11. What is the first step should take in determining the available heads of economic damages and how to measure each one?
12. Who would you consult with take in determining the available heads of economic damages and how to measure each one?
13. As long as a contract is completely legal; where would you look first to determine the correct method to measure economic damages for a claim related to the contract?
14. What types of torts result in economic damages?
15. What does a tort damages award seek to do?
16. Where would you look to determine the methodology required to measure statutory damages?
17. CAVU Air Express (CAVU) enters into contracts with several medical equipment companies to deliver medical equipment to remote locations by air. Under the contracts CAVU is entitled to recover $1 per air mile per equipment package. Each flight typically hauls 10 equipment packages. CAVU's cost to cover aircraft maintenance, fuel, insurance, tie down, reserves, dead legs, and pilot compensation equal to $5 per air mile. Two CAVU employees, who have signed employment agreements prohibiting them from engaging in any non CAVU air transportation related activity, set up a company to refuel CAVU's planes at the destination airports. They buy fuel at $5 per gallon and re-sell it to CAVU at $8 per gallon. CAVU aircraft typically burn .20 gallons of fuel per mile. A typical flight covers 1,000 air miles. How much profit would CAVU earn on a typical flight? How much profit should CAVU have earned on a typical flight?
18. If you are a Certified Public Accountant/Accredited in Business Valuation, what standards are you required to follow in performing a business valuation in litigation?
19. Where would you look to determine the standard of value in a litigation matter? Who would you consult in making that determination?
20. How would an event that occurs after the valuation date, but before you issue your valuation report change the business valuation amount included in your report?

CHAPTER SUMMARY/KEY TAKEAWAYS

So, here are some things to think about:

- Explore settlement with the opposing party in a way that allows you to learn their perception of the strength of their position.
- First, you need to understand the type of remedy that is available in your matter.
- Next, you need to understand the legal standards you will need to satisfy in order to be able to recover economic damages.
- Then you need to identify all of the heads of damages that might represent recoverable economic damages.
- Then you need to identify the best techniques for measuring the economic damages.
- Finally, you must develop a clear and compelling way to communicate your work, conclusions, and opinions related to your measurement of economic damages.

In Chapter 12 you will learn how to present your findings and conclusions internally.

NOTES

1. https://www.nytimes.com/1985/12/19/business/how-texaco-lost-court-fight.html
2. http://www.willamette.com/insights_journal/18/summer_2018_1.pdf
3. http://www.willamette.com/insights_journal/18/summer_2018_1.pdf
4. http://www.willamette.com/insights_journal/18/summer_2018_1.pdf
5. http://www.willamette.com/insights_journal/18/summer_2018_1.pdf
6. http://www.willamette.com/insights_journal/18/summer_2018_1.pdf
7. http://www.willamette.com/insights_journal/18/summer_2018_1.pdf
8. http://www.willamette.com/insights_journal/18/summer_2018_1.pdf
9. http://www.willamette.com/insights_journal/18/summer_2018_1.pdf
10. http://www.willamette.com/insights_journal/18/summer_2018_1.pdf
11. http://www.willamette.com/insights_journal/18/summer_2018_1.pdf
12. AICPA Code of Professional Conduct, American Institute of Certified Public Accountants, Effective December 15, 2014, Updated for all official releases through March 2021, Copyright 2021 Sections 0.300.010, 0.300.020, 0.300.030, 0.300.040, 0.300.050, 0.300.060, 0.300.070. https://pub.aicpa.org/codeofconduct/Ethics.aspx
13. AICPA Statements On Standards For Valuation Services, VS Section 100, American Institute of Certified Public Accountants, Inc. Copyright 2015.
14. Statement on Standards for Consulting Services, American Institute of Certified Public Accountants, Inc., Copyright 2015.
15. Statements on Standards for Forensic Services (SSFSs) are issued by the Forensic and Valuation Services Executive Committee, Effective for engagements accepted on or after January 1, 2020, American Institute of Certified Public Accountants.
16. AICPA Statements On Standards For Valuation Services, VS Section 100, Copyright 2015. https://www.nytimes.com/1985/12/19/business/how-texaco-lost-court-fight.html

12 Presenting Findings and Conclusions Internally

In this chapter, we will talk about presenting your investigative findings internally to management and the board. These can be delicate and difficult communications. I will explain how to manage these interactions in ways that will help you to be successful. It's often the case that you will conduct an excellent investigation and have conclusions based on solid evidence but will encounter terrible difficulty in getting the people who most need to hear your findings to listen. I once worked on an audit committee investigation in which the audit committee refused to listen to the truth until the company's chief accounting officer was convicted in a federal criminal trial.

SECTION I: TO MANAGEMENT

Dear Reader, your own management can be the trickiest audience of all. There are several reasons for this. One is that if what you are investigating is internal misconduct, which misconduct happened on their watch, or worse, is connected to them somehow. Another is that management may have a business or social relationship with the target of the investigation. This situation triggers a strange response in human beings. It goes something like: if my colleague or friend is a criminal, what does that say about me? So, most people have to go through the five stages of grief: denial, anger (at you), bargaining, depression, and acceptance. This is because the revelation represents the death of the relationship. In virtually every case in which I have identified a person engaged in illicit conduct, I get the same reaction from their colleagues, "Sally can't possibly be involved in anything like that; I know her and she wouldn't do anything like that."

Let me tell you a story to illustrate this point:

It all started with a tragic accident and a heroic father laying down his own life to save his children. The president of a large mid-western engineering company, owned by an enormous European concern, had accompanied his two sons on a Cub Scout camping trip. They were canoeing alone one evening when the canoe suddenly capsized. The boys could not swim, and their father valiantly gave his life in order to push them to safety.

The European concern now had no leader for this important American asset. They conducted a search and came up with the perfect candidate for the position. His education and experience aligned exactly with their perception of what would be required to be successful in the position. He told them he was considering offers from other companies. Their need was so great that they decided to put together a compensation package offer, which included a generous signing bonus, that they believed no one else would match. The candidate, let's call him Mr. Deckard, accepted their offer.

The engineering company's key performance metrics began to decline almost immediately. The Europeans chalked it up to key managers still mourning the death of their friend and beloved leader. They also told themselves that this situation was to be expected due to transition period challenges for Mr. Deckard. However, quarter after quarter things got progressively worse. I was brought in shortly after Mr. Deckard's first employment anniversary to investigate the causes of the company's decline. A daunting task to be sure, but even the thousand-mile journey begins with one step. In this case, I focused first on what had changed at the point of the beginning of the company's decline. My preliminary evaluation revealed that just one thing had changed: the hiring of Mr. Deckard as president. So, the next step I took was to run an in-depth background check on Mr. Deckard.

The background check revealed some very disturbing things. First, none of the universities listed on Mr. Deckard's CV had any record of his attendance. Next, Mr. Deckard's experience included a

DOI: 10.1201/9781003121558-14

tour of duty in Vietnam as a helicopter pilot. Once again, the Army had no record of Mr. Deckard's service. At this point I stopped and contacted my client, the European general counsel, to inform him of these concerning findings. My client listened carefully and then told me that my background check results were most certainly incorrect.

Under the heading of: "clients may be incorrect, but they are always clients", I demurred. I told the general counsel that an in-depth background investigation could sometimes be incorrect and that if we had made a mistake, we would take full financial responsibility for it. I then asked what in our findings the general counsel knew to be incorrect. The general counsel responded that the information about Deckard's service as an Army helicopter pilot was clearly wrong; he went on to say that a number of employees of the engineering company had told him that they had seen Mr. Deckard in a History Channel episode devoted to Vietnam helicopter pilots. He said that they said that Mr. Deckard had been interviewed on camera for that episode. He said that they said that they were proud to work for a military hero. So, I asked, "Who are the employees who said this to you? He gave me their names. I interviewed each of them and was told that Mr. Deckard had paid each of them to spread that lie about his military service.

I shared this unfortunate information with the European general counsel. He accepted the findings and terminated Mr. Deckard. He asked me to conduct an exit interview with Mr. Deckard, which I agreed to do. Mr. Deckard would only agree to meet, for lunch, at the local Red Robin; yes, of course, I ordered the never-ending French fries; don't judge me.

Back to our story, Mr. Deckard looked me in the eye and, with a steady gaze and no hint of emotion, said, "So what, you got me. Tomorrow, maybe even today, I will be applying for my next position. You won't know where. So, you won't be there to warn anybody. Most companies don't check; I just don't respond to the ones that do. See you around." With that, he got up and walked out of Red Robin. I was struck by the sense that I had been speaking to a soulless machine that looks human and takes on human identities but is really not human. I have never heard anything more from or about Mr. Deckard. It's terrifying to think about what he might be employed at now: VP Engineering for Boeing; VP Engineering for Pacific Gas & Electric; I mean, who knows?

The moral of this story is simple: "Trust, but, verify." The Mr. Deckards of the world are always seeking to penetrate those organizations, which trust but do not verify; that is their job. Once inside, they are like a cancer which, if left untreated, can kill any organization. You may also want to have all senior officers, in your company, take the Voight-Kampff test.

I will tell you this story to prepare you for the internal backlash your work may trigger. Be prepared for it by being prepared. Make sure to keep potential conclusions within the investigation team only; no leaks. Only tell management conclusions that you can prove from the evidence.

It's very important that you communicate your findings and conclusions in a clear, simple compelling manner using actual evidence to support your findings whenever possible. This is definitely a situation where one picture is worth a thousand words.

Let me illustrate with an actual example from an internal investigation I conducted at a large privately held company. The CFO who later became president of the company set up a bank account with the company's name but his home address as the address of record for the account. He then proceeded to direct proceeds from the company's sales transactions and other cash collections to the fake account. Figures 12.1–12.13 trace one of those transactions from its inception through the funds, due to the company, being directed to the fake account he created.

Kahn Point Escrow
Transactions

Money from the Kahn Point Escrow Account to Mr. Feather

FIGURE 12.1

Kahn Point Escrow ███████ Letter

March 17, ████

Via Facsimile: ████████

████████████ LLC
████████████

Dear ████:

I enjoyed having a chance to have lunch with you and ████████ yesterday; nevertheless, I came away with some concerns. After meeting with our friend, Mr. ████████, these concerns became even more significant.

FIGURE 12.2

Kahn Point Escrow Letter

You also expressed concern that we ████████ perhaps were being over compensated (my term) for merely being a "broker". As I explained, I now have over $1,300,000 in cash in this transaction and have also agreed to reimburse ████████ for an additional $90,000. Hardly the position in which any self-respecting broker would put himself.

You also suggested that it might be appropriate for me to use some of the return that ████████ would receive from this development to perhaps compensate ████████ for the extension requested by ████. I indicated to you that I felt this was an unfair request. I also explained the $3,000,000 front-end fee would be used to buy out several of my partners that have absolutely no interest in being involved in a 10 to 15 year project.

I then will have the privilege of investing $6,000,000 in land that might not even have utilities and roads to it for another five years. Again, I do not wish to belabor the point, but this is hardly the role of a "broker". Incidentally, at ████████ the very upscale product I built on my 85 acres quite frankly set the tone for the entire community.

Further, the 3% kicker on lot sales would not even begin to come into play for at least another three to four years. If this overheated real estate market starts to cool down, then it could be considerably longer.

████, I will be putting a huge amount of my time and significant cash into this project over the next five to ten years. I sincerely feel I will earn every dollar I receive.

FIGURE 12.3

Kahn Point Escrow ███████ Letter

Nevertheless, the key to successful negotiations is that all parties come away feeling that they have made a good deal. I sincerely feel that we have now arrived at that point for everybody concerned. I think we need to put this deal to bed. Obviously, it is your call.

Needless to say, it is imperative that we hear from you as soon as possible.

As usual, my very best regards,

███████████

> However, I cannot find any document, beyond one draft agreement, that references ███████ or ███████ ultimately being a party to the Kahn Point Transaction.

███████

Attachment

FIGURE 12.4

Kahn Point Escrow Account Created Ahead of Closing on Sale

ASSIGNMENT AND ASSUMPTION AGREEMENT

THIS ASSIGNMENT AND ASSUMPTION AGREEMENT (the "Assignment") is made and entered into as of this 1st day of June, ████ by and between ██████ DEVELOPMENT, LLC, a ██████ limited liability company ("Assignor██████ PARTNERS, LLC, a ██████ limited liability company ("Assignee").

WITNESSETH

WHEREAS, Assignor and Assignee are parties to that certain Agreement of Purchase and Sale with an effective date of September 16, ████, as amended by that certain Letter Agreement dated December 20, ████, as further amended by that certain Modification Agreement dated January 7, ████ and as further amended by that Second Amendment dated January 26, ████ (collectively, the "Agreement") for the sale of certain property in ████ County (the "Property"), which Property has been acquired on this date by Assignee from Assignor; and

WHEREAS, Section 3.5 of the Agreement contemplates the assignment by Assignor to Assignee of the "Water and Sewer Agreement", as such term is defined therein; and

FIGURE 12.5

Kahn Point Escrow Account Created Ahead of Closing on Sale

4.   Escrow Funds. Pursuant to the Escrow Agreement attached hereto as Exhibit C, Assignor has delivered the sum of $5,000,000.00 ("Escrow Funds") to ███████████ County ("Escrow Agent"). Upon (i) receipt of the consent of ███ County to the assignment of the Water and Sewer Agreement to Assignee, or (ii) the execution by Assignee (or its assigns or designees) of another agreement with ███ County (or another governmental entity) containing comparable terms whereby water and sanitary sewer service is provided for the benefit of the Property, Assignor shall advise Escrow Agent of the same and the Escrow Funds shall be released to Assignor in accordance with the terms of the Escrow Agreement. Assignor and Assignee agree that, in the event Assignor and Assignee determine it is necessary and appropriate to bring a suit against ███ County to compel ███ County to grant its consent to the assignment herein or to otherwise enter into a substitute water and sewer service agreement for the benefit of the Property, Assignor will fund the legal costs thereof (with counsel selected by Assignee) from the Escrow Funds and will direct Escrow Agent to pay legal invoices form the Escrow Funds. In the event that the conditions of clauses (i) or (ii), above, have not been satisfied on or before the date that is two (2) years after the date hereof, the Escrow Funds will be paid to Assignee.

FIGURE 12.6

Kahn Point Escrow Account Created Ahead of Closing on Sale

EXHIBIT C

ESCROW AGREEMENT

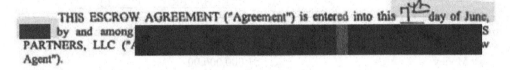

THIS ESCROW AGREEMENT ("Agreement") is entered into this 1ᵗʰ day of June, ███ by and among ███████████████████████████ S PARTNERS, LLC ("█████████████████████████████ w Agent").

WITNESSETH:

WHEREAS, Assignor and Assignee are parties to that certain Assignment and Assumption Agreement (the "Assignment") to which this Escrow Agreement is attached as Exhibit "C"; and

WHEREAS, the Assignment provides for the deposit of $5,000,000.000 to be held, invested and disbursed by Escrow Agent in accordance with the Assignment and this Agreement.

FIGURE 12.7

Kahn Point Escrow Not Part of Cash at Closing

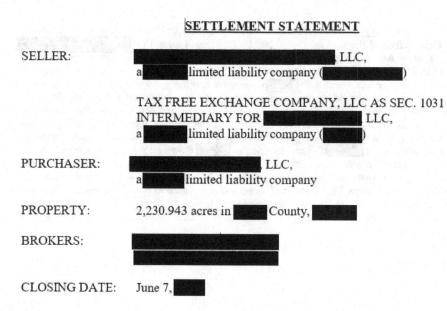

SETTLEMENT STATEMENT

SELLER: ███████████████████████, LLC,
                     a ███████ limited liability company (███████████)

                     TAX FREE EXCHANGE COMPANY, LLC AS SEC. 1031
                     INTERMEDIARY FOR ████████████ LLC,
                     a ███████ limited liability company (███████)

PURCHASER: ███████████████████, LLC,
                     a ███████ limited liability company

PROPERTY: 2,230.943 acres in ██████ County, ██████████

BROKERS: ███████████████████████

CLOSING DATE: June 7, ████████

FIGURE 12.8

Kahn Point Escrow Not Part of Cash at Closing

I.   PURCHASE PRICE AND PRORATIONS

	CREDIT TO PURCHASER	CREDIT TO SELLER
Purchase Price		$41,200,000.00
Earnest Money (See Item 2 below)	$1,000,000.00	
Proration of ████ taxes (See Item 3 below)	$ 9,576.38	
Reimbursement of all costs of the design, engineering and permitting of the Initial Plans pursuant to Section 3.3 of the Agreement		$ 100,000.00
Balance Due Seller	$40,290,423.62	
TOTAL	$41,300,000.00	$41,300,000.00

FIGURE 12.9

Kahn Point Escrow Not Part of Cash at Closing

II.   NET PROCEEDS TO SELLER

Balance Due Seller	$40,290,423.62

Transfer Tax to ▇▇▇ County for Deed to Purchaser	(41,200.00)
Transfer Tax to ▇▇▇ County for Deed to ▇▇	(753.18)
Recording Fees to ▇▇▇ County for Deed to ▇▇	(20.00)
Broker's Commission to ▇▇▇▇▇▇▇▇▇▇	(824,000.00)
Broker's Commission to ▇▇▇▇▇▇▇▇▇▇	(824,000.00)
Escrow Funds to ▇▇▇ Bank of ▇▇▇▇▇▇ Assignment and Assumption of Escrow Agreement	(5,000,000.00)
Attorney Fees to ▇▇▇▇▇▇▇▇	(22,500.00)

NET TO SELLER	$33,577,950.44

FIGURE 12.10

Kahn Point Escrow Not Part of Cash at Closing

Net to Seller disbursed as follows:

▇▇▇▇▇▇▇▇▇:

Wire Transfer to ▇▇▇▇▇▇	$30,220,155.39

▇▇▇:

Wire Transfer to Tax Free Exchange Company, LLC as Sec. 1031 intermediary for ▇▇▇ Holdings, LLC:	$ 3,357,795.05

FIGURE 12.11

Kahn Point Escrow Not Part of Cash at Closing

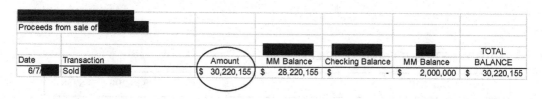

Date	Transaction	Amount	MM Balance	Checking Balance	MM Balance	TOTAL BALANCE
6/7/	Sold	$ 30,220,155	$ 28,220,155	$ -	$ 2,000,000	$ 30,220,155

FIGURE 12.12

Kahn Point Mr. Feather Letter to Bank

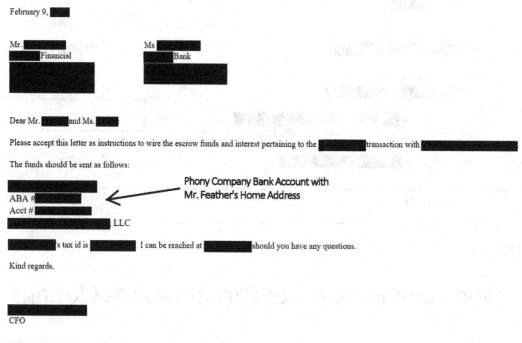

FIGURE 12.13

This was just one of the many transactions in which Mr. Feather directed the company's funds to his phony bank account and then used for personal purposes. What I wanted you to see is that communicating this unpopular information was very difficult and uncomfortable for everyone involved. So, I designed a presentation that was completely objective and based entirely on the actual evidence. It was simple, clear, and used pictures of the actual evidence to tell the story. I included very little narrative and no assumptions or opinions.

This allowed the viewers to react to the information without having to take sides. In order to get the central message of the presentation, you didn't have to for or against Mr. Feather. There was no opportunity for people to take sides. The evidence doesn't take sides. It is what it is and that is the way you need to use it to communicate a difficult message like the one above.

In situations where emotions are likely to run high and people are likely to take sides and entrench themselves in positions that are based on feelings and emotions, it is important for you to design your communications about your findings in ways that are not likely to allow your audience to do those things without first seeing the evidence. In earlier chapters, I described about strategically placing opinions first or early in the report to make sure the readers get those points before they lose attention span. Communicating findings to management requires the opposite approach. Take time to go, in detail, through the process and evidence before presenting conclusions.

SECTION II: TO AUDIT OR OTHER BOARD COMMITTEES

Communicating with the audit committee is an entirely different matter. Most people who serve on corporate boards do so because they really like the company and its management. But, they are keenly aware of their fiduciary responsibility to the shareholders they represent. My experience has been that audit committees can be fickle because of their allegiance to the company and management. They can be very resistant to evidence of wrongdoing in the beginning. They often have to go through the five stages of grief before they are able to accept the conclusions suggested by the evidence presented to them. On the other hand, I have worked for audit committees who embrace the investigation from the outset. Then there can be divided audit committees. I worked on an audit committee investigation where a number of the committee members were in denial and resisting the investigation. Then the head of the audit committee, a very powerful and well-known titan of industry, spoke up. In a booming voice, he shouted, "I do not have time for this horse... (i.e. poop). I want this investigated and I want it investigated now!" His colleagues quickly fell into line.

When making presentations to audit committees you must keep in mind that they are responsible for oversight of the company's financial reporting processes, the independent auditors, internal audit, compliance with legal, regulatory and company policy requirements, and whistleblower processes. However, their role is an oversight role; they do not participate in the operation of any of these processes. So, one of the first things you need to explain to the audit committee is how the conduct you are investigating was able to occur even though the various systems of control that they are responsible for were operating. This will often be because a senior member of management overrode the controls.

Remember though, that audit committee members have very positive feelings toward the company and its management. So, you may initially encounter the same denial and anger that you would encounter when presenting your findings to management. If this is likely to be the case, you should put together a presentation like the management presentation above. Let the evidence tell the story for you. You must be totally impartial regarding the evidence. You must remain a faithful witness to the truth, whatever that truth may be. You must convince the audit committee, through your actions and words, that you will be a reliable messenger communicating the evidence to them in a completely neutral manner. Do not be an alarmist; you must work, instead, to become the audit committee's trusted advisor.

The following is an example of a presentation I created and narrated in a huge internal investigation into management fraud (see Figures 12.14–12.22).

Hot Rod Ltd. Transactions

**Money from the Hot Rod Ltd. Deal Flows To and Through Entities and
Persons Related to Mr. Feather**

FIGURE 12.14

Hot Rod, Ltd. Owned by IndyCar

07/11/   01:23   905983519S   year ended: -03-31   PAGE 84

RELATED AND ASSOCIATED CORPORATIONS

This schedule is to be completed by a corporation having one or more of the following:
- related corporation(s)
- associated corporation(s)

Name [100]	Ctry of resi- dence [200]	Business Number (Note) [300]	Rela- tion- ship Code [400]	Number of common shares owned [500]	% of common shares owned [550]	Number of preferred shares owned [600]	% of pre- ferred shares owned [650]	Book value of capital stock [700]
	US NR		3	0	0.00	0	0.00	0
	US NR		1	0	0.00	0	0.00	0
	US NR		3	0	0.00	0	0.00	0

Note: Enter "NR" if a corporation is not registered.

Relationship code:
- Parent 2 - Subsidiary 3 - Associated 4 - Related, but not associated

The relationship code represents the relationship that the corporation named has to the filing corporation. For example, if the corporation is the parent corporation of the filing corporation, then the relationship code is "1".

Corporate Taxprep / Taxprep des sociétés - T2-03

Schedule 9

FIGURE 12.15

Hot Rod Ltd. Owned by IndyCar

Royalties deductible under Syncrude Remission Order **815** 0

Tax remitted under Syncrude Remission Order

Tax installments paid

Refund code **894** **1** Overpayment 226 **Total credits**

816 0
840 35,000
890 35,000

Balance (line A minus line B) 35,000 B
−226

If the result is negative, you have an overpayment.
If the result is positive, you have a balance unpaid.
Enter the amount on whichever line applies.
We do not charge or refund a difference of $2 or less.

Balance unpaid **896** 1 Yes [ ] 2 No [X] 0

Enclosed payment **898** 0

Direct deposit request

To have the corporation's refund deposited directly into the corporation's bank account at a financial institution in Canada, or to change banking information you already gave us, complete the information below:

[ ] Start [ ] Change information **910** Branch number

914 Institution number **916** Account number

If the corporation is a Canadian-controlled private corporation throughout the taxation year, does it qualify for the one-month extension of the date the balance of tax is due?

Certification

I **950** Last name in block letters **961** First name in block letters

am an authorized signing officer of the corporation. I certify that I have examined this return, including accompanying schedules and statements, and that the information given on this return is, to the best of my knowledge, correct and complete. I further certify that the method of calculating income for this taxation year is consistent with that of the previous year except as specifically disclosed in a statement attached to this return.

955 09-20 Date (yyyy/mm/dd) Signature of the authorized signing officer of the corporation

954 CHIEF FINANCIAL OFFICER Position, office, or rank

956 Telephone number

Is the contact person the same as the authorized signing officer? If No, complete the information below **957** 1 Yes [ ] 2 No [X]

958 Name in block letters

959 Telephone number

Language of correspondence - Langue de correspondance

990 Indicate the language of your choice.
Indiquer la langue de correspondance de votre choix.

1 English/Anglais [X] 2 Français/French [ ]

FIGURE 12.16

Hot Rod Ltd. Owned by IndyCar

87/11/   01:15   ■ CORPORATION INCOME TAX RETURN   PAGE 02

200
Code 0301

Do not use this area

CLIENT'S COPY

This form serves as a federal, provincial, and territorial corporation income tax return, unless the corporation is located in ■ If the corporation is located in one of these provinces, you have to file a separate provincial return.

Parts, sections, and paragraphs mentioned on this return refer to the *Income Tax Act*. This return may contain changes that had not yet become law at the time of printing. If you need more information about items on the return, see the corresponding items in the ■ *Corporation – Income Tax Guide* ■

Send one completed copy of this return, including schedules and the *General Index of Financial Information* (GIFI), to your tax services office or tax centre. You have to file the return within six months after the end of the corporation's taxation year. For more information on when and how to file ■ returns, see items 1 to 5 in the guide.

Identification

Business Number (BN)   ....   001 ■

Corporation's name

502 ■

Has the corporation changed its name since the last time we were notified?   ......   003 □ 1 Yes   X 2 No

Address of head office
Has the address changed since the last time we were notified?   ......   010 □ 1 Yes   X 2 No

011 ■
012 City ■

015 Country (other than) ■

Province, territory, or state

018 Postal code/ZIP code ■

017 ■

Mailing address (if different from head office address)
Has the address changed since the last time we were notified?

020 □ 1 Yes   X 2 No

021 ■
022 ■
023 City ■

026 Province, territory, or state ■

028 Postal code/ZIP code ■

027 US. Country (other than) ■

Location of books and records

If Yes, do you have a copy of the articles of amendment? ......   004 □ 1 Yes   □ 2 No

To which taxation year does this return apply?

Taxation year start   Taxation year-end

050 04-01   061 03-31
YYYY/MM/DD   YYYY/MM/DD

Has there been an acquisition of control to which subsection 249(4) applies since the previous taxation year?   063 □ 1 Yes   X 2 No

If Yes, give the date control was acquired   065 ___ YYYY/MM/DD

Is the corporation a professional corporation that is a member of a partnership?   067 □ 1 Yes   X 2 No

Is this the first year of filing after:

Incorporation?   ......   070 □ 1 Yes   X 2 No
Amalgamation?   ......   071 □ 1 Yes   X 2 No

If Yes, complete and attach Schedule 24.

Has there been a windup of a subsidiary under section 88 during the current taxation year?   072 □ 1 Yes   X 2 No

If Yes, complete and attach Schedule 24.

Is this the final taxation year before

FIGURE 12.17

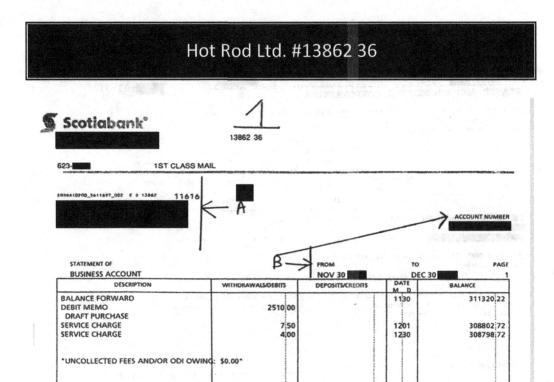

FIGURE 12.18

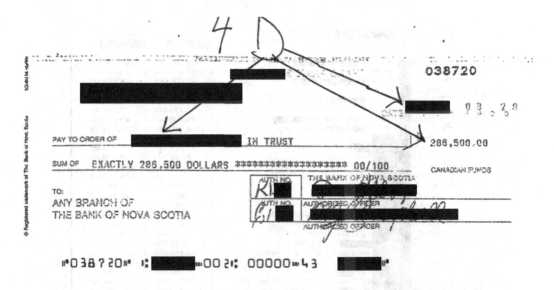

FIGURE 12.19

Hot Rod, Ltd. Owned by IndyCar

07/11/   01:23   9859835195   PAGE 04
ELATED AND ASSOCIATED CORPORATIONS   Year Ended: -03-31

iis schedule is to be completed by a corporation having one or more of the following:
· related corporation(s)
· associated corporation(s)

me [100]	Ctry of resi- dence [200]	Business Number (Note) [300]	Rela- tion- ship Code [400]	Number of common shares owned [500]	% of common shares owned [550]	Number of preferred shares owned [600]	% of pre- ferred shares owned [650]	Book value of capital stock [700]
	US NR		3	0	0.00	0	0.00	0
	US NR		1	0	0.00	0	0.00	0
	US NR		3	0	0.00	0	0.00	0

te: Enter "NR" if a corporation is not registered.
lationship code:
- Parent 2 - Subsidiary 3 - Associated 4 - Related, but not associated

e relationship code represents the relationship that the corporation named has to the filing
rporation. For example, if the corporation is the parent corporation of the filing corporation,
en the relationship code is "1".

chedule 9

Corporate Taxprep / Taxprep des sociétés - TP-09

FIGURE 12.20

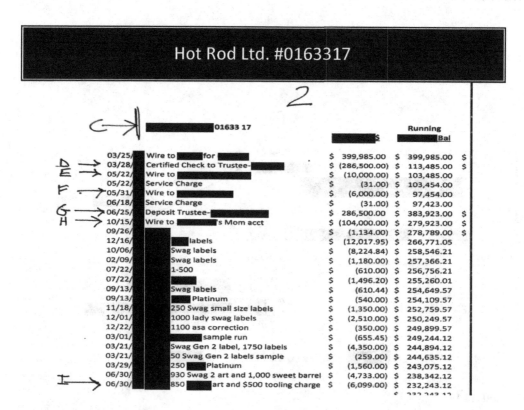

FIGURE 12.21

Payments to the Holmes (Batco GM's Family) and Batco Supplier Ballco

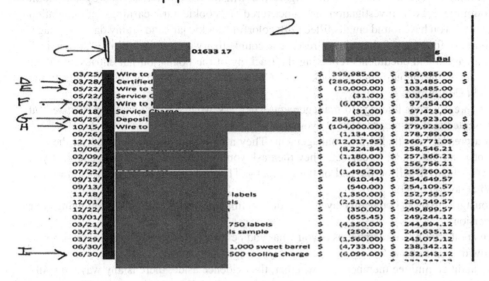

03/25/	Wire to	$	399,985.00	$ 399,985.00 $
03/28/	Certified	$	(286,500.00)	$ 113,485.00 $
05/22/	Wire to	$	(10,000.00)	$ 103,485.00
05/22/	Service C	$	(31.00)	$ 103,454.00
05/31/	Wire to	$	(6,000.00)	$ 97,454.00
06/18/	Service Charge	$	(31.00)	$ 97,423.00
06/25/	Deposit	$	286,500.00	$ 383,923.00 $
10/15/	Wire to	$	(104,000.00)	$ 279,923.00 $
09/26/		$	(1,134.00)	$ 278,789.00 $
12/16/		$	(12,017.95)	$ 266,771.05
10/06/		$	(8,224.84)	$ 258,546.21
02/09/		$	(1,180.00)	$ 257,366.21
07/22/		$	(610.00)	$ 256,756.21
07/22/		$	(1,496.20)	$ 255,260.01
09/13/		$	(610.44)	$ 254,649.57
09/13/		$	(540.00)	$ 254,109.57
11/18/	labels	$	(1,350.00)	$ 252,759.57
12/01/	els	$	(2,510.00)	$ 250,249.57
12/22/		$	(350.00)	$ 249,899.57
03/01/		$	(655.45)	$ 249,244.12
03/21/	750 labels	$	(4,350.00)	$ 244,894.12
03/21/	ls sample	$	(259.00)	$ 244,635.12
03/29/		$	(1,560.00)	$ 243,075.12
06/30/	1,000 sweet barrel	$	(4,733.00)	$ 238,342.12
06/30/	500 tooling charge	$	(6,099.00)	$ 232,243.12

FIGURE 12.22

The preceding was one of many acquisition and other transactions that the CFO diverted to his personal benefit and that of his cronies. Notice that most of the presentation slides contain pictures of the actual evidence. The sparse narrative I include is there only to explain how the pieces of evidence fit together. My oral narrative during the presentation was limited to further explanatory remarks and answering audit committee member questions. My answers to their questions were based on the facts contained in the evidence; I offered no opinions, feelings, suspicions, etc. It was the facts; just the facts. In this way the audit committee members could process the evidence in a space free from my intervention. They could ask questions and use what they learned to come to their own conclusions. I was simply the messenger and trusted advisor making sure that they had accurate information to use in making their decisions.

EXERCISES

1. Why can presenting internal investigation findings to management be difficult?
2. How do people often react to learning that a colleague may have committed a criminal act? Why do they react in that way?
3. What are the five stages of grief?
4. How do people work through them?
5. Should you do attempt to guide them through the five stages?
6. What is the best approach to presenting internal investigations that are bad news to management?
7. How can you sidestep management's initial negative reactions to your findings?
8. Why do people typically agree to serve on boards of directors?
9. How do audit committee members often react initially to negative Audit Committee investigation findings? Why?
10. What is the best way to present the results of your investigation to board members?

11. What should you tell them, early on, if true?
12. What must you become to the board members you are serving?
13. Let's assume a whistleblower has filed a credible complaint that reached the Audit Committee. You are asked to investigate the whistleblower's allegations by the Audit Committee. Your investigation has uncovered a "cookie jar" earnings manipulation scheme. You have found emails filled with colorful "cookie jar" and "rainy day" language. You have found journal entries to reserve accounts that were used to fill the "cookie jar." You have found documents reflecting the tracking of the bogus journal entries and their impact on the amounts in the "cookie jar." Construct a presentation of your findings to the Audit Committee.
14. You present your findings to management. They ask what you believe the evidence you presented to them means. How do you answer?
15. You present your findings to management. They accept your findings, based on the evidence you presented, as correct. They then ask you to bury your findings because, if you reveal them, it will be the end of the company. They ask you to be a good team player. What do you do?
16. You agree to be a good team player. How do you imagine events will unfold following your decision?
17. An audit committee member asks you what you believe your investigation has uncovered. How do you respond?
18. An audit committee member asks whether, the evidence aside, there is any way we could interpret this as not a violation of law or company policy. How do you respond?

CHAPTER SUMMARY/KEY TAKEAWAYS

So, here are some things to think about:

- Remember, when communicating your findings to management, keep in mind that they will often be initially resistant to any negative findings because the conduct occurred on their watch and, even worse, they may be implicated in the conduct.
- No one wants to believe that a work colleague or friend is a criminal. That is because they believe that, if true, it would reflect negatively on their own character.
- Management and colleagues will often have to work through the five stages of grief before they will be open to objectively process the evidence. Give them the space to do that.
- Board members normally agree to serve because they really like the company and its management.
- Board members often have to work through the five stages of grief, also, before they will be open to objectively process the evidence. Create a communication style that allows them to do that. Be a trusted advisor. Let the evidence speak to them directly. Let them process the evidence and reach their own conclusions.

In Chapter 13, you will learn how to present your findings and conclusions to law enforcement.

13 Presenting Findings and Conclusions to Law Enforcement

The following are excerpts from a speech recently given by FBI Director Christopher Wray:

"Fordham University—FBI International Conference on Cyber Security
New York City, New York
January 28, 2021

The FBI and the Private Sector: Battling the Cyber Threat Together

New Cyber Strategy

At the FBI, we've been fighting the cyber threat for many years now. We began our early high-tech crime effort in the mid-1990s, and created our Cyber Division almost 20 years ago, in 2002. We've become known for our efforts to call out destabilizing and damaging cyber activity by nation-state actors, like the indictment last summer of two hackers working on behalf of the Chinese Ministry of State Security, stealing intellectual property from companies in the U.S. and around the world while also targeting dissidents who spoke out against the Communist Party. And the charges we announced last fall against the Russian intelligence officers behind the most destructive cyber campaign ever perpetrated by a single group, including the NotPetya and Black Energy attacks.

But we're also focused on the threat posed by cyber criminals. Schemes like ransomware have caused disruption and financial loss for many years, but today they've escalated to a whole new level—shutting down schools, interrupting key government services, crippling hospitals, and threatening critical infrastructure.

We've put our new cyber strategy in place to stay ahead of this ever-evolving threat landscape. Our goal is to impose risk and consequences on bad actors in cyberspace—whoever and wherever they are. We want to make it harder and more painful for hackers and criminals to do harm. And the way we're doing that is by leveraging our unique authorities, our world-class capabilities, and our enduring partnerships—and using all three in service to the larger cyber community.

It's a shift in mindset, focused on impact. We've got to change the cost-benefit calculus of both criminals and nation-states who believe they can compromise U.S. networks, steal U.S. financial and intellectual property, and put our critical infrastructure at risk—all without incurring any risk themselves.

Our sharpened focus on leveraging our partnerships is key. We might forego a law enforcement action, like an arrest or an indictment, if we can hit the threat harder another way. Information from our investigations gives Treasury officials the means to cut criminals off from the global financial system. It gives our global law enforcement partners the means to seize malicious infrastructure, and locate and arrest criminals hiding over in their jurisdictions. And, vitally, that information arms private sector network defenders around the world with technical indicators they need to protect their companies, as well as the ability to shut down criminal infrastructure and kick bad guys off their platforms and networks.

DOI: 10.1201/9781003121558-15

It doesn't matter whose action leads to that impact. What matters is that we're working together to ensure safety, security, and confidence, for all of us, in our digitally connected world.

Focus on Partnerships

The best way to understand our commitment to working through partners is to look at the institutions we've built to drive that cooperation. We've created unique hubs where members of the cyber community can work alongside each other and build long-term relationships. We're working to build an atmosphere of trust and collaboration, the kind that only comes from sitting across the table from someone you know and really hashing things out.

Within government, that hub is the National Cyber Investigative Joint Task Force, the NCIJTF. Led by the FBI, the NCIJTF includes more than 30 co-located agencies from the Intelligence Community and law enforcement. We've pushed a significant amount of our own operational and analytical capabilities into the NCIJTF to strengthen its role as a core element of this nation's cyber strategy. And last year we invited senior executives from other agencies to lead new threat-focused mission centers there. We also refocused the NCIJTF itself, so that it now coordinates multi-agency campaigns to combat the most significant cyber threats and adversaries.

But we know that government can't do it alone. This fight requires a whole-of-society approach—government and the private sector, working together against threats to our national security and our economic security.

That's why we're co-located with partners in industry, academia, and the financial sector as part of the National Cyber-Forensics and Training Alliance in both Pittsburgh and New York City—not just sharing between government and private sectors, but helping our private sector partners share among themselves, too.

It's why we created another hub to work with and facilitate cybersecurity collaboration among the defense industry, the National Defense Cyber Alliance, where experts from the FBI and cleared defense contractors sit together, sharing intelligence in real time. **And it's why agents in every single FBI field office now spend a huge amount of time going out to companies and universities in their area, establishing relationships before there's a problem, and providing threat intelligence to help prepare defenses.**

That includes information we've obtained from sensitive sources. Now, I'm sure you can appreciate there are times when we can't share as much as we'd like to, but we're working to get better and smarter about that, too. We might not be able to tell you precisely how we knew you were in trouble. **But we can usually find a way to tell you what you need to know to prepare for, or stop, an attack.**

And having a pre-existing relationship with a company or university invariably helps us do that faster. Talking with us before a problem strikes helps you understand how we actually operate, how we protect information provided by victims who face challenges on a whole bunch of fronts in the wake of a major intrusion, and how we work hard not to disrupt their operations. That kind of information is a lot easier to digest when things are calm, rather than in the midst of a crisis. It helps you better understand how we can help. For example, victims often ask us to flag their assistance for regulators like the FTC, the SEC, and state AGs, and when asked we're happy to do so.

Ideally, we can create a flow of information that runs both ways, so we can get helpful information from you, too. We may come to a victim knowing one IP address used to attack them, but not another. If they tell us about the second one, not only can we do more to help them, but we may be able to stop the next attack, too. And we're committed to giving you feedback on what you share with us.

We're in this together, with all our partners. We all face the same dangers, and we won't make any headway if we're each off doing our own thing, instead of working in unison.

Our Unique Capabilities

Just as important as our commitment to partnership is what we bring to those who work with us. Given the gravity of the cyber threats we face, the government employs a whole ecosystem against them. And at the FBI, we play a central, core role in that ecosystem because we offer an unmatched range of abilities.

The FBI is both a law enforcement agency and an intelligence agency—with the range of authorities, capabilities, and relationships to match. Within the U.S. cyber ecosystem, the FBI uses our dual role to focus on threats. Not just investigating discrete incidents, but making it our business to understand who and where our cyber adversaries are, how they operate, and how we can weaken them.

We're collecting and sharing intelligence from an enormous range of sources, to create opportunities for our domestic and international partners, making the most of our strong presence here at home and abroad.

We've got cyber squads with interagency partners in every FBI field office, and cyber agents in embassies around the world, working with both foreign law enforcement and intelligence services.

We've got a rapid-response force, our Cyber Action Team, ready to respond to major incidents anywhere, anytime.

And we're leveraging our decades of experience across the FBI. For example, our Counterintelligence Division is filled with experts in combating a wide range of foreign intelligence threats on U.S. soil. Our Counterterrorism Division helps us anticipate how terrorists might develop the skills and plans to harm us virtually. And our Criminal Investigative Division helps us stop massive online criminal schemes and syndicates.

We're taking all these tools and bringing them to the table to share, because a win for you is a win for us. And anything we can do—together—to put the bad guys on their heels is a victory.

Battling the Threat, Together

With all that in mind, I'd like to illustrate what our strategy looks like in practice, and how we're attacking some of the most dangerous threats on the cyber front.

Against the cyber criminal threat, just in the last 36 hours, we and our international partners announced coordinated disruptions of the vast Emotet criminal botnet. As many of you know, Emotet has for years enabled criminals to push additional malware onto victim networks in critical sectors like healthcare, e-commerce, technology, and government. Emotet is one of the longest running and most pervasive malware delivery services out there. And even more dangerous than that suggests, because it frequently opens the door to the TrickBot Trojan, Ryuk ransomware, and the financial and operational devastation those tools increasingly cause together.

With Europol, national partner services across Europe, and a number of providers, we used the detailed technical information obtained through our investigation to interrupt the botnet administrators' control of their own servers. Applying lessons learned from disruptions of earlier botnets, we broke the server control chain at multiple levels—making it harder and slower for the botnet administrators to regain control. It's the kind of disruption that demands cooperation—Emotet, like other major ransomware threats, spans the globe—and one with immediate, significant benefits for our whole community.

To take another example, the blended threat of state-sponsored economic espionage facilitated by cyber intrusions continues to grow. And we're deploying our own and our partners' tools against it, sequenced and synchronized, for maximum impact.

In September we unsealed charges against five Chinese nationals from the hacking group we call APT 41. They were targeting victim companies around the world from their safe haven in China. With our partners here and abroad, we arrested two of their co-conspirators in Malaysia, and seized or took down hundreds of the hackers' accounts, servers, and domains. We also distributed a FLASH to our private sector and foreign partners with technical information to help detect and mitigate APT 41's malicious activities.

On the Russia front, last year we and our partners at NSA uncovered and exposed highly sophisticated malware developed by Russian military intelligence. We used criminal process to get information that helped us better understand that malware, complementing the great work our fellow intelligence community colleagues at NSA had done. That information allowed us to release an unclassified report to warn the right people, and that public release was a painful disruption to a well-known adversary. It imposed a real cost on Russia, because they'd spent a lot of time and money developing the malware we outed.

Elsewhere on the same front, we're working nonstop on the SolarWinds investigation through a task force, the Unified Coordination Group, with CISA and ODNI, and with support from NSA. As the lead agency for threat response, the FBI's investigation is concentrating on identifying additional victims, collecting evidence, analyzing the evidence to determine further attribution, and sharing results with our government and private sector partners to inform operations, the intelligence picture, and network defense.

Responding to Your Needs

The way we do business today—and so many of the changes we've made to our strategy—are a product of our work with you. We've been listening to your concerns and to your suggestions, and we've taken them to heart. We've shifted the way we think and the way we operate so that we can make a more significant impact on our adversaries. We've taken steps to work better with our partners at every level. From vastly increasing our information sharing with the private sector, to being as unobtrusive as possible when we come out to work with a company, to placing some of our cyber agents at desks right next to their foreign counterparts to make it even easier to collaborate.

We've been listening to what our partners say they need and focusing more on meeting those needs, and all those efforts are paying off. But where do we go from here?

What can we do this year so that when I come back to Fordham again, I can talk about the next evolution in our work with you? That back-and-forth starts with building those before-the-storm relationships with us that I talked about earlier. Any suggestions you have for us will help us be a better partner to you, and to who knows how many others out there who might appreciate the same improvement.

We've got to keep improving our understanding of where we're each coming from. The U.S. government learned after 9/11 that we had no choice but to work together. The threat posed by international terrorist organizations was so large and looming that we had to combine all our resources, our experiences, and our tools.

The same is true of the cyber threat. We knew the government had to do a better job of working together—and we are. Now we have to focus our efforts at working better with you in the private sector, every single day. And that's one of my top priorities.

You may have heard what former Defense Secretary Mattis used to say about the Marine Corps—there's "no better friend, no worse enemy" than the U.S. Marines. We've adopted a similar mentality. **People should be able to say "there's no better partner" than the FBI.** We want that to be the case for all our partners—especially those counting on us to help protect them. We want you to turn to us because there's no better partner in this common fight."[1]

SECTION I: FACTORS TO CONSIDER IN DECIDING TO GO TO LAW ENFORCEMENT

I begin with Director Wray's speech to illustrate that the government wants to work with your company to prevent and investigate high priority crimes like cyber-crimes. With the recent ransomware attacks on pipelines, food processors, financial institutions, and many more, the threat represented by these crimes is great. Also, the resources you would need to investigate these crimes may not be available or might not make sense financially. The FBI wants to be your partner in addressing these crimes. Perhaps it would make sense to take them up on their offer. Recall our discussion of managing risks in Chapter 2? This is a risk that you may want to transfer some portion to the FBI. As you can see, they have awesome international resources at their disposal, armies of personnel expert in investigating these crimes and their help costs you nothing. However, there are some downsides you need to consider. One is that when you get the FBI involved, they take control of the investigation. They also take control of the evidence. They also control the resolution strategy. This is true of any investigation where the government gets involved.

There are some situations where you have no choice. An example would be where you discover criminal conduct that must be reported (e.g. contraband found on an employee's computer). But, in most cases you have three choices: end the conduct (i.e. by terminating all actors involved in the criminal conduct) and move on, investigate the criminal conduct yourself, or get law enforcement involved.

These can be difficult decisions which are impacted by a variety of factors including: regulatory requirements (e.g. financial accounting and reporting fraud); severity of the damage caused by the criminal conduct; company core beliefs and policies; cost; brand image; and many others. The best resolution strategy is often in the eye of the beholder. This is why I always meet with the client before beginning the investigation and ask the following question: If this were to turn out exactly as you would like it to, what would that look like? I then ask them to describe their preferred outcome in as much detail as possible. The reason that I do that is to identify which path is most likely to deliver that result. The path chosen has significant implications for what happens during the investigation and litigation processes.

Reasons that you might decide to go to law enforcement are numerous. First, depending on the criminal conduct, you may be required to turn the investigation over to law enforcement. If, as a result of the conduct, your company has potential criminal liability you may be able to get credit for cooperating with law enforcement and prosecutors. This could be anything from a deferred prosecution agreement (i.e. the company is not prosecuted as long as it satisfies its cooperation requirements) to reduced penalties at sentencing. Next, you may need law enforcement to end the criminal conduct (i.e. bank robbery). Law enforcement may have resources you need to resolve your problem (i.e. international cyber-terrorism). You may not be able to conduct the investigation in a cost-effective manner. Reinforcing company values (i.e. we have zero tolerance for crime) may require prosecuting all criminals identified by the company. There are many other reasons that could cause you to seek law enforcement involvement.

Let's take a look at the reasons to go to law enforcement that are less discretionary. When are you required to get law enforcement involved? The main statute you must consider is Title 18 Section 4 Misprison of a felony:

"TITLE 18—CRIMES AND CRIMINAL PROCEDURE

§ 4. Misprison of a felony

Whoever, having knowledge of the actual commission of a felony cognizable by a court of the United States, conceals and does not as soon as possible make known the same to some judge or other person in civil or military authority under the United States, shall be fined under this title or imprisoned not more than three years, or both."[2]

I learned of a case where the CFO of a private company, which had significant bank debt, discovered that the CEO of the company was creating fraudulent purchases from a fictitious vendor he had created to skim money out of the company. The CEO was doing this because the covenants in the bank debt restricted the amount of compensation, dividends, or other distributions he could receive from the company annually. Before he blew the whistle, the CFO wanted to do his own investigation to gather the evidence necessary to prove his suspicions. The CFO chose not to consult counsel or employ any outside experts. During his investigation he continued to submit monthly financial information, required by the Company's loan covenants, to the bank that included the fraudulent transactions. He decided not to alert the bank until he completed his investigation. At the end of three months, he completed his investigation and called the bank to set up a meeting to present his investigative findings. The bank contacted the FBI who assigned an agent to the case. The investigation moved swiftly and the CEO ultimately plead guilty to bank fraud. The CFO was thanked for his cooperation. Several weeks later the CFO got a call from the same FBI agent who said that he, "Wanted to ask him some questions." The CFO agreed to meet. The CFO dutifully answered the FBI agent's questions truthfully and completely. The CFO was later indicted for misprison of a felony for not alerting the bank or authorities as soon as he became aware of the CEO's criminal conduct. Also, he'd continued to submit the company's fraudulent financial statements to the bank for three months. The CFO plead guilty and is out of prison, but has a felony on his record.

Originally, the misprison of a felony statute required you or your company to report a felony you learn about. Now, there is also a required element in which you must do something to conceal the felony from law enforcement in order to violate the statute. The concealment could be not responding completely and truthfully to a law enforcement officer's questions about the conduct.

That leads me to another section of Title 18. Section 1001 of Title 18 makes it a felony to make knowingly false or incomplete answers in response to questions asked by an agent of the federal government. This crime is punishable by five years in prison. I cannot tell you how many people I have encountered in my investigative career who got themselves into far worse trouble trying to hide their conduct than they would have by telling the truth to the federal agents who questioned them.

I would be remiss if I did not also mention Title 18 USC Section 1510—obstruction of justice.

"§1510. Obstruction of criminal investigations
(a) Whoever willfully endeavors by means of bribery to obstruct, delay, or prevent the communication of information relating to a violation of any criminal statute of the United States by any person to a criminal investigator shall be fined under this title, or imprisoned not more than five years, or both."[3]

INVESTIGATOR NOTES

There are actually a wide variety of ways in which you or others in your company could commit this crime. You could, for instance, hold a seminar in which you instruct your employees not to answer questions, posed by law enforcement agents, under penalty of dismissal. If federal agents arrive at your company's premises with a valid warrant, you could conceal documents or dismiss your employees with instructions to leave the building immediately. You could destroy records that are sought under a search warrant or grand jury subpoena. The list goes on and on. So, your company needs to retain the services of a highly trained and experienced attorney to make sure you never step on any of these land mines.

There are, of course, other situations, which, under federal or state law, require involving law enforcement. Once, again please consult a highly trained and experience lawyer in making these decisions.

Another reason you might want to cooperate with law enforcement is if your company, as a result of the conduct of employees, has potential criminal liability. Let's look at an excerpt from the US Justice Department's Principles of Federal Prosecution of Business Organizations to see how this may arise:

9-28.200—GENERAL CONSIDERATIONS OF CORPORATE LIABILITY

A. General Principle: Corporations should not be treated leniently because of their artificial nature nor should they be subject to harsher treatment. Vigorous enforcement of the criminal laws against corporate wrongdoers, where appropriate, results in great benefits for law enforcement and the public, particularly in the area of white collar crime. Indicting corporations for wrongdoing enables the government to be a force for positive change of corporate culture, and a force to prevent, discover, and punish serious crimes.

B. Comment: In all cases involving corporate wrongdoing, prosecutors should consider the factors discussed in these guidelines.[1] In doing so, prosecutors should be aware of the public benefits that can flow from indicting a corporation in appropriate cases. For instance, corporations are likely to take immediate remedial steps when one is indicted for criminal misconduct that is pervasive throughout a particular industry, and thus an indictment can provide a unique opportunity for deterrence on a broad scale. In addition, a corporate indictment may result in specific deterrence by changing the culture of the indicted corporation and the behavior of its employees. Finally, certain crimes that carry with them a substantial risk of great public harm—e.g., environmental crimes or sweeping financial frauds—may be committed by a business entity, and there may therefore be a substantial federal interest in indicting a corporation under such circumstances.

In certain instances, it may be appropriate to resolve a corporate criminal case by means other than indictment. Non-prosecution and deferred prosecution agreements, for example, occupy an important middle ground between declining prosecution and obtaining the conviction of a corporation. These agreements are discussed further in JM 9-28.1100 (Collateral Consequences). Likewise, civil and regulatory alternatives may be appropriate in certain cases, as discussed in JM 9-28.1200 (Civil or Regulatory Alternatives). When considering whether to enter into a non-prosecution or deferred prosecution agreement with the defendant, prosecutors should consider the interests of any victims and be aware that any fines collected under such agreements will not be deposited into the Crime Victims Fund, but will rather go to the General Fund of the Treasury. See JM 9-28.1400.

Prosecutors have substantial latitude in determining when, whom, how, and even whether to prosecute for violations of federal criminal law. In exercising that discretion, prosecutors should consider the following statements of principles that summarize the considerations they should weigh and the practices they should follow in discharging their prosecutorial responsibilities. Prosecutors should ensure that the general purposes of the criminal law—appropriate punishment for the defendant, deterrence of further criminal conduct by the defendant, deterrence of criminal conduct by others, protection of the public from dangerous and fraudulent conduct, rehabilitation, and restitution for victims—are adequately met, taking into account the special nature of the corporate "person."

---

[1] While these guidelines refer to corporations, they apply to the consideration of the prosecution of all types of business organizations, including partnerships, sole proprietorships, government entities, and unincorporated associations.

[revised July 2020]

9-28.210—FOCUS ON INDIVIDUAL WRONGDOERS

A. General Principle: Prosecution of a corporation is not a substitute for the prosecution of criminally culpable individuals within or without the corporation. Because a corporation can act only through individuals, imposition of individual criminal liability may provide the strongest deterrent against future corporate wrongdoing. Provable individual criminal culpability should be pursued, particularly if it relates to high-level corporate officers, even in the face of an offer of a corporate guilty plea or some other disposition of the charges against the corporation, including a deferred prosecution or non-prosecution agreement, or a civil resolution. In other words, regardless of the ultimate corporate disposition, a separate evaluation must be made with respect to potentially liable individuals.

Absent extraordinary circumstances or approved departmental policy such as the Antitrust Division's Corporate Leniency Policy, no corporate resolution should provide protection from criminal liability for any individuals. The United States generally should not release individuals from criminal liability based on corporate settlement releases. Any such release of individuals from criminal liability due to extraordinary circumstances must be personally approved in writing by the relevant Assistant Attorney General or United States Attorney.

B. Comment: It is important early in the corporate investigation to identify the responsible individuals and determine the nature and extent of their misconduct. Prosecutors should not allow delays in the corporate investigation to undermine the Department's ability to pursue potentially culpable individuals. Every effort should be made to resolve a corporate matter within the statutorily allotted time, and tolling agreements should be the rare exception. In situations where it is anticipated that a tolling agreement is unavoidable, all efforts should be made either to prosecute culpable individuals before the limitations period expires or to preserve the ability to charge individuals by tolling the limitations period by agreement or court order.

If an investigation of individual misconduct has not concluded by the time authorization is sought to resolve the case against the corporation, the prosecution authorization memorandum should include a discussion of the potentially liable individuals, a description of the current status of the investigation regarding their conduct and the investigative work that remains to be done, and, when warranted, an investigative plan to bring the matter to resolution prior to the end of any statute of limitations period. If a decision is made at the conclusion of the investigation to pursue charges or some other resolution with the corporation but not to bring criminal charges or civil claims against culpable individuals, the reasons for that determination must be memorialized and approved by the United States Attorney or Assistant Attorney General whose office handled the investigation, or their designees.

Under the doctrine of *respondeat superior*, a corporation may be held criminally liable for the illegal acts of its directors, officers, employees, and agents. To hold a corporation liable for these actions, the government must establish that the corporate agent's actions (i) were within the scope of his duties and (ii) were intended, at least in part, to benefit the corporation. In all cases involving wrongdoing by corporate agents, prosecutors should not limit their focus solely to individuals or the corporation, but should consider both as potential targets.

Agents may act for mixed reasons—both for self-aggrandizement (direct and indirect) and for the benefit of the corporation, and a corporation may be held liable as long as one motivation of its agent is to benefit the corporation. See *United States v. Potter*, 463 F.3d 9, 25 (1st Cir. 2006) (stating that the test to determine whether an agent is acting within the scope of employment is "whether the agent is performing acts of the kind which he is authorized to perform, and those acts are motivated, at least in part, by an intent to benefit the corporation."). In *United States v. Automated Medical Laboratories, Inc.*, 770 F.2d 399 (4th Cir. 1985), for example, the Fourth Circuit affirmed a corporation's conviction for the actions of a subsidiary's employee despite the corporation's claim that the employee was acting for his own benefit, namely his "ambitious nature and his desire to ascend the corporate ladder." *Id.* at 407. The court stated, "Partucci was clearly acting in part to benefit AML since his advancement within the corporation depended on AML's well-being and its lack of difficulties with the FDA." *Id.; see also United States v. Cincotta*, 689 F.2d 238, 241–42 (1st Cir. 1982) (upholding a corporation's conviction, notwithstanding the substantial personal benefit reaped by its miscreant agents, because the fraudulent scheme required money to pass through the corporation's treasury and the fraudulently obtained goods were resold to the corporation's customers in the corporation's name).

Moreover, the corporation need not even necessarily profit from its agent's actions for it to be held liable. In *Automated Medical Laboratories*, the Fourth Circuit stated:

[B]enefit is not a "touchstone of criminal corporate liability; benefit at best is an evidential, not an operative, fact." Thus, whether the agent's actions ultimately redounded to the benefit of the corporation is less significant than whether the agent acted with the intent to benefit the corporation. The basic purpose of requiring that an agent have acted with the intent to benefit the corporation, however, is to insulate the corporation from criminal liability for actions of its agents which may be inimical to the interests of the corporation or which may have been undertaken solely to advance the interests of that agent or of a party other than the corporation.

770 F.2d at 407 (internal citation omitted) (quoting *Old Monastery Co. v. United States*, 147 F.2d 905, 908 (4th Cir. 1945)).

[updated November 2018]

Notice the discussion of the doctrine of *respondeat superior* and the *Automated Medical Laboratories* above. These discussions make it clear that even if the employee engages in illegal conduct, which benefits the company, in order to receive increased compensation and/or promotions, personal benefits, the company is still criminally liable for the employee's illegal conduct.

In this situation it is usually a good idea to have the company cooperate with law enforcement. Let's take another look at an excerpt from the US Justice Department's Principles of Federal Prosecution of Business Organizations to see how this works:

9-28.300—FACTORS TO BE CONSIDERED
A. General Principle: Generally, prosecutors apply the same factors in determining whether to charge a corporation as they do with respect to individuals. See JM 9-27.220 et seq. Thus, the prosecutor must weigh all of the factors normally considered in the sound exercise of prosecutorial judgment: the sufficiency of the evidence; the likelihood of success at trial; the probable deterrent, rehabilitative, and other consequences of conviction; and the adequacy of noncriminal approaches. *See id.* However, due to the nature of the corporate "person," some additional factors are present. In conducting an investigation, determining whether to bring charges, and negotiating plea or other agreements, prosecutors should consider the following factors in reaching a decision as to the proper treatment of a corporate target:

1. The nature and seriousness of the offense, including the risk of harm to the public, and applicable policies and priorities, if any, governing the prosecution of corporations for particular categories of crime (see JM 9-28.400);

2. The pervasiveness of wrongdoing within the corporation, including the complicity in, or the condoning of, the wrongdoing by corporate management (see JM 9-28.500);

3. The corporation's history of similar misconduct, including prior criminal, civil, and regulatory enforcement actions against it (see JM 9-28.600);

4. The corporation's willingness to cooperate, including as to potential wrongdoing by its agents (see JM 9-28.700);

5. The adequacy and effectiveness of the corporation's compliance program at the time of the offense, as well as at the time of a charging decision (see JM 9-28.800);

6. The corporation's timely and voluntary disclosure of wrongdoing (see JM 9-28.900);

7. The corporation's remedial actions, including, but not limited to, any efforts to implement an adequate and effective corporate compliance program or to improve an existing one, to replace responsible management, to discipline or terminate wrongdoers, or to pay restitution (see JM 9-28.1000);

8. Collateral consequences, including whether there is disproportionate harm to shareholders, pension holders, employees, and others not proven personally culpable, as well as impact on the public arising from the prosecution (see JM 9-28.1100);

9. The adequacy of remedies such as civil or regulatory enforcement actions, including remedies resulting from the corporation's cooperation with relevant government agencies (see JM 9-28.1200);

10. The adequacy of the prosecution of individuals responsible for the corporation's malfeasance (see JM 9-28.1300); and

11. The interests of any victims (see JM 9-28.1400).

B. Comment: The factors listed in this section are intended to be illustrative of those that should be evaluated and are not an exhaustive list of potentially relevant considerations. Some of these factors may not apply to specific cases, and in some cases one factor may override all others. For example, the nature and seriousness of the offense may be such as to warrant prosecution regardless of the other factors. In most cases, however, no single factor will be dispositive. In addition, national law enforcement policies in various enforcement areas may require that more or less weight be given to certain of these factors than to others. Of course, prosecutors must exercise their thoughtful and pragmatic judgment in applying and balancing these factors, so as to achieve a fair and just outcome and promote respect for the law.

[updated July 2020]

9-28.400—SPECIAL POLICY CONCERNS

A. **General Principle:** The nature and seriousness of the crime, including the risk of harm to the public from the criminal misconduct, are obviously primary factors in determining whether to charge a corporation. In addition, corporate conduct, particularly that of national and multi-national corporations, necessarily intersects with federal economic, tax, and criminal law enforcement policies. In applying these Principles, prosecutors must consider the practices and policies of the appropriate Division of the Department, and must comply with those policies to the extent required by the facts presented.

B. **Comment:** In determining whether to charge a corporation, prosecutors should take into account federal law enforcement priorities as discussed above. See JM 9-27.230. In addition, however, prosecutors must be aware of the specific policy goals and incentive programs established by the respective Divisions and regulatory agencies. Thus, whereas natural persons may be given incremental degrees of credit (ranging from immunity to lesser charges to sentencing considerations) for turning themselves in, making statements against their penal interest, and cooperating in the government's investigation of their own and others' wrongdoing, the same approach may not be appropriate in all circumstances with respect to corporations. As an example, it is entirely proper in many investigations for a prosecutor to consider the corporation's pre-indictment conduct, e.g., voluntary disclosure, cooperation, remediation or restitution, in determining whether to seek an indictment. However, this would not necessarily be appropriate in an antitrust investigation, in which antitrust violations, by definition, go to the heart of the corporation's business. With this in mind, the Antitrust Division has established a firm policy, understood in the business community, that corporate leniency is available only to the first corporation to make full disclosure to the government. As another example, the Tax Division has a strong preference for prosecuting responsible individuals, rather than entities, for corporate tax offenses. Thus, in determining whether or not to charge a corporation, prosecutors must consult with the Criminal, Antitrust, Tax, Environmental and Natural Resources, and National Security Divisions, as appropriate.

[updated July 2019]

9-28.500—PERVASIVENESS OF WRONGDOING WITHIN THE CORPORATION

A. **General Principle:** A corporation can only act through natural persons, and it is therefore held responsible for the acts of such persons fairly attributable to it. Charging a corporation for even minor misconduct may be appropriate where the wrongdoing was pervasive and was undertaken by a large number of employees, or by all the employees in a particular role within the corporation, or was condoned by upper management. On the other hand, it may not be appropriate to impose liability upon a corporation, particularly one with a robust compliance program in place, under a strict respondeat superior theory for the single isolated act of a rogue employee. There is, of course, a wide spectrum between these two extremes, and a prosecutor should exercise sound discretion in evaluating the pervasiveness of wrongdoing within a corporation.

B. **Comment:** Of these factors, the most important is the role and conduct of management. Although acts of even low-level employees may result in criminal liability, a corporation is directed by its management and management is responsible for a corporate culture in which criminal conduct is either discouraged or tacitly encouraged. As stated in commentary to the Sentencing Guidelines:

> Pervasiveness [is] case specific and [will] depend on the number, and degree of responsibility, of individuals [with] substantial authority ... who participated in, condoned, or were willfully ignorant of the offense. Fewer individuals need to be involved for a finding of pervasiveness if those individuals exercised a relatively high degree of authority. Pervasiveness can occur either within an organization as a whole or within a unit of an organization.

USSG § 8C2.5, cmt. (n. 4).

[new August 2008]

9-28.600—THE CORPORATION'S PAST HISTORY

A. **General Principle:** Prosecutors may consider a corporation's history of similar conduct, including prior criminal, civil, and regulatory enforcement actions against it, in determining whether to bring criminal charges and how best to resolve cases.

B. **Comment:** A corporation, like a natural person, is expected to learn from its mistakes. A history of similar misconduct may be probative of a corporate culture that encouraged, or at least condoned, such misdeeds, regardless of any compliance programs. Criminal prosecution of a corporation may be particularly appropriate where the corporation previously had been subject to non-criminal guidance, warnings, or sanctions, or previous criminal charges, and it either had not taken adequate action to prevent future unlawful conduct or had continued to engage in the misconduct in spite of the warnings or enforcement actions taken against it. The corporate structure itself (e.g., the creation or existence of subsidiaries or operating divisions) is not dispositive in this analysis, and enforcement actions taken against the corporation or any of its divisions, subsidiaries, and affiliates may be considered, if germane. See USSG § 8C2.5(c), cmt. (n. 6).

[new August 2008]"[4]

So let's break this down. Some factors are beyond anyone's control: nature and seriousness of the offense; pervasiveness of wrongdoing in the corporation; the corporation's history of similar misconduct; the adequacy and effectiveness of the corporation's compliance program at the time of the offense; collateral consequences; the interests of any victims. The company's current actions really can't affect those things. However, there are a number of factors that the company can control: the corporation's willingness to cooperate; the corporation's timely and voluntary disclosure of wrongdoing; the corporation's remedial actions; and remedies resulting from the corporation's cooperation with relevant government agencies. The commentary informs us that the foregoing is illustrative only and that other factors may be considered. But, this gives us a good starting point.

The implications of going to law enforcement and getting them involved are significant. First, you must cooperate fully with them; there could be serious legal jeopardy for not cooperating fully with law enforcement during their investigation. Also, they will take full control of the investigation. They will take full control of any evidence you have gathered. The only things they will not access or take are things that are subject to an attorney client privilege. When criminal litigation begins, any related civil litigation will be stayed until the criminal litigation concludes. They will control the criminal litigation; who is and is not indicted. They will prosecute the criminal litigation. The company may need to enter into a formal cooperation agreement and, depending on the nature of the offense, may be required to enter into a corporate integrity agreement. This could create significant additional costs for the company.

One final thought, law enforcement may not be interested in getting involved in your company's investigation. If your company happens to be a victim of a crime that is not a high-priority crime (i.e. Chris Wray, Director of the FBI, won't be giving any speeches about embezzlement against corporations), if the crime is too small or if it appears that the crime will be too difficult to investigate or prosecute, the Justice Department or other law enforcement agency may not be interested in getting involved. The Justice Department's current criminal investigation priorities include:

"The priorities were established using data from 21 Federal departments and agencies and FBI information on white-collar crimes. Following identification of law enforcement objectives and analysis of each criminal activity's major attributes, seven priority areas for investigation and prosecution were identified. Under crimes against government by public officials, priority crimes include corruption in Federal procurement programs and law enforcement, and corruption of major State and local officials. In the area of private citizens' crimes against the government, priority areas include major Federal procurement or program fraud, counterfeiting of currency or securities, customs violations, major Federal tax violations, and major trafficking in contraband cigarettes. Priority areas for business crimes include insurance fraud, advance fee schemes, bankruptcy fraud, bank fraud and embezzlement, and other major crimes against business. For crimes against consumers, priority areas include major consumer fraud, antitrust violations, and energy pricing fraud and related fraud. For crimes against investors, securities fraud, commodities fraud, and land or other investment frauds are priority areas. Priority crimes against employees include corruption by union officials and major health and safety violations. For crimes affecting the general public's health and safety, priority areas include discharge of excessive toxic wastes and life endangering violations of federally regulated goods and facilities."[5]

So, if the crime against your company was not one of the crimes listed above, you may have trouble getting a prosecutor interested enough to initiate a prosecution. You can improve your odds of getting law enforcement interested in helping you in two ways: you can do an effective preliminary investigation, which demonstrates that the case will be easy to investigate, prosecute, and get a conviction or you could get an influential person to recommend to law enforcement that they get involved in your case. Of course, there is an old saw that the FBI agents really make the charging decisions, so, it might be a good idea for your company to develop a relationship with the local FBI office. The cybercrime partnership Director Wray described above could be a great place to start.

INVESTIGATOR NOTES

Once I was hired by the Justice Department to investigate the use of the proceeds of crime by a person who took valuable assets from wealthy people, on consignment, sold them and spent the proceeds on himself. I was working on the case with a former FBI agent. I asked the agent what federal law could possibly have been violated that would create federal jurisdictional interest in a case like this one. It just seemed like a pretty ordinary crime that would be prosecuted by the local District Attorney. My FBI agent friend made up some Section of Title 18 of the US Code. I asked him what law was codified in that section? He said, "It's the stealing stuff from rich, influential people statute!" We had a good laugh, but, in all seriousness, you are more likely to get a prosecutor's attention if an influential person gets involved.

SECTION II: SHARING FINDINGS, CONCLUSIONS, AND EVIDENCE WITH LAW ENFORCEMENT

Once law enforcement is involved in your investigation, it becomes their investigation; they are in control. This is really an "in for a penny, in for a pound situation" in which you must fully comply with their requests.

Let's begin with the situation where the illegal conduct committed by one or more employees also creates criminal liability for the company. Also, let's assume that the company wants to get credit for cooperation with law enforcement. This could be anything from a deferred prosecution agreement to lower penalties at sentencing. Once again, let's take a look at an excerpt from the US Justice Department's Principles of Federal Prosecution of Business Organizations to see how this works:

9-28.700—THE VALUE OF COOPERATION
Cooperation is a mitigating factor, by which a corporation—just like any other subject of a criminal investigation—can gain credit in a case that otherwise is appropriate for indictment and prosecution. Of course, the decision not to cooperate by a corporation (or individual) is not itself evidence of misconduct, at least where the lack of cooperation does not involve criminal misconduct or demonstrate consciousness of guilt

(e.g., suborning perjury or false statements, or refusing to comply with lawful discovery requests). Thus, failure to cooperate, in and of itself, does not support or require the filing of charges with respect to a corporation any more than with respect to an individual.

A. General Principle: In order for a company to receive any consideration for cooperation under this section, the company must identify all individuals substantially involved in or responsible for the misconduct at issue, regardless of their position, status or seniority, and provide to the Department all relevant facts relating to that misconduct. If a company seeking cooperation credit declines to learn of such facts or to provide the Department with complete factual information about the individuals substantially involved in or responsible for the misconduct, its cooperation will not be considered a mitigating factor under this section. Nor, if a company is prosecuted, will the Department support a cooperation-related reduction at sentencing. See U.S.S.G. § 8C2.5(g), cmt. (n. 13) ("A prime test of whether the organization has disclosed all pertinent information" necessary to receive a cooperation-related reduction in its offense level calculation "is whether the information is sufficient ... to identify ... the individual(s) responsible for the criminal conduct.").[1]

If the company is unable to identify all relevant individuals or provide complete factual information despite its good faith efforts to cooperate fully, the organization may still be eligible for cooperation credit. *See* U.S.S.G. § 8C2.5(g), cmt. (n. 13) ("[T]he cooperation to be measured is the cooperation of the organization itself, not the cooperation of individuals within the organization. If, because of the lack of cooperation of particular individual(s), neither the organization nor law enforcement personnel are able to identify the culpable individual(s) within the organization despite the organization's efforts to cooperate fully, the organization may still be given credit for full cooperation."). For example, there may be circumstances where, despite its best efforts to conduct a thorough investigation, a company genuinely cannot get access to certain evidence or is legally prohibited from disclosing it to the government. Under such circumstances, the company seeking cooperation will bear the burden of explaining the restrictions it is facing to the prosecutor.

To be clear, a company is not required to waive its attorney-client privilege or attorney work product protection to be eligible to receive cooperation credit. *See* JM 9-28.720. The extent of the cooperation credit earned will depend on all the various factors that have traditionally applied in making this assessment (e.g., the timeliness of the cooperation, the diligence, thoroughness and speed of the internal investigation, and the proactive nature of the cooperation).

B. Comment: In investigating wrongdoing by or within a corporation, a prosecutor may encounter several obstacles resulting from the nature of the corporation itself. It may be difficult to determine which individual took which action on behalf of the corporation. Lines of authority and responsibility may be shared among operating divisions or departments, and records and personnel may be spread throughout the United States or even among several countries. Where the criminal conduct continued over an extended period of time, the culpable or knowledgeable personnel may have been promoted, transferred, or fired, or they may have quit or retired. Accordingly, a corporation's cooperation may be critical in identifying potentially relevant actors and locating relevant evidence, among other things, and in doing so expeditiously.

This dynamic—i.e., the difficulty of determining what happened, where the evidence is, and which individuals took or promoted putatively illegal corporate actions—can have negative consequences for both the government and the corporation that is the subject or target of a government investigation. More specifically, because of corporate attribution principles concerning actions of corporate officers and employees, *see* JM 9.28-210, uncertainty about who authorized or directed apparent corporate misconduct can inure to the detriment of a corporation. For example, it may not matter under the law which of several possible executives or leaders in a chain of command approved of or authorized criminal conduct; however, that information if known might bear on the propriety of a particular disposition short of indictment of the corporation. It may not be in the interest of a corporation or the government for a charging decision to be made in the absence of such information, which might occur if, for example, a statute of limitations were relevant and authorization by any one of the officials were enough to justify a charge under the law.

For these reasons and more, cooperation can be a favorable course for both the government and the corporation. Cooperation benefits the government by allowing prosecutors and federal agents, for example, to avoid protracted delays, which compromise their ability to quickly uncover and address the full extent of widespread corporate crimes. With cooperation by the corporation, the government may be able to reduce tangible losses, limit damage to reputation, and preserve assets for restitution. At the same time, cooperation may benefit the corporation—and ultimately shareholders, employees, and other often blameless victims—by enabling the government to focus its investigative resources in a manner that may expedite the investigation and that may be less likely to disrupt the corporation's legitimate business operations. In addition, cooperation may benefit the corporation by presenting it with the opportunity to earn credit for its efforts.

The requirement that companies cooperate completely as to individuals does not mean that Department attorneys should wait for the company to deliver the information about individual wrongdoers and then merely accept what companies provide. To the contrary, Department attorneys should be proactively investigating individuals at every step of the process—before, during, and after any corporate cooperation. Department attorneys should vigorously review any information provided by companies and compare it to the results of their own investigation, in order to best ensure that the information provided is indeed complete and does not seek to minimize, exaggerate, or otherwise misrepresent the behavior or role of any individual or group of individuals.

Department attorneys should strive to obtain from the company as much information as possible about responsible individuals before resolving the corporate case. In addition, the company's continued cooperation with respect to individuals may be necessary post-resolution. If so, the corporate resolution agreement should include a provision that requires the company to provide information about all individuals substantially involved in or responsible for the misconduct, and that is explicit enough so that a failure to provide the information results in specific consequences, such as stipulated penalties and/or a material breach.

[cited in JM 9-47.120]

[updated November 2018]

---

[1] Of course, in addition to cooperation in an investigation, the Department encourages early voluntary disclosure of criminal wrongdoing, *see* JM 9-28.900, even before all facts are known to the company, and does not expect that such early disclosures would be complete. However, the Department does expect that, in such circumstances, the company will move in a timely fashion to conduct an appropriate investigation and provide timely factual updates to the Department."[6]

Let's break this down. First, we have the following requirement:

"In order for a company to receive any consideration for cooperation under this section, the company must identify all individuals substantially involved in or responsible for the misconduct at issue, regardless of their position, status or seniority, and provide to the Department all relevant facts relating to that misconduct. If a company seeking cooperation credit declines to learn of such facts or to provide the Department with complete factual information about the individuals substantially involved in or responsible for the misconduct, its cooperation will not be considered a mitigating factor under this section."[7]

So, the first step is to identify all individuals involved in the illegal conduct. Also, you must provide all of the information you have collected about the involvement of these individuals. Note that the requirement states that you should not fail to include someone based on status, position, or seniority. That's right, if the CEO is involved, then you must identify the CEO and provide all information you have about the CEO and his or her conduct. However, note that the company is not required to provide information subject to the attorney-client privilege to receive credit.

Now, let's turn to the situation where the company is the victim and has no criminal liability as a result of the illegal conduct. Law enforcement will still take control of the investigation, the evidence, and the prosecution of the case. You will be required to comply with law enforcement requests and answer law enforcement's questions. Related civil litigation will be stayed pending resolution of the criminal litigation. You may be required to testify at trial.

Well, that's really all there is to it. The most important thing is to understand when or when not to get law enforcement involved. If you do decide to get law enforcement involved and they agree to get involved then they will take control of the investigation and the prosecution of those involved. Your job will be to cooperate completely with them. Once again, it will be important to get competent, experienced attorneys involved in all decision-making.

EXERCISES

1. What questions must you ask internally before making the decision to take your case to law enforcement?
2. Imagine that you are discussing your approach to resolving allegations of cybertheft with your boss. What questions would you ask him or her in deciding on whether or not to get law enforcement involved?
3. What are reasons to get law enforcement involved in your investigation?
4. When must you get law enforcement involved?
5. How could you commit the crime of misprison of a felony?
6. What are some ways in which you, your colleagues, or your company commit the crime of obstruction of justice?
7. What crime is committed when someone responds to a question asked by a federal agent untruthfully or makes an intentional omission of a significant fact?
8. What are the downsides of involving law enforcement in your investigation?
9. What is the doctrine of *respondeat superior* and what does it mean for your company when someone does something wrong that benefits the company?
10. What factors does the Justice Department consider in deciding whether to indict a corporation for crimes committed by its employees?
11. What benefit is available to companies that cooperate with law enforcement in investigating crimes committed by their employees?
12. What must a company do to receive cooperation credit?
13. Can a company cooperate and maintain its attorney-client communication or work product privilege?
14. Your company has agreed to enter into a cooperation agreement with the Justice Department. Since you led the internal investigation, you are tasked with leading the company's information gathering requirements under the agreement. What must you do first?

CHAPTER SUMMARY/KEY TAKEAWAYS

So, here are some things to think about:

- First, you need to decide whether the matter you are investigating must be shared with law enforcement.
- Next, you need to consult with a competent experienced attorney to make sure you, your team, and uninvolved management do not violate the law in conducting your investigation.
- Then you need to carefully consider the pros and cons of bringing law enforcement into the matter you are investigating.
- If you do bring law enforcement in, you must cooperate with them completely.

In Chapter 14, you will learn how to present your findings at trial.

NOTES

1. https://www.fbi.gov/news/speeches/the-fbi-and-the-private-sector-battling-the-cyber-threat-together-012821
2. https://www.govinfo.gov/content/pkg/USCODE-2011-title18/pdf/USCODE-2011-title18-partI-chap1-sec4.pdf
3. https://uscode.house.gov/view.xhtml?path=/prelim@title18/part1/chapter73&edition=prelim
4. https://www.justice.gov/jm/jm-9-28000-principles-federal-prosecution-business-organizations #9-28.100
5. https://www.ojp.gov/ncjrs/virtual-library/abstracts/national-priorities-investigation-and-prosecution-white-collar
6. https://www.justice.gov/jm/jm-9-28000-principles-federal-prosecution-business-organizations #9-28.100
7. https://www.justice.gov/jm/jm-9-28000-principles-federal-prosecution-business-organizations #9-28.100

14 Presenting Evidence at Trial

I titled this chapter "Presenting Evidence at Trial," but many of the concepts also apply to giving evidence before arbitral panels, regulatory bodies, or other resolution venues. The rules for each venue are different, so you will need to understand and apply the rules for the venue in which you will be testifying. Also, even federal courts have local rules, which you must learn about before you testify. Also, the judge, arbitral panel members, or regulatory agents may impose or change rules as the proceeding progresses.

I was hired by a US Attorney's office to investigate the ways in which a criminal used the proceeds of his crimes for personal benefit. I was scheduled to give expert testimony at his criminal trial in US District Court. The judge was an extremely knowledgeable and talented jurist. I imagine she knew, even then, that she would be chosen to serve on the appellate bench where she sits today. After being sworn in my voir dire (i.e. the examination to determine whether I will be allowed to testify as an expert) began. The defense lawyer began making objections to me testifying. He said that my testimony would be prejudicial and irrelevant; neither argument made any sense. Nonetheless, the judge, I believe to protect her appeals record in light of her aspirations for the appellate bench, sequestered the jury. Then she had the Assistant United States Attorney, who retained me, do my entire direct examination. Then she allowed the defense lawyer to cross-examine me. The judge then took a copy of the transcript of my examinations and went though it with me line by line. The judge would give instructions like, "When you answer this question, don't use this word." and "I will let you answer this question but not this one." After we went through my testimony, in detail, the judge brought the jury back and we did my direct and cross-examination all over again.

My point in telling you this story is that anything can happen at trial. You cannot react to all the distractions that can occur at a trial. You must maintain your emotional intelligence and remain calm. I always think of trial as a situation where you are in extreme danger for a finite amount of time, then it's over and you get to go home. Of course, the finite amount of time can be more than you expect. I once testified in US District Court in upstate New York; my direct examination was four hours long. My cross-examination went on for eight days. But, even so, at the end of it, I got to go home.

I am a pilot. Most people think that pilots are risk takers. Actually, good pilots are not risk takers; they are risk managers. One of the ways they manage risk is to constantly learn about flying and its risks. Then, they regularly practice avoiding extremely dangerous situations and procedures for surviving them if they do occur. Giving expert testimony is like that. To be good at it you must be a constant learner and practice how to deal with difficult situations and questions because they will always come up during your testimony. One of the things I do to prepare myself for giving expert testimony is that I follow a routine that puts me in the right frame of mind to remain calm and emotionally intelligent as the danger and distractions rise on all sides in the courtroom. I never do any studying the night before I testify. Instead, I have a nice dinner and watch my favorite Western movie, which has a character that I channel ahead of and during my testimony. Then I go to bed early and get a good night's sleep. What your own pre-testimony routine includes is less important than having one that you can follow faithfully.

SECTION I: THE JUDICIAL PROCESS GENERALLY

A significant amount of my work has been performed outside the United States. I was once asked to address a large group of lawyers from around the world on the topic of providing expert testimony in different countries. The conference was in Amsterdam and I was delighted to be the guest of lawyers who lived in that lovely city; it's always more fun to hang out with people who live in the city you are visiting. The organization who organized the conference also helped me to research the rules of procedure, evidence, and local rules for a number of different countries. So, I was well prepared. But, I will admit, dear Reader, that I was quite intimidated. I love public speaking, but I was truly dreading getting a question from one of these lawyers that I knew nothing about. However, there was no turning back, so I delivered my speech and opened the floor for questions. I didn't get any that I knew nothing about. The reason was that all the questions were about litigation in the United States. I was quite relieved, but, surprised. That evening I asked my local host why I only got questions about the US litigation. He laughed and said, "It is because you live in the most litigious country on the planet Earth. These guys are all litigators and because they all see their own judicial systems moving in the direction of the U.S., they want to know what to expect."

Of course, criminal and civil litigation systems can be very different depending on where you are giving expert testimony. I can remember working on a large commodity fraud case in Greece. Greece's criminal justice system is based on the Napoleonic Code. The best Greek lawyers attend law school in France. There system has a prosecuting judge who can compel defendants to produce any records requested. The trier of fact at the criminal trial is a panel comprised of one trained lawyer and two lay people who are considered to be virtuous and incorruptible.

But, since the US District Court System is the one I am most familiar with, we will use that one to illustrate the concepts that follow. Most of the concepts will apply in any venue in which you may be required to testify. The only differences will be the procedural, evidence and local rules with which you will be required to observe. Remember, as I have said many times throughout this book: I am not a lawyer. So, my insights about other aspects of the judicial system should not be relied on and you should always consult an attorney before engaging, in any manner, with the judicial system. Also, remember the wise saying: A person who represents himself in litigation has a fool for a client.

So, let's look at the Federal Rules of Civil Procedure, as they pertain to testimony, first:

"TITLE V. DISCLOSURES AND DISCOVERY

Rule 26. Duty to Disclose; General Provisions Governing Discovery
(a) REQUIRED DISCLOSURES.

(1) *Initial Disclosure.*

(A) *In General.* Except as exempted by Rule 26(a)(1)(B) or as otherwise stipulated or ordered by the court, a party must, without awaiting a discovery request, provide to the other parties:

(i) the name and, if known, the address and telephone number of each individual likely to have discoverable information—along with the subjects of that information—that the disclosing party may use to support its claims or defenses, unless the use would be solely for impeachment;

(ii) a copy—or a description by category and location—of all documents, electronically stored information, and tangible things that the disclosing party has in its possession, custody, or control and may use to support its claims or defenses, unless the use would be solely for impeachment;

(iii) a computation of each category of damages claimed by the disclosing party—who must also make available for inspection and copying as under Rule 34 the documents or other evidentiary material, unless privileged or protected from disclosure, on which each computation is based, including materials bearing on the nature and extent of injuries suffered; and

(iv) for inspection and copying as under Rule 34, any insurance agreement under which an insurance business may be liable to satisfy all or part of a possible judgment in the action or to indemnify or reimburse for payments made to satisfy the judgment.

(B) *Proceedings Exempt from Initial Disclosure.* The following proceedings are exempt from initial disclosure:

> (i) an action for review on an administrative record;
>
> (ii) a forfeiture action in rem arising from a federal statute;
>
> (iii) a petition for habeas corpus or any other proceeding to challenge a criminal conviction or sentence;
>
> (iv) an action brought without an attorney by a person in the custody of the United States, a state, or a state subdivision;
>
> (v) an action to enforce or quash an administrative summons or subpoena;
>
> (vi) an action by the United States to recover benefit payments;
>
> (vii) an action by the United States to collect on a student loan guaranteed by the United States;
>
> (viii) a proceeding ancillary to a proceeding in another court; and
>
> (ix) an action to enforce an arbitration award.

(C) *Time for Initial Disclosures—In General.* A party must make the initial disclosures at or within 14 days after the parties' Rule 26(f) conference unless a different time is set by stipulation or court order, or unless a party objects during the conference that initial disclosures are not appropriate in this action and states the objection in the proposed discovery plan. In ruling on the objection, the court must determine what disclosures, if any, are to be made and must set the time for disclosure.

(D) *Time for Initial Disclosures—For Parties Served or Joined Later.* A party that is first served or otherwise joined after the Rule 26(f) conference must make the initial disclosures within 30 days after being served or joined, unless a different time is set by stipulation or court order.

(E) *Basis for Initial Disclosure; Unacceptable Excuses.* A party must make its initial disclosures based on the information then reasonably available to it. A party is not excused from making its disclosures because it has not fully investigated the case or because it challenges the sufficiency of another party's disclosures or because another party has not made its disclosures."[1]

We can see that Rule 26 covers disclosures by both potential fact and expert witnesses. But, then it speaks specifically to disclosure of expert testimony in its own section:

"(2) *Disclosure of Expert Testimony.*

(A) *In General.* In addition to the disclosures required by Rule 26(a)(1), a party must disclose to the other parties the identity of any witness it may use at trial to present evidence under Federal Rule of Evidence 702, 703, or 705.

(B) *Witnesses Who Must Provide a Written Report.* Unless otherwise stipulated or ordered by the court, this disclosure must be accompanied by a written report—prepared and signed by the witness—if the witness is one retained or specially employed to provide expert testimony in the case or one whose duties as the party's employee regularly involve giving expert testimony. The report must contain:

> (i) a complete statement of all opinions the witness will express and the basis and reasons for them;
>
> (ii) the facts or data considered by the witness in forming them;
>
> (iii) any exhibits that will be used to summarize or support them;
>
> (iv) the witness's qualifications, including a list of all publications authored in the previous 10 years;

(v) a list of all other cases in which, during the previous 4 years, the witness testified as an expert at trial or by deposition; and

(vi) a statement of the compensation to be paid for the study and testimony in the case."

The following is an example of a report that satisfies these requirements. These requirements do not need to be set out in the written report in the same order that they are set forth in the Rule 26. They just all need to be addressed in the written report (see Table 14.1).

- The identity of the expert witness. (See Section I in the report below.)
- The qualifications of the expert witness. (See Section I and Exhibit A in the report below.)
- A statement of all opinions to be offered by the expert witness. (See Secton IV in the report below.)
- The facts and data considered by the expert witness. (See Exhibit B in the report below.)
- Any exhibits used to summarize or support facts and data considered by the expert witness. (See Exhibit B in the report below.)
- A statement of the compensation to be paid for the study and testimony. (see Section III in the report below.)

EXPERT REPORT OF WILLIAM L. JENNINGS, CPA

February 5, 2020

IN THE UNITED STATES DISTRICT COURT
FOR THE NORTHERN DISTRICT OF GEORGIA
ATLANTA DIVISION

TABLE 14.1

Report Cover Sheet of Filing

SECURITIES AND EXCHANGE COMMISSION,	)	
	)	
	)	
Plaintiff,	)	
	)	
vs	)	Case No. X: XX-XX-XXXXX-XXX
	)	
XXXX XXXXXXXX, XXX,	)	
XXXXX XXXXXX, XXXX XXXXXXX, and	)	
XXXX XXXXXXX	)	
	)	
	)	
Defendants,	)	
	)	
And	)	
	)	
XXXX XXXX XXXXXXXXXX	)	
	)	
Relief Defendant.	)	

EXPERT REPORT OF WILLIAM L. JENNINGS, CPA

February 5, XXXX

I. Qualifications.

My name is William L. Jennings. My business address is Veritas Forensic Accounting, LLC, 1175 Peachtree Street, NE, Atlanta, GA, 30309.

I am a Member of Veritas Forensic Accounting, LLC. My previous positions included: Principal at AEA Group, LLC; Managing Director at Alvarez & Marsal in the Global Forensic and Dispute Services practice; Managing Director in the Disputes and Investigations Practice at Navigant Consulting, Inc.; Director in the National Forensic Accounting Practice at LECG, LLC; President of FFI, Inc.; Managing Director at Kroll, Inc., in charge of investigative accounting services for the Central Region; Principal-in-Charge of the Atlanta office of Lindquist, Avey, Macdonald, Baskerville, a multi-national independent forensic accounting firm; Director-in-Charge of Coopers & Lybrand's Fraud Investigation Services practice for the Southeast Region; and Partner in the public accounting firm of Brown & Jennings.

I have a Bachelor of Science degree in Accounting from the University of New Orleans and a Master's degree in Business Administration from Auburn University. I have been a Certified Public Accountant ("CPA") since 1981 and a Certified Fraud Examiner ("CFE") since 1991. I am also Certified in Financial Forensics ("CFF"), Accredited in Business Valuation ("ABV"), a member of the American Institute of Certified Public Accountants, a member of the Association of Certified Fraud Examiners, and a member of the Board of Governors for the Center for Ethics and Corporate Responsibility at Georgia State University.

For nearly 40 years, I have provided forensic accounting, investigation, asset recovery, business valuation, and business controls consulting services to a wide range of clients, including public companies, private companies, and government agencies, such as the U.S. Attorney's Office for multiple districts, the U.S. Securities and Exchange Commission, and the U.S. Marshals Service. Over the course of my career, I have been engaged on hundreds of forensic accounting, audit and investigation assignments, including audit assignments for companies that engaged in significant derivative trading activities, such Good Hope (Refinery), Inc. and Freeport McMoRan, Inc., and I have gained substantial experience with and expertise on a variety of accounting, financial and investment-related topics, including U.S. Generally Accepted Accounting Principles ("GAAP"); the Financial Account Standards Board's ("FASB") Accounting Standards Codification ("ASC") which codify GAAP[1]; alternative investment vehicles, such as hedge funds, private equity funds, and venture capital funds; and a diverse range of financial instruments, including options, futures, stocks, and bonds. I have also personally traded stocks, bonds, options and futures in my own account.

I frequently speak and publish articles on accounting, financial and investment-related topics, such as forensic accounting, fraud investigations, white-collar crime, business ethics, and the valuation of financial instruments, among others.

In addition, I have often provided expert testimony in federal and state courts, as well as in many other dispute resolution venues. I have testified in matters that related to

---

[1] According to FASB Statement of Financial Accounting Standards No. 168, "The FASB Accounting Standards Codification (Codification) will become the source of authoritative U.S. generally accepted accounting principles (GAAP) recognized by the FASB to be applied by nongovernmental entities. [...] This Statement is effective for financial statements issued for interim and annual periods ending after September 15, 2009."

a variety of derivatives and hedge fund accounting, including: *Nodvin et al. vs National Financial Services Corporation* (testimony regarding accounting for and reporting of values for IOs, POs, and inverse IO floaters given at NASD Arbitration Hearing); *Piedmont Family Office Fund, LP, et al. vs Robert L. Duncan, et al.* (testimony given at deposition).

Additional details regarding my qualifications, education, publications, speaking engagements and past expert testimony are included in my curriculum vitae, which is attached as Exhibit A.

II.　Case Background.

This case concerns two hedge funds, XXX Xxxxxxxxxxx, XXX ("XXX") and Xxxx Xxxxxxxxxxx, XXX (the "XX Fund") (together, the "Funds"), that primarily traded options on, options on futures on, and futures on broad-based indices, such as the S&P 500 Index.

On May 31, XXXX, the Securities and Exchange Commission (the "SEC") filed a complaint in the United States District Court for the Northern District of Georgia against Xxxx Xxxxxxxx, XXX ("Xxxx") and Xxxxx Xxxxxx ("Xx. Xxxxxx") alleging violations of the Securities Act of 1933, the Securities Exchange Act of 1934, and the Investment Advisers Act of 1940.[2] The SEC filed a First Amended Complaint on January 11, XXXX,[3] and a Second Amended Complaint on August 30, XXXX, which, among other things, added claims against Xxxx Xxxxxxx and Xxxx Xxxxxxx.[4]

The SEC alleges that Xxxx and Xx. Xxxxxx manipulated the trading strategy of the Funds to avoid realizing losses and to generate incentive allocations paid to Xx. Xxxxxx and Xxxx Xxxx Xxxxxxxxxx (the "Xxxx Xxxxxxxxxx") from at least January XXXX through May XXXX.[5] In addition, the SEC alleges that Xxxx and Xx. Xxxxxx misrepresented or omitted details about Xxxx's trading strategy.

III.　Assignment

I have been asked by counsel for Xxxx and Xxxxx Xxxxxx to provide my opinions on the accounting and related issues in this litigation, including background information on derivatives.

For my work on this matter, I am being compensated at my standard consulting rate of $XXX per hour. My compensation is in no way contingent upon or based upon the content of my opinions or the outcome of this matter.

COMPLETE STATEMENT OF OPINIONS:

IV.　Summary of Opinions.

Based on my review and analysis of the information described below, certain empirical analyses I have performed, and my skills, knowledge, education, training, and experience, I am of the following opinions, which are explained more fully in Part XI below:

- The Funds did not enter into any trades that were open for more than 90 days, which comports with the XX Fund's disclosures to investors.
- Xxxx applied correct accounting treatment to the Funds' classification of open and closed trading positions. In particular, as to options that expired and resulted

---

[2] *See generally* Complaint filed May 31, XXXX (Dkt. No. X).

[3] *See generally* First Amended Complaint filed January 11, XXXX (Dkt. No. XX).

[4] *See generally* Second Amended Complaint filed August 30, XXXX (Dkt. No. XX).

[5] Unless otherwise stated herein, this report refers to the time period of January 1, XXXX through May 31, XXXX.

in the assignment of the underlying financial instrument, on the date those options expired, Xxxx correctly classified the expired option as a closed position, and the resulting assignment of the underlying financial instrument as a separate, open position.

- With respect to the Xx Fund and the XXX Fund, the unrealized and net asset value ("NAV") of open positions and of the Funds were not particularly relevant (other than for margin and tax purposes). The XX Fund and the XXX Fund often had open positions in an unrealized loss position, but that was not necessarily reflective of an actual risk of realized losses or the potential for realized gains. As investors in the Funds redeemed based on their percentage ownership of net realized gains and losses on closed positions, unrealized and net asset values that did not reflect the actual risk of realized losses or the potential for realized gains were not particularly relevant.

- Xxxx's investment strategy, in part, relied on the premise that, over time, it could reduce and eliminate trading losses that were caused by periods of unusual and extreme market volatility. This premise is supported by Chebyshev's Theorem and the Empirical Rule, including the tendency of reversion to the mean that is implied by both propositions.

- If the XX Fund utilized a fee structure more in line with the traditional "2 and 20" fee model based on NAV for hedge funds, XX. Xxxxxx and Xxxx Xxxxxxxxxx would have earned approximately $7.2 million *more* in fees and incentive allocations between January XXXX and May XXXX. In other words, the XX Fund's fee structure—with no management fee and an incentive allocation equal to 20% of net realized gains on closed positions—*saved* the investors approximately $7.2 million between January XXXX and May XXXX.

V. The Complex and Volatile World of Options and Futures.[6]

Options, futures, and options on futures are types of financial instruments known as derivatives. According to Accounting Standards Codification ("ASC") No. 815, developed by the FASB, a derivative instrument is a financial instrument or other contract with each of the following characteristics: (a) one or more underlying and/or one or more notional amounts or payment provisions; (b) no or little initial net investment; and (c) the ability to be settled under contract terms, through a market mechanism, or by delivery of a derivative instrument or asset readily convertible to cash.[7]

An underlying may be, among other things, a security price, security price index, commodity price, or commodity price index.[8] In the case of options on S&P 500 Index Futures, the underlying is an S&P 500 Index futures contract. The S&P 500 Index is a market-cap-weighted stock market index that "includes 500 leading companies and captures approximately 80% coverage of available market capitalization."[9]

A notional amount is a number of currency units, shares, bushels, pounds, or other units specified in the contract.[10] Some derivative instruments require an initial net investment as compensation for either or both of the following: (a) the time value of the derivative instrument; or (b) terms that are more or less favorable than market

---

[6] This section provides a general overview of how options and futures work, and it does not and is not intended to address every possible permutation of an options or futures contract.

[7] See ASC 815-10-15-83; ASC 815-10-15-99.

[8] *See* ASC 815-10-15-88.

[9] *See, e.g.,* <http://us.spindices.com/indices/equity/sp-500>.

[10] *See* ASC 815-10-15-92.

conditions.[11] "An option generally requires that one party make an initial net invest-ment ... because that party has the rights under the contract and the other party has the obligations."[12]

An option is the right or obligation to buy or sell a particular underlying financial instrument at a specified price on or before a certain date. A **call option** represents the right to buy or obligation to sell an underlying financial instrument, while a **put option** represents the right to sell or obligation to buy an underlying financial instrument. (*See* Table 14.2.) In the case of options on futures, the underlying financial instrument is a futures contract. The specified price at which an option may be exercised is called the **strike price**, and the date on or before which the option may be exercised is known as the **expiration date**, or expiry.[13]

Each option transaction consists of two parties—a buyer (who subsequently becomes a holder) and a seller (or writer). The buyer of a call option is said to take a "long" posi-tion in the market, while the seller of a call option takes a "short" position in the market. Similarly, the buyer of a put option has a "short" position, and the seller of a put option has a "long" position.[14]

TABLE 14.2

Rights (Obligations) of Option Holders (Writers)

	Call	Put
Holder	Has the **right** to **buy** the underlying financial instrument at the strike price.	Has the **right** to **sell** the underlying financial instrument at the strike price.
Writer	Has the **obligation** to **sell** underlying financial instrument at the strike price.	Has the **obligation** to **buy** the underlying financial instrument at the strike price.

The option buyer pays the seller a price which represents an initial net investment called a **premium**. The amount of premium the buyer pays depends on factors includ-ing the price of the underlying, the strike price, time remaining until expiration (i.e., time decay), and volatility of the underlying financial instrument. An option's premium generally increases as the option becomes further in the money and decreases as the option becomes more deeply out of the money. Generally, volatility of the underlying is positively correlated to changes in the premium. However, time remaining until expira-tion has a negative, exponential correlation to the premium. That is, the closer that an option gets to expiration, the lower the premium paid by the buyer and the faster the rate of reduction in the premium.[15]

At any given point in time, an option may be "**out of the money**" or "**in the money**."[16] For a call option, the option is said to be out of the money when the current market price

---

[11] *See* ASC 815-10-15-94.

[12] *See* ASC 815-10-15-95.

[13] *See, e.g.,* Cordier, James and Gross, Michael. *The Complete Guide to Option Selling: How Selling Options Can Lead to Stellar Returns in Bull and Bear Markets.* McGraw-Hill, 2004; "Fundamentals of Options on Futures." *CME Institute* <https://institute.cmegroup.com/whitepapers/markets/fundamentals-of-options-on-futures>; "CME Group Options on Futures." *CME Group* <https://www.cmegroup.com/education/files/options-on-futures-brochure.pdf>; "Options Pricing." *The Options Industry Council.*

[14] *Ibid.*

[15] *Ibid.*

[16] An option may also be "at the money," meaning that the market price of the underlying financial instrument is the same as the option strike price. However, options that are "at the money" are treated as either in the money or out of the money, depending on the terms of the option.

of the underlying financial instrument is below the option strike price and in the money when the current market price of the underlying financial instrument is above the option strike price. The converse is true for a put option: the option is said to be out of the money when the current market price of the underlying financial instrument is above the option strike price and in the money when the current market price of the underlying financial instrument is below the option strike price.[17]

The value of an option has three components: (a) intrinsic value; (b) time value; and (c) volatility. An option has **intrinsic value** if it is in the money; the magnitude of this intrinsic value is based on the amount by which the option is in the money. The **time value** of an option is based on the amount of time remaining until expiry. Even when all other factors are held constant, time value erodes non-linearly the value of an option with each minute that passes.[18] As explained by the Options Industry Council, "Theta or time decay is not linear. The theoretical rate of decay will tend to increase as time to expiration decreases. Thus, the amount of decay indicated by Theta tends to be gradual at first and accelerates as expiration approaches. Upon expiration, an option has no time value and trades only for intrinsic value, if any."[19] The non-linear decay of the time value of an option is illustrated below (see Figure 14.1). Note, in particular, how the time value of an option decays more rapidly as the expiration date approaches—in this way, time value is always working in favor of the option seller.

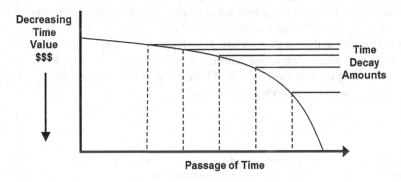

FIGURE 14.1[20]

Volatility measures how quickly and how much an option price moves in relation to the underlying financial instrument and may favor either the buyer or seller of the option.[21] The stock market moves constantly due to temporary differences in supply and

---

[17] See, e.g., Cordier, James and Gross, Michael. The Complete Guide to Option Selling: How Selling Options Can Lead to Stellar Returns in Bull and Bear Markets. McGraw-Hill, 2004; "Fundamentals of Options on Futures." CME Institute <https://institute.cmegroup.com/whitepapers/markets/fundamentals-of-options-on-futures>; "CME Group Options on Futures." CME Group <https://www.cmegroup.com/education/files/options-on-futures-brochure.pdf>; "Options Pricing." The Options Industry Council <https://www.optionseducation.org/getting_started/options_overview/options_pricing.html>.

[18] Ibid

[19] See "Theta." The Options Industry Council <https://www.optionseducation.org/strategies_advanced_concepts/advanced_concepts/understanding_option_greeks/theta.html>.

[20] See "Fundamentals of Options on Futures." CME Institute <https://institute.cmegroup.com/whitepapers/markets/fundamentals-of-options-on-futures>.

[21] See, e.g., Cordier, James and Gross, Michael. The Complete Guide to Option Selling: How Selling Options Can Lead to Stellar Returns in Bull and Bear Markets. McGraw-Hill, 2004; "Fundamentals of Options on Futures." CME Institute <https://institute.cmegroup.com/whitepapers/markets/fundamentals-of-options-on-futures>; "CME Group Options on Futures." CME Group <https://www.cmegroup.com/education/files/options-on-futures-brochure.pdf>.

demand stemming from a variety of reasons and economic indicators, including market sentiment, growth expectations, valuation, momentum, and central bank activity.[22] The value of an option based on the stock market likewise moves constantly due to instantaneous changes in both the price of the underlying and volatility, along with the ever-eroding time value.[23] Thus, option prices have the potential for more volatility than stock prices.

For option sellers, profit potential is limited to the premium collected upon the sale of the option and there is theoretically an unlimited risk of loss. However, a study published by *Futures* magazine in 2003 found that 76.5 percent of options held to expiration expire worthless and the Chicago Mercantile Exchange estimated in 2001 that approximately 74 percent of options held to expiration expire worthless. These proportions of options expiring worthless, along with the fact that the time value of an option is ever-eroding, indicate that the odds of gains on any option trade typically favor the option seller.[24]

There are two main styles of options—American-style options and European-style options. Both styles of options may be traded on American exchanges. The difference between the styles is the time at which they can be exercised. American-style options may be exercised by the option buyer at any time before or at expiration. European-style options, however, may only be exercised at expiration.[25] The buyer or seller of either an American style or European style option may "close" the position at any time. To close a position prior to expiration, an option seller or buyer must make an offsetting transaction; that is, a put or call buyer (seller) must sell (buy) a put or call with the same strike price and expiration date as the purchased (sold) put or call option, respectively.[26] Upon the execution of such an offsetting transaction, the position is closed.[27] Based upon my review of trading records for the Funds, I have found that the options that Xxxx traded were very rarely exercised prior to expiration.[28]

---

[22] *See, e.g.,* Goonatilake, Rohitha. "The Volatility of the Stock Market and News." *International Research Journal of Finance and Economics,* 2007 <http://citeseerx.ist.psu.edu/viewdoc/summary?doi=10.1.1.124.5376>; Kirilenko, Andrei, et al. "The Flash Crash: The Impact of High Frequency Trading on an Electronic Market." February 21, 2014 <http://www.cftc.gov/idc/groups/public/@economicanalysis/documents/file/oce_flashcrash0314.pdf>; "Findings Regarding the Market Events of May 6, 2010." *U.S. Securities and Exchange Commission and U.S. Commodities Futures Trading Commission,* September 30, 2010 <https://www.sec.gov/news/studies/2010/marketevents-report.pdf>; "A Fascinating Look at How the Internet Has Changed the Stock Market." *Vision Computer Solutions,* 2016 <http://vcsolutions.com/a-fascinating-look-at-how-the-internet-has-changed-the-stock-market/>; Baden, Ben. "5 Factors That Drive Stock Prices." *U.S. News,* 2011 <https://money.usnews.com/money/personal-finance/mutual-funds/articles/2011/07/14/5-factors-that-drive-stock-prices>.

[23] *See, e.g.,* Cordier, James and Gross, Michael. *The Complete Guide to Option Selling: How Selling Options Can Lead to Stellar Returns in Bull and Bear Markets.* McGraw-Hill, 2004; "Fundamentals of Options on Futures." *CME Institute* <https://institute.cmegroup.com/whitepapers/markets/fundamentals-of-options-on-futures>; "CME Group Options on Futures." *CME Group* <https://www.cmegroup.com/education/files/options-on-futures-brochure.pdf>; "Options Pricing." *The Options Industry Council* <https://www.optionseducation.org/getting_started/options_overview/options_pricing.html>.

[24] *See, e.g.,* Summa, John. "Sellers vs Buyers: Who Wins? A Study of CME Options Expiration Patterns." *OptionsNerd.com* <http://app.topica.com/banners/forms/900067555/900031275/SELLERSVSBUYERSWHOWINS.doc>; Cordier, James and Gross, Michael. *The Complete Guide to Option Selling: How Selling Options Can Lead to Stellar Returns in Bull and Bear Markets.* McGraw-Hill, 2004.

[25] *See, e.g.,* Cordier, James and Gross, Michael. *The Complete Guide to Option Selling: How Selling Options Can Lead to Stellar Returns in Bull and Bear Markets.* McGraw-Hill, 2004; "Fundamentals of Options on Futures." *CME Institute* <https://institute.cmegroup.com/whitepapers/markets/fundamentals-of-options-on-futures>; "CME Group Options on Futures." *CME Group* <https://www.cmegroup.com/education/files/options-on-futures-brochure.pdf>.

[26] *Ibid.*

[27] *Ibid.*

[28] *See, e.g.,* Trading Records of the XX Fund and XXX Fund, identified in Exhibit B.

At expiry, the seller of an option of either style that is in the money is typically assigned or obligated to perform. When an option holder exercises a long call, an option seller is assigned the obligation to sell the underlying financial instrument at the strike price. This assignment results in a short position in the underlying financial instrument for the option seller. When an option holder exercises a long put, the option seller is assigned the obligation to buy the underlying financial instrument at the strike price. This assignment results in a long position in the underlying financial instrument for the option seller.[29] An assigned short or long position in the underlying financial instrument may be netted by an offsetting position; that is, a short position in the underlying financial instrument may be netted by a long position in the same underlying financial instrument, and vice versa.[30]

A futures contract is a legally binding agreement to buy or sell a specified commodity or financial instrument in a specified amount at a specified date in the future. One who buys a futures contract agrees to purchase the underlying commodity or financial instrument, while one who sells a futures contract agrees to sell the same. A futures contract includes the item being bought and sold, the contract size, the contract month (typically March, June, September, or December), and the manner of settlement. Stock index futures do not call for the delivery of the actual stocks associated with the stock index; rather, a cash settlement mechanism is used wherein subsequent to the final settlement day, positions expire and are settled at the spot (i.e., cash) value of the underlying index.[31]

Stock index futures, including S&P 500 futures, were introduced in 1982 on domestic futures exchanges. The original S&P 500 futures contract was based on a value of $500 times the index value. In 1997, the Chicago Mercantile Exchange found that the futures contract value was too high and halved the contract multiplier to $250. In the same year, realizing that the futures contract value was still high relative to many other futures contracts, the exchange introduced an alternative, electronically-traded "E-mini" S&P 500 contract based on a value of $50 times the index. The E-Mini S&P 500 design was "widely accepted and rapidly grew to become the most popular line of stock index futures available today."[32]

The SEC notes on its website that it "sometimes receive[s] questions and complaints about futures trading." It further notes that "[t]he SEC administers and enforces the federal laws that govern the sale and trading of securities, such as stocks, bonds, and mutual funds, but we do not regulate futures trading. We refer questions and complaints about futures to the Commodity Futures Trading Commission (CFTC)—the federal agency that does regulate futures trading."[33]

---

[29] *See, e.g.,* Cordier, James and Gross, Michael. *The Complete Guide to Option Selling: How Selling Options Can Lead to Stellar Returns in Bull and Bear Markets.* McGraw-Hill, 2004; "Fundamentals of Options on Futures." *CME Institute* <https://institute.cmegroup.com/whitepapers/markets/fundamentals-of-options-on-futures>; "CME Group Options on Futures." *CME Group* <https://www.cmegroup.com/education/files/options-on-futures-brochure.pdf>. Note that the assigned futures position will have a different expiration date than the option itself.

[30] *See, e.g.,* https://www.theocc.com/education/futures/

[31] *See, e.g.,* Cordier, James and Gross, Michael. *The Complete Guide to Option Selling: How Selling Options Can Lead to Stellar Returns in Bull and Bear Markets.* McGraw-Hill, 2004; "Fundamentals of Options on Futures." *CME Institute* <https://institute.cmegroup.com/whitepapers/markets/fundamentals-of-options-on-futures>; "CME Group Options on Futures." *CME Group* <https://www.cmegroup.com/education/files/options-on-futures-brochure.pdf>; "Security Futures: An Introduction to Their Uses and Risks." *National Futures Association* <https://www.nfa.futures.org/members/member-resources/files/security-futures.pdf>; "Stock Indexes: Understanding Stock Index Futures." *CME Group,* May 3, 2013 <https://www.cmegroup.com/education/files/understanding-stock-index-futures.pdf>; "S&P 500 Futures and Options on Futures." *CME Group* <https://www.cmegroup.com/trading/equity-index/files/sandp-500-futures-options.pdf>.

[32] *Ibid.*

[33] *See* "Fast Answers – Commodity Futures Trading Commission." *U.S. Securities and Exchange Commission* <https://www.sec.gov/fast-answers/answers-cftchtm.html>.

VI.   An Overview of Hedge Funds.

A hedge fund is a privately offered fund that is administered by a professional invest-ment management firm. Hedge fund managers seek and assume calculated risks to achieve investment returns. Globally, there are an estimated 8,200 active individual hedge funds with more than approximately $3.1 trillion in assets under management. The US accounts for approximately 72% of the global assets under management.[34]

One measure of value that is common among hedge funds is net asset value, or "NAV," which equals the hedge fund's total assets minus its liabilities. In other words, the NAV of a hedge fund is the value of the fund if it were closed at that moment. Daily changes in NAV occur due to changes in a fund's holdings, as well as mark-to-market accounting of its holdings. Under mark-to-market accounting (fair value accounting),[35] the value of an asset or liability is based on the current market price of the financial instrument, rather than the book value (*i.e.*, the price paid for the financial instrument). The market price of an option moves constantly due to instantaneous changes in both the price of the underlying financial instrument and volatility, along with the ever-erod-ing time value. Accordingly, for hedge funds that trade options, the value of the fund's assets and liabilities (and, thus, its NAV) are constantly subject to change.[36]

For hedge funds that trade financial instruments without expiration or maturity dates, such as the stock of publicly-traded companies, NAV is a relevant data point for investors and it is strongly correlated to the profitability of the fund. If, however, a hedge fund trades financial instruments with expiration or maturity dates, such as options or futures, NAV is not nearly as relevant to investors nor is NAV strongly correlated with the profitability of the fund. For example, when a hedge fund sells an option, there is a potential for the fund to profit at expiration or maturity even if if the option shows a paper loss at the moment NAV is calculated. In other words, an out of the money option may have a paper gain or loss at any given moment, but all else held constant, the option will be worthless at expiration. For example, suppose that the market price of Apple stock was $100 and that on January 1 a hedge fund sold one (1) call option on Apple stock for $20 with a strike price of $150 with an expiration date of February 15. This short call is out of the money by 50 points and has about 45 days until it expires. If, on January 31, the market price of Apple stock increased to $140, I would expect the price of the option to increase; in this case, suppose the price increases to $30. Since the stock price increased and is closer to the option's strike price, the value of the option would have increased. However, there has been 30 days that have passed and been a negative influence on the price of the option. The $10 price increase in the option is the net effect of the market driven increase and the decrease from time decay. Thus, this option is still out of the money, but would result in a $10 loss (−50%) if the fund decided to close it. If the fund chose not to close it, the option has a high probability that it will expire

---

[34] *See, e.g., Herbst-Bayliss, Svea. "Fewer hedge fund managers call it quits in 1st-half 2017." Reuters, September 18, 2017* <https://www.reuters.com/article/us-hedgefunds-closures/fewer-hedge-fund-managers-call-it-quits-in-1st-half-2017-idUSKCN1BT2C3>; *"Preqin Special Report: Hedge Funds in the US." Preqin, October 2016* <http://docs.preqin.com/reports/Preqin-Special-Report-Hedge-Funds-in-the-US-October-2016.pdf>; *Acton, Gemma. "Number of hedge funds continues to shrink as launches fall to financial crisis levels." CNBC, December 16, 2016* <https://www.cnbc.com/2016/12/16/number-of-hedge-funds-continues-to-shrink-as-launches-fall-to-financial-crisis-levels.html>; *"About Hedge Funds" Hedge Fund Association* <http://www.hedgefundassoc.org/about_hedge_funds/>; *Gad, Shan. "What Are Hedge Funds?" Forbes and Investopedia, October 22, 2013* <https://www.forbes.com/sites/investopedia/2013/10/22/what-are-hedge-funds/#7a653ff48ee3>.

[35] *See, e.g.,* ASC 815-10-10-1: "Fair value is the most relevant measure for financial instruments and the only relevant measure for derivative instruments."

[36] *See, e.g.,* <http://www.nasdaq.com/investing/glossary/m/mark-to-market-accounting>; "Fast Answers − Net Asset Value." *U.S. Securities and Exchange Commission* <https://www.sec.gov/fast-answers/answersnavhtm.html>.

worthless in 15 days out of the money. If the option indeed expired worthless out of the money, the fund would realize a $20 gain (+100%) on the option. A calculation of the fund's NAV would not be able to capture or show to investors that, although the fund would lose money on certain positions if they were closed, the fund would be very likely to earn a profit on those positions when they mature or expire.

The traditional fee structure for hedge funds is the "2 and 20" structure based on NAV and subject to a high-water mark. Under this fee structure, hedge fund managers earn an annual management fee equal to 2% of the net asset value of the fund (irrespective of the fund's performance) plus 20% of gains, including both unrealized and realized gains and losses. In addition, many investors pay direct and indirect pass-through fund expenses under the typical hedge fund fee structure, such as administrative, legal, and audit fees.[37]

Despite its prevalence, many market commentators have criticized the traditional "2 and 20" fee structure for hedge funds. Warren Buffet, for example, has said that the "2 and 20" fee structure "borders on obscene."[38] As he explained, "how many hedge fund managers in the last 40 years have said 'I only want to get paid if I do something for you? Unless I actually deliver something beyond what you can get yourself, I don't want to get paid.' It just doesn't happen."[39]

VII. The Xxxx Entities.

Xxxx Xxxxxxxx, XXX ("Xxxx"), is a Xxxxxxxxx Limited Liability Company that was formed on March 23, XXXX. Xxxx is, or was, respectively, the investment advisor to Xxxx Xxxxxxxxxxx, XXX (the "XX Fund") and XXX Xxxxxxxxxxx, XXX (the "XXX Fund") (collectively, the "Funds"). Xxxx is registered with both the Commodity Futures Trading Commission ("CFTC") and the National Futures Association ("NFA") as a commodity pool operator and was registered as an investment advisor with the SEC from July XXXX until September 1, XXXX.[40]

Xxxx is wholly owned by Xxxxx Xxxxxx. Xx. Xxxxxx is an options trader and has served as President of Xxxx since March XXXX.[41] Xx. Xxxxxx received a bachelor's degrees in mathematics and accounting from the University of North Carolina, Chapel Hill, and holds an MBA from Wake Forest University. Xx. Xxxxxx previously held a CPA license, which is no longer active.[42] Xx. Xxxxxx became listed with the CFTC as a Principal of Xxxx, registered as an Associated Person of Xxxx, and became a member of NFA, in such capacities, on January 24, XXXX.[43] Xxxx Xxxxxxx and Xxxx Xxxxxxx are both employees of Xxxx. Xx. Xxxxxxx is a trader and Xx. Xxxxxxx is the controller, and previously served as the chief compliance officer.

---

[37] *See, e.g., Delevingne, Lawrence. "Struggling hedge funds still expense bonuses, bar tabs." Reuters, January 19, 2017* <https://www.reuters.com/article/us-hedgefunds-passthrough-insight/struggling-hedge-funds-still-expense-bonuses-bar-tabs-idUSKBN1530JL>; *Barlow, Joshua. "Hidden Fees in Hedge Funds." FINalternatives, July 30, 2013* <http://www.finalternatives.com/node/24322>; *"Lessons in Clarity: Hedge Funds." CFA Institute* <https://www.cfainstitute.org/programs/investmentfoundations/courseofstudy/Pages/lessons_in_clarity_hedge_funds.aspx>.

[38] *See Gurdus, Elizabeth. "Hedge funds' 'obscene' fees make people rich – just not investors, says Buffett." CNBC, February 27, 2017* <https://www.cnbc.com/2017/02/27/buffett-hedge-funds-fees-border-on-obscene.html>.

[39] *See Buhayar, Noah, et al. "Buffett Says Money Spent on Plumbers Better Than on Hedge Funds." Bloomberg, May 6, 2017* <https://www.bloomberg.com/news/articles/2017-05-06/buffett-says-money-spent-on-plumbers-better-than-on-hedge-funds>.

[40] *See, e.g., Defendants Xxxx Xxxxxxxx,XXX's and Xxxxx Xxxxxx's Answer and Affirmative Defenses to the Second Amended Complaint filed October 16, XXX (Dkt. No. XX), ¶ 6.*

[41] *See, e.g., id. ¶ 7.*

[42] *See* <https://xxxxxxxxxxxxxxxxxxxxxxx.org/team/xxxxx-xxxxxx/>.

[43] *See, e.g., Xxxx Xxxxxxxxxxx, XXX* Confidential Private Placement Memorandum and Disclosure Document dated January 31, XXXX, p. 25 (XX_000681-738 at 711).

Xxxx Xxxx Xxxxxxxxxx ("Xxxx Xxxxxxxxxx") is a Xxxxxxxxx-based tax-exempt 501(c)(3) private foundation.[44] Xx. Xxxxxx was the President of the Xxxx Xxxxxxxxxx in XXXX, XXXX and XXXX.[45] Xxx Xxxx Xxxxxxxxxx pays for all administrative expenses of Xxxx Xxxx Xxxxxxxxxxxxx ("Xxxx Xxxx"), which allows Xxxx Xxxx to use 100% of the donations it receives for project costs.[46]

Xxxx Xxxx is a Xxxxxxxx-based tax-exempt 501(c)(3) charitable organization founded by Xx. Xxxxxx.[47] Formed in XXXX—prior to Xxxx and the Funds—the organization "works to make an impact that lasts by empowering remarkable people to overcome some of the world's most difficult living conditions."[48]

The XXX Xxxx was a Xxxxxxxxx Limited Liability Company formed on or around April 3, XXXX and dissolved on or around August 6, XXXX.[51] On November 1, XXXX, the XXXX Xxxx ceased being a commingled commodity pool and became a single member limited liability company owned entirely by Xxxxx Xxxxx Xxxx, who was also the XXX Xxxx's managing member.[52] Xxx XXX Xxxx was originally formed by three individuals, Xxxxx Xxxxx Xxxx, X. Xxxxxxx Xxxxxx, and Xxxxx Xxxxxx, who previously worked together at Xxxxxxxx Xxxxxxxxxx, Xxx., a limestone company based in Xxxxxxxxx, Xxxxxxxxx.[53] Xxxx became the investment advisor of the XXX Fund in XXXX, and ceased trading for the XXX Fund in XXXX.[54]

The XX Xxxx is a Xxxxxxxxx Limited Liability Company formed on February 16, XXXX.[55] The XX Fund is a hedge fund offered by Xxxx, which is the investment advisor of the XX Fund. The XX Fund is registered with the CFTC as a commodity pool, which subjects its operations to regulation under the Commodity Exchange Act, administered by the CFTC. The XX Fund is also subject to the rules of the NFA.[56]

The XX Fund has three classes of interests although only one, Class A, is offered to investors.[57] The Class B Interests are all held by Xxxx Xxxxxxxxxx and are entitled

---

[44] See, e.g., Xxxx Xxxx Xxxxxxxxxx Form 990-PF (Return of Private Foundation) filings for years ended XXXX-XXXX (accessed through GuideStar).

[45] See, e.g., Xxxx Xxxx Xxxxxxxxxx Form 990-PF (Return of Private Foundation) filings for years ended XXXX-XXXX (accessed through GuideStar).

[46] See, e.g., Defendants Xxxx Xxxxxxxx, XXX's and Xxxxx Xxxxxx's Answer and Affirmative Defenses to the Second Amended Complaint filed October 16, XXXX (Dkt. No. XX), ¶ 10; <https://xxxxxxxxxxxxxxxxxxxxxx.org/xxxx-xx-xxxxx/>; https://xxxxxxxxxxxxxxxxxxxxx.org/our-approach/

[47] See, e.g., id.; Xxxx Xxxx Xxxxxxxxxxxx Form 990 (Return of Organization Exempt from Income Tax) filings for years ended XXXX-XXXX.

[48] See Xxxx Xxxx Xxxxxxxxxxxxx Form 990 (Return of Organization Exempt from Income Tax) filings for year ended XXXX.

[51] See, e.g., Defendants Xxxx Xxxxxxxx, XXX's and Xxxxx Xxxxxx's Answer and Affirmative Defenses to the Second Amended Complaint filed October 16, XXXX (Dkt. No. XX), ¶ 12; Xxxxxxxxx Department of Xxxxx Xxxxxxxx of Business Services Filing Information for XXX Xxxxxxxxxxx, XXX.

[52] See, e.g., XXX Xxxxxxxxxxx, XXX Financial Statements for the Years Ended December 31, XXXX and XXXX (XX_002815-2833 at 2815).

[53] See, e.g., Deposition of X. Xxxxxxx Xxxxxx dated June 8, XXXX, p. 22–24; 27–28.

[54] See, e.g., XXX XXXXXXXXXXXX, XXX Financial Statements for the Years Ended December 31, XXXX and XXXX, p. 8 (XX_002815-2833 at 2824); March 31, XXXX statement for XXX Xxxxxxxxxxx, XXX (Xxxx_NDGA-00019836); January through March XXXX trading records for XXX Xxxxxxxxxxx, XXX (Xxxx_NDGA-00000062, Xxxx_NDGA-00000077, and Xxxx_NDGA-00000079).

[55] See, e.g., Defendants Xxxx Xxxxxxxx, XXX's and Xxxxx Xxxxxx's Answer and Affirmative Defenses to the Second Amended Complaint filed October 16, XXXX (Dkt. No. XX), ¶ 11; Xxxxxxxxx Department of Xxxxx Xxxxxxxx of Business Services Filing Information for Xxxx Xxxxxxxxxxx, XXX.

[56] See, e.g., Xxxx Xxxxxxxxxxx, XXX Financial Statements for the Years Ended December 31, XXXX and XXXX, p. 8 (XX_002834-2855 at 2843); Xxxx Xxxxxxxxxxx, XXX Financial Statements for the Years Ended December 31, XXXX and XXXX, p. 9 (XX_002856-2880 at 2866); Xxxx Xxxxxxxxxxx, XXX Financial Statements for the Years Ended December 31, XXXX and XXXX, p. 9 (Deposition of X. Xxxxxxx Xxxxxx dated June 8, XXXX, Ex. 7).

[57] See, e.g., XXX Xxxxxxxxxxx, XXX Confidential Private Placement Memorandum and Disclosure Document dated January 31, XXXX, p. 1–2 (HA_000681-738 at 687–688).

to a 10% incentive allocation, as defined in various documents described below.[58] This funding to the Xxxx Xxxxxxxxxx, among other things, "provides a permanent source of funds to pay the administrative costs" of Xxxx Xxxx.[59] Class C Interests are held by Xx. Xxxxxx, as the Managing Member of the XX Xxxx, and she is also entitled to a 10% incentive allocation as defined in various documents, described below.[60] Xx. Xxxxxx pays certain of the XX Xxxx's operating expenses as well as certain of Xxxx's operating expenses, including compensation for employees, such as Xxxx Xxxxxxx, Xxxx Xxxxxxx and others, from the 10% incentive allocation that she receives.[61]

For the period that is relevant to this proceeding, certain features of the XXX Fund and the XX Fund were somewhat unique, as compared to other hedge funds. First, many hedge funds operate under a "2 and 20" fee structure, as described above. In contrast, the XXX Fund and the XX Fund paid incentive allocations that were equal to 20% of net realized gains on closed positions. Second, investors who withdrew all or any portion of their investment from the Funds did so based upon capital account values that reflected only net realized gains and losses on closed positions. Thus, withdrawing members did not participate in unrealized gains and losses on open positions. The Funds' redemption practices contrasted with the redemption practices of certain other hedge funds, under which investors redeem at NAV, which includes realized and unrealized gains and losses.[62]

VIII. Information Provided to Prospective Investors in the XX Fund.

It is my understanding that prospective investors in the XX Fund were provided an XX Fund Confidential Private Placement Memorandum ("PPM"), XX Xxxx Operating Agreement (the "XX OA"), and Contribution Agreement (collectively, the "XX Fund Offering Materials"), which explained, among other things, the XX Fund's objectives and risks, the terms of investing in the XX Fund, as well as, fees and redemption terms.[63]

The original PPM was dated March 23, XXXX and updated on January 31, XXXX, January 31, XXXX, January 31, XXXX, and January 31, XXXX.[64] Each of the PPMs contained information that described the fund's investment objective, the manner in which incentive allocations would be earned and paid, the withdrawal process, tax information, suitability standards, and risk factors, among other things. Unless otherwise stated, this section quotes from the PPM dated January 31, XXXX.

---

[58] *The Xxxx Xxxxxxxxxx also owns Class A interests.*

[59] *See, e.g., Defendants Xxxx Xxxxxxxx, XXX's and Xxxxx Xxxxxx's Answer and Affirmative Defenses to the Second Amended Complaint filed October 16, XXXX (Dkt. No. XX), ¶ 10.*

[60] *See, e.g., XXX Xxxxxxxxxxx, XXX Confidential Private Placement Memorandum and Disclosure Document dated January 31, XXXX, p. 1–2 (XX_000681-738 at 687–688); Third Restated Operating Agreement of XXX Xxxxxxxxxxx, XXX, dated January 31, XXXX, p. 29 (XX_000652-680 at 680).*

[61] *See, e.g., Defendants Xxxx Xxxxxxxx, XXX's and Xxxxx Xxxxxx's Answer and Affirmative Defenses to the Second Amended Complaint filed October 16, XXXX (Dkt. No. XX), ¶¶ 8–9.*

[62] *See, e.g., Faccone, Erin. "The Essential Guide to Third-Party Valuations for Hedge Fund Investors." NEPC, LLC (2017) <https://cdn2.hubspot.net/hubfs/2529352/files/Third%20Party%20Valuations-%20White%20Paper-1.pdf?t= 1513697342060>.*

[63] *The early versions of these materials contained the material terms of an investment in the XX Fund. Subsequent versions contained more details but did not alter the material terms describing the XX Fund.*

[64] *The updates to the PPM did not alter the material terms of an investment in the XX Fund or provide any material information not disclosed in the original PPM, dated March 23, XXXX. See Xxxx Xxxxxxxxxxx, XXX Confidential Private Placement Memorandum dated March 23, XXXX (Xxxx_000177-196); Xxxx Xxxxxxxxxxx, XXX Confidential Private Placement Memorandum dated January 31, XXXX (Xxxx_000037 – 58); Xxxx Xxxxxxxxxxx, XXX Confidential Private Placement Memorandum and Disclosure Document dated January 31, XXXX (Xxxx_000059-140); Xxxx Xxxxxxxxxxx, XXX Confidential Private Placement Memorandum and Disclosure Document dated January 31, XXX (XX_000681-738); Xxxx Xxxxxxxxxxx, XXX Confidential Private Placement Memorandum and Disclosure Document dated January 31, XXXX (Xxxx_000115-172).*

Class A investors signed a Contribution Agreement for the XX Fund, wherein the investor, or "Subscriber," certified that he or she has reviewed and understands the risks of an investment in the Fund, has the financial knowledge and experience to evaluate such investment, is able to bear the substantial risks of an investment in the Fund and is able to afford to lose his or her entire investment.[65] Class A investors also certified that they are qualified investors.[66] It is my understanding that there were multiple iterations of the Contribution Agreement, although the material aspects of the document did not change throughout the iterations.[67]

In executing the XX Fund Contribution Agreement, each prospective investor certified that he or she has "carefully reviewed and understands the various risks of an investment in the Fund, including those summarized under 'Risk Factors' and 'Conflicts of Interest' in the [PPM]."[68] In addition, the prospective investor certifies that:

> Subscriber has had the opportunity to review the material documents referenced in the Memorandum, and has had the opportunity to ask questions and receive answers concerning the Fund and the terms and conditions of this offering and to obtain such additional information as Subscriber considers necessary to verify the accuracy of the information in the Memorandum and evaluate appropriately an investment in the Fund.
>
> [...] Subscriber has carefully reviewed and understands the fees and expenses that are directly and indirectly assessed on the Fund and the Class A Members, including, without limitation, the Incentive Allocation.[69]

A. The XX Fund's Investment Objective and Trading Program.

The XX Fund Offering Materials highlight the fund's investment objective and past performance and generally describe the fund's investment strategy. The PPM states, "[t] he investment objective of the Fund is to seek to profit from speculative trading. The Fund was specifically designed to trade in options on, options on futures on, and futures on [...] broad-based equity indexes [...]."[70] The XX OA similarly notes that, "[t]he purpose of the [XX Fund] is to use the funds provided by its Class A Members [...] for the sale, purchase, and trading of options on broad based equity indexes, options on futures on broad based equity indexes, and futures on broad based equity indexes [...]."[71]

The PPM cautioned investors, however, that "[t]here is no guarantee that the Fund will achieve its investment objective, and [investors] may lose [their] entire investment."[72] It continues, "**Investors must be able to bear the substantial risks of an investment in the Fund and be able to afford to lose his or her entire investment.**"[73] In addition, the PPM stated that "[a]**n investment in the Fund is speculative and involves a high degree of risk. Investors should be aware that an investment in the Fund is suitable only for persons who can afford to lose their entire investment.**"[74]

---

[65] *See, e.g., Xxxx Xxxxxxxxxxx, XXX Subscription Booklet, at 2–3 (Xxxx_000253-292, at Xxxx_000260-61).*

[66] *Ibid.*

[67] *See Xxxx_000197-331.*

[68] *See* Contribution Agreement for Xxxx Xxxxxxxxxxxx to be used in conjunction with the January 31, XXXX PPM (Dkt. No. XX-X), p. 3.

[69] *Ibid.*

[70] *See, e.g., Xxxx Xxxxxxxxxxx, XXX Confidential Private Placement Memorandum and Disclosure Document dated January 31, XXXX, p. 9 (XX_000681-738 at 687).*

[71] *See Third Restated Operating Agreement of Xxxx Xxxxxxxxxxx, XXX, dated January 31, XXXX, p. 10 (XX_000652-680 at 661).*

[72] *See Xxxx Xxxxxxxxxxx, XXX Confidential Private Placement Memorandum and Disclosure Document dated January 31, XXXX, p. 1 (XX_000681-738 at 687).*

[73] *Id. at p. 2 (XX_000681-738 at 688) (emphasis in original).*

[74] *Id. at p. 5 (XX_000681-738 at 691) (emphasis in original).*

The PPM further disclosed many specific risks that investors faced with an investment in the XX Fund.[75]

Moreover, the XX Fund Offering Materials cautioned investors that due to "the proprietary nature of the Investment Advisor's trading program, [investors] generally will not be advised if adjustments are made to the Investment Advisor's trading program," except that "to the extent that such changes are material, [investors] will be notified of such material changes, and [investors] will be given the opportunity to withdraw [their] investment."[76] While the XX Fund Offering Materials described the general trading objectives and strategy of the fund to prospective investors, Xxxx further informed its investors of updates to its strategy at various points from XXXX through XXXX, including updates in response to market volatility.[77] In addition, each Class A interest holder had the right to inspect the books and records of the XX Xxxx.[78]

B.   The XX Fund's Fee Structure.
The XX Fund Offering Materials explained that the investors in the XX Fund, holders of Class A interests, do not pay a management fee to Xxxx, the XX Fund's investment advisor.[79] Rather, as described in the PPM, the XX Xxxx's operating expenses are paid for by Xx. Xxxxxx, except for brokerage commissions and trading fees, which are paid for by the XX Fund itself.[80] The PPM further described the incentive allocation, which is paid to Xxxx Xxxxxxxxxx, as the current holder of Class B interests, and Xx. Xxxxxx, as holder of Class C interests:

> An incentive allocation (the 'Incentive Allocation') equal to 20% of the New Trading Profits (as defined below) earned by the Fund accrues and is payable monthly to the holders of the Class B Interests and Class C Interests. [...] The holders of the Class B Interests receive 50% of the Incentive Allocation (i.e., 10% of the New Trading Profits), and the holder of the Class C Interests receives 50% of the Incentive Allocation (i.e., 10% of the New Trading Profits).
>
> The term "New Trading Profits" means net trading profits that have been realized on closed positions of trades made from the assets of the Fund [...], decreased proportionally by the Fund's brokerage fees and other transaction costs and increased by any interest income received by the Fund.[81]

Earlier iterations of the PPM stated the same by disclosing, *inter alia*, that the Class B and C interest holders would be compensated with 20% of "the profit realized by the [XX Xxxx] based upon the trades done by the [XX Xxxx] and/or the Investment Manager."[82]

As the Incentive Allocation was based on "net trading profits that have been realized on closed positions," the PPM further disclosed to investors that "it is possible that the

---

[75] *Id. at p. 18–23 (XX_000681-738 at 704–709).*

[76] *Id.* at p. 22 (HA_000681-738 at 708).

[77] *See, e.g.,* Letter from Xxxxx Xxxxxx to Xxxx Xxxxxxxxxxxx, XXX, Investor(s) dated March 25, XXXX (Dkt. No. XX-8); Letter from Xxxxx Xxxxxx to Members of Xxxx Xxxxxxxxxxxx, XXX, dated December 24, XXXX (Dkt. No. XX-9); Letter from Xxxxx Xxxxxx to Members of Xxxx Xxxxxxxxxxxx dated June 4, XXXX (Dkt. No. XX-10).

[78] *See* Third Restated Operating Agreement of Xxxx Xxxxxxxxxxxx, XXX, dated January 31, XXXX, p. 23 (XX_000652-680 at 674).

[79] "No management fee will be charged to the holders of the Class A Interests." *See* Xxxx Xxxxxxxxxxxx, XXX Confidential Private Placement Memorandum and Disclosure Document dated January 31, XXXX, p. 4 (XX_000681-738 at 690).

[80] *Ibid.*

[81] *Ibid.* It is my understanding that the incentive allocation Xx. Xxxxxx received from the XXX Xxxx was calculated in the same manner.

[82] *See* Xxxx Xxxxxxxxxxxx, XXX Confidential Private Placement Memorandum dated March 23, XXXX, p. 4 (Xxxx_000177-196 at 180).

Fund will pay an Incentive Allocation on New Trading Profits even though there are unrealized losses on open positions":

> The Fund pays an Incentive Allocation based upon the New Trading Profits generated by the Investment Advisor for the Fund. These New Trading Profits only include realized gains and losses on closed positions. Accordingly, it is possible that the Fund will pay an Incentive Allocation on New Trading Profits even though there are unrealized losses on open positions. Thus, there is an incentive for the Investment Advisor to realize gains and defer realization of losses; however, due to the type of trading in which the Investment Advisor engages, it is unlikely that the Investment Advisor will be able to defer realization of losses on positions for any extended period of time since most trades into which the Investment Advisor enters will only be open for 30- to 90-days at maximum.[83]

C.   Withdrawals from the XX Fund.

As noted above, another aspect of the XX Fund that was somewhat unique, compared to other hedge funds, was that withdrawing members do not participate in unrealized gains and losses. That aspect of the XX Fund was also explained in the PPM:

> Upon the Withdrawal Date, the withdrawing Member shall only receive his or her *pro rata* portion of any net realized profits or losses on closed positions. Such Member will not receive the benefit of any unrealized gain that is subsequently realized by the Fund. Similarly, the withdrawing Member will not participate in any unrealized loss.
>
> Following such a Withdrawal by a Member, all other Members remaining in the Fund after the Withdrawal Date will receive the benefit of any gains realized subsequent to the Withdrawal Data; however, the Members remaining in the Fund will also participate in any losses subsequently realized on positions that were outstanding as of that Withdrawal Date and closed after the Withdrawal Date.[84]

The XX Fund Offering Materials note that an investor who wishes to withdraw some or all of his or her investment must give written notice of the withdrawal at least one month prior to a withdrawal of $5,000 to $25,000 and at least three months prior to a withdrawal of over $25,000. This notice requirement provides Xxxx with time to close out positions that "used and/or have relied upon the presence of the withdrawing Member's funds."[85] The PPM continues:

> The Fund will use its best efforts to close out positions that have relied upon the presence of the withdrawing Member's funds; however, upon the Withdrawal Date, the withdrawing Member will receive the *pro rata* portion of the realized gains or losses on all closed positions as of that date.[86]

D.   Open and Closed Positions.

The XX Fund Offering Materials, as described above, disclosed to investors that withdrawals from the XX Fund and the incentive allocation were based on realized gains and losses on closed positions, and excluded any unrealized gains and losses on open positions. It is well-established that an options or futures position is closed when it expires

---

[83] *Id. at p. 18 (XX_000681-738 at 704).*
[84] *Id. at 19–20 (XX_000681-738 at 705–706). It is my understanding that investors in the XXX Fund also withdrew or redeemed from the fund based only on their percentage ownership of the XXX Xxxxx's realized gains and losses on closed positions, excluding unrealized gains and losses on open positions.*
[85] *Id. at 3–4 (XX_000681-738 at 689–690).*
[86] *Ibid.*

or when Xxxx manually closes it by purchasing an offsetting position.[87] Otherwise, the position is open. As for options positions that expire in the money and result in the assignment of the underlying financial instrument, it is well-established that, in such a circumstance, the expired option is closed while the assigned futures position is open.[88]

IX. Account Information Provided to Investors in the Funds

A. Monthly Account Statements.

The XX Fund Offering Materials state that as "promptly as practicable after the close of each calendar month, the Fund will distribute to each Class A Member a monthly Capital Account report with respect to such Class A Member's investment in the Fund."[89] The XX OA further states that, in accordance with 17 CFR 4.22 and 4.25:

> Xxxx Xxxxxxxx, as the Investment Advisor for the Fund, is required to report gains and losses to Investors in its offered Funds monthly and annually based upon realized and unrealized gains and losses. Xxxx Xxxxxxxx will report monthly the Fund's unrealized gains and losses on open positions at month's end. Also, monthly Xxxx Xxxxxxxx will report Net Realized Trading Profits and Losses on closed positions based upon the contractually agreed upon payment of the Incentive Allocation to the Class B and the Class C Members [...].
>
> ....
>
> The first monthly statement will be based upon realized gains and losses on closed positions [...]. Members will also receive a second monthly statement calculated according to the Commodity Futures Trading Commission Rule 4.22 found in 17 CFR Part 4, Subpart B in which unrealized gains and losses related to open positions at month end will be calculated according to accounting principles generally accepted in the United States.[90]

It is my understanding that monthly account statements were distributed to XX Fund investors in compliance with the XX Fund Offering Materials.[91]

From the beginning of the relevant period in January XXXX through August XXXX, Xxxx sent investors in the Funds monthly statements consistent with a contractual accounting method.[92] During this time, a typical XX Fund monthly capital account statement provided the following information, by month: (1) the Beginning Realized Capital Account balance as of the beginning of the month; (2) the amount of Capital Contributions made within the month; (3) the amount of Capital Distributions made within the month; (4) the Revised Capital Account balance; (5) the Member Interest in the Revised Capital Account; (6) the Gross Realized Gain/(Loss) for the month; (7) the 20 percent Expenses paid (or, Incentive Allocation) on the Gross Realized Gain/(Loss); (8) the Net Realized Gain/(Loss) after allocation of the 20 percent Expenses; (9) the Ending Realized Capital Account balance; and (10) the Net Monthly Realized ROI

---

[87] *See, e.g., ASC 815-10-25-9; ASC 815-10-45-9.*

[88] *Ibid.*

[89] *See Xxxx Xxxxxxxxxxx, XXX Confidential Private Placement Memorandum and Disclosure Document dated January 31, XXXX, p. 5 (HA_000681-738 at 691). See also id. at p. 34 (XX_000681-738 at 720).*

[90] *See Third Restated Operating Agreement of Xxxx Xxxxxxxxxxx, XXX, dated January 31, XXXX, p. 17–18, 24 (HA_000652-680 at 668-669, 675).*

[91] *See, e.g., Deposition of Xxxxx Xxxxxxx dated January 11, 2018, p. 246–247; Deposition of Xxxxx Xxxxxxx dated June 19, XXXX, p. 23; Deposition of X. Xxxxxxx Xxxxxx dated June 8, XXXX, p. 64–65.*

[92] *See, e.g., Durak, Robert. "New option a game changer for private companies." Journal of Accountancy, September 1, 2013 <https://www.journalofaccountancy.com/issues/2013/sep/20137921.html>; "Financial Reporting Framework for Small- and Medium-Sized Entities." American Institute of Certified Public Accountants, 2013; AU Section 623 "Special Reports." AICPA <https://www.aicpa.org/Research/Standards/AuditAttest/DownloadableDocuments/AU-00623.pdf>.*

(Return on Investment). In addition to these financial metrics, the statement included a graph showing Cumulative Net Realized Gain/(Loss).[93] A typical XXX Fund monthly capital account statement from the beginning of the relevant period in January XXXX through August XXXX contained substantially the same information.[94]

Xxxx expanded the investors' monthly statements for the XX Fund beginning with the statements for August XXXX to also include a statement prepared under regulatory accounting that showed both realized and unrealized gains and losses, as well as the one prepared under contractual accounting that showed realized gains and losses and an incentive allocation calculated based on the same. Beginning in August XXXX, the second page of a typical XX Fund capital account statement included a Statement of Operations for the period and a Statement of Changes in Net Asset Value for the period, each shown for each of the XX Fund in total, Class A Members, and the individual investor. The second page also includes a shaded box with a bold border that shows the calculation of current Net Asset Value based on: (1) the Realized Capital Account Balance; (2) Pending Contributions for NAV; (3) Pending Withdrawals for NAV; and (4) the Current Month Unrealized balance.[95] Put another way, beginning with the statements for August XXXX, Xxxx issued two-page monthly reports to XX Fund investors, with the first page showing realized gains/losses consistent with the participants' contractual investment terms and the second page showing the XX Fund's net asset value as well as realized and unrealized gains and losses, which complies with Regulation 4.22(d). Beginning with the statements for September XXXX, Xxxx also provided substantially similar two-page statements to investors in the XXX Fund.[96]

B. Year-End Audited Financial Statements and K-1s.

In addition to monthly account statements, the XX Fund Offering Materials indicate that investors would also receive as promptly as practicable after the close of each fiscal year an annual report containing audited financial statements for the fund.[97] It is my understanding that audited financial statements of the XX Fund were distributed to XX Fund investors in compliance with the XX Fund Offering Materials.[98] It is also my understanding that audited financial statements of the XXX Xxxx were distributed to

---

[93] *See Xxxx Xxxxxxxxxxx, XXX July XXXX Account Statements for Xxxx Xxxx Xxxxxxxxxx, Xxxxx Xxxxxx, Xxxxx Xxxxxx Carry and Xxxxx Xxxxxx IRA (Xxxx_NDGA-00004453-4457); Xxxx Xxxxxxxxxxx, XXX August XXXX Account Statements for Xxxx Xxxx Xxxxxxxxxx, Xxxxx Xxxxxx, Xxxxx Xxxxxx Carry and Xxxxx Xxxxxx IRA (Xxxx_NDGA-00004485-4493).*

[94] *See Xxxx_NDGA-00002955-56.*

[95] *See Xxxx Xxxxxxxxxxx, XXX July XXXX Account Statements for Xxxx Xxxx Xxxxxxxxxx, Xxxxx Xxxxxx, Xxxxx Xxxxxx Carry and Xxxxx Xxxxxx IRA (Xxxx_NDGA-00004453-4457); Xxxx Xxxxxxxxxxx, XXX August XXXX Account Statements for Xxxx Xxxx Xxxxxxxxxx, Xxxxx Xxxxxx, Xxxxx Xxxxxx Carry and Xxxxx Xxxxxx IRA (Xxxx_NDGA-00004485-4493).*

[96] *See Xxxx_NDGA-00002964-66.*

[97] *See, e.g., Third Restated Operating Agreement of Xxxx Xxxxxxxxxxx, XXX, dated January 31, XXXX, p. 24 (XX_000652-680 at 675); Xxxx Xxxxxxxxxxx, XXX Confidential Private Placement Memorandum and Disclosure Document dated January 31, XXXX, p. 5–6, 34 (XX_000681-738 at 691–692, 720).*

[98] *See, e.g.,* Deposition of Xxxxx Xxxxxx dated January 11, XXXX, p. 243; Deposition of Xxxxx Xxxxxxx dated June 19, XXXX, p. 27–28; Deposition of X. Xxxxxxx Xxxxxx dated June 8, XXXX, p. 72–73; Letter from Xxxxx Xxxxxx to Investor(s) dated March 25, XXXX (Dkt. No. 18-8); Xxxx Xxxxxxxxxxx, XXX Financial Statements for the Years Ended December 31, XXXX and 2012 (XX_002834-2855); Xxxx Xxxxxxxxxxx, XXX Financial Statements for the Years Ended December 31, XXXX and XXXX (HA_002856-2880); Xxxx Xxxxxxxxxxx, XXX Financial Statements for the Years Ended December 31, XXXX and XXXX (Deposition of X. Xxxxxxx Xxxxxx dated June 8, XXXX, Ex. 7).

XXX Fund investors until it ceased being a pool and became a single member Limited Liability Company managed account.[99] It is my understanding that the audited financial statements were distributed to investors after the close of the pool's fiscal year.[100]

I have reviewed the audited financial statements for XXX Fund and XX Fund for the years XXXX through XXXX. The financial statements of both the XX Fund and the XXX Fund were prepared in accordance with GAAP, as established by the FASB, and were audited by registered independent auditors each year during the relevant time period.[101] The financial statements of both Funds for the year ended December 31, XXXX were audited by Xxxxxxxx CPAs, P.C.[102] The financial statements of the XX Fund for the year ended December 31, XXXX were audited by XxXxxxxxx LLP, now known as XXX XX LLP.[103] The financial statements of the XX Fund for the year ended December 31, XXXX were audited by Xxxxxxx Xxxxx Xxxxxxxx, LLC.[104] Each of the foregoing companies is a public accounting firm currently registered with the PCAOB and was inspected by the PCAOB during the relevant period.[105]

In each audit report prepared for the XX Fund and the XXX Fund, the independent auditors stated that the audited financial statements included the current "statement of financial condition," "condensed schedule of investments," "statement of operations," statement of "changes in members' equity" for the year then ended, and "the related notes to the financial statements."[106] The auditor's opinion in each instance was that

---

[99] *See, e.g., XXX Xxxxxxxxxxxx, XXX* Financial Statements for the Years Ended December 31, XXXX and XXXX (XX_002815-2833).

[100] *See, e.g.,* Staff of the Investment Adviser Regulation Office Division of Investment Management, U.S. Securities and Exchange Commission. "Regulation of Investment Advisers by the U.S. Securities and Exchange Commission." March 2013, p. 34–35 and footnote 181 <https://www.sec.gov/about/offices/oia/oia_investman/rplaze-042012.pdf>; Letter from Xxxxx Xxxxxx to Investor(s) dated March 25, XXXX (Dkt. XX-8); Deposition of Xxxxx Xxxxxx dated January 11, XXXX, p. 243.

[101] *See, e.g., XXX Xxxxxxxxxxxx, XXX Financial Statements for the Years Ended December 31, XXXX and 2012, Independent Auditor's Report and p. 8 (HA_002815-2833, at HA_002818, 2824); Xxxx Xxxxxxxxxxxx, XXX Financial Statements for the Years Ended December 31, XXXX and 2012, Independent Auditor's Report and p. 8 (HA_002834-2855 at 2837-2838, 2843); Xxxx Xxxxxxxxxxxx, XXX Financial Statements for the Years Ended December 31, XXXX and XXXX, Independent Auditor's Report and p. 9 (HA_002856-2880 at 2859-2860, 2866); Xxxx Xxxxxxxxxxxx, XXX Financial Statements for the Years Ended December 31, XXXX and XXXX, Independent Auditor's Report and p. 9 (Deposition of X. Xxxxxxx Xxxxxx dated June 8, 2017, Ex. 7); 17 CFR 4.22; 17 CFR 4.25. According to 17 CFR 4.22, "The financial statements in the Annual Report must be presented and computed in accordance with generally accepted accounting principles consistently applied and must be certified by an independent public accountant."*

[102] *See, e.g., Xxxx Xxxxxxxxxxxx, XXX Financial Statements for the Years Ended December 31, XXXX and XXXX, Independent Auditor's Report and Independent Auditor's Report on the Supplementary Information (XX_002834-2855 at 2837–2838, 2852); XXX Xxxxxxxxxxxx, XXX Financial Statements for the Years Ended December 31, XXXX and XXXX, Independent Auditor's Report and Independent Auditor's Report on the Supplementary Information (XX_002815-2833 at 2818–2819, 2832).*

[103] *See, e.g., Xxxx Xxxxxxxxxxxx, XXX Financial Statements for the Years Ended December 31, XXXX and XXXX, Independent Auditor's Report (XX_002856-2880 at 2859–2860).*

[104] *See, e.g., Xxxx Xxxxxxxxxxxx, XXX Financial Statements for the Years Ended December 31, XXXX and XXXX, Independent Auditor's Report (Deposition of X. Xxxxxxx Xxxxxx dated June 8, XXXX, Ex. 7).*

[105] *See, e.g., Public Company Accounting Oversight Board Firm Summaries for Xxxxxxxx CPAs, P.C., XxXxxxxxx LLP (now known as XXX XX LLP), and Xxxxxxx Xxxxx Xxxxxxxx, LLC (accessed through PCAOB website 02/05/ XXXX).*

[106] *See* Xxxx Xxxxxxxxxxxx, XXX Financial Statements for the Years Ended December 31, XXXX and XXXX, Independent Auditor's Report (XX_002834-2855 at 2837–2838); XXX Xxxxxxxxxxxx, XXX Financial Statements for the Years Ended December 31, XXXX and XXXX, Independent Auditor's Report (XX_002815-2833 at 2818–2819); Xxxx Xxxxxxxxxxxx, XXX Financial Statements for the Years Ended December 31, XXXX and XXXX, Independent Auditor's Report (XX_002856-2880 at 2859–2860); Xxxx Xxxxxxxxxxxx, XXX Financial Statements for the Years Ended December 31, XXXX and XXXX, Independent Auditor's Report (Deposition of X. Xxxxxxx Xxxxxx dated June 8, XXXX, Ex. 7).

"the financial statements referred to above present fairly, in all material aspects, the financial position" of the audited Fund "and the results of its operations for the year then ended, in accordance with accounting principles generally accepted in the United States of America."[107]

The audited financial statements prepared for both the XX Fund and the XXX Fund reflected both realized and unrealized gains and losses for the Funds. The Statements of Operations that were prepared for each of the Funds in each year reflected both the "Net realized gain from derivative contracts" and the "Net unrealized increase (decrease) in value of derivative contracts." Further, the audited balance sheets for the Funds (the Statements of Financial Condition) reflected the fair value of both asset and liability derivative contacts as of the end of each year.[108] It is my understanding that all investors in both the XX Fund and the XXX Fund received the audited financial statements for the fund in which they were invested, and which reported all realized and unrealized gains and losses for the Funds.[109]

Investors in the XXX Fund and the XX Fund were also provided with Schedule K-1s.[110] I have reviewed a sample of K-1s that were prepared for investors in each of the years XXXX through XXXX.[111] The K-1s include the following information, which was specific to each investor: annual gains and losses calculated in accordance with GAAP, the annual increase or decrease in the investor's account based on GAAP accounting, and the investor's percentage ownership of the XX Fund.[112]

X.   Xxxx's Investment Strategy.

Xxxx's investment strategy was to make a profit (realized gains), and minimize losses, for the investors of the XXX Fund and XX Fund.[113] The Funds were specifically designed to trade in options on, options on futures on, and futures on, broad based equity indexes, primarily the S&P 500 Index. The Funds, among other things, traded, bought, sold, spread, or otherwise acquired, held, or disposed of the aforementioned derivatives.[114] During the relevant period, Xxxx traded in options on S&P 500 Index Futures.[115]

To achieve its investment strategy, depending on a multitude of factors, including market conditions, the macroeconomic environment, world events, and the positions

---

[107] *Ibid.*

[108] *See, e.g., XXX Xxxxxxxxxxx, XXX Financial Statements for the Years Ended December 31, XXXX and XXXX (XX_002815-2833); Xxxx Xxxxxxxxxxx, XXX Financial Statements for the Years Ended December 31, XXXX and XXXX (HA_002834-2855); Xxxx Xxxxxxxxxxx, XXX Financial Statements for the Years Ended December 31, XXXX and XXXX (HA_002856-2880); Xxxx Xxxxxxxxxxx, XXX Financial Statements for the Years Ended December 31, XXXX and XXXX.*

[109] *See, e.g., Deposition of Xxxxx Xxxxxx dated January 11, XXXX, p. 243; Deposition of X. Xxxxxxx Xxxxxx dated June 8, XXXX, p. 72; Deposition of Xxxxx Xxxxxxx dated June 19, XXXX, p. 27–28; XXX Xxxxxxxxxxx, XXX Financial Statements for the Years Ended December 31, XXXX and XXXX (XX_002815-2833); Xxxx Xxxxxxxxxxx, XXX Financial Statements for the Years Ended December 31, XXXX and XXXX (XX_002834-2855); Xxxx Xxxxxxxxxxx, XXX Financial Statements for the Years Ended December 31, XXXX and XXXX (XX_002856-2880); Xxxx Xxxxxxxxxxx, XXX Financial Statements for the Years Ended December 31, XXXX and XXXX.*

[110] *See* Deposition of Xxxxx Xxxxxx dated January 11, XXXX, p. 243.

[111] I have reviewed a sample of the XX Fund K-1s produced by the Xxxxxxxxxxxx CPA firm. *See* BCPAS000009-166, 175–332, 334–490, 555–742, 751–938, 940–1127, 1202–1385, 1392–1575, 1578–1761, 1763–1944, 2017–2154, 2163–3200, and 2302–2439. I have also reviewed a sample of the XXX Fund K-1s. *See, e.g.,* Xxxx_NDGA-00003683-84; Xxxx_NDGA-0004801-4802.

[112] *Ibid.*

[113] *See, e.g., Deposition of Xxxx Xxxxxxx dated December 13, XXXX, p. 22–23.*

[114] *See Trading Records of the XX Fund and XXX Fund, identified in Exhibit B.*

[115] *Ibid.*

already in the portfolio, Xxxx deployed various tools that are widely utilized within the industry, including in the money expiration probabilities, analysis of market trends, moving averages, and Bollinger Bands.[116]

Bollinger Bands are, "curves drawn in and around the price structure usually consisting of a moving average (the middle band), an upper band, and a lower band that answer the question as to whether prices are high or low on a relative basis."[117] Xxxx utilized these tools to evaluate the market, consider potential trades, and execute the trades that would create the most benefit for XX Fund and XXX Fund investors.[118]

One of the ways Xxxx executed its investment strategy for both the XX Fund and the XXX Fund was selling out of the money options.[119] But Xxxx also sold in the money options, purchased options, and purchased and sold futures,[120] depending on market conditions, macroeconomic conditions, world events, the positions in the portfolios, and a variety of other factors.[121]

In addition, Xxxx utilized a variety of tools to protect investors and help the Funds recover from periods of extreme or unusual market volatility, such as the October and December 2014 "V-bottom" events. A "V-bottom" event is characterized by a sharp decline in the market followed by a quick, sharp recovery.[122] In October 2014, the S&P 500 experienced such a "V-bottom" event, and the financial markets overall experienced significant turmoil. According to the Wall Street Journal, the October 2014 volatility was, "a 'bloodbath' for hedge funds, inflicting large losses at an array of multibillion-dollar firms in the industry's worst stretch since late 2011."[123] Those "V-bottom" events caused the Funds to experience trading losses, and realizing those losses at the end of the month would have caused a sharp decay in the value of each investor's capital account from which investor withdrawals are made. Xxxx believed that it could reduce and eliminate those losses over time and it executed trades that provided time in which it could work through and reduce the losses to an appropriate level.[124] Xxxx fully reduced the losses associated with the October and December 2014 market events by June XXXX.[125]

---

[116] *See, e.g., Deposition of Xxxx Xxxxxxx dated December 13, XXXX, p. 22–25; Nielsen, Lars Tyge. "Understanding N(d1) and N(d2): Risk-Adjusted Probabilities in the Black-Scholes Model." Finance, Economics, and Mathematics. October 1992.* <http://www.ltnielsen.com/wp-content/uploads/Understanding.pdf>; *Roman, Jan. "Chapter 15: Option Valuation."* <http://janroman.dhis.org/finance/General/Option%20Valuation.pdf>; *"Technical Analysis." University of Cambridge. February 2, 2011.* <https://www.mrao.cam.ac.uk/~mph/Technical_Analysis.pdf>; *Thorp, Wayne. "An Intro to Moving Averages: Popular Technical Indicators." American Association of Individual Investors Journal. August 1999.* <https://www.aaii.com/journal/article/an-intro-to-moving-averages-popular-technical-indicators.touch>; *Fang, Jiali, et al. "Popularity versus Profitability: Evidence from Bollinger Bands." Auckland Centre For Financial Research, August 2014.* <https://acfr.aut.ac.nz/__data/assets/pdf_file/0007/29896/100009-Popularity-vs-Profitability-BB-August-Final.pdf>.

[117] *See, e.g.,* <https://www.bollingerbands.com/bollinger-bands>.

[118] *See, e.g., Deposition of Xxxx Xxxxxxx dated December 13, XXXX, p. 22–23, 33–34; Deposition of Xxxx Xxxxxxx dated December 19, XXXX, p. 14–16.*

[119] *See* Trading Records of the XX Fund and the XXX Fund, identified in Exhibit B.

[120] *Ibid.*

[121] *See, e.g.,* Deposition of Xxxx Xxxxxxx dated December 13, XXXX, p. 20–25.

[122] *See, e.g.,* Deposition of Xxxx Xxxxxxx dated December 13, XXXX, p. 30–31, 41–42; Deposition of Xxxx Xxxxxxx dated December 19, XXXX, p. 41–43; Deposition of Xxxxx Xxxxxx dated January 11, XXXX, p. 72–82; Letter from Xxxxx Xxxxxx to Members of Xxxx Xxxxxxxxxxx, XXX, dated December 24, XXXX (Dkt. No. XX-9).

[123] *See, e.g.,* Chung, Juliet, et al. "Misery Widespread at Hedge Funds: Market Turmoil Inflicts Losses in Industry's Worst Period Since 2001." *The Wall Street Journal,* October 20, 2014 <http://www.wsj.com/articles/misery-widespread-at-hedge-funds-1413849220>.

[124] *See, e.g.,* Deposition of Xxxx Xxxxxxx dated December 13, XXXX, p. 32–33; Letter from Xxxxx Xxxxxx to Members of Xxxx Xxxxxxxxxxxx, XXX, dated December 24, XXXX (Dkt. No. XX-9).

[125] *See* Exhibit 1.2.

XI. Opinion.

Based on my review and analysis of the materials identified above and certain empirical analyses I have performed, and my skills, knowledge, education, training, and experience, I am of the following opinions:

A.   The Funds did not enter into trades that were open for more than 90 days.

Based on my review of the XX Fund's and the XXX Fund's trading records, I have not identified any trades that were open for more than 90 days.[126] With respect to the XX Fund, this conforms to the PPM, which noted that most trades into which Xxxx enters will be open for less than 90 days.[127]

B.   Xxxx applied correct accounting treatment to the XX Fund's and the XXX Fund's open and closed trading positions.

Options contracts and futures contracts are examples of transferable derivative instruments. According to FASB ASC 815 on Derivatives and Hedging, which Xxxx was required to follow, "Derivative instruments that are transferable are, by their nature, separate and distinct contracts."[128] Thus, it was necessary for Xxxx to treat options contracts, on the one hand, and futures contracts that were assigned from options that expired in the money, on the other, as separate and distinct assets and liabilities.

Xxxx appropriately followed this mandatory guidance in preparing the monthly account statements for the XX Fund and the XXX Fund, and in calculating the XX Fund's and the XXX Fund's realized gains and losses on closed positions, as reflected in the monthly account statements. In particular, when Xxxx sold options for the XX Fund's account or the XXX Fund's account that expired in the money at the end of a particular month and resulted in the assignment of futures, Xxxx correctly classified the option as a closed position and the premium it received from the sale of that option as a realized gain, and Xxxx correctly classified the futures position that it was assigned as an open position and the gain or loss (depending on its mark-to-market value) on that futures position as unrealized.

Likewise, the XX Fund's and the XXX Fund's outside auditors appropriately followed this mandatory guidance in preparing annual audited financial statements for the XX Fund and XXX Fund.[129] The XX Fund's and the XXX Fund's outside auditors properly recorded options contracts and futures contracts as separate positions in the Funds' schedules of investments.[130] The schedules of investments were included in the audited financial statements that were distributed to the Funds' investors.[131] Regarding

---

[126] *See Trading Records of the XX Fund and the XXX Fund, identified in Exhibit B.*

[127] *See, e.g., Xxxx Xxxxxxxxxxx, XXX Confidential Private Placement Memorandum and Disclosure Document dated January 31, XXXX, p. 18 (HA_000681-738 at 704).*

[128] *See ASC 815-10-25-9.*

[129] *See, e.g., Xxxx Xxxxxxxxxxx, XXX Financial Statements for the Years Ended December 31, XXXX and XXXX, p. 6 (XX_002834-2855 at 2841); Xxxx Xxxxxxxxxxx, XXX Financial Statements for the Years Ended December 31, XXXX and XXXX, p. 7 (HA_002856-2880 at 2864); Xxxx Xxxxxxxxxxx, XXX Financial Statements for the Years Ended December 31, XXXX and XXXX, p. 7; XXX Xxxxxxxxxxx, XXX Financial Statements for the Years Ended December 31, XXXX and XXXX, p. 6 (XX_002815-2833 at 2823).*

[130] *See, e.g., Xxxx Xxxxxxxxxxx, XXX Financial Statements for the Years Ended December 31, XXXX and XXXX, p. 4–5 (XX_002834-2855 at 2839–2840); Xxxx Xxxxxxxxxxx, XXX Financial Statements for the Years Ended December 31, XXXX and XXXX, p. 5–6 (XX_002856-2880 at 2862–2863); Xxxx Xxxxxxxxxxx, XXX Financial Statements for the Years Ended December 31, XXXX and XXXX, p. 5–6; XXX Xxxxxxxxxxx, XXX Financial Statements for the Years Ended December 31, XXXX and XXXX, p. 4–5 (XX_002815-2833 at 2821–2822).*

[131] *Ibid.*

accounting treatment of gains and losses, ASC 815 states, "Gains and losses (realized and unrealized) on all derivative instruments [...] shall be shown net when recognized in the income statement, whether or not settled physically, if the derivative instruments are held for trading purposes."[132]

C. With respect to the XX Fund and the XXX Fund, Net Asset Value and unrealized gains and losses on open positions were not particularly relevant.

Other than for margin requirements and tax purposes,[133] with respect to the XX Fund and the XXX Fund, unrealized gains and losses on open positions and the NAV of the Funds were less relevant than realized gains and losses on closed positions. As explained in Part VI, the unrealized value or NAV of an open position measures the gain or loss the XX Fund or the XXX Fund would incur if it closed that position by purchasing or selling an offsetting position. In other words, unrealized value or NAV represents the value of a particular position or the Fund as a whole if that particular position or all of the Funds' positions were closed at the moment the unrealized value or NAV was measured.

As the Funds were a going concern and many of the Funds' investors were largely long-term investors,[134] however, the liquidation value of particular positions or the Funds as a whole was not particularly relevant. In addition, although it was not unusual for the Funds to have open positions with a negative unrealized value or NAV, such unrealized values were not particularly relevant because they did not necessarily reflect a risk of future realized losses or a potential for realized gains. As shown by the example in Part VI, even if the unrealized or net asset value of a position is negative, there could still be an extremely high likelihood that, at expiration, the XX Fund or XXX Fund will realize a gain on that position. Or, put differently, even when the unrealized or net asset value of a position is negative, there may be an extremely low likelihood that, at expiration, the XX Fund or the XXX Fund will incur a realized loss. As investor withdrawals from the XX Fund and XXX Fund were based on each investor's respective ownership of the XX Fund's or the XXX Fund's realized gains and losses, unrealized or net asset values of positions were not particularly relevant, since they did not necessarily reflect a risk of future realized losses or the potential for realized gains. Moreover, Xxxx primarily traded options on, options on futures on, and futures on the S&P 500 index, the value of which is constantly changing. As a result, the unrealized value or NAV of positions held by the XX Fund or the XXX Fund could increase or decrease instantaneously, which makes momentary unrealized gains and losses less relevant.[135]

---

[132] *See ASC 815-10-45-9.*

[133] *In accordance with Section 475 of the Internal Revenue Code, Xxxx marked all open positions to market at the close of each year, December 31, recognizing all gains and losses, realized or unrealized, as income. Under this tax election, Xxxx reported such mark-to-market gains and losses to investors through their Schedules K-1, and individual investors reported these mark-to-market gains and losses as income on their tax returns. Because all positions were marked to market at year-end, Xxxx's approach to Incentive Allocation and redemption based upon realized gains and losses did not impact investors' tax reporting See, e.g., Internal Revenue Code Sec. 475; I.R.C. §475: Field Directive related to Mark-to-Market Valuation <https://www.irs.gov/businesses/irc-475-field-directive-related-to-mark-to-market-valuation>; Soled, Jay, et al. "The lure of a Sec. 475 election." Journal of Accountancy <https://www. journalofaccountancy.com/issues/2014/jul/sec-475-election-20149537.html>; Harmon, Michael and Kulsrud, William. "Sec. 475 Mark-to-Market Election." The Tax Adviser <https://www.thetaxadviser.com/issues/2010/feb/sec475mark-to-marketelection.html>; "Mark-to-Market Election for Hedge Funds." Capital Fund Law Blog <http://www. capitalfundlaw.com/blog/2015/05/21/mark-to-market-election-for-hedge-funds>.*

[134] *See, e.g., Deposition of X. Xxxxxxx Xxxxxx dated June 8, XXXX, p. 26; Deposition of Xxxxx Xxxxxxx dated June 19, XXXX, p. 21.*

[135] *See, e.g., Deposition of Xxxxx Xxxxxx dated January 11, XXXX, p. 47.*

D. Xxxx's premise that, over time, it could reduce and eliminate trading losses caused by periods of extreme and unusual market volatility is supported by Chebyshev's Theorem and the Empirical Rule.

As explained in Part X, during periods of unusual and extreme market volatility, such as the October and December 2014 "V-bottoms," the XX Fund and XXX Fund experienced trading losses and realizing those losses at the end of the month would have caused a sharp decay in the value of each investor's capital account from which investor withdrawals are made. Xxxx's investment strategy, in part, relied on the premise that, over time, it could reduce and eliminate trading losses that were caused by periods of unusual and extreme volatility.[136] And, indeed, Xxxx fully reduced the losses associated with the October and December 2014 market events by June XXXX.[137]

This strategy is, in fact, supported by Chebyshev's Theorem, the Empirical Rule, and the tendency of reversion to the mean that is implied by both propositions. Chebyshev's Theorem states that for any set of data, regardless of the shape of the frequency distribution of the data, the proportion of values that lie within k standard deviations ($k > 1$) of the mean is at least $1—(1/k$ squared). The standard deviation of a measurement is a calculation of distance from the mean, or the average of a data set. Given Chebyshev's Theorem, for $k = 2$, at least 75 percent of the data lie within two standard deviations of the mean; for $k = 3$, at least 89 percent of the data lie within three standard deviations of the mean (see Figure 14.2).[138] Of course, all of the trades in stocks included in the S&P 500 index form a population with an easily identified mean.

Further, for data sets with frequency distributions that are symmetric and bell-shaped, these percentages are generally much higher than Chebyshev's Theorem specifies. The Empirical Rule applies to such data sets and predicts that 68 percent, 95 percent, and 99.7 percent of the data lie within one, two, and three standard deviations of the mean, respectively.[139] The following is an illustrates the operation of this principle:

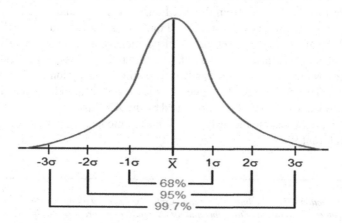

FIGURE 14.2

[136] *See, e.g., Deposition of Xxxx Xxxxxxx dated December 13, XXXX, p. 32–33; Letter from Xxxxx Xxxxxx to Members of Xxxx Xxxxxxxxxxx, XXX, dated December 24, XXXX (Dkt. No. XX-9)*

[137] *See Exhibit 1.2.*

[138] *See, e.g., Jennings, William. "The mathematics of compliance." Compliance & Ethics Professional, December 2014; Evans, James R. and Olson, David L. Statistics, Data Analysis, and Decision Modeling (Second Edition). Prentice Hall: Upper Saddle River, NJ (2003), p. 51–55; University of California, Davis Department of Statistics Lecture regarding Describing Data <http://www.stat.ucdavis.edu/~ntyang/teaching/12SSII/lecture02.pdf>.*

[139] *Ibid.*

When Xxxx evaluated potential transactions involving the sale of out of the money options, it utilized various tools, including Bollinger Bands and in the money expiration probabilities that are based, in part, on Chebyshev's Theorem and the Empirical Rule and the probabilities that each puts forth. In particular, one of the ways Xxxx executed its investment strategy was selling out of the money options with a strike price that was at least two standard deviations from the current market price of the underlying financial instrument, which, according to Chebyshev's Theorem accounts for at least 75 percent of data. When selling that type of option, Xxxx utilized an in the money expiration probability threshold which was based, in part, Chebyshev's Theorem and the Empirical Rule.[140]

Reversion to the mean is "the tendency for stock returns to return to their long-term norms over time—periods of exceptional returns tend to be followed by periods of below average performance, and vice versa."[141] Dr. James Schultz notes that this tendency for reversion to the mean is the reason why options traders execute trades based on the probability of an option to expire in the money.[142] The stock market as a whole and the S&P 500 Index have historically shown an inexorable tendency for investors' returns to revert to the mean. Moreover, the mean returns for both the stock market and the S&P 500 Index are historically positive.[143]

Taken together in light of the S&P 500 Index, Chebyshev's Theorem, the Empirical Rule, and the tendency of reversion to the mean show that observations of extreme stock market returns, whether positive or negative, are infrequent, and that returns over time tend to revert to the mean. Because the historical mean of the S&P 500 Index is positive, it follows that periods of loss tend to eventually be offset by periods of gain, though the timing of reversion to the mean is unknown.[144] In other words, Chebyshev's Theorem, the Empirical Rule and the tendency of reversion to the mean support Xxxx's premise that it would be able to reduce trading losses caused by extreme market events to an appropriate level over time through its investment strategy, which included, among other things, selling options that have a high probability of expiring out of the money.

E.   The traditional "2 and 20" method for hedge fund fees would have yielded approximately $7.2 million more in fees and incentive allocations.

Under the XX Fund fee structure, Xx. Xxxxxx and Xxxx Xxxxxxxxxx collectively received an incentive allocation equal to 20% of month-end realized gains on closed

---

[140] *See, e.g.,* <https://www.bollingerbands.com/bollinger-bands>; *Jennings, William. "The mathematics of compliance." Compliance & Ethics Professional, December 2014; Evans, James R. and Olson, David L. Statistics, Data Analysis, and Decision Modeling (Second Edition). Prentice Hall: Upper Saddle River, NJ (2003), p. 51–55; University of California, Davis Department of Statistics Lecture regarding Describing Data* <http://www.stat.ucdavis.edu/~ntyang/teaching/12SSII/lecture02.pdf>.

[141] *See, e.g., Bogle, John C. The Little Book of Common Sense Investing: The Only Way to Guarantee Your Fair Share of Stock Market Returns. John Wiley & Sons, Inc.: Hoboken, NJ (2007), p. 16.*

[142] *See, e.g., Dr. James Schultz. "From Theory to Practice: The Central Limit Theorem." tastytrade (2016)* <https://www.tastytrade.com/tt/shows/from-theory-to-practice/episodes/the-central-limit-theorem-09-30-2016>.

[143] *See, e.g., Bogle, John Co. "The Telltale Chart: Keynote Speech before the Morningstar Investment Forum, Chicago, IL, on June 26, 2002* <https://www.vanguard.com/bogle_site/sp20020626.html>; *Bogle, John C. The Little Book of Common Sense Investing: The Only Way to Guarantee Your Fair Share of Stock Market Returns. John Wiley & Sons, Inc.: Hoboken, NJ (2007), p. 160.*

[144] *See, e.g., Jennings, William. "The mathematics of compliance." Compliance & Ethics Professional, December 2014; Evans, James R. and Olson, David L. Statistics, Data Analysis, and Decision Modeling (Second Edition). Prentice Hall: Upper Saddle River, NJ (2003), p. 51–55; University of California, Davis Department of Statistics Lecture regarding Describing Data* <http://www.stat.ucdavis.edu/~ntyang/teaching/12SSII/lecture02.pdf>; *Bogle, John Co. "The Telltale Chart: Keynote Speech before the Morningstar Investment Forum, Chicago, IL, on June 26, 2002* <https://www.vanguard.com/bogle_site/sp20020626.html>; *Bogle, John C. The Little Book of Common Sense Investing: The Only Way to Guarantee Your Fair Share of Stock Market Returns. John Wiley & Sons, Inc.: Hoboken, NJ (2007), p. 16, 160; Dr. James Schultz. "From Theory to Practice: The Central Limit Theorem." tastytrade (2016)* <https://www.tastytrade.com/tt/shows/from-theory-to-practice/episodes/the-central-limit-theorem-09-30-2016>.

positions. From January XXXX through March XXXX, the investors in the XX Fund earned $111,352,292 in net realized gains on closed positions, and Xx. Xxxxxx and Xxxx Xxxxxxxxxx were entitled to receive incentive allocations equal to 20% of that amount, which resulted in incentive allocations of $22,270,458.[145] Half of that amount ($11,135,229) was paid to the Xxxx Xxxxxxxxxx. The other half went to Xx. Xxxxxx, but she did not personally retain that amount. Instead, Xx. Xxxxxx used those funds to pay all expenses of the XX Fund (except for brokerage commissions and trading fees). In addition, as the sole owner of Xxxx, the XX Fund's investment advisor, Xx. Xxxxxx was also responsible for all of Xxxx's expenses, and she used her portion of the incentive allocation to pay for certain of Xxxx's expenses as well. I have performed an analysis of the XX Fund's records to determine the amount that Xx. Xxxxxx earned in salary and retained in incentive allocation after paying expenses as described above. I have determined that from January XXXX through May XXXX, this amounted to approximately $4.8 million, or approximately 22% of the $22,270,258 in incentive allocations paid by the XX Fund (see Figures 14.3–14.5).[146]

I have also performed an analysis to determine whether Xx. Xxxxxx and Xxxx Xxxxxxxxxx would have earned more, less or the same amount from January XXXX through May XXXX if (i) the XX Fund charged an annual 2 percent management fee based on the XX Fund's NAV and (ii) the incentive allocation paid by the XX Fund was based on realized gains or losses on closed positions *and* unrealized gains or losses on open positions. This hypothetical fee structure would be more in line with the traditional "2 and 20" fee structure for hedge funds, as described in Part VI above.

As shown in Exhibits 1.1 and 1.2, under that hypothetical fee structure, Xx Xxxxxx and Xxxx Xxxxxxxxxx would have earned $9,976,143 in management fees and $19,521,946 in incentive allocations from January XXXX through May XXXX. In total, Xx Xxxxxx and Xxxx Xxxxxxxxxx would have earned $29,498,088. That is $7,227,630 or approximately 32% *more* than Xx Xxxxxx and Xxxx Xxxxxxxxxx *actually earned* in incentive allocations. In other words, the XX Fund's fee structure—with no management fee and an incentive allocation based on realized gains on closed positions only—*saved* the investors approximately $7.2 million, as compared to a fee structure more in line with the traditional "2 and 20" model that is common among hedge funds.[147]

XII. Other Considerations.

My report is issued in accordance with the Standards for Consulting Services issued by the American Institute of Certified Public Accountants. This report is to be used solely in connection with proceedings in the above-referenced matter, it should not be used for any other purpose, and it is designated Confidential pursuant to the Consent Confidentiality Order. Outside distribution of this report to others is not permitted without the written consent of Veritas Forensic Accounting, LLC. The information in this report is based on information learned through the date of this report. My review and analysis of the facts and circumstances of the case is ongoing, and I reserve the right to supplement and amend my opinions to consider information learned subsequent to the date of this report.

This concludes my report and it is respectfully submitted this fifth day of February XXXX.

By:_____
    William L. Jennings, CPA

---

[145] *See, e.g., Exhibits 1.1 and 1.2. The investors in the XX Fund earned $5,150,703 in net realized gains on closed positions from April through May XXXX, upon which Xx. Xxxxxx and Xxxx Xxxxxxxxxx did not charge an incentive allocation.*

[146] *See Xxxx_NDGA-00015807; Xxxx_NDGA-00015819; Xxxx_NDGA-00015844; Xxxx_NDGA-00015934.*

[147] *See, e.g., Exhibits 1.1 and 1.2.*

XIII.   Exhibits

Exhibit A   CV of Williams L. Jennings

William L. Jennings, BS, MBA, CPA, CFE, CFF

A. Background and Education
1. Present Position
- Veritas Forensic Accounting, LLC, Member

2. Other Positions Held
- Accounting, Economics & Appraisal Group, LLC, Principal, May 2016 to December 2017
- Alvarez & Marsal Global Forensic and Dispute Services, LLC, Managing Director, June 2012 to May 2016
- Navigant Consulting, Inc., Managing Director and Practice Segment Leader, Southeast—Disputes and Investigations, October 2005 to June 2012
- LECG, LLC, Director—National Forensic Accounting Practice, August 2004 to October 2005
- FFI, Inc., President, 2003–2004
- Kroll, Inc., Principal, 1995–2003
- Coopers & Lybrand, L.L.P., Director-in-Charge—Fraud Investigation services, 1989–1994
- Oxford Group, Ltd., Acting Chief Financial Officer, 1989
- Brown & Jennings, CPAs, Partner, 1984–1989
- Coopers & Lybrand, L.L.P., Supervisor—General Audit Practice, 1979–1983
- A.A. Harmon & Co., CPA's, Semi-Senior Accountant, 1978–1979

3. Education and Professional Certifications
- BS, Accounting, University of New Orleans, 1976–1978
- Tulane University 1973–1975
- MBA, Auburn University, 2005
- CPA, American Institute of Certified Public Accountants, 1981
- CFE, Association of Certified Fraud Examiners, 1991
- CFF, American Institute of Certified Public Accountants, 2009
- Private Detective (Class A), 2000
- ABV, American Institute of Certified Public Accountants, 2015

B. Publications
- The Tangled Web: Unraveling the Badges of Fraud. (2007, March). *Investigations Quarterly Newsletter*
- The Mathematics of Compliance. (2014, December) *Compliance & Ethics Professional. (A publication of the Society of Corporate Compliance and Ethics)*

C. Speaking Engagements
- *High In-Fidelity—Corporate Theft and Recovery.* (2009, July)
  - Risk and Insurance Management Society 34th Annual Education Conference, Naples, Florida
- *The New Hard Times: Business Crimes, Ponzi Schemes and Affinity Frauds.* (2009, August)
  - Georgia Society of CPA's 2009 Fraud and Forensic Accounting Conference, Atlanta, Georgia

- *High In-Fidelity—Corporate Theft and Recovery.* (2010, July)
  - Risk and Insurance Management Society 34th Annual Education Conference, Naples, Florida
- *Asset Recovery: How to Get Your Stuff Back.* (2011, April)
  - Georgia Society of CPAs 2011 Spring Decision Makers Conference, Atlanta, Georgia
- *Hands-On, Real-Life Case Study on Succeeding in Tracing and Recovering Assets in a Multinational Fraud Case* (2011, June)
  - International Association for Asset Recovery 2011 Cross-Border Asset Tracing and Recovery Conference, London, England
- *Dissecting Bank, Business and Credit Card Records That Lead You to Hidden Assets and Fronts for Bad Guys* (2011, June)
  - International Association for Asset Recovery 2011 Cross-Border Asset Tracing and Recovery Conference, London, England
- *The Audit Leader's Role in Proactively Addressing Fraud: Keeping your Organization Out of the Headlines* (2013, January)
  - MIS Audit Leadership Institute, Miami, Florida
- *Fraud Prevention and Detection: What Chief Audit Executives Must Know* (2013, April)
  - MIS Training Institute SuperStrategies 2013 The Audit Best-Practices Conference, Orlando, Florida
- *Race to the Top: Issues Related to Rankings and External Data Misreporting in Higher Education* (2013, June)
  - Society of Corporate Compliance and Ethics Higher Education Compliance Conference, Austin, Texas
- *Keep Your Organization Out of the Headlines by Proactively Addressing Today's Threats* (2014, January)
  - Society for Corporate Compliance and Ethics Webinar, Atlanta, Georgia
- *Managing Fraud Risk with the Audit Committee* (2014, May)
  - MIS Training Institute SuperStrategies 2014 The Audit Best-Practices Conference, Chicago, Illinois.
- *Use of Forensic Audit as a Tool in Recovery* (2015, May)
  - FMO Special Operations Seminar 2015, Amsterdam, Netherlands
- *Managing Fraud Risk with the Audit Committee* (2016, May)
  - MIS Training Institute SuperStrategies 2016, Las Vegas, Nevada.

D. Expert Testimony
- U.S. vs Wardlaw and Turpin
  - Evidence given at trial
- Nodvin et al. vs National Financial Services Corporation
  - Evidence given at NASD Arbitration Hearing
- Curtis vs Morgan
  - Evidence given at trial and by affidavit
- Robert Reich, Secretary of Labor vs Davis Acoustical Corporation et al.
  - Evidence given at trial and by affidavit
- U.S. vs David Ramus
  - Evidence given at trial
- Alumax, Inc. vs David Mitchell, et al.
  - Evidence given at trial and by affidavit
- Mitsubishi International Corporation vs Joseph Smith, et al.
  - Evidence given at trial in evidentiary hearings, at depositions and by affidavit

- US vs Healthmaster, Jeannette Garrison, et al.
  - Evidence given by affidavit
- Solnick vs Physicians Health Corporation, et al.
  - Evidence given at American Arbitration Association hearing
- Errol O. Kendall vs Thomas Rosencrants
  - Evidence given at arbitration hearing and by affidavit
- Cimlinc vs Softech
  - Evidence given at arbitration hearing and by affidavit
- Merkel vs Pollard
  - Evidence given at trial and by affidavit
- Madison Gas & Electric vs Wisconsin Power & Light Arbitration Dispute
  - Evidence given at arbitration hearing and by affidavit
- Alla, et al. vs Network Concepts, et al.
  - Evidence given at trial
- Crown Theatres vs Milton Daily, et al.
  - Evidence given by affidavit
- Ralph C. McCullough, III, as Plan Trustee for HomeGold, Inc., HomeGold Financial, Inc. and Carolina Investors, Inc. vs Elliott Davis, et al.
  - Evidence given by written report
- Cox Enterprises, Inc. vs News-Journal Corporation and Others
  - Evidence given at deposition and at trial
- The State of Oregon, et al. vs McKesson HBOC, et al.
  - Evidence given at deposition
- Cendant Corporation, et al. vs Ernst & Young, LLP
  - Evidence given at deposition
- MC Asset Recovery, LLC vs The Southern Company
  - Evidence given at deposition
- Securities & Exchange Commission vs Steven Forman
  - Evidence given at deposition
- Etowah Environmental Group LLC, et al. vs Advanced Disposal Services, Inc., et al.
  - Evidence given at deposition and arbitration hearing
- CSX Transportation, Inc. vs Brian K. Leggett
  - Evidence given at trial
- Darryl S. Laddin, as Liquidating Trustee vs Steven A. Odom, et al.
  - Evidence given at deposition
- Piedmont Family Office Fund, LP; et al. vs Robert L. Duncan; et al.
  - Evidence given at deposition
- Heather Q. Bolinger, et al. vs First Multiple Listing Service, Inc.
  - Evidence given at deposition
- United States of America, ex rel. vs American Intercontinental University, Inc.
  - Evidence given at deposition
- Geveran Investments Limited vs Lighting Science Group Corporation, et al.
  - Evidence given at deposition and hearing
- United States of America vs D. Terry Dubose, et al.
  - Evidence given at deposition and trial
- U.S. Tobacco Cooperative, Inc., U.S. Flue-Cured Tobacco Growers, Inc., and Big South Distribution, Llc, vs Big South Wholesale of Virginia, Llc, d/b/a Big Sky
  - Evidence given at deposition
- Douglas Beal, et al. vs Royal Alliance Associates, Inc., et al.
  - Evidence given at FINRA arbitration hearing

- Alice Caputo, et al. vs Royal Alliance Associates, Inc., et al.
  - Evidence given at FINRA arbitration hearing
- United States of America vs Michael Kipp and Joanne Viard
  - Evidence given at trial
- United States of America vs Mark Hazelwood, Scott Wombold, Heather Jones and Karen Mann
  - Evidence given at trial

FACTS AND DATA CONSIDERED BY THE WITNESS (SEE TABLE 14.3)

TABLE 14.3
Exhibit B—Materials Considered

	Description	Beginning Bates or Range
	Pleadings	
1	XXXX.05.31 Complaint	
2	XXXX.05.31 Consent Preliminary Injunction Order	
3	XXXX.09.01 Defendants' Motion to Dismiss for Failure to State a Claim	
4	XXXX.10.03 Plaintiffs' Opposition to Defendants' Motion to Dismiss	
5	XXXX.10.17 Defendants' Reply in Further Support of their Motion to Dismiss	
6	XXXX.01.11 First Amended Complaint	
7	XXXX.01.11 Order regarding Defendants' Motion to Dismiss	
8	XXXX.07.10 Response to First Interrogatories	
9	XXXX.07.10 Response to First Request to Admit	
10	XXXX.07.25 Redline of First Amended Complaint v Second Amended Complaint	
11	XXXX.07.25 Second Amended Complaint	
12	XXXX.08.22 Affidavit re Motion for Leave to File Second Amended Complaint	
13	XXXX.08.31 Order Granting Motion for Leave to File Second Amended Complaint	
14	XXXX.08.31 Second Amended Complaint	
15	XXXX.10.16 Defendants Xxxx Xxxxxxx and Xxxx Xxxxxxx's Motion to Dismiss	
16	XXXX.10.16 Defendants Xxxx's and Xxxxxx's Answer and Defenses to Second Amended Complaint	
17	XXXX.10.16 Defendants Xxxxxxx and Xxxxxxx's Answer and Defenses to Second Amended Complaint	
18	XXXX.10.20 Plaintiff's Opposition to Motion to Dismiss by Xxxxxxx and Xxxxxxx	
19	XXXX.11.08—SEC's Response to Second Interrogatories of Xxxx Xxxxxxxx, XXX and Xxxxx Xxxxxx	
20	XXXX.11.13 Xxxxxxx and Xxxxxxx's Reply in Further Support of Motion to Dismiss	
21	Letter from Xxxxx Xxxxxx to Xxxx Xxxxxxxxxxx, XXX, Investor(s) dated March 25, XXXX (Dkt. No. XX-8)	
22	Letter from Xxxxx Xxxxxx to Xxxx Xxxxxxxxxxx, XXX, Investor(s) dated December 24, XXXX (Dkt. No. XX-9)	

(Continued)

TABLE 14.3 (*Continued*)
Exhibit B—Materials Considered

Description	Beginning Bates or Range
23	Letter from Xxxxx Xxxxxx to Xxxx Xxxxxxxxxxx, XXX, Investor(s) dated June 4, XXXX (Dkt. No. XX-10)	

Deposition Transcripts and Exhibits

24	Deposition of X. Xxxxxxx Xxxxxx dated June 8, XXXX and Exhibits 1–10	
25	Deposition of Xxxxx Xxxxxxx dated July 25, XXXX and Exhibits 7–9, 11–13	
26	Deposition of Xxxx Xxxxxxx dated December 13, XXXX and Exhibits 14–16 and W1–W9	
27	Deposition of Xxxx Xxxxxxx dated December 19, XXXX and Exhibits R1–R-10	
28	Deposition of Xxxxx Xxxxxx dated January 11, XXXX and Exhibits B001–B004	

Public Documents, Statutes, Rules, Publications, and Books

29	XXXX Xxxx Xxxx Xxxxxxxxxxxxx Form 990—Guidestar	
30	XXXX Xxxx Xxxx Xxxxxxxxxxxxx Form 990—Guidestar	
31	XXXX Xxxx Xxxx Xxxxxxxxxxxxx Form 990—Guidestar	
32	XXXX Xxxx Xxxx Xxxxxxxxxxx Form 990-PF—Guidestar	
33	XXXX Xxxx Xxxx Xxxxxxxxxxx Form 990-PF—Guidestar	
34	XXXX Xxxx Xxxx Xxxxxxxxxxx Form 990-PF—Guidestar	
35	Xxxxxxxxx Secretary of State Filing Information—Xxxx Xxxxxxxxxxx, XXX	
36	Xxxxxxxxx Secretary of State Filing Information—XXX Xxxxxxxxxxx, XXX	
37	15 U.S.C. 77q(a)—Use of interstate commerce for purpose of fraud or deceit	
38	15 U.S.C. 78j(b)—Manipulative and deceptive devices	
39	15 U.S.C. 80b-6—Prohibited transactions by investment advisers	
40	17 CFR 4 (including 4.22 and 4.25)	
41	17 C.F.R. 240.10b-5—Employment of manipulative and deceptive devices	
42	17 C.F.R. 275.206(4)-8—Pooled investment vehicles	
43	17 CFR 279	
44	26 U.S.C. Sec. 475	
45	Form ADV Part 2	
46	ASC 210-20—Balance Sheet Offsetting	
47	ASC 405-20-40—Derecognition of Liabilities	
48	ASC 815-10—Derivatives and Hedging Overall	
49	ASC 815-20—Hedging General	
50	ASC 815-30—Fair Value Hedges	
51	ASC 815-30—Cash Flow Hedges	
52	ASC 820-10-35—Subsequent Fair Value Measurement	
53	ASC 825-10-65—Transition and Open Effective Date of Financial Instruments	
54	ASC 860-10-40—Derecognition of Transfers and Servicing	
55	AU Section 623 "Special Reports." AICPA <https://www.aicpa.org/Research/Standards/AuditAttest/DownloadableDocuments/AU-00623.pdf>	
56	FASB Statement of Financial Accounting Standards No. 133	
57	FASB Statement of Financial Accounting Standards No. 168	

(*Continued*)

TABLE 14.3 (*Continued*)
Exhibit B—Materials Considered

Description	Beginning Bates or Range
58	Public Company Accounting Oversight Board Firm Summaries for Xxxxxxxx XXXx, P.C., XxXxxxxxx LLP (now known as XXX XX LLP), and Xxxxxxx Xxxxx Xxxxxxx, LLC (accessed through PCAOB website 02/05/2018)	
59	http://www.cmegroup.com/trading/equity-index/us-index/e-mini-sandp500_ quotes_globex_ options.html?optionProductId=138#optionProductId=138	
60	http://www.nasdaq.com/investing/glossary/m/mark-to-market-accounting	
61	https://xxxxxxxxxxxxxxxxxxxxx.org/team/xxxxx-xxxxxx/	
62	https://xxxxxxxxxxxxxxxxxxxxx.org/where-we-serve/	
63	https://xxxxxxxxxxxxxxxxxxxxx.org/make-an-impact/	
64	https://xxxxxxxxxxxxxxxxxxxxx.org/our-approach/	
65	https://www.bollingerbands.com/bollinger-bands	
66	www.facebook.com/pg/xxxxxxxxxxxxxxxxxxxxx/about/	
67	http://us.spindices.com/indices/equity/sp-500	
68	https://www.theocc.com/education/futures/	
69	Acton, Gemma. "Number of hedge funds continues to shrink as launches fall to financial crisis levels." CNBC, December 16, 2016 <https://www.cnbc.com/2016/12/16/number-of-hedge-funds-continues-to-shrink-as-launches-fall-to-financial-crisis-levels.html>	
70	Baden, Ben. "5 Factors That Drive Stock Prices." U.S. News, 2011 <https://money.usnews.com/money/personal-finance/mutual-funds/articles/2011/07/14/5-factors-that-drive-stock-prices>	
71	Barlow, Joshua. "Hidden Fees in Hedge Funds." FINalternatives, July 30, 2013 <http://www.finalternatives.com/node/24322>	
72	Bogle, John C. The Little Book of Common Sense Investing: The Only Way to Guarantee Your Fair Share of Stock Market Returns. John Wiley & Sons, Inc.: Hoboken, NJ (2007)	
73	Bogle, John Co. "The Telltale Chart: Keynote Speech before the Morningstar Investment Forum, Chicago, IL, on June 26, 2002 <https://www.vanguard.com/bogle_site/sp20020626.html>	
74	Buhayar, Noah, et al. "Buffett Says Money Spent on Plumbers Better Than on Hedge Funds." Bloomberg, May 6, 2017 <https://www.bloomberg.com/news/articles/2017-05-06/buffett-says-money-spent-on-plumbers-better-than-on-hedge-funds>	
75	Chung, Juliet, et al. "Misery Widespread at Hedge Funds: Market Turmoil Inflicts Losses in Industry's Worst Period Since 2001." The Wall Street Journal, October 20, 2014 <http://www.wsj.com/articles/misery-widespread-at-hedge-funds-1413849220>	
76	Cordier, James and Gross, Michael. The Complete Guide to Option Selling: How Selling Options Can Lead to Stellar Returns in Bull and Bear Markets. McGraw-Hill, 2004	
77	Delevingne, Lawrence. "Struggling hedge funds still expense bonuses, bar tabs." Reuters, January 19, 2017 <https://www.reuters.com/article/us-hedgefunds-passthrough-insight/struggling-hedge-funds-still-expense-bonuses-bar-tabs-idUSKBN1530JL>	
78	Dr. James Schultz. "From Theory to Practice: The Central Limit Theorem." tastytrade (2016) <https://www.tastytrade.com/tt/shows/from-theory-to-practice/episodes/the-central-limit-theorem-09-30-2016>	

(*Continued*)

TABLE 14.3 (*Continued*)
Exhibit B—Materials Considered

Description	Beginning Bates or Range
79	Durak, Robert. "New option a game changer for private companies." Journal of Accountancy, September 1, 2013 <https://www.journalofaccountancy.com/issues/2013/sep/20137921.html>	
80	Evans, James R. and Olson, David L. Statistics, Data Analysis, and Decision Modeling (Second Edition). Prentice Hall: Upper Saddle River, NJ (2003)	
81	Faccone, Erin. "The Essential Guide to Third-Party Valuations for Hedge Fund Investors." NEPC, LLC (2017) <https://cdn2.hubspot.net/hubfs/2529352/files/Third%20Party%20Valuations-%20White%20Paper-1.pdf?t=1513697342060>	
82	Fang, Jiali, et al. "Popularity versus Profitability: Evidence from Bollinger Bands." Auckland Centre For Financial Research, August 2014. <https://acfr.aut.ac.nz/__data/assets/pdf_file/0007/29896/100009-Popularity-vs-Profitability-BB-August-Final.pdf>	
83	Gad, Shan. "What Are Hedge Funds?" Forbes and Investopedia, October 22, 2013 <https://www.forbes.com/sites/investopedia/2013/10/22/what-are-hedge-funds/#7a653ff48ee3>	
84	Goonatilake, Rohitha. "The Volatility of the Stock Market and News." International Research Journal of Finance and Economics, 2007 <http://citeseerx.ist.psu.edu/viewdoc/summary?doi=10.1.1.124.5376>	
85	Gurdus, Elizabeth. "Hedge funds' 'obscene' fees make people rich—just not investors, says Buffett." CNBC, February 27, 2017 <https://www.cnbc.com/2017/02/27/buffett-hedge-funds-fees-border-on-obscene.html>	
86	Harmon, Michael and Kulsrud, William. "Sec. 475 Mark-to-Market Election." TheTaxAdviser<https://www.thetaxadviser.com/issues/2010/feb/sec475mark-to-marketelection.html>	
87	Herbst-Bayliss, Svea. "Fewer hedge fund managers call it quits in 1st-half 2017." Reuters, September 18, 2017 <https://www.reuters.com/article/us-hedgefunds-closures/fewer-hedge-fund-managers-call-it-quits-in-1st-half-2017-idUSKCN1BT2C3>	
88	I.R.C. §475: Field Directive related to Mark-to-Market Valuation <https://www.irs.gov/businesses/irc-475-field-directive-related-to-mark-to-market-valuation>	
89	Jennings, William. "The mathematics of compliance." Compliance & Ethics Professional, December 2014	
90	Kirilenko, Andrei, et al. "The Flash Crash: The Impact of High Frequency Trading on an Electronic Market." February 21, 2014 <http://www.cftc.gov/idc/groups/public/@economicanalysis/documents/file/oce_flashcrash0314.pdf>	
91	Nielsen, Lars Tyge. "Understanding N(d1) and N(d2): Risk-Adjusted Probabilities in the Black-Scholes Model." Finance, Economics, and Mathematics. October 1992. <http://www.ltnielsen.com/wp-content/uploads/Understanding.pdf>	
92	Roman, Jan. "Chapter 15: Option Valuation." <http://janroman.dhis.org/finance/General/Option%20Valuation.pdf>	
93	Soled, Jay, et al. "The lure of a Sec. 475 election." Journal of Accountancy <https://www.journalofaccountancy.com/issues/2014/jul/sec-475-election-20149537.html>	

(*Continued*)

TABLE 14.3 (*Continued*)
Exhibit B—Materials Considered

Description	Beginning Bates or Range
94 Staff of the Investment Adviser Regulation Office Division of Investment Management, U.S. Securities and Exchange Commission. "Regulation of Investment Advisers by the U.S. Securities and Exchange Commission." March 2013, p. 34-35 and footnote 181 <https://www.sec.gov/about/offices/oia/oia_investman/rplaze-042012.pdf>	
95 Summa, John. "Sellers vs Buyers: Who Wins? A Study of CME Options Expiration Patterns." OptionsNerd.com <http://app.topica.com/banners/forms/900067555/900031275/SELLERSVSBUYERSWHOWINS.doc>	
96 Thorp, Wayne. "An Intro to Moving Averages: Popular Technical Indicators." American Association of Individual Investors Journal. August 1999. <https://www.aaii.com/journal/article/an-intro-to-moving-averages-popular-technical-indicators.touch>	
97 University of California, Davis Department of Statistics Lecture regarding Describing Data <http://www.stat.ucdavis.edu/~ntyang/teaching/12SSII/lecture02.pdf>	
98 "A Fascinating Look at How the Internet Has Changed the Stock Market." Vision Computer Solutions, 2016 <http://vcsolutions.com/a-fascinating-look-at-how-the-internet-has-changed-the-stock-market/>	
99 "About Hedge Funds" Hedge Fund Association <http://www.hedgefundassoc.org/about_hedge_funds/>	
100 "CME Group Options on Futures." CME Group <https://www.cmegroup.com/education/files/options-on-futures-brochure.pdf>	
101 "Fast Answers – Commodity Futures Trading Commission." U.S. Securities and Exchange Commission <https://www.sec.gov/fast-answers/answers-cftchtm.html>.	
102 "Fast Answers – Net Asset Value." U.S. Securities and Exchange Commission <https://www.sec.gov/fast-answers/answersnavhtm.html>	
103 "Financial Reporting Framework for Small- and Medium-Sized Entities." American Institute of Certified Public Accountants, 2013	
104 "Findings Regarding the Market Events of May 6, 2010." U.S. Securities and Exchange Commission and U.S. Commodities Futures Trading Commission, September 30, 2010 <https://www.sec.gov/news/studies/2010/marketevents-report.pdf>	
105 "Fundamentals of Options on Futures." CME Institute <https://institute.cmegroup.com/whitepapers/markets/fundamentals-of-options-on-futures>	
106 "Lessons in Clarity: Hedge Funds." CFA Institute <https://www.cfainstitute.org/programs/investmentfoundations/courseofstudy/Pages/lessons_in_clarity_hedge_funds.aspx>	
107 "Mark-to-Market Election for Hedge Funds." Capital Fund Law Blog <http://www.capitalfundlaw.com/blog/2015/05/21/mark-to-market-election-for-hedge-funds>	
108 "Preqin Special Report: Hedge Funds in the US." Preqin, October 2016 <http://docs.preqin.com/reports/Preqin-Special-Report-Hedge-Funds-in-the-US-October-2016.pdf>	
109 "S&P 500 Futures and Options on Futures." CME Group <https://www.cmegroup.com/trading/equity-index/files/sandp-500-futures-options.pdf>	
110 "Security Futures: An Introduction to Their Uses and Risks." National Futures Association <https://www.nfa.futures.org/members/member-resources/files/security-futures.pdf>	

(*Continued*)

TABLE 14.3 (*Continued*)
Exhibit B—Materials Considered

	Description	Beginning Bates or Range
111	"Stock Indexes: Understanding Stock Index Futures." CME Group, May 3, 2013 <https://www.cmegroup.com/education/files/understanding-stock-index-futures.pdf>	
112	"Technical Analysis." University of Cambridge. February 2, 2011. <https://www.mrao.cam.ac.uk/~mph/Technical_Analysis.pdf>	
113	"Theta." The Options Industry Council <https://www.optionseducation.org/strategies_advanced_concepts/advanced_concepts/understanding_option_greeks/theta.html>	
114	"Options Pricing." The Options Industry Council <https://www.optionseducation.org/getting_started/options_overview/options_pricing.html>	

Produced Documents

	Description	Beginning Bates or Range
115	Xxxx Xxxxxxxx, XXX Incentive Fees Schedule (SEC 801-78293, Question 45)	XX_001390
116	Xxxx Xxxxxxxxxxx rate of return schedule	Xxxx_NDGA-00004060-4061
117	December XXXX Xxxx Xxxxxxxxxxx spreadsheet	Xxxx_NDGA-00015807
118	December XXXX Xxxx Xxxxxxxxxxx spreadsheet	Xxxx_NDGA-00015819
119	December XXXX Xxxx Xxxxxxxxxxx spreadsheet	Xxxx_NDGA-00015934
120	May XXXX Xxxx Xxxxxxxxxxx spreadsheet	Xxxx_NDGA-00015844
121	Email string between Xxxx Xxxxxxxx, Xxxxx Xxxxxx, and Xxxx Xxxxxxx (April XXXX)	Xxxx_NDGA-00004412
122	XXXX XXX Year End Statement—Xxxxx Xxxx	XX_003122
123	XXXX XXX Year End Statement—Xxxx Xxxxxx	XX_006688
124	July XXXX XX Fund account statements	Xxxx_NDGA-00004453
125	August XXXX XX Fund account statements	Xxxx_NDGA-00004486
126	XXX Xxxxxxxxxxx, XXX Financial Statements for the Years Ended December 31, XXXX and XXXX	XX_002815
127	Xxxx Xxxxxxxxxxx, XXX Financial Statements for the Years Ended December 31, XXXX and XXXX	XX_002834
128	Xxxx Xxxxxxxxxxx, XXX Financial Statements for the Years Ended December 31, XXXX and XXXX	XX_002856
129	Xxxx Xxxxxxxx, XXX Investment Advisory Agreement dated January 24, XXXX	XX_000017
130	Xxxx Xxxxxxxx, XXX Investment Advisory Agreement dated January 24, XXXX	XX_000006
131	Xxxx Xxxxxxxx, XXX Investment Advisory Agreement dated January 24, XXXX with attached Schedule A	XX_002790
132	Contribution Agreement for Xxxx Xxxxxxxxxxx to be used in conjunction with the January 31, XXXX PPM	Xxxx_000228
133	Contribution Agreement for Xxxx Xxxxxxxxxxx to be used in conjunction with the Second Restated Operating Agreement	Xxxx_000217
134	Contribution Agreement for Xxxx Xxxxxxxxxxx to be used in conjunction with the original Operating Agreement, version 2	Xxxx_000207
135	Contribution Agreement for Xxxx Xxxxxxxxxxx to be used in conjunction with the original Operating Agreement	Xxxx_000197
136	Xxxx Xxxxxxxxxxx, XXX Subscription Booklet (XXXX PPM)	Xxxx_000253
137	Xxxx Xxxxxxxxxxx, XXX Subscription Booklet (XXXX PPM)	Xxxx_000293

(Continued)

TABLE 14.3 (*Continued*)

Exhibit B—Materials Considered

	Description	Beginning Bates or Range
138	Third Restated Operating Agreement of Xxxx Xxxxxxxxxxx, XXX dated January 31, XXXX	XX_000652
139	Amendment to the Third Restated Operating Agreement of Xxxx Xxxxxxxxxxx, XXX dated January 31, XXXX, Amendment dated August 25, XXXX	XX_000650
140	Confidential Private Placement Memorandum dated March 23, XXXX for Xxxx Xxxxxxxxxxx, XXX	Xxxx_000177
141	Confidential Private Placement Memorandum dated January 31, XXXX for Xxxx Xxxxxxxxxxx, XXX	Xxxx_000037
142	Confidential Private Placement Memorandum dated January 31, XXXX for Xxxx Xxxxxxxxxxx, XXX	Xxxx_000059
143	Confidential Private Placement Memorandum dated January 31, XXXX for Xxxx Xxxxxxxxxxx, XXX	XX_000681
144	Confidential Private Placement Memorandum dated January 31, XXXX for Xxxx Xxxxxxxxxxx, XXX	Xxxx_000115
145	January XXXX TD Ameritrade statement for XXX	SEC-AMERITRADE-E-0001504
146	February XXXX TD Ameritrade statement for XXX	SEC-AMERITRADE-E-0001587
147	March XXXX TD Ameritrade statement for XXX	SEC-AMERITRADE-E-0001603
148	April XXXX TD Ameritrade statement for XXX	SEC-AMERITRADE-E-0001590
149	May XXXX TD Ameritrade statement for XXX	SEC-AMERITRADE-E-0001510
150	June XXXX TD Ameritrade statement for XXX	SEC-AMERITRADE-E-0001452
151	July XXXX TD Ameritrade statement for XXX	SEC-AMERITRADE-E-0001554
152	August XXXX TD Ameritrade statement for XXX	SEC-AMERITRADE-E-0001544
153	September XXXX TD Ameritrade statement for XXX	SEC-AMERITRADE-E-0001503
154	October XXXX TD Ameritrade statement for XXX	SEC-AMERITRADE-E-0001507
155	November XXXX TD Ameritrade statement for XXX	SEC-AMERITRADE-E-0001597
156	December XXXX TD Ameritrade statement for XXX	SEC-AMERITRADE-E-0001548
157	January XXXX TD Ameritrade statement for XXX	SEC-AMERITRADE-E-0001599
158	February XXXX TD Ameritrade statement for XXX	SEC-AMERITRADE-E-0001446
159	March XXXX TD Ameritrade statement for XXX	SEC-AMERITRADE-E-0001550
160	April XXXX TD Ameritrade statement for XXX	SEC-AMERITRADE-E-0001442
161	May XXXX TD Ameritrade statement for XXX	SEC-AMERITRADE-E-0001449
162	June XXXX TD Ameritrade statement for XXX	SEC-AMERITRADE-E-0001594
163	July XXXX TD Ameritrade statement for XXX	SEC-AMERITRADE-E-0001456
164	August XXXX TD Ameritrade statement for XXX	SEC-AMERITRADE-E-0001489
165	September XXXX TD Ameritrade statement for XXX	SEC-AMERITRADE-E-0001565
166	October XXXX TD Ameritrade statement for XXX	SEC-AMERITRADE-E-0001463
167	November XXXX TD Ameritrade statement for XXX	SEC-AMERITRADE-E-0001458
168	December XXXX TD Ameritrade statement for XXX	SEC-AMERITRADE-E-0001644
169	January XXXX TD Ameritrade statement for XXX	SEC-AMERITRADE-E-0001468
170	February XXXX TD Ameritrade statement for XXX	SEC-AMERITRADE-E-0001529
171	March XXXX TD Ameritrade statement for XXX	SEC-AMERITRADE-E-0001513
172	April XXXX TD Ameritrade statement for XXX	SEC-AMERITRADE-E-0001181
173	May XXXX TD Ameritrade statement for XXX	SEC-AMERITRADE-E-0001120
174	June XXXX TD Ameritrade statement for XXX	SEC-AMERITRADE-E-0000643
175	July XXXX TD Ameritrade statement for XXX	XX_002008
176	August XXXX TD Ameritrade statement for XXX	XX_002043

(Continued)

TABLE 14.3 (*Continued*)
Exhibit B—Materials Considered

Description	Beginning Bates or Range
177	September XXXX TD Ameritrade statement for XXX	XX_002063
178	October XXXX TD Ameritrade statement for XXX	XX_002094
179	November XXXX TD Ameritrade statement for XXX	XX_002130
180	December XXXX TD Ameritrade statement for XXX	XX_002156
181	January XXXX TD Ameritrade statement for XXX	XX_001857
182	February XXXX TD Ameritrade statement for XXX	XX_001883
183	March XXXX TD Ameritrade statement for XXX	XX_001909
184	April XXXX TD Ameritrade statement for XXX	XX_001932
185	May XXXX TD Ameritrade statement for XXX	XX_001954
186	June XXXX TD Ameritrade statement for XXX	XX_001978
187	July XXXX TD Ameritrade statement for XXX	XX_002014
188	August XXXX TD Ameritrade statement for XXX	XX_002050
189	September XXXX TD Ameritrade statement for XXX	XX_002076
190	October XXXX TD Ameritrade statement for XXX	XX_002106
191	November XXXX TD Ameritrade statement for XXX	XX_002136
192	December XXXX TD Ameritrade statement for XXX	XX_002161
193	January XXXX TD Ameritrade statement for XXX	XX_001874
194	February XXXX TD Ameritrade statement for XXX	XX_001901
195	March XXXX TD Ameritrade statement for XXX	XX_001926
196	April XXXX TD Ameritrade statement for XXX	XX_001948
197	May XXXX TD Ameritrade statement for XXX	XX_001971
198	June XXXX TD Ameritrade statement for XXX	XX_001997
199	July XXXX TD Ameritrade statement for XXX	XX_002034
200	August XXXX TD Ameritrade statement for XXX	SEC-AMERITRADE-E-0001320
201	September XXXX TD Ameritrade statement for XXX	SEC-AMERITRADE-E-0001343
202	October XXXX TD Ameritrade statement for XXX	SEC-AMERITRADE-E-0000860
203	November XXXX TD Ameritrade statement for XXX	SEC-AMERITRADE-E-0001332
204	December XXXX TD Ameritrade statement for XXX	SEC-AMERITRADE-E-0001374
205	January XXXX TD Ameritrade statement for XXX	Xxxx_NDGA-00000062
206	February XXXX TD Ameritrade statement for XXX	Xxxx_NDGA-00000077
207	March XXXX TD Ameritrade statement for XXX	Xxxx_NDGA-00000079
208	April XXXX TD Ameritrade statement for XXX	SEC-AMERITRADE-E-0001133
209	May XXXX TD Ameritrade statement for XXX	SEC-AMERITRADE-E-0001330
210	March XXXX TD Ameritrade statement for XX Fund	SEC-AMERITRADE-E-0001580
211	April XXXX TD Ameritrade statement for XX Fund	SEC-AMERITRADE-E-0001474
212	May XXXX TD Ameritrade statement for XX Fund	SEC-AMERITRADE-E-0001583
213	June XXXX TD Ameritrade statement for XX Fund	SEC-AMERITRADE-E-0001577
214	July XXXX TD Ameritrade statement for XX Fund	SEC-AMERITRADE-E-0001623
215	August XXXX TD Ameritrade statement for XX Fund	SEC-AMERITRADE-E-0001572
216	September XXXX TD Ameritrade statement for XX Fund	SEC-AMERITRADE-E-0001484
217	October XXXX TD Ameritrade statement for XX Fund	SEC-AMERITRADE-E-0001486
218	November XXXX TD Ameritrade statement for XX Fund	SEC-AMERITRADE-E-0001482
219	December XXXX TD Ameritrade statement for XX Fund	SEC-AMERITRADE-E-0001542
220	January XXXX TD Ameritrade statement for XX Fund	SEC-AMERITRADE-E-0001626
221	February XXXX TD Ameritrade statement for XX Fund	SEC-AMERITRADE-E-0001574
222	March XXXX TD Ameritrade statement for XX Fund	SEC-AMERITRADE-E-0001534
223	April XXXX TD Ameritrade statement for XX Fund	SEC-AMERITRADE-E-0001523
224	May XXXX TD Ameritrade statement for XX Fund	SEC-AMERITRADE-E-0001519

(*Continued*)

TABLE 14.3 (*Continued*)
Exhibit B—Materials Considered

	Description	Beginning Bates or Range
225	June XXXX TD Ameritrade statement for XX Fund	SEC-AMERITRADE-E-0001635
226	July XXXX TD Ameritrade statement for XX Fund	SEC-AMERITRADE-E-0001479
227	August XXXX TD Ameritrade statement for XX Fund	SEC-AMERITRADE-E-0001527
228	September XXXX TD Ameritrade statement for XX Fund	SEC-AMERITRADE-E-0001629
229	October XXXX TD Ameritrade statement for XX Fund	SEC-AMERITRADE-E-0001631
230	November XXXX TD Ameritrade statement for XX Fund	SEC-AMERITRADE-E-0001538
231	December XXXX TD Ameritrade statement for XX Fund	SEC-AMERITRADE-E-0001638
232	January XXXX TD Ameritrade statement for XX Fund	SEC-AMERITRADE-E-0001491
233	February XXXX TD Ameritrade statement for XX Fund	SEC-AMERITRADE-E-0001560
234	March XXXX TD Ameritrade statement for XX Fund	SEC-AMERITRADE-E-0001606
235	April XXXX TD Ameritrade statement for XX Fund	SEC-AMERITRADE-E-0000592
236	May XXXX TD Ameritrade statement for XX Fund	SEC-AMERITRADE-E-0000677
237	June XXXX TD Ameritrade statement for XX Fund	SEC-AMERITRADE-E-0001128
238	July XXXX TD Ameritrade statement for XX Fund	XX_002414
239	August XXXX TD Ameritrade statement for XX Fund	XX_002200
240	September XXXX TD Ameritrade statement for XX Fund	XX_002513
241	October XXXX TD Ameritrade statement for XX Fund	XX_002534
242	November XXXX TD Ameritrade statement for XX Fund	XX_002576
243	December XXXX TD Ameritrade statement for XX Fund	XX_002204
244	January XXXX TD Ameritrade statement for XX Fund	XX_002209
245	February XXXX TD Ameritrade statement for XX Fund	XX_002259
246	March XXXX TD Ameritrade statement for XX Fund	XX_002297
247	April XXXX TD Ameritrade statement for XX Fund	XX_002330
248	May XXXX TD Ameritrade statement for XX Fund	XX_002355
249	June XXXX TD Ameritrade statement for XX Fund	XX_002376
250	July XXXX TD Ameritrade statement for XX Fund	XX_002420
251	August XXXX TD Ameritrade statement for XX Fund	XX_002456
252	September XXXX TD Ameritrade statement for XX Fund	XX_002525
253	October XXXX TD Ameritrade statement for XX Fund	XX_002559
254	November XXXX TD Ameritrade statement for XX Fund	XX_002602
255	December XXXX TD Ameritrade statement for XX Fund	XX_002628
256	January XXXX TD Ameritrade statement for XX Fund	XX_002250
257	February XXXX TD Ameritrade statement for XX Fund	XX_002289
258	March XXXX TD Ameritrade statement for XX Fund	XX_002322
259	April XXXX TD Ameritrade statement for XX Fund	XX_002348
260	May XXXX TD Ameritrade statement for XX Fund	XX_002369
261	June XXXX TD Ameritrade statement for XX Fund	XX_002400
262	July XXXX TD Ameritrade statement for XX Fund	XX_002449
263	August XXXX TD Ameritrade statement for XX Fund	SEC-AMERITRADE-P-0000050
264	September XXXX TD Ameritrade statement for XX Fund	SEC-AMERITRADE-P-0000057
265	October XXXX TD Ameritrade statement for XX Fund	SEC-AMERITRADE-P-0000065
266	November XXXX TD Ameritrade statement for XX Fund	SEC-AMERITRADE-P-0000071
267	December XXXX TD Ameritrade statement for XX Fund	SEC-AMERITRADE-P-0000077
268	January XXXX TD Ameritrade statement for XX Fund	SEC-AMERITRADE-P-0000081
269	February XXXX TD Ameritrade statement for XX Fund	Xxxx_NDGA-00000116
270	March XXXX TD Ameritrade statement for XX Fund	Xxxx_NDGA-00000128
271	April XXXX TD Ameritrade statement for XX Fund	Xxxx_NDGA-00000140
272	May XXXX TD Ameritrade statement for XX Fund	Xxxx_NDGA-00000151

(Continued)

TABLE 14.3 (*Continued*)
Exhibit B—Materials Considered

	Description	Beginning Bates or Range
273	June XXXX TD Ameritrade statement for XX Fund	Xxxx_NDGA-00000162
274	July XXXX TD Ameritrade statement for XX Fund	Xxxx_NDGA-00000173
275	August XXXX TD Ameritrade statement for XX Fund	Xxxx_NDGA-00000183
276	September XXXX TD Ameritrade statement for XX Fund	Xxxx_NDGA-00000192
277	October XXXX TD Ameritrade statement for XX Fund	Xxxx_NDGA-00000086
278	November XXXX TD Ameritrade statement for XX Fund	Xxxx_NDGA-00000096
279	December XXXX TD Ameritrade statement for XX Fund	Xxxx_NDGA-00000106
280	January XXXX TD Ameritrade statement for XX Fund	Xxxx_NDGA-00000203
281	Xxxxxxxxxxx-produced XX Fund Tax Returns and K-1s for XXXX	BCPAS000009-166, 175-332, 334-490
282	Xxxxxxxxxxx-produced XX Fund Tax Returns and K-1s for XXXX	BCPAS000555-742, 751-938, 940-1127
283	Xxxxxxxxxxx-produced XX Fund Tax Returns and K-1s for XXXX	BCPAS001202-1385, 1392-1575, 1578-1761, 1763-1944
284	Xxxxxxxxxxx-produced XX Fund Tax Returns and K-1s for XXXX	BCPAS00XXXX-2154, 2163-2300, 2302-2439
285	XX Fund account statements	Xxxx_NDGA-00005286-00015802
286	XXX account statements	Xxxx_NDGA-00019814-00019872
287	August XXXX statement for XXX	Xxxx_NDGA-00002955-2956
288	September XXXX statement for XXX	Xxxx_NDGA-00002964-2966
289	Employment information for Xxxxx Xxxxxx, Xxxx Xxxxxxx, Xxxx Xxxxxx, and Xxxx Xxxxxxx	XX_000002
290	List of Xxxx Xxxxxxxx, XXX employees and others who resigned or were eliminated during SEC examination period	XX_000003
291	List of threatened, pending, and settled litigation involving Xxxx Xxxxxxxx, XXX	XX_000004
292	List of joint ventures and other businesses in which Xxxx Xxxxxxxx, XXX, or its employees participate	XX_000043
293	Xxxx Xxxxxxxx, XXX, current fee schedule	XX_000045
294	Trade blotters for XXX, XX Fund, and Impact Capital fund	XX_000469—XX_000472
295	Schedules of fund returns for XXX, XX Fund, and Impact Capital fund and comparisons to SPX returns	XX_000478
296	Xxxx Xxxxxxxx, XXX, balance sheets as of December 31, XXXX and July 31, XXXX; cash flow statements for January through December XXXX and January through July XXXX; profit and loss statements for January through December XXXX and January through July XXXX; trial balances as of December 31, XXXX and July 31, XXXX	XX_000479—XX_000487
297	Xxxx Xxxxxxxx, XXX, general ledger as of July 31, XXXX and journal for cash receipts and disbursements from July XXXX through July XXXX	XX_000488—XX_000582
298	Schedules of investors (balances, contributions, and withdrawals) for XXX for July XXXX through July XXXX; XX Fund for July XXXX through July XXXX; and Impact Capital for January XXXX through July XXXX	XX_000987—XX_000990
299	XXX, XX Fund, and Impact Capital balance sheets, cash receipts and disbursements journals, general ledgers, income statements, trial balances, audited financial statements, and liquidation statements for various periods from XXXX through July XXXX	XX_000991—XX_001329

EXHIBITS USED TO SUMMARIZE FACTS OR DATA

U.S. Securities and Exchange Commission v. ▮ *et al.*   Exhibit 1.1

Comparison of Actual Fees and Hypothetical "2 and 20" Fee Method Based on NAV

	Actual			Hypothetical "2 and 20" Fee Method Based on NAV			Difference Between Actual and Hypothetical "2 and 20" Method Based on NAV
	Management Fee	Incentive Allocation	Total	Hypothetical Management Fee [1]	Hypothetical Incentive Allocation [2]	Total	
2013	$ -	$ 7,634,408	$ 7,634,408	$ 2,488,255	$ 9,818,382	$ 12,306,637	$ (4,672,228)
2014	-	6,920,232	6,920,232	3,204,658	3,445,286	6,649,944	270,288
2015	-	6,228,960	6,228,960	2,944,674	6,258,278	9,202,952	(2,973,992)
2016 through May	-	1,486,858	1,486,858	1,338,556	-	1,338,556	148,302
	$ -	$ 22,270,458	$ 22,270,458	$ 9,976,143	$ 19,521,946	$ 29,498,088	$ (7,227,630)

Sources: Monthly account statements for ▮ *-00005286-00015802), ▮ -00004061, and ▮ -00015807*

[1] Assumes a hypothetical management fee equal to 2% of the ▮ 's end of month net asset value

[2] Assumes a hypothetical incentive allocation equal to 20% of the ▮ 's end of month gains, including realized gains/(losses) on closed positions as well as the monthly change in unrealized gains/(losses) on open positions, subject to a monthly high-water mark based on the previous month's realized gains/(losses) on closed positions as well as the monthly change in unrealized gains/(losses) on open positions

Note: Immaterial differences may exist due to rounding.

Page 1 of 1

FIGURE 14.3

U.S. Securities and Exchange Commission v. ▮▮▮ et al. — Exhibit 1.2

Comparison of Actual Fees and Hypothetical ''2 and 20'' Fee Method Based on NAV - Detail

Period	Month	Year	End of Month NAV	Realized Trading Gains/(Losses)	Change in Unrealized Gains/(Losses)[1]	Total Monthly Gains/(Losses)[1]	Cumulative Change in Gains/(Losses)	Total Monthly Gains/(Losses) High- Water Mark[2]	Hypothetical Management Fee[3]	Hypothetical Incentive Allocation[4]	Actual Incentive Allocation	Difference Between Actual Incentive Allocation and Hypothetical "2% and 20" Method Based on NAV
Dec-12	Dec	2012	$ 79,379,541				$ 9,848,904	$ (9,261,223)				
Jan-13	Jan	2013	96,409,215	$ 1,919,556	$ 13,887,296	$ 15,806,851	25,655,756	6,545,629	$ 160,682	$ 1,309,126	$ 383,911	
Feb-13	Feb	2013	108,128,047	1,496,309	5,349,303	6,845,612	32,501,368		180,213	1,369,122	299,262	
Mar-13	Mar	2013	104,078,401	3,761,269	(7,430,397)	(3,669,128)	28,832,240		173,464	-	752,254	
Apr-13	Apr	2013	110,033,590	3,739,625	6,157,128	9,896,753	38,728,993	6,227,625	183,389	1,245,525	747,925	
May-13	May	2013	103,593,911	3,486,731	(11,068,491)	(7,581,760)	31,147,233		172,657	-	697,346	
Jun-13	Jun	2013	120,667,510	2,332,347	15,232,886	17,565,233	48,712,466	9,983,473	201,113	1,996,695	466,469	
Jul-13	Jul	2013	129,369,438	3,985,849	231,460	4,217,309	52,929,775		215,616	843,462	797,170	
Aug-13	Aug	2013	132,440,738	3,333,755	(771,655)	2,562,100	55,491,875		220,735	512,420	666,751	
Sep-13	Sep	2013	135,489,321	3,353,810	(146,030)	3,207,780	58,699,655		225,816	641,556	670,762	
Oct-13	Oct	2013	147,449,833	3,590,021	(1,352,276)	2,237,745	60,937,400		245,750	447,549	718,004	
Nov-13	Nov	2013	149,609,681	2,319,449	(1,221,082)	1,098,367	62,035,767		249,349	219,673	463,890	
Dec-13	Dec	2013	155,683,033	4,853,320	1,312,950	6,166,270	68,202,037		259,472	1,233,254	970,664	$ (4,672,225)
Jan-14	Jan	2014	164,668,358	4,382,872	1,245,546	5,628,418	73,830,455		274,447	1,125,684	876,574	
Feb-14	Feb	2014	153,782,500	2,994,120	(13,616,333)	(10,622,213)	63,208,242		256,304	-	598,824	
Mar-14	Mar	2014	158,728,669	4,448,431	1,948,613	6,397,044	69,605,286		264,548	-	889,686	
Apr-14	Apr	2014	168,089,580	1,223,264	2,188,518	3,411,782	73,017,068		280,149	-	244,653	
May-14	May	2014	174,963,675	2,251,901	5,412,352	7,664,253	80,681,321	6,850,866	291,606	1,370,173	450,380	
Jun-14	Jun	2014	167,871,366	3,390,133	(9,736,809)	(6,346,676)	74,334,645		279,786	-	678,027	
Jul-14	Jul	2014	174,657,357	5,008,227	2,647,491	7,655,718	81,990,363	1,309,042	291,096	261,808	1,001,645	
Aug-14	Aug	2014	161,574,286	2,413,014	(14,603,286)	(12,190,272)	69,800,091		269,290	-	482,603	
Sep-14	Sep	2014	177,313,801	5,578,087	10,050,289	15,628,376	85,428,467	3,438,104	295,523	687,621	1,115,617	
Oct-14	Oct	2014	144,118,572	1,833,768	(34,954,186)	(33,120,418)	52,308,049		240,198	-	366,754	
Nov-14	Nov	2014	138,658,823	864,279	(4,851,346)	(3,987,067)	48,320,982		231,098	-	172,856	
Dec-14	Dec	2014	138,367,876	213,065	191,429	404,494	48,725,476		230,613	-	42,613	270,287.90
Jan-15	Jan	2015	147,349,745	1,489,590	12,114,637	13,604,227	62,329,703		245,583	-	297,918	
Feb-15	Feb	2015	151,284,176	1,729,670	4,501,695	6,231,365	68,561,068		252,140	-	345,934	
Mar-15	Mar	2015	159,253,903	2,413,443	7,127,901	9,541,344	78,102,412		265,423	-	482,689	
Apr-15	Apr	2015	156,877,561	1,344,383	(630,921)	713,462	78,815,874		261,463	-	268,877	
May-15	May	2015	161,043,128	2,627,381	2,776,693	5,404,074	84,219,948		268,405	-	525,476	
Jun-15	Jun	2015	167,162,478	2,575,922	18,098,737	20,674,659	104,894,607	19,466,140	278,604	3,893,228	515,184	

CONFIDENTIAL

Page 1 of 2

FIGURE 14.4

U.S. Securities and Exchange Commission v. ▬ *et al.*

Exhibit 1.2

Comparison of Actual Fees and Hypothetical "2 and 20" Fee Method Based on NAV - Detail

Period	Month	Year	End of Month NAV	Realized Trading Gains/(Losses)	Change in Unrealized Gains/(Losses)	Total Monthly Gains/(Losses)[1]	Cumulative Change in Gains/(Losses)	Total Monthly Gains/(Losses) High-Water Mark[2]	Hypothetical Management Fee[3]	Hypothetical Incentive Allocation[4]	Actual Incentive Allocation	Difference Between Actual Incentive Allocation and Hypothetical "20 and 20" Method Based on NAV
Jul-15	Jul	2015	176,499,345	3,227,226	8,598,022	11,825,248	116,719,855		294,166	2,365,050	645,445	
Aug-15	Aug	2015	118,138,653	4,102,702	(58,760,854)	(54,658,152)	62,061,703		196,898	-	820,540	
Sep-15	Sep	2015	140,778,692	2,805,003	20,501,036	23,306,039	85,367,742		234,631	-	561,001	
Oct-15	Oct	2015	122,440,810	2,856,734	(20,937,122)	(18,080,388)	67,287,354		204,068	-	571,347	
Nov-15	Nov	2015	135,013,807	2,938,797	9,954,600	12,893,397	80,180,751		225,023	-	587,759	
Dec-15	Dec	2015	130,962,278	3,033,950	(6,347,632)	(3,313,682)	76,867,069		218,270	-	606,790	(2,973,991.89)
Jan-16	Jan	2016	136,961,159	2,596,009	4,288,325	6,884,334	83,751,403		228,269	-	519,202	
Feb-16	Feb	2016	135,552,222	2,268,780	(2,446,275)	(177,495)	83,573,908		225,920	-	453,756	
Mar-16	Mar	2016	129,589,412	2,569,500	(7,749,460)	(5,179,960)	78,393,948		215,982	-	513,900	
Apr-16	Apr	2016	196,502,534	2,141,979	2,837,690	4,979,669	83,373,617		327,504	-	-	
May-16	May	2016	204,528,057	3,008,724	6,232,300	9,241,024	92,614,641		340,880	-	-	148,302
				$ 116,592,995		$ 82,765,737			$ 9,976,143	$ 19,521,946	$ 22,270,458	$ (7,227,630)

Sources: Monthly account statements for ▬ *-00005286-000015802), ▬ -00004061, and* ▬ *-00015807*

[1] Total monthly gain/(loss) is the sum of monthly realized trading gains/(losses) and the change in unrealized gains/(losses)

[2] Assumes a hypothetical monthly high-water mark, including realized trading gains/(losses) and the change in unrealized gains/(losses). Prior to January 2013, the total monthly gains/(losses) high-water mark was approximately $19,110,127, which occurred in May 2012. The cumulative gain/loss of approximately $9,848,904 in December 2012 was approximately $9,261,223 below the high-water mark.

[3] Assumes a hypothetical management fee equal to 2% of the ▬'s end of month net asset value

[4] Assumes a hypothetical incentive allocation equal to 20% of the ▬'s end of month gains, including realized trading gains/(losses) as well as the change in unrealized gains/(losses), subject to the total monthly gains/(losses) high-water mark

Note: Immaterial differences may exist due to rounding.

Page 2 of 2

CONFIDENTIAL

FIGURE 14.5

The following section deals with what occurs with respect to experts ahead of trial.

"(4) *Trial Preparation: Experts.*

(A) *Deposition of an Expert Who May Testify.* A party may depose any person who has been identified as an expert whose opinions may be presented at trial. If Rule 26(a)(2)(B) requires a report from the expert, the deposition may be conducted only after the report is provided.

(B) *Trial-Preparation Protection for Draft Reports or Disclosures.* Rules 26(b) (3)(A) and (B) protect drafts of any report or disclosure required under Rule 26(a)(2), regardless of the form in which the draft is recorded.

(C) *Trial-Preparation Protection for Communications Between a Party's Attorney and Expert Witnesses.* Rules 26(b)(3)(A) and (B) protect communications between the party's attorney and any witness required to provide a report under Rule 26(a)(2)(B), regardless of the form of the communications, except to the extent that the communications:

(i) relate to compensation for the expert's study or testimony;

(ii) identify facts or data that the party's attorney provided and that the expert considered in forming the opinions to be expressed; or

(iii) identify assumptions that the party's attorney provided and that the expert relied on in forming the opinions to be expressed.

(D) *Expert Employed Only for Trial Preparation.* Ordinarily, a party may not, by interrogatories or deposition, discover facts known or opinions held by an expert who has been retained or specially employed by another party in anticipation of litigation or to prepare for trial and who is not expected to be called as a witness at trial. But a party may do so only:

(i) as provided in Rule 35(b); or

(ii) on showing exceptional circumstances under which it is impracticable for the party to obtain facts or opinions on the same subject by other means.

(E) *Payment.* Unless manifest injustice would result, the court must require that the party seeking discovery:

(i) pay the expert a reasonable fee for time spent in responding to discovery under Rule 26(b)(4)(A) or (D); and

(ii) for discovery under (D), also pay the other party a fair portion of the fees and expenses it reasonably incurred in obtaining the expert's facts and opinions."[2]

Now let's look at the federal rules of evidence. This first section deals with both fact and expert witnesses. It lays out the requirements that must be met before someone will be allowed to testify in a federal civil trial.

"ARTICLE VI. WITNESSES

Rule 601. Competency to Testify in General

Every person is competent to be a witness unless these rules provide otherwise. But in a civil case, state law governs the witness's competency regarding a claim or defense for which state law supplies the rule of decision.
(As amended Apr. 26, 2011, eff. Dec. 1, 2011.)

Rule 602. Need for Personal Knowledge

A witness may testify to a matter only if evidence is introduced sufficient to support a finding that the witness has personal knowledge of the matter. Evidence to prove personal knowledge may consist of the witness's own testimony. This rule does not apply to a witness's expert testimony under Rule 703.

(As amended Mar. 2, 1987, eff. Oct. 1, 1987; Apr. 25, 1988, eff. Nov. 1, 1988; Apr. 26, 2011, eff. Dec. 1, 2011.)

Rule 603. Oath or Affirmation to Testify Truthfully

Before testifying, a witness must give an oath or affirmation to testify truthfully. It must be in a form designed to impress that duty on the witness's conscience.
(As amended Mar. 2, 1987, eff. Oct. 1, 1987; Apr. 26, 2011, eff. Dec. 1, 2011.)"[3]

The following rule is important to keep in mind. The scope of cross-examination is limited to the subjects covered in the direct examination of the witness. This applies to fact and expert witnesses.

"Rule 611. Mode and Order of Examining Witnesses and Presenting Evidence

(a) CONTROL BY THE COURT; PURPOSES. The court should exercise reasonable control over the mode and order of examining witnesses and presenting evidence so as to:

(1) make those procedures effective for determining the truth;

(2) avoid wasting time; and

(3) protect witnesses from harassment or undue embarrassment.

(b) SCOPE OF CROSS-EXAMINATION. Cross-examination should not go beyond the subject matter of the direct examination and matters affecting the witness's credibility. The court may allow inquiry into additional matters as if on direct examination.

(c) LEADING QUESTIONS. Leading questions should not be used on direct examination except as necessary to develop the witness's testimony. Ordinarily, the court should allow leading questions:

(1) on cross-examination; and

(2) when a party calls a hostile witness, an adverse party, or a witness identified with an adverse party.

(As amended Mar. 2, 1987, eff. Oct. 1, 1987; Apr. 26, 2011, eff. Dec. 1, 2011.)"[4]

This next thing comes up often at trial. The judge will often ask you questions while you are on the stand under oath. Do not be flustered by this. It just means the judge is paying attention and is interested in what you have to say.

"Rule 614. Court's Calling or Examining a Witness

(a) CALLING. The court may call a witness on its own or at a party's request. Each party is entitled to cross-examine the witness.

(b) EXAMINING. The court may examine a witness regardless of who calls the witness.

(c) OBJECTIONS. A party may object to the court's calling or examining a witness either at that time or at the next opportunity when the jury is not present.

(As amended Apr. 26, 2011, eff. Dec. 1, 2011.)"[5]

This following section deals with opinions and expert testimony. There is a common misconception that if you are a fact witness, you are not able to offer opinions as part of your testimony. Fact witnesses are allowed to offer rational opinions that are helpful in understanding the witness's testimony. However, they must not offer opinions based on specialized knowledge; that testimony is reserved to qualified (i.e. by the court) experts.

"ARTICLE VII. OPINIONS AND EXPERT TESTIMONY

Rule 701. Opinion Testimony by Lay Witnesses

If a witness is not testifying as an expert, testimony in the form of an opinion is limited to one that is:

(a) rationally based on the witness's perception;

(b) helpful to clearly understanding the witness's testimony or to determining a fact in issue; and

(c) not based on scientific, technical, or other specialized knowledge within the scope of Rule 702.

(As amended Mar. 2, 1987, eff. Oct. 1, 1987; Apr. 17, 2000, eff. Dec. 1, 2000; Apr. 26, 2011, eff. Dec. 1, 2011.)"[6]

Now let's turn to expert testimony. This first section covers what the expert's opinion must be based on. First, the whole reason for expert testimony is to help the trier of fact understand the evidence and/or issues that are related to the subject of the litigation. Those opinions must be based on sufficient facts of data that has been subjected to a reliable method in the expert's field of expertise. The expert must also demonstrate that he or she reliably applied those principles and methods to the facts and data in forming the expert opinions being offered in testimony.

"Rule 702. Testimony by Expert Witnesses

A witness who is qualified as an expert by knowledge, skill, experience, training, or education may testify in the form of an opinion or otherwise if:

(a) the expert's scientific, technical, or other specialized knowledge will help the trier of fact to understand the evidence or to determine a fact in issue;

(b) the testimony is based on sufficient facts or data;

(d) the testimony is the product of reliable principles and methods; and

(e) the expert has reliably applied the principles and methods to the facts of the case.

(As amended Apr. 17, 2000, eff. Dec. 1, 2000; Apr. 26, 2011, eff. Dec.1, 2011.)"[7]

There are some additional requirements that have been added by jurisprudence that resulted in something called a Daubert Challenge. This is the most important change in the admissibility of expert testimony during my career. When I began testifying in the early 1980s, anyone could be qualified as an expert. My favorite "experts," at that time, were phrenologists who offered "expert opinions" regarding mental faculties and character traits based on the configurations of a person's skull. Most forensic accountants, at that time, would base their "expert opinions" on their experience. So, the trier of fact was left to decide which expert to believe based on their perception of the expert. An older, attractive, and likeable expert was more likely to prevail with triers of fact; a very dubious standard for evaluating the veracity of expert testimony. The following is the Supreme Court opinion that established the Daubert challenge:

"DAUBERT ET UX., INDIVIDUALLY AND AS GUARDIANS
AD LITEM FOR DAUBERT, ET AL. vs MERRELL DOW PHARMACEUTICALS, INC.

CERTIORARI TO THE UNITED STATES COURT OF APPEALS FOR THE NINTH CIRCUIT

No. 92–102. ARGUED MARCH 30, 1993—DECIDED JUNE 28, 1993

Opinion of the Court

Justice Blackmun delivered the opinion of the Court.

In this case we are called upon to determine the standard for admitting expert scientific testimony in a federal trial.

I

Petitioners Jason Daubert and Eric Schuller are minor children born with serious birth defects. They and their parents sued respondent in California state court, alleging that the birth defects had been caused by the mothers' ingestion of Bendectin, a pre-scription antinausea drug marketed by respondent. Respondent removed the suits to federal court on diversity grounds.

After extensive discovery, respondent moved for summary judgment, contending that Bendectin does not cause birth defects in humans and that petitioners would be unable to come forward with any admissible evidence that it does. In support of its motion, respondent submitted an affidavit of Steven H. Lamm, physician and epidemiologist, who is a well-credentialed expert on the risks from exposure to various chemical sub-stances.[1] Doctor Lamm stated that he had reviewed all the literature on Bendectin and human birth defects—more than 30 published studies involving over 130,000 patients. No study had found Bendectin to be a human teratogen (*i.e.,* a substance capable of causing malformations in fetuses). On the basis of this review, Doctor Lamm concluded that maternal use of Bendectin during the first trimester of pregnancy has not been shown to be a risk factor for human birth defects.

Petitioners did not (and do not) contest this characterization of the published record regarding Bendectin. Instead, they responded to respondent's motion with the tes-timony of eight experts of their own, each of whom also possessed impressive cre-dentials.[2] These experts had concluded that Bendectin can cause birth defects. Their conclusions were based upon "in vitro" (test tube) and "in vivo" (live) animal studies that found a link between Bendectin and malformations; pharmacological studies of the chemical structure of Bendectin that purported to show similarities between the structure of the drug and that of other substances known to cause birth defects; and the "reanalysis" of previously published epidemiological (human statistical) studies. The District Court granted respondent's motion for summary judgment. The court stated that scientific evidence is admissible only if the principle upon which it is based is "'sufficiently established to have general acceptance in the field to which it belongs.'" 727 F. Supp. 570, 572 (SD Cal. 1989), quoting *United States vs Kilgus,* 571 F. 2d 508, 510 (CA9 1978). The court concluded that petitioners' evidence did not meet this stan-dard. Given the vast body of epidemiological data concerning Bendectin, the court held, expert opinion which is not based on epidemiological evidence is not admissible to establish causation. 727 F. Supp., at 575. Thus, the animal-cell studies, live-animal studies, and chemical-structure analyses on which petitioners had relied could not raise by themselves a reasonably disputable jury issue regarding causation. *Ibid.* Petitioners' epidemiological analyses, based as they were on recalculations of data in previously published studies that had found no causal link between the drug and birth defects, were ruled to be inadmissible because they had not been published or subjected to peer review. *Ibid.*

The United States Court of Appeals for the Ninth Circuit affirmed. 951 F. 2d 1128 (1991). Citing *Frye vs United States,* 54 App. D. C. 46, 47, 293 F. 1013, 1014 (1923), the court stated that expert opinion based on a scientific technique is inadmissible unless the technique is "generally accepted" as reliable in the relevant scientific community. 951 F. 2d, at 1129–1130. The court declared that expert opinion based on a methodology that diverges "significantly from the procedures accepted by recognized authorities in the field ... cannot be shown to be 'generally accepted as a reliable technique.'" *Id.,* at 1130, quoting *United States vs Solomon,* 753 F. 2d 1522, 1526 (CA9 1985).

The court emphasized that other Courts of Appeals considering the risks of Bendectin had refused to admit reanalyses of epidemiological studies that had been nei-ther published nor subjected to peer review. 951 F. 2d, at 1130–1131. Those courts had found unpublished reanalyses "particularly problematic in light of the massive weight of the original published studies supporting [respondent's] position, all of which had undergone full scrutiny from the scientific community." *Id.,* at 1130. Contending that reanalysis is generally accepted by the scientific community only when it is subjected to verification and scrutiny by others in the field, the Court of Appeals rejected petitioners' reanalyses as "unpublished, not subjected to the normal peer review process and generated solely for use in litigation." *Id.,* at 1131. The court concluded that petitioners' evidence provided an insufficient foundation to allow admission of expert testimony that Bendectin caused their injuries and, accordingly, that petitioners could not satisfy their burden of proving causation at trial.

We granted certiorari, 506 U. S. 914 (1992), in light of sharp divisions among the courts regarding the proper standard for the admission of expert testimony. Compare, *e.g., United States vs Shorter,* 257 U.S. App. D. C. 358, 363–364, 809 F. 2d 54, 59–60 (applying the "general acceptance" standard), cert. denied, 484 U.S. 817 (1987), with *DeLuca vs Merrell Dow Pharmaceuticals, Inc.,* 911 F. 2d 941, 955 (CA31990) (rejecting the "general acceptance" standard).

II

A

In the 70 years since its formulation in the *Frye* case, the "general acceptance" test has been the dominant standard for determining the admissibility of novel scientific evidence at trial. See E. Green & C. Nesson, Problems, Cases, and Materials on Evidence 649 (1983). Although under increasing attack of late, the rule continues to be followed by a majority of courts, including the Ninth Circuit.[3]

The *Frye* test has its origin in a short and citation-free 1923 decision concerning the admissibility of evidence derived from a systolic blood pressure deception test, a crude precursor to the polygraph machine. In what has become a famous (perhaps infamous) passage, the then Court of Appeals for the District of Columbia described the device and its operation and declared:

> "Just when a scientific principle or discovery crosses the line between the experimental and demonstrable stages is difficult to define. Somewhere in this twilight zone the evidential force of the principle must be recognized, and while courts will go a long way in admitting expert testimony deduced from a well-recognized scientific principle or discovery, *the thing from which the deduction is made must be sufficiently established to have gained general acceptance in the particular field in which it belongs.*" 54 App. D. C., at 47, 293 F., at 1014 (emphasis added).

Because the deception test had "not yet gained such standing and scientific recognition among physiological and psychological authorities as would justify the courts in admitting expert testimony deduced from the discovery, development, and experiments thus far made," evidence of its results was ruled inadmissible. *Ibid.*

The merits of the *Frye* test have been much debated, and scholarship on its proper scope and application is legion.[4] Petitioners' primary attack, however, is not on the content but on the continuing authority of the rule. They contend that the *Frye* test was superseded by the adoption of the Federal Rules of Evidence.[5] We agree.

We interpret the legislatively enacted Federal Rules of Evidence as we would any statute. *Beech Aircraft Corp. vs Rainey,* 488 U.S. 153, 163 (1988). Rule 402 provides the baseline:

> "All relevant evidence is admissible, except as otherwise provided by the Constitution of the United States, by Act of Congress, by these rules, or by other rules prescribed by the Supreme Court pursuant to statutory authority. Evidence which is not relevant is not admissible."

"Relevant evidence" is defined as that which has "any tendency to make the existence of any fact that is of consequence to the determination of the action more probable or less probable than it would be without the evidence." Rule 401. The Rules' basic standard of relevance thus is a liberal one.

Frye, of course, predated the Rules by half a century. In *United States vs Abel,* 469 U.S. 45 (1984), we considered the pertinence of background common law in interpreting the Rules of Evidence. We noted that the Rules occupy the field, *id.,* at 49, but, quoting Professor Cleary, the Reporter, explained that the common law nevertheless could serve as an aid to their application:

> "'In principle, under the Federal Rules no common law of evidence remains. "All relevant evidence is admissible, except as otherwise provided .... " In reality, of course, the body of common law knowledge continues to exist, though in the somewhat altered form of a source of guidance in the exercise of delegated powers.'" *Id.,* at 51–52.

We found the common-law precept at issue in the *Abel* case entirely consistent with Rule 402's general requirement of admissibility, and considered it unlikely that the drafters had intended to change the rule. *Id.,* at 50–51. In *Bourjaily vs United States,* 483 U.S. 171 (1987), on the other hand, the Court was unable to find a particular common-law doctrine in the Rules, and so held it superseded.

Here there is a specific Rule that speaks to the contested issue. Rule 702, governing expert testimony, provides:

> "If scientific, technical, or other specialized knowledge will assist the trier of fact to understand the evidence or to determine a fact in issue, a witness qualified as an expert by knowledge, skill, experience, training, or education, may testify thereto in the form of an opinion or otherwise."

Nothing in the text of this Rule establishes "general acceptance" as an absolute prerequisite to admissibility. Nor does respondent present any clear indication that Rule 702 or the Rules as a whole were intended to incorporate a "general acceptance" standard. The drafting history makes no mention of *Frye,* and a rigid "general acceptance" requirement would be at odds with the "liberal thrust" of the Federal Rules and their "general approach of relaxing the traditional barriers to 'opinion' testimony." *Beech Aircraft Corp. vs Rainey,* 488 U.S., at 169 (citing Rules 701 to 705). See also Weinstein, Rule 702 of the Federal Rules of Evidence is Sound; It Should Not Be Amended, 138 F. R. D. 631 (1991) ("The Rules were designed to depend primarily upon lawyer-adversaries and sensible triers of fact to evaluate conflicts"). Given the Rules' permissive backdrop and their inclusion of a specific rule on expert testimony that does not mention "general acceptance," the assertion that the Rules somehow assimilated *Frye* is unconvincing. *Frye* made "general acceptance" the exclusive test for admitting expert scientific testimony. That austere standard, absent from, and incompatible with, the Federal Rules of Evidence, should not be applied in federal trials.[6]

B

That the *Frye* test was displaced by the Rules of Evidence does not mean, however, that the Rules themselves place no limits on the admissibility of purportedly scientific evidence.[7] Nor is the trial judge disabled from screening such evidence. To the contrary, under the Rules the trial judge must ensure that any and all scientific testimony or evidence admitted is not only relevant, but reliable.

The primary locus of this obligation is Rule 702, which clearly contemplates some degree of regulation of the subjects and theories about which an expert may testify. *"If scientific,* technical, or other specialized *knowledge will assist the trier of fact* to understand the evidence or to determine a fact in issue" an expert "may testify *thereto."* (Emphasis added.) The subject of an expert's testimony must be "scientific ... knowledge."[8] The adjective "scientific" implies a grounding in the methods and procedures of science. Similarly, the word "knowledge" connotes more than subjective belief or unsupported speculation. The term "applies to any body of known facts or to any body of ideas inferred from such facts or accepted as truths on good grounds." Webster's Third New International Dictionary 1252 (1986). Of course, it would be unreasonable to conclude that the subject of scientific testimony must be "known" to a certainty; arguably, there are no certainties in science. See, *e.g.,* Brief for Nicolaas Bloembergen et al. as *Amici Curiae* 9 ("Indeed, scientists do not assert that they know what is immutably 'true'—they are committed to searching for new, temporary, theories to explain, as best they can, phenomena"); Brief for American Association for the Advancement of Science et al. as *Amici Curiae* 7–8 ("Science is not an encyclopedic body of knowledge about the universe. Instead, it represents a *process* for proposing and refining theoretical explanations about the world that are subject to further testing and refinement" (emphasis in original)). But, in order to qualify as "scientific knowledge," an inference or assertion must be derived by the scientific method. Proposed testimony must be supported by appropriate validation—*i.e.,* "good grounds," based on what is known. In short, the requirement that an expert's testimony pertain to "scientific knowledge" establishes a standard of evidentiary reliability.[9]

Rule 702 further requires that the evidence or testimony "assist the trier of fact to understand the evidence or to determine a fact in issue." This condition goes primarily to relevance. "Expert testimony which does not relate to any issue in the case is not relevant and, ergo, non-helpful." 3 Weinstein & Berger ¶702[02], p. 702–18. See also *United States vs Downing,* 753 F. 2d 1224, 1242 (CA3 1985) ("An additional consideration under Rule 702—and another aspect of relevancy—is whether expert testimony proffered in the case is sufficiently tied to the facts of the case that it will aid the jury in resolving a factual dispute"). The consideration has been aptly described by Judge Becker as one of "fit." *Ibid.* "Fit" is not always obvious, and scientific validity for one purpose is not necessarily scientific validity for other, unrelated purposes. See Starrs, *Frye vs United States* Restructured and Revitalized: A Proposal to Amend Federal Evidence Rule 702, 26 Jurimetrics J. 249, 258 (1986). The study of the phases of the moon, for example, may provide valid scientific "knowledge" about whether a certain night was dark, and if darkness is a fact in issue, the knowledge will assist the trier of fact. However (absent creditable grounds supporting such a link), evidence that the moon was full on a certain night will not assist the trier of fact in determining whether an individual was unusually likely to have behaved irrationally on that night. Rule 702's "helpfulness" standard requires a valid scientific connection to the pertinent inquiry as a precondition to admissibility.

That these requirements are embodied in Rule 702 is not surprising. Unlike an ordinary witness, see Rule 701, an expert is permitted wide latitude to offer opinions, including those that are not based on firsthand knowledge or observation. See Rules 702 and 703. Presumably, this relaxation of the usual requirement of firsthand knowledge— a rule which represents "a 'most pervasive manifestation' of the common law insistence upon 'the most reliable sources of information,'" Advisory Committee's Notes on Fed. Rule Evid. 602, 28 U. S. C. App., p. 755 (citation omitted)—is premised on an assumption that the expert's opinion will have a reliable basis in the knowledge and experience of his discipline.

C

Faced with a proffer of expert scientific testimony, then, the trial judge must determine at the outset, pursuant to Rule 104(a),[10] whether the expert is proposing to testify to (1) scientific knowledge that (2) will assist the trier of fact to understand or determine a fact in issue.[11] This entails a preliminary assessment of whether the reasoning or methodology underlying the testimony is scientifically valid and of whether that reasoning or methodology properly can be applied to the facts in issue. We are confident that federal judges possess the capacity to undertake this review. Many factors will bear on the inquiry, and we do not presume to set out a definitive checklist or test. But some general observations are appropriate.

Ordinarily, a key question to be answered in determining whether a theory or technique is scientific knowledge that will assist the trier of fact will be whether it can be (and has been) tested. "Scientific methodology today is based on generating hypotheses and testing them to see if they can be falsified; indeed, this methodology is what distinguishes science from other fields of human inquiry." Green 645. See also C. Hempel, Philosophy of Natural Science 49 (1966) ("[T]he statements constituting a scientific explanation must be capable of empirical test"); K. Popper, Conjectures and Refutations: The Growth of Scientific Knowledge 37 (5th ed. 1989) ("[T]he criterion of the scientific status of a theory is its falsifiability, or refutability, or testability") (emphasis deleted).

Another pertinent consideration is whether the theory or technique has been subjected to peer review and publication. Publication (which is but one element of peer review) is not a *sine qua non* of admissibility; it does not necessarily correlate with reliability, see S. Jasanoff, The Fifth Branch: Science Advisors as Policymakers 61–76 (1990), and in some instances well-grounded but innovative theories will not have been published, see Horrobin, The Philosophical Basis of Peer Review and the Suppression of Innovation, 263 JAMA 1438 (1990). Some propositions, moreover, are too particular, too new, or of too limited interest to be published. But submission to the scrutiny of the scientific community is a component of "good science," in part because it increases the likelihood that substantive flaws in methodology will be detected. See J. Ziman, Reliable Knowledge: An Exploration of the Grounds for Belief in Science 130–133 (1978); Relman & Angell, How Good Is Peer Review?, 321 New Eng. J. Med. 827 (1989). The fact of publication (or lack thereof) in a peer reviewed journal thus will be a relevant, though not dispositive, consideration in assessing the scientific validity of a particular technique or methodology on which an opinion is premised.

Additionally, in the case of a particular scientific technique, the court ordinarily should consider the known or potential rate of error, see, *e.g., United States vs Smith,* 869 F. 2d 348,353–354 (CA7 1989) (surveying studies of the error rate of spectrographic voice identification technique), and the existence and maintenance of standards controlling the technique's operation, see *United States vs Williams,* 583 F. 2d 1194, 1198 (CA2 1978) (noting professional organization's standard governing spectrographic analysis), cert. denied, 439 U.S. 1117 (1979).

Finally, "general acceptance" can yet have a bearing on the inquiry. A "reliability assessment does not require, although it does permit, explicit identification of a relevant scientific community and an express determination of a particular degree of acceptance within that community." *United States vs Downing,* 753 F. 2d, at 1238. See also 3 Weinstein & Berger ¶702[03], pp. 702–41 to 702–42. Widespread acceptance can be an important factor in ruling particular evidence admissible, and "a known technique which has been able to attract only minimal support within the community," *Downing,* 753 F. 2d, at 1238, may properly be viewed with skepticism. The inquiry envisioned by Rule 702 is, we emphasize, a flexible one.[12] Its overarching subject is the scientific validity—and thus the evidentiary relevance and reliability—of the principles that underlie a proposed submission. The focus, of course, must be solely on principles and methodology, not on the conclusions that they generate.

Throughout, a judge assessing a proffer of expert scientific testimony under Rule 702 should also be mindful of other applicable rules. Rule 703 provides that expert opinions based on otherwise inadmissible hearsay are to be admitted only if the facts or data are "of a type reasonably relied upon by experts in the particular field in forming opinions or inferences upon the subject." Rule 706 allows the court at its discretion to procure the assistance of an expert of its own choosing. Finally, Rule 403 permits the exclusion of relevant evidence "if its probative value is substantially outweighed by the danger of unfair prejudice, confusion of the issues, or misleading the jury ...." Judge Weinstein has explained: "Expert evidence can be both powerful and quite misleading because of the difficulty in evaluating it. Because of this risk, the judge in weighing possible prejudice against probative force under Rule 403 of the present rules exercises more control over experts than over lay witnesses." Weinstein, 138 F. R. D., at 632.

III

We conclude by briefly addressing what appear to be two underlying concerns of the parties and *amici* in this case. Respondent expresses apprehension that abandonment of "general acceptance" as the exclusive requirement for admission will result in a "free-for-all" in which befuddled juries are confounded by absurd and irrational pseudoscientific assertions. In this regard respondent seems to us to be overly pessimistic about the capabilities of the jury and of the adversary system generally. Vigorous cross-examination, presentation of contrary evidence, and careful instruction on the burden of proof are the traditional and appropriate means of attacking shaky but admissible evidence. See *Rock vs Arkansas*, 483 U.S. 44, 61 (1987). Additionally, in the event the trial court concludes that the scintilla of evidence presented supporting a position is insufficient to allow a reasonable juror to conclude that the position more likely than not is true, the court remains free to direct a judgment, Fed. Rule Civ. Proc. 50(a), and likewise to grant summary judgment, Fed. Rule Civ. Proc. 56. Cf., *e.g., Turpin vs Merrell Dow Pharmaceuticals, Inc.,* 959 F. 2d 1349 (CA6) (holding that scientific evidence that provided foundation for expert testimony, viewed in the light most favorable to plaintiffs, was not sufficient to allow a jury to find it more probable than not that defendant caused plaintiff 's injury), cert. denied, 506 U.S. 826 (1992); *Brock vs Merrell Dow Pharmaceuticals, Inc.,* 874 F. 2d 307 (CA5 1989) (reversing judgment entered on jury verdict for plaintiffs because evidence regarding causation was insufficient), modified, 884 F. 2d 166 (CA5 1989), cert. denied, 494 U.S. 1046 (1990); Green 680–681. These conventional devices, rather than wholesale exclusion under an uncompromising "general acceptance" test, are the appropriate safeguards where the basis of scientific testimony meets the standards of Rule 702.

Petitioners and, to a greater extent, their *amici* exhibit a different concern. They suggest that recognition of a screening role for the judge that allows for the exclusion of "invalid" evidence will sanction a stifling and repressive scientific orthodoxy and will be inimical to the search for truth. See, *e.g.,* Brief for Ronald Bayer et al. as *Amici Curiae*. It is true that open debate is an essential part of both legal and scientific analyses. Yet there are important differences between the quest for truth in the courtroom and the quest for truth in the laboratory. Scientific conclusions are subject to perpetual revision. Law, on the other hand, must resolve disputes finally and quickly. The scientific project is advanced by broad and wide-ranging consideration of a multitude of hypotheses, for those that are incorrect will eventually be shown to be so, and that in itself is an advance. Conjectures that are probably wrong are of little use, however, in the project of reaching a quick, final, and binding legal judgment—often of great consequence—about a particular set of events in the past. We recognize that, in practice, a gatekeeping role for the judge, no matter how flexible, inevitably on occasion will prevent the jury from learning of authentic insights and innovations. That, nevertheless, is the balance that is struck by Rules of Evidence designed not for the exhaustive search for cosmic understanding but for the particularized resolution of legal disputes.[13]

IV

To summarize: "General acceptance" is not a necessary precondition to the admissibility of scientific evidence under the Federal Rules of Evidence, but the Rules of Evidence—especially Rule 702—do assign to the trial judge the task of ensuring that an expert's testimony both rests on a reliable foundation and is relevant to the task at hand. Pertinent evidence based on scientifically valid principles will satisfy those demands.

The inquiries of the District Court and the Court of Appeals focused almost exclusively on "general acceptance," as gauged by publication and the decisions of other courts. Accordingly, the judgment of the Court of Appeals is vacated, and the case is remanded for further proceedings consistent with this opinion.

It is so ordered."[8]

"by *Donald N. Bersoff;* for Alvan R. Feinstein by *Don M. Kennedy, Loretta M. Smith,* and *Richard A. Oetheimer;* and for Kenneth Rothman et al. by *Neil B. Cohen.*

[1] Doctor Lamm received his master's and doctor of medicine degrees from the University of Southern California. He has served as a consultant in birth-defect epidemiology for the National Center for Health Statistics and has published numerous articles on the magnitude of risk from exposure to various chemical and biological substances. App. 34–44.

[2] For example, Shanna Helen Swan, who received a master's degree in biostatistics from Columbia University and a doctorate in statistics from the University of California at Berkeley, is chief of the section of the California Department of Health and Services that determines causes of birth defects and has served as a consultant to the World Health Organization, the Food and Drug Administration, and the National Institutes of Health. *Id.,* at 113–114, 131–132. Stuart A. Newman, who received his bachelor's degree in chemistry from Columbia University and his master's and doctorate in chemistry from the University of Chicago, is a professor at New York Medical College and has spent over a decade studying the effect of chemicals on limb development. *Id.,* at 54–56. The credentials of the others are similarly impressive. See *id.,* at 61–66, 73–80, 148–153, 187–192, and Attachments 12, 20, 21, 26, 31, and 32 to Petitioners' Opposition to Summary Judgment in No. 84–2013–G(I) (SD Cal.).

[3] For a catalog of the many cases on either side of this controversy, see P. Giannelli & E. Imwinkelried, Scientific Evidence § 1–5, pp. 10–14 (1986 and Supp. 1991).

[4] See, *e.g.,* Green, Expert Witnesses and Sufficiency of Evidence in Toxic Substances Litigation: The Legacy of *Agent Orange* and Bendectin Litigation, 86 Nw. U. L. Rev. 643 (1992) (hereinafter Green); Becker & Orenstein, The Federal Rules of Evidence After Sixteen Years—The Effect of "Plain Meaning" Jurisprudence, the Need for an Advisory Committee on the Rules of Evidence, and Suggestions for Selective Revision of the Rules, 60 Geo. Wash. L. Rev. 857, 876–885 (1992); Hanson, James Alphonzo Frye is Sixty-Five Years Old; Should He Retire?, 16 West. St. U. L. Rev. 357 (1989); Black, A Unified Theory of Scientific Evidence, 56 Ford. L. Rev. 595 (1988); Imwinkelried, The "Bases" of Expert Testimony: The Syllogistic Structure of Scientific Testimony, 67 N. C. L. Rev. 1 (1988); Proposals for a Model Rule on the Admissibility of Scientific Evidence, 26 Jurimetrics J. 235 (1986); Giannelli, The Admissibility of Novel Scientific Evidence: *Frye vs United States,* a Half-Century Later, 80 Colum. L. Rev. 1197 (1980); The Supreme Court, 1986 Term, 101 Harv. L. Rev. 7, 119, 125–127 (1987).

Indeed, the debates over *Frye* are such a well-established part of the academic landscape that a distinct term—"*Frye*-ologist"—has been advanced to describe those who take part. See Behringer, Introduction, Proposals for a Model Rule on the Admissibility of Scientific Evidence, 26 Jurimetrics J. 237, 239 (1986), quoting Lacey, Scientific Evidence, 24 Jurimetrics J. 254, 264 (1984).

[5] Like the question of *Frye's* merit, the dispute over its survival has divided courts and commentators. Compare, *e.g., United States vs Williams,* 583 F. 2d 1194 (CA2 1978) (*Frye* is superseded by the Rules of Evidence), cert. denied, 439 U.S. 1117 (1979), with *Christophersen vs Allied-Signal Corp.,* 939 F. 2d 1106, 1111, 1115–1116 (CA5 1991) (en banc) (*Frye* and the Rules coexist), cert. denied, 503 U.S. 912 (1992), 3 J. Weinstein & M. Berger, Weinstein's Evidence ¶702[03], pp. 702–36 to 702–37 (1988) (hereinafter Weinstein & Berger) (*Frye* is dead), and M. Graham, Handbook of Federal Evidence § 703.2 (3d ed. 1991) (*Frye* lives). See generally P. Giannelli & E. Imwinkelried, Scientific Evidence § 1–5, at 28–29 (citing authorities).

[6] Because we hold that *Frye* has been superseded and base the discussion that follows on the content of the congressionally enacted Federal Rules of Evidence, we do not address petitioners' argument that application of the *Frye* rule in this diversity case, as the application of a judge-made rule affecting substantive rights, would violate the doctrine of *Erie R. Co. vs Tompkins,* 304 U.S. 64 (1938).

[7] The Chief Justice "do[es]" not doubt that Rule 702 confides to the judge some gatekeeping responsibility," *post,* at 600, but would neither say how it does so nor explain what that role entails. We believe the better course is to note the nature and source of the duty.

[8] Rule 702 also applies to "technical, or other specialized knowledge." Our discussion is limited to the scientific context because that is the nature of the expertise offered here.

[9] We note that scientists typically distinguish between "validity" (does the principle support what it purports to show?) and "reliability" (does application of the principle produce consistent results?). See Black, 56 Ford. L. Rev., at 599. Although "the difference between accuracy, validity, and reliability may be such that each is distinct from the other by no more than a hen's kick," Starrs, *Frye vs United States Restructured and Revitalized: A Proposal to Amend Federal Evidence Rule 702,* 26 Jurimetrics J. 249, 256 (1986), our reference here is to *evidentiary* reliability—that is, trustworthiness. Cf., *e.g.,* Advisory Committee's Notes on Fed. Rule Evid. 602, 28 U. S. C. App., p. 755 ("'[T]he rule requiring that a witness who testifies to a fact which can be perceived by the senses must have had an opportunity to observe, and must have actually observed the fact' is a 'most pervasive manifestation' of the common law insistence upon 'the most reliable sources of information'" (citation omitted)); Advisory Committee's Notes on Art. VIII of Rules of Evidence, 28 U. S. C. App., p. 770 (hearsay exceptions will be recognized only "under circumstances supposed to furnish guarantees of trustworthiness"). In a case involving scientific evidence, *evidentiary reliability* will be based upon *scientific validity.*

[10] *Rule 104(a) provides:*

> "*Preliminary questions concerning the qualification of a person to be a witness, the existence of a privilege, or the admissibility of evidence shall be determined by the court, subject to the provisions of subdivision (b) [pertaining to conditional admissions]. In making its determination it is not bound by the rules of evidence except those with respect to privileges." These matters should be established by a preponderance of proof. See Bourjaily vs United States, 483 U.S. 171, 175–176 (1987).*

[11] *Although the Frye decision itself focused exclusively on "novel" scientific techniques, we do not read the requirements of Rule 702 to apply specially or exclusively to unconventional evidence. Of course, well-established propositions are less likely to be challenged than those that are novel, and they are more handily defended. Indeed, theories that are so firmly established as to have attained the status of scientific law, such as the laws of thermodynamics, properly are subject to judicial notice under Federal Rule of Evidence 201.*

[12] *A number of authorities have presented variations on the reliability approach, each with its own slightly different set of factors. See, e.g., Downing, 753 F. 2d, at 1238–1239 (on which our discussion draws in part); 3 Weinstein & Berger ¶702[03], pp. 702–41 to 702–42 (on which the Downing court in turn partially relied); McCormick, Scientific Evidence: Defining a New Approach to Admissibility, 67 Iowa L. Rev. 879, 911–912 (1982); and Symposium on Science and the Rules of Evidence, 99 F. R. D. 187, 231 (1983) (statement by Margaret Berger). To the extent that they focus on the reliability of evidence as ensured by the scientific validity of its underlying principles, all these versions may well have merit, although we express no opinion regarding any of their particular details.*

[13] *This is not to say that judicial interpretation, as opposed to adjudicative factfinding, does not share basic characteristics of the scientific endeavor: "The work of a judge is in one sense enduring and in another ephemeral.... In the endless process of testing and retesting, there is a constant rejection of the dross and a constant retention of whatever is pure and sound and fine." B. Cardozo, The Nature of the Judicial Process 178–179 (1921)."*[9]

So, if expert testimony is challenged based on the Daubert standards, the trial judge must determine whether the expert is proposing to testify to (1) scientific knowledge that (2) will assist the trier of fact to understand or determine a fact in issue. This requires a preliminary assessment of whether the reasoning or methodology underlying the testimony is scientifically valid and of whether that reasoning or methodology properly can be applied to the facts in issue. If you are offering expert testimony, you must make sure that the methodology you employ in arriving at your opinion is one that is generally recognized as an appropriate methodology in your field of expertise and that it has been peer reviewed. Also, you must make sure that you applied the methodology to and considered all available, relevant, and reliable facts and data. You must also establish a link between the harmful conduct and the damages. You must demonstrate that your theory of damages matches the legal remedies available for the type of action you are testifying about.

Rule 703 allows experts to rely on facts and data that have not been admitted into evidence. The only requirement is that they must be the types of facts and data that other experts in the field would rely on.

"Rule 703. Bases of an Expert's Opinion Testimony

An expert may base an opinion on facts or data in the case that the expert has been made aware of or personally observed. If experts in the particular field would reasonably rely on those kinds of facts or data in forming an opinion on the subject, they need not be admissible for the opinion to be admitted. But if the facts or data would otherwise be inadmissible, the proponent of the opinion may disclose them to the jury only if their probative value in helping the jury evaluate the opinion substantially outweighs their prejudicial effect.

(As amended Mar. 2, 1987, eff. Oct. 1, 1987; Apr. 17, 2000, eff. Dec. 1, 2000; Apr. 26, 2011, eff. Dec. 1, 2011.)"[10]

Rule 704 allows an expert to opine on an ultimate issue before the trier of fact. However, before agreeing to give this testimony, check your own professional ethics guidance. This type of testimony is forbidden by some professional organizations.

"Rule 704. Opinion on an Ultimate Issue

(a) IN GENERAL—NOT AUTOMATICALLY OBJECTIONABLE. An opinion is not objectionable just because it embraces an ultimate issue.

(b) EXCEPTION. In a criminal case, an expert witness must not state an opinion about whether the defendant did or did not have a mental state or condition that constitutes an element of the crime charged or of a defense. Those matters are for the trier of fact alone.

(As amended Pub. L. 98–473, title II, § 406, Oct. 12, 1984, 98 Stat. 2067; Apr. 26, 2011, eff. Dec. 1, 2011.)"[11]

Rule 705 requires that all facts and data relied on in forming your opinion must be available in court for cross-examinations. Remember what we described in Chapter 9. You want to make sure that your workpapers are cross referenced in a way that will allow you to quickly locate any document or other materials that contain a fact or data that you relied on in forming your opinions.

"Rule 705. Disclosing the Facts or Data Underlying an Expert's Opinion

Unless the court orders otherwise, an expert may state an opinion—and give the reasons for it—without first testifying to the underlying facts or data. But the expert may be required to disclose those facts or data on cross-examination.

(As amended Mar. 2, 1987, eff. Oct. 1, 1987; Apr. 22, 1993, eff. Dec. 1, 1993; Apr. 26, 2011, eff. Dec. 1, 2011.)"[12]

So, these are the rules that you would be required to follow in offering expert testimony in federal court. It is important that you be familiar with them so that you can plan and execute your investigation or forensic analysis in a manner that will satisfy them.

SECTION II: FACT WITNESS TESTIMONY

The key to understanding the difference between fact witness testimony and expert testimony is that fact witness testimony is based on first-hand observation and ordinary knowledge. Expert testimony, on the other hand, is based on the application of specialized knowledge to facts or data to help the trier of fact to understand them. Also, the expert can rely on facts and data that are normally relied on by other experts in their field of study. There is no requirement for first-hand observation or admissibility of the facts and data they rely on.

Fact witnesses are usually deposed ahead of trial. The Federal Rules of Civil Procedure state:

"Rule 27. Depositions to Perpetuate Testimony
(a) BEFORE AN ACTION IS FILED.

(1) *Petition.* A person who wants to perpetuate testimony about any matter cognizable in a United States court may file a verified petition in the district court for the district where any expected adverse party resides. The petition must ask for an order authorizing the petitioner to depose the named persons in order to perpetuate their testimony. The petition must be titled in the petitioner's name and must show:

(A) that the petitioner expects to be a party to an action cognizable in a United States court but cannot presently bring it or cause it to be brought;

(B) the subject matter of the expected action and the petitioner's interest;

(C) the facts that the petitioner wants to establish by the proposed testimony and the reasons to perpetuate it;

(D) the names or a description of the persons whom the petitioner expects to be adverse parties and their addresses, so far as known; and

(E) the name, address, and expected substance of the testimony of each deponent.

(2) *Notice and Service.* At least 21 days before the hearing date, the petitioner must serve each expected adverse party with a copy of the petition and a notice stating the time and place of the hearing. The notice may be served either inside or outside the district or state in the manner provided in Rule 4. If that service cannot be made with reasonable diligence on an expected adverse party, the court may order service by publication or otherwise. The court must appoint an attorney to represent persons not served in the manner provided in Rule 4 and to cross-examine the deponent if an unserved person is not otherwise represented. If any expected adverse party is a minor or is incompetent, Rule 17(c) applies.

(3) *Order and Examination.* If satisfied that perpetuating the testimony may prevent a failure or delay of justice, the court must issue an order that designates or describes the persons whose depositions may be taken, specifies the subject matter of the examinations, and states whether the depositions will be taken orally or by written interrogatories. The depositions may then be taken under these rules, and the court may issue orders like those authorized by Rules 34 and 35. A reference in these rules to the court where an action is pending means, for purposes of this rule, the court where the petition for the deposition was filed.

(4) *Using the Deposition.* A deposition to perpetuate testimony may be used under Rule 32(a) in any later-filed district court action involving the same subject matter if the deposition either was taken under these rules or, although not so taken, would be admissible in evidence in the courts of the state where it was taken."[13]

Persons or organizations (through designated representatives) may be deposed orally. However, they can also be deposed by written questions.

"Rule 31. Depositions by Written Questions
(a) WHEN A DEPOSITION MAY BE TAKEN.

(1) *Without Leave.* A party may, by written questions, depose any person, including a party, without leave of court except as provided in Rule 31(a)(2). The deponent's attendance may be compelled by subpoena under Rule 45.

(2) *With Leave.* A party must obtain leave of court, and the court must grant leave to the extent consistent with Rule 26(b)(1) and (2):

(A) if the parties have not stipulated to the deposition and:

(i) the deposition would result in more than 10 depositions being taken under this rule or Rule 30 by the plaintiffs, or by the defendants, or by the third-party defendants;

(ii) the deponent has already been deposed in the case; or

(iii) the party seeks to take a deposition before the time specified in Rule 26(d); or

(B) if the deponent is confined in prison.

(3) *Service; Required Notice.* A party who wants to depose a person by written questions must serve them on every other party, with a notice stating, if known, the deponent's name and address. If the name is unknown, the notice must provide a general description sufficient to identify the person or the particular class or group to which the person belongs. The notice must also state the name or descriptive title and the address of the officer before whom the deposition will be taken.

(4) *Questions Directed to an Organization.* A public or private corporation, a partnership, an association, or a governmental agency may be deposed by written questions in accordance with Rule 30(b)(6).

(5) *Questions from Other Parties.* Any questions to the deponent from other parties must be served on all parties as follows: cross-questions, within 14 days after being served with the notice and direct questions; redirect questions, within 7 days after being served with cross-questions; and recross-questions, within 7 days after being served with redirect questions. The court may, for good cause, extend or shorten these times.

(b) DELIVERY TO THE OFFICER; OFFICER'S DUTIES. The party who noticed the deposition must deliver to the officer a copy of all the questions served and of the notice. The officer must promptly proceed in the manner provided in Rule 30(c), (e), and (f) to:

(1) take the deponent's testimony in response to the questions;

(2) prepare and certify the deposition; and

(3) send it to the party, attaching a copy of the questions and of the notice.

(c) NOTICE OF COMPLETION OR FILING.

(1) *Completion.* The party who noticed the deposition must notify all other parties when it is completed.

(2) *Filing.* A party who files the deposition must promptly notify all other parties of the filing.

(As amended Mar. 30, 1970, eff. July 1, 1970; Mar. 2, 1987, eff. Aug. 1, 1987; Apr. 22, 1993, eff. Dec. 1, 1993; Apr. 30, 2007, eff. Dec. 1, 2007; Apr. 29, 2015, eff. Dec. 1, 2015.)"[14].)

Of course, this is all subject to the judge's rulings regarding the nature of fact witness testimony. Some judges can become biased against one party in litigation and allow testimony that violates the rules. I was retained by counsel representing criminal defendants on trial in federal court for white collar crimes. The prosecutor played a tape of one of the defendants singing a song that was highly offensive to the judge. After that the judge consistently ruled against all defendant motions. Then, the judge allowed a prosecution "fact witness" to offer opinion testimony based on specialized knowledge. Fortunately, the jury could see what was going on and came to the correct decision in the end. Incidentally, during my testimony, I could see the judge's computer screen. Instead of listening to the testimony he was shopping online, a rather irresponsible approach to discharging one's duties when someone's freedom is at stake. My only point in telling you this is that, at trial, the judge is the ultimate authority on application of the rules.

So, let's break this down. Looking at the rules above, a fact witness can be anyone who has relevant first-hand knowledge about the subject of the criminal or civil litigation. The only other requirement is that the witness be competent to testify. A fact witness is allowed to offer opinions that will help the trier of fact to understand their testimony as long as those opinions are based on general knowledge.

If you are called as a fact witness, your job will be an easy one. Just tell the truth about what you observed. I have given testimony as a fact witness. It is the easiest testimony I have ever given. Of course, there will be cross-examination, but, as long as you have told the truth and have no personal issues (i.e. character flaws, criminal record, and conflict of interest), there is very little that can be done to impeach your testimony. However, do not let yourself be drawn into a situation where you are offered as a fact witness and later asked, by the attorney, to try to offer expert testimony as part of your fact witness testimony. This has the effect of alienating the judge who normally views this (my example above being the exception) as an attempt to put one over on the court. You will end up in a very uncomfortable position if you attempt this.

SECTION III: EXPERT WITNESS TESTIMONY

Rule 702 sets out the rules related to expert witness testimony. Rule 703 states that a witness who is qualified as an expert by knowledge, skill, experience, training, or education may testify in the form of an opinion or otherwise if:

- The expert's scientific, technical, or other specialized knowledge will help the trier of fact to understand the evidence or to determine a fact in issue;
- the testimony is based on sufficient facts or data;
- the testimony is the product of reliable principles and methods; and
- the expert has reliably applied the principles and methods to the facts of the case.

In addition to this you must be aware of the standards imposed by the Daubert Supreme Court decision.

In terms of required disclosures, an expert must normally provide a written report which contains required information. The report must contain:

- a complete statement of all opinions the witness will express and the basis and reasons for them including the facts or data considered by the witness in forming them;
- any exhibits that will be used to summarize or support them;
- the witness's qualifications, including a list of all publications authored in the previous 10 years;
- a list of all other cases in which, during the previous 4 years, the witness testified as an expert at trial or by deposition; and
- a statement of the compensation to be paid for the study and testimony in the case.

A party must make these disclosures at the times and in the sequence that the court orders. Absent a stipulation or a court order, the disclosures must be made:

- at least 90 days before the date set for trial or for the case to be ready for trial;
- or if the evidence is intended solely to contradict or rebut evidence on the same subject matter identified by another party under Rule 26(a)(2)(B), within 30 days after the other party's disclosure.

Further, Rule 26 states:

> "(4) *Trial Preparation: Experts.*
>   (A) *Deposition of an Expert Who May Testify.* A party may depose any person who has been identified as an expert whose opinions may be presented at trial. If Rule 26(a)(2)(B) requires a report from the expert, the deposition may be conducted only after the report is provided."[15]

So, after you have submitted your expert report and it has been produced to the opposing party(ies) and before trial you will be deposed. A deposition is not a trial. The parties present will likely consist of attorneys for both sides (you will have an attorney present to defend your deposition who will make objections when necessary to the opposing attorney's questions), opposing party's representatives and a court reporter. The court reporter will place you under oath and create a written transcript of your deposition. While you are under oath, you should not have conversations about your testimony with anyone.

Note that no representative of the trier of fact will be present. So, no one who can decide the outcome of the case will be present. Therefore, in most circumstances, it is best to wait before you answer a question to make sure you understand the question and to give the lawyer defending your deposition time to object to the question. In most cases, the lawyer's objections are made to create a record for later appeals. So, even though the lawyer objects to the question, in most cases, you will be instructed to answer. When you answer it is best to give the shortest complete truthful answer. The following is an excerpt from a deposition I gave. I want you to pay attention to my answers:

Deposition of William L. Jennings

1 Q. I assume you have reviewed the Receiver's Report.

3 A. Yes.

4 Q. The documents referenced in the Receiver's Report?

6 A. Yes.

7 Q. Have you reviewed the transcript of any depositions in this case?

9 A. Yes.

10 Q. Which depositions have you reviewed in this case?

12 A. Mr. X, Mr. Y, Mr. Z. I think that's it.

15 Q. And I think there might be some confusion, given the overlap in the cases. Specifically in the case we are here for today in the XXXX case, are all of those answers for Mr. A was deposed both in the ABC case and in the Sutherland case. Did you review his deposition testimony in the Sutherland case?

23 A. You know, sitting here, I don't know.

Notice where a one-word answer will suffice, I give a one-word answer. Also, do not be afraid to answer a question with "I don't know." when, in fact, you do not know the answer to the question. A deposition is not a test; you won't receive a bad grade for answering, "I don't know."

I never bring any documents with me to a deposition. The reason is that anything you bring with you is subject to discovery by the opposition. However, a deposition is not a memory test. If you need to review a document to answer a question, ask to be shown the document.

There are lawyers who treat the deposition like a trial cross-examination. They will often become antagonistic, raising their voice, and gesticulating in threatening ways. This seems very foolish to me. Again, there is no one present at the deposition who can decide the outcome of the litigation. Plus, in taking that approach, they learn very little about me or the bases for my opinions and they provide me with a great preview of what to expect from them at trial.

With this type of lawyer, it is important to maintain emotional intelligence and to hang in there. Do not react to their outbursts. Continue to follow the routine: listen carefully to the question; wait for your lawyer to object; and give the shortest complete truthful answer. These lawyers will try to push you out of your routine; do not let them do it. I have had several lawyers try to push me off the shortest complete truthful answer approach with a threat. They will say, "Mr. Jennings, if you keep answering my questions that way, we are going to be here a long time." I always give the same response to that threat, "Well, I bill by the hour, so, I am happy to be here as long as you like."

The opposing lawyers who are worthy adversaries take a completely different approach to depositions. They are very quiet and respectful. They use the early part of the deposition to create a friendly relationship with me. They try to learn everything they can about me and the bases for my opinions. A deposition with this type of lawyer is a more pleasant experience, but be very careful. Remember that these lawyers are the advocates for opposing parties. They can lull you into a false sense of security which can lead to you letting down your guard and making mistakes that you will regret when you testify at trial.

Finally, remember that it is your deposition. If you need something to drink or to take a bio break, etc. just ask; you should not be told no.

Back to Rule 26:

> "(B) *Trial-Preparation Protection for Draft Reports or Disclosures.* Rules 26(b)(3) (A) and (B) protect drafts of any report or disclosure required under Rule 26(a)(2), regardless of the form in which the draft is recorded."[16]

So, your draft reports do not have to be produced to the other side.

And,

> "(C) *Trial-Preparation Protection for Communications Between a Party's Attorney and Expert Witnesses.* Rules 26(b)(3)(A) and (B) protect communications between the party's attorney and any witness required to provide a report under Rule 26(a) (2)(B), regardless of the form of the communications, except to the extent that the communications:
>
> (i) relate to compensation for the expert's study or testimony;
>
> (ii) identify facts or data that the party's attorney provided and that the expert considered in forming the opinions to be expressed; or
>
> (iii) identify assumptions that the party's attorney provided and that the expert relied on in forming the opinions to be expressed."[17]

Your conversations with attorneys supervising you do not have to be disclosed to opposing counsel with some important exceptions. Those exceptions include: discussions about your compensation, facts, and data you considered in forming your opinions and assumptions provided to you by the lawyer.

Preparation to provide expert testimony should be extensive. Everything is on the line at trial. Do not try to wing it. You should make sure that your work has been independently math-checked and fact-checked. Internally, you and your team should think through every way your opinions or work might be attacked. Then, you should make sure that you have answers for all those possible attacks. You should then schedule time with the trial lawyers to work with you to prepare for your testimony at trial. You know your area of expertise far better than the lawyers do, but the lawyers are experts at what will likely happen at trial. You need their help to get ready for your trial testimony.

The usual order of your testimony is that you will answer direct examination questions that will take the trier of fact through an introduction to you, your education, licensing, experience, your opinions, the bases for your opinion, and your compensation. Your introduction will include your name; what you do; where you do it, and the areas you specialize in. Next, the lawyer will ask questions that will allow you to go through your qualifications in a way that allows you to personalize your bona fides in a way that allows the trier of fact to view you as a trusted advisor. Then, you give your opinions using straightforward, compelling language; no jargon, please. Then tell the trier of fact what you did to arrive at your opinions. This would include the generally accepted methodologies you applied to the facts and data that were available to you. Again, use straightforward, compelling language to communicate these things. The trier of fact must view you as a reliable, transparent expert that he, she, or they can rely on. Do not be afraid of your compensation. Every professional involved in the litigation is being compensated for their role in the litigation. The only important thing here is to make sure that the trier of fact does not view any part of your compensation as a factor that could affect your expert testimony.

Let's talk about the audience for your expert testimony. This could be a judge, a jury, an arbitrator, a regulator, etc. The important point here is to tailor your communication of your expert testimony to the trier of fact. In any case, please leave the jargon at the door. Your job is to develop a way to communicate your opinions, methodology, facts, and data relied on in the simplest, most straight forward way possible. Make your opinion testimony compelling, especially on direct examination, do not put your audience asleep by droning on about details that are not necessary to communicate your opinions and the basis for your opinions.

Juries, in particular, can be intimidated by experts. They believe experts will either be boring or will be condescending; absolutely do not be either. You want to be the kind teacher who is interested in the jury understanding the issues upon which you have been asked to opine.

Be the teacher who helps the trier of fact to understand your opinions and the basis for those opinions. Use simple compelling language. Be knowledgeable, interesting, and, if possible, entertaining. You want the trier of fact to view you as a trusted advisor. Someone who they can trust and rely on to give them the information they need to reach a correct verdict. You must make sure that the trier of fact views you as eminently qualified, objective and having applied a generally accepted method to reliable facts and data in order to arrive at your opinions. You must make sure that there are no errors in your work that could be exploited by opposing counsel to impeach your testimony.

When giving expert testimony, it is important to maintain your emotional intelligence. Some lawyers will attempt to fluster you on cross-examination by snarling their questions and speaking disrespectfully to you. They may also feign disbelief or disgust at your answers. Do not be drawn into their trap. Stay in your routine, listen carefully to the question, give the lawyer time to object, formulate an answer, and deliver it in a calm clear voice. Maintain eye contact with the trier of fact as you deliver your answer. Lawyers who employ bullying tactics with expert witnesses will usually only damage themselves if the expert remains calm, cool, and collected. Triers of fact typically do not react well to bullies.

INVESTIGATOR NOTES

Once I was testifying for the defense in a criminal trial. Two executives were indicted for allegedly bribing an official to obtain a desired outcome for their company. The federal prosecutors based the indictment on a bill of information that alleged a specific amount, in cash, that was used to bribe the official. I used a variation of the IRS's indirect method to conclude and opine that, at the time of the alleged bribe, the defendants did not have the requisite amount of cash included in the indictment.

I had put up a demonstrative exhibit summarizing my work and showing a significantly lower amount of cash available to defendants than alleged in the indictment. The prosecutors had documents that they did not produce to defense counsel that had the effect of increasing the amount of cash available to defendants. The federal prosecutor instructed me to write the additional amounts on my exhibit. Each time I did that he would snarl, "And you didn't include this amount in your analysis; did you Mr. Jennings?"

When he finished handing me documents, I realized that the amounts he had me add to my analysis still resulted in an insufficient amount of cash. So, I began drawing a line under the newly added amounts. Realizing what I was about to do, the prosecutor ordered me to stop and return to the witness stand. At that point the Judge intervened and instructed me to finish what I was doing. I calculated the new total and reported to the prosecutor and the jury that the amount was still significantly lower that the amount alleged in the indictment.

At that point the prosecutor became very belligerent. He snarled, "Isn't it true, Mr. Jennings, that one of these defendants could have won the lottery and you didn't take that into account in your analysis?" Before I could respond, the Judge looked the prosecutor in the eye and asked, "Mr. Smith, do you believe that one of these defendants won the lottery?" The prosecutor answered, "No, Your Honor." Then the Judge asked, "Well, who are you trying to fool; me or this jury?" Then the Judge said, "Now move on and stop asking foolish questions in my Court."

The defendants were both acquitted of all charges.

SECTION IV: RULES OF CIVIL PROCEDURE GENERALLY

Let's spend some time looking at the more significant aspects of the Federal Rules of Civil Procedure:

"AUTHORITY FOR PROMULGATION OF RULES
TITLE 28, UNITED STATES CODE

§ 2072. Rules of procedure and evidence; power to prescribe

(a) The Supreme Court shall have the power to prescribe general rules of practice and procedure and rules of evidence for cases in the United States district courts (including proceedings before magistrate judges thereof) and courts of appeals.

(b) Such rules shall not abridge, enlarge or modify any substantive right. All laws in conflict with such rules shall be of no further force or effect after such rules have taken effect.

(c) Such rules may define when a ruling of a district court is final for the purposes of appeal under section 1291 of this title.

(Added Pub. L. 100–702, title IV, § 401(a), Nov. 19, 1988, 102 Stat. 4648, eff. Dec. 1, 1988; amended Pub. L. 101–650, title III, §§ 315, 321, Dec. 1, 1990, 104 Stat. 5115, 5117.)"[18]

So, the Supreme Court of the United States prescribes these rules for the District Courts, Magistrate Courts, and Appellate Courts.

"TITLE II. COMMENCING AN ACTION; SERVICE OF PROCESS, PLEADINGS, MOTIONS, AND ORDERS

Rule 3. Commencing an Action

A civil action is commenced by filing a complaint with the court.

(As amended Apr. 30, 2007, eff. Dec. 1, 2007.)"[19]

The civil litigation process begins with a complaint. So, the first thing you should do when you are retained to provide expert testimony is to read the complaint.

"TITLE III. PLEADINGS AND MOTIONS

Rule 7. Pleadings Allowed; Form of Motions and Other Papers

(a) PLEADINGS. Only these pleadings are allowed:

    (1) a complaint;

    (2) an answer to a complaint;

    (3) an answer to a counterclaim designated as a counterclaim;

    (4) an answer to a crossclaim;

(5) a third-party complaint;

(6) an answer to a third-party complaint; and

(7) if the court orders one, a reply to an answer.

(b) MOTIONS AND OTHER PAPERS.

(1) *In General.* A request for a court order must be made by motion. The motion must:

(A) be in writing unless made during a hearing or trial;

(B) state with particularity the grounds for seeking the order; and

(C) state the relief sought.

(2) *Form.* The rules governing captions and other matters of form in pleadings apply to motions and other papers.

(As amended Dec. 27, 1946, eff. Mar. 19, 1948; Jan. 21, 1963, eff. July 1, 1963; Apr. 28, 1983, eff. Aug. 1, 1983; Apr. 30, 2007, eff. Dec. 1, 2007.)"[20]

The preceding are the pleadings and motions allowed in federal civil litigation. There can also be an amended complaint. You should also read the amended complaint and any pleadings or motions that relate to you and the subjects that you were retained to address. In most venues you can keep track of these by regularly reviewing the docket which is a list of all the pleadings and motions filed in a civil litigation case.

"Rule 16. Pretrial Conferences; Scheduling; Management

(a) PURPOSES OF A PRETRIAL CONFERENCE. In any action, the court may order the attorneys and any unrepresented parties to appear for one or more pretrial conferences for such purposes as:

(1) expediting disposition of the action;

(2) establishing early and continuing control so that the case will not be protracted because of lack of management;

(3) discouraging wasteful pretrial activities;

(4) improving the quality of the trial through more thorough preparation; and

(5) facilitating settlement.

(b) SCHEDULING.

(1) *Scheduling Order.* Except in categories of actions exempted by local rule, the district judge—or a magistrate judge when authorized by local rule—must issue a scheduling order:

(A) after receiving the parties' report under Rule 26(f); or

(B) after consulting with the parties' attorneys and any unrepresented parties at a scheduling conference.

(2) *Time to Issue.* The judge must issue the scheduling order as soon as practicable, but unless the judge finds good cause for delay, the judge must issue it within the earlier of 90 days after any defendant has been served with the complaint or 60 days after any defendant has appeared.

(3) *Contents of the Order.*

(A) *Required Contents.* The scheduling order must limit the time to join other parties, amend the pleadings, complete discovery, and file motions.

(B) *Permitted Contents.* The scheduling order may:

(i) modify the timing of disclosures under Rules 26(a) and 26(e)(1);

(ii) modify the extent of discovery;

(iii) provide for disclosure, discovery, or preservation of electronically stored information;

(iv) include any agreements the parties reach for asserting claims of privilege or of protection as trial preparation material after information is produced, including agreements reached under Federal Rule of Evidence 502;

(v) direct that before moving for an order relating to discovery, the movant must request a conference with the court;

(vi) set dates for pretrial conferences and for trial; and

(vii) include other appropriate matters.

(4) *Modifying a Schedule.* A schedule may be modified only for good cause and with the judge's consent.

(c) ATTENDANCE AND MATTERS FOR CONSIDERATION AT A PRETRIAL CONFERENCE.

(1) *Attendance.* A represented party must authorize at least one of its attorneys to make stipulations and admissions about all matters that can reasonably be anticipated for discussion at a pretrial conference. If appropriate, the court may require that a party or its representative be present or reasonably available by other means to consider possible settlement."[21]

The point of the foregoing is let you know that you have no role in making scheduling decisions. Illness and emergencies aside, you basically need to show up where and when you are told to appear.

Next, let's talk about interrogatories and requests for production of documents. The Federal Rules of Civil Procedure state:

"Rule 33. Interrogatories to Parties

(a) IN GENERAL.

(1) *Number.* Unless otherwise stipulated or ordered by the court, a party may serve on any other party no more than 25 written interrogatories, including all discrete subparts. Leave to serve additional interrogatories may be granted to the extent consistent with Rule 26(b)(1) and (2).

(2) *Scope.* An interrogatory may relate to any matter that may be inquired into under Rule 26(b). An interrogatory is not objectionable merely because it asks for an opinion or contention that relates to fact or the application of law to fact, but the court may order that the interrogatory need not be answered until designated discovery is complete, or until a pretrial conference or some other time.

(b) ANSWERS AND OBJECTIONS.

(1) *Responding Party.* The interrogatories must be answered:

(A) by the party to whom they are directed; or

(B) if that party is a public or private corporation, a partnership, an association, or a governmental (C) agency, by any officer or agent, who must furnish the information available to the party.

(2) *Time to Respond.* The responding party must serve its answers and any objections within 30 days after being served with the interrogatories. A shorter or longer time may be stipulated to under Rule 29 or be ordered by the court.

(3) *Answering Each Interrogatory.* Each interrogatory must, to the extent it is not objected to, be answered separately and fully in writing under oath.

(4) *Objections.* The grounds for objecting to an interrogatory must be stated with specificity. Any ground not stated in a timely objection is waived unless the court, for good cause, excuses the failure.

(5) *Signature.* The person who makes the answers must sign them, and the attorney who objects must sign any objections.

(c) USE. An answer to an interrogatory may be used to the extent allowed by the Federal Rules of Evidence.

(d) OPTION TO PRODUCE BUSINESS RECORDS. If the answer to an interrogatory may be determined by examining, auditing, compiling, abstracting, or summarizing a party's business records (including electronically stored information), and if the burden of deriving or ascertaining the answer will be substantially the same for either party, the responding party may answer by:

(1) specifying the records that must be reviewed, in sufficient detail to enable the interrogating party to locate and identify them as readily as the responding party could; and

(2) giving the interrogating party a reasonable opportunity to examine and audit the records and to make copies, compilations, abstracts, or summaries.

(As amended Dec. 27, 1946, eff. Mar. 19, 1948; Mar. 30, 1970, eff. July 1, 1970; Apr. 29, 1980, eff. Aug. 1, 1980; Apr. 22, 1993, eff. Dec. 1, 1993; Apr. 12, 2006, eff. Dec. 1, 2006; Apr. 30, 2007, eff. Dec. 1, 2007; Apr. 29, 2015, eff. Dec. 1, 2015.)

Rule 34. Producing Documents, Electronically Stored Information, and Tangible Things, or Entering onto Land, for Inspection and Other Purposes

(a) IN GENERAL. A party may serve on any other party a request within the scope of Rule 26(b):

(1) to produce and permit the requesting party or its representative to inspect, copy, test, or sample the following items in the responding party's possession, custody, or control:

(A) any designated documents or electronically stored information—including writings, drawings, graphs, charts, photographs, sound recordings, images, and other data or data compilations—stored in any medium from which information can be obtained either directly or, if necessary, after translation by the responding party into a reasonably usable form; or

(B) any designated tangible things; or

(2) to permit entry onto designated land or other property possessed or controlled by the responding party, so that the requesting party may inspect, measure, survey, photograph, test, or sample the property or any designated object or operation on it.

(b) PROCEDURE.

(1) *Contents of the Request.* The request:

(A) must describe with reasonable particularity each item or category of items to be inspected;

(B) must specify a reasonable time, place, and manner for the inspection and for performing the related acts; and

(C) may specify the form or forms in which electronically stored information is to be produced.

(2) *Responses and Objections.*

(A) *Time to Respond.* The party to whom the request is directed must respond in writing within 30 days after being served or—if the request was delivered under Rule 26(d)(2)—within 30 days after the parties' first Rule 26(f) conference. A shorter or longer time may be stipulated to under Rule 29 or be ordered by the court.

(B) *Responding to Each Item.* For each item or category, the response must either state that inspection and related activities will be permitted as requested or state with specificity the grounds for objecting to the request, including the reasons. The responding party may state that it will produce copies of documents or of electronically stored information instead of permitting inspection. The production must then be completed no later than the time for inspection specified in the request or another reasonable time specified in the response.

(C) *Objections.* An objection must state whether any responsive materials are being withheld on the basis of that objection. An objection to part of a request must specify the part and permit inspection of the rest.

(D) *Responding to a Request for Production of Electronically Stored Information.* The response may state an objection to a requested form for producing electronically stored information. If the responding party objects to a requested form—or if no form was specified in the request—the party must state the form or forms it intends to use.

(E) *Producing the Documents or Electronically Stored Information.* Unless otherwise stipulated or ordered by the court, these procedures apply to producing documents or electronically stored information:

(i) A party must produce documents as they are kept in the usual course of business or must organize and label them to correspond to the categories in the request;

(ii) If a request does not specify a form for producing electronically stored information, a party must produce it in a form or forms in which it is ordinarily maintained or in a reasonably usable form or forms; and

(iii) A party need not produce the same electronically stored information in more than one form.

(c) NONPARTIES. As provided in Rule 45, a nonparty may be compelled to produce documents and tangible things or to permit an inspection.

(As amended Dec. 27, 1946, eff. Mar. 19, 1948; Mar. 30, 1970, eff. July 1, 1970; Apr. 29, 1980, eff. Aug. 1, 1980; Mar. 2, 1987, eff. Aug. 1, 1987; Apr. 30, 1991, eff. Dec. 1, 1991; Apr. 22, 1993, eff. Dec. 1, 1993; Apr. 12, 2006, eff. Dec. 1, 2006; Apr. 30, 2007, eff. Dec. 1, 2007; Apr. 29, 2015, eff. Dec. 1, 2015.)"[22]

You will likely be asked to assist in answering interrogatories and assembling documents to provide to your attorneys for their review prior to responding to these requests. The opposing party will also be responding with their own answers to interrogatories and documents responsive to document requests. Many of these will be made available to you to use in your forensic accounting analyses including damages calculations. The documents will typically be marked with a unique letter and number referred to as a Bates number. This number will be used to identify each document admitted into evidence and those not admitted into evidence but used in your forensic accounting analysis.

Witnesses, documents, electronic data, and other things can be compelled to be made available for examination by an adverse party by the issuance of a subpoena. The Federal Rules of Civil Procedure lay out the rules related to the issuance of and compliance with subpoenas:

"Rule 45. Subpoena
(a) IN GENERAL.
(1) *Form and Contents.*
(A) *Requirements—In General.* Every subpoena must:
(i) state the court from which it issued;
(ii) state the title of the action and its civil-action number;
(iii) command each person to whom it is directed to do the following at a specified time and place: attend and testify; produce designated documents, electronically stored information, or tangible

things in that person's possession, custody, or control; or permit the inspection of premises; and

(iv) set out the text of Rule 45(d) and (e).

(B) *Command to Attend a Deposition—Notice of the Recording Method.* A subpoena commanding attendance at a deposition must state the method for recording the testimony.

(C) *Combining or Separating a Command to Produce or to Permit Inspection; Specifying the Form for Electronically Stored Information.* A command to produce documents, electronically stored information, or tangible things or to permit the inspection of premises may be included in a subpoena commanding attendance at a deposition, hearing, or trial, or may be set out in a separate subpoena. A subpoena may specify the form or forms in which electronically stored information is to be produced.

(D) *Command to Produce; Included Obligations.* A command in a subpoena to produce documents, electronically stored information, or tangible things requires the responding person to permit inspection, copying, testing, or sampling of the materials.

(2) *Issuing Court.* A subpoena must issue from the court where the action is pending.

(3) *Issued by Whom.* The clerk must issue a subpoena, signed but otherwise in blank, to a party who requests it. That party must complete it before service. An attorney also may issue and sign a subpoena if the attorney is authorized to practice in the issuing court.

(4) *Notice to Other Parties Before Service.* If the subpoena commands the production of documents, electronically stored information, or tangible things or the inspection of premises before trial, then before it is served on the person to whom it is directed, a notice and a copy of the subpoena must be served on each party.

(b) SERVICE.

(1) *By Whom and How; Tendering Fees.* Any person who is at least 18 years old and not a party may serve a subpoena. Serving a subpoena requires delivering a copy to the named person and, if the subpoena requires that person's attendance, tendering the fees for 1 day's attendance and the mileage allowed by law. Fees and mileage need not be tendered when the subpoena issues on behalf of the United States or any of its officers or agencies.

(2) *Service in the United States.* A subpoena may be served at any place within the United States.

(3) *Service in a Foreign Country.* 28 U.S.C. § 1783 governs issuing and serving a subpoena directed to a United States national or resident who is in a foreign country.

(4) *Proof of Service.* Proving service, when necessary, requires filing with the issuing court a statement showing the date and manner of service and the names of the persons served. The statement must be certified by the server.

(c) PLACE OF COMPLIANCE.

(1) *For a Trial, Hearing, or Deposition.* A subpoena may command a person to attend a trial, hearing, or deposition only as follows:

(A) within 100 miles of where the person resides, is employed, or regularly transacts business in person; or

(B) within the state where the person resides, is employed, or regularly transacts business in person, if the person

(i) is a party or a party's officer; or

(ii) is commanded to attend a trial and would not incur substantial expense.

(2) *For Other Discovery.* A subpoena may command:

(A) production of documents, electronically stored information, or tangible things at a place within 100 miles of where the person resides, is employed, or regularly transacts business in person; and

(B) inspection of premises at the premises to be inspected.

(d) PROTECTING A PERSON SUBJECT TO A SUBPOENA; ENFORCEMENT.

(1) *Avoiding Undue Burden or Expense; Sanctions.* A party or attorney responsible for issuing and serving a subpoena must take reasonable steps to avoid imposing undue burden or expense on a person subject to the subpoena. The court for the district where compliance is required must enforce this duty and impose an appropriate sanction—which may include lost earnings and reasonable attorney's fees—on a party or attorney who fails to comply.

(2) *Command to Produce Materials or Permit Inspection.*

(A) *Appearance Not Required.* A person commanded to produce documents, electronically stored information, or tangible things, or to permit the inspection of premises, need not appear in person at the place of production or inspection unless also commanded to appear for a deposition, hearing, or trial.

(B) *Objections.* A person commanded to produce documents or tangible things or to permit inspection may serve on the party or attorney designated in the subpoena a written objection to inspecting, copying, testing, or sampling any or all of the materials or to inspecting the premises—or to producing electronically stored information in the form or forms requested. The objection must be served before the earlier of the time specified for compliance or 14 days after the subpoena is served. If an objection is made, the following rules apply:

(i) At any time, on notice to the commanded person, the serving party may move the court for the district where compliance is required for an order compelling production or inspection.

(ii) These acts may be required only as directed in the order, and the order must protect a person who is neither a party nor a party's officer from significant expense resulting from compliance.

(3) *Quashing or Modifying a Subpoena.*

(A) *When Required.* On timely motion, the court for the district where compliance is required must quash or modify a subpoena that:

(i) fails to allow a reasonable time to comply;

(ii) requires a person to comply beyond the geographical limits specified in Rule 45(c);

(iii) requires disclosure of privileged or other protected matter, if no exception or waiver applies; or

(iv) subjects a person to undue burden.

(B) *When Permitted.* To protect a person subject to or affected by a subpoena, the court for the district where compliance is required may, on motion, quash or modify the subpoena if it requires:

(i) disclosing a trade secret or other confidential research, development, or commercial information; or

(ii) disclosing an unretained expert's opinion or information that does not describe specific occurrences in dispute and results from the expert's study that was not requested by a party.

(C) *Specifying Conditions as an Alternative.* In the circumstances described in Rule 45(d)(3)(B), the court may, instead of quashing or modifying a subpoena, order appearance or production under specified conditions if the serving party:

(i) shows a substantial need for the testimony or material that cannot be otherwise met without undue hardship; and

(ii) ensures that the subpoenaed person will be reasonably compensated.

(e) DUTIES IN RESPONDING TO A SUBPOENA.

(1) *Producing Documents or Electronically Stored Information.* These procedures apply to producing documents or electronically stored information:

(A) *Documents.* A person responding to a subpoena to produce documents must produce them as they are kept in the ordinary course of business or must organize and label them to correspond to the categories in the demand.

(B) *Form for Producing Electronically Stored Information Not Specified.* If a subpoena does not specify a form for producing electronically stored information, the person responding must produce it in a form or forms in which it is ordinarily maintained or in a reasonably usable form or forms.

(C) *Electronically Stored Information Produced in Only One Form.* The person responding need not produce the same electronically stored information in more than one form.

(D) *Inaccessible Electronically Stored Information.* The person responding need not provide discovery of electronically stored information from sources that the person identifies as not reasonably accessible because of undue burden or cost. On motion to compel discovery or for a protective order, the person responding must show that the information is not reasonably accessible because of undue burden or cost. If that showing is made, the court may nonetheless order discovery from such sources if the requesting party shows good cause, considering the limitations of Rule 26(b)(2)(C). The court may specify conditions for the discovery.

(2) *Claiming Privilege or Protection.*

(A) *Information Withheld.* A person withholding subpoenaed information under a claim that it is privileged or subject to protection as trial-preparation material must:

(i) expressly make the claim; and

(ii) describe the nature of the withheld documents, communications, or tangible things in a manner that, without revealing information itself privileged or protected, will enable the parties to assess the claim.

(B) *Information Produced.* If information produced in response to a subpoena is subject to a claim of privilege or of protection as trial-preparation material, the person making the claim may notify any party that received the information of the claim and the basis for it. After being notified, a party must promptly return, sequester, or destroy the specified information and any copies it has; must not use or disclose the information until the claim is resolved; must take reasonable steps to retrieve the information if the party disclosed it before being notified; and may promptly present the information under seal to the court for the district where compliance is required for a determination of the claim. The person who produced the information must preserve the information until the claim is resolved.

(f) TRANSFERRING A SUBPOENA-RELATED MOTION. When the court where compliance is required did not issue the subpoena, it may transfer a motion under this rule to the issuing court if the person subject to the subpoena consents or if the court finds exceptional circumstances. Then, if the attorney for a person subject to a subpoena is authorized to practice in the court where the motion was made, the attorney may file papers and appear on the motion as an officer of the issuing court. To enforce its order, the issuing court may transfer the order to the court where the motion was made.

(g) CONTEMPT. The court for the district where compliance is required—and also, after a motion is transferred, the issuing court—may hold in contempt a person who, having been served, fails without adequate excuse to obey the subpoena or an order related to it.

(As amended Dec. 27, 1946, eff. Mar. 19, 1948; Dec. 29, 1948, eff. Oct. 20, 1949; Mar. 30, 1970, eff. July 1, 1970; Apr. 29, 1980, eff. Aug. 1, 1980; Apr. 29, 1985, eff. Aug. 1, 1985; Mar. 2, 1987, eff. Aug. 1, 1987; Apr. 30, 1991, eff. Dec. 1, 1991; Apr. 25, 2005, eff. Dec. 1, 2005; Apr. 12, 2006, eff. Dec. 1, 2006; Apr. 30, 2007, eff. Dec. 1, 2007; Apr. 16, 2013, eff. Dec. 1, 2013.)"[23]

So, let's break this down. A subpoena must state the following: issuing court, title of the action and its number, command each person to whom it is directed to do whatever is required (e.g. provide testimony, physical and/or electronic documents, etc.) by a specified date and time. However, a subpoena must not create an undue burden or expense for the respondent (i.e. a subpoena for every record ever created by a company would usually be seen by a court as unduly burdensome). Generally, in responding to a subpoena, you must produce the requested records in the form in which they are kept in the ordinary course of business. You will likely be involved in assembling the information that is responsive to the subpoena. Your attorneys will review all this data prior to production for privileged information and other reasons.

The process of civil litigation often takes a long time to unfold. I am working on a matter now that started in 2012. So, be patient; the wheels of justice turn, albeit slowly.

SECTION V: THE CHESS GAME

Chess players intuitively know danger exists behind every move. The perception of ever present danger can cloud the mind. Only when you feel confident that you are aware of all the threats that exist in the game will you be able to think calmly and clearly about your position. The only way to do this is to be strategic and not transactional in your game. You must be able to anticipate the actual danger that lies ahead. When your opponent makes a move, you must identify not his or her next move, but the move that will be made two or three moves ahead.

In giving expert testimony cross-examination is a lot like a chess game. First, you must understand that the lawyer cross examining you is trying to impeach your testimony. He or she is trying to find a weakness that can be exploited to either have the judge rule that your testimony is incredible (i.e. not credible) or to erode the trier of fact's faith in your testimony. Every question is important and you must pay careful attention to each, just as you would pay careful attention to your opponent's moves and your counter moves in a chess game. In either case, one error could destroy hours of work and, perhaps, your client's case.

I cannot overemphasize the need to maintain your emotional intelligence in this situation. If you get lulled into a false sense of trust with the opposing lawyer or you become angry, nervous, frightened of the opposing lawyer, you will make a mistake. Even one mistake can be devastating. Just as in chess where every move provides information about your opponent's strategy and next moves, each question in cross-examination provides information about the upcoming questions. Of course, you should get into the routine of listening carefully to the question, making sure you understand what is being asked, wait for the lawyer who retained you to object and then answer the question. But, you want to slow the process down to a speed at which you have enough time to prepare for the questions that you anticipate will be coming based on the last question asked.

Here is an example of an attorney trying to anger an expert witness on cross-examination:

Q: You are a forensic accountant, right?
A: I am.
Q: Let me understand what you are. You are a doctor?
A: No.
Q: You are a crime investigator?
A: No.
Q: You are an amateur detective?
A: No.
Q: But a forensic accountant?
A: Yes.

Don't let the cross-examining lawyer get under your skin. It's not personal. You are a professional. Do not fall into the anger trap. You will make a mistake and look unprofessional to the trier of fact.

The following is an example to illustrate the point I am making about anticipating future questions based on the current question:

Q. As I understood your testimony a minute ago, you were engaged to develop an expert opinion as to whether any of the loans in this case failed to meet minimal standards for prudent lending. Did I hear that right?
A. That's correct.
Q. And so you wouldn't have evaluated whether any of the loans at issue in this case involved speculative land loans or land banking, for example, is that right?
A. That's correct.
Q. So you didn't evaluate whether any of these lenders—any of these developers at the time the loans were made were already facing a cash crunch or severe liquidity issues; is that a fair statement?
A. I think that's a fair statement. That wasn't my role.
Q. So you can't list for us which loans reflected developers who, at the time the loans were approved, had severe cash crunch and liquidity issues; is that a fair statement?
A. That's correct.
Q. Okay. You can't identify whether any of these projects at the time the loans were approved were known to be near foul-smelling animal rendering plants, for example, can you?
A. I don't know if that occurred, but that's correct, that wasn't part of my analysis.
Q. So you didn't evaluate whether irresponsible loan approval set in motion a series of events that led to the losses on any particular loans, did you?
A. I did in an overall sense by comparing the different economic circumstances between the period when the loans were approved and when the losses occurred, but if you mean did I look at a specific loan, that was really other experts that studied that.

Notice that this cross-examination begins with what the expert was asked to do. What follows are a series of questions about what the expert was not asked to do. So, the lawyer conducting this cross-examination is seeking to limit the scope of the expert's opinion. When you hear a question about what work you were asked to do followed by a question about what you were not asked to do, be prepared for a series of questions about what you were not asked to do. The purpose of these questions is to attempt to limit the scope of your expert opinions. You must listen very carefully to each question; if the lawyer states you didn't do something that you actually did do, it is important to get that answer on the record. Do not let the opposing attorney get you into a rhythm that makes it more likely that you will answer incorrectly. However, if you do answer one of these types of cross-examination questions incorrectly, all is not lost; the lawyer who retained you will clean those types of mistakes up in redirect which we will discuss next.

Now let's look at what happens when an expert does not prepare well, gets sloppy, and then tries to cover it up with ridiculously false answers.

"A: It's what I said at my deposition. Today it's 40 to 60, you know. Including that would be record reviews as well.

Q: Okay. So just so we're clear, 48 to 60 defense cases a year, right?

A: Correct.

Q: Okay. And you still contend that you do 60 percent defense and 40 percent plaintiff?

A: I do.

Q: Okay. But in your deposition you said you only handle three to five plaintiffs' cases a year?

A: It goes up and it goes down.

Q: Yeah. You said that. But then you said that your average is three to five a year of plaintiffs' cases?

A: Right.

Q: I mean, according to my math, that's about 7 percent plaintiffs' cases?

A: You asked me for an estimate. It was an estimate at the time.

Q: Okay. But you haven't done a plaintiff's deposition in years, right?

A: It's been a few years, yes.

Q: To do even just a sit-down for a plaintiff's deposition, right?

A: Right. Because they typically settle before they get to that point.

Q: Okay. So you—your estimate is three to five plaintiffs' cases a year, but yet you do 48 to 60 defense cases a year. That math is 7 percent plaintiffs' cases and the rest defense cases. Right? Is that fair math?

A: That's the way you calculate it. I gave you an estimate. That was the estimate I thought at the time.

Q: Three to five plaintiffs' cases and 60 defense cases. That's not 60–40, is it?

A: Not those particular numbers, no.

Q: Those are the numbers you gave me.

A: Right. But that was the numbers I gave you that day. That changes from week to week.

Q: Well, I know, and I asked you that, because you said the same thing in your deposition. And I asked you, well, is that your average over the years? And you said it was the same in 2015, three to five plaintiffs' cases a year?

A: Right.

Q: Okay. So do you still contend that you do 60 percent defense and 40 percent plaintiff?

A: I do."[24]

Obviously, never do what this expert did. First, he didn't take the time to review his deposition testimony before trial. So, his trial answers are not consistent with his deposition testimony. The next mistake he makes is misstating the percentage of times he works for plaintiff's attorneys versus defendant's attorneys. Now, at this point, if you get into this unfortunate situation, the best strategy is just to own it. But, that's not what this expert chooses to do. Instead, he just reaffirms his ridiculously incorrect answer. This is a recipe for completely losing the confidence of the trier of fact. Look, this is an adversarial proceeding and you will be subjected to rigorous cross-examination. Be prepared, be truthful, don't guess and please never, never lie. The sad part is this lie has nothing to do with the subject matter of the expert's testimony; it is a completely unforced error.

The final phase of questioning is called redirect; this is where both sides get to ask you questions that are designed to correct or clarify you earlier testimony. This is a good place to remember that the shortest correct truthful answer is often best.

Following redirect you will typically be excused. My practice is to get up from the witness chair and walk directly out of the courtroom.

That's really all there is to it.

EXERCISES

1. What can you expect at trial?
2. What can you do to improve your performance as an expert witness?
3. How long can you expect to be on the stand?
4. Imagine what your routine to prepare to give expert testimony might include?
5. You need to arrive for your expert testimony grounded in emotional intelligence and prepared for anything. What do you need to do to get yourself in that place?
6. What must you disclose in your written expert report?
7. When must your expert report be disclosed to the other side?
8. Using notes from an investigation or forensic accounting analysis you worked on, construct a written expert report that satisfies all the requirements of Rule 26.
9. What knowledge must you have to qualify as an expert witness?
10. What is a Daubert challenge?
11. What must you demonstrate to successfully defend against a Daubert challenge?
12. If you have been qualified as an expert witness, when may you opine on the ultimate issue(s) before the trier of fact?
13. In what instances are you precluded from opining on the ultimate issue(s) before the trier of fact?
14. What's the single most important thing to remember if you are called as a fact witness?
15. What is the best answer to give in a deposition?
16. What do you do in a deposition if you do not know the answer to a question?
17. What should you do if you are asked a question about a specific document or documents?
18. How much time should you spend with counsel preparing for your trial testimony?
19. What should you consider when preparing for your direct examination?
20. What will you do the night before your testimony?
21. What characteristics should your direct examination answers possess?
22. What should you do to prepare for cross-examination?
23. What should you do before answering any cross-examination question?
24. What should you do if the attorney asking you cross-examination questions begins to bully you?
25. What should you do when you are released by the judge?

CHAPTER SUMMARY/KEY TAKEAWAYS

So, here are some things to think about:

- Anything can happen during your testimony, so be ready for anything.
- Emotional intelligence is the most important competency you can possess.
- The court is in control of the timing of your testimony.
- Give the shortest complete truthful answers to deposition questions.
- Fact witness testimony is easy. Just tell the truth.
- Preparation for expert testimony is extremely important. Prepare like your career depended on it because it does.
- Do not fall into the trap of getting angry or getting flustered. Remain calm, cool, and collected.

- Cross-examination is like a chess game. Every question you are asked reveals important information about questions to come. Slow the pace and use the information you are given to prepare for upcoming questions.
- Some mistakes can be fixed in redirect.
- When you are dismissed get up and walk out of the courtroom.

NOTES

1. https://www.uscourts.gov/sites/default/files/federal_rules_of_civil_procedure_-_december_2020_0.pdf
2. https://www.uscourts.gov/sites/default/files/federal_rules_of_civil_procedure_-_december_2020_0.pdf
3. https://www.uscourts.gov/sites/default/files/Rules%20of%20Evidence.
4. https://www.uscourts.gov/sites/default/files/Rules%20of%20Evidence.
5. https://www.uscourts.gov/sites/default/files/Rules%20of%20Evidence.
6. https://www.uscourts.gov/sites/default/files/Rules%20of%20Evidence.
7. https://www.uscourts.gov/sites/default/files/Rules%20of%20Evidence.
8. https://www.supremecourt.gov/opinions/opinions.aspx
9. https://www.supremecourt.gov/opinions/opinions.aspx
10. https://www.uscourts.gov/sites/default/files/Rules%20of%20Evidence.
11. https://www.uscourts.gov/sites/default/files/Rules%20of%20Evidence.
12. https://www.uscourts.gov/sites/default/files/Rules%20of%20Evidence.
13. https://www.uscourts.gov/sites/default/files/federal_rules_of_civil_procedure_-_december_2020_0.pdf
14. https://www.uscourts.gov/sites/default/files/federal_rules_of_civil_procedure_-_december_2020_0.pdf
15. https://www.uscourts.gov/sites/default/files/federal_rules_of_civil_procedure_-_december_2020_0.pdf
16. https://www.uscourts.gov/sites/default/files/federal_rules_of_civil_procedure_-_december_2020_0.pdf
17. https://www.uscourts.gov/sites/default/files/federal_rules_of_civil_procedure_-_december_2020_0.pdf
18. https://www.uscourts.gov/sites/default/files/federal_rules_of_civil_procedure_-_december_2020_0.pdf
19. https://www.uscourts.gov/sites/default/files/federal_rules_of_civil_procedure_-_december_2020_0.pdf
20. https://www.uscourts.gov/sites/default/files/federal_rules_of_civil_procedure_-_december_2020_0.pdf
21. https://www.uscourts.gov/sites/default/files/federal_rules_of_civil_procedure_-_december_2020_0.pdf
22. https://www.uscourts.gov/sites/default/files/federal_rules_of_civil_procedure_-_december_2020_0.pdf
23. https://www.uscourts.gov/sites/default/files/federal_rules_of_civil_procedure__-_december_2020_0.pdf
24. The "Money" Cross-Examination Of The One-Sided Expert, Attacking the credibility of the one-sided expert on cross examination, Dan Kramer, Teresa Johnson, 2017 October

Index